THE BUILDINGS OF ENGLAND

FOUNDING EDITOR: NIKOLAUS PEVSNER

CORNWALL

PETER BEACHAM
AND
NIKOLAUS PEVSNER

Cornwall

Boundary of Cornwall & Devon — 'A' roads — Railways

0 · 5 · 10 · 15 miles
0 · 10 · 20 km

Atlantic Ocean

Pentire Head
Trevone · St Enodoc
Trevose Head · Prideaux Place
Harlyn
Constantine Bay · Padstow
St Merryn · Porthilly
Little Petherick · St Issey
St Ervan
St Eval
Mawgan-in-Pydar
Trevelgue Head · St Columb Major
Newquay · St Columb Minor
Colan
Rialton
Crantock · Indian Queens
Trerice · St Enoder
Cubert
St Pirin's Oratory · St Newlyn East
Perranporth · Mitchell · St Stephen-in-Brannel
Peranzabuloe · Ladock
St Agnes · Mithian · St Allen · St Erme
Porthtowan · St Clement · Grampound
Mount Hawke · Probus · Creed
Portreath · Blackwater · Tresillian · Trewithen · Golden
Godrevy Island · Illogan · Chacewater · Kenwyn · Merther · Cornelly · Tregony
Gwithian · St Day · Baldhu · Truro
Tehidy · Pool · Kea · Ruan Lanihorne
St Ives · Tuckingmill · Redruth · St Michael Penkevil · Treothnan
Carn · Carnon · Lanner · Treslissick · Lamorran · Portloe
Zennor · Carbis Brea · Gwennap · Perranarworthal · Philleigh · Veryan
Towednack · Bay · Penponds · Pencoys · Devoran · Come-to-Good
Camborne · Phillack · Gwinear Treslothan · Stithians · Penryn · St Just-in-Roseland
Lelant · Hayle · Ponsanooth · Mylor · Gerrans
Pendeen · Morvah · Crowan · Campus Penryn · Flushing
Geevor · Levant · Mabe · St Mawes
Botallack · St Erth · Budock · St Anthony-in-Roseland
Cape Cornwall · Madron · Ludgvan · Godolphin · Wendron · Pendennis
St Just-in-Penwith · St Hilary · Truthall · Constantine · Porth · Castle
Penzance · Gulval · Germoe · Sithney · Navas
Sancreed · Tereife · Newlyn · Marazion · Helston · Mawnan
Paul · Perranuthnoe · Breage · Gweek · St Anthony-in-Meneage
Mousehole · St Michael's · Prussia · Porthleven · Mawgan-in-Meneage · Manaccan
Sennen · St Buryan · Mount · Cove · Penrose · Helford · St Martin-in-Meneage
Porthcurno · Pengersick · Trelowarren
Castle · Gunwalloe · Cury · Goonhilly · St Keverne
St Levan · Mullion · Coverack
Poltesco
Ruan Major · Ruan Minor
Grade · Cadgwith
Landewednack

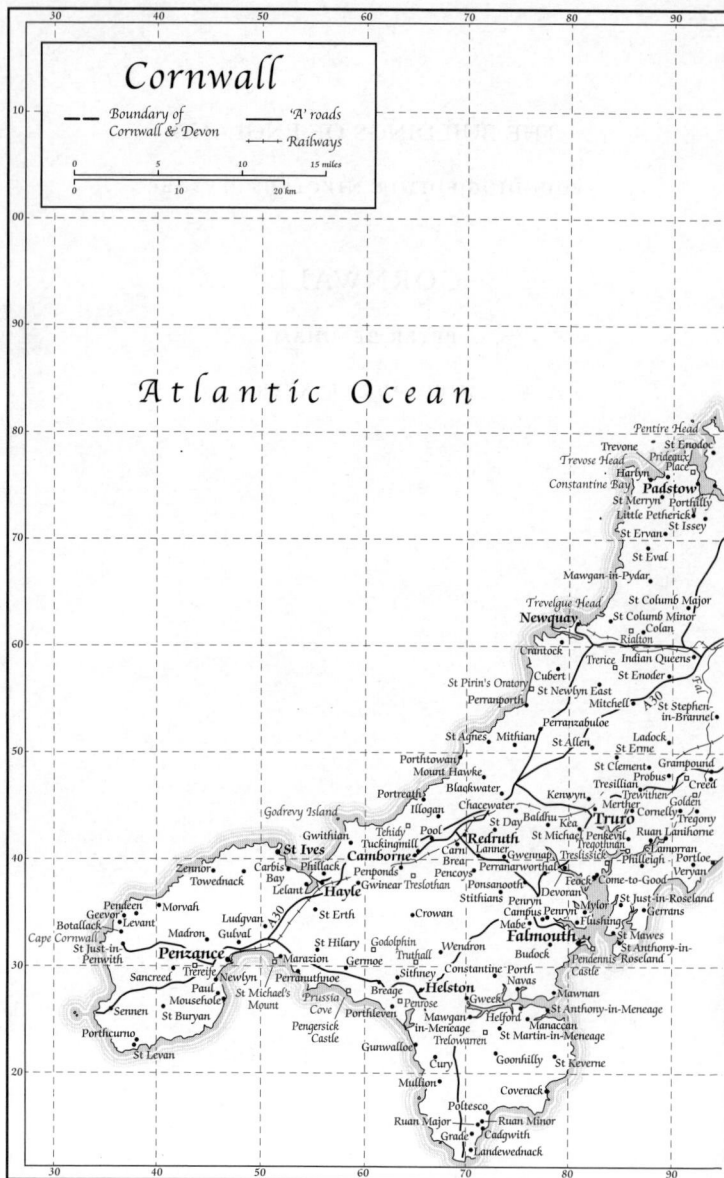

For the Isles of Scilly *see* map p. 705

00
10
20
30
40
50
60
N
DEVON
A30
A39
A38
Tamar
Camel
Fowey
Lynher
Inny
English Channel
Morwenstow
Tonacombe Manor
Kilkhampton
Poughill
Bude
Stratton
Launcells
Marhamchurch
Poundstock
Whitstone
St Gennys
Week St Mary
Jacobstow
North Tamerton
Boyton
St Juliot
Boscastle
Forrabury
Otterham
Warbstow
Trevalga
Lesnewth
Tremaine
Penheale
Tintagel
Trethevy
Minster
Treneglos
Tresmeer
Werrington
North Petherwin
Davidstow
Egloskerry
Delabole
St Clether
Laneast
Launceston
Camelford
Trewen
Lawhitton
Lanteglos-by-Camelford
Port Quin
Port Isaac
St Teath
Advent
Roughtor
Altarnun
South Petherwin
Port Gaverne
Lewannick
Roscarrock
Michaelstow
Brown Willy
Lezant
St Endellion
Trewarne
Trecarrel
St Minver
St Kew
St Tudy
St Breward
Bolventor
North Hill
St Mabyn
Stoke Climsland
St Breock
Wadebridge
Blisland
Linkinhorne
Temple
South Hill
Gunnislake
Croan
Kit Hill
Egloshayle
Pencarrow
Helland
Minions
Warleggan
Callington
Dupath
Washaway
Cardinham
St Cleer
Calstock
Bodmin
St Neot
St Ive
St Dominic
Cotehele
Withiel
St Mellion
Newton Ferrers
St Wenn
Lanivet
Liskeard
Quethiock
Pentillie Castle
Lanhydrock
Pillaton
Hatt
Landulph
St Benet's
Restormel
Braddock
St Pinnock
Menheniot
Landrake
Botus Fleming
St Nectan
St Keyne
Catchfrench Manor
St Erney
Roche
Lostwithiel
Boconnoc
Herodsfoot
Tideford
Saltash
St Dennis
Lanlivery
St Winnow
Duloe
St Germans
Burrell House
Trematon
Treverbyn
Luxulyan
Ethy
Lerryn
Hessenford
Shillingham
Nanpean
Lanreath
Morval
St Martin-by-Looe
Erth Barton
Ince Castle
Antony
St Blazey
Golant
St Veep
Sheviock
Torpoint
Eden Project
Tywardreath
Pelynt
Looe
St John
PLYMOUTH
Tregrehan
Par
Trelawne
Downderry
Millbrook
Mount Edgcumbe
St Austell
Fowey
Bodinnick
Talland
St Mewan
Lansallos
Portwrinkle
Kingsand
Maker
Charlestown
Carlyon Bay
Polperro
Cawsand
Porthpean
Polkerris
Polruan
Lanteglos-by-Fowey
Rame
Pentewan
Menabilly
Heligan
St Ewe
Mevagissey
St Michael Caerhays
Gorran
Gorran Haven

PEVSNER ARCHITECTURAL GUIDES

The Buildings of England series was created and largely written by Sir Nikolaus Pevsner (1902–83). First editions of the county volumes were published by Penguin Books between 1951 and 1974. The continuing programme of revisions and new volumes was supported between 1994 and 2011 by research financed through the Pevsner Books Trust. That responsibility has now been assumed by the Paul Mellon Centre for Studies in British Art.

The costs of research and publication of this volume have been generously supported by

THE CORNWALL HERITAGE TRUST

with major donations from
The Carew Pole Charitable Trust,
The Jane and David Cornwell Charitable Trust,
The Esmée Fairbairn Foundation,
The Hunting Charitable Trust, The Piet Mendels Foundation,
The Lord Myners, The Tim Rice Charitable Trust,
The Michael Trinick Foundation,
The Trusthouse Charitable Foundation,
The Elize Hele Charity,
The Viscountess Boyd Charitable Trust,
The Lord Lieutenant's Committee,
and other individual supporters

THE TANNER TRUST
AND
ENGLISH HERITAGE

Cornwall was the first volume of the *Buildings of England*. It was published in 1951, at the same time as *Nottinghamshire*. Work on the series had begun in 1945 and Nikolaus Pevsner made his research trips to Cornwall three years later. The guide was an experiment in every sense and as Pevsner wrote in his foreword to the second edition, revised by Enid Radcliffe in 1970, 'we were all beginners at the job then'. Yet it established a pattern for the forty-five volumes that followed before coverage of every English county was completed in 1974. Now fully revised and expanded, Pevsner's series has outlasted all its competitors and Yale University Press is delighted to celebrate publication of the first extensive revision and expansion of the pioneer volume.

Cornwall

BY

PETER BEACHAM

AND

NIKOLAUS PEVSNER

WITH CONTRIBUTIONS FROM

ERIC BERRY

SARAH BUCKINGHAM

PETER HERRING

AND

JOHN STENGELHOFEN

THE BUILDINGS OF ENGLAND

YALE UNIVERSITY PRESS
NEW HAVEN AND LONDON

YALE UNIVERSITY PRESS
NEW HAVEN AND LONDON

302 Temple Street, New Haven CT 06511
47 Bedford Square, London WC1B 3DP
www.pevsner.co.uk
www.lookingatbuildings.org.uk
www.yalebooks.co.uk
www.yalebooks.com

Published by Yale University Press 2014
Reprinted with corrections 2014
2 4 6 8 10 9 7 5 3

ISBN 978 0 300 12668 6

Printed in China
through World Print
Set in Monotype Plantin

CONTENTS

LIST OF TEXT FIGURES AND MAPS

MAPS

PHOTOGRAPHIC ACKNOWLEDGEMENTS

The following photographs were taken by:

Eric Berry: 8, 11, 15, 16, 17, 27, 29, 32, 35, 46, 48, 50, 55, 56, 63, 66, 67, 69, 72, 79, 82, 83, 86, 87, 89, 90, 92, 97, 100, 101, 104, 105, 106, 107, 108, 109, 110, 118, 120, 121, 122, 123, 125

Peter Curno (© Peter Curno): 2, 12, 14, 18, 28, 30, 34, 37, 49, 57, 58, 68, 71, 74, 81, 91, 102, 103, 115, 119, 126, 127

James O. Davies (© James O. Davies): 1, 9, 13, 20, 22, 23, 24, 25, 26, 31, 33, 38, 40, 42, 43, 44, 45, 47, 60, 61, 62, 75, 80, 84, 88, 94, 98, 111, 112, 113, 114, 116

We are grateful for permission to reproduce the remaining photographs from the sources as shown below.

© Country Life: 95

Courtesy of Peter & Elisabeth Prideaux-Brune: 78

© Dae Sasitorn/www.lastrefuge.co.uk: 53

Diana Marriott: 39

© English Heritage: 19, 21, 36, 41, 52, 54, 64, 65

© Historic Environment Record, Cornwall Council: 4, 6, 7, 10, 51

Jane Cox: 5

© Julian Love/JAI/Corbis: 124

© Latitudestock/Getty Images: 99

© National Trust Images: 93

© National Trust Images/Aerial-Cam: 73

© National Trust Images/Andreas von Einsiedel: 59, 77

© National Trust Images/Andrew Butler: 70, 85

© National Trust Images/Jerry Harpur: 76

Peter Herring: 3

© Robert Down/fotoLibra, 2013: 96

© Vince Bevan: 117

MAP REFERENCES

The numbers printed in italic type in the margin against the place names in the gazetteer of the book indicate the position of the place in question on the index map (pp. ii–iii), which is divided into sections by the 10-km. reference lines of the National Grid. The reference given here omits the two initial letters which in a full grid reference refer to the 100-km. squares into which the county is divided. The first two numbers indicate the *western* boundary, and the last two the *southern* boundary, of the 10-km. square in which the place in question is situated. For example, Advent (reference 1080) will be found in the 10-km. square bounded by grid lines 10 (on the *west*) and 20, and 80 (on the *south*) and 90; Zennor (reference 4030) in the square bounded by the grid lines 40 (on the *west*) and 50, and 30 (on the *south*) and 40.

The map contains all those places, whether towns, villages, or isolated buildings, which are the subject of separate entries in the text.

FOREWORD AND ACKNOWLEDGEMENTS

The starting point for this book was Nikolaus Pevsner's account in the first edition of 1951 which remained a constant source of inspiration. Preparatory research had been undertaken by Mrs R. Schilling. For this new edition I was fortunate that the publishers agreed to my suggestion that, given the vast amount of new material to be assembled and assessed, the writing should be supported by a researcher. I was richly blessed in the choice of Jo Cox of Keystone Historic Building Consultants, ably supported by Sandi Ellison, for this task. The hundreds of parish files which they prepared for me were not only mines of essential information but sifted the evidence to point me in the most fruitful directions for my visits: their judgement calls about relative significance were unfailingly helpful and this book would not have been possible without their commitment and enthusiasm which went well beyond the call of duty. Jo Cox also accompanied me on early expeditions, was an enduring source of wisdom, and made many helpful comments on much of the text.

I was fortunate, too, in the choice of the specialist contributors, who not only wrote their introductory essays and relevant gazetteer entries but assisted me in numerous other ways. Sarah Buckingham, my former colleague at English Heritage, also accompanied me on my travels, checked some of the perambulations, commented on sections of the text and wrote the gazetteer entries for the Egyptian House and Jubilee Pool at Penzance. Peter Herring was an infallible source of information about all matters of Cornish landscape history on which he is such an authority: he also introduced me to the richness of Bodmin Moor's archaeology. Eric Berry has been of great help on much more than vernacular buildings, not least in sharing his extensive knowledge of the greater houses and especially Cotehele and Trerice in memorable guided tours. John Stengelhofen has been equally generous with his unrivalled knowledge of industrial history and especially its technical detail as shown in his excellent drawing of the working of the Cornish engine house. He also contributed some of the gazetteer entries on C20 buildings. All of them have been patient with my incessant queries and understanding about the need for selectivity of their expert material.

On country houses Paul Holden of the National Trust has been my mainstay. He has not only readily shared the results of his meticulous research but has also read, discussed and commented constructively on my draft entries for all the major houses. Joanna Mattingly has been similarly generous in sharing her wide-ranging research: her perceptive observations have been invaluable especially in revising the accounts of medieval churches and their fittings. Michael Swift kindly allowed me access to his database on Cornish stained glass which proved indispensable in allowing me to make a selection from the vast amount of C19 glass: his database is a remarkable achievement which will be of enduring importance for future research. Canon Michael Warner, an old friend from our days at Salisbury Theological College, has been equally generous in sharing his pioneering research into the Faculty records of the Diocese of Truro as well as his unrivalled knowledge of J. P. St Aubyn. Paul Cockerham and Geoffrey Fisher have been most helpful on church monuments. The latter's attributions are denoted (GF) in the gazetteer.

I have had much help from national and local authorities. The staff of the National Trust have been unfailingly generous in their assistance at their many Cornish properties. English Heritage allowed me access to their assessments of architectural and historic significance of buildings for grant purposes. I should like to record the debt I owe to their architect, the late David Sumpster, who first introduced me to some of the major buildings of Cornwall. His perceptive reports and especially his sketch plans of buildings showing their evolution, often compiled on the train back to London after a brief visit, have often proved my best guide to the interpretation of a house. The staff of the Cornwall Record Office has been unfailingly helpful in answering our many queries. My greatest debt, however, is to Nicholas Johnson, former County Archaeologist, under whose inspirational leadership the Cornwall Archaeological Unit was established in the 1970s and gained a national and international reputation in subsequent decades for its work on all aspects of Cornish archae-ology and history. Its remarkable and influential output, the work of many dedicated and talented colleagues, is reflected in many places in this book: inter alia, it laid the foundations for the successful bid for World Heritage Site status for the Cornish Industrial Landscape. One hopes that the relatively new unitary Cornish Council will continue to recognize what a major contribution the Historic Environment Service (as it has now become) has made to the cultural life of Cornwall so that its vital work can continue. The Service has subsumed all the Conservation Officer expertise of the former District Councils: I have learned much from them, especially Nick Cahill, Terry Clark and Alyson Cooper. Their achievement deserves more recognition than it is usually given since they have often had to work in an inauspicious political climate.

There were other great helps. My early conversations with Veronica Chesher and Professor Charles Thomas, veteran contributors to the earlier editions of this book, proved highly instructive. My old friend, John Schofield (famously, and accurately, described in one report of the Historic Buildings Council in the 1960s as 'son of Godolphin') has been an indefatigable and perceptive researcher, commentator and correspondent about numerous buildings other than Godolphin, reflecting his lifelong passion for Cornish architecture and buildings represented not least in his joint founding of the Cornish

Buildings Group. I hope he will feel that something of the huge amount he has taught me over the years has found its way into these pages. That the statutory list for Cornwall contains such full descriptions of buildings owes much to him, Colin Harvey and Paul Richold of Architecton who supervised the re-survey of Cornwall in the 1980s with a distinguished team of investigators headed by Peter Chapman. John Thorp of Keystone has made available his excellent reports on several major buildings including Godolphin, Menabilly, Roscarrock and Star Castle.

Others who gave me help, either on specialist building types, architects, particular places or their own houses, included John Allan, John Armstrong, Sir John and Lady Banham, Julian and Isabel Bannerman, the late Andrew and Darcie Baylis, Elizabeth Bolitho, the Hon. Evelyn Boscawen, Favell and Helen Briggs, Neil and Ruth Burden, James and Fiona Colville, Ted and Sarah Coryton, Jim Edwards, Earl Falmouth, Anthony and Elizabeth Fortescue, James and Rebecca Fox, Richard Garnier, Jeremy and Caroline Gould, Andrew Harbert, Hazel Harradence, Elain Harwood, Richard Hewlings, Lady Mary and Geoffrey Holborow, Jill Hunter, Francis Kelly, John and Anthea Kendall, Tim and Elizabeth Le Grice, Amanda Le Page, Vanessa and Andrew Leslie, Liz Luck, Peter Mansfield, Lady Iona Molesworth St Aubyn, Nicholas Orme, Jeremy Pearson, Ronald Perry, Peter and Elizabeth Prideaux Brune, Sir Richard and Lady Rashleigh, Richard and Jill Richardson, Matt Robinson, Earl and Countess St Germans, Lord and Lady St Levan, Robert and Kate Sloman, Bill Sowerby, Father Theo and Mrs Jenny Thomas, Peter Tunstall Behrens, Stephen Tyrrell, Sir Ferrers Vyvyan and Michael and Sarah Williams.

There are a great number of other people to whom I am indebted, too many to mention here: I hope they will accept this general note of my gratitude. Cornwall is of course a delight to visit and, as an outsider, I should like to record how warm a welcome I received and how generous people have been with their time, knowledge and hospitality: I was refused access to only one major house. I should like to pay special tribute to the many people whose faithfulness and devotion keep Cornish churches open and welcoming to pilgrim and visitor. When I started on this book, the first to offer me hospitality were Felicity and Peter Pennycard at Treventon, St Columb Major, which proved a wonderful base from which to begin. Later on, Giles and Ginnie Clotworthy made me equally welcome at Trethew, Lanlivery, and introduced me to a wide range of owners and experts. When I began to explore the eastern part of the county Viscount and Viscountess Boyd at Ince were equally generous hosts: Alice Boyd, like Giles Clotworthy, also drove me all over Cornwall and facilitated access to many owners and houses that otherwise I do not believe I would have met or seen. Diana Marriott has been both hugely hospitable and a major support throughout: she accompanied me on many expeditions, became expert at negotiating access to locked churches, tested out some of the perambulations and offered me valuable critiques of some of my draft texts. Sir Richard and Lady Carew Pole kindly had me to stay at Antony and Richard drove me around the Rame penin-sula. Barbara Hargreaves gave me welcome hospitality while I was exploring the Helford area while Tessa Phipps arranged access to houses in that area. Rachel Hunt was similarly welcom-ing at Cotehele, Charles and Caroline Fox at Glendurgan, and the late General Sir Richard and Lady Trant at Lostwithiel.

Gavin Watson of the Buildings Books Trust raised funds and helped to establish connections, as well as supporting the project in numerous other ways. I owe a debt of real gratitude to Bridget Cherry who initiated me into the privilege of writing for this series through my contribution to the *Devon* volume. At Yale University Press Charles O'Brien has been an understanding and supportive editor whose wise critiques have greatly improved my text. As copy editor Katy Carter asked perceptive questions and clarified my draft. Sally Salvesen has always been encouraging, and working with Phoebe Lowndes, Production Editor, and Alice Winborn, Picture Researcher, has been a pleasure. At very short notice we were lucky to recruit Eric Berry, Peter Curno and James O. Davies to take the photographs. Their work is a major contribution to the picture of Cornish architecture I have tried to present in this book. The maps were expertly drawn by Martin Brown. But not a word I have written would have seen the light of day without the Herculean labours of Liz Page, my friend and former colleague at English Heritage, who has had the unenvi-able task over the last ten years of translating what she and my other colleagues used to call my hieroglyphics into a text. I shall be eternally grateful for her skill, patience and good humour.

This book has been over a decade in the making partly because of my preoccupation with other matters until 2011 and I am very conscious of the patience exercised by those in Cornwall who have assisted with the funding of its publication, especially the Tanner Trust and the Cornish Heritage Trust, which raised and co-ordinated many generous donations from within and without Cornwall. But the accolade for the most patient and persistent of all my supporters must go to my wife, Chrissie, and our daugh-ter, Rachel, who have endured my frequent and prolonged absences in Cornwall while they were left looking after our dogs – and so much more – as well as my virtual absence when I was at home writing day after day.

Despite all these extraordinary helps I must take full respon-sibility for the result which I am only too aware is far from perfect. As usual we invite readers to draw our attention to errors and omissions for a future revision.

Peter Beacham
December 2013

I have taken the opportunity offered by the need for an early reprint to make some minor corrections and am indebted to everyone who kindly sent suggestions for this purpose.

August 2014

INTRODUCTION

Cornwall is still a land apart, even if crossing the Tamar on the modern A30 at Launceston or by the rail and road bridges at Saltash has lessened the significance of the historic river border. Visitors soon sense this is different country, a perception reinforced as one travels westwards, the peninsula narrows, and both Atlantic and Channel coasts become visible from the higher ground. As the sky widens and the air becomes more luminous, the sea seems ever more present until the land runs out to leave only the faint prospect of the Scillies on the distant horizon. It is a land which has much in common with its Celtic neighbours Brittany, Ireland and Wales, has its own language, and has had a strong sense of its separate identity throughout history.

The sea has shaped Cornwall, its fisheries of huge importance over the centuries, the south coast and the Scillies historically significant in the defence of Britain, and its shining sands and blue seas in bays and coves between awesome cliffs long the lure for visitors. Inland Cornwall has an astonishing variety of landscape and townscape. Its geological complexity, discussed below, underlies the contrasts of scenery. The comfortable pastoral landscape of the Lizard is as different from the intricate ancient fieldscape of West Penwith as is the remote wildness of Bodmin Moor from the gently rolling hills and valleys of east Cornwall, or as the inhospitable grandeur of the north coast cliffs, broken only by the Camel and Hayle estuaries, is from the sheltered luxuriance of the tropic gardens in the south coast's long and deep estuaries of the Tamar, Lynher, Fowey, Fal and Helford. Here too are some of the richest prehistoric and medieval landscapes in Britain, on the granite uplands that stretch down the spine of the peninsula from Bodmin Moor to Land's End. And threaded through almost every landscape and the pattern of dispersed settlement is the pervasive evidence of Cornwall's industrial history that provided much of its wealth from the medieval period to the late C19, symbolized in the familiar forms of ruined engine houses, Methodist chapels and terraces of miners' houses. It is an illustrious history that has earned the Cornish industrial landscape World Heritage Site status, and which continues today in the raw beauty of the china clay country's vast spoil heaps near St Austell.

For most of its history Cornwall has not been an especially rich county and, especially after the collapse of the tin and copper industries in the mid to late C19, there was a tradition of outward migration, including emigration to the New World. This has been decisively reversed since the mid C20, the population increasing by 56 per cent between 1961 and 2011 to over 532,000. Contrary to its image as a predominantly rural county, the majority of the population lives in urban areas, of which the largest are the Camborne–Pool–Redruth conurbation at 55,000, St Austell (the largest single town) at 35,000, and Falmouth–Penryn at 33,000. Truro, the county town, stands at 23,000, Penzance 21,000, Newquay 19,000, Saltash 16,000, and the former capitals of Cornwall, Bodmin and Launceston, 15,000 and 12,000 respectively. Of the other resort towns St Ives is the largest at 12,000 but most of the others, like Fowey, Padstow and Looe, are 5,000 or less, and there are many other historic towns – Hayle, Liskeard and Lostwithiel for example – with populations far less than 10,000.

Cornwall's urban history is as rich and varied as its landscape and, because almost all its historic towns have survived the late C20 population surge remarkably intact, they are very rewarding in their architecture and townscape. They range from places like Fowey, Launceston, Lostwithiel and Penryn with their medieval town plans, through East Looe with its streets of C16 and C17 town houses, Truro's gracious C18 streets, to the surprising variety of C18–C20 Penzance buildings, and the exuberance of Newquay's resort architecture: large or small, they are consistently visually delightful. Architecturally the C19 is especially well represented, and not just in the towns that were the centres of the major industrial areas like Redruth and St Austell. But most visitors will start their exploration in the countryside, in the medieval religious landscape of inscribed stones, crosses, holy wells and churchtowns – the isolated church, and a farmhouse and perhaps a few cottages – or in the picturesque Cornwall of the small fishing port gathered round its little harbour. The C17–C19 mansions of the mining magnates like the Boscawens' Tregothnan or the Robartes's Lanhydrock are spectacular, but Cornwall is also the county of the small C16–C17 gentry house that has often survived as a farmhouse. It is true, as Pevsner observed in the first edition of this book, that in Cornwall the setting is often as memorable as the architecture, but this only makes it the more enjoyable, for as he said, there is 'much that is lovable and much that is moving'.

GEOLOGY AND BUILDING MATERIALS
BY SARAH BUCKINGHAM

In this most untypical of counties, where timber was not available in any great amounts and the use of brick is not widespread, STONE is the dominant theme. Yet it is not the usual limestones and sandstones of other counties, but a mellow palette of grey, cream and even pink granites; beige, ochre, brown and purple slatestone; and the dark blue-grey and silver of Delabole slate. The rolling Cornish landscape's turbulent and complex geological history has been the subject of many extremely competent and detailed accounts, but some interpretation is required to understand its effect on building traditions.

It is worth beginning by noting the local names for building stones: besides their obvious poetry these provide useful terms for groups of rock types. WHITE ELVAN refers to a group of fine-grained, acid igneous rocks, sometimes known generically as Pentewan stone after one particularly famous source, notwithstanding the fact that in varied forms they are quarried in a number of locations across the peninsula, and may also be known by the names of those sources. There is also KILLAS – slatestone – and BLUE ELVAN or 'greenstone', which encompasses a number of unusual basic igneous rocks. Some earlier attributions of building stones in Cornwall may have misidentified them as types seen more typically elsewhere in England; for instance, white elvans have on occasion been mistaken for limestones, and indeed may perhaps have been used with that intent in fine C18 town houses such as those in Lemon Street in Truro. Both the unusual pink porphyry seen in a few contexts in Cornwall and serpentinite have sometimes historically been described as 'marble', although they are technically nothing of the sort. 90

Medieval churches are a rich source for understanding of the characteristic usage of building stones in Cornwall, and often reveal the relationship between the components of a building and choice of material. For those built or extended before the arrival of the railways the bulk of the masonry tends to be representative of local materials, as stone is heavy and hard to transport by land, while window tracery and arcading, slightly more portable, may be a more unusual or decorative choice – a fine granite or white or blue elvan, for instance. Fonts and fine funerary sculpture may represent the most prestigious building stone within the wider locale, but being more portable still may also come from a distance within Cornwall or south-west England. Places with good access to rivers or the sea reveal materials from even further afield, including imports from France such as Caen limestone.

Cornwall is justifiably famous for its GRANITES. Generally hard and resistant to weathering, they appear throughout the peninsula in the masonry of domestic and agricultural buildings, often as small, roughly dressed blocks laid to course and of a granular, grey appearance, or more finely dressed and regular coursed blocks in churches, larger houses and public buildings. The same granite, often of highly polished appearance, was later exported from the county for use in prestigious architectural or engineering projects such as bridges, harbours or public buildings. Although often too coarse and hard for fine carving, granite is seen again and again in simple decorative capitals in the arcades of typical Cornish churches and in medieval carved fonts: its use in the profuse decoration of St Mary Magdalene, Launceston,

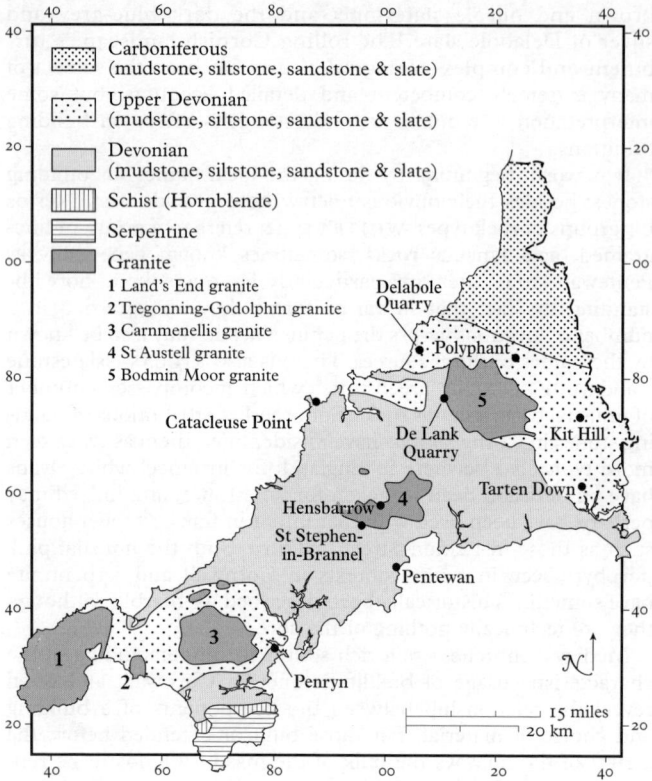

Geological map of Cornwall

the S aisle of the cathedral at Truro, and the tower of Probus church is entirely exceptional.

Granites are crystalline rocks which formed from the cooling of molten magma, and typically contain white or pink feldspars, grey quartz and dark biotite mica or pale muscovite mica, with a texture dependent on the rate at which they cooled. In Cornwall they were intruded when the Cornubian granite batholith thrust up from below into the existing rocks, mainly Devonian mudstones, during the Late Carboniferous/Early Permian period. This now breaks the surface along the spine of the peninsula in a series of five huge bosses, or plutons which, from E to W, are Bodmin Moor, St Austell, Carnmenellis, Land's End and the Isles of Scilly, plus a number of smaller outcrops including Carn Brea, Godolphin, Kit Hill and Hingstone Downs. Upland areas often display tors, characteristic features of a granite landscape created by a distinctive pattern of granite decay along the vertical and horizontal joints which, when exposed by erosion, resemble stacks of huge flat pebbles: the Cheesewring on the SE flank of Bodmin Moor near Minions is an especially memorable example. The debitage around them may also have been an early source of portable building material. Various schemes for classifying Cornish granites have been developed, but the majority are characterized by black biotite flakes and an overall grey appearance, of which De Lank granite, seen in the church at St Breward, is a typical example. In all the granite locations a range of textures from coarse to fine are present, although the particularly distinctive granites with large elongated crystals, phenocrysts, created by slow cooling, are found only in the Land's End and St Austell plutons, visible, for example, in a number of buildings in Chapel Street, Penzance. Fine-grained examples include St Stephen's granite, a lithium mica variety, which is white in colour and can be seen in church arcading in St Columb Major, Charlestown and Duloe churches and Truro cathedral, and Tregonning granite, best observed in the colonnade of Godolphin House. Luxulyanite granite is an attractive aberration of pink feldspar phenocrysts set in a matrix of fine black tourmaline and biotite, which is used for internal ornamental work, including in the Porphyry Hall at Place, Fowey, and the Duke of Wellington's tomb in St Paul's Cathedral.

Chemical decay of granite has given rise to the bounteous mineral deposits which were a source of Cornwall's early richness and later industrialization. Hydrothermal mineralization in and around the cooling masses in some places deposited metaliferous lodes in fissures in the surrounding rocks, notably the Great Flat Lode south of Carn Brea, which, as the name suggests is vast and of a low angle of tilt, and which gave rise to a landscape punctuated with engine houses, the residium of its industrial heyday. In other places the granite has decayed to create china clay, which began to be exploited in the mid C18, beginning with the Tregonning deposits identified by William Cookworthy of Plymouth, to feed a hunger for Chinese-style porcelain. The extensive mining of china clay in the C19 is the source of the otherworldly landscape of conical spoil tips N of St Austell, dwarfed now by the vast plateaus and scarps of modern extraction. Another chemical alteration was tourmalinization, where mica and eventually feldspar were replaced by tourmaline to form dense, dark quartz-schorl, of which Roche rock is the best example.

Loose blocks and pieces of granite, 'moorstones', often very large and easily found on the surface of the Cornish uplands, were used from earliest times in the many standing stones, stone circles and chambered tombs of the Cornish uplands, in early field boundaries and enclosures, as single slabs for packhorse bridges, and for that most iconic of Cornish features, the Celtic cross. The remains at Chysauster indicate a very early and relatively sophisticated use for domestic structures. With the development in the medieval period of cleaving using 'wedge and groove' and improved dressing, larger moorstones and shallow local workings could be exploited for more finished pieces, including door jambs and window surrounds. More commercial quarrying began to take off in the C18 with the work of the Trelevens at Hensbarrow quarry and of others, while the development of Penryn Quarries in the Carnmenellis district created a market for engineering granite in the first half of the C19. However, following rapid expansion it was the latter half of the C19 which saw the zenith of granite extraction and export in Cornwall, peaking around 1880. There were major quarries such as the Cheesewring (Minions), Kit Hill, NE of Callington, De Lank, near St Breward, and numerous small quarries, all serviced by the railway, river and canal infrastructure. Increasingly mechanized, they quarried and dressed blocks for use throughout the world. Competition from Scandinavian quarries at the beginning of the C20 saw activity wane, hastened by the outbreak of the First World War, and the story of the rest of the century was one of decline. Although some quarries remain in use today, mainly for the extraction of roadstone, it is the sheer cliffs and abandoned blocks of disused quarries, rapidly reclaimed by nature, that stand as an imposing reminder of past glory.

The WHITE ELVANS are closely associated with granite masses, extruded around them in straight, often long, dykes, and are of similar composition but generally very finely grained. The best known is Pentewan stone, although similar stones from other sources are also widely used. They can range in colour from creamy to a banded russet caused by iron staining. They are generally resistant to weathering and easily carved, and so used to great effect internally, as in the nave arcading at St Columb Major. Externally, they are employed for fine carved decoration, as in the tower of St Austell parish church, while their fine texture encouraged the use of Newham stone, another variety, in the polite architecture of the C18 and C19 houses of Lemon Street in Truro. A coarser variety is found in the SE of the county where it appears in a number of churches, including Linkinhorne and St Germans, while another variation is the distinctive yellowy-orange 'Growan', seen exclusively at Trerice and Newquay. Tremore stone is 'porphyritic', that is with phenocrysts of white feldspar and quartz in a pink matrix, and used to great aesthetic effect for internal work alongside Luxulyanite such as the Porphyry Hall, Place, Fowey.

The BLUE ELVANS, or greenstones, also derive from dykes or sills, but differ considerably in composition from granite, being rich in dark ferromagnesian minerals, and lacking the light colouring of quartz and feldspar. They tend too to be fine-grained and resistant to weathering. The most famous variety is CATACLEUSE (or Cataclews) stone, a dense rock which when freshly broken, polished or unweathered is a dark green colour and when weathered can take on a browny-red tinge. In its unpolished form it may exhibit a 'talcy' bloom. It is found in a single outcrop at Catacleuse Point near Padstow, where it was extracted from a cliff quarry. Its use is largely confined to the north coast and parishes in that vicinity, but more portable items such as fonts in Catacleuse have been found further afield. Its attractive appearance and facility for fine carving made it the choice for a number of surviving virtuoso works commissioned for churches in north Cornwall, including the chest tomb – now reused as a reredos – at St Issey, and the chest tomb at St Endellion, both

70

31, 41

of around 1400. The slightly later font at Padstow is another outstanding example. The most spectacular monumental use of Catacleuse is in the tomb of Prior Vivian at Bodmin of 1533. 65 Catacleuse was also deployed more substantially and unpolished in church interiors, for instance in arcading at Mawgan-in-Pydar and St Merryn, and in exteriors such as the window tracery in St Petroc, Padstow, now thickly coated in a bloom of red and yellow lichen. The contrast between dark Catacleuse and paler granite was employed to decorative effect, for instance in the distinctive banded church tower at St Eval, which similarly displays an unusual chequered effect in its porch. Still crisp exterior carving in this stone includes the angels with shields at St Merryn, stops on the hood moulding of the w door at St Issey, and detailing to the porch of St Petroc in Padstow.

POLYPHANT, another blue elvan, is an attractive greenish-grey stone with small pink phenocrysts. When unpolished it too shows a talcy bloom, and it polishes lustrously. It weathers very poorly, characteristically delaminating, but nonetheless has been used in exteriors, as at Altarnun church. However, it is in interior work that it comes into its own, for instance in the south arcade of Lewannick church, the delicate foliate carving of the s arcade at 13 St Swithin and St Andrew, Launcells, or the highly polished South African War Memorial by the w door of Truro Cathedral. Promotion of local building materials in the Arts and Crafts tradition by the *Seddings* in the late c19 saw extensive use of Polyphant, for instance at Roche and in St Elwyn, Hayle, while the early c20 saw *Comper* use this material to great effect for decorative elements in the interior of St Michael, Newquay.

KILLAS – slatestone – sits alongside granite as one of the most commonly seen building stones in Cornwall. It is the Devonian mudstone metamorphosed by heat and pressure to exhibit a compressed, fissile form. It can vary hugely in quality, texture and colour, and is extensively used in rubble walling as flat pieces, but can be seen more carefully dressed and coursed or laid to course: the relatively fine buff to russet coloured killas, for example, is prevalent in the priory, church and secular buildings of all ages in Bodmin. Often used in association with quoins and dressings in brick or granite, it very occasionally occurs in ashlar form in large houses, such as Menabilly, where variations in colour are also exploited to decorative effect. Biscovey stone, seen in St Mary the Virgin, Par, and nowhere else, and distinguished by its pink colour, is a unique variation.

A very distinctive use of killas is in the Cornish hedge, which is in fact an earth bank enclosed with stone walls and then allowed to become grown over with vegetation. Although local stone types predominate according to location, in killas areas it is most conspicuously used by taking advantage of the naturally flat and narrow form of individual stones to create attractive herringbone patterning.

SLATE, or helling or healing stone as it was also known in Antiquity, is part of the Devonian group of rocks, differing only from killas in its ability to be split into denser and better defined layers, ideal protection from rainwater. There are a number of different sources of slate, including Carnglaze, Tintagel and, most famously, Delabole. Dark blue-grey, almost navy at times, Delabole slate weathers to a silvery sheen and was extracted from at least the C15 for export to the rest of Cornwall, and later to London, the South of England and abroad. Slate roofs were laid as scantles, in carefully calculated diminishing courses, and pegged to timber battens, or rags, wider than they are deep, or in small random pieces. Failing roofs were sometimes treated with a cement or bituminous slurry. Slate-hanging was also used in parts of the county as an additional layer of weather proofing both on solid walls and especially on the slight timber-framed fronts of later C18 and C19 houses, sometimes with decorative elements and normally nailed into wooden battens with mortar bedding at the top – good examples can be seen in St Columb Major, Launceston and Padstow. Floors of large slate slabs are a familiar later element of many traditional pubs, farmhouses and churches. Exquisitely carved late C16 and early C17 slate monuments are a speciality of Cornwall, while beautifully lettered headstones of the C17, C18 and C19 abound in churchyards.

The Lizard peninsula presents a localized highly distinctive complex of rocks which have been metamorphosed by the upward thrust and heating of a section of ocean floor. Many, such as hornblende schist, are unsuited to extensive use in building; of those that have been used, SERPENTINITE, or serpentine, stands out because of its distinctive speckled and squamous appearance and exotic red, green or black colouring, reminiscent of snakeskin. It is, however, flawed, literally, as a building stone, shot through with bands and spots of different serpentine minerals, and likely to crack when exposed to extremes of temperature. Nonetheless, dressed serpentinite blocks have been successfully used in the Lizard, notably in Grade and Landewednack churches, and in the C19 serpentine factories at Poltesco and Penzance. Its history of use for souvenirs and decorative items means it is seen extensively in internal use locally: the lectern and pulpit at Grade church and the font, lectern and pulpit in Coverack church are fine examples, and further afield, examples include mantelpieces and pedestals at Osborne, Queen Victoria's house on the Isle of Wight. GABBRO is a hard, coarse to medium-grained stone, dark blue-grey, found around St Keverne, and capable of dressing to an angular finish. It was used historically in buildings, walling and sea defences.

The SE of the county also exhibits very characteristic variations. Around Saltash a number of peculiarly local stones are often seen in use together, including grey-green volcanic TARTEN DOWN STONE, geologically identical to the Hurdwick stone of the Tavistock area of Devon E of the Tamar; a very rough vesicular white elvan; and a pale grey Polyphant-like stone with pink phenocrysts. The palette of stones in St Germans church is an early example, particularly of the use of Tarten Down stone, but many other churches in the area, including that at Saltash itself, also show this combination. Further S and E, around

Kingsand, a deep red, fine-grained rhyolite lava and deep red sandstone are ubiquitous in roughly dressed blocks and rubble masonry.

Indigenous LIMESTONE is rare in Cornwall, and only used in extremely localized circumstances; where limestone is used, it is more often than not imported. Fine creamy Caen stone was an early import from France, brought in on the back of trading in tin, as seen in Lostwithiel church. Beer stone from Devon, a grey-white chalk, became more common in the C14 and C15, particularly in churches with a close connection with the Exeter Cathedral workshop, where it is used extensively for discrete architectural elements such as window tracery, nook-shafts, sedilia and funerary architecture (St Ive, St Germans and Sheviock): it was also employed at Glasney College and Launceston Priory. Coarser yellow Ham Hill stone from Somerset may also be seen in later buildings, such as the Public Rooms in Bodmin, while distinctive red-veined, grey Plymouth limestone was brought in for use as dressed blocks in C19 houses, chapels and banks. Of the occasional early uses of Plymouth limestone, the C15 exterior masonry of St Mary, Botus Fleming, and the flags in the kitchen at Cotehele House are notable. Bath stone and Portland stone are rarely present.

SANDROCK, a very young Quaternary rock, is seen in the N of Cornwall around Newquay. Unlike sandstone, it consists of beach sand cemented together with calcium carbonate, and has a rough open-pored texture and yellowy or grey appearance. Not perhaps the most attractive, nor the hardest of building stones, its most visible use is in the masonry of Crantock church.

Although limited, the use of BRICK in the Cornish building tradition may have been underestimated. While brick was a late arrival, in the pre-railway age most towns had a small brickworks, and large brick chimneystacks can often be noted rising above the roofs of C18 shops and town houses, for example in Fore Street, Bodmin. There is a scatter of significant buildings in brick. Probably the oldest is The Keep at Golden Manor, of small red C16 bricks with diaper work formed from burnt headers. Other examples include the remains of the great C17 house of the Grenvilles at Stowe, Kilkhampton, comprising a fine and well-jointed stretch of garden wall in dark orange brick; the mellow mid-C17 brick of Ince Castle; and the dark red pavilions and wall at Trewithen, an C18 house constructed in brick made from the brickearth extracted to form the ornamental lake. By way of contrast is the later creamy-buff brickwork of the China clay districts, for instance the C19 Hicks Brewery building in St Austell. Brick and decorative terracotta, sometimes imported especially from Ruabon in Wales, were to become much more prevalent in the C19, especially significant in the commercial streets of towns like Newquay, and used to great effect by Silvanus Trevail. 74

A dearth of suitable trees and the prevalence of a handy alternative in the form of stone meant that the use of TIMBER in Cornwall was never ambitious; smaller scantlings allowed smaller spans and much lighter framing, so timber buildings and substantial roof structures are limited. Such was its scarcity that tales of timbers being reused from salvaged ships may not be entirely apocryphal, as is suggested by the survival of wooden pegs, 'treenails', in timber members with no apparent relationship to the current structure in alignment or spacing. An interesting use of timber is in the composite construction seen in merchants' housing of the late C16 and early C17 in Fowey and East Looe, where timber-framed frontages, jettied and with horizontal windows of evident quality, rest on a stone ground floor, flanked by solid side walls. This construction of show frontages is an expression of prestige: much more extensive and workaday are the slighter, timber-framed front walls of C18 and C19 town buildings covered in slate cladding or render, widespread but most noticeable in Bodmin, Launceston and St Columb. Both at Fowey and Looe, the trading connection cannot be accidental.

Though not found as ubiquitously as it is in Devon, COB, a mixture of mud, chopped straw and small stones or slate fragments, was also often used in composite structures to create the upper floors on a substantial stone base, as well as alone in houses and walls. Once rendered over and painted, it is difficult to detect unless wall finishings are removed, and its use may therefore have been more extensive than is immediately obvious. The traditional method of construction was in stages, or lifts, with no shuttering, and walling was finished with limewash or clay render to protect it from weathering. It is often associated with slate capping or thatch, where the broad eaves would throw rainwater away. Obvious examples of cob construction may be seen in Helston, and on the Lizard, where a tradition of modern cob construction is developing. Although the use of THATCH seems counterintuitive in such a warm and damp climate as that of Cornwall, it would have been extensively used alongside slate, and employed the wheat reed common to the West Country, plain ridged. Good examples can be seen in Crantock, Cadgwith and Helford.

Render was used extensively to cover rough masonry, while STUCCO too was used in the C18 and C19 to present a good face on polite domestic and commercial architecture constructed in stone rubble, a fine example being the late C18 and early C19 resort suburbs W of the medieval centre of Penzance.

Part of the local distinctiveness of many places in Cornwall is derived from the use of characteristically local materials for street or path surfaces. In Penzance, for instance, granite paving is incised with distinctive honeycomb or fishnet patterns, presumably to reduce slipping. The use of grey and white banded or red gneiss and troctolite cobbles is a distinctive feature in the paths and walls of Lizard coastal settlements. Large irregular crystals of quartz or feldspar, 'sparstones', perhaps by-products of mining or quarrying, were also used to create slightly uneven surfaces to yards and paths, and in walling and Cornish hedging, as seen in the Boscastle area.

Another notable industrial material is SCORIA, a waste product of metal smelting and casting. Very dark brown or blue-black, with a vitreous sheen, it is ubiquitous in Hayle in the quayside, foundry and various industrial buildings. It was cast in large rectangular moulds to form regular blocks, which are used in Phillack churchyard building and walls. 'Mundic' is a term used to describe the deterioration of CONCRETE building blocks which incorporated poor quality aggregates including pyrites and iron sulphide, residues from the mining industry, which caused premature deterioration by generating sulphuric acid on contact with water. Such blocks were used in Cornwall from the early to mid C20, in the absence of mass concrete or brick.

THE CORNISH LANDSCAPE:
PREHISTORIC TO EARLY MEDIEVAL
BY PETER HERRING

Prehistory

Prehistoric life and land use in what is now Cornwall developed throughout its diverse landscape. The quantity and quality of what has survived later change has long been appreciated and celebrated. Studies made since 1970, including large-scale surveys (especially of Bodmin Moor, Scilly and West Penwith), and analysis of artefacts, structures and landscape, including in lowland Cornwall, have deepened knowledge and understanding of Cornish prehistory. It is now thought that population levels might have reached the tens of thousands by the end of the second millennium B.C. and over one hundred thousand by the end of the first. Prehistoric Cornwall can no longer be regarded as a fairly empty and simple place where people, from the Mesolithic period to the later Iron Age, endured 'nasty, brutish and short' lives. As early as the fourth millennium B.C., many were mastering various crafts and industries, undertaking increasingly long-distance exchange and, of particular interest to this volume's readers, building substantial and elaborate structures and creating complex earthworks.

While much prehistoric behaviour is no longer seen as determined by survival, understanding motivations is not easy. Prehistoric Cornwall's structures are better recorded and more closely dated, but, most intriguingly for their visitors, the reasons for their construction and the stories of their use and reuse are often less certainly known. 'Huts' are now seen as houses, and tombs as more than simple repositories for the dead, while forts (like medieval castles) are increasingly regarded as places of gathering and arenas for pleasure, rather than retreats from danger. Few sites can be regarded as purely ritual, ceremonial, domestic, industrial or defensive. Visitors are encouraged to be both cautious in their assumptions and imaginative in the way they participate in understanding the past by pondering ranges of interpretive possibilities, many of which lie well beyond the obvious definitions suggested by antiquarian labelling.

Well-preserved prehistoric complexes survive best in the granite uplands, especially Bodmin Moor and West Penwith. Middle Bronze Age lanes lead from houses through fields to surrounding commons where stone rows and circles stand in apparently understandable relationships with cairns and standing stones, hills and tors. Such is their coherence that walks through prehistoric complexes can be devised (one perambulation, at Roughtor, is included within the gazetteer). These may replicate how prehistoric people also moved through their inherited and created worlds; monuments, again like buildings, are often best understood when experienced in their landscape, itself partially a mental construction in prehistoric and modern minds.

One delight of exploring prehistoric sites is observing or imagining the ways early people responded to the particularities of place, or landscape. Some of these responses were broadly functional, like establishing viable farms on reasonable land and orienting house doorways away from wet weather and towards the light. But there are also examples of the thoughtfully designed inclusion in structures and views (including from doorways) of valued features inherited from ancestors or predecessors, and apparently significant natural elements of the world. Although emphases changed from the Neolithic to the Iron Age, nature and the past clearly always had special meaning and value to prehistoric people in Cornwall. Care was often taken to arrange buildings and monuments so that, as they were either approached or used, older monuments or significant natural features like rocks, tors and hills were revealed or highlighted, celebrated or revered. One result is that we rarely find simple single-episode prehistoric sites: they usually reveal several phases, such as episodically constructed monuments or complexes in which elements were introduced in succession.

Simple handaxes – a few chance finds – show that PALAEO-LITHIC people moved, while gathering and hunting wild food, around Cornwall's tundra, prairie or forest in the hundreds of thousands of years of glacial and interglacial periods. No occupation or activity sites have been found. During the first half of the ten thousand years since the last Ice Age, MESOLITHIC people continued to gather food and hunt, creating sophisticated flint tools (scatters are found in all parts of Cornwall) as they increasingly manipulated nature (encouraging, burning and guiding). They would probably have remarked on, remembered, and created meaningful or reverential relationships with 'natural monuments', like granite tors, and may even have created simple cultural monuments, like some of the PROPPED STONES, which are slabs manoeuvred onto smaller stones to create permanent visual relationships (through pointing or framing) with those natural monuments.

The earliest Neolithic people of the early fourth millennium B.C. apparently mimicked nature's monuments, the tors, when using larger slabs for supports and capstones of chambered tombs (known locally as QUOITS), whether these were simple boxes like Chun (Morvah) and Mulfra (Madron) or more complex 'portal dolmens', like Zennor and Trethevy. Quoits were often carefully located just where significant tors could be seen protruding above intervening hills: Mulfra and Chun quoits are sited precisely where the topmost rocks of Carn Galva, a broadly contemporary tor enclosure, are distantly skylined. Move just a few steps from these quoits and those rocks disappear. The more limited views from lower-lying quoits suggest these may have been used and perceived differently from those on the higher ground. Early prehistoric chambered tombs are found along western Europe's Atlantic fringe and our understanding of their use depends in part on excavations in other areas where soils less acid than those in Cornwall allow human bone to survive. They seem to have been ancestral resting places, ossuaries in which selected bones from numerous individuals were placed, perhaps after excarnation. Dead bodies may have been laid on the quoits' capstones to have their flesh stripped by carrion birds.

3

Quoits and propped stones were of local significance when compared with TOR ENCLOSURES, the Early Neolithic's pre-eminent gathering places. The Cornish equivalents of the cause-wayed enclosures found further E in England, these had banks or lines of stones, piled or set up on edge, running between tors and boulders, to define irregular spaces within which scooped platforms may have contained simple wooden buildings. Excavations of enclosures at Carn Brea and Helman Tor confirmed fourth millennium B.C. dates and unearthed artefacts of types which were traded over very long distances and whose manufacture was associated with especially dramatic places: axe-heads of greenstone prised from Cornish coastal outcrops, pottery of gabbroic clay dug from the furthest corner of the Lizard, and flints gathered from Cornwall's beaches or brought hundreds of miles from England's chalk cliffs and downs. Stories of hazardous procurement were probably passed on with, and gave additional value to, these objects.

Their wide spacing, the effort required for their construction and the capacity of the spaces enclosed suggest that tor enclosures were used by extensive communities. Hundreds or even thousands of people may have descended on them at certain moments in the year, possibly fixed by solar events and marked by rituals associated with seasons and tors, and through them with ancestors and territory. As well as exchanging material, these gatherings provided opportunities for a range of activities, such as resolving disputes, feasting, socializing, finding life partners, making friends, gossiping, and performing rites of passage and initiation ceremonies. Another function might have been defence against other communities or groups, as suggested by evidence of an attack upon Carn Brea.

Trade, ceremony, and the communal effort required to construct Early Neolithic structures indicate an organized society that may also have been at one with the natural environment, most food still being obtained by nomadic gathering, hunting, fishing and trapping. People were not yet living in permanent settlements. Chambered tombs and LONG CAIRNS, trapezoidal stony mounds surviving in upland Cornwall (like Catshole, *see* Bolventor, and Louden Hill, *see* Roughtor), were important fixed points within extensive territories around which individuals and groups moved as the seasons offered changing opportunities. The façades and antechambers at one end of the long cairns and PORTAL DOLMENS (like Zennor, Trethevy and Lanyon) suggest people returned for performances we might characterize as rituals. These presumably attracted more local gatherings than those at tor enclosures, the denser distributions of quoits and long cairns suggesting they belonged to smaller communities. Rituals honouring the dead or their spirits, the ancestors, helped secure individuals within communities, themselves tied to place and thus territory via carefully placed monuments.

The Neolithic has customarily been regarded as the period when agriculture arrived in Britain, but recent reviews of evidence suggest that domestication in Cornwall was at first, and for over two thousand years, largely confined in practice to greatly reducing woodland in order to create extensive open grazings, effectively commons, for domesticated livestock. There is, however, a little excavated evidence for Neolithic small-scale cultivation (charred grains, querns, rubbing stones) and even a few early small stone-banked garden-sized fields high on the NW slopes of Roughtor on Bodmin Moor. That mountainous hill seems, from the numerous monuments set up on it and in relation to it, to have been the secular and religious focus of Neolithic and Bronze Age east Cornwall. Builders of a fine tor enclosure and a 1,263-ft (385-metre) long Neolithic BANK CAIRN, unaware of geological processes, appear to have paid homage to what they imagined to be their fantastically powerful forerunners, effectively giants, who constructed the massive tors along the mountain's summit ridge.

Cultivation may itself have been regarded as magical by people accustomed to gathering wild food. Placing tiny seeds into the earth of their most special hill might have represented another potentially fruitful ritual; but it was a false dawn for agriculturalists, and nomadic pastoral life persisted.

The later third and early second millennia B.C. saw the construction of great numbers of remarkably varied ritual and ceremonial structures. Those monuments indicate the continued importance to early communities of meanings in their worlds that transcended the mundane. With some revealing exceptions, they less obviously incorporate and mimic natural features, and are more clearly distinguishable as human constructions. They are generally found on open ground, usually some distance from tors, referencing them only by orientation and revelation. Many are more architectural, involving careful design, and most are of broad types constructed over large parts of Britain.

HENGES, circular enclosures defined by a ditch inside a broad bank, are generally regarded as gathering places used in ways similar to the earlier tor enclosures. The Stripple Stones henge on Bodmin Moor has a subtle but certain relationship with Roughtor. It contains one of Cornwall's largest STONE CIRCLES. Found mainly in western Britain, stone circles again seem designed for ceremonial and ritual gatherings, but the great variety among even the Cornish circles warns against imagining consistent rituals. Most, but not all, were erected south of significant tor-topped hills and while most are single circles, there are also four examples of multiple rings. Circles vary in size – 49 ft to 148 ft (15 to 45 metres) in diameter, with stones 1 ft to 6 ft (0.3 to 2.0 metres) high – and in circularity, with some perfect circles (perhaps laid out with peg and rope), but many others quite irregular, it having been sufficient simply to form a ring that made the ground within more special than the ground without. The Merry Maidens in St Buryan is a perfect circle of equally spaced stones of remarkably similar height and shape, but Fernacre (Roughtor) and Stannon (St Breward) are highly irregular on all counts. Most circles have stones spaced so that people can pass easily between them, but in others some stones virtually touch, blocking movement. Some circles have higher stones in certain parts of their rings, creating architectural emphases which suggest that different things were done in these parts of the site. A few have large central stones, again suggesting activities at the heart of the site.

STONE ROWS, e.g. the Nine Maidens, near St Columb Major, are sometimes associated with cairns and standing stones, beginning or ending at them. It seems likely that they were intended to be walked along, as significant tors or monuments appear or disappear from view when doing so. Terminal stones are often taller than the others and are sometimes set transversely to the line, closing it, but many rows have tiny stones, just a few inches high, indicating use when vegetation levels were lowest, perhaps in springtime. They also suggest grazing levels high enough to keep commons clear of scrub. Indeed, given their typical positions near downland edges, rows may have been used in ceremonies celebrating the important annual movement of livestock to upland commons.

Fewer STANDING STONES or menhirs are found in Cornwall's eastern uplands than in West Penwith, where their distribution is denser than anywhere else in Britain. Most are granite or quartzite, usually carefully selected slender triangles or pointed pillars, and most are between 5 ft and 11 ft (1.5 and 3.5 metres) high, but reach 16½ ft (5 metres) at the Pipers (St Buryan). Found from valley side to hilltop, they may be either isolated or incorporated in complexes of other prehistoric ritual and ceremonial monuments. This variety, coupled with excavated evidence, emphasizes that menhirs form another artificial classification. Burials or depositions (usually in pots) are rare and appear to be secondary (although some west Cornish menhirs investigated by C19 antiquarians apparently had cremations in their stone-holes). The axe-shaped and axe-carved menhir around which Boscawen-Un's stone circle (St Buryan) was arranged was probably intentionally angled, as it still is, like an axe-head chopping into the earth. Other standing stones may also have been decorated; a small number are perforated, most famously the Men an Tol (Madron), part of a stone circle. Small groups of standing stones forming no coherent pattern (circle, row, etc.), often apparently associated with other monuments, are sometimes referred to as STONE SETTINGS.

Excavations indicate that TIMBER MONUMENTS, either free-standing posts or rings or other arrangements of them, were also common, and not just in lowland Cornwall. The now removed Longstone Downs menhir (St Austell) replaced an earlier stone, itself replacing a large timber post. The surviving monuments with standing stones (menhirs, stone circles, stone rows, stone settings) appear to be the most permanent portion of a large suite of sites comprising vertically set objects. In addition, recent excavations have emphasized the importance of ritual PITS, often dug close to significant natural features, and usually backfilled with meaningful material including artefacts.

ENTRANCE GRAVES, found solely within West Penwith on the mainland and in larger numbers on Scilly, were once thought to be earlier Neolithic. They are now seen to date from this later phase of monument construction. These stone and earth mounds retained by kerbs could be revisited, having a drystone-walled passage reaching into the heart. This passage widened near the innermost end where the roof of large capstones was also slightly heightened, apparently to allow two or three people to crouch or sit, presumably to perform significant activities. Later prehistoric field systems were sometimes developed around entrance graves, which were often low-lying, and were carefully positioned in relation to other monuments or landscape features, including (on Scilly) the sea. Several in Zennor, like that at Pennance, were placed where the rocky peak at the seaward end of Gurnard's Head promontory was visible poking above the coastal plateau.

BARROWS (mounds of earth) and CAIRNS (mounds of stones), mainly of the first half of the second millennium B.C., again display great variety of form, scale and location. Over 3,500 have been recorded in Cornwall and thousands more will have been removed. Most survive as simple circular mounds of earth and stone, some kerbed with upright or laid stones, but most not. Mounds were sometimes constructed with alternating layers of distinctively coloured materials (yellow or white clay, black peat, brown earth), each colour on display for a period until covered by subsequent ones. They can range from 10 ft to 130 ft (3 to 40 metres) in diameter and from 1 ft to 21 ft (0.3 to 6.5 metres) in height; the larger ones are usually also the most prominently positioned, on hilltops or on false crests so that they are skylined when seen from the slopes below. Such mounds, like the Caradon (Minions) group, dominate and appear to mark places presumably regarded as territories.

Other cairns and barrows have more complex forms, and were clearly created in stages. Many are low circular platforms, some with narrow banked rims, some with smaller mounds placed centrally or eccentrically upon them. These platform cairns tend to be relatively inconspicuously sited, but in places from which significant views can be best appreciated, often incorporating Roughtor or other hills with Early Neolithic tor enclosures (Helman Tor, Carn Brea, Carn Galva). These were monuments to climb onto, return to and gather at for rituals and ceremonies to do with geographies that had accrued meanings, even sacredness, over the preceding centuries and millennia. Cairns at Leskernick (*see* Altarnun) were tied into arrangements first established two thousand years before, and those that referenced revered Neolithic hilltops may have had similar links. A few cairns actually incorporated tors and boulders, their builders treating these natural features with great respect, encircling the great cheesewring of Showery Tor (*see* Roughtor) with a large ring cairn, incorporating the tors of Tolborough and Little Roughtor into kerbs and encircling a prone stone at Craddock Moor to form a kerbed boulder.

Recent excavations of cairns and barrows have greatly extended their interest. Once simply regarded as places of burial, many cairns and barrows contain no sign of the disposal of the dead, which appears to have been just one of a wide range of rituals performed on the ground that was to be later sealed and marked by a mound. A circular area was often demarcated, but it was variously bounded (by posts, upright stones, ditch, bank and wall). What went on within left archaeological remains which are rarely, if ever, precisely repeated elsewhere, and these no doubt included elements of a wider liturgical suite of which some have left no trace. Much of the activity seems to have involved symbolism, and especially the reworking of material brought to the site from elsewhere, drawing the apparently mundane or domestic into the sacred. Some sites had their turf removed; some had one or more pits dug, into all or some of which objects (potsherds, stone, flint and metal artefacts) were placed; some had material, including earth and charcoal brought from elsewhere, scattered over parts of the area. Some did indeed have burials or cremations, the burials often contained within stone boxes or CISTS. Incorporated into a few entrance graves and cairns are CUP-MARKED STONES, slabs of granite or slatestone that have been carefully decorated with small circular or elliptical hollows. These appear to have been created and originally used elsewhere, being brought to the monuments as parts of the suite of symbolic reuses.

In west Cornwall several ring cairns lie within HILLTOP ENCLOSURES formed of low stony banks – Bartinney Castle (St Just-in-Penwith), Caer Bran (Sancreed), Castle an Dinas (Ludgvan) – the enclosure extending and also containing the area made sacred by the cairns.

While domestic material was drawn into cairns and barrows, there is still hardly any evidence of settlement in Cornwall before *c*. 1500 B.C. (just a single third millennium shelter excavated in Sennen and an early second millennium house at Gwithian). The second half of the second millennium saw a radical change, with construction of overtly ritual monuments falling away while permanent settlements of ROUND-HOUSES were widely established.

Recent excavations have confirmed what was long suspected, that Middle Bronze Age houses and fields were common in lowland Cornwall as well as on the granite uplands, where well-known extensive settlements survive. Moorland houses are stone-walled, but those in the lowlands tend to be set in shallow excavated hollows; the superstructures of all were of timber, and roofing was of organic material (probably thatch or hides). Some smaller buildings may have been non-domestic, but dwellings were usually large and well built, with evidence for separation of activity areas, some partitioning, levelled floors and careful drainage.

There is again variety in settlement and associated field and boundary patterns forms. This is best seen on Bodmin Moor where settlements may be embedded within either curvilinear or rectilinear field systems, while in the heart of the moor they may have either no field systems or just small pens. This variety suggests both specialization and seasonal use of resources like rough grazing. Analysis of Bodmin Moor's surviving complexes, including the long pasture boundaries progressively closing in the commons, reveals a complex multi-layered rural society, evidence for which is also seen in the variety and quality of pottery, carpentry and metalworking. Local production of tin, copper and other metals may have been carefully controlled to maintain their elite value.

Close examination of houses and settlements indicates that these were drawn into a ritualized world view. Excavated houses normally include evidence of formalized abandonment: meaningful artefacts (often deliberately broken) placed within pits, floors covered with stones, doorways blocked. But there is also evidence that houses were built with ritual in mind: most houses at Leskernick have an outsize stone, possibly a household shrine, built into the wall directly opposite the entrance. Some houses were carefully positioned in ways familiar from earlier prehistoric monuments: each of the hundred or more on the w side of Roughtor was placed so that the Neolithic bank cairn was sky-lined to their N. Inherited monuments – the quoits, circles, rows, cairns, etc., that would still have dominated the Middle Bronze Age landscape – may have been more than merely respected and curated: they may have also been revisited and reused.

The first millennium B.C., when the later Bronze Age ran into the Iron Age, saw commons extended again, with consequent emptying of upland settlements. People continued to live in loose hamlets of round-houses, set within lowland field systems that were reorganized, used more intensively, and even extended onto cliffs. Much of today's anciently enclosed land, covering about 60 per cent of Cornwall largely in the lowlands, was established by the end of this period when resources were being stretched as populations (of livestock as well as humans) increased. The earliest, simplest and most irregular HILLFORTS (like Trencrom, Lelant) may date from the first centuries of the millennium. Later examples are more regular, sometimes forming good circles, and often having several circuits of substantial banks and ditches (as at Killibury Castle). Many are not on hilltops but instead are HILLSLOPE FORTS on higher slopes, overlooking particular sectors of the landscape, presumably local territories: Pencarrow is tilted towards the Camel valley, and Warbstow Bury towards the Ottery and Upper Tamar.

Unlike some English hillforts, Cornish examples do not appear to have been large defended settlements; excavations find at most just a handful of buildings. Defence may well have formed one of their several functions (perhaps as refuges), but they are now widely regarded as later equivalents of the gathering places represented by Neolithic tor enclosures and Bronze Age stone circles. Indeed, the builders of several Cornish hillforts carefully respected surviving remains of earlier gathering places: ramparts were run concentrically around earlier hilltop enclosures at Caer Bran and the western Castle an Dinas (Ludgvan); barrows were contained within several others; and Chun Castle's original entrance was carefully oriented on nearby Chun Quoit. Hillforts thereby created signals of continuity, legitimizing their control or organization of those territories. As well as containing early equivalents of fairs, hillforts may have also hosted local parliaments at which decisions were taken regarding the organization of agricultural and other resources.

CLIFF CASTLES, promontories cut off by one or more lines of ditches and ramparts, were also built through the first millennium. Cliff castles were long seen as coastal equivalents of hillforts, and their interpretation reflects interestingly on understanding of the inland sites. Many cliff castles isolate highly inhospitable land, unlikely to have supported permanent settlement, although they could have been refuges when needed. Those adjacent to safe beaches may have been, in part, secure neutral ports used by Continental traders, best exemplified by the tin entrepôt *Ictis*, described by Diodorus Siculus. Such occasional use seems most likely, but the principal functions of cliff castles distant from beaches may have related more to the liminal or threshold qualities of rocky places jutting out from land to link with the weather and sea. Some, like Treryn Dinas (St Levan), have portions reached by passing through inner ramparts where activities took place in dramatic rockscapes often lashed by wind, rain and spray. Here are natural monuments, par excellence. Hillforts, hoisted high into Cornwall's rushing air, might also have also enclosed special, sacred places, and ritual and ceremony probably figured among the many other functions of gatherings at these enclosed sites.

From around the middle of the first millennium B.C. enclosed hamlets, known as ROUNDS, were created, usually in the anciently enclosed land where there were also unenclosed or open settlements. The round's encircling bank and ditch, *in extremis* a form of defence, must on most days have performed another function, that of distinguishing the hamlet's occupants from those who lived in the unenclosed settlements. Consequently they are now generally regarded as symbols of higher status within an increasingly hierarchical society. Some excavated rounds have yielded evidence of metalworking, tin and iron, but most appear to have been the homes of farming groups.

In west Cornwall are found FOGOUS, underground passages which were occasionally concealed within both enclosed and unenclosed settlements. These were either stone-walled with great roofing capstones (reminiscent of entrance graves) or tunnelled into the soil (or both, as at Pendeen) and had narrow, steeply sloping entrances, easily concealed. Passages curve so that activities at their further ends could not be seen and some fogous have two or more conjoined sections linked by constricted entrances, emphasizing secrecy. Carn Euny even has an underground corbelled circular chamber with a shrine-like alcove reached by the fogou. The effort expended in constructing these architecturally impressive communal structures indicates their importance. They may have been used for ritual, storage and defence (or refuge).

The Roman period

The Romans did come to Cornwall. Sites of FORTS have been identified at Nanstallon, near Bodmin, Calstock and near Restormel Castle, and two more have been suggested, at Lelant and St Hilary churchyards. All but Lelant (commanding St Ives Bay) are near the tidal limits of important rivers (the Camel, Tamar, Fowey and Hayle) that brought coastal traffic towards Cornwall's spinal ridgeway, good places for an invading power to establish authority and control. These discoveries reinforce the suggestion that the Romans first subdued and then worked with the people W of Exeter as a sort of client state, permitting many aspects of Dumnonian life to continue. They tolerated Cornish farming communities continuing to establish rounds (*see* above), complete with their apparent defences, and they created no towns. The only villa is the later C2 example with portico and projecting wings at Magor near Camborne. It is of irregular, almost vernacular, form and may have been built by someone who had only a generalized idea of what constituted a villa.

Significantly, no new hillforts and cliff castles appear to have been created in this period and most were abandoned, though not slighted. It seems that the use of hillforts and cliff castles as refuges and as organizational, ceremonial and ritual centres ceased and that Roman power, ideologies and ways held sway. On Scilly a Roman temple was established on St Mary's and a shrine on Nornour, but on the mainland the placement of several large collections of Roman coins in liminal, watery places like heads of creeks, or on tors, suggests continuation of some Cornish practices.

Rural settlements remained predominantly hamlets, some being enclosed as rounds, some open, and all usually set within intensively worked field systems, many of which were established in the first millennium B.C. Houses became more sophisticated, either ovoid with partially ridged roofs or multi-cellular, as in the C2 to C4 COURTYARD HOUSES of west Cornwall and Scilly. In these, a massive stone-faced earth bank up to 10 ft (3 metres) thick enclosed an irregularly oval structure up to 115 ft (35 metres) across, in which several conjoined rooms (dwellings, animal houses, workshops and stores) were arranged around a paved courtyard.

The early medieval landscape

In the post-Roman period (C5–C7), Cornwall continued with Devon as a society distorted by its experience of Mediterranean imperialism. When Devon was drawn into England, Cornwall was left for around a hundred years as an independent self-governing entity, before it too was gradually assimilated into England (C9–C11).

A post-Roman citadel established on Tintagel Island received imports from as far away as the eastern Mediterranean, and another may have been created on St Michael's Mount. These topographically distinctive and secure ports of trade were probably associated with those who administered post-Roman Cornwall, and post-Roman graves excavated in Tintagel's cliff-top churchyard suggest that they were to some extent Christianized. Archaeological evidence from elsewhere indicates continuation of pagan rites. STANDING STONES, inscribed and uninscribed, may have marked burials of important post-Roman individuals, but most people seem to have been interred in extensive unenclosed graveyards.

Distributions of early Cornish place-names and Christian remains indicate that people still dwelt largely in the anciently enclosed land, the well-drained lowlands and more sheltered upland valleys. Some rounds were in use until the C6 but from then on only Christian communities occupied the thick scatter of circular enclosures known as *lanns*. Farming communities probably lived in unenclosed hamlets. Around the C7 or C8, the cultivated parts of their land appear to have been subjected to an enormous reorganization, the brick-shaped fields inherited from later prehistory being dismantled and replaced with wholly new patterns. Small open fields subdivided into narrow unenclosed strips were possibly established when hundreds of settlements were given names prefixed with Cornish *tre*, 'farming estate', perhaps referring to the blocks of land worked communally by the hamlet's handful of households. Dwelling houses developed from the oval or sub-rectangular forms of the Roman period, so that by the end of the early medieval period there were rectangular PROTO-LONGHOUSES with cattle at the lower end and people at the upper, exemplified by those excavated at Mawgan Porth. Transhumance (in which individual members of the household accompanied grazing livestock to summer pastures), probably originating in the Middle Bronze Age, appears to have ceased in Cornwall in the later part of the first millennium A.D.

The ruins of several groups of up to a dozen small sub-rectangular single-person TRANSHUMANCE HUTS survive on Bodmin Moor. King Arthur's Hall (St Breward) was probably an impressively built pound, used for distraining livestock found grazing without permission on the extensive moorland pastures of Trigg hundred.

Early medieval Cornish economies are glimpsed rather than clearly seen. They can be discerned in the extensive and intensive farming systems and in the remains of complex diets on excavated settlements at Gunwalloe, Mawgan Porth and Gwithian, in the coastal workshops at Gwithian and Duckpool, near Bude, and in the substantial changes to local pottery styles and the sources of their clays. It seems likely that the diversified economy that characterized later medieval Cornwall had deep early roots. The rich late C9 hoard placed in a then operational tin streamworks at Trewhiddle, near St Austell, indicates not only that extractive industry was active, but also that great wealth could be accumulated in Cornwall. In the following century there is the earliest evidence of a Cornish town, at Bodmin. Other markets and thus proto-urban centres had been established by the time of the Norman Conquest at Marazion, Helston, Liskeard, St Germans and St Stephens by Launceston, and there may have been others, probably at important Christian centres.

MEDIEVAL TO MID-SEVENTEENTH-CENTURY ARCHITECTURE

Early Christianity in Cornwall

Christianity probably reached Cornwall in the C5–C6, of which the most visible evidence is in the form of the numerous INSCRIBED STONES of the C5–C11. Of the eighty or so stones known in Cornwall and Devon* around sixty are found in Corn-wall, with a particular concentration in West Penwith and a smaller cluster on Bodmin Moor around Cardinham. The inscriptions are mostly cut on pieces of undressed or roughly dressed stone (usually granite) known as PILLAR STONES with some other inscriptions on CROSS-SHAFTS and CROSS BASES. The earliest are in Ogham, the Irish stroke alphabet, inscribed along the margins of the stones, with later examples in both Ogham and Latin, and the latest in Latin only: they cannot be more precisely dated. Often lichen-covered, they are difficult to read: two of the most legible are inside the churches at Lewan-nick and St Kew. The texts prove that many of the pillar stones and some of the crosses commemorate important individuals.

---

*Only about nine stones are known elsewhere in England, in Dorset, Somerset, Hampshire, Shropshire and the Channel Islands.

Those bearing a cross, the chi-rho (XP) symbol or the formula *hic iacet* are clearly Christian, but it is far from certain that all of them belong to that tradition. Comparable stones occur in Wales and it likely that a major source of the Christianization of Cornwall came through settlers of Irish descent from SW Wales.

The wealth of Cornish church dedications to Celtic saints such as Piran, Petroc, Goran, Mewan, Winwaloe and Winnols has often been cited as suggesting missionary activity from Brittany and Ireland as well as Wales, though this too is far from certain. But in the C7 *Vita Sancti Samsonis* we have an insight into the life of a nomadic Welsh missionary, St Samson, who arrived from Wales in the Camel estuary, and made his way overland via the Camel and Fowey (known today as the Saints' Way) to sail across the Channel to Brittany. There are a few early MONASTIC CELL sites in remote locations known in Cornwall that bear some comparison with other Celtic cells of the period, of which the most evocative is the (now re-buried) C6–C7 St Piran's Oratory in lonely isolation among the massive dunes of Perran Sands; others are known archaeologically at Gwithian and St Levan. But evidence of early medieval church structures in Cornwall is scanty indeed.

It is, however, the CELTIC CROSSES, found in their hundreds at the roadside, in churchyards, towns, and in the open landscape, that are the most pervasive and memorable evidence of the presence of Christianity across medieval Cornwall. They were long considered to be pre-Conquest, but it is now believed that they began to be erected in the C9 with the majority dating between then and the C13, though documentary evidence suggests that some were still being put up as late as the mid C15. Two of the best pre-Conquest examples are St Piran's Cross near St Piran's Oratory, mentioned in a charter of 960, and King Doniert's Stone – a cross-shaft – near St Cleer, commemorating Doniert's death in 875. Most crosses are of granite and they are especially numerous on and around Bodmin Moor in the Cardinham area and in West Penwith around Sancreed, with smaller clusters in the parishes of Wendron and Lanivet. The most distinctive is the Celtic WHEEL-HEAD design, which has many variants, but there are significant numbers of HOLED CROSSES that are pierced right through, and numerous LATIN CROSSES. The most elaborate are the larger and more decorated CHURCHYARD CROSSES, the most finely sculpted being the late C15 LANTERN CROSSES as at Mawgan-in-Pydar and St Michael's Mount, both in Catacleuse stone. The shafts of earlier examples often display intricate patterns of interlace and knotwork designs. Their purpose is varied: the most common is the wayside cross to mark directions, and there are also a large number of boundary crosses. As noted above, some are memorial crosses and a few are true village or market crosses, though some of the latter have been adapted from wayside crosses. *In situ* crosses are rare, with many rediscovered, relocated and re-erected since the later C19, and more still coming to light today.

Cornish resistance to the Anglo-Saxon advance from Wessex is bound up with the half-legendary stories of the Cornish kings like Doniert as well as myths and legends like those of Tristan and Iseult (cf. the so-called Tristan stone near Fowey) and, most powerfully of all, with King Arthur, associated with Tintagel since Geoffrey of Monmouth's C12 *History of the Kings of Britain*. Tintagel is certainly now seen as a centre of royal power in early medieval Cornwall, though the castle buildings visible today are C14 and later. Of ANGLO-SAXON building in Cornwall nothing is visible. The most significant mark the Anglo-Saxons made on Cornwall was King Athelstan's establishment of the Tamar as the border between Cornwall and England in 936 accompanied by a separate Cornish diocese. It was a brief independence, the diocese being re-incorporated into that of Crediton in 1046.

The NORMAN Conquest saw the foundation of significant numbers of MONASTIC HOUSES in Cornwall. The first was the Benedictine priory of Scilly on Tresco in *c.* 1114, with other Benedictine houses at Tywardreath, Minster and St Michael's Mount in the first half of the C12. Five others were founded in the second half of the C12 and early C13: St Anthony-in-Roseland (Augustinian), St Carroc near Fowey (Cluniac), Lammas on Looe Island (Benedictine) and Tregony (Augustinian). All were small cells of a few monks, sometimes as few as two. Cornwall's three largest post-Conquest monastic foundations

Map of religious houses in Cornwall, 1100–1560

were pre-existing monasteries converted into Benedictine priories: Bodmin 1123–4, Launceston 1127 and St Germans in the early 1180s. Franciscan friars established a house at Bodmin between 1240 and 1260 while the Dominicans arrived at Truro in 1259. Three pre-Conquest minsters survived at Crantock, St Buryan and Probus. Of greater significance was the foundation of Glasney College at Penryn by Bishop Bronescombe in 1265, intended as a smaller version of the cathedral at Exeter.

There is hardly any evidence of almost all these Norman monastic houses, which makes what survives at St Germans the more exceptional. It is the most ambitious medieval church in Cornwall, and in its earliest parts wholly Norman. Although we have only a part of the C12 building, it is of impressive scale and design inside and out: a W front with the richest portal in the county flanked by N and S towers; the W end of the interior with the towers opening into the nave and aisles and the beginnings of the S aisle arcade on massive round piers with square scalloped capitals; and a clerestory whose windows with rich zigzag ornament are placed, most oddly, above the spandrels and not the apexes of the arcade, an arrangement taken up by a group of Cornish masons in the C14 (*see* Callington, Fowey and Lostwithiel).

Churches and furnishings

While not comparable in scale to St Germans, the parish churches of Cornwall offer a relatively rich repository of Norman work. Almost 209 parishes or parish-like areas are recorded in the first surviving list of Cornish churches of 1291 and about 140 churches still display Norman architecture or features, clear evidence of widespread construction or reconstruction at that period. Many were built or rebuilt within the earlier sub-circular *lann* enclosures that are comparable to the *lans* (holy enclosures) of Wales: the origin, evolution and purpose of *lanns* is a subject of continuing debate but many parish church sites show continuity of Christian occupation from the early medieval period. The most characteristic image of the rural Cornish church is of it standing almost alone in the landscape in its small churchtown with only a farm or a few cottages.

Many Norman churches were indeed in remote locations but this did not imply a lack of ambition in their builders. The simplest were of two-cell – nave and chancel – plan, but others were built cruciform, or became so, and could have a tower over the crossing as formerly at Crantock and Tintagel: the latter gives a good idea of the unaisled Norman church with small round-headed windows. In other cases we find W towers (St Gennys and St John), or towers attached to one of the transepts or above one of the transepts (Blisland, Bodmin, Duloe, Lawhitton, St Enodoc, Saltash, Veryan, etc., altogether about a dozen). Aisled Norman churches were not absent either, as at North Petherwin, Morwenstow and St Breward with their arcades on circular piers,

18

19

20

their capitals scalloped: the decoration of the Morwenstow arcade with beakheads, beasts and men is especially rich and enjoyable. Other churches retain traces of previous Norman arcades in the responds of their W walls when the aisle was reconstructed later on (St Teath). Some chancel aisles were built to accommodate the more numerous clergy of collegiate churches like Crantock or St Buryan, the latter's arcade still visible embedded in the N wall. Indeed the N walls of nave and chancel particularly, and transepts if they survive, often contain some Norman masonry, sometimes indicated by exceptionally thick walls and with
26   TYMPANA set above blocked doors as at Egloskerry. Here, and at nearby Treneglos, the S doors have Norman tympana re-set above them. Where Norman churches were replaced during the following centuries, decorated DOORWAYS were quite often pre-served, the best at Cury, Kilkhampton, Landewednack, Mor-
21   wenstow, Mylor, St Anthony-in-Roseland, St Martin-by-Looe and South Petherwin. Kilkhampton is the most ambitious, closely rivalled by Morwenstow, even though the latter's was divided up between inner and outer S doorways.

Norman FONTS were treated with special respect by later centuries, with about 115 surviving: they offered irrefutable evidence of parochial status. Some are of primeval rudeness, an eggcup with no structural elaboration. Two of the earliest, of the same size and indistinct vaguely circular shape, are at Washaway (from Lanteglos-by-Camelford) and Morwenstow: the former is decorated with interlacings and probably other early motifs including animals, while the latter is very plain with only a cable moulding at its base. But other Cornish fonts of this period are surprisingly monumental and elaborately adorned with heads or busts and animals or foliage motifs in relief: together they con-stitute the most exuberant Romanesque sculpture in Cornwall, and are exceptionally rewarding to study. They fall clearly into
22   groups and will be mentioned accordingly. The following are the most remarkable: Bodmin, with five shafts, heads at the corners of the square bowl, and big ornamental motifs between; Altar-
25   nun, with one shaft, faces at the corners and rosettes, serpents,
24   etc., between; Fowey, with a roughly hemispherical bowl and bands of decoration with crosses, saltire, etc., on it; and Egloshayle, of Purbeck marble and table-top shape, with shallow blank arcades as its only decoration. The late C12 ivory CASKET or RELIQUARY at Bodmin, reputedly once containing the relics of St Petroc, is unique.

The arrival of the GOTHIC style in Cornwall sometime in the C13 is not well represented in architecture of the EARLY ENGLISH PERIOD, and, where it exists, is more in structure than architec-tural detail. The tower of Lostwithiel church with its lancet windows is its most substantial expression, the spire an addition of the early C14. SPIRES are rare in Cornwall and the other examples – Cubert, Gerrans, Menheniot, Rame, St Anthony-in-Roseland, St Enodoc, St Ewe, St Hilary, St Minver, St Keverne,
28   and Sheviock – point to late C13 and early C14 dates; the Lost-
27   withiel spire is by far the most elaborate. St Anthony-in-Roseland

is the best example of a church of this period, complete with its crossing tower, the foliage capitals of its arches genuine C13. Early Gothic arcades are rare, the C14 chancel aisles at Crantock replacing their smaller C13 predecessors, the N aisle arcade at St Minver exceptionally narrow with a lean-to roof. The most sophisticated E.E. interior work is in the N and S chancel arcades at St Austell, especially the N arcade with a handsome octagonal pier with four slim attached shafts in the diagonals. But otherwise C13 Gothic detail remains rudimentary, most widely characterized by simple lancet windows, sometimes grouped at the E end. There are good examples of C13 windows in some of the Lizard churches (cf. Manaccan, Mawgan-in-Meneage and St Anthony-in-Meneage).

Of the C14 there is more extensive evidence, best seen in three groups of churches which demonstrate the considerable variety that pre-dates the late C15 to late C16 rebuilding of Cornish churches with their ever-recurring themes. Fowey and Lostwith-   30 iel are the main representatives of the first group, and its char- acteristics (octagonal piers without any capitals, and clerestory windows in line with the spandrels and not the apexes of the arches) are odd and call for explanation. Connections with Brit- tany, with which these medieval ports had substantial trading links, have often been cited and are entirely plausible but it is equally, if not more, likely that the influence is English, where piers without capitals existed in the south-west at Bristol, and clerestory windows of the same peculiar type at St Germans. A second group in south Cornwall displays the best Cornwall has to offer of the DECORATED style, with its ogee arches and luxuri- ant crocketing on image niches, sedilia and funerary recesses, in the S aisle at St Germans, St Ive and its nearby sister church at South Hill, Sheviock, St Michael Penkevil and North Hill. She-   29 viock gives the best impression of what a C14 Cornish church was like, complete with its S transept arch, the inner arches to all the S windows, the fine slender shafts supporting the inner arch of the chancel E window, and the tracery of the S and E windows with cusped lights, pointed and cusped little quatrefoils, and a five-pointed star in a large circle. The most sumptuous Dec window in Cornwall is the five-light E window at Lostwithiel; the three-light E window of the Chapel of St Thomas Becket at Bodmin is another fine example. A third group consists of Lizard churches – Cury, Gunwalloe, Mullion and Sithney – which all display remarkably similar late C14 to early C15 windows with cusped tracery. Window tracery of the flamboyant 'palm tree' pattern can be found at Padstow and St Just-in-Penwith.   32

The outstanding SCULPTURE of the early C14 is the Lostwith-   33 iel font, and of the C15 the carvings in Catacleuse stone at St Endellion, St Issey and St Merryn, all of superb quality. The alabaster fragment of a St Christopher at St Ive is also of   40 excellent quality. MONUMENTS of this period are not especially remarkable (cf. the late C14 effigies at St Teath, Sheviock and Stratton). As before, of course, what is lost is the evidence that the larger monastic foundations, especially Glasney and

Launceston, would have provided, but recent archaeological analysis of both sites has confirmed that their churches were of highly sophisticated C14 design and execution on a par with the cathedral at Exeter, with whose workshop they had close artistic links: Launceston's Lady Chapel was comparable in length and window design to the cathedral's, and its reredos, of Beer stone from the cathedral's quarries (as used at Glasney also), was of very high quality.

What has been described so far, however, represents less than a quarter of Cornwall's pre-Victorian churches, because the vast majority date predominantly from the PERPENDICULAR period. This intense period of adaptation, extension and rebuilding, paralleling what happened in Devon, began in the second half of the C15 and in some cases continued into the second half of the C16, well into the post-Reformation period, somewhat later than was once thought:* it probably represents Cornwall's enduring sense of its independent identity, especially its Catholic tradition and veneration of local saints, as much as its relative isolation. The model seems to have been the ambitious rebuilding of Bodmin between 1469 and 1492, replicated all over the county at different scales from the larger towns to the small village or remote churchtown. The Perp reconstruction is often so comprehensive that complete rebuilding is assumed, but caution needs to be exercised: apparently uniform or very similar fabric can have a complex evolution, as the few thorough archaeological investigations and dendrochronological datings have demonstrated (Lanlivery, Minster and St Veep).[†] At Lanlivery the foundations of a N transept tower were discovered, posing the question of whether the transeptal tower was once more widespread.

The Perp achievement in Cornish churches is impressive in scale and spread but highly standardized in its principal characteristics and detail, from the plan form to the profile of the piers, the mouldings of the arcades, and the buttressing of towers. The PLAN is best considered first. The most common enlargement of existing churches was by adding aisles to one or other, or both, sides of the nave; but the special feature of the Perp period in Cornwall (as in Devon) is that the aisles were often carried through to flank the chancel so as to form eastern chapels, sometimes used as chantry chapels: indeed some extensions started from the E end and worked W. The aisles were of the same height and width as the existing nave and chancel (very different from their C12–C14 predecessors), resulting in three parallel ranges – the three-hall church – presenting the E elevation of three parallel gables and three large windows so typical of the West Country: even so, many churches remained lop-sided, with only one aisle built even if a matching aisle had been planned but abandoned

---

*Documentary research by Joanna Mattingley and archaeological analysis by John Allan, Eric Berry and the Cornwall Historic Environment Service has been especially significant.
[†] By Warwick Rodwell, John Allan and Eric Berry respectively.

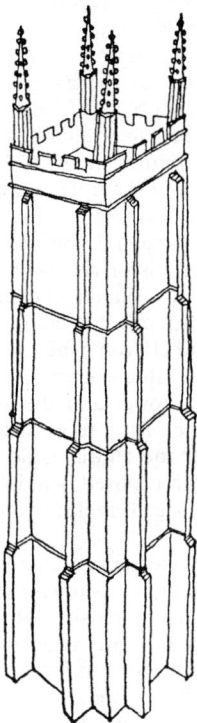

(a)

(b)

Standard Cornish tower
a) Standard Cornish pier
b) Square pier with four
   attached demi-shafts

after the Reformation. Existing transepts were removed, though their ghosts can sometimes be traced in the odd spacing of piers on the arcade bay where the transept once stood. Occasionally short transepts were added outside the new aisles (Breage). In almost all the rebuildings the older chancel arch was eliminated with the roof continuous from E to W end. In the largest or richest churches the whole church (or at least the show elevation) was buttressed and embattled as at Callington, Launceston and St Germans, and the smaller churches at North Hill and St Neot were similarly treated. But wall surfaces were sparsely ornamented: the profuse carvings of the whole of the exteriors of St Mary Magdalene, Launceston, the S chapel at the cathedral at Truro, and the W tower at Probus are wholly exceptional. 34 63

The standard Cornish Perp TOWER is generally at the W end, though they are occasionally found in other positions when they are adaptations of older towers, and there are also detached towers (Feock, Gwennap, Lamorran, Mylor and, most romantically, on the cliffs above the beach at Gunwalloe); the tower at Talland is S of the church but connected to it by a later C15 or early C16 porch. It is usually of three stages and has either no buttresses at all or slim, set-back buttresses leaving the angles free: notable exceptions are the low two-stage serpentine towers of the Lizard. Heavier buttresses with one or more set-offs, diagonal buttresses, and buttresses meeting at right angles at the corners are usually indications of earlier construction. Towers in four stages are rare (Fowey, Linkinhorne, St Buryan, St Columb Major, St Columb Minor, St Ives). The rarity of spires, and their earlier date, has already been mentioned but it should not be forgotten that some spires, like the lofty examples at Bodmin and Truro, have been lost. The tower at St Columb Major is still open at ground-floor level, as was the case at Lostwithiel until the 35

C19. Rarely, the ground floor of the tower opened into the nave and aisles (Lanteglos-by-Fowey and St Keverne), the aisles carried W to flank the tower. With the exception of Probus, already mentioned, and Fowey, most Cornish towers are of a plain dignity especially if of fine granite ashlar blocks. Their stair-turrets sometimes give a defensive-like profile when they rise above the parapet. That makes tower sculpture, where it rarely occurs, the more remarkable, the outstanding example being the stocky figures at St Austell. St Dominic and South Hill have rudely carved figures in panels below the parapet. Other decoration is limited to a single band of quatrefoils or similar at the base (Poughill, North Tamerton, Week St Mary); occasional image niches; earlier medieval heads incorporated as label stops to the W door or window; and large angel corbels from which octagonal turrets and crocketed pinnacles rise. But everywhere the contrast between the upright block of the tower and the lower horizontal blocks of nave and aisles is one of the most striking architectural motifs in Cornwall, whether the churches lie in a town or village, on their own on the hills in exposed, windswept positions, or also on their own in dips or close to creeks, sheltered by trees.

The standard Cornish PIER has a very elementary moulding and probably evolved to avoid delicate detail in a county with so intractable a building material as granite. It consists of four attached shafts in the main axes and four hollows in the diagonals (a). The same pier type is one of the most frequent in Devon too. Square piers with four attached demi-shafts (b) are also often to be found in Cornwall. They seem to be of earlier introduction (Stratton) even if they were carried into the C15 (Callington). Circular piers with four attached shafts or a similar-looking form with four major and four minor shafts appear occasionally too. Finally there are a dozen or so churches with octagonal piers, developed straight from C13 precedent. Some of the most prominent churches have their own exceptional pier shapes (Launceston, St Austell chancel aisle, St Ives). CAPITALS are on the whole also very elementarily moulded but the leaf-frieze capitals of Devon (there called Devon Standard), with a band of large horizontal fern-like leaves, were also in use. Even when stone more amenable to carving is found there is rarely any attempt at more elaborate decoration, though the execution may be sharper (cf. the Catacleuse at St Merryn or the Polyphant at Lewannick), which makes the exquisite flower and foliage work in the arcade of the Colshull Chapel at Duloe and the vines, leaves and grapes in the Trenwith chapel at St Ives the more exceptional. The arches of the arcades seem at first to have simply had two chamfers, then two concave curves instead of the chamfers, and then more complex mouldings, the arch shapes ranging from quite pointed to nearly semicircular and four-centred, the last probably an indication of later date.

Perp window TRACERY is relatively uniform and has often suffered severe restoration or complete replacement, so is of dubious use for dating or stylistic analysis. The standard Cornish

Perp window of three, four or five lights was introduced at Bodmin in 1469 and continued in use until at least the 1530s and 1540s: there are evolved examples at Egloshayle (1529), Lanlivery (1520), Padstow and St Erth. Late Perp windows with flatter heads and no tracery occupying larger wall areas are often found (e.g. in the N aisle at Camborne, 1538–40). Many churches exhibit very domestic-looking windows, usually of three lights, and often on the N side of the church, but there are some prominent examples like those of the 1540s or later in the S wall of the S chapel at St Germans.

Stone vaults are not found in Cornwall's Perp naves, chancels or aisles but simple versions can be found occasionally in some of the more ambitious PORCHES. Those at Creed, North Hill and St Neot all have pointed tunnel-vaults with transverse arches. The latter two porches are two-storeyed as are the large examples at Bodmin, Launceston and Liskeard. All are buttressed, pinnacled and embattled, as are the West Penwith porches at St Buryan and St Just-in-Penwith. Some of the most charming have simple panelled jambs (Breage). The most spectacularly decorated is, of course, Launceston. ₆₄

The character of the Cornish Perp interior owes much to the almost universal use of the timber common rafter WAGON ROOF, a roof type found only in churches, and sharply different from the roofs of domestic buildings in south-west England where the cruck predominates. John Thorp[*] has suggested the possibility of the early derivation of the wagon roof from northern European prototypes in the C12 and C13. Some West Country church roofs have been dated by dendrochronology to the mid C14 but relatively few have yet been investigated and more research is needed which might show that some are earlier than the C15. The distinctive feature of a curved rib to every rafter, especially if the space between the timbers is ceiled,[†] does indeed give the impression of the canvas of a wagon or, as Betjeman noted in the three-hall church at Lanteglos-by-Fowey, 'like three upturned boats'. Such ₃₇ roofs certainly add to the feeling of comfortable spaciousness and breadth. Ribs, purlins and wall-plates are commonly moulded and sometimes enriched with foliage decoration, the elaboration often increasing in the chancel and chancel chapels, and in the S aisle. Most have decorative bosses at the main intersections of the timbers, displaying a variety of motifs including fruits, flowers, faces, shields, emblems and the occasional green man. Shield-holding angels sometimes appear at the intersections of the ribs and the wall-plates, those at St Ives being especially memorable.

Of LATE MEDIEVAL CHURCH FURNISHINGS in Cornwall there is nothing to compare with the hundred or so lavishly decorated ROOD SCREENS of Devon, at least in quantity. But the quality of the screens at Budock, Lanreath, St Buryan, St Ewe,

---

[*] 'The Wagon Roofs at St James' Priory, Bristol', *Vernacular Architecture* 44, 2013.
[†] Whether such roofs were originally ceiled (with plaster or boards) is the subject of continuing debate.

St Levan and St Winnow is excellent, and merits connection with the leading Devon workshops. Some, like Budock and St Levan, only survive as bases, but others are complete, even if they have been skilfully restored in the late C19 and C20 (*see* C19 church restoration below, p. 76). The outstanding examples are St Buryan and St Ewe, both with large quantities of surviving medieval fabric and with rood beams exuberantly enriched with birds, beasts, grotesque heads, etc., all hiding in and peeping out of foliage scrolls. The St Buryan screen also has a good quantity of lovely original colouring, which is also seen at Budock, on the beautifully painted screen at Lanreath, and on the two surviving panels at Gunwalloe. A simpler version, but still impressive in its scale, is the screen at Altarnun, which runs right across the considerable breadth of this large church, each section of two-light panels with Perp tracery with panels of blank tracery at the base.

If Cornwall lacks many of the glories of Devon screens, it can boast a much richer display of its own speciality, late C15 to late C16 BENCH-ENDS. They are of the same type as in the neighbouring county, square-ended without the sloping or pointed tops and poppyheads found elsewhere in England (there are only a handful of these).* At least eleven churches have bench-ends with original backs – Gorran, Kilkhampton, Lansallos, Lanteglos-by-Fowey, Launcells, Michaelstow, Morwenstow, Mullion, St Eval, St Minver and St Veep. Some churches retain almost complete furnishings of bench-ends – seventy-nine at Altarnun, sixty at Launcells, fifty-three at Gorran, over forty at Mullion etc. Those with abbreviated motifs of the Instruments of the Passion with Perp tracery were long considered late C15 while the introduction of Renaissance imagery and arabesque designs was dated to *c.* 1530–5. Modern research† now suggests that these dates may be too early and that bench-ends were introduced relatively late to Cornwall. It is now reasonably certain that there are rare examples of the end of the C15 at Bodmin, of the first half of the C16 at Altarnun, Launcells, Lewannick, Poughill, St Ives and Stratton, for the second half of the C16 at Morwenstow and probably Kilkhampton, and for the early C17 at Camborne, Illogan and Towednack, the latter dated 1633. It is a feature of Cornish churches that their bench-ends show that the transition from medieval to Renaissance motifs is free-flowing and without a break, with the Perp-style tracery, shields or roundels in the middle and quatrefoils at the base continuing the most common type until the second half of the C16, and still found at Morwenstow in 1575. At Altarnun only about a sixth of the bench-ends employ Perp tracery and only a seventh have any religious context at all, with Renaissance motifs dominating, in contrast to Launcells and other churches where the two intermingle freely; at Mullion Passion symbols

---

* Early benches of the desk type appear at Kilkhampton and Madron with animals and birds as finials, while angels form the finials of the St Ives stall-end, and carved figureheads can be seen at Talland.
† Especially the work of Joanna Mattingly.

occur on the front of one set of benches and Renaissance imagery on the front of another set. Both medieval and Renaissance designs produce the most vivid depictions, those of the Passion sometimes almost macabre, those of the Renaissance sometimes entertaining. Memorable examples include the mermaid at Zennor with mirror and comb; the Last Supper, Resurrection and Ascension at Launcells (the latter depicted by footprints below the lower part of the ascending Christ's robes); ship in a storm at St Winnow; a portrait of St James with his pilgrim's hat at St Levan; monks, soldiers, jesters and grotesques at Mullion; a green man at Laneast; and musicians, shepherds and sheep at Altarnun.

Of other furnishings and fittings, the rare survival of four MISERICORDS at St Buryan should be noted. The introduction of PULPITS can sometimes be associated with the installation of bench-ends at the end of the C15 and first half of the C16. By far the finest is the splendidly carved example in wood at Launceston, its original colouring now restored: it is considered to be pre-Reformation. Stone pulpits are rare: the best is at Egloshayle, octagonal with carved shields etc. Good examples of other wood pulpits are Camborne, 1549–50; Mawgan-in-Pydar, c. 1530; and St Kew, uncommonly good Elizabethan. Many pulpits incorporate bench-ends and some panels of former rood screens. WALL PAINTING is not of the highest aesthetic merit, but the representations of the Warning to Sabbath Breakers,* their tools displayed as the instruments of the wounds to Christ's body, are worth recording for other reasons (Breage, Lanivet, Poundstock, St Just-in-Penwith). Breage has the most interesting display of wall painting with a St Christopher and other saints and figures on the walls in the window splays. The Linkinhorne painting of the Seven Works of Mercy, though faint, is the most accomplished in Cornwall, with Christ beneath an unusual canopy and small scenes showing the Works including a depiction of a medieval house. FONTS are often octagonal and rather dull, but the St Ives type with large, severely stylized shield-bearing angels on the circular bowl connected by bands and on a circular base with attached corner supports is of more interest. Launcells' display of ENCAUSTIC TILES from Barnstaple is among the most attractive C17 church decoration in Cornwall.

There are few pre-Reformation BRASSES in Cornwall, and fewer of special note. The most spectacular is that to Margery Arundell of 1420 at Antony, large in scale with a surround with ogee arch and finials. The figure of a rector of c. 1400 at Cardinham is a rare example of a cleric in civil dress. Many other brasses are fragmentary or palimpsests of once more sumptuous monuments (cf. the Arundell set at Mawgan-in-Pydar).

The most spectacular late medieval MONUMENT is the grand effigy and chest tomb of Prior Vivian, 1533, the last prior of Bodmin but two, now in St Petroc, Bodmin, but originally at the priory church. It is of exceptional interest for the appearance of

___

* Not Christ blessing the trades, as was once mistakenly suggested (E. Clive Rouse).

RENAISSANCE motifs (cherubs with shields, coarse Italianizing balusters, the earliest example of the effect on Cornwall of metropolitan work of the period), purely as an ornamental fashion (cf. bench-ends above). Earlier examples are the chest tomb and effigy of Sir John Colshull †1483 at Duloe, attributed to the influence of the Bristol workshop; the alabaster monument of 1502 to Sir Robert Willoughby de Broke at Callington; and the exceptionally large incised slab with cross at St Stephen, Launceston,

Talland, slate tomb to John Bevill, 1579
Drawing

of 1528. There are excellent examples of elaborate early C17 chest tombs in slate at North Hill, Duloe, Lansallos, St Tudy, Talland and many other churches because of another Cornish speciality, the beautifully incised SLATE FIGURES boldly carved in relief, which date from 1500 to 1727. The craft was evidently at its peak between 1575 and 1650 and its most eminent practitioner was *Peter Crocker* of Looe. These monuments, mostly in Delabole slate, are among the most distinctive examples of local art in England, and are thoroughly enjoyable.

Of medieval STAINED GLASS, St Neot is of national importance. So much is preserved (fourteen windows in all) that a live impression can still be obtained of what the coloured glass of the late medieval period gave to the church interior. The earliest window here dates from the early to mid C15, and the last ones are dated 1528–30. Only two other churches now contain complete pre-Reformation windows, St Kew and St Winnow, both of excellent quality and state of preservation. The St Kew window of the Passion probably dates from the 1480s (the Jesse window in the s chapel may also be C15). The St Winnow window, clearly an assemblage of glass from elsewhere in the church (two Virgins etc.), can be assigned to the 1460s. Fragments of medieval glass occur frequently elsewhere, usually in the tracery, though occasionally larger pieces appear as in the chancel E window at Laneast. Otherwise, the medieval glass in the chapel at Cotehele should not be missed.

No account of the medieval church in Cornwall would be complete without some account of the numerous HOLY WELLS, sometimes accompanied by BAPTISTERIES and CHAPELS and occasionally by HERMITAGES, which, with the inscribed stones and crosses described earlier, complete the population of the medieval religious landscape. Often located in remote positions by rivers or watercourses, they offer some of the most atmospheric architecture, albeit in usually a minor key, of any buildings in Cornwall. Almost all are of medieval origin and though frequently restored or rebuilt, especially in the C19 (*see* below), they have an authenticity of their own that is quietly compelling. They range in scale and sophistication from the clearly architectural forms like St Cleer in the village street, through the major sites like St Clether, with its large chapel alongside the well exquisitely sited against rocks in the remote upper reach of the Inny valley, to the delightful simplicity of little gabled well-houses with stone-vaulted roofs like Linkinhorne, reached across fields in the river valley, and to ruined sites of great spiritual power, like those at Madron hidden in woodland, and St Levan perched on the cliff above the beach. Of hermitages, the sight of St Michael's Chapel, licensed in 1409 and perched on top of the fantastic outcrop of jagged schorl at Roche, is unforgettable.

Major secular buildings

Cornwall has a significant place in the history of military architecture in England through both its medieval castles and its

C15–C16 coastal defences. The roll call of major CASTLES may be brief – Launceston, Restormel, Tintagel and Trematon – but they are an eminently interesting group, augmented by a number of other archaeologically informative if less architecturally demonstrative examples. Modern research has much enriched our understanding of their functions other than the solely military, enhancing the interpretation of excavated sites as well as standing buildings.

The consolidation of power by the Earls of Cornwall (Richard and his son Edmund) in C13 and C14 Cornwall is especially vividly illustrated at Tintagel and Launceston. The most dramatically sited is Tintagel, half on an island, half on a sheer cliff with a narrow neck of land between. The ambitious scale of the castle, with an outer and upper courtyard on the inland portion and the heart of the castle with its great hall on the island, is still apparent in the curtain walls and excavated and consolidated remains of the buildings. The impractical nature of the site lends weight to the evidence that it was probably primarily a symbolic venture to demonstrate and reinforce Richard's authority by consciously drawing on the Arthurian legend, no doubt reflected in its early abandonment, the roof of the great hall being removed in the C14. As the gateway to Cornwall from the E, the castle at Launceston still conveys the sense of a border fortress in the way the steep motte crowned by its shell-keep towers over the town. Its origins in C11 earthworks are overlain by Richard and Edmund's C13–C14 ambitious reconstruction, which is still visible in the substantial earthworks, curtain walls, N and S gatehouses and keep, as well as the foundations of the great hall and chapel in the SW part of the bailey. Even here, however, other functions come into play, as the construction of the earls' palatial administrative centre diminished the defensive capacity of the keep with the building of the high tower which created a spectacular position, among other things, to view the deer park.

This evolution of purpose is even more clearly demonstrated at Restormel. Here the most perfect example of C13 military architecture in Cornwall is now seen to have become, by the end of the C13, less a military stronghold and more a splendid fortified hunting lodge in a deer park, the largest in Cornwall, which extended far down the Fowey valley towards Lostwithiel. Its complete set of domestic buildings, familiar from the standard medieval house, is arranged around the internal wall of the shell-keep, including large windows giving extensive views over the park and towards the town to which the earls had moved their administrative base from Launceston, and a chapel projecting beyond the wall. These are not, as long considered, additions to the keep but an integral part of Edmund's C13 reconstruction. Trematon, also connected with an early deer park, has the most impressive standing fabric of them all, with its great motte-and-bailey defended by a formidably tall curtain wall reconstructed in the C12, and a shell-keep even more substantial than those of Launceston or Restormel. It also has the single most complete architectural component of any of the Cornish castles in its C13 gatehouse, with excellent stiff-leaf capitals to the columned fire-places to both upper floors.

The most substantial architectural evidence of medieval forti-fication elsewhere is at St Michael's Mount where much more of the C12 castle has been identified in the W range than was once thought. Its N and S square towers, steps to the entrance, a guard-house and a vestigial curtain wall around the summit still convey much of the sense of the fortified monastery, while the interior shows the medieval plan of cross-passage, hall to the S and service rooms to the N. Of other castle sites, impressive mottes can be seen at Boscastle and Kilkhampton. That at Boscastle, like the low motte or ringwork at Week St Mary, was associated with the market place of the medieval settlement, while Kilkhampton demonstrates that such castles populated the countryside as well. Bury Court, *see* Week St Mary, is a rare example of a medieval moated site. Of the fortress at Cardinham, the motte has been reduced but the bailey is well preserved. Many other settlements had castles that have long disappeared. Though it was not a castle, mention must be made of the Duchy Palace at Lostwithiel, the still imposing remnant of the C14 administrative centre of the Earls of Cornwall: its massive, buttressed construction, originally three-storey and virtually windowless above a stone-vaulted base-ment, suggests a defensive function, possibly as the treasury of the duchy. Similarly the Fowey Museum was originally a first-floor hall over an undercroft, which might indicate a stronghouse necessary for a building so near the waterfront.

But the most memorable of all Cornish castles are the Henri-cian defences at Pendennis and St Mawes, guarding the entrance to the magnificent deep-water harbour of the Fal estuary and Carrick Roads. They present some of the best Tudor architecture in Cornwall, as well as being of considerable significance in English military architecture. St Mawes, 1540–5, is the most perfectly preserved of the Henrician castles. Here we see the radical replacement of the high keeps of the previous age by low bastions spreading out like trefoil leaves from the taller circular central tower, a strikingly un-medieval symmetrical composition and convincingly of the Renaissance. It was one of the most up-to-date fortifications of its date, though at that very moment on the Continent round bastions were being replaced by angular ones. Pendennis shows this change: the castle keep of 1539–45 is surrounded by a sixteen-sided inner curtain wall, but it was transformed between 1597 and 1600 by vast new fortifications to control the whole headland employing the Italian angle bastion system. The remarkable Star Castle on St Mary's in the Scilly Isles of 1593–1600, so called because of its plan in the form of an eight-pointed star, is a belated successor to St Mawes rather than the radically remodelled Pendennis. Of earlier coastal defences, the late C15 blockhouses for a chain stretched across the estuary at Fowey are notable, as is Henry VIII's stronger fort at St Catherine's Castle just S of the town.

When it comes to medieval DOMESTIC ARCHITECTURE we must start by noting the paucity of any visible evidence of the domestic ranges of the more significant monasteries. The most substantial is the undercroft of the C13 priory with its lancet windows at Port Eliot (*see* St Germans): the refectory walls above have been subsumed into the later rebuilding, as is the case with the monastic cellars and refectory at St Michael's Mount. In the earliest Cornish houses that possess easily recognizable early features and fabric a semi-fortified or at least defensive element can occasionally be found. At Godolphin the great hall, built *c.* 1475, had high and low cross-wings closed off by an early C16 curtain wall to form a courtyard with square corner towers. Cotehele's S entrance range and gatehouse of the late C15 to the mid C16 has a definitely defensive character with only a few small openings, reinforcing the inward-looking character of this, the best-preserved Tudor house in Cornwall. A similarly protective air can be sensed in smaller gentry houses like Roscarrock and Tonacombe, and in vulnerable locations it lasted well into the mid C16: the tower at Pengersick of the 1550s, a suite of residential accommodation, nevertheless has a clearly defensive basement with gunloops. Arwenack, Falmouth, the great house of the Killigrews, was possibly fortified in its medieval phase.

Many of Cornwall's GREATER HOUSES, their sites often recorded in Domesday, started as the standard medieval hall with some subsidiary accommodation and evolved into the familiar single or double COURTYARD-PLAN complexes from the C15 to 73 mid C17, though sometimes, as at Godolphin which became a double courtyard plan, a courtyard can subsequently be lost. The most rewarding place to study this transformation is Cotehele, where the Edgcumbes gradually developed a relatively simple medieval range into a three-courtyard plan between the late C15 and the early 1650s; but the same process can be discerned over and over again in other houses where improvement and extension have heavily or completely disguised the medieval building, such as Lanherne (Mawgan-in-Pydar), Lanhydrock, Morval, Place at Fowey, and Trelowarren. Sometimes even if the medieval building has been substantially rebuilt or even demolished, its ghost may still be discernible in the plan of the present house. The same evolution can be seen in many mid-to late C16 gentry houses too: Roscarrock is an especially well-preserved gentry house on a courtyard plan, and Trecarrel was either intended to be of that form but never completed, or was subsequently reduced. Marsland Manor, Morwenstow, is a rare example of a double courtyard plan at this social level. C16 Pengersick was built on a double courtyard plan, but only fragments survive apart from the tower. One of the most visually delightful is Tre- 56 nethick, Wendron, its courtyard approached through its Tudor-arched gatehouse.

Even so, Cornwall has nothing to compare with Devon's rich array of medieval architecture which ranges from the great buildings of Exeter Cathedral close to the hundreds of farmhouses with C14–C17 roofs. The contrast is nowhere better demonstrated than in the comparable scarcity of MEDIEVAL ROOFS, and the even rarer appearance of smoke-blackening from the open hall phase of the central chimneyless hearth. The most common roof form was arch-braced with high, sometimes cranked, collars, its most impressive survival the great open hall roof of the 1520s at Cotehele: it is of seven bays with four tiers of intersecting wind-braces. At a slightly lesser scale a similar roof occurs, of ten bays with wind-braces, over the still open hall at Trecarrel. The roof over the C15 E range at Godolphin is also arch-braced, of four bays. Roscarrock has two medieval roofs, of the early C16 in the SE range and of the mid to late C16 in the SW range: the former, originally over the open hall, is of fourteen bays with three tiers of wind-braces, all very like Cotehele. The principals of this roof are on short curved feet, giving a cruck-like appearance, though the jointed cruck, so ubiquitous in Devon, is curiously absent in Cornwall. But other cruck derivatives are found. One of the earliest examples is Penfound Manor, Poundstock, where the still open-hall roof has four smoke-blackened trusses of a base-cruck type. The earliest medieval roof is at Food for Thought, Fowey, of three phases with crown-posts as well as base crucks, and arched- and wind-braced: it is stylistically similar to a Devon roof dated by dendrochronology to 1299–1300. Rectory Farm, Morwenstow, has a C14 spere-truss relating to a former aisled hall and three smoke-blackened and arch-braced C15 trusses with crown-post detail. The barn at Cargoll, St Newlyn East, all that remains of the C14 palace of the Bishops of Exeter, has raised cruck-trusses to each of its eight bays, subdivided by intermediate trusses of raised base crucks, with long curved wind-braces. Such roofs may well also have been found in smaller gentry houses; for which *see* p. 47–8. The decorated wagon roof of the late C15 hall of Prior Vivian's house at Rialton Manor is wholly exceptional on a domestic building.

58

55

There is little external ARCHITECTURAL DECORATION to compare with the ornamentation of the (re-erected) two-storey early C16 bay at Place, Fowey, where all the lights are cusped and the stonework richly patterned. The porch to the great hall at Godolphin has panelled jambs like those on the S porch at nearby Breage and other local churches, but architectural features are mostly limited to windows and doorways. This is best enjoyed in the exceedingly picturesque early C16 hall and parlour range of the Hall Court at Cotehele with windows of massive mullions and transoms all with ogee-arched heads. The S elevation of the great hall at Trecarrel has a similar window arrangement. The ambitious early C16 extension in front of the hall at Rialton has a stone tunnel-vaulted porch, unique in domestic buildings of this period, with large transomed-and-mullioned windows above to light the prior's private apartment, the windows with panels of blind cusped arches between. Surviving INTERIOR DECORATION is equally scarce from the period, generally limited to relatively plain doorways and chimneypieces. The finest ceiling of this date is that of *c.* 1500 in the hall of the E range at Godolphin, formed of richly decorated intersecting beams. The earlier arrangement of

57

private apartments is usually overlain by later C16 and subsequent improvements (discussed below) but some PRIVATE CHAPELS survive, the earliest (C13) at Erth Barton, the finest at Cotehele complete with medieval glass; a very charming small chapel stands SE of the great hall at Trecarrel and the ruinous example at Shillingham retains remnants of C13 tracery. Of SERVICE ROOMS the most striking is the kitchen at Cotehele, still an open hall with a massive early C16 fireplace.

Before discussing later C16 and early to mid-C17 developments at the greater houses, two other medieval building types of special significance in Cornwall should be noted. As might be expected in a country deeply dissected by rivers and estuaries there are some important early BRIDGES, often associated with causeways. The most spectacular is that over the Camel at Wadebridge of *c.* 1468, the longest in Cornwall and one of the finest in England, with thirteen of its seventeen arches still visible. Yeolmbridge w of Werrington has two mid-C14 arches with three ribbed vaults to each. Lostwithiel Bridge over the Fowey is one of the most attractive with the five pointed-arch w spans dating from a reconstruction of 1437 of an earlier structure. Nearby, Respryn Bridge below Lanhydrock is similar in age and beauty. It is, however, the close sequence of C15 crossings of the lower part of the Tamar that is the most a remarkable survival: Greystone, Lezant (1439); Horse Bridge, Stoke Climsland (1457); and New Bridge, Gunnislake (*c.* 1500). The first two are of remarkably similar design, with four segmental arches; New Bridge is the most impressive, 182 ft (55.5 metres) long with six slightly pointed arches. Many smaller medieval bridges survive, often in exquisitely picturesque settings: Trekelland, Lewannick, over the little River Inny, is a delightful example of *c.* 1500.

A building type special to the SW is the CHURCH HOUSE, the precursor of the village hall, usually sited very near the church, often on the edge of the churchyard. The Cornish examples are generally modest and have often been converted to domestic use but they are usually still recognizable because of their close association with the church and their characteristic end stacks: a good simple example, now a house, stands just outside the s gate of the churchyard at North Tamerton, while an even more modest example is on the N edge of the churchyard at St Teath. But for once Cornwall can outdo Devon in the scale and completeness of preservation of the guildhouse at Poundstock with its early to mid-C16 ten-bay open hall.

The gradual transformation of the LATER MEDIEVAL GREAT HOUSE is well illustrated in Cornwall. As the hall continued to decrease in importance with the increasing emphasis on privacy and comfort, the wings at either end of the hall were often rebuilt to provide separate rooms and apartments with more generous access to the upper rooms by new wide staircases: the sequence is well demonstrated at Cotehele. But it was a process characterized more by piecemeal improvement and additions throughout the later C16 and well into the early C17. Godolphin's w range is an excellent example of the sequential improvement of the medieval private apartments off the higher end of the great hall into a prestigious state apartment. At gentry level the early C16 SW wing of Roscarrock was upgraded in the mid to late C16 to provide highly sophisticated accommodation at first-floor level, including a fine granite bay window overlooking pleasure gardens with views down to the sea, a far cry from Cotehele's inward-facing atmosphere. 69

As has already been noted with churches, the transition towards RENAISSANCE PLANS and DECORATION in the greater houses was also very gradual, first appearing in the addition of classical details rather than wholesale reconstruction. Indeed the symmetrical classical exterior that characterizes England's great Elizabethan and Jacobean houses rarely puts in an appearance in Cornwall. The best Elizabethan house is Trerice, relatively small-scale but exquisitely pretty, the Arundells' early 1570s rebuilding and remodelling of the substantial C15 to early C16 house. Its front is almost, but not completely, symmetrical with a central three-storeyed porch between slightly projecting end wings with highly decorative scrolly gables, large trefoil gables between, and to the l. of the porch a vast hall window filled with a beautiful lattice of mostly original glass. More typical is the Arundells' Elizabethan refronting of their great house at Lanherne, an asymmetrical composition with a splendidly showy two-storey bay with windows of eight lights, the upper level corbelled out. Nicholas Prideaux similarly remodelled the E range of Prideaux Place in the late C16 or early C17 to provide a richly decorated great chamber and an up-to-date elevation to the town. At Trelowarren Sir Richard Vyvyan (1611–65) built wings at either end of the central medieval range, flanking the W entrance court; the S wing was a chapel, granted a licence in 1636. The Robartes mansion at Lanhydrock, greatly extended 1634–44, has all the quality of the grand Jacobean style. With its enchantingly pinnacled gatehouse standing before the house in its lush setting, it is one of the most rewarding of the great houses of Cornwall. Planned around a central courtyard with an outer forecourt that originally incorporated the gatehouse, it is lavish in scale but highly disciplined in external detail. 70 78 76

The GATEHOUSE is a component of the composition of houses of this period in Cornwall, and a remarkably similar example appears at Trewan Hall, St Columb Major, to terminate the r. wing of an early C17 house of U-plan with a double-depth hall range flanked by far-projecting symmetrical wings. Penheale Manor was rebuilt and extended between the late C16 and mid C17 on a courtyard plan, and was also approached through a gatehouse with a five-bay loggia (cf. Godolphin below) on its inner face; its smart N entrance front of granite ashlar has a splendid array of mullioned windows and is dated 1636. Penheale also has an impressive detached STABLE RANGE completed in 1620 with a symmetrical nine-bay front. The finest stable block in Cornwall, perhaps reflecting the influence of *Robert Adams*, is of *c.* 1600 at Godolphin, with a sophisticated façade of triple symmetry: a remarkable design and a very rare survival.

73, 74 Two of Cornwall's greater houses, Godolphin and Ince Castle, are, however, of exceptional importance in tracing the coming of the Renaissance to Cornwall. Sir Francis Godolphin's remodelling of the former *c.* 1630 was clearly intended to result in one of the most ambitious houses of the new style in England, a daring essay in Renaissance planning and architecture, all the more remarkable for being in such a remote position in the far west: here we can see the successful infusion of classical influences into the Cornish medieval building tradition. The tightly disciplined symmetrical N range of eleven bays, the only completed part of the intended reconstruction, with transomed-and-mullioned windows and hoodmoulds drawn into a continuous string course (as at Lanhydrock), actually incorporates the N and S corner towers of the earlier house and its curtain wall as the spine of the central range. The latter supports a suite of first-floor apartments consisting of a spacious central reception room flanked by paired chambers with service rooms that were accessed by separate stairs, one of the earliest examples of such an arrangement in England. Ince, *c.* 1630–40, represents the radically new, a complete break with the Cornish tradition, different in materials, planning and design, and also highly unusual nationally. It is a brick house of square plan with four square corner towers and the principal apartments on a *piano nobile* accessed by a high wide flight of steps and through a doorway treated in the later medieval manner but surmounted by a classical pediment, probably the earliest Cornish appearance of classicism. Its influences must surely be traced first to the Edgcumbes' new house at Mount Edgcumbe of 1547–53, of which Ince can perhaps be seen as a more modern version, and to Lulworth Castle, Dorset, of 1610 as well as the plans (though certainly not the elevation) of some early C16 French chateaux.

With regard to ELIZABETHAN and JACOBEAN INTERIORS, Cornwall is once again the poor relation to Devon in joinery, with few examples of elaborate decoration to doorcases, and screens usually of the simple sturdy stud-and-panel type. The most sumptuous SCREEN is that to the hall at Prideaux Place, late C16 or early C17, with fine inlaid panels and a frieze decorated with fantastic beasts and monsters, with more on the panels, set against formally treated plants and flowers. Another outstanding screen, of *c.* 1640, is that to the hall at Penheale, columned and richly ornamented with deep undercutting and vigorous figure carving including Adam and Eve. Of PLASTERWORK of this period there is perhaps more than might be expected, and some of very high quality comparable to the best Devon work. Trerice has some of the earliest and finest, of the late C16. The ceiling of the hall is in a large open strapwork pattern of thin ribs ornamented with oak leaves and scroll designs, supported on corbels and with splendid pendentives. The great chamber has the richest display, an elaborate barrel ceiling in fine interconnecting strapwork with Tudor rose motifs and scroll designs, large pendants and a deep frieze; an Arundell coat of arms; and a massive overmantel incorporating the Arundell arms supported by telamones.

It has remarkable similarities with Collacombe, Devon. The most spectacular is the Long Gallery at Lanhydrock, where the whole 116-ft (35-metre) length of the barrel-vault is completely covered with a densely patterned design springing from twelve pendants with large panels of Old Testament scenes and smaller panels of flora and fauna; the composition is linked by interconnecting ribs enriched with running vines and pomegranates. The ceiling is almost exactly replicated, at a less ambitious scale but of equally accomplished execution, in the ceiling of the great chamber at Prideaux Place, where the fully modelled panels are linked by elaborate strapwork. In scale and quality too the ceiling of the barrel-vault above the gallery at Penheale is comparable, also with pendants and a charming frieze of mermaids and dolphins. Of overmantels there are excellent examples in the long gallery and morning room at Lanhydrock, the hall at Trerice (in addition to the chamber mentioned above) and, especially charming, to the chimneypiece in the Specott Room at Penheale.

Medieval towns

Little has yet been said about Cornwall's MEDIEVAL TOWNS, partly because despite their variety, interest and substantial degree of preservation in morphology if not in surviving secular buildings, Cornish urban history has not received the attention it undoubtedly deserves. Harold Fox has pointed out that by 1350 in Cornwall, with the third largest proportion of boroughs in relation to land in England, 'few people would have been without easy access to a town of moderate size'.* Launceston, the C13 capital, was created by the Earls of Cornwall as their administrative centre because their castle commanded the land gateway to the county, but generally castles had little influence in the later shaping of most towns. Most were C13 and early C14 creations by major landowners, planting urban settlements at locations most favourable for trade. For this reason most were ports, either on the coast or near the mouths of rivers (Boscastle, East and West Looe, Fowey, Padstow, Penryn, Penzance, St Mawes, etc.) or at the highest navigable points or lowest crossing places (Lostwithiel, Helston, Tregony, Truro). Inland towns like Camelford, Grampound and Mitchell took advantage of being on major thoroughfares across the county. Most were street towns, that is one long street, sometimes following the spine of a ridge or spur as at Boscastle, Helston, Penzance, Tregony and Truro, and with burgage plots running back from narrow frontages on both sides. Subsequent medieval development, for example at Bodmin, Launceston, Lostwithiel and Penzance, added extensions either lineally on to the main streets or at angles to it. More research would be likely to reap rich rewards, not least because in so many towns the detailed investigation of standing buildings would

* 'Medieval Urban Development', in *Historical Atlas of South West England*, 1999.

reveal the survival of much earlier fabric than their later, often C19, façades suggest.

One other aspect of Cornwall's medieval urban history requires special mention, the significance of the stannaries and the stannary towns. The exploitation of the county's rich mineral resources, especially tin, reaches back deep into prehistory, and by the Roman period Cornish tin was a considerable export. But tin's importance burgeoned in the medieval period and by the late C14 the focus of its production had begun to move from east Cornwall, where moorland tin-streaming predominated on and around Bodmin Moor, to more westerly areas, where new open-cut, shaft and adit mining was developing. When the Duchy of Cornwall was created in 1337 the income from tin (coinage) became a significant part of the duchy revenues and the stannaries – essentially the main mining districts – became an integral part of the administration of the duchy. The four stannaries, which had emerged from the ancient rights enjoyed by Cornish tinners and had their own law, courts and parliament, were Foweymore (modern Bodmin Moor), Blackmore (the Hensbarrow Downs above St Austell), Tywarnhaile (the Truro and St Agnes area), and Penwith-with-Kerrier in the far west. In this context, the status of being a stannary or coinage town – where tin was assayed, stamped and taxed – was of considerable importance. Bodmin, Lostwithiel, Truro and Helston were awarded this status by 1305, Liskeard by the late C16, and Penzance in 1633. It is hardly too much to say that it was tin which provided so much of the wealth that lay behind the development of medieval Cornwall.

VERNACULAR BUILDING, 1400–1800
BY ERIC BERRY

The traditional buildings of Cornwall are of a highly varied character which reflect the county's rich history, geology and topography. Early buildings are rarer than in most other counties of England, for many reasons. The wet climate produced fast-grown timber of poor quality and of limited scantling, timber that was also susceptible to rot and woodworm degradation. Available timber sizes also meant that many early buildings were of inadequate scale to be easily upgraded, often leading to complete rebuilding rather than remodelling. Pressure for change was also brought about by good coastal communications that successively brought fashionable features into play. Typically these were grafted onto buildings with earlier, more local, traditions. Land ownership has also been a strong factor. Farmhouses were often leased from large estates where the lessees were often expected to carry out their own improvements, sometimes with highly individual results. In many cases, even where much of the core masonry of an early building survives, at least the front wall has been rebuilt or refaced. Consequently, compared to Devon, Cornwall has a relatively poor heritage of late medieval vernacular buildings. Cornwall also has fewer longhouses, much less thatch and fewer early roof structures associated with this tradition. There is a greater concentration of earlier buildings in North and East Cornwall, particularly where the economy was more dependent on agriculture than industry or fishing. It is very rare to find a house with pre-1700 origins that has not been refashioned many times. These layers of construction are often of considerable interest in their own right and result in buildings where the standing archaeology they contain can be 'read' and admired.

MERCHANTS' HOUSES of the type with stone side walls and timber jettied gable-ends to the street front can be found in some of the towns (especially Fowey, Launceston, East Looe and Penryn). These can be compared to those found in Devon towns such as Exeter and Totnes and also share a strong stylistic relationship with merchants' houses in Brittany and elsewhere in France. Arguably the best examples of this type in Cornwall are Nos. 11, 13 and 13A High Street, Launceston.

PLAN FORM is an important factor in assessing the date, type and evolution of historic houses. Early plans were simple and usually built end-on to the slope of the land. TWO-ROOM and THROUGH-PASSAGE PLANS were most common, with the OPEN HALL (the living room) on higher ground (the higher end) to one side of the passage and an unheated service room at the lower end on the other side of the passage, as for example at Truthall. This was also the common plan type for LONG-HOUSES where the lower end was used for farm animals. Except for ruined examples in upland areas this building type was until fairly recently considered to be almost unknown in Cornwall. However, limited archaeological investigation of recent years has produced a high percentage yield rate of houses that started life as longhouses. Good examples of genuine longhouses include Cullacott in Werrington parish, Halbathick near Liskeard, and Codda, Altarnun. Codda is in the middle of Bodmin Moor and the other examples are in nearby upland areas. As in Devon, the location of these examples indicates a relationship between upland areas and surviving longhouses which may be connected with transhumance but further investigation is needed. Cullacott is near the Devon border and suspected longhouses like Penfound, Poundstock, and Well Farmhouse in North Tamerton may indicate that this building type is more numerous nearer to the Devon border.

Higher-status houses sometimes also had an inner room (a room beyond the hall), the result usually called a THREE-ROOM and THROUGH-PASSAGE PLAN, and many houses that started life as a two-room plan were extended by adding an inner room later to provide a more private and prestigious room space. This

71

plan type evolved so that the 'inner room' was added as a projecting wing (a PARLOUR WING). As time went on houses were designed to have integral parlour wings and sometimes they also had balancing service wings forming a U-plan courtyard at the front.

Because of the limits imposed by their central hearths relating to open halls, many earlier houses were one storey high throughout, the rooms divided by low timber screens, like the earliest identified phase of the Old Post Office at Tintagel. When wall fireplaces with chimneys were added many of these houses were provided with upper floors under steeply pitched original roofs. Often this happened as a phased scheme. Sometimes a room was added above the lower end and a small room above the passage. This room over the entry was often JETTIED over the still open hall. However, there are now very few surviving houses with this feature in an easily recognizable form. Good examples include Truthall, Methrose in Luxulyan parish, and Cullacott.

The difficulties and limited effectiveness of radical conversions often led to a decision for total rebuilding instead. There are many examples in Cornwall where houses that had existed at the time of the Domesday Survey in 1086 were completely rebuilt in the C16 and C17 as two-storey houses, usually with generous provision of windows and with fireplaces fitted to most room spaces. Despite this revolution in house design many houses continued in use as open halls until the latter part of the C17, late within the national pattern. Some late C17 glebe terriers descriptions show that a few rectories, relatively high-status buildings, survived as open halls. A very small number of open halls even survived into the C20, when they became properly recognized; sometimes their survival was a result of being reused as farm buildings in the C19, as at Cullacott, where a new farmhouse was built in 1884.

At many higher-status houses from the late C16 until well into the C17, two-storey porches were being added to the front of through passages, or were a feature of the original design of the house. Occasionally porch chambers were heated and it is likely that they were often used as the private office for the owner or tenant. A good example of a heated porch survives at Trerithick, Altarnun, dated 1585 for John Hecks. Many such porches are probably early examples of 'count houses', particularly where they are related to local industry. At Trenethick, Wendron, a pair of strongrooms, fitted with narrow lights to their mullioned windows, and also with dressed granite floors and ceilings, were added to the front of the lower end of the house, probably in the late C16. The provision of windows to the strongrooms suggests that the rooms were also used as count houses by the Hill family, who made money out of tin mining. A striking stone gatehouse with a jettied dressed granite front reinforced the security needs of the house.

Fully developed plans include Tregarden, St Mabyn, which has an E-plan front with central porch and a forward projecting wing at either end. Great houses were sometimes provided with extensive new plan forms, as for example at Trerice where a fashionable E-plan front almost totally replaced the earlier house. At the more vernacular level ambitions were more modest, but there are often surprising pretensions to grandeur. A Renaissance-inspired colonnade at Pendeen Manor was probably influenced by the grand scheme at Godolphin.

During the C17 and C18 the plan form of rural houses continued to be one room deep with extra accommodation being provided in the form of wings, including stairs housed in small wings. However, there was an increasing fashion for providing shallow rooms under an outshut roof and the staircase was usually included within this part, or as a short wing sand-wiched between. Generally, double-depth plans become more common in the latter half of the C18, partly owing to the development of the king post roof and the greater span that this could provide. Alternatively, double-depth plans were accommodated under parallel roofs, one behind the other, or with U-plan roofs that drained via a central valley. As privacy became more important internal passages were provided at first-floor level so that each bedchamber could be accessed without going through another room space as had been accepted, even in houses of high status, since two-storey houses had become more common.

ROOFS can often provide the best evidence for dating a build-ing. In some instances a roof structure is older than many of the walls that support it. This usually occurs where walling was rebuilt under an existing roof structure to accommodate more fashionable features. Medieval (pre-1485) roofs in secular buildings are extremely rare in Cornwall and are mostly of a BASE-CRUCK derivative type. Houses where good examples of base-cruck roofs survive include Truthall and Methrose, Luxu-lyan. This roof design combines architectural display with engin-eering principles, the latter adapted to make use of the relatively short lengths of timber available. All surviving examples display similar design characteristics with raised base crucks rising to collar level, arched bracing, square-set purlins and reduced prin-cipals above collar level. The lack of availability of suitable timber is a probable reason why, except for one known example at the Abbey House in Padstow, there are no jointed crucks in Cornwall, whereas in Devon this is the main type of roof struc-ture employed for buildings from the C14 right into the C17. In Cornwall, C16 and C17 roof structures survive in reasonable numbers and are represented by a small number of identifiable designs. ARCHED-BRACED and WIND-BRACED ROOFS are used during the first half of the C16 for high-status buildings (*see* above, p. 39). At the less ambitious level, roofs had RAISED CRUCK-TRUSSES, sometimes with THREADED PURLINS and MORTISED and CRANKED COLLARS. Good examples of this kind of roof structure can be seen at the Old Post Office at Tintagel, 59 and the guildhouse (a former church house) at Poundstock. 60 Usually of slightly later date, many roofs had collars fastened to the principals by halved and lapped fishtail (or dovetail) joints, as employed in the 1579 (datestone) parlour wing at Cullacott. As the fashion changed from open roofs to plaster ceilings, roof structures were designed in a much simpler way with no need to use carpentry detail for display. Dendrochonology has provided some confident and reliable dating evidence, including an approximate date of *c.* 1510 for the roof of the great hall at Cotehele House; a probable *c.* 1540 date of construction for the guildhouse at Poundstock; a *c.* 1613 date for roofs with dovetail joints at Keigwin and the Old Standard in Mousehole; and a *c.* 1620 date for the roof of the Convocation Hall at the Duchy Palace in Lostwithiel. These latter results show that this particular tradition carried on into the early part of the C17.

CHIMNEYSTACKS are an important part of the character of many rural houses in Cornwall. The materials of their construction, as well as their design and location, can tell us much about their age and status. Pre-1700 chimneys are usually built from local stone or dressed granite. Many chimneys project externally from the walls either as LATERAL STACKS, at the front or rear of a house, or as GABLE-END stacks. The lateral stack is usually an early feature and often associated with houses that began life as open halls with central hearths. Lateral stacks were commonly added to open halls when upper floors were added, or to improve the smoke removal from the building as at Pennellick, near Pelynt. However, the tradition for lateral stacks continued long after the construction of two-storey houses became common. Higher status chimneys of the C16 and C17 were built from dressed granite and had shaped tops above a weathering course. Special features included the incorporation of battlements, as at Pendeen Manor House. Lower down the social scale stone rubble stacks and simpler dressed granite stacks are more difficult to date as the tradition for building stone chimneys sometimes continued well into the C19, particularly in the granite areas of Cornwall.

WINDOWS and DOORWAYS are significant architectural features that not only provide visual punctuation but also present good dating evidence. Medieval windows and doorways are usually constructed from dressed freestone or oak and finished with moulded or chamfered detail. Small early windows were constructed from a single piece of stone or oak, sometimes with multiple narrow lights. The Old Post Office at Tintagel has many examples of small windows cut from single pieces of stone. Dressed granite became the most common material from the early C16 and its use sometimes resulted in some very fine features like the ogee-headed MULLIONED WINDOWS at Trecarrel. Oak continued to be used, but because of the more fragile nature of this material few examples survive externally. However, oak windows with arched lights at the guildhouse at Poundstock testify to the high quality that could be achieved. External oak doorways are now rare but moulded doorways at No. 13 High

Street in Launceston and No. 8 St Thomas Street, Penryn, are good C17 examples. Internal oak doorways are more common and even survive from the late medieval period, as the arched doorway from the through passage to the lower end room at Methrose, Luxulyan, exemplifies.

The pointed-arched doorway design gave way to the four-centred arch *c*. 1500. Later came the basket arch, and then the round arch resulting from Renaissance influence, all usually with moulded or chamfered detail. Simpler doorways with flat heads are more difficult to date. Sometimes all that survives from an earlier scheme is the stone doorway.

Moulded or chamfered mullioned windows were the dominant window type until about 1700 when SASH WINDOWS became fashionable, and mullioned windows were often removed in order to fit them. Alternatively, whole sections of walling were rebuilt or refaced to accommodate them. As a result of this process Cornwall now has a rich heritage of early sash windows with thick glazing bars, as for example at late C17 Lancarffe, Helland, and in the early C18 refronting of C17 Cusgarne Manor, Gwennap. Alternatives to sash windows were casement windows and horizontal-sliding sash windows. Early examples of all these designs survive in Nos. 11, 13 and 13A High Street, Launceston. From the late C18 thinner glazing bars became common.

72

Turning to interior decoration at the vernacular level, WALL PAINTINGS are now extremely rare. Such poor survival is compensated for by the high quality of what remains, as for example the C16 wall paintings in the hall, and in the room over the entry, at Cullacott, and a remarkable painted frieze at Trevelver, St Minver, which depicts the landscape surrounding the house as it was in the C17. DECORATIVE PLASTERWORK is represented by some nationally important examples at the higher social level (*see* p. 42), where in the C16 and C17 ornate plaster ceilings, friezes and overmantels were superseding the earlier fashion for decorative timber ceilings and open roofs. At a slightly lower social level the fashion for decorative plasterwork generally came slightly later. However, many plaster barrel ceilings were added under earlier roofs or were designed into a more fashionable scheme, as at Pendeen Manor. Much earlier plasterwork has been lost through refashioning or decay but many good examples of C17 plaster overmantels survive, as at Pengenna, St Kew. Sometimes early plasterwork tells a particular story, as for example at Penrose, Sennen, where a C17 wall plaster panel depicts an apple tree associated with a tragic incident. It is the first half of the C18 that sees the wider distribution of plasterwork, particularly with respect to plaster ceilings in the Baroque or Rococo styles, usually fitted to the parlour of a house. Rosteague, near Gerrans, for example, has fine early C18 plasterwork added to the parlour within its C17 parlour wing. WALL PANELLING is rare from the earlier period but as with ceiling plaster there is a strong fashion for full wall panelling or simple dado panelling and for panelled doors during the C18. Bolection mouldings are common in the early part of the century, as represented at Kerris Manor, Paul, but raised and fielded panels or ovolo-moulded panels become fashionable later or were used earlier in rooms of slightly lower status. In simple farmhouses the survival of the two-panel door with HL hinges is sometimes all that is left from an C18 scheme.

Farm buildings

Early farm buildings are extremely rare in Cornwall. In the medieval period the longhouse had been a self-contained farmstead but what survives of purpose-built detached farm buildings of the medieval period is limited to very few known examples. Domed stone DOVECOTES (or CULVER HOUSES), probably dating from the C16 or possibly earlier, are represented by a few surviving examples; the best-known one is at Cotehele.

Two THRESHING BARNS that retain medieval roof structures are Maer Barn, Bude, and Cargoll Barn, St Newlyn East, both related to ecclesiastic ownership. There is a medieval barn at Trerice too, a house that once had its own chapel. The great barn at Cotehele is a complex early C16 design that includes a two-storey part at one end. A less-known example of a C16 barn survives at Bokelly, St Kew. Most surviving pre-1700 farm buildings are single-storey threshing barns that typically date from the latter half of the C17 or the early C18. During the C18 the two-storey threshing barn became the more established type: some of these were built from cob and originally had thatched roofs, but many of those that survive were well constructed from stone and had slate roofs. These barns had their threshing floors on the first floor, which was also a drier place to store grain and to protect it from vermin. Initially designed for hand threshing, many of these barns were later provided with HORSE ENGINE HOUSES where threshing and other machinery was driven by whims powered by horses or cattle. A C19 open-sided polygonal-plan example of this building type can be found attached to the rear of an C18 barn at Tregithew, Manaccan. The first use of STEAM POWER in the world for driving farm machinery took place at an C18 brick barn at Trewithen Home Farm, where an engine designed by Richard Trevithick was installed in 1811. This engine survives in the Science Museum.

Despite the fashion for large lofts in two-storey barns, detached GRANARIES carried on STADDLE STONES continued to be built in Cornwall: the best survival of these is in St Kew parish, as for example at Bokelly. Another building type added to farmsteads, usually in the C18, common in Devon but rare in Cornwall, was the LINHAY, a building with an open front used as a shelter shed or shippon on the ground floor and with hay and straw storage in a squat loft above. WATERMILLS had existed from medieval times and these continued to be updated as the technology relating to them advanced. A consequence of this is that very few mills retain early machinery. However, chamfered granite doorways or other pre-1700 features provide clues to earlier origins. Many watermills were totally rebuilt, as for example at Addicroft Mill, Linkinhorne, where there is a purpose-built early C19 mill with its original machinery and a miller's house.

MODEL FARMS became more common as the C19 progressed but more commonly a more planned layout of farm buildings of specialist function was added to an existing farmstead. A good example of a model-farm group is Methleigh, near Porthleven, where a three-storey watermill was a key element in a complex system of water function within the farmstead. At Coombshead, Lewannick there are two parallel ranges flanking the large yard, both of which include barns, one a bank barn with a waterwheel. At Botallack Manor there is a good example of a planned but informal layout of C19 farm buildings added at a distance from the C17 house and its associated C17 barn. The later buildings include a PIGSTY RANGE that has feeding hatches in its rear wall, a design that became increasingly common in line with scientific advances made to this and other building types.

ARCHITECTURE FROM 1660 TO 1800

That Cornwall remained essentially conservative in its building traditions long into the second half of the C17 is demonstrated by the architecture of the first CHURCH built after the Reformation: King Charles the Martyr, Falmouth, begun in 1661. It is still Gothic in some of its external detail with two tiers of typically Cornish Perp windows, while the interior is indisputably classical with the aisles divided from the nave by tall granite columns with Ionic capitals in plaster. The dedication is characteristic: Cornwall had been one of the most Royalist counties in England, and the Royal Arms, modelled or painted, which appear in so many Cornish churches are evidence of that. The most spectacular are a plaster group in the N of the county (Kilkhampton, Launcells, Marhamchurh, Poughill, Poundstock and Stratton) which were erected for Charles I (that at Poundstock was dated 1638), with strapwork decoration. Some appear to have been updated for Charles II and in the case of Poundstock for George IV. Another of this group is found miles away at Boconnoc. A letter of thanks written by Charles I in 1643 is also recorded in many churches in one way or another.

Kilkhampton also has some splendid early C18 monuments by *Michael Chuke* (1679–1742), a native of the town, to whom the royal arms mentioned above were erroneously attributed in the previous editions of this book. Chuke had been a pupil of Grinling Gibbons and worked with Gibbons for John Grenville on his great house at Stowe in Kilkhampton parish: had it survived it would have remained Cornwall's finest COUNTRY HOUSE. Grenville had been created 1st Earl of Bath in 1660 as a reward for his assistance with the Restoration and in 1675 began building a house of astonishingly ambitious scale on a dramatic hillside site near the sea. On a rectangular plan with two principal floors above a basement, it was seven bays deep with a magnificent eleven-bay E front looking inland towards Kilkhampton castle and church. It was demolished as early as 1739, but so sumptuous were its features that much was moved elsewhere including the grand staircase with openwork carving in the style of Gibbons to Cross near Great Torrington, Devon, and an entire room with lavish plasterwork and decoration to the Town Hall at South Molton, Devon. The rich plasterwork at Marhayes Manor, Week St Mary, rebuilt in brick in the late C17, is probably another example of post-Restoration reward since its likely builder, John Rolle, was made a Knight of the Bath for his loyalty. The plasterwork at both Stowe and Marhayes is of the highest quality, comparable to Devon, which is perhaps unsurprising in view of the proximity of both properties to the border.

One of the first later C17 houses to abandon Tudor precedent in favour of classical design is Newton Ferrers. Two-storey over a basement but still of H-plan, it has a seven-bay centre wholly occupied by a saloon on a *piano nobile* accessed by a graciously proportioned flight of steps, an arrangement reminiscent of the earlier Ince Castle. A rare example of the DOUBLE-PILE house of this period is Tregrehan, of *c.* 1680, almost symmetrical with the principal rooms arranged to look towards St Austell Bay. Croan is an especially complete house of *c.* 1690 with a symmetrical seven-window front. At the level of the smaller gentry house Trewarne near St Kew is an interesting example of mid-C17 rebuilding to create a symmetrical front, with a four-centred central doorway flanked by pairs of unusually tall four-light windows with king mullions and transoms, and with a generously proportioned stair to the originally three-storey accommodation built at the rear of the through passage. It also has fine contemporary plasterwork. Trereife near Penzance is a slightly later version of the remodelling of an earlier house to produce the same desired symmetry in its charming and well-proportioned seven-bay front of 1711, with an impressive staircase, if of conservative detail, at the rear.

The greatest GEORGIAN HOUSE in the grand manner in Cornwall is Antony, 1718–24. Long attributed to *James Gibbs* on account of its consummately disciplined classicism, it is now considered more likely to have been overseen by *John Moyle* of Exeter, possibly following a Gibbs design: it is likely that the brick pavilions and forecourt to the S entrance front are based on a design by Gibbs or are by Gibbs himself. The interior echoes the exterior in its strict geometry of plan and restrained decoration. Trewithen, on the other hand, shows how even at the scale of the great house a stately symmetrical mansion could be achieved by gradual but radical remodelling and extension. *James Gibbs* had prepared a scheme for a new four-storey seven-bay house of a plain English PALLADIAN form, but the decision of successive members of the Hawkins family to transform the existing U-plan house incrementally meant that the Gibbsian masterplan took over thirty years to reach fruition. The process involved a number of architects, beginning with *Thomas Edwards* of Greenwich in 1737 and continued after Edwards's departure in 1761 by one or other of the *Brettinghams* who worked with *Sir Robert Taylor*, to whom the splendid interior, the epitome of Georgian design in Cornwall, is attributed. Each side of the house was built or rebuilt at a different time and each range planned separately from the rest in a fascinating demonstration of how architects adapted existing architectural fashions as well as responding to successive patrons setting different priorities. The five-bay central range of the s front most closely adheres to Palladian rules: though without a basement podium or classical ornament, it has a dominant relationship to its flanking ranges, its windows are twice as tall as wide, it has a classical cornice, and there are architrave surrounds to the windows and doorways. The brick pavilions on either side of the N forecourt are reminiscent of Antony of a few decades earlier. The result is that Trewithen exudes the character of the Cornish gentry house in scale and proportions rather than a purer Palladian appearance.

Thomas Edwards is by far the most interesting (and prolific) architect working in Cornwall in the mid c18. Although little is known of his life, except that he died in Greenwich in October 1775 as a man of considerable wealth, it is possible that he was a pupil of John James, Clerk of Works to the construction of the Greenwich Hospital under Nicholas Hawksmoor. He received payments for work on the remodelling of Trewithen 1738–46 and up to 1761. It is certain that he built up a substantial Cornish practice in which the principal influence was his relationship with the Rev. William Borlase and his circle. It was undoubtedly through the influence of Borlase that Edwards owed his introduction to the Vyvyans' great house at Tre-lowarren. Between 1756 and 1760 he transformed the multi-gabled and irregularly windowed house without and within. The elevations were regularized by reproducing the extant Tudor mullioned windows, introducing a shallow hipped roof with a continuous crenellated parapet, rendering and colour-washing the rubble walls, and extending the chapel w in Bath stone. Inside, the hall was subdivided and an elegant cantilevered stone stair was provided in the new entrance hall.

86

That Edwards was eminently capable both of working classical forms into existing houses and building in a more pure Palladian style is abundantly clear from his other work, and especially Tehidy, Nanswhyden and Carclew (*see* Mylor). It is one of the great regrets about Cornwall's architecture that none of these houses has survived, though something of each remains. Fortunately all are illustrated in Borlase's *Natural History of Cornwall* of 1758. Tehidy is where Edwards's presence is first recorded in 1734 building a new house for the Bassets, one of the great Cornish mining dynasties. It was an imposing Palladian mansion, a square central block of three storeys over a podium with a three-bay pedimented centre set within four quadrant pavilions. Nanswhyden, 1740, was also an elegantly proportioned square of three storeys above a basement and of nine bays, with a graciously proportioned double flight of steps giving access to the principal rooms. Carclew, *c.* 1750, had a splendid Palladian front in granite ashlar with a central Ionic portico to full height linked by Tuscan colonnades to pavilion wings with pediments. Other Cornish houses of this period with originally detached pavilions (e.g. Chyverton, Perranzabuloe, and Trewarthenick, Cornelly) saw them incorporated into the main house in later remodellings. At Werrington the new mid-C18 range is across the courtyard from the old hall: it has the progressive features of a central canted bay and, behind the main rooms, a spacious corridor intended as a sculpture gallery.

Of the later C18 the small group of castellated houses in west Cornwall (Acton Castle, Perranuthnoe; Tregenna Castle, St Ives; and possibly the embattled Manor Office at Marazion, all *c.* 1775) has previously been attributed to *John Wood the Younger* but more likely to have been by *William Wood* of Truro (Paul Holden). Although much reduced from its late C18 zenith, Boconnoc remains of considerable interest because of its substantial remodelling by *Thomas Pitt* working with *Charles Rawlinson*: Pitt had advised Walpole on the decoration of Strawberry Hill and designed garden buildings at Mount Edgcumbe as well as Stowe and Hagley Hall outside Cornwall. The majestic imperial stair of *c.* 1774 with richly decorated walls in the Neoclassical style and fine C18 plasterwork in the drawing room still give a flavour of its former grandeur. Both at Prideaux Place, where Humphrey Prideaux replaced the E front gables with hipped roofs and castellations, and at Port Eliot, St Germans, where *John Johnson* extended the s front and built the round room at the E end of the house, the houses were awaiting their early C19 transformation.

Cornish TOWNS are also rewarding places to enjoy C18 architecture, Truro most of all, contemporary observers comparing it in its elegance and society with Bath and London, albeit on a lesser scale. It can boast the two best C18 town houses in the county, Princes House and Mansion House, Princes Street: they are both by *Thomas Edwards*, and are remarkably grand mansions of metropolitan quality. The former, 1739, is Gibbsian outside and Baroque within; the latter, 1755–62, is Palladian outside and Rococo within: characteristically both are highly restrained in external detail with sumptuous interiors. Only the front façade of the former Assembly Rooms survives, felicitously the centrepiece of the square outside the w front of the cathedral, but it is enough to show that both in proportions and detail it would not have looked out of place in Bristol or Dublin: it is *c.* 1780 by *Christopher Ebdon*, a pupil of James Paine. That Truro was striving to be a proper Late Georgian town is reflected both in the demolition of a row of buildings in the middle of Boscawen Street in the 1790s to create a dignified civic space and especially the laying out of Lemon Street, begun *c.* 1790. It is the most gracious street in Cornwall, rising wide and spacious from the waterfront and lined by the unified frontages of its Georgian buildings, most faced in honey-coloured Pentewan stone. Most towns have some good C18 houses and a few have similarly gracious streets, though not on the same scale: Castle Street, Launceston, has three excellent brick houses of the early to mid C18 all with fine contemporary plasterwork and other detail; Cross Street, Helston, is a mid-C18 suburb of villas in leafy gardens cheek-by-jowl with the town centre; and Chapel Street, Penzance, has a nice mix of brick and stucco houses of the mid to late C18. Some of the best are the former town houses of the gentry like Edgcumbe House, Fore Street, Lostwithiel, and Bank House, Bank Place, Falmouth, the home of the Fox family; there are several other brick houses in Arwenack Street also built by the Foxes. Of PUBLIC BUILDINGS, the outstanding survival is the Guildhall and Cornmarket at Lostwithiel, its 1740 date remarkably early for Cornwall, while Fowey has its dignified Town Hall, dated 1787, in very fine granite ashlar near the historic waterfront. Penzance has the rare survival of a (now converted) C18 theatre behind the Union Hotel, Chapel Street, of almost exactly the same dimensions as the extant example at Richmond, North Yorkshire. GEORGIAN CHURCHES are rare. The most interesting is St Michael, Helston, 1756–61, again by *Thomas Edwards*, here turning away from Palladianism back to *Wren*, *Hawksmoor* and *James* models: indeed the exterior at Helston bears comparison with James's St George, Tiverton, 1714–33. The body of the church of St Euny, Redruth, 1768, is eloquently classical, reflecting the town's mid-C18 ambitions, two-storey divided by a plain band with small sashes below and tall round-headed windows above with a spacious, lofty interior. Some classical features that had been installed in medieval churches like the late C17 Tuscan s arcade at Crowan were swept away by C19 restorations, leaving the stately Doric columns of the N arcade at Pelynt of c. 1680 as a rare survival. Many medieval churches were also re-windowed at this period with sashes replacing the old tracery, only of course to be in turn replaced by medieval styles in the C19 (*see* below on C19 restorations). A rare example of an C18 sash window survives in the E window of the N aisle at Paul, and at St Ewe the disturbance to the s wall occasioned by the restoration of Gothic tracery to replace the sash windows (shown in a painting in the church) can be clearly seen in the masonry.

Georgian FUNERAL MONUMENTS, though not rare, are on the whole less distinguished than the C18 architectural achievement in Cornwall might have been expected to produce. There is little to compare with the grand scale of *Rysbrack*'s Eliot monument of 1722 at St Germans, the most ambitious C18 monument in Cornwall. He worked more modestly at St Michael Penkevil in 1763 in a monument designed by *Adam*. Other noteworthy examples are the splendid Pyper and Wise memorial at St Mary Magdalene, Launceston, of 1731, uncommonly classical and uncommonly good; the Molesworth monument, 1735, at Egloshayle, of metropolitan workmanship; the Mohun monument,

1737, at St Ewe, excellent London work attributed to *Sir Henry Cheere* with first-rate fruit and flower decoration complementing the life-sized bust between broken pediments below and above; and the Hawkins monument at Probus, 1766, attributed to *Nicholas Read*, with a very good epitaph with seated pointing figure holding a medallion, and a flying angel above. Monuments entirely of *Coade* stone, the terracotta-like material with which mechanical production of art begins in England, are found at Lawhitton and St Michael Caerhays.

The old Dissent in Cornwall is principally marked by the activities of the Quakers, with MEETING HOUSES recorded in a number of places by the end of the C17 including some of the major towns (they were later rebuilt, as at St Austell). The oldest Friends meeting house to survive is their delightful and typically modest building at Marazion, built in 1688, but the most outstanding in situation, design and fittings is Come-to-Good, Kea, of 1710, representative in every aspect of the unassuming simplicity and integrity of the Quaker endeavour. The early introduction of METHODISM to Cornwall in the 1740s was to transform the religious experience of the Cornish (*see* The Nineteenth Century below) but little that is recognizable survives of their pre-1800 chapels: the best place to feel something of the character of early Methodism is Wesley's Cottage, Altarnun, where a society had met since 1740s. However, the preaching pit at Gwennap, in use from 1762, and the slightly later examples at Indian Queens and St Newlyn East are powerful and evocative reminders of Wesley's practice of open-air preaching.

So far nothing has been said about the GARDENS, PARKS and LANDSCAPES that complement the greater and gentry houses. Cornwall's mild climate, almost frost-free along the coast, especially along the sheltered S estuaries penetrating far inland, provided the most beneficent environment for the creation of gardens, which were to reach their exotic peak in the C19 (*see* below). It is noteworthy that so many of the major houses are found in or around these estuaries: their landscaped settings are increasingly essential components of the estate, and one of the most enjoyable and distinguishing features of Cornish houses. Many had evolved from medieval deer parks through the formalism of the C16 and C17 but the C18 saw more extensive formal and landscaped gardens designed and created, adorned with classical buildings and sculptures. Werrington was ambitiously landscaped in the mid C18. One of the most charming and complete gardens is at Prideaux Place, which includes a temple of 1738–9 in Bath stone from Ralph Allen's Combe Down quarries. Mount Edgcumbe is one of the most extensive and richly architectural. At Boconnoc, the chief attraction is really the grounds, which are extensive and were laid out with the generosity and the sensitivity to landscape effects that the C18 so easily possessed. It is worth noting that in Cornwall, so far W, *Humphry Repton* produced Red Books for Antony, Catchfrench, Pentillie, Port Eliot (St Germans), Tregothnan and Trewarthenick, Cornelly.

THE INDUSTRIAL ARCHAEOLOGY OF CORNISH MINING AND TRANSPORT
BY JOHN STENGELHOFEN

As has already been mentioned, the long history of the mining industry in Cornwall saw the creation of much of the wealth of the medieval county, but things changed irrevocably from around 1700 as mining achieved a truly industrial scale with inevitable social and economic repercussions. The rural population was depleted as the mining parishes offered greater opportunities. Real fortunes were made by landowners with minerals on their estates, and the proceeds resulted in impressive mansions like Carclew, Tehidy and Tregothnan – as well as philanthropic works. Although Cornish mining is popularly associated with tin, it was copper that dominated the mining scene for a century from the mid c18. Cornwall was producing three-quarters of the world's copper and this was responsible for the largest mines, employing huge numbers of miners, and great prosperity – until its decline forced the mass emigrations of the 1860s. Copper's sudden rise and equally sudden descent were over in less than 200 years, but tin continued to be mined from prehistoric times until the end of the c20.

Over time, tin and copper lodes were traced back further into hillsides or deeper into the ground so that flooding became an increasing problem; if adits could not be dug, horsepower or manpower soon proved of limited use. Various methods of dewatering in the more advanced German mines were published in the mid c16 (in Georgius Agricola's *De Re Metallica*, 1556)

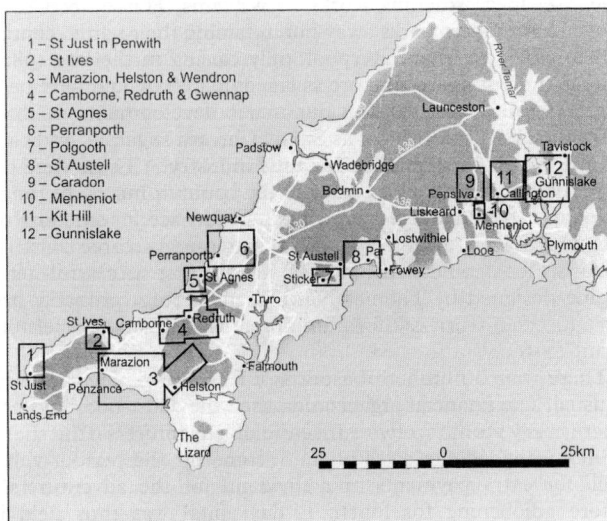

Map of major mining districts in Cornwall

with detailed woodcuts. Agricola's most sophisticated system used pumps operated by waterwheels, although the difficulty of accurately boring timber pump pipes limited their effectiveness. Richard Carew's *Survey of Cornwall*, 1602, suggests that water-powered pumping was known in Cornwall, and the waterwheel continued in use until the mid C20 in some situations, such as at Tolgus stream works near Redruth. But it was another century before deep pumping – and deep mining – became practical, with the introduction of the steam engine.

The basis of ORE TREATMENT for both tin and copper until the C20 relied on gravity to separate out the heavier metal content. After breaking up the rock containing these minerals, crushing with STAMPS reduced it to the consistency of coarse sand. In the stamps a waterwheel turned a drum with cams that raised heavy timber or iron vertical beams, which dropped back to crush the ore, as at Tolgus. Various methods were then used to allow the metal to settle while the waste was washed onwards. These processes are best seen at King Edward Mine, Camborne, and Geevor, St Just, where much of the machinery can be seen working. On many derelict mine sites remains of rectangular settling pits, and concave and convex BUDDLES – shallow circular concrete pits, introduced in the mid C19 – can be seen. Copper processing was simpler, but historically was based on the same principles. TIN SMELTING from the early C18 in reverberatory furnaces took place in over thirty works at one time or another, on a larger scale than was possible using charcoal in old blowing-houses; little remains, however, other than derelict walls and chimneys. A few furnaces continued working into the C20 and the remains of the last to close, in 1931, Seleggan (*see* Carn Brea) are accessible, with extensive walled enclosure and chimneys. The Mellanear smelting works of Williams, Harvey & Co. in Hayle moved their works away but, retaining their name, continued to smelt tin near Liverpool, only closing in the late 1980s. The method of processing ore as late as *c.* 1700 would have been largely familiar to Agricola, but major developments in three fields then occurred which, as Sandy Gerrard suggests, 'radically altered the character and scale of the industry'.* These were the introduction first of gunpowder to the county's mines, begun in 1689, and secondly of the reverberatory furnace for smelting tin with coal in 1705, avoiding the use of increasingly scarce charcoal. Of far wider significance, however, was the first successful steam engine designed by Thomas Newcomen in 1712, probably first introduced to Cornwall for pumping at Wheal Vor (*see* Helston) about 1716.

There were a number of aspects of Cornish mining that were unusual. The financial organization used the 'Cost-book' system, where every month or two a meeting of 'adventurers' (the share-holders) divided the costs or the income for the period with a 'call' for extra payments or a dividend for the adventurers – before adjourning for lunch. Little capital was thus held in

---

* *The Early British Tin Industry*, 2000.

reserve, which was potentially disastrous in metal mining where wildly fluctuating returns alternated with a sudden need for investments, though surprisingly the system survived until the late C19. Another peculiarity in the county was the division of underground workmen into 'tutworkers', taking an agreed sum for sinking a shaft or similar specified work, and 'tributers', groups of independent miners who worked a 'pitch' for a period, following a Dutch auction. They worked independently, being paid so much in the pound for the tin they raised offset by various costs for candles, gunpowder and other items. Surface workers breaking and processing ore included women known as 'balmaidens'. Unlike in other mining areas women were never asked to work underground, although they were capable of breaking up large rocks. Dolcoath Mine in the 1860s employed 691 men and 352 women as well as 161 children, with most of the boys going underground to join their fathers or other relatives.

During the C18 copper increased in importance, overtaking tin tonnages by the 1760s. This position of supremacy was maintained for almost 100 years, although copper values, per ton of metal, tended to be lower. Following some attempts to smelt copper in Cornwall, notably at Copperhouse, it proved advantageous to take the ore to south Wales for the large quantities of coal required in smelting. This had considerable implications for transport, because copper, being sent away as unrefined ore, entailed moving twenty times the tonnage of smelted tin for transport across the Bristol Channel. The scale of copper mining largely financed the greatest engineering achievement of the period, the COUNTY ADIT. A tunnel driven from the Carnon valley eventually drained 100 mines around Redruth, St Day and Chacewater up to 150 ft (45 metres) below ground, achieving huge savings in pumping costs. Commenced in 1748, it was promoted by two landowning mining families, the Lemons of Carclew and the Williams of Scorrier, and entailed 40 miles of tunnelling. The rebuilt portal can still be seen 1,500 ft (450 metres) s of Twelveheads, but no longer carrying the peak flow of some 14 million gallons (65 million litres) a day.

For the first half of the C19 both copper and tin production continued to increase, mines becoming deeper and deeper, with a few ultimately reaching depths of around 2,500 ft (750 metres), helped by major improvements in opening up new shafts and levels with the introduction of the compressed-air rock drill around 1880. Copper is more widely distributed than tin and today's reserves are still substantial, while tin is far more localized; as a result, Cornwall remained a prime source of the metal over a much longer period. But new sources of minerals in South America resulted in catastrophic price reductions in copper and mine closures across the county during the 1860s; tin was then increasingly faced with competition from Malaysia and Indonesia from the 1870s and 1880s. Cornwall's copper production had peaked at 12,000 tons a year in the 1840s and 1850s, but had virtually ceased by 1900; tin had peaked at 10,000 tons in the 1860s and 1870s, but had halved by 1900. Major tin mines closed in the 1870s and the decline, less abrupt than for copper, simply continued despite an occasional better year, attempts to rework old mines and even a few over-optimistic new developments. The decline dragged on for most of the C20. A few new large mines were tried using modern techniques in the 1970s and 1980s but these had all closed by 1991. Finally South Crofty, working a vast area E of Camborne, having absorbed many other historic mines, closed in 1998 ending all metalliferous mining in the county – at least for the present.

Beam engines and mine buildings

Cornwall's iconic industrial monument, the ENGINE HOUSE, well illustrates the extent of C19 mining activity across a large part of the county, although only 300 engine houses remain in some recognizable form from the 3,000 installations known to have taken place. The steam engine finally solved the water problems – and then much more – albeit requiring huge quantities of coal, which often arrived as return cargo in the ore ships from south Wales. After many experiments with steam Thomas Newcomen, a Devon ironmonger, had built the first workable pumping engine near Dudley in 1712, at a colliery where coal was plentiful. In the 'Atmospheric Engine' condensing steam created a vacuum to draw the piston down in the cylinder, pulling the pivoted beam down, so lifting the outside end up; the weight of the pump rods then descended, by gravity, forcing water up the pumping pipes. This was to be the basis, incorporating future developments, of beam engines, and it dictated the form of the engine house for almost two centuries, with a pivoting beam on the end wall connecting the engine to the shaft outside the house. Sixty Newcomen engines had been erected in Cornwall by the 1770s, but more efficient engines were required to cut the coal costs in Cornwall, far from any collieries. James Watt's patent engines began to replace Newcomen's, introducing a separate condenser so that, rather than heating and cooling the cylinder for each stroke, the steam cylinder remained hot throughout the cycle.

Cornish engineers were still looking for more efficiency, and outstanding among these was Richard Trevithick, who proved the possibilities of higher steam pressure. He could then build more efficient engines which were also easier to adapt to other uses, creating the first road carriage (1801), the first railway locomotive (1804), and the first steam threshing machine for the Trewithen farms at Probus in 1811. This engine is in the Science Museum collection and the engine house is still standing. Improved manufacturing techniques in boilers made increased steam pressures feasible and resulted in the 'Cornish Boiler', which Trevithick installed first at Dolcoath in 1812. There were variations in engines depending on their intended use. James Watt's patented 'sun and planet' motion (1781) converted the reciprocating engine action to rotative for driving factory machinery with line shafting and to raise ore in mines as a winding engine. Later

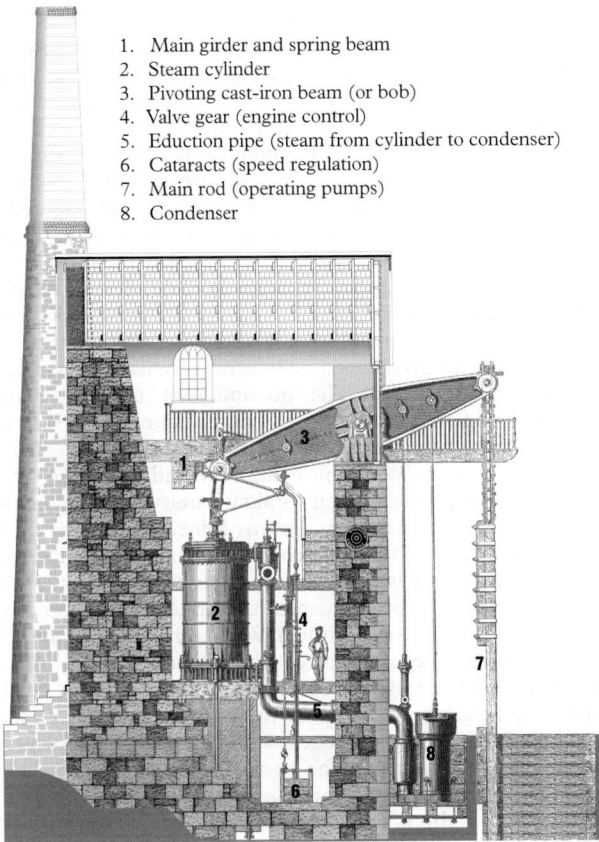

1. Main girder and spring beam
2. Steam cylinder
3. Pivoting cast-iron beam (or bob)
4. Valve gear (engine control)
5. Eduction pipe (steam from cylinder to condenser)
6. Cataracts (speed regulation)
7. Main rod (operating pumps)
8. Condenser

Engine house. Typical section

reciprocating engines would replace waterwheels powering larger Cornish stamps for ore crushing, from 1813.

With a beam up to 50 tons, pivoted three floors up, tipping back and forth (so locally called the 'bob'), the engine house needed to be substantially built so even on an exposed cliff or hilltop, many of these monuments remain, some almost intact after 100 years or more. The constructional requirements were specified by the engine's designer and built by specialist local masons, but the engine houses were almost devoid of architectural embellishments, using locally sourced random stone, with stone or timber lintels, or brick and occasionally even round-headed or pointed windows. Bob-walls tended to be better built with dressed quoins, some even with granite ashlar. On the 'bob' level a cantilevered platform gave access to the end of the beam, and from here up into the gable was timber weatherboarding up to the slate roof. On the back wall a larger opening at ground level gave access for the cylinder and other heavy components. The size of engines is quoted as the diameter or bore of the cylinder, in inches. This varied typically from 18 inches (45 cm) up to 80 inches (2 metres) or more, depending on the task to be performed.

BOILER HOUSES have rarely survived despite being stone-built, as they provided little more than weather protection. Great Wheal Busy, Chacewater, is one of the best, with three arches for its three Cornish boilers. The chimneystack was usually built against a back corner for structural advantage, but occasionally was free-standing. It was almost invariably built tapered in random stone, with iron tie bands, for two-thirds of its height, the top invariably in brickwork on a corbelled brick or granite collar; it is thought that this change in material was to avoid working with large stones at such heights, whereas bricks, small and precise, were easier to lay as the diameter diminished.

Among these utilitarian engine houses there were a few exceptions and eccentricities. The proximity of the landowner's mansion could require a more picturesque engine house: two, fully castellated and with Gothick windows, stood near Camborne, one visible from Pendarves and the other from Tehidy. In a few cases cast-iron window frames could be the only exotic feature, as at Hingstone Downs Mine, Gunnislake, to the E of Kit Hill. Nothing in Cornwall, though, compared with similar engines supplied to municipalities for water or sewage pumping, when civic pride dictated elaborately decorated buildings. Two engine houses of the 1880s, both still standing, are supposed to have been designed by an architect, at East Wheal Rose, St Newlyn East, and Tregurtha Downs, St Hilary. They use narrow slit windows to maintain the structural integrity of the walls, rather than being weakened with the usual large openings.

Experiments to improve the performance of engines led to numerous different arrangements, some successful, that could affect the house, though very few examples survive. Avoiding the use of a beam some had an inverted cylinder pumping directly from the shaft below, all within the engine house. These would look similar to some smaller engines completely enclosed in the house, as the preserved Levant winding engine. Saved from destruction in 1935, a very early example of industrial preservation, it resulted in the formation of the Cornish Engine Preservation Society, later to evolve into the Trevithick Society. In 1804 Camborne engineer Arthur Woolf patented a 'compound' engine with two cylinders; steam was used at high pressure, then at low pressure, in a big cylinder, a principle later developed into the marine 'triple expansion' engine. In the impressive ruined Marriott's engine house on Basset Mines, Carn Brea, an 'inverted compound' had cylinders above the beam, one powering each end. However, a comparatively small number of these variations were built and none survive in the county.

In the early C19 it was increasingly realized that a cold walk home after a climb up 1,000 ft (300 metres) or more of ladders, following a long shift in near-tropical temperatures, was

100

unhealthy. The Royal Cornwall Polytechnic Society campaigned for improvements and, based on earlier German installations, the MAN ENGINE was first introduced at Tresavean, near Lanner, in 1842, followed by other larger mines; that at Levant continued until a major accident in 1919. As with pumping, the beam engine operated heavy timber rods in the shaft, but every 12 ft (3.6 metres) or so platforms were attached to rise and fall; similar fixed platforms were installed in the shaft so that miners jumped alternately from stationary platforms to the moving platforms, to progress either up or down. The engine house, however, was commonly the sole survivor on a mining site, for invariably the rest has been swept away, leaving a very false impression of a mine site. The picturesque cliff-top engine house could be totally obscured by buildings piled up around, as can be seen at Geevor.

In 1855 a visitor wrote of:

A hungry landscape, everywhere deformed by small mountains of many-coloured refuse; traversed in all directions by narrow paths and winding roads, by streams of foul water, by screaming locomotives with hurrying trains; while wheels and whims and miles of pumping rods, whirling and vibrating, and a forest of tall beams, make up an astonishing maze of machinery and motion. Giant arms of steam-engines swing up and down; and the stamping mills appear to try which can thunder loudest, proclaiming afar the progress made in disembowelling the bountiful old earth.*

Every mine was surrounded by lighter structures of timber, which have long disappeared, housing many of the tin refining processes that did not take place in the open. An impression of this landscape and buildings can best be found in preserved sites, especially Geevor Mine, Tolgus (see Redruth) and King Edward Mine, which give a better idea of the reality of working above ground in a mine. Photographic records of the late C19 in museums show the extensive sheds, timber-clad with timber or corrugated iron roofs, invariably in a dilapidated condition even while in use. Other surviving buildings include circular stone explosives stores and, outstandingly, the rare and vast stone-built carpenters' and blacksmiths' workshop at Wheal Busy, Chacewater.

Other metals

It was said everything could be mined in Cornwall except coal. Among the complex mineral deposits of the county were several where extraction could be viable, as well as traces of others such as GOLD, found occasionally in association in some mines but never in sufficient quantities to justify mining alone. Mining for LEAD was locally important until the mid C19 and, in some places, SILVER, as an important by-product. Lead from

* Walter White, *A Londoner's Walk to the Land's End*, 1855.

mid-Cornwall mines resulted in the over-optimistically large lead smelter at Par Harbour. The 'Great Perran Iron Lode' was also a disappointment, but in the 1870s the prospects encouraged the building of the railway line to Newquay, which led to the financial ruin of the great railway contractor Sir Morton Peto. ZINC was localized but was found in the same areas as lead, while as late as 1981 Wheal Jane, near Baldhu, produced over 10,000 tons of zinc concentrate. Other minerals have been by-products or of short-lived importance, such as wolfram (the ore of tungsten), when it was required for light bulbs and steel making and when Marie Curie first isolated radium it was from pitchblende from Trenwith Mine, St Ives.

ARSENIC, commonly found with tin and copper, contaminated ores and was simply burnt off until, in the C19, uses were found for it, in glass making, tanning, chemical dyes and cosmetics, while its poisonous properties made it a constituent of insecticides and wood preservatives into the mid C20. It was first produced commercially in 1812 in the Bissoe valley, Perranarworthal, and then on larger mines. In the 1830s William Brunton developed his calciner, which was soon widely adopted: a small number of examples survive (*see* Botallack and Geevor, St Just). In an early 'environmental health' action the Crown won a case in 1851 against the leading arsenic producer for carrying on a trade 'detrimental to the health, well-being or comfort of his neighbours'. Despite the potential dangers in recovering arsenic some mines continued working it when tin could no longer pay the mine's costs, as in Wheal Busy, delaying its closure until 1922. The Brunton calciners at South Crofty continued working until 1962, the last arsenic works. Fumes from calciners were inevitable, despite precautions, and prevailing winds left large areas devoid of vegetation for decades and occasionally caused the death of a cow or horse.

Foundries

Casting large cylinders for engines required skills that were confined to places like Coalbrookdale in the early C18. By 1800 engines had become more complex, cast-iron beams had replaced timber, and demand was increasing, providing opportunities for a foundry in the county. John Harvey, a blacksmith from Gwinear, moved to Hayle in 1779 to establish a small foundry to make cast-iron flanged mine pump pipes to replace bored-out tree trunks. Just thirteen years later he was building complete pumping engines, on the Newcomen principle to avoid Boulton & Watt's patent royalties. Rapidly establishing a reputation, Harvey expanded and diversified with help from his son-in-law, Richard Trevithick. Then at the E end of Hayle, the Copperhouse Foundry (1819–67), or Sandys, Carne & Vivian, replaced their declining copper smelting business to compete with Harvey's. Earlier, Perran Foundry (1791–1879) had been set up on the River Kennal at Perranarworthal by the Fox family of Falmouth. These three major foundries were capable of building large beam engines or, when required, a ship, a railway locomotive, or almost any other foundry work, and all three exported beam engines around the world. Harvey's built twenty-nine large engines pumping 70 per cent of London's water by the mid C19; two of these engines are preserved *in situ* at Kew Bridge Steam Museum, one of them working again. The Harvey-built Cruquius engine, with a 144-in. (3.65-metre) diameter cylinder (1849) built to drain the Haarlemmermeer, part of a contract in which the Perran Foundry built the pumps, is now preserved as a National Monument in Holland. Additionally some half-dozen smaller foundries in the county were capable of building beam engines up to about 60-in. (1.5-metre) cylinders in size, as well as often continuing general foundry work.

Later foundries specialized: so Holman Bros in Camborne (1801–2003) became noted for their widely exported pneumatic rock drills and their expertise was applied to their pneumatic grenade launchers during The Second World War. They also built beam engines, but survived in the C20 concentrating on portable compressors. The Rock Drill Showroom, Camborne, is now almost all that remains of their works. J. & F. Pool in Hayle (1848–2000) produced perforated metal sheet, required for grading ore in crushing mills, using the former parts of the Copperhouse Foundry buildings in Hayle. Charlestown Foundry (1827–2002) manufactured the last steam engine built for use in Cornwall in 1911; from 1935 it was owned by the major clay company and produced pumps, filter presses and special equipment for use in clay works.

Dealing with castings on such a scale required some large spaces. The second Dutch engine's cylinder was cast at Copperhouse for Perran Foundry as it was beyond their capacity – the job entailed pouring 30 tons of iron in three minutes, a considerable achievement in the 1840s. It is tragic that so little remains of the foundry buildings. A number of buildings, associated with their diverse interests, remain at Harvey's in Hayle, but of the foundry itself there are only ruins – although they are still impressive. At Copperhouse the dock and the canal were much earlier than the foundry, of which none of the works buildings have survived. Only at Perran are recognizable remains extant, now carefully converted for residential use, and retaining the lettered cast-iron lintels and many other features.

Explosives

Fire had long been used in mines to burn dry gorse twigs to split cracks in rocks, but the introduction of gunpowder was a considerable advance, enabling mine shafts and levels to be opened up more easily and quickly. Thomas Epsley introduced gunpowder in 1689 following its use in mines in the Midlands, although he was buried the next year at Breage, his death probably demonstrating the risks of using fuses made by filling quills or straws with powder. The rapidly increasing demand for gunpowder resulted in it being manufactured in Cornwall from the beginning of the C19. For safety reasons sites were then in remote wooded valleys, with a stream capable of working 'incorporating' mills for grinding and mixing the constituents, as at Kennal Vale, Ponsanooth: there six water-powered edge runner mills which ground gunpowder remain, together with other structures, along the wooded banks of the River Kennal. By the late C19 new explosives such as cordite and nitroglycerine were introduced, with larger works set up, ideally among sand dunes where individual buildings of light timber construction were protected by enclosures of sand banks to confine the spread of any explosion. This can be seen on an impressive scale amongst the sand dunes between Hayle and Gwithian, and a smaller site close to Cligga Head, Perranporth. The risks involved with fuses in mining was finally solved when William Bickford invented the safety fuse in 1831 and established a significant industry centred in Tuckingmill, where a complex of industrial buildings survives. Bickford's inspiration came on visiting a friend's ropewalk: he developed the idea based on gunpowder being poured into the centre as a cover of jute was woven on a rope-making machine. The specification for different uses incorporated additional jute covers, varnish, tape or a tar cover for use in wet mines, under water, or in extreme temperatures. The quantity of jute required led to the establishment of a spinning plant that employed fifty people. Bickford-Smith & Co., later part of ICI, established factories all over the world and continued as the leading manufacturer well into the C20 – still producing 40,000 miles of safety fuse in Tuckingmill in 1930.

China clay

China clay occurs in all the granite outcrops of SW England, but chiefly N of St Austell; the feldspar component (aluminium silicate) softened into a fine white powder known as kaolin in China, where it had been used for centuries for manufacturing fine porcelain. William Cookworthy, a Quaker chemist from Plymouth, identified a source in the late 1740s, SW of Tregonning Hill, Germoe, and then around St Austell. Cookworthy experimented in his pottery in Plymouth in the 1760s but rapid expansion began as Staffordshire potters saw opportunities to compete with Meissen – and the Chinese. Kaolin could be washed from hillside pits and as these deepened washing continued with hoses; the 'slurry' was raised to ground level first by waterwheels and then, from a greater depth, by steam engines and then electric pumps. It was then realized that slurry could be piped by gravity from pits in the hills above St Austell to the roads, railways or ports, for refining and drying. After kaolinization the remaining constituents of granite remain solid, so refining relied on settling out waste from liquid clay. This was carried out by slowing the flow to deposit coarse quartz and mica, clay alone being carried onward to settle in stone-lined tanks until it was almost solid. From the mid C19 final drying was carried out in coal-fired PAN-KILNS or 'drys'; these distinctive long stone sheds, with a chimneystack at one end, are a fast disappearing feature in the local landscape.

Each ton of clay produced about 8 tons of waste, so conical 'sky-tips' long dominated the area above St Austell; few now remain, as they have been superseded since the 1960s by larger flat-topped tips designed for later landscaping, but some historic conical tips were swallowed up by environmental improvement schemes. At one time this landscape was popular as a sci-fi film location, made famous by *Dr Who*. Waste sand was increasingly used as concrete aggregate, for blocks and bricks and in road construction (*see* Building Materials). During the C19 other uses for clay were found particularly in paper manufacture, cosmetics and illegally in the early C19 as a whitener in bread. Its use increased as a filler in plastics, and pharmaceuticals including toothpaste and pills as a tasteless inert white powder.

Gradually improvements in processing were made, so that those shown in the museum at Wheal Martyn, St Austell, have long been superseded. The quantities of clay produced, together with the requirements for coal to fire kilns and pumping engines, stimulated the early C19 building of Pentewan, Charlestown and Par harbours, as well as railways in the district. From the earliest days clay was shipped out and taken to the Mersey for the canal to the Staffordshire Potteries. In the C20 up to 80 per cent of production was exported all over the world, mostly from deepwater quays at Fowey. Despite Cornwall and west Devon producing the highest quality clay production has continued to decline after peaking at 3.26 million tons in 1988.

Transport

Travelling in Cornwall has always been slow and difficult, with little evidence of wheeled transport before the C18. The county was remote from the rest of the kingdom, and ROADS were poor and hilly; so the quickest route to London might include a paddle steamer to Bristol as late as the 1850s. It was mining that made more critical demands for efficient transport: the lines of packhorses or mules carrying copper ore down narrow tracks from inland mines to harbours became increasingly impractical, though unavoidable, until they were replaced by the first mineral railways. Road transport was slow to keep pace with developments elsewhere: the first Turnpike Trust was not set up until 1754, and the last was as late as 1863. Their routes are marked by many surviving toll houses, a quarter of all those 180 built.

CANAL projects mostly failed owing to the terrain and resulting engineering problems, with two exceptions. The Bude Canal (1823–91) was established for the import of lime and sea-sand for agricultural improvement in the hilly NE corner of the county: its sea-lock entrance at Bude Haven is still an impressive sight.

It required six incline planes (one in Devon) with one rising no less than 225 ft (68 metres). The Liskeard and Looe Union Canal (begun 1827) was more profitable, serving the inland mines and quarries around Caradon Hill, until the canal company built a link to the mineral railway at Liskeard, so avoiding trans-shipment.

RAILWAYS were soon established from mining districts to the coast, not to connect with the rest of the country but to bring coal inland to the mines and quarries and export their products. The horse-drawn Poldice Tramway, linking Portreath with copper mines in Gwennap, was operating by about 1812 and continued working until about 1866. The Redruth and Chasewater (*sic*) Railway connected mines s of Redruth to Devoran (1826) and the Pentewan Railway connected St Austell to the port at Pentewan for exporting china clay (1829). The Bodmin and Wadebridge Railway (1834) opened with steam locomotives, and passengers – two years before London's first public railway. Built primarily for agricultural purposes, in 1895 it was joined to the North Cornwall line, providing services to Waterloo Station until 1967. More lines built for mining traffic followed with the Hayle Railway (1837), later to become part of the mainline through Cornwall. Newquay (1846) and Par (1847) were developed by J. T. Treffry, joining his harbours to the mines, quarries and clay works he owned in mid-Cornwall. Penzance was served by an extension of the Hayle Railway in 1852, as were Portreath and Truro, forming the West Cornwall Railway, the first line in the county where receipts from passengers exceeded those from goods. Railways reached both Par (1855) and Looe (1860) to replace canals that had links to inland mineral railways. All these ports therefore had railway access before the 'main line' out of the county opened in 1859.

Brunel's Great Western Railway subsidiary reached Plymouth in 1848 and his magnificent 7-ft ¼-in. (2.14-metre) gauge would continue to Truro and Falmouth as the Cornwall Railway. The West Cornwall Railway linked to this at Truro, but remained in the 'economy' standard gauge – with no through trains and trans-shipment of goods. Main railways in the county were costly to build, with modest potential returns. The Cornwall Railway route avoided the high moors, but its south coast route crossed deep river valleys after a high-level crossing of the Tamar, an Admiralty requirement to clear the highest masts. To save money Brunel developed his earlier viaduct designs using an elegant 'fan' of timber members spanning between stone piers. This was an economic solution, when close to 6 miles of viaduct were required, but costly maintenance led to replacement stone viaducts being built alongside between 1871 and 1934, the original piers usually left standing. Cornwall became the last county to have access to the national railway system with the completion of Brunel's famous Royal Albert Bridge at Saltash in 1859.

99   Much remains to be seen on the lines still open, although few stations have retained the original structures in Brunel's favoured Italianate style; only St Germans now remains and a platform

shelter at Menheniot. Many stations were replaced as traffic increased at the end of the C19 and more have gone following contraction of the system. The original Cornwall Railway Carriage and Locomotive Works, often attributed to Brunel, remains at Lostwithiel, although now converted to flats. Engineering works provide interest in hilly terrain, with bridges and viaducts, and a dozen railway inclined planes. A favoured method in the 1830s and 1840s for hauling trains up steep lines was on a rope or chain pulled by a stationary steam engine. In many instances a straight hedgerow can still be seen from afar marking an incline in the landscape, as at Portreath or Angarrack.

The C20 saw an increasingly busy period for the railways with the Great Western Railway promoting holidays on the 'Cornish Riviera' – a term invented in the publicity department at Paddington in 1904. Paid holidays after the Second World War brought a final short boom, with crowded Saturday 'special' trains and extra carriages arriving at Newquay, where platforms required lengthening. Soon, however, a combination of Dr Beeching's axe and increasing car ownership closed many branches on the Great Western Railway and all the routes in north Cornwall, built by the London & South Western Railway to Bude and to Padstow. Stations were sold off, and the much promoted 'Atlantic Coast Express' was forgotten.

THE NINETEENTH CENTURY

The C19 saw the profound transformation of Cornwall. The great engine of change continued to be the vast wealth from mining, described above, now accelerated by the phenomenal rise in copper production alongside tin and accompanied by the opening up of the county through the early development of the railway system. Later, as copper crashed in the 1860s and tin started its slower decline, the Cornish economy diversified into new enterprises like the nascent tourist industry, aided by a resurgence of Cornish identity spurred on by the Celtic Revivalists. The effects on the architecture of Cornwall were formative on the character and appearance of the county as we see it today. The great mining dynasties used their fortunes to aggrandize their houses and estates, still mostly preferring to remodel and improve, often spectacularly, than building *de novo*. They also helped to fund the improvement of Cornish towns including the major expansion of ports and harbours, the spirit of improvement combining with burgeoning trade to see the erection of proud new civic buildings and the provision of public health, educational and cultural facilities: this included technical schools, scientific institutes and polytechnics as well as working men's institutes, reading rooms and libraries, many architect-designed like those by *Silvanus Trevail* for his patron John Passmore Edwards (1823–1911) the Cornish born newspaper proprietor and philanthropist. A religious revival

saw the astonishing growth of Methodism in all its diversity,
accompanied by energetic Anglican programmes to revitalize the
church's presence and mission: the result was the building of
hundreds of new chapels and substantial numbers of new
churches as well as the restoration of medieval churches, often
long neglected. Truro epitomizes the transformation, becoming
the new capital of Cornwall with city status in 1877 and the see
of the new Cornish diocese, with England's greatest Victorian
cathedral rising at its centre.

Early nineteenth-century country houses

Tracing these changes can begin with the design of the COUNTRY
HOUSE in the early C19. The earliest sign of the coming of the
GOTHIC taste had been the recasting of the former Lady Chapel
at St Michael's Mount into the charming pre-Strawberry Hill
89   Rococo Gothic suite of the Blue Drawing Rooms in the 1740s.
91   *Sir John Soane* was refashioning Port Eliot (*see* St Germans)
between 1804 and 1809, putting right the 'Islington Gothic' of
his predecessor *John Johnson* with his picturesque battlemented
and Gothic windowed S and E elevations and his elegant interiors.
His stables and coachhouse of 1802–6 are of a characteristically
unusual Soanian design. On a smaller scale the gracious proportions and restrained ornament of the interior of *Benjamin Tucker*'s
castellated house of 1807–8 at Trematon Castle are reminiscent
of Soane. The epitome of the picturesque is *John Nash*'s sublime
Caerhays Castle of 1808, his largest surviving essay in castellated
Gothick, a breathtaking composition of square and round towers
and battlemented walls set against a hillside with exotic planting
and surrounded by Nash's terraced and walled gardens, in a
magical position overlooking the sea. The early C19 Gothicking
of Prideaux Place produced the satisfyingly picturesque S front
but even better the nobly proportioned and exquisitely decorated
stair hall with richly crocketed canopies ornamenting the stair;
Harlyn House has a scaled-down version of the stair hall of great
86   charm. The radical reworking of the W entrance front at Trelowarren included the extension of the chapel with a new Gothic
W gable with an ogee-headed and traceried blank window, while
95   the interior was fitted up with a sumptuous display of Gothic
plasterwork including crocketed canopies exactly like those at
Prideaux Place; the arcaded wall of the Lady Garden was
imported from Nanswhyden at the same time. And J. T. Treffry's
extravagant remaking of Place at Fowey between 1813 and 1845,
an overwhelming display of Romantic Gothic, produced an especially memorable ensemble with the noble tower of the parish
church.

But even Treffry's extravagance was outdone by the palatial scale
of the Boscawens' Tregothnan. *William Wilkins* was employed in
1816–18 to create a spectacular new mansion which he achieved
by encasing the C17 house, of which two complete rooms survive,
in an elaborate East Anglian Tudor Gothic, with elevations of

extreme picturesqueness articulated by castellations, turrets and a forest of elaborately decorated chimneys. All this was ramped up to new levels of magnificence by the dramatic enlargement of the house in 1845–8 by *Lewis Vulliamy*. The *Wilkins* also worked at Pentillie *c.* 1810–15 where they Gothicked the elevations, the garden front again in Tudor Gothic, of eleven bays divided by stepped buttresses with an embattled parapet and clustered polygonal chimneys.

The alternative in the battle of styles of the early C19 was, of course, the NEOCLASSICAL. The most distinguished example in the Grecian taste is Trelissick by *P. F. Robinson*, of *c.* 1825 onwards. Once again the core of the earlier house, here mid-C18, was retained, but completely refashioned into the severest neo-Grecian mansion in Cornwall by adding a giant six-column Ionic portico in the style of the Erechtheion at Athens to screen the recessed front of the original, with a single-storey Doric portico on the w front. In a similar but plainer vein was *Henry Harrison*'s *c.* 1830 remodelling of Trewarthenick (*see* Cornelly), *R. F. Brettingham*'s earlier composition, raising the single-storey flanking wings to the centre to full height. Harrison also worked at Enys (*see* Mylor) and Heligan in the Neoclassical style, though his most arresting achievement is his theatrical Gothic w entrance front to Port Eliot of 1829 with its huge porte cochère and magnificent full-height entrance hall. One of the most interesting architects working at this period was *George Wightwick* of Plymouth (1802–72), the partner of *John Foulston*; despite that pedigree, he was capable of working in a variety of styles. His supremely accomplished Palladianization of the E elevation of Pencarrow in 1844–6 is typical of his skill, also demonstrated in his classical recasting of Tregrehan in 1848–9 by the addition of a two-storey range in front of the s front of the late C17 house, with an Ionic colonnade; he also moved the entrance to the w front with a graciously proportioned entrance hall. His equally ambitious classicization at Trewarne of 1834 is now sadly reduced.

Early nineteenth century public, commercial and military buildings

The Neoclassical style was prominent in PUBLIC BUILDINGS of the early to mid C19, embodying the gravitas required of town centres now being rebuilt on a grander scale. It makes an early appearance, in the Greek Revival style, in the Falmouth Custom House (1814), its severe single-storey stucco front with Doric portico, plain frieze and triangular pediment above the parapet cornice, all strongly reminiscent of *Foulston*'s work at Devonport and Tavistock. Falmouth has another Greek Revival façade in the Arts Centre, built as the Royal Cornwall Polytechnic by *George Wightwick c.* 1835–6, two-storey, the first floor recessed behind fluted Doric columns. The style reaches its apogee in the Market House and Town Hall at Penzance by *William Harris*, 1836–8, where a large Greek temple dominates the prospect up Market

Jew Street towards the town centre – the main approach from the E – perfectly symbolizing the town's ambition to be seen as the capital of the far west; Harris designed other market houses in the same style, but at a smaller scale, at Bodmin and Helston. He also built the Guildhall at Helston, 1837–8, a strong design with an especially good front, the triangular pediment elaborately infilled with decoration in Bath stone. The granite ashlar front of the Shire Hall at Bodmin by *Henry Burt*, 1837–8, is an appropriately severe and imposing presence for the Assize Court at the centre of the then county town, complemented by the nearby Shire House, the former Judges' Lodgings by *Joseph Pascoe*, c. 1840, a more elegant stucco classical composition. At Truro, in contrast, an up-to-date Italian Renaissance style was employed by *Christopher Eales* for the City Hall, 1846–7, a grander version of his palazzo Market Hall at St Austell of 1844. Designed as a suite of buildings between Boscawen Street and Back Quay, it had civic, judicial and market functions, the two-storey front originally an open arcade on tall vermiculated columns that gave into an interior of Piranesian proportions. Many COMMERCIAL BUILDINGS of this period were also Neoclassical, like *Philip Sambell's* (a pupil of Wightwick) Truro Savings Bank of 1845 (now the Royal Institution of Cornwall), but the most astonishing

96 is the Egyptian House, Penzance, the outstanding early C19 survival of Egyptianizing commercial architecture in Britain, clearly inspired by the Egyptian Hall in Piccadilly and *Foulston's* Civic and Commercial Library in Devonport.

Among the most impressive public works of the mid C19 are the MILITARY BUILDINGS erected after the Royal Commission on the Defences of the United Kingdom recommended a ring of strong detached forts around Plymouth Sound, each capable of containing a small garrison. Sited about a mile apart (bombardment range was estimated at the time at *c.* 8,000 yards, or 7,300 metres), they were intended to offer protection from attack by land and sea, and were the most ambitious British C19 land defences to be built, even more extensive than the smaller ring built at the same time around Portsmouth. Most of the land forts were on the Devon side but there are two in Cornwall, Tregantle and Scraesdon. Outer sea defences were provided on the Cornish side by Cawsand, Picklecombe and Polhawn, with Mount Edgcumbe Gardens providing additional defence within the Sound. Elsewhere, the former barracks of the Cornwall Light Infantry at Bodmin of 1881 incorporated the impressive militia keep of 1859 in the French Renaissance style.

Churches and chapels

Early C19 Anglican CHURCHES include three Commissioners' churches by *Charles Hutchens*, a native of St Buryan: St Day,
101 1826–8, Redruth, 1827–8, and Penzance, 1832–5, the latter by far the most ambitious and, in granite ashlar, substantial-looking, with stylistic similarities to St Luke, Chelsea. They were designed

as preaching spaces with galleries, a feature that had been installed in many Cornish churches in the C18 and C19 but was particularly detested by the later C19 High Church restorers and so swept away: the C18 W gallery at Helston is a rare survival. *Philip Sambell* built St John, Truro, in 1828 as a plain rectangle with apsidal chancel in the Greek Revival style. *George Wightwick* was again the most accomplished and versatile, ranging from his remarkable first church in E.E. at Bude, 1834, a rare example of low church, liberalist architecture, through the plain Italianate of Lanner, 1838–40, and the Romanesque of Flushing, 1841–2, and back again to E.E. at Treslothan, 1840–2.

The great church and chapel builders in Cornwall of the early to mid C19 were the NONCONFORMIST denominations. Cornwall holds a special place in the development of Nonconformity and its relationship to Britain's transition into an industrial economy and society. The Quakers were the strongest of the Old Dissent – Presbyters, Baptists and Independents (Congregationalists) – that maintained a modest following in the C17 and C18.* It was, however, the arrival of Methodism in the 1740s, with the first Methodist society formed at St Ives, that transformed the religious experience of the Cornish. John Wesley captured the 'free-church' audience in the C18 and for the whole of the C19 and the first half of the C20 Methodism was the effective established church in Cornwall with nearly a thousand chapels, an especial irony given Wesley's original intention, as an ordained Anglican minister, to reinvigorate the Church of England from within. It was an extraordinarily diverse and vital movement, with endless subdivisions. By 1850 chapels had become a prominent feature of the Cornish landscape and townscape, with chapel building continuing strongly into the second half of the C19 even after the Cornish economy, especially fishing and mining, had started its long decline.

The earliest CHAPELS were adaptations of existing vernacular buildings, and some chapels remained of the simplest form: the cob and thatch chapel at Gwithian and the small, humble chapel at Penrose (St Ervan) are rare survivals. But the diversity of Methodism is reflected in the extraordinary range and variety of chapel architecture, impossible to represent fully in this book. The plan was standard: a rectangle with the main entrance in the W gable and galleries along the side walls, and the W end facing the liturgical E end furnished with a pulpit that later evolved into a rostrum. If any degree of architectural elaboration was employed it was concentrated on the front elevation with standardized or local interpretation of classical and Gothic. The vast majority of pre-1850 chapels drew their architectural features from the classical vocabulary, including the largest, the 'thousand seaters' of Penzance, 1814, Redruth, 1826, St Mary Clement, Truro, 1829–30, by *Philip Sambell*, and St Just, 1833. The Gothic style

109

---

*The Quakers rebuilt their meeting houses in the early C19 with plain, dignified simplicity (Redruth, Truro and St Austell) while *Philip Sambell* built two Neo-Norman Baptist churches at Helston and Penzance in 1836–7.

gathered momentum after 1850, especially among the Wesleyans, though still only as the application of a small number of Gothic features and steeper proportions: such chapels really stand in the Picturesque Gothic tradition of the C18, without its whimsical detail. The E.E. style was favoured, not only as more economical to build but as a deliberate contrast to the more studious and archaeologically correct Dec of High Church Anglicans. A notable exception is *Hine & Norman*'s 1870 chapel at Launceston, a robust Gothic composition with nave, aisles, transepts, and apsidal chancel (and originally with a spire), the interior decorated by *Harris* of Plymouth and *Hems* of Exeter, and complemented by the Romanesque schoolroom by *Hine & Odgers*, 1890. Another is the strikingly spiky French Gothic chapel at Porthleven by *James Hicks*, 1881–3, all elevations strongly expressed and its buttressed bays soaring above the town to a cluster of open bellcotes and pinnacles. The most idiosyncratic Methodist Gothic is at Flexbury Park, Bude, 1905, an exuberant and dramatic display of 'builder's Gothic' with strongly buttressed N and S corner towers set at an eccentric angle to the W front. Chapel interiors are universally decorous and dignified, the seating characteristically of a conservative panelled design preserving an C18 flavour, the decoration limited to an often spectacular central plaster ceiling rose, sometimes exquisitely painted, and, later in the C19, some STAINED GLASS with naturalistic patterns, representations of church saints, and biblical scenes increasingly employed in remodelling schemes (Marazion and Leek Seed, St Blazey, Par). The social importance of Methodism is often evident in the chapels' extensive ancillary halls and school buildings: like the chapels themselves, many are fast being converted to other uses.

This brief summary of Methodist architecture has touched on the effect of the GOTHIC REVIVAL that began in the 1840s, of particular importance in Cornwall because of its role in the Anglican church's campaign from the mid C19 to recover the religious initiative it had long lost to Nonconformity. The growth of the High Church Tractarian movement was paralleled by the development of a scholarly interest in medieval architecture which saw the C14 church in the 'second pointed' or Dec style as the ideal, following its advocacy by Pugin and the Camden Society. In this respect it is vital to recall that at this time the established church in Cornwall was still, as it had been since its brief period of ecclesiastical independence in the C10 and C11, ruled from Devon as part of the Exeter diocese. Exeter had in Henry Phillpotts a High Church bishop and a strong if residual High Church tradition, so it is unsurprising that it was one of the earliest dioceses to respond positively to these new religious and architectural ideals: the Exeter Diocesan Architectural Society, established in 1841 to promote Camdenian principles, was the first such organization outside the universities. Phillpotts's recognition that remote Cornwall had long been a neglected part of his vast diocese led to his determination to promote the building of churches* to serve the expanding new communities created by the mining industry, the restoration of medieval churches that had often fallen into serious disrepair, and eventually the re-establishment of a separate Cornish see.

This helps to explain the appearance in Cornwall from the 1840s of two architects, *William White* (1825–1900) and *George Edmund Street* (1824–81), who were pioneers of the Gothic Revival. Both had been in *G. G. Scott*'s office and both had started their ecclesiastical architectural careers in Cornwall. *White*'s first church was at Baldhu, 1847–8, a design of striking simplicity with Dec tracery and a broached spire, the corbels of the tower arch with portrait heads of Bishop Phillpotts and the young Queen Victoria. His St Philip and St James, Maryfield, 1864–71 (*see* Antony), for the Pole-Carews on their estate at Antony, is pictur- 103 esque without and richly decorated within; he had previously built the school, chapel and vicarage at Maryfield in 1847–8. His rebuildings and restorations of Gerrans, 1849–50, Phillack, 1850–7, and St Hilary, 1853–5, are marks of originality, thought- fulness, and clarity. He also worked at St Columb Major for the Rev. Samuel Walker, the rector and London property speculator who was keen to persuade the authorities that a new Cornish see should be based there. To that end he commissioned White to build an ambitious new rectory that could serve as the bishop's palace, resulting in one of White's earliest and most important houses. Begun in 1851, and theoretically a restoration of the medieval rectory, it is an entirely new house, a brilliant essay in Victorian Romanticism, its charmingly irregular elevations highly picturesque C14 Gothic, the planning of the interior innovative and beautifully detailed; the main rooms, including the chapel, are on the first floor. St Columb has another of White's outstand- ing early buildings, Bank House, North Street, 1856–7, an eye- 110 catching essay in Venetian Gothic at the heart of the town.

Street's first church is St Mary the Virgin, Par, 1848, closely followed by his second at Treverbyn, 1848–50: both are of great charm and originality, strong design, comfortable proportions, and pleasing appearance, with highly effective use of local mater- ials. The former is E.E., the latter early Dec, but both employ a vocabulary that is purely architectural rather than simply decor- ative, the restrained and disciplined detail especially striking in their bold internal scale. His restorations of Cubert, 1846–9, Ladock, 1862–4, and St Michael Penkevil, 1863–5, are similarly memorable, that at Ladock especially notable as being his first collaboration with *William Morris*, his former pupil, which resulted in the best display of *Morris & Co.* glass in Cornwall; 104 there was a similar collaboration at St Michael Penkevil. Near Lostwithiel, Street built the former House of the Sisters of Mercy, now Peregrine Hall, 1862–75 in stages, a composition of great power if also angular austerity in the earliest central phase, miti- gated by the later E.E. chapel and the mellow W domestic extension.

*Fifty-one new churches were built between 1840 and 1900.

A reassessment of the damning verdict that the C19 RESTORA-
TION of Cornish churches was an almost wholly negative process
is now possible. It is difficult to assess their state of disrepair
accurately, but Sir Stephen Glynn's survey of 106 of the then
c. 240 Anglican churches between 1849 and 1870 established that
many of them were sadly neglected. The combination of Bishop
Phillpotts's determination to remedy this situation and the intel-
lectual energy of the Gothic Revival provided the impetus for
successive campaigns of restoration – a term which embraced
repair, rebuilding, extension and embellishment – from the 1840s
sometimes into the first decades of the C20. Canon Michael
Warner's pioneering research* has demonstrated how long and
sustained restoration programmes were; most of them stalled
through lack of funds and were only completed over one or two
decades. Though many of the earlier restorations were undoubtedly destructive, the habit of ripping out earlier fabric was gradually replaced by the more conservative approach advocated by
William Morris and his followers. The result is that the corpus
of C19 Cornish ecclesiastical architecture is all the richer.

Two of the earliest and exemplary practitioners, *Street* and
White, have already been mentioned but restorations were carried
out by almost all the architects working in Cornwall at the time.
The most well-known and prolific restorer was *James Piers St
Aubyn* (1818–95), whose practice was in London but who worked
extensively in Cornwall where his aristocratic family connections
(cf. Clowance, Crowan, and St Michael's Mount) were undoubtedly helpful. St Aubyn made his mark on ninety-eight churches,
restoring seventy-eight and building twenty new. He was an
accomplished deployer of Gothic in his new churches, most of
which are relatively small, but the largest – St John-in-the-Fields,
St Ives, 1857–8, Marazion, 1861, Gunnislake, 1880, and St John
Penzance, 1879–81 – are impressively composed, often on difficult sites. His smaller churches are worthy of more appreciation
than they have often received: Hessenford, 1871, is a typically
well-detailed E.E. example, entirely un-Cornish but charming,
with a complete set of *Clayton & Bell* windows. He worked on
some of the major churches, including St Austell and St Columb
Major, and could produce sensitive interiors like the beautifully decorated chancel at St Issey. But many, if not most, of his restorations
were unnecessarily destructive: he had a fondness for inserting
new and somewhat assertive arch- and wind-braced roofs to
replace the simple Cornish wagon roof and for moving features
such as tracery and piscinas around between churches. The
heavy-handed character of a St Aubyn restoration becomes weari-
some because of the sheer volume of his work.

The most accomplished ecclesiastical architectural name of the
later C19 in Cornwall is *Sedding*, a small but important dynasty.
John Dando Sedding (1838–91) started work with his elder brother,

*I am greatly indebted to Canon Warner for generously sharing his unpublished
Gazetteer of Works in Cornish Anglican Churches 1700–2000 with me, and discussing
the work of J. P. St Aubyn in particular.

Edmund Sedding (1836–68) of Penzance, and also worked with Edmund's son *Edmund Harold Sedding* (1863–1921): it is often difficult to be certain about precise attributions. All three were highly skilled in Arts and Crafts Gothic and together worked on sixty-five churches. *J. D. Sedding's* new builds at Hayle, 1886–8, All Saints, Falmouth, 1887–90, and St Paul, Truro, 1868 (completed in stages 1882–1910 by *E. H. Sedding*), show his versatility from the simple E.E. of Hayle, through the cathedral-like proportions of the interior at Falmouth, to the varieties of Perp at St Paul, Truro. The Seddings are especially memorable for thoughtful and sensitive restoration. They were advocates of the use of local materials, especially of Polyphant, and were careful repairers of old fabric as at Lawhitton, 1860–75, Wendron, 1867–9, Towednack, 1869–70, South Hill, 1871–2, Lelant, 1872–3, St Erth, 1873–4 and 1900–16, and St Winnow, 1874–1907. Where rebuilding was undertaken, as with *Edmund Sedding* at Gwithian, 1865–7, or *E. H. Sedding* at Chacewater, 1892, and Crantock, 1899–1901, the results are both disciplined and delightful.

106

Many other architects, mostly local, made significant contributions to the Gothic Revival in Cornwall. Of the earlier period *Christopher Eales*, familiar from his Renaissance palazzo Town Hall and Market Halls at St Austell and Truro, built Charlestown in 1848–51 in an adapted E.E. style reflecting the early influence of the Ecclesiological movement. *John Hayward*, architect to the Exeter Diocesan Architectural Society, is represented by skilful E.E. at Tuckingmill, 1843–6, and Herodsfoot, 1848–50. At Pendeen the vicar, *Rev. Robert Aitken*, designed an ambitious cruciform E.E. church in 1851. *J. L. Pearson* experimented with a restrained E.E. at Devoran in 1855; the vicar was a nephew of Bishop Phillpotts. Of the later C19 there is *Hine & Odgers's* Delabole, 1878–82, a severe E.E. design; *Silvanus Trevail's* inventive rebuilding of Temple, 1882–3; *James Hicks's* free E.E. at St Andrew, Redruth, 1881–6, and *G. H. Fellowes Prynne's* All Hallows, Kea, 1894–7 in a strongly Arts and Crafts-influenced late Perp.

Of FURNISHINGS AND FITTINGS for these new and restored churches, both the *Seddings* and *Fellowes Prynne* are notable for their sensitive treatment of woodwork old and new. There are several examples of excellent restoration of medieval screens, as at St Buryan and St Ewe, and their substantive recreation of screen and bench-ends at Crantock. Fellowes Prynne's embellishment of Holy Trinity, St Austell, is perhaps the most important example of later Victorian ecclesiastical art in Cornwall. His restoration of Poundstock, 1892–8, is a simpler but equally accomplished scheme. Much of the craftsmanship in wood was undertaken by *Violet Pinwill*, the daughter of the rector of Ermington, Devon, and her school of carvers: they worked in the medieval tradition, distinguished by a charming if somewhat studied naturalism. *Harry Hems* of Exeter was also active in Cornwall as at St Erth and his pulpit at St Austell. Notable schemes of embellishment by local practitioners can be enjoyed at St Just-in-Roseland, 1872, St Anthony-in-Roseland, 1850, and Philleigh, 1867, where *Rev. C.W. Carlyon*'s vigorous carpentry stands out. The outstanding ensemble is at Quethiock, 1878–88 by *Rev. William Willimott*, including his excellent array of stained glass, a richer version of his earlier work at St Michael Caerhays.

Of STAINED GLASS there is a vast array. For the C19 the stained-glass window became the most common form of memorial and one of the principal means of achieving the desired medieval atmosphere for devotion. The Index of Artists at the end of this book will lead the enthusiast to the work of the leading firms, all of which are represented here including *Wailes*, *Westlake*, *Hardman*, *O'Connor*, *Clayton & Bell*, *Lavers, Barraud & Westlake*, *Heaton, Butler & Bayne* and *Kempe*, as well as *Percy Bacon Bros* and *Fouracre & Watson*. The important early window by *Morris & Co.* of 1863 at Ladock has already been mentioned but the church also has windows by this firm of 1869–70 and 1897, including designs by *E. Burne-Jones* and *Ford Madox Brown* that demonstrate the stylistic developments of the period. The largest display of *Morris & Co.* glass is at St Germans with two exceptionally fine *Burne-Jones* designs of 1896 and 1902. Other glass by this firm can be seen at St Michael Penkevil St Peter, Flushing and some pretty relocated roundels at Polruan.

The crowning glory of the Gothic Revival in Cornwall is, of course, Truro Cathedral, *J. L. Pearson*'s masterpiece designed in 1878 and completed in 1910. Its dramatic rise above the streets of the town is unforgettable and Pearson's genius is immediately apparent in his deployment of Normandy Gothic for the towers and spires, underscoring Cornwall's links with its Celtic neighbours and asserting its distinct and separate identity from England. The fact that, when studied in detail, the most pervasive influences are English with particular echoes of Lincoln and Peterborough simply enhances one's appreciation of Pearson's design, every element skilfully re-scaled to make a virtue of concision. The emphatic verticality of the exterior is taken up in the soaring height of the interior, which is powerfully reinforced by Pearson's brilliance with stone vaulting and his strict discipline of ornament to demonstrate the structural logic of Gothic. Of the generally impressive furnishings, the outstanding feature is the stained glass by *Clayton & Bell*, one of the finest and certainly the largest scheme of Late Victorian glass in England.

Late nineteenth-century country houses and gardens

Most of the important C19 work on COUNTRY HOUSES has already been described but some late C19 examples merit mention. One is the restoration of Lanhydrock by *Richard Coad* and *James M. MacLaren* after the disastrous fire of 1881. Although the N range survived, the rest of the house needed major reconstruction in 1882–5, and the remodelling of the S and W ranges, including the building of two new service courtyards behind, created one of the most impressive service ranges of this period in England. MacLaren's interiors are of considerable interest, showing the introduction of Aesthetic Movement motifs within the overall Jacobean style required by the Agar-Robartes. *J. P. St Aubyn*'s Pencalenick, St Clement, in an eclectic Palladian style, was the last great Victorian house built in Cornwall with two-thirds of the accommodation given to service functions and staff quarters. But St Aubyn's greatest work is his E wing of St Michael's Mount, an astonishingly ambitious building on a highly constrained site, skilfully devised so that its vast scale does not interfere with the celebrated silhouette of the monastery and castle.

Cornwall is, of course, renowned for its great GARDENS which provide the settings for the houses often as memorable, or more so, than the architecture: their detailed history and description are beyond the scope of this book but the gazetteer provides brief summaries of the most important. Suffice it to say that the C19 saw the creation of magnificent parks and gardens, many exotically planted by their mining magnate owners some of whom became keen plantsmen, like the Williams at Caerhays or the Foxes at Glendurgan. Other great estates witnessed radical remodelling and enhancement, such as the continuous development of the exquisite landscape of Mount Edgcumbe or at a smaller scale the delightful C19 gardens at Pencarrow, which include one of the earliest grottos in England. On the grand scale the Vyvyans at Trelowarren and the Boscawens at Tregothnan were implementing vast landscaping schemes that included the creation of long Reptonian approach drives, connecting their estates to the wider landscape.

Late nineteenth-century public and commercial buildings

The later C19 saw a plethora of new PUBLIC AND COMMERCIAL BUILDINGS especially, but not exclusively, in towns: the self-confidence and civic pride of the period are frequently on display, as in the monumental Italianate civic palace that is the Public Buildings of 1864–7 by *John Matthews* at Penzance, or the more quietly assertive Gothic of *Hine & Odgers*'s Guildhall and Town Hall at Launceston of 1881–7. A feature of these developments is the rise of local architects to prominence in their towns, making the distinctive character of each rewarding and enjoyable to study. The most prolific is *Silvanus Trevail* (1851–1903) who undertook over 300 commissions between 1870 and 1903. Like his local contemporaries he was extraordinarily versatile, capable of working over the entire functional and stylistic range, but Trevail was among the most inventive. Most towns have at least one Trevail building – a bank, shop, school, technical college, Passmore Edwards library or institute, hospital, hotel or housing. As an entrepreneur willing to risk funding his own developments he played a major role in the late C19 development of the Cornish tourist industry, seeing it as having an important potential role

in the reinvigoration of the Cornish economy. Though his dream
of a string of large hotels around the coast linked by the railway
remained unfulfilled, his King Arthur's Castle Hotel (now The
Camelot) at Tintagel and the Atlantic and Headland Hotels at
Newquay are memorable for the way they take full advantage of
their romantic sites, their monumental scale, and their accomplished architecture inside and out. There are particularly good
ranges of Trevail buildings in Newquay, St Austell and Truro. Of
other distinguished local figures, *James Hicks* (1846–96) was so
prominent in Redruth that a part of the town was dubbed 'Hicksville': he also built the highly original Arts and Crafts-influenced
Newlyn Art Gallery, 1894, and examples of his work can be found
in most other towns. At Liskeard *Henry Rice* (1808–76) built so
extensively that over 100 of his works survive. Other examples
are *Otho B. Peter* at Launceston and *Oliver Caldwell* in and around
Penzance.

Finally, special mention must be made of the expansion of
Cornish PORTS AND HARBOURS during the C19. One of the
delights of Cornwall is the small fishing port gathered around its
small harbour, the harbour wall probably dating from the medieval period even if rebuilt and extended over successive centuries.
The processing of fish started in small domestic fish cellars
beneath fishermen's houses, of which the best examples survive
at St Ives. The development of seining – the setting out of a long
net stretched between a number of boats around a large shoal
and bringing it to shore – necessitated the development of larger
purpose-built fish cellars (good examples survive at Port Gaverne
and Port Isaac); and later, as fish processing became almost
industrial in scale, much more substantial warehouses were
required. This went hand in hand with the expansion and diversification of trade from Cornish ports, necessitating entirely new
harbours and the enlargement of many existing port facilities.
Some of the new early C19 ports were created by the great landowners – Charlestown by the Rashleighs, Devoran by the Agar-
Robartes, Newquay and Par by the Treffrys, and Pentewan by
the Hawkins – for the export of the products of the mining
industry. Others, like Hayle, which was developed from the late
C18 for the foundry, were expanded in the early to mid C19 as
trade boomed. The later C19 saw the most dramatic developments as in the vast new harbour facilities at Penzance and
Newlyn, but other smaller ports like Mousehole, Mevagissey and
Looe also had impressive new piers and quays dwarfing the scale
of the original medieval harbour walls.

ARCHITECTURE SINCE 1900

The early years of the C20 saw the continued diversification of
the Cornish economy in which the growth of the TOURIST
INDUSTRY, facilitated by the spread of the railway network,

played an increasingly significant role. It is enjoyably illustrated in the Edwardian architecture of resorts like Bude, Newquay, Penzance and St Ives. Silvanus Trevail had seen Newquay as an English version of the great European spas, the centrepiece of his plans for a 'Cornish Tourism', and from 1897 the Urban District Council embarked on an ambitious expansion of the C19 town including a large new suburb, a new public park along the Trenance valley and the purchase of the remaining common land on the headlands to preserve the town's setting. It almost exactly replicates the achievement of the Corporation at Penzance a few decades earlier which laid the foundations for that town's early C20 makeover as a modern resort, the eye-catching centrepiece being the Art Deco Jubilee Pool. Both towns featured prominently in the Great Western Railway poster campaign to promote the 'Cornish Riviera'.   118

Among CHURCHES Newquay has the only major C20 example in Cornwall, the supremely assured St Michael, 1909–11 by *Sir Ninian Comper*, a successful re-interpretation of Cornish Perp skilfully composed on an awkward, sloping site with a cool, spacious interior using much Polyphant stone. The town also has the excellent Wesleyan Methodist Church, 1904 by *Bell, Withers & Meredith* in a forceful Tudor Gothic, as well as the fine Gothic United Reformed Church of 1926. The continued vitality of Methodism is seen elsewhere, as in the Richmond Wesleyan Chapel of 1907 by *Gunton & Gordon* at Penzance which combines Arts and Crafts influences with a free Gothic style. The enrichment of churches continued too, especially where the local economy was defying the general economic decline that had so devastated the older mining areas. A significant impetus for this new work was the desire to reorder churches as settings for Anglo-Catholic liturgy, strikingly demonstrated by the transformation of *Wightwick*'s low church St Michael and All Angels, Bude, between 1900 and 1940 with the installation of stained-glass windows, well-designed, well-crafted and well-decorated furnishings, and the addition of an elaborate baptistery. At St Austell the continued success of the china clay industry helped fund a substantial programme of embellishment overseen by *G. H. Fellowes Prynne*, continuing from the late C19 well into the 1930s. The character of St Peter, Newlyn, is defined by the work of *Martin Travers* begun in the 1920s and flourishing under the long incumbency of *Rev. Allan Wyon* from 1936 until 1955, reflecting their engagement with the Newlyn school. That artistic tradition found its supreme expression at St Hilary in the long campaign by *Father Bernard Walke* from 1913 to 1936, creating an outstanding and nationally important ensemble of religious art of the first half of the C20. Even so, Anglo-Catholicism found its most astonishing setting in *Comper*'s sumptuous realization of a Puginesque vision in miniature at Little Petherick, carried out   107
from 1908 to 1947, with breathtakingly rich colours and fine craftsmanship.

Enthusiasts for Edwardian COMMERCIAL ARCHITECTURE will find the resort towns already mentioned rewarding, but self-confident banks, purpose-built emporia and elaborate shop-fronts are a feature of most Cornish towns. A flash of the *moderne* is a delightful feature of Penzance, which also has the suitably dramatic façade of the former Pavilion Theatre of 1911 by *Cowell & Drewitt* where crouching caryatids hold up the corner towers. PUBLIC BUILDINGS of the first half of the century are, however, generally unremarkable: a notable exception is a group of POST OFFICES at St Austell, 1920, Bodmin, 1924, and Falmouth, 1930, by *H. M. Office of Works*, all sensitive exercises in contextual design, and therefore in very different style, but characteristically finely detailed. *Richardson & Gill*'s buildings for the Duchy of Cornwall, Home Farm at Stoke Climsland, 1913, are a rare example of early C20 model farm buildings: the same firm designed various buildings for the Duchy in Hugh Town, St Mary's, Isles of Scilly at that period.

There are comparatively few early C20 PRIVATE HOUSES of any distinction, somewhat surprisingly given the increasing popularity of Cornwall as a second home for the wealthier middle class: the most spectacular work is Sir Edwin Lutyens' new wing and court at Penheale Manor which echoes his contemporary work at Castle Drogo, Devon. Less surprisingly perhaps, the preferred style for the most notable examples is the ARTS AND CRAFTS tradition and its many variables. A good group can be found around Daymer Bay. *G. L. Kennedy*'s Little Parc Owles, Carbis Bay, is a more interesting example: he also built an impressive group of farm buildings at Tremedda, Zennor, *c.* 1910. But the best houses in this tradition are at Chapel Point, Mevagissey, 1935–8 by *John Campbell*, a highly original interpretation: he built Pentyr at Helford Point in 1939 in a similar style after its owner had seen Chapel Point while sailing past. There is also the remarkable Porth-en-Alls, Prussia Cove, 1910–14 by *Philip Tilden*, only a partial realization of the intended great house, and the much more modest Wheal Betsy, Newlyn 1910 by *Arnold Mitchell*. Of decorative art, the outstanding example is the set of seventy-three pieces of stained glass by *Veronica Whall* at King Arthur's Halls, Tintagel, 1928–33, one of the best schemes of its date in England. The MODERN MOVEMENT, on the other hand, clearly did not find great favour in Cornwall at this time, despite its apparent suitability for exotic seaside locations. The best is *Marshall Sisson*'s small development at Carlyon Bay, especially Gull Rock House, 1934. Tregannick, Sancreed, by *Geoffrey Bazeley*, 1935, makes a striking appearance in the landscape of the far west of Cornwall, as does *Colin Drewitt*'s Jubilee House, 1935, in the intimate townscape of Queen Street, Penzance. Polventon, Mother Ivey's Bay, by *Crowe & Careless*, 1936, is highly theatrical in its streamlined presence on its cliff-edge site.

The greatest opportunity for PUBLIC ARCHITECTURE by local authorities came in the decades after the Second World War, and it was this period that saw the most sustained Modernist campaign in Cornwall through the notable work of *Cornwall County Council Architect's Department*. The finest achievement of their

considerable output is New County Hall, Truro, 1963–6, one   122
of the best county halls of the mid C20 in England, grand in scale,
rigorous in design and meticulously detailed, including the furnishings of the council suite. Often described with reference to
Le Corbusier's monastery of La Tourette, 1953–60, it is a telling
contrast to the quiet Neo-Georgian of McMorran's County Hall
at Exeter, 1957–64, seeming to represent the perennial Cornish
determination to be different and to surprise. Its dramatic siting
and imaginative landscaping on a s facing slope on the sw edge
of the city owe much to the influence of *Sir Geoffrey Jellicoe* who
was the inspiration of the project. The talented and often changing group of architects, early practitioners of system building,
produced many excellent new schools, colleges, libraries and
court buildings. Most of the schools and colleges have been
compromised by later extensions so that their original clarity of
design has been obscured: the seven-storey tower of the 1968
building at Cornwall College, Pool, for example, originally had
exposed concrete and Brutalist detailing now hidden behind
smart flush cladding. Some of the highlights are the libraries
at Saltash (1963, job architect *Royston Summers*) and St   119
Austell (1959–60, job architect *Michael Kirkbride*); Sandy Hill
Community Primary School, St Austell, (1972, job architect
Lionel Aggett); and the Magistrates' Court, Bodmin (1984, job
architect *Michael Way*). Of other public buildings of the period,
the daringly contrasting Chapter House at Truro Cathedral was
built by *John Taylor* of *Marshman, Warren & Taylor* in 1967 and
the firm later designed many of the new civic buildings in Pydar
Street, Truro, the earlier work more assured than the latter.

Of mid-to late C20 HOUSING there is disappointingly little,
most of the extensive estate and private housing depressingly
familiar from the rest of England. A delightful bright spot is a
late flowering of the Arts and Crafts tradition at *Dawber, Fox &
Robinson*'s Homeyard Homes 1956 at Veryan which takes up the
round-house form for which the village is renowned. A notable
exception to the dearth of good design in public housing is
Fielden & Mawson's Rialton Heights, St Columb Minor, 1974,
an ingenious scheme that exploits the difficulties of the site to
great effect around a pedestrian street focused on the church
tower. Of private housing, *John Taylor*'s Redannick, Chapel Hill,
Truro, of the 1950s is excellently conceived, a large estate using
simple geometric shapes and showing Scandinavian influence.
His Alverton Court NE of the city, 1963, takes the same concept
to a more refined level. Of the many holiday villages scattered
over the Cornish landscape, an outstanding exception to their
general mediocrity is Headland Cottages, 1999, at the Headland
Hotel, Newquay, a skilful contemporary interpretation of Cornish
vernacular, beautifully detailed inside and out, by *David Judson*
of *Workhouse Design*.

There is a sprinkling of individual houses of note, the most
outstanding being a group at Feock that includes the inspirational Creek Vean by *Team 4*, 1964–7 (their first work), a brilliant   121
realization of the potential of the superb creek-side site in Frank

Lloyd Wright style, the understated exterior giving onto a dramatic interior with not a single right angle. Pillwood House on the opposite side of the creek by *John Miller* with *Su Rogers* 1971–4 is a pioneering High-Tech structure, a striking contrast to the solid, sculptural form of its neighbour. Nearby at Restronguet Point, The Boathouse, 1973 by *John Crowther & Associates*, is a cool glass box when viewed from the river, the landward side solid with a circular stair drum. Not far away at Calenick Creek, Kea, are two good smaller Modernist houses, Otter Creek of 1961 by *Giles Blomfield* of *John Crowther & Associates* and Shooldarry of 1962 by *MichaelWhitham*. Both Crowther's and Blomfield's work can be found around Cornwall and is among the best of its kind: similarly in west Cornwall the work of *Cowell, Drewitt & Wheatly* and *Poynton Bradbury Wynter Cole*. A rare example of domestic Postmodernism is *Graham Ovenden*'s lively and colourful Barley Splatt, Warleggan, of 1970.

Truro demonstrates all too graphically how easy it is to erode a graceful and elegant town's character by inappropriate development. It is still a fine town but deserves better buildings than it has often received in the last few decades: the clumsy faux industrial monolith at the SW end of Lemon Quay is especially damaging to views of the cathedral. A development that is exemplary in its skilful articulation on a prominent site is the Courts of Justice of 1986–8 by *Evans & Shalev*, marking the firm's transition from New Brutalism towards Postmodernism. It also marks the start of a renaissance in Cornwall's fortunes in the late C20 and early C21 that was greatly assisted by the flow of significant European Union funding after the recognition that Cornwall was one of the most deprived parts of the Community. The recent regeneration of Camborne, Redruth and Hayle are some of the best fruits of this investment, though the redevelopment of the 1960s shopping precinct at St Austell, which was the first in Cornwall, has proved architecturally disappointing.

There are some very good PUBLIC BUILDINGS. *Evans & Shalev* reprised some of their Courts of Justice motifs in their Tate St Ives of 1989–93, a design that imaginatively links the art inside with the townscape and landscape that were its inspiration, employing an organic Modernism that draws on the town's C20 tradition. In a different way *Long & Kentish*'s National Maritime Museum of 2003 at Falmouth successfully takes up the maritime motifs of the historic town, as does *Bill Dunster*'s Jubilee Wharf at Penryn of 2006. At a smaller scale, the intimacy of Bernard Leach's pottery at St Ives is sensitively echoed in the thoughtful extension by *Gilmore Hankey Kirke*, 2008. A growing concern about the environment has led to the significant evolution of eco-building for sustainable development in Cornwall, imaginatively interpreted in Bishop Cornish Education Centre, Saltash, 2010 by *ARCO2 Architects*. Explaining human interaction with the natural world has rarely been so engagingly demonstrated than at the Eden Project, symbolically utilizing a disused china clay pit from 1998 onwards to create a spectacular set of buildings using pioneering technology by *Nicholas Grimshaw*. But perhaps the greatest contemporary expression of Cornwall's ability to renew itself and reassert its identity is to be seen in the vast new Penryn Campus of the Combined Universities of Cornwall, where development has proceeded at breathtaking pace in the last decade with some excellent large-scale architecture, and which continues to evolve.

A defining element of Cornwall's C20 and C21 identity has been its artistic tradition, of national and international importance, and still vibrant. The county's intense natural beauty, not least around its coasts, its ancient landscapes, the traditional life of its fishing communities, its relative remoteness and the extraordinary luminosity of the air drew artists westward, first to Newlyn in the later C19 and then from the early C20 to St Ives. Figures like Barbara Hepworth, Ben Nicholson, Peter Lanyon and Bernard Leach made St Ives and its artistic community a major influence on mid-C20 art, recognized by the establishment of Tate St Ives in the late C20.

Cornwall has come a long way economically from the nadir of the mid to late C20 when the tourist trade, then a rare economic lifeline, was struggling with the competition from cheap foreign holidays and the proud tradition of deep mining had finally ground to a halt. It has come a long way too in an evolving consciousness that it would be all too easy to lose what makes it special. It was the Council for the Preservation of Rural England's *Survey of Cornwall* of 1933 that first voiced concern about the spoliation of the Cornish coastline, which later resulted in Enterprise Neptune, the National Trust's ambitious and successful campaign to save its coasts from development. The Trust in Cornwall took the conservation initiative forward in many exemplary ways in the second half of the C20 under the energetic leadership of its then Regional Director, Michael Trinick, which included the acquisition of a large number of major historic houses and estates. The Cornish Buildings Group has a proud record of encouraging good design as well as opposing the destruction of the historic environment, no easy task in a county that was slow to appreciate its architectural and buildings heritage, some of the former District Councils not appointing conservation officers until the 1990s. Cornwall County Council played a significant role from the 1970s in raising consciousness about the importance of its archaeological, architectural and industrial past through the distinguished work of the former Archaeological Unit. Nothing better symbolizes their success and the welcome change of understanding than the recent granting of World Heritage Site status to the Cornish Industrial Landscape, which only a few decades ago was seen as an unwelcome reminder of the county's decline and fall.

Considerable though these achievements are, Cornwall will need to be ever more vigilant to safeguard its identity if its recent welcome renaissance continues. There are worrying signs, like the wholesale replacement of seaside bungalows in spacious gardens and modest hotels in resort towns like Newquay and St Ives by densely packed residential blocks too large and assertive for their context, or the proliferation of wind farms across so much of the Cornish landscape. So little of the huge surge of new development sweeping across the county is of a design worthy of its setting: Cornwall, so rich, complex and beautiful deserves better.

FURTHER READING

Of GENERAL WORKS the best modern introduction is Philip Payton's masterly *Cornwall: A History* (1996 and 2004); his *The Cornish Overseas* (1999 and 2005) gives a vivid account of Cornish emigration. Of older sources, the most valuable are Richard Carew's *The Survey of Cornwall* (1602); W. Borlase's *Observations on the Antiquities, Historical and Monumental, of the County of Cornwall* (1754); John Maclean's *The Parochial and Family History of the Deanery of Trigg Minor* (1872–9); Richard Polewhele's *The History of Cornwall*, 3 vols (1803–8); and Joseph Polsue's *A Complete Parochial History of the County of Cornwall*, 4 vols (1867–72). Many Cornish houses are depicted in Borlase and in the amateur but instructive early C18 topographical drawings by Edmund Prideaux, published by J. Harris in *Architectural History* 7, 1964.

Of GUIDEBOOKS, *Murray's Handbook for Devon and Cornwall* (1859) offers a good picture of the mid-C19 county. John Betjeman's *Shell Guide* (1964) is still incomparable in its evocation of the character of Cornwall: it is worth noting that Betjeman's sense of place so impressed Pevsner that the *Shell Guide* descriptions of Marazion and Polperro were used in the second edition of this book (1970). Of modern regional surveys, Roger Kain (ed.), *English Landscape: The South West* (2006) is a good general introduction, while the most comprehensive compilation of later C20 research can be found in Kain and William Ravenhill (eds), *Historical Atlas of South West England* (1999). The principal county antiquarian periodicals are the *Journal of the Royal Institution of Cornwall* (*JRIC*) and *Cornish Archaeology* (*CA*). The former has long published major papers on architectural history, while the latter increasingly reflects the modern continuity between below- and above-ground archaeology: its Silver Jubilee Volume 25 (1986) and Golden Jubilee Volume 50 (2011) cover modern research across the antiquarian range with extensive bibliographies.

For GEOLOGY AND BUILDING MATERIALS a technical overview of Cornwall's geology is given in C.M. Bristow's *Cornwall's Geology and Scenery* (2004) and E.B. Selwood, E.M. Durrance and C. M. Bristow (eds), *The Geology of Cornwall and the Isles of Scilly* (1998). The *Strategic Stone Study: A Building Stone Atlas of Cornwall and the Isles of Scilly* (English Heritage, 2011) clearly relates geology and building stones, while P. Stanier's *Cornwall's Geological Heritage* (1990) is an accessible introduction. Volumes dedicated to specific stone types include P. Stanier's *South West Granite: A History of the Granite Industry in Cornwall and Devon*

(1999), a thorough investigation of the quarries, industrial processes and economics of the granite industry, and Michael Sagar-Fenton's account of the use of serpentine in *Serpentine* (2005). J. Ferguson and C. Thurlow, *Cornish Brick Making and Brick Buildings* (2005), provides a comprehensive overview of the manufacture and use of Cornish brick.

There is a wealth of published material on Cornish PREHIS-TORY, too voluminous to summarize here: the reader is referred to the county antiquarian publications for modern sources. Malcolm Todd's *The South West to AD 1000* (1987) is an excellent general introduction. Of other works, J. Barnatt, *Prehistoric Cornwall: The Ceremonial Monuments* (1982) and W. C. Borlase, *Nænia Cornubiæ, a descriptive essay, illustrative of the sepulchres and funereal customs of the early inhabitants of the country of Cornwall* (1872) are full of interesting information. P. Dudley's *Goon, hal, cliff and croft: The Archaeology and Landscape History of West Cornwall's Rough Ground* (2011) is a good example of a detailed study of a specific area, here of the striking landscape of West Penwith. Much of the outstanding work of the former Cornwall Archaeological Unit, now the Historic Environment Service, is available online at http://www.historic-cornwall.org.uk. Of their prodigious output an outstanding example is Nicholas Johnson and Peter Rose's *Bodmin Moor: An Archaeological Survey, vol. I: The Human Landscape* (2008). Peter Herring's extensive work is represented in his 'Commons, fields and communities in prehistoric Cornwall' in A. Chadwick (ed.), *Recent Approaches to the Archaeology of Land Allotment*, British Archaeological Reports (2008).

For the background to Cornwall's RELIGIOUS HISTORY, Nicholas Orme's *A History of the County of Cornwall*, vol. II: *Religious History to 1560*, VCH (2010) is a scholarly account with a gazetteer of religious houses that covers their often complex documentary history with sections on surviving buildings; the popular version, *Cornwall and the Cross: Christianity 500–1560* (2007), has many excellent illustrations. Orme also edited *Unity and Variety: A History of the Church in Devon and Cornwall* (1991), a general survey up to the end of the C20. Sam Turner's *Making a Christian Landscape* (2006) traces the evolution of the religious landscape of medieval Cornwall alongside other SW counties.

On MEDIEVAL CHURCHES, E.H. Sedding's *Norman Architecture in Cornwall* (1909) remains indispensable and thought-provoking: it covers far more than the Norman period for the churches included. C.J. Cox's *County Churches in Cornwall* (1912) and Charles Henderson's *The Cornish Church Guide and Parochial History of Cornwall* (1925) are still useful sources for Anglican churches, the latter incorporating some primary (translated) late medieval documentation. Warwick Rodwell's 'Lanlivery church: its archaeology and architectural history', *CA* 32, 1983, is an object lesson in revealing the wealth of information that becomes available when stripping of finishes accompanied by partial excavation allows the full investigation of a church. For the period before the creation of the Cornish see in 1876, the *Transactions of the Exeter Diocesan Architectural Society* (from 1841) included articles on Cornish churches and their fittings, some beautifully illustrated: some volumes are online, and there are plans to digitize the first series. An easily searched source of plans and the names of architects of church restorations can be found at www.churchplansonline.org. For CHAPELS, Jeremy Lake, Jo Cox and Eric Berry's *Diversity and Vitality: The Methodist and Nonconformist Chapels of Cornwall* (2001) is a comprehensive history of Nonconformist building that includes a useful gazetteer and bibliography.

On CHURCH FIXTURES AND FITTINGS there are William Lack, H. Martin Stuchfield and Philip Whittemore's *The Monumental Brasses of Cornwall* (1997); H. Lee's *Cornwall's Churchyard Heritage* (1996); Joanna Mattingly's 'The dating of bench-ends in Cornish churches', *JRIC*, 1991; Joanna Mattingly and Michael G. Swift's 'Pre-Dissolution stained glass in Cornwall' at http://vidimus.org/issues/issue-31/features; and C.B. Newham and Rosemary Pardoe's *Royal Arms in Cornish Churches* (1982 and 2007). *The Slate Figures of Cornwall*, by Alice C. Bizley, 1965, is a valuable account of this remarkable Cornish tradition of figure carving, illustrated with exquisite line drawings by the author of the surviving sixty-five slates. Andrew Langdon's five-volume *Cornish Cross Series* (1992–2006) is an authoritative guide and gazetteer to the wealth of stone crosses, as is Elisabeth Okasha's *Corpus of Early Christian Inscribed Stones of South-west Britain* (1993) to inscribed stones. SCULPTORS of church monuments are the subject of A. White's 'A Biographical Dictionary of London Tomb Sculptors *c.* 1560–*c.* 1660', *Walpole Society* 61, 1999, and supplement in vol. 71 (2009). For the ensuing period up to the mid C19 the information previously provided by Rupert Gunnis's *Dictionary of British Sculptors* (1953) is now to be found, greatly expanded and supplemented, in I. Roscoe et al., *A Biographical Dictionary of Sculptors in Britain 1660–1851* (2009), also available as a searchable database on the Henry Moore Institute website (www.henry-moore.org/hmi/library/biographical-dictionary-of-sculptors-in-britain).

Country Life remains a major resource on individual COUNTRY HOUSES of all periods. Helen McCabe's *Houses and Gardens of Cornwall* (1938) is a useful general survey, but it is much to be hoped that Paul Holden's long-standing researches into the history of country houses in Cornwall will soon result in a major publication: his 'Situation, contrivance, receipt, strength and beauty: the building of Lanhydrock House 1620–51', *JRIC*, 2005, and 'Trewithen and the Brettingham plans', *Georgian Group Journal* XXI, 2013, whet the appetite. His collaboration with Peter Herring and Oliver Padel on *The Lanhydrock Atlas* (2010) brought to a wider audience this remarkable survey of the 1690s of every field on the vast Robartes estate. Pamela Dodds's extensive research into Cornish country houses is represented in 'The Hawkins of Trewithen and Thomas Edwards of Greenwich', *JRIC*, 1999.

Information on other architects can be found in Howard
Colvin, *A Biographical Dictionary of British Architects 1600–1840*
(4th edn, 2008). Of individual biographies, Gill Hunter, *William
White: Pioneer Victorian Architect* (2010), is especially valuable on
White's early career and work in Cornwall. Ronald Perry and
Hazel Harradence, *Silvanus Trevail: Cornish Architect and Entrepreneur* (2008), is invaluable on the prodigious output of this
most inventive and versatile of architects. Ronald Perry and
Sharron Schwartz's 'James Hicks: architect of regeneration in
Victorian Redruth', *JRIC*, 2001, is important not only for the
survey of Hicks's works in the town but also for its account of
how its regeneration was founded by Cornish émigrés. Rosa-
mund Reid's 'The architectural work of George Wightwick in the
county of Cornwall', *JRIC*, 1999, is the most significant account
available of this highly accomplished and prolific architect. *The
Life and Work of Henry Rice*, by George Vaughan-Ellis, Eileen
Crouch and John Rapson, 2010, is an album of this architect's
work, principally in Liskeard.

As to VERNACULAR BUILDINGS, Cornwall was the subject of
one of the most influential and pioneering regional studies of the
subject in England in Veronica and Frank Chesher's *The Cornishman's House* (1968): it remains essential reading, not just for its
breadth of vision in placing Cornish houses in a wider national
context, but for its perceptive analysis of their relationship to the
smaller gentry houses that are so characteristic of the county.
Surprisingly little in the way of more detailed vernacular studies
has been published subsequently, though much survey work has
been undertaken on individual buildings. P.S. Barnwell and
Colum Giles's *English Farmsteads 1750–1914* (1997) includes ana
lysis of the farm buildings in east Cornwall contrasted with four
other areas of England. The rich resource of Cornwall's town
buildings has scarcely been investigated. Notable exceptions are
the early surveys of Penryn and Truro inspired by Veronica
Chesher, and the more recent studies of Mousehole and Newlyn
in Joanna Mattingly (ed.), *Cornwall and the Coast*, VCH (2009).
Peter Laws's essay on the architecture of Penzance in P.A.S.
Pool's *History of the Borough of Penzance* 1974 and *The Buildings
of Scilly*, 1980, are valuable accounts that include assessment of
c20 buildings up to the time of their publication. Of more general
historical surveys, those of nineteen towns covered in the Cornwall and Scilly Urban Survey Project (2002–5) include an account
of each settlement's development with maps and references to
key buildings and a list of published sources: they are available
at www.historic-cornwall.org.uk/csus/project.htm.

Descriptions of individual buildings, archaeological sites and
historic parks and gardens can be found in the National Heritage
List for England at www.list.english-heritage.org.uk. The building descriptions for Cornwall are more detailed than usual
(though some towns were not covered in the 1980s re-survey)
and the parks and gardens entries contain good summaries of
the principal buildings. The National Trust's series of guides to
the *Coast of Cornwall*, 1986 onwards, initiated by Giles

Clotworthy, provides a wealth of good historical information and description of local buildings. Liz Luck's *South Cornish Harbours* (1995) also has excellent descriptions of coastal buildings.

As should be expected, there is an extensive literature on Cornish INDUSTRIAL HISTORY, though surprisingly there is, as yet, no comprehensive survey. A notable localized exception is Frank Booker's *Industrial Archaeology of the Tamar Valley* (1967) which places that area in the wider context. On MINING, the outstanding reference work is still H. K. Hamilton Jenkins's *The Cornish Miner* (1927). His *Cornwall and its People* also covers FISHING, while his *Miners and the Mines of Cornwall* in sixteen slim volumes (1961–70) covers specific areas and mines. The earlier period of mining up to 1700 is related in Sandy Gerrard's *The Early British Tin Industry* (2000). D. Bradford Barton's *The Cornish Beam Engine* (1965), *History of Tin Smelting and Mining in Cornwall* (1967) and *History of Copper Mining in Devon and Cornwall* (1968) are invaluable overviews. There are many excellent local studies, including the Trevithick Society's publications from the 1970s onwards.

On RAILWAYS, E. T. MacDermot's classic official *History of the Great Western Railway* (reprinted 1964) remains unsurpassed, while the SWR lines in north Cornwall are covered in C.F. Dendy Marshall's *History of the Southern Railway* (reprinted 1963). Frank Booker's *Great Western Railway* (1985) and David St J. Thomas's *The West Country* (1973) in David and Charles's Regional Railway Series are good general surveys. There are a number of publications on local lines. John Binding's *Brunel's Cornish Viaducts* (1993) and *Brunel's Royal Albert Bridge* (1997) describe these outstanding railway structures. On CHINA CLAY, Ruth Barton's *History of the Cornish China Clay Company* (1966) is an excellent overview while Kenneth Hudson's *The History of English China Clays* (*c.* 1968) includes sections on subsidiary industries including BRICKMAKING and HARBOURS.

The MILITARY HISTORY of the Cornish coast w of Plymouth is admirably described in Andrew Pye and Freddy Woodward's *The Historic Defences of Plymouth* (1996). The Henrician defences at Pendennis and St Mawes are fully covered in their joint guidebook, and the military history of Scilly in Mark Bowden and Allan Brodie's *Defending Scilly* (2011).

The research notes compiled for this edition and its predecessor will be deposited with the English Heritage Archive, Swindon, and may be freely consulted by prior arrangement with the public search room.

GAZETTEER

ACTON CASTLE *see* PERRANUTHNOE

ADVENT

ST ADWEN. In a lonely spot just off the w edge of Bodmin Moor. It was a medieval chapelry to Lanteglos-by-Camelford (q.v.). Slim late C13–C14 w tower, three-stage and unbuttressed, but crowned by eight pinnacles (a number only exceeded in Cornwall by the twelve at St Ive). w door arch with multiple mouldings, like nearby Michaelstow (q.v.), blocked when the ground outside was raised. The body of the church was extensively restored 1847–9 and 1973–5. The earliest part, the N transept, was substantially rebuilt but retains its E.E. lancet windows. The s porch and s aisle are in large granite blocks. The porch has a fine ceiled wagon roof with large bosses, one with three T-crosses. The s door has a pretty motif of isolated stylized fleurons in jambs and voussoirs, the spandrels of the four-centred doorhead with tracery decoration. The five-bay s aisle arcade is of standard granite design but with a rare E window with a flamboyant centre motif in the tracery (cf. Lanteglos-by-Camelford). Beyond this was until 1870 a s transept whose C15 entrance arch, identical with that to the N transept, is still visible; the E window of the transeptal chapel is in the blocked wall. Ceiled wagon roofs to nave, chancel and s aisle, only the aisle roof original with carved wall-plate, moulded ribs and carved bosses, the others reusing some C15 timbers. – FONT. Plain, circular; Norman with a (renewed) octagonal shaft with bold mouldings. – MONUMENTS. Elizabeth Bennett †1643.

TRESINNEY CROSS, ¼ m. s, *in situ* beside an ancient track. One of the tallest complete round-headed wayside crosses, the shaft slim, the head with an equal limbed cross in relief and expanded ends.

NEW HALL, 1 m. SSE. An especially picturesque example of the Cornish vernacular farmhouse, characterized by the use of local materials. Of the through-passage hall-house type, with a possibly open hall floored in the C16. Large front lateral stack, half-bay with gabled projection, mullioned windows and pigeon holes. Lower end rebuilt as a short wing.

TRETHIN, ¼ m. N. C16 moorland farmhouse near the remains of a prehistoric settlement. Parlour wing added 1655 for Matthew Vivian (dated fireplace) and two-storey porch of similar date. Stone winder stair in rectangular turret next to the porch.

MOORGATE STANDING STONE, ¾ m. ENE. Late Neolithic or Early Bronze Age. The tallest standing stone on Bodmin Moor, over 9 ft (2.7 metres) high and dynamically asymmetrical. The slender granite slab is positioned on a hill crest so that its point thrusts into the sky when viewed from below.

2080

ALTARNUN

The village street with picturesque stone cottages climbs down the hill to a little stream and bridge, the church rising large on the other side.

ST NONNA. One of Cornwall's best Perp churches whose impressive scale and presence are matched by an interior of uncommon interest. The W tower is 109 ft (33 metres) high, one of the highest in Cornwall, though this is not as noticeable as at Probus or St Columb Major, for example, because it stands against the hillside. The lower stage was probably started in the late C14 but the second and third are early to mid-C15. It is relatively plain with the usual set-back buttresses to just above the second stage, a battlemented parapet with crocketed finial, and NW stair-turret rising above the pinnacles. The body of the church is C15 and early C16 with N and S aisles and N and S porches, both of the latter with their old wagon roofs. Both N and S aisles have almost complete Perp tracery of the same design which takes two lights together under one pointed arch, specially popular in this district. Datestone above the W window of the N aisle, DV:DC:1795. The spacious, light interior is a

36   fitting setting for some of the best early to mid C16 fittings and furnishings of any Cornish church. The aisle arcades are of only five bays but they are wide and airy, the piers of standard design with capitals with very multiform mouldings. Each pier, capital, and base consists of a single piece of granite. C15 wagon roofs to N and S aisles, partly restored, with carved bosses and wall-plate. The church was carefully restored 1865–7 by *Edmund Sedding* with new roofs to nave and chancel. – FONT.

25   A magnificent piece of Norman decoration, one of the largest in Cornwall, with bearded faces at the corners bearing traces of colouring, large rosettes with serpents between, and cable moulding around the stem. – ROOD SCREEN. Exceptionally

fine, running right across nave and aisles. Each section has two lights only with Perp tracery and at the base three panels of blank tracery alternating with three traceried panels. Restored 1888 by *Harry Hems* of Exeter, who replaced the lost groining in the one and a half bays at each end. The screen was never painted. – BENCH-ENDS. Seventy-nine in total, forming one of the most important and interesting sets of this Cornish speciality. They probably date from *c.* 1535 and demonstrate the transition from the predominance of symbols of the Passion of the late medieval period to the more universal Renaissance designs: indeed only a seventh of the benches have any religious content, here mainly the five wounds of Christ depicted as pierced hands and feet, arranged in pairs above and below a pierced heart and carried on shields held by angels. There is no obvious stylistic break between the two types. Among the liveliest Renaissance depictions, especially in the S aisle, are a fool, a Cornish bagpiper with dog, a musician with ville, a sexton asperging holy water, some sheep grazing on the moor, a green man and a possible merman, and two sword dancers. One is inscribed 'Robert Daye maker of this worke and William Bokyngham Curate, John Hodge, Clarke, on MDXX', the last figures illegible. – ALTAR RAIL. Running the full width of the church. Inscribed JOHN RUDDLE MINISTER OF LAUNCESTON PREBENDARY OF EXON AND VICAR OF THIS PARISH 1684 and WILLIAM PRIDEAUX AND SAMPSON COWL CHURCHWARDENS, still completely Jacobean in the shape of its fine balusters. – PAINTINGS on wood on the E wall, early C17, one a depiction of communion, the other a Crucifixion. – SCULPTURE. Carved head of Norman pedestal PISCINA set low in the N wall at the W end of the church.

38

The churchyard has a large medieval WAYSIDE CROSS, restored on a modern shaft 1905. Also many good slate HEADSTONES, mostly C18 and C19, including an endearing memorial signed '*N. N. Burnard** aged 14' to his father and mother, George †1805 and Elizabeth Burnard †1819: it has a slate patch where he has mistaken one of the letters. – Stone CHEST TOMB with wrought-iron spearhead railings with urn finials to Digory Isbell †1795 (q.v. Wesley's Cottage, Trewint, below).

PENHALLOW MANOR, the former vicarage, N of the churchyard. Early C19, two-storey, double-depth plan with symmetrical elevations with canted bays.

METHODIST CHURCH, off the village street. 1859 datestone, plain except for the more elaborate symmetrical gabled front with two entrance porches with finials.

In the village THE OLD CHAPEL, built or bought 1826, enlarged 1836 (datestone) as a Wesleyan chapel, later a Sunday school.

---

*Nevill Northey Burnard, 1818–68, the celebrated society sculptor, was especially renowned for his portrait busts including one of Richard Trevithick. Among his larger works the best known are the Lander memorial at the top of Lemon Street, Truro, and the memorial to Ebenezer Elliott in Sheffield of 1854. Other examples of his work can be seen in the Royal Cornwall Museum, Truro.

Originally with stables and storeroom on ground floor and meeting room above, the door flanked by thirty-six pane sashes, and approached by a flight of steps from the street. Of special interest the carved relief BUST of John Wesley dated 1836, by *Burnard* when he was sixteen: his birthplace is commemorated by the plaque on the adjacent PENPONT MILL.

At Trewint, ½ m. SSW, WESLEY'S COTTAGE, built probably in the early C18 as a very small two-room plan cottage, extended in the mid C18 with a two-room plan wing by *Digory Isbell* (*see* churchyard above) to provide accommodation for visiting Methodist preachers, including Wesley in 1744.

CODDA, 3 m. SSW. In a remote moorland setting, within a group of ruined longhouses. One of the very few former longhouses still in domestic occupation. The house has the classic plan of a domestic higher end and a lower end for animal shelter divided by a through passage. A four-centred arched doorway between through passage and hall suggests a late C16 or early C17 date.

TRERITHICK, 2 m. ENE. A long evolution reflected in a complex plan and delightfully varied elevations. The principal late C16 phase is recorded in the lintel over the porch inscribed ANNO DOMINI 1585 by M + IH and a mullioned window dated 1575. Much of the house was built for John Hecks (a Thomas Hecks was mayor of Launceston in the early C16). Good C17 and early C18 interior. Small medieval window resited in farm building at the rear.

LESKERNICK HILL, 2½ m. W. On the plain S of the hill a 340-yd (310-metre) long Early Bronze Age STONE ROW runs to a point between two STONE CIRCLES. Most stones are fallen. Excavation confirmed that the row's western terminal stone, the tallest, was set transversely, closing the line. Stone-built ROUND-HOUSES are embedded in curvilinear enclosures on the hill's S slopes and in remarkably stony ground on W side. Above the western houses is a structure like a QUOIT on a small natural tor. Supporting stones and capstone form a tunnel through which the summer solstice sun can be seen setting behind High Moor. The midsummer sun sets behind it when viewed from a Neolithic LONG MOUND on Beacon Hill, ¾ m. away. The long mound, quoit and sunset were last perfectly aligned in the fourth millennium B.C.

BUTTERN HILL, 3 m. WNW of Bowithick. Five Early Bronze Age CAIRNS top one of the rounded downs buttressing West Moor's N edge. One is kerbed, one a platform and a third a ring. The largest contains a well-preserved CIST, its capstone leaning on the box's edge. Short STONE ROW low on the hill's NW side.

NINE STONES, 2½ m. SSE. Bodmin Moor's smallest Late Neolithic or Early Bronze Age stone circle, just 49 ft (15 metres) across. In open moorland. Restored in 1889. Seven stones standing, one fallen, a pit indicates a removed ninth. Centre stone is C19.

ANTONY

The village and its medieval church lie quite separate from the house and its C19 church.

St James. Standing high in the centre of the village. It was re-dedicated in 1259. One chancel window and the SEDILIA and PISCINA prove that the E part belongs to that phase in the building history. The next phase is established by the tower, two-storey, with diagonal buttresses, C14 windows, and the top battlements (without pinnacles) corbelled out. In the C15 aisles were added, first on the S (square piers with four demi-shafts), then on the N (standard Cornish pier profile). The S windows are straight-headed; those of the N side have Perp tracery. N porch of *c.* 1700. The church was thoroughly restored in the mid C19 with an arch-braced roof, the E bay with painted figures of the saints, and other decoration and fittings. – PULPIT. With four carved panels of the Evangelists; *c.* 1500, not English, perhaps Spanish. – STAINED GLASS. A fine array of mid to late C19 glass. – Chancel and S aisle 1848 by *Clayton & Bell.*– N aisle W 1888 by *Kempe.* – N aisle N 1847 by *Wille-ment.* N aisle E 1886 by *Percy Bacon Bros.* – MONUMENTS. Brass to Margery Arundell, †1420, the most spectacular early brass in Cornwall, large, with a thin architectural surround with ogee arch and finials. – Good Carew monuments, especially to Sir John Carew †1692, and his son and daughter, †1703, †1705. Fine decorative wall epitaph. Mary Carew †1731, a pretty portrait medallion against drapery and other paraphernalia, signed *Thomas Carter* of London. Sarah Carew †1671. Jemima Pole-Carew 1804 by *Sir Richard Westmacott.* – Admiral Jones †1755 by *Joseph Wilton*: a Roman *columna rostrata* and two urns standing on a Doric entablature. On corbels, the inscription between the corbels.

Antony House. In an exquisite position on the S shore of the River Lynher just to the W of its confluence with the Hamoaze within its extensive grounds. It has been a Carew property since the late C15. Sir William Carew (1689–1744) built the house as it now stands between 1720 and 1724. It is without doubt the best example of its date in Cornwall. The elegant simplicity of its composition and proportions long suggested an attribution to *James Gibbs* (Lysons) since a design included in Gibbs's *Book of Architecture* (1728) has been identified as corresponding to Antony. It is more likely that it is the work of *John Moyle*, a master mason (sometimes 'bricklayer') of Exeter who was also responsible for the accomplished Puslinch, Devon, of 1720–6. Moyle had been contracted to build garden walls at Antony in 1713 and in 1718 had agreed to build the shell of the house 'according to a Draught agreed upon in a good and workmanlike manner and to the satisfaction of Sir William Carew' (Colvin). Was this his own design or was he following one by another hand? It is, however, much more

85
p. 96

Antony House. Drawing by E. Prideaux, 1727

likely that the pavilions and forecourt to the s entrance front of the house are based on a Gibbs design or were by Gibbs himself: the wings are shown as complete in Prideaux's drawing of the house of 1727. A two-storey Italianate wing was added to the NE of the house in the mid C19, replaced by a Neo-Jacobean wing in stone and red brick in 1905 which was removed by *Philip Tilden* in 1948.

The house stands on an artificially levelled terrace near the centre of its estate overlooking a gentle N facing slope down to the Lynher. Rectangular in plan, two-storey over a basement, under a hipped slate roof with pedimented attic dormers. It is constructed of brick faced with Pentewan ashlar, a stone suited to the building's perfect proportions and almost austere lack of ornament. This is best seen on the nine-bay N front, the central three bays slightly advanced under a pediment, but, with the exception of rusticated end pilasters and the door surround, with no decoration whatever. The W front is of five bays. The s front is similar to the N except that its proportions are obscured by a giant porte cochère on Doric columns added in 1871. The enclosing forecourt has a symmetrical pair of arcaded two-storey pavilions in warm red brick flanked by single-storey arcades which terminate at the four corners in smaller pavilions with almost Chinese-looking little pointed domes contributing just one note of gaiety. The forecourt is bounded to the s by a brick wall with regularly spaced stone piers surmounted by ball finials and centrally placed wrought-iron gates with scrolled and leaf decoration between stone piers with vase finials.

The interior is of almost unaltered early C18 character and exceptional quality, the discipline evident in the exterior carried through in strict geometry of plan and restrained ornament. The centre of the s front is the square entrance hall flanked W by the present library and E by the staircase hall.

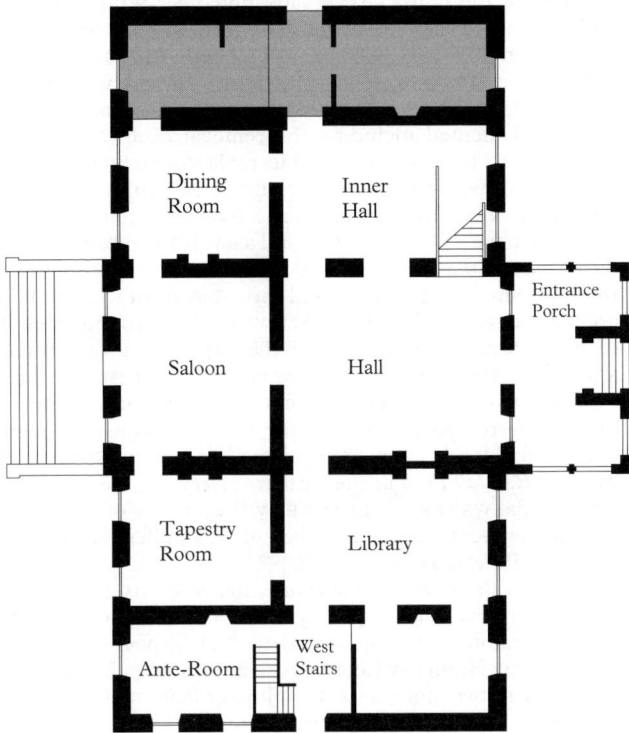

Antony House. Ground-floor plan

From the rear of the entrance hall a spinal corridor runs E–W to the secondary staircases at either end (a feature repeated on the first floor), with the shallower saloon in the centre of the N front flanked by two rooms either side. The house exudes warmth from the plain but well-proportioned panelling, the ground floor in oak, the first floor in pine, some painted, and the simple wood-panelled arches that link the rooms and spaces. Marble chimneypieces to each room, of different coloured marbles, mostly with simple bolection mouldings. The staircase with barley-twist balusters and columnar newels retains original glass globe lights on shaped brass bases: it was reconstructed in 1808–9 to rise in two flights from an arch nearest the s wall from its original design which started from the central arch and rose in three flights.

SE of the house, the STABLE COURT. An early to mid-C18 group with later C19 and C20 alterations including a combined former STABLE AND COACH HOUSE, CARPENTER'S SHOP, SMITHY, and BARN with HORSE ENGINE SHED attached.

The delightful GARDENS, PLEASURE GROUNDS and PARK demonstrate sustained development by the family since the building of the house. As already noted Sir William Carew had begun to remodel the gardens from *c.* 1710, under the supervision of *Humphry Bowen* of Lambeth. In 1792 Reginald Pole-Carew (1753–1835) commissioned *Humphry Repton* to produce a Red Book. Some of Repton's recommendations were implemented including the removal of an C18 formal garden to the N of the house and its replacement by lawns with trees and shrubs framing views to the river.* To the NE of the house, an early C18 circular brick DOVECOTE complete with potence; to the NW near a tidal pond a BATH HOUSE of 1788–90 by *Thomas Parlby*, a simple building of two compartments, a robing room with a symmetrical three-bay front with shallow arched recesses and a plunge set well below ground level. W of the house the brick walls of the KITCHEN GARDEN and NURSERY, 1793 to the designs of the Milanese architect *Placido Columbani*. Of more recent date a monumental BELL in an ogee-roofed pavilion to the W of the house, brought back from Mandalay in 1886; of the late C20 a SCULPTURE by *Peter Randall Page* in the former quarry; on the W terrace a pyramidal WATER SCULPTURE by *William Pye* of 1996; and, closing the avenue to the E of the house, a millennial classical ARCH by *Ptolemy Dean* of 2002.

On the S boundary of the estate, the early C19 ENTRANCE LODGE, originally a simple square one-room plan building with a pyramidal roof attributed to *J. A. Repton* on the site suggested by Humphry Repton. Also attributed to J. A. Repton the early C19 two-storey LODGE at Jupiter Point N of the house. On Ferry Lane nearby, BROOMHILL COTTAGE, a picturesquely gabled late C19 lodge.

ST PHILIP AND ST JAMES, Maryfield, ESE of the house. 1864–71 by *William White* for W. H. Pole-Carew as a private chapel for the Antony estate. Picturesque outside and rich inside. It is the most complete of White's smaller churches in warm red sandstone from the Pole-Carews' quarry at Sheviock Wood with yellow limestone dressings, and all Dec. Three-stage W tower with angle buttresses with finials to top of third stage and octagonal spire with crocketed pinnacles with gabled dormers at the base and upper lucarnes, a fine composition designed to be visible from the park E of the house. Nave with lean-to N aisle and a separately gabled chancel aisle which projects E from a tall N transept for the family pews. The interior shows White's consummate skill in re-creating pre-Reformation polychromy, the patterning and colouring intense, the overall effect resonant with mystery. The arches of the arcade are of alternate red and yellow stone, the walls painted with geometric patterns with scenes from the life of Christ: the chancel arch has a painted

103

---

* This was succeeded by an early C20 formal garden with a *clairvoie* modelled on a C17 gate screen at Beddington Manor, Surrey. The garden was removed in 1948 by *Philip Tilden* and the *clairvoie* re-erected on the skyline at the end of the S avenue.

scene of the Annunciation, apparently of patterned tiles. As Gill Hunter has observed, 'even in a pictorial scene of the Resurrection, White utilises geometric forms by placing the figure of Christ within an aureole composed of red and blue triangles. Although White's figures are stiff and medievalised, his abstract patterns are a *tour de force*. They display a development from the purely geometric diapering of Bishops Court (Devon) into a freer, more open arrangement.' Most of the fittings and furnishings including FONT, CHOIR STALLS, REREDOS, LECTERN and IRONWORK were designed by White (some of the woodwork carved by *Violet Pinwill*) as was the STAINED GLASS, conceived as an integral part of the overall character of the church. An exceptionally fine scheme by *Clayton & Bell*, richly coloured and figured. – ALTAR, N aisle, made in Normandy in 1944 by troops from the bar of a ruined café. – TOWER SCREEN. 1993 by *John Phillips*. – In the churchyard a CROSS, *c.* 1870, probably by White with chamfered and crocketed shaft.

N of the church MARYFIELD HOUSE, begun 1847 as a school house and parsonage with part of the schoolroom screened to serve as a chapel. White's second executed work, subsequently much extended to serve as the vicarage, first in 1853 to the S with two storey and attic gabled bays, later to S and E including a three-storey circular stair-tower, possibly not to White's design. The result is a picturesque, rambling composition around a small courtyard, the original schoolroom marked by a spired bellcote and a six-light mullioned-and-transomed window, the irregular elevations multi-gabled with large external stacks and a variety of lancet windows. Remarkably complete interior, many characteristic White features including a staircase with quatrefoil pierced balustrade.

TREGANTLE FORT, 1 m. SW. The mightiest of the forts of the Western Defences of Plymouth, intended with Scraesdon (*see* below) and another (unbuilt) fort between to command the western approach between the St Germans River and the coast. Built 1858–65, and by far the most complete and impressive fortress surviving on the Cornish side. A hexagonal work containing a keep at the apex of the gorge and barrack casemates along the S and E flanks and in the keep, surrounded on all sides except the S by a *c.* 20-ft (6-metre) deep dry rock-cut ditch defended by bombproof *caponiers* and an extensive *glacis* beyond. The keep is semicircular in plan. On the N flank the rampart was constructed in zigzag form, allowing more guns to be mounted. Much of the evidence of its armament survives inside.

SCRAESDON FORT, ¼ m. NW. With Tregantle (*see* above) one of the two forts of the Western Defences of Plymouth. Built 1858–68. A polygonal work surrounded by a 30-ft (9-metre) deep rock-cut ditch on all sides except the gorge, which is fronted by a shallower ditch. The upper parade is a dramatic feature of the interior and many of the gun emplacements survive.

BALDHU

A former mining parish (the name means 'black mine').

Former ST MICHAEL AND ALL ANGELS, now PORCH HOUSE
and TOWER HOUSE. 1847–8 by *William White*, his first building. In an isolated spot on a wooded hill reached by a narrow
road, its prominent spire a local landmark. Its simplicity of
form, satisfying composition, use of local materials and fine
detail remain constants in White's later work. Three-stage NE
tower with single-light cusped openings to the second stage
rising to a broached spire with two-light openings. Nave and
chancel under one roof, S aisle under parallel roof. Dec style
tracery. The capitals of the two-centred pointed arch and
arcade are carved with lily, convolvulus, oak and vine, the
corbels of the tower arch with portrait heads of Bishop Phillpotts and the young Queen Victoria. – STAINED GLASS. E
window by *Beer* of Exeter. Converted in 2009, inserted first
floor lit by large triangular dormer windows.
S of the church, an OBELISK memorial for Billy Bray †1868, on
inscribed pediment with moulded base and impressive inscription in incised grotesque lettering. Bray, a miner and Bible
Christian, was one of the most renowned figures of Cornish
Methodism, famous beyond Cornwall.
WELL HEAD, W of the church, *c.* 1847, possibly by *White* or by
the incumbent *Rev. W. Haslam*. In the style of a C15 holy well
with corbelled gabled roof with cross on E gable.
MELODY HOUSE. Former vicarage, built 1848 for *Rev. W. Haslam*
and possibly designed by him or helped by *White*. L-shaped
plan, irregular three-window SE front with one wider hipped
projecting wing.
Former SCHOOL, by *James Hicks*, late C19.

BISCOVEY see PAR

BLACKWATER
1 m. N of Chacewater

Former WESLEYAN CHAPEL. 1822 (date plaque), slightly remodelled in the late C19. Two-storey front with wide central
doorway and late C19 round-headed windows with marginal
lights.
BLACKWATER LITERARY INSTITUTE, on the main road SW of
the chapel. 1890 for J. Passmore Edwards, the first of his benefactions to Cornwall, and in his birthplace. A small but dignified building with symmetrical four-window front with paired
segmental arched windows flanking the central entrance in a
projecting gabled bay.

BLACKWATER COMMUNITY PRIMARY SCHOOL, North Hill.
A remarkably intact Board School. Dated 1877 with later C19
extension. The original school is on a U-shaped plan, symmetrically arranged with entrance lobbies either side of the
main schoolroom and projecting classroom wings at either
end. Wooden mullion windows with tracery in pointed-arch
heads. Thoughtful early C21 extension to l. with tall glazed
entrance under a projecting porch on slender columns and
pointed-head windows echoing the originals.

BLACKWATER POST OFFICE AND STORES, East Hill. A rare
survival of a late C19 shop with complete shopfront and interior
fittings around a columned floor space with spiral staircase
at rear.

BLISLAND   *1070*

ST PROTUS AND ST HYACINTH. One of the loveliest churches
in Cornwall, of compelling and varied interest. Unusual plan
with the tower to the N of the N transept, of three stages, the
second stage recessed, the third more, with clasping buttresses
rising to crocketed finials. NE stair-turret of rectangular plan
finishing above the embattled parapet. The tower has C15 and
C16 features but probably incorporates earlier fabric in the
thick walls of its lower stage: an early tower with a Norman
first stage stands in this position at St Enodoc and another is
known from archaeological excavation at Lanlivery (qq.v.).
The essentially Norman character of the church, known to
have been cruciform by the C12, is immediately apparent in
the N and W walls of the nave end N transept: there is a blocked
door of that date in the N wall with a surviving semicircular
label, and the W wall is strongly battered with no W door. Of
later development, the E window of the chancel is an E.E.
triplet of lancets; the N chancel aisle has a fine four-light C16
Perp E window; the S aisle has C16 and C19 Perp tracery, the
W window especially good; and the S wall of the S transept,
whose E wall probably incorporates Norman work, was rebuilt
in the C19 as the Moorshead and Lavethan Chapel, with a
separate door. The S aisle of six bays, the arcade very visibly
leaning to the S and supported by a striking late C19 decorative
scissor-brace, is of standard Cornish granite design. A rare
feature is the special 'chancel arch' which opens into the N
transept from the N chancel aisle. Good C16 wagon roofs,
ceiled, with carved ribs, wall-plates and bosses. The glory of
the interior is *F. C. Eden*'s restoration of 1894–6, continued in
stages until 1930: once seen its numinous luminosity is indel-
ibly etched in the memory, as captivating in its recreation of
the character and atmosphere of the medieval church as Comper's slightly later achievement at Little Petherick and E. H.
Sedding's at Crantock (qq.v.). This was Eden's first important

work, remarkable for its early date, and shows the influence of Bodley & Garner in whose practice Eden had worked with Comper. The scheme at Blisland also shows Eden's architectural inclusivity in his confident use of different styles in a way that somehow respects and enhances the Cornish church's character. His magnificent ROOD SCREEN of 1894–6 runs the whole width of the church in a blaze of colour, rising to a rood loft and large rood: Eden had been critical of Blomfield's plans for Swaffham Prior because of 'the vulgar error of making the rood far too small'. It is accessed by the original rood loft stair, and the capitals of the piers on which it sits clearly display the bearings for its medieval predecessor. The effect is further enhanced by the HIGH ALTAR in the Italian Renaissance style, oddly incongruous yet wholly successful in its glinting gold presence below the small C13 lancets and the decorative plasterwork panels of the chancel roof. – FONTS. One Norman, circular, of Polyphant stone, with four times a motif of concentric Vs and a herringbone moulding across the top. The other octagonal, C15, with shields in quatrefoils. – PULPIT AND CANOPY. Extensively restored in 1912, incorporating carvings in the *Grinling Gibbons* style. – STAINED GLASS. E chancel window 1911 by *Sir Ninian Comper*, by him also the E window of the S chancel chapel, 1894, and its S windows, 1901, all in the C15 style. – MONUMENTS. In the chancel floor, brass to John Balsam, rector of Blisland, †1410 (cf. the brass of similar date at Cardinham, though this figure is in contrast fully priestly vested). – Several good slate memorials, the best in the chancel to the Kempe family with six kneeling figures, †1624.

The churchyard has a number of exceptionally good C19 patternwork slate HEADSTONES and the fragment of a WHEEL-HEAD CROSS W of the tower.

The churchtown is grouped prettily around a treed green and its buildings, of generally modest scale and often of C17 origin, are well worth a gentle perambulation. At the entrance to the churchyard CHURCHGATE COTTAGE, C17, with the frames of former mullioned windows still visible around later glazing, and a plain rear elevation. It adjoins THE OLD SCHOOL, 1842 datestone, with two long three-light windows with cusped heads and diamond-leaded glazing to front and rear. At the NW corner of the green the OLD COACH HOUSE, 1869 datestone, originally a central coachhouse with loft above and flanking stables. An especially good group along the N side including the BLISLAND INN, 1911(?), Tudor but not incongruous. Towards the E end POPE'S COTTAGE was built as a pair of cottages with central paired doors under round-headed arches with datestone above 'AD 1833 S Pope'. The NE corner is framed by the MANSION HOUSE, a substantial though much altered late C16 and early C17 house arranged around a courtyard on an overall U-shaped plan with ranges on the S, W and N. Its impressive embattled gateway, a demonstration of its high original status, was removed to Lavethan (*see* below) in the late C18. The main elevation faces S and is of five irregular bays with a central two-storey gabled porch, its upper stage rebuilt 1972–4, with a deeply moulded arched doorway. The striking, and unifying, features of the house are the scrolled granite kneeler stones (cf. Trerice, Pendeen Manor, and houses at St Just-in-Penwith). The N range has a C12 arch, clearly re-set, in its N wall. In the chamber in the W wing a large fireplace with roll mouldings and large ball and spade stops, plasterwork above with a floral motif dated 1636, and remnant plasterwork indicating a barrel-vaulted ceiling.

CLAPPER BRIDGE, Bradford, 2 m. NNE. One of a number of good examples in the large moorland parish along with other medieval bridges, many C17 farmhouses and mills.

JUBILEE ROCK, Pendrift Downs, 1 m. N. Inscribed to commemorate the jubilees of George III, Victoria and Elizabeth II.

LAVETHAN, ½ m. W. In a lovely position on a SW slope of a tributary valley of the River Camel. A substantial house in the early C16, marked by Norden as the residence of Humphrey Kent *c.* 1584. The original layout is uncertain after extensive remodelling in the C17 and early C18. The present house has a central hall range facing SE with wings l. and r. at front and back. The hall range has eight unsooted early C16 roof trusses of high quality; mostly C17 roofs elsewhere. Two-storey porch added to the SE front in the early C17. In the late C17 or early C18 the house was reorientated to face NW, the new front refenestrated with twelve pane sashes with thick glazing bars, and the interior remodelled: the ground- and first-floor principal rooms and bedchambers received fine panelling and the inner room was partially subdivided to create a stair hall with a grand open-well stair.

The SE entrance has a beautiful pitched-stone courtyard; built into walling on the N approach is the embattled GATEWAY brought from The Mansion House in the churchtown (*see* above). In the grounds the remains of a HOLY WELL and three WAYSIDE CROSSES.

TREWARDALE. 1 m. S. Comfortably set on a S-facing valley slope. William Browne settled here in 1680 (cf. datestone in gateway in garden) but the present house is mostly late C18 to mid C19 with later alterations. Imposing eleven-window stucco front with a central two-storey range of seven bays flanked by two-storey pavilions, that to the l. rebuilt 1932, with dining room and service ranges to the rear. Fine and complete interior with late C18 and mid-C19 fittings. Wide central entrance hall with late C19 open-well stair. The kitchen has complete C19 fittings including a range by *Martyn* of Wadebridge.

BOCONNOC

1060

Boconnoc was one of the great estates which the Conqueror attached to the earldom of Cornwall, subsequently passing

during the later medieval period through the Carminows, Cour-
tenays, Russells and Mohuns before acquisition by the Pitts in
1717. The comfortable ensemble of house and church enjoys the
most generous of landscaped settings: over 300 acres of gardens,
pleasure grounds, parkland, ornamental plantations, and picturesque walks and rides. They are principally the creation of *Thomas
Pitt* (1737–93), first Lord Camelford, nephew of William Pitt and
friend of Horace Walpole. He was a distinguished amateur architect and landscape architect who had advised Walpole on the
decoration of Strawberry Hill and designed garden buildings at
Mount Edgcumbe and outside Cornwall at Stowe and Hagley
Hall, Worcestershire. Working with *Charles Rawlinson* of Lostwithiel, he substantially remodelled the early C18 house created
by his grandfather, another Thomas Pitt (1653–1726), and what
remained of the medieval building: his additions included a long
s gallery wing and there were later alterations by *Sir John Soane*.
The house then passed to the Fortescues of Devon and was
reduced to its present form by the demolition of most of the s
wing in 1971. It stood derelict during the later C20 until restored
by Anthony Fortescue with *Stephen Tyrrell*★ in the early C21.

The principal elevation of the HOUSE is the E entrance front, a
    restrained but dignified almost symmetrical arrangement of
    eight bays around an off-centre doorway, the N and S ends
    breaking forward as a pair of bays treated identically with
    graceful first-floor Venetian windows, and unified by a continu-
    ous modillion cornice to the parapet. To the N, and slightly set
    back, a three-storey tower, the E end of a C19 N wing reduced
    from four storeys in the C20. To the S, a single-storey range
    and a C20 screen wall, remnants of the gallery wing. The out-
    standing feature of the interior is the ENTRANCE HALL and,
    to its l., the STAIR HALL. The former has a deep carved cornice
    and moulded ceiling with an Ionic screen with coupled
    columns. The latter contains a majestic imperial stair and,
    above a ground floor of painted ashlar, is richly decorated in
    Neoclassical style with caryatids and porticos to the sides, a
    coffered niche with Nike on the landing, and a ceiling of panels
    with grotesques and illusionistic reliefs of classical sacrifices; a
    very strongly architectural composition. The stair is *c.* 1774 by
    Rawlinson, but what is the date of the decoration? The staircase
    seems to run over it. To the r. of the entrance hall, an impres-
    sive four-bay DRAWING ROOM with excellent C18 details
    including an elaborate plaster ceiling of perimeter ribs above
    an enriched pulvinated and modillion cornice. Two aedicules
    with shell heads, each below an entablature on consoles, break
    forward above the dado, and flank a doorcase which is set
    inside a pedimented entablature of fluted Ionic pilasters. This
    room is probably the medieval hall since eight sets of late C15
    principals, originally arch-braced, survive in the roof above.

★ I am grateful to Stephen Tyrrell for his observations on the evolution of the house.

Elsewhere simpler C18 decoration, mostly panelling to dado level.

The CHURCH (dedication unknown) is set above and just NE of the house, the relationship as intimate as at Lanherne (Mawgan-in-Pydar) and Lanhydrock. No tower, only a SW turret of 1877, but the body of the church is substantial: nave, S aisle, S porch and N chancel aisle. The S aisle arcade is of six standard bays, mostly rebuilt in a restoration of 1873 when much re-windowing was done. Original wagon roofs to nave, chancel, N aisle (partly restored) and porch. Late C19 scissor-braced roof to S aisle. Musicians gallery at W end of S aisle. – FONT. The most interesting object in the church: five supports, as in the C13, but the tracery decoration clearly of the C15 and of good quality. – REREDOS. 1888 by *Harry Hems* of Exeter, reusing carved wood from the house. – PULPIT. 1629, octagonal, decorated with cherubs holding musical instruments. Panels of carved naturalistic foliage. – Massive oak ALTAR TABLE inscribed 'Made by me, Sir Raynold Mohun 1621'. – ROOD SCREEN. Probably early C16, possibly taken from Braddock, used as a N parclose screen: two sets of three tracery panels as at St Winnow. No floral or foliage carving. Only part of the base preserved with banded quatrefoils and blind arches. – ROYAL ARMS. Painted plaster, Charles I, reputedly dated 1639 though this is not visible, with some strapwork decoration. (cf. Kilkhampton, Launcells, etc.). – STAINED GLASS. Three windows in the S aisle by *Burlison & Grylls*, 1900. – MONUMENT. Penelope Mohun, 1637, kneeling against an aedicule background. At high level above S arcade in nave, two fine carved reliefs, one on W of kneeling woman, one on E with figures of time with hourglass and death standing by sleeping figure.

Immediately N of the house and church, a large quadrangular COURTYARD of C18–mid C19 date, in an E-plan range of estate buildings, carriage houses and stables, now offices. W block with bellcote and clock tower flanked by arcaded link wings. On S side, reused medieval arches set in a rubble wall, probably from the medieval house. – DOVECOTE, probably mid C18, part of an outer group of farm buildings beyond the stables. Squat cylinder with raised central cupola.

Though it is Thomas Pitt's late C18 achievement that defines the Boconnoc landscape, its C17 origins, early C19 picturesque improvements, and C19 gardens and pleasure grounds all make significant contributions. The pleasure grounds are to the S and E of the house, with further areas on the higher ground to the NE, N and NW. From the S terrace there are extensive views across the park to the LAKE, constructed in the mid C19. A complex network of drives permeates the whole park so celebrated by C18 and C19 visitors for their exploitation of the picturesque scenery and features of the Lerryn valley. The most significant architectural incident is the OBELISK, 1 m. NE. 1771, designed by Thomas Pitt in memory of his uncle, Sir Richard Lyttelton. It stands 123 ft (37.5 metres) high on a grassed square, possibly a Civil War battery, a tall square plinth from which the obelisk rises square and slightly tapered, and surmounted by a pyramidal cap. The approach along the 1 m. drive from the NE is framed by two classical shrines: two rectangular piers with blind round arches with Gibbs surrounds below pediments with recessed tympana. The obelisk was repaired in 1787 by *Soane* after a lightning strike.

BODINNICK

A very picturesque group, especially seen across the estuary from Fowey, with the village street of modest cottages climbing steeply from the ferry slip. The jettied twin gables of FERRY-SIDE and the three-storey slate-hung OLD FERRY HOUSE INN are the eyecatchers, the latter with a smart early C18-looking panelled room. Its former stables were converted into ST JOHN'S CHURCH in 1949: small but exquisite carving of Christ in Glory by *Violet Pinwill* (q.v. Lanteglos-by-Fowey). Further up the street BLUE COTTAGE, probably the smallest C17 jettied house in Cornwall.

HALL CHAPEL, ½ m. above the village on the coastal footpath. A significant remnant of the former manor of the Mohuns, otherwise largely demolished in the Civil War. C14 walls, much adapted, but retaining a small embattled W bell-turret like a tiny tower, its lower stages engaged in the W wall. Good N doorway, now in store.

BODMIN

Bodmin lies at the centre of Cornwall and has played a central role in its history. It was one of the county's earliest and most important religious centres, probably its earliest urban settlement, its largest town throughout the medieval and post-medieval period, and the county town during the C18 and C19. In the second half of the C20 it was also the only Cornish town to undergo major planned expansion.

Its history begins *c.* 800 with the cult of St Petroc, perhaps moved here from Padstow (q.v.). By the later C10 a monastic foundation devoted to the saint had grown around the site of the present parish church, re-established as a powerful Augustinian priory in 1123–4 with a large new complex developed to the S of the church. A Franciscan friary was founded on the adjacent site of Mount Folly Square by 1260 and there were also three hospitals and a number of medieval chapels in or near the town. Almost all has vanished save the Norman base of the church

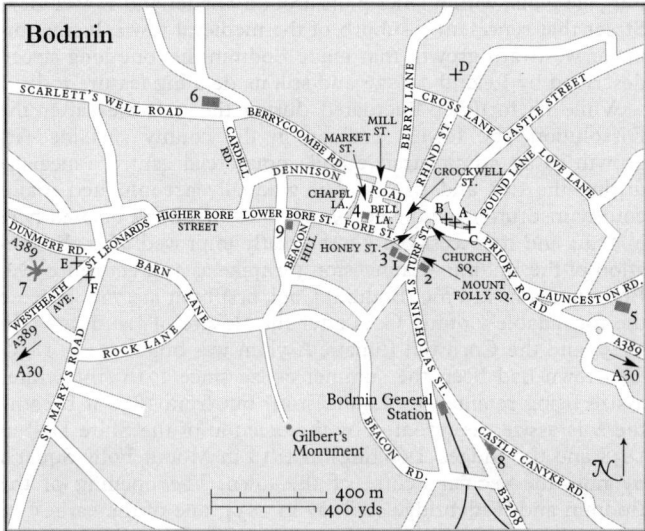

```
Bodmin
```

A   St Petroc
B   Well of St Guron
C   Chapel of St Thomas
    Becket
D   Berry Tower (Chapel of
    the Holy Rood)
E   St Lawrence
F   St Mary and St Petroc
    (R.C.)

1   Shire Hall
2   Shire House
3   Bodmin Town Museum and
    Public Rooms
4   Market House
5   Magistrates Court
6   Bodmin Jail (former)
7   Cornwall Lunatic Asylum (former)
8   Bodmin Barracks (former)
9   Passmore Edwards Free Library

tower which was part of the earlier monastery, the chapel of St Thomas Becket to the E of the church, and the NW corner of the late C12 or early C13 priory church excavated in the 1980s. Some sense of the architectural import of the priory can, however, be gleaned from the fragments of carved stone assembled in Priory Park, and especially from the tomb of Prior Vivian, now in the parish church. The church was almost entirely rebuilt between 1469 and 1475 and is the largest church in Cornwall, but 750 years ago was clearly of secondary importance.

The prior was the *de facto* proprietor of Bodmin and developed the secular settlement recorded as already having sixty-eight houses and a market in 1086. The priory had substantial estates in north Cornwall including Lanhydroc, Padstow, Rialton and Withiel, and from 1198 was a coinage town trading tin directly with Bordeaux and La Rochelle through Lostwithiel. The dominating presence of the priory precinct meant that expansion had to be westward. The area of Fore Street between Crockwell Street and Market Street was probably a planned C12 development of

burgage plots, with further plots around Higher and Lower Bore
Street that represent a suburb of the medieval town. It was this
linear westward growth that made Bodmin the 'one long street'
described by Leland *c.* 1536 and still its defining feature today.

While its fortunes fluctuated during the centuries after the
Dissolution, the town's position in the county sustained its
growth as an administrative and commercial centre, especially
during the C18 and C19, and it gradually accumulated major
county institutions and roles. Cornwall's first bank opened here
in 1744 and its accessibility was greatly improved after the creation of the Bodmin–Launceston turnpike as a direct route over
Bodmin Moor in 1769. Bodmin Gaol, first built in 1779, became
the formidable County Gaol after the closure of Launceston in
1829, and the Cornwall Lunatic Asylum was built here in 1820.
The town had been the summer assize since 1716 (the winter
assize being retained by Launceston) but from 1836 it became
the sole assize, represented by the erection of the Shire Hall in
1838 and the Judges' Lodgings in 1840 in Mount Folly Square,
by now the secular centre of the town. The opening of the
Bodmin and Wadebridge Railway in 1834, one of the earliest in
England, was a further stimulus, and a new Market Hall opened
in 1840. The town's population doubled to 4,200 between 1811
and 1841, and was further boosted by the erection of a militia
barracks in 1877 and the rail connection to the Great Western
Railway mainline in 1887. There are substantial Late Victorian
suburbs of villas and the grammar school of 1895 around Bodmin
Central Station, and of municipal housing around the late C19
former priory, convent and orphanage at West End.

Yet throughout its history Bodmin never enjoyed unchallenged
pre-eminence, and the choice of Truro in 1876 as the see of the
new Cornish diocese symbolized the decisive shift westward of
the county's economic centre of gravity, confirmed by the
building of the new County Hall there in 1912, though it was not
until 1988 that Bodmin finally ceded the assize court to Truro.
Despite these blows, Bodmin doubled its population to over
12,000 between 1961 and 1981 as a result of planned expansion
for London overspill with major public housing developments around the historic centre and a light industrial estate to
the NE.

After a period of relative decline in the late C20, the town is
benefiting from the recent economic resurgence of Cornwall.
Most of the former major institutional buildings have found new
uses and, though the later C20 expansion more than doubled the
spread of the town, the historic centre is remarkably intact.

CHURCHES

ST PETROC. Mostly rebuilt in 1469–75 and in that renewed form
probably more ambitious and impressive than the priory,
which had by then long since passed its glory. Building accounts
survive which demonstrate that all except the W end, tower and

chancel was reconstructed.* It is the earliest Cornish Perp church designed with high parallel aisles the full length of the building, the plan form that became the aspiration for so many churches in the county. The scale of the building, exceptionally large by Cornish standards, is not immediately apparent as the church is built into the steep hillside to the N: it is 151 ft (46 metres) long, 65 ft (20 metres) wide and has a tower which, before the spire was destroyed after a lightning strike in 1699, was 150 ft (45.7 metres) high. The tower is of massive construction, the walls of the lower stage over 8 ft (2.4 metres) thick, and is Norman up to the third storey, unbuttressed, and strongly receding from floor to floor. Large quoins, small masonry and small windows enhance its commanding presence. The S porch is two-storeyed with niches for sculpture on the upper wall and a little fan-vault on the ground floor. The rest of the outside is characterized by battlements and stair-turrets and bears the heavy imprint of successive C19 restorations which included the complete reconstruction of the W front in 1841, extensive re-windowing reusing some C15 tracery, re-tooling or refacing of the local elvan stonework, and the addition of the battlements in 1871.

The interior reveals the truly noble scale of the late C15 rebuild, immensely more lofty and spacious than the standard Cornish church. Nine bays for nave and chancel with no separation of the two in plan, but in elevation the three chancel arcades are lower than those of the nave. N and S aisles are the same width as the nave, the piers are slim and tall, of standard Cornish section, the small capitals with a little carving: the openings are wide with depressed two-centred arches. The system and detail are so much like St Andrew's, Plymouth, that E. H. Sedding suggested they might be designed by the same masons. The roofs are all C19 renewals except the S chancel aisle wagon roof with the 1475 date carved on. – FONT. An outstanding piece, C12, the best of its type in Cornwall and of impressive scale. Deep bowl on stumpy shaft, slimmer shafts in the four corners with busts of angels as capitals, interlaced and undercut foliage, scroll ornament, and lower down symmetrical beasts with 'trees of life' between. – CRESSET. Just inside the S door, as a collecting vessel. It is octagonal, C15, and has an eight-foiled depression in its top (cf. Mylor). – For the PULPIT and BENCHES contracts of 1491 exist with *Matthew More*, the benches to take as their model those of St Mary's, Plympton, the pulpit that of Moretonhampstead. The carving

22

* Four hundred and sixty people – nearly every adult in the parish – subscribed to the rebuilding, in addition to contributions from the guilds. The vicar gave a year's salary. There were gifts of building material and other goods, and those who were too poor to give anything else gave their labour. The total sum expended was £268 17s. 9½d. About twenty masons were employed; skilled men received 6d. a day. A workshop was set up at the quarries where the stone was shaped and dressed before it was sent to Bodmin. The N and S walls cost £22. Nine shillings was paid for carving capitals, nineteen shillings for ironwork. See G. H. Cook, *The English Medieval Parish Church*, London, 1954, p. 252.

of the pulpit is good but is made up of pieces of the original;
other fragments of former stalls and misericords are incorporated in its base, the lectern and prayer-desk. Also some panels
from these and the former rood screen reused in screens to the
N and S aisles and in CHOIR STALLS and REREDOS by *Sir
Charles Nicholson*, 1932, constructed forward of the E wall and
thus obscuring most of the 1894 scheme of mosaic panels
behind. – LANTERN CROSS. Head of probably the churchyard
cross excavated from the churchyard in the C19. Well-carved
Crucifixion, the figures in relief, with single figures to the sides.
– STAINED GLASS. Many by *Clayton & Bell*, dedicated to the
Duke of Cornwall's Light Infantry in various wars. Particularly
striking the Boer and First World War windows in the N aisle.
Tower W by *Heaton, Butler & Bayne*, 1868, and S chapel E
with heavy Pre-Raphaelite influences. – N chapel E by *A. K.
Nicholson*, 1936.

MONUMENTS. Sepulchral slab with foliated cross outside
the S wall of the church: inscription in French (cf. St Breock,
Little Petherick, St Merryn, St Buryan). – Between chancel
and N aisle free-standing monument in black Catacleuse
stone to Thomas Vivian, the last Prior of Bodmin but two,
†1533 (cf. Rialton). It comes from the priory church. Of outstanding interest as the most significant survival of the priory
and a testament to its importance, and the finest pre-
Reformation monument in Cornwall. Recumbent effigy on a
chest decorated with figures of the Evangelists. Cherubs and
shields, and coarse Italianizing balusters (the earliest example
of the effect on Cornwall of such metropolitan work as the
tomb of Henry VII, completed fourteen years earlier). – John
Vyvyan †1545, very fine and remarkably preserved, an important example of a surviving pre-Reformation monument in
Cornwall, and in slate rather than imported stone. – Richard
Durrant †1632 and his wives and twenty children, slate
slab. – Peter Bolt, 1633, one of the finest incised slabs in the
county. – Michael Bennet, 1821 by *William Behnes*. – Capt.
Oakley, 1835, also by *Behnes*, very restrained, with Greek
helmet and shield. – Displayed in the S aisle, the BODMIN
CASKET, ivory, of Spanish Mudéjar style, C12. It may be the
casket in which relics of St Petroc were handed back to the
Prior of Bodmin in 1177, after having been stolen.

WELL OF ST GURON. Outside the W end of the church. C19
well-head with dressed granite roof simulating slate courses.
Above the four-centred doorway a carved panel depicting St
Guron kneeling in front of the well. The water supply flows to
a granite water trough with 1545 datestone at the SW entrance
to the churchyard, issuing through two lions' heads as water
spouts. The well niche has two re-set granite columns flanking
its doorway, possibly from the former priory. W of the well an
octagonal COLUMN with moulded base and cap, from the
friary church.

CHAPEL OF ST THOMAS BECKET, in the churchyard, E of the
church. An eloquent ruin. Of the building licensed for worship

in 1377, the crypt and large sections of the upper walls survive. Fine Dec E window of three lights, triple sedilia with three cinquefoil arches within pointed hoodmoulds, and ogee-headed cinquefoil aumbry.

BERRY TOWER, Cemetery Road. The ruins of a three-stage tower, the only survival of the late C15 Chapel of the Holy Rood. Immediately W a WHEEL-HEAD CROSS with flared Greek cross in relief to each face.

CHURCH OF ST LAWRENCE, Westheath Avenue. Built 1859–61 as the chapel for the County Asylum (q.v.) following its mid-C19 expansion. Early Pointed style, clearly influenced by the Ecclesiological Movement. Apsidal chancel, five-bay nave with S transept and aisle, porches, bellcote over transept, and deeply splayed lancets.

CHURCH OF ST MARY AND ST PETROC (R.C.), Westheath Avenue. Foundation stone 1937, but not completed until 1965 by *Vyvyan Salisbury*. Plain, simple interior; glass from the *Buckfast Abbey* workshop. Part of the large site of the adjoining former ST MARY'S PRIORY AND ORPHANAGE, established 1881. Outside the E front of the church, fragments of medieval carved stone assembled as a shrine.

CARMINOW CROSS, 1½ m. SE of Bodmin at the centre of a roundabout near the A30. One of the most impressive crosses in Cornwall, 12 ft (3.7 metres) high and the second largest in the county. Pre-Conquest or medieval, a four-holed wheel-head flared Greek cross; the outer ring is a perfect circle. Noted by Langdon as in use as a boundary stone between the parishes of Bodmin and Lanhydrock.

CASTLE STREET HILL CROSS, at the top of Castle Street, ½ m. NE of the parish church. Pre-Conquest or medieval wayside wheel-head cross. Castle Street Hill was the medieval route N out of Bodmin across Bodmin Moor to Launceston. Each face displays a flared Greek cross in low relief.

PUBLIC BUILDINGS

SHIRE HALL, Mount Folly Square. The former Assize Court, 1837–8 by *Henry Burt* of Launceston. Severe Neoclassical, the defining building of Bodmin's former status as the county town. Granite ashlar with channelled rustication to basement. Symmetrical 2:3:2 front with central bays broken forward under pediment, and with round-headed openings at the base. Original wrought-iron gates with cast-iron spearhead finials. Remarkably complete inside; the entrance hall leads to a wide cantilevered imperial stair with round-headed openings to two smaller staircases either side. They lead to identical double-height courtrooms with U-plan galleries, one with original judges' seats, jurors' and other benches, docks, etc. The principal benches are panelled and enclosed like box pews. Below a set of thirty cupboard-like cells with ventilated doors.

SHIRE HOUSE, Mount Folly Square. The former Judges' Lodgings, now offices, c. 1840 by *Joseph Pascoe* of Bodmin. Tall and elegant Neoclassical, with giant pilasters in stucco above granite plinth. Square plan with two nearly symmetrical five-bay fronts to W and N, both with central doorways and very tall first-floor windows. Interior stripped.

BODMIN TOWN MUSEUM AND PUBLIC ROOMS, Mount Folly Square. 1891 by *Ralling & Tonar* of Exeter. A striking design in free Gothic style that admirably exploits the dramatically sloping site. The elevation to Mount Folly Square is especially lively and full of incident, a successful complement to the austere Shire Hall. Square polychrome local elvan and slate-stone with Hamstone and granite dressings to a 1:5:1 bay front, gabled cross-wings flanking the central five bays of tall three-light windows to the principal floor above a round-arched windowed basement. The l. gable-end has a canted first-floor oriel, the r. a rose window with a central figure over a canted and balustraded stone balcony, backed by a pointed-arched opening with a traceried tympanum rising from a central shaft. The gables have octagonal corner finials. The interior has an octagonal column from the former Franciscan friary on this site, exactly like that in the churchyard, and a loftily impressive public hall.

MARKET HOUSE, Fore Street. 1840, by *William Harris*, District Surveyor for Bristol. One of his three Greek Revival market houses in Cornwall (cf. Helston and Penzance) and based on a building on the island of Delos illustrated in Stuart and Revett's *Antiquities of Athens* (vol. 3, 1794). A remarkable design, distinguished by its severe façade and carving. Symmetrical 1:3:1-bay front, the central bays originally open, and framed by flat Doric pilasters with carved bulls' heads to the frieze above, and a small window to each side. Interior completely remodelled in the C20.

MAGISTRATES' COURT, Launceston Road. 1984 by *County Architect's Department*, project architect *Michael Way*. Rectangular plan around a small courtyard. Modest looking in unusually good reddish-brown brick, the public entrance reached around an impressive curved SW corner with a concrete ramp from the lowest part of the site. W and S walls to the entrance with narrow full-height windows, only interrupted on the curved corner by a semicircular oriel corbelled out and capped with a half-dome glass roof-light. The courts are in the centre and offices and secure areas at the E end under a shallow slate pyramidal roof.

POLICE STATION, Priory Road. 2009 by *Stride Treglown*. Strikingly sited on the skyline E of the town, on a boomerang-shaped plan with an oversailing roof, supported on slender columns all round, which slopes steeply down from front to rear.

BODMIN JAIL, Berrycoombe Road. The grim roofless cell blocks that loom over the town's northern suburbs stand on the site of the original gaol opened in 1779 as the first prison in England built to the reformist principles of John Howard

(1726–90). It was by *Thomas Jones* of Exeter for John Call, High Sheriff of Cornwall. Built on a steep southern-facing hill-slope with good light, air and water supply, it was an elegant classical design with the cells raised on arcades either side of a two-storey central block. It accommodated a hundred prisoners but after it became the County Gaol from 1829, successive alterations and additions were eventually followed by an entirely new prison in 1859 of vastly larger scale, with 250 cells. The architect was *F. W. Porter* of London. Although closed as a prison in 1929, almost all of it survives.

Its plan is best appreciated from the s. From above its fortress-like walls rise the tall main CELL BLOCK running E–W and the NAVAL PRISON N–S, each with parallel ranges of cells flanking a central hall (formerly with slate walkways). At their intersection a CROSSING TOWER of striking design, in fact a vast chimney for an innovative heating system: it is recessed at the top of the first stage and the third stage is a giant tapered cap corbelled out over the second stage. At its E end the main cell block continues as the former CHAPEL, marked by tall windows with dormers, and ends as a three-bay EAST ENTRANCE FRONT with a bellcote over the central gable. The entrance is only less intimidating in its smaller scale, the GATE-HOUSE of two storeys in Scottish Baronial style with end drum towers, all under one steep roof with multi-corbelled deep eaves to the central section resembling machicolations. To the s the former GOVERNOR'S HOUSE and CHAPLAINCY, a semi-detached pair in a simple Baronial style with stepped gable copings. In front of the governor's house a cast-iron open porch. On Berrymore Road the former NAVAL OFFICERS' QUARTERS, an asymmetrical pair of lodges flanking a carriage gateway, the parapet continued over the entrance with a recessed rectangular porch below.

Former CORNWALL LUNATIC ASYLUM, Westheath Avenue. Later St Lawrence Hospital, now partly demolished and converted to housing with much new building over the vast site: the Church of St Lawrence was its chapel (*see* Churches). The asylum was begun in 1817. The original layout is now difficult to read but at the E end is the earliest and most interesting building: *John Foulston's* 1817–20 panoptical building with six wings radiating out from a central core, to aid supervision of the inmates. All the wings have additions by *George Wightwick* c. 1838 and later in the C19. Between the front wings a tapered entrance with segmented ends to the front. The original two window fronts of the central building with their first-floor oriels survive between most of the wings, as do some iron windows and doors for fire-proofing. This innovative plan was the first in England but from the start was considered unsuitable: in an 1846 *Builder* article on asylums, Charles Fowler used Bodmin as an example of the disadvantages of the radial plan, resolved by his Exminster asylum (Devon) with curved corridors. The superintendent's house by Wightwick was added in 1838 with alterations and extensions of 1898 by *Silvanus Trevail*. The large free-standing blocks to the w were built by Wightwick in 1842–5 as the Williams Building, a double E-plan and by Trevail as the Foster Block, a 250-bed unit begun in 1897 and opened in 1906. Trevail also built the Isolation Hospital of 1897. Trevail's work characteristically employs much Ruabon terracotta.

Former BODMIN BARRACKS, St Nicholas Street. The impressive French Renaissance style front block is the former MILITIA KEEP, 1859, for the Royal Cornwall Rangers Militia, now the regimental museum. It was incorporated into the depot barracks as the main entrance and quartermaster's department in 1881 under the Cardwell reforms which aimed at local recruitment to the county regiment. Steep hipped slate roof with central dormer with steep pyramidal roof rising to a finial on each elevation of the rectangular double-depth plan. Enclosed by a perimeter wall with musket loops and central entrance under a narrow steep gable as a pediment. Single storey stables inside. In front the WAR MEMORIAL, 1922, a fine bronze of a soldier in battledress by *L. S. Merrifield*. Behind the keep on the extensive site a rare example of Cardwell's localization depots, designed by *Major H. C. Seddon*, which replaced the bilateral symmetry and parade-centred layout that had dominated British barracks since the early C18 with more functional arrangements dictated by internal logistics and local considerations. Two matching BARRACK BLOCKS, 1881, tall stone buildings symmetrically arranged around their central three bays which are slightly broken forward, their austere and disciplined character now severely compromised by the proximity of a crescent of town houses in faux Georgian style. Also former SERGEANTS' MESS and HOSPITAL, sturdy two-storey blocks.

PASSMORE EDWARDS FREE LIBRARY AND INSTITUTE, Lower Bore Street. 1895 by *Silvanus Trevail*. An eclectic combination of Gothic and Dutch Renaissance styles, with shaped gables to the street elevations.

BODMIN GENERAL STATION, St Nicholas Street. Built 1887 as the terminus of the GWR branch that finally connected the town to the mainline at Bodmin Road. A fine example of a country terminus, almost unaltered. Single-storey frontage building with ticket office and r. hand wing with waiting rooms etc. The signal box is a replica. Now the headquarters of the Bodmin & Wenford Railway.

PERAMBULATIONS

Bodmin's character and interest are as much about its very readable medieval town plan and its development as its later buildings and architecture. Mount Folly Square makes a good starting point for both perambulations, one to the e around the former religious precinct, the other w up the mile-long main street of the secular settlement.

1. Mount Folly Square and the medieval religious precinct

The square is the heart of the historic county town and occupies
the site of the C13 friary. It is of two contrasting halves. The
principal civic buildings of the Shire Hall, Shire House and
Museum and Public Rooms (*see* Public Buildings) make an
imposing group at the upper end of the steeply sloping space.
They are joined to the E by the solidly reassuring Italianate
BARCLAYS BANK, 1874 by *Henry Rice* of Liskeard as the East
Cornwall Bank. The lower half of the square is formed of late
C18–late C19 houses and shops, mostly stucco, like much of
the rest of the town centre. Above the Shire Hall on Crinick's
Hill the excellent Neo-Georgian POST OFFICE, 1924 by
A. Bullock of *H. M. Office of Works* (cf. Falmouth and St
Austell), a fine design for its prominent position and steep site,
in Neoclassical style with a large bay window overlooking the
town. Next door THE FRIARIES, a town house of *c.* 1820–40,
tall symmetrical four-window front and wide porch with four
slender columns.

Entering PRIORY PARK between Shire House and Barclays
Bank, the extensive open space that fossilizes the site of the
former priory is immediately revealed. E of the Edwardian
pond (probably on the site of the priory fish ponds) is an
impressive array of large fragments of carved medieval stone.
Then PRIORY HOUSE, 1766–72, slightly remodelled and
extended in the mid C19, with a three-storey five-window front,
originally with flanking single-storey wings, and a large Doric
porch. To its immediate N the excavated NW corner of the
priory church, demonstrating that the house occupies the
church site. N of Priory Road, widened with the loss of the S
part of the churchyard in 1929 and again in the 1960s, lies the
parish church and chapel of St Thomas Becket (*see* Churches)
on the site of the former monastic precinct. At the W end of
the churchyard, CHURCH SQUARE, are Nos. 4 and 5, a pair of
two-storey early C19 town houses, both doorways under a
single porch with Tuscan granite columns, and No. 2, a late
C18 town house of three storeys and a five-window front. These
houses, those in Castle Street to the NW of the churchyard and
others around Priory Park, show that the E end of Bodmin
became the more prestigious part of town in the C18 and C19.
CASTLE STREET has houses of various scale of that period but
also TOWER HILL FARMHOUSE, a vernacular survivor from
the C17 with a deep T-shaped plan, remodelled *c.* 1700 and in
the early to mid C18: its former farmyard buildings also survive
to the W. ST GURONS is a large undistinguished villa of 1899
by *Silvanus Trevail*.

Returning to Church Square, the triangle of development
between Turf Street and Honey Street probably represents the
infilling of the medieval and later market place. The narrow
HONEY STREET, entered past a column from the priory, is a
delightful mix of C18 and C19 former town houses like No. 11
(now THE WEAVERS pub) and purpose-built later C19 retail

premises opposite, built as a post office and three shops by *Silvanus Trevail* in 1884. The most striking building, Nos. 15 and 16, a tall shop and warehouse with rich Baroque-style red terracotta detailing as tympana over the first-floor windows and a long panel above the central doorway. Behind the granite arched central passage of Nos. 23–27 is the former INDEPENDENT CHAPEL, dated 1804.

2. *Fore Street, Lower and Higher Bore Street, St Leonards and West End*

FORE STREET is a long, gentle rise with many side streets and alleys (known as opes locally), fundamentally the street pattern of the medieval town. Given its length the street is an exceptionally complete ensemble of C17–C19 buildings, mostly former town houses and later commercial buildings with a few larger institutional buildings, but remarkably little later C20 redevelopment. It repays detailed study, not least because many of the later fronts hide earlier fabric. As in other Cornish towns there is much disguised timber framing to the frontages, identifiable by the thinness of the walls and the placing of the windows right on the wall face with no reveals.

The CLOCK TOWER at the junction of Mount Folly Square, Fore Street, and Honey Street is the place to start. It is of 1845 by *George Wightwick*, a slender Italianate tower in granite ashlar, starting with a giant first stage with a round-arched vermiculated doorway below a half-domed niche and plaque, surmounted by a clock face with a scrolled pediment and rising to a bellcote with panelled corner acroteria and a central dome. Opposite, No. 2, mid-C19 with a splendid seven-bay shopfront subdivided by Ionic columns. Off to the r., CROCKWELL STREET is the first of the small medieval side streets. In this area N of Fore Street there is some sense of the town's intensely built-up character before C20 demolition and the construction of Dennison Road. Back in Fore Street, No. 8 is an example of an obviously earlier house of the C17, its timber-framed front jettied out at the second floor, as is No. 33 further up the street on the r. (cf. similar jettied town houses in Fowey, Looe and Penryn). In BELL LANE, the EYEWATER SPRING, datestone 1700 and inscription D/GEORGE/DEMOUNFRYART/MAYOR. No. 22 Fore Street is C17 with a contemporary rear wing, its former status as the Guildhall signified by the doorway flanked by two granite columns with moulded capitals and the royal arms over. No. 24 is a disguised C17 merchant's house with a timber-framed front. Of the later period of town houses, No. 42, early C19 stucco with channelled rustications and hoodmoulds with keys to the ground floor, and a carriage entrance to former stables behind, and No. 64, late C18–early C19 with a smart elvan ashlar front, pilastered doorway with Doric entablature and spoked fanlight, also with a carriage entrance.

The Market House (*see* Public Buildings) is a dramatic incident in the street scene as is the MANOR HOUSE (No. 84), the
former Methodist Sunday School, its Italianate style well
suited to its large scale and steeply sloping site to the E side of
the former METHODIST CHURCH, 1840, drastically altered
and enlarged 1885–6 and tactfully converted to a pub in 2008.
The latter is imposingly set high above the street and
approached by a wide curved and converging flight of granite
steps with lanterns on square piers. Three central bays of two
tiers of round-arched openings with moulded pediment,
flanked by two wings broken forward with smaller pediments.
Among the little side streets, Market Street offers a lovely
curving view downhill and Beacon Hill a similar view uphill.
Fore Street ends with No. 96, a tall late C18 town house with
a three-storey canted bay, partly slate-hung, and a massive
early brick stack.

As Fore Street runs into LOWER BORE STREET there is a notable
diminution of scale from three- to two-storey buildings, the
appearance of more stone fronts among the stucco, and a
widening out of the street that reflects the former market and
fair area of this medieval suburb. The last major public building
is the Passmore Edwards Library (*see* Public Buidlings).
Despite their unpretentious character and late-looking fronts,
some of these buildings at least are earlier town houses, e.g.
No. 20 which dates from *c.* 1610, adjoining the curiously
narrow late C19 No. 22. No. 45 is a fine C18 town house set
back from the street with a good triple doorcase. No. 4 HIGHER
BORE STREET is a large late C18 or earlier town house with a
late C19 five-window front, the central bay broken forward with
a deep moulded arched doorway and vermiculated quoins and
window surrounds. Courtyard to the rear with C18 wing and
earlier buildings. There is evidence of burgage plots still trace-
able behind the mostly C19 fronted houses. A good point to
return to the centre.

OBELISK, The Beacon. 144 ft (44 metres) high, erected to commemorate Lt. Gen. Sir W. R. Gilbert, 1856–7. Slender tapering
column of granite ashlar on a moulded pedestal base with
inscription to each side. It still dominates the approach to the
town.

TULIP FOODS FACTORY, Newtons Margate Industrial Estate,
Cooksland Road. By *Pearn & Proctor*, 2001. Large and spreading but excellently modulated, its sleek lines accentuated by its
cladding in vertical grey sheeting.

BOLVENTOR

1070

The parish, in the centre of Bodmin Moor, was created in
1846 from parts of Altarnun, Cardinham and St Neot, the once

remote little village now adjacent to the dual carriageways of the modern A30.

JAMAICA INN at the centre has been an inn of that name since at least the first decade of the C19. Probably built as a coaching inn on the 1769 turnpike. Originally of a two-room through-passage plan between end stacks, greatly extended in the C19 by two rooms either side and a rear range slightly later. Stables at the front converted to residential and commercial use.

Former HOLY TRINITY CHURCH, SW across the A30. Now residential. A simple cruciform whose accurately replicated Perp-style tracery gives it a more venerable appearance than its 1846 date might suggest. Corbelled octagonal bellcote at the junction of nave and chancel with four pierced openings under a conical roof with finial.

CATSHOLE, 1¼ m. NW. Early Neolithic LONG CAIRN. The wider NE end of this 52-ft (16-metre) long trapezoidal kerbed mound retains two central upright portal stones and two fallen slender granite corner posts. Diagonal to contours, the long cairn appears designed to mimic Brown Willy's long ridge (q.v.) when viewed from Tolborough Tor.

TOLBOROUGH TOR, 1 m. NW. Early Bronze Age CAIRN, a prominent mound distinguishing the hill from other rounded downs along the upper Fowey. A fine laid-stone kerb merges with the natural rock face of a small tor. To the S is a landscape of rounded downs; but from the short STONE ROW on the cairn's SE side Cornwall's great rocky mountains, an ancestral landscape, are suddenly visible, with Roughtor's topmost tors poking above Brown Willy's long dark flank.

BOSCASTLE
including Forrabury and Minster

Visitors frequent the picturesque harbour where the sea snakes in through formidable cliffs at the confluence of the Jordan and Valency rivers. But fewer explore the rich history of the settlement above, surprisingly complex in its morphology for such a relatively modest place. Boscastle straddles the parishes of Forrabury and Minster but their medieval churches are quite separate from the urban settlement: that began on the higher ground above the steep-sided Jordan valley where a castle, market and chapel of ease dedicated to St James were established by the C14. The castle, the principal residence of the Bottreaux family,[*] one of the most important in medieval Cornwall, was in decay by the C15 and the chapel was finally demolished in the late C19. But the town grew steadily, peaking in the C19, the harbour area (Quaytown and Bridgetown) becoming a significant port, while

---

[*] It is from the family and castle that Boscastle is named.

Upper Town's amiable little streets are full of good examples of buildings from the C15–C19 with much excellent vernacular detail.

CHURCHES

St Mertherian, Minster, 1 m. e. The mother church of Boscastle, almost hidden below the road on the steep slopes of a ferny dell among luxuriant trees: indeed it is best approached on foot from the wooded Valency valley, from which its remoteness is striking. The location, dedication and churchyard enclosure are characteristic of an early Christian site (the place name is pre-Conquest) and may suggest a small C8 monastery. The church was rebuilt after the Conquest, the monastery becoming the cell of an alien priory, with possible remains of other monastic buildings in the valley below. But preserved in the NE corner of the chancel is part of the early building, with one small lancet (with later head), a two-light E.E. window, and a blocked doorway. Sedding considered the tower C13 and remodelled in the C15 but it was much rebuilt and given a saddleback roof in an extensive restoration by *J. P. St Aubyn* 1869–71. C16 s aisle of five bays with standard Cornish piers and four-centred arches and s porch. Two C13 windows reset in s wall. – FONT. Norman, of the simplest design, a round bowl with diagonal criss-cross lines (cf. Forrabury, Tintagel). – MONUMENTS. Fine assemblage of slate plates at the w end of the s aisle. – Two good little monuments with kneeling figures opposite each other as usual about 1600 in s aisle: one William Cotton †1656 and wife Elizabeth, with three sons and five daughters below, the other John Hender †1611. – John Cotton †1703, indifferent. Endearing brass to the infant Hender Roberts †1602 in chancel. – CURIOSUM. Shears or scissor carving on NW corner of the tower, its significance unexplained.

St Symphorian, Forrabury. As prominently exposed on the bare hill above Boscastle as the church is at Tintagel. A sturdy, low, plain w tower, the upper part rebuilt 1760. The little church retains traces of the Norman building in the lower part of the s wall and the Norman imposts to the s transept; a mullioned window was added to the transept in the early C16. The s porch is roofed by huge slabs of granite. The simple, low interior is a curious blend of the small early church and a major restoration of 1868 that added a N aisle with an arcade of thick, vaguely classical columns, replacing the N transept in the process. – FONT. Norman, cup-shaped, with diagonal criss-cross decoration like Minster and Tintagel. – Several BENCH-ENDS incorporated into the altar, credence table, and pulpit. In the s of the churchyard a WHEEL-HEAD CROSS.

Methodist church, Fore Street. Built *c.* 1825, partly remodelled in the early C20 when a two-storey entrance tower was added. Interior with w gallery and rostrum pulpit. Datestones from other converted or demolished local chapels re-set in tower.

PERAMBULATION

Start an exploration of Quaytown and Bridgetown from the HARBOUR. The gently curving pier of vertically set slatestone projecting from the SW side dates from *c.* 1584 and continues between natural outcrops of rock to the landward. The outer bar from the N side was built in the C18, destroyed in the Second World War and rebuilt 1962 using stone from the demolished Laira Bridge at Plymouth. A QUAY runs inland from the pier. Many of the buildings spreading (inland) above the steep-sided watercourse originated as industrial and commercial structures of the former port, including FISH CELLARS (National Trust shop and Penally Terrace), a LIME-KILN, FORGE, BLACKSMITH'S SHOP and WAREHOUSES (the Cobweb Inn). Most are later C18 and C19, some rebuilt after the great flood of 2004. Just E of the bridge the C19 OLD MILL with an overshot waterwheel, and the WELLINGTON HOTEL, the most imposing building in the town, a C17 coaching inn largely rebuilt 1853. Front range three-storey with attic dominated by a four-storey curved and castellated corner tower. Inside, four windows of armorial glass from the Royal Hotel, Bodmin, that commemorated Queen Victoria's visit in 1846, and three glass lamps either designed or given by Thomas Hardy, possibly from St Juliot's Church (q.v.).
Now for the steep climb up Old Road to Upper Town. Just behind the Wellington Hotel MARINE TERRACE, built *c.* 1844 for the Admiralty as accommodation for their revenue men, with remarkably narrow half-doors. Rising up on the r. on New Road above – built in the mid C19 to improve access – seven VILLAS of 1889 in a robust Neo-Georgian style: they present single-storey elevations to the road but dignified two-storey fronts on high battered plinths to the valley. Upper Town (or Top Town) is essentially one long street running up the hill as Dunn Street, Fore Street and High Street successively with a few other lanes or footpaths off them. Halfway up Fore Street a small footpath leads l. to the still impressive remains of the motte of BOTTREAUX CASTLE with its ramparts below. Slightly further up the street on the r. a characteristically robustly detailed SCHOOL by *Silvanus Trevail*, 1879. On the corner with Gunpool Lane off r., the VILLAGE HALL of 1888–9, built as a mission church on the site of the chapel of St James and incorporating a two-light cusped-headed window from the medieval building in the gable-end. The principal claims of Upper Town are, however, the delightful street scenes provided by the variety of good vernacular detail in their small buildings with wavy roofs of local slate, many lateral stacks, and the frequent reuse of older features. Some of the houses, e.g. TINKERS and SMUGGLERS, Fore Street, are medieval in origin. And all remarkably unspoiled.

FORRABURY STITCHES, Forrabury Common. Immediately N of the churchyard of St Symphorian. A remarkable survival of forty-two of the original sixty 'stitches', long, gently curving strips of land up to the cliff edge tenanted individually and cropped on a four-year rotation, in cultivation from Lady Day to Michaelmas but reverting to common grazing in winter. Probably post-medieval in their present form. Immediately W of the Stitches, WILLAPARK, a bold promontory defended in the Iron Age as a cliff castle, now surmounted by an early C19 whitewashed TOWER. Its history is uncertain, variously described in early guidebooks as a 'pleasure house', 'prospect house' (cf. Doyden Castle, Port Quin), or 'observatory': it later served as a coastguard look-out. A magnificent viewpoint.

WELLTOWN MANOR, ¾ m. SW. One of the most recognizable 61 yeoman houses in Cornwall. Early C16, for the Tinke family with initials OT on the hall window and BT in the spandrels of the porch doorway. Probably originally an open hall, extended and remodelled in the early C17. The extremely picturesque front elevation includes granite mullioned windows, first-floor windows within gabled dormers, a two-storey gabled porch, and a tall lateral stack. Medieval roof with morticed collar joints and threaded purlins.

WORTHYVALE MANOR, 3 m. S. A house demonstrating the transition from the single room depth plan to the double depth plan. Lobby entrance to hall and parlour but with an integral one-and-a-half-storey lean-to back block. Exceptionally large fireplace in the hall, implying cooking still done there, but with service rooms in the rear. Probably mid-C17, despite the date 1703 above the front door. Nearby an INSCRIBED STONE: LATINI IC IACIT FILIUS MAGARI, the lettering transitional between Roman and Hiberno-Saxon.

WATERPIT DOWN, 2 m. S. CROSS-SHAFT. Decorated on all four sides and inscribed CRVX INBVRGE (Hiberno-Saxon), 'The Cross of Inburga'.

BOTALLACK 3030
1½ m. N of St Just-in-Penwith

The area near the steep cliffs provides a dramatic setting for an exploration of the mining landscape, the track from the village first passing the plain, dignified COUNT HOUSE, 1862, to the extensive remains of the 1906 TIN MILL (later reused as ARSENIC WORKS), including a 1908 CHIMNEY, 1980s steel HEAD FRAME and a Brunton ARSENIC CALCINER. This was the last gasp of mining at Botallack, which had continued since at least the late C16 and was, with nearby Levant (q.v.), the most important mine in the St Just area. The most spectacular reminder that the shafts of the mines reached far out under the Atlantic is offered by the two ENGINE HOUSES perched just above the sea on Crowns Rocks, Botallack Head: the lower house 1835, the higher 1862, with the remains of their boiler houses also visible.

BOTALLACK MANOR HOUSE, ¼ m. inland. C17 L-plan house plus an C18 stair wing. Scrolled kneelers to the coping of the gable-ends, stacks with moulded granite caps, and datestone 1665. A C17 BARN next to the house has an original granite doorway and the good group of farm buildings also includes a small C18 BARN and a C19 PIGSTY RANGE.

4060

BOTUS FLEMING

ST MARY. Nothing special about the three-stage W tower, probably later C15, with diagonal buttresses (roughcast alas) and tall embattled parapet with pinnacles, nor about the rest of the exterior whose walling is of Plymouth limestone. But inside it has a handsome five-bay arcade between the N aisle and the nave on octagonal piers whose capitals are studded with stylized fleurons, an unusual and very successful treatment: the arcade is in stone of a vesicular texture found in this area. Moreover the second pier has on its W side, carved out of the pier, a projecting base and canopy for a figure, and the two adjoining piers also have brackets for statues. The same motif occurs in Devon. Restored 1872 by *Henry Elliott*, with new arch-braced roofs, pews, floors and glazing. – FONT. Of Polyphant table-top type; with seven flat little blank niches with pointed heads on each side, probably C14. – STAINED GLASS. Chancel E by *Osborne Phillips*, replacing a window destroyed in 1941. Chancel S, 1902 by *Fouracre & Son*, and a striking window in abstract crystalline patterns depicting a tree and doves of peace, 1976 by *Father Charles Norris* of Buckfast. – MONUMENTS. In a recess in the N aisle, a cross-legged knight carrying a shield, possibly late C14–early C15, badly preserved, probably one of the Moditons (*see* below). – Other monuments to the Symons of Hatt (q.v.), including William Symon †1766, oval marble tablet on slate ground with pediment, by *R. Isbell* of Stonehouse. – Mark Batt †1753 with festoons of fruit. – Elizabeth Bray †1747, with draped flaming urn, by *Veale* of Plymouth.

In the churchyard, slate MONUMENTAL INSCRIPTIONS from 1737 onwards (others now in the church) reveal that many parishioners went to Devonport but were buried in their birthplace. In a field NE of the church an OBELISK 12 ft (3.7 metres) tall to William Martyn, †1762, who, being 'a Catholic Christian, in the true, not depraved Popish sense of the word' knew 'no superstitious veneration for church or churchyard' and therefore preferred to be buried in unconsecrated ground.

THE BIDWELL, near the church. A small rectangular well-house, probably C15, built into the bank. Four-centred doorway, C19 wrought-iron gate with trefoil finials to shafts and image niche with C19 statue of the Virgin.

CHURCHTOWN FARMHOUSE, just W of the church. Tall three-room and through-passage house part of a former great house, possibly for Digory Wills (re-set label stops with DW initials) who lived at Moditonham in the early C17.

MODITONHAM, ¼ m. E. Of the medieval castle of the Moditons nothing is preserved. The present house is early C18 with later C18 and C19 alterations. Smart three-storey seven-bay front in 2:3:2 bays, the outer bays slightly advanced with rusticated quoins, in Plymouth limestone ashlar with granite dressings, and a central Roman Doric portico with fluted columns. Fine C18 interior including entrance hall plasterwork incorporating rustic motifs of rake, billhooks, wheatsheaf and barrel, a rear stair hall with late C18 imperial stair and one room with late C18 plasterwork with Greek maidens in the central roundel. The approach is through a pair of late C18 two-storey LODGES with granite GATEPIERS surmounted by ball finials.

BOYTON   3090

HOLY NAME. The church belonged to Tavistock Abbey before the Conquest. Unbuttressed C14 W tower, partly rebuilt 1692–4 (cf. the round-headed top windows). Nave and S aisle only with five-bay arcade of Cornish standard. Wagon roofs, good in the aisle, especially over the S chancel chapel. Windows straight-headed. Restored 1876–7 by *J. P. St Aubyn*. – FONT. Plain Early Norman, of the same irregular oval shape as Morwenstow and Washaway. – ROOD SCREEN. Base only, and much restored, with tracery of *c.* 1500, similar to that on so many Cornish bench-ends. – STAINED GLASS. Chancel E, 1876 by *Jones & Willis*, incorporating a kaleidoscope of medieval and Georgian fragments. – Nave N, 1896 by *Fouracre & Son*.

BRADDOCK   1060

ST MARY. Small, remote, and in a lovely position close to Bocon-noc Woods. A post-Conquest foundation as a chapelry to St Winnow but a separate parish by 1331. Two-storeyed W tower without buttresses, battlemented with crocketed finials: it may incorporate earlier fabric but was rebuilt in the C13 or C14 with late reticulated tracery in the W window. The N side still has the early transept and no aisle, the S side an aisle of five bays with standard Cornish piers on elongated bases and with octagonal flat capitals. The odd arches between nave and N transept with a pier in the middle could be the beginnings of an aborted N aisle; alternatively they could be C19, reusing heavily moulded C16(?) piers with renewed capitals. Original wagon roofs to nave, chancel, S aisle and porch, restored in 1926. – FONT. Norman with four corner faces, tree of life on one side, palmettes on the other three. – PULPIT. Elizabethan with panels with round arches, intertwined foliage and heraldic arms. – ROOD SCREEN. Two sections of the base remain (the upper part was removed to Boconnoc, q.v.): four narrow panels on the N side, six on the S, subdivided by later twisted columns with castellated capitals. Exuberant carving with pomegranates and foliage with figures including a monkey, a pig playing bagpipes, and a dragon's head breathing out a scroll. The carved motifs have enough allusions to the coming of the Renaissance to make a date before 1530 unlikely. – Unusual carved SCREEN at W end with beakhead figures at the base of the posts and a curious set of panels. What can they be? They look like *Volkskunst* of the C18, little carved groups in relief of two figures opposite each other, very stiff and quaint, one panel with three faces, one *en face*, two in profile, one panel with a woman holding a snake's tail, and the whole surrounded by panels with Celtic-looking animals. – BENCH-ENDS. Very cut about, but obviously originally an interesting set, with a figure of St Sidwell, two small figures of saints on shields with their emblem on a neighbouring shield: one is of St Sidwell with her scythe. – STAINED GLASS. E window, 1878 by *Burlison & Grylls*.

The church sits within an oval raised churchyard or *lann*, entered from the S through a re-set *c.* C16 four-centred arch and from the NW by a charmingly rustic LYCHGATE, probably C18.

BREAGE

6020

ST BREAGE. The splendid W tower, tall and strong and visible for miles around, draws one to a church of exceptional interest, a model of C15–C16 perfection. It was the mother church of the area by *c.* 1170 with dependent chapelries at Cury, Germoe and Gunwalloe. The tower, like the entire church, is of ashlar granite and has set-back buttresses to its three stages, the buttresses finishing below crocketed corner pinnacles which are corbelled out on angels holding shields (cf. Germoe, Gulval and St Ives), with grotesque heads and gargoyles sticking out from the string course below the battlements. C14 chancel E window. Unusually ambitious S porch with panelled jambs, buttresses and battlements; it compares well with the porch to the former hall at Godolphin with which the church has strong connections. That may suggest the existence of a 'Godolphin workshop' in the C15.* Unusual too are the N and S transeptal chapels, also battlemented and with uncusped and untraceried windows, like Egloshayle, of c. 1530.

The interior has two identical seven-bay aisles to the nave with standard Cornish granite piers, plain capitals, and decorated abaci: the arches to the transeptal chapels are of the same type. The jambs to the tall tower arch are panelled like the porch and there is decoration in the reveal of the w door like the E window at Padstow. C15 wagon roofs to the aisles, and a fine panelled timber ceiling of hefty section in the N chapel (a rarity in Cornwall). The C15–C16 sequence is likely to have started with the construction of the aisles, followed by the tower and porch c. 1460, with the transeptal chapels coming some time later, by perhaps as much as sixty years on the evidence of their late windows: the E windows of the aisles, with their uncusped oval tracery like St Erth and St Eval, are insertions c. 1520–40. The church was restored 1890–1 by *Rev. Ernest Geldart*,[†] with some work by *E. H. Sedding*, with new roofs to nave and chancel, a fine ROOD SCREEN in the West Country medieval tradition running the full width of the church, a vast REREDOS that almost blocks the E window, and good, workmanlike pews. – WALL PAINTINGS. C15. The outstanding feature of the interior, of the highest importance including the best preserved of the three examples in Cornwall of the Sunday Christ (as a warning to Sabbath breakers), here with a St Christopher, and one of the very best in England and Wales. The figures, on the N wall, are 9 ft (2.7 metres) high and of arresting vigour. Among the unusual features, most notable are the arrangement of the tools to relate directly to the blood flowing from Christ's wounds, and the range of items, some of local provenance, depicted, which include an anchor, gun, lute, two different types of axe and saw, and playing cards. The St Christopher has a charming mermaid holding a mirror, and a large flat fish. Smaller single figures of (from the w) St Hilary, St Corentine, St Augustine and St Michael on the N wall and window splay; and on the window splays of the S aisle, identified (from the w) as Henry VI, Thomas Becket and St Giles. – ROMAN STONE with an inscription referring to Marcus Cassianus Posthumus, a usurper who ruled Gaul and Britain 258–68: the full inscription reads 'For the Emperor Caesar, our Lord, Marcus Cassianus [Latinus Posthumus]. . .' – SCULPTURE. In the S aisle (Godolphin) chapel, a C14 stone with pointed head representing the Crucifixion. – STAINED GLASS. A few medieval fragments in the E window of the S chapel. – Chancel E, 1854 and S aisle W, 1863 by *William Wailes.* – S aisle, Three Marys at the Tomb, and N aisle, Faith, Hope and Charity, both 1900, by

50

*I am indebted to John Schofield for this and other suggestions in this account.
[†] Geldart, rector of Little Braxted, Essex, was a friend of the incumbent and reviser, in 1882, of Edward Cox's *Art of Garnishing Churches*, first published 1868.

Heaton, Butler & Bayne. – N aisle, The Good Shepherd, 1909, by *Hardman.* – In the Godolphin chapel, three HELMETS with wooden replicas of dolphin crests (the dolphin is the principal feature of the Godolphin crest).

The churchyard stands in a likely *lann.* Outside the S porch a four-holed WHEEL-HEAD CROSS of red sandrock, with very worn decoration.

RINSEY HOUSE, Rinsey, 3 m. WSW. Perched above the headland. 1928 by *Cowell, Drewitt & Wheatly.* Arts and Crafts style, stone walls with complex slate roofs.

BROWN WILLY

1070

4 m. SE of Camelford on Bodmin Moor

Cornwall's highest hill, at 1,378 ft. (420 metres). Its W side contains one of Britain's best-preserved medieval strip field systems, with low stony banks defining narrow plots in which the ridges of spade-dug lazy beds survive alongside small heaps of the stones cleared during cultivation. Near the centre lies the ruined medieval hamlet where the workers of the fields lived. Documented by the C13, it contains the remains of six LONGHOUSES, their long axes running down the slope. Each house has its own group of farmyard enclosures and small outhouses. The ruins of two small CORN-DRYING BARNS stand at either end of the straggling group of farmsteads, each apparently communally maintained and used. Post-medieval farmhouses were superimposed on two longhouses.

BROWN WILLY CAIRNS. Two large, simple Early Bronze Age CAIRNS. One at summit is surmounted by a triangulation pillar; the other, on a third peak, is placed where it is invisible from the summit cairn.

BUDE

2000

Atlantic breakers roll in endlessly over wide sands towards the low, spreading town, Cornwall's most recent holiday resort. Its heyday was the first half of the C20 when the Atlantic Coast Express brought holidaymakers from London Waterloo in less than five hours, and the unassuming charm of its modest buildings and streets is familiar from other English seaside resorts of the period rather than reflecting anything distinctively Cornish.

Yet this is also a place with an important and unusual pre-C20 history. The medieval town and mother church lie on higher ground just inland at Stratton and for most of its life Bude Haven was a small port at the mouth of the small River Neet, a rare

refuge in the hostile N Cornish coastline. It was long owned by
two of Cornwall's great families, the N side by the Grenvilles of
Stowe, the s around Ebbingford Manor by the Arundells of
Trerice. Its transformation began in the early C19 when the
Aclands of Killerton in Devon acquired Ebbingford. Their energetic and philanthropic patronage greatly expanded the port,
with the construction of a new breakwater, look-out tower,
wharfs, and a hugely successful canal from a sea lock that carried
lime-rich sand for use inland as an agricultural fertilizer. They
also strongly promoted the early tourist trade, an 1836 town map
aspirationally titled 'Bude Haven . . . Lately become the fashionable Watering Place of the West'. The many new amenities
included a church (Bude becoming a separate ecclesiastical
parish in 1836), The Falcon (a large coaching inn, later the
present hotel), a steam laundry and the town's first swimming
pool. The town grew steadily during the C19 until the arrival of
the London & South Western Railway from Holsworthy in 1898
provided the impetus for the growth of the modern resort. It is
now becoming a major holiday destination again, like Newquay
drawing visitors for its magnificent surf, while imaginative early
C21 investment has brought the area around the sea lock, canal
and wharfs back to life.

St Michael and all Angels, Church Path. 1834 by *George
Wightwick* for Sir Thomas Dyke Acland, transepts added and
chancel rebuilt 1878 by *Edward Ashworth*. Significant as one of
the few examples of low church, liberalist architecture in Cornwall or Devon: Wightwick used illustrations of this, his first
church, to argue for 'the reviving Taste for Pointed Architecture' in the *Architectural Magazine* in 1835.* The strength of his
design shines out from the original building: while the transepts are sympathetic in scale, they lack his assured touch. The
church is built in a warm yellow stone (from Trerice), tall and
with elegantly proportioned long lancets in deeply splayed
reveals, single to the N and s walls, triple to the w end, which
rises to a gabled bellcote. The interior is lofty and spacious,
the fine nave roof of an adapted queenpost design with every
timber moulded. What is remarkable is the wholly successful
way in which the church was transformed for Anglo-Catholic
ritual in the first four decades of the C20, the sustained quality
of the enrichments reflecting the continued prosperity of the
town at that time: e.g. the BAPTISTERY (1913) with a richly
moulded two-bay arcade and large, finely carved FONT, both
in Polyphant, the latter square with angels at the corners, their
wings spreading along the sides. – PULPIT, 1903, on a Polyphant base with timber traceried panels. STATUE of St Michael
in niche above baptistery arcade. PRAYER-DESKS, 1944 and
angel-bearing columns either side of the High Altar. – STAINED

---

* His anti-Tractarianism was severely to diminish his future ecclesiastical work in
the strongly Tractarian Exeter Diocese.

GLASS. An interesting display with good examples from 1897 to the mid 1930s. Chancel E by *Percy Bacon Bros*, 1901. – Nave W, 1898 by *James Powell & Sons*, a rich composition with biblical texts enfolded in vines. – Nave N, 1934 by *Veronica Whall*, the lower panel especially fine.

CENTRAL METHODIST CHAPEL, Ergue-Gabaric Way. 1878–80. A large complex in a sombre Romanesque style which, because of its prominent position, is a powerful presence in the town.

FLEXBURY PARK METHODIST CHURCH, Flexbury. 1905 by *John Pethick*, a local builder. A highly idiosyncratic example of 'builder's Gothic', its dramatic massing taking full advantage of its corner site on the edge of the park and perfectly expressing the confidence and vitality of the new resort. Large complex of church, schoolrooms and meeting rooms. The arresting W front has buttressed corner towers at the angles, one with clock, belfry and spire, the other a truncated version for a stair to a W gallery never constructed, all given added verticality by tall pyramidal pinnacles.

PERAMBULATION. The chief architectural and historic interest of the town (in effect the Aclands' 'new town' of BUDE HAVEN) is the area around the SEA LOCK, CANAL and WHARFS, 1823 by *James Green*, enlarged in 1835 by *James Meadows Rendel*. The lock's outer walls are rounded, projecting like military bastions towards the sea, with two sets of massive lock gates and cast-iron hand winches for the sea gate in Gothick arched frames. Sand was taken from the beach on a narrow gauge tramway alongside the canal (a section of the track is still visible) for loading into 'tub boats' on the wharf: these were fitted with wheels so that beyond Helebridge 2 m. inland they could be pulled up two-track incline planes (instead of locks) to a summit 433 ft (132 metres) above sea level, and on inland for a total length of 35 m.* Water for the canal was supplied from a header reservoir at the Tamar Lake Dam. From the sea lock the view seaward makes it possible to appreciate what a great feat of engineering this is. With little natural protection, shelter had to be provided by a BREAKWATER between the cliff and Chapel Rock (so called because it was crowned by a medieval chapel until the late C19). The breakwater was made in 1839–43 by *George Casebourne*, engineer to the canal and harbour company. Low deeply battered wall with a sloping seaward side, replacing the original 1819 breakwater destroyed by a storm in 1838. On the SW seaward side of the lock EFFORD CELLARS, originally fish cellars converted into a holiday house for the Aclands in the 1820s, and inland along BREAKWATER ROAD a pretty group of *c.* 1900 semi-detached houses. Along the wharf itself some small single-storey buildings including the former canal FORGE. Then l. to THE CASTLE, protected by large banks of sand but only just back

*Only the section to Helebridge survives.

from the tidal reach of the sea. 1830 by *Sir Goldsworthy Gurney*.*
Built on an early form of concrete raft to counteract the in-
stability of the sands. Irregular castellated elevations with *piano
nobile* over basement, the main range flanked by wings l. and
r., the latter connected by a turret tower. In view of the castle
the BUDE LIGHT, 2000 by *Carole Vincent* and *Anthony Fanshawe*, a millennium homage to Gurney. Tall coloured concrete
cone incorporating fibre optic star patterns which sparkle at
night, with a light at the top. Back to the wharf, with some
small early C19 former WAREHOUSES, including a BARK
HOUSE and AGRICULTURAL MERCHANTS, tactfully converted
and with good modern infilling between.

Now over the bridge to the UPPER WHARF. It is worth
walking a little way along the towpath for a sense of the scale
of the canal enterprise. On the opposite side the OLD LIFE-
BOAT HOUSE of 1863 with pretty gable-ends, buttressed and
with decorative bargeboards. A little further up on the same
side the OLD STEAM LAUNDRY, 1840, with a fine canalside
elevation of a ten-bay round-headed open arcade to the ground
floor and a large square stack to the rear. Return to the bridge
and cross over to the FALCON HOTEL, Breakwater Road.
Originally established in 1798, it became the Falcon Crest Inn
in 1824–5 as part of the canal development and was extended
in 1826 as the Falcon Hotel. By far the most prominent building of the area, three-storey with deep eaves in a long front
elevation distinguished by an asymmetrically placed four-
storey tower with pyramidal roof. A good finale is the parish
church (*see* above), from where it is possible to walk across
Efford Down to Compass Point to the STORM TOWER of 1835
by *George Wightwick*, a coastguard refuge designed ornamen-
tally as a striking eyecatcher for visitors to the town: the architect justifiably described it as 'after the Temple of the Winds at
Athens' and it is indeed a tall octagon with low pyramidal roof,
its entrance with entablature and pediment on pilaster columns,
the points of the compass carved as a frieze in sans serif below
the moulded cornice.

LIFEBOAT STATION, overlooking Summerleaze Beach. 2002 by
the *Bazeley Partnership*. The form is dictated by a circular look-
out room over the ground floor that is extended inland to
merge with the lifeboat and tractor house.

EBBINGFORD MANOR, Vicarage Road. Late C16 manor house,
radically remodelled 1758 when much earlier fabric was reused,
with C19 and C20 additions and alterations. Passed to the
Arundells in 1433, inherited by the Aclands in 1802. Elongated
H-plan with long two-storey front, irregularly windowed, with
massive central stack and another projecting at the E end of
the N wing.

---

*A polymath and inventor. His inventions included the Bude Light, a very bright
light source created by injecting a stream of oxygen into an oil flame, then reflected
by a series of mirrors. It was used to light this house and several places in London,
including the Houses of Parliament.

At MAER, 1 m. N, a BARN with probable C14 origins and some
evidence of medieval rebuilding. Part of a large tithe barn
with four C14(?) arch-braced trusses surviving: the principals
are upper crucks. Two tiers of purlins, square-set ridge on
yoke. Floor of massive beams. A rare survival of a Cornish
medieval roof.

BUDOCK

ST BUDOC. The mother parish of Falmouth, the church set in
its churchtown above the village. C15 W tower with diagonal
buttresses, a motif not usual in Cornwall, of three stages,
embattled and pinnacled. The C15 or early C16 S porch has the
panelled jambs familiar in this part of Cornwall (cf. Breage,
Constantine, Ruan Major, etc.), much-eroded cusping to the
outer doorway, and remains of a traceried head over the inner
doorway. The S transept is C13 with one lancet window at the
E: its pointed arch towards the nave is double-chamfered and
rests on shafts with moulded capitals. The N aisle is of Cornish
granite standard of seven bays. Extensive mid-C19 restoration
replaced the existing Venetian windows with stone tracery
within the Perp outer frames and installed new arch-braced
roofs, only retaining the C18 plaster barrel-vault over the N
aisle. – ROOD SCREEN. The base remains across N aisle and
chancel, with charming carving and painted saints (cf. Gunwalloe, St Winnow, and Devon); it was thoughtfully restored
in 1909 with a new upper section to the chancel by *Harry Hems*
of Exeter to designs by *E. H. Sedding*. – Other carving, including a GREEN MAN, of this period by *Violet Pinwill*. – STAINED
GLASS. A large quantity of mid-C19–early C20 glass, with many
tracery painted armorials but also including a S transept
window of female saints by *Fouracre & Watson*, 1891, and the
tower W window of 1925 by *Leonard Pownall* (cf. All Saints,
Falmouth) of Christ's call to the fishermen. – MONUMENTS.
Large brass to John Killigrew, 1597, and wife in chancel floor.
– Fragment of a monument to Sir John Killigrew, erected in
1617. Limestone and alabaster, with kneeling figures and finely
carved ornament.

In the churchyard a pretty early C19 slate-hung VESTRY with
Gothick windows over former traphouse and stables. The
LYCHGATE has C16 tracery reused as a ventilator. Nice C19
wrought-iron RAILINGS to the churchyard.

ROSEMERRYN, 1½ m. S. Small country house, *c.* 1720, of
U-shaped plan, two-storey with fine seven-bay front; rather
heavy pedimented central doorway with Gibbs style rustications and Ionic capitals. C18 sash windows with wide glazing
bars and much original crown glass.

PENJERRICK, 1 m. SSW. One of the Fox family houses (cf.
Mawnan) with mid-C19 gardens like Glendurgan and Trebah.

QUAKER COTTAGE, 200 yds s on Penjerrick Hill, was built in
1862 in the style of a Swiss chalet for R. Were Fox.
At TREWOON, 1 m. W, ruins of C16 manor house remodelled in
1634. The late C17 GATEPIERS survive.

BURRELL HOUSE   3050
2½ m. W of Saltash

Of this once important house with a four-centred arched door,
mullioned-and-transomed windows, and datestones of 1621
and 1636, only part of a roofless ruin remains. It had a first-
floor hall open to an arch-braced roof, later given a C17 ornamental plaster ceiling.

CADGWITH   7010

The little fishing port is gathered around a natural harbour with
its boats beached on the foreshore and the buildings of the
fishing industry on the shoreline above. A WINCH HOUSE,
FISH CELLARS, BOATHOUSES and SAIL LOFTS survive, some
in their original use. Modest cottages and houses, mostly C17–
C19-looking with a remarkable amount of thatch over walls of
serpentine blocks, rise from the beach up the steep slopes of
the sheltered valley behind, past the early C19 CADGWITH
COVE INN. A path between the cottages to the car park leads
by ST MARY, the epitome of the fisherman's church, c. 1900,
surely the simplest and yet one of the most atmospheric Anglican churches in Cornwall. Blue gloss painted corrugated iron
with a little bellcote and gabled porch. Another path leads high
above the settlement to a former COASTGUARD LOOK-OUT
and a fine viewpoint where the seaward panorama W includes
a long view of the LIFEBOAT STATION at Kilcobben Cove (cf.
Landewednack). This is one of the best places to see a working
fishing village and local building traditions at their unselfcon-
scious best, and is utterly enchanting.
HOLY WELL OF ST RUAN. ¼ m. W. Just below the road, little
C15 well-house of serpentine with stone-vaulted roof and small
image niches.

CALLINGTON   3060

The little town, not specially attractive, is dominated by the
great chimney of a disused mine at Kit Hill to the NE, looking

from the distance like one more Wellington Testimonial. Located
at the junction of important routes between the Lynher and
Tamar, it was probably a planned medieval borough, granted
a market charter in 1267, and in succeeding centuries became
a service and residential centre for the surrounding mining,
quarrying and agricultural industries, trading through the ports
of Calstock, Cotehele and Halton Quay. Its strongly C19 character reflects its period of greatest prosperity, first from 1841
to 1870 when the Tamar valley was one of the richest copper
mining areas in the world, and then in the later C19 and C20 from
the continued success of its quarrying industries, with the
Kit Hill granite company supplying granite to London and
Plymouth.

St Mary. The mother church of Callington is South Hill (q.v.),
3 m. N – just as St Stephen is the mother church of Launceston, St Martin of Looe, Lanlivery of Lostwithiel, Wendron of
Helston etc. St Mary was consecrated in 1458, an ambitious
building that still dominates the town centre. Three-stage W
tower whose buttresses are set back and end at the top of the
second stage. They are there replaced by three-eighths projections on demi-figures of angels with shields, and on these
projections are turrets rising to crocketed pinnacles. The body
of the church is all battlemented and buttressed with a fine S
porch, and mercifully is only marginally compromised by an
ill-conceived NW extension of 2003–4. The interior is lofty and
spacious, the more surprising because the clerestory is hardly
visible from outside behind the battlements: its windows are
ranged with the spandrels of the arcade, not with the apexes
of the arches, a feature common to the other rare examples of
Cornish clerestories (cf. Fowey, Lostwithiel and St Germans).
Its spaciousness derives from its possession of an outer N aisle,
skilfully added by *J. D. Sedding* in 1882, as well as N and S aisles.
The medieval arcades are of four tall, wide bays and they seem
early, for they have the simple square piers with four attached
shafts that characterize C15 work in Cornwall. The capitals are
simply moulded; the arches have two concave chamfers. Wagon
roof to nave with carved bosses and moulded ribs. Sedding's
aisle is elegantly designed, its arcades taller and more slender-
looking than the originals. Outside it is difficult to detect as a
late C19 addition because the medieval N wall was reconstructed as its outer face. There was an earlier restoration, of
1858–9, by *J. P. St Aubyn*. – font. A good example of the type
of Altarnun, St Thomas Launceston etc., with faces at the
corners and large rosettes in circles. – Medieval altar slab
in S aisle chapel. – south door of the C15 with simple hinges
and closing ring. – reredos, early C20 with canopy added
1919, over-dominant. – Elaborate parclose screens, 1882.
– stained glass. 1882–9, mostly by *Ward & Hughes*, including the Sermon on the Mount, 1883, in S aisle. – monuments.
Brass to Sir Nicholas Assheton and wife, †1466, now beneath

the modern raised chancel floor. – Splendid alabaster monument, the outstanding feature of the church, to Sir Robert Willoughby de Broke, Steward of the Duchy of Cornwall and lord of the manor of Callington, †1502. The effigy, beneath a slightly lower arch of the N arcade, is in armour with Garter robes and folded hands, with feet against a lion; two tiny figures of friars appear beneath it. Evidently imported, possibly from the Bristol workshop.* – Large slate ledger stone with a relief of a kneeling woman to Ann Holiday †1753, signed by *John Burt* of Callington, on external E wall of S porch.

In the S of the churchyard, a LANTERN CROSS-HEAD, probably contemporary with the consecration of the church, very damaged and worn but still impressive in both its scale and evidence of its original decoration: it had sculpted figures (of the Crucifixion, Virgin etc.), beneath canopied ogee arches on its four faces supported at each corner by angels with wings outstretched beneath the figures, and with corner pinnacles. It sits on a later and plain octagonal shaft.

The town centre is worth a brief exploration. The medieval plan is still readable in the streets around the parish church, though its buildings are predominantly late C18 to late C19-looking, with much stucco and slate hanging. The triangular space in front of the church is the site of the medieval market place, and CHURCH STREET, FORE STREET and LISKEARD ROAD offer pleasantly varied townscape, if with no individually outstanding buildings. Exceptions are CHEQUETTES HALL, just N of the church in Church Street, a smart early C18 three-storey five-window front house with rusticated granite corner pilasters and deep modillioned eaves, robbed of its dignity by a specially clumsy projecting shop front added in 1959; and the PIPE WELL, Well Street, rebuilt 1816, a nice survival with a hipped roof of two courses of granite slabs.

HERITAGE CENTRE, Liskeard Road. 1877, built as the mortuary chapel for the cemetery. A plain, almost barn-like building with nearly solid side walls and a steeply pitched roof and central opposing full-height door arches, now infilled, within slightly projecting gables.

NEW BRIDGE, 1¼ m. SW, over the River Lynher. Late C15, mentioned by William of Worcester in 1478. Partly rebuilt in 1698, widened on the S side with rebuilt parapets 1875, both recorded by datestones. Four original segmental arches with cutwaters rising to refuges, further arch to E.

CADSON BURY, ½ m. SW of Newbridge. Simple Iron Age HILL-FORT crowning a steep-sided hill above the River Lynher. The rampart follows the contour to create a rounded diamond plan. Inturned entrances at W and E angles.

DUPATH HOLY WELL. *See* p. 178.

KIT HILL. *See* p. 262.

---

*I am indebted to Paul Cockerham for the suggestion of the Bristol connection.

CALSTOCK

A parish of great scenic variety on the long winding loops of the upper navigable reaches of the Tamar, which includes the Cotehele estate and its great Tudor house. Its C19 development in the peak years of mining in east Cornwall is evident in a landscape scattered with former mining settlements, mission churches, chapels and chimneystacks and, most memorably, in the drama of a railway viaduct of improbably slender proportions soaring above the steep-sided river valley and the little port town of Calstock.

ST ANDREW. Away from the settlement on a lofty site commanding fine views from the churchyard. Late C15 W tower of three stages of regular granite blocks with set-back buttresses to the second stage from where octagonal turrets are corbelled out and carried above the embattled parapet. Late C15 S porch with diagonal buttresses and four-centred arched outer doorway with clustered piers, a fireplace in the W wall, and a large granite ledger to the Griffin family dated 1625 set in the floor. The body of the church has mostly Y-tracery with some C19 Perp windows but its E end is highly unusual in having for its N and S sides two very domestic-looking windows of three lights with straight tops, hoodmoulds with label stops, and transoms: they light chapels added to their aisles (cf. the straight joints), the N one the Edgcumbe Chapel of 1588 with R and E on the label stops and on the label of its N door. Inside both chapels are walled off from the body of the church. The aisle arcades of four bays are different in a historically significant way: early and late C15 – the N arches with square piers with attached demi-shafts, the S arches on piers of standard Cornish design; the N arches plain double-chamfered, the S with much more complex moulding. Nave and N aisle have ceiled wagon roofs with carved bosses and wall-plates; the S aisle has a ceiled wagon roof, possibly C16 or C17, with moulded ribs and wall-plates. Restored 1886–8 by J. P. St Aubyn with new wagon roofs to the chancel and porch, tiled floors at new levels, pews, and stone pulpit and font. – WALL PAINTINGS. On the arcade of the N aisle, much damaged and faded but seeming to include a St George. – ROYAL ARMS dated 1816. – Fine PAINTED BOARD of a letter from Charles I at Sudeley, dated 1643 and signed by the churchwardens, 1736. – CURIOSUM. Fine RINGERS BOARD with painting of ringers in their best attire and instructions in verse, dated 1773. – STAINED GLASS. Chancel E, 1885, by *Fouracre & Watson*. S aisle, two windows of 1890 by *Moore & Co.* – MONUMENTS. In the Edgcumbe chapel, to Piers Edgcumbe †1666/7, good white and grey work without figures, attributed to *Jasper Latham* (GF), and to Jemima, Countess of Sandwich, †1674, with two mourning figures and a large coronet, also attributed to *Latham* (GF). – Elegant slate to John Strick †1814, by *Lobb* of Calstock.

Former METHODIST CHURCH, Sand Lane. Dated 1910. Strong
Gothic front with angle buttresses surmounted by turrets, two-
light cusped windows flanking a central porch, also buttressed,
and above a large four-light window with Perp style tracery
and an ogee hoodmould with finial.

VIADUCT. 1904–7, designed by *W. R. Galbraith* and *R. Church*,
contractor *J. C. Lang*, to carry a branch line from Gunnislake
to join the South Western Railway's Exeter to Plymouth route
at Bere Alston. The twelve semicircular arches of 60 ft (18
metre) span, 108 ft (33 metres) above ground level, constitute
one of the most elegant monuments to the railway era in
Cornwall, best seen from the quayside where glimpses of
Cotehele can be gained beyond. Constructed of eleven thousand pre-cast concrete blocks, manufactured on site on the
Devon bank.

The town gathers comfortably around the quayside and the
TAMAR INN, with a smart early C19 front range, two-storey
with hipped roof and tall window openings (filled by C20
replacements) to the four bays with a central entrance. The
ground-floor windows have wedge-shaped lintels and keystone
with a granite band above and a granite pilaster to the l. The
narrow streets that climb the hill behind are worth a brief
exploration for a nice variety of C18–C19 buildings including
several good former shopfronts of the later C19–early C20.

RAVENSCOURT, ¼ m. N of the church. 1853–4 by *Decimus Burton*
as the rectory. Two-storey asymmetrical front with gable-end
and full-height canted bay to r., and lower service wing to l.

COTEHELE. *See* p. 159.

CAMBORNE   6040

The town, which lies at the w end of the Camborne–Redruth
conurbation,* is in comparison to its architecturally richer
eastern neighbour plain, almost to the point of austere. At its
centre large chapels and a few substantial public buildings rise
above streets of modest two-storey terraces, against a backdrop
of the occasional deserted engine house and chimney and the
talismanic presence of the South Crofty tin mine, the last tin
mine to close, and at the time of writing perhaps preparing to
reopen. That Camborne has more of the authentic character of
an industrial town than any other in Cornwall is fitting, for this
was the epicentre of Cornish mining and its engineering expertise; it was the home of Richard Trevithick and other distinguished engineers, and latterly of the Camborne School of Mines,
the only school of metaliferous mining in Britain.

* See Tuckingmill and Pool for some of the closely related buildings, and Redruth,
Portreath, Illogan and Carn Brea for a fuller picture of the conurbation.

Camborne, Dolcoath Copper Mine. Lithograph, 1831

Norden had found only 'A churche standing among the bar-
reyne hills' in 1584 but by 1814 Lysons was describing a small
market settlement with 'the whole parish scattered over with cottages belonging to the miners': it had developed around the E
side of the churchtown in the area of Church Street, Commercial
Street and Fore Street. The rest of the C19 saw Camborne's
booming expansion on land owned by the Vyvyans of Trelowarren and the Bassets of Tehidy, primarily to the SE around the
triangle of streets bounded by Trelowarren Street, Centenary
Street, Trevenson Street, Basset Street and Basset Road. Its
growth was strongly assisted by its early railway connections with
Redruth, Hayle and Portreath from 1837. No less than three new
parishes were created out of the town's boundaries as part of this
boom, Tuckingmill and Treslothan in 1845 and Penponds in 1854.

With some of the greatest of all Cornish mines in or near the
parish, including the Dolcoath group and the South Crofty area,
the town continued to grow in the later C19, as these mines were
more resilient than most to the collapse of the industry elsewhere
and also bolstered the development of ancillary engineering
industries with worldwide markets. The most famous firm was
Holman Bros which employed over three thousand workers at its
peak, producing specialist mining equipment such as rock drills
as well as some of the last Cornish beam engines on a site of
more than 20 acres of works. As in Redruth, a number of new
public buildings were constructed around the turn of the century,
the most notable a civic group in Trevenson Street near the
station as a new town centre. Modest but attractive villas of the
managerial class were also built along the approach to the centre,
such as those in Pendarves Road, Roskear and Tehidy Road.
Similarly Dolcoath Avenue was built as part of a massive early
C20 investment programme to attract skilled workers to the
mines. But even Dolcoath could not survive the collapse of the

tin market and it closed in 1921. Nearly a century later the centre of Camborne remains remarkably much as it was then.

CHURCHES

St Meriadoc, Church Street. The low, spreading, granite church stands at the w end of the town. Mostly late C15–mid-C16 but incorporating some earlier C15 fabric. Restored in 1861–2 and enlarged in 1878 with an outer s aisle by *J. P. St Aubyn*. Three-stage w tower with double set-back buttresses, embattled parapet and corner pinnacles. The nave is flanked by two identical aisles, the s late C15, the N *c*. 1538–40, each of five bays, with two lower bays for the chancel (cf. Bodmin), on standard Cornish piers with large horizontal leaves to the capitals (cf. Gwinear) and four-centred arches with cavetto and roll moulding: all this is imitated by the added aisle. The four- and five-light windows have late Perp four-centred heads to each light and no tracery, not an unusual feature in this part of Cornwall. Restored arch-braced collar-truss roofs. Chancel added *c*. 1540, one of the latest in Cornwall. – ALTAR SLAB in the present altar, almost certainly C10. It comes from Chapel Ia, Troon, and has a key border, Anglo-Saxon lettering referring to the donor Leuiut, and five crosses* on the present under-surface. – REREDOS. Fine Siena marble tripartite piece in classical style with commandment tables in shouldered panels under an open pediment, flanked by Lord's Prayer and Creed in lugged panels under swan-neck pediments with three cherubs' heads above; lettered medallions in the dado state that it was given by Samuel Percival of Pendarves in 1761. The side walls of the chancel have a dado made up of early C17 carved BENCH-ENDS. – PULPIT. 1549–50 with Tudor coat of arms, though with some restoration. – STAINED GLASS. Mostly 1960s by *J. P. Wippell* designed by *Cooper-Abbs*, but chancel E by *Frederick Cole*, 1960 and s aisle w by *Alexander Gibbs*. Oddfellows window in N aisle w 1863, with vivid iconography. – MONUMENTS – Sir William Pendarves †1683. – Sir William Pendarves †1726, with a medallion bust by *James Paty the Elder* of Bristol. – Anne Acton †1780, with gracefully carved urn, by *F. Robins* of Bath. – Mrs Grace Percival †1763, founder of the Charity School in Camborne. – Edward William Wynne Pendarves †1853, with a large bust at the top, by *E. H. Baily*. – In the exterior E wall of the s aisle a CROSS-HEAD, and just inside the s door a CROSS-SLAB.

In the churchyard, sw of the porch, 6-ft (1.8-metre) tall wheel-headed WAYSIDE CROSS, the shaft divided into two vertical panels decorated with incised triangles and zigzags forming a chevron-like pattern. Another CROSS, w of the tower, is a roughly hewn granite monolith 6 ft (1.8 metres) tall tapering to a small wheel-head. Nearby, the VIVIAN

---

*They refer to the C12(?) change from frontal to mensa. Not now visible (Professor Charles Thomas).

MONUMENT, a late C18 chest tomb on a very large base with a raked surface, the chest with moulded plinth with sunk panels in the sides commemorating various members of the Vivian family.

CHURCH OF ST JOHN THE BAPTIST (R.C.), Trevu Road. 1858–9. Simple Gothic. Served a substantial Irish population.

CAMBORNE METHODIST CHURCH, Chapel Street. 1828, altered 1911. Severe classical five-bay front with a pediment over the three central bays and parapet with swept shoulders. The original porch has been extended to make a continuous portico with two pairs of fluted Doric columns. The interior has a horseshoe gallery on iron columns with stiff-leaf capitals and fluted Corinthian pilasters to the basket-arched apse. In the forecourt, WHEEL-HEAD CROSS. To the l. the SMITH MEMORIAL WESLEYAN INSTITUTE of 1887. Granite ashlar, two-storey, five-window front. A memorial to the eminent Methodist educationalist George Smith, representative of Methodist provision for adult education after the 1870 Education Act.

CENTENARY METHODIST CHURCH, Wesley Street. The striking eyecatcher at the end of Trelowarren Street, rising majestically above the vernacular scale of the town. Dated 1839 but enlarged in 1860 and refronted in 1890. Two storeys and five bays. The original façade was a simple composition with six giant Doric pilasters and plain pediment with flanking single-storey porches with pedimented doors. The Roman Doric porch giving emphasis to an inserted central doorway and Corinthian pilasters are of 1890. Interior has a horseshoe gallery of 1861 with cast-iron columns and basket-arched apse.

Former UNITED METHODIST CHAPEL, Trelowarren Street. 1909 by *Sampson Hill*. Strongly Free Gothic front.

PUBLIC BUILDINGS

Former COUNCIL OFFICES AND FIRE STATION, Trevenson Street. 1903. An expression of civic pride, following Camborne's establishment as an Urban District Council, rising imposingly from its modest surroundings. Renaissance style, the eight-bay façade housing the main entrance in the third bay, which is slightly broken forward with a wide segmental-headed doorway furnished with diamond-panelled doors framed by stout Ionic columns of polished granite with an open pediment; it is carried up to an elaborately shaped gable with a vertical *œil de bœuf* flanked by panelled stacks. The former fire station's large doors are to the r.; it was a slightly later addition.

LIBRARY, The Cross. 1895, by *Silvanus Trevail*, funded by Passmore Edwards. One of Trevail's best buildings, with strong Arts and Crafts motifs. It exploits an awkward corner site with great flair in an asymmetrical composition in which the l. range is set back and the r. range presents as a gable against a unifying central tower. The r. range gable has a canted oriel on corbels springing from the ground-floor window. The entrance is in the base of a richly detailed three-storey tower that rises to an elaborate parapet. In front, a STATUE of Richard Trevithick (1771–1838), of 1922 by *L. S. Merrifield*. Striking figure in forward striding pose with a pair of dividers in his raised hand and a model of a steam locomotive cradled in his l. arm. Each side of the plinth has a small bronze relief plaque: that on the back depicts a sail ship, the others have kneeling female figures holding examples of the application of steam power – a Cornish boiler on the front, locomotive on the l. side, and iron steam and sail ship on the r.

CAMBORNE COMMUNITY CENTRE, 100 yds W of The Cross. Early C19, built as the Tehidy Estate Office, and attributed to Lord de Dunstanville's agent. Four bays and two storeys with lower wings, with V-jointed ashlar and quoins, its size and quality reflecting the wealth of its owner.

Former PUBLIC ROOMS, Trevenson Street. 1891, by *Trevail*, and at that time the largest public rooms in Cornwall. Originally a vast first-floor hall, later subdivided by insertion of another floor to which the windows of the side walls relate. Projecting corner stair-towers, showing a faint Arts and Crafts influence, in rusticated stonework under pyramidal roofs, lower than the doors and roof of the hall. Restored as part of the regeneration of the larger Trevithick View site (*see* below) and converted into housing association apartments 2012 by *Lilly Lewarne Practice*.

OLD MARKET, Church Street. A rather lumpen Italianate palazzo pile on the corner with Commercial Street. Erected 1866 by John Francis Basset of Tehidy, as recorded by an inscription on the tower. The façade to Commercial Street, originally the Town Hall, is of two storeys and seven bays. The taller Church Street section, originally a single-storey market house, was raised to three storeys with twelve bays in 1911.

Former LITERARY INSTITUTE, Chapel Street. Now a community centre. 1842 by *Philip Sambell*, enlarged 1852 and internally altered by conversion. The most distinguished building in the town, if a little old-fashioned for its date. Greek Revival style, recalling one of Decimus Burton's park lodges. A severe granite ashlar composition, single-storey with the main hall entered through a giant Doric portico *in antis*, flanked by lower wings set at right angles, their gable walls pedimented and with a triglyph frieze like the front. To the rear of the r. wing is a former lecture hall added in 1852 in stucco with vermiculated quoins. The Camborne Literary Institute was founded in 1829 in the heyday of steam technology. In the forecourt is a medieval wheel-headed CROSS with a raised figure in a circular granite panel.

Former CAMBORNE BOARD SCHOOL, Basset Road. Dated 1893 in the gable, by *James Hicks*. Fine symmetrical front elevation in free Gothic style, of two high storeys and nine bays. The elaborate three-bay centre breaks forward around a central ground-floor window in a basket arch with a deep chamfered surround flanked by pinnacled buttresses, carried up to a canted bay window with a deep embattled parapet, and rising in a steeply pitched gable to an apex finial. The flanking tran-somed-and-mullioned windows are also crowned by steep gablets.

PERAMBULATION

Start at the w end of the town in CHURCH STREET with St Meriadoc church (*see* Churches, above), to the e end of which the bulk of the Old Market looms (*see* Public Buildings). Opposite, TYACKS HOTEL has an c18 granite ashlar front, three storey and five bays, with three two-storey canted bays. Now incorporated into the hotel to the l. is the former UNICORN HOTEL, late c18, with a lower two-storey five-bay front with a small Doric porch in the centre.

Now e into COMMERCIAL STREET with on the s side the former CORNWALL & DEVON BANK (now Lloyds Bank), 1893 by *James Hicks*. Three-storey, granite and Polyphant. Off to the street's s side COMMERCIAL SQUARE, with a FOUNTAIN of 1890, given by John Holman of Holman Bros, engineers, one of the major benefactors of the town in the c19 and early c20. The continuation of the square is CHAPEL STREET, with the former Literary Institute (*see* Public Buildings), the POST OFFICE, 1899 by *Oliver Caldwell* in severe classical style, the Methodist church (*see* Churches). Then on into CROSS STREET, a good example of late c19 terraced housing with typical Camborne detail like bay windows and panels of ver-miculation. The MASONIC HALL of 1899, as similarly sober as other late c19 industrial buildings in the town. In VICTORIA STREET to the N, other plainer and smaller terraced houses.

At the SE end of Cross Street at its junction with TREVENSON STREET is the civic group of the library, Trevithick statue, former council offices and former Public Rooms (*see* Public Buildings): it can still be read as a striking exercise in town planning to create a new centre away from the old churchtown, and has recently been much improved. The former HOLMAN BROS SHOWROOM opposite the station, *c.* 1912 with five bays of display windows between plain granite pilasters and beneath a heavy projecting cornice, was restored 2011–12 when the elaborate panel of lettering was replicated. The area between The Cross and the railway, now known as TREVITHICK VIEW, underwent comprehensive regeneration including four-storey apartments that curve around the corner next to the Public Rooms, helping to form a more enclosed space around the Trevithick statue. Behind, further residential development incorporating some c19 and early c20 buildings, by *Lilly Lewarne Practice*. Now down Basset Street into Basset Road which has a good series of early to mid-c19 stucco two-storey villas with large sash windows, the houses of the managers and owners of the industrial and engineering works in and around the town. On the E side of Basset Street the assertive former BOARD SCHOOL (*see* Public Buildings). At the S end of the street, PENDARVES ROAD has other, generally more modest, C19 villas.

Back in the centre TRELOWARREN STREET begins its long E stretch towards the Centenary Methodist Church (*see* Churches), drawing the eye at the end of the street. As one progresses E, an increasing proportion of the buildings are domestic, not commercial, and of cottage scale, indicating that the commercial Victorian rebuild petered out. There is otherwise little of special note in the buildings save the Wesleyan chapel (*see* Churches) but it is worth walking and taking diversions off to see more of the C19 terraces between here and TREVENSON and CENTENARY STREETS. To complete the picture of industrial housing, go further E down WESLEY STREET beyond Tesco's store (on the site of Holman's main engineering works) and then r. into the early C20 DOLCOATH ROAD. Looming up on the r. is the heavy and uninspired office block of Holman Bros of the 1960s, in five storeys of rock-faced granite blocks.

An extended walk E leads to the sparse remains of DOLCOATH, *p. 136* 'the queen of Cornish mines': a major copper mine in the C18, its deeper tin deposits made it consistently the richest, and, at 3,300 ft (1,005 metres), the deepest. First is the ENGINE HOUSE of New Sump Shaft and a large COMPRESSOR HOUSE. Off LOWER PENEGON the ENGINE HOUSE of Wheal Harriet's Shaft and a large MINERS' DRY for Dolcoath of 1880. To the SE on the slope of Carn Entral the ruins of the WINDING HOUSE of Williams' Shaft, the deepest. Returning towards the town centre, the miners' housing in DOLCOATH AVENUE of 1907, a pioneering venture in a county with no tradition of company housing.

Finally, N of the centre in Tehidy Road is ROSEWARNE HOUSE. A ponderous Greek Revival house of *c.* 1815, the central block with gabled projecting wings joined by a Doric colonnade, its roof forming a balcony protected by an elegant wrought-iron balustrade of intersecting circles with Greek key standards. The interior has a fine cubic entrance hall with front and rear screens of polished red granite Corinthian columns and beyond an elegant geometrical staircase with delicate wrought-iron balusters. The panelled doors also have Greek key decoration. Also in Tehidy Road, LOWER ROSEWARNE, a complete C16 hall and cross-passage house, with another hall added longitudinally *c.* 1500, now largely enclosed in C18 additions.

BETHANY HOMES, Tregenna Lane. 1935 by *C. R. Corfield* for C. V. Thomas. A delightful post-Arts and Crafts group of almshouses, arranged around a small green and entered through a charmingly rustic gatehouse with rounded ends and roof. The group comprises three pairs of semi-detached and two detached single-storey cottages with hipped slate roofs, canted bay windows, and prominent chimneystacks.

KEHELLAND, 1 m. NW. SCHOOL by *James Hicks*. Large central gable for the main hall, with flanking smaller gables labelled 'Boys' and 'Girls and Infants'.

KING EDWARD MINE MUSEUM, 1 m. S. A unique set of buildings of a small but complete mine, acquired by the Camborne School of Mines in 1902 and re-equipped to give practical experience to students. The most striking features of the site are the examples of those lesser structures, timber-framed and clad, that would once have surrounded the more substantial stone buildings of any mine. The ENGINE HOUSE, ARSENIC CALCINER, COUNT HOUSE, MINERS' DRY and various WORKSHOPS mostly dating from the 1860s. The WINDER HOUSE, rebuilt to match the original timber buildings, houses a horizontal steam engine supplied by *Holman Bros* in 1907.

CAMELFORD

An ancient town that started at a crossing-point of the River Camel, was granted a borough charter by Earl Richard in 1258, had sixty-two burgesses in 1300 and had built a chapel of St Thomas the Martyr by 1311 (demolished after the Reformation). By the end of the C17 it had developed into a small market and coaching town on the main route between Launceston and Bodmin, functions that remained its mainstays from the C18 to the mid C20 despite the opening of the turnpike road across Bodmin Moor in 1769. It retains something of its former character in the generally unpretentious C17–C19 buildings which line the long main street that is its core.

ST THOMAS OF CANTERBURY, Victoria Road. 1937–8 by *Sir Charles Nicholson*. A minor delight. It sits well on a slightly elevated site above the main road, its modest scale and use of local Delabole slate combining well with an understated Romanesque style, with round-headed windows and a small bellcote at its W end. The interior is pleasingly simple too, of a light and gracious character, with a round-headed blank N arcade and a shallow barrel roof with ceiled panels between the ribs and purlins. – FONT. Medieval, small and circular, given by the Cowland family of Launceston. – ALTAR. Elegantly plain, a long Delabole slab on satisfyingly proportioned slate corner posts. – STAINED GLASS. Two good windows of 1938. Chancel E by *Martin Travers*, the figures strongly modelled, including St Thomas holding a model of Canterbury Cathedral. S chapel E by *Theodora Salusbury*, a charming miniature of the Blessed Virgin Mary with the infant Jesus.

METHODIST CHAPEL, Market Place. Dated 1837. Lanky lancet style with main gabled central range set slightly forward of Sunday School to the l. and room to the r. Nice cast-iron grills.

TOWN HALL, Market Place. 1806, financed by the Duke of Bedford. Very much the centrepiece of the town. The hall is at first-floor level over the former market house. Round-headed windows, small to the ground floor, large sashes above, and a Venetian window with armorial glass at the w end. The hipped roof is surmounted by a tall cupola with clock and weathervane.

There is more to Camelford to be found in the many narrow opes that punctuate the main street but the centre has a number of substantial buildings, especially those that originated as hostelries. The most striking of these is the DARLINGTON HOTEL, Fore Street. Late C16 or C17 origins in the main range with a later wing at the higher end, three storey and slate-clad. The front seems to have had a first-floor jetty over a walkway with an arcade of granite piers, now obscured by outshots on the main range, but represented by a nice C19 wrought-iron balcony to the wing. Another is the MASON'S ARMS, Market Place, its irregular three-storey front elevation recording its C17–C19 evolution. Interior retains a C17 fireplace and an C18 stair. No. 13 Fore Street, early C19, with a three-storey three-window ashlar front, was also built as a coaching inn. Some good C19 buildings in Market Place, like WALKEYS, No. 25, and COLLINS CHEMISTS, shops with accommodation over. In Victoria Road Nos. 1, 3 and 5, late C16, probably originating as a courtyard plan house, extended and partly rebuilt in the C17 and C18, now subdivided. Five-window front with deep overhanging eaves on console brackets. The front range has a largely intact late C17–C18 interior including bolection-moulded panelling, plasterwork ceiling, and open-well stair. No. 2 is a mid-C17 house remodelled in the late C18, with a three-storey four-window front and doorway to l. of centre with segmental-arched hood on moulded console brackets. C19 cast-iron railings and gates.

CAPE CORNWALL

1½ m. w of St Just-in-Penwith

3030

The promontory is crowned by a CHIMNEY of c. 1864 of the relatively unsuccessful Cape Cornwall mine, though it is such a prominent landmark that from a distance it appears as a memorial obelisk (cf. Kit Hill): indeed it is consciously architectural in its design, on a tall octagonal base with round-headed blind arches with corbelled cornice above, surmounted by a tapering cylindrical shaft. On the E slope, the fragmentary remains of the medieval ST HELEN'S CHAPEL, long converted to a farm building.

The large granite house occupying the splendid site overlooking Cape Cornwall is PORTHLEDDEN, c. 1910 for Francis Oates, a local boy from St Just who worked in the mines from the age of twelve but emigrated to South Africa and rose to become chairman of de Beers. He purchased Cape Cornwall in 1900 and promoted various schemes to employ miners. The walled structures on the s side of the promontory below the mine's former COUNT HOUSE, the remains of TERRACED GARDENS of greenhouses and vineries built on the old tin floors, were part of this.

CARBIS BAY

ST ANTA AND ALL SAINTS. Begun 1929 to designs by *R. F. Wheatly* of Truro, built in stages and completed 1965–9. A surprisingly large and ambitious church for this period but curiously conservative in its neo-Gothic style. Much mid to late C20 STAINED GLASS, the best the little w porch windows, 1970 by *Joan Fulleylove*.

LITTLE PARC OWLES, Pannier Lane. Commenced *c.* 1919, extended in the late 1920s. By *G. L. Kennedy*, then in partnership with *F. B. Nightingale*. Closely associated with leading figures of the St Ives artistic community, and the home successively of Adrian Stokes and Peter Lanyon. The steep slope towards St Ives Bay is skilfully used by extending the single-storey entrance level over a terrace to create a floor below, a well-composed elevation that sits comfortably in the landscape. In a version of Arts and Crafts with broad gables with semi-dormers, punctuated by chimneys and a decorative louvre. One ridge tile, of a modelled horse, by *Bernard Leach*.

CARDINHAM

ST MEUBRED. The church sits serenely on a hill in its small churchtown, its noble w tower visible for miles. The tower is C15 in fine granite ashlar, of three tall stages on a moulded plinth with thin set-back buttresses from which clasping pinnacles rise at each stage, and is crowned by an embattled parapet with large octagonal pinnacles with crocketed spirelets. Four-centred arched w doorway with roll mouldings and recessed spandrels with carved leaves and four-light w window, its sill with a panel carved with quatrefoils, stars and a central shield: there are similar quatrefoil panels either side of the door. The body of the church is Perp, nave and chancel in one, N and s aisles, and s porch. Especially good and complete Perp window tracery. The aisles are wide and light, the arcades on tallish piers of Cornish standard design, the s aisle of six bays, the N of five. Original wagon roofs with carved ribs, bosses and wall-plates to aisles and porch; C19 scissor-truss roof to nave and chancel. In the N wall of the chancel a low E.E. sepulchral niche with colonettes and trefoil moulded niche over. Below is a (sepulchral) slab with a mutilated inscription which Sedding read as 'Here lies buried . . . [possibly Goodman or Truebody] rightly so called. He died on the 3rd day of May after the feast of the Aerial Flight, 1404. God stand by to have mercy on his soul.' The church was gently treated in a series of C19 restorations, one in 1907–8 by *G. H. Fellowes Prynne*, and another in 1921 by *E. H. Sedding*. The E end of the chancel was damaged in the Second World War and rebuilt thereafter. – FONT. A square bowl with blank arcade to sides, carved with trefoils and stars. – Triple SEDILIA in chancel. – BENCHES AND BENCH-ENDS. A specially good set of the early C16. – ROYAL ARMS, 1661, with strapwork decoration, finely modelled. – STAINED GLASS. Good mid-C20 ensemble. Spirited realist designs in N and S chancel windows by *Francis Keate* with well-executed scenes of local life, buildings and landscapes and in chancel E by *Christopher Webb*. – S aisle, St Francis by *Wippell*, and good Grylls armorial, late C18, in N aisle. – MONUMENTS. In chancel, floor brass to Thomas Awmarle, rector *c.* 1400, in belted cassock and hood, with sword, an exceedingly rare example of a cleric in civil dress. – In S aisle, Glynn family monument, 1699. Epitaph on oval tablet with swags. Corinthian columns to entablature, very conservative for its date. – William Glynn, C17, remains of slate tablet.

In the churchyard opposite the S porch, perhaps the finest sculptured CROSS of its type in Cornwall, found in 1872 built into the external wall of the chancel. 8½ ft (2.6 metres) high with a four-holed head and knotwork on the front face. Shaft in three panels, the top one with a vestigial inscription, AR THIT, below plaitwork. Back face with beautiful interlace, back shaft with coarse scrolls. C9 or C10.

Several INSCRIBED STONES: one at the E gate of the churchyard as the shaft of an equal-limbed cross, also found in the chancel wall in 1872, the inscription RANOCORI FILI NESGI; at the crossroads ¼ m. NW of Welltown, VAILATHI FILI URO-CHANI, C6 or C7, and beside it another, OR P EP TITUS, C6 or C7.

Of the scatter of other medieval crosses in the parish, the best is TRESLEA or WHYDEYEAT CROSS, ½ m. E. *In situ*, marking the E boundary of the glebe. Wheel-headed cross with projections on the top and sides, a feature only found in this parish and Blisland. On each side of the shaft a bead extends full length from the lower limb of the cross.

HOLY WELL, ½ m. N, just S of the entrance to Trezance. Set into the hillside in a little coombe with an unusually large rectangular chamber roofed with granite monoliths.

OLD CARDINHAM CASTLE, 1 m. SSE. Motte-and-bailey, built by the Fitz Turolds: Richard Fitz Turold was one of the largest landowners in Cornwall at Domesday with twenty-eight manors. The motte has been substantially reduced on its top and E side but the bailey is well preserved.

BURY CASTLE, 1 m. NE. Well-defined Iron Age HILLFORT on ridge protruding SW from Bodmin Moor, affording fine panoramic views. Main enclosure with rampart and external ditch, with two additional lines at the vulnerable N end, both reduced by later farming. Low broad bank indicates possible earlier inner enclosure.

GLYNN, 4 m. S. The house occupies a comfortable position on the N side of the steep Fowey valley, best appreciated from the road near Bodmin Parkway station. There was a C17 house here but Tonkin attributes a 'handsome new house', which was illustrated by Edmund Prideaux in 1727, to William Glynn (†1727) and his wife, Rose Prideaux of Prideaux Place. It was damaged by fire in 1819 and substantially rebuilt by *John Eveleigh* of Lostwithiel. Subdivided in the late C20. Of L-plan with principal rooms on the S entrance and W garden fronts and service rooms to the N and E. Symmetrical entrance front with deep eaves on stone brackets with the central bay slightly broken forward with a Doric portico (an 1830s addition), the end bays also broken forward. The garden front is of nine bays, the central three under a pediment with four attached Doric columns, probably added after the early C19 fire. To the W end, an octagonal TEMPLE with engaged Doric columns at the angles. Interior extensively remodelled by subdivision but four ceilings with plasterwork of copies of Sir Hussey Vivian's medals from the Peninsular War survive in the W range.

0050

CARLYON BAY

An area of extensive C20 residential development with a few hotels mixed in along SEA ROAD, the earliest the large Art Deco CARLYON BAY HOTEL on a butterfly plan. Only its central three-storey entrance tower, staircase and geometric glazing survives substantially unaltered. The notable buildings further W along the road are a group of Modern Movement houses. The largest and best is GULL ROCK HOUSE by *Marshall Sisson*, 1934, overlooking the sea. Of white-painted reinforced concrete, flat-roofed with railings defining the roof terrace and almost continuous glazing to the seaward elevation, its streamlined nautical character perfectly suited to its site. On the other side of the road Nos. 55–61, detached and semi-detached houses, the latter with first-floor balconies on pilotis: No. 61 proved beyond repair and is an inspired re-creation of 2012 by *ALA Architects*. These were part of a larger planned development eventually continued in conventional suburban styles.

A major residential development is currently proposed which includes a massive sea wall and the building over of a significant section of the beach.

RAILWAY BRIDGE, ½ m. N across the road to Par. Built 1859 for the Cornwall Railway. Small but more architecturally ambitious than most, detailed in Gothic with twin turrets and machicolations.

CARN BREA

6040

sw of Redruth

The summit of Carn Brea is one of the great viewpoints of Cornwall with the sea visible on both N and S horizons on a good day. The eastern two of three tors constitute the most fully excavated Early Neolithic TOR ENCLOSURE in SW England. The E tor, its steep slopes falling away on three sides, was the core of a complex of stone-walled enclosures, some with discontinuous ditches. A substantial wall 6½ ft (2 metres) high and wide with some large granite slabs on edge formed an irregular inner enclosure incorporating several large granite outcrops. Within are around twelve levelled platforms, two of which were stances for rectangular wooden structures. The larger outer enclosures have more earthen ramparts containing granite orthostats and external ditches with numerous narrow entrances; some may have been reused in the Iron Age period when a small settlement of twelve round-houses was established between the two tors.

On the summit is the MONUMENT of 1836 to Francis Basset of Tehidy (Lord de Dunstanville), its scale a suitably imposing testimony to the power and wealth of one of the greatest of all the Cornish mining dynasties. It is in the form of a massive tapering octagonal Celtic cross on a plinth and octagonal broached pedestal, all in large dressed granite blocks. The cross-head has concave sides and is pierced by a diamond-shaped opening. Just E the Gothick pile of CARN BREA CASTLE rises sheer from the boulder-strewn summit like a Norman keep. Built by the Bassets as a folly, possibly starting as an earlier hunting lodge in their walled deer park; it is almost completely C18 and C19. Four irregular rectangular turrets enclose a square core of the same height, with two-centred arched openings and an embattled parapet. Huge granite boulders form the ground floor of the NW turret in a self-consciously picturesque manner.

Carn Brea is the best starting point for an exploration of the greatest of all Cornwall's mining areas, with the long stretch of the Camborne Redruth conurbation immediately below to the N, and to the S a thick scatter of deserted engine houses and chimneys, sometimes in dramatic clusters. Looking S from the top of Carn Brea, it is possible to see the extent of mining activity leading away to the SW on the Great Flat Lode, an area where several thousand miners would have toiled in the late C19. Across the valley can be seen the WHEAL BASSET STAMPS where two engines sat next to each other in one house, and below, the three-storey BASSET COUNT HOUSE with hipped slate roof. Further to the E, surrounded by an extensive wall and with two chimneys, is the site of SELEGGAN, the last tin smelting works in the county, which closed in 1931.

Leaving the hill, almost in CARNKIE village are the engine houses of LYLE'S SHAFT, where looking back up the side of Carn Brea are the extensive ruins that mark the main processing area developed on the 1896 amalgamation of the Basset and Frances Mines to form BASSET MINES. On this slope can be seen the remains of steam-powered stamps, concave and convex buddles, arsenic calciners and roofless buildings that housed vanning tables and other tin processing equipment – similar to that at King Edward Mine (*see* Camborne) but on a much larger scale. The areas of this extensive mine were connected by a narrow gauge railway tunnelled under the road W of Carnkie old school to bring ore from the W part for processing.

From Carnkie, ½ m. SW is the most impressive complex of mine buildings, dating from the last years of the C19 and centred on Marriott's Shaft at the SOUTH WHEAL FRANCES MINE section of the Basset Mines. This was a state-of-the-art mine, on a large scale, although hardly typical. The engine house is massive, planned to house two large inverted compound beam engines, although only one was installed. The group also includes the great boiler house adjoining the engine house, a large miners' dry, with a separate section for management and directors, winding engine house, ore crusher, and compressor house. The structures are all roofless remains now, but generally walls stand to their full height, all slightly reminiscent of a ruined abbey.

From Marriott's, 200 yds W is a pair of more conventional engine houses on PASCOE'S SHAFT, and beyond for a further 1½ m. a sprinkling of engine houses track the line of the Great Flat Lode. About 350 yds towards the Carn Brea monument, at THOMAS'S SHAFT engine house, the datestone AD 1854, set in a fine warm ashlar granite bob wall, is an unusual feature.

100

3050

CATCHFRENCH MANOR

1¼ m. N of Hessenford

Late C18 by *Charles Rawlinson* of Lostwithiel, on part of the site of the earlier manor house. Entrance front with central porch tower flanked by single bays with Gothick windows and other decorative detail: it was originally surmounted by a castellated parapet, removed in the early C19. In the C20 the S end of the house was demolished. To the S the ruins of the earlier house with a three-storey porch tower with four-centred arched doorway of the C16, a six-light mullioned-and-transomed hall window with king mullion and a re-set doorway, dated 1580 and inscribed GEORGE KEKEWYCHE.

Humphry Repton visited in 1792, while working on neighbouring Port Eliot (q.v.), and produced a Red Book in 1793. He considered the site and surrounding scenery to be of such high quality that little improvement was required beyond screening the nearby public road. The informal gardens and pleasure grounds around the house remain.

CAWSAND AND KINGSAND   4050

These two historic fishing villages, separated only by a tiny stream, are among the most picturesque and unspoiled in Cornwall. For centuries they were on different sides of the county boundary, Cawsand in Cornwall, Kingsand in Devon, until the latter was brought into Cornwall in 1844. They were centres of the pilchard industry, with remains of PILCHARD CELLARS dating from the late C16 still visible on the shoreline just beyond Kingsand, and also of smuggling in the C18 and early C19, when over fifty smuggling vessels operated out of Cawsand Bay. Though there are few individual buildings of special note, the character of the place is so much more than the sum of its parts with hardly a jarring note in its intimately scaled streets of small houses running down to the sea. On the seafront in Kingsand THE INSTITUTE, its clock tower of 1911 and balconies of the later C20 added to a C19 building. In Cawsand ST ANDREW, a chapel of ease of 1878, plain E.E., and the eye-catching PENLEE LODGE, a *rundbogenstil* tower built *c.* 1860 on the basement storey of a Napoleonic fortification as a gatehouse for the Mount Edgcumbe estate. Round-headed windows, the second floor with three-bay arcades with plain columns on plinths, the roof with deep eaves brackets. Probably by *G. Wightwick.*

In dramatic contrast to all this is CAWSAND FORT, towering above the settlements on the high spur between. Built 1860–3 as part of the Plymouth Defences to act as a keep for ten or so guns, on the site of a battery of 1779. Its massive bulk and sheer walls still impress despite the domestication of its once severe skyline by the erection of housing in the late C20 right on top of the ramparts, creating a bizarre clash of images. Within the fort much survives, including two gun platforms from the C18 battery.

CHACEWATER   7040

The village occupies a narrow tributary valley near the head of the Carnon River, an early focus of mining and tin-streaming, with the 'Great Works', later Wheal Busy, active by the C16 and continuously important thereafter until the early C20. On the turnpike from Truro to Redruth, Chacewater developed as a marketing and service centre as well as a purely industrial settlement, its importance reflected in the name of the Redruth & Chasewater (old spelling) Railway of 1824 that was to link the local mines to the new port at Devoran (q.v.). Earlier sporadic development along the valley sides surrounds a planned mid-C19 centre along the main road.

ST PAUL. The church stands to the S and apart from the village, separated by fields and up a short steep hill. A Commissioners' church of 1826–8 by *Charles Hutchens* (cf. St Mary, Penzance, and St Mary, Redruth) was rebuilt by *E. H. Sedding* in 1892 in a restrained Perp style. The impressive NE tower rises in four stages, gaunt and bare of windows except in its uppermost stage, to an embattled parapet, its striking verticality reinforced by an octagonal NE stair-turret that finishes above the parapet. Nave with clerestory and a wagon roof 43 ft (13 metres) high, the aisles with lean-to roofs.

John Betjeman's description is best: 'The lofty interior is remarkable for the colour of the unplastered walls of local stone, buff, grey, yellow and brown setting off the shallow-sea-water green of the octagonal shafts of Polyphant stone and granite arches of the five-bay arcades. There are lancets in the clerestory and square-headed windows in the aisle walls which have shallow recesses inside and corresponding projections without. A satisfying sense that Sedding here knew what effect he wanted to get; and got it.' – STAINED GLASS. Five-light E window with bright glass by *William Warrington*, 1850, moved from St Mary, Truro, in 1892. S aisle by *Wippell*, designed by *Cooper-Abbs*, 1963, and N aisle by *G. Maile*, 1986.

LYCHGATE. N of the W end of the church. Probably also 1892 and by *E. H. Sedding*. N gable-end of elvan ashlar with a four-centred arch rising to an octagonal finial with a moulded pendant base surmounted by a Latin cross.

CHACEWATER METHODIST CHURCH, Station Road. Erected 1832, renovated 1895 (inscription). A plain rectangle, the quoins of the front elevation now painted a bright red.

CHACEWATER PRIMARY SCHOOL, Church Street. National School and school house. 1847, altered and enlarged in 1861 by *William White* with the addition of a NW wing, and further extended by *Silvanus Trevail* in 1896. Tudor style. Symmetrical E front with central coped gable-end of the original two-storey school house with 1847 datestone, surmounted by bellcote, flanked by single-storey schoolrooms with mullioned windows, that to the l. original.

Former CHACEWATER LITERARY INSTITUTE, Fore Street. Now two dwellings. 1893 by *W. J. Wills*. A strong Late Victorian architectural statement in a street with many good C19 buildings. The two principal rooms are arranged either side of a central passage, giving a symmetrical street frontage, the central doorway flanked by tall gables. Elaborate decoration above the doorway with building name plaque surmounted by a scrolled plaque with the donor's initials, and scrolled pediment with finial and date within the tympanum. This is the second of four such institutes in Cornwall donated by J. Passmore Edwards.

The later planned centre, represented by FORE STREET, HIGH STREET, THE SQUARE and STATION ROAD, remains remarkably intact, lined with modest C19 houses and cottages, former public houses, and some good C19 shopfronts including early C19 bow windows at Nos. 5 and 8 Fore Street. SUNNY CORNER NURSERIES, The Square, is the early to mid-C19 market house, with a colonnade of plain Doric columns, largely rebuilt in the C20.

WHEAL BUSY, ¾ m. W. The mine's wealth is demonstrated by the succession of technological innovations here: a Newcomen pumping engine in the 1720s, Smeaton's much improved 72-in. (180-cm.) engine of 1775, the first Watt engine in Cornwall in 1778, and many later Cornish engines. ENGINE HOUSE, c. 1850, with separate stack and boiler house. Nearby a massive WORKSHOP, probably a unique survival, with a 42-ft (12.8-metre) kingpost roof: the pair of inscribed cast-iron lintels unequalled in the county, except in foundries, the outside reading GREAT WHEAL – 1872 – BUSY MINES, inside PERRAN 1798 FOUNDRY. S of this the remains of the Brunton ARSENIC CALCINER with derelict zigzag condensing floor of 1907. The panorama of engine houses and stacks to the S includes the unmistakable stack of KILLIFRETH MINE, with brick-heightened upper stage of c. 1914.

WHEAL BUSY CHAPEL. Bible Christian chapel, 1863. One of the best surviving and most complete examples of the simple wayside chapel in Cornwall. Small single-storey rectangle with a symmetrical two-window front centred on a later C19 porch, the windows small-paned sashes. The unaltered interior has a wealth of good original detail including a plaster ceiling cornice; panelled dado; a gallery supported on slender columns with a panelled front carried on brackets; box panelled pews (in the gallery and the central area below, and similar for choir and leaders); and decorative rostrum. Front courtyard bounded by low walls surmounted by ornate cast-iron railings with a central gateway with a fine cast-iron gate.

CHARLESTOWN   0050

One of Cornwall's most remarkable places – a virtually intact C19 working port and estate settlement set in fields and woods against the cliffs and sea.

Charles Rashleigh of Duporth, a younger son of the Rashleighs of Menabilly, decided to create a harbour and settlement here from 1790. Its promotion was, like that of the Treffrys at Par and the Hawkins at Pentewan (qq.v.), the act of a landowner turned entrepreneur who saw the potential of the rapidly developing fishing, copper and china clay industries. The original settlement of Polmear, no more than a farm and a few small houses, was almost immediately renamed Charlestown in honour of its founder. The harbour took nine years to build and is a major feat of engineering requiring the construction of a breakwater and outer harbour, an inner harbour basin deeply incised into the slope of the land, and a seven-mile leat to bring water from the Luxulyan valley to scour the harbour and keep the wet dock full. A battery was built on the cliffs w of the harbour, a rare defence made specifically for a mineral port in Cornwall, and a range of housing and industrial buildings were developed for the varied trade the port handled – exports of copper, china clay and fish, imports of coal and lime, and shipbuilding in the inner harbour.

By 1820 the settlement had grown to nearly one hundred houses with many specialist buildings. It had acquired hotels in the early 1800s, one of the earliest large Methodist chapels by 1827 and an ambitious new Anglican church in 1851. Proximity to the source of clay for the Staffordshire potteries allowed it to expand even after the collapse of copper mining to become one of the county's leading C19 china clay ports. As late as 1906 a large new china clay dry was constructed to process clay from the Carclaze area. Only after the First World War did Charlestown finally begin losing out to Fowey and Par with their easy access to rail transport. It remains a microcosm of C19 industrial Cornwall.

ST PAUL, Church Road. A church of more than usual interest, its interior of understated power and mystery. 1851 by *Christopher Eales*, architect of the market and town halls at Truro and St Austell, and his only church design. Slatestone walls with granite dressings. A confident essay in an adapted E.E. style reflecting the early influence of the Ecclesiological Movement. Cruciform plan with aisles and N porch, tower at W end of N aisle heightened in reconstituted stone, with fibreglass spire added in 1972. The interior has a convincing early Gothic ambience – lofty nave with clerestories, tall narrow aisles, tall pointed arch crossing between nave and chancel, lower to the transepts, set off by arcades of alternate round and square piers – the more so for being on a relatively intimate scale. A sensitive reordering in 1951 by *Stephen Dykes Bower*, an early expression of the Liturgical Movement, enhances its simple but moving character. – Granite ALTAR on Delabole slate dais in front of an elegant wrought-iron chancel SCREEN with large rood beam and striking rood figures above. The screen rises from low walls of green slate quarried from the Rashleighs' quarries at Duporth Bay ½ m. S of the church; the chancel is also paved with Duporth stone and a red limestone from south Devon. – STAINED GLASS. An interesting didactic scheme mostly by *Mayer* and *Fouracre & Watson*, 1886–1901.

In the churchyard, Celtic cross WAR MEMORIAL of Luxu-lyan granite, and former CHURCH HALL of Carn grey granite.

Former WESLEYAN CHAPEL, Charlestown Road. 1827. Its early date, ambitious scale and fine fittings make it one of the most important chapels in Cornwall, though sadly neglected at the time of writing. Refurbished 1889 and re-windowed 1907. Pentewan ashlar front with distyle Doric porch. The interior retains its original plaster ceiling cornice and central rose with acanthus leaves and a gallery on scrolled wrought-iron brackets linked to wooden columns. Schoolrooms added at the rear 1865. Two parallel ranges with unusual clerestory lights running their full length.

PERAMBULATION. The ensemble of port and settlement in its unspoilt setting can be seen from the BATTERY on the cliff w of the harbour. Built in 1795 as a semicircular crenellated walled enclosure, its insubstantial construction suggests it was at least partly an ornamental incident in views from the Rashleigh estate at Duporth. The HARBOUR is one of the best examples of late C18 and C19 harbour works in Britain, showing the civil engineer coming into his own. Rashleigh consulted *John Smeaton* on its design. Construction commenced in 1791 with the protective western arm of the outer harbour, followed by the eastern arm in 1793, both with large granite ashlar block facings and granite block paving to the quays and the floor of the outer basin. On the E quay the HARBOURMASTER'S HUT of *c.* 1885, octagonal with conical roof and a ship weathervane; built on top of a former limekiln. The inner harbour was also begun in 1791 and required immense excavation of the steep hillside. Even today it seems a mighty work. It was extended further inland in 1871. Visible in its steep eastern wall are four CHINA CLAY CELLARS, each with a trap door at road level for pouring clay into the cellars before it was loaded onto ships. There are also ORE HUTCHES for the temporary storage of copper ore before shipping.

A tour of the settlement should start around the harbour. On the w side the most prominent building is the PIER HOUSE HOTEL, built 1782 and recorded in 1825 as a hotel, stables and garden: its three-storey height is rare in Charlestown. All its twelve windows look over the harbour and out to sea. On the E side of the harbour former FISH CELLARS, first recorded in 1825, overlook the beach: the sockets for the press poles for pilchard presses are still clearly visible. On QUAY ROAD, over-looking the inner harbour, are the earliest cottages, lovely plain Late Georgian. No. 10, a slightly larger detached house, and Nos. 12–17, a terrace of mainly double-fronted cottages, are first recorded in 1842: all have wrought-iron open piers to their simple porches, a local speciality. The SHIPWRECK AND HERITAGE CENTRE was adapted from early C20 china clay cellars. Behind these are more mid-C19 cottages and then POLMEAR, a former farmhouse, the most significant survivor from the original settlement. L-shaped, partly brick. Probably early to mid-C18, on an earlier site, although its outbuildings, including a long linhay, look late C18. Rising dramatically behind is the tall chimneystack of the 1906 CHINA CLAY DRY, its long main stone-built range currently roofless. Clay slurry was piped 1½ m. from the hills above St Austell and after drying was dropped from storage bins into a tramway tunnel below, the wagons pushed out directly to the quayside above awaiting ships below. At the head of the harbour basin are two WEIGH-BRIDGES, the front one of c. 1936, the original of 1882 behind, both with cast-iron platforms and single-storey offices.

CHARLESTOWN ROAD starts on its E side with No. 6 (T'Gallants Guest House), a three-storey mid-C19 house recorded as the coastguard station in 1882. Then the RASH-LEIGH ARMS of 1842, whose car park of large granite cobbles is the best surviving example of an ore floor, laid down for the storage of copper and later china clay: in the mid C19 some 5 acres of the village were reserved for this use. Adjacent, more pretty early cottages with open cast-iron porches. The W side of the road begins at the upper end with Nos. 111 and 113, an imposing construction of granite blocks with external stairs to the first floor, probably intended for other industrial uses as much as its recorded function as a threshing barn. Nos. 91–99 are another group of earliest cottages of 1825. Nos. 51–65, at right angles to the main road behind No. 45, were originally a terrace of back-to-back cottages of 1795 known as the Front and Back Rows, the buildings of the former still intact in front, the latter demolished in the 1960s; their gardens and some privies still survive on the W side of the street. Back on the main road, the former COUNT HOUSE, a single-storey painted brick building, much extended. Then within the public car park on the site of a former coal yard, a group of special inter-est: three LIMEKILNS of 1825, originally two back-to-back kilns, the third added to the front of the eastern kiln, all fronted by a two-storey GUN SHED built for the storage of guns for the battery (*see* above). To the rear of the car park and in BARK LANE, late C20 housing by *Alan Leather*, the former an unwieldy 1970s bulk, the latter a more successful 1980s blend of indi-vidual units and terrace.

COLAN

ST COLAN. A small church in a lonely sheltered spot with its former vicarage, set among trees. W tower of two stages, with embattled parapet and pinnacles, in granite ashlar with the lower stage banded in darker stone. It was rebuilt in 1879. The body of the church is essentially C13 and can be connected with the date 1276 when a Cardinham gave it (through the bishop) to Glasney College, Penryn. Of the C13, probably cruciform, church are the S wall, S chancel wall, and S transept (cf. its single-chamfered arch into the nave). On the N side a standard Perp arcade of three bays plus two for the chancel, the latter built in two stages with the E end at a higher roof level. The chancel part of the aisle is separated from the nave part by an arch just like those of the nave arcade: the aisle seems to have been rebuilt with this arch inserted, since the arcade pier is complete on its N side. C16 wagon roof over the nave with carved bosses, ribs and wall-plates; the other roofs late C19, the S transept arch-braced. – ROOD SCREEN. The base and lower section only of a C16 wooden screen with cusped heads to panels and quatrefoil panels along the base. – STAINED GLASS. Six windows by *Gibbs & Howard*: E and S windows of chancel, S window of nave, three in N aisle, *c.* 1884. – MONUMENT. William Glannel, 1726, slate with low relief carved flowers and foliage. – BRASSES. In chancel, John Coso-warth and family, 1575, the same composition of inscription, figures and shields as on the Arundell brasses at Mawgan-in-Pydar and St Columb Major (qq.v.). – In N aisle, the Bluett family, with twenty-two children, *c.* 1580.

In the churchyard, STONE CROSS outside the S porch. Pre-Conquest, re-sited here in 1970. Roughly hewn stone with four identical circles at the top on the front. CROSS BASE, S of the tower. C15, the socket set in an octagonal frame with cushion stops.

To the E of the church, former VICARAGE, with a modest late C18–early C19 slate-hung front.

COME-TO-GOOD
Kea

FRIENDS MEETING HOUSE. 1710. Pleasantly set in its small burial ground, from the outside it is the archetype of the ver-nacular cottage, the steep thatch sweeping low over white-washed cob walls and extending out over a linhay at the E end, a C19 addition for the shelter of the horses of the congregation. Three latticed windows to the S front with oak mullions, wooden saddlebars, lead cames, and external shutters. The original entrance was the central bay between the buttresses which formed a rudimentary porch before the new entrance was made in the early C19, displacing the W window to its present position. The interior is homely, loveable, and almost completely intact. The seating consists of plain boarded wall settles, raised up only slightly by two steps for the stand at the E end; the other seating is tall and slender open-backed benches. The roof of trussed rafters with pegged apexes and collars is open to the underside of the thatch. A W gallery was added in 1716, originally approached by a staircase against the N wall, now re-sited in the NW corner. Whatever the derivation of the place name, the building perfectly captures the compel-ling simplicity and integrity of the Quaker endeavour.

CONSTANTINE

A large and diverse parish, rich in prehistory, and once an important medieval religious centre with a possible pre-Conquest monastery on the site of the church, a pre-Conquest chapel at Budock-Vean (gone), and two later medieval chapels at Bonallack and Carwythenack (also both gone).

ST CONSTANTINE. An impressive church in a commanding position on the hills N of one of the N creeks of the Helford River – large, and all of regular granite blocks, reflecting the historical importance of the parish's famous granite quarries. Of the C12 church only a reused section of chevron moulding above the W window of the S aisle and another in the internal jamb of its E window. The church was rebuilt and enlarged between c. 1420 and the early C16 with first the S aisle and S porch, then the N aisle, and finally the W tower and the additional N chapel (the Bosahan aisle). The stately tower is tall, of three stages, with buttresses set back from the corners, panelled and crocketed pinnacles, a lozenge decoration of the top cornice, and heads carved at the tops of the buttresses. The W door has leaf-scroll decoration exactly as nearby Mawgan-in-Menage, with small heads at the base, a hoodmould with heads as label stops, and a carved head in the voussoir. The four-light W window has Perp panel tracery. Shallow N porch (reconstructed) with trefoil-headed niche above the door. The whole church has slender buttresses, except for the chancel, rebuilt in 1862. The fine S porch is also buttressed with truncated shafts over the buttresses, and a four-centred arched door with its tracery broken away, panelled jambs (usual in this area of Cornwall), a canopied image niche above and a wagon roof with carved ribs and wall-plates. The character of the interior reflects a series of five restorations between 1859 and 1901, the earliest by *J. P. St Aubyn*, the latest by *E. H. Sedding*: all the roofs were replaced and the plaster stripped. The tall tower arch is provided with shafts to the responds as at Mawgan-in-Meneage and angel corbels with shields at the springing of the arch. The six-bay S arcade and the seven-bay N arcade are standard Cornish granite: the former was extended E by one bay beyond a short section of wall that Sedding discovered contained the entire pier of the original E end of the aisle, thus demonstrating an intention to extend for some reason abandoned. The three-bay arcade of the Bosahan aisle is the variant with four attached demi-shafts. – Small section of the ROOD SCREEN wainscot with the usual floral carving. – CHEST with some finely carved C16 panels showing Renaissance influence. – STAINED GLASS. Some medieval fragments in the W window. – Chancel E and chancel S, both 1879 by *Lavers, Barraud & Westlake*. – S chapel E, 1973 by *John Hall, Glass Co.* of Bristol, designer *J. A. Crombie*. – N aisle E, 1870 by *Alexander Gibbs*. – BRASSES. To Richard Gerveys, 1574, and family, a palimpsest with, on the reverse, the upper part of a large Flemish C14 brass with knight in armour. – Small brass in the Bosahan aisle to John Pendarves †1616. – MONUMENTS. Small alabaster wall monument in Bosahan aisle to Jane Penticost †1597. – Marble wall monument with urn to William Nicholls †1803 by *R. Isbell.*

The parish has an exceptionally large number of medieval WAYSIDE CROSSES including one in the NW side of the churchyard reconstructed on a cross base that had been reused in the lychgate. Of the others, the best is TREVEASE CROSS, 2½ m. NW at Trevease Farm, with a very primitive Crucifixus with horizontally stretched-out arms, the feet standing on a cross with two top bars.

To the N of the church, a pretty CHURCH ROOM, of late C16 or early C17 date, altered in 1733 (datestone), with the room at first-floor level accessed by external steps. In the large village, the Italianate METHODIST CHURCH, Fore Street, 1880, with earlier-looking VESTRY and STABLES alongside. VICARAGE TERRACE has GREEN DALE, the former vicarage, c. 1830, the CHURCH HALL, formerly the National School dated 1864, and No. 8, a late C18 thatched house of two-room plan with central entrance and gable-end stacks.

TREWARDREVA. 1 m. NW. An E-plan manor house of c. 1600 for Thomas Rise, radically remodelled 1719–49 (datestone); W wing demolished 1860. It is nevertheless one of the most delightful early to mid-C18 houses in Cornwall. Smart S front in ashlar granite with later sash windows (the original sashes with thick glazing bars survive in the rear elevation), the two-storey porch and projecting two-bay E range flanking the now central three bays. The remodelling shows clearly in the gable of the porch, where the early C18 cornice intrudes into the earlier coping which is surmounted by an elaborate C17 scrolled finial. The interior is remarkably complete with many fully panelled rooms with contemporary early to mid-C18 plasterwork and two chambers with high vaulted ceilings: the SE chamber has decorative plasterwork in the central panel and a painted overmantel of an Italianate landscape. Graceful staircase with ramped balusters, panelling, and plasterwork ceiling over. N wing of the 1930s. Handsome STABLES W of the house, also early C18.

MERTHEN, 2 m. S. Shown on a chart of the S coast of the mid C16 as Reskymer, with four round towers standing in a wood, no doubt a pictorial device, but mentioned by Leland as a 'ruinous manor place in a fair park'. Acquired by the Vyvyans of Trelowarren in 1629. The house presents a picturesque N front with an exceptionally wide two-storey porch with the Reskymer arms dated 1575 above the doorway, flanked by many mullioned windows, those at the higher end with king mullions under a gable. E front has three two-storey C19 bays. The other elevations and interior radically altered in the mid C19 and C20.

Other good C16–C17 houses include TREVIADES BARTON, 2 m. E, late C16 around a courtyard plan; BONALLACK BARTON

COTTAGES, 2 m. SSW, converted into two cottages probably from the parlour wing of a C16 house; and TRENARTH BARTON, 2½ m. E, another C16 courtyard plan house.

BOSVATHICK, 2 m. NE. A severe classical house of 1896 by F. J. Bellamy on a courtyard plan subsuming a house of c. 1760. The entrance drive is announced by a LODGE of that date and two crouching stone lions just like those at Trerice (q.v.).

GWEEK. See p. 226.

PORT-NAVAS. See p. 451.

CONSTANTINE BAY
1 m. NE of St Merryn

ST CONSTANTINE. The ruins of the medieval church, some of whose features may have been removed to the churches at St Merryn and Little Petherick, and to Prideaux Place, Harlyn House etc. (qq.v.). What survives, in the middle of a golf course, is the remains of the W tower with a high slatestone arch. The dimensions of the church were apparently 40 ft by 24 ft (12 metres by 7.3 metres). Fragments of C15 Catacleuse tracery stored at the nearby WELL (*see* below) demonstrate its considerable status.

ST CONSTANTINE'S WELL, N of the church. Medieval, possibly C14, low well-house with remains of a pointed stone vaulted roof and a pointed arch opening to the rear with a niche above. Recovered from the sand in 1917 and now under a mid-C20 shelter.

CORNELLY
1½ m. W of Tregony

ST CORNELIUS. All on its own with a wide view S towards the woods of Trewarthenick, the former Gregor house, in the distance. A slender little W tower, as Mylor would be if it did not have its heavy buttresses, the ground-floor slate with a tiny lancet W window, no doubt C13, the second and third stages of the early C16 in granite ashlar and of receding width, surmounted by battlements and crocketed pinnacles. The body of the church, also charmingly diminutive, is a double-cell plan of the C13, the N wall of that date with one lancet window, with a short N chancel aisle. On the S side the windows were replaced by Perp windows with cusped heads and a S porch added in the early C16. The N chancel aisle of two bays was built in 1720 over the Gregor family vault with standard Cornish responds and pier and at a slightly higher level. Chancel rebuilt by J. P. St Aubyn in 1866, the remainder thoroughly restored in 1900; the wagon roof of the porch is made up of salvaged sections from the rest of the church. In its humble scale and simplicity of plan it still gives a good impression of the C13 Cornish church. – FONT. Octagonal, as primitively carved as if it were Norman, yet no doubt post-Reformation, and hardly intended to be revivalism – just a rustic carver's handiwork. – PULPIT with crudely painted panels with coats of arms; C17. – MONU-MENTS. Two Gregor monuments of note – Jane Reeves, a Gregor daughter, †1783. The best feature of the church, an exquisite portrait bust of the young woman in an oval medallion. – Elizabeth Gregor †1703. Baroque cartouche with an oval border and carved angels.

The church is built in the middle of a round that may have been a Bronze Age burial mound.

TREWARTHENICK, 1 m. SW. Of interest as much for its landscape as the house: this is one of the Cornish estates (cf. Antony, Catchfrench, Pentillie, Port Eliot and Tregothnan) for which *Humphry Repton* produced a Red Book, in this case for Francis Gregor in 1792. Now a plain house with an E front of seven bays in two storeys, the three central bays slightly broken forward with a pediment over, with a reset 1686 datestone. It was once the centrepiece of a more prestigious composition: a Prideaux drawing of *c.* 1727 and a watercolour by Repton of 1793 show the E front, then the entrance front, with a steeply pitched pediment and a pair of loggias N and S. Repton, working with *Robert Furze Brettingham* (Paul Holden), remodelled the loggias as single-storey flanking wings, that to the S with a conservatory, that to the N as the new entrance. These were subsequently altered and raised to full height by *Henry Harrison c.* 1830 (cf. Enys and Heligan) but demolished in 1925.

The shelter belts and plantations that define the Trewarthenick LANDSCAPE are of Repton's scheme, much of which was implemented. This included replacing the earlier E, W and N approaches with the principal approach via the present N drive.

COTEHELE

4060

The most extensive, complete and important Tudor house of Cornwall, picturesquely set among woods high above the Tamar, is also sublimely picturesque in its architecture. The latter is not the result of early abandonment or late reinvention but the product of sustained investment by the Edgcumbe family, from 1353, when they acquired the house by marriage, until 1947, when it passed to the National Trust. The Edgcumbes, rich and important gentry with court connections, deliberately sought to embellish Cotehele's ancient fabric and character as a way of demonstrating their own deep roots in the past. They achieved this first by transforming an earlier medieval house into a complex three-courtyard plan house through several major phases of

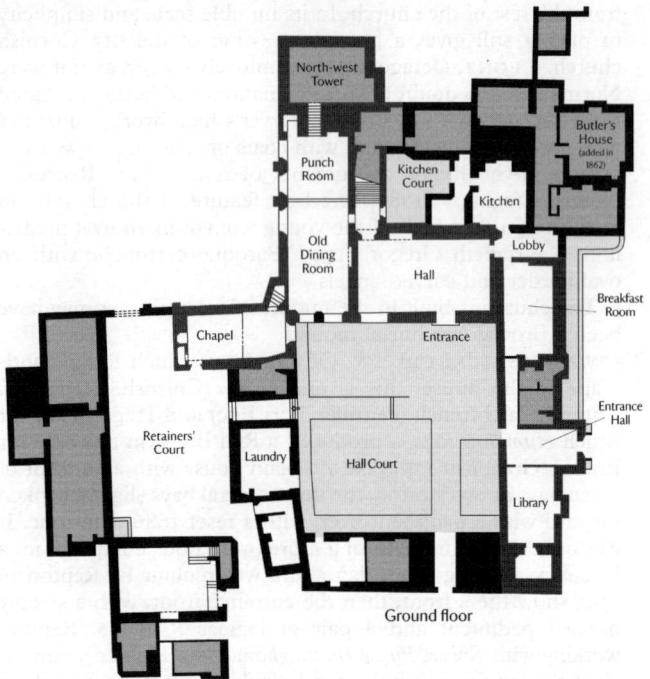

Cotehele House. Ground-floor plan

reconstruction and extension between the late C15 and the 1650s, even after their new house at Mount Edgcumbe had been built; continued the process in the C18 with subtle changes in the spirit of the Romantic movement; and finished with some meticulous medievalizing in the C19. It is the combination of their early and persistent antiquarianism with an almost complete absence of classicism that makes Cotehele such a contrast to most of Cornwall's other great houses.

Such an evolution has produced a succession of the most pleasing architectural vistas built in a harmonious combination of slatestone, granite and slate, enhanced by silver-grey patinas of age and the Cornish weather. But it has left very few wall surfaces with their original architectural features intact. So although Cotehele has far more early features than any comparable house in Cornwall, many have been reused, replicated, or replaced: as early as 1652 a letter refers to a window (in the little parlour) 'that is polled down to be converted for a window in the great parlour'. The visitor must therefore enjoy the puzzles that almost every elevation presents.*

*I owe my understanding of the house to major research of 2004 commissioned by Rachel Hunt of the National Trust and undertaken by Eric Berry, James Gossip, Joanna Mattingley, and Nigel Thomas; Jo Cox and John Thorpe's report of 1985; and Stephen Docksey.

EXTERIOR. The approach from the S presents the strong impression of a semi-fortified great house with the three-storey embattled GATEHOUSE flanked by ranges with small windows at first-floor level only. This reflects its late C15–early C16 inward-looking arrangement, the main ranges opening onto the enclosed courtyard with only small windows in the rubble outer walls that were originally rendered. The S walls of the flanking ranges are among the least altered parts of Cotehele* and include early features like the pair of slit ventilators under a single lintel to the l. of the tower. In contrast the mid-C16 tower shows clear evidence in its granite ashlar upper storeys of having been added above an earlier gateway of which the jambs survive on its inner face. The tympanum over the robustly moulded entrance is filled by a shield and two large leaves, a motif replicated above the hall door. Inside, a fine granite tunnel-vault, divided by transverse ribs as if it were a timber wagon roof.

The HALL COURT is the epitome of Tudor picturesque, all four elevations irregular, and full of architectural incident. In another contrast with the exterior, the slatestone walling is generally of square and coursed blocks. The gatehouse entrance is aligned directly opposite the door to the GREAT HALL with the PARLOUR WING to its l., both built forward into the court in the early C16. The high level ashlar granite of the hall represents a mid-C16 heightening when the large doorway was inserted and all the windows in the hall and the Parlour Wing were replaced. The three windows above the door are disposed symmetrically (cf. Trecarrel), the great window of the hall and the windows of the Great Parlour and Great Chamber transomed and mullioned with massive king mullions, a single monolithic lintel over the parlour window, and ogee-headed lights. 57

The WEST RANGE begins with the CHAPEL's three-light Perp E window with reticulated tracery of the late C15, its dignity somewhat diminished by the intrusion of the Parlour Wing. This range has early architectural features including two pre-Tudor pointed-arched doorways and a scatter of single lights, as well as some later ogee-headed windows. The WEST GATE has a wide four-centred arch, curiously on rubble jambs, with a tall stack rising above. The SOUTH RANGE wall was rebuilt or refaced when the range was developed as a continuous frontage, interrupted by the inner face of the gatehouse. The EAST RANGE shows evidence of its original function in the low four-centred doorways that gave access to the cellarage, and of heightening in the 1550s when the windows were inserted.

Through the W gate is the RETAINERS' COURT, the passage to it with an C18 plaster ceiling with cornice and its face a

*The S range roof has been dendrochronologically dated to the late C15. The W end of range was truncated when the S range of the Retainers' Court was built and a smaller infill erected.

replacement doorway of the 1550s with a gunloop on its S side, probably an antiquarian addition. The eye is immediately drawn to the delightful pinnacled bellcote of Breton character of the 1520s over the W end of the CHAPEL (cf. Dupath Holy Well); the chapel door and the two-light window are of the 1550s. To its W the EMBATTLED WALL and four-centred arch of the NORTH GATE, c. 1520, give some sense of the curtain wall that once surrounded the court: it survives in the N and W walls of the W range. A pair of mid-C16 four-centred arched doorways share a central jamb in the W range and there is a four-centred arched door at the l. of the S range, evidence of the construction of these ranges in the 1560s. C19 heightening is obvious in the three gabled dormers in the W range, and there are several C19 windows.

Through the N gate to the W wall of the Parlour Wing, its N end incorporated in the NW tower. Constructed in the 1520s, this wall would have been blind or only sparingly windowed, the large four-centred and ogee-headed windows probably being insertions of the mid C16. The NORTH-WEST TOWER, added in the 1560s, is the most imposing single component of the Cotehele exterior, its three storeys surmounted by an embattled parapet above a striking cable-moulded cornice (cf. Boringdon Hall, Plympton) and with large four-light windows to the upper floors of the N and S elevations with king mullions and basket-arched lights. The string courses are employed as hoodmoulds over the windows, which are filled with late C18 or C19 casements. Smaller windows to the ground floor and staircase, the staircase windows, which are later insertions, daringly close to the corner. The E elevation has a wide chimney-breast projection into which a spiral staircase was inserted with an embattled stair-turret c. 1652 rising above the main battlements. To the E of the tower, the NORTH RANGE with one small window of the 1520s, the date of its roof established by dendrochronology. To its l., a SERVICE WING added in 1862.

Finally, the E front of the EAST RANGE. Though this range was remodelled in 1862 to provide a self-contained suite for Caroline, dowager Countess of Mount Edgcumbe, it is substantially C16 (cf. the survival of small single-light windows at first-floor level). The gable towards the N end that defines the E end of the hall range is mid-C16, when the wall was heightened. The C19 additions include: the projecting porch, dated 1862 on the labels to the doorway, rising to a large transomed four-light window with ogee heads; the insertion of large windows at the N end and l. of the porch; and the rebuilding of a former latrine projection to create a lateral stack. Even these radical late alterations seem entirely harmonious.

58   INTERIOR. The GREAT HALL is the most impressive Tudor room in Cornwall, twice as long as wide, immensely tall and open to the roof. Dated by dendrochronology to the 1520s, the roof structure was apparently re-assembled at the higher level when the walls were heightened in the 1550s. Seven bays with eight

arch-braced trusses with high cranked collars, producing a steep four-centred arch form. Between the trusses are four tiers of intersecting carved wind-braces. Except for the common rafters, all the timbers are heavily moulded. The hall has no screens passage, the door from the court leading directly into the room about a third of its length from the E end. At the E end are three doorways with simple four-centred arches with convex outer mouldings: the N door accessed the service passage to the kitchen and service stair, the central door is likely to have led by stairs to the principal chamber of the E range, and the S door originally gave access to the cellars on the ground floor of the E range. The hall is heated by one large fireplace in the N wall inserted during the mid C16 and heightened c. 1652 (see the bases of the jambs). The large roll-moulded doorway in the NW corner, also heightened at the same date, leads via the Great Stair to the Great Chamber and NW tower. At high level in the E and W walls are quatrefoil vents, probably serving as squints, probably more examples of antiquarian invention of the C18. – STAINED GLASS. Heraldic shields set within a border of yellow/gold silver stain, some medieval but much Victorian replacement.

Through the NW door to the PARLOUR WING, a cross-wing to the hall containing the Edgcumbes' private apartments, which originally comprised the Great Parlour on the ground floor and the Great Chamber above, both lit by splendid six-light S windows and with an open arch- and wind-braced roof to the chamber.* Both ground- and first-floor rooms were subdivided in the mid C17 and the first-floor rooms given plaster ceilings with coved cornices. The rooms are richly furnished with TAPESTRIES covering all the wall surfaces, ruthlessly cut to suit the spaces: most are late C17 with some C16 pieces.

The SW corner of the parlour wing is linked to the CHAPEL by a tapered link added in the mid C16. The chapel has a ceiled early C16 wagon roof. In the S wall a window looking into the chapel from the first-floor room. – In the W wall, a recess enclosing a medieval CLOCK. – Nave floor of C16 glazed TILES, much worn. – PEWS, probably late C19 or early C20, incorporating some C16 BENCH-ENDS and LINENFOLD PANELLING. – C16 SCREEN with cusped heads, with pretty C18 delicate tracery work above the panels and on the cresting. – TRIPTYCH. Flemish, dated 1589, the central panel the Adoration of the Magi, the wings with kneeling portraits of the donor and his wife with their painted shields and their ages, thirty-four and twenty-eight. – ALTAR FRONTAL/DORSAL, displayed on the S wall, c. 1500, a beautiful piece of appliqué work, silver on purple, with Christ and the twelve apostles and the arms of Sir Piers Edgcumbe †1539. – STAINED GLASS. Some of the best medieval glass in Cornwall. In the E window the Crucifixion with the Blessed Virgin Mary and St John. The glass was

* In the late C19 this roof was 'restored' in the manner of church roofs of that period.

extensively restored *c.* 1880 by *J. T Fouracre* who replaced the upper half of Christ and the head of Mary, but the figure of John is late C15 and complete. At the base of each light are heraldic shields, insertions of 1530–40: their frames are almost identical to those at Lytes Cary, Somerset. In the S window, St Anne and the Blessed Virgin Mary in the l. light, St Catherine in the r. Late C15, similar to the St John of the E window, all probably of Somerset origin: the painted patterns on the diamond quarries are identical to those in Somerset glass of that date.* The glass must have belonged to the earlier S window and been re-fitted when the 1550s window was inserted.

Back to the GREAT STAIR, a wide wooden staircase built 1652 to replace a previous spiral. It leads to the NORTH-WEST TOWER, private chambers which could also be used as an independent suite of rooms. By comparison with the original scale of the Great Parlour and Great Chamber the rooms are small and easily heated, with their own stair between first- and second-floor rooms. The ground-floor chamber has a pretty C18 Jacobean-style ceiling with panels divided by moulded wooden ribs. The first-floor chamber has a fine internal porch formed of a linenfold panelled oak screen. The upper floor was divided into two rooms *c.* 1700 with bolection-moulded doorways with basket-arched heads and moulded plaster ceiling cornices. As in the Parlour Wing, the rooms are hung with C17 TAPESTRIES incorporating some C16 pieces.

To the KITCHEN COURT and the KITCHEN, which survives as an open hall. Its principal feature is the massive early C16 chamfered fireplace in its W wall; another large fireplace in the N wall with three ovens is an C18 addition.

Finally to the EAST RANGE. Its principal feature is the first-floor drawing room with a fine arch- and wind-braced roof, a skilful 1862 replica of the Tudor roof, and some linenfold panelling incorporating some C16 panels. In the breakfast room below, a CUPBOARD front, of Welsh Marches origin, made in 1550 and imported into the house in the 1860s. Of three tiers with the two rows of panels separated by a tier that once contained drawers, and an inscription. The panels depict Welsh minstrels, Adam and Eve and the Tree of Life, etc., with huntsmen and animals in the framework. Also a copy of the MONUMENT to Sir Richard Edgcumbe †1489 at Morlaix, France.

The extensive and beautiful GARDENS and PARK contain several buildings of interest. On the approach to the house, the large BARN, of two builds, the three bays nearest the house late C15, the rest C16–C17, with later extensions and alterations. The W elevation is the least altered, with buttresses, four-centred arched doorways, and ventilation slits. The roof is an C18 replacement. In the Terrace Garden E of the house a late C16 DOVECOTE, circular, with a domed corbelled slatestone roof

---

*I am grateful to Alfred Fisher and Caroline Atkinson for this observation.

surmounted by a central lantern. It overlooks a FISH POND
shown on the plan of 1731. In the mid to late C19 walks were
developed in the wooded valley below, one of which leads ¼ m.
E to the little CHAPEL (St George and St Thomas a Becket),
perched on the edge of a cliff above the Tamar. Built by Sir
Richard Edgcumbe in the late C15 in memory of his escape
from Sir Henry Trenowth of Bodrugan in 1483; restored in
1769 and the C20. The simple interior has a small fragment of
medieval GLASS in the tracery of the E window and furnishings
that incorporate C15 BENCH- and PRAYER-DESK ENDS. To the
N of the house, ¼ m. beyond more terraces and the embattled
CURTAIN WALL of the garden, a late C18 three-stage PROS-
PECT TOWER. Triangular on plan, dished on all sides, giving
the illusion of greater proportions.

The wider ESTATE demonstrates something of the historically
large-scale industrial and commercial activity of the Edgcumbes. Near the house, mid-to late C19 FARMHOUSE and
LODGE. At COTEHELE QUAY, ½ m. S, an especially picturesque group of C18–C19 buildings, reflecting the primary
importance of the Tamar for the economy of Cotehele, which
includes LIMEKILNS, WAREHOUSES, the EDGCUMBE ARMS,
a MALTHOUSE, LODGE and the restored Tamar sailing barge,
the SHAMROCK, built at Stonehouse in 1899. An early C19
BRIDGE in C15 style leads to COTEHELE MILL, ½ m. SW,
with a range of mostly mid-C18 and C19 buildings including
a working WATERMILL. Other buildings are scattered over
the estate including the attractive hamlet of BOHETHERICK,
1 m. S.

COVERACK

7010

The little fishing village gathers comfortably around its small
harbour, bounded in part by natural rock and part by retaining
walls and a QUAY with a stone inscribed 'T Ellis 1724'. Above
are former FISH CELLARS, some behind the PARIS HOTEL
still in use, and pretty C17–C19 cottages; many thatched.

ST PETER. 1885, splendidly situated overlooking the sea, plain
but dignified with a small W bellcote. – FONT, LECTERN and
PULPIT in polished red and green serpentine from the former
serpentine works at Poltesco (q.v.). – Good set of late C19
STAINED GLASS by *Clayton & Bell.*

CHYNALLS CLIFF CASTLE, 1 m. S. Substantial ditch with discontinuous stony bank or rampart using natural outcropping
at the neck of an elegant rocky promontory. Entrance causeway
reused by modern track.

LANKIDDEN CLIFF CASTLE, 2 m. WSW. On a wedge-like promontory dominating a beautiful bay. Bank and ditch with a
slightly angled entrance gap and causeway.

CRANTOCK

As at St Columb Minor, the old parish was subdivided in 1894 to cede part to Newquay, but the centre remains pleasingly villagey with an unusual number of thatched cottages.

ST CARANTOC. One of the few Cornish churches to retain major Norman fabric, and of curious proportions reflecting its interesting history. Its walls contain more sandrock, a rare building material, than anywhere else in Cornwall. Small W tower, a chancel higher than the nave with catslide roofs for N and S aisles, an aisleless nave but with N and S transepts, and S porch. There was a church here in 1086 on a former monastic site. Bishop Brewer of Exeter founded a college of nine prebends and a dean here c. 1236, which necessitated enlargement of the chancel. Of the Norman church of cruciform plan there remain the narrow nave, the shallow transepts and some masonry including a blocked door in the W wall of N transept. The foundations of the chancel aisle arcades and much of the chancel E of the arcades (now rendered over) are Norman too. The Norman arches of the transepts open into the chancel aisles but in its present form the chancel is C14 with arcades on octagonal piers and two-centred, single-chamfered arches. There was formerly a central tower which collapsed onto the nave in 1412 after which the W tower was built or reconstructed: it is roughcast with battlements but no pinnacles. It has buttresses on the lower stage which meet at right angles at the corners and not, as was usual in the SW of England, leaving the corners free: this suggests that the lower stage is earlier, perhaps C13. The interior owes its entirely convincing medieval character to sensitive and imaginative reconstruction by *E. H. Sedding* in 1899–1901. It is richly embellished with high quality carved WOODWORK, much of it the work of *Violet Pinwill* and her school of carvers, especially the bench-ends and other furnishings (cf. Lanteglos-by-Fowey and Launceston). The ROOD SCREEN is especially accomplished with large rood figures carried above a second tier of fine woodwork high in the chancel arch. It incorporates five plain uprights of the medieval screen in the N transept: it is clear that the original had no tracery at all between the uprights and can therefore be compared to that specially airy and graceful type to be seen at Mawgan-in-Pydar. – FONT. Of the Norman style, like Mawgan-in-Pydar, St Columb Minor, St Wenn, the date 1474 inscribed in large script: is this a C15 re-tooling or a copy after the tower fell and destroyed the original? – COMMUNION RAIL. C17 with turned balusters. – PANEL. In S transept, a wooden arch with a painted and carved low relief scene of Abraham, probably Dutch C17. – STAINED GLASS. Fragments of medieval glass with a Latin text in the sacristy, the rest a full didactic scheme of the Gospel Narratives and St Carantoc by *C. E. Tute*, 1901–4.

In the village centre a ROUND GARDEN, thought to be the site of one of seven Celtic oratories of the former college.

CREED

The churchtown of Grampound (q.v.), of church, former rectory and farm.

ST CRIDA. In a lovely position below the road overlooking meadows sloping down to the Fal. Highly attractive exterior. w tower of three stages with buttresses set back from the corners, embattled parapet and large crocketed pinnacles; rebuilt 1734. By 1291 the church was cruciform, of which the N transept and traces of Norman masonry in the N wall survive. The s transept was replaced in the mid C15 by an ambitious s aisle with very lavish windows, especially the E window: the w window is Dec. s porch of unusual richness, early C16, with fluted jambs, decorated capitals and a pointed tunnel-vault with transverse arches inside, rare in Cornwall (cf. St Cuby, Luxulyan and St Germans). Badly carved heads as the boss of the central arch. Early C16 three-light square-headed mullioned windows in N transept. Light and airy interior, the plain glazing accentuating the fragments of medieval glass in the tracery of the E and S windows of the s aisle. The arcade of the aisle is of five bays, tall and spacious, with standard Cornish piers. The aisle retains its C15 wagon roof with carved ribs, bosses and wall-plates, partly reconstructed in 1904. Nave and chancel have a late C19 wagon roof, part of the restorations by *J. P. St Aubyn* in the 1870s, and *Otho B. Peter* of Launceston in 1903–4. – PISCINA. In the N transept. For the antiquarian the most interesting object in the church – a Norman pillar piscina with chevron decoration of the pillar, placed under a C13 trefoil arch. Fragment of medieval WALL PAINTING above, with Gothic script. – The chancel PISCINA looks early C14. – FONT. C13, a miscellany, of Catacleuse stone, octagonal, with two shallow blank niches with pointed heads to each side. – ROOD SCREEN. Only a little preserved, but of interesting design, with flamboyant blank tracery of the panels. – ALMS BOX. Probably C18 using earlier wood, on chamfered wooden pillar, by s door. – STAINED GLASS. C15 fragments in the s chapel and s aisle tracery, an important collection with many interesting details, including a finch wearing a chain of office and carrying a staff. – MONUMENTS. Thomas Denys, 1589, and his wife Margaret, 1578. A chest tomb with carved slate inscription plate and low relief shield of arms, in s aisle. – Robert Quarme, 1708. Marble tablet with Latin inscription with good lettering.

PENNANS, 2 m. NE of Grampound. A substantial late C17 house fronted in granite ashlar, remodelled and extended *c.* 1700–20. Now a farmhouse. The original part is the five-bay centre with pedimented doorway to entrance hall and principal rooms to

l. and r., each heated by a rear lateral stack. At the rear of the
entrance hall, a projecting stair-tower. In the early C18 wings
were added to the front l. and r. to form a U-plan, though the
l. wing may never have been completed and is now gutted. The
interior has excellent late C17 fittings including a fine open-well
stair of *c*. 1680 with barley-sugar twist balusters and ramped
moulded handrail. Bolection-moulded panelling with dado
and plasterwork with rosettes and cornice in the front ground-
floor r. room; similar decoration in the chamber above. The r.
wing has good features of the early C18 including an open-well
stair with turned balusters, wide moulded handrail and ramped
dado panelling, and closets to the main chamber with fielded
panelling.

Behind the house, fragmentary but tantalizing remains of
once extensive GARDENS and pleasure grounds, defined by
remnant brick walls, recorded in 1757 by a visitor as having
'several statues remaining in the garden as well as pleasant
walks, and plantations, likewise iron gates, but they are all
neglected'. They were the creation of *Philip Hawkins*, the father
of Philip Hawkins of Trewithen (q.v.).

GARLENICK, 2 m. N of Grampound. Large symmetrical five-bay
fronted house with embattled parapet. Probably of late C17
origin but substantially rebuilt in 1812 for Gwennap Moore,
dated GM1812, and subsequently little altered. Double-depth
plan with central entrance giving to principal rooms l. and r.,
and a large central hall behind with stair hall to the l. Good
contemporary fittings.

CROAN
1 m. NW of Washaway

An unusually complete late C17 or early C18 house owned by the
Roscarrocks until 1654, rebuilt *c*. 1690 by Edward Hoblyn:
datestone on rear wall of 1696. The house is L-shaped, the s
front of three-room plan with a NW wing of two rooms and
passage. Symmetrical seven-window front under a hipped roof,
the central three bays set slightly forward. Early C18 sashes with
heavy glazing bars and dressed stone flat arches; central doorcase with pulvinated frieze in cornice and console brackets.
Extensive late C17 interior fittings of fine quality, including
bolection-moulded panelling, cornices, doors and chimneypieces. Good open-well stair with contemporary *trompe l'œil*
painting on the ceiling.

The house occupies the summit of deeply wooded hilly
countryside and is approached through early C18 brick GATE-
PIERS. The high walled gardens have two PAVILIONS, and the
remains of a DOVECOTE of the same date, probably by Edward's
son, Edward, Sheriff of Cornwall in 1722.

CROWAN

ST CREWENNA. The church suffered three major restorations between 1828 and 1891, the impetus for the earlier campaign the need to accommodate the increasing mining population. The architect for the 1872 and 1891 work was *J. P. St Aubyn*, an unsurprising choice given that this was the home parish (cf. Clowance below) of the St Aubyn family. This is the architect at his most severe. The only part to escape intact was the fine C15 W tower of three stages, unbuttressed, with embattled parapet and corner pinnacles. There are medieval carved heads over the buttresses that flank the W window of the N aisle. St Aubyn added the S porch and a large organ chamber as a S transept in unattractive rock-faced granite: the transept also has a chimney, striking another discordant note. The S arcade, which had been added in the late C17 on Tuscan columns (cf. Pelyn where they survive), was swept away and replaced by a lifeless one of Cornish standard. Fortunately the remarkable N arcade was retained with standard Cornish granite piers, but capitals of sufficient height to house shield-holding angels on all four sides (similar to St Ives). Their escutcheons allude to a St Aubyn marriage of 1398. The arches are steep and two-centred. There are three of these bays; the following three are lower. – FONT. Granite; plain, square bowl, quatrefoil section of shaft, base with extremely primitively carved lions *passant*; probably late medieval, not Norman (cf. St Ives). – STAINED GLASS. Chancel E, 1907, and chancel N, 1891, by *Heaton, Butler & Bayne*; S aisle W, 1872 by *Lavers, Barraud & Westlake*; N chapel N, 1932, by *Heaton, Butler & Bayne*. – MONUMENTS. A generally fine assemblage of St Aubyn memorials in the N aisle. – Brasses, re-set in slate by St Aubyn, to Geoffrey St Aubyn and wife, *c.* 1420, Geoffrey St Aubyn and wife, *c.* 1490, Thomas St Aubyn and wife, *c.* 1550. – Damaged monument to Col. Thomas St Aubyn with a small standing figure, *c.* 1650. – Sir John St Aubyn †1714. Tomb-chest with black marble inscription plate on top. – Sir John St Aubyn †1772, by *Joseph Wilton*, with two life-size putti and an urn. – Sir John St Aubyn †1839, with a life-size mourning woman by an urn: dull. By *Behnes*. – A marble Ionic aedicule with dove in the tympanum commemorates the 1872 restoration.

There were once at least eight Nonconformist chapels in this mining parish, including examples at LEEDSTOWN, datestone 1862, and TOWNSHEND, datestone 1871, and a large number of medieval CROSSES, including a very eroded one outside the S wall of the church tower.

TRENOWETH HOUSE, ½ m. W. The former vicarage, dated 1888 and probably by *J. P. St Aubyn*. An interesting example of a medium-sized house built in the Scottish Baronial style, unusual for Cornwall. Many mullioned windows, steep-pitched roofs, gable parapet, and massive chimneystacks.

CLOWANCE, ¾ m. W. The house of the St Aubyn family, now a resort, the setting severely compromised by holiday homes. It was largely destroyed in fires of 1837 and 1843, and mostly rebuilt after 1845. Plain granite front of seven bays and two storeys with a Doric porte cochère on four columns. Much more handsome are the former COACHHOUSE and STABLES, late C18, with central range with central pediment and a cupola with pagoda roof with ball finial directly behind, and two long projecting flanking wings; and the ORANGERY, late C18, with five large twenty-four pane sash windows. These buildings indicate the high quality of the former C18 house. To the W of the house, Nine Maidens Down Cross, with unusually richly decorated shaft similar to that at St Dennis (q.v.)

BINNERTON MANOR, 2 m. WSW. Former C17 manor house extended to form an L-plan in the C18. Good quality features including an C18 Rococo ceiling in the parlour. C19 DOVECOTE in walled forecourt.

CUBERT

ST CUBERT. The spire is such a landmark for miles across the bare, windswept country W of Newquay that the small scale and unassuming character of the church come as a surprise. Of the Norman building the W part of the N wall of the nave and the very thick responds of the S chancel arcade. Low W tower with bold buttresses on the lower stage only just set back from the angles and an octagonal broached spire, an unusual feature in Cornwall. *G. E. Street* rebuilt it in 1852, following his extensive but sensitive restoration of the church 1846–51.* The moulding of the tower arch confirms that the whole tower was built originally *c.* 1300 (cf. St Ewe). Of the same date and moulding the arch into the N transept, which has piers of Catacleuse, and the plain N door into the nave. Then in the C15 the S aisle was added, of six bays, with a S transept, the piers with wave and hollow mouldings, the capitals with the stiff horizontal leaf decoration of Devon. The S side of the transept has a niche for a tomb. Chancel, aisle and N transept have their original wagon roofs. Much mid-C19 re-windowing, but a two-light C14 window in the N wall of the chancel and one of three lights in the S wall of the aisle. Street's low chancel screen and simple pews seem entirely appropriate for the modest proportions of the interior. – FONT. C13, circular, on the usual five supports (the outer with shaft-rings), the sides of the bowl with chip-carving of rosettes, stars, etc. – PULPIT. Made up of bench-ends with symbols of the Passion, including a shroud. – STAINED GLASS. S aisle windows by *F. Drake*, 1886,

---

*The spire has strong resonances with St Mary Biscovey, Par (q.v.), Street's first church of 1848.

and *A. O. Hemmings*, 1902. – N transept by *Ward & Hughes*, 1888. – MONUMENTS. Extremely pretty slate plate for the 'exuviae Arthuri Lawrence plebei' and his sons. They died in 1669 and 1699. The inscription is flanked by boldly incised columns, with a rich scrolly pediment with plenty of floral decoration above. – Fine, sharp inscription plate with urn above to John Hoskin †1810, by *J. Isbell* of Truro. – INSCRIBED STONE in the W wall of the tower: CONETOLI FILI TEGER NOMALI. Date C7 at the earliest (note the Hiberno-Saxon letters). Pre-Conquest WHEEL-HEAD CROSS against the W wall of the N transept with a wide-limbed cross in relief within a narrow bead.

HOLY WELL OF ST CUBERT, 1 m. NW. Probably C15, restored 1936. Small well-house built into the bank with round-arched doorway with moulded and stopped surround, fronted by a screen wall stepped up over a two-centred arched doorway.

KELSEY HEAD CLIFF CASTLE, 2¼ m. NW. Iron Age. Tightly curving simple bank and ditch rampart pierced by entrance E of apex. Ditch clearly cut in stages. Island (The Chick) immediately offshore possibly originally part of the castle. Bronze Age BARROW on rising ground inland reused as early modern beacon.

CURY

6020

ST CORENTIN. The church stands on a raised oval enclosure or *lann*. C15 W tower of two stages, low and unbuttressed in the Lizard tradition, with a stair-turret rising in the NW corner to above the pinnacles. Simple W door and W window, both with reused heads as label stops (cf., for example, Manaccan): they could be late C12 or C13 and are excellently preserved. The S wall of the church has the earliest features otherwise, Norman and C14 probably. The main point of interest is the fine Norman S door (the r. side partly obscured by a clumsy C19 porch) with a specially varied range of decorative motifs: there is one order of columns, with a key band on one side and chevron on the other side of the columns, and tympanum with interlaced rings surrounded by chevron and beads. The interior bears the stamp of severe Victorian restoration which installed heavy hammerbeam roofs, except the N aisle which retains parts of its wagon roof. A squint connects S transept and chancel: it consists of an octagonal pier taking the place of the corner, just as at Landewednack and Mawgan-in-Meneage. The N aisle is of six bays; the tracery of the E window is of the same design as at Gunwalloe, Mullion and Sithney, the points of the cusps enriched with cylindrical mouldings with fleurons, and the charming decoration of the inner arch, with quatrefoils in panels and Tudor roses, is the same as at Sithney. The piers of the arcade are Cornish standard, with the familiar horizontal leaves along the abaci. – FONT. Probably C12, a variety of the Bodmin type with crude corner shafts and shallowly carved star or rose as medallions between. – In the churchyard, s of the church, a WHEEL-HEAD CROSS, one of the tallest and best preserved in Cornwall.

BONYTHON, 1 m. E. Late C18. An exceptionally elegant granite house of basement and two storeys. Five bays. Eight wide steps with curving handrails rise to the doorway (cf. Pengreep), with fanlight above and wide rusticated surround. The central bay is brought slightly forward. Venetian window above, and a slight pediment with small fan-shaped window. Four stone balls on hexagonal pillars cap the pediment (as at Clowance).

BOCHYM, ¾ m. ESE. Large and irregular, of C16 and C17 origins with wide mullioned windows, substantially but handsomely remodelled in the mid C19. Open-well staircase, some bolection panelling and a plaster ceiling with a large elliptical wreath. To the E on the main road, the delightfully fanciful LODGE, 1851, its walls of serpentine blocks, on a cruciform plan, each wing with a gable-end and ball finial and central bay window with transoms and mullions. The porches in the angles also have gables with ball finials. Inside a hammerbeam roof (cf. St Corentin).

DAVIDSTOW

ST DAVID. Fine Perp W tower of three tall stages with buttresses that leave the corners free, an un-embattled parapet, and rectangular N stair-turret. The rest was effectively rebuilt by *J. Hine* in 1875 so that little original work remains. What prevails, however, is the generous scale of the original, with some good C19 detail (e.g. the rich S porch with its decorated outer doorway in Polyphant, reflecting the Polyphant inner door). The interior is uncommonly spacious with an unusually wide nave and wide five-bay N and S aisles with Cornish standard piers. The three E windows all of five lights each, also wider than the standard. – Three C16 BENCH-ENDS fixed to the front pews in the nave, one a bagpiper. – STAINED GLASS. The otherwise rather sombre interior is enlivened by the vigorous, bright and colourful chancel E and S and S chapel E windows by *Taylor & O'Connor*, 1875–6. – S aisle W 1985 by *David Gubbins* of Exeter. N aisle 1877 by *Fouracre & Watson*. – MONUMENTS. Fine large slate ledgers include Richard Bettenson †1668, Thomas Bettenson †1693, John Parlon †1693, Francis Nicholls †1674, and William Pearse †1638.

In the s of the churchyard a C17 SUNDIAL on a baluster stem: to the E the former SUNDAY SCHOOL, probably 1875; immediately W CHURCHTOWN BARTON, rebuilt 1849 in the

Elizabethan style by *John Pearse*. One window lintel inscribed THE YEAR OF OUR LORD 1607 TP, another Pearse. The family funded the restoration of the church, as recorded in a large plaque in the S porch.

In a field to the NE, a HOLY WELL of medieval origin but rebuilt in the later C19 reputedly with material from a ruined chapel. The well-house has an unusually wide, low front in granite ashlar that rises to a gable over the central entrance.

DELABOLE   *0080*

A long straggling village of three conjoined hamlets – Rockhead, Medrose and Pengelly – on the W edge of the famous slate quarry, all set in a treeless coastal landscape exposed to Atlantic gales.

ST JOHN, High Street. 1878–82 by *Hine & Odgers* of Plymouth. A severe E.E. design that suits the rather bleak industrial character of the settlement. Tower of two stages with set-back buttresses and pyramidal roof, placed at the W end of the S aisle. Triple lancet windows to nave, chancel and S aisle with squat pillars and moulded capitals. – FONT. Octagonal. – PULPIT. C19, painted in the 1920s. – Striking ALTAR and RIDDEL-POSTS, mid-C20, in Delabole slate by *Reginald Wheatly*.

PRIMARY SCHOOL, High Street. 1878 by *Silvanus Trevail*. A long spreading composition of school and school house, the entrance originally through a central towered porch, very similar to the school at St Teath (q.v.).

DELABOLE SLATE QUARRY. The vast scale of the quarry takes some moments to grasp. Sheer cliffs drop 160 ft (49 metres) to terraced workings as deep again and a central lake of alchemical blue-green, at over 1½ m. in circumference one of the biggest human-made holes in Europe. The name, which could be derived from the Cornish 'delyow' meaning leaves or flakes (i.e. of slate) and 'pol' meaning pit, was in use by 1284, and may imply the presence of slate workings by that date. Duchy of Cornwall records reference it as a source of roofing slates by the C15. A number of small concerns quarried from the late C15 under lease from the Roscarrock family and after 1596 the Trevanion estate. Enterprising lessees began to amalgamate smaller workings during the C18, until all leases were concentrated in the hands of the Old Delabole Slate Quarry in the 1840s. Murray's handbook of 1851 describes an industrial, steam-powered scene employing gunpowder, engines and machinery and animated by about a thousand workers, extracting 120 tonnes of slate a day for export from Port Gaverne (summer) and Boscastle (winter) to the SW peninsula, southern England and the Continent.

DELABOLE WIND FARM, I m. NE. Britain's first commercial
wind farm, operational from 1991. The original ten turbines
were replaced in 2010 by four turbines nearly twice as tall,
325 ft (99 metres) to the tip of the blade, dramatically increasing the energy output. They look entirely at home in this
windswept landscape. The former GAIA CENTRE, 2001 by
Edward Cullinan Architects, enclosed by a protective bund, built
to demonstrate and promote renewable energy sources, is an
admirably low-key structure of timber-clad walls under a
sweeping curved roof. Now a school.

DEVORAN

A pretty former port town near the head of Restronquet Creek
at the E end of the Carnon valley, created between 1840 and 1880
during the heyday of Cornish mining. The stimulus was the
establishment of the Redruth & Chasewater Railway here from
1826 to connect the principal Cornish mining areas with the sea,
principally exporting copper ore and importing coal. A prospectus for a floating harbour and new town was published in 1832
by the Agar-Robertes of Lanhydrock, envisaging two symmetrical
triangles of streets either side of the market, school and church
between parallel roads running W–E along the side of the valley;
the curiously lop-sided form of the C19 settlement is the result
of only partial realization of this plan. The town was not simply
to house the industrial workforce but to appeal to the aspiring
middle classes, the prospectus describing the streets as 'possess-
ing a southern aspect on a gentle declivity ... commanding the
most picturesque scenery ... few situations present such advan-
tages for the *Retirement of the Wealthy*, or for the spirited *Enterprise
of Trading and Commercial Men*.' As a consequence, after the collapse of Cornish mining, Devoran was well placed to become a
residential community strategically situated between Falmouth
and Truro, a function it has subsequently retained.

ST JOHN, Devoran Lane. 1855 by *J. L. Pearson*. Promoted by the
vicar, Rev. Thomas Phillpotts, nephew of Bishop Phillpotts and
another example (cf. St Mary Biscovey, Par and Treverbyn) of
the latter's enthusiasm for church building in new industrial
communities. Comfortably sited in its leafy churchyard. A
design of striking verticality in restrained E.E. that nevertheless, as Anthony Quiney has noted, shows Pearson's 'hesitating
steps towards the High Victorian style'.* The SW tower rises
beside the steep gable of the S porch to a belfry with triple
openings on each face, surmounted by a pyramidal granite

---

*Quiney also draws parallels with St Germain, Amiens, and the church at Ober-
wesel which Pearson had just visited.

spire, above a corbel course decorated with masks. The chancel is a semi-octagonal apse, the roofs of nave and chancel very steep, the windows all lancets. The impressively lofty interior has a high arch-braced nave roof and a polygonal timber vault to the chancel carried on slender marble shafts on corbels. The FITTINGS are contemporary. – Painted polygonal PULPIT with blind arcade of pointed arches on short marble shafts. – Simple pine PEWS. – STAINED GLASS, a good ensemble, all of 1857, by *William Wailes*, mostly grisaille.

VICARAGE, next door to the church, *c.* 1850s, probably by *Pearson*. Faintly Tudor vernacular, with the porch set diagonally in the angle of a T-shaped plan and massive end stacks. First-floor oriel window on moulded granite corbel.

Former PRIMARY SCHOOL, Market Street. 1846, probably by *Pearson*, with major extensions of 1871, later C19 and early C20. Tudor style. Originally one large schoolroom with a smaller room to the l. and entrance, slightly projecting from the schoolroom gable-end, surmounted by a gabled bellcote (cf. the very similar example at Feock). The MARKET HOUSE, later incorporated into the school, is *c.* 1850; plain Italianate; two storeys with round-headed sash windows and doorways.

Neat mid-C19 terraces define the new town; the more prestigious ST JOHN'S TERRACE with its views over the water originally had servants quarters. Detached and semi-detached two-storey houses, of killas stone with granite dressings, sash windows under wide eaves, and enjoyably varied porches, verandas, conservatories and bay windows. Behind this street are the more modest, and more varied, houses of BELMONT TERRACE. In its own grounds opposite the church, DEVORAN HOUSE, early–mid C19. The home of John Taylor, the great mining entrepreneur, who was the driving force behind the Redruth & Chasewater Railway. At the bottom of MARKET STREET, with its modest terraced houses and former shops, QUAY ROAD retains some remnants of Devoran's industrial development. The long plain VILLAGE HALL was built as the railway workshop, *c.* 1854. Beyond, OLD QUAY HOUSE, also *c.* 1854, was the railway office and engine shed, the latter with its large round-headed entrance arch still visible. The line continued 1 m. further S to POINT QUAY, formerly the chief shipping place on the creek, with a tin-smelting works. The most intact of the three main quays is NARABO QUAY with its copper ORE HUTCHES and MOORING BOLLARDS.

DOWNDERRY

ST NICHOLAS. 1883–4 by *J. P. St Aubyn*. A less expensive church than Hessenford to which it should be compared. A competent-enough exterior, again not at all Cornish, but a dull interior.

DULOE

St Cuby. A church of exceptional and varied interest, prominently sited within a large raised oval churchyard or *lann* in the high country between the East and West Looe rivers. There was a church here by 1286, re-dedicated by Bishop Bronescombe in 1321. Its plan – nave, N and S transepts, N aisle, N chancel chapel, and tower not at the W end but attached to the S transept – is rare though not unique in Cornwall (cf. Mawgan-in-Pydar). The tower stands strong and solid, dating from the C13 and exceptionally well preserved, with sturdy two-stage buttresses at the foot and lancets in the W, S and E elevations; a Perp upper stage (possibly originally with a steeple) was removed during a restoration of 1861–3 by J. P. St Aubyn and replaced with a pyramidal roof. The S door into the tower, mid-C19 with engaged columns and simply moulded capitals, is within an opening with a pointed relieving arch above, which was probably made when the arch between transept and tower was blocked at an early date. The S transept walls, chancel, and E and W nave walls were wholly or substantially rebuilt by St Aubyn. The NE Colshull Chapel is remarkably elaborate for Cornwall, singled out on the exterior by buttresses, battlements, pinnacles and well-executed grotesques and gargoyles and a rood stair-tower projecting above the battlements; its tall windows are of unusually high quality with tracery with ornate cusped lights, the four-light E window specially good.

The interior also has richer architectural detail than usual, the four-bay N aisle arcade and the arch from the nave to the S transept of a variation on the standard Cornish design: it is in white St Stephen's granite and instead of the simple shaft-hollow-shaft profile of the piers there are two fillets l. and r. of the hollow (cf. St Martin-by-Looe, St Cleer and Lewannick). The two bays of the Colshull Chapel adjoining the chancel are a little lower but much more sumptuous, 'by far the most delicate and beautiful stone carving that Cornwall possesses' as E. H. Sedding observed. They are in Beer stone with exquisitely and deeply carved detail of flowers, leaves and grapes with heraldic devices and image niches, and include a green man with his tongue out looking heavenwards. The E arch rests on a large demi-figure of an angel, for this was the original position of the MONUMENT of Sir John Colshull †1483 so that his effigy looked up to it: he was one of the three most important men in Cornwall in the mid C15. The tomb is now at the E end of the chapel, a tomb-chest with shields in quatrefoils in circles in squares as its chief decorative motif (exactly the same as in the octagonal FONT); on the W side of the tomb this decoration is replaced by a Crucifixion. On the chest lies a thick plate of dark Purbeck marble, and on this is Sir John in armour. The carving of the figure, in limestone, is disappointing compared to that of the arcade. The unusually high quality

Duloe, St Cuby, memorial to Ann Smith, 1592. Drawing

of decoration of the chapel and tomb may represent a combination of different workshops, especially Exeter (cf. St Ive etc.). The chapel retains two-thirds of its PARCLOSE SCREEN, the other third having been moved to the N transept prior to 1861. The W side is clearly not in its original position, but incorporates armorial devices that prove its connection with the Colshull family. – STONE BASIN. Near N transept. Circular, possibly carved with figures of griffin and dolphin, by tradition from the nearby Holy Well of St Cuby (q.v.). – OAK

STALLS in the chancel, brought from Balliol College, Oxford, in 1937. – REREDOS. Late C19 by *Harry Hems* of Exeter. – STAINED GLASS. E chancel window by *Ward & Hughes*, 1871, with unusual narrative arrangement. Three in S wall of the nave, by *Percy Bacon Bros*, 1894–1906. In the Colshull Chapel, three scenes of the Good Samaritan by *Fouracre & Watson*, 1887. – OTHER MONUMENTS. Slates in the Colshull Chapel, one of the best groups in Cornwall: to Ann Smith, 1592, in Elizabethan dress; to two unknown wives and their children, also Elizabethan, and especially pretty in the way the figures kneel on cushions floating nowhere, with foliage trails as a surround; to John Killiow †1601 and his wife, tomb-chest with coat of arms; and to Mary Arundell, who died young in 1629 (Marie Arundell\Man a dry laurel\Man to the marigold compar'd may Bee\Man may be likened to the laurel tree\Both feede the eye, both please the optick sence\Both soone decay, both suddenly fleet hence\What then inferre you from her name but this\Man fades away, man a dry laurel is). – Henry Bewes, 1793 by *William Adam*. His best work: relief of a woman with portrait medallion of the dead man.

HOLY WELL, ½ m. down the hill on the r. side of the road to Looe. Charming well-house, built into the bank, the outer structure altered and partly rebuilt in 1822 when the road was constructed, leading to an inner cell or chapel, probably C15, with corbelled walls and a flat granite roof which is believed to have contained the circular basin now in the parish church (q.v.).

STONE CIRCLE, ¼ m. NE of the church, and delightfully situated across a field, is Cornwall's smallest Early Bronze Age stone circle, just 33 ft 6 in. (10.2 metres) across. Also the only circle wholly of quartz. Lichens now dull the eight stones, 1 to 2.4 metres high, whose largest four mark (roughly) the cardinal points. N stone broken during an attempted Victorian re-erection when a hedge bisecting the circle was removed. A Bronze Age urn containing bones found beside it may support a suggestion that the circle was an outsize kerb of a small barrow.

TRENANT PARK, 2 m. SE. Large house, subdivided in the C20, of possible early C17 origins, substantially remodelled in the early C18 and mid C19. H-shaped plan, with much C18 and C19 fenestration especially on the front elevation. Set in extensive parkland. The TEMPLE at Trenant Point, overlooking the entrance to Looe Harbour, is now in ruins.

DUPATH

3060

62   HOLY WELL. Set below a farm looking towards Kit Hill. One of the most loveable in Cornwall, built early C16 by the canons of St Germans and dedicated to St Ethelred, to serve as a baptistery and oratory, and constructed entirely of granite. Above

regular block walls the gabled roof is of courses of large slabs that form a steep pitched tunnel-vault supported by one transverse arch. Bellcote-like turret over the W door, a delightfully rustic version of that on the chapel at Cotehele, rising from a moulded base via sides of irregular single slabs to a battlemented cornice with four crocketed stumpy corner pinnacles and a taller central pinnacle. More pinnacles at the corners of the building, possibly later, two small slit openings in the side walls, and a two-light mullioned window in the E end. The water flows in from the W end, running in a narrow conduit to a sunk rectangular basin at the E end, and out into the open through the E wall into a moulded bowl.

EDEN PROJECT

0050

3 m. NE of St Austell

No visitor could fail to be astonished by their first glimpse of Eden. Hidden from view until the last moment, the spectacular scale and ambition of the Project are suddenly revealed: spreading out across the crater of the disused Bodelva china clay pit, almost 300 ft (91 metres) deep, the compellingly organic form of the structures seems to grow out of the ground and the steep cliff behind. It is a highly original architectural solution that implements a unique concept of how to explore and explain human interaction with the natural world, and one that is thrillingly successful.

The Project was conceived by *Tim Smit* (cf. Heligan) in the mid 1990s with initial architectural advice from *Jonathan Ball*. Such a large and complex scheme, depending on much pioneering technology as well as the use of recycled materials on a sustainable basis, required an inter-disciplinary approach to design and implementation, which began in 1998. It was led by *Nicholas Grimshaw & Partners* with *Anthony Hunt Associates* as structural engineers, *Ove Arup & Buro Happold* as service engineers, and *Land Use Consultants* for the masterplan and landscape design.

The initial phase comprised the two huge BIODOMES (the Humid Tropics Biome and the Warm Temperate Biome), constructed by *MERO* in 1998–2001. They are the largest greenhouses in the world, and the designers cited as influences Paxton's Great Conservatory at Chatsworth and Palm House at Kew; Buckminster Fuller's geodesic domes; and especially Frei Otto in Germany, who studied the interconnection of domes from the way soap bubbles form together and who designed the tent-like structures of the German Pavilion at Expo '67.

The domes are so engagingly reflective of natural forms that it is tempting to see them as consciously designed images of nature rather than what they are, drawing their inspiration not from the way nature looks but from how it works. Rather than two monumental structures, each is composed of four inter-connecting spherical caps of differing sizes, made out of two-dimensional hexagons and pentagons. The structural components are of tubular steel joined by spherical nodes, with an outer compressive grid linked to an inner tensile grid, and scaled according to the size of each cap. The result is an amazingly light structure for such enormous spans, made possible because of the then novel use for glazing of ETFE (ethylene tetrafluoroethylene plastic) in air-filled triple-layered pillows. It is these that give the domes their unique appearance. Especially in the largest of the domes (the Humid Tropical Dome), the combination of structure and tropic planting with a waterfall cascading from the high back wall is breathtaking.

Adjacent to the domes is the CORE (education centre) of 2005, also by the same teams, where the role of plants in the ecosphere is explained. Markedly different in its form and materials, it is an equally arresting design, this time echoing the spiral pattern arrangement of seeds in a pine-cone or sun-flower. It falls across three levels, each having a ground floor, the roof springing from a central trunk, of criss-crossing timber arches supporting each other, the roof grid dipping to ground level at three equidistant points around the perimeter where it terminates in concrete feet. The roof of copper panels has openable roof-lights taking the form of small pyramids popping up from the roof surface. At the centre, almost hidden, a monumental seed-shaped SCULPTURE (2006) by *Peter Randall Page*, of granite from the De Lank quarry, St Breward, intended by the sculptor as 'fossil and seed … uniting concept and form, object and structure, art and architecture in a unique and cohesive whole': it does so.

The ancillary buildings of the site are deliberately under-stated, well judged and elegant, including the turf-roofed LINK between the biomes and the ARRIVAL BUILDING with its walls of rammed earth. Holding the vast site together is subtle landscaping with a network of apparently meandering paths that all lead to the centrepieces of this extraordinary achievement.

EGLOSHAYLE

The N bank of the Camel was favoured as a place of residence long before the later C19 rise of Wadebridge, and the parish is rich in manors and larger houses like Croan and Pencarrow (qq.v.). Egloshayle's history as a bridge town is nicely reflected in the long row of pleasant C18 and C19 houses and cottages overlooking the estuary that joins the bridge with the parish church.

ST PETROC. A noble W tower 82 ft (25 metres) high, especially
impressive from the other side of the estuary, of three stages
with buttresses set back from the corners, battlemented parapets, crocketed finials and a NE stair-turret. It was built *c.* 1477
in the time of John Lovebond, vicar from 1461 (†1477) and
builder of the bridge (*see* Wadebridge). The W door is of
unusual interest: it is of Catacleuse with roll mouldings in the
jambs in the form of ascending and descending serpents and
shield-carrying angel labels, to the l. carved with three hearts
banded together with a ribbon and inscribed 'Loveybond', and
to the r. with the arms of Kestell impaling Ravenscroft (cf. the
less elaborate but similar Cataceluse W door at St Mabyn).
Nave and chancel, N transept, part N chancel aisle, S aisle and
S porch. Of the C12–C14 church some masonry in the N wall,
the N doorway with its flanking two-light windows of *c.* 1300,
and possibly the E wall of the transept. The S aisle, begun 1529,
is of exceptionally fine proportions, of six bays with piers of
the usual Cornish profile, simple moulded capitals and pointed
arches; its range of Perp windows, four-light in the S side, five-
light in the E end, is lovely, the tall E window exceptionally
grand for Cornwall. The aisle retains its original finely carved
wagon roof with richly decorated purlins and ribs and twelve
angel corbels surviving from the original forty. A similar N aisle
may have been intended but only two and a half arches opening
up the transept were completed before the Reformation. Of
the restoration by *J. P. St Aubyn* of 1867 the arch-braced roofs
of nave, chancel and transept, E and W windows and furnishings. – Pedestal STOUP, by S door, Norman. – FONT. Norman,
Purbeck table-top type: the square bowl has plain blank arcading on the sides, restored in the C19. – PULPIT. Octagonal,
Caen stone, early C16, with carved shields, etc. and some more
emblems referring to John Loveybond, with remains of earlier
colouring on W and E sides. – STAINED GLASS. Striking E
window by *G. Cruttwell* and *T. Hamilton,* 1930; the heavenly
city etc. Forceful design with strong figures and colours. – Nave
two-light windows by *William Morris & Co.* of Westminster,
1952, and *J. Hall,* 1956. – N transept, three-light window
by *Francis Skeat,* 1980, St Nicholas with swamped boat. –
MONUMENTS. Dame Barbara Molesworth †1735. Large, of
white and grey marble, with bust, and obelisk in relief behind;
evidently of metropolitan workmanship, although the inscription says, not very complimentarily: 'To deliver to Posterity a
Description of the Beautys of her Mind would be as equally
Vain as the Sculptor's Attempt in the above resemblance of
her face. The one was superior to Art, the other to Imagination.' – Sir A. D. Molesworth †1824 by *Sir Richard Westmacott.*
– Also minor Neoclassical wall monuments, for example by
Shepherd of Plymouth. – Large good slate slab and back plate
to the Kestell family late C16 etc., in base of tower.
  The CHURCHYARD has an excellent range of C18 and C19
slate headstones and two medieval CROSS-HEADS outside the
porch.

GONVENA HOUSE. Prominently set above the estuary near the
N end of the bridge. An impressive three-storey five-window
front in Flemish bond red brick under a hipped roof with
end stacks. Built *c.* 1790 for Edward Fox, a Wadebridge merchant. Smart details such as rubbed brick flat arches with
dressed stone key blocks and original C18 sashes with crown
glass.

THREE HOLE CROSS, 1½ m. NE. Probably pre-Conquest, the
wheel-head pierced with three holes, the fourth only partly cut
through, like St Piran's Cross, St Piran's Oratory (q.v.).

KILLIBURY CASTLE, 1½ m. NE. Small Iron Age HILLFORT
commanding prehistoric ridgeway routes: the Wadebridge road
passes through the original entrances. Two close-spaced ramparts and ditches. Rectilinear outwork guarding the w entrance.
Excavations on the s part established third century B.C. date
and found timber round-house and storage structures.

CROAN. *See* p. 168.

PENCARROW. *See* p. 401.

WASHAWAY. *See* p. 694.

2080

EGLOSKERRY

ST KERIA. Standing in the middle of the village within a probable *lann*. There must have been an important Norman church
here, of which the N wall and N transept survive. The blocked
N doorway has a tympanum with a dragon snapping at its own
tail. w tower C16, of three stages and unbuttressed. s porch of
ashlar granite with wagon roof. C15 s aisle, most of the window
tracery renewed in a severe restoration of 1887 by *Otho B. Peter*.
The interior has more evidence of the Norman building.
Another tympanum was found in the s wall during the restoration and was re-sited above the Perp s door. Also a plain FONT,
with cable moulding at the top, and a PISCINA s of the altar
(a rarity). It is a block capital on a short shaft, with a little
palm-leaf decoration in the corners between the characteristic
lunettes of the block capital. Finally the jambs of the transept
arch towards the nave are also Norman. C15 s aisle five-bay
arcade of standard Cornish design. Much of the window
tracery renewed in the restoration. – STAINED GLASS. Chancel
E, 1886 by *Percy Bacon Bros.* – MONUMENT to a layman, in
niche at the E end of the aisle. Alabaster effigy of high quality
but in a bad state of preservation.

TREGEARE, 2 m. w. Built *c.* 1790, with mid- and late C19
additions and alterations after a fire in 1983. Two-storey,
symmetrical 2:1:2 bays, outer bays advanced. Central Ionic
portico. Late C18 interior details include plaster cornices,
open-well stair, and first-floor landing screen of fluted Ionic
columns.

PENHEALE. *See* p. 407.

ERTH BARTON

3050

3 m. SW of Saltash

A medieval manor house but in its present form almost entirely
C17 with major C20 extensions and alterations. Two-storey and
L-shaped with two-storey porch and mullioned windows
including a six-light window to the hall. The C20 work incorporated a former farm building to the r. and added a round
stair-tower at the rear, the latter by *Lewis Lightfoot*. To the l. of
the house a CHAPEL above an undercroft with dressings of
Tarten Down stone. Late C13, the earliest extant domestic
chapel in Cornwall. Three-light E window with the simplest
tracery under a straight-sided pointed arch, two trefoil-headed
lancets in the N wall, another in the S, and a PISCINA. The S
wall retains fragments of WALL PAINTING showing parts of
two figures and a diaper background.

ETHY

1050

½ m. NE of Lerryn

Finely set in a landscaped park sloping down towards the River
Lerryn; a sheltered walled garden behind with rich ornamental
planting. Of medieval origins, the estate was developed in the
C16 by the Courtneys of Devon. The present house, with some
likeness to Colquite, is a mid-C19 remodelling of an C18 house
that had similarities with Carnanton and may possibly have
been by *John Eveleigh* of Lostwithiel. Plain two-storey SE front
of seven bays, the centre flanked by giant pilasters: there is C18
brickwork behind at least some of the rendered elevations.
Good C18 features in several rooms, especially plasterwork.

FALMOUTH

8030

Every facet of Falmouth's rich and absorbing character reflects
the sea and the town's splendid position near the mouth of the
Fal estuary and Carrick Roads, one of the finest deep-water
havens in the world. Yet medieval urban settlement was sheltered
further inland around the estuary's upper navigable limits at
Penryn, Tregony and Truro, with St Mawes the only significant
coastal settlement, and it was not until the late 1530s, when the
strategic value of the Fal was realized, that the building of the
artillery forts at Pendennis and St Mawes created the defensive
preconditions for the founding of Falmouth as a C17 new town.

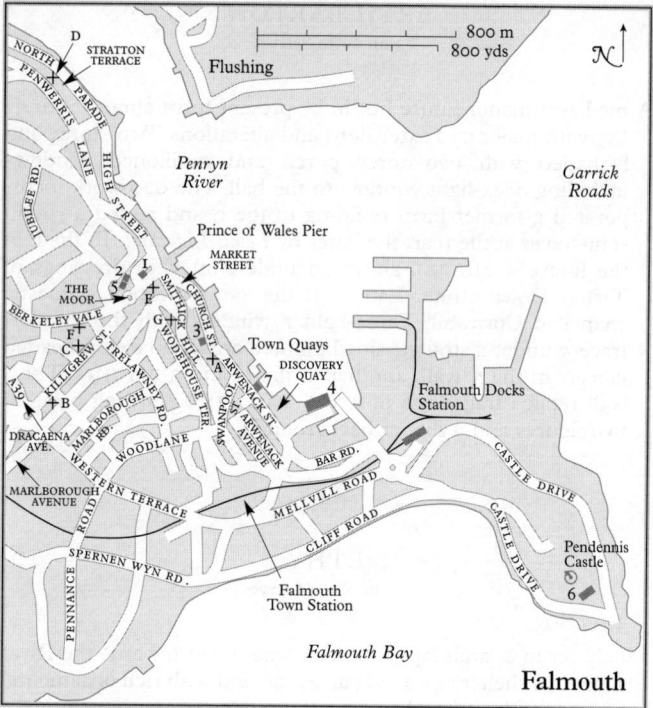

Falmouth

A   King Charles the Martyr
B   All Saints
C   St Mary Immaculate (R.C.)
D   St Michael
E   Falmouth Methodist
    Church
F   United Reformed Church
G   Synagogue (former)

1   Town Hall and Court (former)
2   Falmouth Art Gallery and
    Library
3   Falmouth Arts Centre
4   National Maritime Museum
    Cornwall
5   Post Office
6   Maritime Rescue Centre
7   Custom House

Mid-C16 maps of the area occupied by modern Falmouth record only Arwenack, an estate with a manor house just NW of the Pendennis promontory acquired by the Killigrew family in the late C14; and it was the early C17 Killigrews who saw the potential of this W shore of the estuary as a victualling base and shelter for shipping. Other than Arwenack, the earliest settlement, known as Smythycke, was around a small cove and beach at the sea end of the Moor, Market Strand and Smithick Hill. It must have developed quickly because in 1613 Helston, Penryn and Truro petitioned against a proposal for a new town, and by 1620 the Killigrews were asking for an additional six inns. After the Civil War, Sir Peter Killigrew obtained permission for the transfer of customs from Penryn to Falmouth, a weekly market, and two annual fairs, and in 1661 a royal charter was granted for

Smythyke to become the town of Falmouth, with a mayor and corporation.

The town expanded rapidly along the shoreline, first s, probably to bring development closer to Arwenack. Church Street was laid out in the early 1660s with the erection of the new parish church of King Charles the Martyr, and the Town Quays – Custom House, King Charles and North Quays – were built c. 1670 with Arwenack Street behind. By the late C17 the town had also extended N to form the present High Street, associated with the rise of the hugely important Packet Service* from 1688, which was concentrated on the N quays, especially Greenbank. This trade ushered in a period of sustained growth right through the C18 and into the 1820s, with Falmouth established as an international mercantile centre, including a substantial pilchard trade with Italy. By the early C18 its population at 2,000 made it Cornwall's largest settlement and by 1801 it had reached 4,850, still the most populous.

It is this thin shoreline spread of the town, hemmed in by the steep hill behind, from Penwerris in the N to the docks at the s, that characterizes Falmouth in C17–C19 descriptions as 'one very long strete stretched out†', and is still immediately tangible today. The pattern of residential development was first of small courts of houses off narrow opes from the main streets, and later of terraces on the steep slopes behind the shoreline, the earliest built to obtain views across the harbour like those facing Flushing at Penwerris and Bar Terrace at the s end, with subsequent development infilling behind. Growth was arrested when the packet trade declined in the 1820s with the advent of steam-powered shipping and the eventual transfer of the service to Liverpool and Southampton, but boomed again when the arrival of the railway from Truro in 1863 sparked Falmouth's rejuvenation as a major dock town and a seaside and residential resort. Two dry docks were built in 1859, and there was also major C20 expansion in the 1930s and 1960s, the latter including the Queen Elizabeth dock, capable of handling vessels of 90,000 tons. The resort town grew around its s end and the beaches overlooking Falmouth Bay, beginning with the Falmouth Hotel (completed in 1865), with easy access to the walks and gardens on the slopes of Pendennis. Castle Drive, one of the most spectacular coastal drives in England, was laid out in the same year, Cliff Road was constructed soon after, and other parks and gardens with rich tropic planting were provided generously elsewhere in the town.

A surge in population from 9,400 in 1861 to over 12,000 by 1881 was reflected in a suburban building boom. Between 1840 and 1880 a grid of terraced streets was laid out over the hilltop area from Killigrew Street in the N to Woodlane in the s: Albert

---

*Falmouth was preferred by the Post Office as a packet port to Fowey or Plymouth. The packet ships first carried only to Spain and Portugal but later expanded to the Mediterranean, North and South America, and the West Indies.
†Davies Gilbert, *The Parochial History of Cornwall, founded on the manuscripts of Mr William Hals and Mr Thomas Tonkin* (1788).

Cottages with its pointed arched doors and windows, Cambridge Place, and Florence Place and Terrace are especially pretty examples. There was also some rebuilding in the town centre, and a plethora of institutional buildings both in the centre and to serve the new suburbs, including churches by J. D. Sedding and J. A. Hansom. In the 1890s a new centre was created in The Moor, with major new public buildings around a wide civic space, a striking contrast with the narrower shoreline streets.

The C20 saw major changes that dramatically extended the spread of the town, and, at over 33,000 with Penryn, it is now the third largest in Cornwall. The most pervasive later C20 change has affected the historic shoreline with residential developments comprehensively replacing the distinctive waterfront buildings of fish cellars, warehouses, rope stores and sail lofts. But, with the notable exception of the alien presence of the Ships and Castles leisure centre on the N slopes of Pendennis, historic Falmouth has been spared major disruption, and the town can claim one of the county's best modern buildings, the National Maritime Museum Cornwall, that triumphantly reasserts Falmouth's enduring dependence on the sea.

CHURCHES

CHURCH OF KING CHARLES THE MARTYR, Church Street. Built 1661–5 by Sir Peter Killigrew, part funded by Charles II. The oddly diminutive W tower, strikingly narrower in its E–W than its N–S dimension, was built about 1684, the top stage and pinnacles added in 1800. The interior, unlike any other Cornish parish church, is a synthesis of the late C17 original modified by a succession of major later interventions, notably by *E. H. Sedding* in 1897–8. The nave was originally 66 ft by 66 ft (20 by 20 metres) and separated into nave and aisles by tall granite columns with Ionic capitals in plaster. In the strangest contrast to this classical splendour are the windows, in two tiers of typically Cornish Perp design. A chancel was added in 1684, but this was replaced in 1813, lengthening the church by about one-third. Its Venetian E window has full Ionic details. Galleries were inserted in 1686, 1695 and 1702, somewhat spoiling the simplicity of the former interior. Sedding added side chapels to the chancel and a S organ chamber, which entailed the addition of the marble columns and E responds of the chancel, copying the 1662 granite columns and moving the two existing easternmost further E to make the bays equal. He also removed the N and S galleries; rebuilt the W gallery; completely re-roofed and re-ceiled the church; inserted the Ionic entablature above the columns;* and re-seated throughout. The N porch is by *William White*, 1853. – PULPIT, incorporating C16 and C17 English and German carvings acquired by the Rev. William Coope. – SCREEN. The central part of the base is from St Paul,

79

---

*An enlarged and extended version of the original.

Penzance, where it served as a communion rail, surmounted by late C19 to early C20 wrought-iron work. – CREDENCE TABLE. 1759, with the Killigrew arms. – The hexagonal FONT has similar carved detail of the same date. – STAINED GLASS. Lady Chapel window incorporating figures by *Robert Morrow*, *c.* 1850 – E window by *Taylor* and *Clifden*, 1913 – S aisle by *Wippell*, designed by *C. Atchley* with interesting Cornish iconography and inscription. – MONUMENTS. Thomas Corker †1700. Prettily written inscription on a convex oval shield. – Richard Lockyer †1789. Standing mourning woman by an urn against a dark obelisk: by *Paty* of Bristol. – Capt. James Bull †1821, exactly the same composition in reverse, by *J. Isbell* of Truro. – Rev. Lewis Matthias †1837 by *Jacob* & *Thomas Olver* of Falmouth. Attached to the NE vestry and on the street, the CHURCH INSTITUTE, 1925 by *C. Russell Corfield*.

ALL SAINTS, Killigrew Street. 1887–90 by *J. D Sedding* in an E.E. style and considered by the architect to be among his best work: Betjeman's verdict that it is 'almost a triumph' is apt. The exterior is more impressive than loveable, characterized by the strong E and W ends with five lancets and two bold buttresses to the former and three lancets and four buttresses to the latter, very much in Sedding's style. But the interior is profoundly satisfying: a spacious and lofty nave of almost cathedral-like proportions, enhanced by flanking arcades of very tall piers connected to the narrow aisles by round arches which spring from the piers without capitals, its simplicity a contrast to the richly adorned E end; the composition is so serene that the pointed Gothic windows of the aisles seen through the semicircles of the arcades seem slightly odd. The fittings of the E end are of excellent quality, many later and designed by *E. H. Sedding*: large and elaborate stone and alabaster REREDOS, 1909, surmounted by PAINTED PANELS, 1924 by *L. A. Pownall* of Falmouth. He also designed and made the striking STAINED GLASS E window, 1912, one of his first works, an unusually glorious and celebratory depiction of the Apocalypse, and N transept window, 1923, a vivid St John the Baptist. Pretty cobweb glazing to the aisle windows. Tower window by *Clayton & Bell*, 1893. Lady Chapel ALTAR, 1947 by *Violet Pinwill*.

ST MARY IMMACULATE (R.C.), Killigrew Street. 1868 by *J. A. Hansom*, tower and spire 1881 by *J. S. Hansom*, baptistery and porch 1908 to the original designs. A blend of Gothic and Burgundian Romanesque producing picturesque elevations with deliberately irregular eaves lines, window types and sizes, and different motifs, supremely expressed in the eye-catching tower. It rises from a square, buttressed lower stage through an octagonal second stage to an arcade of round-arched louvred lights at the upper stage, and is surmounted by a dressed granite spire with steep gabled lucarnes, accompanied almost to full height by a circular stair-turret with conical roof. The effect, as intended, is very French, not English. – Two STAINED GLASS windows in exquisite mosaic in the baptistery

106

by *Father Charles Norris* of Buckfast Abbey, important early examples of the artist's work. w rose by *A. K. Nicholson*, 1897.

St Michael, Stratton Terrace, Penwerris. 1827 by *R. Crout*. A simple Commissioners' church in Tudor Gothic with a curious castellated façade with embattled octagonal turrets and corbelled central turret towards the water. Very simple interior with open-well staircase to panel-fronted gallery on unfluted columns. – Stained glass. e window by *Fouracre & Son*, 1904. Attached parish hall, 1926–32 by *Cowell, Drewitt & Wheatly*, an odd contrast in large concrete blocks.

Falmouth Methodist Church, Killigrew Street. Rebuilt 1874–6, twice bombed in the Second World War, reconstructed 1956 with three-storey interior. What matters is the street façade, one of the grandest expressions of Methodism in Cornwall, of familiar tripartite form and Italianate style but here on a monumental scale with imposing presence. – Stained glass. Light of the World, 1956, and war memorial, 1958, by *John Hall & Sons Ltd* of Bristol and London.

United Reformed church, Berkeley Vale. Built 1867 as a Bible Christian Chapel. Classical style, symmetrical pedimented front, the central three bays broken forward with three linked round-headed lights and two round-headed doorways. Complete galleried interior, a rare survival.

Former Synagogue, Smithick Hill. 1816. One of the oldest surviving synagogues in England, in use until 1879. The front elevation is of red brick with burnt headers and granite quoins. Simple, rectangular plan. Large sash windows with spoke fanlight heads. It bears striking similarities to contemporary Nonconformist chapels.

PUBLIC BUILDINGS

Former Town Hall and Court, The Moor. Now a bar. 1864 by *Charles Reeves*, Surveyor to the County Courts in England and Wales. It replaced the former Town Hall in High Street (q.v.). A quirky Italianate stucco composition around a taller central two-storey range that rises to a squat attic storey, the attic windows squeezed between grouped consoles to the moulded eaves cornice. Flanking lower ranges. The curved corner doorway is the principal feature of the former Town Hall with flanking Tuscan half-columns and dentilled cornice surmounted by a royal coat of arms. Fine cantilevered stone staircase inside. Fire station in matching style added 1895, on Webber Street.

The Municipal Buildings (Art Gallery and Library), The Moor. 1896 by *W. H. Tresidder* as the Passmore Edwards Free Library. One of the most stylistically eclectic buildings of Passmore Edwards benefactions in Cornwall, here with a combination of Italianate, Renaissance, Neoclassical and Flemish motifs. Two-storey symmetrical 1:3:1 layout, the cross-wings with Venetian windows and surmounted by finials, flanking a central columned, loggia surmounted by a squat balustrade.

Central octagonal lantern. The interior retains most of its
original layout and features. – STAINED GLASS. Three windows,
2009, one over the staircase, two in the gallery shop, in striking
abstract designs inspired by Matisse's chapel at Vence. They
originated as part of a community project engaging *Falcare*
(formerly Mencap) and the *Kerrier Pupil Referral Unit*, the glass
made by *Mike Welch*. A SPOT TILE WALL, with tiles designed
by *Linda Styles* with children's imprints in the centre of each
tile, was an associated project.

FALMOUTH ARTS CENTRE, Church Street. Formerly the Royal
Cornwall Polytechnic. Refronted and altered by *George Wightwick c.* 1835–6. Another Greek Revival façade of two storeys,
symmetrical, three bays, the first floor recessed with fluted
Doric columns and triglyphs to frieze, and original sashes. It
fronts a building with an exceptionally interesting history.* It
was constructed with a large hall to stage exhibitions with the
rooms at the front housing a public dispensary, savings bank,
and subscription library.

NATIONAL MARITIME MUSEUM CORNWALL, Discovery
Quay. 2003 by *Long & Kentish*. A spectacular building that
realizes the potential of a prominent and challenging site where
the town meets the docks. It is at once profoundly contextual
yet always dramatic and surprising: the memory of the ship-
builders' and timber merchants' sheds that previously occupied the site is immediately evoked in the English oak that
clads the whole building, yet the design is entirely contemporary. From the town the building is skilfully articulated into tall
shed-like components that culminate in a free-standing tower
at the N end; from the sea its large scale is dramatically
expressed in a vast monopitch slate roof, laid in diminishing
courses, that spreads out obliquely like a giant sail above the
water. Outside, a walkway wraps around the building from the
docks to the harbour, with water lapping against its walls;
inside the water laps against the huge glass windows in the
Tidal Gallery at the base of the tower. To offer further engagement with the elements, the walls of the main Daylight Gallery
are open in summer. This gallery is the epitome of the arresting
spaciousness that pervades the building, enhanced by a curved
wall of beechwood panels like the hull of an ocean liner. The
architects' conceptual consistency is equally evident in the
planning, design and cladding of the two neighbouring buildings that graciously enclose the large yet comfortable square
through which the museum is approached.

Former POST OFFICE, The Moor. 1930 by *A. Bullock* of *H. M.
Office of Works* (cf. Bodmin and St Austell). A tall, dignified
three-storey building, Neo-Georgian but with Arts and Crafts

---

*The Royal Polytechnic Society was founded in 1833 by Anna-Maria and Caroline,
daughters of Robert Were Fox, who, as Quakers, sought to create means by which
the artisans of the Perran Foundry (q.v.) could exhibit their ideas. It was the first
in Britain to use the word 'Polytechnic' as meaning 'of many arts and techniques'.
It pioneered many inventions, including photography, and made an important
contribution to the Industrial Revolution.

touches, somewhat reminiscent of Clough Williams-Ellis. The ground floor's rusticated granite is carried up over the round-headed windows and central door, with Gibbs surrounds to the first-floor windows, hipped dormers to the steep roof, and a square latticed central lantern. A worthy C20 contribution to the gravitas of the centre and an excellent example of Office of Works contextualization at this period.

FALMOUTH SCHOOL (formerly Trescobeas School), Trescobeas Road. 1953–8 by *Lyons, Israel & Ellis* (associate architect *Allan Park*). A fine example of a school designed on uncompromisingly Modernist lines, its bold monolithic form following the contours down the slope of the strong topography of its site so that it becomes four storeys at its lower end under an even roof level. It is tough, too, in its materials: grey blockwork and reconstructed stone with china clay aggregate. It seems at home in its setting.

FIRE STATION, Trescobeas Road. Of *c.* 1970 by the *County Architect's Department*, job architect *Mike Way*. Functional with neat, regular shapes and consistent detailing in light grey fine textured brickwork relieved by the four large red doors. Clearly influenced by brick Scandinavian buildings of the period.

MARITIME RESCUE CO-ORDINATION CENTRE. Below the tip of Pendennis Castle on Pendennis Point. 1981 by *PSA Architects* for H.M. Coastguard. Suitably designed like a military look-out, the overhanging roof shielding the continuous windows of the control room on the upper floor, with reflections and glare further reduced by inward-sloping glazing.

TOWN QUAYS: KING CHARLES QUAY fronts the foreshore, NORTH QUAY has a slender hammerhead end, and CUSTOM HOUSE QUAY runs parallel SE with a N return to enclose the harbour. The vertically set killas stone quay walls are of 1670, with later granite ashlar sections and several flights of steps. Running down from QUAY STREET on to North Quay the three ranges of the MARINE HOTEL, SHIPWRIGHTS and CHAIN LOCKER, probably part C18 but mostly early to mid-C19: their irregular elevations form picturesque backdrops to the harbour with the rear of the Custom House and Harbourmaster's Office (*see* below).

PRINCE OF WALES PIER. Only a small vertically set killas stone NW section of the C17 quay walls survives, the rest extended and refaced in granite in 1873, and the pier built 1903–5 and reconstructed 1951, of pioneering Hennebique reinforced concrete construction on drum piers, to the designs of *L. G. Mouchel*.

CUSTOM HOUSE, Arwenack Street and Custom House Quay. 1814 and, like several other public buildings of this period in the town, in the Greek Revival style.* Severe single-storey stucco front to Arwenack Street with Doric portico, plain frieze with royal arms in the centre, and triangular pediment

---

*There are strong similarities with John Foulston's work at Devonport and Tavistock of the same period.

above the parapet cornice. The original round-headed arched doorway with spoked fanlight is centrally placed within the portico behind iron railings between the columns. The rear elevation, single-storey over a basement, is a seven-window range with original sashes, the l. end enclosed by courtyard walls giving access to the KING'S PIPE, *c.* 1814, a three-storey brick flue on a granite ashlar plinth for the burning of contraband tobacco. To the l. of the Arwenack Street front is the HARBOURMASTER'S OFFICE, an early C19 town house and later shop of double-depth plan with a two-storey three-window front with original sashes and a similar rear elevation over a basement.

PERAMBULATIONS

1. The south waterfront and adjoining streets: Grove Place, Arwenack Street and Church Street

The obvious place to start is the KILLIGREW MONUMENT in Grove Place, a severely plain pyramid of dressed granite erected to Sir Peter Killigrew in 1737 and re-sited (for the second time) in 1871. It stands opposite ARWENACK MANOR, the much reduced, altered and subdivided remains of the Killigrews' great house, of medieval origins and possibly fortified but substantially rebuilt by Sir John Killigrew in 1571. What survives is fragmentary and much disguised by C18–C20 rebuilding, but it was probably originally of E-shaped plan of which the far l. wing has vanished, with the r. hand part fully enclosed by a curtain wall. Most prominent from Grove Place are the C18 front ranges, with a semicircular stair-turret between the cross-wing and the front wing. Some impression of the former grandeur of the house can be gained from the surviving front wall of the great hall with its flanking semi-octagonal turrets and a pair of enormous six-light transomed-and-mullioned windows with king mullions. Other notable survivals are the C16–C17 four-light oriel window on the front elevation and C17 fireplaces inside.

To the estuary side of Arwenack are DISCOVERY QUAY and the National Maritime Museum of Cornwall (*see* Public Buildings). To the E, beyond Bar Road, is BAR TERRACE, a nice example of the residential evolution of the C18 and C19 town, once commanding a view across the water; pretty, with a nice variety of porches, and occasionally quirky, especially Nos. 3–5, paired houses with extraordinary giant end columns. PORT PENDENNIS, a large late C20 residential development of a banality that could be anywhere but belongs nowhere, occupies a large site between here and the docks.

Back to Grove Place. Nos. 1–7 a terrace of large stucco houses of the 1840s, of double-depth plan and three storeys over basements, their porches with square columns and anthemion-decorated pediments. Next is BANK HOUSE, 1788, the large stucco town house of Robert Were Fox (cf. Falmouth Arts

Centre). Three storeys and five-bay front, remodelled and refronted *c.* 1868. Then Nos. 1–3 BANK PLACE, a smart red brick contrast with all the stucco, *c.* 1770. Designed as a unified front, each house with a symmetrical five-window front, the central house with three central bays broken forward and pedimented. The overall impression is, however, curiously institutional rather than domestic.

To the l. up SWANPOOL STREET, the substantial late C17 gatepiers that formed the approach to Arwenack Manor by ARWENACK AVENUE. Back into ARWENACK STREET, developed after Church Street from the later C17 as part of the Killigrews' efforts to pull commercial expansion towards their end of their new town. It is a mix of modest C18 and C19 two- or three-storey former town houses interspersed with more substantial buildings. The eyecatchers are the Custom House leading down to the Town Quays (*see* above) and No. 48, a pair of splendid red brick town houses of *c.* 1770, built for George Crocker Fox (1727–1782). The symmetrical 2:1:2 bay front has a central canted bay carried up to a turned balustrade, flanked by open-pedimented half-column pilastered doorways with panelled reveals and round-arched cobweb fanlights. The houses are approached by granite steps with wreathed wrought-iron handrails. Towards the N end of the street, No. 14, *c.* 1870 with a granite ashlar front in Italianate style; next door, No. 11, a late C18 town house in stucco with channelled rustication, flat arches and dropped keys to the four-window front. As the street elbows around its junction with Church Street, Nos. 7–9, a good terrace of three early C19 town houses with later C19 shops with pretty glazing bar patterns.

Now into CHURCH STREET, with the parish church of King Charles the Martyr (*see* Churches) set high above. Developed as the first street of the new town, and now its most architecturally interesting street with a rich mix of former town houses and institutional buildings, together with many good C19 and early C20 shopfronts, a feature of the town generally. Next to the church, the KINGS HEAD HOTEL, C17–C18, remodelled and extended mid C19, with a three-storey porch in incised stucco. No. 26, an imposingly tall three-storey Italianate building, the ground floor with three round arches, was purpose built as the post office in 1867. Next door is the Falmouth Arts Centre, formerly the Royal Polytechnic Society (*see* Public Buildings). Opposite, No. 34, built as the National Provincial Bank *c.* 1870 in a richly detailed Italianate style in Plymouth limestone with Hamstone dressings. Nos. 36 and 37 were built as a grander late C18 house with an ashlar stone front. Nos. 47 and 48, a pair of C18 stucco town houses, with quoin strips and modillion cornice under a deep soffit. Between Nos. 48 and 49, UPTON SLIP, steps down to the river offering a good sense of the old waterfront. Nos. 49 and 50 are a pair of C19 two-storey stucco houses, No. 50 with an unusually detailed late C19 shopfront. No. 53 projects into the street on fluted Doric columns. It was opened in 1826 as the Falmouth Subscription Rooms, a meeting place for local merchants and visiting ships' officers; some of the columns were removed when the shopfronts were inserted. Opposite, the former FREEMASONS HALL, 1885, and SAVINGS BANK, 1887, in granite ashlar with rusticated pilasters; the oldest purpose-built lodge in Cornwall. On the other side the especially jaunty bow windows of Nos. 54 and 55. ST GEORGES ARCADE opposite was built as a cinema in 1912 with enjoyably exuberant swagged decoration to the street frontage.

Another distinct elbow marks the junction of Church Street with MARKET STREET. It starts with the former ROYAL HOTEL on the w side, of three-storey elevations to the corner site with giant end pilasters and a large pedimented window with four Doric half-columns to the upper floor. But does not sustain such grand pretensions and the street is now mostly mid- to late C19 fronts with some early to mid-C20 rebuilding. Off the w side is an ope to BELLS COURT, an intriguing survival of an early court with C17 houses of some substance, the l. house with original two-storey porch on Tuscan columns, the r. house mostly rebuilt c. 1980. The street now ends ignominiously with the shoddy 1980s replica of the former KING'S HOTEL that turns the corner to the Prince of Wales Pier, the large Doric porch of the original unconvincingly attached over the street.

2. The North Quays, High Street and Penwerris

Begin at the Prince of Wales Pier (*see* Public Buildings). Arrival by sea offers the best appreciation of the long waterfront spread of the C17–C19 town and its many quays and slips stretching N towards Greenbank. Of the area around MARKET STRAND that was the early settlement of Smythyke, the only indication is an insignificant set of steps on the N side that marks the earliest road from here to Arwenack. On the sw side are steps to SMITHICK HILL, a street that preserves the old settlement's name and includes the former synagogue (*see* Churches) near the top. The present buildings are of late C18 or early C19 appearance, mostly modest three-storey stucco with simple moulded details.

Market Strand merges imperceptibly into HIGH STREET, developed by the later C17 in association with the packet trade quays: evidence of c. 1700 quays can be found at the foot of the several opes leading off the waterfront side. The middle of the street suffered a major fire in 1862 and was rebuilt 10 ft (3 metres) wider. It is a pleasingly coherent street of mostly three-storey stucco houses and shops of early to late C19 appearance: No. 42 has a C19 cast-iron shopfront. Of the more substantial buildings, No. 51 is an altered survival of a probably late C17 town house with good internal contemporary features including a moulded ribbed plaster ceiling and stairwell with heavy barley-twist balusters. Enclosing CAMES YARD are mid-C19 walls and gatepiers to the former stable yard of a brewery. The outstanding building is the OLD TOWN HALL (now a shop), built as a Congregational chapel *c.* 1700, one of the earliest purpose-built Nonconformist chapels in Cornwall. The digni-fied tall single-storey front is of painted brick with rusticated stucco quoins, Gibbs-surround central door and round-headed windows. The interior retains fine C18 features including a coved and moulded plaster ceiling, the centre in deep relief. Opposite, the STAR AND GARTER INN with fine tiled lettering advertising harbour views. Such a good street deserves better than the feeble GATEWAY building at its N end, as insubstantial as a stage set but not as convincing, part of a large late C20 development striding down to the waterfront where the new blends more successfully with the old.

Beyond are GREENBANK and PENWERRIS, and some of Fal-mouths's most enjoyable buildings in terraces looking out over the quays and the Penryn River to Flushing. Many of the houses were built as packet commanders' houses, like the ROYAL CORNWALL YACHT CLUB, 1810–30, two-storey and double-depth plan with Doric porch and sash windows. The GREENBANK HOTEL, with pretty late C19 veranda, was one of the earliest catering for visitors. GREENBANK GARDENS, opened 1914, occupy the site of the workshops of *William Olver*, Falmouth's leading builder until the mid C19, who prob-ably built DUNSTANVILLE TERRACE, developed from *c.* 1800. Engagingly varied detail, many houses embellished with later bays, bows and porches: the most elaborate No. 10, a good early C19 three-storey house in Pentewan stone, the front remodelled *c.* 1910 with a central first-floor bow window with moulded cornice over a bowed glazed porch. On into STRAT-TON TERRACE, a group of gracious *c.* 1810 stucco villas like No. 14, the end pilasters with floral decoration and an anthemion mid-floor band, and No. 13, built as a Catholic church to resemble a villa, the floor with central half-dome statue niches between two-storey bowed bays. Past St Michael's church (*see* Churches), Nos. 1–9 TEHIDY TERRACE in pretty early C19 stucco is a worthy finale.

3. The Moor and Killigrew Street

After the long stretch of shoreline streets, THE MOOR offers a sense of arrival at the centre of the town. It is still just possible with the help of history to read this area, a steep-sided valley, as the focus of the pre-C17 settlement: JACOB'S LADDER, a long steep flight of mid-C19 steps on the S side, offers an immediate sense of the topography. The surprise is The Moor's spaciousness and the ambitious scale of its principal buildings grouped at the lower end. The former Town Hall and Courts are flanked to the S by the giant façade of the Methodist church, and to the N by the Art Gallery and Library and the Post Office (*see* Churches and Public Buildings). Among other buildings of interest, the SEVEN STARS, a rare survival of a market pub, with a late C19 refronting and internal planning and fittings, and a 1912 wing. w of the Post Office, the MARKET FOUNTAIN, early C19, a strikingly large semi-spherical bowl on a saucer-like base under a square shelter on plain granite columns. In the centre of the street towards its upper end the PACKET MONUMENT, 1818, a granite obelisk on a panelled pedestal.

Off the top of The Moor to the r. is BERKELEY VALE with the former CORNWALL CONSTABULARY building, 1902, the former DRILL HALL, 1874, with a large rose window, and the United Reformed church (*see* Churches). KILLIGREW STREET continues a long gentle tree-lined ascent to the top of the hill, with pleasant early to late C19 houses. The point in view is the spire of the church of Hansom's St Mary Immaculate, beyond which, near the crest of the hill, is Sedding's All Saints (*see* Churches). TRELAWNEY ROAD climbs steeply s of Killigrew Street. At the crest of the hill, the EARLE'S RETREAT almshouses of 1869, by *Alexander Lauder* for George Earle, to accommodate thirty-two residents. A stylish essay of the Gothic Revival, the E-shaped front with loggias linking gabled wings to a centrally placed chapel. The loggias are of five bays of pointed arches on round piers, which have carved capitals with moulded entablatures to their balustrades. The chapel has a large Dec window above three trefoiled niches with compressed shafts. E of this in VICTORIA COTTAGES, the former OBSERVATORY of 1862 for the Royal Cornwall Polytechnic Society (q.v.). A three-storey octagonal stucco tower rising to an observation room above a parapet with deep coving. ALBERT COTTAGES are another group in the Gothic style.

Further out, s of Western Terrace and off MARLBOROUGH AVENUE, a pretty PAVILION with lantern, the front with an Ionic colonnade, the interior a handsome curved staircase. It was built 1805–15 by Captain Bull for Marlborough House, now BENTON LODGE, the original relationship compromised by intrusive modern housing.

PENDENNIS CASTLE. See p. 404.

FEOCK

8030

An unusually pretty village, of Devon rather than Cornish character, overlooking Carrick Roads.

ST FEOC. The striking feature is the sturdy detached BELL TOWER built well above the church at the top of the steeply sloping churchyard as a beacon for shipping (cf. Mylor and Talland). C13, the bell storey over a basement, with battered walls, a low simple pointed-arched E doorway, small louvred ventilators to the bell storey, and a pyramidal slate roof. The church was practically rebuilt by *J. P. St Aubyn* in 1875–6 in his Perp style but retaining some C15 windows, S aisle arcade, and doorways: the arcade is of five bays of standard Cornish design with plain capitals and four-centred arches. Two-bay C19 arcade to N aisle. Arch-braced roofs with angled struts over collar- and wind-braces. The chancel was expensively furnished with a low alabaster screen, painted decoration to the roof, and a richly ornamented REREDOS: it has crocketed pinnacles over battlements with a cusped ogee arch to the centre filled with gold mosaic, flanking pointed-arch panels with the commandments, and painted panels of the Evangelists above. – FONT. Late Norman, of Catacleuse, and of exceptional quality: crisply carved, circular, with a frieze of two tiers of diagonal crosses above and circles with trees of life below (cf. the similar fonts at Ladock and Fowey). – PULPIT. With four late C16 Flemish Renaissance panels with religious scenes. – STAINED GLASS. Fine E window designed by *William de Morgan*, 1876. – S aisle E window by *Beer* of Exeter, also 1876. S aisle S window nearest the porch by *Kempe & Co.*, 1930. – N transept by *J. Hall*, 1959, a striking angel at the empty tomb.

CROSS. S side of the churchyard. Late C12–early C13. A remarkable example. On the NW face a figure of the crowned Christ with arms outstretched within a narrow bead, the legs of the figure appearing to end at the knees, flanked and carried below as a double bead. The reverse face has a foliated cross of a design unique in Cornwall but familiar elsewhere on C13 cross-heads. LYCHGATES. One S of the church, plain early C19, remodelled late C19, with slate-hung upper storey as a vestry room; another to the NW, *c.* 1900, with moulded granite jambs with engaged shafts surmounted by moulded corbelled kneelers.

OLD SCHOOL. NE of the church. Former National School, probably by *J. L. Pearson*, 1846, extended twice in the later C19. Tudor style. Originally one large schoolroom and smaller room to r. of front with adjoining entrance porch with granite ashlar bellcote. Schoolroom and classroom extension parallel to original schoolroom with small open courtyard to rear, later built over as another classroom. The design is similar to Devoran, also by Pearson (q.v.).

The sheltered Fal estuary provided ideal locations for shipping of copper ore from inland mines, and this former industrial character of the parish is reflected in a number of METHODIST CHAPELS, as at Carnon Downs, Goonpiper and Penpolls, and also some historic QUAYS: Roundwood, late C18; Pill Quays, *c.* 1760 for Thomas Daniell of Trelissick (q.v.), with boat shed; Marble Head, 1783; and Point, late C18 for Sir William Lemon of Carclew and Truro (q.v.).

The village expanded considerably in the C20 with a number of detached houses taking advantage of the splendid views over Restronguet Creek and towards Carrick Roads. Most are undistinguished but opposite each other at the head of Pill Creek are two that in contrasting yet complementary ways are

the most important C20 houses in Cornwall, and of significance far beyond:

CREEK VEAN, on the E side of the creek, is of 1964–7 by   121
Team 4 (Norman & Wendy Foster, Richard & Su Rogers, and
Georgie Wolton) for Marcus and Rene Brumwell, Su Rogers's
parents. It was the first built work by Team 4 and an example
of the influence of Frank Lloyd Wright on the Rogers following
their return from studying at Yale. A brilliant realization of the
potential of its splendid steeply sloping site overlooking the
small creek, the orientation towards the view governing
the plan, the steep site the section. The building, surprisingly
small scale, is articulated into two masses divided by the
entrance from the road over a small bridge, both displaying
unwindowed 'Forticrete' concrete block walls;* a wide external
flight of steps between them leads down to the garden. The
deliberately understated exterior heightens the contrast with
the dramatic interior, the views penetrating the spaces; as Alan
Powers describes it, 'in a succession of light and dark cullises
in perspective, corresponding to the discrete yet continuous
phasing of access, reserve and privacy in the house'.† There
are many surprises created by imaginative detailing including
the use of unusual geometry with not a single right angle anywhere. The entrance door is in the two-storey l. hand block in
an oblique wall, and one then crosses an internal bridge just
below the level of the studio/living room, which itself bridges
the kitchen and dining room on the level below. The lower
block has a sloping clerestory roof against the rear wall with
continuous glazing to the creek. All the external doors are
frameless glass.

PILLWOOD HOUSE, on the W side of the creek, is of 1971–4,
by John Miller with Su Rogers, also for Marcus Brumwell. A
striking and no doubt deliberate contrast to Creek Vean's solid
sculptural form, this is a pioneering high-tech structure ('using
industrial components' was Miller's preferred description)
with a steel frame and glass walls, also arranged to take advantage of the sloping site and the views of the creek and estuary
beyond. The first impression is that the house is all glass, with
a roof like a giant greenhouse sweeping downhill. This superstructure is set on and against a solid, white L-shaped box.
The accommodation is arranged with the living rooms on the
first floor, in an entirely glazed gallery, looking down into a
fully glazed studio behind which are the bedrooms and bathroom. Miller's vision of a 'holiday perch' in a clearing in the
forest is triumphantly realized in this jewel-like house shining
in the trees of its sylvan setting.

THE BOATHOUSE, Restronguet Point. 1973 by John Crowther &
Associates. Almost a glass box on the river elevations, the glazing
in timber frames on a strict module. Landward side with few

---

* The architects had so much trouble with this conventional heavyweight construction that they decided never to use it again.
† Alan Powers, The Twentieth Century House in Britain (2004).

windows, white rendered walls with circular stair drum, all very disciplined and simple enough not to date.

KILLIGANOON. 2 m. NW. of *c.* 1750, remodelled 1874–5 after a serious fire in 1873. Two-storey, five-window NW entrance front with Doric porch; long SE garden front with canted central bay. Late C19 interior almost intact.

DUCHY GRAMMAR SCHOOL. 1¼ m. NW. Formerly Tregye. 1809 for William Penrose, extended and remodelled late C19. Two-storey over basement, four-window S entrance front, the original entrance obscured by C20 extension. Five-window E garden front with central canted bay; the room behind is octagonal. Ceiling with trailing rose band and central rose with carvings of harvest fruits.

FLUSHING

A serene waterfront place across the Penryn estuary from Falmouth. The original fishing settlement, said to have been given its name by the Dutch, was greatly improved in the early C18 by Samuel Trefusis who, according to Lysons in 1814, 'levelled the ground, constructed quays, and erected numerous buildings at a great expense'. Trefusis had obtained a condition from the Falmouth Post Master (his father-in-law) that all commanders, officers and crew of the Falmouth packet service had to live in Flushing. Though this was soon rescinded, the employees mostly going to live in Greenbank on the Falmouth side of the estuary, it accounts for the genteel building of the first half of the C18 that sets the architectural tone of the waterfront, with more modest but attractive early to mid-C19 buildings in the few small streets behind.

ST PETER. 1841–2 by *George Wightwick*: though restored in 1871, 1893 and 1906 it retains much original detail. Romanesque style on an aisleless plan with a chancel apse. The dignified SW front, approached through a pretty wrought-iron overthrow with flanking railings, rises from a generous porch with a parapet cornice to the wide gable-end, its central round-headed window flanked by recessed panels with small windows and sloping machicolated cornices, and is surmounted by a gabled bellcote: the twin-gabled vestry to the l., an extension of 1871, only marginally impinges on the strong symmetry of Wightwick's design. Light and spacious interior lit by long round-headed cast-iron windows. Tall chancel arch and blind reredos arcade with four-leaf enrichments to the cornice. – STAINED GLASS. Fine E window, 1917, by *Morris & Co.* to designs by *Burne-Jones*. Window of N side, 1995 by *Alan Younger*, a striking and successful abstract design, the best in Cornwall. – CROSS-HEAD outside the W front. Medieval. Each face has a simple carved figure of Christ with outstretched

arms and an indeterminate pattern behind the head and
shoulders.

On the waterfront are several Trefusis QUAYS, mostly of the
familiar vertically set rubble walls with granite copings. The
best ensemble of early C18 houses is in TREFUSIS ROAD (e.g.
Nos. 1 and 2, CLANMORE, and CLINTON HOUSE), parts of
a stuccoed terrace with sash windows, simple classical doorcases and doors, and moulded cornices. Nos. 25 and 26 and
Nos. 32 and 32A are similar with part brick and part slate
hanging respectively. At the S end, NEWQUAY LODGE is a
three-storey example with very deep eaves, while NEWQUAY
HOUSE has a slate-hung bowed end. Further SE near KILN
QUAY some larger Victorian villas and a curiosity, a timber-
framed Wealden house from Kent re-erected here c. 1919 by
Joan Beech, who had married a sea captain. C15–C16, typical
plan with hall, inner room with solar and former service end
with chamber above and the first floor jettied externally at both
ends of the house. Returning to the NW end, in ST PETER'S
ROAD some good later C18 to early or mid-C19 houses, mostly
three-storey stucco with some slate cladding. LAWN CLIFF is
a Regency classical house. In TREGEW ROAD, GROVE
COTTAGE, also early C19, built as the dower house for the
Trefusis family: pretty stucco SE elevation with pointed arched
lights.

FORRABURY *see* BOSCASTLE

FOWEY   *1050*

First impressions of Fowey on crossing by ferry from Bodinnick   2
or Polruan, or coming in from the open sea, are indelible. The
little town runs along the western side of the estuary, almost one
long street on either side of the memorable ensemble at its heart
– the noble C15 tower of St Fimbarrus, rising close to the towers
and battlemented walls of Place, seat of the Treffrys, all set in
pine trees and Cornish vegetation against the steep hillside.

Fowey is one of Cornwall's most historic ports, promoted from
the late C13 by Tywardreath Priory. It is so remarkably intact that
it is essentially still confined by its geography to the layout and
street pattern of the late medieval town, when Fowey was the
busiest and most important port on the estuary, exporting tin,
cloth, hides and fish, in return for wine, salt and cloth from Brittany, Bordeaux and Normandy. By the mid C14 it had overtaken
Lostwithiel (q.v.) as the county's leading outlet for tin and by the
late medieval period was Cornwall's premier port. Though eventually overtaken by the growth of Falmouth from the late C16,
Fowey remained commercially buoyant throughout succeeding
centuries, its fine Town Hall demonstrating its late C18 prosperity.

Fishing was still of major importance into the late C19 when the industry was in general decline.

Its C13–C15 growth had been stimulated during the wars with France and Spain when the strategic significance of a deep-water harbour in the SW peninsula was first realized, and from 1300 onwards it became a supply port for the navy. But its position near the mouth of the estuary made it vulnerable to attack. In 1437 a Breton fleet raided the town, sacked the church and badly damaged Place. Blockhouses were built SE of the town and opposite at Polruan, partly at the Treffrys' expense, to hold a chain to close the channel between them, as at Dartmouth and Kingswear further E in Devon. The town's fortifications were strengthened during the C16 and C17 by a small artillery fort, St Catherine's Castle, and reinforced during the Napoleonic Wars and the two C20 world wars.

The mid to late C19 saw Fowey rise as a china clay port and tourist resort, the result of the extension of the railway from Lostwithiel and St Blazey in 1869. By 1876 china clay exports from Fowey had already overtaken those from the shallower St Austell bay harbours. From 1890 steamers were offering visitors excursions to Mevagissey, Looe and other south coast fishing ports with a regular service to Falmouth and Plymouth. Fowey's population nearly doubled between 1871 and 1901, from 1,344 to 2,258, and has remained almost static since. The town centre remains a dense concentration of C14–C19 buildings, tightly packed along both sides of narrow streets with only the occasional glimpse of water around the working quays.

ST FIMBARRUS. In the first rank of the county's churches but in most stylistic respects very untypical of Cornwall. Its large scale and noble proportions are not immediately apparent, set as it is immediately below the walls of Place (*see* below) rising dramatically to the N and W. Only the plan is Cornish standard – nave and chancel, N and S aisles, S porch and W tower – otherwise the execution differs from the usual pattern in many ways. The C15 tower is one of the most beautifully proportioned in Cornwall, of four rather than the usual three stages, and with buttresses which leave the corners free. It is richly decorated (cf. Launceston and Probus): plinth with two bands of ornament, first string course with two bands of ornament, second and third string courses also two bands, pinnacles in relief against the top part of the buttresses, panelled and crocketed top pinnacles, ornamented battlements. The S porch is also C15 and of unusual interest, not least being open to E and W. It is large, two-storeyed and battlemented. The four-centred arches to E and W have moulded spiral decoration to their outer shafts with octagonal capitals to their inner faces. The roof is an eight-ribbed groin-vault with central boss, the ribs springing from shafts in the corners.

30   It is the interior, however, that is most strikingly different: the influence of the friaries of Brittany is apparent and parallels with Lostwithiel spring immediately to mind. Nave and chancel

continuous and immensely tall, the height emphasized by the soaring tower arch, the five C14 arcades opening into the N and S aisles, plain octagonal piers running without any capitals into the plain double-chamfered pointed arches; they fit the early C14 and the known re-dedication of the church in 1336. The contemporary clerestory windows range with the spandrels, not the apexes of the arches (cf. Callington, St Germans and Lostwithiel) and start below these. The year 1336 seems to mark the rebuilding of an earlier church on the site by 1170 but whose plan is unclear: the rebuild probably had narrow lean-to aisles, later extended to their present unusual width. The S aisle was extended E to form the Treffry chapel in 1500–10 and refurbished (as at Bodmin) with standard Cornish Perp four-light windows with colonettes on their inner jambs; similarly the five-light chancel window. The fine C16 wagon roof of twenty bays is supported by angels at the ends of the principal rafters and decorated with bosses and shields of the founders and benefactors of the church, the shields painted by *Dr Drake* of Fowey in 1876 as part of a major restoration under *J. P. St Aubyn*. It was extraordinarily expensive for the time at £5,000 and included the renewal of most of the window tracery, the replacement of the N aisle roof and the removal of the W gallery. Vestry added at the NE corner by *Silvanus Trevail* in 1894. Roofs of nave, chancel and S aisle extensively repaired 1932–4 but using much of the medieval roof timber.

FITTINGS. – FONT. Norman, of Catacleuse; with rosettes in   24
circles and an upper border of crossed chevron lines, a section on the N face roughed out only, the base a C20 copy. Good workmanship. The same workshop supplied very similar fonts to Ladock and Feock. – PAINTING. In the base of the tower, of bellringers and ringer's rhyme, 1732. – PULPIT. Handsome, hexagonal, dated 1601. – REREDOS and PARCLOSE SCREEN 1896 by *Harry Hems* of Exeter and SCREEN 1909 by *E. H. Sedding*, all in the C15 style. – STAINED GLASS. Chancel E window and S aisle E window by *Charles Gibbs*, good colour and figures. – Tower W by *Heaton, Butler & Bayne*, 1876. – Nine clerestory windows of Cornish saints by *Fouracre & Watson*, 1881. – C14 Agony in Gethsemane, inserted into N aisle from the Rashleigh town house (*see* below). – MONUMENTS. A rich display, especially of the Treffrys in the S aisle and the Rash-leighs in the N aisle. Very large granite grave slab with three Treffry brothers in armour inscribed 'YE FIRST YEAR OF THE RAYNE OF KYING HENRY THE EYGHTH, HERE LIE THE BODIES OF SIR JOHN TREFFRY, KNYGHT, WILLIAM TREFFRY & THOMAS'. – Another large granite slab standing against the chancel wall, John Treffry †1590. – Small slate memorial to Thomas Treffry †1635. – On S wall gilded and painted cartouche to John Treffry †1684 in the form of a will leaving his estate to his nephew William Toller, who took the Treffry name; complete cadaver above. – Against N aisle wall, large marble and freestone chest monument to John Rashleigh †1624 in ruff and beret; fine effigy of his son John kneeling on

w side. – Another Rashleigh monument of 1683 with an architectural background, columns, garlands, and a broken segmented pediment. – Small marble monument to Thomas Rashleigh †1662. – In chancel rich columned and garlanded memorial with angels to John Goodall and his son William †1686, first mayor of Fowey under charter of James II, kneeling facing each other, William in his mayoral gown. – Susannah Graham †1779 and Thomas Graham †1792, urn on a chest. – BRASSES. In the floor near the pulpit four small brasses: Richard Rashleigh †1591 and his wife Agnes, another to a civilian †1450, John Rashleigh †1582, Alice Rashleigh †1591. – Four small C15 brasses on the sill of the E window of the S aisle: Thomas Treffry, his wife and son, also Thomas and his wife, Elizabeth, who defended Place in 1457.

PLACE. Set immediately above and NW of the church and with its towers, high walls and battlements forming a delightful ensemble with it. The Treffry house is first recorded in 1457 when, after the French raid on the town, Thomas Treffry is reported by Leland as building 'a right fair and strong tower in his house and embattling all the walls, in a manner made it a castle'. The present character of Place is, however, an overwhelming display of early C19 to Early Victorian Gothic, the fruit of over thirty years reconstruction by Joseph Thomas (Austen) Treffry between 1813 and 1845. Here this industrial pioneer, responsible for building the harbours at Newquay and Par, the mineral tramway to Newquay, the Treffry viaduct in the Luxulyan valley, and the lower rock-cut road into Fowey, turned his indefatigable energies to a radical remodelling of his own house.

Not much was left untouched and the extent of the medieval survival beneath the comprehensive Gothic dressing is unclear. There had been earlier reconstruction after 1500 by William Treffry, High Sheriff of Cornwall, and the C18 had seen at least two major phases of remodelling of the E side to build a Georgian wing. But Treffry's campaign was all-embracing, costing the prodigious sum of over £120,000. He seems to have designed for himself, using stone mason *Edmund Rickett* and carver *George Gauntlett*, both recorded as suffering from drink problems, with possibly *Neville Northey Burnard* of Altarnun for some of the carved work. The results, inside and out, are sometimes curious but always audacious: as Mark Girouard has pointed out, 'it is extraordinary that such a man as Treffry should have made so public his dream world'. *Country Life*, (1962).

The house is built around a courtyard plan. The present S range seems to correspond with the Tudor S range of the hall (now the dining room) and the solar (now the library). The Pentewan stone entrance and killas stone hall are probably part of the 1457 rebuild. The best late medieval feature of the house is the two-storeyed early C16 bay in the courtyard with transoms and all the lights cusped, apparently the only part of the W range not altered by J. T. Treffry, though it only lights the back hall. The Romantic Gothic treatment of the s front is especially fulsome with two ornate two-storeyed canted bays and two tall towers with soaring chimneyshafts to give exaggerated height. The taller tower looks like a solid cube from the s but is built in two halves joined at the top. There is another two-storeyed bay on the E front. The w bay on the s front is a reconstruction of an existing c16 bay and has strong similarities in the richness of its granite carving to Launceston church; the others are mid-c19 and of remarkable workmanship.

The interior was similarly remade by Treffry: even the pretty Rococo ceiling of the library was considered too low and was lifted 16 in. (41 cm.) higher. The ceiling's designer was probably *Thomas Edwards*, the plasterer *William Lorrington* and the carver *Heyden*, who did the chimneypiece. The room was converted into a library about 1827 and lined with Gothic fittings in oak from the *Bellerophon*, the ship that carried Napoleon from France after the Hundred Days War. The drawing-room ceiling, based on the Tudor panelled ceiling of the dining room but with an over-large central boss, is of plaster painted by *Robert Whale* to look like wood. The cornice is decorated with weird heads and animals, probably by *Gauntlett*, but they are nothing compared to the riot of monsters and beasts that stare from the main staircase with serpents coiling around tree trunks, angular dolphins forming the balusters, and toads and crabs facing up to each other. As time went on, Treffry's building became more odd, culminating in the showpiece Porphyry Hall of 1841–3 above the library accessed from the w by a porch between the two halves of the granite tower. It is a grand curiosity of Cornish geology with walls of polished red porphyry, darker polished Luxulyanite and polished Luxulyan granite.

T. H. Mawson prepared a plan for the gardens in 1907 and, although the design was not fully implemented, the series of terraces looking out over the river, and the summerhouse, are by him.

PERAMBULATION. Fowey's rich history resulted early on in an intensively built up waterfront by the infilling of small inlets like Town Quay: around two-thirds of the present waterfront is comprised of quays of medieval origin. On TOWN QUAY are gathered a selection of Fowey's best buildings, including some of the earliest town buildings in Cornwall. The showy centrepiece is the KING OF PRUSSIA inn, its three-storey mid-c19 front elevation raised over an open basement of c17 Doric granite columns. This is the latest phase of a complex history, clearly suggested by its N elevation to Webb Street where at ground floor are two granite moulded mullioned windows, one with cinquefoil-headed lights, and a pointed-arched granite doorway. The commanding position indicates its origin as a late medieval merchant's house; the colonnaded area was later used as a market. To its l., the TOWN HALL, dated 1787, distinguished by exceptionally fine but very austere granite ashlar.

Scale

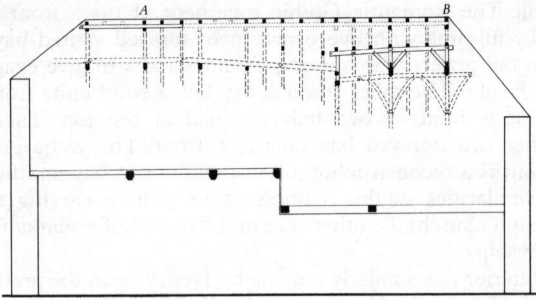

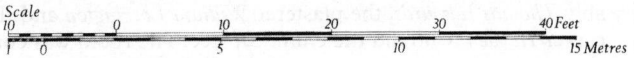

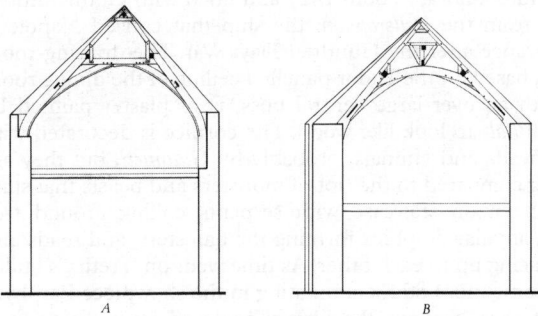

—— surviving members through centre of building

----- surviving members along plane of purlin

·········· presumed members now missing

Fowey, Food for Thought. Sections of medieval roof

The best C18 building in the town. The hall is at first-floor level lit by three twenty-four pane sashes over a seven-bay closed arcade of round arches. At the rear, granite steps retain some late C18 iron railings. There is also a blocked first-floor doorway and a later doorway in an enlarged window opening. The interi ior with a kingpost roof suggests a medieval structure remod-elled. Restored in 1896 for 'dramatic performances'.

Facing the Town Hall's principal front is a smart, three-storey late C18 house with sliding sashes, rusticated quoins, and modillion eaves cornice. Adjoining to the rear, completely disguised by bland C20 elevations, is FOOD FOR THOUGHT, possibly the earliest surviving town building in the south-west, a late medieval merchant's hall of major status, originally open to the roof but floored in the C17 with chamfered cross-beams. It was originally of two-room plan, much altered subsequently, but remarkably the medieval roof survives, of nine bays constructed in three phases. It is stylistically very similar to the roof at the Old Rectory, Cheriton Bishop, Devon, dated by dendrochronology to 1299–1300.* The front three bays incorporate crown-posts, only found elsewhere in Cornwall at Rectory Farm, Morwenstow (q.v.), with two arch-braced trusses and wind-bracing. Though the feet of the trusses are hidden they are presumed to be of the base-cruck type. This section of the roof is also smoke blackened. In the adjoining section is a truss with three sets of straight collars with a vertical post between and angled straight braces in the upper part. It too is smoke blackened. The E section of the roof has three arch-braced trusses with square-set purlins (cf. Penfound, Poundstock; Pennellick, Pelynt; Methrose, Luxulyan, and Truthall). As a contrast on the opposite side of the quay and completing the enclosure is the straightforward red and yellow brick of *Silvanus Trevail*'s WORKING MAN'S INSTITUTE, dated 1878.

Forming the backdrop to the quay are the church tower and Place (qq.v.) on the higher ground above the narrow streets of the town, typified by FORE STREET, with the continuous weave of pleasing buildings that gives the town its consistently intimate character. Mostly C18 and C19 with rendered, stone, or occasionally brick fronts to the street with sash windows and many traditional shopfronts, but there are frequent hints of rich histories hidden deep in fabric behind. Among those which display their history more directly are the C16 and C17 part timber-framed merchants' houses with jetties at first and second floors, e.g. the LUGGER HOTEL, extensively remodelled in 1900 in half-timbered style but with a genuine and rare twelve-light ovolo-moulded window running the full width of the first floor and a six-light oriel window on three brackets to the second floor. A ground-floor room has a panelled and embossed ceiling with moulded cornice with anthemion enrichment of the early C17. Nos. 27 and 29 are even more eye-catching, a pair of gabled late C16 to early C17 merchants, houses again with jettied timber-framed fronts, the first floor with ovolo-moulded mullioned oriels carried on carved brackets. Opposite is the Queen Anne style LLOYDS BANK, originally the Devon & Cornwall Bank, of 1906 by *Silvanus Trevail*. Three tall storeys, end bays slightly advanced, with Trevail's characteristic use of yellow terracotta for the rusticated architraves and pediments to windows and mullioned cornice above a ground floor of rusticated granite. Next door OLD QUAY HOUSE of 1889, an eclectic design with interesting variations of glazing bars: almost every window is different. Beyond and to the r. another glimpse of the estuary at ALBERT QUAY. It has the CUSTOM HOUSE with its irregular C18 and C19 elevation and, opposite, VICTORIA STEPS, 2003 by *Alan Leather*, a

*I am indebted to John Thorp for this comparison.

rare essay in good contemporary infilling as a canted three-storey house on plain round concrete columns with oriel windows facing the estuary: a thoughtful interpretation of the local vernacular. The street is closed gracefully by the POST OFFICE, an early C18 house later adapted to its present use. Five-window front with double-hung sashes, moulded glazing bars, architraves and sill brackets, a modillioned eaves cornice and three pedimented dormers. Large shell-hood over the door.

On up Custom House Hill into NORTH STREET and a sudden jump in scale to the tall front of the former WESLEYAN CHAPEL, 1894, on the site of an earlier chapel. Tall three-light pointed-head windows subdivided by wide pilaster columns with foliage capitals and wrought-iron finials, just like Mevagissey (q.v.). Further N into PASSAGE STREET, No. 1 is an early C19 three-storey house in red brick with burnt headers built over a coursed stone ground floor. The walk from here to the Bodinnick Ferry is crammed with good small buildings, the earlier buildings on the estuary side a mix of houses, fish cellars, boat yards and sail lofts, with narrow passages diving down to the waterside. The whole composition is, of course, best seen from the river. At CAFFA MILL QUAY is an OBELISK, originally erected on Albert Quay to commemorate Victoria and Albert's visit in 1846, re-erected here in 1977.

Back to the centre via BULL HILL, walking immediately below the battlemented walls of Place to No. 9 SOUTH STREET, another remarkable late C16 to early C17 jettied timber-framed fronted house, this time with three jetties and early C19 sashes to the first floor. The interior has a stone newel staircase with round arch doorways to access two garderobes, good C17 panelling and C18 dog-leg staircase.

W of the church and the vicarage in COBBS WELL are the RASHLEIGH ALMSHOUSES, the first eight erected before 1626 by John Rashleigh, the others by Jonathan Rashleigh 1663 as a thanksgiving for surviving the Civil War.

Finally, TRAFALGAR SQUARE, SE of the church at the junction of South Street and Lostwithiel Street, has two important early survivals. On the W side is a complex group (now the SHIP INN and KITTOW BROS), with three gabled wings to the street of varied dates. Its development is unclear but it appears to have been rebuilt in 1578 for John Rashleigh, incorporating an earlier C15 house. This period is represented by the three-storey wing to the l., facing Lostwithiel Street, which has at first floor a two-light mullioned window with cinquefoiled heads, enclosing an inner C17 ovolo-moulded frame. This is mirrored in the four-light, hoodmoulded window in the house opposite (No. 1 Lostwithiel Street) to which it was originally connected by a gallery over the street (removed in the early C20). This was also the position of the town's medieval S gate. Inside this early part is a C17 panelled room with later C16 or early C17 chimneypiece: with flanking caryatids with Ionic capitals supporting a pedimented overmantel, the Ionic pilasters of which frame three large heads, the central one with a bust assumed to be John Rashleigh. The two-storey central wing, containing the entrance, is also C17 with staircase hall behind and a late C17 chamber of exceptional quality and intactness: a barrel ceiling with moulded cornices, the ends of the barrel moulded as pediments each containing a tree decoration, the wall moulded with large panels, and with a bolection-moulded chimneypiece. The r. wing, C19, has its main front to the churchyard, a wide three storeys with a frieze of ogee arches continued on the gable-end, and at first floor a central pilastered arched panel containing the inn sign. The other building of note in the square is the FOWEY MUSEUM, originally a first-floor hall over an undercroft (another Breton influence?), floored to create an extra storey in the C17 and subsequently used as the guildhall and courtroom; the precise sequence of development is unclear but the elevation to Trafalgar Square is the most instructive. Four original openings still visible: from the l. a round-arched window and a tall two-light mullioned window with cinquefoil heads, to the r. a basket-arched doorway with remains of square hoodmould, approached by small granite steps, and another small round-arched window on its r. Basement with two small C17 chamfered cell windows. Irregular rear elevation to Market Street with numerous window openings of various dates, the only original towards the l., probably a former doorway at the end of a former cross-passage to the front doorway. Interior with C17 chamfered cross-beams above first floor and boarded barrel ceiling above, also C17.

LOSTWITHIEL STREET rises steeply uphill. Nos. 5 and 7 are good corner buildings, early C19 stucco with late C19 shopfronts. Next the former CONGREGATIONAL CHAPEL of 1887. Three-light pointed-arched windows and a striking corner tower with pyramidal slate roof over Lombard frieze. The street is full of good buildings, most now with pleasant C18 and C19 fronts but given the importance of this main route inland there is likely to be much of interest behind. No. 20 (Treffry Estate Office) was built as the Masonic Lodge in 1882 by *Silvanus Trevail*; red brick with stone dressings. Nos. 62–66 form a pretty row of C19 cottages including a nice corner building, while Nos. 74 and 76 are good examples of C18 and early C19 town houses. Off Lostwithiel Street is THE ESPLANADE, which stands on the site of the former ropewalk. Rather like Passage Street at first with modest two-storey cottages on the riverside and larger Late Victorian and Edwardian houses on the inland side, some with cast-iron verandas and balconies. But then the story of Fowey's expansion as a resort unfolds as the street widens out and larger later C19 villas and hotels appear as the vistas open out across sheltered gardens over the estuary to Polruan (q.v.) and onwards towards the open sea. At the water's edge the ruinous remains of the small square tower of a BLOCKHOUSE, late C15, a pair with that on the Polruan side for the slinging of a chain across the estuary.

FOWEY HALL HOTEL, Hanson Drive. 1898 for Sir Charles Hanson, a Lord Mayor of London and native of Polruan, in a commanding position above the town looking across the estuary towards his birthplace. A pleasing and generously scaled composition in the Queen Anne style, set in a planned garden. Large, nearly symmetrical plan with square domed towers projecting at the corners. Five-bay entrance front with pedimented Doric porch and central first-floor window under an open segmented pediment on Ionic columns. Symmetrical garden front, the central bays set back behind a Doric round-arched arcade to ground-floor loggia surmounted by a stone balustraded balcony. Very high-quality interior in a robust early C18 style including Baroque-style plasterwork.

In the grounds a former WINDMILL. Squat tower standing on a site recorded as a windmill in 1290. Present building converted into a folly in the C19.

POINT NEPTUNE, Readymoney Road. Mid-C19 Italianate villa, extended 1864 for William Rashleigh of Menabilly, retaining the smaller early C19 house as a service wing. A significant, early example of Fowey's growing reputation as a resort from the mid C19.

ST CATHERINE'S CASTLE, 1 m. SW. A small artillery fort built by Thomas Treffry in 1540 as part of the Henrician coastal defences (cf. Pendennis and St Mawes castles) covering the headland on the W side of the estuary entrance at St Catherine's Point. What remains is a D-plan blockhouse and bastioned curtain wall on the tip of the rocky headland. The blockhouse is two-storey with three gun-ports on the ground floor, and two more (one blocked) and five narrow windows on the first floor. The castle was refurbished in 1855 as a gun battery during the Crimean War and modified as an emplacement in a more extensive battery occupying the Point during the Second World War. The gun emplacements lie below the blockhouse.

TRISTAN STONE, 1 m. NW beside the main road. Large memorial stone recorded by Leland in 1542 1 m. S of Castle Dore (*see* Golant), and with a chequered subsequent history before its erection here in 1971. On the S face a very worn C6 Latin inscription carved vertically, said to read DRUSTANUS HIC IACIT CUNOMORI FILIUS (Here lies Drustanus, son of Cunomonus). On the N face a T-shaped cross. A mortice in the top of the shaft indicates that a cross-head was once attached, presumably at a later date.

GEEVOR
¼ m. W of Pendeen

An unprepossessing set of industrial buildings gathered around its steel headgear represents the largest preserved C20 TIN MINE in the world. Established in 1911, it worked some three square miles underground at depths of up to 2,100 ft (650 metres), including much of the old Levant mine (q.v.), until 1990. The character and atmosphere of a working mine have survived as a visitor attraction, with much original equipment and ephemera in the simple buildings. The site slopes down towards the cliff edge. The HEADGEAR marks the position of Victory Shaft. The entrance area includes the WINDING ENGINE HOUSE, MINERS' DRY and COMPRESSOR HOUSE. Below, in a series of buildings comprising THE MILL stepping down the hillside, the ore was passed through a series of processes that crushed and refined it: there appear to be timbers in all directions, the effect like walking through a massive medieval roof. The mill leads directly into the underground area of WHEAL MEXICO, a small mine of late C18 origin. Among the other buildings on the site is a well-preserved Brunton ARSENIC CALCINER.

GERMOE

5020

ST GERMOE (St Germoc). A church of strong appeal, comfortably sited alongside the village green at the centre of the little settlement, of unusual interest for its architectural detail. The fine C15 W tower shows features similar to Breage (q.v.), of which this was a chapel: Tregonning granite blocks, three stages, with the same panelled and crocketed pinnacles on angle corbels and two gargoyles under the parapet on each face. The body of the church retains much pre-C15 fabric: the S wall of the nave and the lower parts of the chancel walls Norman, the S transept C13, remodelled in the C15. Late C14 S porch, the outer and inner doors pointed, with original coping and Crucifixus and kneeler stones, the latter depicting long-tailed monkeys. C13 or C14 trefoil-headed stoup. C14 windows in the S wall and S transept but the transept's W window C12, re-set. Pretty C19 Gothic-style bellcote over chancel arch. Light, serene interior with low four-bay N arcade with Cornish standard piers; similar arch to N transept. S transept has two-bay arcading, the E impost C14, the rest C19 in Perp style. C12 head and two C13 or C14 heads in W wall of S transept. Restored 1891–2, probably by *E. H. Sedding*: of that date the collar rafter roofs incorporating fragments of C15 wagon roofs. Large chancel arch carried on rood beam, panelled above with pierced and cusped decoration. Chancel roof *c.* 1850, of panelled polygonal vault construction. An unusual combination of roof styles that works remarkably well. – FONT. C11, strikingly primitive-looking, with irregular round bowl with three faces, one hardly recognizable. – FONT BOWL (W end of nave). C12 with cable moulding. – C18 painted WALLBOARD TEXTS.

ST GERMOE'S CHAIR. A remarkable and interesting little building NE of the church built into the churchyard wall. Like an C18 covered seat but clearly medieval, perhaps C13 or C14 in origin, possibly (imaginatively) reconstructed later. It is entered by a twin arch with a circular pier and has three seats at its back, with blank pointed arches separated by shafts with moulded capitals. The central arch has a C13 crowned head, badly carved, at its top. Another head, C12, above the apex of the gable outside.

GERRANS

St Gerrans (St Gerent). At the centre of an open hilltop village, in a raised oval churchyard or *lann*. The handsome spire, a rarity in Cornwall, is octagonal with one ring of quatrefoil decoration midway up, rising from a two-stage tower with diagonal buttresses and granite ashlar to the w ground floor only, all probably C14. Nave and chancel under one roof, N transept and s aisle mostly the product of *William White*'s restoration of 1849–50 which started his career in Cornwall. According to *The Ecclesiologist* of 1851, 'the work here has been a literal rebuilding, the very stones of the almost Debased piers and arches have been replaced and the old windows, as far as possible, used again'. The church's appearance successfully suggests continuous development since the C13. As Gill Hunter has observed, it 'reflects White's antiquarian picturesque aesthetic as well as his appreciation of vernacular style and use of local materials that would imbue all his work': cf. his use of variously coloured slatestone in the voussoirs. The N wall has two small C13 lancets, the transept E window is of C13 triple lancets and the s aisle has C15 windows; the finely proportioned aisle arcade of seven bays on piers with four attached shafts, dice capitals and depressed arches. The trussed rafter roofs are all 1850, with fragments of C15 wall-plate in the s porch. – FONT. Of the Egloshayle type, Norman, square, with four blank niches on each side, a simplified version of that at Egloshayle (q.v.). – Six BENCH-ENDS, early C16 of the standard square-topped kind with tracery and various devices such as Catherine of Aragon's pomegranate, symbols of the Passion, etc. – Some BENCHES by White, simple and solid with crisply rolled tops, prefiguring William Morris's furniture of 1856 onwards. – ALTAR RAIL, also by *White*, with curving iron supports. – STAINED GLASS. Two E windows by *Clayton & Bell*, 1896 and 1906. – MONUMENTS. In N wall of transept, C13 sepulchral coffin slab with quatrefoil-headed cross with arched recess. – Edward Hobbs, 1737 by *Weston* of Exeter, with two allegorical figures in garments as chastely understated as if they were of 1820.

CROSS. s of s porch. Medieval. A large solid wheel-head with incised Latin cross to both faces.

The village extends E to the coast at PORTSCATHO, a former fishing village open to Gerrans Bay. Above the harbour is THE LUGGER, a pretty row of early C19 houses, some stuccoed, with symmetrical three-window fronts around central door-ways with simple porches on round columns or doorcases with consoles. Beyond, the UNITED REFORMED CHURCH, 1822, also stucco, with long E.E. windows and pretty Gothic porch.

ROSTEAGUE HOUSE, I m. S. C15–C16 house remodelled *c.* 1700 and extended 1820. Two-storey symmetrical five-window E front with identical flanking wings two bays deep and one bay wide, with a small chapel to N of main range (first mentioned in 1401). Parlour has fine moulded plaster ceiling of *c.* 1700 with oval bayleaf and oakleaf garland, bolection-moulded pan-elling and re-sited C16 fireplace. To the SE a WALLED GARDEN originating in the C17 with a re-sited C17 Baroque carving of Abraham and Isaac, and a late C19 summerhouse. To the NW of the house, ST NUN'S WELL, probably a holy well with a medieval core and reused C16–C17 doorway lintel.

TREWINCE, I m. SSW. Mid-C18 incorporating remnants of earlier C15–C17 building phases; extended *c.* 1930. Neatly pro-portioned Georgian five-window granite ashlar E front with modillion cornice and rusticated quoins; the sills were lowered in the C19. Interior has much good mid-C18 detail including plasterwork to main stairwell, vestibule and parlour. To SW, early C19 QUAY for the house with cobbled slipway.

TREWITHIAN HOUSE, I m. N. Remodelling *c.* 1700 of an earlier house. U-shaped plan, symmetrical three-window E front with flanking projecting wings of equal length. Interior has open-well stair and dog-leg second stair. Clover-leaf moulded plaster ceiling in parlour of r. wing.

GODOLPHIN

6030

Former CHURCH OF ST JOHN THE BAPTIST. Now residential. 1850 by *J. P. St Aubyn*, one of his best churches. A delightfully simple design realizing the ideas of the early Ecclesiological Movement in E.E. style. The form is striking, the steep scantle slate roofs carried down over the aisles at a lower pitch and a lower roof over the chancel. Double bellcote over W gable. Single or paired lancets, the chancel E window with three trefoil-headed lights. The lofty nave has an arch- and scissor-braced roof springing from corbels in the spandrels of the four-bay arcade. Pointed arches, the arches carried on round piers with moulded capitals. Entrance GATEWAY with square gatepiers, wrought-iron gates and round-arch overthrow with lamp holder, and cyma-shaped walls of vertically set granite either side.

GODOLPHIN. The most westerly major house on the mainland. Its haunting solitude, encircled in woods below Godolphin Hill, makes arrival at its *c.* 1630 colonnaded entrance front all the more astonishing: for here, so far west, is a daring essay in

73

p. 213

Renaissance planning and architecture that has remained almost unaltered.

There was a house here by the early C14 but this was reported ruinous in the later C15 and a new house was begun c. 1475. The approach at that time was from the W but it must have been at least partially reconstructed by Sir William Godolphin I in the 1530s, since Henry VIII's *Great Map of the West* of 1538 shows a fortified house (now entered from the N), and an early C18 Borlase drawing (copying a then extant depiction of the house on panelling at nearby Pengersick Castle) shows a hall flanked by two wings and closed by a castellated N curtain wall with E and W corner towers. Throughout the C16 and early C17 the Godolphins advanced at the Tudor and Stuart courts and increased their influence in Cornwall, becoming Governors of the Isles of Scilly from the mid C16. Tin mining further enhanced their fortunes, leading to a major programme of remodelling between c. 1585 and c. 1635 by Sir Francis I (1535–1608), his son Sir William IV (†1613) and his son Sir Francis II (†1667). This, Godolphin's formative period, saw the gradual and successful infusion of classical influences into the medieval Cornish building tradition. At its fullest extent the house comprised a double courtyard plan divided by a great hall, but most of the hall and the buildings of the S court were demolished c. 1805. It became a tenant farm until purchased by Sidney Schofield in 1937. The Schofield family began a long campaign of repair, taken forward in the late C20 and early C21 by *John Schofield** and *Architecton* (project architect *Paul Richold*) until the estate passed to the National Trust in 2008.

EXTERIOR. The house, of three wings around a square courtyard, is approached from the N into a FORECOURT created by Sir Francis II c. 1630. Closing the approach is the impressive ashlar-faced NORTH RANGE of this date, the only part completed of the intended reconstruction of the house. It is castellated and incorporates at each end the corner towers of the outer wall of the earlier house. Between these on a stylobate of two steps a seven-bay centre is raised on a colonnade of six sturdy Tuscan columns of monolithic granite from Tregonning quarry (*see* below) on both front and courtyard elevations. Between the columns are flat keystoned lintels with surprisingly advanced fascia detail. The windows are transomed and mullioned and have the same hoodmoulds drawn in a continuous string course as at Lanhydrock (q.v.). The elevation to the inner courtyard is the same. The spine of this range is the old curtain wall and the inner courtyard is still reached through the splendid ARCHWAY built into the wall c. 1575–80 by Sir Francis I. This is so remarkably similar to that at Collacombe, Devon, as to appear to be a copy, if not an entirely correct one. It is flanked by two cylindrical attached columns with multimoulded capitals and bases on pedestals, above which the

---

*This account is much indebted to John Schofield's research into the house and estate.

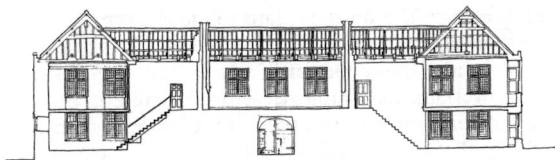

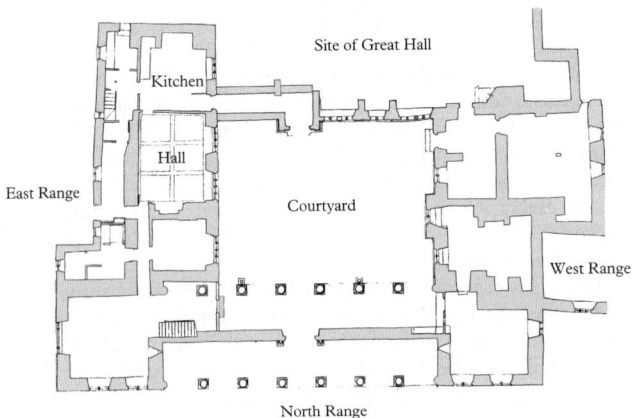

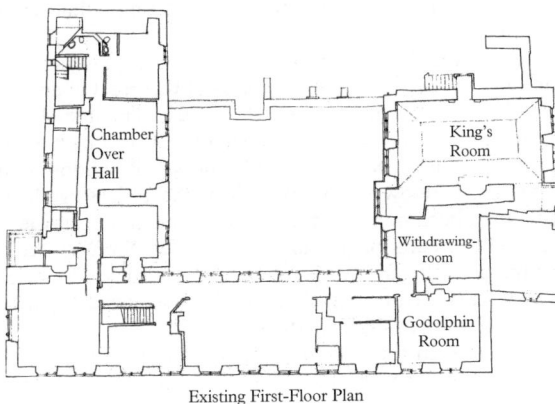

Godolphin House. Section, looking south.
Ground and existing first-floor plans

capitals become bases for short upper columns also terminating in capitals: outsize guttae prove more existed above. It is complemented by contemporary oak gates with pilasters and cornices, their tops forming a large scallop shell. The N range was designed as a suite of apartments and is one of the earliest examples in England of an arrangement of paired chambers with service rooms accessed by separate stairs and a spacious reception room in the centre. Its Renaissance conception must surely reflect the Godolphins' connections at the Stuart court.

That Francis's ambitious plans to make a symmetrical house were abandoned, perhaps at the Civil War, is apparent immediately inside the courtyard, where the pre-existing EAST RANGE overlaps the N range (leaving one column free-standing inside the present entrance hall); it is also demonstrated by the toothing of the uncompleted ashlar on the E elevation of the range. The E range is the most recognizable survival of the house begun after *c.* 1475. This had possibly started as an independent set of lodgings to the main house with its own hall and great chamber, but the varied assembly of post-medieval windows, all uncusped, and the centre ground-floor window taller than its neighbours, suggest that Sir William upgraded it to a private hall. Separate access from the lower end of the great hall was made by bringing forward the N wall of the hall into the courtyard. The S end of the range was remodelled *c.* 1805 reusing two three-light mullion windows and a four-centred arched doorway.

On the S side of the courtyard are the puzzling remains of the demolished great hall, now reduced and its battlemented parapet lowered. The late C15 porch with blind panelled jambs, very similar to the S porch at Breage church and other local churches, projects only slightly from the hall wall, because the wall of the hall was rebuilt further into the courtyard *c.* 1600 to align with the connecting wall to the E range that had been brought forward earlier.

The courtyard elevation of the WEST RANGE was refaced *c.* 1630 but still displays the high status of the great chamber and the high end of the hall in the earlier house. The first-floor suite has tall mullioned windows and a slightly projecting bay carried over cellars with C18 barrel stands and small windowed storerooms: the windows of the W wall of the cellars are late C15. This range became a prestigious state apartment in the series of embellishments begun in the 1530s by Sir William I and continued by the later C16 and early C17 family. The oriel and porch were added by Sir William IV, who moved the fireplace from the S to the N side of the chamber.

INTERIOR. In the hall (now dining room) of the E range, a fine *c.* 1500 ceiling, the best of its date in Cornwall, its intersecting beams richly moulded with vine trails, bosses and leaves. Also much contemporary linenfold panelling. The chamber above has a four-bay arch-braced roof with carved wall-plate and a barrel ceiling revealed and restored in 1985. In the kitchen an elliptical arched fireplace (cf. Star Castle, Isles of Scilly). The King's Room, on the first floor in the W range has a canopied ceiling with two C17 pendants of ornamental plasterwork, and two bays symmetrically placed on the N side, one with an early C17 cornice and frieze; with its porch and oriel, the arrangement suggests a presence chamber. On the S wall, the spectacular early C17 oak chimneypiece from the great hall, placed here in the 1980s: intricately carved Renaissance detail, paired Ionic columns with amulets and pineappling on patterned pedestals supporting a deep pulvinated and scaled frieze, above which are three large niches set back from matching smaller columns and round arches with rusticated splats between. A deep gadrooned frieze with wide cornice on hart's-tongue brackets completes the composition. The large fireplace has roll and cavetto mouldings and diabolo stops; there is a similar one in the next room which also has a C17 plasterwork frieze of large flowers. In the N range, also at first floor the Godolphin Room (w) has a C17 plasterwork frieze and a mid-C17 fireplace behind early C18 Delft tiles of sea creatures, surrounded by an overmantel with pilasters flanking a bolection-moulded panel with articulated cornice. The early C17 layout of the first-floor rooms in this range was masked by an early C19 corridor running along the s side until its recent restoration.

STABLES. Adjoining the NW end of the house. A long range whose back is a solid C15 wall enclosing the King's Garden (*see* below). Built by Sir Francis I *c.* 1600, a remarkable design and rare survival. A sophisticated façade of triple symmetry, (revealed inside as three interlinked sections), the side sections with arched doorways between low mullioned windows, the central doorway raised on steps at mezzanine level, and first-floor loading doors either side; at both ground and first floor two long equal compartments flanking a smaller central compartment. Pigeon holes below the eaves. This is the finest stable block of its date in Cornwall and may reflect the influence of *Robert Adams** who was at that time designing Star Castle on St Mary's for Sir Francis (q.v.).

GARDENS AND PLEASURE GROUNDS. There is nowhere better in Cornwall to see the survival of Tudor and Stuart outdoor arrangements. At the SW corner of the W wing, the KING'S GARDEN, so named for its proximity to the King's Room, created as an enclosure in the early C16. Its late C15 N wall (the s wall of the stables) has four BEE BOLES. The SIDE GARDEN, E of the house, dates from the late C15 and is of nine square compartments separated by cross walls, rising to the SE and bounded by raised walls to N, E and s. The three W compartments appear from archaeological evidence to survive from the layout of the early C14 precinct. The six E compartments are now divided from the present garden by a C19 wall but the late C15 and C16 layout survives as banks and archaeological features. The SW compartment contains a rectangular pond that has been truncated by the construction of another pond in the late C17 or early C18. The s wall is likely to have been used as a stand for viewing the C16 DEER COURSE running E–W parallel to the garden boundary, on a line now occupied by a C17 avenue. The once extensive ORCHARD lay to the N with a rectangular late C17 or early C18 CIDER HOUSE at its centre. THE MOWHAY, SW of the house, is probably the SW compartment of the C14 precinct and appears to have been a significant garden in the late C15 and early C16. The WATER GARDEN lies to the NW of the house N of the stableyard.

*I owe this suggestion to John Schofield.

PARK. The deer park, disparked in 1830 and now known as Godolphin Hill, occupies an area of heathland and the summit of the hill. Stone park pales survive to the s and NW with stone walls enclosing The Slips – a track and remnants of an avenue leading SW from the house – and a C16 watering complex SW of the house. A series of C16 and early C17 pillow mounds, built to house rabbits, survive N and E of the summit. The C14 park which originally reached down to the Hayle river was later extended NE in a series of compartments adjoining the Side Garden and the Far Orchard NE of the house. The deer course s of the house appears to date from this phase and comprised a level E–W course with a square STAND W of the house overlooking it; its solid stone base of the late C16 or early C17 survives adjacent to the C18 stone walled POUND, which incorporates an earlier structure with the remains of two or more slab-roofed cells.

Of other estate buildings, an extensive range of mostly C19 FARM BUILDINGS to the W of the house, including BARN, SHIPPONS and PIGSTIES. To the NE of the house a late C16 BLOWING HOUSE and the ruins of another. These were the key buildings of the Godolphin tin works where Sir Francis I employed German or Dutch advisers to improve the refining process: their innovations were important to the history of tin mining in Cornwall. The N gable-end contains an upright hearth and locker arrangement similar to Dartmoor blowing houses. The adjacent BLOWING HOUSE STAMPS, a late C17 and C18 structure, is now a private house. The former three-storeyed COUNT HOUSE, N of the house, is now also a residence.

At GREAT WORK, 1 m. SSW, the prominent ENGINE HOUSE on Leeds Shaft, its distinctive stack of two brick stages with no batter above the stone base and a separating granite string course.

TREGONNING HILL, 2 m. S. An important granite quarry for the great house and other important buildings (e.g. Breage church), within an oval bivallate Iron Age hillfort, Castle Pencaire, with close-spaced ramparts on the N summit. Two well-preserved Iron Age or Roman ROUNDS on the E side, the s one remarkably intact with strong bank and ditch, SE entrance, and earthworks of round-houses against the inner side of the bank. Set within extensive medieval outfield strips. William Cookworthy of Plymouth discovered a source of china clay to the SW of the hill in the late 1740s.

GODREVY ISLAND
1¾ m. NNW of Gwithian

There are few more memorable images of Cornwall than the prospect across St Ives Bay of the LIGHTHOUSE, its mystique heightened by its frequent appearance in the paintings of Alfred Wallis and the St Ives School as well as its identification as the likely inspiration for Virginia Woolf's *To the Lighthouse* (1927). 1859 by *James Walker*, built by *Thomas Eva* of Helston. Five-storey and lantern, octagonal plan, enclosed in an almost oval perimeter wall, with single storey keepers' cottages and stores.

GOLANT
St Samson

ST SAMSON. Wonderfully situated high above the village, the E side overlooking the Fowey estuary. A small church but full of interest. W tower, nave, S aisle and S porch. A chapel of Tywardreath Priory from 1281, rebuilt almost in one go in the early C16; consecrated in 1509, although the square-headed windows on the N and S elevations seem more like *c.* 1520. Low tower of rough granite blocks, in two stages, battlemented but not pinnacled. Small late C15 HOLY WELL in the corner between tower and S porch with stone-vaulted roof. The porch, open W to the well, is dated 1856MR (Martha Rashleigh) and was probably rebuilt at that time. The interior is a delight, light and airy with white plastered walls and ceiled wagon roofs over nave, chancel and S aisle. A restoration of 1842 removed the screen and repaired the roofs which have richly moulded ribs, bosses and wall-plates; the latter carry inscriptions but are a mix of original and mid-C19 in the wrong order. The seven-bay arcade between nave and chancel and S aisle has low standard piers, the five nave piers of Pentewan stone with ring capitals, the chancel piers of granite with faceted capitals. Tower and W end restored by *Hine & Odgers* in 1891. – BENCH-ENDS, early C16, later made up into a PULPIT, LECTERN, READING DESK and SANCTUARY CHAIR. They are uncommonly varied: especially noteworthy is a series with little figures of apostles on one shield and their emblems on the other; also one large figure of St Sampson. Other motifs include two carved heads on little castles, a fool's head, a coat of arms of the Colquite family, and an angel issuing from a pomegranate flower. – SCULPTURE. Head of Christ, looking up; marble; Italian Baroque? – ROYAL ARMS. Of James II, dated 1685, painted on board. – STAINED GLASS. In N window of chancel, late C15 figures of St James the Great and St Anthony, well preserved. Two E windows by *Burlison & Grylls*, 1891 and 1907, and S aisle by *Fouracre & Watson*, 1891. – MONUMENT. Slate plate to Edmund Constable †1716 ('Short blaze of life, meteor of human pride / Essayed to live but liked it not and died').

Former METHODIST CHAPEL, Cowshit Lane. Built *c.* 1875 incorporating an earlier building as a schoolroom, with two tall round-arched windows to the road.

PENQUITE. ½ m. N. 1848 by *George Wightwick*, the same year he
enlarged Tregrehan (q.v.). Plain two storeys, symmetrical five
windows and N front, the N front with the three centre bays
broken forward under a pediment with *œil de bœuf*. Double-
depth plan with central stair hall and fine open-well stair with
moulded wreath handrail and cast-iron balusters. Single-storey
service block around small courtyard with bellcote over.

CASTLE DORE, 1¼ m. W. Small bivallate HILLFORT on ridgeway with extensive views. Excavated 1936–7. Two major Iron
Age phases; postulated post-Roman association with King
Mark (Tristan and Iseult stories) dissolved on recent review of
evidence. Numerous Iron Age ROUND-HOUSES, of both
phases, excavated within circular inner enclosure. Original
earthen rampart heightened and revetted with stone in second
phase when houses also built in outer enclosure. Parliamentar-
ian soldiers made a vain stand against the Royalists here
in 1644.

GOLDEN MANOR

9040

The intriguing group of buildings is consistent with Leland's
description 1542, that 'John Tregian' hath a manor place richly
begun and amply but not ended called Wulvedon, alias Goldoun'.

The HOUSE faces N and is divided into three parts, each of which
show details of early C16 construction, with ruined fragments
in early brick in the SE range: it is possible that what survives
is just the N range of a larger (or planned but uncompleted)
courtyard house. As it stands, however, it is tempting to inter-
pret the three sections of the house as the usual medieval
arrangements of the hall at the centre, the services at the W
end, and the solar at the E end, with a first-floor chamber with
two-light pointed windows. The hall was remodelled in the
early C17 in granite ashlar as a three-bay two-storey block with
three-light square-headed windows in ovolo-moulded surrounds, and has a fireplace with Renaissance decoration in four
panels of tritons and candelabra. Soon afterwards a giant new
fireplace was built at the W end of the hall backing onto the
former screens passage and partly blocking the new window
of the N front. The symmetrical three-bay E elevation and the
whole of the rest of the house show a Late Georgian character
that was probably achieved at more than one period.

To the E, THE KEEP, a small rectangular Tudor brick building
with a C19 wing, the earliest use of brick in the county. It may
have been the gatehouse to the main house. Its E gable wall
has diaper work at first-floor level, also the earliest known
instance of such patterning in Cornwall. The extensive use of
brick here (it also occurs in the house as backing to the early
C17 granite ashlar of the N range and in a fireback) is of unusual

significance given its rarity and must be a local tradition that continues in the mid C18 at Trewithen (q.v.), of which estate Golden is part.

ICE HOUSE and ASH HOUSE, SW of the house. Early to mid-C18, partly brick.

BARN, NE of the house. C15–C16 with extensive later rebuilding, including some C18 brick. L-plan with quadrant newel stair-turret in the angle leading to both blocks. A variety of late medieval features but many re-set: the round-headed window at first-floor level in the W wall is one of the few *in situ*. The datestone 1879 indicates the rebuilding of the S part of the building, the gable-end incorporating many reused C16 fragments from the house, including door and window arches reversed to create pointed arches and a fireplace used as a doorhead. The former eight-bay roof was of upper cruck trusses (cf. the Old Post Office, Tintagel). The newel stair raises the question of whether this barn was a house with a first-floor hall (cf. Neadon Upper Hall, Manaton, Devon).

GOONHILLY EARTH STATION

Between Cury and St Martin-in-Meneage

7020

The giant parabolic dishes rising above the bare and windswept Goonhilly Downs mark the birthplace of satellite communication; a site that received the first transatlantic television pictures via Telstar and became for a time the largest satellite station in the world, with sixty-four dishes. The first dish, Antenna No. 1, was designed *c.* 1958 and built 1960–2 by *Husband & Co.*, engineers, design consultant *Mr Kington* and the *GPO*. It was dubbed Arthur, with other dishes named after characters from the legend. The dish is 85 ft (26 metres) in diameter, of framed stainless steel, fully mobile on twin bipods mounted on roller bearings. The station was a companion to the GPO Tower in London, serving the communications revolution of that period. Antenna No. 3, 1972, is reminiscent of a windmill with its reinforced concrete tapered tower and counterbalance weights, the dish held within a frame of interconnected and braced metal girders.

GORRAN

9040

ST GORRAN. A stately W tower 90 ft (27.4 metres) high signals a large church of great dignity and more than usual interest. Tower of three stages with buttresses set back from the corners, wholly late C15 or early C16, with pierced slate ventilators and louvres to third stage, embattled parapet, and large crocketed

pinnacles. S porch also C15 with embattled parapet, two pinnacles, panelled jambs and wagon roof with foliated ribs,
bosses and wall-plates. S aisle has C19 Perp three-light windows
and a four-light C15 E window, the chancel a C14 three-light E
window. Of most interest, however, are the lancet windows of
the N transept and especially the blocked door in the N side of
the nave, clearly of the C13 with a head at its apex and two
heads as label stops. A church was here by 1086, possibly a
monastic foundation, and the evidence for its originally cruciform plan is strongly suggested by the N wall of the nave, the
N transept with a C14 arch from nave to transept, and the
retention of the responds of the former S transept when the S
aisle was built in the early C15; the parallels with the sequence
of development at nearby St Ewe (q.v.) are striking. The S aisle
has an eight-bay arcade, the five most easterly bays of Pentewan stone, the most westerly three of granite and more crudely
carved, with three different forms of base suggesting the aisle
was built in stages. The piers have the same variation of the
standard section as St Ives, namely a concave–convex–concave
curve instead of the usual single hollow. The moulded
capitals and two-centred arches also point to the early C15.
Restorations by *J. P. St Aubyn* 1890–5 included the arch- and
wind-braced roofs to nave, chancel and S aisle, much re-
windowing and re-flooring. – FONT. Norman, on five supports,
with corner faces and, as chief ornamental motifs between, the
unusual motif of streaking flowing hair alongside rosette, tree
of life etc. Partly reworked, probably in the C14, to incorporate
the Bodrugan arms (*see* Bodrogan Farmhouse below): a
curious un-Norman faced monster lies at the base. – BENCH-
ENDS. Fifty-three, an unusually large number, attached to late
C19 pews. Some have two motifs, some one. There are many
initials and also some ornamental motifs clearly belonging to
the Renaissance including a triple face. – PARCLOSE SCREEN.
1945, part of a major reordering of the chancel including choir
stalls, panelling etc., good mid-C20 craftsmanship. – STAINED
GLASS. Fragments of medieval glass in the E window of the S
aisle. – Two windows in S aisle by *William Wailes*, 1875. –
MONUMENTS. Head of a coffin-shaped slab with raised carved
foliated urns. – Brass of a kneeling female figure *c.* 1510, said
to be the 'lady of Brannel'. – Monument in the nave to Richard
Edgecumbe of Bodrugan †1604. A purely Italian frame with
scrolly broken pediment, the inscription panel with strapwork
and corbels, impossible in England at that time: either foreign
or later, say *c.* 1670.

In the CHURCHYARD, a large granite VAULT attached to the
S aisle with segmented arch with ball finial on a shaped stem
and carved inscription: 'Resurgemus 1813 WSG'. Capped
SUNDIAL with gnomon dated 1708 on granite pier set into wall
at E end of churchyard, and C19 LYCHGATE with simple
wrought-iron overthrow.

The small churchtown is a good group of modest local buildings, including the former SCHOOLROOM of *c.* 1840 immediately W of the lychgate and opposite, across the road, a handsome late Georgian INN.

BODROGAN FARMHOUSE. Of the once great medieval house and chapel of the Bodrugan family, immensely powerful in C14 and C15 Cornwall, nothing remains. The present house is a largely C19 and C20 remodelling of a late C17 to early C18 building with some fragments from the original.

GORRAN HAVEN

0040

The village, known as Portheast in the medieval period, was once important for pilchard fishing.

ST JUST. The small scale and tightly constrained site among whitewashed cottages above the beach bestow a charmingly intimate character. Probably built in the C15 by the Bodrugans as a chapel of ease to Gorran (q.v.). Sold in 1568, recorded as ruinous in 1745 and later used as a pilchard cellar with a Wesleyan chapel over, but restored by *J. P. St Aubyn* in 1885. The W tower is roughly pentagonal in plan, the extra angle incorporating the stair-turret with a four-centred arched doorway and three-light Perp window above. The two windows in the S side of the nave are of two and three lights with cusped lights with square heads. The best feature is the S door which has a four-centred arch with roll mouldings and recessed spandrels with carved heads; above it is an image niche with moulded ogee arch and foliated sill decoration. Interior with late C19 wagon roof with C15 bosses, tall three-centred tower arch, a C15 PISCINA and a well-carved IMAGE STAND, not *in situ.* – ALTAR RAILS. Of C15 roof timbers, said to be from St Gorran. – STAINED GLASS. Naïve but charming E window and tower window by *W. Willimott c.* 1870s.

The small harbour is protected by a single PIER, rebuilt in 1888 by J. C. Williams, Lord Lieutenant, to replace the medieval one constructed by the Bodrugans. STEP COTTAGE and CLIFF COTTAGE in CHURCH STREET retain former pilchard cellars at ground-floor level, with the living accommodation above accessed by an external stair. The cluster of cottages and little streets struggle to retain their identity as a small enclave around the harbour now engulfed inland by C20 suburban housing.

THE DODMAN, 1½ m. S. Two closely spaced ramparts of later Iron Age CLIFF CASTLE secure south Cornwall's most massive headland. Inner rampart largely intact. Traces of outer rampart along most of its length. Two Bronze Age BARROWS survive among the former medieval strip fields within the enclosure.

GRADE

St Grade. In a lovely remote position alone in fields and visible for miles around. Late C14 or C15 w tower of regular serpentine blocks, two stages and unbuttressed, just like the neighbouring Lizard churches. The rest of the church was rebuilt in 1861–3 by *E. W. Godwin* of London and Bristol in un-Cornish proportions with roof pitches so steep as to almost overwhelm the low walls of the nave and chancel, a contrast with the diminutive dignity of the tower. A pointed-arched s door, a blocked N door of serpentine, and a small cusped-headed image niche on the s porch, all of the C14, were re-set in the new building. – FONT. C13, a simplified version of the Bodmin type, similar to nearby Cury: thick, short corner shafts and four shallowly carved stars, rosettes etc., in circles. – Fine mid-C19 serpentine LECTERN, serpentine PULPIT of lesser quality, from the Poltesco factory (q.v.). – STAINED GLASS. The Good Shepherd, 1865 by *Wailes*, in the s wall, excellent. – E window 1862 and other s aisle windows of 1865 and 1870. – MONUMENTS. The best feature in the church is the fine large BRASS to James Erisey †1522 and his wife, Margaret, with their ten children below and shields at the corners of the slab. Erisey's armour is especially detailed. It is an early example of a type found elsewhere in Cornwall (cf. Mawgan-in-Pydar, etc.). – Two Erisey tablets in the tower, Armiger Erisey †1692 and his wife, Marie, †1699 with inscription in rectangular frame and arms surrounded by foliage, and Richard Erisey †1722. – Large slate slab on external N wall of the chancel to Hugh Mason, †1671. Coat of arms with inscription below.

GRAMPOUND

From the bridge and toll house at the crossing of the Fal the little township climbs gently uphill as not much more than a single street towards its charming centrepiece, the diminutive Town Hall and small church. Grampound was a medieval borough with a charter granted in 1332, and its medieval plan is still readable in the settlement's layout of houses and burgage plots behind. But the borough never grew large and, although sending two members to Parliament, was extinguished even before the 1832 Reform Act. A complete small town street survives, lined with Pentewan stone houses and cottages, most presenting C18 and C19 fronts with good period details.

St Naunter. A chapel of ease to Creed (q.v.), licensed in 1421, ruinous by *c.* 1820, and completely rebuilt in 1869 in a reticent E.E. style with lancet windows, apsidal E end and gabled w bellcote. The interior is surprisingly lofty, the arch- and wind-braced nave roof rising from stone corbels, the chancel with a wooden vault. Good C19 fittings and furnishings. – STAINED GLASS. A touching S aisle window by *Fouracre & Watson*, 1882. – Excellent ironwork at the entrance to the church with twisted iron railings with trefoil finials, cable-moulded stanchions, and cross finials to the pedestrian gateway, all of 1869. Against it stands the 12 ft (3.7-metre) tall late medieval CROSS, on steps and pedestal, unadorned.

TOWN HALL. The perfect expression of Grampound's transition from borough to parish status. A small rectangular building of single ground-floor room with a chamber above is transformed by its slate-hung clock tower with eye-catching ogee cupola and golden ball into the classic C18 town hall in miniature. The chamber has pleasing early C19 plasterwork with central elliptical rosette and moulded cornice.

In Fore Street, the MANOR HOUSE (now subdivided into Nos. 1–3). C16 to early C17 house with later C17 additions, thatched roof. External front lateral stack with carved stone gargoyles to the cornice. Plain plaster barrel ceiling in the chamber over the hall with central pendant and moulded cornice. Fine bolection-moulded chimneypiece inside No. 3. To the E, a DRYING SHED and attached PIT SHED, dated 1839 on internal plasterwork, part of the former tannery.

TOWN MILLS, Mill Lane. Mid-C19 watermill with overshot waterwheel, three-storey with gabled sack hoist.

At GRAMPOUND ROAD, 2 m. NW, the VILLAGE HALL. 1933 by *Cowell, Drewitt & Wheatly*. Sweeping overhanging slate roofs over rough-rendered walls, battered and slate-topped buttresses, and excellent Arts and Crafts detailing. A good example of how the radical style of one generation became acceptable to the conservative architectural taste of the next. It was the gift of Sir Robert Harvey of TRENOWTH, 1 m. W, a Neo-Georgian house of 1929 by the same firm. Below the house the remains of a CHAPEL mentioned in 1405.

GRIBBIN TOWER *see* POLKERRIS

GULVAL

4030

ST GULVAL. At first sight C19, the church fitting well with the Victorian-looking churchtown in which it sits. Only the tower is obviously old: of regular granite blocks, in three stages, with no buttresses, and plain except for image niches corbelled out at the corners below the parapet that are filled with squat figures, possibly of the Evangelists. We are here in the rare position of knowing its date: it had just been completed in 1440. The rest was extensively renewed and enlarged in a series

of restorations of 1858, 1885 and 1891–3 when the C13 N transept was rebuilt and a N aisle added by *J. P. St Aubyn*: one is
inclined to agree with Henderson that, as a result, 'its interest
and antiquity have fled before the invading forces of modern
munificence'. The S aisle has octagonal piers, their capitals
decorated with shield-holding angels, as at St Ives. The date
there would compare to that of the tower at Gulval. Similar
piers and arches spanning the transept indicate a N aisle was
intended. – FONT. Also of the St Ives type but with only
one severely stylized angel holding a shield, and the Kymiel
arms impaling St Aubyn. – C14 SEDILIA and PISCINA in
chancel. – STAINED GLASS. Much of the mid to late C19.
Chancel E by *Ward & Hughes*. – S chancel chapel and S aisle
mostly 1858–69 by *Lavers, Barraud & Westlake* with one of 1874
by *Ward & Hughes*. – N aisle some by *Heaton, Butler & Bayne*
and again *Ward & Hughes*. – MONUMENTS. Fragmentary
monument with two kneeling figures: John Davills †1627
and Arthur Harris †1628. – William Harris †1766, prettily
Rococo. – William Arundel Harris †1826 by *Scott* of Penzance:
rather reactionary for its date. – Outside the S wall of the
church l. of the porch, INSCRIBED STONE. A churchyard
cross-shaft, set upside down. On its front face plaitwork in the
uppermost panel and the letters VN and VI in the middle and
lower panels; key patterns on the sides. Alongside, a very
eroded LANTERN CROSS-HEAD on a large granite block with
a kneeling figure with a halo, holding a bible, on its main face.

METHODIST CHURCH, Trevarrack Road. 1884. Curious mix of
classical and Gothic on the main road elevation, where the
large central Gothic window is flanked by round-headed
windows.

7   CHYSAUSTER, 1 m. NE of Newmill. An unusually large settlement, primarily Romano-British but with some Iron Age elements (ROUND-HOUSE and FOGOU), comprising at least eleven
courtyard houses, of which five are partly excavated and
restored (between 1873 and 1939). Eight edge a street-like
trackway. Small garden plots are attached to the houses. Only
the two simplest houses appear identical. They had a gateway
into a probably un-roofed courtyard, onto which opened two
standard buildings, or rooms (probably individually roofed).
The round room opposite the entrance was probably the
main dwelling, with stone-lined rectangular hearth, while the
curving long room was a cowhouse. Other courtyard houses
contain these elements plus other cells including additional
round rooms and open-sided lean-to structures, perhaps for
workshops.

NINE MAIDENS (Dans Maen), ½ m. NW of Boskednan. Early
Bronze Age STONE CIRCLE, the positions of its eleven standing stones suggesting a perfect circle, even spacing and an
original total of twenty-two or twenty-three stones. Cairns and
a broken menhir mark a line leading NW towards Carn Galva's
Neolithic tor enclosure. The circle's two tallest stones, 6 ft 6 in.
(2 m.) high, in the NW quadrant also frame Carn Galva when

viewed from the Bronze Age CAIRN just S of circle, emphasizing that tor's importance to the circle's builders and users.

BODRIFTY, 1 m. NW of Newmill. Group of well-built ROUND-HOUSES, their walls faced inside and out. Excavations showed continuous occupation from later Bronze Age to later Iron Age, some houses being substantially rebuilt. The Iron Age enclosure of the settlement is entered through a surviving W gateway. Earlier prehistoric CUP-MARKED STONE beside farm track to W.

GUNNISLAKE

4070

A straggling mining parish just above the tidal reach of the Tamar whose scenery, including a 300 ft cliff face on the Devon side of the river, was dramatic enough to inspire Turner on his 1813 tour, and which remains largely unspoilt.

ST ANNE, Sand Hill. 1880–91, by *J. P. St Aubyn*, as a chapel of ease to Calstock. Built into a steeply sloping site, skilfully designed to emphasize its tall proportions using an E.E. style with additional lancets to the basement and clerestory. The two-stage NW bell-tower, open at the ground floor as a porch, rises to a pyramidal roof with finial, and has a circular stair-tower. Five-bay N and S arcades with chamfered four-centred arches.

NEW BRIDGE. The most impressive of the medieval Tamar crossings. Built *c.* 1500, 182 ft (55.5 metres) long, of six slightly pointed arches with triangular cutwaters rising to refuges. The granite ashlar is carried up to the string course and built out in rubble at parapet level, the latter rebuilt in the C20.

TAMAR VALLEY CENTRE, Cemetery Road. 2010 by *Bill Dunster Associates* and *ZEDfactory*, using local materials, especially timber, as a low-energy building. Striking design, simple and workmanlike, with the architect's signature wind cowl above a sedum roof. It complements the ruined engine houses among which it is set.

Bealswood Road leads to the S end of the 300 metre long TAMAR MANURE NAVIGATION CANAL *c.* 1808, part of a proposal to join the Bristol Channel at Bude with the English Channel. Remains of LOCKGATES and WALLING in granite ashlar: the canal entrance here formed a widening of the river to allow Victorian and Edwardian paddle steamers to turn round. The higher ground to the W and N, from Hingstone Downs to the Tamar valley, is an area rich in mining remains, quarries, brickworks and arsenic stacks, the most prominent GREENHILL, with scattered groups of small miners' cottages.

WHIMPLE FARM, 1 m. S, is a good example of a high-quality C17 vernacular house with a two storey porch added (and dated) 1670, and stair-towers either side of the through passage at the rear. Carefully repaired and restored (including the reconstruction of the upper storey of the porch) by *Van der Steen Hall Architects*, 2012–13.

GUNWALLOE

St Winwaloe. Even for Cornwall an especially romantic site for a church, on its own on the edge of a sandy cove but sheltered from the sea by a bluff. It was one of the three medieval chapelries to Breage. The unusual feature is the detached BELL-TOWER to the W of the church (cf. Feock, Gwennap and Lamorran), built over a natural recess in the rock, two-storeyed, with a pyramidal roof and no buttresses; it might be C13 in origin but was much rebuilt in the C19. The CHURCH itself was rebuilt in the C14 to C16, only the W gable-end of the nave surviving from the earlier structure. The S porch has the panelled jambs familiar from other Lizard churches, and the N aisle an E window with bulbous cusped decoration as at Cury, Mullion and Sithney, a more elaborate form of the C15 windows in the N wall. N and S aisles are of five bays and identical design, with standard Cornish piers, plain capitals, and thinly decorated abaci. Fine wagon roofs to porch and S aisle: the roof of the nave and N aisle belong to an extensive restoration of 1869–71 that also renewed the E windows of the chancel and S aisle and the W window, and extended the chancel slightly E. – Two FONTS, one early C12 with a shallow round bowl and barbaric chevron, the other a C19 copy of a C15 type. – ROOD SCREEN. Two panels of the rood screen, C15, are the most important feature of the church, with painted figures of apostles below (cf. Budock, St Winnow, and many Devon examples) and beautiful flamboyant tracery above. They are used inside the N and S doors. – Handsome PAR-CLOSE SCREENS, BENCHES and BENCH-ENDS in the Cornish tradition *c.* 1920–30 by *Herbert Read* of Exeter. – Granite ALTAR with deep *mensa* by *Sir Ninian Comper*, also early C20. – In the churchyard just E of the S aisle a wheel-headed WAYSIDE CROSS, medieval, with slightly flared cross on each face.

GWEEK

An ancient port at the head of a little creek off the Helford river. It is probably of Roman origin and was acquired by Helston before 1301 after the Loe bar had blocked the harbour there. Its long industrial history included its role as a major port for the export of tin from the Wendron district in the C18. Still with a busy boatyard and working QUAYS, the settlement gathers loosely around an early C18 BRIDGE with a pretty village street of C18 and C19 HOUSES and COTTAGES, a former early C19 CORN MILL and a large TIMBER STORE and OFFICES, now converted to residential and commercial use, a former METHODIST CHAPEL dated 1887, and THE LODGE, an especially good little *cottage orné* of the early C19 with an octagonal thatched roof carried over an open veranda supported on wooden columns with Gothick windows, originally a lodge for Trelowarren (q.v.).

GWENNAP

The area was renowned as 'the richest square mile in the Old World' in the late C18 and early C19, the wealth coming from the hugely important Consolidated, United and Poldice mines: by the 1820s the parish's mines produced more than a third of the world's copper and its population of 10,794 in 1841 was only exceeded by Penzance and Truro. The settlement pattern is a scatter of small hamlets mostly grown up around former mines; the landscape still clearly displays the effects of extensive mining.

St WENEPPA (St Gwennap), Churchtown. Set at the top of an extensive churchyard. The rare feature is the detached BELL-TOWER (cf. Feock and Gunwalloe). Rebuilt in the C15 on older, possibly Norman, foundations. Two stages with a pyramidal roof, round-headed N doorway, two-light mullioned windows and single-light windows. The CHURCH is substantially C15, incorporating part of the C13 building in the SW corner, and is of three parallel ranges of nave, N and S aisles, all extended E to show as triple gables. N and S porches. Thoroughly restored in successive C19 campaigns including by *J. P. St Aubyn*: the Perp tracery replaced the early C19 sashes inserted when the medieval tracery was removed. The interior has tall, dignified seven-bay granite arcades of standard Cornish design except for the two W piers of the S arcade and the E respond of the N arcade, which are moulded as if they were round pillars with four engaged shafts (cf. Philleigh). – FONT BASE. Norman, originally with large round central shaft and four corner shafts. – PISCINA. In S wall, probably C13 or C14, trefoil-headed. – STAINED GLASS. E window by *William Wailes*, 1870. – Two N aisle windows by *James Powell & Sons*, 1893 and 1927. – MONUMENTS. Slate tablet over the N door with shaped pediment, angels and vine, 1829 by *Neville Northey Burnard* of Altarnun. – Some nice monuments of the 1840s, some by *Pearce* of Truro, to the Williams family, including to Caroline Elizabeth Williams †1849, carved figure with urn on pedestal. – Benjamin Sampson of Tullimar, Perranarworthal (q.v.), †1840, a marble aedicule with carved sarcophagus over a tree. – Slate slab to James Pearrowe of St Buryan, †1691.

LYCHGATE. Strikingly set in the middle of the churchyard. Late C19, robust Gothic, with cusped pointed arches flanked by tiered corbels that carry arch-braced trusses. s of the church, a CROSS. Principal face with relief carving of Christ with arms outstretched enclosed in a bold bead, with a Latin cross below extending down the shaft; the reverse face has a broad-limbed Latin cross with the lower limb again extending down the shaft.

TREWENNA, Churchtown. Early C19, former vicarage, possibly by *George Wightwick*, in Tudor Gothic. Two phases, the second the rather grander wing with a four-window garden front overlooking the church. Fine stair hall and good interior fittings.

TREVINCE HOUSE. ¼ m. N. Large and rambling, mostly rebuilt and remodelled *c.* 1870 but incorporating C17 to early C19 parts. The main elevations are of the late C19 with a large Doric porch to the entrance front. Fine C19 stair hall.

83   GWENNAP PIT. 2 m. NNW near Busveal. The largest and most famous of the three surviving open-air preaching pits (cf. Indian Queens and St Newlyn East), first used by John Wesley in 1762. Oval pit made in a fallen-in mine shaft, reduced in size in a remodelling of 1806 but still an impressive 360 ft (110 metres) in circumference with thirteen tiers of turfed seating (Wesley either mis-remembered or exaggerated its capacity at 22,000). A pair of stone posts on the fourth tier down on the N side probably marks the pulpit. To the E, METHODIST CHAPEL, early C19, a small simple square building, single-storey with two square-headed windows with wooden glazing bars making central arched lights.

Of the settlements away from Churchtown, there are several good early to mid-C19 houses and a Methodist church in CAR-HARRACK; at BURNCOOSE, Burncoose House, mostly of around the early C19, extended and remodelled in the mid C19 with its lodge, *c.* 1830–40, single-storey with a central projecting gable; at COMFORD, the Fox and Hounds Inn, dated 1742, and Comford House, early to mid-C19, possibly once part of the inn; and at SUNNY CORNER some late C18 thatched cottages with outbuildings that might have been detached kitchens or washhouses.

CUSGARNE, 1 m. E. CUSGARNE MANOR, Higher Cusgarne, is possibly C16 at its core but was partly rebuilt in 1629 (datestone in W wall). The handsome front, remodelled at least once in the C17 and definitively in the early C18, is of five bays with a central door. The windows are twenty-four-pane sashes with wide glazing bars and internal ovolo mouldings; the window over the door is wider with thirty panels. Much original glass. The early C18 plan survives with contemporary joinery largely intact. At the rear a central stair-tower flanked by service outshoots unaltered since the early C18. CUSGARNE HOUSE, Lower Cusgarne, is similar, probably C17 with a three-bay mid-C18 front with twelve-pane sashes – sixteen in the wider window over the door – again with wide glazing bars, internal ovolo moulding and much original glass. The house was rented by James Watt between 1781 and 1800 when he was supervising the installation of his engines into local mines.

PENGREEP. 1 m. SE. Early C18 and extended in the early to mid C18 for the Beauchamps (Joseph Beauchamp was Sheriff in 1784) with good quality additions of *c.* 1865 for the Williams family. Dignified SE entrance front of ten bays and two storeys over basement, the early C18 five-bay house in the centre. It was originally symmetrical with a wider middle first-floor window over the door, which was later moved one bay r. Original twelve-pane sashes – sixteen in the wider window – with wide glazing bars, ovolo-moulded internally, and much original glass. The door is approached by a wide flight of steps with ramped iron railings and finials. The three bays to the r. are the slightly later mid-C18 extension, the taller two bays to the l. of the *c.* 1865 additions. The five-window NE front has similar mid-C18 detail. The interior is exceptionally complete, especially the entrance hall, which is one of two surviving early C18 reception rooms, with moulded plaster ceiling, cornice, fielded dado panelling, eight-panel door and mid-C18 fireplace. There is similar detail in other rooms and equally intact Victorian detail in the later parts including an open-well open-string staircase.

GWINEAR

ST WINNEAR. A large church with several unusual features of uncommon interest. W tower of granite ashlar, under construction in 1441, of three stages, with buttresses set back from the angles and a NE stair-turret rising above the battlements and pinnacles. The windows at the bell-stage are straight-headed. Two earlier heads on the W face. The chancel window is typical of *c.* 1300, five lancet lights and tracery of the intersecting type. S aisle windows late Perp, of four lights with four-centred heads and no tracery at all, very similar to Camborne. Other windows late C19 Perp (replacing sash windows) from an extensive restoration of 1881 by *Hingerston Randulph.* N and S doorways with Tudor roses to the spandrels of the four-centred heads. N porch partly built over an additional doorway to an outer N aisle incorporating two earlier heads. This, the Arundell Aisle, confuses the interior to interesting effect, making the E end of the church as wide as it is long. The N aisle follows the nave all the way, the two W bays of the six-bay arcade Cornish standard with large horizontal leaves on the capitals, the further bays with octagonal piers and capitals showing four angels holding shields (cf. Crowan and St Ives), repeated in the three bays of the Arundell Aisle which also has a stag on the W pier. The S aisle starts two bays from the W with piers of four major and four minor shafts and unusual bulbous capitals. The sequence of development starts in the early to mid C15 with the creation of two N chapels (either at the same time or one not long after the other) at the E end of the church. A two-bay S chapel was also built (cf. the different capital decoration of the E pier and the simpler bays). This was followed by the later extension W of the aisles, N first, then S. The S aisle windows may be a refenestration of the 1530s. – FONT. Granite, dated 1727, an early case of antiquarian imitation of the Norman style, with earlier base. – PULPIT. Made up of bench-ends and rood screen, with one motif for each end. – LECTERN and READING DESK also made from bench-ends. – ROOD SCREEN. The much altered base is left, with especially richly and well-carved ornament, chiefly in each panel a vertical foliage serpentine but also symbols of the Passion etc. – Part of a CRESSET STONE, fragments of a Norman TOMB, and a wayside CROSS-HEAD. – STAINED GLASS. Six 1880s windows of vine leaf grisaille by *Hingerston Randulph*. – Chancel E, 1882, and N aisle windows, 1888, by *Harwood Bros* of Frome. – Marble WALL MONUMENT to Elizabeth Arundell †1683.

In the CHURCHYARD, three medieval CROSSES. Beside the path to the N porch, a tall WHEEL-HEAD CROSS on a long shaft: relief carving of Christ with arms outstretched on the W side and an equal-limbed cross on the E side. Opposite, another with a short shaft and Latin cross on its front face. E of the church an unusual geometric CROSS-HEAD, with an equal-limbed cross in relief, the parallel arms enclosed in a foliated head with small projections at the neck. At the SE corner, a C19 DOORWAY to the former vicarage incorporating fragments of C15 cusped tracery.

LANYON MANOR. ½ m. ENE. Fine C17 house with two-storey eight-bay N front. Two-storey porch to l. of centre, dated 1668, with scrolled kneelers and Lanyon coat of arms over the doorway incorporating motto VIVE UT VIVAS. Porch doorway with dressed granite piers. One C18 sash survives, the rest early C19 sashes, all of twelve panes.

At ANGARRACK, ¾ m. NW, one of the most impressive of all the GWR VIADUCTS in Cornwall. 1888, eleven spans of round arches on tapered piers over a deep valley, road and stream.

GWITHIAN

As at St Piran's oratory and church (q.v.) there was first an ORATORY in the sands, unsurprising given the proximity of the Hayle estuary, the disembarkation point for the Celtic saints. Of C5 or C6 origin, it was abandoned in the C13 after being overwhelmed by the dunes, but was shown by C19 excavation to have been a substantial rectangular building of nave and chancel. The site, just SE of Gwithian bridge, still exists, but has once again been left to itself and was last visible in 1940.

ST GWITHIAN. Late C15 or early C16 three-stage W tower in granite blocks with embattled parapet and panelled pinnacles. Much of the body of the church was rebuilt 1865–7 by *Edmund Sedding* in a straightforward E.E. that rather suits the character of the small churchtown perched above the dunes. Sedding retained the N transept and chancel walls but removed the C16 S aisle, returning the church to its C13 cruciform plan. The interior is most pleasingly proportioned under barn-like roofs, lit by clear glass windows, and furnished with pews of honest carpentry. The striking chancel arch and N and S transept arches carried on impost corbels are copied from the original N transept arch, shown in a sketch by J. T. Blight of 1863.* – FONT. C13 but so tampered with as to be wholly unrecognizable as medieval. It is square, with neat motifs of snake, rosette, and cross, in medallions (cf. Phillack). – Fragments of carved C16 ROOF CARPENTRY from Phillack church incorporated in chancel roof. – STAINED GLASS. S chancel window by Sedding, the most memorable feature of the church. A fine design with unusual composition, dense iconography, and jewel-like colours.

Sedding reused piers and arches from the former S aisle in the charming LYCHGATE, beyond which in the churchyard is a C13 TOMB-SLAB, re-tooled, used as a coffin rest. In the middle of the churchyard, a medieval CROSS bearing equal-limbed crosses in low relief with beaded circular borders.

VILLAGE HALL, next to the church. Late C19, intended as the Sunday School. Almost cottage-like with steep gabled roof, prominent front stack and square-headed mullioned windows with leaded lights, the bellcote the only non-domestic touch.

METHODIST CHURCH, Churchtown Road, S of the church. 1810. A rare survival. One of the most homely and appealing of Methodist buildings in Cornwall, of cottage-like scale with painted rubble and cob walls under a hipped thatched roof and with one sash window in each wall. The simple interior retains its gallery, rostrum, choir stalls and pews, and is a place of quiet dignity.

JAM POT CAFÉ, Gwithian Towans. Former coastguard look-out. Early C19, a small single-storey building of circular plan with two round-headed windows.

HARLYN   *8070*

HARLYN HOUSE. The understated Late Georgian E front masks the complicated plan and structural history of a house that belonged to the Tregrewes (Richard de Tregrewe was MP for Cornwall in 1448) and passed to the Peters (relatives of the

* I am indebted to Professor Charles Thomas for this and other information about the parish in his booklet *Gwithian* (1964).

c16 and c17 courtier Petres) from the 1630s to 1851. The house is roughly T-shaped, larger than it first appears, with older ranges, low built and rambling, extending W from the rear of the E range. The E range is two rooms deep, the show elevation of 2:3:2 bays, the three centre bays broken forward under a wide, low pediment with a Venetian window at the centre of the first floor: it is early c18, with bold mouldings and carved ceilings in the first-floor end rooms and corridor. The interior was transformed in the early c19, the most architecturally ambitious phase of the house, by the construction of a splendid stair hall to the rear of the front set of rooms: it is one of the best of its date in Cornwall with excellent Regency Gothick detail including cast-iron balustrade, plaster vaults and vaulted alcoves, and a tall octagonal lantern above. At the same time, the house was fitted out with a fine library with fielded panelling and giant pilasters, a dining room with a bold curvilinear ribbed ceiling, and a drawing room with excellent joinery and plasterwork. All this has close similarities to the contemporary work in the stair hall at nearby Prideaux Place, Padstow (q.v.). The much altered older ranges, also two rooms deep, date from Thomas Peters' early c17 rebuilding. This is evident in the surviving roof construction but more visible in a ground-floor room with plasterwork friezes of roses and fleurs-de-lys dated 1635 and a frieze of sea serpents of the same period in a first-floor chamber. On the N side of the c17 range, a c15 pointed arch in Catacleuse, which is either evidence of the status of the medieval house or was imported from the ruined church at Constantine (q.v.).

Immediately NW of the house, a pillar DOVECOTE, a rare if not unique example in Cornwall. Probably c18, an octagonal stone pillar supporting a lantern-shaped cote of red brick with four tiers of pigeon holes with slate ledges.

4060

HATT

HATT HOUSE. The residence of the Symons since *c.* 1700. In the early c18 they built a new house on to the front of the c16 house, a small-scale but handsome addition, on roughly square plan, of high quality Flemish bond brickwork. Two-storey, the E elevation of five bays, the N originally of three, later extended by one bay to accommodate the main entrance moved from the E. Fine c18 interiors including complete fielded-panelled front l. room, bolection-moulded panelling in front r. room, and stair hall with open-well stair rising to the attic. The lower earlier building, which was retained as a service range, may have been truncated by the new house. It comprises a central range with a late c17 or early c18 wing with bellcote over and a two-storey porch in the angle between. These ranges have good c16–c18 details including a large later c16 or early c17 fireplace and C17 plasterwork ceiling oval with fruit and leaves in a ground-floor room, and a fluted shellback cupboard of *c.* 1710 with painted cherubs in a first-floor chamber. Outside there are C18 WALLS and GATEPIERS with ball finials and a late C18 to early C19 GRANARY, timber-framed and weather-boarded, on nine granite staddle stones.

HAYLE   5030

Though the modern A30 by-passes the town, the traveller's eye is caught by the towering sand dunes (towans) at the E end of the settlement and, on a good day, a gleam of white sand and turquoise sea marking the mouth of the Hayle estuary, the setting for one of Cornwall's most atmospheric places. C19 Hayle was one of the county's greatest industrial ports, home to two of the three great Cornish iron foundries, and a major commercial centre. The industry and commerce have vanished, and the harbour has become a modest fishing port, but the story of Hayle is still evoked in the town's curious morphology, its surviving industrial and commercial infrastructure and buildings, and, most memorably, in the vast expanses of its waterfront.

The estuary has been a focus of settlement and trade from prehistory onwards, the medieval church towers of Lelant and Phillack (qq.v.) prominent on its opposite sides. But modern Hayle* is the result of an explosion of industrial activity between the late C18 and mid C19, aided by an early rail link to the mines of the Camborne–Redruth area, that saw the growth and eventual coalescence of two major centres at Copperhouse to the E and Foundry to the W, converging on the earliest, smaller focus at Penpol between. The centres were the domains of two great and rival companies, the Cornish Copper Company (CCCo.) and Harvey and Company (Harvey's), both of which developed international reputations for iron founding and engineering, for manufacturing steam engines that were the largest ever built, and for a brief period in the early C19 as world leaders in technological and commercial innovation: Harvey's drew on the genius of great engineers like Richard Trevithick, William West and Arthur Woolf. Both had diversified but after 1869 only Harvey's survived, with shipbuilding and various engineering and commercial activities continuing even after the closure of the foundry in 1903; they continued to dominate the W of Hayle well into the late C20.

Copperhouse is the earliest settlement. The CCCo. established a copper smelter on Copperhouse Creek in 1758, constructed the Copperhouse Canal and Dock by 1769, and by 1779 was building houses for its workforce along what is now Fore Street, with much use of scoria, cast blocks of vitreous copper slag. From the early C19 Copperhouse grew into the main commercial and

---

*Hayle was created as a civil parish out of Phillack (q.v.) in 1888.

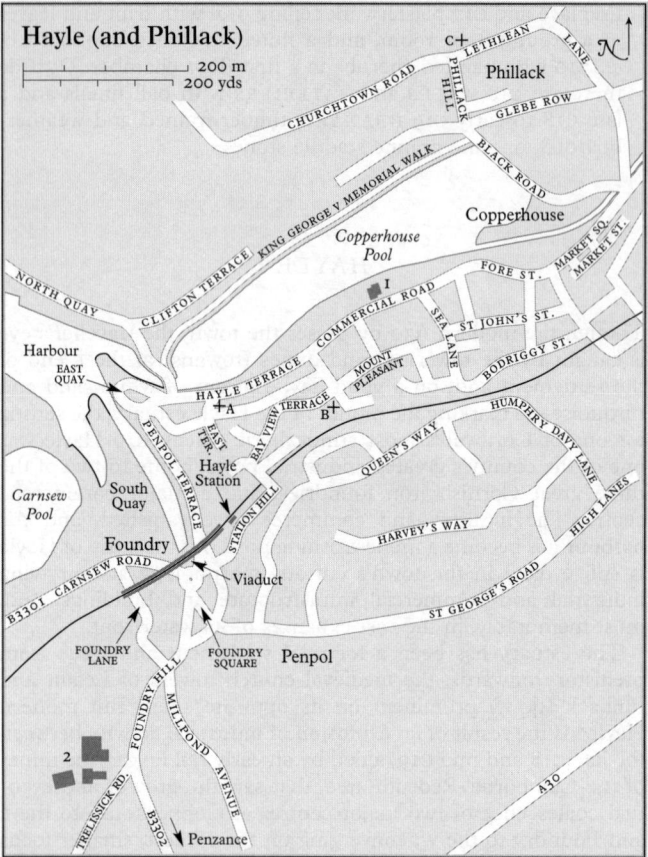

Hayle (and Phillack)

200 m
200 yds

Phillack

LETHLEAN LANE

CHURCHTOWN ROAD

PHILLACK HILL

GLEBE ROW

BLACK ROAD

KING GEORGE V MEMORIAL WALK

Copperhouse

Copperhouse Pool

CLIFTON TERRACE

NORTH QUAY

FORE ST.

MARKET SQ.
MARKET ST.

COMMERCIAL ROAD

ST JOHN'S ST.

SEA LANE

Harbour

EAST QUAY

HAYLE TERRACE

MOUNT PLEASANT

BODRIGGY ST.

A

EAST TER.

BAY VIEW TERRACE

B

HUMPHRY DAVY LANE

PENPOL TERRACE

QUEEN'S WAY

Hayle Station

Carnsew Pool

South Quay

STATION HILL

HARVEY'S WAY

HIGH LANES

Foundry

B3301 CARNSEW ROAD

Viaduct

ST GEORGE'S ROAD

FOUNDRY LANE

FOUNDRY HILL

FOUNDRY SQUARE

Penpol

MILLPOND AVENUE

2

TRELISSICK RD.

B3302

Penzance

A30

A   St Elwyn
B   Methodist church
C   St Felicitas, Phillack

I   Passmore Edwards
    Literary Institute
2   The Downes
    (St Michael's Hospital)

residential centre of the area with a market house by 1814 and a grid of streets of industrial housing behind Fore Street. Foundry started in 1770 when John Harvey, a blacksmith, set up a small foundry and engineering works to supply the expanding local mining industry. At the peak of its prosperity, between 1820 and 1870, the company occupied a huge site that extended from the estuary to Foundry Square, to Foundry House and Foundry Hill, and around the Millponds; its prestige was reflected in the gracious villas built for the Harvey family and its senior employees in Millpond Avenue and Trelissick Road, and the range of commercial and public buildings erected around Foundry Square. Between the two centres East Quay and Custom House Quay divided the estuary into two extensive creeks, the rising ground to the s distinguished by the dramatic landmark of J. D. Sedding's church of St Elwyn.*

In the C20 Hayle experienced mixed fortunes. New industries, including an explosives company and a large electricity generating station, came and went. Serious decline set in from the 1960s, Harvey's finally losing its identity to a merger of 1969. The town's glorious natural setting and proximity to St Ives make it potentially attractive to developers but the later C20 saw successive over-ambitious schemes foundering. The early C21 saw the restoration and sensitive new build of parts of the Foundry site. The latest (2013) redevelopment proposals are again large scale with a scheme for 700 houses on North Quay and, controversially, a supermarket on South Quay.

CHURCHES AND PUBLIC BUILDINGS

ST ELWYN, East Terrace, Penpol. 1886–8 by *J. D. Sedding*, one of his last works. Commenting on the design, *The Builder* described it as 'defiantly original'. Strikingly sited on a steep slope high above and back from the waterfront, its strong verticality and satisfying massing bestow an architectural benediction on the whole town. It is built in a subtle polychromy of granite, local brown killas and bands of green Polyphant. Its vertical proportions are reinforced by the buttressing of all elevations, including the w window, divided by a central buttress, and the treatment of the nave windows, whose large pointed-arched three-light openings are blind except for the central lights. Sedding's composition of the NE side, the steep approach from the waterfront, is especially pleasing (and reminiscent of the comparable elevation of Comper's St Michael, Newquay, of twenty years later), the apse of the N aisle thrusting forward like a bastion, w of which the tower rises splendidly in three stages. The lower stage is square with buttressed corners, the second and third stages octagonal, finishing in a short octagonal spire. A projecting octagonal NW stair-turret accompanies the first and second stages. The interior is more austere than one might expect since the original polychrome has been painted white, though the resulting simplicity is strangely moving, with low six-bay arcades of round arches on fat round piers in Bath stone to N and S aisles. Unusual E window design with two pairs of three-light lancets and a large roundel above. The high point is the NE part, where the subtle articulation of different levels expressed externally is used to create a N chapel accessed via a dramatic flight of steps over the first floor of the tower, and a second-floor musicians' gallery looking into the chancel. – FONT. Polyphant, Norman style with corner shafts and round bowl with blind Perp tracery. – Good original REREDOS, CHOIR STALLS and PEWS. – STAINED GLASS. An almost complete scheme to Sedding's

*The ecclesiastical parish of St Elwyn was formed out of Phillack in 1870 to serve Foundry, Copperhouse having been served by Phillack.

design, by *Curtis, Ward & Hughes*. Of special note the W window, by *Clayton & Bell* 1933, an unusual treatment using a stylized tree as a background that weaves the images together and gives the whole a quilted appearance.

To the N of the church, below on Hayle Terrace (Commercial Road), the CHURCH HALL. Datestone 1905. An appropriately Gothic approach to the church, and similarly vertically proportioned. The street front has two pairs of buttressed gabled windows of three stepped lights with trefoil heads flanking a central stack. At the E end a central pointed-arched buttressed doorway in a full-width lean-to, surmounted by a turret with trefoil-headed single-light windows.

METHODIST CHURCH, Bay View Terrace. A period piece of 1972 by *George Vaughan-Ellis*. Octagonal, the roof rising W to E to finish as a jutting point, like the prow of a ship with two metal columns at the E end framing a cross at the high point.

PASSMORE EDWARDS LITERARY INSTITUTE, Commercial Road. 1893 by *Silvanus Trevail*, his first Passmore Edwards commission and the largest of the four similar institutions in Cornwall. Two deep parallel wings under pedimented gables linked by a central entrance porch with parapet. Tripartite ground-floor windows with central triangular pediments, Venetian windows to first floor flanked by pairs of pilasters, all in different granite finishes. Interior has fine open-well stair and other good original fittings.

PERAMBULATIONS

1. Foundry

The best way of gaining an impression of the town's geography is from the summit of THE PLANTATION off Carnsew Road W of Foundry Square. It is now a park, the result of landscaping in the late C19 of the Iron Age Carnsew hillfort, by the partly paralysed Henry Harvey. Ramped walkways, one through a splendid Roman ARCH, dated 1844, skilfully built on the skew through embankments either side. Nearby is the earliest Christian MEMORIAL STONE known in Cornwall, probably mid-C5 and of an Irish woman, Cunaide: the indistinct Latin inscription reads 'Here [in] peace, lately went to rest Cunaide. Here in the grave she lies. She lived years thirty three' (the modern slate panel is a misreading). The summit offers a panorama of the estuary, with its mouth into St Ives Bay to the N, Lelant on the W bank across Carnsew Pool, the long stretch of South Quay, Penpol Creek and East Quay in the centre with Hayle harbour beyond and North Quay on the Phillack shore, and, just visible, the entrance to Copperhouse Pool running E with the noble silhouette of St Elwyn's church above.

Now across Carnsew Road towards the quays, past a C19 TIMBER STORE with brick ventilation panels, still in use for its original purpose. SOUTH QUAY of *c.* 1819 is built like most of the Hayle waterfront of a mix of granite, killas and, on the Copperhouse side, scoria. To the w is CARNSEW QUAY, 1758, extended 1834, its timber SLUICE GATE partly buried (but scheduled for restoration), which originally opened to fill the huge expanse of CARNSEW POOL, 1834, a sluicing pool to flush out the harbour. Opposite the gates an impressive curved wall directed the water seaward. C20 dumping has buried much of the C18 harbour front, the site of Harvey's shipyard, slips and docks. But something of the awesome power of the water can still be seen when the pool is draining through the two TUNNELS under the quay. The end of South Quay affords views of the HARBOUR and NORTH QUAY, and EAST QUAY on the e side of Penpol Creek, the latter built by the CCCo. after a bitter dispute with Harvey's over the construction of South Quay. It is possible to walk right around Carnsew Pool and further N out into the estuary on the NEW PIER, where St Ives unexpectedly comes into view.

Return towards Foundry Square, passing under the VIADUCT. The growth of Hayle was facilitated by the standard gauge mineral railway running from Redruth to the town from 1837 (the second steam-powered railway in Cornwall), via the N side of Copperhouse Creek, with its terminus in Foundry Square. The viaduct over Foundry Square, the defining feature of Foundry today, dates from 1852 and the opening of the new line connecting Truro and Penzance, its original timber supports replaced in 1886 by the present stone piers with wrought-iron girders. As a fire precaution brick piers were used for the section spanning the Foundry.

Into FOUNDRY SQUARE, the public face of the Harvey empire. Immediately abutting the viaduct on the r., No. 25, a late C19 bakery, later warehouse, with a large stilted round-arched second-floor window rising into the gable. Next, with its slate-hung clock turret, the FOUNDRY OFFICE, incorporating the C18 carriage entrance to the foundry. The frontage building became the main office range, with a rear SW wing added as a drawing office in the early to mid C19. On the street front a panel with the names of ships owned by Harvey's, part of the 2007 restoration programme. Then BARCLAYS BANK, built as an emporium in the early C19, with giant Ionic pilasters, the first floor on squat square Doric columns with tall sash windows. Beyond, the imposing façade of Nos. 18, 19 and 20, 1896, converted from Harvey's retail premises and stores to the designs of *James Hicks* as the CORNUBIA BISCUIT FACTORY, linked to the great Hayle milling firm of W. Hosken & Son (cf. Loggans Mill below). Three-storey and ten bays, built to fit an almost triangular site: brick piers divide the bays as engaged columns with stucco mouldings, the first-floor windows round-headed and also with stucco mouldings. Forming a grand presence on the s side of the square is the WHITE HART HOTEL, built by Henry Harvey in 1838 to provide suitable facilities for entertaining customers. Three-storey stucco elevations with strong classical detail, the front corners with panelled pedestals carrying a giant order of clasping square fluted columns, the three bays of the upper floor with four giant engaged round columns surmounted by a plain entablature. The columns are debased Roman Doric with Egyptian influenced capitals. Entrance and stairwell retain original architectural features including a fine open-well stair. Abutting to the l. is its predecessor, the older White Hart Hotel, also built by Henry Harvey, *c.* 1824, to support his sister Jane who had married Richard Trevithick. It became the FREEMASONS HALL. A much more modest building, two-storey, three-window front under an almost pyramidal roof. Nearer the centre of the Square is LLOYDS TSB, *c.* 1869, its curiously single-storeyed form for such a prominent site the result of a fire in 1935 that removed the public hall from over the ground floor of what was built as a market house; the heavy classical detail looks overscaled as a consequence. Further E in Chapel Terrace the former FOUNDRY CHAPEL, now Pratts' Market. Date plaque 1845, a grander example of the classical style of Methodist chapel, stucco, with an elaborate full-width porch. The interior retains its panelled gallery, with Corinthian pilasters at the E end.

Now to FOUNDRY YARD, unfortunately fronted by early C21 terraced housing dressed up with pseudo-historical motifs. The scale of the Harvey enterprise is apparent in the tall gaunt remains of the MANUFACTORY, built in stages between *c.* 1825 and *c.* 1875. From l. to r. it housed a granary, machine shop, boiler room and engine room: a range of two-storey shippons, part of the large FOUNDRY FARM, lies to the rear. Nearer the viaduct the remains of the PATTERN SHOP. Early C19, two-storey, seven bays each with a large round-headed doorway. Some windows are iron casements with glazing bars. Adjacent are two-storey ranges connected by a drum staircase, tactfully inserted OFFICE and SMALL BUSINESS UNITS of 2007 by *Lacie Hickie Caley.* The high C19 WALLS of Foundry Farm survive W of the main industrial area and lead to the grandiose FOUNDRY ARCH, a Roman triumphal arch erected in 1845 to celebrate the contract for pumping engines for draining the Haarlemmer Meer, Holland. Further up the footpath towards The Plantation, the BRIDGE, built over the West Cornwall Railway in 1852.

Return down to FOUNDRY HILL. No. 5, now residential, was built as a school for foundry workers' children with a large rectangular schoolroom on each floor and schoolmaster's accommodation in the rear wing. Across the road THE MILLPONDS, the extension of the Harvey industrial complex, with the walls of the former HAMMER and GRIST MILLS, ROPEWALK and BRASS FOUNDRY still extant. The Millponds supplied the motive power. It is possible to continue around the ponds and return along MILLPOND AVENUE with gracious stucco villas of the 1840s. LADBROKE HOUSE is the best preserved, with giant Corinthian corner capitals, flanked l. by LANE END and r. by THE GLADE, all with good classical detail. Nearer Foundry Hill Nos. 7, 8 and 9, a nice terrace of three early to mid-C19 cottages. Up Foundry Hill and off Trelissick Road, THE DOWNES in the grounds of St Michael's Hospital (*see* below).

2. Penpol and Copperhouse

Start from Foundry Square along PENPOL TERRACE and the E side of Penpol Creek, the route of the 1837 railway from Redruth that terminated in the square. This area was the beginning of the CCCo. domain, Penpol Terrace of better quality housing laid out in the 1820s after the company had built EAST QUAY to rival Harvey's construction of South Quay opposite. Later in the C19, after Harvey's were forced to allow trading other than in their emporium, single-storey shops were built in the front gardens of the terrace: good examples of later C19 and early C20 shopfronts, the best CARNSEW GALLERY, built as a butcher's shop. 1893 by *Sampson Hill* of Redruth with Mannerist-style columns, terracotta panels with sheeps' heads to the stall riser, and a tiled mosaic panel of a bull. Some fragmentary remains of C19 buildings on the quay, principally of the former GAS WORKS, and NORTH QUAY opposite with some surviving sections of vertically set mid-C18 walling and the CHIMNEY of the former arsenic works. Of greater significance to the E the iron SWING BRIDGE for the road to cross the Copperhouse Canal, with associated walls and brick ENGINE HOUSE of 1877 with its machinery intact. On the bridge's W side the battered walls with corbelled parapet of the abutments to the former RAILWAY BRIDGE, 1852. Over the N side of the bridge is the OLD CUSTOMS HOUSE, the date 1862 carved in the lintel over the doorway. Two-storey with flanking lean-tos with rusticated quoin-strips, alternate quoins vermiculated, similar detail around the doorway. The threshold stone of the doorway has incised compass points for the calibration of ships' instruments. On the hill above, CLIFTON TERRACE, proudly looking over towards Foundry, so named by the CCCo. in honour of the company winning the contract for the links of the Clifton Suspension Bridge in 1840. The vast expanse of COPPERHOUSE POOL, the sluice pool for the CCCo. quays, stretches away E beyond the new NORTH QUAY BRIDGE, 2011–12.

Back across the bridge to HAYLE TERRACE with the CHURCH HALL on the road and St Elwyn's church rising above (*see* Churches and Public Buildings). E along COMMERCIAL ROAD past No. 36, with its elaborate Renaissance-style granite shopfront dated 1891, and on the other side the Passmore Edwards Institute (*see* Churches and Public Buildings), the canal continuing behind, to FORE STREET and the heart of Copperhouse. Mostly modest two-storey houses with shops,

which makes the grand scale of the early C20 St George's
Hall with its exuberant terracotta façade and large blind oriel
window the more striking. No. 1 Market Square is the former
Market House, datestone 1839, five-window stucco front
with dressed granite rustications. The Cornubia Inn of 1867,
with a large six-bay stucco façade, was named after a fast
Harvey-built paddle steamer. Some good late C19 or early C20
shopfronts as at Nos. 55 and 57 Fore Street. Little survives of
the CCCo. buildings except its C18 office, now No. 10 Market
Street. But what does remain of the firm's enterprise makes
a fitting finale to this perambulation: Copperhouse Quay
with a stretch of the Copperhouse Canal and Dock
behind the N side of Fore Street, the dock with walls of
vertically set blocks of scoria. It is possible to take a circular
walk around Copperhouse Pool by walking across the causeway to the Phillack side (q.v.), returning across the swing
bridge.

The Downes, Trelissick Road, a convent from 1902–2002 and
now part of St Michael's Hospital. Small country house
c. 1870s, for W. J. Rawlings, a partner in Harvey's. The first set
of plans was prepared by *Edmund Sedding* but the project was
taken over after his death by *J. D. Sedding* and greatly altered
in execution.* The house was extended in 1902 when it became
a convent, was further extended in the early C20, and given a
Tudor-Gothic chapel on the SW elevation in 1927. It occupies
a fine hilltop site with commanding views, though its original
approach and setting have been compromised by the extensive
late C20 and early C21 development of the hospital. Fortunately
the essence of the intimate relationship of house and formal
garden as envisaged by the Seddings survives remarkably
intact. The HOUSE is an accomplished essay in Tudor-Gothic,
of irregular plan ranged around a central entrance and stair
hall, with well-detailed elevations full of incident including a
four-light timber-framed gabled bay over the lean-to porch
with pargetted plasterwork, trefoil-headed lights, quatrefoil
tracery, and an arch-braced kingpost on a corbel to the gable.
The interior retains fine original fittings including a timber-
framed oriel overlooking the stairs, and a dining room with
richly moulded panelled ceiling, Gothic fireplace, and plaster
frieze, all coloured.

The formal GARDENS begin to the N front of the house in
a terrace bounded by a low granite wall with trefoil-headed
openings with a Tudor-Gothic SUMMERHOUSE at the E end,
which has an oriel in its N face. To the W the terrace is terminated by a low granite parapet with ball finials. From the
terrace a flight of steps descends to a lawn which was the site
of Sedding's 'geometric garden', originally with thirty-nine

---

* A perspective of The Downes was included in J.D. Sedding's posthumously published but highly influential *Garden Craft Old and New* (1891).

brick-edged flowerbeds, the planting scheme for which was sent to the architect twice a year for his approval. The central axis of the garden is terminated by a stone ARBOUR which has an arcaded s façade with arched openings, its gabled roof supported by granite Tuscan columns; its design was inspired by St Germoe's Chair at Germoe (q.v.).

GLANMOR HOUSE, Trelissick Road. Built *c.* 1862 by Harvey's for their transport manager. A classical villa, two-storey, stucco, with giant engaged corner pilasters and Tuscan porch. Interior with fine original fittings including plasterwork ceilings and chimneypieces, and a cast-iron stair balustrade by Harvey's.

BODRIGGY HOUSE, Bodriggy Street. The house was rebuilt *c.* 1718 incorporating C17 or earlier fabric, slightly extended in the late C19. U-shaped plan with three large rooms to the front with large central hall and earlier wings l. and r. at rear. The Victorian wing was added to the r. of the r. rear wing. Excellent early C18 architectural details, including open-well stair with canopied ceiling over with central oval with winged putto blowing a pipe.

LOGGANS MILL, Loggans Lane. Prominent at the E approach to the town. Four- and five-storey with a taller tower to the rear. An early C19 watermill extended 1852 and 1884 by William Hosken as a flour mill, which became part of the renowned West Country HTP flour milling firm, producers of 'Cornubia' biscuits (cf. Foundry Square). This was the largest mill in Cornwall in the later C19 and early C20. Much of the main structure, though derelict, survives, but the rest of the extensive site has been demolished.

FAIRGLEN, off Loggans Road. A pioneering development of twenty-eight low-energy houses, first phase 2007–8 by *Lilly Lewarne Practice*, project architect *John Stengelhofen*, developer *Percy Williams & Sons Ltd.* Two-storey solid-wall construction with aluminium roofing, imaginatively planned on a s facing slope, and crisply detailed.

HELFORD

A pretty hamlet gathered around a small creek on the s shore of the Helford river. It is a good place to see cob and thatch cottages and Cornish slate roofs among the C18 and C19 buildings rising from the quays.

PENTYR, on higher ground at Helford Point, is by *John Campbell*, 1939, and very similar to his houses at Chapel Point, Mevagissey (q.v.): indeed it was built after the original owner had seen them while sailing down the coast. The Arts and Crafts motifs are similarly employed to create irregular elevations in

a picturesque composition, perfectly at home with the little
settlement below.

HELIGAN
2 m. NW of Mevagissey

A Tremayne estate from the C16 until the late C20, now renowned
for its gardens and pleasure grounds. The HOUSE is on the site
of an earlier dwelling of c. 1600, which was rebuilt and extended
from 1697 and extensively remodelled and further extended
c. 1830 by *Henry Harrison* for J. H. Tremayne. Three-storey
symmetrical entrance front, the centre three bays advanced,
central Doric portico with paired columns to front. Similar
garden elevation with a two-storey service wing beyond. The
windows are all C19 sashes. Entrance hall with early C18
marble bolection-moulded chimneypiece, panelling and plaster
cornice; the stair hall to the rear has two fluted Doric columns
and pilasters forming a screen, and an imperial stair with
moulded wreathed handrail, stick balusters in triplets and
Greek key frieze. First-floor landing has a cast-iron lattice
screen with fluted composite columns, second-floor columns
in the form of fasces, and a domed lantern over. – STABLES
and COACHHOUSE. A well-preserved two-storey early to
mid-C18 ensemble around a symmetrical U-plan with central
clock cupola.

The extensive GARDENS and PLEASURE GROUNDS in the
wider parkland setting were restored from dereliction during
the 1990s under the supervision of *Tim Smit* and *John Nelson*,
revealing one of the most interesting designed landscapes and
botanical and horticultural ensembles in Cornwall. The late
C17–early C18 house was complemented by a large walled
garden, parterres and terraces. It was around this framework
that the later C18 and C19 Tremaynes made extensive alterations and improvements, establishing shelter belts to enclose
parkland N of the house, creating a new approach from the N
and a network of walks, drives and rides, and making new and
exotic plantings including rhododendrons, bamboos and tree
ferns. All of this was lost when the estate fell into decay after
the First World War, and remained hidden until its rediscovery
in the late C20.

The gardens and pleasure grounds lie principally to the N
and S of the house: three grass terraces from the C18 formal
gardens survive immediately around the S and E of the house.
The Jungle, the Lost Valley, Flora's Green and the Ravine are
crammed with exotic planting and are part of the extensive C19
reworkings and improvements of the C18 design. Of the structures and buildings, the most notable are: THE MOUNT,
believed to be the beacon mentioned in an account of 1623;
the late C18 brick SUMMERHOUSE with open three-arched

front and sea views; a GROTTO incorporating quartz crystals; and an early C20 Italianate SUMMERHOUSE in the Italian garden. Of exceptional interest are the buildings of the KITCHEN GARDENS, two linked late C18 brick enclosures with the full array of specialist structures necessary for the wealthy C19 Victorian horticultural enthusiast. The southern garden, designed around a central circular dipping pool and now known as the Flower Garden, has a range of fruit-growing glasshouses against its N and E walls, including a vinery of Paxtonian form, citrus and peach houses, a bothy and office and a small square glasshouse for growing bananas. To the N the second brick enclosure, approximately segmental on plan, has pineapple pits, melon houses, cold frames and other bothys and stores. All are now in working order. To the NE of this, an early C19 brick wall contains three tiers of bee boles.

HELLAND   0070

ST HELENA. The originally cruciform C13 church, extended in the late C15 or early C16 with S aisle, in 1646 with N transept (date on gable), was substantially rebuilt by J. P. St Aubyn 1870–5, and the nave refitted by him in 1878. Scrolled granite kneeler stones to nave, transept and aisle gables (cf. Mansion House, Blisland). The w tower was rebuilt by *Silvanus Trevail* in 1888: two stages with embattled parapet and pinnacles but lacking the presence and originality of his tower at Temple (q.v.). The only substantial medieval architecture surviving is the S aisle with its four-bay arcade, the capitals with fleurons; the four S wall windows; a two-light window with cusped lights and square head on the S side; and a similar one on the N side. – FONT. Circular C13 bowl on later stem. – STAINED GLASS. Fragments of medieval glass in the E window of the S aisle. – MONUMENT. Ledger stone with figure and inscription to Humphrey Calwodley, early C16.

HELLAND BRIDGE, over the River Allen. Early C15. Four pointed arches with double rings of thin slate voussoirs and large cut-waters, one of the best medieval bridges in Cornwall, comparable to Lostwithiel (q.v.).

LANCARFFE, 1⅜ m. SSE. C17, extended and remodelled *c.* 1680. The late C17 range forms a symmetrical S-facing entrance front with a central entrance and principal rooms l. and r. Forty-pane sashes with very small panes, thick glazing bars, bolection-moulded on the inside. At the same period a stair-tower was added to the rear in the angle to the pre-existing range with large open-well stair. The original W range is the garden front, a symmetrical three-bay elevation with projecting wings each end. The interior retains an unusually complete set of bolection-moulded panelled rooms. C17 roof trusses over the main range.

HELSTON

Architecturally among the most rewarding of small Cornish towns, exhibiting in a limited scale a wonderful variety of confident public and domestic buildings of the early C18 to mid C19, set in typically Cornish up-and-down topography, and woven together around the cruciform main streets by a network of pedestrian alleys and granite-lined water channels.

Helston* sits on the E side of the River Cober astride a minor side valley, a strategically important location through which routes connecting Falmouth and Penzance have to pass to avoid Loe Pool to the S, the largest body of fresh water in Cornwall; this is also the boundary between the historically rich mining area to the N and W and farming country to the S and E. Its topography can also be interpreted as a castle town, the reputed site of the castle being at the lower S end of the town on the historic bowling green overlooking the Cober valley, which in turn determined the line of its grandest street, Coinagehall Street, which rises graciously E. It was an important medieval town with a charter of 1201 confirming an earlier one, became a coinage town in 1492, and sent two MPs to Parliament from 1294 until 1832. Its medieval church occupied a commanding site across the tributary valley from the castle and it had two medieval hospitals, one near the river for non-lepers, with a lazar house nearby.

The town continued to prosper in the post-medieval period, closely linked with the great Godolphin tin mines, with major expansion in the late C17 and early to mid C18 along Meneage Street, the laying out of a new wealthy suburb around Cross Street between the town and the church, and a new church erected on the site of the medieval building in 1761. By the early C19 there were over one hundred mines in the area including Wheal Vor, owned by H. M. Grylls, a lawyer for the Godolphin estates, claimed as the largest tin mine in the world at that time. To this period belong the major public buildings of the town including the Guildhall and Market House, both 1837–8, several chapels, schools and institutes, and most of the larger houses, with much by *George Wightwick*. The railway, a branch line from Gwinnear Road, reached Helston in 1887 with its terminus some distance NE of the centre in Station Road, prompting development in that area and on Godolphin Road.

The disappearance of the mining industry and the contraction of agriculture in the first half of the C20 was reflected in the town's gentle decline, but after 1945 the rapid development of nearby RNAS Culdrose saw the construction of large residential estates on the greenfield sites to the N and E. The airbase is still the largest employer, and though the later C20 and early C21 have seen further extensive residential development around the town's modern by-pass, the centre remains intact and delightful.

---

*The ecclesiastical parish of Helston was created out of Wendron in 1865.

CHURCHES AND PUBLIC BUILDINGS

ST MICHAEL, Church Street. 1756–61 by *Thomas Edwards** of Greenwich (cf. Trelowarren, Trewithen, Tehidy, etc.), at the expense of the Earl of Godolphin. Restored and extended 1837–8 by *George Wightwick*. Within a *lann* which may have been an earlier settlement separate from the town. The medieval church had been struck by lightning in 1727 and remained ruinous: a C15 gable cross is the only visible remnant. A typical classical town church of the mid-Georgian period, an aisleless rectangle with first-floor round-headed windows over ground-floor windows with flat arches. To this Wightwick added a low chancel, s porch and N chapel. The tower is charming Georgian Gothic, Cornish in feeling but with pilasters instead of buttresses, round-headed windows, and obelisks instead of pinnacles. The interior is, however, profoundly disappointing, stripped not only of its N and S galleries but of pulpit, chancel screen, panelling and pilasters in a 1970s reordering. The w gallery remains with a rear stair and grained seating, though somewhat reworked. Panelled ceiling, the central panel an oval with richly carved arabesques and cornice interrupted by an arcade of round arches. – FONT. serpentine shaft, Beer stone bowl, arcaded. – REREDOS. Tripartite mosaic, central panel depicting the Last Supper by *James Powell & Sons*, 1883. – CHANDELIER. Brass, dated 1762, recording the generosity of the Earl of Godolphin. – BRASSES, in N chapel, to Thomas Bougins †1602, his wife and children. – MONUMENTS. John Trevener, 1825, and Peter Hill, 1837, by *Thomas Denman*. – STAINED GLASS. Chancel E by *G. Kruger Gray*, 1937, depicting the Helston Floral Dance, in disappointingly muted colours. – Over s door, the Transfiguration, 1843, in painted enamel by *Hedgeland*, originally in the E window.

In the CHURCHYARD, many MEMORIALS with the huge lettering characteristic of the mining area (cf. Redruth and St Day) and three CAST-IRON PLAQUES (cf. Phillack). The TRENGROUSE MEMORIAL, mid-C19 by *Spargo* of Helston, commemorates Henry Trengrouse, 1772–1855, the inventor of rocket life-saving apparatus for shipwrecks.

METHODIST CHURCH, Coinagehall Street. By *Morley & Woodhouse* of Bradford, 1889. An imposing presence even in this splendid street, designed to seat one thousand. Heavy classical front with large central portico with two-bay arcade of polished pink granite columns and granite balustrade above. Horizontally divided and completely refurbished 1995. Behind, the much simpler early C19 chapel.

Former ALL SAINTS MISSION CHURCH, Meneage Road, now a community centre. 1882 by *W. J. Winn*. Simple Gothic.

GUILDHALL, Market Place. 1837–8, by *William Harris*, District Surveyor, of Bristol. Council chamber, mayor's parlour and offices above a corn market. A fittingly dignified centrepiece to the town in a strong, almost severe Neoclassical design, the

*Some at least of the rebuilding was overseen by *Bland*, an architect from Truro.

front especially striking: ground floor has three pilastered door-ways with solid triangular pediments on consoles rising to a first floor of fluted Doric columns framing three tall windows. This is surmounted by a triangular pediment elaborately infilled with clock and town arms between carved winged figures over a Doric frieze in Bath stone. The other elevations, though simpler, are equally well detailed. Original plaster ceiling in council chamber. The slope of the ground means it has a basement storey to the rear, which is rusticated.

Behind the Guildhall in Church Street and built at the same time is the former Market House (now HELSTON FOLK MUSEUM), one of three Greek Revival market houses designed by *Harris* in Cornwall (cf. Bodmin and Penzance). A remarkable survival. Single-storey with a front screen wall with two segmental-arched doorways framed by plain pilasters, the l. to the market, the r. to the open courtyard. Courtyard elevation of eleven bays with segmental-arched window openings and tripartite windows, and a central round-arched doorway with tympanum. The museum extends into the former DRILL HALL, 1838–9, which has Venetian windows and round-arched doorways with spoked concentric fanlights, and is surmounted by a bellcote. In front of the museum a CANNON from HMS *Anson*, wrecked on Loe Bar in 1807.

GRYLLS MONUMENT, Monument Road. 1834 by *George Wightwick*. Memorial gateway by public subscription to H. M. Grylls, whose Wheal Vor mine sustained the prosperity of the town in the early C19. A hefty Gothic design worthy of its position as the splendid point-in-view at the w end of Coinagehall Street. Granite ashlar and richly detailed with identical front and rear elevations. Central four-centred arched doorway flanked by buttresses to bays that have tall trefoil-headed niches and quatrefoils above, angle buttresses with gablet, all with finials, and embattled parapet between tall crocketed pinnacles.

Former PASSMORE EDWARDS INSTITUTE, Penrose Road. Now Helston Community Centre. 1889 by *James Hicks*, as the Passmore Edwards Science and Arts Schools, extended 1905 as Cornwall's first County Secondary School, enlarged again 1913–14 by a r. wing. Two-storey central range with flanking projecting wings, the latter with first-floor Venetian windows.

GODOLPHIN HALL, Wendron Street. The tall frontage building was erected as public rooms in 1888–9. Granite ashlar with corbelled first-floor buttresses rising through tall coped gabled parapet entablature with shorter intermediate buttresses, all with finials. Set back to the r., the former GRAMMAR SCHOOL, 1834, by *George Wightwick*, in a more assured Gothic with a segmental three-bay centred front with central trefoil-headed louvred vent to finialed gable. Heavily moulded central doorway with four-centred arched head and coat of arms.

OLD MATHEMATICAL SCHOOL, Penhallaz Hill. Datestone 1799. Former literary and scientific institute, now part of the Freemasons Hall. Plain rectangular two-storey; triangular

pediment to front with scrolled kneelers. Principal accommodation at first-floor level with round-headed windows.

OLD TOWN PRISON, Shute Hill. Dated 1835, by *Henry Penberthy*. A rare and complete example of a small early C19 prison
(the first floor now residential). The ground floor has four open
arches, behind which are a passage and cells with studded
doors and barred windows. Former exercise yard to NW.

PERAMBULATION

Start at the Grylls Monument (*see* Churches and Public Buildings) to gain some sense of the layout and setting of the town.
Looking W, the putative CASTLE SITE on the bowling green,
with the Cober valley falling away steeply beyond; the bowling
club, one of the oldest in the country, was founded in 1760.
But the glory of Helston is the view E up COINAGEHALL
STREET, after Lemon Street, Truro, the most handsome street
in Cornwall. It climbs, pleasingly wide, in a gracious curve up
towards the Guildhall, with water flowing in granite-lined
channels either side and sections of granite paving with curved
grooves in an almost foliate pattern. Its generous width reflects
the probable site of the market place, later infilled by the
coinage hall, Duchy Office and other buildings, all demolished
c. 1830. And it is lined with houses of pleasant scale. Occupying
a corner site on the junction with Monument Street is No. 58,
early to mid-C18, its relatively plain but dignified exterior of
five bays to both streets fronting a rich interior with most of
its original features surviving. Fine open-well, open-string
staircase with egg-and-tongue and scrolled brackets, turned
balusters, ramped handrail, wreathed over the fluted newels.
Several panelled rooms with moulded ceiling cornices including in the rear parlour a moulded ribbed ceiling with incised
shields, garlands and rosettes, and niches with shaped shelves.
Further up, the BLUE ANCHOR, a remarkable vernacular survival in such an urban street. Diminutive, thatched, and with
sliding sashes, of C15 origin but much reconstructed in the
early C18. The interior retains the layout and character of an
authentic old inn, with its own brewhouse in use at the rear,
the oldest continuously operating brew pub in the country.
Opposite, CHYMBER HOUSE, a smart early to mid-C19 stucco
town house on the corner of Lady Street with good elevations
to both and rich detail. Further up on the same side, BAR-
CLAYS BANK, a 1933 reconstruction of a 1755 town house (date
on reused rainwater goods), in granite and pink elvan. On the
opposite side, the huge presence of the former METHODIST
CHAPEL (*see* Churches and Public Buildings). Beyond, the
awkward 1960s POST OFFICE, the one discordant note in the
street. Then the ANGEL HOTEL, reputedly the C16 Godolphin
town house, refronted in the early C19: the deep plan incorporates the core of the earlier house. Central C16 moulded granite
four-centred arched doorway with an early C19 Doric porch.
Original beams and joists in l. front room and four-centred

arched doorway to the rear of the former through passage. At
the rear a late C18 ballroom with bowed balcony. At various
points up this street, and throughout the town, it is worth
exploring the pedestrian alleys (opes) that sometimes lead to
courts of smaller houses, many of them C18 and C19: CHAPEL
ROW is a good example. Further up again, the SEVEN STARS
HOTEL, now the Fitzsimmons Arms. Mid to late C18 front
with canted oriels flanking the former central carriage entrance,
and deep rear wings. The grand finale is the Guildhall (*see*
Churches and Public Buildings), with LLOYDS BANK a strong
presence on the corner of Wendron Street, 1891 by *Silvanus
Trevail*. It was reduced to two storeys from the architect's ambitious four-storey original design. Fine bay window to the
banking hall looking down the street.

CHURCH STREET leads down and across the tributary valley and
up to the church, making for an engaging townscape with a
good range of buildings and enhanced by open conduits like
Coinagehall Street. Several good C19 shopfronts, a feature of
the town generally. Of special note No. 14, a smart three-storey
C17 town house largely rebuilt in the early C18; No. 20, late
C17 or early C18, with a central first-floor bow window; No. 35,
THE WILLOWS, 1776, with Victorian bay windows; No. 48,
early C19, has engagingly over-scaled panelled chimneystacks
with octagonal shafts on the street four corners; and Nos. 43
and 45, a *c.* 1700 town house refronted in the early C19 as a
pair of houses. Just below the church (*see* above), a charming
group of the OLD NATIONAL SCHOOL, dated 1828, with symmetrical three-bay gabled front, flanked by SCHOOL HOUSES
of the same date and with the courtyard enclosed by wrought-
iron railings and gatepiers.

Return down the street and r. into CROSS STREET, the third of
Helston's best streets, this a prosperous C18 suburb of large
villas set in generous grounds. At the corner, No. 50 Church
Street, an early C18 stucco town house, its front remodelled
in the early C19. Two-storey over basement and symmetrical
three-window front with Doric porch. Early C19 twelve-pane
sashes over two-light granite mullioned basement windows.
Interior retains most of its C18 features including open-well
staircase and parlour with bolection-moulded panelling and
chimneypiece with C18 overmantel painting of ships. Outside,
the early C19 wrought-iron gateways with open gatepiers in
spirals, characteristic of Helston in this period, and in front of
the garden wall a wheel-headed granite CROSS. Now to Nos.
3 and 5, GREAT OFFICE, built 1788 as the Helston Union
Bank, later legal offices used by H. M. Grylls and the Godolphin estates. Three-storey bay front with second-floor bowed
sash, decorative wrought-iron balcony to the projecting central
bay, and Doric porch. No. 7 is a symmetrical three-bay town
house with giant panelled end pilasters, extended l. in the C20.
Its principal feature is an elaborate central canted oriel carried
on arch-braced brackets as part of an integral porch which has

square end columns. Opposite, LISMORE, c. 1820, for Glynn Grylls, extended c. 1840, probably by *George Wightwick*. Plainish dignified two-storey exterior, except for a portico with fluted Doric columns and frieze from No. 21 Meneage Street on E front. Fine interior of the early to mid C19 on double-depth plan. It is set in spacious grounds looking towards the town and is bounded to Cross Street by a wall with wrought-iron piers that have clusters of fir cones as finials; cast-iron water pump, dated 1844, set into the wall. Early C19 COACH-HOUSE and STABLES, datestone 1839, attributed to *Wightwick*, incorporating part of a building with Gothic windows marked on a 1792 survey. Next door, No. 4, the former VICARAGE, 1790s, possibly by *Thomas Edwards*, slightly remodelled early C19. Late Georgian style, double-depth plan, two storeys and attic. Almost complete interior with large open-well staircase, plaster cornices and chimneypieces. Further along on the r. on a splendid elevated site PENHELLIS, c. 1840s by *George Wightwick*. The best of the town's villas, in Italianate stucco, with a two-storey three-bay symmetrical entrance front around a central porch on paired Corinthian columns. Early C20 bowed window to garden front. Complete interior including segmental vault to entrance hall, vault to stair hall with cross-ribs, and oak open-string staircase with an acanthus ceiling cornice and petalled central rose over.

Back along Cross Street to a r. turn down TANYARD LANE, with the immensely tall garden walls of the former vicarage on the l., to LADY STREET and LESLIE HOUSE, built 1810 for a wealthy tin merchant. Smart, restrained ashlar granite with tall sashes and fine interior. Again, the wrought-iron railings and gatepiers with spiral finials in the front wall are most pleasing. For an experience of the network of little side streets, return to the centre by FIVE WELLS LANE and pass the Guildhall into MENEAGE STREET. Another good intact street, of mostly small houses with C19 shopfronts and a few larger former town houses. Of special note: Nos. 4 and 6, probably a C17 merchant's house with C18 and later alterations, tiered oriels to first and second floors, and an early C18 ribbed plaster ceiling, panelling and chimneypiece to a first-floor room in No. 6; NATWEST BANK (No. 29), formerly a mid-C18 town house, stucco, five-bay front; and Nos. 21 and 23, a mid-C18 town house, red brick in Flemish bond, with rusticated granite quoins and a splendid Art Deco shopfront in black vitrolite. Continue as far as the former UNION WORKHOUSE, of 1855 by *F. W. Porter*, now residential. Single-storey entrance screen with tall central entrance with entablature flanked by three-bay lodges, the bays divided by pilaster piers. The main range within is characteristically austere and on a long E-shaped plan of fifteen bays to the front elevation with a central porch tower. A small diversion up TRENGROUSE WAY leads to TRENGROUSE HOUSE, c. 1972 by the *County Architect's Department*, project architect *Mike Way*. Designed for elderly residents, single-storey on a cruciform plan with low monopitch roofs, the two long wings in a sweeping curve broken by communal rooms and a central circular courtyard.

Return along Meneage Street r. into WENDRON STREET. The most prominent building is Godolphin Hall with the former GRAMMAR SCHOOL behind (see Churches and Public Buildings). Almost opposite, the former BAPTIST CHAPEL, now a cinema. 1836–7 by *Philip Sambell*, in a robust Norman style, similar to his chapel in Clarence Street, Penzance (q.v.). The ground floor is obscured by an ill-conceived C20 extension but the arcade of five arches with engaged columns above, rising to a three-bay gable with a deeply recessed central rose and pseudo-machicolation, shows the quality of Sambell's design.

BAR LODGE, Penrose Hill. 1895 by *G. H. Fellowes Prynne*. Strong Arts and Crafts style. Irregular square plan, with two-storey range to l. and single-storey range to r. with early example of roof terrace. Picturesque elevations with gabled and hipped roofs, tall stacks and varied fenestration.

TRENETHICK. *See* Wendron.

PENROSE. *See* p. 410.

2060

HERODSFOOT

ALL SAINTS. 1849–50 by *John Hayward*. Accomplished E.E.: a difficult site skilfully deployed, the proportions of the church handsome, architectural detail spare but effective.* It is best approached from below, where it appears perched dramatically above the small former C19 mining hamlet on the steep E slope of the West Looe valley, its strong verticality expressed in a w end of tall lancets between buttresses and a tall gabled roof surmounted by a bellcote. (On entry to the churchyard it presents as a quieter building with the one sweep of its slate roof encompassing nave and chancel, more lancets and buttresses, and a similarly vertically proportioned s porch with a richly moulded doorway. The surprise is the interior, whose lofty, elegant proportions effortlessly accommodate the chancel at a significantly higher level than the nave, reached up a flight of four steps and under a dignified two-centred chancel arch. – FONT. C14. Of interesting design with a circular bowl and a frieze of foliage scrolls along the upper rim. It is either from the ruined chapel of St Martin, Respryn, St Winnow, or a chapel of St Martin, Bosmaugan, St Winnow. – FURNISHINGS. Mostly by Hayward, simple and well made. – STAINED GLASS. A reglazing scheme of 2007 by *Jim Swingler* and *Lucy Gregory* reused much of the original glass but introduced a wider

---

* So much so that Betjeman was persuaded it must be by G. E. Street.

colour palette in a way that sensitively complements the character of the church.

HESSENFORD

St Anne. 1871 by *J. P. St Aubyn*, showing how skilful the architect could be, even if the result is not at all Cornish. The E.E. style is deployed in a satisfyingly composed exterior with a steeply pitched roof accented by a slim, tapering spirelet and swept low over narrow N and S aisles with lancet windows. The interior is lofty and dignified with four-bay aisle arcades on plain circular piers with four-centred arches. Nave, chancel and aisles have common rafter roofs; the aisles also have windbraces, and the chancel is roofed at a lower level beyond a tall chancel arch. Complete set of contemporary or early C20 furnishings including elaborate REREDOS with mosaic inlay. – STAINED GLASS. An excellent and complete ensemble by *Clayton & Bell*, 1880–1901.

ILLOGAN

The historic parish stretched from the heights of Carn Brea through Pool to Portreath on the N coast. Engine houses and chimneys are prominent in the landscape, visible reminders of the mining industry that dominated this area from the C18, much of it promoted by the Bassets of Tehidy (q.v.). The parish church lies in what was once a small churchtown now connected to the main urban area.

St Illogan. A late C14 granite WEST TOWER is all that survives of the old church, retained as a navigation landmark when the rest was demolished in 1846. Of two small stages with diagonal buttresses to the W side of the first stage, small angle buttresses to the E side, and an embattled parapet. Small two-centred W windows of two cusped lights to the first stage, two trefoil-headed lights to the belfry, and a blocked depressed tower arch to the former small narrow nave, its roof scar above. The new CHURCH, built away from it in 1846 by *J. P. St Aubyn*, has an impressive presence, though of a more urban than rural character. The nave and N and S aisles are all of equal height with a short chancel, all much buttressed and with Perp windows, the E end an especially effective composition. After this the interior is disappointingly dull, with five-bay arcades to N and S aisles on octagonal piers, and plain arch-braced roofs; the proportions are compromised by a clumsy W end subdivision of the 1980s. – FONT. Granite, with the old Cornish motif of faces at the corners, completely re-tooled in the C19. – PULPIT, incorporating Early Renaissance bench-ends. – STAINED GLASS. E window 1894 by *C. Elliot*. N aisle, Martha and Mary, 1898, by *Fouracre & Watson* of Plymouth. – MONUMENTS. A good ensemble, mostly removed from the former church. – Incomplete set of small BRASSES to James Basset and his wife, 1603. – Stone relief in the chancel to Rev. John Collins, rector 1632–84. Four kneeling figures with excellent draperies though with strangely coarsely carved hands and over-large heads. – Mary Collins †1743, elaborate cartouche with open pediment and putti. – Several other Basset monuments – Francis Basset †1769. Good medallion portrait above a sarcophagus in relief. – Francis Lord de Dunstanville †1835, with frontal bust medallion by *Sir Richard Westmacott*. – John Basset †1843, his disconsolate children standing by a locked door. – Frances Baroness Basset †1855, a touching depiction of a young woman feeding the poor. – John Francis Basset †1869. Standing angel in a plain, rather dull frame by *J. S. Westmacott*.

INCE CASTLE

74　　In the first rank of all the greater houses of Cornwall, and one of the most eminently picturesque. A perfect square of warm C17 brick – a very early occurrence in Cornwall, but not the earliest cf. The Keep, Golden Manor. It not only differs in so many ways – style, design, planning and materials – from its C17 Cornish contemporaries but is highly unusual nationally. The exquisite setting is a tongue of land in the tidal reaches of the Lynher opposite Antony (q.v.). The central two-storey range is embattled, with four square corner towers projecting from its main faces, their upper stages slate-hung and topped by pyramidal roofs. High, wide flight of steps leading to the principal entrance on a *piano nobile* in the W elevation; the doorcase is in the late medieval manner but it is surmounted by a large-scaled pediment containing a shield in a strapwork cartouche.

Ince was almost certainly built *c.* 1630–40 by Henry Killigrew, though probably not completed, and acquired by Edward Nosworthy in 1653; it is Nosworthy's arms which have been restored in the pediment. Killigrew was a staunch Royalist, and Ince was garrisoned in 1645–6 against Parliamentary forces in Plymouth. Architecturally, however, the house's function was clearly not primarily defensive. The towers were originally battlemented, as shown in Edward Prideaux's drawing of *c.* 1720, and there are gunloops in the sides of its front flankers to guard the stair to the main entrance, just as Godolphin's nearly contemporary front was embattled and its entrance covered by gunloops from the corner towers. Some degree of

Ince Castle, west front. Drawing by E. Prideaux, 1727

protection would indeed have been prudent in the troubled years leading up to the Civil War, but of much greater significance is the way in which the design and planning of the house show a synthesis of the need for protection with an understanding and care about style and comfort and a conscious desire for the picturesque effect.

For its antecedents, therefore, we may look first to nearby Mount Edgcumbe (1547–53) of which Ince could be regarded as a more modern version, and to Lulworth, Dorset, a hunting lodge and mock castle of 1610. Perhaps, though, the more direct influence should be seen as French chateau design, following the prevailing fashions of *c.* 1620 in its central two-storey range with higher corner towers, especially the work of Philibert de l'Orme in his *Le Premier tome de l'architecture* (1568).[*]

The suspended pediment with no supporting columns or pilasters is, however, highly unusual for its date and may well be the earliest Cornish appearance of classicism, pre-dating even Godolphin's entrance colonnade. And it is in its interior planning that Ince clearly represented the very latest in style and convenience for a gentleman's residence. Though it is impossible to reconstruct the interior in detail because of major c20 interventions,[†] a detailed record made after the serious fire of 1988 demonstrated that it was planned as a double-pile house with the ground and principal floors divided into six equal cells by a spine wall running N–S and two cross walls.[‡] There was no central hall or staircase between the two floors, the only stairs being in the corner of the house. Of the

---

[*] I owe this suggestion to Paul Holden, to whom I am grateful for other observations about the significance of Ince.

[†] There was a major restoration of the 1920s, very substantial alterations in 1960–2 by *S. R. Edwards* for Viscount Boyd, and substantial reconstruction in the 1990s, after the fire, by *Antony Jaggard* of *John Stark & Partners.*

[‡] The record was made by Nicholas Cooper of the former RCHME, to whom I am most grateful for this information and other commentary.

unresolved oddities that the house presents, the most curious is the fact that the two central rooms, including that forming the principal entrance, were unheated. The late c20 reconstruction contrived a gracious cantilevered staircase within this room that now connects it with the ground floor, and re-invented the principal rooms in well-judged proportion and detail. Only one plaster overmantel survived (in the SW room), and that heavily restored, with strapwork panels and two small figures blowing trumpets; the strapwork is like that within the entrance pediment. A section of a frieze of mermaids and mermen with forked tails terminating in dolphins' heads also survived, now replicated to continue around the room and repeated elsewhere.

Given the radical changes to the interior, the extraordinarily unaltered appearance of most of the exterior at Ince is remarkable, later additions only adding to the romantic character of its original conception. The brickwork is in slightly irregular English bond with granite dressings, with a flat band running around the house 2 ft (61 cm.) above the level of the principal floor and, below parapet level, a handsomely proportioned and generously scaled eaves cornice of moulded brick plastered in imitation of stone. The ground floor has retained most of its granite mullioned windows, some of them replaced, but the larger transomed-and-mullioned windows (probably of timber in brick surrounds) of the principal floor were replaced by sashes in the early c18, when the house was recorded as being in poor repair. This was also the time when the roofs of the corner towers were altered. In the 1920s a range was constructed between the N and E towers.

The GARDEN has a SHELL HOUSE of 1963 SW of the house, the interior decorated with shells collected by Viscount Boyd when Secretary of State for the Colonies.

INDIAN QUEENS

PREACHING PIT, off Pocahontas Crescent. Opened 1850. One of three surviving open-air Wesleyan preaching pits (cf. Gwennap and St Newlyn East). Four tiers of seating, semicircular preaching platform, and steps between the grass terraces. It was constructed within a disused openworks in one of the most historic tracts of mining country.

JACOBSTOW

ST JAMES. Pleasantly situated in a hollow in its small remote churchtown. Finely proportioned unbuttressed W tower of three stages with trefoil-headed niche with engaged finial at second stage and substantial octagonal turrets with crocketed finials, all very like Poundstock. The plinth is carved with mouchettes in roundels and quatrefoils in squares (cf. North Tamerton and Week St Mary). Late C15 or early C16. Castellated S porch with plain tunnel-vault and trefoil-headed image above S door of the same date. Nave and N and S aisles a little earlier. Arcades of four bays, Cornish standard shafts, rather low, and four-centred arches. The aisle windows are original, the three-light standard Cornish. Chancel rebuilt and nave roof replaced 1886 by *Otho B. Peter* of Launceston. Plain but pleasingly light and dignified interior. – FONT. Norman, a fine example of the Altarnun type with faces at the four corners and stylized six-petalled flowers in niches on the four sides. – PULPIT. Made up of C16 bench-ends. – ALTARS. High Altar an Elizabethan communion table with bulbous legs; S chancel chapel a stone *mensa* with consecration crosses. – The inner NORTH DOOR, with vertical and horizontal battens, is C15. – MONUMENT. Good slate to Susannah and Mary Clark †1745 and 1748 on exterior E wall of chancel.

KEA

OLD CHURCH OF ST KEA, Old Kea. Only the WEST TOWER survives, ivy-clad and ruinous, standing above a creek in a remote E corner of the large parish; it was retained as an eye-catcher for Tregothnan when the rest was pulled down after the construction of a new church in a more central location in 1802–3. C15, possibly remodelled in the C16 or later. Three-storeyed with thin diagonal buttresses, battlements and crocketed pinnacles. Four-centred W door, E arch of two orders with evidence of the nave roof above.

To the NE within the churchyard the MISSION CHURCH OF ST KEA, 1862, enlarged 1869 and re-seated and improved subsequently. A charming little essay in simple Gothic, incorporating some material from the old building. Nave, chancel, S aisle and miniature three-stage W bellcote. Interior with four-bay arcade of reused pointed arches on cut-drawn octagonal piers, and simple arch-braced roofs. – FONT. C15. Octagonal with very weathered decorative panels to each side. – STAINED GLASS. E and W nave early windows by the enthusiastic amateur *Rev. William Willimott,* and four windows by *Alexander Gibbs.* S of the church, a large tapered round CROSS-SHAFT, undecorated except for a raised band above the base. Professor Charles Thomas has suggested it might have been a menhir.

ALL HALLOWS. One of the most attractive late C19 churches in Cornwall (though very un-Cornish), beautifully situated in its sylvan landscape, the park of Killiow. 1894–7 by *G. H. Fellowes*

Prynne and of greatest interest among his churches, in a strongly Arts and Crafts-influenced late Perp style. The massing is most satisfyingly composed: three-stage w tower with weathered diagonal corner buttresses, embattled parapet, and a striking broached spire in copper; the nave roof swept out over the aisles; the s transept roof parallel to the nave. The walls are of a lovely cream killas stone in large and small blocks, with granite dressings and prominent diagonal corner buttresses, bestowing an appropriately rustic character enhanced by a timber-framed porch on a stone plinth. The interior is especially handsome, of generous and spacious proportions, with a wide nave, narrow N and s aisles with lean-to roofs, and walls of a mellifluous polychromy: dressed killas stone brought to course with bands of red Paignton sandstone and yellow Ham Hill stone. The aisle arcades are of three wide bays of Bath stone on octagonal piers, the corbelled chancel arch of alternately Bath stone and Catacleuse blocks. The low wall between nave and chancel was removed in 1988 and reused below the organ chamber in the s transept. Arch-braced roof with widely spaced trusses. – FONT. Norman, a notable example of the Bodmin type, from the old church. Bowl on five supports, heads at the four corners, and on the sides the tree of life twice, and once a cross and a lion *passant*. – ALTAR, a classic Fellowes Prynne design with five panels, a step and a central tabernacle, enhanced by a complete scheme of tiled flooring. The panels house paintings by *E. A. Fellowes Prynne* of angels, seraphim and the Lamb. – POOR BOX. 1739, of the pillar type, from the old church. – STAINED GLASS. Fine chancel window by *Percy Bacon*, designed by Fellowes Prynne, 1926. N wall of nave, 1917, by *Heaton, Butler & Bayne*.

LYCHGATE, N of E end. Of *c.* 1896. Probably by *E. A. Fellowes Prynne*. Steep slate roof with open arch-braced gables.

CHURCH COTTAGE. The former National School of 1849–51 by *William White*. Simple Gothic with steep slate roof, louvred flèche and deep eaves; the decorative bargeboards are later. Originally a single-storey schoolroom with large N porch. Adjacent are the plainer MASTER'S HOUSE, 1852 but not to White's design, and MEMORIAL HALL, 1896.

The large parish* was an important mining and industrial area in the C18 and C19, reflected in the number of Nonconformist chapels. At Kerley Downs, BILLY BRAY'S THREE EYE CHAPEL, originally built *c.* 1835, with 'three windows, one on one side, and two on the other', giving it its nickname. The present chapel is an enlargement or substantial rebuilding of the mid C19, with fittings including a chair with a flat wooden seat inscribed BILLY BRAY BALDHU 1839. At Porthkea, METHODIST CHAPEL, three-bay gabled front with pointed-arch windows and trefoiled tablet dated 1869.

---

*Chacewater and Baldhu were created out of it in 1828 and 1847 respectively.

At PLAYING PLACE, ¾ m. SSE of All Hallows, MR LANYON'S ALMSHOUSES, Halvarras Road. 1726. A remarkable survival of almshouses in their original function and design. Symmetrical six-window E front arranged as two pairs with two doorways in the middle of each; tall end stacks and a central axial stack. Much interior detail remains including stud-and-panel screens and ovolo-moulded beams. It is thought that originally the ground floor was for men, the first floor for women.

At CALENICK, ¾ m. ENE of All Hallows, Nos. 1–6 ROPEWALK ROW is a rare example of a symmetrical terrace of workers' housing of c. 1760. Originally four houses, paired either side of a passage with central stair and shallower service wings to rear. Built to serve the smelting works formerly nearby. CALENICK HOUSE, 100 yds N, was rebuilt 1702, incorporating traces of an earlier building. A pretty Queen Anne house, very similar to Trereife (q.v.) but smaller. Beautifully proportioned two-storey, seven-window front around a simple central door with pediment, the upper storey slate-hung. Interior little altered on plan of two reception rooms flanking a l. of centre stair hall, leading to a stairwell between narrower service rooms. Dog-leg closed-string column-on-vase baluster staircase with moulded handrail, square newel caps and pulvinated string. In a first-floor room a fine c. late C18 fireplace, which has tapered fluted pilasters with entablature broken forward over pilasters and to centre, and with Adam decoration to frieze. Used during most of the C18 and C19 as an account house for a nearby smelting works. A brick CLOCK TOWER groups prettily with the house to the SW. Mid-C18, of two stages surmounted by an open bellcote, the second stage greatly reduced. Interior virtually complete with original clock works by *Richard Wallis*, 1756, and bell inscribed 'William Lemon 1749'. S of the house, a WEIGH HOUSE, for the weighing of iron, probably early C19. Simple single-cell building, the interior with a heavy weighing beam spanning E–W.

SW of Ropewalk Row, overlooking Calenick Creek, two small Modernist houses built into the slope one above the other. The upper is OTTER CREEK (formerly LANTEGLOS), 1961 by *Giles Blomfield* of *John Crowther & Associates*, the lower SHOOLDARRY, 1962 by *Michael Whitham*. Both are strongly disciplined designs on 3-ft (0.9-metre) and 4-ft (1.2-metre) grids under flat and monopitched roofs respectively, employing full-height glazing to the seaward views between whitewashed rendered blockwork side and back walls. They sit well in their sheltered maritime context.

KILLIOW, ½ m. SW of All Hallows. Splendidly situated overlooking its informal parkland landscape. C18 and earlier, remodelled c. 1850, possibly by *Paxton*. Now a golf club. Two-storey square granite ashlar house, the SW entrance front with a wide central doorway with Doric porte cochère, the SE garden front with a shallow two-storey bay flanked by tripartite windows on the ground floor. The interior has two equal reception rooms either side of a central entrance vestibule leading to a spacious stair hall with two further reception rooms beyond the r. hand room. Very fine fittings of the early and mid C19 including doors and doorcases, ceiling cornices and bands. The entrance vestibule has a moulded coffered ceiling and a good C18 chimneypiece. Cantilevered open-string stone stair with ornate cast-iron splat balusters. COACHHOUSE of seven bays with cupola. The parish contains several former gentry houses, indicating its proximity to Truro. SEVEOCK is mid-C18 with contemporary sash windows and glass and a virtually intact interior. PENEL-EWEY BARTON, 1¼ m. SSE, an early to mid-C18 remodelling by William Lemon (cf. Truro) of an earlier house, also has almost complete contemporary glazing and good interior including a fine mid-C18 Chinese Chippendale dog-leg stair, and gatepiers and garden walls of the same date in English bond brick. To the N a very intact C19 planned farm group around a yard with barns, shippons, linhays and stables.

COME-TO-GOOD. *See* p. 155.

See p. 155.

8040

KENWYN

The mother parish of Truro of which Kenwyn is now a suburb. The close relationship is vividly demonstrated from the E end of the churchyard with its fine view of the city, the viaduct in front, the cathedral in the centre, and the river beyond.

ST KEYNE (St Kenwyn). Consecrated in 1259 and appropriated to Glasney College in 1270, extended in the C15 and C16 with S aisle and tower, but greatly rebuilt in a series of restorations between 1820 and 1880. The 1820s work was by *John Foulston* of Plymouth, the 1850s rebuilding of the N transept was by *William White*, and an 1862 campaign by *J. P. St Aubyn*. The C13–C14 church was cruciform, of which the N side and the foundations of the N transept survive. The W tower of three stages has buttresses set back from the angles, embattled parapet and crocketed corner pinnacles. The S aisle and chapel are separated from the nave and chancel by a tall arcade of seven bays with slim standard Cornish piers and four-centred arches. The arcade to the N transept is later still. Figures of a bishop and an angel attached to the capitals. C19 wagon roofs to nave, chancel and aisle. – STAINED GLASS. A good C19 ensemble. E window by *Alexander Gibbs*, 1864, a splendid array of blues, reds and golds with medallions, and two in S chapel of the same date. S chapel W by *Lavers & Barraud*, 1859, bright and lively, also chancel N, 1850, and tower 1857. S chapel E, 1845 by *Robert Beer* of Exeter.

LYCHGATE. SW of the church. Reputedly C14 but much rebuilt, with slate-hung upper storey, probably a schoolroom, and a cottage attached. – HOLY WELL OF ST KEYNE. At the SW corner of the church. Early medieval origin, late C19 structure of dressed granite and rubble with steps down to well. – Outside SE corner of church. Agnes Jenney †1769. Granite ashlar square-on-plan CHEST TOMB with chamfered plinth and cornice surmounted by inscribed urn. – HEAD-STONE. 100 yds NE. Joseph Emidy †1835, with moulded top framing a raised central lozenge containing a garlanded urn in relief with inscription. A former slave, Emidy was the first African composer in England. – PINNACLE. NE of the church, just outside the churchyard. Octagonal in granite ashlar. The top of the spire from the former church of St Mary, Truro (demolished save for the S aisle for the building of the cathedral (q.v.)), re-sited here *c.* 1890.

EPIPHANY HOUSE, Kenwyn Church Road. Formerly Copeland Court. An C18 house on an older site, extended and remod-elled 1878 as the bishop's palace for Bishop Benson (cf. the cathedral), with chapel and further extensions of *c.* 1906 by *E. H. Sedding* for Bishop Stubbs. Large irregular plan with remains of the double-depth C18 house somewhat overwhelmed by the later work in a mix of styles. The entrance front is full of incident, including a three-bay colonnaded loggia, an octag-onal cupola and an extravagantly detailed gable-end to the chapel. This has a semicircular broken and scrolled pediment containing a niche with a small triangular pediment over, sup-ported on three-quarter columns on consoles that flank a round-arched window. Late C18 or early C19 open-well stair. The CHAPEL has a stone-coffered barrel vault and fittings from the former convent (now the Alverton Manor Hotel, Tregolls Road, Truro), including REREDOS and STALLS by *Ninian Comper.* – Relief of John Wesley, a copy by *J. Harvey* of that at the Old Chapel, Altarnun (q.v.). – STAINED GLASS. E window, 1914 by *Powells* of Whitefriars.

CAUSILGEY, 3 m. N. 1870, reputedly by *George Devey.* A small country house in Tudor vernacular style with deliberately irreg-ular plan and elevations to create a romantic pile. Charming SE front, two-storey with central range flanked by projecting wings of differing height and varied granite mullion windows including a six-light window in the main range and canted bays to the l. wing.

KILKHAMPTON

2010

A large village that originated as a medieval borough and market closely connected with the Grenvilles, whose great house at Stowe (*see* below) lay in the W of the parish near the sea.

ST JAMES. A stately church, unexpectedly large for this remote part of north Cornwall and testimony to the former impor-tance of Kilkhampton and the Grenvilles. That there was a

substantial church here in the C12, when it belonged to Tewkesbury Abbey (its patronage passed to the Grenvilles in 1237), is
shown by the magnificent Norman s doorway, though the rest
of the building is Perp. Tall three-stage w tower with buttresses
set back from the corners and battlemented with crocketed
pinnacles: it is visible for miles around. N door with re-set
beakhead. Small segmental-arched s door to the Grenville
chapel with Grenville arms and cusped niche over. s porch
built by John Grenville, rector 1524–80, and inscribed 'Porta
Celi 1567'. The outstanding feature of the church is the
Norman inner s doorway (cf. Morwenstow), the second largest
in Cornwall after St Germans. It consists of four arches carried
on three colonettes which have waterleaf feet and varied capitals including fir cones and heads. Inner arch has beakheads
holding a roll moulding and chevrons on soffit; second arch
has chevrons and further chevrons on soffit in an unusual
design (cf. Morwenstow); third arch similar but with lozenges
on corner between soffit and outer arch; outer arch has chevrons with roll moulding on soffit.

Lofty, spacious aisled INTERIOR: N and s arcades of seven
bays on tall piers with standard shafts and four-centred arches,
and tall tower arch. Fine unceiled wagon roofs throughout with
carved ribs and bosses, partly but skilfully renewed. Chancel
roof slightly lower with angels carved on wall-plates: the church
was restored 1858–60 by *George Gilbert Scott* who rebuilt the E
end. – BENCHES AND BENCH-ENDS. A remarkable sight, 157
in all, filling the interior. A few early examples but mostly C16,
and late C16 at that; the installation of some documented in
1567. The subjects include a large number of Symbols of the
Passion (cf. especially the N aisle); heraldic and armorial
devices, especially the Grenville arms; arabesques and occasional grotesques, some with unconventional borders; and
emblems of trades (e.g. shovel, scythe and flail in N aisle). At
the sw and NW corners of the aisles two of bishops and priests,
probably part of an early priests' stall. Those benches facing
the chancel have fine profiled heads. – ROOD SCREEN AND
ROOD. 1905 by *G. H. Fellowes Prynne*. – FONT. C16. Octagonal
bowl with curious inscription in inverted Lombardic letters.
Continuous frieze below, armorial panels below again, and
blind panels on stem. It is likely that the document 'setting up'
of the font in 1585 refers to this, given by Richard Grenville
(of the *Revenge*). – NORTH, SOUTH and WEST DOORS. Probably. C16. – ROYAL ARMS. Large, plaster, for Charles I with
strapwork decoration (cf. Boconnoc, Launcells, Marhamchurch, Poughill, Poundstock and Stratton). – STAINED GLASS.
Many examples of good C19 glass, mostly by *Clayton & Bell*,
including a fine E window and the w window of the tower, the
latter an outstanding Empire memorial window with rich iconography and deep colours, reminiscent of the firm's work in
the cathedral at Truro. – Numerous early C18 WALL MONU-
MENTS (e.g. John Warminster †1700; Richard Westlake †1704;
John Courtis †1705), are attributed to *Michael Chuke* (1679–1742)

of Kilkhampton who was a pupil of Grinling Gibbons. Most of them are badly repainted: retaining earlier colouring the monument above the vestry door to Rev. John Coryndon †1711. – On s wall of Grenville chapel, Sir Bevill Grenville †1643, erected 1714 ('Thus slain thy valiant ancestor did ly / When his one Bark a Navy did defy', etc.) and also attributed to *Chuke*, who worked for the Grenvilles at Stowe, carving a pulpit and wainscoting for the chapel (now at Stowe School, Bucks). He may also have executed the fine Grenville arms above the rood screen. – Algernon Carteret Thynne †1917 by *W. Goscombe John*. Bronze reliefs of Palestine and bronze statue of horse and rider above.

The churchyard is full of good C19 slate memorials. LYCH-GATE, 1860 probably by *Scott*.

Former RECTORY. Mid-C19, probably also by *Scott*, with C17 rear outshuts. Two-storey three-bay symmetrical front with open pediment to central bay. Later addition of one bay at l. end. Overhanging eaves with modillion cornice. Interior with mid-C19 detail.

The buildings of the village are unpretentious but the atmosphere is distinctly Cornish and the medieval street pattern is still discernible, centred on THE SQUARE with WEST STREET leading off towards the castle, the site of Stowe, and the sea. Less easily observable on the ground is the survival of burgage plots but Kilkhampton is possibly the best example in Cornwall of a medieval borough layout.

KILKHAMPTON CASTLE, 1 m. w. Small triangular motte to w of Kilkhampton, with two small baileys to E. All three contain the mounds of now collapsed buildings, the motte's probably a small stone tower. C12 pottery found in mid-C20 excavations may support a theory that this was an adulterine castle held by Robert, Earl of Gloucester, half-brother of Empress Matilda. It appears, however, not to have been slighted at the civil war's end, suggesting another possibility, that it was the Grenville family castle. A hollow way connecting castle and town passes through an outwork to the castle's E. The main front of Stowe was carefully aligned on this castle rather than the church tower, Stowe's long straight eastern roadway running directly towards it.

STOWE BARTON, 3 m. w. Little remains of the Grenville house, though the site, dramatically perched on the high hillside with views of the sea, still conveys something of the astonishing achievement of building such a sumptuous complex in so exposed a location. A Buckler drawing of 1827, copied from an unknown original depiction, shows a house with a magnificent eleven-bay front facing inland and seven bays deep, on a rectangular plan with two principal floors above a basement. Built 1675* by John Grenville, created 1st Earl of

* Several articles in the *Journal of the Royal Institution of Cornwall* by Michael Trinick discuss the house, one attributing it to *John Fitch*, a prominent London builder; his brother Thomas provided the brickwork for Kingston Lacy, Dorset.

Bath 1660 as a reward for his assistance in the Restoration; demolished in 1739. Some of the principal features were moved to other buildings: carved woodwork to the Grenville Room in Prideaux Place, Padstow (q.v.); the grand staircase with openwork carving in the style of Grinling Gibbons a (tumbling putti entwined in scrolls of foliage) in Cross House, Little Torrington, Devon: and an entire room with elaborate plasterwork and decoration used as the Mayor's Parlour at the Guildhall, South Molton, Devon. The most striking surviving feature is the BRICKWORK to the courtyard wall of Stowe Barton, partly in English bond; a possible REAL TENNIS COURT used as a shippon, also in brick; and a reputed CARRIAGE WASH.

ALDERCOMBE BARTON, 1 m. ENE. One of the most complete early courtyard houses in Cornwall. It originated in the C16 and was extended to a courtyard plan in the C17, with ranges to the W, N and E sides. The most arresting feature is the splendid S gateway of *c.* 1500, its wide four-centred archway with quatrefoils in the spandrels, rising to a crown of C17 pyramids, the central pyramid raised on the pyramidal plinth and square classical cornice, possibly reused. The charming S front has many mullioned windows, one with a king mullion. Paul Orchard, Sheriff of Cornwall, lived at Aldercombe in 1760, and by his marriage to a Luttrell heiress came into possession of the former Hartland Abbey.

3070

KIT HILL
2 m. NE of Callington

The CHIMNEY that crowns the summit of the hill, an outcrop of Bodmin granite, is one of the most prominent landmarks of east Cornwall, and has the architectural qualities of a memorial monument, for which it is often mistaken. Built by Sir John Call of Whiteford (cf. Stoke Climsland) in 1858 of granite, the circular shaft with moulded plinth and projecting square slab cap, sited on a pentagonal earthwork, it formed part of the Great Consols mining complex. The QUARRY to the N, seemingly the work of giants, is a sublime landscape of sheer granite faces, machinery foundations, and abandoned blocks, some finished, others simply fallen. Developed from the 1870s, abandoned in 1955, it was the apogee of the quarrying industry on Kit Hill and one of the sites that made Cornwall's reputation in the late C19 and early C20 as a supplier of granite to Britain and the world. Finished blocks were moved down the slope by tram for loading on the East Cornwall Minerals Railway, to be sent via Gunnislake to the Tamar for distribution to major London projects, including Battersea Bridge and Embankment and County Hall, and the National Library of Wales.

LADOCK   8050

St Ladoc. A specially well-proportioned w tower of regular granite blocks, in three stages, with buttresses leaving the corners free and finishing in tall crocketed pinnacles. It was added in the late C15 or early C16 to a church that was cruciform by the C13, of which the n wall of the present nave survives, and was enlarged by a s aisle and a s porch at the same date. The porch has its old wagon roof, heavy decoration, and a curious, very primitive face boxed in a narrow frame over the s door. Is it Norman? And what did it belong to? The s aisle arcade of six bays has slim piers of standard design and unusually elaborate arch mouldings. Nave and s aisle have C16 wagon roofs. The church was restored 1862–4 by *G. E. Street*: the chancel was embellished with an elaborate cusped, arch- and wind-braced roof, an e window with French Gothic detail flanked inside by shafts of polished serpentine, and rich marble, alabaster and tile polychromy, the ALTAR with three painted panels by *E. A. Fellowes Prynne* added in 1907. Also in 1907 the n transept was extended e by *E. H. Sedding* to form an ambitious n chancel aisle with stone vaulted roof and a charming bay-windowed vestry of almost domestic character. – FONT. Exactly as at Feock, of Catacleuse stone, sharply carved. Late Norman, circular, with an upper border of two tiers of crosses, and trees of life in circles below (cf. Fowey, St Mewan and Lanlivery). – ROOD SCREEN. C16. The massively carved base survives, across nave and aisle, with two entrances, and altogether sixteen panels, rather broad and with large, heavy leaves. – BENCH-ENDS. A few made up into a lectern. – STAINED GLASS. The best display of *Morris & Co.* glass in Cornwall, of outstanding interest in demonstrating the development of the workshop, the designs mostly originals not replicated elsewhere. Sequence of three windows. The e window, 1863, is the earliest known instance of Street collaborating with *William Morris*, his former pupil (Dr Royston Lambert), and is characteristically different from his firm's later work: simpler, less rich in colour range, and forming a band in the centre of the window with angels in circles below; above, in the tracery, Christ in Majesty, seated on a rainbow with sun, moon and stars. Central panel of St Mary Magdalene washing the feet of Jesus by *E. Burne-Jones* – touching, without a hint of sentiment – flanked by Morris windows, l. of St Mary Magdalene with Mary the wife of Cleopas, and r. the Virgin with St Ladoca. – s chancel aisle e window, 1869–70, the glass richer in colour and filling the whole window. Central panel of St Luke by *Ford Madox Brown*, flanked l. by St Raphael and r. by St Peter, both by *Morris*, with lovely textured robes. – w window of s aisle, 1897, by Burne-Jones, of Moses, St John the Baptist, and Isaiah, against blue backgrounds with foliage and fruit above and a foreground of grass, of Pre-Raphaelite character.

104

Adjacent to the church and churchyard the SCHOOL of 1867 by
J. P. St Aubyn. Schoolrooms and school house in the medieval
vernacular style, a pretty composition with the church. Opposite the church, LADOCK HOUSE, the former rectory. 1832,
extended 1850. Stucco with granite dressings, U-shaped plan,
granite Tuscan porch. Interior has cantilevered stone staircase
with iron balusters.

LAMORRAN

ST MORAN. In a lonely position on a tidal creek of the Fal. A
small cruciform church with a detached bell-tower. It was
cruciform when re-dedicated in 1261, restored in 1845, and
partially rebuilt in 1854 by *William White* for 6th Viscount Falmouth. The reworking of the C13 fabric has undoubtedly been
extensive, with some features (e.g. the Perp three-light window)
re-set, but it is always thoughtful. The interior with its pointed
chancel arch on pillars, plastered walls, low oak benches, and
Georgian choir arrangement is of pleasing simplicity. – FONT.
Circular, Norman, on five supports with four corner figures
and no other ornament. – STAINED GLASS. An interesting collection of Victorian glazing for such a small church. – In the S
transept, a bright three-light window by *Thomas Willement*, also
1854. – Some pieces of medieval glass in the S aisle E window.
E window early *Lavers & Barraud*, 1858, unusual Crucifixion
iconography. – W window *Clayton & Bell*, 1893, allegoric
figures of Christ. N transept, amateur roundels of Evangelists,
possibly by *Lady Falmouth*. – MONUMENT to John Verman
†1658 and his wife, uncommonly large, with four arches, two
for the figures and two for the inscriptions, deeply cut.

The diminutive BELL-TOWER is in the SW corner of the
churchyard. Late medieval and late C16 to early C17. Two-
storey with gable roof, semicircular doorway and small square
two-light oak mullion window to first floor. Entrance to first
floor and bell-tower by ramp to narrow doorway in W gable-
wall. Small corbelled arched openings to the E and W walls of
the ground floor. Interior has oak bell-frame with carved
braces and one bell *in situ*; there were formerly three bells, one
of which is now at Tresillian. CROSS, S of the church. Gothic,
specially fine, with foliated head broken, on octagonal tapered
shaft.

MANOR HOUSE. L-shaped plan, C16–C17 with C18 wing to S.
Large gable-end of E front has early C16 four-centred arched
doorway with moulded spandrels and hoodmould, probably
resited.

SETT BRIDGE, ½ m. NE, across the River Fal. 1850. Four-span
with segmental arches and cutwaters.

LANDEWEDNACK

The most southerly parish in Britain, of magnificent cliff scenery, small coves and improbably blue sea around Lizard Point.

ST WINWALOE, Church Cove Road. Low early C15 W tower of contrasting blocks of granite and 'blue, glossy green and velvet black' serpentine; of two stages without buttresses, like all the surrounding churches. The S porch, which adjoins the transept as at nearby Mawgan and St Anthony-in-Meneage (qq.v.), is battlemented and has a rib-vault inside, resting on angel shield-bearing corbels and with a larger angel holding a scroll as a boss: it may be of C13 (Sedding) or C14 (Henderson) origin but has been extensively restored – there were major restorations in 1860–2 and in the 1920s. The S door sheltered by this porch is Norman, uncommonly lofty, with chevron decoration to the outer arch and circles in the voussoirs of the inner; its columns are C19, of black serpentine with cushion capitals, and there is a Perp doorway inserted within. The S transept, chancel and E end of the N aisle have C14 windows. The N aisle is of five bays with plain Cornish standard arcades and Perp windows without tracery in the N wall. From the S transept a squint opens into the chancel much like Cury and Mawgan; the corner is simply cut off and replaced by a squat pier of standard Cornish design. There is a low-set lancet window behind, its function uncertain. Wagon roofs to nave, chancel, S transept and N aisle, with carved ribs and bosses. – Late C13 PISCINAS in chancel and transept. – FONT. A simplified version of the Bodmin type with short C19 serpentine corner columns and inscription 'IHC and D RIC BOLHAM ME FECIT 1404': Bolham's dates as rector at Landewednack are 1404–15. – PULPIT and LECTERN. 1860, of polished serpentine, the pulpit of strikingly simple design for the period. – STAINED GLASS. Mostly of the 1860s, some geometric patterns, chancel S 1869 and N aisle W 1887 by *Lavers, Barraud & Westlake*.

At CHURCH COVE, some C18 thatched cottages and former buildings of the fishing industry now converted to residential use, including FISH CELLARS, WINCH HOUSE and a former LIFEBOAT HOUSE of 1887. The present LIZARD LIFEBOAT STATION is S off Church Cove Road in Kilcobben Cove. 2010–11 by *Poynton Bradbury Wynter Cole*, structural engineer *Royal Haskoning*. An impressive structure, dramatically sited in one of the most rugged and remote locations in Britain. It perches above a long slipway and below a cliff railway with a winch house above.

LIZARD TOWN, arranged around a large green ½ m. W of the church, is the place from which to explore the area. Here, and at the S end of the road to the lighthouse near LIZARD POINT, SERPENTINE WORKSHOPS, simple timber-clad huts, established here in the late C19 after the closure of the serpentine works at Poltesco (q.v.). Just to the E the LIZARD LIGHTHOUSE, the oldest mainland lighthouse in Cornwall, with its two hexagonal towers flanking a terrace originally for offices and accommodation. The towers were built in 1752, their symmetry slightly upset by the dismounting of the W light in 1903. Above the white walls rise tall black chimneystacks, cowls, fog horn and the circular lantern of the E tower: diagonal latticework with grills and railings and a conical roof with ball finials.

MARCONI WIRELESS STATION, ½ m. SSE on the Pen Olver headland. A pair of simple timber-framed huts where Marconi set up his experimental wireless station to work in conjunction with his larger station at Poldhu (*see* Mullion). On 23 January 1901 a new record for wireless communication of 186 miles was set between the Lizard and the Isle of Wight, paving the way for the famous transatlantic signals transmitted from Poldhu a year later. On the adjoining E headland above Bass Point the former LLOYDS SIGNAL STATION, 1872. Erected by *G. C. Fox & Co.*, Falmouth shipping agents. A white battlemented square, two-storey with small rectangular seaward look-out windows. Communication with ships was by semaphore, and with the ships' owners by telegraph, obviating the necessity for calling at Falmouth; more than one thousand ships per month were using the facility by 1877.

WINDMILL TOWER, 2 m. NNW, near Rose-in-the-Valley. Circular base of the tower, of serpentine and elvan, its origins pre-1695. One of the few windmill remains in Cornwall.

KYNANCE GATE, 1½ m. NW. Middle Bronze Age SETTLEMENT, redeveloped in the Iron Age and Roman periods when the surviving circular and ovoid buildings were constructed. Excavated 1952–63. Group of eight houses tightly clustered around a prominent outcrop of serpentine and linked by curving banks to form three small enclosures. Second looser group of seven houses on flatter ground to N, again linked by low field banks.

LANDRAKE

ST MICHAEL. The narrow streets of the hilltop village away from the busy main road gather around the church with its tall, elegant tower – 100 ft (30 metres) high – which can be seen from far away. It is late C14, of the usual three stages with buttresses set back from the angles that fade gracefully into the battlements, and, like the rest of the church, is entirely of the lovely sage-green Tarten Down stone from quarries in the parish. In the NE is a stair-turret of three-eighths plan rising above the pinnacles. The S side of the church must still contain Norman masonry; at any rate it contains a S doorway with Norman colonettes, a pointed arch substituted when the S porch was added in the C16. The church is entered by a shallow, pinnacled N porch with two medieval heads. The interior is lofty and spacious, if rather short, with a tall C15 N aisle. The arcade is of four wide bays, the piers of an unusual variety of the standard Cornish profile, with three-quarter instead of demi-shafts. The S transept arch belongs to the same date. From the transept to the chancel and the rood-loft stairs runs a squint-like cut. A restoration of 1877 by *Henry Elliott* re-roofed the nave, chancel and transept and installed a new chancel arch on C15 shafts with ring capitals and mask corbels; there was also much replacement and renewal of windows. The wagon roof of the aisle is C15 but thoroughly restored. – FONT. Norman, of the Altarnun type, with corner faces and large rosettes in circles. – STAINED GLASS. Chancel E, 1878, by *Jones & Willis*. – Chancel S, 1888, by *Fouracre & Watson*. – Tower W, 2002, by *Andrew Johnson*, a striking design in somewhat strident colour. – MONUMENTS. Small BRASS to Edward Courtenay, Lord of Wotton in Landrake, †1509. – Several excellent C18 and early C19 slate LEDGER PLATES in nave and transept, and a specially fine pair of 1607 in the chancel to Nicholas Mylls and his wife, with carved figures in relief and strapwork.

LANDULPH

ST LEONARD. There was a church here by 1086 but only the massive base stones of the W door of the strong W tower are Norman: the lower two stages are late C14, the upper stage early C15. It has buttresses only just leaving the angles free, replaced by thin diagonal buttresses at the top stage. A three-eighths stair-turret rises above the embattled parapet and pinnacles. The exterior of the body of the church is roughcast, not a very pleasing treatment. The outer arch of the S porch is a reconstruction of late C13 stonework, the inner doorway C14. C15 tracery. The interior has five-bay arcades to the aisles with octagonal piers and a fairly simple profile of the arches (two concave chamfers). A restoration of 1901–2 by *G. H. Fellowes Prynne* reconstructed the wagon roofs, retaining C15 bosses in both aisles and principal rafters and pendants in the S aisle, and raising the nave roof to form a clerestory with three-light cusped dormers; this was probably an earlier arrangement, the much steeper pitch of the medieval roof being recorded in the scar on the E face of the tower. As a record of the church's connection with the Lower family of Clifton, the CHEST TOMB to Sir Nicholas Lower †1655, with a beautiful large black marble plate with inscription and coat of arms; a pair of BRASS TABLETS in stone ovolo-moulded surround with some ancient colour and stone skull and hourglass to Sir Nicholas Lower, 1695, and Dame Elizabeth Lower, 1638; and the panelling of the FAMILY PEW, dated 1621, now displayed against the W walls of the N and S aisles, with linenfold ornamental carving, many coats of arms, and unicorn finials. The pew was at the E end of the S aisle, beyond the ROOD SCREEN, which was restored in phases between 1914 and 1932, including the late addition of the rood figures; the base is original, with comparatively simple carving of the panels, quatrefoils, and the blank tracery with mouchettes which is so characteristic of C16 Cornish bench-ends. The church has a number of such BENCH-ENDS with the usual motifs – and a few unusual ones: a boar's head, bear-baiting, a fox and goose, a rabbit, a bat and an eagle. – FONT. Plain, octagonal, on five supports and a restored Norman base. Letter inscription and date, 1660, around the bowl. – Two Norman CARVED HEADS as corbels either side of the entrance to the chancel. – C18 ALMS BOX. – ROYAL ARMS of George II. – CURIOSUM. Early C18 RINGERS' VERSES in tower, in bolection-moulded frame. – STAINED GLASS. S aisle window retains fragments of medieval glass, including the Courtenay balls, and C17 shields of arms and unicorn crest of the Lower family of Clifton. – S aisle E, 1913, by *Fouracre & Watson*, of Bishops Benson, Gott and Wilkinson. – MONUMENTS. Besides those of the Lowers (*see* above), in the S aisle an inscription recording the death and burial of Theodore Palaeologus, a descendant of the medieval Christian Emperors of Byzantium, who died at Clifton 1636. – Stone TABLET to Elizabeth Roberts, 1654. – In the tower, slate TABLET with shaped head and trumpeting angel carved in relief to FitzAntony Pennington, bell-founder of Lezant, with quatrain, 1768.

In the churchyard SW of the porch, base of a SUNDIAL, dated 1690, a granite shaft, chamfered, with pyramid stops at the top.

LANDULPH METHODIST CHURCH, 1 m. N, near Cargreen. Datestone 1874. An unusually attractive ensemble of church, Sunday School (added to the rear in 1893), and two-storey tower with diagonal buttresses and a pyramidal roof, all fronted by a long wall surmounted by cast-iron railings. The church is entered through the ground floor of the tower, and also has buttresses with a three-light window to the road and paired lancets to the sides.

LANEAST

ST SIDWELL. 'One of the most pleasing (churches) in the diocese, both within and without' (Henderson). A chapelry founded and maintained by the Augustinian priory of Launceston. It sits within a *lann* in the churchtown of the village above the delightful valley of the little River Inny. Of the cruciform Norman church the masonry of chancel, N wall and N transept remains. In the N transept is an E window with the original jambs and a small E.E. triple-lancet N window. The

C14 W tower has diagonal buttresses; its third stage is C15 as are the S aisle and S porch, completely of granite. The porch has a good wagon roof; the S doorway has a fine C17 studded door with fleur-de-lys strap hinges. Four-centred tower arch with triple shafts. Wide moulded four-centred arch to N transept. The aisle arcade is of five low bays, simple Cornish standard, with four-centred arches, the aisle windows of three lights with standard Cornish tracery, and there is a wagon roof. A careful restoration of 1848 retained some bosses in the new roofs of nave and chancel. – FONT. Norman, a fine example of the Altarnun type, with bearded faces at three corners, a long oak leaf at the SE corner and stylized six-petalled flowers in circles on the four sides. – Two C15 Polyphant PISCINAS. – BENCHES. A remarkable sight, a nearly complete set, though restored. The bench-ends are carved in the usual Cornish way but mostly with interlaced knots, stars, coats of arms and a green man, and a few symbols of the Passion. – ROOD SCREEN across nave and aisle. About 9 ft (2.7 metres) high with unusually wide bays, each of four lights. – Some good remains of C15 STAINED GLASS. Crucifixion, roses, crowns, and an unidentified face, in the chancel E window. St Christopher and St Etheldreda of Ely in the chancel S window. – S aisle E 1902. Painted insets in the plain glass of the S aisle windows, possibly early C19, symbols of the Passion etc. – C18 ALMS BOX at the W end of the S aisle carved with oak leaves. – MONUMENTS. John Squier †1694, slate ledger. – William Edgcumbe †1679, slate with marble surround and Gothic lettering. – Marble memorial to John Couch Adams †1892, the astronomer who discovered Neptune.

In the churchyard opposite the S porch, a four-holed CHURCHYARD CROSS, discovered buried in the churchyard in 1952 and restored in 1954 on a new base and lower section of the shaft by De Lank Quarry.

To the E of the church the OLD VICARAGE, a classic 1840–50 parsonage with Gothic details.

HOLY WELL. In the middle of a field ¼ m. S. C16 with vaulted stone roof and three-centred arched doorway. The basin takes up the whole of the floor area with niche at the rear.

BRIDGE over the River Inny at Gimblett's Mill, 1 m ESE. 1847, odd with six square openings.

LANHYDROCK

The first prospect of Lanhydrock is enchanting: the C17 gatehouse crowned by a profusion of stumpy obelisks stands as the most exquisite of garden follies in front of the great house of the Robartes family, set below a heavily wooded skyline and looking out over the Fowey valley. It is among the grandest houses in Cornwall, third after Godolphin and Port Eliot (*see*

St Germans) in the Hearth Tax assessment, and certainly the
grandest of its century, largely the creation of John Robartes
(1606–85), later 1st Earl of Radnor, who between 1634 and
1644 built an impressive mansion round a central courtyard,
with an outer court and gatehouse. Its N range incorporated
the house of his father, Richard Robartes, which may in turn
have reworked the buildings of a grange of Bodmin Priory on
this site (cf. the church). Richard (c. 1580–1634), a man celebrated as 'the wealthiest in the west', had been created a peer
by Buckingham in 1624 in return for a payment of £10,000.
It is a house in scale with the family's prodigious wealth yet
sufficiently restrained in style to reflect John's convinced Pres-
byterianism; its nearest Cornish equivalents are Penheale and
Trewan, St Columb Major (qq.v.).

The E range was demolished in c. 1784 creating a fashionable
U-plan house with a central porch. There were some mid-C19
improvements first by *Joseph Pascoe* and then by *George Gilbert
Scott* but the greatest change came after much of the house
was extensively damaged by fire in 1881. The N range survived
virtually intact, but the rest of the house required major reconstruction between 1882 and 1885, during which Thomas
Charles Agar-Robartes★ took the opportunity to remodel the
S and W ranges and construct two new service courtyards
behind them to create some of the most impressive service
accommodation of its date anywhere in England. The architect
was *Richard Coad* and his chief assistant *James M. MacLaren*.
Coad, Liskeard-born, had worked with Scott, while MacLaren
was Coad's protégé: the former worked on the exterior and
engineering work, the latter on some of the more chic interiors.[†] The eventual cost was £73,000, an astonishing sum for
its time. Yet the result was never simply opulent: MacLaren's
interiors are of interest in their own right, introducing
Aesthetic Movement motifs among more eclectic contributions within the overall Jacobean style required by the up-and-
coming Agar-Robartes.

76   The GATEHOUSE is a symmetrically composed rectangular block
flanked by octagonal towers and was originally crowned by a
cupola. It was completed in 1651 as a lodge to survey hunting
in the largest C17 deer park in Cornwall. Its obelisks with ball
finials and its delightful fusion of Gothic substance with
Renaissance motifs give it an almost fanciful air, especially on
the outward elevation with its columns and niches and large
semicircular doorway; the detail of the inner doorway might,
however, come straight from a Perp Cornish church, perhaps
reflecting that the family were inwardly looking back towards
ancestry while outwardly open to modernity. Forecourt walls
would have originally attached it to the former E range: the

★The family affixed the name Agar to Robartes in 1822.
†This account owes much to Paul Holden's research: see especially his *Of Things
Old and New: The work of Richard Coad and James M. MacLaren* in J. Edwards and
I. Hart (eds), *Rethinking The Interior, c 1867–1896* (2010).

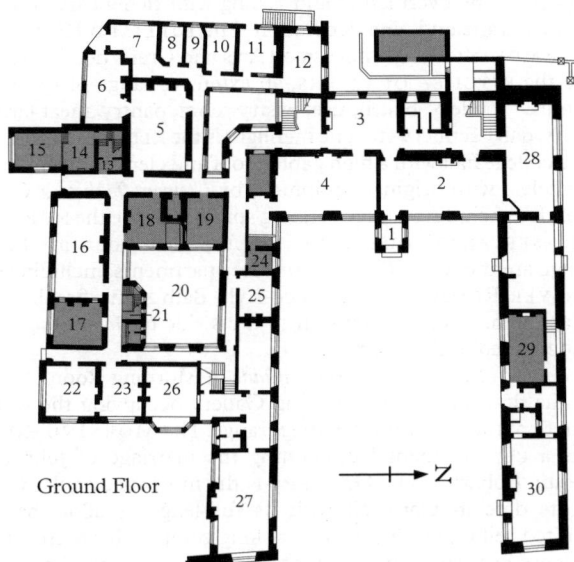

Ground Floor

Lanhydrock House. Ground-floor plan

1. Porch	11. Dairy Scullery	21. Women's Staircase
2. Outer Hall	12. Dairy	22. Housekeeper's Room
3. Inner Hall	13. Men's Staircase	23. Housemaids' Room
4. Dining Room	14. Lamp Room	24. Wine Cellar
5. Kitchen	15. Gun Room	25. Lady Robartes's Room
6. Scullery	16. Servants' Hall	26. Smoking Room
7. Bakehouse	17. Still Room	27. Billiard Room
8. Dry Larder	18. Butler's Parlour	28. Music Room (formerly Library)
9. Fish Larder	19. Butler's Pantry	29. Schoolroom
10. Meat Larder	20. Pantry Court	30. Lord Robartes's Room

Shaded area shows rooms not open to the public

present low crenellated garden walls punctuated by more obelisks are dated 1857.

The composition of the C17 HOUSE is completely symmetrical.
The windows are mullioned on the upper floor, all of six lights,
but all without transoms. The roof disappears partly behind
battlements. All this is still entirely pre-classical. The N range
may contain earlier or even medieval fabric but its evolution
is not fully understood. The W range was completed between
1636 and 1640 with the Robartes arms over the door. The S
range was completed in 1642 but entirely rebuilt by Coad both
to reorder the living space and create the double courtyard
service accommodation. The PORCH has a C17 panelled door
carved with the Robartes arms, the inner door displaying one
of the many Arts and Crafts touches introduced after the fire.
The OUTER HALL retains the original fireplace, some of the
plasterwork frieze and much oak panelling, while the DINING
ROOM has excellent features of the Aesthetic Movement,

especially the overmantel and ceiling with richly carved intertwined grape and vine decoration. The BILLIARD ROOM and
the SMOKING ROOM have good Arts and Crafts detail. Behind
are the KITCHEN QUARTERS, an extensive range of specialist
rooms – scullery, bakehouse, pastry room, pantry, meat larder,
dairy, dairy scullery etc. The highlight is the KITCHEN, designed
as a college hall with a high gabled roof and clerestory windows,
complete with original equipment by *Clement Jeakes & Co.* of
London including a huge rotating spit. Above are the NURSERY
and SERVANTS' QUARTERS. On the first floor in the W
range are the Agar-Robartes' private apartments, including the
PRAYER ROOM with a Rococo-style Bath stone fireplace by
MacLaren. A small extension to the S side by *John Sansom* in
1902 added a gun room.

The climax of the house is the *enfilade* of Morning Room, N half
of the drawing room and Long Gallery occupying the whole
length of the upper floor of the N range. The MORNING ROOM
has a C17 overmantel celebrating the marriage of John and
Letitia Robartes. The GALLERY is the most spectacular room
of its date in Cornwall with its full-length shallow barrel-
vaulted ceiling 116 ft (35 metres) long completely covered with
a dense pattern of moulded, cast and modelled plasterwork, a
hugely ambitious design (cf. its closest Cornish parallel at
Prideaux Place, Padstow, and the now demolished gallery at
Trewan). It is divided into twelve bays with an overall repeating
pattern of intersecting ribs enriched with running vines and
pomegranates. The pattern, in deep relief, springs from the
twelve pendants into panels on each side filled with Old Testament scenes, surrounded by lesser panels containing flowers,
birds and beasts. The biblical imagery is meant to be read in
sequence from the E end, the original access from the demolished E wing (where there was another gallery). On the S side
Adam and Eve fill the first five panels, Cain and Abel the next
two, Noah and the Flood the next four, finishing with Abraham
and Isaac. On the N side, there are twelve panels of the life of
Jacob running W to E, all of two scenes usually divided by a
tree. Three scenes from the life of David decorate the E end
tympanum and the two fireplace overmantels, while the W end
tympanum is filled by the Robartes arms set in an elaborate
strapwork cartouche. As an entity the decoration of this room
is a masterpiece, one of the finest examples of Jacobean plasterwork in England and powerfully expressive of the Presbyter-
ian culture of the period.*

The small parish church of ST HYDROC is raised immediately
behind the house, very similar to the close arrangement of
church and house at Boconnoc and Lanherne, Mawgan-in-
Pydar. Its main charm is its position in the great house's
shadow as a quiet benediction on the whole grey granite
ensemble. A chapel of Bodmin Priory by 1299, the present

77

---

*I am indebted to John Thorp's perceptive account of the Lanhydrock plasterwork
in *Apollo* (April 1998).

church dates from the mid C15 but was much restored for the Agar-Robartes in 1886–8 by *George Vialls* of London. The restoration was probably very radical: it was one of the most, if not the most, expensive of this period in Cornwall. It included extending the chancel to allow the insertion of a new E window, clearly designed to read with the main house though it oversails the family door in the process. Nave and aisles, the unbuttressed W tower of three stages noticeably offset from the nave. N and S aisle arcades of four bays with standard Cornish piers and four-centred arches, the capitals of the S aisle of lighter coloured granite.* The tracery of the S aisle windows looks like a C17 interpretation of Perp, but could even be later (indistinct datestone of WS:CWD 1756(?) on S aisle W wall); the windows have moulded architraves running down to floor level, the W window to a seat. Aside from a surviving thick E wall to the S aisle, the very regular granite ashlar of the arcades and new roofs (except for the S porch) suggests that much of the church may have been reconstructed. Of the 1880s are the MOSAIC FLOOR by *Burke & Co.* of London and Paris, FONT, PULPIT and an alabaster and serpentine REREDOS of the Last Supper by *Earp & Hobbs* of Kensington. – STAINED GLASS. E window, 1886 by *Clayton & Bell*. – ROYAL ARMS, N aisle, of 1621, a rare example of James I, elegant and unpainted with strapwork similar to that in the gallery of the house. – MEMORIALS. S aisle: George (†1599) and Jane (†1609) Carminow below the Carminow arms. Slate. N aisle: Lady Essex Speccot (†1689). Marble with Corinthian columns, arms, shields and lion masks. Not of specially remarkable design but of fine, certainly not local, workmanship.

CHURCHYARD CROSS restored and re-erected here in the early C19, a former wheel-head Latin cross re-set on a rectangular shaft with plaitwork to the front and scrolls to the rear.

To the S of the house is the service courtyard with the COACH-HOUSE of 1857 by *Scott* in the modern Gothic style and the STABLE and HARNESS HOUSE by *Coad* in a style similar to the service accommodation. The former KENNELS by *John Sansom*, 1905, are ½ m. NE.

The GARDENS are first depicted in the *Lanhydrock Atlas* of 1694–7, a remarkable survey of the 50,000 acres of the Robartes estate, as a typical C17 layout including a flower garden, pheasantry, kitchen garden, bowling green and wilderness. By the early C19 the formality has been replaced by a Reptonian landscape of parkland flowing up to the house in which the gatehouse had become a true folly. In 1824 *George Truefitt* prepared a geometric layout with water features, terracing, gravelled walkways and a promenade walk, which Coad adapted in his formal garden layouts executed between 1857 and 1864, adding features of his own like the flight of steps to the church. The Front Court is a terraced parterre at the E front, with lawns and a further parterre to the N. To the W are

---

*The mouldings are contemporary with the rebuilt St Petroc Bodmin (q.v.).

the higher gardens, originally laid out in the 1860s and altered and enhanced in the C20.

The precision of the formal gardens contrasts strongly with the informality of the PARKLAND, of which the outstanding feature is the double AVENUE stretching nearly a mile to the E and aligned with the axis of the gatehouse and the porch of the W wing. It was originally a single avenue of sycamores planted by John Robartes *c.* 1648, but in the early C19 an outer row of beeches was added, along with plantations, drives and an arboretum elsewhere in the park. This later planting overlays and extends the C17 landscape and was designed to enhance views towards the Fowey valley. Two estate lodges are of interest: DOUBLE LODGES at the head of the N drive, which dates to *c.* 1760, and the curious castellated NEWTON LODGE which dates to the mid C19 and is most likely by Richard Coad.

RESPRYN BRIDGE, 1 m. E over the River Fowey. One of the most beautiful medieval bridges in Cornwall. There was a bridge here by 1300; this long structure is C15 with later adaptations. The small central four-centred arch is the oldest. The two W are modern.

LANIVET

CHURCH. Surprisingly ambitious with a tall ashlar granite W tower of three stages, very sheer, with buttresses set back from the angles, and without pinnacles, and with N as well as S aisles of six bays. There was a church here by 1268, the High Altar and four other altars were dedicated in 1318, and the church re-dedicated in 1338; the present church is, however, largely early C15 to early C16. Tall tower arch into nave. The piers of the arcades are circular with four attached shafts, the S arches late C15 and simply double-chamfered, the N arches with the earlier concave rather than straight chamfers. The E ends of the chancel and aisle were rebuilt in the late C15. Large Perp windows of varying design. A severe restoration of 1864 by *J. P. St Aubyn* defines the character of the interior: it included new arch- and wind-braced roofs (the chancel roof with stencilled decoration), E window, re-flooring and re-furnishing. – FONT. Octagonal, with elaborate C14 tracery panels. – ROOD SCREEN. In N aisle, two sections with cusped panels and quatrefoil frieze. – REREDOS, late C19 by *Harry Hems* of Exeter. – WALL PAINTINGS. Destroyed during the restoration: one of them was the familiar Warning to Sabbath Breakers (*cf.* Breage, Poundstock, St Just-in-Penwith). – PISCINA. A hollowed-out large late C12 capital, about 31 in by 29 in. (78 cm. by 74 cm.), probably from Bodmin Priory: cf. the similar fragments in Priory Park, Bodmin. In 1539 the parishioners bought four bells from the dissolved priory. – PILLAR STONE. In S aisle, inscribed in Roman capitals: ANNICU FIL (ANNICUS, son of . . .), C5 or C6. – STAINED GLASS. Good set of six by *Fouracre & Watson*, 1890–3. Fragments of medieval glass in the tracery of two N aisle windows. – MONUMENTS. Slate plate to John and Richard Courtenay, with life-size bearded figure; 1632. – Marble monument to Roger Henwood, 1815, by *Kitt* of St Austell. – Marble monument to Mary Magor, by *Edgcombe* of Truro.

The church sits in a raised CHURCHYARD and is one of the most rewarding places to see monuments of pre-Conquest Cornwall. – CROSS-SLAB, adjacent to the S side of the tower. A cross partly in relief, partly incised. A rare type; cf. Temple, Towednack, Wendron. – COPED STONE. Outside S aisle. A hogback-shaped tombstone. Top and sides with key patterns; at head and foot of the top, four dog-like or bear-like beasts; knots at the ends. C10? cf. St Tudy, Phillack, St Buryan. – CROSS, on the N side of the churchyard. 10 ft (3 metres) high and the most elaborately decorated wheel-head cross in Cornwall, almost entirely incised on all four sides. The decoration is divided into panels, several with punch-dot ornamentation (cf. the Market Cross at Penzance). The most extraordinary panel, about 3 ft (0.9 metres) high, shows a man with a tail (cf. Penzance). The iconography is not sufficiently understood and although connections to pagan fertility rites have been suggested there are also six panels with incised crosses of varying forms: two diagonal, one equal-limbed, two Latin, and a small wheel-head. – CROSS, W of the tower. Similarly tall at 10½ ft (3.2 metres) high, but completely different in style. Knot decoration on all four limbs enclosed in a narrow bead with a central boss, the E face of the shaft with foliated scrollwork, the W face with an interlaced figure of eight knots, the S face more foliated scrollwork, the N face poorly executed plaitwork. Ten other medieval CROSSES are known in the parish.

ST BENET'S. *See* p. 504.

LANLIVERY

0050

The modest churchtown is the perfect foil to the church. At the church gate the BOARD SCHOOL of 1877, a fine Victorian flourish, with the Gothic tympani infilled with red encaustic tiles. Opposite, the CROWN INN, substantial multi-phase vernacular from the C17 with very wide gable-end fireplace and unusually deep oven. At the E end of the churchyard former early C19 school, converted to VILLAGE HALL in 1982–4, and to the S CHURCHTOWN HOUSE, the former vicarage, a handsome mid-C18 house with C19 additions, now subdivided.

ST BRYVYTA (St Brivet). An exceptionally proud church, its noble tower, 97 ft (29.5 metres) tall, a landmark for miles over the far-stretching valley of the Fowey. Almost entirely C15 on

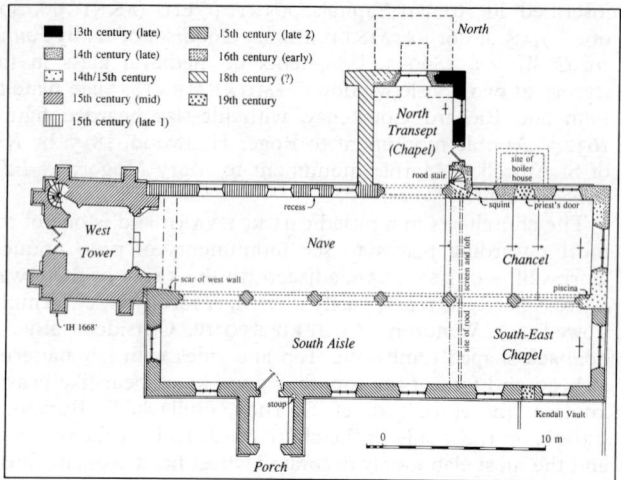

Lanlivery, St Bryvyta. Plan showing C13–C19 phasing

the standard plan of nave and chancel, S aisle and porch, N transept and W tower. But its evolution, instructive for understanding the development of the medieval Cornish church, can be demonstrated because of a detailed investigation facilitated by major repairs and excavation, including re-roofing and the removal of plaster from the interior walls, in 1992–3.* Tower of the mid C15 in three stages with Perp windows and buttresses set back from the angles, including the E elevation indicating construction structurally independent of an earlier W nave wall. As at St Austell the buttresses cease at the top of the second stage and the polygonal corner turrets/pinnacles, on corbels finely carved with lions, angels and crowned human faces, start as low down as that and accompany the whole third stage, the pinnacles finishing as castellated and crocketed spirelets. The W door and window are architecturally ambitious and finely sculpted but the door is curiously squat and poorly related to both window sill and tower plinth, probably evidence of manufacture at the quarry and the rectifying omission of one course from the door jamb mouldings (in different stone) on site; further evidence of such 'kit assembly' is offered by the uncarved label stops of the window. Next the body of the church and differences in external walling: tower, nave, S aisle and porch in large ashlar blocks, N transept and part of the chancel of rubble construction. Similarly the windows: large late Perp, the four-light E window of the aisle the most complex with the reticulation interrupted by a form of Y-tracery, the E window of the chancel early C16. But the transept is different,

---

*The analysis of results of the investigation is published by Warwick Rodwell, 'Lanlivery church: its archaeology and architectural history', *Cornish Archaeology* 32 (1993). Joanna Mattingley thinks work may have continued into the C16.

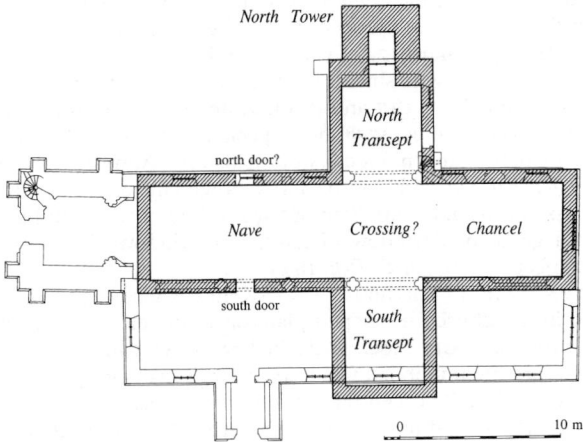

Lanlivery, St Bryvyta.
Reconstruction of late C13/early C14 plan

the E wall with a small C13 triple lancet window, the N wall
with a C14 Dec window identical to the W window of the aisle.
The lancet window is *in situ* in C13 walling incorporating the
slightly later rood-loft stair projection, confirming the transept
as the earliest part of the church, but the Dec window is prob-
lematic because excavation revealed the foundations of a small
C14 transeptal tower in this position which was demolished by
the mid C15 and replaced by the present window. It is likely
that this window and the aisle W window were reused during
the general C15 reconstruction of the church.

Now for the INTERIOR, entered through the S porch with a
heavily moulded outer opening, roof renewed 1879, and four-
centred inner arch with C15 door. Nave and chancel undivided,
aisle of similar length of six bays with wide arches on slim
Cornish standard granite piers and four petal low-relief motifs
on the abaci; a slightly curved stub of walling at the W end
resolved the misalignment of aisle arcade and tower when the
former W wall of the nave was removed. Although the masonry
of arcade and aisle is one late C15 build, the wagon roof is three
separate structures. The latest is the elaborately decorated E
end with running leaf scrolls to the wall-plates and purlins
framing square ceiling panels, which have carved bosses in leaf
and rosette decoration and grotesques; there were once also
shield-bearing angels to the wall-plates (cf. Blisland). Then
the plainer middle section with wall-plates and purlins with
running scrolls, moulded ribs and low relief bosses: this could
be a replacement of an earlier transept roof. Finally, the earliest
and plainest W section. The arch to the transept belongs to the
general later C15 rebuilding, superseding an earlier opening: it
only differs from the arcade in having rope-moulded decoration on the imposts. In the E wall of the transept the rood-loft

stair and, alongside, the loft entrance a small squint. – FONTS. In the vestry three pieces of hemispherical bowl of the ornate Fowey type, mid-C12. – In the church an uncommonly large octagonal font with shields in quatrefoils. C15. – MONUMENTS. Several good late C17 and C18 monuments to the Kendalls of Pelyn. Mary Cotes, 1758, not especially interesting design but of good, probably not local, workmanship. – Anne Wynter, 1839 by *J. Theakston*. – STAINED GLASS. Fragments of blue medieval glass in central tracery light of E window in chancel, and medieval glass in N window of nave. Two windows in N wall of chancel by *Clayton & Bell*, 1879.

PELYN, ¾ m. E. The house of the Kendalls whose monuments lie in the church. E-shaped plan, on a fine elevated site. The central early C18 block is flanked by lower wings of *c.* 1600 with granite mullioned windows, a very satisfying symmetrical composition. The central section was originally three-storey but was reduced to two after a fire in 1860 when it seems as if the front was brought forward by 6 ft (1.8 metres), the sash windows were heightened on the first floor and deepened on the ground floor, and the level of the ground floor also dropped to leave a very shallow cellar. A ballroom was created in 1836 (attributed to *Harrison*) between the centre and the E wing, of excellent proportions with a shallow barrel vault and lit by long wooden mullioned-and-transomed windows. The E wing was converted into stables about this time. After a long period of neglect, the house was thoughtfully restored for John Kendall 2006–8 by the *Bazeley Partnership*, work that included an imperial stair in a new rear staircase wing on the (smaller) footprint of the destroyed C18 stair, reconverting the stables back into domestic use, reinstating the C18 glazing to the sash windows of the central range, and re-fitting much period detail that had been stripped out.

TRETHEW, ½ m. SW. Of medieval origins with reused Tudor doorways, by tradition thought to be from the priory at Tywardreath, and a fireplace boldly dated 1676 between the initials W and K for Walter Kendall of Pelyn. Remodelled in the C18 and sympathetically adapted and extended 1976 by *Gordon Collins*.

HELMAN TOR, 2 m. NW. Early Neolithic TOR ENCLOSURE. A tumbled stony bank, including slabs on edge, links granite outcrops to isolate and enclose the summit of the tor-topped hill. Within the irregular enclosure are several roughly level platforms. Excavation of one found numerous post- and stake-holes and much early Neolithic material. A broadly contemporary Early Neolithic CHAMBERED TOMB, now ruinous, lies 1 m. NE at Lesquite.

LANNER

A large mining village with many terraces of C19 two-storey cottages and several former chapels along the main road. In

CHURCH ROAD a large sombre Methodist chapel 1905 and hall 1904, and further up CHRIST CHURCH, 1838–40 by *George Wightwick*. A delightful surprise, a plain Italianate building, dignified and well proportioned without and within, with shallow chancel and three-bay s aisle added 1883; of that date also the E window of the chancel by *A. Gibbs*. – FONT. Octagonal, with winged figure on each face, from the church of St Dunstan, Fleet Street: it must be C19.

LANREATH

1050

ST MARNARCK (St Manac). A church whose present appearance is wholly Perp and specially complete and satisfying. It was tactfully restored by *G. F. Bodley* in 1887. W tower of three stages with thin buttresses set back from the angles and battlements with crocketed finials on octagonal pinnacles. Nave and chancel in one, N transept, S aisle and S porch. The nave N wall and the transept walls are Norman with traces of Norman masonry but later windows; of the time of the re-dedication of 1321 nothing survives. Aisle arcade of five bays, piers of standard Cornish section, capitals with elementary ornamental carving, arches low and four-centred. Good wagon roofs, with large unusual star-shaped bosses in the nave. – FONT. Norman, of the Fowey cup-shaped type. Uncommonly rich, with elaborate zigzag decoration to the base, a plait around the waist, and palmettes on the bowl. – COVER. Jacobean. Handsome octagonal shape decorated with Renaissance stylized foliage. – ALTAR STONE. Norman. On the sill of the E window of the S aisle, the front and one end carved with a geometric pattern similar to the font. – ROOD SCREEN. The outstanding feature of the church. Ten four-light traceried bays right across nave and aisle of a more Devonian than Cornish type (cf. in Cornwall Budock, St Buryan, St Ewe, St Winnow). Richly carved, with painted saints on the bottom panels *c.* 1520 (cf. St Winnow). Cornice of three carved strips. Sensitively restored by *T. R. Kitsell* of Plymouth in 1905 with new coving. – CHANCEL STALLS. With excellent crowning figure sculpture, much of it Jacobean, the rest *c.* 1500. – PULPIT, good Elizabethan. – BENCH-ENDS. Two at the E end of the nave with heraldic shields of the Grylls and Bere families and carved bearded heads, C16, incorporated into later stalls. Early C17 bench-ends in s aisle chapel. – Painted ROYAL ARMS, 1660, CR. – STAINED GLASS – Chancel E window, 1886, *Clayton & Bell*. S aisle w, the Ascension by *W. D. Snell*, †1927. – Elaborate MONUMENT to Charles Grylls and wife, 1623. Husband and wife kneel frontally on a tall chest with a relief of eight children. Four Corinthian columns support a canopy with arms, cherubs and cartouches. It is all carved in wood (a great rarity), in imitation of current stonework. – John Grylls †1649 and his wife Grace †1653, erected 1666 and repaired in 1794.

Inscription in frame and in roundels with heraldic arms surmounted by a hedgehog.

COURT BARTON FARMHOUSE, S of the church. A small manor
house, formerly of the Grylls family. Early C17 with two later
C17 wings forming a U-shaped plan and projecting two-storey
gabled porch, much restored in 1899. The scattered fenestration of the front includes low six-light windows l. and r., four-
light windows above them and a two-light window over the
entrance arch which is four-centred with hoodmould and
carved trefoils in the spandrels. An elaborately carved panelled
chamber on the first floor has a fireplace with carved overmantel supported by herms.

RABBIT WARREN WALLS, S of Court Barton Farmhouse. C18 or
earlier. Roughly coursed slatestone with original capping of
a slate course corbelled out to prevent the rabbits from
escaping.

BURY DOWN HILLFORT, 2 m. N. Small hillfort on NW crest of
locally dominant hill, the site of an early modern fire beacon.
The fort's two circuits may not be contemporary: the outer
one, lower and more irregular, may be either unfinished or
considerably earlier than the Iron Age inner line.

LANSALLOS

ST ILDIERNA. The three-stage W tower is of slatestone with
granite dressings and unusually its angle buttresses have flamboyant tracery decoration at their feet. An image niche above
the W window incorporates a Norman head at its base. Battlemented parapet with turrets and crocketed pinnacles. The
tower is also earlier than most: the lower two stages may be
C14, reworked in the C15 when the third stage was added. The
body of the church – nave and chancel in one, six-bay S aisle
and S porch and three-bay N aisle – looks C15, but there was a
church here by 1086 with a dedication recorded in 1331: *E. H.
Sedding*, the early C20 restorer, noted reused Norman stonework in the N and S walls and the W wall of the N aisle, which
survived from the former transept. The piers to both aisles are
of Cornish standard section with coarsely carved capitals and
low four-centred arches. The late C15 to mid-C16 wagon roofs
are of high quality throughout with richly carved ribs, arcade
and wall-plates; some of the bosses were restored in a series of
late C19 and early C20 restorations begun in 1884 by *Richard
Coad* and continued by Sedding and *Wheatly*. There was
another after a major fire in 2005. – FONT. Norman, Bodmin
type; the square bowl on renewed Polyphant columns with tree
of life and odd fleur-de-lys ornament. Remains of an earlier
font nearby. – BENCH-ENDS. Thirty-four of the early to mid
C16, especially finely carved with heraldic arms, figureheads
and Renaissance detailing. – Remains of ROOD SCREEN

incorporated into BENCHES in the chancel and at the W end
of the nave: ogee-headed lights with Renaissance detail, intertwined foliage and moulded rails. – PULPIT mounted on a
pinnacle fallen from the tower in 1923. – MONUMENTS. Large
stone fragments of C14 knight and lady. – Margaret Smith
†1579, slate slab signed by *Peter Crocker* of Looe. Shallow but
finely detailed relief of woman in period costume.

LANTEGLOS-BY-CAMELFORD   *1080*

ST JULITTA. The parish church of Camelford until the town's
own church was consecrated in 1938. It sits comfortably in a
wooded valley and large churchyard, its generous scale and tall
W tower quietly impressive. Of the probably cruciform C12
church the early masonry in the N wall of the nave and chancel
and E and W walls of the N transept. The C14 tower is unbuttressed, embattled with crocketed finials, with a NE stair-turret
and a nice two-centred W doorway with heads as label stops
of the hoodmould, similar to Egloshayle. C15 s aisle and s porch
in granite ashlar, the latter with a large cinquefoil-headed niche
and wagon roof. The S aisle S windows, of three lights, have a
tracery pattern different from the usual, with an E window of
five lights: the E window of the chancel, also of five lights, has
the unusual flamboyant motif in a circle at the centre of the
tracery only to be seen elsewhere in Cornwall at Advent.
Inside, the six-bay aisle arcade is carried on slim piers of
Cornish granite standard, with depressed four-centred arches.
C15 wagon roofs with crenellated wall-plates which have
moulded ribs and carved bosses displaying arms. The original
imposts of the transept arch indicate its C12 origins but it
was at least partly rebuilt, as was the N wall of the transept,
in heavy-handed restorations of 1864 and 1873 that left
the interior with an unexpectedly austere character. – FONT.
C15, octagonal, with traceried panels. – STAINED GLASS.
Some C15 fragments in the tracery of the S aisle and N
chancel windows, for example Christ, St Andrew, St James,
somewhat overwhelmed by especially strident coloured C19
glass borders. – Pretty MONUMENT to W. Inch †1815 by
R. Isbell, with a relief of a woman standing by an urn under a
weeping willow.
   Outside the S wall of the church an assemblage of four
medieval WHEEL-HEAD CROSSES and an INSCRIBED STONE.
The inscription on the latter, probably C10, reads 'Aelselth 7
Genereth wohte thisne sybstel for Aelwines soul 7 for heysel'
(Alseth and Generth wrought this personal memorial for
Aelwine and for themselves): it was first recorded in the 1870s
in a farm building at Castlegoff Farm NW of the churchyard
and resited here in 1900. The small cross close by was once
fixed to the top of the inscribed stone: it has the unusual

decoration of five small bosses. One of the other crosses is remarkable for the large scale of the cross-head.

St Julitta's Holy Well, ¼ m. NE. Rebuilt 1891. Two-centred Catacleuse arch to the well-house built into the bank.

1050

LANTEGLOS-BY-FOWEY

St Wyllow. 'Spacious, solitary, beautiful for situation and full of interesting features', wrote *E. H. Sedding*, who restored the church sensitively in 1904–6 and to whom the furnishings owe much of their character. Built into the hillside, the unbuttressed tower rises through four stages and is finished with battlements and pinnacles: inside it opens in tall arches of simple double-chamfered section into the N and S aisles as well as the nave, very unusual for Cornwall (cf. St Keverne). The nave, of five bays, has octagonal piers of Pentewan stone (cf. Fowey) with very simple capitals and bases and plain round arches: like the tower arches, they look C14. Four-light aisle windows, probably C16. Sedding compared them to Somerset churches, possibly reflecting the appropriation of the church to the Hospital of St John at Bridgewater from 1284. What the pre-C14 church was like we cannot say, but Sedding thought he discerned traces of Norman work in the corners of the tower piers: the jambs of the S doorway are certainly Norman. Built into the doorway is a chi-ro (XP) stone; C8 at the latest. Sedding also suggested that the S porch may have been rebuilt in the C17. The roofs give a rare sense of what the complete medieval ensemble in such a church looked like: starting with the chamfered timbers of the N aisle; then the naves which is moulded; and finally the more elaborately carved S aisle.

FONT. Early C13. Purbeck base with moulded capitals and bases. The Pentewan stone bowl has stiff-leaf foliage and is hollowed out octagonally, a rare feature. Font cover by Sedding. – ALTAR TABLE. A Mohun gift, of 1634. – BENCH-ENDS. A considerable number of *c.* 1500. Much carving of the early 1900s by *Violet Pinwill* and her school of carvers (cf. Crantock, Launceston and St Winnow): CHOIR STALLS, TOWER SCREEN, PULPIT, ALTAR RAILS and LADY CHAPEL ALTAR, to Sedding's designs. – STAINED GLASS. A little of late Perp date in the E window of the S aisle, pretty figures of the Annunciation and Coronation of the Virgin; their style is similar to the figures at St Winnow (q.v.). – E window, Adoration of the Shepherds and Saints, and N and S chancel windows, by *Kempe*, 1905. W – window and S aisle window by *Kempe & Co.*, 1907. – MONUMENTS. Tomb-chest in a canopied recess in the S chancel aisle. On the chest a small brass to Thomas de Mohun, laid down *c.* 1440. Above, traces of contemporary WALL PAINTING depicting the Resurrection with the tomb resembling volumes of books – the gospels? – and vestiges of text on the supporting scrolls. – BRASS. Close by, of *c.* 1525 to John Mohun and his wife, who died 'ex infirmate vocata sudye' (the sweating sickness) in 1508. The chancel aisle was probably a Mohun chapel: Bodinnick and Boconnoc (qq.v.) were both seats of the Mohuns, and Sedding re-erected PANELLING with coats of arms from the former family pews at Boconnoc at the w end of the s aisle. – LANTERN CROSS. Outside the s porch. Gothic, on an octagonal shaft, elaborately carved: N face crowned Christ crucified; s face Virgin and Child; w face St Peter seated and holding his key; E face St Paul standing with sword. The central finial and corner pinnacles are lost. – CROSS. Near SE entrance to the churchyard. Latin cross of Pentewan stone discovered in Pont Pill Creek in the late C19 and reunited with its shaft, found in the churchyard in the early C20.

LAUNCELLS

2000

ST SWITHIN AND ST ANDREW. Delightfully placed in a wooded valley away from all traffic with the HOLY WELL OF ST SWITHIN opposite the s entrance across a little bridge. Typical Cornish Perp exterior with an unbuttressed w tower and four very tall and boldly sculpted corner pinnacles. The interior is serene and light, with clear glass (some of it ancient), white walls and a white-painted wagon roof to the nave and chancel giving something of an early C19 character, and of unusual interest for its furnishings and fittings. Nave of five bays with tall slim shafts of standard Cornish design, with standard capitals that have pretty fleur-de-lys crenellation, and four-centred arches. The s arcade is of Polyphant, the N of granite. The windows have Perp tracery, some of it renewed. Wagon roofs to the aisles with carved wall-plates, purlins and bosses, the N aisle specially good with three examples of the Granville arms. – The pride of Launcells, and especially enjoyable, are the carved BENCH-ENDS AND BENCHES, over sixty of them, with abbreviated representations of the Passion and other New Testament scenes, for example table with flagon and loaves for the Last Supper; flagon, dish and towel for the Washing of the Feet; open coffin and spice boxes for the Resurrection; Easter Day, with a spade representing Christ as the gardener and a spicebox for Mary; footprints and, higher up, cloud with two feet and the end of a robe for the Ascension. Fronted with continuous carving of blind tracery and quatrefoils filled with various symbols. The same workshop supplied bench-ends to Kilkhampton and Poughill. – Specially notable also the extensive array of ENCAUSTIC TILES in the chancel, C17 Barnstaple ware, with conventional designs of fleurs-de-lys, Tudor roses, lions *passant* and *rampant*, pelican, and profile head with foliage. – REREDOS. Of pleasingly simple carpenter's Gothic

39

framing C18 marble commandment and communion tablets given by Sir John Call (*see* Launcells Barton below). – Similar COMMUNION RAILS. – PULPIT. Gothick tracery applied to a drum of C17 style. – Late C18 BOX PEWS in N aisle. – C17 PANELLING of friezes of round-headed arches and vine decoration on the E and part of the S wall of the S aisle. – ROYAL ARMS. Charles I, plaster with strapwork decoration, the same design as at Boconnoc, Kilkhampton, Marhamchurch, Poughill, Poundstock and Stratton. – FONT. Very plain, one of the earliest in Cornwall, early Norman with cable mouldings. – WALL PAINTING of the Sacrifice of Isaac, large but faint on the W wall of the S aisle: 1680–90, a rare example of post-Reformation date. The various components are of extremely variable artistic quality. Some very rustic figures but competent and detailed depictions of Isaac, Abraham and the ass. The whole scene is within a painted surround of classical architecture with the Vault of Heaven at the top. – MONUMENT. Sir John Chamond †1624: standing wall tomb with semi-reclining stiff effigy in armour, and two small kneelers at head and feet. – Many good C17–C18 monuments.

LAUNCELLS BARTON, NE of the church. Once in the possession of Hartland Abbey, purchased by the Chamond family 1553 (see Sir John's monument in the church). Sir John Call (cf. Whiteford Temple, Stoke Climsland) built the main block of the present house 1765–77. It is two-storey over a basement, its three-bay front with a double flight of steps up to front door that retains original balusters and ramped handrail. Basement lit by two oculi, Venetian windows flanking doorways above with small entablature on tall consoles. Central staircase hall with open-well staircase and contemporary landscape painting in fixed frame on W wall, and ground-floor room with *c.* 1720 panelling. Two ranges of the earlier house were retained as service rooms to the W. They have an C18 plaster barrel ceiling over the linking stair with the main house, concealing a *c.* 1600 roof above. Remains of medieval carp ponds below the house.

ANDERTON, 2 m. E. House of C15 origin with C17 remodelling. Four-bay solar to l. of through passage with four arch-braced roof trusses. Two-storey porch, many mullioned windows, and C15–C17 interior details. Anderton is illustrated in the Spoure Book which shows that the barn projecting from the r. end formed part of an enclosed courtyard: the opening in the barn shown on the drawing survives.

Parts of the BUDE CANAL (*see* Bude) run through this parish.

LAUNCESTON

2   Travellers crossing into Cornwall from Devon sense they are in different country when they reach Launceston. High above the little River Kensey, its buildings gathered tightly around the

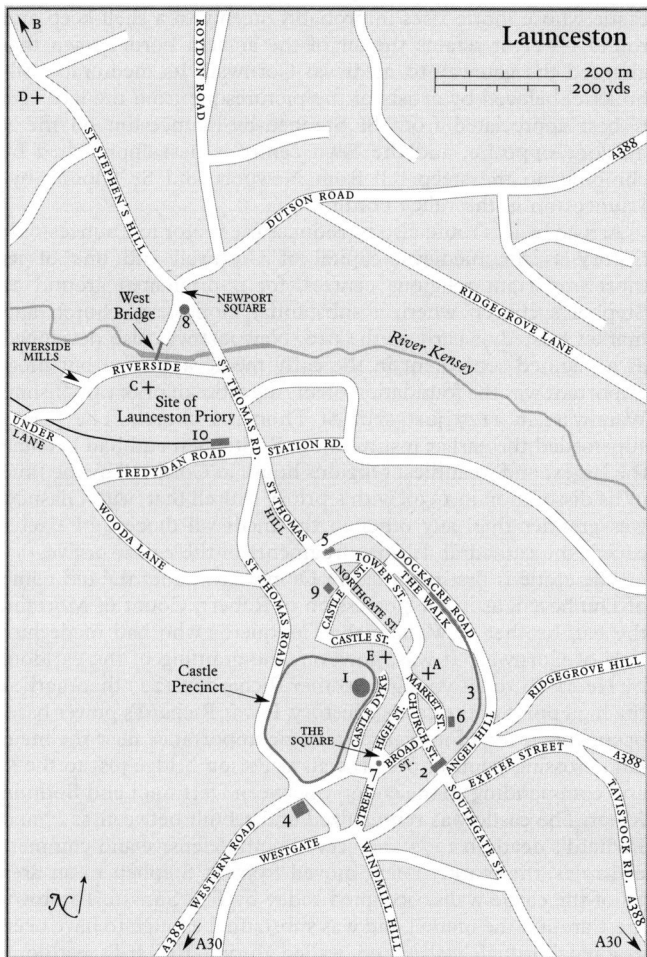

Launceston

200 m
200 yds

A	St Mary Magdalene	I	Launceston Castle
B	St Stephen	2	Southgate
C	St Thomas	3	Town Walls
D	St Cuthbert Mayne (R.C.)	4	Guildhall and Town Hall
E	Methodist church	5	Passmore Edwards Institute (former)
		6	Market House
		7	War memorial
		8	The Roundhouse
		9	Lawrence House Museum
		10	Launceston Steam Railway

castle whose motte rises improbably steeply to a shell-keep and round tower, it retains the air of the ancient border town that guarded the gateway to medieval Cornwall. Its memorable silhouette, beloved by artists of the picturesque from the late C18, is best appreciated from St Stephen-by-Launceston on the N hillslope opposite, and the town centre is best approached by climbing up the steep hill from Newport and St Thomas-by-Launceston in the valley bottom.

Arrival by this route also introduces the visitor to Launceston's history as the medieval capital of Cornwall and one of its most important religious centres, for it originated around St Stephen's church where a substantial monastery, church and market existed as early as the C10. Newport was also developed as a planned settlement in the early medieval period but most important was the foundation of an Augustinian priory by Bishop Warelwast in 1127 just S of St Thomas's church. The priory superseded the earlier institution at St Stephen and had become the largest and wealthiest religious house in Cornwall by the time of its dissolution in 1539, with a priory church that, with Glasney, was grander than any other in the medieval diocese of Exeter except the cathedral. Elegiac fragments of the ruins survive.

The castle is first recorded in Domesday, under the old name of Dunheved, as in the possession of Robert, Count of Mortain, the half-brother of William the Conqueror who had made him Earl of Cornwall. It was, however, the granting of the earldom by Henry III to his younger brother Richard in 1227 that marked the high point of the castle's history. It was Richard's power base, occupying a site of immense strategic importance near the main land crossing point into Cornwall at Polson bridge just to the E, and commanding all the country between Dartmoor and Bodmin Moor. The castle was reorganized and rebuilt between 1227 and Richard's death in 1272 and served both defensive and commercial roles, the market being moved from St Stephen to an area SE of the castle walls, occupied today by The Square. The town grew around the market and was substantial enough to have been granted borough status and walled during Richard's earldom. The Southgate and parts of the walls survive.

Though Richard's son Edmund moved the administrative functions of the castle to Lostwithiel, a rich array of C16–C18 buildings – including the parish church of St Mary Magdalene which has the most spectacular exterior of any late medieval church W of Exeter – reflects Launceston's post-medieval prosperity, its prestige consolidated by its role as the county assize town from 1177. But the steep and difficult access, such an asset in earlier defensive times, proved disadvantageous later. So the C18 saw a new bridge over the Kensey and the early C19 the start of a major road-building programme. The arrival of the Launceston and South Devon Railway in 1865 connecting to Plymouth and onward to London Paddington was followed in 1886 by the North Cornwall Railway from Halwill Junction, giving a direct route to London Waterloo.

Better communications laid the basis for Launceston's later C19 and early C20 renaissance as the commercial, civic and political centre for its large rural hinterland, compensating for the loss of its assize and county town status to Bodmin in 1838. The result was a building boom that enriched the centre and the immediate suburbs with a complete range of C19 buildings that included new market halls, banks, commercial premises, schools, hospital, chapels and villas, the town's self-confidence perfectly demonstrated by the ambitious Town Hall and Guildhall of 1881 and 1887 opposite the s gate of the castle. As in other Cornish towns, the sustained quality of building in this period reflects the work of accomplished local architects, here Otho B. Peter, antiquarian and artist, and James Hine.* And while the later C20 saw the spread of suburbs into the Kensey valley and up the hill towards St Stephen, and some lacklustre development in parts of the centre, Launceston remains essentially intact, visually delightful, and the most fascinating of all Cornwall's inland towns.

CHURCHES

ST MARY MAGDALENE, Church Street. Given the splendour of the church exterior it is tempting to give the SW tower only brief consideration: it is unexpectedly plain and not of spectacular height. Yet it is of great interest as the only survival of the town chapel, the predecessor of the present church. It dates from the late C14 with the standard Cornish buttresses set back from the angles and a SE stair-turret rising above the embattled parapet. The chapel, obviously not a mean building, had a steeper roof pitch than the church of today, as can be seen by the scars of its roof-line on the E face of the tower. Church and tower are connected rather incongruously by a plain room of 1851, the intention to build a tower at the W end of the nave of the rebuilt church never having been fulfilled.

The church as we see it now was built 1511–24, wholly of granite, 103 ft (31.4 metres) long, and externally decorated with barbarous profuseness. It can with certainty be ascribed to the generosity of Henry Trecarrel (*see* Trecarrel), whose arms, quartered with those of his wife, Margaret Kelway, appear on the porch and elsewhere, with their heads as label stops on the first window E of the porch. But its sumptuous appearance is also likely to reflect the prosperity of the C16 town whose corporation seems to have been more than usually involved in the affairs of its church: as early as 1395, when the priory had agreed to maintain the town chapel, the corporation had undertaken the upkeep of the rest of the church. Work began, unusually, at the W end, the roofs were made in 1521–2 and the church consecrated in 1524, though the E window was glazed as late as 1543.

The s porch is particularly thorough in its ornamentation   64
and is the best place to start a detailed study. It is two-storey

*I am indebted to Jim Edwards for much information on Launceston.

with diagonally set buttresses enriched with panelled and foliate-headed engaged shafts at the second stage, large gargoyle beasts, and crocketed pinnacles at the corners of the embattled parapet. Above the door is a foliated canopied niche filled with a terracotta figure of the patron saint of 1911. On the base of the niche is an inscription in a ribbon design supported by two angels, AN.DOM.MCCCCCXI. Flanking the niche are lively reliefs, St George to the l. and St Martin to the r.

The church's outer walls are panelled all the way through without any caesura. Most of the panels are repetition work, impressive as much by their number as by their quality. The motifs are partly familiar from contemporary bench-ends of the special Cornish type but with some curiously Renaissance-looking vase finials. The style and extreme lavishness are not wholly original either. Trecarrel evidently went to masons busy on such elaborately decorated exteriors as St Mary, Truro (begun 1504), and the tower at Probus (where work was under way in the early 1520s), and told them that he wanted his decoration still bigger and better.

The main motifs of the carving are fully detailed by Cox: on the plinths the familiar quatrefoils, with coats of arms and fleurs-de-lys alternately, then above these tracery with letters alternating with coats of arms. The letters, from the chancel door eastwards, read: AVE MARIA GRACIA DOMINUS TECUM. SPONSUS AMAT SPONSUM. MARIA OPTIMAM PARTEM ELIGIT. O QUAM TERRIBILIS ET METUENDUS EST LOCUS ISTE. VERE ALIUD NON EST HIC NISI DOMUS DEI ET PORTA CELI (Hail Mary full of grace. The Lord is with thee. The bridegroom loves the bride. Mary chose the best part. O how terrible and fearful is this place. Truly this is no other than the house of God and the gate of heaven). Above the legends a course of rose and thistle ornament. Then come the large three- and four-light windows, flanked by ornamental buttresses. By the sides of the windows are unfurling fern leaves, and there are roses in the spandrels. Above the windows is some scroll ornament. The battlemented parapet has rose, thistle and pomegranate. At the E end in a niche below the chancel window is a recumbent figure of the Magdalene with a vase of ointment beside her and, though eroded, she is movingly graceful. She is flanked by four kneeling figures, choristers and minstrels with their instruments including clarion, lute, harp and a kind of hand organ, the conductors with chains of office. At the top of the gable are the royal arms.

After such sustained exuberance, the interior is altogether more sober. The eight-bay N and S arcades are carried on slender circular piers with four groups of three attached shafts, a unique pattern in Cornwall, with capitals of the usual Cornish Perp type. The arches are pointed, with the exception of the fifth bay which is wider than the others and has a depressed four-centred arch (a hint at a transeptal centre). As the piers are slim and the windows large, the church has an even light and a feeling of comfortable width. Wagon roofs with shield-holding angels on the wall-plates. Its character owes much to mid-C19 to early C20 restorations and embellishments: of 1850–3 by *Decimus Burton* of uncertain extent; and of 1892–4 by *J. D. Sedding*, implemented after Sedding's death by *H. Wilson* and supplemented by *E. H. Sedding c.* 1911, who was chiefly responsible for the excellent woodwork of the period. This is entirely fitting because the outstanding feature of the interior is the PULPIT, probably pre-Reformation at least in its 67 panels, of splendidly and delicately carved woodwork, with original colouring revealed after cleaning of its black coating in 1970. It is easily the best in the county. Of the later C19 and early C20 furnishings, the BENCH-ENDS in the nave, 1892–4 by *Arnold Fellows* on the theme of the Benedicite, and the N and S PARCLOSE SCREENS of 1904 and 1913 respectively, with delicate flowers, fishes and animals, all in an accomplished Art Nouveau style and of exceptional quality; the CHANCEL SCREEN, 1911, designed by *E. H. Sedding* and executed by *Violet Pinwill* of *Rashleigh Pinwill & Co.*, who also carved the canopied frame of the REREDOS of 1911 – the large alabaster figure of the Transfiguration of Christ after Fra Angelico is by *Harry Hems* of Exeter; and CHOIR STALLS by *John Northcott* of Ashwater. – FONT. 1914, with an upturned Norman font bowl used as the base. – ORGAN FRONT. Fielded panels, 1723, possibly by *Thomas Schwarbrick*, rebuilt and enlarged 1904 by *John Northcott*. – LECTERN, 1895 by *Rattee & Kett* of Cambridge. – STAINED GLASS. All of the mid C19 to early C20: the best the pair of windows by *William Wailes* in the S chapel E and N chapel E, both of 1853. – Chancel E, 1894 by *Hardman*. – S chapel S, 1910 by *Percy Bacon Bros*, and another of 1863 by *Gibbs*. – S aisle, 1880 by *Lavers, Barraud & Westlake*. – MONUMENTS. Fragments of a monument to Sir Hugh Piper †1687 with Sir Hugh and his wife facing each other with praying-desk between. – Captain Philip Piper †1677. Not up to much: the same pattern with columns, swags and a broken curved pediment. – Granville Pyper and Richard Wise (ceno-   84 taph; they are buried in Bath), †1731. Sumptuous, uncommonly classical, and uncommonly good. Tall plinth and two storeys, white and a little dark marble. Busts of Wise on the l., Pyper on the r., and two tiers of standing allegorical figures above: Faith and Charity with three little children, and Hope on the upper tier; Justice and Fortitude on the lower. – Carved ROYAL ARMS. – In the churchyard E of the S aisle a Catacleuse LANTERN CROSS-HEAD.

St STEPHEN, St Stephen's Hill. The mother church of Launceston, with its noble W tower, stands serene high on the N side of the Kensey valley looking over towards castle and town. It has the appearance of a typical late C15 to early C16 Cornish church but at its core is essentially the substantial cruciform church of the Norman priory, with N and S transepts and N

and S chancel chapels.* There is little visible evidence of this
period except fragmentary Norman SCULPTURE outside on
the E wall of the chancel: a seated Saviour, and Virgin and
Child (probably from an Adoration of the Magi), 2 ft 3 in.
(69 cm.) and 2 ft 9 in. (84 cm.) high; and inside, traces of
round-headed arches in N and S walls of chancel. A S aisle was
added in 1419 and the tower and solid two-storey buttressed
S porch in granite ashlar in the early C16. Probably at the same
time some of the walls were rebuilt, at least all their upper
levels, to enable embattled parapets to be introduced. The
windows are mostly Perp, the tracery renewed. The three-stage
tower has buttresses set back from the angles with pinnacles
in relief, and an embattled parapet with panelled octagonal
turrets surmounted by tall crocketed corner pinnacles. Inside,
the four-bay nave arcade has Polyphant piers of the earlier
Cornish type, square with attached demi-shafts, and plain,
double-chamfered arches. Similar single bay to N chancel
chapel with fleurons to capitals. An extensive restoration of
1883 by *Hine & Odgers* re-roofed and re-furnished the church.
Three C16 BENCH-ENDS with the usual quatrefoils were incorporated in the new pews, and part of the medieval screen in
the ROOD SCREEN, sufficient to show that the original was of
the type still extant at Mawgan-in-Pydar and of which there
are remains at Crantock. – FONT. Large, Norman, ornamented
with three cable mouldings at the top, the lower part with a
band of running ornament in bold relief, and another cable
moulding at the top of the circular stem. – Small stone COFFIN,
C12. – S DOOR, C15 or early C16, studded. – STAINED GLASS.
Chancel E, 1920 by *Percy Bacon Bros*, a First World War
memorial. – MONUMENTS. Incised slab with cross, †1528. –
Two slate slabs, well carved, †1631 and †1675.

ST THOMAS, Riverside. Originally a chapel to St Stephen, and
adjacent to the great Augustinian priory, to the ruins of which
the churchyard is joined (*see* below). Slender, plain two-stage
unbuttressed W tower, probably C14 in its lower stages. The
rest is standard Cornish Perp, though a cut-down Norman
tympanum and a much eroded figure, presumably from the
priory, are incorporated in the S wall of the S porch. Five-bay
S aisle with piers of the usual profile. Heavily restored by *J. P.
St Aubyn* with new roofs and mostly new windows. – FONT.
The outstanding feature of the church, Norman, the largest in
Cornwall. It is of the Altarnun type with superbly carved
corner faces and very large rosettes in circles. – TOWER
SCREEN, incorporating C16 linenfold panels, of which there are
others inside S door. – WALL PAINTINGS. Two fragments at
the E end of the S aisle. – S DOOR with C14 ironwork. – STAINED
GLASS. Some C15 fragments used as marginal glazing in the
late C19 scheme.

*I am indebted to Eric Berry's account in the *VCH History of Cornwall*, vol. II
(2010).

LAUNCESTON PRIORY. The path s of St Thomas' church to the
priory ruins passes the base of a CI3 MOULDED PIER, with
three engaged shafts, from the priory church. The priory was
ruinous by the end of the C16, extensively robbed, and subsequently levelled. It was rediscovered by *Otho B. Peter* in excavations 1886–92, during construction of the railway to the s and
gasholders to the E. Peter's plan of 1893 shows the impressive
scale of the Augustinian foundation and is by far the fullest
record of any monastic house in Cornwall. The remains visible
today – choir, altar steps, High Altar, N and S choir aisles, and
a room to the N of the N aisle – represent only a small part of
the excavated site but are sufficient, when augmented by the
large collections of architectural fragments, floor tiles and

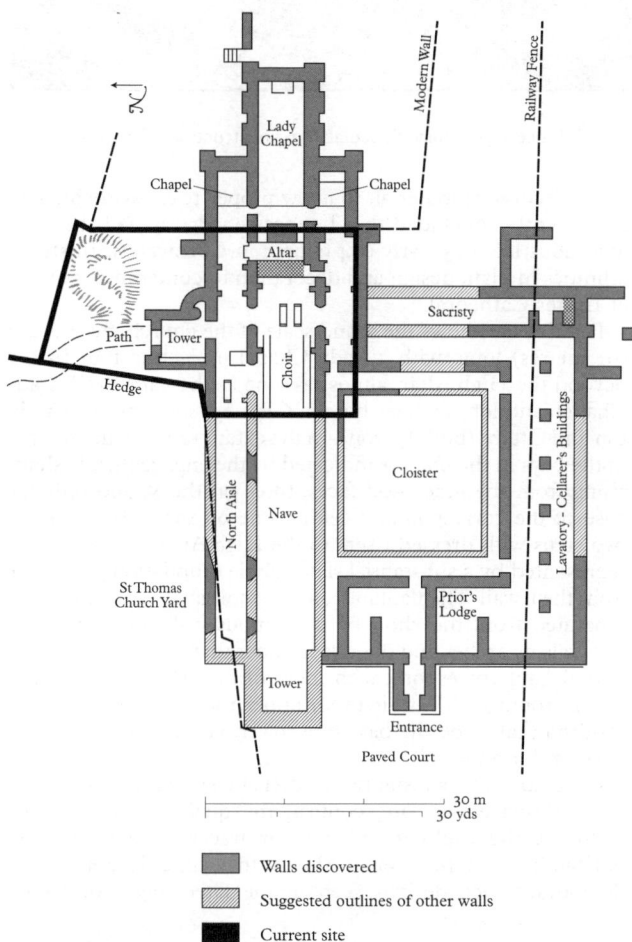

Launceston Priory, plan of excavated site, 1893

Launceston Priory. Speculative reconstruction of *c.* 1500

other decorative material, to allow proper re-assessment. This has recently concluded that Launceston Priory had the most ambitious late C13–early C14 church in Cornwall, with strong affinities in plan, design and decoration to contemporary work at Exeter Cathedral.*

Peter's plan shows the grand scale of the church, over 200 ft (61 metres) long, with a Lady Chapel projecting four bays E beyond the High Altar, almost as long as the cathedral's Lady Chapel, and longer than those at Glasney (*see* Penryn), Crediton and Ottery (both Devon). In the extant remains the rhythm of the bays in the choir is indicated by the engaged triple shafts rising from the inner wall faces, three on the N, and only the base of the corresponding central one on the S. To the E are two steps with dressed risers to the High Altar, whose base is represented by a substantial slate rubble foundation projecting from the E wall. The flanking N and S choir aisles are, unusually, separated from the choir by continuous walls punctuated at intervals by arches and doorways rather than arcades, and their bays do not correspond with those of the choir. To the N is a square room with a stair to an upper room; its walls are too insubstantial to be the base of a tower, and it is in the wrong position for a porch.

Over 300–400 substantial ARCHITECTURAL FRAGMENTS, many displayed on site, confirm the quality of the design, including the vaulting and window tracery: the latter is of outstanding interest for it shows the same inventive and flamboyant Dec designs seen in the later stages of Exeter

*This account is greatly indebted to John Allan's 'Notes towards an architectural history of Launceston Priory', in *Launceston Priory: Clearance and Archaeological Recording in Advance of Consolidation*, Cornwall Council (2011).

Cathedral's building programme of *c.* 1310–40, each of the choir windows different as there. The collection of floor tiles is probably the largest and most significant of its type in Cornwall, with some originating from Exeter. But the most eloquent testimony to the richness of the church's interior are small but exquisitely carved fragments of Beer stone recovered from near the High Altar, which indicate a grand reredos as at Exeter (*c.* 1313–26), Ottery (1330), and Christchurch Priory, Dorset (1330s–40s). In these respects at least the priory church at Launceston was in the vanguard of early C14 architecture in England.

ST CUTHBERT MAYNE (R.C.), St Stephen's Hill. 1910–11 by *Arthur Langdon,* completed by *Ralling & Tonar* of Exeter. A church of uncommon interest for its date, modest in scale but handsomely proportioned using a free Byzantine style and resembling in many of its fine details the cathedral at Westminster. The exterior is skilfully articulated with an apsidal E end surmounted by a dome, apsidal baptistery at the W end and bellcote over the SW corner, with a more domestic elevation incorporating vestry and meeting rooms to the N. Serene interior with a simple plaster barrel-vault over solid walls with round-headed openings, the chancel arch with detached columns with carved imposts, and reticulated tracery over the Diocletian vestry door. Round FONT of polished Polyphant, by Langdon, with interlaced carving on the bowl and fishes on the shaft, of superb quality.

METHODIST CHURCH, Castle Street. 1870 by *Hine & Norman* of Plymouth. One of the most ambitious churches of Cornish Methodism, on the site of 1810 and 1862 chapels. Its strong early Gothic composition, with the tall steep gable-end of the nave flanked l. by the Romanesque-style HALL and r. by the SCHOOLROOM of 1890 by *Hine & Odgers,* makes it a powerful presence in the street immediately below the castle, despite the demolition of its fine spire in 1984, leaving only a stumpy tower base. Triple entrance loggia with pointed arches over polished granite piers and large Dec-style window above. The interior is spacious and impressive: apsidal chancel, transept and aisles with four-bay arcades with pointed arches, lit by clerestory windows. Fine fittings including carved woodwork by *Harry Hems* of Exeter and painted panels by *Harris* of Plymouth.

On the corner of Castle Street and Northgate Street the former CONGREGATIONAL SCHOOL, dated 1884, by *Otho B. Peter* with a good Gothic front.

LAUNCESTON CASTLE

Towering above the rooftops of the town, the ruined castle still conveys the sense that this was the *raison d'être* of Launceston. The most impressive features are the high motte and massive earth ramparts that fortify the rectangular bailey, which is contrived on a steeply sloping ridge. The earthworks originate in the C11 but were later consolidated and reinforced by the walls and buildings, of which significant parts survive, mostly dating from Earl Richard's remodelling.

The SOUTH GATEHOUSE, the principal entrance today, faced away from the town in the medieval period when it was the entrance to the castle park, which lay either side of the steep valley to the W. The gate was created in the C12 through and over the original bailey rampart and modified by Earl Richard to make an imposing entrance, with the addition of two shallow drum towers. A fortified bridge was constructed in the C14 to carry the entrance to the site of the present Guildhall: the first pair of arches of this bridge, blocked with masonry, can be seen just inside the pavement. But the rest of the medieval arrangement is difficult to read because the entrance was 5 ft–6 ft (1.5 metres) above the present level, reduced by the construction of St Thomas Road in 1834 which destroyed the moat and all but the inner end of the bridge: fortunately, the bottom of the portcullis slot, representing the original threshold, can still be seen on the r. Access to the rooms over the gatehouse was by an external stone stair on the E side of the gatehouse, which survives at high level only.

Less remains of the NORTH GATEHOUSE, the medieval town gate, except the gate passage itself and the ground-floor room alongside it, and nothing of the ditch or bridge lost during the construction of the adjacent Eagle House. The inner gate arch, of three simple chamfered orders with a portcullis slot inside and a ribbed vault of two complete bays and part of a third, is also of Richard's reconstruction. A pointed-arched doorway leads into a rectangular room below what was probably the castle constable's chamber, lit by three narrow rectangular loops; it later served as a prison.

The BAILEY's NE corner is occupied by the huge motte, from which a high earth rampart runs E and then S, interrupted by the inserted S gate, to slope away to a steep scarp to the W. The C13 curtain wall was built along the crest of the rampart, at its highest where it overlooks the town. Late C20 excavations revealed evidence of several C13 buildings in the SW part of the bailey, including the great hall and chapel. The C19 cottage is a survival of the landscaping by the Duke of Northumberland, lessee of the castle and much of the town, of 1840, when the castle was made a public park.

The startlingly steep MOTTE achieved its present height and shape in several stages, the earliest motte being considerably lower. It is approached by a modern bridge over a C13 ditch built on medieval bridge piers and abutments. The bridge was guarded by a D-shaped tower of which three voussoirs of the relieving arch over its gateway survive. The motte was then accessed by a walled and roofed stair. At the summit is the early C14 stone KEEP: originally it had rooms within it, of which the jambs of a window on the W side are the only evidence, because the round HIGH TOWER was then constructed inside it, and one storey higher, with the intervening space roofed over at wall-walk level. The tower contained two rooms,

the upper one lit by a large window with window seats and
heated by a large fireplace.

TOWN WALLS

Launceston was the only Cornish town to be walled. The SOUTH-
GATE is the principal surviving portion of its circuit. The first
recorded reference is to two keepers in 1381. On its outer side
two massive buttresses flank a lofty rib-vaulted passage and
above the arch the face is recessed to receive a drawbridge. The
upper two storeys belong to the late C16, the rooms lit by plain
square-headed mullioned windows. An original doorway has
been adapted on the S, with remains of another on the opposite
wall indicating an extension of the gatehouse to the N. Until
1884 the upper rooms were used as the town prison, the prison
doors remaining. It was refurbished in 1887 by *Otho B. Peter*
who, having purchased some property here, demolished the
adjacent buildings to the W and added the pedestrian routeway
to prevent the gatehouse from being demolished as an obstruc-
tion to traffic. The gatehouse was re-roofed and the battlements added at this time. Substantial lengths of the C13 WALLS
run from a little to the NE of the Southgate round Dockacre
Road.

PUBLIC BUILDINGS

GUILDHALL and TOWN HALL, Western Road. The former 1881   111
by *Hine & Odgers* assisted by *Otho B. Peter*, the latter 1887 by
Peter alone. A splendid display of civic pride with impressive
presence at the W entry to the town, an accomplished essay in
the Gothic Revival style. Handsome three-stage entrance tower
with round SW stair-turret, the four-centred Polyphant doorway
arch approached by wide granite stairs, with the arms of the
town in red sandstone by *Harry Hems* of Exeter, and rising to
an embattled parapet with pyramidal roof. Guildhall to the l.
with three gabled windows, Town Hall to the r. with tall gable-
end and very large seven-light window. Splendidly detailed, e.g.
the chimneys as miniature castles and the fine hoppers to the
rainwater goods of the Guildhall of almost Burges-like quality.
The interior of the Guildhall has excellent medievalized council
chamber with a chimneypiece dated 1881 and arch-braced roof
springing from corbels. The vast Town Hall has a similar roof
with tie-rods. Memorial window with royal portraits and arms
of the town etc. by *J. T Fouracre* of Plymouth. Very good interior
details throughout. At the rear is an additional services block
in the same style and, set back to the r., a former fire engine
house.

Former PASSMORE EDWARDS INSTITUTE, Wooda Road/Tower
Street. Now residences. 1900 by *Silvanus Trevail*, for library and
reading room, but an uncharacteristically dull building from
this inventive architect, which even his trademark use of
red terracotta dressings fails to light up. The explanation is

probably that Passmore Edwards, never convinced Launceston was committed to his library, was only willing to fund a cheap building: it had to be repaired by *Hine* not long after its completion.

MARKET HOUSE, Market Street. 1838 by *George Wightwick*. Large rectangular plan, single storey with central clerestory. Plain exterior, spacious interior, ten bays long, three-bay ends, now fitted with modern shopfronts. When first built the centre was the butchers' market, the outer bays for fish and vegetables.

WAR MEMORIAL, The Square. 1921. Elegant, in the style of a medieval market cross or lantern. Octagonal in plan, rising from a stepped plinth to inscribed panels below an open stage with traceried lights, which is surmounted by buttress finials and radiating ribs to a cross. It replaced the upper market by *George Wightwick*.

WEST BRIDGE, Riverside. Late medieval foot and packhorse bridge over the Kensey, of five spans with two cutwaters to the upstream side, one downstream. Only the arches are now visible because of the silting up of the river.

LAUNCESTON STEAM RAILWAY. Opened 1983. The STATION BUFFET is a timber-framed bungalow, exhibited at the Ideal Home exhibition of 1919 and originally erected in Surrey.

PERAMBULATIONS

1. *The town centre*

Start from the castle (*see* above), the best place from which to grasp the town's topography and morphology. To the NW the land falls steeply away to the Kensey valley and Newport, the tower of St Thomas's church marking the site of Launceston Priory, before rising steeply again up St Stephen's Hill to the church of St Stephen. To the W the park of the medieval castle. And from the S round to the NE are the slate roofs* of the town, with its medieval street pattern evident beyond the castle precinct.

Leave the castle by the S gatehouse to view an area of impressive late C19 civic buildings, starting with the Guildhall and Town Hall (*see* Public Buildings). Further W along WESTERN ROAD No. 14, the former ODDFELLOWS HALL of 1880, with robust and stylistically eclectic stucco detailing, and at the junction with Westgate Street the unassuming stone façades of the former LAUNCESTON HOSPITAL of 1862 (enlarged 1900), and ROWE DISPENSARY of 1871 by *Otho B. Peter & Wise*. Return towards the centre by WESTGATE STREET past the former COUNTY POLICE STATION of 1886 with round-headed red brick openings; ST JOHN'S AMBULANCE HALL, 1924 by *Arthur G. Peter*; the former DRILL HALL of 1907 with

---

*Launceston is one of the best places in Cornwall to see local slate roofing and wall cladding.

its buttressed front; and the rear of the Town Hall and Guild-hall. Further up, where the street bends l., the handsome WESTERN BUILDINGS of 1881 by *Hine & Odgers* with Gothic ground floor and transomed-and-mullioned upper floors, one of many purpose-built commercial premises of the period. The best building of the street is the NATWEST BANK, built in 1868 as the Launceston Bank, accomplished High Victorian with transomed-and-mullioned windows, corbelled oriel with large gable over, and two pointed-head doorways with trefoils to inscribed tympanae and an inner order of nook-shafts.

Into THE SQUARE, the town's principal civic space, bounded by BROAD STREET and a delightful variety of buildings and with the WAR MEMORIAL (*see* Public Buildings) at its centre. On its E side the WHITE HART. Its five-window painted brick front of 1762 incorporates a mid-C12 doorway (possibly from the castle or priory) with two orders of colonettes and a frieze of lozenges to the round-arched head: the interior includes good C18 features including a wide open-well staircase. Next is LLOYDS BANK, a solid example of early C20 banker's classical. Then Nos. 9 and 11, 1840, a handsome and substantial pair of stucco town houses with later shops, three-storey with central pediment over giant pilasters framing the central bays. No. 8 is probably an early town house with a jettied first floor. Nos. 1–7 are an early C18 town house with later shops, the upper storey timber-framed and slate-hung with hornless sashes with thick glazing bars. Opposite, Nos. 2, 4 and 6 and BARCLAYS BANK, the most prominent example of High Victorian Gothic in the town, *c.* 1870s by *Peter*. Satisfyingly composed and articulated as it turns the corner from The Square, subtly varied in its elevations as it runs down Broad Street and turns the corner into Church Street, and skilfully detailed including Ruskinian banding in the polychrome walling and dressings. At the junction of The Square and High Street, Nos. 11, 13 and 13A, one of the most picturesque groups of town buildings in Cornwall. On the corner is the jettied timber-framed end of a C16 building whose stone side wall, with the outer frame of a granite mullioned window, faces The Square: the label stops to the window's hoodmould carry the initials TH for Thomas Hecks, mayor of Launceston at the Reformation, and whose family were connected with Trerithick, Altarnun (q.v.). Adjoining in HIGH STREET is the jettied elevation of a three-storey C17 house with an exceptionally well-preserved moulded oak door frame and square-panelled studded door, and first-floor oriel windows in which the intermediate mullions have been replaced by paired C18 horizontal sliding sashes. Both properties retain C16 and C17 roof structures and good C17 and C18 features. Further down High Street, No. 4 and the JUDGE'S KITCHEN, a rare survival of a C16 courtyard-plan town house, the three-storey elevation with pseudo-jetties and moulded cornices. Many good C16–C18 interior features including open-well staircase with pulvinated frieze and bolection-moulded chimneypiece. Next is No. 5, C18, one of the few town houses

72

whose ground floor has not been wholly converted to retail use. No. 10, by *Otho B. Peter*, was built as a temperance hotel. Now back to the N side of The Square. WOOLACOTTS (No. 14) is *c.* 1700, with excellent panelling and plasterwork of that period, refronted by *Hine* after fire damage in 1878. Hine also rebuilt the next two buildings after the fire, giving No. 18, now HSBC, a splendid Italianate palazzo front. Further along the playful intrusion of Art Deco, as the CAFÉ parapet inscription proclaims. Next to this, another good corner building by *Peter*, 1901, as a bakery.

Return down Broad Street and l. into CHURCH STREET, packed with C17 to late C19 buildings, many earlier structures with later fronts; much slate cladding and some good C19 shop-fronts, the latter another feature of the town. No. 28, for example, is an early C19 refronting with a bowed front of a C17 house. No. 26, a former C17 inn, has a double-gabled jettied front and remarkably complete interior. The architectural highlight is No. 22, built *c.* 1870 by *Hine* as Hayman's piano-forte warehouse: a rich Italianate composition with a cast-iron balcony that returns around the building, which runs through to High Street where the elevation has a carving of angels with lutes. Turning the corner between Church Street and High Street is No. 20, which has the town's most exuberant shop-front with pilasters, carved decoration, capitals, elaborate consoles, and a moulded entablature with frieze and acanthus-decorated cornice. At the top of Church Street, at its corner with Market Street, LOKAROMA, late C19 commercial prem-ises by *Henry Burt*. Opposite is the S flank of St Mary Magdalene (*see* Churches). W of St Mary in Church Street, and facing the Methodist church (*see* Churches), the spirited double-gabled and oriel-windowed former LIBERAL CLUB, 1897 by *Otho B. Peter*, with a charming first- and second-floor round bay turret at the l. end.

From Church Street, Northgate Street (*see* below) descends steeply into CASTLE STREET, the most gracious street in the town with a group of large C18 brick town houses. First is CASTLE HILL HOUSE, early to mid-C18, two-storey and attic over basement, five-window front with the three central bays slightly advanced and pedimented over. Elegant interior with open-well stair and excellent C18 plasterwork, the best being in the ground-floor parlour. Across the street the similar but more showy EAGLE HOUSE HOTEL, *c.* 1764 for Coryndon Carpenter, the castle constable and mayor. Two-storey and attic over basement, five-window front, the three central bays broken forward under a pediment that is surmounted by a Grecian-style figure flanked with urns, its gracious proportions somewhat disturbed by a very large late C19 porch. Another fine interior, of several C18 and C19 phases including stair hall with open-well staircase (with later fretted woodwork simulat-ing an iron balustrade) and Rococo plasterwork. The rear l. room has similar plasterwork and doorways with carved archi-traves, the rear r. room an early C19 heavily moulded coffered

88

ceiling. Modillion cornices in small front rooms and cornices in chambers. Nice brick enclosing walls and ironwork to front. In contrast the adjacent No. 5 presents a modest, low, rendered front, but it conceals one of the oldest houses in the town, with a late C16 roof. The house was remodelled in the early C18 with a bolection-moulded panelled room and other good details. Next No. 7, 1761 (inscription), partly rebuilt 1931, with dog-leg staircase. Then the LAWRENCE HOUSE MUSEUM, 1753 (inscription), rebuilt wing to r. with 1913 inscription. Two-storey and attic over basement. Again a good C18 interior, with plasterwork similar to that at Castle Hill House and the Eagle House Hotel, Doric columns and Doric frieze to the former stair hall (1913 replica columns on r.), panelling and chimneypieces. Opposite, the site of a mid-C19 Congregational chapel, with its former SCHOOL (see p. 293) on the opposite corner of the pedestrianized section of Northgate Street. Turn r. up Northgate Street towards the tower of the parish church, past Nos. 26 and 24 (formerly the RING OF BELLS) with nice slate cladding. The OLD BELL INN has slate cladding and two Gothic doorways, one C19, the other medieval reused. Before the tower is the former SUNDAY SCHOOL, 1886 by *Peter*, a handsome two-storey Tudor-style building.

In MARKET STREET, E of St Mary, CHURCH STILE, a five-bay late C18 stucco house raised from two to three storeys *c.* 1900 with Greek heads over the windows. The focal point of the street is the MARKET HOUSE (see Public Buildings). Market Street leads back to SOUTHGATE STREET. No. 1 (HALIFAX) is another good corner building by *Peter*. Then KING'S HOUSE (Nos. 5–7), a splendid early C19 brick house, with its five-bay front and central pediment. Big early C20 shopfront. Interior much altered but retains good C18 features including ribbed plaster ceiling with quatrefoils and arabesque, and stair window with columns. The second-floor windows slide up into the wall. Opposite, No. 8 is another brick house of similar date, of one build with Nos. 2–6. Finally, the Southgate (see Town Walls), a powerful reminder of the defences of the medieval town.

Beyond the gate is EXETER STREET, cut through in the 1820s. No. 1 is a lively Italianate corner building of *c.* 1860, and further along is BANK HOUSE, 1857 by *Henry Crisp*, an unusually early savings bank. Then back to Angel Hill, at the bottom of which sections of the medieval TOWN WALLS are visible, continuing for some distance NE along Dockacre Road. On the E side of the road is DOCKACRE HOUSE, of C16 origins with a pretty garden front of five gables, each gable above a jettied bay. C17 transomed-and-mullioned windows and good C17 and C18 interior features. Above the W side of Dockacre Road, on the wide ramparts of the town walls, THE WALK, the town's promenade, with at one end the Italianate NORTHERN-HAYE HOUSE, 1878, the first dated building by *Otho B. Peter* in Launceston, and at the other end a delightful early *cottage orné* (1756 datestone), the house of the Peter family. Behind

17

this the PARADE GROUND, created during the Napoleonic
Wars, its extensive views over the surrounding countryside a
fitting finale.

2. St Thomas-by-Launceston, Newport, and St Stephen-by-Launceston

The steep ST THOMAS HILL, lined with C18- and C19-looking
modest houses (some no doubt of earlier origin), still gives a
sense of having been the principal N route up into the town.
Turn l. into RIVERSIDE past St Thomas's church and the ruins
of Launceston Priory (see Churches), and cross the River
Kensey by the medieval footbridge to NEWPORT, with THE
SQUARE at its centre. The centrepiece of The Square is the
ROUNDHOUSE of 1829, possibly by George Wightwick, built as
a market house for the Duke of Northumberland: a pretty
Gothick octagon in stucco with buttressed angles and embat-
tled parapet. Within is a medieval CROSS BASE.

Then up ST STEPHEN'S HILL, another street of great interest
with a variety of building from the C15–C19, including some
C17 houses with lateral stacks and some refronting of earlier
fabric, to the church of St Cuthbert Mayne, and then on to
the top of the hill and the church of St Stephen (see Churches).
The little green (the former market place) with its late C19
former inn, the NORTHUMBERLAND ARMS, and a group of
four estate-looking cottages facing the church and DUKE
STREET,* the main village street, convey something of the
medieval settlement here, where Launceston originated on the
main N route into Cornwall.

HOLY WELL OF ST STEPHEN, ½ m. W of St Stephen's church.
Two well-houses, one behind the other. The tall front house is
probably C19, incorporating an earlier door frame and with a
stone vaulted roof. The other, built into the bank, is possibly
earlier.

DUNHEVED CROSS, Landrake Road. At the end of a cul de sac,
on the S side of the A30. Gothic cross-head, impressively
sculpted, on tall octagonal shaft.

KESTLE RINGS, 3 m. W. Iron Age bivallate hillfort on stubby
spur dominating the Kensey valley. Inner rampart reduced to
rounded earthworks.

LAWHITTON

ST MICHAEL. The parish was given to the Bishop of Sherborne
by King Egbert in 830. The church, sited within a lann, is small

---

*More evidence of the Duke of Northumberland's influence on C19 Launceston.

and of an unusual plan, with a C13 S tower that originally stood at the end of a S transept before the S aisle was added in the C15. The tower is of three stages (Henderson and Cox considered the base Norman), diminishing in dimensions from stage to stage, without buttresses, and with a NE stair-turret. The C15 porch comes close to the tower: it has an old wagon roof, a Polyphant stoup and ogee-arched image niche above the C19 inner door. The nave N windows are straight-headed, the S aisle windows Perp, of three lights. Inside, the S arcade of five bays is relatively tall, with piers of standard section and multiple moulded capitals. The church was restored in 1860 and more extensively in 1873 by *J. D. Sedding*, and it is the latter restoration that has given it its satisfyingly well-ordered character and finely detailed features such as the hammerbeam roof to the chancel with large angels, the decorative tiling of the chancel floor, and the traceried panels l. and r. of the altar. – FONT. Norman, of the Altarnun type, but with unbearded corner faces. – BENCH-ENDS. Just a few, not specially interesting. – PULPIT. Elegantly simple, dated 1665, yet still entirely in the Jacobean style. – STAINED GLASS. Chancel E, 1873 by *Clayton & Bell*, very similar to that at North Hill. – S chapel E 1888, S aisle 1899, and three windows in N nave 1882–1900 by *Bell & Beckham*. – MONUMENT. R. Bennet †1683, slate, with ornamental writing and a handsome coat of arms. – Richard Coffin †1796, of Coade stone, the patent terracotta ware made by *Coade & Sealy*, whose signature is on the monument. Figures such as the mourning woman on the sarcophagus and the two somewhat oversized putti, now broken but originally standing l. and r., could be ordered from the catalogue (cf. the putti at St Michael Caerhays).

The WHITE HOUSE, immediately SW of the churchyard, has an elaborate late medieval FINIAL in the shape of a bishop's mitre on an end stack, probably a remnant of the small (and little-used) medieval bishop's palace that occupied the site of the present C18 house.

LELANT

5030

ST UNY (St Euny). Lelant was a considerable medieval seaport until outdone by St Ives and this was the mother church of both St Ives and Towednack. It stands sentinel above the dunes on the W side of the Hayle estuary in sight of the sea. W tower of three stages with diagonal buttresses, going very thin higher up. Fine S porch like St Erth, buttressed and with panelled jambs, the inner door with nice fleurons in jambs and voussoirs with tracery decoration in the spandrels. The surprise of the interior is the survival of part of a Norman N arcade, one round arch on two short circular piers with scalloped capitals of an unusual variety, the scallops tied together by bands above and below. The bay to the w of the Norman one has a plain two-centred arch, just to connect the Norman part with the tower; the three bays to the E and the whole s arcade on square piers with four attached demi-shafts and two-centred aches. A few capitals are more decorated than usual, with horizontal leaves in the Devonshire pattern. The windows are mostly Perp, those on the s partially restored, on the N with quite plain three-light openings without tracery. The E window is C19, with C15-style tracery. The church was extensively but sensitively restored in 1872–3 by *J. D Sedding* who renewed the roofs of chancel and N aisle and repaired the nave and s aisle roofs; the latter is the more richly decorated and original. – Simple, workmanlike PEWS, also by Sedding. – FONT. Octagonal, with the simplest of ornament, almost undateable: it was found in a farmyard and restored on its nine supports and base by *J. P. St Aubyn* in 1889. – STAINED GLASS. Chancel E, 1973 by *M. C. Farrar-Bell* with local iconography. – N chapel E 1850, an early window by *John Hardman*. – One of 1924 by *Powells* of Whitefriars. – MONUMENTS. Two slates on wall near font. – William Praed †1620 and his family, with kneeling figures and flowers, sand-glass, skull; strapwork as decoration. – Stephen Pawley †1635. – In the churchyard against the s wall a large, severely plain sarcophagus to William Praed †1833, some good slate cutting including an C18 sundial, and memorial slab in church wall with flowery border signed *Richard Osman* of Truro. Good memorial in the newer section of the churchyard to Olive Bivar †1976 by *Joe Hemming* of Sancreed. – MORTUARY CHAPEL, 1879. – There are also five CROSSES in the churchyard and new cemetery.

WESLEYAN CHAPEL, Lower Lelant. 1834. Handsome front with central entrance flanked by blind round-headed window recesses, three round-headed windows above, surmounted by a gable parapet swept up at the eaves and rising to a square clock tower.

TREVETHOE HOUSE, 1 m. SW. C19 stucco disguising an older house. Seven-bay two-storey entrance front with central pediment above the three centre bays which are slightly advanced. Lower two-storey range behind linking to the taller rear wing. SE LODGE, two-storey, C19 with good contemporary railings and gates; N LODGE, single-storey, early C19, round bays with Gothic lights.

TOR ENCLOSURE and HILLFORT, Trencrom, 2 m. WSW. A stone-faced ditchless rampart links the several granite summit tors of this steep hill rearing above travellers entering West Penwith. It creates a pear-shaped enclosure with w and E entrances and slighter enclosures attached to N and NE. Leaf-shaped flint arrowheads found in the early C20 match those found at Carn Brea (q.v.). Three Early Bronze Age kerbed CAIRNS indicate second millennium B.C. use while pot sherds date the rampart's strengthening to the Early Iron Age. Other sherds indicate later Iron Age, Roman period and early medieval reuse of the hilltop.

LERRYN

A former port on the upper reaches of the Fowey, active until
the early C20. Two C16 BRIDGES, both of two arches, the one
at the head of the creek originally of three, mentioned by
Leland in 1542 and rebuilt in 1573. Modest cottages, a few
former shops with unaltered mid-C19 shopfronts, and a large
early to mid-C19 rectangular top-loaded LIMEKILN by the
roadside, built into the hillside.

LESNEWTH

ST MICHAEL AND ALL ANGELS. In a very pretty position in a
valley, the churchyard so steeply sloping down to a little stream
below that only the fine w tower is visible from the road above.
The tower is tall, of three stages and unbuttressed, and C15,
with its stair-turret (with tiny quatrefoil openings) on the N
side. The rest extensively rebuilt by *J. P. St Aubyn* 1865, before
which it had both its Norman transepts (a rarity in Cornwall),
though compared to some of this architect's work the result is
pleasingly simple and well detailed. The s porch was rebuilt w
of the earlier porch and a vestry added as a s chancel aisle with
two gables, its two-bay arcade with a pier reusing a C12 base
and capital. A shallow projection was added to the N wall of
the chancel to accommodate a reset C13 lancet window with a
mensa, reputedly moved from the former N transept, below. In
the s wall a re-set C14 piscina. At the w end of the church, on
the floor, a C12 scalloped capital, hollowed out. – STAINED
GLASS. s and N windows of the nave, 2000 and 2003 roundels
by *Caroline Henderson*. – MONUMENTS. Several C17 and early
C18 slate ledgers with good lettering. – In the churchyard the
head of a WAYSIDE CROSS with a narrow bead around the edge
and an equal-limbed cross on its principal face. Another
WHEEL-HEAD CROSS and a C13 GRAVE-SLAB with an incised
foliated cross, found in the stream bed after the 2004 Boscastle
flood, are displayed in the porch.

LEVANT

½ m. w of Pendeen

The earliest reference to mining here is in 1670 and by the 1820s
the Levant MINE became, with nearby Botallack (q.v.), the
most important of the St Just area and one of the ten most
significant in all Cornwall.* As at Botallack, an extensive area

***

*It was also the scene of one of the worst Cornish mining tragedies in 1919.

of the ruinous yet eloquent remains of the latest C19 and early
C20 mining – engine houses, stacks, miners dry, tin floors,
arsenic calciners, settling tanks and buddles, etc. – can be seen
just above the cliff edge. At the heart of the area are two
ENGINE HOUSES clustered around the mine's principal shafts
that extended far out to sea. The smaller roofed house contains
the oldest surviving Cornish BEAM ENGINE, 1840 by *Harveys*
of Hayle, restored to working order in the 1980s.

2080

LEWANNICK

A small hilltop village in the parish of the famous Polyphant stone
quarries.

ST MARTIN. In the centre of the village within a probable *lann*.
Fine late C15 to early C16 W tower of Polyphant, in three stages
with buttresses set back from the angles and ending on the
second stage: on the third the three-eighths plan of the pinnacles starts. The W side is one of the most charming in Cornwall: a W door with fleurons in jambs and voussoirs, flowers
and scrolls in the spandrels, and above it a W window with a
crocketed ogee canopy and elongated finials on the sides. The
oddest thing architecturally about the exterior is the tracery of
all but one of the S and N aisle windows with two mullions and
one transom high up in the earlier four-centred arches: it probably belongs to the C18. The E windows of the chancel and S
aisle have their four-light Perp tracery of the design which
unites two lights under one main arch and is especially popular
in this district (cf. Altarnun, etc.). The church has large N and
S porches with wagon roofs with some C19 bosses: the S porch
has a charming depiction of chasing animals – a rabbit, hare,
deer and fox – carved below the W side bench, and a multiple-
moulded S door of Polyphant. Inside the N aisle is of five bays
and one small and narrow one for the chancel. The piers are
standard. The S aisle has five bays and the Polyphant piers
show an unusual section, the same as found at St Cleer (q.v.):
they belong to a partial reconstruction following a devastating
fire in 1896 which destroyed the original roofs (except the
porches) and almost all the interior timberwork. The work was
undertaken by *Otho B. Peter* (cf. Launceston) who was
instructed 'to re-design the interior to be as near the original
as funds would allow'. – FONT. Large, octagonal, Norman with
some unusual ornamental motifs including a coil (labyrinth?),
a maze, and (twice) a pentagram. – INSCRIBED STONES.
Two with inscriptions partly in Roman capitals, partly in
Ogham lettering, that curious script used mainly in south
Ireland and occasionally used in England in the C5 to C7. It
consists entirely of unconnected vertical strokes (cf. St
Clement, St Kew). One stone is in the church with the Roman

13

inscription . . . ( )C IACIT VIIAGNI . . . (here lies the body of Ulcagnus), between the Ogham inscriptions on the front face: it was found in two pieces in 1894 built into the porch walls. The other, in the churchyard S of the church, has the Roman inscription INGENVI MEMORIA on the face and the Ogham script reading INGENAVI MEMOR (the monument of Incenvus). – CRESSET STONE. A great rarity, with seven cups, six arranged symmetrically around a central cup and supported on an octagonal pillar, to hold tallow, with wicks to give light (cf. the smaller one at Marham church). – STAINED GLASS. All early C20. Chancel E, 1903 by *Herbert Davis*. – Chancel S 1920. – S aisle E, 1910 by *C. G. Archer*. – S aisle, 1904 by *Jones & Willis*.

COOMBSHEAD, ½ m. E. A model farm begun 1839 (datestone) and extended in phases as the home farm of the nearby Trelaske estate, of which the house was demolished in the late 1950s. Planned around a very large yard with the farmhouse at the higher N end and bounded by ranges of farm buildings E and W. Both ranges include large BARNS, the E a BANK BARN originally powered by a waterwheel, and an unusually large variety of specialist buildings.

TREKELLAND BRIDGE, 1½ m. E over the River Inny. Built *c.* 1500, this is possibly the nameless bridge near Launceston for which Bishop Oldham granted an indulgence in 1504. One of the best-preserved and most beautiful of medieval Cornish bridges, in a picturesque setting. Granite ashlar, of two large arches and a smaller arch, with recessed arch rings and keystones and deep cutwaters carried up to the parapet as refuges.

LEZANT

3070

ST BRIOCHUS. There was a church here by the early C12, sited within a *lann*, its High Altar re-dedicated by Bishop Grandisson in 1336. Fine late C15 or early C16 W tower much like others locally (cf. North Hill, South Petherwin and Stoke Climsland), of regular granite blocks in three stages, deeply recessed and moulded W window and door (the latter with giant label stops), set-back buttresses, and large octagonal corner turrets with crocketed pinnacles. Of the Norman building scalloped capitals reused in the outer doorway to the porch, and probably the N and S walls of the chancel with the two lancets in a deeply splayed opening in the S wall. The masonry of the N aisle must also be early – see the N door with its plain chamfered arch and the cusped little lancet window in the W wall (Sedding regarded the window opening itself as Norman but, at least in its present form, it cannot be earlier than the end of the C13). Re-set C12 animal corbel at SW corner of S aisle, which has C15 Perp windows. The N aisle has square-headed windows that suggest an early C16 date. The interior bears the stamp of a

restoration of 1869 by *J. P. St Aubyn* but the early character of
the chancel remains obvious, helped by some good STAINED
GLASS by *Clayton & Bell* of 1883 and 1871. The N and S arcades
are Cornish standard and St Aubyn spared the old ceiled
wagon roofs. – FONT. Norman, of the Altarnun type, but with
the corner faces carved off so that the shape is now octagonal.
– Square AUMBRY in N wall and C14 trefoil-headed PISCINA
in S wall of chancel. – MONUMENTS. Trefusis family. An altar
tomb at the E end of the S aisle, with slate front and top, a slate
back, and also an upright backplate against the S wall. The
kneeling figures appear there; otherwise there are inscriptions,
coats of arms, and ornament. – MONUMENT to a lady stiffly
reclining, in an aedicule, with two small allegorical figures on
the top cornice.

GREYSTONE BRIDGE, 2 m. ENE, spanning the Tamar and the
Devon border. 1439, partly paid for by Thomas Mede, Abbot
of Tavistock. Remarkably similar to Horse Bridge, downstream
in Stoke Climsland parish. Four segmental arches to river with
two flood-water arches on each bank. Arches recessed with
single chamfering and double voussoirs; cutwaters rise to
refuges on the parapet.

GREYSTONE FARMHOUSE, ⅓ m. NW of the bridge. Rare L-plan
former open-hall house, floored in the C16 and with a C17 wing.
Five-bay moulded arch-braced and wind-braced roof with
slight smoke blackening. C16 ceiling beams and stone spiral
staircase.

LANDUE, 1 m. NE. Late C17 with C18 and C19 alterations and
extensions. Nine-window front, two-storey and C18 hood to
central entrance. Rear range has three two-light cinquefoil-
headed windows with king mullions forming a large six-light
window. Late C17 newel stair, ground-floor rooms with plaster
cornices. Picturesque Gothick LODGE, dated 1823, with
veranda on rustic posts, and gables with decorative slate cladding, fretted bargeboards and pendants. Early C19 GATEPIERS
with large ball finials.

TRECARREL. *See* p. 636.

LINKINHORNE

ST MELOR. 'There are few man-improved sights in Cornwall so
satisfying as the way the stately church tower rises out of an
amphitheatre of trees on the hill slope, as one approached
the church town from South Hill.'* The tower is the second
highest (next to Probus) in the county at 120 ft (36.6 metres),
of four storeys rather than the usual three, with buttresses set
back from the angles, embattled parapet, and crocketed pinnacles; its large scale and fairly sumptuous quality (cf. the deep

---

*John Betjeman, *Shell Guide to Cornwall* (1964).

moulding of the w door and window surround) are said to be
due to the generosity of a Trecarrel (cf. Trecarrel and Launceston). The whole church is entirely of the large regular
granite ashlar blocks characteristic of the last fifty years of the
Perp style. Fine s porch, its entrance with a curious interlaced
figure-of-eight ornament in the jambs and voussoirs, like
Maker (q.v.), the ends of the labels to the hoodmould supported on little square shafts, and a wagon roof with moulded
ribs and purlins. C15 door with excellent ironwork. Nave of five
bays, N and S aisles with piers of standard section and four-
centred arches but with slightly different capital decoration:
the N with scroll and interlace like the porch, the s with trefoil,
quatrefoil and flowers, more sharply carved. The s aisle arcade
is an attractive mix of granite and a warm yellow-brown local
stone. Wagon roofs to nave and N and S aisles. The aisle
roofs are of more than usual interest for their bosses that
include: a mermaid holding a mirror and comb in the s aisle
and several heads; angels with scrolls and shields on the wall-
plates in the N aisle; and traces of early colouring in red and
dark green and black. Tower ceiling framed with intersecting
moulded ribs and massive bosses. A restoration of 1891 by *Hine
& Odgers* renewed the chancel roof and stripped most of the
plaster from the walls. – FONT of Polyphant. C13, cf. Egloshayle, that is, a large square top with narrow pointed blank
arcades, and with a base with blank arcading in higher
relief. – ALTAR SLAB with five crosses, beneath the altar in the
s aisle. – Part of a Norman CAPITAL discovered during the
restoration, on a window sill in the s aisle. – Two small C16
PEWS and BENCH-ENDS. – Other furnishings late C19 to early
C20, including OAK PEWS in the chancel by *Harry Hems*. –
WALL PAINTINGS. In the s aisle. The outstanding feature of
the interior. Between the second and third windows, the Seven
Corporal Works of Mercy, the most accomplished painting
now remaining in Cornwall: even in the late medieval period
it must have been one of the best. The haloed Christ stands
clad in loose drapery beneath an unusual canopy like the ceremonial tent of a medieval king, and is surrounded by small
scenes showing the Works. These begin at the top l. with
Feeding the Hungry; Clothing the Naked, one of the clearest,
is immediately below. The clearest scene on the r. is at the top,
Giving Drink to the Thirsty, with Receiving the Stranger
immediately below: though faint, this shows a large gabled
house with a round window and tiled roof, painted in yellow
ochre. The remaining scenes, very faint, are Visiting Prisoners,
bottom l.; Visiting the Sick, bottom centre; and Burying the
Dead, bottom r. Further w, a very obscure painting, possibly
a Doom, too fragmentary to ensure certain identification. –
STAINED GLASS. A few small fragments of medieval glass in
the tracery of N and s aisles. – s chapel E, 1844, decorative
roundels in tinted glass. – N aisle, Faith, St Melor, Hope etc.,
1876, and Abraham and the Four Evangelists, 1890, by *Fouracre
& Watson*.

In the churchyard several STONES with charming folk art decoration and fine lettering by *Daniel Gumb* who lived with his wife and children in a lonely cottage near Cheesewring rock and died in 1776.

HOLY WELL OF ST MELOR. In an archetypal setting by the side of a stream in a field ¼ m. SW of the church. A little C15 building, exceptionally well preserved, entirely of granite, the roof of horizontal slabs, with image niches in the gabled front above the round-arched door and inside in the rear wall and l. side wall.

PLUSHA BRIDGE, 1½ m. SW. Late C15, granite, of three round-headed arches.

ST PAUL, Upton Cross. 1885–7 by *Silvanus Trevail*, as a mission church. Plain E.E. with lancets.

WESTCOTT, 1½ m. W. Late C16 to early C17 house, remodelled and extended 1653 by Edward Kneebone: what survives may be the remnant of a larger house, or an uncompleted one. L-plan with later parlour wing to r., and projecting wing to l. of the earlier building. Six-light granite mullion window and three- and four-light mullions to first floor, all with king mullions. Datestone 1653. Fine plasterwork ceiling of that date with knot pattern, acorn and oak leaf bosses and fruit sprays in the parlour wing; the chamber over has a plain plaster barrel with honeysuckle plasterwork frieze and overmantel with vase of flowers and bird perching on a stem.

ADDICROFT MILL, 1½ m. WSW. Rare example of early C19 three-storey mill and two-storey mill house on L-plan, the mill's machinery still in working order.

LISKEARD

The town's gentle charm owes much to the hilly topography of its site, with the medieval church on an E eminence, the spacious C18 and C19 Parade on the W hill, and a cluster of small streets that constitute its historic commercial heart in the steep valley between. The sequence of development, probably pre-Conquest in origin, began around the church with a market immediately adjoining, a castle (or more likely a fortified manor house) nearby NW on the hill, and a settlement in the valley below. Liskeard was granted a charter in 1296 and in 1307 became a stannary town, one of five in Cornwall, to serve the rapidly developing local tin industry. The market had migrated to the valley around Market Street by the late medieval period and the original market site was infilled. Leland describes it as 'the best town in Cornwall save Bodmin' in 1542 although Norden and Carew were reporting its decline by the end of the C16. But it remained relatively prosperous through the C17 and C18 as a service centre for its rich rural hinterland, helped by its position on the main southern route into Cornwall and the development of the turnpikes around the mid c18 bringing better road access from the east. By that time the later market site had itself begun to be built over and a new market had been established on the high ground now occupied by the Parade.

The c19 saw the making of the modern town. The building of the Looe–Liskeard Union Canal in the late 1820s with its terminus at Moorswater just west of the town further improved its trading links, based on the import of coal. But it was the discovery of a rich copper lode at South Caradon Mine in 1837 (cf. Minions), leading to the opening of the Liskeard and Caradon Railway in 1844 linking Moorswater to the Caradon Hill mines with a branch to the Cheesewring granite quarries, that made Liskeard a boom town. The arrival of the Great Western Railway in 1859 sealed its prosperity and an extensive programme of public and private development produced some fine, if generally modest, civic, commercial and institutional buildings in the town centre and pleasant terraces, houses and villas in the immediate suburbs. After the decline of mining in the late c19, its growth continued into the early c20 when it was still sustained by its service and secondary industries.

As a result Liskeard is a town with a strong c19 architectural personality. Some of the best c19 Cornish architects of the period – Foulston, Wightwick and Hicks – are represented but an unusual number of buildings were designed by one talented Liskeard architect, Henry Rice (1808–76), who was Borough Surveyor and whose practice flourished in the boom years; other more local architects – Richard Coad (cf. Lanhydrock), John Sansom and John Paul – all began as his assistants. Like Hicks at Redruth and Trevail at St Austell and elsewhere, Rice was versatile, inventive, and capable of working across the range from modest houses and terraces to larger villas, banks, shops and civic buildings. Over a hundred of his buildings remain in and around the town centre which, mercifully by-passed by the Plymouth–Bodmin road since 1977, has survived remarkably complete and repays patient exploration.

CHURCHES

St Martin. One of the largest parish churches in Cornwall, with an overall length of 140 ft (42.7 metres) (Bodmin is 151 ft (46 metres)). From its hilltop site its tower dominates the town, though not happily: it was rebuilt in a harsh neo-Cornish style in 1900–3 by *John Sansom*, incorporating fragments of the Norman church, principally a doorway in the (internal) N wall of the tower with double chevron decoration, five reworked windows in the second stage, and thirty-three late c12 corbels supporting the parapet. A deeply splayed opening in the w wall of the present N aisle, its apex only about 7½ ft (2.3 metres) from the ground, is also Norman. The rest of the exterior is Perp and impressive in its unusual features as much as its scale, with nave, N and S aisles, N and S porches and an extra outer S aisle (Lady Chapel). The S porch is remarkably fine, comparable to Bodmin and Launceston, with an upper storey with a small cinquefoil-headed window flanked by statue niches and a smaller niche above. The N porch is the first of three curious bay-window-like projections which accompany the outer wall of the aisle from W to E, as high as the aisle and battlemented like both aisles: they are chantry chapels erected at the expense of various town guilds. There are also thirteen CONSECRATION CROSSES on the outer walls of the N and S aisles, unique in Cornwall. The dates of the S aisle (1428–30), and N aisle (1477) are recorded in agreements between the prior of St Stephen, Launceston, and the mayor of Liskeard.

The interior is airy and lofty, the five-bay nave arcade tall with slim piers of Cornish standard moulding and two-centred arches. The chancel is of two bays, lower than the nave and separated from it by a chancel arch, an arrangement very unusual in Cornwall (cf. Bodmin and Crantock); there are similar arches to the aisle chapels. The arcade between S aisle and Lady Chapel is of three bays. The windows are all Perp (some restored), of four and five lights, except the E window of the chancel which is 1899. The chantry chapels do not tally with the nave arcade and are covered with depressed tunnel-vaults with three stone arches across. The church was re-roofed in restorations of 1870 and 1877–9 by *Richard Coad*: two richly carved fragments of the medieval roof are preserved on the W wall of the Lady Chapel. – FONT. Plain, probably C16. – Norman bowl font set in E wall of N porch as a STOUP. – Re-set Norman heads below the responds of the chancel and E end of the aisle. – Beautifully carved octagonal PULPIT, dated 1636, by *Peter Short*. – Large early C19 slate COMMANDMENT BOARDS, LORD'S PRAYER and CREED, with ornamental script, relegated to the N exterior walls. – The interior continued to be embellished in the later C19 and early C20 (like St Austell), with new VESTRIES, 1888 and 1912, PARCLOSE SCREENS, 1897, and SCREENS in the Lady Chapel, 1927 and 1935. – STAINED GLASS. An especially rich array of late C19 and early C20 glass. Chancel E and three in N chapel by *Clayton & Bell*, 1889 and 1890. – Lady Chapel E by *Ward & Hughes*, – 1879, S by *Clayton & Bell*, 1904. – Three in S chapel by *Clayton & Bell*, 1905–20. – S aisle, interesting iconography of Protestant martyrs including Ridley etc., by *Clayton & Bell*, 1920. – Tower W and N, *Clayton & Bell*, 1920. – N aisle by *Ward & Hughes*, 1879; and W window of N aisle by *Osmond Caine*, 1980, in an attractive Arts and Crafts style. – MONUMENTS. Many minor Neoclassical works by the usual regional purveyors, though none of major importance: *R. Isbell* of Stonehouse (Lieut. Hawkey 1809, quite elaborate and rather tasteless), *Shepherd* of Plymouth, *Crocker* of Plymouth.

In the churchyard, SE of the church, a medieval WAYSIDE CROSS, brought from a nearby farm and restored in 1908. In the shape of a Latin cross with Latin crosses incised on each face.

OUR LADY AND ST NEOT (R.C.), West Street. The first site of an R.C. church in the Plymouth diocese after Catholic emancipation in 1829. The present church, by *J. S. Hansom* in the plainest E.E. style, was built in 1862–3 to accommodate an influx of Irish miners during the mining boom, the original building retained as a small hall alongside.

METHODIST CHURCH, Windsor Place. 1846 by *Henry Rice*, enlarged by him 1861 and further altered in 1891 and 1907. A powerful presence, in Italianate style, the street elevation with two taller bays brought forward under a pediment on the r., with recessed pairs of round-headed lights with turned shafts under corbelled heads, and a very large porch. The stucco pilasters to the main range windows were added in 1925. The interior has a fine moulded and carved ceiling above a gallery running around three sides on slender Doric columns. Elaborate rostrum of 1889 by *John Ugalde*. To the r. of the church, former SCHOOLROOM, 1890, Italianate with large Venetian window at first floor.

GREENBANK CHRISTIAN CENTRE, Greenbank Road. Originally a simple and elegant Methodist chapel of 1838 by *Henry Rice*, refronted with a ponderous entrance lobby in 1925.

PUBLIC BUILDINGS

GUILDHALL, Fore Street. 1859–68 by *Henry Rice* and *Charles Reeves*, as town hall and county court. Its clock tower is the focal point of the small streets of the old town, and its large scale and grand Italianate style contrast sharply with the generally modest buildings around. An awkward corner site on a steep slope is used to create a striking piece of civic architecture, a fine example of its type, that speaks of the town's prestige at its mid-to late C19 zenith. Above the open loggia arcade with rusticated rock-faced dressings and cast-iron gates to the l., the Fore Street front rises to the first (main) storey with tall large round-headed windows and vermiculated rustications, finishing in a squat attic storey with deeply recessed windows. The elaborate clock tower has two round-headed lights to each stage, the first with cast-iron grilles, the second with squat engaged columns with Ionic capitals, and a clock face to each side under open segmented pediments. The interior has a fine open-well staircase and quatrefoil tracery supporting the second flight and landing above. Council chamber with panelled ceiling.

LISKEARD AND DISTRICT MUSEUM, Pike Street. Originally built as a lecture room and East Cornwall Savings Bank in 1835 by *Henry Rice*. It became the Foresters Hall in 1896 and the museum in 2000. The eye-catching street façade in Ruskinian Venetian style is the prettiest in the town, in a lively polychromy, the loggia of three pointed arches on chamfered columns above a tall plinth with the central doorway breaking an inscribed band. Row of 1:3:1 small lancets above. At the rear of the loggia are four trefoil-headed lancets flanked by pointed-arched doorways with planked doors.

PUBLIC LIBRARY, Barras Street. Datestone 1896, by *Symons & Sons* for John Passmore Edwards. Fine street elevation in Flemish Renaissance style with three bays broken forward at first-floor level under coped gables with ball finials. Central bay with round-headed doorway with rusticated voussoirs flanked by fluted Ionic pilasters, and an inscribed panel above, rising to a five-light mullioned oriel window with double transoms. Similar windows to the flanking bays.

PUBLIC ROOMS, West Street. 1890 by *Otho B. Peter*. The plain stucco Gothic front leads to a large hall at the rear which has an imposing chapel-like Gothic elevation to Barras Place with a seven-light pointed window with two central mullions (blank below) and round corner turrets.

Former WORKHOUSE, Station Road. 1837–9 by *Scott & Moffatt*; later Lamellion Hospital, dem. 1960s. Only the LODGES survive. Single-storey, stuccoed, originally linked by a stone arch with pediment.

DUCHY HOUSE, Station Road. 1914 by *Sir Albert Richardson* for the Duchy of Cornwall. Quietly imposing Neoclassical with prominent semicircular entrance porch.

RAILWAY STATIONS, Station Road. An unusual arrangement of two separate stations. The simple mainline station building, 1859 for the Cornwall Railway, is high up above the platform with a curved glazed canopy overlooking the line, 2004 by *Robert Allen Architects*. The pretty little timber-clad station building for the branch line to Looe, below at right angles at the E end of the platform, and originally incorporating the offices of the Liskeard and Looe Railway Co., is 1901 by *John Sansom*.

PERAMBULATION

It is worth starting at the E end of the town with the parish church (*see* Churches). This high part of the town offers good vantage points to appreciate its development, first in the medieval period into the steep valley below W, and then in the C18 and C19 onto the higher ground beyond. There is no trace of the castle or manor in Castle Park NE of CASTLE STREET, so it is better to go straight down the steep CHURCH GATE and CHURCH STREET to the heart of the old town. Much of Liskeard's character comes from its little streets and tightly packed buildings, mostly C19 and C19 fronted, modest in scale and architectural detail, some slate-hung and many with good early C19 shopfronts, now domesticated. This is the area of the late medieval market after it had moved down from the higher land near the church: the Market Hall of 1822 was demolished in 1956 but MARKET STREET, FORE STREET, BAYTREE HILL, PIKE STREET and adjoining streets have the character of the town's older commercial core. Dominating the area is the Guildhall (*see* Public Buildings) but there are other buildings worth noticing. The PIPE WELL is tucked away behind Fore Street in WELL LANE, the present mid-C19 well-house and late C19 wrought-iron gates replacing the medieval building. Opposite the well, a substantial late C19 WAREHOUSE with hoist and deep bracketed eaves. More than a few of the premises in this part of the town are by *Henry Rice*, displaying his range of style and type: e.g. No. 1 Market Street, 1853, one of his best, an ornate classical town house with enriched modillion eaves cornice, rusticated quoins and cartouches; and No. 7 Market Street, another nice example of his enriched upper-storey detailing. End this part of the perambulation by going up Pike Street, past the splendid Venetian Gothic of the Museum (*see* Public Buildings), to reach The Parade.

THE PARADE is the best civic space and the most architecturally ambitious group of buildings in the town. At the centre is an elaborate stone FOUNTAIN, 1871 by *Henry Rice*, surmounted by an ornate cast-iron lamppost on four arched feet. It commemorates Michael Loam, inventor of the man-engine, a mechanical ladder for miners. The most imposing single building on the E side is WEBB'S HOUSE, 1833 by *John Foulston*, built as a hotel (now offices). Its large scale, simple stucco classical detailing, three-storey height and symmetrical five-window range around a distyle porch in granite, with a bold Egyptianized-lettered name, give it a commanding presence. Foulston was an innovator in hotel design in Plymouth at the Royal Hotel (now demolished). To the N, BARCLAYS BANK, of 1851 for the East Cornwall Bank by *Henry Rice*. Disciplined classicism in granite ashlar. Three-storey, three-window front, the ground floor with round-headed arched openings with arches on impost bands and tall keystones, and tall first-floor windows with pediments. Across Greenbank Road, No. 2, also by *Rice*, c. 1837, originally double-fronted before road widening. Stucco with channelled rustication to ground floor. On the W side, PARADE HOUSE, large and classical, probably of mid-C18 origin with alterations by *Rice* c. 1835 and 1850. Two storeys and attic over basement, symmetrical five-window front and central round-arched doorway to distyle porch with engaged columns. Inside mid-C18 stairs and cornices. Also LISKERRIT HOUSE, c. 1840, with arched glazing bars in top sashes, a *Rice* feature. Downhill the MASONIC HALL, dated 1872, by *John Paul*. Attractive Venetian Gothic in polychromy (cf. the Museum, Pike Street). Ground floor with segmented-arched openings and doorway with nook-shafts and open pediment with Masonic symbols. Stilted round-headed first-floor windows with nook-shafts, slender hoodmoulds, key blocks and coloured glass. Next to this, LLOYDS BANK, 1867 by *Rice*. Neoclassical front, of pink granite ashlar on a white granite plinth, with rusticated end pilasters and similar flanking the central entrance, channelled rustications to ground floor, and entablature with consoles under the parapet. All the openings have recessed architraves and key blocks.

Now S into BARRAS STREET with the Library (*see* Public Buildings) and next door STUART HOUSE, one of the few houses in the town that display pre-C18 origins. Late medieval, remodelled and extended in the C17 and C18 with C20 alterations to the interior. An attractive composition, two- and three-storey, with three-storey porch projecting to the street, slate-hung. Porch has reused C15 two-centred doorway, the similar arch to the inner door in its original position. Two-room and cross-passage plan with a pair of three-storey wings added to the S end. The interior has some features from most phases of the house's complex development. On again into WINDSOR PLACE. Opposite the Methodist church (*see* Churches) Nos. 7 and 8, *c.* 1864 by *Henry Rice*, excellent examples of classical town houses, fronted in cement mortar, the ground floor rusticated. Flat pedimented porches, a Rice invention, and modillioned eaves brackets with turned ends. Next door in contrast is a plain commercial building, originally built by *Rice c.* 1864 for Blamey & Morcom, agricultural merchants.

For Rice enthusiasts there is much more to see, especially his terraced housing and villas to the W of the town centre. The most ambitious of the terraces, in a generally modest range, is DEAN TERRACE in New Road, W off Dean Street. This was a speculative project of 1838–47 born out of the mining boom, of plain classical style and external stuccoed consistency, but with interesting variations of plan and detail. Opposite are three of his best villas, INVERSAID, OAKDEAN and DEAN MEADOW, of the mid 1850s and with more architectural detail. Other more modest terraces are Nos. 1–8 MANLEY TERRACE, 1860, and Nos. 10–14 ASHPARK TERRACE, *c.* 1865, Station Road; Nos. 1–6 RUSSELL STREET, *c.* 1965; and Nos. 1–6 VARLEY TERRACE, Dean Street, 1853. One of his most charming buildings is WESTBOURNE LODGE, Dean Street, the lodge for WESTBOURNE HOUSE for which Rice designed a new S front in 1864. Finally, ¼ m. NE, No. 2 GREENBANK LANE, 1847–51, a modest stone villa, was Rice's own house and office.

LUXSTOWE MANOR (COUNCIL OFFICES), Greenbank Road. 1831–2 by *George Wightwick* for William Glencross, the Plymouth builder. Wightwick's essential romantic conception, in a castellated Tudor Gothic style with tall hexagonal and diamond chimneyshafts in groups, is just strong enough to have survived the multi-phase extensions that have spread over the site except for the original NE entrance and SE garden front elevations, which still make a dignified approach to the complex. NE elevation with a four-centred arch doorway, corbelled four-light oriel window over and tall finials on the angles. To the l. a tall gable-end with mullioned windows with four-centred arched lights and dated coat of arms to gable. SE front of 1:1:1:2 gabled bays with projecting l. wing. The interior retains good original detail including an open-well staircase, moulded and carved plasterwork, and Tudor Gothic doors and doorcases.

MOORSWATER VIADUCT, ¾ m. SW. One of the most spectacular and elegant of the Great Western Railway viaducts, even for Cornwall, 1881 by *P. J. Margary*, engineer. Seven tapering piers of snecked rock-faced slatestone and eight semicircular arches with granite voussoirs spanning the wide valley of the East Looe river at 147 ft (45 metres) high. Moulded corbel course with moulded stone brackets supporting an iron lattice parapet railing. The remains of the piers of the earlier viaduct of 1859 by *I. K. Brunel* stand alongside. The canal from Looe terminated on the site of the MOORSWATER INDUSTRIAL ESTATE, and was connected after 1846 with the railway from the Caradon copper mines and Minions quarries: some remains of LIMEKILNS, WAREHOUSES and COTTAGES.

HALBATHICK FARMHOUSE, 1½ m. N. A C16 former hall house and longhouse, rescued from dereliction in the late C20. Occupied 1655–88 by Thomas Mounce, a Quaker who remodelled the parlour wing as an occasional meeting house with accommodation for a visiting elder above. Probably the oldest purpose-adapted Quaker meeting place in Cornwall.

LITTLE PETHERICK

ST PETROC. The modest, mildly quirky exterior hardly suggests that this church is one of the architectural highlights of Cornwall: its scale is tiny, the nave roof has two full dormers, and the immediately striking feature is a life-size bronze monument visible through a window of the C20 chantry chapel on the path from the SE entrance to the churchyard. It tells an intriguing story of C19 and C20 high church patronage. In 1858 the modest C14 church was rebuilt by *William White* for Sir Hugh Molesworth, the Tractarian rector, with a new N aisle – the E bay Catacleuse, the rest granite. The Molesworths (*see* Pencarrow) were also patrons of the church, and from 1876 to 1898 another Molesworth was rector. In 1898 Athelstan Riley (later Seigneur de la Trinité, Jersey) became patron. To him we owe the introduction of *J. N. Comper* to the church. Comper restored it in a long campaign that started in 1908 and continued until 1947. He began with the ROOD SCREEN and LOFT across the aisle and nave, carved by *John Parsons* of St Teath and decorated under the supervision of *H. A. Bernard Smith*, with characteristically large rood and seraphim figures carved by *W. D. Gough* of London. Work continued with the addition of the RILEY CHANTRY CHAPEL in 1920 to commemorate the Hon. Mrs Andalusia Riley (*née* Molesworth) with her rich bronze MONUMENT and a C17 Flemish RELIEF behind. In 1947 Comper added the High Altar REREDOS and the Lady Chapel ALTAR and REREDOS. Comper also designed the organ loft gallery at the W end and gave the church (except the chancel) plaster panelled roofs. It is an ensemble of some of his finest work, the realization of a Puginesque vision in miniature, the scale perfectly judged for such a constrained space with rich colours and fine craftsmanship, the effect astonishing. Compare this with Comper's very different, but equally accomplished, simple calm Gothic at St Michael, Newquay. – FONT. C15, plain. – BENCH-ENDS. Some C16, usual motifs. – STAINED GLASS. Chancel E by *Comper*, 1908. – S aisle windows by *Edwin Horwood* of Frome, 1870s. – SEPULCHRAL SLAB. C13 in Purbeck marble to Sir Roger Lemporn ('gist ici') with a foliated cross and a human head above it. – Catacleuse ANGEL CORBEL on S side of the tower, just like those at St Merryn (q.v.), and CORBEL in the sanctuary to the N of the altar, brought by Molesworth from St Constantine. In the churchyard, three features dating from William White's restoration: SOUTH EAST GATEWAY of a pair of gatepiers, gates and tapered coffin rest, the piers summated by C15 crocketed pinnacles; the SOUTH GATEWAY with a single wrought-iron gate between square piers; and to the N, above the church, a reset C15 Catacleuse stone ARCH with a C15 crocketed finial surmounted by a small Celtic cross.

The narrow ROAD BRIDGE to the E of the church is of 1820, with dressed stone segmented arch and key block. Immediately N of the bridge, the VILLAGE HALL and CARETAKER'S COTTAGE, 1907 datestone, designed by or for Athelstan Riley. A charming sub-Arts and Crafts design, the slate roof continued over a deep veranda with diagonal glazing, well-carved bargeboards of C15 character, and a small carved figure of St Petroc in a niche at the apex of the gable. Immediately W of the church, a pair of pretty mid-C19 mirror-image COTTAGES with gabled porches, cusped bargeboards, crested ridge tiles, and diagonally set brick shafts to the shared central chimneystack.

MOLESWORTH MANOR. Dated 1854. The former rectory, by *William White* for Sir Hugh Molesworth. A large confident house in Gothic style, the front elevation an especially pleasing composition: it was designed as asymmetrical, with a tall gabled bay at the l. end set slightly forward and the gabled entrance porch to its r. In the early C20 it was extended with a cross-wing in similar style built on to the l. end, and two bay windows were added to the front elevation. Three gabled dormers in its steeply pitched roof (cf. Bank House, St Columb Major) with fish-scale slate-hanging. Good Gothick plasterwork frieze in the hall and a handsome open-well stair with irregularly alternating barley-sugar twist, turned and moulded balusters, and moulded rail. The stair window incorporates the Molesworth arms and initials and date.

At the head of Petherick Creek, 1 m. N, an impressive three-span steel VIADUCT of 1899 that carried the railway from Wadebridge to Padstow. On the S side of the creek, SEA MILLS. Quay, slip, retaining walls and sea walls of the millpond for a former tide mill of the C18 or earlier. It ceased operation when the viaduct restricted access to the mill.

LIZARD LIGHTHOUSE see LANDEWEDNACK

LOOE

So steep and thickly wooded are the river valley approaches to Looe that the sudden appearance of the twin towns, joined by their bridge across the estuary below Looe Pool, comes as a surprise. Built facing each other rather than the sea, these are the medieval boroughs of East and West Looe which notoriously sent no fewer than four members to Parliament before the Reform Act, and whose contrasting yet complementary character has drawn visitors for centuries.

Looe was one of the busiest medieval ports in the south-west until overtaken by Fowey and Plymouth, its fleet large enough to provide ships for the Crown on thirteen occasions during the C14. A small medieval settlement 1 m. E inland at Shutta was soon overtaken by East Looe whose principal charter was granted in 1320: although the earthworks and walls of its barbican have vanished its medieval plan of narrow streets is strikingly intact with a C16 guildhall and some of the best early town houses with timber-framed fronts in Cornwall. West Looe's layout is different but just as well preserved, essentially a small hub of streets by the river from which one long medieval street, also rich in early buildings, leads westwards uphill. Both settlements were recorded in C16 surveys as inhabited by wealthy merchants whose trade was based on tin exports and imports of wine from Gascony, salt from Spain, and timber and tar from the Hanseatic ports, further boosted by the development of the Newfoundland trade in that century. Even so their churches remained chapels of ease to St Martin-by-Looe and Talland until 1845.

Looe saw major expansion in the C19 when it became the main outlet for copper and granite from the rich mining area N of Liskeard, while importing coal, building materials, manure and limestone. The construction of the Liskeard & Looe Union Canal in 1827 and the completion of the railway link to Liskeard in 1860 were complemented by the extension of the harbour quays to handle the vastly increased tonnage. In the late C19 tourism started to flourish, with the railway now carrying passenger traffic and sea excursions from Plymouth and other south-west ports; hotels, guest houses and villas had begun to appear on the steep hillsides above both towns. By the end of the century East Looe had a grand new guildhall and a rebuilt church, while in West Looe the construction of the Hannafore Viaduct had enabled a planned development of the promontory overlooking Looe Island, and a new road had been opened to Polperro. The C20 was not kind to Looe's dramatic setting, especially its skylines,

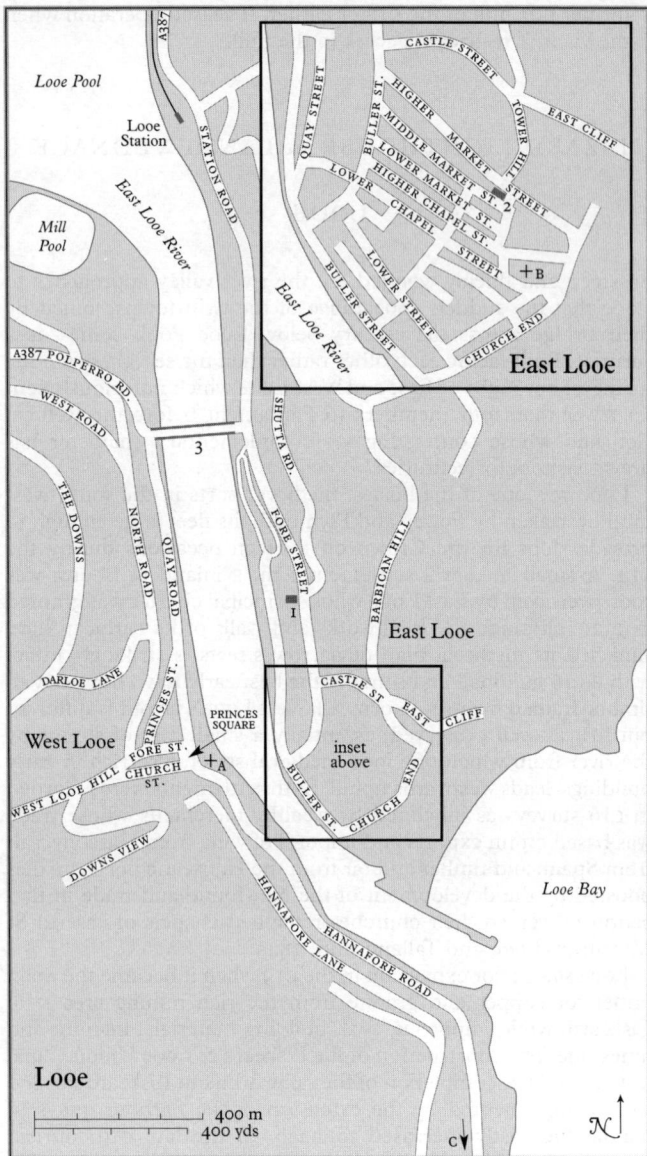

Looe Pool

Looe Station

East Looe River

Mill Pool

A387 POLPERRO RD.

WEST ROAD

THE DOWNS

DARLOE LANE

West Looe

WEST LOOE HILL

DOWNS VIEW

STATION ROAD

NORTH ROAD

QUAY ROAD

PRINCES ST.

FORE ST.

CHURCH ST.

PRINCES SQUARE

+A

3

SHUTTA RD.

FORE STREET

1

East Looe River

BARBICAN HILL

East Looe

CASTLE ST. EAST CLIFF

inset above

BULLER ST. CHURCH END

HANNAFORE ROAD

HANNAFORE LANE

Looe Bay

Looe

400 m
400 yds

C

N

QUAY STREET

CASTLE STREET

HIGHER MARKET STREET

BULLER ST.

MIDDLE MARKET ST.

LOWER MARKET ST.

TOWER HILL

EAST CLIFF

2

HIGHER CHAPEL ST.

LOWER CHAPEL STREET

LOWER STREET

BULLER STREET

CHURCH END

+B

East Looe Street

East Looe River

East Looe

A	St Nicholas, West Looe	1	Guildhall
B	St Mary, East Looe (former)	2	Museum
C	Site of St Michael's (Lammana) Chapel	3	Bridge

but in recent decades a revived fishing industry has brought new buildings to East Looe's waterfront and sustained the working harbour that has always been its *raison d'être*.

CHURCHES AND PUBLIC BUILDINGS

St Nicholas, West Looe. Very small and picturesquely sited on the waterfront, the eyecatcher from across the water its slim C14 tower surmounted by a late C19 Italianate cupola. Endowed as a chapel of ease to Talland before 1330, it was used after the Reformation as guildhall, prison and school before being restored as the parish church in 1852. Later restorations in 1862 and, sensitively, by *E. H. Sedding* in 1915–17. Of the early building a possibly C12 round-headed W door and similar door to return wall of tower, C13 lancet above W doorway and C14 PISCINA. The S wall and windows partly C15, rebuilt in 1917. C16 wagon roof to nave and chancel, of five bays with curved feet to the trusses (cf. the Museum, East Looe), the tie-beams inserted in 1917. Three-bay N aisle arcade with posts and braces of timbers from one of Napoleon's battleships, *St Joseph*. – Good late C19 and C20 furnishings include PEWS in N aisle and FONT SCREEN by *Violet Pinwill* and her school; later C20 carving by *Rev. John Harvey* in the same late medieval style.

St Mary, Church End, East Looe. Former parish church, inelegantly converted to residential use in the late C20. A chapel was dedicated on this site by Bishop Bronescombe in 1259. The present building has a C15 tower surmounted by a parapet on moulded corbels; the rest was rebuilt 1882–3 in Plymouth limestone in a harsh and dull Gothic style by *Edwin J. Munt*.

St Michael's (Lammana) Chapel, ¾ m. SW of West Looe. Foundations of a small C12 chapel, a cell of Glastonbury Abbey and a pair with the site of the chapel on the summit of Looe Island opposite, both rebuilds of earlier sites. Nave and chancel 35 ft (10.7 metres) long and 16 ft (4.9 metres) wide, with S porch. It was abandoned at the Reformation. The fragmentary remains of a wall with slit windows, possibly part of a monastic building, survive 200 yds SE.

Guildhall, Fore Street, East Looe. 1877 by *J. P. Gould* of Barnstaple. The landmark building of the town, a substantial and successful essay in the Gothic Revival style and an imposing composition, the tall hall range raised over the ground floor with pointed arched openings, the adjoining clock tower rising to a machiolated cornice and very steep pyramidal roof with weather vane and hipped dormers with finials to each face. The clock is 1880.

Museum, Higher Market Street, East Looe. The former guildhall. Probably C16, remodelled in the C17, restored 1972. A first-floor hall (cf. Fowey) accessed by external stairs under a pentice roof. Late C17 three-light oak mullioned windows to first floor, much C16 and C17 carpentry, some reused. Above the ground-floor windows the truncated corbels of a former pentice roof. Two small barred windows in the SE end wall. The C16 roof has high morticed collars, trenched purlins and slightly curved feet to the trusses (cf. St Nicholas, West Looe). Magistrate's bench of 1705 with bolection-moulded panelling and coat of arms above dated 1705, painted on boards.

BRIDGE, across the estuary. 1853, of seven bays with segmented aches. It replaced the early C15 bridge (earlier than Wade-bridge) described by Defoe in 1724 as 'beautiful and stately', of fifteen arches. This stood 100 yds seaward of the present bridge, its position marked by a stone in Fore Street, East Looe, recording its repair in 1689.

PERAMBULATIONS

1. East Looe

The core of the old town is best enjoyed after the harbour and seafront have been explored. Starting from the bridge, the fish quay with its FISH MARKET, 1988 by *Bartram Deakin Associates*, and PACKING SHEDS, 1990, honest workmanlike buildings which sit well with the tall and robust C19 granite warehouses beyond, tactfully converted to commercial use. The length of the quay stretching seaward offers some sense of the scale of the harbour at its C19 peak, ending in BULLER QUAY, 1860, and BANJO PIER, 1896 by *Joseph Thomas*,★ so called because of its shape. The pier also shelters East Cliffe beach, protected at its E end by finely conceived COAST PROTECTION WORKS of 1974, of monolithic tiered pre-cast concrete blocks with steps between, both functional and sculptural. Behind the seafront in Church End the Italianate former WATCH TOWER and LIFEBOAT SHED of *c.* 1860 with exaggerated projecting eaves.

Inland from this point the more intimate character of the early town is immediately apparent and its narrow streets repay close study. The buildings range widely in type, materials and construction, style, and date, and are closely packed into the medieval layout behind QUAY STREET and BULLER STREET in five parallel streets: from W to E LOWER STREET, LOWER CHAPEL STREET, HIGHER CHAPEL STREET, LOWER MARKET STREET and MIDDLE MARKET STREET. Among the most interesting C16–C17 building types are: houses where the living accommodation is raised above former fish cellars and sometimes accessed by external stairs (cf. St Ives); merchants' houses of mixed construction sometimes jettied out over the street (cf. Fowey); early houses with C18 or C19 fronts; and more substantial town houses with stone rather than timber fronts. There is much good C16 and C17 detail, worth looking for even when later alteration has obscured most of

---

★ He had assisted with the construction of Looe Bridge, worked on the harbours at Mevagissey and St Ives and was also engaged in the Bovisand and Crownhill forts of the Plymouth defences. Outside Cornwall he worked on St Katharine Dock in London.

the original. The finest jettied house is LANTAU, Higher Chapel Street, three-storey on a double-depth plan with canted oriel windows on carved brackets to the first floor, pentice roof over and good interior fittings. For detail a good example is the FISHERMANS ARMS, Higher Market Street, with steep twin gables carried on moulded oak corbels: the ground floor has a chamfered early C17 oak doorway with original panelled door flanked by two-light mullioned windows and a second-floor chamber with a 1611 date in plasterwork. The oldest jettied building is the C16 YE OLD COTTAGE, Middle Market Street. Of the more prestigious stone houses, the best is CHURCH HOUSE, Higher Chapel Street, with a C16 four-centred arch doorway with hoodmould with labels, and a similar hood-mould with shorter labels over the l. window. In a small compass it is one of the richest assemblages of early urban building in Cornwall and offers the most delightful variety of street scenes.

Finally into FORE STREET where the scale of building is larger, later, or refronted. The OLD SALUTATION INN is a smaller C17 survival, remodelled in the C18 with an incised stucco front on a timber frame with rusticated quoins and central pilastered doorway. The mock timber framing on the front of DOWLING & BAY disguises an early merchant's house, with a 1666 inscription. Opposite is the most recognizable of the former merchants' houses, the GOLDEN GUINEA RESTAURANT. Early C17, the first floor with two wide canted oriel windows on brackets of six lights and sidelights with moulded sills, transoms and mullions and central king mullions. Stud and panel screen to l. of central passage; in the room to the r. a moulded plaster ceiling cornice with trailing vine. First-floor chamber has plaster panel in crude relief with figures and angel, plants and beasts with inscription 'To obey is better than sacrifice EEE'. Another plaster relief in the same room dated 1652.

2. West Looe

Best approached by ferry from East Looe, a quieter and simpler place than its busy neighbour. From the water good views of the 1930s quays towards the bridge with the mostly C19 buildings of QUAY ROAD behind, and seawards towards HAN-NAFORE ROAD, the VIADUCT of 1895 by *Joseph Thomas* of three bays of elegant segmental arches built against the cliff and terminating each end in turrets corbelled out at the top. Also best appreciated from across the water the former COAST-GUARD STATION AND COTTAGES, North Road, a distinctive symmetrical composition of eight houses in Plymouth lime-stone around a central carriage entrance under a projecting gable with similar end gables.

The heart of West Looe is the cluster of small streets behind the church and FORE STREET, with much of interest in the long climb up WEST LOOE HILL towards Portloe. Many good examples of small C18 and C19 houses and cottages, mixed in with more substantial three-storey mid-C19 town houses around PRINCES SQUARE and the lower part of Fore Street. In Princes Square, the JOLLY SAILOR INN, the lower range C16 and C17 with a large front lateral stack, on a three-room cross-passage plan. The charming former BUTTER MARKET, datestone 1853, of hexagonal plan rising to a central bellcote, is the appropriately diminutive centrepiece of this intimately scaled town centre. Among the earliest houses are the three-storey C17 ELIZA COTTAGE with a slate-hung timber-framed front, originally jettied, and among the more substantial later properties the late C18 DARLOE, set back above the street with a three-window symmetrical front around a central round-headed doorway with spoked fanlight, and under a hipped roof. Several buildings display large C17 lateral or end chimneystacks. The climb to the top of the street gives good views back into the town and across the estuary to East Looe.

GRADNA, Plaidy, East Looe. 1930. Modernist house sited on the cliff top, crisply designed as a tall three-storey block with windows set at the corners. Commissioned by the Wills (tobacco) family and reputedly by an unknown French architect. Virtually rebuilt 1992–2002.

LOSTWITHIEL

Lostwithiel is the most unassuming of Cornwall's major historic towns, but among the most rewarding. Secluded in the deep wooded valley of the Fowey, it is still so remarkably compact that the visitor comes across it suddenly and unannounced via modern suburbs. Its clearly defined plan of small medieval streets and burgage plots, the graceful and omnipresent spire of the C13–C14 parish church, and a subtle blend of pre-C20 buildings and townscape in a small compass result in a town of exceptionally coherent and richly engaging character.

This modest place was the epicentre of power in C14 Cornwall, for Lostwithiel lies only a short distance from the Norman castle of Restormel, and it was the Cardinhams of Restormel who first developed the town out of the mother parish of Lanlivery sometime between 1086 and 1189. The settlement evolved from a single street, Fore Street, into the grid pattern between Fore Street and North Street, with Queen Street at its western end and the river to the east. This was the lowest bridging point of the Fowey, where the road from Liskeard to St Austell could cross, so was the ideal site to develop a port for the medieval tin industry on Bodmin Moor – Lostwithiel ranked seventh of all English ports for the value of its export trade in the customs return of 1203–5. The town was granted to Richard Earl of Cornwall in 1260 but it was during his son Edmund's earldom (1272–99) that Lostwithiel became the administrative and commercial capital of Cornwall, and its major buildings – the church, the Duchy Palace and the bridge – date from this time. This was the town's high point: there were periods over the next few centuries when, as the headquarters of the duchy, Lostwithiel was the only town in Cornwall where tin could be assayed, stamped and weighed for export.

But what had given Lostwithiel its *raison d'être* also aided its eventual decline, as the streaming of tin upstream on the moor contributed to the gradual silting up of the Fowey estuary. Although Leland in 1542 could still describe Lostwithiel as the shire town of Cornwall, he also remarked that 'by the shire hall appear ruins of ancient buildings, a house of the Duke of Cornwall'. Norden in 1584 and Carew in 1602 both noted its continuing demise, and it suffered badly during the Civil War when in 1644 the Parliamentarians under the Earl of Essex first took and then were besieged in the town. Many buildings, including the church and Duchy Palace, were extensively damaged. After the Civil War there seems to have been some revival in the town's fortunes, now based on tanning and wool as well as tin, as several late C17 datestones suggest.

It was not until the advent of the Edgcumbes of Mount Edgcumbe from 1730 that Lostwithiel regained something of its former prestige. Between 1730 and 1781 the Cornmarket, Guildhall and Grammar School were constructed under Edgcumbe patronage, as well as the Edgcumbe's own town house. But after the Reform Act of 1832, the Edgcumbes lost interest in Lostwithiel and the town seems to have gone quietly to sleep: even the arrival of the Cornwall Railway Company with its carriage works in 1859 did little to alter its essential character. The greatest and most beneficial C20 change was the construction of a new bridge in 1939 that by-passed the heart of the town, though Queen Street still suffers grievously because it now takes all the through traffic. That apart, one can still explore Lostwithiel and find hardly a single jarring note.

St Bartholomew. A church of outstanding interest, and in a style very untypical of Cornwall: commentators' references to Breton influence seem apt. Its C14 spire, 'the glory of Cornwall' to *G. E. Street* who skilfully repaired it in 1883, is a presence that permeates the whole town and acts as a constant reference point in any perambulation. And its striking interior – simple, lofty and dignified C14 – is very different from the standard C15 and C16 Cornish church. The tower with its lancet windows is clearly C13: through its base a public way passed (as one does at St Columb Major still) until 1878. The spire was added in the early C14 with the interposition of a bold, ruthless transition from square to octagon, an extraordinarily skilled achievement. It is broached and has lucarnes on four of its eight sides. Round its foot is an octagonal screen with on each side double lights, quatrefoil tracery and a gable. The double lights are divided horizontally (transom fashion) by a panel of four

28

p. 324

Lostwithiel, St Bartholomew. Lithograph, 1850

diapers. The NE side has a wheel (St Catherine) motif instead.
The body of the church, with nave of four bays, N and S aisle,
chancel with narrower and lower arcades, and S porch, is C14
too, though later than the spire: in the same unusual style and
plan as Fowey lower down the river. The great E window of
five lights is one of the most sumptuous in Cornwall, evidently
of the same date as the spire with trefoils and quatrefoils,
mostly round but also pointed. The S doorway, with colonettes
with shaft-rings and hoodmould on two head corbels, also
looks C14.

The nave arcade piers are octagonal and have no capitals,
the arches are double chamfered, and the clerestory, a rarity
in Cornwall, has groups of three lancet windows placed in line
with the spandrels, not with the apexes of the arches (cf. also
St Germans, Callington and Fowey). Not all is quite as it first
seems, however. The E end of the N aisle was originally separated from the chancel by a solid wall, replaced in 1775 by an
arch to match the five bays of the S arcade; the N aisle may
post-date the S aisle, the E wall of the former being set back

from the continuous build of the chancel and s aisle. Following damage from an explosion during the Civil War, the nave roof was replaced at a lower level than originally (the earlier pitch visible as a scar on the tower's E face) and the clerestory windows lowered. There was a major campaign of restoration in 1879 by *Joseph Clarke*, however, when all the roofs were renewed, the w gallery and pews removed, the church re-floored throughout and the passage through the tower closed. The E window of the N aisle is an addition of 1843; the plain square-headed windows are from a later C19 restoration. The vestry was added in 1893.

The FONT displays the pre-eminence of C14 Lostwithiel, 33 octagonal and of outstanding quality. On the bowl, panels with carved figures: from the E, Crucifixion, hunter with hawk, lions, grotesque animal head, square with geometric figures, dog and hare, square with geometric figures, and a bishop. The style of the carving is so metropolitan it reminds one that the Earls of Cornwall were at one time challengers for the throne. Only the Crucifixion is of a distinctly inferior quality, perhaps recarved later. For the date of the font the tracery panels are instructive: their use of ogees makes a pre-C14 date impossible. – ALMS BOX. Oak, 1645, in the shape of a sturdy figure with shield, folk art, inscribed *W. T. Maier*. – ALABASTER PANEL. Flaying of St Bartholomew. – PULPIT by *Harry Hems*, 1880: he also undertook the carvings of the new ceiling. – STAINED GLASS. After two previous interventions in 1843 and 1864, the great E window was reglazed by *Clayton & Bell* in 1886. Crucifixion above the entombment, of high quality and worthy of its setting. – N aisle: easternmost windows by *Wailes*, next window near N door by *Thomas Willement*, 1848, Faith, Hope and Charity. – S aisle E end: window by *Wailes*, next by *Clayton & Bell*, next by *Hardman*. – MONUMENTS. Brass of Tristram Curteys 1423 on N wall, esquire in armour. Also two pretty Elizabethan wall tablets and Neoclassical monuments, for example to Thomas Hall †1806 by *J. Bedford* of London, Lieutenant Hawkey †1809 by *Robert Isbell* of Stonehouse, and Jane Mickel †1824 by *Edward Shepherd* of Plymouth. In the outer S wall between porch and tower, two sepulchral recesses, opened in 1890. – CHURCHYARD. Medieval CROSS (cf. Launceston) on C19 shaft, a lantern with crocketed gablet and pinnacles, with figures on all four sides including a Crucifixion and Virgin and Child. Several good table tombs, e.g. William Taprell near S door, and many finely carved slate headstones of the C18 and C19, e.g. against the E wall of the chancel.

DUCHY PALACE, Fore Street and Quay Street. The enigmatic remains of buildings that served as the administrative centre of the duchy and commanded the port when Lostwithiel was at its C13–C15 peak.* To anyone expecting a palace, first

p. 326

*This account is indebted to N.J.G. Pounds, 'The Duchy Palace at Lostwithiel, Cornwall', *Archaeological Journal* 136 (1979), pp. 203–17, and Eric Berry, *Convocation Hall*, Cornwall Buildings Preservation Trust (2009).

Lostwithiel, Duchy Palace. Engraving by S. and N. Buck, 1774

impressions disappoint: on the corner of Fore Street and Quay Street is a much altered but substantial medieval building followed to the s by a range (now divided into five separate properties) mixing ancient and modern fabric. Evidence for its medieval appearance can be discerned from a Buck engraving of 1743,[*] which shows a ruinous great hall of eight strongly buttressed bays, longer than Dartington Hall Devon, with a rose window set high in the N gable wall and a smaller roofed building with narrow lancet windows immediately to the N, its front elevation set back from the main building line.[†] This smaller building survives substantially intact and later became successively the Convocation Hall where the Stannary Court met, the office of the Duchy of Cornwall between 1852 and 1873, and a Masonic Hall from 1878 until 2008. It is of immensely solid and heavily buttressed construction, originally three storeys above a barrel-vaulted undercroft (probably a wine cellar), the floor of which is now 4 ft (1.2 metres) below street level. The N elevation to Fore Street has blocked openings at first and second floor below a later stack with a shaped granite cap and has a C19 door to the undercroft; there is also a carved stone coat of arms with fifteen besants in pile, flanked by lions. So the elevation to Quay Street comes as a surprise, the result of the building's conversion to the Duchy offices when the second floor was removed, two large Gothic windows inserted, and the N gable hipped. The porch was added when the Masons took on the building and the windows were also reglazed with Masonic glass. But one of the narrow lancet windows shown by Buck survives blocked between the two C19 windows and others, also blocked, with cusped heads, survive in the rear wall. That this building was added to the Great Hall is confirmed by the survival of the Great Hall's rose window

---

[*] It is likely that this drawing is based on an earlier depiction of the building as it appeared after the Civil War.
[†] The set-back is exaggerated by Buck's perspective.

inside the present s gable-end, its originally external outer frame now internal. The roof is *c.* 1620, evidence of a major reconstruction following the Great Hall's demise. What was its original purpose? Its massive construction and originally almost windowless elevations suggest a secure strongroom, perhaps used as the Duchy treasury.

The rest of the remains of the Great Hall have been absorbed in other buildings on Quay Street. The stretch of wall incorporating No. 8 (Old Palace Antiques and Palace Printers) is easily recognizable from Buck's engraving as part of the Great Hall's E wall. It contains the vaulted arched passage which carried the Cob Brook under the building, another former passageway marked by a blocked arch in the COINAGE HALL, and the remnants of two buttresses or walls probably enclosing a forecourt. Set back from this medieval building line is the DEBTORS' PRISON, probably a mid-C18 conversion of an earlier part-reconstruction, whose barred cell windows at second-floor level are still visible. It shares the original rear wall of the Great Hall with SHIRE HALL; its front elevation on the street line is incongruously clad in artificial stone.

GUILDHALL AND CORNMARKET, Fore Street. Erected, as the datestone on the front records, by Richard Edgcumbe in 1740, remarkably early for Cornwall. The Guildhall was placed over the (formerly open) arcade of the ground-floor Cornmarket; the latter was converted into the town museum in 1971. The former town prison is at the rear. The Guildhall is splendidly fitted out with fielded dado panelling and reused linenfold with a deep, coved plaster cornice. At the W end is the central mayoral seat with flanking benches on a raised dais, enriched with mid-C18 pilasters and broken pediment with dentils and egg-and-dart mouldings.

PERAMBULATION. It is worth starting from the medieval BRIDGE and walking to its eastern end to enjoy the view back into the town. From here there is still some sense of medieval Lostwithiel gathered tightly around the spire of the parish church and comfortably set against the steeply rising hills to the W. The course of the Fowey has altered considerably over the centuries and the bridge is now much reduced from its original form. The five pointed-arch W spans, however, are impressive and rare survivals of the narrow medieval crossing, probably dating from major repair and restoration in 1437 to an earlier core; the parapets were added in 1676. Next E are a round arch and its diminutive neighbour, probably C18 rebuildings, then a small island, and beyond, two further C18 arches that replaced a timber bridge. The eastern edge of the bridge leads to the C20 brick STATION building which replaced the original of 1859 by *Brunel*. Dominant on the E riverside are the remains of the GWR carriage works, possibly to designs by Brunel. Long range, part single- part two-storeyed, in stone with brick dressings to round-headed openings and continuous ridge ventilator, its muscular character successfully complemented by extensive but tactful infilling during conversion by *Tony Howes*, 1999–2005.

Now return across the bridge to the town and follow along the riverside into THE PARADE and MONMOUTH SQUARE which have good groups of modest early to mid-C19 houses. Forming an eccentric but not unhappy point-in-view at the bottom of Fore Street is a DRILL HALL of 1914–18. Opposite, running s from the corner of Fore Street along QUAY STREET from the Masonic Hall to Shire House, are the remains of the Duchy Palace (*see* above), even in its battered and fragmentary form evocative of its former grandeur. Further along Quay Street are mostly modest C19 houses, the best being NORWAY HOUSE, all granite ashlar. Also two early C19 LIMEKILNS.

Return along Quay Street as far as the Duchy Palace and pass under the arch next to Palace Printers into SOUTH STREET, where huge granite slabs have been used to culvert the former Cob Brook under the building and right up the street. It is possible to see something of the burgage plots leading back from Fore Street, and something too of the complex building history of the houses behind their mainly C18 and C19 fronts. From the junction of South Street and Church Lane there is one of the best views of the church tower and spire soaring above the modest scale of the street and its houses.

Now into FORE STREET, the heart of the town and its best street. Betjeman's assessment that this street 'spans the whole gamut of English domestic and public architecture for six hundred years' is not wide of the mark if one starts with the Duchy Palace (*see* above) at the E end and works slowly up to Queen Street at the W end. What is so engaging is the endlessly varying treatment of frontages: Nos. 1–5, for example, show render, slate cladding, granite and brick successively, with much surviving C18 joinery and glazing and good C19 shop-fronts. In the churchyard, BOSEGLOS (No. 29), a mid-C18 house enlarged in the mid C19 and then extended by *G. E. Street* in the 1890s as the verger's cottage: the gabled Street addition slightly set back with ground-floor Gothic window with trefoil head and a delightful Venetian porch, its triple lancet window with diminutive colonnettes and corbels. Opposite the W side of the churchyard the former WORKING MAN'S INSTITUTE, an unlikely but characterful contribution to the street scene. Founded 1872, rebuilt 1890 by *Skantlebury* in a cheerful combination of red brick with yellow brick dressing. On the corner of Church Lane No. 9, datestone 1688 TBA. There are many late C18 to mid-C19 fronts to earlier (late C17 and early C18) houses e.g. Nos. 10, 15, 17, 24–26 and 34, mostly with double-depth plans. Nos. 11 and 12 are among the grandest in the street: late C17 five-window front with central door and fanlight, revamped in the late C18 with good C18 and early C19 interior and fittings.

The street ends with a grand mid-C18 granite flourish thanks to the Edgcumbes who erected both their town house here and the civic buildings of the Guildhall and Cornmarket opposite (*see* above). EDGCUMBE HOUSE incorporates the remains of the former mansion of the Taprell family, mayors of Lostwithiel in the later C17 and early C18. Their house formerly extended the whole length of the burgage plot between Fore Street and North Street. The Edgcumbe house is of five bays, of small scale but fine quality, in ashlar granite with moulded plinth and cornice returned at both ends. The central double doors are probably mid-C19 but the interior has a sustained show of high-quality mid-C18 joinery and plasterwork. Double-depth plan. The r. hand room on the ground floor, now the mayor's parlour, is the showpiece, the panelling here enriched with egg-and-dart, the ceiling with a modillion cornice and foliage, doorcase with pulvinated frieze and a marble fireplace with shell cartouche above: a fine example of a provincial best chamber of the period. Elegant C18 open-well stair in rear stair-tower. Behind (and now accessed from North Street) the older block, TAPRELL HOUSE, is an impressive survival from the C16 and C17, including on the ground floor a full-width kitchen chimney and a curious large granite block below a window in the E wall with three funnel-like bowls or sinks: their function is unclear. On the first floor a substantial garderobe with window and stone seat. Sensitively repaired and converted by *John Carter* in 1993 to provide a public library and a small Methodist chapel.

Next to Edgcumbe House is the simpler DOWER HOUSE, another mid-C18 front block of double-depth plan with an earlier range behind. Ground-floor rooms with C18 panelling and cornice and a similar C18 open-well stair to rear. The back range probably incorporates parts of the C17 buildings that originally formed part of the Taprell house; the exact relationship between the buildings is far from clear.

Uphill to the corner of Fore Street, the KINGS ARMS HOTEL, owned by the Taprells in the C17, rebuilt *c.* 1800. Despite the traffic it is worth a brief excursion into QUEEN STREET. Closing Fore Street's view is No. 8 Queen Street, a good C18 house with broad five-bay front but rendered over rubble walls, cornice, hipped roof and heavily moulded dormers: it has a similar double-depth plan to Edgcumbe House, with the stair-tower at the rear. On the E side, a house with the datestone 1682 STE, and finally on the W side the imposing granite front of the OLD GRAMMAR SCHOOL. Another Edgcumbe gift to the town, this time by George Edgcumbe, 1781. Well set back from the street in a small forecourt with little side gates to former classrooms. Smart symmetrical front of ashlar granite of 1:3:1 bays, with the three central bays broken forward and a ground-floor arcade of three round arches. Only the façade was retained in the redevelopment for housing by *Marshman, Warren & Taylor* in 1981. Back N along Queen Street past the former BANK CHAPEL, ambitiously built for the Methodists in 1900 in a collision of Gothic and classical styles by *Sampson Hill*. Converted to housing in 1987.

Now up DUKE STREET to the ROYAL OAK, behind which is KING STREET. The Royal Oak, the terraced houses to both sides of King Street and the former chapel at the N end are a small early C19 artisan suburb, another example of Edgcumbe patronage.

Anywhere up the steeply rising Duke Street and then BODMIN HILL affords glimpses of more C19 terraces and fine views across the town. Further up Bodmin Hill, LOSTWITHIEL SCHOOL. Built *c.* 1870 with classroom and headmasters house of later C19, a good example of a Victorian school where the functions of the buildings are still clear and the later C19 additions contribute positively to the asymmetrical Gothic style.

Return down Bodmin Hill to Queen Street and then into NORTH STREET, one of the original medieval streets with a good range of mostly modest C18–C19 houses. The OLD MALT HOUSE has a datestone of 1658 recording Walter Kendall's 3,000-year lease. No. 16 opposite has fragments of a medieval window in the front wall. The best group is Nos. 21–25, three good town houses opposite the church: No. 21 (WOODCLOSE), No. 22 with red encaustic tile-decorated Gothic tympani, and No. 23 (LOWENNA HOUSE), the former vicarage, six window front in ashlar granite with good late C18 panelling and cornices – a classy provincial finale.

Prominent on the skyline E of the town is PEREGRINE HALL, formerly St Faith's House of the Sisters of Mercy (closed 1948, now a house). Founded in 1862 on land given by the Robartes of Lanhydrock as a penitentiary 'for girls and women who have strayed from the paths of virtue'.

Built by *G. E. Street*, in three phases, the original and best is the three-storey centre block of 1864. Grey slatestone with Bath stone dressings. A strong, even severe, asymmetrical composition with square-headed windows randomly placed, articulated by heavy buttresses and a large chimneyshaft now truncated at eaves level. It culminates at the E end in a large canted bay to the ground and first floors, dramatically reinforced by a central buttress rising to an overhanging gable at second-floor level, marking the original chapel which has larger windows. The whole effect is hard, austere, angular and original, genuine Victorian rather than re-interpreted Gothic. Less happy the treatment of the ground-floor chapel, added to the E *c.* 1870. In the later C20 its E.E. windows were either blocked or enlarged. Inside, the impressively scaled crown-post roof has been ceiled over and the E window by *Clayton & Bell* has been removed. Only delicately coloured tilework of angel musicians, St George and the Dragon etc. survives. Quieter domestic-scale W extension of 1875 in yellow slatestone with simple windows.

LUDGVAN

St Ludgvan and St Paul. Fine C15 w tower of three stages
in granite blocks with buttresses set back from the angles and
panelled pinnacles corbelled out on angel heads with gargoyles
between, all reminiscent of Breage. The tower arch inside has
panelled jambs. The rest of the church was extensively restored
and partially rebuilt 1912 by *H. J. Wadling of St Aubyn &
Wadling*, e.g. the completely new s arcade and new openings
in the walls between chancel and s chancel chapel, and chapel
and s aisle; it was so harshly treated then (or in a previous
restoration of 1840) that the character of the interior is unexpectedly austere. s aisle of four bays, n aisle of six, the piers
with four major and four minor shafts. Two blocked windows,
possibly C12, in s wall of chancel. – FONT. A C19 copy of a
Norman design. – MONUMENTS. Slate to John South †1636
and family, very appealingly infantile. – Christopher Borlase
†1749. Brass plate with fine engraved script. ('By the smallness
of this table / judge not, Reader, of the loss which it deplores',
etc.). – Also memorials to William Borlase, the great Cornish
antiquarian, rector 1720–72, and the parents of Sir Humphry
Davy. – Three WAYSIDE CROSSES in the churchyard, and a
CROSS-SHAFT with Hiberno-Saxon knotwork built into the
steps of the belfry.

HOGUS HOUSE, formerly the rectory, opposite the church
behind high walls. Late C18 with early C19 alterations. Symmetrical five-window s front, two-storey over basement. C18
reception rooms and early C19 open-string stair.

CASTLE AN DINAS, 2 m. NW. The outer three of four roughly
circular and concentric prehistoric circuits enclosing the top
of the rounded hill are probably elements of a later Iron Age
HILLFORT, but the inner one, a low stony bank, is possibly a
Late Neolithic or Early Bronze Age HILLTOP ENCLOSURE
with the low central mound possibly a Bronze Age CAIRN. The
second circuit from the centre is a fallen vertically faced stone
wall; the third a stone and earth bank; and the fourth and most
substantial, on the w side only, a rampart with external ditch.
ROGERS' TOWER, a square castle-like folly constructed in
1798, has an arched opening to the SE, facing Mount's Bay – to
be appreciated from John Rogers's home at Treassowe.

LUXULYAN

St Ciricius and St Julitta. A large all granite church, especially impressive for the huge ashlar blocks of the tower and
the remarkably even surface of the E end. A chapel of Lanlivery
by *c.* 1150, rebuilt in the C15 and early C16 with W tower, nave

and chancel, N and S aisles and S porch. The three-stage tower rises without buttresses to an embattled parapet without pinnacles and a very tall embattled NE stair-turret; the whole effect is rather military-looking. The S porch is also battlemented with an exceptionally handsome tracery-panelled pointed tunnel-vault inside, uncommon in Cornwall (cf. Creed, St Cuby, St Germans). Above the door an image niche with cusped head and brattished top, and three turrets carved below. The interior has N and S aisles of six bays and very similar design, both with standard Cornish piers and the same arch mouldings, except the two E piers of the N aisle which have slightly different capitals. The wagon roofs of the N and S aisles are substantially intact with carved bosses, the nave roof a replacement in a restoration of 1893. *Silvanus Trevail*, whose home parish this was, undertook further work in 1902–3; the chancel SCREEN is by him and the STAINED GLASS of 1906 in the E window his memorial. There are fragments of medieval glass in the W tower window. – FONT. Norman, *c.* 1150, of the Bodmin type and almost identical with St Austell (q.v.), vigorously carved. – MONUMENTS. In the N aisle, Joseph Carveth, vicar, 1728. Fine Baroque design with pilasters, broken segmental pediment with shield of arms and helm, batwinged skull on apron and oval panel with Latin inscription. Several other late C18 slate tablets with winged cherubs, verses, etc.

The GATEWAY to the churchyard is probably late C15, with granite benches and coffin stand and a C19 wrought-iron overthrow and gates. Beside it a WHEEL-HEAD CROSS, medieval or earlier, with raised carved Maltese cross on each face, set on a large uncut boulder. – SUNDIAL. S of the S aisle. Shaft dated 1687, sundial dated 1902, the gift of Silvanus Trevail. – MONUMENTS. Tall Celtic cross to Silvanus Trevail and other members of the family, relief carved with interlace decoration in panels. Several other Trevail memorials including small OBELISK to Joseph Trevail, 1903.

In the grounds of the now subdivided former VICARAGE, W of the church, the remains of a luxuriant garden laid out by Richard Grylls, vicar, in the 1830s, including three granite GROTTOS with shell decoration.

ST CYOR HOLY WELL, ¼ m. SE of the church by the road to the Luxulyan valley. Small well-head with nice little narrow moulded doorway and stone-vaulted roof.

The large and varied parish has several good Methodist churches including EBENEZER, dated 1859, with round-headed sashes and Gothic interlace glazing; GUNWEN, dated 1869, round-headed sashes and radial glazing: and, most important, INNIS, near Innis Downs, a rare survival of the simple single-storey type of Bible Christian chapel, *c.* 1820, with plain interior, large pulpit at W end and leaders' seats in front with open-backed benches.

TREFFRY VIADUCT, 1 m. S. The now tranquil wooded Luxulyan valley, once a busy industrial area, is the setting for one of Cornwall's most impressive industrial monuments. Designed by *William Pease* and completed in 1842, it is built of huge granite

blocks and is 650 ft (198 metres) long, 98 ft (30 metres) high
and carried on ten 40-ft (12-metre) span arches. The first large
granite viaduct in Cornwall, it was part of a local industrial
transport system devised by Joseph Treffry of Fowey (q.v.),
whose arms it bears, to carry china clay from workings N of St
Austell to Treffry's port of Par. The system originally comprised
a mile of canal from Par to Ponts Mill, followed by a standard
gauge wagon track to Bugle. Beneath the deck an aqueduct
carried the water supply to operate a waterwheel on the incline.

PRIDEAUX HOUSE, 1½ m. SE. In 1808 Sir John Colman Rashleigh
built his new house lower down from the C16 manor house (*see*
below) with views towards St Austell Bay. A square, handsome
granite block of three by three bays, the centre bay broken
forward, with a niche in the centre and tripartite windows l. and
r. On the entrance front the central bay is carried on two pairs
of granite columns supporting the wide unmoulded arch of the
porch, its archivolt recessed into the house. Double-depth plan,
the entrance giving to rooms front l. and r. with oval stairwell
to rear r. Charming open-well stair with open-string and
wreathed handrail; rectangular lantern above with swagged plasterwork. A screen wall extends from the r. of the entrance front
with the service yard behind terminated by a two-storey gazebo.
Large contemporary service wing to the rear, of three storeys
over vaulted cellars. On the higher ground behind is PRIDEAUX
OLD MANOR, the much altered remains of the C16 house. It
was used as stables in the C19. Two-storey gabled porch with
four-centred arch doorway with roll mouldings and hollow-
chamfered hoodmould, three-light window above with arched
lights and hoodmould, and Rashleigh coat of arms in a recess
in the gable apex. Three other ground-floor three-light windows
and another four-centred arched doorway of similar style.

METHROSE, 1 m. S. One of the best medieval farmhouses* in
Cornwall, of great interest because of the survival of most of
its early C16 features, including the open hall. Its small scale
adds to its delightful character. A four-centred arch in a regular
granite wall leads into a small courtyard of the L-shaped house
with the hall to the r. and the C17 wing ahead. The hall range
is low built, its roof dipping to no more than 8 ft (2.4 metres)
above the ground, and has a tall lateral chimneystack of ashlar
granite blocks, with a bay window to its l. The C17 wing is in
granite ashlar and has a drip-course instead of hoodmoulds, a
feature occasionally found in Cornwall in the C17. The hall roof
is of two bays with an arch-braced truss as at Truthall (q.v.).
The chamber beyond the hall has been absorbed into the later
parlour wing which is said by Henderson to have been built
by Nicholas Kendall sometime between 1622 and 1649. The
service end apparently always had an upper floor extended over
the cross-passage and jettied into the open hall. On the first
floor of the C17 wing there was a four-bay open roof with
mouldings along the principals, collars and purlins, remodelled

---

* Sub-divided into two houses since 1952.

in 1676 with a plaster ceiling and a fireplace, of which only the dated overmantel survives.

MABE

St Laud. The church lies far from the village, alone in fields above the Argal reservoir. c15 w tower of regular granite blocks, in three stages, with no buttresses, embattled parapet and crocketed pinnacles (cf. the towers at Mawgan-in-Meneage and St Anthony-in-Meneage). The chief interest is the decoration of the w doorway, its mouldings enriched with foliate carving and pyramid ornament with carved heads as label stops to the hoodmould (like nearby Constantine and Mawgan), and the outer and inner doorways of the s porch, which has cable decoration outside and a repeated motif, emblematic of the Virgin, of a lily in a vase, inside up the joints and along the arch. The inner doorway is specially fine, of yellow limestone uncommonly richly decorated and finely worked, with leaf scrolls along two orders of jambs and voussoirs and decoration in the spandrels too. c15 window tracery throughout, the cusping precisely similar to Cury and St Anthony-in-Meneage. N and s aisles separated from the nave by octagonal piers with capitals evidently made for standard Cornish piers. The tower arch has responds with attached shafts and heads instead of capitals. In the N wall of the chancel an arched recess, probably for an Easter sepulchre. The church was restored in 1869 by J. P. St Aubyn with new arch- and wind-braced roofs and the N aisle rebuilt. – To the l. and r. of the reredos of 1928 are fragments of an alabaster reredos of the c15 (Visitation, Presentation in Temple, etc.). – stained glass. Chancel e 1880, s chapel e 1880, and N aisle 1883, all by Lavers, Barraud & Westlake.

In the churchyard to the l. of the porch a wheel-head cross with a broad-limbed Latin cross on both faces.

MADRON

St Madern. A large and uncommonly interesting church, as befits the mother church of Penzance, with lovely views out over Mount's Bay from the churchyard. Unbuttressed w tower of only two stages, but the lower one very tall. At its upper end a corbel table. Two of the s aisle windows have very primitive carved heads as keystones. The s porch is a copy of St Buryan, by J. D. Sedding who restored the church sympathetically 1886–9 and extended the chancel a few feet e. Spacious and lofty interior with a C14 S aisle arcade of six bays in Beer stone: the piers are of four major and four minor shafts with two-centred arches. In the chancel is a one-seat SEDILIA with PISCINA next to it which probably belongs to the same date (re-dedication of altar, 1336). The six-bay N aisle is C15, also in Beer stone, with taller piers and unusually rich foliage carving around some of the capitals. Much of the old carving is incorporated into the restored wagon roofs which have angels on the wall-plates of nave and chancel (cf. St Ives). An unusually rich ensemble of furnishings and fittings. – FONT. Damaged Norman font bowl on floor near the modern font. – ROOD SCREEN. Some panels of the base are original, discovered during the restoration, and keep some of their original colours. Each panel is of two lights, with a tall crocketed gable, the design reminiscent of Dunster, Somerset, as Bligh Bond observed. – BENCH-ENDS in S chancel chapel, of standard two-shield design, but with crouching beasts on the tops (cf. St Newlyn East, Kilkhampton). – PULPIT. Plain, good C18 oak, with tester. – ALTAR RAILS. Good, solid C18 work. – TOWER SCREEN. Jacobean, the balustrading characteristically coarser than that of the altar rails. – C15 ALABASTER PANEL of nine orders of angels (from a former reredos) and a royal COAT OF ARMS (from the former rood screen). – STAINED GLASS. Much mid- to late C19 glass, including chancel E, 1894 by *Lavers, Barraud & Westlake*; two interesting windows of the 1840s in the S aisle, the middle window of the S wall by a Paris firm, the W window with very obvious Tractarian iconography; and S chapel and N aisle (Virgin and Child), 1850s by *William Wailes*. – INSCRIBED STONE. Against W wall of S aisle. C7–C8 with a mix of Roman capitals and later lettering, reading VIR/QONFAL/FILIVS/VENNORCIT, 'My husband Qonfal, son of Vennorcit' (Professor Charles Thomas). – MONUMENTS. Large brass to John Clies, mayor of Penzance, and his family, 1623 (S chancel chapel floor). – Slate plate to John Maddern †1621, very *Volkskunst*, and to Thomas Fleming and his family †1631, with two couples carved on top of each other and their children kneeling below, just like playing cards. – The Rev. Duke Pearce, 1720. Two kneeling figures facing each other across a prayer-desk, a type which had been in fashion in the C16 and must in 1720 have appeared extremely outmoded. – In the churchyard the very heavy, severely Greek PRICE MAU-SOLEUM, *c.* 1820 to Rose Price of Trengwainton, and enormous MEMORIAL to Scobell Armstrong †1929 with upper figure of blindfolded maiden playing a lyre and sitting on a large granite ball. – Wheel-headed WAYSIDE CROSS close to the tower and Gothic CROSS-SLAB near the S porch. Many other crosses in the parish.

HOLY WELL and BAPTISTERY OF ST MADDERN, ½ m. NW. One of the most atmospheric well sites, even for Cornwall, where the medieval religious landscape seems tangible. The ruinous C14 plain BAPTISTERY occupies a much earlier site. It was desecrated at the Reformation but restored for its curative properties as late as 1640. It contains an altar still *in situ*. It is fed from the WELL, 100 yds away, the water flowing into the S wall of the baptistery and across the W wall.

Nos. 1 and 2 FOLNAMODRY, Fore Street. 1924, probably by *G. L. Kennedy* for the Bolitho estate. A pair of semi-detached staff cottages. Plain, granite, with simple handed plans, storeyed porches, round-headed doorways, and good internal joinery.

ROSEMORRAN, 1 m. E. Late C18 *cottage orné*, one of the most picturesque in Cornwall. Wheat reed thatch, said to be the longest thatched roof in Cornwall, over a long range of five rooms with central entrance porch. Two-storey except for third bay which is full height and has a pointed-arch window. First-floor dormers with arched heads. Some original internal features.

TRENGWAINTON, ½ m. SW. On site of a Tudor house, part of front probably C18, remodelled *c.* 1810, extended early to mid C19, but practically rebuilt for the Bolitho family in 1882 (date stone) and again in 1887 by *J. P. St Aubyn*. Two-storey, central entrance with columned porch. Flanking bays surmounted by triangular pediments with a balustraded parapet between. The GARDENS were created by *T. R. Bolitho* with advice from *J. C. Williams* of Caerhays (q.v.) and *P. D. Williams* of Lanarth, with plants from New Zealand, Australia, Chile and the Himalayas. Extensive OUTBUILDINGS include coachhouse, stables, courtyard and garden walls, bothy, potting-shed, gardeners' cottages and lodge.

MULFRA QUOIT, ¾ m. NW of Newmill. Early Neolithic. Chambered tomb 440 yds SE of the rounded hill's summit. Careful placement means the contemporary Carn Galva tor enclosure comes into view as the quoit is reached. 5 ft 7 in. (1.7-metre) high upright slabs form three sides of a simple box; SE stone missing. Large capstone now leans against chamber. Low mound around quoit. 1749 excavation found pit inside chamber.

MEN AN TOL, 2½ m. NW of Madron. Probably Early Bronze Age. First recorded as Men-an-Tol (holed stone) in 1613. Possibly fragment of Bronze Age STONE CIRCLE; three standing stones and several fallen ones form 59-ft (18-metre) diameter ring. Perfectly circular hole, 1 ft 8 in. (0.5 metres) in diameter, largely eroded by natural processes when horizontal, probably as part of tor.

LANYON QUOIT, 1¼ m. NW of St Madern. Early Neolithic. Well-known chamber tomb with the probably contemporary Carn Galva tor enclosure dominant to its N. Present arrangement established in 1824 (dated on S upright). Large horizontal granite capstone on three supports. Additional uprights to N probably originally formed ante-chamber to main rectangular chamber. Quoit at N end of low stony mound, probably two Bronze Age round CAIRNS, possibly containing remains of several CISTS.

MAKER

St Mary and St Julian. The church stands quite on its own on the high ground adjoining the far w end of the Mount Edgcumbe estate. It has a heavy w tower built of local red sandstone with contrasting granite buttresses and pinnacles, the latter ornate and on large octagonal turrets, all of a more Devonian than Cornish character. The buttresses leave the angles free and end halfway up the third stage in little pinnacles in relief. The body of the church has n and s aisles, n transept, s porch, and an outer s aisle added as an Edgcumbe family chapel at a slightly higher level. The piers of the five-bay arcades n and s are Cornish standard of identical design; the three bays of the Edgcumbe aisle have a slightly different (later) moulding, with more pronounced points between the shafts and the hollows, and more finely moulded capitals and arches. Original wagon roofs except porch and Edgcumbe chapel, the latter with arch- and wind-braced roof from a major restoration of 1874–6 which included much window replacement. Image niches with trefoiled heads diagonally set in the sides of the s aisle e window. – FONT. Brought from St Merryn when that church acquired the Catacleuse font from Constantine. Norman, large and excellent, of Bodmin type, with five supports, corner busts, and the snake convolutions in between especially wild and disorderly. – STAINED GLASS. Chancel e, 1844 by *Warrington*. – s aisle e, tower w, and two vestry windows by *Fouracre & Watson*, 1874–83. – n aisle windows, early c20. – MONUMENTS. Among the extensive array of Edgcumbe monuments, the best to Richard Lord Edgcumbe †1758, a standing wall monument with a bust above a sarcophagus and against a pyramid. – Sir Richard Hunt †1787, by *Kendall* of Exeter. Large grey oval plate with white laurel wreath, and inside it a framed inscription plate with urn on top.

St Julian's Well, ¼ m. NE. Chapel over holy well, c14–c15, restored *c.* 1890. Very steeply pitched corbelled stone roof supported by a single chamfered rib springing from moulded corbels. Lancet-shaped niche in e wall with ogee head, and ogee-headed aumbry in s wall. All in the lovely sage-green Tartan Down stone.

Fort Picklecombe, ½ m. SE. A battery of the 1860s, one of only two of this multi-tier type built in England, designed for sixty guns in two tiers with sixteen more on an open platform above. Dramatic curving frontage of forty-two granite-faced casemates. The late c20 residential conversion included the apartments on the roof. Above is the impressive Tudor-Gothic barracks of 1848 and on its approach a Schinkelesque LODGE for Mount Edgcumbe. At the top of Pickle Combe a Gothic seat, one of the miscellaneous structures in Mount Edgcumbe's landscape.

At MAKER HEIGHTS, I m. sw, five REDOUBTS started in the late c18, BARRACKS begun 1804–8, remodelled and extended 1858–9, and later c19 and early to mid-c20 BATTERIES.

MOUNT EDGCUMBE. *See* p. 363.
RAME and RAME HEAD. *See* p. 464.

MOUNT EDGCUMBE. *See* p. 363.
RAME and RAME HEAD. *See* p. 464.

7020

MANACCAN

ST MANACCA. The church sits at the centre of its pretty little churchtown within its raised churchyard or *lann*. Bishop Bronescombe acquired the manor and advowson in *c.* 1270 and conveyed the latter to Glasney in 1275. The present building has much of interest from the C12–C14. Of the cruciform Norman church the walls of nave, chancel and S transept survive. Plain C14 W tower of two stages, unbuttressed, with C15 pinnacles and battlements. The W door has heads as label stops (cf. e.g. Cury). Norman S door, with three little orders of columns and curious fluted voussoirs: it was carefully restored in 1888, the jambs seemingly undisturbed, the arch rebuilt. Re-set corbel and cross above. The triple lancet E window of the S transept and the chancel lancets are C13: Sedding considered the latter converted from Norman windows. The interior retains much pre-C15 character. The N aisle is late C15 or early C16, six bays of standard Cornish granite design with square-headed mullioned windows in the N wall. C19 open wagon roofs with narrower roof over chancel carried on moulded C15 granite corbels on the N side. The top of a Norman shaft is reused as a quoin at the NW corner of the transept and there is a squint between chancel and transept. – FONT. Round, probably a late medieval copy of the Norman original. – CHAIRS. Chancel. Made of C15 carved timber from the roof or rood screen. – STAINED GLASS. Chancel E, 1861 by *Wailes*, excellent. Two windows in S transept, one in S nave wall, and W tower, 1889 by *Horwood Bros* of Frome. N aisle E, 1889 by *Heaton, Butler & Bayne*.

KESTLE BARTON, ¾ m. NW. A C16–C17 house, originally of U-plan. Remodelled 1772 and 1744 (dated on E front and S end), and possibly also when barns were built S and E, one of which incorporates *c.* 1600 features reused from the house. Impressive lateral stacks dominate rear elevation. The later farm buildings are of the model farm type.

TREGITHEW, ¾ m. WSW. C17 house refronted and extended 1726 (inscribed plate) incorporating C17 doorway, with original sash windows with thick glazing bars on the front. Good C18 interior with panelled parlour and chamber above with coved ceiling. Associated outbuildings include an C18 BARN with C19 HORSE ENGINE HOUSE.

5030

MARAZION

The indelible memory of Marazion is the spectacular series of vistas of St Michael's Mount afforded throughout the long shoreline settlement, perfectly expressing their enduring historic relationship. The town owes its origins to the Benedictine priory, is the oldest of the Mount's Bay ports probably opening by the CII, and became a major port by the CI4, a borough by 1594 and a charter town in 1614, its corporation only dissolved in 1883. It retains the authentic ambience of an ancient town, its pleasant streets of mostly modest buildings prettily grouped around the harbour, The Square and Fore Street, and occasionally enlivened by an engaging fashion for castles and Gothic in the CI9, no doubt reflecting what was happening on the Mount.

ALL SAINTS, Fore Street. 1861 by *J. P. St Aubyn*. A well-composed church that fits comfortably enough into its intimate townscape, its relatively large scale mitigated by the street elevation of buttressed N aisle, N porch and W bellcote, all added in 1891. Dec style. Apsidal chancel, four-bay N and S aisle arcades on octagonal piers and pointed arches, the chancel arch carried on heavy corbelled imposts, arch- and wind-braced roofs. – Large CRUCIFIXUS, tenderly sculpted, and CANDLESTICKS in N chapel by *Martin Travers*, *c.* 1930. – STAINED GLASS. Much late CI9 or early C20, including S aisle windows by *Lavers, Barraud & Westlake*, one a memorial to J. P. St Aubyn (†1895) depicting the building of Solomon's temple. The best glass, of 1861, is to be found in the centre three single lancets of the chancel, the W window, and the N aisle chapel window, the latter two by *William Wailes*.

FRIENDS MEETING HOUSE, Rosehill. A delightful example of Quaker simplicity, one of the best in Cornwall (cf. Come-to-Good, Feock). Built 1688, remodelled 1742 and *c.* 1880, a small single storey has rare CI8 sashes. Charming interior has original elders' bench with splat balusters and newel posts with ball finials, and original settle. Other settles and simple benches.

METHODIST CHURCH, Fore Street. 1893–4. Good Gothic front, the buttresses that divide the three bays rising to pinnacles, excellent Dec-style tracery, and a cruciform finial over the apex.

TOWN HALL, Market Place. 1871. An extraordinary irruption of chateau-style architecture into the centre of the town. Imposing entrance front with tall square clock tower flanked by lower round turrets with steep roofs, rising to a steep sprocketed lead roof and iron balustrade with fleur-de-lys detail. The clock tower is elaborately detailed below with a tall traceried blind niche.

MARAZION (or THE CODE) INSTITUTE, The Square. Dated 1883. A memorial to Theophilus Code. Gothic style, two-storey, four-bay N front with splayed corner bay that has an oriel window on moulded corbels.

CHY-AN-SCOL and OLD SCHOOLHOUSE, Turnpike Hill. 1861 in Tudor style, with schoolroom on l. with entrance porch and cross-wing of school house on r.

OLD BRIDGE, over the Red River. CI8, two-span with semicircular refuges. Incorporates parish boundary stone.

MANOR OFFICE, West End. A house of *c.* 1775 for John Blewett, probably by *William Wood* of Truro: it invites comparison with Acton Castle (Perranuthnoe) and Tregenna Castle (St Ives). Three-storey, three-bay front, central bay broken forward, flanking pilasters, embattled parapet, paired pilasters flanking central doorway. Inside, excellent C18 detailing including an open-well open-string stair through three floors and late Rococo plasterwork with arabesques and swagged friezes under egg-and-dart cornices.

TRELAWNEY LODGE, by the gates to Manor Office. Pretty pair of lodges, dated 1887, of Jacobean style with large central stack with tall panelled brick shaft.

OLD MANOR HOUSE, Fore Street. Built *c.* 1775 for William Cornish and later for a time the home of J. P. St Aubyn. Granite ashlar front with rusticated quoins, two-storey over basement, first floor with tripartite Venetian windows. Interior has fine C18 Rococo plasterwork. Extended to the rear, and to the E with canted bay in the mid C19. The interior was altered in the C19 and the stair is of this date.

GODOLPHIN ARMS, West End. Large early to mid-C19, classical front, possibly remodelled from an older house, with five-bay front. Former coachhouse set back on l.

GAZEBO, Leys Lane. Mid- to late C19. Small, octagonal, embattled, prominently sited above the shoreline opposite the Mount, another Gothic flourish.

2000

MARHAMCHURCH

A pleasant village on a high E–W ridge, the church attractively placed at the W end of the wide village street.

ST MARWENNE. A church of modest size with a sturdy tower of modest height. E. H. Sedding, who seems to have worked here, considered that substantial Norman work survived in the thick walls of the S and E walls of the chancel, the S walls of nave and transept, and the plinth of the N aisle. Of the C14 cruciform church the chancel, S transept (the N transept is absorbed into the C15 aisle), and the lower stage of the tower. The tower was completed in the C15, with diagonal buttresses climbing up in four stages, and a polygonal NE staircase turret. C15 S porch with moulded arch-braced roof and foliage decorated wall-plates. Late C15–early C16 studded S door of overlapping vertical planks and original ironwork, a rare survival. The four-bay aisle arcade is low, of standard Cornish appearance. Aisle and nave are of about the same width, the N aisle roof mostly C15–C16 with some original bosses, the nave, chancel and transept roofs late C19 renewals. – Curious WINDOW built into a niche high up in the W wall of the aisle. It is of Polyphant with a cusped head but a transom and mullion below: it may be the opening of an anchorite's cell, the construction of which adjacent to the church for Cecilia Moyes is recorded as 1403–5. – FONT. Probably a late C19 re-cutting of a Perp original. – PISCINA, trefoil-headed, C14, in s wall of chancel. – PULPIT. A fine C17 piece, with two tiers of round-headed arches with demi-figures of saints above and eagles and a lion below, surmounted by strapwork and cartouches, and completed by a contemporary tester. – Large plaster ROYAL ARMS with strapwork decoration (cf. Boconnoc, Kilkhampton, Launcells, Poughill and Stratton), originally of Charles I with Charles II repainting (information from Anna Hulbert). – CRESSET STONE with four holes on an octagonal pier. – STAINED GLASS. A large quantity of mostly early C20 glass. Chancel E, transept s, and two N aisle windows of 1907 and 1910 by *Kempe*. – Nave s and N chapel E, 1907 by *Lavers, Barraud & Westlake*. Nave N by *Robert Beer* 1843. – MONUMENTS. Four good C17 slate slabs below chancel step. In the churchyard, a charmingly simple LYCHGATE with a pyramidal slate roof.

In the village street the former NATIONAL SCHOOL of 1873 incorporating two C17 granite doorways from almshouses demolished in the late C19. The most notable building is the impressive Arts and Crafts BRAY INSTITUTE, dated 1913, skilfully composed on a sloping corner site with a grand corner entrance rising between steeply pitched roofs over flanking wings: the wings each have large transomed-and-mullioned windows rising to gables.

BRIDGE, 1 m. W at Helebridge, over the Bude Canal, probably by *James Green* (q.v. Bude).

LANGFORD HILL, 2 m. SSW. C16 origins, probably as an L-shaped house, incorporated in an C18 remodelling into a double-depth plan with the addition of projecting front wings E and W of the main range; the latter were rebuilt as chapel and billiard room in the early C20. Eight-window front, asymmetrical, with large Gothick conservatory. Early C18 panelling and other contemporary fittings, and early roof over the C16 section with raised crucks and wind-braces.

MAWGAN-IN-MENEAGE

7020

ST MAWGAN. A church of more than usual interest set within an oval churchyard or *lann*. Fine three-stage C15 W tower of regular granite blocks with ribbed pinnacles on angel corbels (cf. e.g. St Anthony-in-Meneage). The W door has a charming leaf-scroll decoration all over one order of jambs and voussoirs. Close to the door the coats of arms of the Carminow, Reskymer, Ferrers and Bodrugan families. The body of the church, cruciform by the C13, has E.E. work in the s wall and parts of the s transept, the latter attached to the porch as at St Anthony-in-Meneage. The chancel has two E.E. windows, the chancel s and E windows are Dec. The N aisle is clearly Perp with a fine E window, the jambs decorated with stylized foliage. Inside, the N aisle has an arcade of seven bays with piers of Cornish standard design and distinctive capitals (like Cury) with a little decoration of the abaci. N transept c. 1500. The s transept is connected to the chancel by an elaborate squint similar to those at Landewednack, etc. The cut-off corner is replaced by a three-eighths shaft with a badly carved shield-holding angel. The tower arch has shafts attached to the responds and angels as capitals. C15 or early C16 wagon roofs to porch, nave, N transept and N aisle, the latter especially richly carved. The church was restored 1894–5 by E. H. Sedding, including partial rebuilding of the s transept. – FONT. Octagonal, with corner shafts coming out in a stove-pipe fashion. – MONUMENTS. In the s transept, a cross-legged knight, Sir Roger Carminow and his wife wearing a wimple, c. 1300 but moved here from elsewhere. – Sir Vyell Vyvyan †1820. Two children and urn, a large relief signed in Greek letters by Bartolini. Other good Vyvyan memorials of 1665 and 1696 in the floor. – LECTERN, C20, of lovely red and green serpentine. – STAINED GLASS. Two windows in the s wall of the chancel, 1895 and 1908, by James Powell & Sons, the latter an interesting and imaginative design. – s transept E, 1895, Martha and Mary, still Pre-Raphaelite.

At MAWGAN CROSS, ¼ m. SW of the church, an INSCRIBED STONE: inscription CNEGUMI FILI GENAIUS, with Hiberno-Saxon letters, perhaps as late as the C10 and originally with a cross-head. The position at the meeting of three roads seems original.

TRELOWARREN. See p. 644.

8060

MAWGAN-IN-PYDAR

Sheltered below Atlantic gales, and nowadays Newquay airport's runways, is the welcome surprise of the Vale of Lanherne, a lovely wooded valley running along the River Menahyl with church, house and village embedded in trees at its heart.

ST MAWGAN. Beautifully situated below the house and of major interest for its substantial C13 core, C15–C16 additions and restoration in 1860–1 by William Butterfield. A large church of nave and chancel, N and s transepts, s nave and chancel aisles, Butterfield vestry N of chancel, and a service extension tactfully inserted between this and the N transept by Richard Church, 2000. The handsome tower is unusually placed to the s of the s transept, of three stages with buttresses set back from the angles and a NE stair-turret rising to above parapet height: the embattled parapet has polygonal turrets surmounted by obelisks and ball finials, of which the stair-turret has a larger version. The lower part of the tower, the nave, N transept and its arch from the nave are C13, when the church was of cruci-

form plan. S chancel aisle of Catacleuse stone, two bays with
two-centred arches, added before the mid C15. S nave aisle of
four wide bays, yet the piers of the earlier bays are already of
standard Cornish design. The nave arcades are also standard
with four-centred arches and horizontal leaves carved along
the abaci, as in Devon. The nave W window of three narrow
lights is c. 1300, the other windows good Perp of three, four or
five lights, apart from Butterfield's Dec E window of the chancel.
A C13 squint leads from the N transept into the chancel.
Except for the medieval roof of the N transept and the reused
bosses in the S porch, all the roofs are Butterfield's, the ribs
of the chancel roof with delicate stencilled polychrome
decoration.

The fittings are of unusual range and interest. – FONT. Of
the Bodmin type, circular bowl of the C12, on four Devon
marble columns and a Bath stone shaft, all Butterfield repairs.
The corners with faces, the four sides with a zigzag border
and shields below (cf. St Wenn, Crantock, St Columb Minor).
PULPIT. Of c. 1530, with panels with large Instruments of the
Passion. – ROOD SCREEN. Tall (with loft), painted and, unusually, the openings have no tracery; their heads are freely cusped.
For this specially graceful and airy type of screen cf. Crantock.
Cornice incorporating animals preserved on the back. Before
1860, a finer screen crossed the S aisle. – PARCLOSE SCREEN
by Butterfield. Delicately cusped and painted to complement
the rood screen. – BENCH-ENDS. Forty-two, mostly C16, the
usual two shields with monograms, Instruments of the Passion,
and Arundell, Carminow, Rous and Vyvyan arms. – Also by
Butterfield the COMMUNION RAILS, the sanctuary TILES in
diaper pattern with zigzag border and ALTAR TABLE in the S
chancel aisle with open cusped panels. – BRASSES. In the floor
at the E end of the S chancel aisle. An array of C15 and C16
brasses, especially of the Arundells, much reduced from their
original form: they were removed from the chancel and dispersed in 1860. All are incomplete: some are palimpsests
of C14–C16 Flemish brasses, and parts of some are now at
Wardour Castle. The following deserve notice: priest, early C15;
George A. †1573 and his wife, two figures and verses (palimpsest of early C16 Flemish brass); Jane A. †1577 and Mary A.
†1578, inscriptions and shields only, figures at Wardour
(palimpsest of Flemish brass of 1374); Cecily A. †1578, figure,
verses and shields (palimpsest of 1374, as above); unknown
man, late C16, in long-sleeved robe. – STAINED GLASS. NW
window of nave, 1879, and E window of S chancel aisle, 1887,
by *Clayton & Bell*. – E window of chancel, 1902, and one of
three lights in N wall of nave, 1905, both by *Percy Bacon*. –
MONUMENTS. Henry Stephen †1611 and his wife, Dorothy,
†1630, figures in low relief in Jacobean costume; Thomas
Coad †1731, slate with carved panels in low relief with hourglass, skull and crossed bones; Humphrey Noye †1679, slate;
John Willyams †1800, marble on slate ground with urn, by
Isbell of Plymouth.

In the churchyard, the LYCHGATE. By *Butterfield*. A quietly assertive announcement of the import of the church, the walls buttressed and with imposts for an arch-braced roof, hipped with shaped ridge tiles and cast-iron finials. Near the E end of the chancel, CROSS-HEAD, medieval, very worn. To NW of church, a LANTERN CROSS. One of the finest of this type of C15 canopied cross-head, in Catacleuse stone set on a chamfered shaft, filled with figures of the Annunciation to the N, Trinity to the S, and bishops. Crocheted ogee arches to truncated gable-heads, the filled dowel holes indicating the sites of lost pinnacles. Further up the path, a BOAT STERN, a memorial to ten men washed ashore frozen to death near Mawgan Porth in 1844; this is a replica of 1922 by *Alan Goss* of Newquay.

LANHERNE. Standing serene and mysterious among the trees, this was the house of the Arundells (cf. St Columb Major) that since 1794 has been an enclosed convent and a historic centre of Roman Catholic worship in Cornwall. The high walls of the enclosure have long hidden most of the building from public view but what is visible, the two-storeyed Elizabethan S front, conveys strong hints of the complex history of the house behind. The elevation is asymmetrical with the gables of the E and W ranges of a large courtyard plan showing at either end. First to the l. a four-window section around a wide arch with panelled double doors and fanlight above and hollow-moulded granite windows with cusped heads. A pair of fine lead rainwater heads and downpipes dated 1717 flank the door. Next a splendidly showy bay of one eight-light window at ground floor and a similar window corbelled out above. Then, fronting the r. gable-end, a five-light window on ground and first floor (lighting the chapel) with a C19 single-storey chapel porch beyond.

Only a few tantalizing glimpses are possible of the rest of the house. But even these – early C18 sash windows, brick arcaded and panelled stacks, and a cupola with clock, ogee lead roof and weathervane – testify to its impressive scale and high status. The courtyard plan has two parallel ranges at the S front of which the inner range is the earlier. The rear of the courtyard is closed by a N range of *c.* 1700 with a symmetrical nine-bay front of two storeys above a cellar. The house is said to contain good plasterwork and an arch-braced roof over the W range.

In the garden by the entrance to the chapel, a WHEEL-HEAD CROSS, one of the best in Cornwall, with Christ crucified dressed in a simple tunic and on the r. side an interlaced beast. All four sides are richly sculpted and the Hiberno-Saxon inscription and beast are very similar to Sancreed (q.v.).

The enclosure WALLS date from the late C17, heightened in some places. Uphill to the W of the house, the walls of the KITCHEN GARDEN, early C18, enclosing about an acre, with a single gateway on the SW side. The gatepiers are square with a limestone cornice and acorn finials. The gate is blocked, access from the convent being by a tunnel under the road.

Near the church the FALCON INN, *c.* 1840, with pretty marginal glazing of Chinoiserie character; the BRIDGE, dated CGWW 1748 and 1865 JP, the date of its widening, of two spans; plain METHODIST CHURCH of 1870, and the SCHOOL, by *Butterfield*, 1863. A simple, sturdy building of main schoolroom and cross-wing and typical Butterfield details – porch set in the angle with buttresses, two tall lancets in the gable-end of the crossing, large mullion-and-transom in the main range gable-end, and corbelled bellcote. Uphill to the W a FOUNTAIN, dated 1904, an unusually grand affair in granite ashlar. The fountain is set into the inside rear wall through a central four-centred arch opening with swept gable and cross finial, flanked by stone basins set in niches either side and another basin inside. Wrought-iron gate across the central bay by *Worrall* of Liverpool.

OLD RECTORY, by *Butterfield*, *c.* 1858. In a commanding position overlooking the village. A typical purpose-built rectory plan of the simpler type with two staggered parallel ranges and a cross-wing at the S end. High Victorian Gothic, the elegant vertical proportions emphasized by steeply pitched roofs and tall chimneys. The entrance front is an especially satisfying composition with the two-storeyed gabled and buttressed entrance porch placed in the angle between the main range and the wing: a two-centred outer arch, originally with cast-iron gates, and four-light trefoil-headed windows to each side. Lively Gothic details, harmoniously resolved. The interior has excellent joinery throughout and several marble chimneypieces of simple but assured design. A nice prelude to arrival at the entrance front is the former STABLE and COACHHOUSE, now residential, on an L-shaped plan with similar motifs to the house.

CARNANTON. Protected below shelter belts of weather-beaten trees, the house is exquisitely set in extensive parkland and gardens. It belonged to the Noyes (William Noye was Attorney-General to Charles I) and since then theWillyams (Thomas Willyams †1566 was Speaker of the Commons). The present building is essentially a fine early C18 house with several phases of C19 remodelling. The well-proportioned, relatively unadorned house of *c.* 1710 survives as the present S garden front of two storeys and seven bays: it was originally of double-depth plan with a central entrance to a large entrance hall, principal rooms to the l. and r. and service rooms and stair hall to the rear. In the early C19 it was dramatically reordered to make the E end the entrance front with a grand granite Ionic portico with paired columns and cornice and a flight of steps leading to an inner pair of doorways with pilasters and cornices. At the same time a single-storey range of three service rooms was added immediately N of the new entrance, an arrangement which makes for an intriguing initial impression. More extensive alterations and additions were made in the mid C19 behind these C18 and early C19 ranges.

The interior retains good features and details of all the main phases. The early C19 entrance hall, reworking the original C18 build, has a screen of Ionic columns dividing it from the stair hall, the open-well mahogany stair with turned balusters, moulded swept handrail, ramped dado panelling and closed string with Greek key frieze. Fine C18 and early C19 plaster-work with statue niches and plaster surrounds to paintings on side and rear walls including plums, pomegranates, grapes etc. with excellent vigorous modelling. The C18 rooms along the s front have good C18 marble chimneypieces, plaster-work and joinery. Extensive service buildings to the N of the house include a STABLE BLOCK with a clock tower over the entrance to the inner yard, a former LAUNDRY, KENNELS and SCHOOLROOM.

LOWER DENZELL, 1½ m. NE. Farmhouse with w cross-wing, central entrance door on s side and pent-roofed kitchen entrance further E by *William White* sometime before 1899. To the E, model farm buildings also by *White*, including a two-storey mill, granary, and associated buildings forming a double quadrangle with separate stable block. Though all converted to residential use, characteristic White touches like the high relieving arches and voussoirs of thin collared stones (cf. Gerrans church).

7020

MAWNAN

ST MAUNAN. Far from the village, among trees and within an oval enclosure or *lann* overlooking the mouth of the Helford River. Low w tower of two stages, unbuttressed, with window tracery of the Dec style: the base is probably C14, largely rebuilt or heightened in granite ashlar in the C15. The chancel is, at least in its s wall, C13 (cf. the narrow lancet window). The two aisles are of identical C15 design, with granite piers consisting of four major and four minor shafts. A drastic restoration in 1880 renewed the roofs, heightened the chancel, and enlarged and wholly or partially rebuilt the s aisle (in the N aisle the wall-plate of the former wagon roof survives): it bears all the hallmarks of *J. P. St Aubyn* at his most severe. – Excellent C13 PISCINA in the chancel wall with finely carved heads as label stops. – The FONT is octagonal, C15. – Of the ROOD SCREEN only a few painted panels of saints remain (cf. Budock and Gunwalloe). – STAINED GLASS. Chancel E, 1892 by *Lavers, Barraud & Westlake*; N aisle, Christ with Mary Mag-dalene, 1880 by *Mayer*. Mid-C20 windows include w window of N aisle, 1946 by *William Aikman*, with a depiction of Saint Sophia, Istanbul, and a good Arts and Crafts style window of the Virgin and Child, 1957, in the s aisle. – C17 pillar ALMS BOX. – Near the font a C13 COFFIN SLAB with the remains of a foliated cross. – In the exterior of the w wall a medieval CROSS-HEAD.

In the village of Mawnan Smith, ST MICHAEL, 1873–4 by *J. P. St Aubyn*, dull E.E. with canted E end and contemporary STAINED GLASS by *Lavers, Barraud & Westlake*; METHODIST CHAPEL, Carwinion Road, *c.* 1815 with symmetrical road front, the centre broken forward under a triangular pediment, and round-headed sashes to the first floor; and ST EDWARD THE CONFESSOR R.C. CHURCH, ¼ m. SE in Old Church Road. 1964 by *Waldo Maitland* (cf. former chapel at Tremough). Simple white exterior with no ground-floor windows, the church lit by dormers and a large W window by *Harry Clarke Stained Glass Ltd* of Dublin.

The parish has a number of small- to medium-size country houses, reflecting its favoured position on the Helford River and its proximity to Falmouth, including several of the early C20. The Fox family of Falmouth (q.v.) were especially prominent not only in building substantial houses but developing exquisitely beautiful gardens in the C19 including GLENDURGAN and its neighbour TREBAH; these and PENJERRICK (cf. Budock) share many characteristics of design and planting. BOSLOE, 1880 and 1903 in a Vernacular Revival style with Renaissance features and terraced gardens. BOSVEAL and CARWINION are other neighbours. At the foot of the Glendurgan gardens the pretty hamlet of DURGAN, with its former school, 1876, right on the river and an C18 QUAY.

Of other early C20 houses the most noteworthy are NANSIDWELL, ¼ m. SE, *c.* 1905 by *Leonard Stokes*, Georgian style on a U-shaped plan with C18-style interior, and HEYLE, Helford Passage, 1914, another Vernacular Revival example. Of earlier houses BAREPPA, 1 m. NNE, early C18 with early C19 remodelling to create a new entrance front but retaining good early C18 features in the original front rooms; and PENWARNE, 1 m. NNW, late C18 extended in the early C19 with five-window stucco front, the central bay broken forward under a triangular pediment and an Ionic porch.

MENABILLY

2 m. W of Fowey

1050

The Rashleigh mansion sits secluded in parkland and gardens running down to the sea and Gribbin Head. The Cornish Rashleighs originated from Devon (cf. Rashleigh Barton, Wembworthy) and it was John Rashleigh, a successful Fowey merchant, who purchased Menabilly in 1573: his Fowey house survives as the Ship Inn (q.v.). The substantial late C16 to early C17 courtyard plan house, which served as the headquarters of Lord Essex during the Civil War, was radically remodelled by Philip Rashleigh in 1723–5, and it is the early C18 house that shines out from the earlier and later work, which included alterations after a major fire in 1815 and extensive reworking and enlargement in 1878–9 by Jonathan Rashleigh.*

Facing s and seawards with the principal rooms in the s and e wings, Menabilly is built of green-purple ashlar slatestone to the s and e elevations. The s and e fronts are understated but assured, their early c18 rhythm only interrupted by a small library of 1878–9 at the se corner in the c18 style. s front, a symmetrical 2:3:2 elevation with sliding sashes,† the centre slightly advanced, and a central doorway framed by Ionic columns to a moulded entablature with a broken segmental pediment and the Rashleigh arms: surprisingly unpretentious. Ornamental lead rainwater heads and downpipes, dated 1733 with the initials PR, flank the central section. e front of nine bays, three storeys at the N end with two granite two-light hollow-chamfered cellar windows surviving from the earlier house and two fine lead downpipes with ornamental rainwater heads dated 1713 with the initials PR. The ground-floor window of the library is filled by a large limestone plaque in the form of a leafy tree, two heraldic shields, a biblical text, the initials JR and date 1878–9: it is of fine workmanship, by *Harry Hems* of Exeter. In front, a lead water tank with pretty decoration dated 1689 JR, for an earlier Jonathan Rashleigh. The courtyard has been encroached on all four sides since the early c17 but the early c18 N elevation is still impressive and deserves a better setting than the late c19 utilitarian brick extensions provide. It is a three-storey red brick loggia rising to a clock tower surmounted by a cupola. Only three of the original five bays of the loggia survive, and only one is open. The W range was destroyed by the fire and substantially rebuilt with reordered service accommodation.

The interior shows little evidence of the late c16 to early c17 house, though the roof structure demonstrates that the courtyard plan was achieved by 1624 in two or more phases and also that there was a stair-tower in the sw corner of the courtyard c. 1680–90. The internal arrangement of the s and e wings survives from the early c18; some of the rooms were refurbished in the late c19 in c18 style, the detail mixed but generally so expertly achieved that it could pass for the original. s range has central entrance hall leading to a gloomy inner entrance lobby with painted glass of c. 1855 and flanked by drawing room and library, while the e range has a Long Parlour flanked by two smaller rooms. The large open-well stair hall at the s of the e range is of 1878–9, in Queen Anne style with a fine plaster ceiling and elaborate modillion cornice over. The 1877–8 N wing was demolished in 1981.

The GARDENS were laid out in their present form from the 1820s and were celebrated for their splendid landscaping with sea

---

* This account owes much to research by John Thorp of Keystone, 1998.
† The windows were restored by Daphne du Maurier during her tenancy in the 1950s; the house was the inspiration for Manderley in *Rebecca*.

views and a wealth of sub-tropical planting. Though much decayed, the elements of the original design are discernible in the remnants of the pine and palm walks and the site of the fernery. At the foot of the grounds near Polridmouth is a roof-less circular GROTTO of 1750–60, or possibly of the 1730s.

MENHENIOT

St Lalluwy (St Lallu). One of the rare Cornish churches with a spire: plain, octagonal, on a two-storeyed tower with battle-ments and strong three-stepped buttresses set back from the angles to the top of the lower stage. The windows are small, and the battlements project on a corbel table. The whole is early looking, probably early C14. Inside there is a difference between the arcades of the N and S aisles, though both are Perp. The S aisle is later (cf. its more elaborately detailed capitals and four-centred elaborately moulded arches). Mostly C15–C16 Perp windows. The ceiled wagon roofs of nave and aisles are specially complete and enjoyable. A restoration by *J. P. St Aubyn* of 1865–6 extended the chancel E and installed the over-dominant arch- and wind-braced chancel roof. Fortu-nately its impact was considerably softened and the interior enhanced by subsequent restorations, including one of 1922–4 by *G. H. Fellowes Prynne*. – PULPIT. 1891 by *Harry Hems* of Exeter, one of his best pieces, a beautifully carved depiction of the polar exploits of Vice-Admiral Trelawney-Jago of Coldrennick (q.v.), and his ship the *Enterprise* (e.g. the detail of the ship's rigging). – Of the Fellowes Prynne work, the excel-lent furnishings and floorings of chancel and sanctuary, includ-ing the PARCLOSE SCREENS, CHOIR STALLS and REREDOS, and probably the ORGAN LOFT which sits on elegant fluted columns in the tower arch. Much of this by *Dart & Francis* of Crediton. – The WAR MEMORIAL in the S porch is probably also by Fellowes Prynne. – STAINED GLASS. Chancel E, *Clayton & Bell*. Three good windows in the N wall of the N aisle by *Percy Bacon* of the 1920s, and another by *Fouracre & Sons*, 1908. S aisle E by *Hugh Easton* 1951. N aisle E, 1868. S wall of S aisle by *David Peace*, 1997, a fine example of his work in engraved glass, depicting a Celtic cross and grains of wheat (cf. St Merryn and Porthilly). – Beautifully engraved BRASS INSCRIPTION to Sir Ralph Carmynow †1386, set in the floor at the base of the pulpit, the earliest in Cornwall. – Other Trelawny MONUMENTS. Semicircular top of a slate tomb to I.T., with good decoration, in particular two oversized, fat putti. – Jonathan Trelawny †1653, and his wife †1674, classical with broken pediment and heraldic arms. – Edward Trelawny, Dean of Exeter, †1726, with a good bust on the pediment, and Darell Trelawny †1727, by *Rysbrack*, whose design is in the V&A (GF). – L. Stephens †1724. A large black marble slab with superb lettering and achievement. – Tablet to Lady Charlotte Carr, by *M. Eames* of Exeter.

The church is pleasantly and spaciously set within a probable *lann* at the centre of the large village and a good group of buildings, including the former SUNDAY SCHOOL, *c.* 1860s, in the NE corner of the churchyard, its windows with round-cusped heads; to the E the POADS TRUST ALMSHOUSES, early C19, restored and extended 1960s, with triangular-headed windows and doors; and to the W a late C19 SCHOOL, HALL of 1911, and modest terraced houses. To the S, HOLYWELL, dedicated to St Lalluwy in C13 and C14 documents, rebuilt in the C19 when the C16 four-centred arch was re-set to form a pointed head.

COLDRENNICK, I m. SE. The half-timbered black and white mansion by *C. F. Hayward*, 1870, was demolished *c.* 1950. It had replaced an C18 house, three-storey and ten bays, shown on a plan of 1760; the STABLES of this earlier house survive, very plain but dignified classical, converted to residential use, as do extensive WALLED GARDENS.

MERTHER

ST COAN. Ruinous and overgrown after gradual abandonment in the C20 in favour of Tresillian (q.v.). A chapelry of Probus by 1327 and restored in 1843–4. Slender W tower of two stages, more like Mylor than Cornelly (q.v.) because of the heavy diagonal buttresses, with a pointed W doorway. In the N wall two Norman window embrasures, the stonework of the windows removed; other windows late Perp with cusped lights and hoodmoulds. Early C16 S aisle, its standard Cornish arcade now fallen but the W respond with traces of its four-centred arch.

MEVAGISSEY

At heart a picturesque fishing port despite C20 residential expansion that spreads from the sea up to the skyline. A significant medieval settlement with an excellent deep-water harbour, it became one of the major centres of the Cornish pilchard industry. To accommodate the industry's expansion the medieval pier was replaced by the present inner harbour in the late C18 and the quayside buildings were adapted or rebuilt. By 1850 the port had eighty registered fishing vessels employing three hundred fisherman and ten fish-curing businesses. Further expansion came as late as the end of the C19 when the outer harbour walls and pier were constructed, more than tripling the size of the harbour. The pilchard industry may have vanished but tourism has advanced. The narrow streets around the harbour and climbing the steep slopes to N and S are full of modest C18 and C19 buildings of enjoyable variety – cottages and small houses, converted fish cellars, warehouses and sail lofts – enhanced by an array of different building materials – much slate cladding, red brick (often painted), local stone, and render. And with little redevelopment and careful conversions of existing buildings, there is still hardly a false note in the core of this engaging place.

St Peter. A church of unusual but endearing appearance with a clearly shortened tower and a disproportionately large S transept, its prominence accentuated by the steep rise of the churchyard to the NE. There was a church here by 1230, re-dedicated in 1259, originally cruciform but subsequently reworked in the C14 to C16 to the present plan of nave and chancel, N aisle, S transept, S porch and W tower. The tower was reported as ruinous in the mid C17 and when Glynne visited in 1853 he described 'a miserable church in bad repair and altogether dirty and neglected'. The subsequent restoration by *J. P. St Aubyn* in 1887–8 at a cost of £2,000 was inevitably extensive. The unbuttressed tower had by then been reduced to below the height of the nave roof and St Aubyn restored it in its shortened form with a saddleback roof. The interior has a surprisingly intimate scale. The N aisle of four bays is of Pentewan stone. The piers are of standard section but the abaci are octagonal and decorated. Earlier traces are the trefoil PISCINA in the nave, W of the S transept, and the three-light Dec S window of the transept. Apart from two small three-light medieval windows in the N aisle, the others are late C19 replacements, as are the roofs. – FONT. Norman, circular, with chip-carved rosettes, etc., a herringbone moulding above, a zigzag moulding below, and a cable moulding on the base. – STAINED GLASS. Three windows by *Heaton, Butler & Bayne*, 1887–8. – MONUMENTS. Otwell Hill †1617 and wife Mary ('Stock Lancashier, Birth London, Cornwall gave/to Otwell Hill Inhabitance and Grave/Franck, Frugall, Plaissannt, Sober, Stout and Kinde . . .'), an uncommonly ambitious composite with the two effigies reclining above and behind each other (cf. Truro Cathedral) and columns l. and r. with a semicircular top, with inscription plate and strap and fruit ornament. – Lewis Dart †1632 and family, in contrast a humble, local slate with ten kneeling figures.

PERAMBULATION. Start at the HARBOUR and walk along East Wharf to the North Pier, or West Wharf to Victoria Pier, to appreciate both the impressive scale of the outer harbour and the jagged cliffs, seaward of which some rugged outcrops are incorporated in its walls. The outer harbour works are of 1897, the inner harbour 1770–5. The harbour is also the best place to capture a sense of the pre-C20 settlement clustered tightly around the quays. On EAST WHARF some former fish cellars, sail lofts, and boat-building premises, one of the latter recorded in 1745 now the MUSEUM. Rising steeply from the quay are THE CLIFF and other little streets with slate-hung cottages tumbling over each other. Set back in OLIVER'S QUAY is a pointed arched WELL, of 1937, a replica of Towan Holy Well (q.v.). Fronting the harbour are attractively irregular groups of c18 and c19 buildings, several of which are former warehouses, fish cellars and net lofts, e.g. the SHARKSFIN RESTAURANT, a four-storey warehouse building with central loft doors.

The commercial heart of Mevagissey is the maze of little streets immediately inland behind the harbour, reached by narrow lanes like JETTY STREET with more former fish cellars and warehouses. FORE STREET, MARKET STREET, MARKET SQUARE and CHURCH STREET are all worth exploring to see the pleasing variations of local building, mostly c18 and c19, with hardly a c20 building to be seen. There are few buildings of exceptional interest but the whole townscape is coherent and intimate. Of the buildings that stand out, the SHIP INN is a good c18 example, with round-headed door and fanlight and eaves cornice. Up PILKIRT HILL No. 2 has a smart late c18 Pentewan ashlar front and rusticated voussoirs. Nos. 5–9 are of similar date with pretty round-headed doors and intact glazing with very thin glazing bars. No. 27 is the best, c. 1730 and very prominently sited above the harbour, with a three-storey five-window front, modillion cornice and demi-columned door, entablature and pediment.

Further up Church Street and on the corner with CHAPEL STREET is ST ANDREW'S UNITED REFORMED CHURCH, 1883 by *Silvanus Trevail*, formerly Congregational. Rather ponderous composite Gothic, tall three-light windows with cinquefoil heads and plate tracery and curious gablets to both sides of the front. To the rear, SUNDAY SCHOOL, datestone 1873, and to the l. a former BOARD SCHOOL of 1881. At the other end of Chapel Street is the former BIBLE CHRISTIAN CHAPEL, 1896, pretty front with triple lancets between Corinthian pilasters, foliated buttresses and quoins and cast-iron finials like Fowey (q.v.). Back into Church Street up CHURCH LANE, LAWN HOUSE, good c18 symmetry, the central three-window bay slightly advanced with a large low pediment, central lunette and eaves cornice and prettily slate-hung between ground and first floor and in the pediment.

Other *Trevail* buildings are the CEMETERY CHAPEL, Chapel Hill (1882), POLPIER, Tregoney Hill (*c.* 1890), and SCHOOL HOUSE, School Hill, the former Board School of 1877.

PORTMELLON, ¾ m. w. Once a small hamlet of c18 and c19 cottages at the head of a delightful beach, now joined from over the hill by the outskirts of modern Mevagissey.

PENWARNE MANOR, ¼ m. w. Fine c16–c17 house built into the slope with a dignified ten-window front, the hall and inner room at the higher end and a very long three-storey lower end. Rear wing has a blocked window with ogee head, said to be from the former house of the Polruddens nearby. A good ensemble with its complete C18 walls, gatepiers, stables, barns and outbuildings.

At CHAPEL POINT, 1½ m. SE, three houses of 1935–8 by *John Campbell*, among his last and finest designs and intended as part of a larger planned development on a dramatic promontory site. Simple and direct, innovatively composed, and with hardly any ornament, they show Campbell's highly original interpretation of Arts and Crafts. The GATE HOUSE is the most picturesque, at the highest point of the site and reached through a courtyard guarded by round corner turrets. Its tower-house form springs from a compact plan, reinforced by a large semicircular stair-turret: the seaward elevation is especially pleasing, springing from a four-arched loggia through a ground floor with asymmetrically disposed windows to a steeply gabled and dormered roof of the narrow tower which has narrow round-arched windows with balconies. POINT HEAD is the smallest, on falling ground near the E tip of the promontory. A large lateral stack rises from a solid base of boiler room and coke store. The use of materials is striking: rubble stone for the chimney, plinth and outbuildings, the main house walls of concrete block. CHAPEL POINT HOUSE was built for Campbell's own use. It is impressive in its presence, though only the cross-wing with its W-facing blank wall is two-storey, contrasting with the lower E workshop wing. The interior is made spacious by Campbell's use of the roof spaces in a boarded barrel vault in the living room and exposed roof timbers in the bedroom, and in his creation of vistas through the internal arched openings, including a sequence of three at the entrance to the living room that look out to sea.

MICHAELSTOW

0070

The church stands beside the green at the centre of its small churchtown within its raised churchyard.

ST MICHAEL. Unbuttressed C15 W tower of three stages with rectangular NE stair-turret (cf. Lanteglos-by-Camelford), rising to embattled parapet with crocketed finials surmounted by crosses. There was a church here by 1269 and the N wall of the chancel may be of this date: on its exterior face is a low-set C13 piscina, associated with a quatrefoil opening above on the inside (blocked externally) which is reputed to have been the window of an anchorite cell grafted on to the exterior. Nave, chancel, N and S aisles and S porch with good evidence of the likely sequence of development. The N aisle is of four bays, stopping short of the anchorite cell site, of standard Cornish granite design of the C15. The S aisle of similar design is of five

bays, but the w respond and pier have standard capitals in blue
elvan, not granite, and the three e piers and respond have
limestone capitals carved with large horizontal leaves. It seems
the arcade was built in two stages, the w first, and completed
in the early c16: the s door certainly looks of that date and is
of Polyphant stone with hollow chamfer with floral motifs and
a hoodmould. Original wagon roofs to nave, n and s aisles and
porch, with carved ribs, wall-plates and bosses and evidence
of pendants in the n aisle. – FONT. c15, plain, octagonal, on
Norman base. – BENCHES AND BENCH-ENDS. An exceptionally fine pre-Reformation set, rescued from St Tudy. Other
benches, pulpit and reredos (now at the rear of the church)
are from an extensive but sensitive restoration begun in 1870
and completed in 1889 by *Hine & Odgers*. – ROYAL ARMS,
dated 1727, painted on timber board. – STAINED GLASS. Some
medieval fragments. Pretty Arts and Crafts e window, 1906 by
Louis B. Davis, manufactured by *Powells*. – MONUMENTS.
Several good slate plates, for example Jane Merifield, 1663,
with nice scrolly lettering and two standing figures in the
costume of the period, incised as primitively as if they were
done by a child.

HOLY WELL, s of the church on the edge of the churchyard. The
small well-house built into the hillside may have been part of
a larger medieval building indicated by the low walls in front.

CROSS, w of the tower. A four-holed cross of excellent workmanship on an impressively long shaft. It was rediscovered in 1883
at the bottom of the flight of steps.

METHODIST CHAPEL, Treveighan, 1 m. NW. 1828, built by
Edward Hocking, and SCHOOL with SCHOOL HOUSE: the latter
is interesting as the school was adapted from an c18 cottage
in 1852 (datestone) when the schoolhouse was built.

MILLBROOK

An ancient settlement around the Millbrook lake looking out to
the Hamoaze. In the c17 it had a large fishing fleet, tide mill and
gunpowder factory that expanded over time, with a ropewalk,
limekilns, boat building, a large brewery and other industries
along the n side of the lake. The narrow streets of small houses
and some former industrial buildings around the infilled quay
and a scatter of waterside villas beyond survive from its considerable expansion in the c20.

ALL SAINTS. 1893–5, possibly by *Hine & Odgers*. A large church,
partly reflecting its role as a garrison church for the nearby
military establishments, in solid but dull Perp and built of
Plymouth limestone with Polyphant dressings. Nave, n and s
aisles and s porch, the aisles with buttresses and angle buttresses, the heavily buttressed two-storey porch the base of an

intended tower. Spacious interior with five-bay N and S arcades and single bays to chancel and N and S chapels, all in Poly-phant. C15-style wagon roofs. – STAINED GLASS. Chancel E 1905, S chapel E 1899, and S chapel S, all by *W. G. Taylor*.

MILLBROOK METHODIST CHURCH, New Street. Dated 1873. A powerful presence rising above the modest houses of the settlement's centre. Two-storey with two-storey porch, the latter with rounded gable below the main gable.

Ruined CHAPEL, off Chapel Way, ¼ m. N. Gaunt but still impres-sive remains of the vanished Champernowne manor house at Insworke. Two-storey, the chapel at first-floor level with trefoil-headed E window, the tracery gone, and trefoil-headed lancets to N and S walls. It is likely that this was the building licensed by Bishop Grandisson in 1331.

Along and above the delightful waterside road to Cremyll some nice stuccoed villas. ST ELMO and TREGENNA with pretty verandas, were built 1847 as a speculative venture by *William Joseph Little*; Tregenna's former gazebo, THE ROUND HOUSE, octagonal with pointed-headed windows, is on the road nearby. POINTFIELD and ELMSLAKE HOUSE are similar. Also ANDERTON HOUSE, a mid-C19 refronting of an earlier build-ing and HIGHER ANDERTON HOUSE, *c.* 1830 with few altera-tions, two-storey and attic with symmetrical front of 1:3:1 bays, the ground floor with horizontal rustication, the first-floor bays divided by pilasters and tall panelled parapet. Fine interior including richly decorated plaster cornices with wheat-ears, poppies and vine leaves to the two principal ground-floor rooms.

Of the former industry, the only recognizable feature is the TIDE MILL, rebuilt on a C16 site in 1801, its mill pond to the N infilled in the early C20. All that remains of the Admiralty's Southdown Victualling Yard (1733–1835) is the C18 SOUTH-DOWN QUAY.

MINIONS

2070

In 1840 there was no village but between 1860 and 1880 this was the scene of the nearest thing to a gold-rush seen in Cornwall, after a significant copper find fuelled major investment, with a complex of railway lines running down to Liskeard and the quays at Looe. A boom village, like no other in Cornwall, completely of granite, pleasant terraces, two former chapels, and a village green and inn.

PERAMBULATION. The Minions area is one of the best places to see a microcosm of the Cornish landscape at its C19 peak. Start from the car park on the E approach to the village. To the NW is South Phoenix Mine with HOUSEMAN'S ENGINE HOUSE, now the information centre. Past Houseman's the footpath along an old railway line leads to CHEESEWRING QUARRY, ½ m. N, named after the tor that stands prominently above.

An impressive site, with public access into the quarry and the vast area of waste stone to the E. Drill holes for blasting can be seen in the rock face, as well as various remains of cranes and railway track into the quarry. Outside the quarry are remains of a smithy, powder store and workers' housing. Barclays Bank and other buildings in Liskeard used Cheesewring granite. Closing in 1882, the quarry was opened again to supply granite for Tower Bridge and then other prestige projects until finally closing in 1934.

The Prince of Wales engine house, about ½ m. NE of Houseman's, was built for a reworking of PHOENIX UNITED (1907–14). It housed the last large Cornish-built pumping engine, and was started by the Prince of Wales in July 1909. Despite profitable working from 1844 to 1898 it only worked for four years. Prince of Wales shaft reached 1,193 ft (364 metres), and left an imposing monument: the chimney is large, built with a square base in random rubble granite to halfway up the gable; then changing to red brickwork, it reduces to the circular form which then tapers up to a decorative brick cornice. Extensive ruined remains of other buildings around the engine house in the same style have survived, including a winding engine house and boiler, a compressor house and engine house for the processing mill.

A lengthier walk from Minions over 4 m. around the S side of Caradon Hill includes the Gonamena railway incline, and the complete circuit is almost entirely on the former Liskeard & Caradon Railway route. It passes through SOUTH CARADON MINE, where the initial copper discovery of 1836 took place, and where for an outlay of £640 dividends of £10,000 per annum were paid from 1840 onwards, making it the richest of all the Caradon mines. It raised over 200,000 tons of ore. Many fine ruined engine houses and buddles are visible.

This area of Bodmin Moor is also rich in prehistory. Some of the major sites are:

THE HURLERS, ¼ m. NW. Early Bronze Age. A line of three perfectly circular stone rings, whose stones are evenly spaced and regularly shaped. The diameters vary – 108 ft (33 metres), 105 ft (32 metres) and 115 ft (35 metres) from S to N – but each circle apparently had twenty-nine stones, with the tallest placed in the southern arcs. Such shared characteristics may suggest sequential construction, but paving linked northern and central circles, indicating movement between functioning elements of the one site. The circles also align with Rillaton Barrow, on the skyline uphill, and lie within an extensive ritual complex. A possible fourth circle with fallen stones has been noted 47 yds N of The Hurlers.

CARADON HILL, 1 m. SE. Straggling line of nineteen CAIRNS of various sizes, 43 ft (13 metres) to 115 ft (35 metres) diameter, running from the summit down the W side of a large rounded hill. Some platform cairns, some incorporating natural tors and some with internal structures.

RILLATON BARROW, ½ m. N. Early Bronze Age. Large cairn 112 ft (34 metres) in diameter and 9 ft (2.7 metres) high on Rillaton Common's rounded ridge. Long views across SE Cornwall to Dartmoor. When a secondary CIST built into the E side of the main cairn was opened in the early C19 it revealed a skeleton and decorated pot, inside which was the famous ribbed Rillaton gold cup (now in the British Museum).

STOWE'S POUND, ¾ m. N. Neolithic and Early Bronze Age. Two conjoined HILLTOP ENCLOSURES, one with outworks, on a bulky hill with naturally sculpted tors and rocks. The smaller summit enclosure has the more substantial rampart, up to 15 ft (4.5 metres) high, with no ditch, but numerous stones on edge. It links tors and encloses naturally sculpted boulders, some with fine rock basins, but excludes the famous Cheesewring rockpile. The later larger enclosure on the hill's slightly lower N back has a less massive rampart, again un-ditched. Contains over 110 house 'stances', cleared and levelled sub-circular spaces on which circular or squarish buildings probably stood. They are probably Early Bronze Age, like the two PLATFORM CAIRNS in clitter (loose boulders) at the enclosures' N end. The N enclosure has complex E and W entrances, but no gateway links it to the earlier, possibly Neolithic, summit enclosure, which contains no house stances and whose stony bank is carefully positioned to obscure all sight of the tors when viewed from the N. Apparently reused as a medieval pound for restraining livestock trespassing on Rillaton Common.

CRADDOCK MOOR ROUND HOUSES, ½ m. NW. Probably Middle Bronze Age. The houses are so distributed that each appears to have controlled two or three fields in a well-defined curvilinear system, a pattern which grew with one field attached to another. Downhill lynchets indicate cultivation while broad lanes from houses to fields to open pasture beyond suggest mixed farming.

MINSTER *see* BOSCASTLE

MITCHELL   8050

Now a small village with a few good houses but formerly a rotten borough sending two members to Parliament until 1832. The PLUME OF FEATHERS is an C18 inn, much but well remodelled with a gabled porch room on granite columns. Tactfully converted stables at the rear; RALEIGH HOUSE is C17 with a similar porch; THE PILLARS also C17 (dated 1683 v/F.P); and WELLESLEY, early C19 with good Pentewan ashlar front. Plain METHODIST CHAPEL of 1845.

MITHIAN

2 m. N of Chacewater

ST PETER. 1846–51 by *William White*, following the creation of the ecclesiastical parish in 1847 to serve the growing population of the mining district. The gaunt, severe Gothic cruciform church stands in bleak country on a hilltop site, the body of the church of tall proportions, but lacking the command of the landscape that its original spire was designed to bestow. *The Ecclesiologist* considered the window tracery 'very commendable and by no means commonplace', with groups of two, three or four lancets within pointed-arched openings with plate tracery. The interior is of bare early Tractarian austerity and of lofty proportions under a high arch-braced roof. The spire and tower were removed in 1898, the tower rebuilt in 1928 to designs by *Cowell, Drewitt & Wheatly*. Now redundant with permission for residential conversion.

In the village, 2 m. N, the MINERS ARMS INN. C17 with early C18 extensions and further extended in the C19. The early C18 parlour wing on the r. has an excellent interior, including a geometric-patterned ribbed plaster ceiling of two concentric ovals with a central diamond and a large moulded cornice, dado panelling and a corner cupboard with shaped shelves. Another plaster ceiling in the passage behind the parlour with dentilled cornice and arabesques, dated 1775, fielded panelling and stair with turned balusters. Just w in the village street the OLD POST OFFICE and WHITEWALLS COTTAGES, built in the early C18 as a row of four one-room plan dwellings.

ROSE-IN-VALE HOTEL, ¼ m. E. Built *c*. 1770, with compact but elegant six-bay front, greatly extended to the rear.

HARMONY COTTAGE, ½ m. N. A row of an C18 house and two later cottages with rubble and cob walls under a thatched roof. The house of John Opie (1761–1807), the painter, born in St Agnes.

MORVAH

ST MORVETH. The interest of this church is less its humble, two-staged, unbuttressed w tower of the C14 than its rebuilt nave and chancel of 1828. In spite of their date these are not in the Commissioners' style (cf. Penzance, St Day): rough, granite, unaisled, and certainly meant to be Cornish Medieval from outside, though the window tracery does odd things. Simple interior with boarded ribbed barrel ceiling. Contemporary walls, stile, piers, and wrought-iron gates with patterned bracing and finials to the churchyard.

CHUN CASTLE, 1 m. S. A small bivallate later Iron Age HILL-FORT, with an unusual drystone inner rampart that was apparently still 15 ft (4.6 metres) high in the early C19. Excavations in the 1920s found four round-houses, a well, furnace, tin slag and iron suggesting a tinners' fort protecting ores and ingots. But the builders evidently were also concerned with antiquity and territory, for the inner enclosure's entrance faces W to the much earlier Chun Quoit, as did the original entrance in the lower outer rampart (marked by upright granites). Reuse, perhaps post-Roman, included shifting the outer entrance S, offsetting it from the inner. Ruined segmental stone structures built against inside of inner rampart appear to be late.

CHUN QUOIT, 1 m. S. Beautiful Early Neolithic CHAMBERED TOMB. Large, curved-topped capstone, 12 ft (3.6 metres) square, supported by four inward-leaning granite slabs forming a simple box. Visible on the skyline when viewed from Woon Gumpus Common to W. When it was excavated in 1871, a shallow pit in the chamber had already been emptied. Stony mound probably secondary to the chamber it surrounds. Medieval pasture and parish boundary incorporates the quoit.

MORVAL

2050

As at Lanhydrock and Boconnoc, the church and house lie close together, here in a small landscaped park set in a steep valley that slopes down towards Looe and the sea. The estate was owned by the Glynns (1436–1512), Coodes (1512–1629) and Bullers (1659–1890).

ST WENNA. Small and low behind the rhododendrons. The priory of St Germans held the rectory between 1224 and 1539. The church is probably of Norman cruciform origin but there is no certain evidence of Norman work, though Sedding considered the S wall of the nave massive enough to be of that date. It was re-dedicated in 1318. The three-stage unbuttressed W tower with battlemented cornice, square turrets and crocketed finials could be C14. The body of the church, of nave, chancel, N aisle, S transept and S porch, shows substantial remodelling in the C15 and C16: the tracery is predominantly that of the latter period (partly renewed in late C19 restorations), save the S window of the chancel which looks as though it might have been C13 originally. The transept was appropriated by the Bullers in the later C17, with a private entrance on the W side under a two-centred arch with hoodmould and initial and date IB 1671. S porch sundial also 1671. The N aisle arcade is of five bays, with standard Cornish piers on tall moulded bases, the capitals decorated with large horizontal leaves (as in Devon), and wide two-centred arches: it was added in the early C16 with windows of the latest Perp type (cf. Morwenstow) set unusually high in the wall, presumably because of the steep rise of ground to the N. The aisle retains its original wagon roof, of good quality with carved ribs, wall- and arcade plates and ornate carved bosses. Sealed wagon roof to S transept with moulded wall-plate. – FONT. Octagonal, C13. – C17 ALMS BOX with iron hinges and mountings at W end of nave. – STAINED GLASS. Chancel E by *Clayton & Bell*, 1891. – S transept E by *Thomas Willement*, 1849. – N aisle W by *Julian George*, 2001, with interesting iconography including the Hale-Bopp comet. – MONUMENT in S transept to Walter Coode †1637. Slate, with kneeling parents and children allegorically expressed by fruits growing out of branches issuing from the parents. Skulls above the fruits show the death of children before their parents.

The serene S front of the HOUSE presents one of the best C16 or C17 elevations in Cornwall, a symmetrical composition with a long two-storey central range flanked by projecting wings with hipped roofs. But this disguises a long sequence of develop- ment since the C15, with major C16, C17 and C19 extension and rebuilding, the complexity markedly more evident from the main approach from the N with its charmingly irregular assem- blage of building gathered around the clock tower. The plan of the house is arranged around a courtyard, with a double-depth range to the N. Its evolution is not fully understood but the oldest fabric is on the E side, of a truncated C15 hall with four surviving bays of lightly smoke-blackened roof trusses. A second hall was built to the W of this, which was extended S in the early C16 by a first-floor hall or parlour with a four-bay arch-braced roof. By the late C16 the S front had been made symmetrical with the building of the SE wing, and slightly later the courtyard was enclosed to the N with a through passage aligning with the wide passage in the central range. In the C19 a nursery wing was built to the SW, much of the N range rebuilt, and the clock tower added.

The S elevation is profoundly satisfying, its symmetry enhanced by the regular disposition of windows, the central range with two six-light mullioned windows with king mullions flanking the C19 remodelled central entrance under a two- centred arch and smaller three four-light mullioned windows with king mullions above. Similar window arrangements in the projecting wings. A highly distinctive feature is the glazing of the windows with late C18 diagonal glazing bars with lambs' tongues and crown glass. On the S side of the courtyard is a slate-hung loggia supported on Doric columns reused from the former S porch demolished in *c.* 1970. Though much fine C17 plasterwork is known to have been lost, the interior retains good C17 features including many fireplaces, bolection- moulded panelling and a *c.* 1670 stair re-set as a dog-leg with square panelled newels, ornate carved finials and carved closed strings; it is believed to have come from Keveral Barton, St Martin-by-Looe (q.v.), which also belonged to the Bullers.

Former ALMSHOUSES, ¼ m. N on the road to Looe. 1860 for J. F. Buller of Morval. Two-storey symmetrical front, built as four one-room plan cottages, two entered at the centre, the others by lean-to porches either end, and with two large lateral stacks.

MORWENSTOW

To R. S. Hawker, the remarkable poet-parson and antiquary who was vicar here between 1834 and 1875, Morwenstow was 'the end of the world'. Even now there is still something strangely arresting about this parish, the most northerly in Cornwall, remote and high above precipitous cliffs, that owes much, as Betjeman perceptively noted, to Hawker's 'strong, Celtic, catholic and compassionate personality'.

St Morwenna. One of the most atmospheric of churches, even for Cornwall. Its position is incomparably romantic; the way the tower stands four-square and silent above the coombe, facing the sea beyond, is unforgettable. The tower is of three stages, unbuttressed, with tall corner pinnacles with crocketed finials, its lower stage probably C15, the upper stages *c.* 1550. That there was a substantial Norman church here is immediately obvious from the s porch whose outer doorway is the reused outer arch of the C12 s doorway, removed when the s aisle was added, with zigzag carving below an order of flowers in heavy relief. The four grotesque corbel heads at the gable-ends are also Norman, as is the Agnus Dei with two dragons at the gable apex. The rest of the C12 doorway was re-set as the inner door (q.v. Kilkhampton) minus the outer arch, for which the colonettes remain with a variety of capitals including birds and pine cones. Inner arch of striking beakheads, chevron on soffit, outer order of chevron with more chevron on soffit. Before examining the interior it is worth noting the early chancel, solid-walled with small C13 lancets. Most of the windows are C19 replacements. Inside, the most important feature is the survival of three bays of the Norman arcade to the N aisle, with round-headed arches on thick circular piers with cushion capitals, one carved with chevron. Unchamfered double arch to W with some carvings at apex and either side. Next arch E has three orders of carving including beakheads, chevrons and pellets. The final C12 E arch is also richly moulded with orders of decorative and sculpted chevrons. The most interesting Norman features are the crude heads of men and beasts both in the porch and the arcade arches, and, of especially strong appeal, the beasts' heads projecting from the spandrels of the arches. The three Norman bays are followed by two E.E. bays also with circular piers: they have double-chamfered pointed arches. The s arcade and s aisle on the other hand are standard Cornish late medieval. One bay has the date 1564 and initials on capitals and abaci, another example of substantial post-Reformation church building. Fine wagon roofs of naves and aisles with flat bosses and wall-plates with vine foliage and carved angels; the chancel bosses are carved and of higher quality. The church was restored in the 1850s under Hawker's direction, with further campaigns in 1878–87 by *J. P. St Aubyn* and in the early C20, possibly by *E. H. Sedding*. – FONT. Very primitive Norman, egg-shaped, with a simple cable moulding round the centre and remains of carving below on plinth made up of stone with carved fleurons, possibly the remains of a tomb. – BENCH-ENDS. Complete set of fixed benches and ends with moulded rails and Gothic tracery above Renaissance arabesques. One has 'TK' for Thomas Kempthorne, vicar 1539–94, another has the date 1575 and inscription. – The dark and mysterious chancel is entered through the SCREEN, originally constructed by Hawker but replaced in 1908: it includes fragments of C16 and C17 carving including some fine depictions of birds and animals. The metal tracery dates from Hawker's original design. – Large REREDOS, 1908, designed by *E. H. Sedding*, carved by the *Pinwills*: it contains a CARTOON by *Giovanni Battista Piazetta* (1683–1734) and three engravings by *John Baptist-Jackson* (1701–80). – Fragment of late C15 or early C16 WALL PAINTING on N wall of chancel, near a fragment of CARVING, probably C16, of profile head, dove and dragon. – SHIP'S FIGUREHEAD from the *Caledonia of Arbroath*, wrecked in 1842, on N wall of nave. – STAINED GLASS. Chancel E, 1849 by *William Warrington*. – Several early C20 windows by *Lavers, Barraud & Westlake* including S aisle, 1904, depicting R. S. Hawker with his dog, church, and various other features in the parish associated with him. – MONUMENTS. Large floor slate to Charlotte Hawker, his first wife, in front of the pulpit. – Slate to Grace Coryndon †1731.

In the churchyard several good C17 CHEST TOMBS; the HOLY WELL OF ST JOHN (documented as early as 1296) SE of the church, with well-house with steeply gabled stone roof; and LYCHGATE, STILE and former MORTUARY. Stile probably designed by *Hawker*, lychgate C17, rebuilt C18, and mortuary C19.

OLD VICARAGE, NE below the churchyard. 1837, designed for himself by *R. S. Hawker*. 'I begin my house in a few days', he wrote to the Rev. H. T. Ellacombe, 'and if you have access to Hunt's "Designs for Parsonage Houses", you may see a sketch of mine for it is the first in the Series of Engravings. The Style Old English, coeval with that of part of my Church . . . The only objects then perceptible from my two fronts will be the Church and the Sea, the suggestions of both which are boundless.' Picturesque gabled composition, the windows Gothick throughout with arched timber lights and, most distinctive, six prominent chimneystacks in the form of church towers. They are said to be modelled on churches with which Hawker had an association but have proved difficult to identify: there are similarities with North Tamerton, Stratton and Whitstone at least.

On the cliffs W of the church HAWKER'S HUT, designed by *Hawker* for himself, built of timber from the wreck of the *Alonzo* with a turf roof; he used it for reflection and writing poetry.

The parish has a remarkable number of medieval manor and other large houses, a unique assemblage in Cornwall.

RECTORY FARM, just S of the church. An unpretentious gabled front with a large two-storey C17 porch disguises a medieval house which was substantially rebuilt in the C15. Its roof is one of the earliest in the country and includes a C14 spere truss relating to a former aisled hall and three smoke-blackened and arch-braced C15 trusses with crown-post detail (cf. Food for Thought, Fowey). C17 staircase in porch.

STANBURY MANOR, 1 m. S. Documented in 1296, the birthplace of John Stanbury, Bishop of Hereford 1453, passing to the Manning family in the C15. Hall fireplace inscribed to John and Christian Manning dated 1585 indicates substantial C16 rebuilding. Originally on a courtyard plan, its present front with projecting lateral stacks has a defensive appearance. C16 roof structure and many C16 and C17 features.

MARSLAND MANOR, 1 m. NNE. A well-preserved and extremely rare example in Cornwall of a double-courtyard-plan yeoman's house, a less genteel version of Tonacombe (*see* p. 633). Walled forecourt with gatehouse and other offices enclosing an inner court in a quasi-defensive manner. Much C19 alteration including replacement of roofs and windows.

Other former open-hall houses include GOOSEHAM BARTON, Gooseham, 2 m. NE, and LOWER CORY, 1 m. NNE.

At COOMBE, 3 m. S, a delightful hamlet around a ford at the seaward end of the Combe valley, including HAWKER'S COTTAGE, a C17 cob-and-thatch house with a cross-shaped window designed by Hawker, other cottages, and a former WATERMILL dated 1842.

MOUNT EDGCUMBE

4050

The magnificence of Mount Edgcumbe's situation, spectacular even for Cornwall (in fact in Devon until 1854), is first best appreciated from the Plymouth side of Plymouth Sound and then from the ferry crossing to Cremyll, where the house appears in its elevated and stately position up a grassy slope of the headland. Though gutted by bombs in 1941 and partly reconstructed 1958–64, leaving an interior of little interest, it endures as the centrepiece of one of the earliest and most richly ornamented landscaped estates in Cornwall.

The HOUSE was originally built as a villa for Sir Richard Edgcumbe in 1547–53. The contractor was *Roger Palmer* of North Buckland, Devon, 'followynge ... the devyse advyse and platt of the seyd Sir Richard Eggecombe and his assignes'. It was a very modern, indeed audacious, mansion for the Tudor period, its shape of great significance historically, for it was outward-facing, utterly different in conception from the conventional courtyard plan of Cotehele, the Edgcumbes' principal seat. From the first it had corner towers, round and slender, a feature found in French royal houses by this date but exceptional in England. It also had a central clerestoreyed hall just as at Michelgrove, West Sussex (*c.* 1540) and Wollaton, Nottinghamshire, thirty years later, though here the hall was the same size and shape in plan as Cotehele and it had no fully symmetrical front. The hall was heightened in the late C17 and the corner towers rebuilt to an octagonal plan in 1749 for Richard Edgcumbe, former Lord of the Treasury who was raised to the peerage by Walpole in 1742. C17, C18 and C19 alterations included to the w a banqueting house of 1675, perhaps by *Robert Hooke*, linked to the house by a wing of 1788, and added to, with a conservatory by *George Wightwick c.* 1840. All of this was destroyed after 1941, but the late C17 front door remains and has been attributed to *William Taylor*. The post-fire reconstruction by *Adrian Gilbert Scott* was around the shell of the external walls only, including a lower central hall and revealing the red sandstone rubble walls which had been lime-washed or stuccoed since at least the late C17. One tower retains a mid-C16 fireplace, and some ogee-headed windows (cf. Cotehele).

The GARDENS, PLEASURE GROUNDS and PARK are of great interest and beauty, enhanced by splendid views over the Sound and the Hamoaze as well as along the coast. Celebrated by visitors and artists from the C16 onwards, Mount Edgcumbe's fame ensured its depiction on Catherine the Great's 'Frog' dinner service. Sir Piers Edgcumbe first enclosed a deer park here in 1539 and it was landscaped in the early C18 and early C19 (and admired by Repton). *Thomas Hull,* gardener and surveyor, received huge sums between 1731 and 1772. In the early C19 a coastal ride was developed through the villages of Kingsand and Cawsand to Penlee Point (*see* Rame) and the whole landscape is thickly populated with picturesque features and structures.

E of the house in the Earl's Garden, the EAST LAWN SUMMER-HOUSE, an early C19 arcaded structure, and overlooking the Cedar Lawn a late C18 SHELL SEAT encrusted with shells, fossils and crystalline stones. The formal gardens further N of the house begin with the Italian garden, containing a fine classical ORANGERY dated 1785, by *Thomas Pitt, Lord Camelford,* of Boconnoc (q.v.). It has a seven-bay front, the bays articulated by plain Doric pilasters, paired to the outer bays. Triglyph frieze. Lodge nearby, also dated 1785. The fountain was 'recently erected' in 1803. Also an early C19 monumental double STAIRCASE of Italian Renaissance inspiration supporting C19 statues, several after the antique and an C18 bust of Ariosto. S is the single-storey ENGLISH GARDEN HOUSE. The

centre part was built by 1729, with a pediment on Doric
columns, triglyph frieze and tapering pedimented doorcase
copied from Serlio's and Palladio's illustrations of the Temple
of Vesta at Tivoli (cf. the Deerhouse at Chiswick of *c.* 1728).
The bays l. and r. with lugged and tapered surrounds added
by 1809. The marble-lined plunge bathroom behind the l. addition is probably mid C18. In the adjoining garden, the FRENCH
GARDEN HOUSE, here by 1784 at least, a summerhouse and
conservatory with a central octagonal room flanked by a pair
of plant houses. Also the MONUMENT to Countess Sophia
†1806, an urn on a pedestal. Just outside the garden, a MONU-
MENT to Timothy Brett †1791, a friend of the 3rd Lord Edgcumbe. Concave-sided triangular stone pedestal on tortoises
with roundels on each face and fluted urn on top. It reproduces
James Wyatt's Sarsfield memorial at Lucan, Dublin (1772, cf.
the Frankland monument, Stanmer Park, East Sussex and
others). E beside the coast, THOMSON'S SEAT, a temple with
an inscription from James Thomson's poem *The Seasons* of
1730. It has a back-to-back plan with pediments and on the
front, baseless Roman Doric columns in antis (cf. the 1730s
Temple of Piety, Studley Royal). Nearby to the S, a mid-C16
single-storey crenellated BLOCK HOUSE. Immediately E is a
terrace which began as an C18 saluting platform but was rebuilt
along with the segmental plan GARDEN BATTERY, dated
1862, as part of the Palmerstonian defences.

Along the coastal path S of the house is, first, the DRIPSTONE,
a rock arch with an anthropomorphic keystone; then the
TEMPLE OF MILTON, an Ionic rotunda with an inscription
from *Paradise Lost*, built 1755. High on the ridge above a
FOLLY, an intentionally ruined stone tower incorporating
medieval fragments from the churches of St George and St
Lawrence in Stonehouse, Plymouth. Constructed 1747 as a
picturesque feature in place of a navigation obelisk. Finally, a
ROMAN ARCH above Redding Point. *See* also Picklecombe,
p. 337 and Rame.

The grandest of the entrances is the TRIUMPHAL ARCH at Higher
Lodge, built to commemorate the visit of George III in 1789,
the arch supported by giant moulded volutes and flanking
walls terminating in piers with ball finials; the lodge is probably
contemporary but in an archaic style. At Cremyll Quay, the
picturesque early C19 LOWER LODGE, with canted crenellated
porch with pointed windows, and monumental rusticated
stone gate piers surmounted by ball finials in the ENTRANCE
SCREEN. The whole ensemble makes an impressive entrance
from the ferry approach from Stonehouse. Near Maker church,
MAKER LODGE, *c.* 1850, two-storey Gothic, marking the
entrance to the deer park.

At CREMYLL a pretty C18 and C19 group by the QUAYS (by *J.
M. Rendel*, 1836–7), and one of the best views across The
Narrows to the Royal William Yard at Plymouth. FERRY
TICKET OFFICE, crenellated and with battered elevations. In

the nearby Admiralty playing fields, a late C18 to early C19 OBELISK.

At EMPACOMBE ½ m. W, a remarkable Gothick wall with two towers overlooking Millbrook Lake, built as part of the construction of the kitchen gardens supervised by *Thomas Parlby*, c. 1775–6.

MOUNT HAWKE

7040

ST JOHN THE BAPTIST. 1878 by *A. C. Hancock*. Plain, E.E. style with Bath stone dressings to lancets, and simple bellcote.

Former BOARD SCHOOL, Rodda's Road. 1874 datestone. Usual U-plan and pretty Gothic details including traceried windows of early Perp pattern.

MOUSEHOLE

4020

A former fishing port whose exceeding picturesqueness remains remarkably unspoiled. Its buildings may be mostly modest C18 and C19 houses with few of individual note but they populate a pattern of streets around the harbour and the hillside behind that dates from the late C13 when the town, then part of the parish of Paul (q.v.), was the pre-eminent port in Mount's Bay. Even as late as the early C16 it was the second largest place in West Penwith after St Ives. In decline by 1595 when sacked by the Spanish, it continued to prosper on fishing and related industries in the C18 and C19. It is a distinguished history that still infuses a place conspicuously less commercialized than usual in modern Cornwall.

ST CLEMENT'S METHODIST CHURCH, Chapel Street. Founded 1784 and enlarged and remodelled at several periods in the C19, it is Mousehole's grandest building, two-storey, stucco, the ground floor rusticated, with round-headed sash windows, four to each floor on the side elevations, three to the ends. Fine and complete mid-C19 interior with horseshoe gallery on slender Ionic columns, and elaborate pulpit. Good late C19 and early C20 patterned glass including the figures of Wesley, Bunyan and Wycliffe.

An exploration should begin at the heart of the town, the HARBOUR and its SOUTH QUAY, started before 1392 and extended several times subsequently, latterly in the C19: substantial sections of the medieval pier remain embedded in the present structure. The NORTH QUAY was constructed in the 1860s. From the harbour walls it is possible to enjoy a panorama of the whole settlement spreading along the waterfront and up the slope behind. Much of the town is built of Lamorna granite walls with slate roofs and relatively little of the white render and colour wash of other Cornish fishing ports. The one building whose large scale and imposing presence stands out from the rest is Mount Zion Methodist Church (*see* above). In complete contrast, and much more typical of the Mousehole streetscape, are the humble C19 cottages along THE WHARF on the edge of the waterfront. Just inland in KEIGWIN PLACE, KEIGWIN and OLD STANDARD, both probably C17 in their present form though occupying medieval house plots, their principal features – mullioned windows and moulded stone door surrounds – dating from that later period. The porch of Keigwin, carried on four granite posts with unusual square cushion heads, necks and bases, dates from *c.* 1700 when a set of grand upper rooms with plaster barrel ceilings was created. Both became inns in the late C18. FAIRMAIDS COTTAGE, Keigwin Place, has the external stairs associated with former fish cellars below the domestic accommodation, of which there are several other examples in neighbouring streets. Continue along FORE STREET, which runs along the waterfront, past the C18 and C19 OLD SHIP INN, and the HARBOUR OFFICE, early to mid-C19 with a gabled brick clock tower perched on its roof. All the other little streets and courts around the water-front repay brief exploration, with nice plain cottages in CHAPEL STREET and GERNICK STREET.

MULLION

ST MELINA. In the centre of its large village, within a possible *lann*. The C15 W tower is a specially mellifluous blend of large serpentine and granite blocks. It is of two stages, unbuttressed, very similar to nearby Cury with the same reuse of earlier heads as label stops (the r. one a bishop) to the W door and a little relief of the Crucifixion above the window. The S porch has the familiar panelled jambs of the Lizard churches, and the S aisle the same E window with bulbous cusped tracery as at Cury, Gunwalloe and Sithney. The N and S arcades are identical, late C15 to early C16, of Cornish standard design and undecorated capitals. Fine ceiled C15 wagon roofs throughout with angels on the wall-plates of the chancel. The N and S doors are original too, the S door with a curious small opening set low down (suggested as designed for the expulsion of dogs). Restorations in 1840 and *c.* 1880 were followed by a thoughtful embellishment by F. C. Eden (c. f. Blisland) in the 1920s. – FONT. Good C13 work, octagonal, three of the sides with two very shallow blank trefoiled arcades, the fourth with a serpent motif. – BENCHES and BENCH-ENDS. This is one of the best churches for the study and enjoyment of these characteristi-cally Cornish furnishings, with a remarkably complete array occupying most of the nave and aisles. Though somewhat rearranged and altered, they are a visual and iconographic delight, meriting close inspection. Some benches have two motifs, some one, for each end; others form the fronts and backs of the blocks of pews; and others are in the centres of the blocks. Among the representations are the usual Gothic motifs of the Instruments of the Passion and initials and many engaging profiles of, *inter alia*, monks, soldiers, jesters and grotesques. The date range must be *c.* 1530–50 for there is a wealth of detail to indicate the coming of the Renaissance, as at Altarnun and Launcells (qq.v.): see for example the panel at the rear of the S aisle with the two cherubs with chalice and barrel. – LECTERN, incorporating two Elizabethan female figures. – ROOD SCREEN. Only small sections of the base survive but they are worked into a splendid screen complete with rood loft and large rood of 1925–31 to Eden's design by *Herbert Read* of Exeter, the S section completed in 1961: all very reminiscent of Eden's screen at Blisland (q.v.), though here without the colour. – ROYAL ARMS of Charles II, well carved. – Near the S porch the head of a medieval CHURCH-YARD CROSS, octagonal in section, on a well-executed modern shaft and base.

At MULLION COVE, 1 m. SW, a good example of a small fishing harbour protected by a QUAY of 1895, including a WINCH HOUSE and a small COTTAGE perched on the rocks overlooking the harbour.

At POLDHU COVE, 1 m. NW, strikingly set near the cliff edge above the S side of the cove, the MARCONI MEMORIAL. Erected 1937 by the Marconi Company of London, designed by *Kelly & Co. (Cramb Bros) Ltd* of London. Ashlar granite shaft, slightly tapered, rising from a stepped base and surmounted by a globe in a double triangular frame. Four plaques on the sides of the plinth commemorate Marconi's research between 1900 and 1933 at the Poldhu Wireless Station, which stood NE of the memorial: from here the first transatlantic signals were transmitted by wireless telegraphy on 12 December 1901, evoking reflection on the momentous consequences of Marconi's work that ushered in the communications revolution of the C20. Adjoining the site to the N, the MARCONI CENTRE, 2002 by the *Barlow, Schofield Partnership*.

8030

MYLOR

The churchtown overlooks Carrick Roads at the mouth of Mylor Creek, well away from the modern village spreading from the former port at Mylor Bridge.

ST MELOR. In a lovely waterside position, standing within a lushly planted *lann* churchyard that extends N towards the creek. Remarkable in several ways which distinguish it from the standard Cornish church. First it has two towers. One is the turret on its W gable supported by immense buttresses l. and r., the width of the nave behind, with crisply carved bell-openings that suggest an early to mid-C14 date. The other is detached a little further W and higher up, and is a belfry of c. 1636 with a C19 weatherboarded upper storey which, like the towers at Feock and Talland, is likely to have served as a land-mark for shipping. Moreover, the church possesses two fine Norman doorways: one is on the N in its original position with a Maltese cross in the tympanum, zigzag moulding up the jambs and along the lintel, and an outer hoodmould in the form of a serpent, its mouth visible on the W impost; the other, clearly assembled from different fragments, was transferred to the W tower entrance and has one order of colonettes and a cross in the tympanum. The lower parts of the N walls, includ-ing those of the transept, still have masonry from the Norman cruciform building but the rest of the church is predominantly C15 with a later C15 S aisle. Of unusual interest also is the early C16 porch with its exceptionally well-carved doorway with octagonal jambs panelled with trefoil-headed niches and a pretty ogee openwork tracery head (cf. St Austell). A flared cross in the gable above the doorway is probably part of another Norman tympanum.

The interior bears the heavy imprint of a severe restoration of 1869–70 with plain roofs of this date. S aisle arcade of six bays on slim piers of standard Cornish design and standard decoration of the abaci, all in Caen stone, which is also used for the outer and inner porch doors, the window of the S aisle gable, and the columns of the N door. Two niches in the N wall of the N transept incorporate Norman fragments and on the E wall of the chancel aisle are two Perp corbels found and resited here in 1870, one plain and the other part of an angel holding a shield with traces of original colour. – FONT. Octagonal, with a plain decoration of crosses. Base and shaft C13; bowl later, and rough, possibly C17. – PISCINA. Octagonal pillar with octagonal bowl, a larger version of the same design at Bodmin. – PULPIT. C17 with panels of the usual kind and others with lozenges. – ROOD SCREEN. Only the dado survives, reassem-bled but well preserved and well and broadly carved in an early Renaissance style. To each section belong four narrow upright panels with undulating foliage; some of its original colour, red and black, is still clearly visible. Above the l. panels runs an inscription: IARYS IONAI JESW CREST (Mary, John and Jesus Christ). Joined to the dado, and now forming part of the choir stalls, are two C16 BENCH-ENDS. – The REREDOS has a central panel of glass mosaic by *Salviati*. – STAINED GLASS. Chancel E and S transept by *Alexander Gibbs*. – MONUMENTS. Francis Trefusis, 1680, kneeling in front of an aedicule with a classical segmented pediment, a cartouche with large angels below. Of more interesting design than good quality. – Reginald Locks, 1805, signed by *Richard Westmacott Jun.* – Several minor monuments. – Richard Bonython †1697, his wife †1710 and Samuel Kempe, the husband of their only daughter †1803, by *Pearce* of Truro, a largish Gibbsian wall tablet. – Edward Jescombe †1803, a white inscription tablet surmounted by an urn on a grey marble oval with a sarcophagus below. Others by *J. Isbell* of Truro, *Olvers* of Falmouth, *Pearce* of Truro and *T. King* of Bath. – In the churchyard what would be the tallest Cornish CROSS at 17 ft 6 in. (5.4 metres) if 7 ft (2.1 metres) of its shaft were not buried in the ground. Found in use as a flying buttress against the s wall of the church during the restoration. A wheel-headed cross, deeply cut but not pierced. Little ornament, chiefly incised circles and concentric circles. – HOLY WELL. On the N of the church. Medieval in origin, rebuilt in C19. – LYCHGATE. W of the church, early C19, re-roofed 1928 with arch-braced trusses.

HARBOUR QUAY, NE of the church, is late C18 and early C19. L-shaped plan with rounded end to W. Vertically set slate rubble with short sections of granite ashlar, with granite ashlar copings. Site of the smallest Royal Navy Dockyard, established 1805, to provide water to the Navy.

At MYLOR BRIDGE, 1 m. NW, is an C18 QUAY fronting the creek, of vertically set rubble with granite copings and some pleasant early to mid-C19 houses in LEMON HILL, with a CLOCK TOWER built *c.* 1850 for Charles Lemon of Carclew. Three stages on square plan, the clock face on the middle stage and an upper bell-stage with round-arched openings to each side and squat pyramidal stone roof surmounted by ship weathervane. Gates and cast-iron fence to r., richly decorated, in front of the former SCHOOL of the same date. Nearby VILLAGE PUMP, 1852.

PANDORA INN, Restronguet Passage, 1 m. NE of Mylor Bridge. Idyllically sited on the waterfront with long sweeps of wheat-reed thatch unifying a C17–C20 ensemble and sustaining an authentic vernacular character. The older waterfront range probably started as a C17 three-room cross-passage house with a lateral stack, enlarged in the early C19 by a service wing to the rear of the l. room and by a cellar with room over at the further l. Extended by a large, irregular r. wing with a lateral stack in the C20. The remodelled interior retains C17 ceiling beams, floorboards, and old clay tiles in the l. room. The inn is named after the ship that captured some of the mutineers from the Bounty. Severely damaged by fire 2010 but meticulously restored 2011–12.

ENYS, ½ m. W of Mylor Bridge. First mentioned in the C15, remodelled and extended in the early C18 by Samuel Enys, the house rebuilt 1833–6 by *Henry Harrison* (cf. Heligan, and Trewarthenick, Cornelly) for John Samuel Enys. An engraving by Borlase of 1758 shows the C18 house as E-shaped with a walled forecourt to the s and extensive walled gardens to the E; Harrison retained part of the C18 building as a three-storey service wing. This is set back to the l. from his plain granite

Mylor, Carclew. Engraving after W. Borlase, 1758

ashlar block of two storeys in a restrained classical style. The tall ground-floor windows rise directly from a low stone plinth, the first-floor windows of smaller proportions. The service wing retains its C18 dog-leg staircase, the house most of its 1833 features. To the l. of the service wing a late C19 three-stage Italianate CLOCK TOWER. Harrison's scheme included extensive landscaping, removing the walled forecourt, reducing the walled gardens and developing the park: Enys had been celebrated in the C18 for its gardens and became famous in the C19 for its many rare and tender plants, a tradition continued into the C20. ½ m. SW, an early C19 single-storey LODGE, remodelled in the late C19, the central bay set back under an elaborate open gable, and with cusped headed windows and door.

CARCLEW, 2 m. NW of Mylor Bridge. One of the most beautiful and important houses in Cornwall before it was gutted by fire in 1934 and left a fragmentary but romantic ruin. It was built in a commanding position overlooking Restronguet Creek and Carrick Roads in the centre of a large medieval estate that had been acquired by Samuel Kempe in 1677. He began a new house and planned extensive formal gardens from *c.* 1720 which were left uncompleted when the estate was sold in 1749 to William Lemon (cf. Truro). Lemon employed *Thomas Edwards* of Greenwich to complete and enlarge the house: Edwards had already built Princes House, Truro, for Lemon, would go on to build Mansion House (also in Truro) and had also remodelled Trewithen (qq.v.). The splendid Palladian front in granite ashlar had a central Ionic portico to full height with pavilion wings with pediments and Venetian windows, joined by Doric colonnades to the main block. The house was further extended w in the late C18 and early C19 by *Henry Harrison* in stuccoed granite rubble to include a clock tower. The central block was square in plan, three rooms wide, with reception rooms flanking the entrance hall, the stair hall behind and service wings to the side and rear. The staircase was similar to the Mansion House, the balustrade design almost identical, while the back stair had a Chinese Chippendale balustrade like that at Trewithen. Like the Mansion House too, it was liberally enriched with decorative plasterwork.*

The ruins comprise the portico and adjoining walls to the W, rising through two storeys above a basement. To the W the four-stage clock tower. The E half was extensively damaged by the fire but elements of the plan and even decoration survive, with architectural fragments and masonry scattered around.

The estate had other buildings of note, some of which survive converted to other uses. Outstanding is a GARDEN PAVILION, now a house, N of the ruins. Pretty mid-to late C18 granite ashlar front in a curious mixture of Gothic and classical. The three-bay symmetrical front has weathered diagonal corner buttresses with bays punctuated by fluted consoles under a Gothic-style cornice, surmounted by a blind parapet with cross-bracing and quatrefoils with four obelisk pinnacles as finials. Batty Langley appears to be the source of this doorway, trimmed of some of the detail. It is possible this is also by Edwards.

Former COACHHOUSE AND STABLES, sympathetically converted to a modern house. Mid to late C18. Three-bay coachhouse with accommodation over flanked by three-bay stable blocks. Palladian style in Flemish bond brick with granite dressings. The coachhouse is broken forward under a granite pediment, the stables each have a central doorway with rusticated Gibbs surrounds; possibly also by Edwards. The BARN nearby also has a Palladian front.

The Lemon family were leading importers of rhododendrons and camellias and developed extensive gardens and pleasure grounds in wooded valley parkland. To the W of the house ruins, a series of linked rectangular enclosures with WALLS and TERRACES on four levels stepping down to an ornamental pond, with a kitchen garden at the N end. The walls are in Flemish bond brick using some earlier bricks. The parkland shows well in estuary views.

9050

NANPEAN

ST GEORGE. 1877 by *Silvanus Trevail*. Plainest E.E. with single lancets, buttresses and W bellcote. The GATEPIERS are made from sections of the C15 arcade removed from St Dennis in 1847 (q.v.) with late C19 caps.

---

*For a full description see Laurence Weaver's account in *Country Life*, May 1916, repeated in April 1934.

NEWLYN

Visitors expecting to find the small fishing village so luminously portrayed by the painters of the Newlyn school discover instead one of Britain's largest fishing ports. The transformation was already under way in the second half of the C19 at the same time that Walter Langley and Stanhope Forbes were establishing the artists' colony in the town and it was being opened up to the wider world. Newlyn today still fascinates precisely because it combines the vibrancy of a large working harbour and fishing fleet with the survival of much of the street pattern and buildings of the old town, quietly suffused with the enduring legacy of its artistic tradition.

For most of its pre-C19 life Newlyn Town, the settlement around and above the small medieval quay (first recorded in 1437), was simply a densely settled fishing village. Sheltered by the Penwith peninsula to the W and with panoramic views E across Mount's Bay towards Penzance and St Michael's Mount, its narrow streets and closely packed buildings climb steeply up the hill from the shoreline. From the C17 it was linked with two other small medieval settlements just to the N, Street-an-Nowan on the narrow but more level coastal strip, and Tolcarne on the N side of Newlyn Coombe, which carries the River Newlyn to the sea. Those links were cemented in the later C19 when the huge growth of the fishing industry fuelled the need for a major harbour in the far SW as a port of refuge and call for other British and foreign fishing fleets as well as the town's own rapidly growing fleet. A massive new harbour was built between 1885 and 1894, enclosing the historic quay, accompanied by a vastly improved road network connecting the harbour to Penzance and the town's hinterland: the junction of roads at the lower end of Newlyn Coombe became the new centre of the expanded settlement. In the early C20 these facilities encouraged a number of new industries including the large-scale export of granite from quarries to the S at Gwavas and Penlee and to the N at Castle an Dinas (*see* Ludgvan).

Though little of this transformation was recorded by the Newlyn artists, the reputation of Newlyn as an artistic centre persisted, encouraged by a second generation of the 1920s and 1930s that included Alfred Munnings, Lamorna Birch, Harold Harvey and Laura Knight. But to find the places that so inspired them, persistence is required. Slum clearances from the 1930s to the 1960s removed some of the smaller streets and houses close to the waterfront, and the larger scale of the buildings of the fishing industry that dominate the harbourside makes it difficult at first sight to believe there is much left to see. Yet more than enough survives to convey the intimate character of the older settlement, while several buildings of the later C19 and early C20 reflect its later artistic connections.

ST PETER, The Coombe. 1859–66. *Rev. F. C. Hingeston* drew up initial proposals, *James Perrow* prepared final plans, and *J. W.*

Trounson signed the certificate. E.E. style, with a skilfully composed s elevation of high roofed nave, lower chancel, transept, s aisle and s porch, and octagonal bell-turret. N aisle 1886 by Trounson. Surprisingly spacious and lofty interior with four-bay nave arcade of steeply pointed arches on circular piers on high square bases. Its character is shaped by the work of *Martin Travers* of the Newlyn school, starting in the 1920s and flourishing under *Rev. Allan Wyon*, vicar 1936–55, himself an accomplished sculptor and engraver. Travers designed the splendid E end with its finely carved ALTARPIECE of the Last Supper and the soaring REREDOS that rises to a BALDACCHINO with Wyon's large CRUCIFIX above the altar. By Travers also the FONT COVER, PASCHAL CANDLE and CANDLESTICKS, by Wyon the tenderly carved large MADONNA AND CHILD in a niche on the N wall of the chancel. The ensemble is an outstanding example of Anglo-Catholic embellishment of the period. – PULPIT. serpentine and granite by *Edmund Sedding*, 1866. – STAINED GLASS. A rich assembly of some major firms' work from 1866 to the early C20. Of special note the N aisle windows of Faith, Hope and Charity, and Dorcas, both 1889 by *Burlison & Grylls*, and Lady Chapel windows by *George Ostrehan, c.* 1890. In the churchyard a medieval CROSS-HEAD from Trereife.

Former TRINITY METHODIST CHAPEL, Chywoone Hill. 1834–5, enlarged 1866. One of the best and most complete early C19 chapels in Cornwall. Plain, dignified exterior, rich interior of 1866 with grained box pews and box pulpit – a rare survival – incorporated in later rostrum, oval gallery on marbled cast-iron columns with stencilled decoration to panelled front, and stencilled frieze.

NEWLYN ART GALLERY (formerly Passmore Edwards Memorial Art Gallery), New Road. 1894, promoted by Stanhope

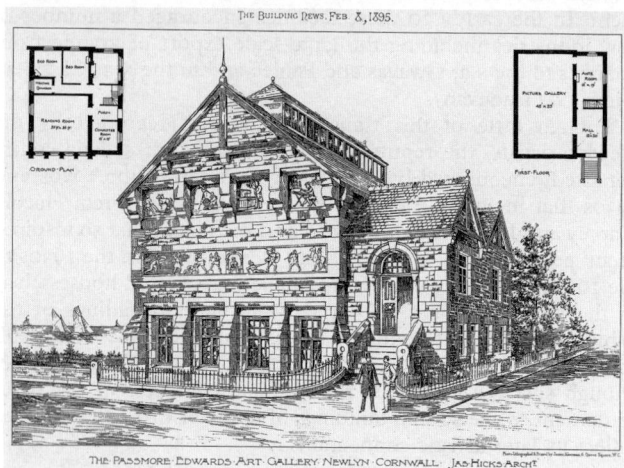

Newlyn, Art Gallery. Engraving, 1895

Forbes, founded by Passmore Edwards, and designed by *James Hicks*, for the Newlyn School of Art. A highly original and striking main façade dominated by a set of four copper repoussé panels framed by carved granite brackets and an ovolo lintel, and surmounted by a quirky timber A-frame supported on granite corbels. The building is crowned by a long glazed lantern. The panels, representing earth, fire, air and water and depicting birds, mammals, reptiles and fish, were made by *Philip Hodder* of Newlyn and students to the design of *J. D. Mackenzie*, the renowned Arts and Crafts copper craftsman, with artistic direction from *T. C. Gotch*, one of the Newlyn school painters. Small but exquisitely sculptured panel of Stanhope Forbes by *Rev. Allan Wyon*, 1948. A low-key slate-hung extension 2007 by *MUMA* (*McInnes Usher McKnight Architects*) successfully complements the lively original.

HARBOUR. The picturesquely curving medieval quay (Old Quay) looks curiously diminutive in comparison with the massive later C19 piers that define the present harbour. It has been rebuilt at several periods since the C15 though parts of the original structure remain. S pier 1865 with a lighthouse at its extremity. The N (or Victoria) pier 1888, extended 1894; in turn the extension was widened in the early C20. Within the harbour also the Mary William pier, 1980. FISH MARKET, with new small boat pontoons, 2006.

SEAMEN'S MISSION (Royal Maritime Mission to Deep Sea Fisherman), Strand. 1911 by *Edward Warren*. A building of considerable presence at the seaward end of the modern centre, a typically understated composition by this architect with interesting fenestration (first-floor windows set tight under the eaves line), the large roof enlivened by dormer, gable and cupola with fine galleon weathervane in copper by *Tom Batten* and *Francis Clemens*, members of the Newlyn Industrial Class started by J. D. Mackenzie. In the area in front of this building a striking WAR MEMORIAL of 1920, the stonework by *W. A. Snell* and bronze sculpture by *L. S. Merrifield* of exceptional quality.

PERAMBULATION. The Newlyn Art Gallery (*see* above) announces Newlyn on the approach from Penzance along NEW ROAD into TOLCARNE, the most northerly of the three medieval settlements that comprise Newlyn today. From the gallery down ART GALLERY TERRACE the path leads seaward to a strongly modelled MEMORIAL to fishermen lost at sea by *Tom Leaper*, 2007, and then into little streets and via Creeping Lane over the early C19 BRIDGE towards the C19 centre of Newlyn in THE COOMBE. Apart from some shops, the street is dominated by the buildings of the fishing industry including several large fish WAREHOUSES and the former PILCHARD WORKS, dated 1874. In the other direction, where the street is called STRAND, a BARCLAYS BANK of 1910, before the Seamen's Mission and war memorial herald the vast extent of the harbour (*see* above). S of these, the early C20 POST OFFICE AND SAVINGS BANK. Off Strand into FOUNDRY PLACE and

into the little streets of tightly packed terraced houses like
CHAPEL STREET off ORCHARD PLACE, which still resonate
with the character of the medieval settlement of STREET-AN-
NOWAN. Forming the inland boundary to this area is the late
C19 road up CHYWOONE HILL on which the former Trinity
Methodist Chapel stands (*see* above).

On the upper side of Chywoone Hill some of the late C19
and Edwardian terraces that define the skyline of Newlyn from
Penzance. At the top (S) end is BELLE VUE, a genteel mid-to
late C19 suburb above Newlyn Town which became an enclave
for the Newlyn school artists. Further S their larger houses like
LA PIETRA of 1895 for Lionel Birch, the Jacobean-style granite
HIGHER FAUGAN of 1903–4 for Stanhope and Elizabeth
Forbes, and WHEAL BETSY of 1910 by *Arnold Mitchell* for the
Gotch family, a quiet Arts and Crafts design with deeply overhanging swept eaves and slate-clad. Now down Belle Vue and
into the maze of densely packed streets and houses of Newlyn
Town, like HARBOUR VIEW TERRACE, TREWARVENETH
STREET, BOASE STREET and CHURCH STREET. The frequent
glimpses down to the harbour are entrancing, with wonderful
views back over the town and towards Penzance and Mount's
Bay. Eventually descend to the harbour again where the small
medieval quay is a suitable finale.

NEWQUAY

The splendour of Newquay is its spectacular natural setting
extending along the cliff tops of Newquay Bay and Fistral Bay
and sheltered by the three headlands of Pentire Point, Towan
Head and Trevelgue Head. The earliest reference to a quay here
is 1440 and the medieval economy was based on pilchard seining;
a fish market is first recorded in 1571 but the settlement remained
modest until Richard Lomax, a London speculator, started
building the present harbour in 1832. In 1838 the manor was
purchased by Joseph Treffry of Place, Fowey (q.v.), who completed the harbour and made Newquay the premier port of north
Cornwall. This included the construction of a mineral tramway
in 1849 to connect the harbour with his tin mines in Newlyn East
and his china clay sites in St Dennis.

The tramway was to prove vital to Newquay's emergence as a
seaside resort when, after Treffry's death, the port declined in the
later C19 with the collapse of the Cornish mining industry. This
led the Cornwall Mineral Railway to diversify into carrying
passenger traffic from 1873 onwards. A stone viaduct was built
over the Trenance valley in 1874, a passenger station opened in
the town in 1877, and the railway was eventually purchased by
the GWR in 1896. The tourist industry had started earlier in the
C19 when wealthy families had built summer villas but was now
promoted assiduously by the GWR, epitomized in its early to

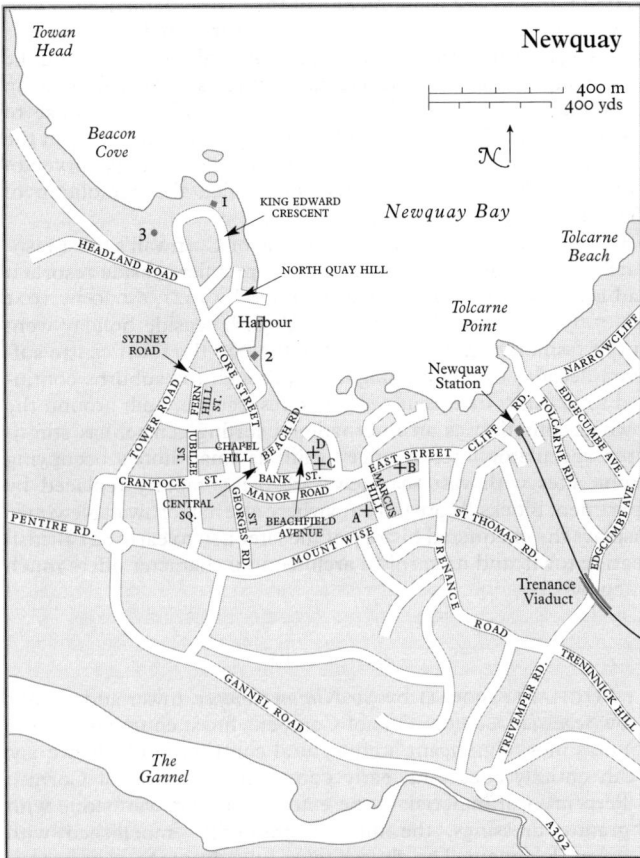

A   St Michael
B   Wesley Methodist church
    and hall
C   United Reformed church
D   Claremont Methodist Church

I   Huer's House
2   Lifeboat station
3   War memorial

mid-C20 poster campaigns where Newquay was packaged as a vital part of the 'Cornish Riviera'.

Silvanus Trevail had seen Newquay as key to realizing his vision for a 'Cornish Tourism', aiming to transform the town into an English version of the great European spas by planning hundreds of mansions, villas and terraces with boulevards, recreation grounds, public gardens and a church. Though this grand project was to fail, he built three of the resort's important Victorian hotels as well as a variety of other buildings. His vision was, however, taken up by Newquay Urban District Council, established in 1868. By 1897 the UDC's surveyor, John Ennor, was planning an ambitious new development s of the C19 settlement on a grid pattern, with E–W routes running along the contours and N–S routes against the gradient. The UDC also laid out a large public park along the floor of the Trenance valley and later bought up the remaining common land on the headlands in response to concern about the spoliation of Newquay's natural setting in the Council for the Preservation of Rural England's 1933 survey of Cornwall. The same survey had demanded the demolition of Trevail's Atlantic and Headland Hotels.

By the early 1930s Newquay was one of Cornwall's most fashionable shopping centres as well as its premier seaside resort. It had grown from 2,000 in 1890 to 3,000 by 1921, 6,000 by 1921 and 7,651 by 1931. But when the English seaside holiday went out of fashion in the second half of the C20 the town centre suffered decades of relative stagnation, though the suburbs continued to expand. Its recent economic resurgence, built around the town's reputation as an international surfing centre, has stimulated speculator interest once again, as small hotels occupying prime sites with vast sea views are being rapidly replaced by apartment blocks. More than anywhere else in Cornwall Newquay displays the chequered history of the later C19 to early C21 British seaside town, and its carnival architectural character offers much to enjoy.

CHURCHES

St Michael. 1909–11 by *Sir Ninian Comper*, tower added 1961 by *Sebastian Comper*. One of Comper's finest churches and the C20's most significant architectural contribution to Newquay. An entirely successful early C20 reinterpretation of Cornish Perp in local materials – the exterior in Pentewan stone with granite dressings, the interior gracefully embellished with green Polyphant. The church takes full advantage of its prominent and steeply sloping site to gently flex the muscle of its large and ambitious scale – nave and chancel continuous, N and s aisles and porches and sw tower – as a presence over the whole town. Comper senior's achievement is best appreciated coming up Marcus Hill in the satisfying free grouping of chancel projecting forward of the N aisle, an octagonal bellcote rising in the junction of chancel and N aisle, and a two-storeyed battlemented N porch with basement dramatically emphasizing the slope, the whole seen against the tall sw tower: Comper originally intended it to stand at the SE corner but the site proved unstable. Tower of four stages with tall pyramidal pinnacles above the battlements and octagonal stair to third stage, its presence as a landmark more than compensating for the discovery close up that it is built of reconstituted stone. The interior is light, spacious and understated. Polyphant piers and arcades of nine arches have type A piers modified with a more prominent concave section between the attached shafts; Polyphant also for door surrounds, piscinas and the base of the NE bellcote. White-painted wagon roofs with plain moulded ribs over the aisles, foliage-enriched bosses in the nave and only light polychrome with angel bosses over the chancel. – ROOD SCREEN, 1930. A delightfully light and delicate filigree of unpainted wood skilfully refining the medieval type, though radically different in its striking simplicity compared to Comper's screen at Little Petherick (q.v.). Huge gold rood figures and seraphim above, the latter larger versions of those at Little Petherick. – CHOIR STALLS and PEWS plain but high quality. – FONT. Octagonal stone with carved sides and base. – STAINED GLASS. Chancel E and S chapel E characteristic *Comper*, 1930 and 1945. – Three by *J. Hardman* in S wall, 1914–18.

The whole interior bestows a cool, calm, assured character, so rightly judged in juxtaposition to the plethora of building styles and materials in the town's adjacent streets. Restoration by *Richard Church* in 1996 after extensive fire damage in 1993 which destroyed the fine organ case in the N aisle. Most of the original dado panelling around the walls and the more sombre dark floor were removed, a narthex was created from the westernmost arcade and the W end slightly extended to introduce meeting rooms, achieved with admirable respect for Comper's original conception.

WESLEY METHODIST CHURCH and HALL, East Street. 1904 by the London firm of *Bell, Withers & Meredith*. One of the most accomplished examples in Cornwall of the application of the free Gothic style, here an interpretation of Tudor Gothic to offer a quietly forceful presence set back from and above a busy commercial street, articulated into porch, auditorium, tower and hall, the latter recessed. Three-stage tower with set-back buttresses and embattled parapet. The church two storeyed to the street, the principal feature the unusual five-light window under a four-centred arch subdivided by two large mullions and further subdivided by tracery.

UNITED REFORMED CHURCH, Bank Street. 1926. Quiet Gothic front to Bank Street, nicely modulated between granite pilasters and unusual local stone walls rising to a three-storeyed corner tower. More modest elevation with yellow brick dressings to The Crescent.

CLAREMONT METHODIST CHURCH, Beachfield Avenue. 1895–6. Loose E.E. style, the central bay of the church broken forward at ground-floor level between pilasters, which carry up to roof level as corbelled pyramidal pinnacles with finials, a striking addition to the street scene.

PERAMBULATIONS

1. West of the town centre: the Harbour, Towan Head and Upper Fore Street

The HARBOUR is set in a sheltered natural cove and surrounded to W and E by sheer cliffs reinforced by rubble revetment walls and surmounted high above by later C19 and early C20 villas and terraces. The present harbour, on the site of the medieval New Keye, was commenced in 1832 by Richard Lomax and completed by Joseph Treffry by 1840. N and S piers, the latter with rotunda and look-out. The stub of a middle jetty added in 1872 survives unconnected to the shore. The working harbour has a LIFEBOAT STATION of 1994 by *Poynton, Bradbury & Wynter*: gabled front in robust rustic squared granite echoing the original on Towan Head (*see* below) and incorporating the NEWQUAY HARBOUR MISSION, successor to the Seamen's Mission established in 1891. Visible in the cliff wall behind are the blocked exit of Treffry's MINERAL TRAMWAY and, higher up, several ORE CHUTES. To the N of the N pier, the promontory sites of three of the once numerous former FISH CELLARS.

Up the coastal path N off KING EDWARD'S CRESCENT is the HUER'S HOUSE, the most significant and evocative witness to the pilchard seining industry in Cornwall. Probably remodelled in the late C18 but with earlier, possibly C14 fabric. Single-storey and almost circular with a small tower reached by an external stair; the tower is a stack for heating the room, which is open towards the sea. The whole effect of this little white-washed structure perched on the cliff edge with commanding views of the sea is so much more than picturesque: here it is easy to imagine the watching huer waiting for approaching shoals of pilchards and then crying 'Heva, heva' and with signals directing the fishermen in the boats. Prominently sited above on a natural eminence to the W is the WAR MEMORIAL of 1921, a large Celtic cross on a tor-like mound of huge granite boulders.

From here, the resort's late C19 development is dramatically revealed in the powerful presence of two of *Silvanus Trevail's* huge hotels, The Atlantic above King Edward Crescent and, further W, The Headland. THE ATLANTIC of 1892 is like a promontory fortress on its raised site, visible for miles and, as Trevail intended, a major presence in views throughout the town. Close up it is now impossible to appreciate Trevail's original design because it is completely disguised by later external alterations, which included raising the parapet to create a fourth storey, so hiding the original hipped roof, large extensions to the entrance front and N and W elevations, and re-windowing. The interior retains more of Trevail including a majestic full-height imperial staircase and main reception rooms with large marble Ionic columns.

THE HEADLAND of 1898 sits lower, on the isthmus of the promontory, and because one comes across it almost unexpectedly, is the more startling – one can understand why its construction occasioned a riot, not just because the site was used by local fishermen for net drying. Externally this is the best preserved of Trevail's hotels, and the perfect expression of the ambition of the man as architect/entrepreneur, its daring worthy of its setting, the better for not trying to dominate all in the manner of The Atlantic and Trevail's similar enterprise at Tintagel (q.v.):

here the concept is more chateau than castle. Red terracotta, a Trevail speciality, is employed for the architectural highlights in various eclectic styles: the terracotta cost nearly £5,000 out of a total building cost of £25,000. Almost square on plan, its vast horizontal spread modulated by skilful vertical articulation, best seen on the entrance front. 2:4:2:4:2 bays, the central and end bays advanced, with Lombard frieze. Central towers to entrance and rear fronts have tall pyramidal roofs with square cupolas, the end bays terracotta gables with obelisk finals. Central entrance leads to a large entrance hall with stair hall to l.: full-height imperial staircase with cast-iron balustrade and Ionic columns in dusky pink marble. More similar marble columns on the first-floor landing and in the main reception rooms with plain plaster cornices. Adjacent is a HOLIDAY VILLAGE by David Judson of Workhouse Design, 1999. A most skilful and accomplished contemporary interpretation of Cornish vernacular on a very exposed site with high quality detailing and landscaping. By the same hand plans for a conference centre overlooking Fistral Beach but almost completely hidden underground.

It is worth a walk to the end of the promontory for views of the town, the Atlantic rolling in over its vast beaches, and the long ribbon of hotel development stretching eastwards towards Porth: best seen from such a distance are the BEACH HUTS, tiered and cast into the base of the cliffs, at Tolcarne Beach ½ m. E. Past the former LIFEBOAT HOUSE (1899), granite gable with oriel and finials, and the late C20 PUMP HOUSE, a sculptural spiral of rubble stone walls built into rising ground, to the former COASTGUARD LOOKOUT, octagonal with pyramidal roof. Then back along Headland Road where late C19 and Edwardian villas (Nos. 12–18 are unremarkable Trevail) are now making way for larger apartment blocks. Best seen across the golf links is the white-rendered TOWER HOUSE of 1835, now the golf clubhouse, formerly the summer villa of the Molesworths, a leading Catholic family (it originally had a private chapel). Once a charming Gothick group around a castellated round tower but no longer: the chapel has lost its castellated parapet and pyramid roof and the house is diminished both by later extensions and recent apartment blocks nearby.

Now r. along TOWER ROAD and l. into CRANTOCK STREET to the former MADAME HAWKES WORKS, the most substantial survival of the early C20 knitwear industry (now housing), its long grey slate-roofed profile visible all over the town. This is a good area to appreciate late Victorian and Edwardian terraced housing, nicely detailed and enclosed by low boundary walls with planted tops, so return down Tower Road towards the harbour via JUBILEE STREET, FERN HILL ROAD, SYDNEY ROAD and FORE STREET. Above the harbour the RED LION, an early tourist inn whose cast-iron veranda has been incorporated into the main building. Nearby is the grand granite arched former entrance to PENTOWAN, Trevail's tall gabled villa for

George Hicks, now compromised by an oversized apartment block in its grounds.

At the start of UPPER FORE STREET, CLIFF COTTAGE (No. 83) is one of the pre-resort town's early former inns. This end of Fore Street and adjacent streets are the best places to see examples of smaller C19 houses, some with modest carved granite gatepiers. Off to the r. Nos. 2–11 DEER PARK, a complete terrace of early C19 cottages, is an especially remarkable survival that offers a sense of the modest character of the early settlement. The change of scale ramping up to the S end of Fore Street is marked by the FORT INN of the 1870s, another of the early summer villas for summer lettings, this time with Elizabethan gables, transomed-and-mullioned windows and tall chimneystacks. Modern extensions to the rear have preserved more of the original house than one expects, one panelled room with moulded cornice and tiled Jacobean-style fire surround, transomed-and-mullioned bay window and a staircase with painted panel over the window. From here it is best to return to the S side of the harbour via South Quay Hill, or continue down Lower Fore Street with the next perambulation.

2. *Town centre and East Street*

CENTRAL SQUARE is the site of the medieval hamlet of Towan Blystra and the centre of Newquay. The defining building is THE CENTRAL, a two-storey eight-window fronted inn with offset former carriage entrance. Early to mid-C19, a rebuilding of the former Old Inn, an early recorded place of trade. From the square, head up LOWER FORE STREET for good examples of Late Victorian and Edwardian shops. Especially good are Nos. 2–6, the large half-timbered emporium on the corner of Chapel Hill, the corner marked by an octagonal cupola and weathervane dated 1911, the shopfronts elegant Art Deco with polished red granite stall risers and pilasters. Further up, Nos. 14–16, a pair of late C19 shops which have a low cast-iron first-floor balcony and central round bay over one intact shopfront with glass rounded corners. Also Nos. 24 and 26 with a slightly earlier and more elaborate first-floor veranda. Opposite, rounding the corner with BEACH STREET is ROUND HOUSE with a semicircular tower surmounted by a Dutch gable, tall three storeys in yellow brick with terracotta tile decoration. More showy the NEWQUAY INSTITUTE CLUB with terracotta cornucopia panels on the E side of Beach Street. Further down towards Towan Beach a good view of THE ISLAND, a house precariously perched on an outlier of cliff and connected to the mainland by a miniature SUSPENSION BRIDGE of 1911.

Now E along BANK STREET and the sequence of buildings most expressive of the Edwardian town's commercial self-confidence and prosperity. The banks mostly in sober granite, the shops, emporia and offices in yellow brick with much exuberant terracotta embellishment and all manner of bay, oriel and rounded corner windows, gables, coloured glass and the occasional cupola: their dignity often compromised at ground-floor level by over-sized modern fascias and gaudy shopfronts. But this is a seaside town and only the odd later C20 rebuild really jars. Among the banks, LLOYDS BANK, tall two-storeyed with giant pilasters to the four-window front; HSBC, part bank, part shop, strong rusticated pilasters and window surrounds, plainer ground floor with heavy dentilled frieze; FIRST CHOICE, the most striking of all, is a tall single-storey in severe Roman style and over-sized pediment decorated with fasces; and finally YORK BUILDINGS, thorough-going Edwardian bombast with clumsy exaggerated detail and huge corbels. Among the other commercial buildings, No. 1 BANK STREET is at the top of the scale in the competition for the most elaborate elevation, encrusted with red and yellow terracotta. Nos. 33–41 are another almost intact example of a former Edwardian department store. Earlier stone buildings include the early to mid-C19 NEWQUAY ARMS, a three-storey four-bay front with rusticated quoins, and W. H. SMITH, two-storey early C19 front in Pentewan stone with granite quoins and round-headed double doors. Down BEACHFIELD AVENUE is the front of the former NEWQUAY STEAM BREWERY, identifiable by granite-dressed full-height ground-floor openings and a decorative terracotta panel above the door depicting cherubs frolicking among hop vines.

The junction of Bank Street and EAST STREET is the best point to note the route of Treffry's MINERAL TRAMWAY as it swings in from the W in an arc S of Bank Street on the line of MANOR ROAD, across the junction to curve away N of East Street, eventually emerging again at East Street's junction with CLIFF ROAD. Up MARCUS HILL, a group of three former chapel buildings, the earliest the United Methodist Free Church of 1866. Further up is St Michael's church (*see* above). Returning to East Street, TREBARWITH CRESCENT is worth a brief diversion to see the ornate early C19 cast-iron veranda and canopy to TALAVERA LODGE. Back to East Street and a gradual transition to more modest two-storey buildings. Soon the HOTEL VICTORIA looms up eastwards. The third of the resort's very large late C19 hotels, this time promoted by the District Council and a rival to Trevail's ventures but lacking their forceful character. Three-storey with attics, the central bay broken forward, ponderously detailed and with poor replacement windows, partly redeemed by a pretty cast-iron Gothic canopy and veranda over the entrance; the late C19 interior with good staircase and principal rooms largely intact. Opposite and further E, good examples of three-storeyed Edwardian terraces. The determined can complete the tour by going as far as the RAILWAY STATION of 1877, a disappointingly utilitarian shelter with the original stone front now completely hidden by later development, and the GREAT WESTERN HOTEL, the third of *Trevail*'s purpose-built hotels in the town, but so altered in the 1930s and 1970s as to be unrecognizable from the two-storey gabled original.

Trevail enthusiasts may wish to go even further to EDGECUMBE GARDENS and EDGECUMBE AVENUE, where Trevail laid out the TOLCARNE ESTATE for Edward Pearce in 1883. Some large detached and semi-detached villas survive, with much decorative woodwork including first-floor verandas, best seen in Nos. 2, 4 and 6 Edgecumbe Gardens.

TRENANCE VIADUCT, over Edgcumbe Avenue. Rebuilt 1939, replacing the original timber and then cast-iron viaduct for the mineral tramway. Seven round-headed arches on immensely tall piers carry the railway over the Trenance valley to the town station, the central piers massively chamfered to take the road diagonally through Trenance Gardens.

BARROWFIELDS. Three surviving barrows from a Bronze Age cemetery (*c.* 1500 B.C.) and medieval ridge and furrow earthworks.

3060

NEWTON FERRERS

In a lovely secluded position high above the River Lynher. Built for Sir William Coryton *c.* 1685–95, it is one of the earliest gentry houses in Cornwall to abandon Tudor precedent in favour of classical design. The handsomely proportioned plain granite mansion, two-storey above a basement and of H-plan, has a seven-bay centre flanked by two little projecting cross-wings of two bays each with a dentilled cornice and roofs hipped to the wings: an earlier W range was shown on a Prideaux drawing of *c.* 1735. Two-thirds of the house – the centre and W wing – were gutted by fire in 1940; while the centre was partly reconstructed, the W wing was left ruinous until 1993–7 when the whole house was meticulously restored to its late C17 form by Andrew and Darcie Baylis.

The central entrance on the S elevation, approached up a graciously conceived flight of ten segmental granite steps, is flanked by rusticated pilasters with tall moulded bases and decorated capitals surmounted by a projecting moulded cornice. It gives into the saloon which occupies the whole of the centre of the house, for the principal rooms are on this *piano nobile,* an arrangement closely comparable to Ince Castle (q.v.). A second entrance in the E elevation of the E wing, at basement level at this side, leads into a staircase hall, with a staircase up to the principal rooms; the hall has two large marbled columns and bolection-moulded panelling. The remade staircase is modelled on one at Powderham Castle, Devon, and incorporates fragments of the fire-damaged handrail of the original: it has square newels, the rail ramped at the corners, and carved balusters. The E wing retains high-quality late C17 fittings including bolection-moulded panelling and very plain marble chimneypieces in ante-room, library and parlour; these were replicated in the restoration of the house. The gardens descend into the valley by a delightful series of late C17 TERRACES linked by more flights of segmental steps, bounded by a balustrade on the upper terrace and by walls around and below and decorated with a profusion of ball finials. A pair of tall late C17 GATEPIERS have incised decoration on their plinths and the de Ferrers and Coryton arms above. To the W of the house the STABLES, dated 1688, with a seven-window front, the centre bay set very slightly forward.

NORTH HILL   2070

The pretty churchtown with slate-clad cottages is set in lovely country beneath some of Bodmin Moor's most dramatic eastern tors and against the park landscape of the extensive Trebartha estate (see below).

ST TERNEY. One of Cornwall's most enjoyable churches, specially ambitiously decorated without and rich in interest within. Its W tower, N and S aisles, and S porch are all of ashlar granite blocks. Indeed the embattled S aisle and S porch are so comparable in design and quality to those at Liskeard and St Neot (qq.v.) that perhaps the same masons worked on all three: the former has the same buttresses with crocketed pinnacles rising from their set-offs and the same large, wide windows (though of only three lights), the latter the same two-storey form and decoration and the same pattern of the vaulting ribs inside. The plain tower, like several others locally, is of three stages with buttresses set back from the angles, deeply recessed and moulded W door and window with a very unusual decoration of carved roundels at the sill, and battlemented parapets with large octagonal turrets with crocketed finials. The interior is spacious and graciously proportioned with especially finely carved ceiled wagon roofs in the nave and N and S aisles (the panels of unusually small dimension in the nave and S aisle); the chancel roof was restored in 1868 when it was decorated and painted. The four-bay aisle arcades rest on wide and lofty arches which in turn rest on slim piers of Cornish standard design. All of this is of the C15 or early C16. But the chancel must be C14 as is obvious in its many Dec features: a richly crocketed (if very restored) ogee niche – an EASTER SEPULCHRE in the N wall and the small ogee statuary niches to the l. and r. of the E window and also E of the N and S windows. Moreover the N window has a curious shelf at its base with little traceried niches against its back. A squint connects S aisle and chancel. Also a much restored SEDILIA, PISCINA and CRE-

DENCE in the S wall. There was a series of restorations by *Rev. C. Rodd*, rector 1832–83, an extensive restoration of the chancel in 1870 by *Otho B. Peter* of Launceston, much exterior work in 1892, and re-seating with oak benches in 1897. The overall effect of these campaigns is dignified and enhancing (e.g. the finely carved BENCH-ENDS in C16 patterns), and it was during the chancel restoration that much of the C14 work was discovered. – FONT. Norman, circular, undecorated. –The Trebartha FAMILY PEW in the S chancel has doors with inlay woodwork dated 1724 set in later panelling. – STAINED GLASS. Nice set of three *Clayton & Bell* windows in the chancel, 1865 and 1882 (N chancel), giving rich light. – Three in S aisle by *Herbert W. Bryans*, 1889–1920. – MONUMENTS. More, and more interesting, than in most Cornish village churches. – Slate to Henry Spoure †1603. Skull (imago mortis) and coat of arms. –Against the N wall at the W end of the church Thomas Vincent †1606, wife, and fifteen children. A rare example of an elaborate altar tomb that has survived virtually intact with slate front and top and a prettily upcurved slate back, with an allegorical representation of the Resurrection and, below, a figure of death. The carving is exquisitely detailed, e.g. the oak tree on the E side. – Richard Spoure †1653, also still slate, with three arches: still wholly of Jacobean proportions. – Henry Spoure †1688, with sister and parents. One of the most endearing monuments in Cornwall: father and mother kneeling opposite each other, still in the old Elizabethan and Jacobean tradition, the children standing in niches behind. The four figures realistically coloured. Standing wall monuments with columns l. and r. and an elaborate entablature and pediment. – V. Darley and wife †1791 by *Emes* of Exeter. – F. Hearle Rodd and wife †1836 and †1833, identical monuments by *E. Gaffin* of Regent Street.

On the E edge of the village BATTENS MILL. Late C16 watermill, possibly of earlier origins. C19 overshot wheel to rear and late C19 machinery. Lean-to porch supported on two octagonal granite piers with moulded bases and caps. The MILL HOUSE has a 1702 datestone.

TREBARTHA, ½ m. NW. The estate was the seat of the Spoures and Rodds (*see* above). The main house including additions by *Sir Jeffry Wyattville* was demolished in 1948 but two late C19 LODGES with decorative bargeboards, GATEPIERS, and some small C16–C18 houses including TREBARTHA BARTON survive. The latter, late C18 or early C19, is of an unusual arrangement whereby a tall three-storey central range flanked by two-storey lean-to ranges and gabled axial stacks present impressive symmetrical gable-end elevations, the rest slate-hung.

STONAFORD, 1 m. NW. A medieval hall house and former longhouse, truncated and remodelled at the lower end as parlour with chamber above. A *c.* 1600 two-storey porch adjoins a *c.* 1700 pantry extension to the road front.

BERRIOWBRIDGE BRIDGE, 1 m. S. Mid-C16 road bridge over the River Lynher, repaired 1640 (datestone), widened on the upper side 1890. The piers are as thick as the four-centred arches are wide.

TREWORTHA MARSH, 3 m. w. Deserted medieval hamlet of four LONGHOUSES arranged along the contour, some with outhouses and small enclosures. Downhill, across a long broad townplace and beside a lane to the stream, a small CORN-DRYING BARN. The Rev. Sabine Baring-Gould's excavation of this and two of the longhouses in the 1890s was Britain's earliest archaeological examination of a medieval settlement.

NORTH PETHERWIN   *2080*

ST PATERNUS. A surprisingly large church on an elevated position in its churchtown. Its chief architectural feature is the survival of a Norman N aisle with thick circular Norman piers *20* with many-scalloped capitals (cf. Morwenstow, St Breward). Double-chamfered pointed arches. Small clerestory windows (a rarity both in Cornwall and Devon) not above the apexes of the arches but above the piers. This oddity appears also at St Germans and later at Callington, Lostwithiel and Fowey. The style of the clerestory windows (and the aisle windows) is *c.* 1300. The rest of the church Perp. w tower with diagonal buttresses, gargoyles below the battlements, and big cusped pinnacles. Lofty s aisle with Perp windows and granite arcade of five bays with standard Cornish piers and capitals only to the main shafts. The Norman piers are followed on the N side by a chancel chapel of two more bays identical with the s arcade. C16 roofs to aisle and s porch. s porch door with early C16 ironwork scroll hinges. The chancel much embellished by *Rev. T. B. Trentham*, vicar 1867–1909. – SCREEN. Only the lower part survives. – COMMUNION RAILS. Now under the tower arch, with big balusters and other ornamental motifs which make the initially surprising date 1685 quite convincing. – BENCH-ENDS. Only a few, with Instruments of the Passion. – STAINED GLASS. Chancel E 1876. N aisle w, 1876 by *Lavers, Barraud & Westlake*. – BRASS. Leonard Yeo †1621. Inscription and two shields. – INCISED SLABS. Dorothy Killigrew †1634. – Three daughters of Edmund Yeo †1638.

NORTH TAMERTON   *3090*

ST DENIS. High on a hill close to a bridge across the Tamar looking into Devon with Dartmoor in the far distance. It is a setting that enhances the noble, plain dignity of its tall C15 w tower. This is of granite ashlar, three stages, and unbuttressed. There are crude carvings on the plinth: squares with trefoil, quatrefoil, star etc., with leaves as infillings (cf. Jacobstow, Week St Mary). The exterior of the s aisle has two granite bands at window-sill and window-arch-springing level. Nave, s aisle, s porch and chancel, the latter rebuilt in 1875. Five-bay aisle arcade of the standard Cornish C15 type with ceiled wagon roof, as is the porch roof: the nave roof heavily restored. The interior was richly embellished in the long incumbency of Rev. R. S. Smith between 1849 and 1901, e.g. the colourful tiled ROOD SCREEN. – FONT. Circular bowl, plain, C12. – BENCH-ENDS. A large and interesting collection, with the usual symbols of the Passion and some more unusual motifs including woodcock and partridge. Also charming animal tops like Madron and St Newlyn East. – STAINED GLASS. Good w window of s aisle, 1906 by *Maurice Drake* of Exeter, and a very Kempe-style window, 1923 by *A.L. Moore*, in the s aisle. – MONUMENTS. Small but good BRASS to Leonard Loves of Ogbeare Hall (*see* below), 1576, Receiver General to Elizabeth I. – Pretty slate SLAB to Walter Robins †1706.

CHURCH HOUSE, in front of the church. Late C16 to early C17.

WELL FARM, ¼ m. E. A probable longhouse with remains of medieval smoke-blackened thatch on its roof: the earliest part of the roof is that over the inner room, the two-bay hall roof slightly later, and the much simpler lower end roof C17 or later. Datestone 1660, the probable date of the gable. C18 shippon wing at right angles to lower end.

OGBEARE HALL, 1 m. SW. A large gabled late C19 Gothic house encasing the C15 great hall of a substantial medieval house; the Victorian part, radically reduced in size in the 1930s, has a three-storey tower with pyramidal roof in the angle over the entrance porch. Hall roof rebuilt using medieval arch braces, wall-plate and bosses. Screen also of reused timber with carved foliage, with gallery jettied over into hall on carved bressumer. Large fireplace with moulded elliptical arch, carved foliage spandrels, and frieze of sunken quatrefoils.

OTTERHAM

ST DENIS. In its small remote churchtown. The tower must be Norman in part, for the arch into the nave rests on Norman imposts. From outside, however, there is nothing in the two stages of the tower which indicates so early a date, and the upper part was rebuilt in 1702. The church was severely restored in 1889 after a previous restoration of 1850 had removed the Norman N transept. Four-bay C16 s aisle on standard Cornish piers; with contemporary tracery in the E window. – FONTS. One plain, octagonal, possibly C13. Remains of two probably Norman fonts at w end of nave, one with a round bowl, the other a hexagonal bowl: the former is ornamented with a simple pattern of large lozenges and a kind of

incised roll, not unlike a cable roll, round the base. – MONU-
MENTS. Slate ledgers, including to Mary French †1652 and
Alice Grigg †1684. – Several more mid C17 ledgers re-set on
outer wall of chancel.

PADSTOW

The town embraces its harbour, sheltered on the western side
of the wide Camel estuary below the church and Prideaux Place,
the Prideaux mansion and its deer park. The cult of St Petroc
started here in the C6 but had moved further inland to Bodmin
by the C10 because of raids on this more vulnerable site. As a
manor of Bodmin Priory and a rare safe haven on the inhospitable N coast, it became a considerable medieval fishing port and
township with nine chapels (more than Bodmin) and was leased
by the last prior to the Prideaux family before the Dissolution.
Padstow prospered through trade with the ports of the Bristol
Channel, Wales and especially Ireland and in 1579 it became
a post town for that country. Its later trading links were far-
reaching: in return for exports of copper, tin and lead, slate, cured
fish and dairy products came timber from Norway and Sweden,
salt and wine from France, and hemp, iron and jute from Russia.
During the first half the C19 it was one of the major points for
Cornish migration, especially to Canada, and then developed a
significant shipbuilding industry with five shipyards: one yard
alone launched twenty-nine ships between 1858 and 1870, though
the industry was in decline by 1900. The arrival of the railway in
1899, the associated construction of a large hotel, and the revival
of its fisheries (the port had 150 registered vessels in 1912) helped
it survive the vicissitudes of the first half of the C20, and it has
prospered in the later C20 and early C21 as a centre for tourism
and the development of the shellfish industry. It offers some of
the best townscape of any of Cornwall's historic fishing ports on
an intimate but dignified scale and in a gentle polychromy of
slate, brick and colourwash.

CHURCHES AND PUBLIC BUILDINGS

ST PETROC, Church Street. In a lovely embowered situation
above the town and so built into the steeply sloping site that
its sizeable scale and handsome proportions are not immediately apparent. Of the monastery founded before 981 nothing
remains. The sturdy W tower has a heavily buttressed first stage
of the C13, strongly receding to the later upper two storeys (cf.
Bodmin), with battlements but no pinnacles. There is no W
door but a wall enclosing the entrance to the Prideaux vault

on which is a re-set medieval cross recovered from Prideaux Place in 1833. The body of the church is of nave and N and S aisles. Impressive five-light Perp chancel window and four-light Perp windows to the aisles in Catacleuse stone, partly restored in the C19; the flamboyant tracery of the S chancel chapel windows, of the palm pattern of the early to mid C15, is a rarity in Cornwall (cf. St Just-in-Penwith). The buttresses to the chapel have two animals and one figure with a shield as support, all damaged. Good late C17 raised-and-fielded panel doors to N and S entrances. The interior is lofty and spacious with a tall C13 two-centred tower arch and aisles of five bays plus two lower bays for the chancel chapels (cf. Bodmin and St Austell). The S chancel chapel is furthermore separated from the aisle by a 'chancel arch'. The nave piers, in limestone, are tall late C15 of standard Cornish section; the S chancel chapel has hollow chamfered piers of the earlier type like Mawgan-in-Pydar and St Austell, the capitals have leaf decoration and stylized flowers on the abacus. In the nave, however, most of the capitals are plain and there is only a fleur-de-lys crenellation to the abacus. Fine ceiled wagon roof to nave. That to the S chancel chapel also especially good with carved corbelled angels. An early restoration in 1847–55 when the W gallery was removed was followed by another in 1888–9 by E. H. Sedding, principally of the chancel. – FONT. Of the Bodmin type. One of the group of outstanding pieces of Cornish medieval sculpture, the bowl in Catacleuse, the columns of granite. C15 with demi-figures of angels at the corners and the twelve apostles in the niches between, the carving of the figures sophisticated and detailed. It must be the template for the strikingly similar, though lesser, font at St Merryn (q.v.). – PISCINA. Early C14 with ogee design, restored 1888. – BENCH-END. In the chancel, of the fox preaching to the geese (cf. St Austell). – PULPIT of c. 1530 with panels with symbols of the Passion, restored in C19. – STAINED GLASS. Chancel E, 1958 by Gerald Smith with Cornish iconography. – Two attractive windows in the Lady Chapel by A. K. Nicholson, 1932. – Interesting fragments of the 1840s glazing by William Warrington in N aisle. – MONUMENTS. Brass to L. Merther, †1421, demi-figure of a priest, re-set on sanctuary step. – Fine standing wall monument on the W wall of the S aisle to Sir Nicholas Prideaux, 1627. Base with inscriptions, ornament, and a chubby child stepping on an old man's shoulder. Above, the four life-sized figures of Sir Nicholas's children, and yet a little higher and further behind, Sir Nicholas and Lady Prideaux. The parents and children are facing each other, with prayer-desks between. – Dignified simple monument to Edmund Prideaux †1693, attributed to William Stanton (GF).

At the NE and SE entrances to the churchyard, fine C18 ironwork GATES, that to the NE of kissing-gate form. By the SE gate, CROSS-SHAFT AND BASE, decorated with interlaced plaitwork in the Hiberno-Saxon style; on one side a curious motif similar to a fleur-de-lys. Discovered buried in the churchyard in 1869; its scale would make the cross one of the largest in Cornwall. – CROSS outside s porch, four-holed, the smallest of its type in the county, re-erected on a modern shaft and base in 1897.

INSTITUTE, LIBRARY and MUSEUM, Broad Street. 1881 with a lively street elevation including a canted oriel with slate turret roof.

Former BOARD SCHOOL, New Street. 1880 by *Silvanus Trevail*. School and school house as one long range, the continuous roof enlivened with shallow projecting bays and double and triple lancets with alternating stone and brick dressings.

OBELISK, Dennis Hill. 1 m. s. Erected 1889 to celebrate Victoria's Jubilee of 1887. Tall rusticated granite obelisk on pedestal with deep coved cornice and stepped rusticated plinth.

WINDMILL, 1 m. W. Base of a windmill tower, probably C17, circular in plan and tapering, capped with a C20 water tank. Dressed stone arch entrance and two opposing lancet windows to first floor.

DAYMARK, 2 m. N. Probably early C19. Tapering circular tower, originally limewashed, standing high on the cliffs at Stepper Point to aid navigation into the Camel estuary.

PRIDEAUX PLACE

In 1602 Carew wrote: 'Mr Nicholas Prideaux from his new and stately house thereby taketh a full and large prospect of the town, haven and country adjoining.' C18 and C19 shelter belts have long secluded the house from the town but its splendid late C16 E front, guarded by mock fortifications of the mid C18, with glimpses of charming early C19 Gothick in the extensive service ranges to the NE, still overlooks the deer park. This memorable ensemble is an apt introduction to the rich and complex architectural history of one of Cornwall's great houses.

Padstow, Prideaux Place. East front. Drawing by E. Prideaux, 1727

Four principal periods of Prideaux construction can be discerned in the main elevations. The E elevation, of E-shape, is the front of the house attributed by Carew to Nicholas Prideaux who inherited in 1581, which was of H-plan: though heavily disguised, it remains the essential structural skeleton of the present house. The hall to the s of the central porch and the great chamber above are the clearest survivals, while the N wing contained a state bedroom at its E end with the kitchen in the middle of that range. The second significant phase is by Edmund Prideaux who inherited in 1728 (†1745). A well-travelled scholar and artist, he was the author of a remarkable set of topographical and architectural drawings of the early to mid C18, including records of, and proposed alterations for, Prideaux Place. He remodelled the s wing, created the present reading room at its w end, and added the NW bakehouse range to the N wing. His creation of formal gardens in a small compass was one of the earlier English arcadias, of which several structures survive (*see* below). His son Humphrey was responsible for the third period of major change, including replacing the original gables to the E front with hipped roofs and castellations, improving circulation by building linked extensions to the rear of the N and s ranges, building a new two-storey NE wing to match Nicholas Prideaux's original, and remodelling the N wing to link with this new wing. He also constructed the mock fortifications to the E front shown in a Borlase drawing of 1758. But the most memorable period at Prideaux Place is the work of Charles Prideaux-Brune, who inherited in 1793 (†1833). His Gothick transformation of the house is accomplished inside and out, even if it is somewhat archaic – rather 1760 than early C19. The s front owes its picturesque composition to him with a huge tall castellated bay (taller and pinnacled until the 1960s) in the centre with an oval bedroom above and a drawing room below. The sw block was remodelled as a library with a stair leading to it: it is possible that the Catacleuse Gothic window of this room was from the ruined church at Constantine (q.v.). The most impressive change of all was the construction of a fine new staircase hall to the rear of the Elizabethan hall, a much grander version of the more modest stair at Harlyn House (q.v.).

The INTERIOR is resplendent with fittings and decorations that represent of all these phases and more. The hall and through passage were given a new ceiling and cornice by Edmund Prideaux in the early C18. The richly carved hall screen is of the late C16 or early C17 and was probably imported during the early C19 alterations when the hall became a dining room: it contains fine inlaid panels and the frieze is decorated with fantastic beasts and monsters, with more on the panels set against backgrounds of formally treated plants and flowers. The hall panelling is of at least three periods. Both the steward's room to the r. of the through passage and the reading room in the s wing have bolection-moulded panelling, by tradition from Stowe Barton, Kilkhampton (q.v.). The stair hall is nobly proportioned and exquisitely detailed with a delicate Gothick ceiling echoed by a fine cast-iron balustrade that reflects the lightness of the cantilevered stairs. An exciting aspect of the design is the division at the head of the first six steps, the main flight turning r. upstairs, the lesser leading up to the library. The crocketed canopies above exactly match those in the chapel at Trelowarren (q.v.). The drawing room has a Gothick moulded plaster cornice with quatrefoils, the library a vaulted Gothick ceiling. Even so, the most splendid feature of the interior remains the early C17 shallow barrel-vaulted plaster ceiling of the great chamber of *c.* 1614, with remarkable similarities to that in the long gallery at Lanhydrock (q.v.). They share the same design of fully modelled panels, rectangular here, linked by elaborate strapwork. And as at Lanhydrock, the main panels depict Old Testament scenes, here the story of Susannah and the Elders, with beasts and birds in subsidiary panels.

The extensive range of garden and service structures and buildings are of major interest. The principal entrance is now by the s drive through the SOUTH GATE, containing the MOCK FORTIFICATIONS to the e elevation shown in the Borlase drawing of 1758. It comprises a crenellated stone arch flanked by square crenellated turrets. Of Edmund Prideaux's garden structures: the SOUTH TERRACE and GARDEN SEAT, the former an early C19 reconstruction of the late C16 terrace, with a crenellated central section with a grotto niche and scattered rocks before it, the latter (dated 1740) a vermiculated and pedimented portal flanked by low quadrant walls each with four shallow niches, terminating in piers surmounted by vase-capped urns. This forms an EXEDRA OF ANTIQUITIES for inscriptions and portable shrines of the C1 A.D. brought from Rome by Prideaux in 1739. The TEMPLE, to the sw of the house, 1738–9, is a tetrastyle Ionic pedimented structure approached by steps and in Bath stone, which Prideaux acquired from Ralph Allen.* SE of the house is an C18 LEAD BUST of a Roman emperor. The mock fortifications were extended to the N in the early C19 to form crenellated wings screening the stable yard and the bridge to the estate yard. The STABLES are another expression of Charles Prideaux-Brune's Gothick embellishment, a long rectangular structure with ten quatrefoil windows to the upper floor and internally a set of five Batty Langley-style looseboxes and good heraldic plasterwork in the lobby. At right angles to the stables, a charming combination of DAIRY and GROTTO, set against the pleasure garden wall. In Tudor Gothic style, the dairy roof on slender iron colonettes. The dairy is of oval shape with slate tables and Gothick plasterwork, with an ante-room to the s with coved ceiling; both chambers are approached from a splendid rockery/grotto. The ESTATE YARD behind the

---

*Allen, born at St Blazey, had worked in the Cornish postal service before becoming postmaster at Bath and subsequently one of the major developers of the C18 city. In 1727 he purchased the Combe Down quarries, the greatest source of Bath stone.

stables includes the 'Cow Palace' of 1909 as well as lesser earlier buildings and a fine horse trough, an early C19 GRANARY above a STABLE with a quatrefoil overlooking the mock fortifications, and an ENGINE HOUSE of 1911.

PERAMBULATION

The HARBOUR is the place to start. The s end of FERRY QUAY affords a good view of the town and its setting, comfortably contained in a deep coombe stretching up towards the church within a semicircle of skyline trees and fields. The inner harbour dates from the construction of the NORTH QUAY c. 1534 followed by the gradual building of the slips and walls of SOUTH QUAY and THE STRAND along the harbour's w side; it was deepened and much rebuilt in 1854, and in 1990 a tidal gate was installed across the harbour mouth. The outer harbour – Ferry Quay and the long Commissioner's Quay to the s – is mostly the product of 1930s improvements to the port.

Now for the buildings on or around the quays. On North Quay the RED BRICK WAREHOUSE, a 1991 replica of a former C19 warehouse in hard red brick, with an incongruous granite colonnade. Many of the buildings along the water's edge originated in the C18 or C19 as warehouses, net lofts, stores and workshops of the former shipbuilding industry: e.g. on North Quay THE SHIPWRIGHTS, C18 brick in Flemish bond; the red brick and slate-hung former warehouses, now shops, at the s end of The Strand; and the OLD CUSTOM HOUSE on the corner of South Quay and Riverside, a former bonded warehouse which stood originally on the waterside until the mid-C19 remodelling of the s side of the harbour. But there are also buildings of much earlier origin and more substantial status. Outstanding is ABBEY HOUSE on North Quay, with its intriguing slate-hung front behind simple C18 railings: it has a central shallow projection in the form of a three-storey porch with an entrance to a raised basement, flanked to the l. by a straight flight of steps to the ground floor. At first floor an eye-catching Catacleuse stone four-centred arch (probably re-set) with carved spandrels and a hoodmould with carved headstops. This elevation seems to have been the front range of an irregular courtyard-plan house of the C15, with a first-floor hall over a basement and open to the roof, before being floored in the late C16 or early C17; the wings to rear are C18 or C19. The surviving joinery includes roof principals with curved feet, at least one jointed cruck truss, and evidence for an original barrel roof.

Another large house survives, although subdivided, on RIVERSIDE, s of the harbour, as Court House, Raleigh House and No. 8. This is of late C16 origin with major late C17 and C19 extensions. Of L-shaped plan, the earlier range is at right angles to the road: it was truncated by one bay during the mid-C19 port improvements but had previously fronted the water's edge. Early C18 shell-hood porch. Good C17 and C18 interior fittings including a room of raised and fielded panelling and a chamber with evidence for a barrel ceiling originally decorated with C17 plasterwork. Up r. into ST EDMUND'S LANE and l. into a small lane that leads to the METROPOLE HOTEL, whose grey-rendered mass presides over the s end of the old town. It was built in 1900 by the London & South Western Railway to encourage tourism after the arrival of the railway in 1899, as the GWR was successfully doing at Newquay; part of the former STATION building survives in the car park below near the workmanlike SCHOOL OF COOKERY, 1988 by *ADG* of Plymouth. Then back into St Edmund's Lane and at the top r. into NEW STREET, climbing uphill. No. 4 (ST PETROC'S HOTEL) is one of the best examples of the larger early C18 merchants' houses around the town, with a painted five-window front retaining its original sashes with thick glazing bars and fine dormers. Almost opposite, the WHITE HART, originating in the early C17, an important coaching inn on the main approach to the town.

Now back down New Street into the centre and the web of little streets behind the waterfront like STRAND STREET, DRANG, MARKET SQUARE, MILL SQUARE and BROAD STREET. All have a varied range of C18 and C19 fronts with much slate cladding and sash windows, sometimes with earlier C16 and C17 fabric behind. Opposite the Institute on the corner of DUKE STREET, the tactfully plain 1970s BARCLAYS BANK incorporates C15 ridge tiles with two horses and riders. Then up LANADWELL STREET to the CINEDRONE, a rare survival of a small local cinema of 1921, probably designed by its owner, *E. J. Pope*. The auditorium is elaborately decorated with a modillion cornice, panelled walls, fluted pilasters, lion heads, small swags, and drop motifs. The proscenium is flanked by engaged columns and above the suspended ceiling is a painted ceiling of clouds. Into MIDDLE STREET, and the ALMS-HOUSES, datestone 1870, of diminutive scale and in red brick in English bond. Courtyard plan with two rows of four origin-ally one-room plan houses. The street elevation is prettily con-trived with large boards to deeply projecting verges on the gable-ends around a stepped walled central entrance with a dressed stone trefoil arch.

Away from the centre, Padstow is a quieter town as the streets climb up the valley towards the church and Prideaux Place, with here and there large houses and the occasional villa. CHURCH STREET, the best street in the town, offers continu-ously picturesque streetscape with many C18 and C19 houses of good proportions complete with original sash windows, doorcases and doors making an appropriately dignified approach to the church. Duke Street, Church Lane and High Street also have much of similar character. At the top of Church Street, turn r. along TREGIRLS LANE for a view of the E front of Prideaux Place: its sudden appearance on the small country lane comes as a surprise. Then back along FENTON-LUNA LANE. On the corner of High Street and Fentonluna

Lane, the DOWER HOUSE, *c.* 1860, a large plain Gothic house with mullion-and-transom windows. Here, high above the town, the prevailing ambience is entirely rural as the lane runs below the walls of the deer park. Set into the wall of Fenton-luna Lane, a WELL, probably of medieval origin, with a Prideaux arch re-set and reversed to form a pointed arch: although the arch is probably late C16 the 1592 datestone must have been carved in the C19. In ST SAVIOUR'S LANE, No. 1 is a good later C18 house. Begin the descent to the harbour via CROSS STREET, where No. 7 (Polyphant) has a tall late C18 front with rusticated ground floor and a fine doorcase with fluted pilasters and carved entablature. The early C18 CROSS HOUSE provides a pretty elevation at the junction of Cross Street and Church Street with its symmetrical five-window front behind its triangular enclosure of garden walls. Return to the waterfront via DUKE STREET and MILL SQUARE with more closely packed C18 and C19 inns, shops and houses.

PAR

Par owes its existence to Joseph Treffry of Place, Fowey (q.v.). Like Rashleigh at Charlestown and Hawkins at Pentewan (qq.v.) Treffry saw the need for a seaport for the mineral and china clay industries and by 1840 constructed a breakwater and quays to convert the open bay into a safe harbour, connecting it with the mines and quarries inland by railways, canals and leats. This resulted in considerable development around Par and St Blazey during the C19, spurred on by the establishment of the headquarters of the Cornwall Minerals Railway which served the china clay country. Because of its mainline rail connections, Par continued to expand in the C20, along with Fowey, as the principal port for the export of china clay, though shipping from here ceased in 2007. Treffry's original harbour has been much expanded: it is the largest artificial harbour in Cornwall, its straight E quay 1,200 ft (366 metres) long, and its immediate environs are dominated by the huge china clay drying sheds of the modern industry. There are enclaves of mid to late C19 industrial housing such as at Par Green with its late C19 little mission church.

102   ST MARY THE VIRGIN, Biscovey. The parish church of the ecclesiastical parish of Par, created out of St Blazey and Tywardreath in 1845. *G. E. Street's* first church, 1848. A remarkable work for a beginner, immediately loveable and of a freshness and charm typical of his best early work. An original and subtle adaptation of the E.E. style in a design of engaging simplicity, the epitome of the early Ecclesiological movement. Walls of pink Biscovey stone from the adjacent quarry with Pentewan

dressings bestow a mellow glow to the strong, quietly assured composition. Nave, chancel, s aisle culminating in a low comfortable steeple placed at the w end of the aisle, all of reassuringly good proportions. The spire rises from the buttressed first stage of the tower through a broached second stage and an octagon – strong echoes of a combination of Cubert and Lostwithiel: Street was restoring the former between 1846 and 1849 and went on to repair the latter in 1878. The windows are plain lancets, single or paired but tripartite at the e end of the chancel and of differing lengths, achieving an especially fine effect at the se corner. The entrance is through the base of the tower, its intended dramatic effect somewhat reduced by the introduction of later screens to create an internal porch, but the simple, honest dignity of the interior is striking. The nave roof is an arresting timber construction of tie-beam, crown-post and open rafters, mirrored by a lesser version over the aisle; in contrast the chancel roof is a painted barrel with ribbed panels. Delightful touches include the two different piers – one round, one octagonal – in the three-bay arcade between nave and aisle, the deep rear arches to the e window of the chancel, and a little triangular window in a niche above the three-bay sedilia. – PEWS. Robustly designed, plain, square ended and moveable. – STAINED GLASS. In the sanctuary, by *Wailes*, deep colours, good figures and medallion motifs, very enjoyable. – Two windows in s aisle by *Charles Gibbs*. – CROSS-SHAFT. In the churchyard, moved from a roadside position in Biscovey in 1896, a sepulchral monument with very worn inscription, ALRDRON ULCUI FILIUS, with Hiberno-Saxon plaitwork.

CHURCH OF THE GOOD SHEPHERD, Par Green. 1896, by *E. H. Sedding*. E.E., granite with Polyphant dressings, and single and double lancets with a five-light lancet chancel e window. Sanctuary skilfully embellished by *Stephen Dykes Bower* in 1948. – STAINED GLASS. Chancel e by *Francis Stephen*, 1954, a celebration of the Diocese of Truro. – w window by *Geoffrey Robinson*, 1985.

LEEK SEED CHAPEL, St Austell Road, St Blazey Gate. Wesleyan chapel. 1824, restored and re-furnished by *F. C. Jury* in 1904. One of Cornwall's best chapels, with a dignified exterior and richly furnished and unaltered interior. Three-window front with moulded cornice and corner finials and taller central gable with open pediment, round-headed first-floor windows and distyle Tuscan porch. Fine mahogany and pine fittings, the gallery front with paired panels between Ionic pilasters. Rostrum with shaped front, segmented-arched panels, Ionic pilasters and dentilled cornice. – STAINED GLASS. John Wesley in central w window tracery. – MONUMENT. John Williams †1849 and family. Arched marble wall monument by *Bovey and Co.* of Plymouth.

ROUNDHOUSE BUSINESS PARK, St Blazey Road. Formerly the headquarters of the Cornwall Minerals Railway, of 1874 by *Sir*

Morton Peto, one of the last great Victorian railway contractors. A remarkable and significant survival, one of the best-preserved examples of a classic planned small railway company works anywhere in England. The complex consists of nine engine sheds, arranged in a segment around a working turntable, and connected by a small link to the long single-storey workshop range, with a two-storey administration block in the centre and a tall tapered stack with moulded entablature. This is proper railway architecture, all in red brick with much decoration, culminating in the three-bay pilastered front of the administration block, with round-headed keyed windows and modillion parapet cornice. All very intact, including the original cast-iron windows, large V-jointed doors to the engine sheds, and iron trusses and column stanchions to the interior.

PAR RAILWAY STATION, Eastcliffe Road. The junction for the Newquay branch line. One of the least altered examples of a small late C19 station. The downside buildings date from 1879. Full canopies on both platforms. Signal box and mechanically operated signals still in use, and a typical *Brunel* design road BRIDGE at the N end of the station.

MID CORNWALL GALLERIES, 100 yds SW of St Mary. 1877. Former Biscovey Board School, partly by *Silvanus Trevail*.

THE OLD VICARAGE, St Austell Road. 1842 by *Silvanus Trevail*.

RASHLEIGH ALMSHOUSES, Polmear Hill. Built *c.* 1800 for William Rashleigh. A simple but delightful set of seven former almshouses each with gabled stone porch over four-centred arched doorway and a large lateral stack between. Original four one-room plan dwellings, early on extended by another three and then in 1855 by a small hospital wing at right angles to the r. Converted into three cottages in 1977–8.

TREGREHAN. *See* p. 640.

MENABILLY. *See* p. 347.

PAUL

ST POL-DE-LEON. The churchtown is half a mile inland from Mousehole, the principal settlement of the historically extensive parish, on the summit of a hill overlooking the port and Mount's Bay. Probably an early Christian site and C13 church with a re-dedication by Bishop Grandisson in 1336. It was severely damaged by fire in the raid of 1595 by a Spanish force (cf. Mousehole and Penzance) though the extent of the destruction is disputed, Carew claiming that 'it utterly ruined all the great stonie pillers', others suggesting the church was simply gutted. The fine C15 W tower is of three stages, with buttresses leaving the corners free, and a stair-turret rising above the pinnacles. There are heads as stops to the hoodmould over the W door and two niches flank the W window, with another above it. In the interior

Launceston (p. 284)
Fowey (p. 199)

7	10
8	11
9	

12	13	17
14	15	
	16	

| 18 | 20 |
| 19 | 21 |

34. St Neot, parish church, c14 to early c16 (p. 595)
35. St Ives, St Ia, early–mid c15, outer s aisle, c. 1500 (p. 557)

Altarnun, St Nonna, interior, C15 to early C16 (p. 92)
Lanteglos-by-Fowey, St Wyllow, interior, C14 and C15 (p. 282)

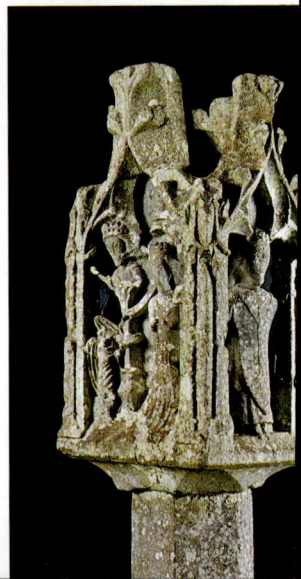

		48	49
45		48	49
46	47	50	

55. Rialton Manor, porch to Prior Vivian's house, early c16 (p. 479)
56. Wendron, Trenethick Barton, gatehouse, early c16 (p. 697)
57. Cotehele, Hall Court, late c15–early c16 (p. 161)
58. Cotehele, Great Hall, c. 1520 (p. 162)

3. Probus, St Probus and St Grace, tower, early C16 (p. 461)
4. Launceston, St Mary Magdalene, porch, 1511 (p. 287)
5. Bodmin, St Petroc, tomb of Prior Vivian, †1533 (p. 110)

66. St Buryan parish church, rood screen, early C16, restored by E.H. Sedding, 1910 (p. 510)
67. Launceston, St Mary Magdalene, pulpit, early C16 (p. 289)
68. St Neot, parish church, Noah window, mostly mid to late C15 (p. 597)

66 | 68
67 |

. Roscarrock, SW range, oriel window, mid to late C16 (p. 483)
. Trerice, SE front, *c.* 1570s (p. 649)
. Fowey, 9 South Street, jettied town house, late C16–early C17 (p. 206)
. Launceston, 11, 13 and 13A High Street, jettied town houses, late C16–early C17 (p. 297)

76. Lanhydrock, gatehouse, completed 1651 (p. 270)
77. Lanhydrock, Long Gallery, plasterwork, completed *c.* 1640 (p. 272)
78. Padstow, Prideaux Place, plasterwork in Great Chamber, *c.* 1640 (p. 272)

79. Falmouth, King Charles the Martyr, interior looking E, 1661–5 (p. 186)
80. North Hill, St Terney, monument to Henry Spoure, †1688 (p. 386)
81. St Germans, priory church, monument to Edward Eliot by Rysbrack, 1722 (p. 546)

79 | 81
80 |

82. Come-to-Good, Friends meeting house, 1710 (p. 155)
83. Gwennap, Gwennap Pit, mid c18, re-modelled 1806 (p. 228)
84. Launceston, St Mary Magdalene, cenotaph to Granville Pyper and Richard Wise, 1731 (p. 289)

85. Antony, Antony House, N front, probably by John Moyle to a design by James Gibbs, 1718–24 (p. 95)
86. Trelowarren, W front, central medieval range and chapel re-modelled by Thomas Edwards, 1756–60, chapel W front, c. 1830 (p. 644)

7. Trereife, s front, *c.* 1711 (p. 648)
8. Launceston, Eagle House Hotel, Castle Street, *c.* 1764 (p. 298)

89	91
90	92
	93

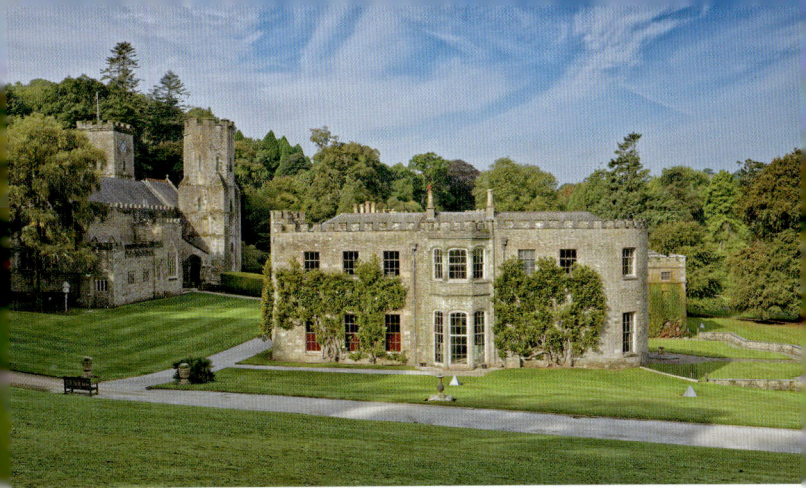

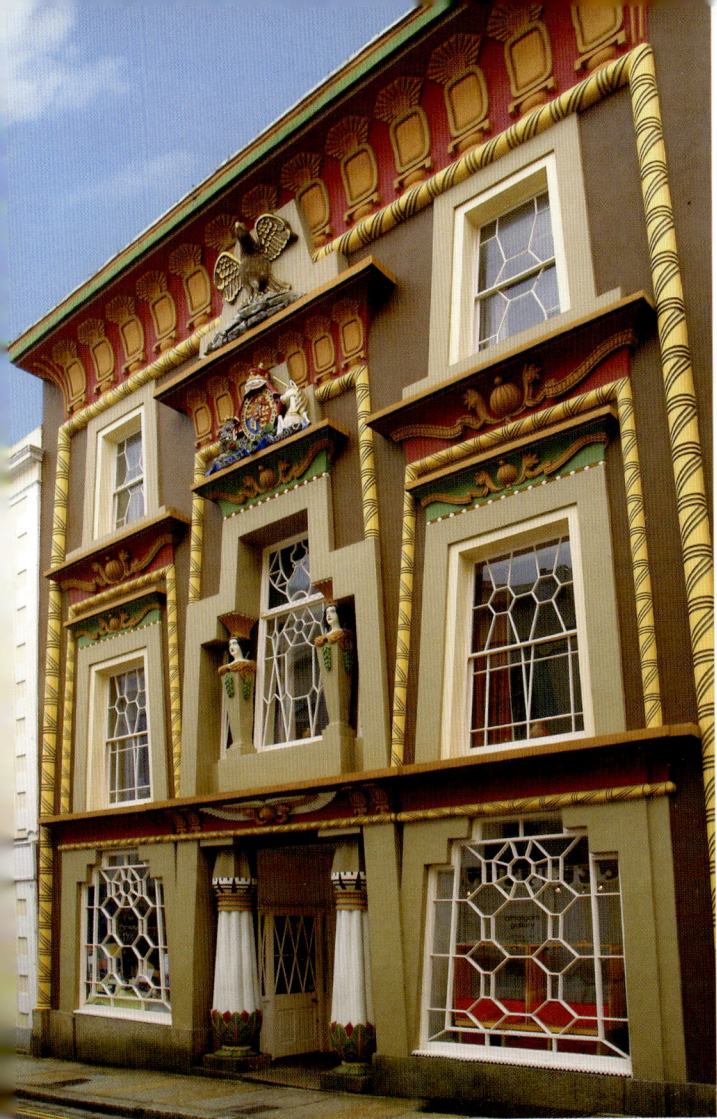

4. Pencarrow, E front, by George Wightwick, 1844–6 (p. 40)
5. Trelowarren, chapel, plasterwork, c. 1830 (p. 645)
6. Penzance, The Egyptian House, Chapel Street, 1835–6 (p. 432)

97. Penzance, Old Town Hall and Market House, Market Jew Street, by William Harris, 1836–8 (p. 428)
98. Bude, sea lock to the Bude canal, by James Green, 1823 (p. 128)
99. Saltash, Royal Albert Bridge, by I. K. Brunel, 1847–59, with Tamar Bridge behind, by Mott, Hay & Anderson, 1959–61 (p. 611)
100. Carn Brea, Marriott's Shaft, South Wheal Frances, c.1896 (p. 148)

101. Penzance, St Mary, Chapel Street, by Charles Hutchens, 1832–5 (p. 426
102. Par, St Mary the Virgin, St Blazey Gate, by G. E. Street, 1848 (p. 39
103. Antony, St Philip and St James, Maryfield, chancel, by William White
    1864–71 (p. 98)
104. Ladock, St Ladoc, chancel E window by William Morris, central
    panel by E. Burne-Jones, 1863 (p. 263)

120. Goonhilly Earth Station, 'Arthur' (Antenna No. 1), by Husband & Co. et al., 1960–2 (p. 219)

121. Feock, Creek Vean, by Team 4 (Norman and Wendy Foster, Richard and Su Rogers, and Georgie Wolton), 1964–7 (p. 197)

22. Truro, New County Hall, by F. K. Hicklin and A. J. Groves, County
    Architects, 1963–6 (p. 669)

23. Truro, Courts of Justice, by Evans & Shalev, 1986–8 (p. 672)

124. St Ives, Tate St Ives, Porthmeor, by Evans & Shalev, 1989–93 (p. 560

25. Penryn, Jubilee Wharf, by Bill Dunster of ZED factory, 2006 (p. 414)
26. Saltash, Bishop Cornish Education Centre, Lynher Drive, by ARCO2
   Architects Ltd, 2010 (p. 611)

127. Eden Project, Biomes and Core (Education Centre), by Nicholas Grimshaw & Partners et al., 1998–2001 and 2005 (p. 179)

there are N and S aisles of seven bays with octagonal piers and double-chamfered arches, identical with one exception: on the N side, where the rood screen originally went across, the arch is narrower, is built up from the floor as if it were a recess with no back,* and is formed of a curious arrangement of sections of piers of quite different design and of Polyphant not granite; they are of unusual section with moulded capitals of an unusual design. Are these the remnants of the pre-1595 church and are the rest of the arcades late C16 or early C17 replacements, even if in their design the latter look more C15 than C17? – A rare example of an C18 SASH WINDOW survives as the E window of the N aisle – Pre-Conquest SHAFT with interlace decoration built into base of N wall. – STAINED GLASS. Excellent E chancel window with good colours by *R. Anning Bell*, 1918. – MONU-MENTS. To Capt. Stephen Hutchens †1709, with two cherubs on the cornice and a cartouche with ships in relief below. – John Badcock †1784, long inscription and some fine minor decoration by *Golden* of Holborn. – Grace Marrack, 1810 by *J. Isbell* of Truro. – To the crew of the Penlee lifeboat drowned 1981. Strikingly simple, a vast sea-smoothed granite boulder from the beach at Lamorna. – In the churchyard, near the SE gate, an OBELISK set up by Prince Lucien Bonaparte to com-memorate Dolly Pentreath †1778, who was said to have been the last person to speak Cornish. The Hutchens monument has part of its inscription in Cornish. – Fixed to the top of the SW boundary wall, a wheel-headed CHURCHYARD CROSS with figure of Christ with nimbus or halo on the front and five bosses in high relief on the reverse, of pre-Conquest date. Many other crosses in the parish. In the churchyard extension and cemetery, fine examples of modern MEMORIALS by *Joe Hemming* of Sancreed.

The pleasant and unspoiled churchtown gathered around the church includes HUTCHENS HOUSE, Mousehole Lane, to the W of the churchyard. Dated 1709, a long two-storey range with first-floor granite mullions repositioned from the ground floor. A private almshouse, known as the Hutchens Gift House, to house six poor men and six poor women of the parish. Immediately N, former STABLES, C18, now residential, the stables originally on the ground floor with loft above. They form a good group with the church, churchyard and early C19 former VICARAGE.

KERRIS MANOR, 1½ m. W. C17 house, refronted early C18, built around a small courtyard with projecting C17 wing set back on the l. Symmetrical seven-bay E front of granite ashlar, as are the gable-end stacks with moulded caps and rear lateral stack. Dated 1721 RP (Richard Pearce) over central door. Interior reflects the phasing, including good early C18 features with a bolection-moulded panelled parlour.

---

* It has been suggested it might be an Easter sepulchre, though it is in an unusual position.

TREVELLOE, 1½ m. SW. Small country house, 1911 by *Arnold Mitchell* for W. E. T. Bolitho. A fine design in a free Arts and Crafts style, three-storey but disguised by a steep central gable that sweeps up dramatically from the ground floor. Interior with C18-style features but many Art Nouveau details. Service wing with central dovecote.

PELYNT

ST NUN (St Nunit). Prominently sited within an oval raised churchyard or *lann*. Fine C14 W tower, partly remodelled in the C15, of three stages with corner buttresses, one ogee-headed light at the second stage, three-light Perp belfry openings, and battlemented parapet with octagonal turrets and ball finials. The base of the buttresses are carved with quatrefoils (cf. the more flamboyant decoration at Lansallos). The body of the church is Perp with Perp windows throughout. Its chief feature is its N arcade of stately granite Doric columns and depressed segmental arches, erected *c.* 1680 to replace the medieval piers. The ceiled wagon roof of the nave has some carved medieval bosses, some C19, awkwardly applied. A harsh restoration of 1879–83 by *J. P. St Aubyn* rebuilt much of the S transept, restored the nave masonry, replaced tracery, and installed new pews, tiles, dado and cathedral glass, leaving little of architectural interest but a fine selection of MONUMENTS. – William Achym †1589. Slate slab, part of a chest tomb with large recumbent figure in armour in high relief; probably by *Peter Crocker* of Looe. – John Buller of Tregarrick †1615. Tomb-chest with ornamented top slab against the wall surmounted by backplate with husband, wife, and twelve children in flat relief. – Edward Trelawny, by *Robert Wills*, 1639; chiefly ornamental. Inscription 'Here lies an honest lawyer, wot ye what A thing for all the world to wonder at'. – Elizabeth Vyvyan †1640; poor. – Pretty slate plate with inscriptions of homespun poetry, 1654 and 1675. – Slate slab to Cordelia Trelavnia, anagram 'O, illa creditavrnae'. Flanked by two heraldic shields and surmounted by a floral trail signed by *Anthonius Collie*, 1634. – Sir Jonathan Trelawny, the famous Bishop of Exeter and Winchester (†1721), is buried at Pelynt. The PASTORAL STAFF carried at his funeral is exhibited in the church with the BISHOP'S CHAIR, possibly from Trelawne (q.v.), which was constructed by St Aubyn from pieces of the bishop's chair from Winchester. – Large CROSS-HEAD on N wall of aisle. C11, trefoil-shaped.

In the cemetery NW of the churchyard, large Delabole slate HEADSTONE to William Stackforth Grigson †1930, inscribed by *Eric Gill*, 1931.

Former SCHOOL and SCHOOL HOUSE, N of the church. 1842 by *George Wightwick*. Two-storey Tudor style, with central canted oriel on moulded corbel surmounted by a gabled bellcote to the satisfyingly composed front elevation. Schoolroom extension to r. c. 1908.

PELYNT HOUSE, s of the church. Former rectory, 1841, also by *Wightwick*. Tudor-style stuccoed two-storey house with three-window garden front.

PENNELLICK FARMHOUSE, 1 m. s. A medieval house retaining the smoke-blackened remains of two raised base-cruck trusses over the hall, now heated by a tall C17 lateral stack. The lower end has gone but the cross-passage is fronted by a two-storey C17 porch. C17 wing behind the hall.

ST NONNA'S HOLY WELL, about 1½ m. NE at Hobb Park. The other centre for the cult of the saint, originally with chapel licensed in 1400. Well-house built into the side of the bank, chamber with corbelled stone roof and circular stone basin, possibly Norman, with a deeply moulded rim and series of rings enclosing a Greek cross or ball.

TRELAWNE. *See* p. 641.

PENCARROW

0070

The best approach to Pencarrow is from the s down the mile-long carriage drive. The visitor passes successively through the encircling shelter belts, an extensive Iron Age hillfort – Pencarrow Rounds (*see* below) – and generous ornamental planting before gaining a first prospect of the house set comfortably in its amphitheatre of formal gardens. From here the drive passes around the rear to arrive at the E entrance front, slowly revealing the house and offering an insight into the building history behind the stuccoed E and s show fronts.

A substantial Jacobean house was built here for Sir John Molesworth II (†1716), High Sheriff of Cornwall, of which the present two-storey w elevation and the two-light mullion windows of the brick vaulted cellars survive. In contrast are the fine Palladian E and s show fronts, both seven bays: the E with a slightly projecting pedimented three-bay centre and pediments to the first-floor windows; the s front longer and with a different rhythm of windows, but also the window pediments. Their evolution is interesting. The three-storey s garden wing was begun c. 1730 as the first stage of an ambitious rebuilding planned by Sir John Molesworth IV (†1766). It was in the Italian palazzo style, possibly by *Allessandro Galilei* (†1737), since it has strong similarities to his design of Castletown, Ireland, in elevation and floor plan, both having an axial corridor with rooms either side, similar plasterwork, and comparable cantilever staircases.* The wing was built directly

---

*I am indebted to Paul Holden's research for this and other suggestions in this account.

onto the outside side wall of the earlier house, the linkage resulting in complicated floor levels. The rebuilding was not completed until 1765–75 for Sir John Molesworth V, and is attributed to *Robert Allanson*, an otherwise unknown architect from York, who died at Egloshayle in 1773. Of this time is the accomplished E wing with its especially good mid-Georgian dining room and drawing room. In the 1820s a Palladian-style extension to the E wing created a three-room-deep plan with the music room at its N end.

But it was *George Wightwick* who finally Palladianized and rendered the E elevation between 1844 and 1846. Wightwick is also known to have formed the present arrangement on the E front, of a central entrance hall flanked by the music room and drawing room, replacing the original 1770s entrance on the S front. The ENTRANCE HALL doubles as the library with bolection-moulded panelling and overmantel, brought in the 1770s from the family's demolished house at Tetcott in north Devon. The splendid MUSIC ROOM has a Rococo stucco ceiling and an intriguing tripartite alcove extension, also by Wightwick, to house a statue of Aphrodite bought in Rome about 1830, with maple-grained panelling and more reused earlier joinery. Fine C18 chimneypiece in DINING ROOM. Inner STAIR HALL has a groin-vaulted corridor supporting a stone first-floor landing reached by the cantilever open-well stair, now supported on two C20 columns, with early C19 wrought-iron balustrade, winding around a vast combined stove and colva oil lamp standard by *Heardens* of Plymouth c. 1845. The staircase has a Venetian window to the N.

The house is immensely enhanced by its setting in extensive early and mid-C19 formal gardens, informal pleasure grounds and C18 parkland. The former were developed from the 1830s by Sir William Molesworth (†1855), who had oversight of Kew Gardens in his capacity of First Commissioner of Works, and renewed and reinforced by the family during the C20, notably by Lt Col. Sir Arscott Molesworth-St Aubyn (†1998). Sir William set out the S drive as a picturesque approach to the house, exploiting the antiquarian interest of Pencarrow Rounds, and created the spectacular sunken ITALIAN GARDEN centred on a magnificent FOUNTAIN, a single bowl supported by four caryatids, copied from the Piazza Navona in Rome. The grounds include numerous specimen plantings displaying the family's links with prominent C19 nurseries and plant collectors, including the monkey puzzle tree that is said to have given rise to the epithet of that name. The ROCK GARDENS of 1831 are among the earliest in England. Massive granite boulders from Bodmin Moor incorporating a GROTTO lined with quartz and crystals: presently roofless PALMHOUSE created from an earlier building in the 1840s, and an early C18 brick-lined ICE HOUSE. NE of the house, STABLES AND YARD with BEE BOLES in N wall lead to two brick and stone WALLED KITCHEN GARDENS.

PENCARROW ROUNDS. Well-preserved but unfinished Iron Age HILLSLOPE FORT overlooking land on E side of the Camel valley. Simple bank and ditch defences.

PENCOYS

ST ANDREW. 1881 by *Thomas Goodchild* of London. Simple Gothic, steeply pitched roof to nave that partly obscures the lower chancel. E.E. details, cusped lancets and bellcote over W end.

PENDEEN

ST JOHN THE BAPTIST. It is a surprise to find such an ambitious church among the modest terraces of this C19 mining village. Built by local people to the design of their evangelical vicar *Rev. Robert Aitken* in 1851, it is a remarkable period piece. On a large scale, with NW tower and cruciform plan; the exterior is plain and dignified in E.E. style with lancets and steeply pitched roofs. The interior is exceptionally lofty, the roof of scissor trusses springing from high-set corbels, its impressive verticality accentuated by the narrow pointed chancel arch and a fine five-light E window of long lancets with pretty decorative glass. Pews and choir stalls of simple, honest workmanship. Some Flemish roundels set in patterned glazing of the S transept and S nave wall.

The church is set within a churchyard bounded by a high embattled wall, the entrance arch charmingly pinnacled: Betjeman's description of it as 'like a toy fort' is apt. Similar entrance to the cemetery opposite. Aitken's energetic ministry also built a sober classical VICARAGE to the N of the church, and SCHOOLS on the adjoining site, now the village hall, all of the mid C19.

PENDEEN MANOR HOUSE, ¾ m. N. The reputed birthplace of William Borlase, the great Cornish antiquary, in 1695. Rare C16 and C17 courtyard-plan house, dated 1670 on the front. Smart main front in ashlar granite with round-headed arched doorway to the through passage, mullioned windows to the l. with linked hoodmoulds, large lateral stack and gable-end stacks with crenellated chimneys, and nice scrolled kneelers to the lower gable-ends of the roof. Courtyard accessed via remains of gatehouse from l. return wing. The r. return wing retains remains of a formerly open colonnade, like Godolphin and Penheale Manor (qq.v.). Interior with C17 fireplaces, plaster barrel ceiling and unusual C17 doors with reeded detail.

Behind the house, and accessed from the yard, an Iron Age FOGOU with a sloping passage running NE for 23 ft (7 metres) before turning NW for a further 33 ft (10 metres), terminating in a partially blocked entrance opening on to a field. The main passage is stone faced and roofed with lintels. At the angle of this passage is a second chamber 24 ft (7.3 metres) long.

PENDEEN LIGHTHOUSE, 1 m. N. 1900 by *Arthur Carkeek* of Redruth, but to a design by *Sir Thomas Matthews*, engineer-in-chief of Trinity House. The sturdy tower is surmounted by a lantern by *Chance* of Birmingham with a lattice of diamond and half-diamond glazing panels. Much original equipment including the lens floating in a trough of mercury, still in use. The tower is linked to flat-roofed KEEPERS' COTTAGES. Detached ENGINE HOUSE, also with original equipment. The whole attractive cliff-top group surrounded by white rendered walls.

8030

PENDENNIS

Falmouth

Seen from the sea or silhouetted against the western sky from St Mawes, the mighty promontory fortress of Pendennis stands sentinel over the great natural anchorage of the Fal estuary and Carrick Roads, a role it played in the defence of Britain for over four hundred years. It was founded, a pair with St Mawes, as one of the chain of artillery forts which Henry VIII erected from 1538 onwards under the menace of a French invasion. They extend along the south coast from Kent to Cornwall and are designed with a great deal of variety, modifying the theme of the circle and polygon in all-round symmetrical combinations. On their position in the history of architecture and fortification *see* St Mawes. Pendennis was begun in 1539 and completed in 1545, with a blockhouse below on the SE tip of the promontory as at St Mawes. The setting of the castle at Pendennis was transformed in 1597–1600 by vast new fortifications to command the whole headland. They were constructed to the design of *Paul Ive*, an experienced engineer who had built fortresses in the Low Countries in the 1570s and the Channel Islands in the 1590s, employing the Italian angle bastion system. The summit of the headland was enclosed within an elongated polygon of bastions surrounded by steep ramparts and a deep ditch, with a full or half-bastion to each angle and a large triangular S bastion at the S end overlooking Pendennis Point; the Tudor castle was retained as a keep within the S end and the blockhouse incorporated into a small fort. The fortress endured in this form with only relatively minor changes through its subsequent eventful history, including its siege as a Royalist stronghold during the Civil War and repeated re-armament up to and including the 1939–45 war.

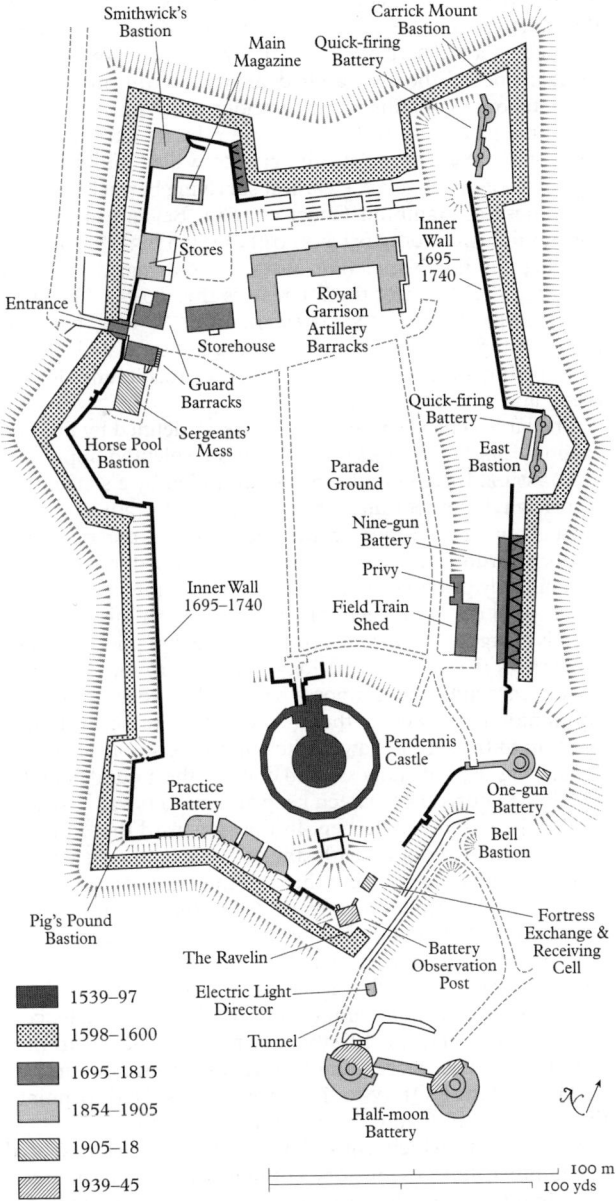

Smithwick's Bastion

Carrick Mount Bastion

Main Magazine

Quick-firing Battery

Main Magazine

Stores

Inner Wall 1695–1740

Entrance

Royal Garrison Artillery Barracks

Storehouse

Guard Barracks

Quick-firing Battery

Sergeants' Mess

Horse Pool Bastion

East Bastion

Parade Ground

Inner Wall 1695–1740

Nine-gun Battery

Privy

Field Train Shed

Practice Battery

Pendennis Castle

One-gun Battery

Bell Bastion

Pig's Pound Bastion

Fortress Exchange & Receiving Cell

The Ravelin

Battery Observation Post

1539–97

Electric Light Director

1598–1600

Tunnel

1695–1815

1854–1905

1905–18

Half-moon Battery

1939–45

N

100 m
100 yds

Pendennis. Plan

Connected to the mainland by a narrow neck of land, the castle is entered on its NW side through the ramparts of the Elizabethan fortress. The very Italian GATEHOUSE of *c.* 1695–1700 is reached by a BRIDGE of *c.* 1845 that replaced a previous drawbridge: one of the two arched alcoves at the inner end of the gatehouse contains the drawbridge mechanism. Inside the castle the gatehouse is flanked l. and r. by GUARD BARRACKS, also of *c.* 1695–1700, sturdy granite-walled buildings with hipped roofs, probably the earliest surviving barracks in Britain after those at Hampton Court of 1689. Beyond to the l. is a substantial two-storey brick STORE, built 1793–1811 to house supplies for the Napoleonic Wars. Beyond again, and commanding the N end of the fortress, is the ROYAL GARRISON ARTILLERY BARRACKS, datestone 1901, a long two-storey range with projecting end wings and a tall central clock tower with pediment and an octagonal stair-turret and look-out rising above its SE corner.

The large central space of the fortress* defined by five of the original Elizabethan BASTIONS makes a splendid approach to the CASTLE. Its circular keep is surrounded by a sixteen-sided Henrician inner curtain wall and entered (rather curiously through an arch which is the rear wall of the demolished Tudor guardhouse) at first-floor level over a drawbridge with a completely preserved portcullis. This gives into a forebuilding coeval with the main keep. The main room on this floor of the keep is octagonal, with walls 16 ft (4.2 metres) thick and ceiling timbers 35 ft (10.7 metres) long and of a 16 in. (40 cm.) by 16 in. scantling. The gunposts have widely splayed sides and ammunition recesses in them. A spiral staircase in a similar position to that at St Mawes leads up to the second floor, with a matching array of gunposts, and down to the ground floor, from which the courtyard between keep and curtain wall is reached, and to the basement kitchen. In the courtyard the heavy guns were placed in gunports with smoke vents; on the curtain walls stood the musketeers firing through the battlements.

Among the various batteries added in the C18 and later C19, HALF-MOON BATTERY below the S end of the fort was first built in 1793 on a curved half-moon plan so that its guns covered a wide arc of fire; it was last modified for the Second World War. The most important of the outer defences is LITTLE DENNIS, the Elizabethan fort remodelled from the 1539 blockhouse, more complete than its opposite number at St Mawes. CRAB QUAY to the E was the best landing point on the headland, probably defended from the C16.

CASTLE DRIVE, which runs around the lower slopes of the promontory, links the history of the fortress to the emergence of Falmouth as a resort (q.v.). The landward approach from the town is now sadly compromised by the green-glazed bulk of the meretricious SHIPS AND CASTLES LEISURE CENTRE, 1993.

---

*It was not always so open, the buildings that came and went including a C17 windmill.

PENGERSICK CASTLE

1 m. SSE of Germoe

A remarkable and important survival, and a surprise to find so noble a four-storey tower suddenly appearing on the road close to the holidayland of Praa Sands. What we see is the most prestigious part of a mid C16 fortified manor of double court-yard plan, probably built by William Worth of Worth, Devon, whose initials appear on the tower's label stops. It stands on the site of a C13 building.* The principal court to the E contained the great hall with the service court to the W, the tower occupying the external angle between them to defend the house from the seaward direction; only fragments of the rest survive. The tower is battered with a single square room on each floor, the lower floor with dumb-bell gunloops, the upper three lit by four-light mullioned widows with king mullions and four-centred heads. A square-newel stair-turret projects from the NE corner of the tower and reaches above its roof: it also has gunloops, and two-light mullioned windows. Both tower and turret are strongly embattled, and there are more gunloops on the other elevations. That this was designed for residence but with a strong element of defence, a self-con-tained refuge within the house (a unique arrangement in Corn-wall and perhaps the south-west generally), is also strongly suggested by the austere character of the interior: a reflection of the vulnerability of this coastal site to French and Spanish raids in the C16. A painted panel recorded by Borlase presents a view of the castle from near the entrance gate with the E court in false perspective. One-and-a-half storey accommoda-tion block of 1928 to the N.

To the NW FARM BUILDINGS that incorporate the early C16 three-storey block which formed the NW corner of the service court, with the remains of a newel stair and a pistol loop. Just W of the castle, PENGERSICK FARMHOUSE, late C17 to early C18, remodelled late C19, retains a four-centred door frame with foliage-decorated spandrels that came from the castle's porch, reused here in the late C19 with its label straps reversed.

PENHEALE MANOR

1 m. NW of Egloskerry

One of the best gentry houses in Cornwall, of uncommon interest for both the sustained quality of the early C17 house, exempli-fying the best of the strong Cornish provincial style of the period (cf. Lanhydrock, Godolphin, Prideaux Place (Padstow) and Trewan (St Columb Major)) and its spectacular early C20 extension by *Edwin Lutyens*. The Domesday manor was

114

*This account is much indebted to John Schofield's research.

acquired in 1592 by George Grenville, whose son sold it to Sir John Specott, a relation by marriage, in the early C17. The medieval house was rebuilt and embellished between the late C16 and mid C17 with impressive new stables completed in 1620 and a gatehouse constructed c. 1636: a small C14 window and a door to a cellar are the only visible evidence of the earlier building.

The HOUSE stands within an enclosed forecourt and is approached through the GATEHOUSE which has a five-bay loggia on its inner face. The smart N entrance front of granite ashlar has a splendid array of mullioned windows and an embattled parapet, and is dated 1636. Inside, a hall screen of c. 1640, one of the most sumptuous in the county, columned and with the whole inner face richly ornamented with deep undercutting and vigorous depictions, including Adam and Eve. To the other side of the screens passage, the dining room with handsome bolection-moulded panelling and plaster ceiling of the late C17 or early C18. Behind the hall an oak-panelled parlour of c. 1625–30. The first floor over the hall is a gallery with fine late C16 to early C17 plaster barrel-vault with pendentives and a frieze with mermaids and dolphins: in scale and quality of execution it compares with the plasterwork at Prideaux Place, Padstow. In the Specott Room above the dining room more excellent plasterwork including another barrel-vaulted ceiling and an especially delightful chimneypiece with spiral columns and three vases with sprays of flowers.

The Specotts continued at Penheale until 1920 when it was acquired and restored by *Captain Norman Colville*, who commissioned Lutyens to undertake major extensions. Lutyens was working at Castle Drogo, Devon, at that time and the similarities are striking. His large-scale additions are brilliantly conceived,* contrasting yet complementary to the original house and experienced as a surprise because they are hidden from the entrance court on the SE side downslope as a second court. In a typical Lutyens touch, they are built of a lovely combination of silver grey Delabole slate walling with sage green Polyphant dressings, though the latter have not weathered well. Its main accent is asymmetrical and very bold, a tower-like structure, four storeys, sheer and with two bay windows, like a London block of flats. Yet it stands up perfectly to the old work, by virtue of its obstinate originality.

The splendid STABLES, remodelled in 1676, stand to the NW of the house. Symmetrical nine-bay front around a central entrance with a loft opening above; the door and loft opening have round-headed arches, the former with a segmental arched pediment, the latter with a triangular one, a motif repeated over two of the ground-floor transomed-and-mullioned

---

*Lutyens wrote to Colville on 9 September 1920: 'Here are my proposals. It all seems to come simple enough now, but it was a difficult job, and I have been a long time over it.' Quoted by Diana Colville, 'Penheale – The Rebirth of a House', *Journal of the Royal Institution of Cornwall* (1989).

windows. In contrast the first floor has ventilation slits only. To the rear an C18 octagonal DOVECOTE, its roof with deeply overhanging eaves and a slate cap. To the W a row of three COTTAGES and a WASHHOUSE, also by *Lutyens*, simple, with deep overhanging eaves. Lutyens also designed one of the formal gardens and a semicircular flight of steps modelled on those at Newton Ferrers. The GATE LODGE is Tudor Gothic, *c.* 1850.

PENPONDS

The parish was formed out of the W edge of Camborne in 1847.

HOLY TRINITY, Church Road. 1854 by *J. P. St Aubyn*, comprehensively refitted by *Canon J. S. Carah* from 1896 to 1935. E.E. style, simple lancets with trefoil heads, a triple lancet at the E end, a gabled bellcote over the W gable and the roof swept out over the N aisle. The four-bay granite aisle arcade has double-chamfered two-centred arches and circular piers with plain moulded capitals. Large double-chamfered two-centred chancel arch and scissor-braced roofs. The early C20 refitting was, as Betjeman observed, 'a complete period piece of High Church good taste' with much gilding, marble and rich furnishings, including spiritedly carved BENCH-ENDS by *Hunt* of Plymouth and a DADO by *William Mitchell* of Penponds. The AUMBRY incorporates a fragment of a medieval bench-end. – STAINED GLASS. Mostly by *Clayton & Bell*, 1907–33.

METHODIST CHURCH, Church Road. Dated 1844. An example of the smaller Bible Christian chapel; the gabled front with two tall round-headed windows.

In CHURCH ROAD, Nos. 15 and 17 are a rare survival of a pair of simple early C19 cottages with central coupled doorways.

TREVITHICK'S COTTAGE, Higher Penponds Road. C18, a symmetrical two-storey thatched house with a stable attached at the r. end. The home of Richard Trevithick (cf. Camborne).

PENPONDS CHURCH INSTITUTE AND CHAPEL HOUSE, Higher Penponds Road. 1849. Built as the church school, with four tall sash windows. The house is lower with three sashes.

MENADARVA, 2 m. NW. The former seat of an important branch of the Arundells of Trerice. The C12 font from its former chapel is now at Tuckingmill (q.v.). The house is still shown as a large assemblage of buildings on a plan of 1783 by which time it had been acquired by the Bassets of Tehidy. What now remains is an interesting fragment, probably with medieval fabric incorporated in the present mostly C17 and early C18 buildings, two-storey on an L-shaped plan partly enclosing a courtyard. Hints of its former high status are offered by the exceptionally large end stack of the main range and a fine panelled parlour with raised bolection-moulded panels, a bolection-moulded corniced fireplace and overmantel, and matching architraves to the doors.*

PENROSE
1½ m. SW of Helston

In a splendid position overlooking Loe Pool as if it were an artificial serpentine lake specially made as a vista for the house. The C17 house, on a medieval site, was probably built for John Penrose (†1679) but was subsequently much remodelled and extended in several phases under the ownership of the Rogers family. The principal campaigns were from c. 1788 by John Rogers, c. 1823 by Rev. John Rogers, 1867–8, and 1927–8 when the centre of the Loe elevation was rebuilt. The result is uncommonly attractive, with irregular elevations to all four fronts in rambling ranges on a roughly square plan around a small courtyard. The charming Loe front has the rebuilt six-bay centre with twelve-pane sashes and off-centre recessed doorway. It is flanked r. by a large two-storey C19 bow window with twelve-pane sashes divided by granite mullions, and l. by the most endearing feature of the exterior, a taller two-storey two-bay range with a steeply pitched hipped roof and embattled parapet. The nearly symmetrical NW front incorporates the original 2:3:2 bay C17 front and has a central doorway with pilasters surmounted by a carved eagle formerly above the parapet. The SW front has a resited late C18 window. The interior retains good C18 features with C19 plasterwork.

The extensive ranges of outbuildings include handsome pre-1788 STABLES SE of the house, with attached BANK BARN of 1833–4, subsequently extended and remodelled. U-shaped plan stables, the central bay broken forward with side buttresses, low-pitched gable with central oculus, and bellcote. To the E an unusual BATH HOUSE, 1840, in Tudor Gothic style, with well-head and sunken slate-lined bath.

EAST LODGE. 1834, designed by *Henry Harrison*, in Tudor style.

PENRYN

Even for a county rich in good historic towns Penryn is astonishingly intact: a medieval foundation on a dramatic promontory site with a dense concentration of C17–C19 buildings offering some of the most delightful streetscape in Cornwall. The prom-

---

*I am grateful to Stephen Tyrrell for his observations on the evolution of the house, and to Professor Charles Thomas who considers the site, or a closely adjacent one, was the shrine of St Derva.

ontory runs w–e towards the Penryn River between two valleys, the town climbing steeply from the waterfront along the spine of a ridge as did medieval Tregony and Truro further up the estuary. Bishop Brewer of Exeter planted the town here in the early c13, just w of the c6 *lann* on which the church of St Gluvias stands, to create a port much nearer the mouth of the Fal: its first charter was in 1236 and its first market and fair were granted in 1259.

Extensive c20 suburbs have not diluted Penryn's historic integrity. Much of its early c13 layout survives including the principal street pattern with the central spine of Higher and Lower Market Streets and remnant burgage plots descending to the valleys, especially complete to the n. The fork of West Street and Helston Road formed its western extent while eastwards it probably continued along Broad Street as far as The Square and the junction with Bohill. The developing town, rapidly diverting trade from Truro, greatly enhanced its status in 1265 when Bishop Bronescombe founded the collegiate church of St Thomas at the head of Glasney Creek on its southern outskirts. Glasney College, one of the earliest collegiate churches in England, became one of the most important religious institutions in Cornwall: only Tywardreath, Launceston Priory and Bodmin Priory could vie with it. With a provost, thirteen canons, thirteen vicars choral, and a bishop's palace within a walled enclosure and park, it was a Cornish version of Exeter Cathedral and its substantial buildings were described at the Dissolution as 'well fortified with towers and ordinance for the defence of the town and river'. The buildings have vanished but surviving architectural fragments, some dispersed through the town in subsequent rebuilding, are of Beer stone and show close connections with the Exeter Cathedral workshop.

Though the Dissolution dented Penryn's prestige and economy, the town continued to grow into one of Cornwall's principal

Penryn, Glasney College. c19 reconstruction based on a plan of
c. 1580–1640

ports as the first and last victualling call on the English Channel coast. By the early C17 it was trading as far afield as Constantinople, and its oyster beds were supplying London. Despite the rise of Falmouth in the C17 it continued to sustain a diverse economy sufficient to justify the building of the Exchequer Quay in 1676. Its position allowed it to service the vast number of mines between the town and Redruth with imports of timber, coal and cattle and exports of tin. It was also a major centre of shipbuilding and repair, engineering, fishing, and later the granite trade. Granite export may have begun very early but the trade developed with hefty harbour works during the C18 and C19 when Penryn granite was exported all over the world. With a rail link to Falmouth opened in 1859, mid-C19 Penryn and its extensive waterfront was a busy industrial place.

Penryn's appearance today, its friendly streets packed with C17–C19-looking buildings often incorporating or refronting earlier fabric,* reflects its sustained prosperity during these centuries: it remained a favoured residence for wealthy merchants until the early C19 when superior society began to gravitate towards Falmouth, leaving it less altered by later C19 development than its near neighbour. But the collapse of the Cornish mining industry triggered a steep decline of the town's population from its 1861 peak and by 1870 a Board of Health report found it poverty-stricken and insanitary. The decline continued during the C20 until a report in 1975 found such dereliction that a Housing Action Area† was declared to repair 270 out of 384 buildings, with a unique combination of housing and conservation grants. It is not too much to say that this saved a complete town, large parts of which would otherwise have been demolished. The scheme, which continued into the early C21, laid the basis for the rejuvenation of Penryn, now strongly boosted by the development of the Tremough Campus (*see* 417) for the Combined Universities of Cornwall and the imaginative conservation and development of the waterfront.

CHURCHES

St Gluvias, Church Hill. The parish church, though separate from the town across the eastern valley. A church was here by 1291, re-dedicated in 1321, and closely connected with Glasney College with four successive late C15 and early C16 vicars becoming provosts. Three-stage C15 w tower with angle buttresses and a NW stair-turret rising above the embattled parapet. Extensively rebuilt, except perhaps for the E end, by *J. P. St Aubyn* in 1883 in the Perp style using Ham Hill stone dressings. Six-bay pointed-arch arcade to N and S aisles. E wall of N aisle

---

*The town's building history was the subject of exemplary investigation by the Penryn Buildings Survey Group. I am grateful to its founder Veronica Chesher, Eric Berry, June Palmer and members of the group for much useful information.
†Such a small place was not originally intended for such treatment under the 1974 Housing Act which had targeted inner cities.

has two arcades of three pointed- and round-arched image niches. C15 piscina in porch, striking oval medieval head over the S door, pointed-arched aumbry to the E end of the S aisle and reused carved C15 ribs in the chancel roof. Some Y-tracery, probably introduced in 1744, when the S aisle was widened, or later. The calm limewashed interior, small elegant chandeliers, simple wood altar rails and organ gallery on Tuscan columns at the W end of the S aisle are of the 1950s by *Sir Ninian Comper*. – STAINED GLASS. S window of chancel by *Lavers, Barraud & Westlake*, 1890. – E window of S aisle by *Leonard A. Pownall* (cf. All Saints, Falmouth), 1910. – W window N aisle by *G. Maile*, 1963. – MONUMENTS. Brasses to Thomas Kyllygrewe, *c.* 1500, and his wives (one wife only on the brass), six daughters, and shields, already of the arrangement of figures and inscriptions which remained typical right through the C16. – Wall monuments to Samuel Pendarves †1643 and his wife and to William Pendarves †1671 and wife. These two were originally of the earlier C17 type with two kneeling figures facing each other and columns l. and r., the only remarkable thing being that even after 1670 this old convention was still preserved. Now, however, they are strangely arranged against the E wall of the S aisle so that two of the four figures kneel in the window jambs round the corner from their respective husband or wife (cf. Harris monument, Plymstock, Devon). – Samuel Ennys of Ennys (now Enys), 1611–97 and his wife, plaster pediment and marble shelf on bracket with lion's head flanking cherub. – J. Kempe †1711, bust with wig under drapery between Corinthian columns.

PENRYN METHODIST CHURCH, The Terrace. 1891–3 by *J. W. Trounson* of Penzance. The imposing Italianate front, in showy variations of granite, has a tall central coped gable with a three-light central window over two wide gabled doorways with moulded arches forming a loggia. Flanking bays with moulded parapets and paired windows with polished nook-shafts and mullions. – STAINED GLASS by *Fouracre & Son.* of Plymouth.

Former CONGREGATIONAL CHAPEL, New Street. Now Sterling House. 1805. Granite ashlar front in classical style with tall round-headed windows flanking a central elliptically arched doorway with smaller round-headed window above.

PUBLIC BUILDINGS

TOWN HALL AND MUSEUM, Market Street. The clock tower, dated 1839, on an island site between Higher and Lower Market Streets, is the splendid centrepiece of the town.* Approaching it from the W it looks like a heavy variation on the theme of St Mary-le-Strand in London. It is of granite

---

*The site is not that of the C14 Chapel of the Blessed Virgin Mary, shown on a map of 1545 with a square embattled tower in the middle of the main street, then called Mary Street.

ashlar in three stages, with a square third stage and octagonal clock stage under a domed lead roof with weathervane. Behind is the former C16 market building adapted as the Town Hall in the C18, with ground-floor arcades of twelve closely spaced basket-arches to both street sides, originally over shuttered shopfronts, and early C18 and C19 windows above. The stucco bowed E end is also a C19 extension, of country-town appearance with end pilasters, moulded parapet entablature, a triple round-headed window to first floor, and large Doric porch. The Town Hall has an early to mid-C18 barrel-vaulted plaster ceiling with dentilled cornice, dado panelling and rostrum.

TEETOTAL HALL, Lower Market Street. Datestone 1852, and name inscribed on frieze below pediment. The plain front could be a Methodist chapel with round-arched openings under a simple triangular pediment.

PENRYN (or COLLEGE WOOD) RAILWAY VIADUCT. 1909. On a graceful curve to the SW of the town, eleven round-headed brick arches on rock-faced granite piers with corbelled refuges at alternate bays. The twelve piers of *Brunel*'s viaduct survive alongside.

PERAMBULATION

Start at the waterfront which still offers a strong sense of Penryn's *raison d'être* as a port, though fast changing as its rejuvenation gathers pace. The promontory EXCHEQUER QUAY, 1676, and the INNER HARBOUR, cut off from the river by a 1930s road bridge, have sections of vertically set killas stone walls like the C17 quays at Falmouth. Opposite Exchequer Quay is JUBILEE WHARF, 2006 by *Bill Dunster* of *ZEDfactory*, London. A striking new gateway to the town, prominently sited on the waterfront, uncompromisingly contemporary and entirely suited to the functional character of the area. A mixed-use development of community, workshop, retail and residential components on a low-energy design pioneered by Dunster in his earlier BedZED housing for the Peabody Trust in Sutton, London. Built above the historic quay level but retaining a strip of the original height at the water's edge. Two blocks frame a sheltered court looking across the creek, the S wall of the lower two-storey block leaning back and sweeping up wave-like on laminated timber beams into the curved roof, clad, as are all the roofs, in zinc. The four-storey block has maisonettes above two levels of workshops. The colourful angular roof cowls complement the wind turbines along the edge of the quay which recreate the character of a working waterfront, totemic of the town's early C21 vitality. Beyond is COMMERCIAL ROAD, completed *c.* 1840, its industrial character partly surviving in C19 warehouses including two with modest Art Deco fronts.

The older waterfront area behind Exchequer Quay and around the Inner Harbour that formed the medieval waterway of Glasney Creek has seen comprehensive later C20 and early C21 residential development of the wharfs once occupied by industry, notably the granite works. The new build has generally, and successfully, taken its cue from the retained warehouse buildings like ANCHOR WAREHOUSE and DANIEL'S SAIL LOFT. The former was built 1843–4 as a bone mill, altered in the late C19 for the manufacture of fertilizer from imported guano, and tactfully converted to residential in 2005. The scale and character of the buildings, interlaced with walkways and the waterfront, seem naturally woven into the texture of the older town.

The town centre is best approached up QUAY HILL which rises steeply from the waterfront, its surprising openness the consequence of demolition following the bombing of Penryn during the 1939–45 war and later road widening. The town starts graciously at THE SQUARE. Nos. 1–3, c. 1770, are a terrace of three town houses built to resemble a mansion house (cf. Truro and Falmouth), eloquently expressing the aspirations of the later C18 town. The central bays of the seven-window front are broken forward under a triangular pediment with an oculus and modillion cornice. The elaborate central pedimented doorway has fluted columns and moulded entablatures with dentils and modillions; the flanking houses have pilastered doorways with ornate cast-iron railings to No. 2. On the E side of the square, Nos. 4–6 are another terrace of three houses of C17 origin, remodelled in the early C18, on a large courtyard plan. No. 5 has good C17 features including an open-well closed-string staircase with heavy turned balusters and an unusual roof structure with principals with curved feet. The S side of the square was destroyed by bombing in 1941.

On into BROAD STREET, like the town centre generally rich in good town houses, some three-storey and quite grand, and displaying an attractive range of building materials; some granite but much coloured stucco and render, sometimes to timber-framed fronts, and slate cladding. Nos. 16 and 18 have an C18 front, pedimented doorcase to a through passage with stud and panel screen, and C16 roof. Of special note in Broad Street are the OLD LIBRARY, early C18 with an incised stucco ground floor and lovely shallow bows to the ground and first floors, and further W on the other side No. 6, a late C18 town house with a splendid Pentewan ashlar front and a good pedimented doorcase. Opposite, the KINGS ARMS HOTEL, C17 on a U-shaped plan with two rear wings behind a mid-C19 three-storey four-window front with an open porch on square granite columns supporting a small first-floor chamber surmounted by decorative ironwork. Facing, on the corner with St Thomas Street, the OLD FIRE STATION dated 1899. Delightfully quirky front elevation with a crow-stepped gable surmounted by a crested finial.

The junction of Broad Street and ST THOMAS STREET was the site of the medieval fish market; the street linked the medieval town to Glasney College and may have been an earlier route to a pre-existing crossing point of the river. It starts with Nos. 4–6, C18 three-storey town houses. No. 8 is a notable survival this far w in Cornwall of a C17 mixed construction merchant's house (cf. Fowey and Looe), probably built for Thomas Melhuish according to a lease of 1656. The timber-framed front is jettied out between rubble side walls corbelled out at each floor level and there is an ovolo-moulded door to the l. fronting a through passage. Opposite is the 1980s LIBRARY, a worthy addition to the street scene, part slate-hung, part stone (somewhat compromised by its ugly snail pointing), with central glazed triangular pediment. No. 28 has a large piece of Beer stone tracery from Glasney at second-floor level above an incised date, 1625. Nos. 32–34 were built as a late C18 town house, remodelled in the early C19 to create a pair, with a smart three-storey brick front with granite quoins. No. 36 is an early C19 house on the site of a gateway to Glasney College, through which runs the narrow COLLEGE OPE leading to the site of Glasney College (now a playing field). At the s end the very fragmentary and fragile remains of the COLLEGIATE CHURCH. All that survives above ground is a moulded Beer stone respond and its abutment rising above impost level with a hint of stone vaulting above it, but it is just sufficient to evoke the architectural achievement of the medieval foundation.*

Returning to St Thomas Street, No. 38 is early C19, granite ashlar front with a central first-floor recess with a *c.* 1950 frieze of St Thomas Becket. At the bottom of the street the late C18 FAMOUS BARRELL INN. Into BOHILL, No. 44 has a granite beast corbel, probably from Glasney, at first-floor level in the front elevation and No. 33 has a late C18 brick front with tuck pointing. At the top of the street CHARTER CLOSE is an excellent housing development of the 1970s on a difficult site with a prominent but well-judged external stair-tower.

Now w of St Thomas Street along the main street where the charming C19 front of the Town Hall (*see* Public Buildings) soon beckons, sitting comfortably in the width of the former market place between HIGHER and LOWER MARKET STREETS and enhanced by their split levels and their fall E. Both streets have good ranges of town houses, Late Georgian or Georgian fronted, and many good unaltered C19 shopfronts, a notable feature of the town centre. Behind, and accessed by opes, are rare survivals of back courts, like EASOMS YARD between Nos. 19 and 21 and BANK COTTAGES between Nos. 27 and 29 Higher Market Street, and BENNETT'S COTTAGES between Nos. 68 and 70 Lower Market Street; the rear wall of the latter has another fragment of Glasney, a Beer stone carving of a greyhound under a pomegranate branch. Nos. 19 and 21 Higher Market Street started as a C16 town house (the roof trusses survive), remodelled with a late C17 or early C18 front. No. 25, now LLOYDS BANK, was built as a mid-C18 town house, with

---

*Excavations in 2005 revealed the buttressed corner of a chapel at the NE end of the church, the E wall of the probable chapter house, and the junction of the S aisle and transept. Finds included architectural fragments in Beer stone and the best collection of medieval tiles ever found in Cornwall.

round-arched windows to ground and first floors. No. 31 has C17 origins, remodelled in the late C18, with two rare survivals of C18 projecting shop windows under a deep jetty. No. 33 has giant cabled pilasters with curved capitals and carved frieze under the eaves. Nos. 35–37 have Gothick stucco decoration. The grandest building is No. 39, THE MANOR HOUSE, described as new in 1770, with a 1768 datestone inscribed RB at the rear. The high-status pattern of building continues in THE TERRACE, announced by the assertive front of the Methodist church (*see* Churches). Opposite the Town Hall in Lower Market Street is the Teetotal Hall (*see* Public Buildings). Further up, a surprise: behind the single-storey C20 shops built in the forecourt of Nos. 52–56 is a mid-C18 mansion house, three-storey over a basement and with a five-window front in granite ashlar. It is worth walking the upper parts of the street for more good C18–C19 houses like Nos. 91–101 and the best views back down over the town centre towards Falmouth.

The smaller streets off the centre – WEST STREET and HELSTON ROAD at the W end and NEW STREET and ST GLUVIAS STREET s of Lower Market Street – are mostly lined with more modest and generally C19 granite houses, greatly enhancing the all-pervasive sense of Penryn's completeness as a town. They should not be missed.

TREMOUGH CAMPUS
½ m. W of Penryn

A settlement at Tremough was first recorded in 1208, with archaeological evidence of a much earlier enclosure including a possible Romano-British settlement. From the 1720s it became a small country house estate and in the C20 a convent and school. But the name now belongs indisputably to the campus of the Combined Universities of Cornwall* created with impressive vigour since the 29-acre site was acquired for that purpose in 2003. It is a hugely ambitious project, still under construction at the time of writing, the single most significant legacy, both culturally and architecturally, of the Cornish renaissance of the late C20 and early C21. It may also prove to be the last of the great campus universities in England, arresting in its architectural ambition and responsiveness to its dramatic site.

The campus occupies a magnificent site above Penryn with extensive views towards Falmouth, Carrick Roads and the sea, the terrain sloping down away from its W high point, sometimes very steeply.† Development has been guided by a masterplan prepared by *Capita Percy Thomas* in 2003–4 and evolved

---

*It embraces Falmouth University, the University of Exeter in Cornwall, the Camborne School of Mines, and the Dartington College of Arts. I am grateful to Andrew Harbert of Falmouth University for his assistance with the history of the development.
†A landscape and arts strategy by *Gillespies* of Oxford has been implemented for the whole site since 2010.

in three significant phases, successfully subsuming the C18–C19 house and gardens at the heart of the campus among the new buildings of much larger scale. The masterplan envisaged arrival at the high W end with development cascading down from it, a concept largely implemented, with the major exception that the entrance has been moved to the NE mid-point of the campus. The result is that the first impression the visitor receives is not of a wide panorama but the somewhat forbidding E wall of the DAPHNE DU MAURIER CENTRE, 2003 by *Capita Percy Thomas* (project architect *Jonathan Adams*), the key building of Phase I. This approach emphasizes the centre's vast scale as it thrusts forward dramatically from the top of the slope, with fortress-like walls of render over rough granite pierced sparingly by small, narrow slit windows, and oversailed by a top storey contrastingly clad in blue glass panels. It is only by going to the top of the hill that one can see how different the initial experience would be had the original concept of arrival at the W end been realized: here the building is encountered as a sedum-clad carpet of flat roofs, the intended roof walkways uncompleted, though the view is still magnificent.

The centre is, nevertheless, a major architectural achievement, especially successsful in its S elevation where it gradually unfolds, stepping down in a series of almost wave-like extensions off the main E–W spine to form a complex that houses a huge variety of functions including library, museum, workshops, reading rooms, lecture theatres, refectory and administration, with courtyards and interconnected by high-level walkways and flights of steps: the lower courtyard is partly defined by especially elegant pilotis. The walling materials to this side are also softer, using vertical timber cladding and white render which, with slate cladding, is employed extensively elsewhere on the site. In the upper courtyard a SCULPTURE, Cornish Building Blocks by *Kurt Jackson*, 2008, four cubes set on the diagonal above each other and of diminishing size, of Penryn granite, Delabole slate, Cornish oak, and Cornish tin and copper. Outside the Camborne School of Mines, another sculpture by Jackson, Cornish Trembling Sea Matt, 2010, a water feature with a rough-hewn granite bowl lined in bronze reliefs to simulate a rock pool, on a rectangular granite base. See below for the EXCHANGE at the N side.

To the E end, and below the Du Maurier Centre, is the second major building of the initial phase, the MEDIA CENTRE, 2003 by *Feilden Clegg*. One of the best buildings on the campus, again skilfully using the steeply sloping site to create the initial impression of a single-storey building at the W entrance that opens out downslope as a three-storey structure. Crisply detailed, the exterior in coursed regular granite blockwork and fair-faced concrete with deeply recessed windows, the cool interior thoughtfully planned around an airy stairwell with sculpturally conceived fair-faced concrete walls, slate floors and a full-height glazed window. It is now linked E to the

PETER LANYON BUILDING, 2008–9 by *Capita Percy Thomas* with *Grainge Architects* of Exeter, part of Phase 2, a large complex spreading around three sides of a courtyard open to the N with a central porch canopy on slender pilotis, deep eaves and brise-soleil screens.

Now NE, past the pointed glazed angle of the PORTERS' LODGE, 2003, by *Capita Percy Thomas* with *Grainge Architects*, extended 2006, to GLASNEY PARC, the student village, developed from 2004 in three phases. Phase 1, SE of the Porters' Lodge, by *Capita Percy Thomas* with *Grainge Architects*, is the most appealing because of its relatively intimate scale of mostly two-storey buildings under monopitch roofs planned along an undulating street. Good, simple detailing with doors set within full-height recesses and a judicious mix of coloured render, slate-hanging and timber cladding. These motifs are employed in the subsequent phases, though not ultimately as successfully when the building height increases to three- and four-storey on ever steeper slopes.

Return S along the path below the Peter Lanyon Building to TREMOUGH HOUSE, the original building on the site, built for John Worth, a local merchant, *c.* 1720 but much altered and reworked in the C19 and C20. Dull ashlar granite front to H-shaped plan, what remains of the C18 double-pile house at the centre of two cross-wings, the r. perhaps a slightly later addition, the l. a C19 extension. The interior has late C19 or early C20 features in C18 style including panelling and plasterwork, and a large former C19 ballroom with Ionic columns. The most striking part of the building is the former convent CHAPEL, 1969 by *Waldo Maitland*, a rare example of mid-C20 Modernism in Cornwall, with a curved monopitch roof sweeping up high to the E end (which is concave externally), dramatically lit by flanking N and S full-height windows with *dalle-de-verre* glass by *Father Charles Norris*. Immediately to the W of the house, the ITALIAN GARDEN, late C19, and, below it, the WALLED GARDEN, their environs embowered with an important collection of camellias and rhododendrons.

To the S of the gardens, the PERFORMANCE CENTRE, 2010 by *Nicholas Burwell*, part of Phase 3 and the most architecturally accomplished building to date. Again, initial impressions are of a relatively small-scale structure which, when approached downslope, is experienced as two separate two-storey buildings with walls of brown killas and vertical timber cladding, and tall stone ventilator stacks rising above the flat roof-line. The drama is on entry when the building is revealed as a large multi-storey complex built into the hillside, brilliantly unfolding around an elegant full-height stair hall with galleries on four floors. The best is kept to last, where the SE elevation finally expresses its true scale in two projecting wings framed by black steel portals with bands of Delabole slate cladding, glazing and timber cladding between which the stair hall is recessed with external stairs rising the full height of the building.

Otherwise Phase 3, most recent at time of writing, consists of two major buildings at the upper (w) end of the site nearest the roundabout. Unlike the main Du Maurier campus, purposely tucked below the skyline, these stand three storeys high, the only part of the campus visible from the A39. Rising up the access road to the r. is Cornwall Council's TREMOUGH INNOVATION CENTRE (TIC) by *Aedeas*, 2011, and opposite the University of Exeter's ENVIRONMENTAL SUSTAINABILITY INSTITUTE, *BDP Architects*, 2012, which almost wraps around the top end of the Du Maurier Building. Both these buildings appear to be more restrained than some of the earlier phases, the ESI particularly neat with the N and short W sides of the upper floors brought forward on circular concrete columns with a rain screen of polished aluminium tiles. The TIC appears more a conventional office block: the S side has glazed strips below overhanging eaves from which the brise-soleil appears to hang, but again much white render to the ends and around the central entrance where the block bends slightly. The limited variety of materials and palette of white through greys and silver blend well, the two blocks forming a good stop at the top of the hill, but the N side is treated differently, as four overlapping timber-clad slabs each with a glazed end looking over the valley.

Returning down from the TIC is a smaller building, the ACADEMY OF INNOVATION AND RESEARCH, sitting under a curved roof supported on substantial laminated arched beams, apparently a single-storey building, the walls set back, in timber above stone. The entrance, a rather discordant grey aluminium box, projects out between laminated beams, and the sedum roof covering leads through to a mezzanine level open to the curved ceiling and looking down to an open-plan working area as the land drops away into the valley.

In a very prominent position in front (N side) of the lower end of the Du Maurier Building is the EXCHANGE, 2012, by *Burwell Deakins*. A long narrow wedge building with free standing I-beam columns set in pairs as a portico, the glazing set back under a continuous overhanging flat roof itself tucked under the projecting top floor of the Du Maurier Building. As the ground drops, so the building increases from a single floor to two and then three levels. Inside, a spacious pedestrian route runs from end to end, with spaces leading off, some forming links to the Du Maurier Building, sometimes mini-atriums. Designed as a central meeting place for the campus, it is proving an interesting and exciting space. Externally the building is an excellent solution and handles the downward increases in height in a very accomplished manner. The juxtaposing with the Du Maurier Building alongside is the drawback: they are too obviously the work of different architects.

LODGE and GATEPIERS. ¼ m. NE. Late C19, with ornate cast-iron panels with fleur-de-lys detail set in wooden railings between the piers, incorporating the initials RS, so probably for R. Sampson.

PENTEWAN

Entered by a narrow bridge from the St Austell road, Pentewan is an atmospheric little place of small village square, a few modest terraces and a decayed harbour. But, as so often in Cornwall, this has a long history as an industrial settlement set in its own local industrial landscape. Pentewan stone – from quarries on the cliffs E of the village and in a seam inland into the Glentowan valley – is one of Cornwall's best building stones and was exported from the C13 onwards. In 1744 Sir Christopher Hawkins of Trewithen built a harbour and fish cellars, but the major expansion of the settlement occurred in the early C19 when the Hawkins estate rebuilt most of the harbour to take advantage of the rapidly growing china clay and pilchard industries. Between 1818 and 1830 major development included specialist harbour buildings, housing for different social groups, churches, a school, the construction of a reservoir in the Glentowan valley to flush out the harbour, and the development of a horse-drawn tramway from St Austell, Cornwall's only true narrow-gauge railway (later converted to steam traction). But the construction of four more flushing reservoirs in the main St Austell valley and extensions to the pier failed to solve the problem of continuous silting and this, combined with competition with the mainline railways from the 1880s, resulted in the gradual decline of the port. It finally closed in 1945 despite the early C20 establishment of one of the first manufacturers of concrete blocks and exporters of sand on land W of the harbour, now occupied by a large holiday camp.

PERAMBULATION. Start from THE SQUARE, where the medieval settlement was grouped around its W side and HIGHER WEST ROAD, and from it expanded both E and W and up the Glentowan valley. The earlier more modest buildings are now inter-mixed with more substantial early to mid-C19 houses. Westwards around the early C19 BRIDGE is a good group of buildings including the SHIP INN, probably late C18, the former BONE MILL (now the garage), the former BOARD SCHOOL of 1873 by *Silvanus Trevail*, and an early C19 PUMP HOUSE W of the bridge. Back towards the square, the tranquil HARBOUR BASIN is highly evocative of former industrial activity. The buildings along its eastern side are an especially good group including, from the sea end, the LOOK OUT, DOCK MASTER'S HOUSE, COUNT HOUSE and COAL YARD and STORES. BOLLARDS, LOCK GATES (of 1945), RAILWAY LINES, GRANITE JETTIES and PIER leading towards the beach; a large granite stone, crudely carved with the Hawkins arms and dated 1826, is set in the pier wall. The railway lines date from the concrete block works of the 1960s; the breakwater extension in concrete belongs to the same sequence.

Up NORTH ROAD from the square is a long terrace of small houses built of Pentewan stone with casements or sash windows: Nos. 32 and 34 have round-headed doors with key-stones. This and the shorter row in GLENTOWAN ROAD were built around the early C19 flushing reservoir which today forms their gardens. A short distance further up the valley are the disused quarries. The architectural surprise of Pentewan is THE TERRACE above the square: a pretty group of HILL-CROFT, Nos. 1–4 CHURCH ROW and the granite bow-fronted church of ALL SAINTS, intended to be the centerpiece of a symmetrical composition of the early 1820s. A delightful ensemble, Hillcroft a slightly superior house with wide Palladian window, the Pentewan stone-terraced houses with square-headed stone-mullioned windows, heavy studded doors and a continuous slate-roofed veranda on Doric columns, and the church with a Venetian window above the central bowed doors flanked by round-headed windows. Was Hawkins here consciously vying with Rashleigh and his almost contemporary development at Charlestown (q.v.) to create a superior port?

₄₀₆₀

PENTILLIE CASTLE
1 ½ m. ESE of St Mellion

The house enjoys the most splendid of sites on a wooded eminence high above a wide loop of the Tamar looking into Devon. It was built in 1698 by Sir James Tillie, steward to Sir John Coryton (cf. Newton Ferrers and St Mellion), who acquired the estate and Coryton's widow when Sir John died. Its complex and chequered building history, not fully understood, includes major phases of remodelling and enrichment during the C18, followed by considerable expansion by *William Wilkins Sen. c.* 1810–15, completed by *Wilkins Jun.*, by when it had accidentally returned to Coryton ownership. The Wilkinses Gothicked the house and added an impressive new main entrance and a square tower at the E end. These were demolished in a remodelling of 1966–8 when the house was stripped back to its pre-Wilkins core and end-stopped by new pavilions on the W entrance front. After further late C20 neglect it was restored by Edward and Sarah Coryton with *Jonathan Mansfield* and *Graham Locke* in 2007–9. The two-storey entrance front is symmetrically composed around a five-bay centre with an arcade of granite Doric columns with brick arches of *c.* 1700: the l. and r. bays are carried up to embattled attic storeys and are flanked by the C20 pavilions. From the pavilions, walls project forward to form a courtyard with a fine late C17 statue of Sir James Tillie (resited) in the centre. At the S end is a C20 porte cochère with a slate sundial dated 1693. To the l. a single-storey service wing with an arcade of three round brick arches. The E garden front is wholly Tudor Gothick; eleven bays divided by stepped buttresses with an embattled parapet and clustered polygonal chimneys. At the N end a projecting wing, reputedly for a chapel.

The character of the interior is chiefly C18. The principal rooms are arranged along the garden front above C17 cellars with a corridor, entrance hall and other rooms along the entrance front. The panelled stair hall with open-well stair with stick balusters has six-panelled doors with eared architraves and Greek key surrounds, a Greek key frieze, and moulded cornice. On the passage side of the dining room is another doorway with Greek surround, eared architrave and a lion mask set as a keystone. The cellars have a granite doorway with a three-centred arch, roundel and pyramid stops with initials ST IT (probably James Tillie) and the dates 1698 and 1699.

The extensive gardens and parkland, enhanced by *Humphry Repton* who produced a Red Book for Pentillie in 1810, include terraces descending to the Tamar. On the quay a mid-C19 BATHING HOUSE, using C17 features. On Mount Ararat, ½ m. N, an early C18 TOWER, erected as a mausoleum for Sir James Tillie, whose statue looks out from the upper room.* At PAYNTERS CROSS, close to one of the gates to the estate is the former ESTATE OFFICE, a charming Regency building, only three bays, connected by walls to little wings: Palladio's villa plan *en miniature*. The first-floor veranda is a nice English enrichment of Palladio. Opposite is a group of HOUSES for retainers, stone, in the Tudor style, nicely grouped somewhat like almshouses, but in their detail heavy if compared to the Regency elegance across the lane.

PENZANCE

4030

There is something immediately captivating about the most south-westerly town in Britain. Beautifully set within the generous arms of Mount's Bay, with St Michael's Mount rising spectacularly from the sea to the E and the promise of Land's End and the Scillies beyond the western horizon, Penzance feels like a place set apart, the end of the line, as indeed it is of the railway from London Paddington. Exploration reveals it to be one of the most surprising of all Cornwall's historic towns with an enjoyably diverse architectural personality.

Penzance is first recorded in 1284 with St Mary's Chapel in existence by 1327 (probably on the site of the present parish church) and the granting of markets and fairs in 1332. It was a substantial harbour and urban settlement by the early C15, important in the fish export trade as well as the ferrying of pilgrims from St Michael's Mount to Santiago de Compostela. By the time of the Spanish raid in 1595, when at least part of the town was burned, it had become a major market and had outstripped the rival ports of Marazion and Mousehole. As at

---

*Investigation in 2013 confirmed that Tillie had, as he had wished, been entombed sitting upright looking out over the Tamar.

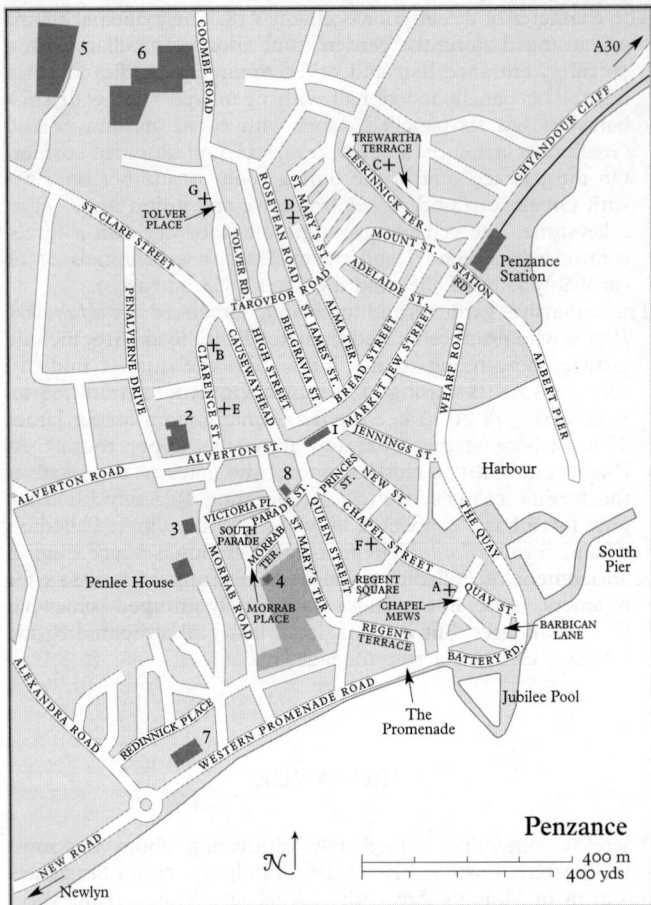

Penzance

A	St Mary	I	Market House and Old Town Hall
B	St Paul	2	Public Buildings (St John's Hall)
C	St John the Baptist	3	Penzance School of Art, Library
D	Church of the Immaculate		and Science School
	Conception (R.C.)	4	Morrab Library and Gardens
E	Baptist church	5	Penwith College
F	Methodist church	6	Humphrey Davy School
G	Richmond Wesleyan Chapel	7	Pavilion Theatre (former)
		8	Acorn Theatre

Helston, Penryn, Tregony and Truro, a medieval settlement was laid out along the ridge rising up from the harbour, represented by present day Chapel Street, with the market at its upper end around the present Market Place and parts of Queen's Square and The Greenmarket. In turn this led to the building up of Market Jew Street, the long, curving road climbing up the steep slope from the W and Marazion (Marazion = Market Jew). In 1663 it became a coinage town (at the expense of Helston) for the expanding tin industry of the St Just area, setting the seal on its enduring role through subsequent centuries as the commercial, administrative and cultural capital of the far west.

It was the closure of Europe to English travellers during the Napoleonic Wars that laid the foundations of Penzance's emergence as an early resort. W. G. Maton had, as early as 1794, observed: 'The mildness of the air, the agreeableness of the situation, and the respectability of its inhabitants render Penzance particularly inviting to residence, and, with regard to invalids, it may justly be considered as the Montpelier of England.' By the mid C19 an extensive new suburb of genteel houses, mostly stucco terraces, but with some granite ashlar, had been developed around squares and parades W of the old town centre. The new interest in the benefits of sea bathing led to the laying out of the Promenade in 1843 as part of the new resort, while the best houses of the town had been built, some in brick, along Chapel Street from the late C18, with a splendid new church constructed on the old St Mary's Chapel site in 1832. This, and the huge and imposing new Greek Revival Market House at the top of Market Jew Street, proclaimed the enhanced status of the town, its cultural sophistication also evident in the diversity of architectural styles in other buildings of this period, not least the astonishing Egyptian House in Chapel Street.

The arrival of the railway in 1852, with the through link to London in 1859, heralded a new phase of expansion. The resort was now accessible to a wider social range, with the first large hotel, the Queen's, built in 1861. The railway enabled the export of flowers, fruit and early vegetables to London and stimulated the growth of both industries and commercial activities like smelting, tanning, saw mills, flour mills, rope making, foundries and shipbuilding and repairing, and new enterprises like serpentine works, of which there were five by 1881. The harbour continued to grow: earlier in the century it had been hugely expanded with the construction of the Albert Pier and now a new wet dock was built. Most significantly for the layout of the town the corporation, under its first Borough Surveyor, *John Matthews*, promoted an ambitious new road-building programme including Alexander Road (1865) and Morrab Road (1880) to the W, the major improvement of Taroveor Road in the 1860s to the NW, and Wharf Road around the harbour in 1886.* This provided the framework for another major phase of town expansion, especially in the grids of highly packed streets of small terraced houses N of Market Jew Street and Taroveor Road and rising up the slope of Lescudjack Hill to the NE. All this brought a plethora of new buildings, civic, religious, educational, commercial, philanthropic, cultural and residential, in a rich variety of architectural styles, with many by good local architects. Penzance was espe-

---

*The Penzance Corporation also dramatically improved the town's cultural amenities (*see* Public Buildings).

cially fortunate in having several distinguished practitioners like *Oliver Caldwell, J. W. Trounson* and *F. G. Drewitt*, with significant buildings by architects from further afield in Cornwall such as *James Hicks* and *Silvanus Trevail*.

There was a flourish of modernization in the 1930s with some good Art Deco buildings, especially the eye-catching lido, the Jubilee Pool. But the town suffered decades of decline through the second half of the C20. Slum clearance had started in the 1930s, Betjeman noting the erosion of the little streets around the harbour by the 1960s and some clumsy redevelopment in the town centre. A particular casualty was the s side of Market Jew Street, which has a damaging number of the most lacklustre commercial buildings of that period. The early C21 has, however, seen sensitive conversion and adaptation of former warehouses and other industrial buildings that sit cheek-by-jowl with the main streets, and many good examples of tactful infilling. This has gone a long way to recover and reinforce the town's delightfully varied character.

CHURCHES

101 St Mary, Chapel Street. 1832–5 by *Charles Hutchens*, a native of nearby St Buryan (cf. his other churches at Redruth and St Day). A good example of Commissioners' Gothic and, built of granite ashlar, more substantial-looking than most. Handsomely set on the headland above the harbour, its striking presence the defining feature, with the cupola of the Market House, in views of the town. There are stylistic similarities to St Luke, Chelsea, with a slim w tower (Cornish in detail) placed tightly between the low-pitched gables of the aisles, the aisles as tall as the tall nave, and six long lean windows on the N and s sides with their pinnacled buttresses between them, not buttressing anything, for inside the tall wooden piers support only the shallow curves of ceilings. Five s aisle windows replaced 1920–1, E window stonework replaced with a large untraceried circle above five lancets in 1986–7 after a fire in 1985. Lofty interior, light and spacious, with gallery running round three sides, the E end with a tall shallow apse. Five-bay arcades of four-centred arches on slim piers rising through the gallery fronts. Well executed plaster vault in the entrance porch with the Commissioners' portcullis at its centre. Plaster fan-vault also below the w gallery, the space rather unhappily divided off with charmless metal and glass screens in 1986–7. Otherwise the church was thoughtfully restored and re-furnished after the fire in a pleasantly understated way by *George Vaughan Ellis*.* – ALMS BOX dated 1612, from the former

---

*The fire sadly destroyed the REREDOS and ALTAR, the latter described by Pevsner as 'a spectacular affair of 1934 by *Ernest Procter*, with a whole prospect including the heavenly host, a corrugated silvery backcloth, jagged rays; all smacking a little of the Wurlitzer'.

chapel of St Mary. – FONT. 1874, octagonal, of fine red and green serpentine with quatrefoil panels. – Gothic three-seater MAYORAL CHAIR (or is it a SEDILIA?) *c.* 1835. – ORGAN CASE, from the University Church of St Mary the Virgin, Oxford, with Gothic rebuilding by *Thomas Plowman,* 1827. – Striking and vibrantly colourful E window by *Alfred Fisher,* 1987. Of other STAINED GLASS a window in the N aisle of 1864, very much in the Gibbs style. – MONUMENT. John Tremenheare †1761, a Baroque tablet from the previous chapel. Many minor TABLETS, mostly early C19 in the Greek Revival style. – Sarah Bedford, 1832 by *J. Bedford* of London. – In the churchyard at the SE corner of the church a mutilated LANTERN CROSS, the W face with the Crucifixion, the E with Virgin and Child.

ST PAUL, Clarence Street. Now closed. 1843 by *John Matthews,* N aisle 1893 by *J. W. Trounson,* exactly matching the original. Porch added 1886 by *Silvanus Trevail.* Originally built for supporters of the Oxford Movement. E.E. style, W front with two gables, the aisle recessed, the nave rising to an elaborate bell-cote. Lancet windows throughout. Spacious interior with plastered walls and gilded arch-braced roof on false hammerbeams. – FONT, serpentine. – STAINED GLASS. Significant Tractarian scheme by *Thomas Willement* 1843. – pillar POOR BOX dated 1612 in the entrance porch.

ST JOHN THE BAPTIST, Trewartha Terrace. 1879–81 by *J. P. St Aubyn.* An austere exterior in E.E. style embedded in the narrow streets of late C19 terraces, but a lofty and dignified interior with four-bay nave arcades with lean-to aisles, clerestory, tall transeptal arches and arcades to N and S chapels with no capitals to the columns and a high crown-post roof: St Aubyn at his best. A tower was intended over the S porch but only the ground floor was built. – Fine ALTAR and REREDOS, 1902 by *G. H. Fellowes Prynne,* made by *H. H. Martyn* of Cheltenham with paintings by *E. A. Fellowes Prynne.* The CHOIR STALLS and ORGAN GALLERY woodwork may have been to Fellowes Prynne's specification, as also the excellent wrought-iron SCREEN and GATES to chancel, 1905. – STAINED GLASS. A rich assemblage of late C19 and C20 glass including some of the major firms of the period; especially good the E window of long lancets, 1901 by *Clayton & Bell.* – S transept S window 1955 by *William Morris & Co.* of Westminster. Some 1970s glass by *G. Maile* in the N aisle. (Also one by *Kempe,* 1901).

CHURCH OF THE IMMACULATE CONCEPTION (R.C), Rosevean Road. 1843. An interestingly early post-Emancipation church, rising impressively sheer from the surrounding little C19 streets. Tall W front rising to a bellcote, its verticality emphasized by pinnacled buttresses, with richly canopied statue niche above the door. Dignified interior with splendid granite, serpentine and marble REREDOS and ALTAR,

1869. – STAINED GLASS. Chancel E, 1991 by *Roy Mead* of Falmouth.

BAPTIST CHURCH, Clarence Street. 1836 by *Philip Sambell*. Remarkable Neo-Norman front, in robust stucco, with plenty of zigzag (cf. Sambell's other church in the style in Wendron Street, Helston): an unusually early example of this style. Almost intact interior with GALLERY supported on slender columns with Romanesque capitals, and fine arcaded ROSTRUM with bowed centre and flanking turned balusters, in front of which is a large tiled BATH for complete baptismal immersion.

METHODIST CHURCH, Chapel Street. Erected 1814, enlarged 1864. One of the largest and most important in Cornwall, seating 1400. Imposing seven-bay front with Doric portico. The only Cornish chapel remaining that uses the City Road internal plan with the communion area beyond the high pulpit and rostrum. Full gallery with panelled front cantilevered out on slender columns. Original box pews to ground floor. Good cast-iron railings to forecourt and large SCHOOL, 1884, to l.

RICHMOND WESLEYAN CHAPEL, Tolver Place. 1907 by *Gunton & Gordon* of London. A striking composition in free Gothic style with Arts and Crafts influences. Unusual Methodist plan of nave and chancel. Strongly modelled entrance front with deeply recessed windows and a gabled porch on r. Fine hammerbeam roof.

PUBLIC BUILDINGS

97 MARKET HOUSE AND OLD TOWN HALL, Market Jew Street. 1836–8 by *William Harris*, District Surveyor for Bristol. One of the three Greek Revival market houses he designed in Cornwall (cf. Bodmin and Helston), and by far the most ambitious in scale and prominence in the townscape: a dignified granite temple that greets the traveller from the W as Market Jew Street climbs up towards the town centre. It must have set the seal on Penzance's re-invention of itself as the capital of the far west. Unusually for the time the corporation held a competition, which Teulon as well as Harris entered, which was won by *H. J. Whitling*, a London architect. The cost of Whitling's scheme proved prohibitive, however, so the job went to Harris. Skilfully contrived on an awkwardly narrow site, with a giant Ionic portico to the first and second upper storeys above a grand plinth/basement. The E end contained the Guildhall with steps to cells below, with grammar school and theatre above; The ground floor, entered from the W, was the market. The building is surmounted by a handsome dome, a defining landmark of the Penzance skyline, with Doric columns around the drum. In 1922–5 the market end was remodelled as Lloyds Bank by *Cowell, Drewitt & Wheatly* when it was shortened, the columned portico added, and Harris's dome remodelled. The

interior of the market became a magnificent banking hall with tall marbled columns: its dignified scale and gracious proportions survive.

PUBLIC BUILDINGS (ST JOHN'S HALL), Alverton Road. 1864–7 by *John Matthews* at the huge cost of £13,000. A monumental Italianate civic palace with an eleven-window front, the five-bay centre flanked by three-bay projecting wings, two-storey over semi-basement, all in granite ashlar from Lamorna. Approached by a grand flight of steps with flat Doric entrance and Palladian window above, heavy eaves cornice and parapet. The central block, a concert hall, seated 850, the w wing the Royal Geological Society, and the E wing civic offices and Natural History and Antiquarian Society.

PENZANCE SCHOOL OF ART, LIBRARY AND SCIENCE SCHOOL, Morrab Road. 1880–1 by *Silvanus Trevail*, doubled in size 1892 by *Henry White* who changed the roof-line and added the front with terracotta dressings.

LIBRARY, Morrab Gardens. Formerly MORRAB HOUSE, built in 1841 by Samuel Pidwell, a wealthy brewer, on a 3-acre strip of land between the town centre and seafront (Morrab = Cornish: from *mor* sea and *app* shore). Small, stuccoed and of pleasing classical proportions, four-window entrance front, two-storey, panelled end pilasters, and off-centre granite porch on Tuscan columns. In 1899 the corporation purchased the house and laid out its gardens as a municipal park to enhance the town's appeal for visitors as well as residents. *Reginald Upcher* was largely responsible for the gardens, though its reputation for a splendid array of sub-tropical plants came slightly later. It contains the BOER WAR MEMORIAL of 1904; a fine BANDSTAND of 1905 with ornate cast-iron balustrade and slender cast-iron columns supporting a wrought-iron finial and cresting; and delightful FOUNTAIN in the form of a large pedestal with relief friezes of sea shells, dolphins at the corners, and cherubs between riding turtles spouting water, and upper basins crowned by a globe with an otter holding a fish.

PENWITH COLLEGE. A small campus of Truro College, developed around the former County Girls' School, of 1912 by *Oliver Caldwell*. It incorporates the remaining grounds of TRENEERE MANOR. This is of 1758, the former home of the Robyns family, and a neat square granite ashlar mansion, two-storey over basement, of three bays, the E front with centre bay advanced under a pediment, and a late C19 mansard roof. The new buildings, and the restoration from near dereliction of the manor, are by *Poynton Bradbury Wynter Cole*, 2009–11, and very large scale with massive overhanging monopitch roofs of steep pitch and the firm's characteristic 'port-hole' windows. Just s, on Coombe Road, the HUMPHRY DAVY SCHOOL, similarly developed around the former County School for Boys, of 1909 by *Sampson Hill*.

Former PAVILION THEATRE, The Promenade. 1911 by *Cowell & Drewitt*. A suitably dramatic façade, an early example of the 'hacienda' style, of five-bay centre with Doric columns, origin-ally open, flanked by taller square corner towers incorporating crouching caryatids and short square pilasters. The loss of the original leaded ogival roofs has reduced its flamboyance. Now an amusement arcade.

ACORN THEATRE, Parade Street. Methodist chapel by *Oliver Caldwell*, 1889–90, good Italianate front. Sensitively converted to a theatre in 1970.

118 JUBILEE POOL, Battery Road. 1935 by *Captain Frank Latham*, Borough Engineer. It rests sleekly like a liner at anchor project-ing into the sea between The Quay and Promenade, its con-crete walls and streamlined triangular shape designed to resist extremes of storm and wave. Britain's largest and southern-most surviving lido, replenished with seawater as required, it is a subtle Art Deco composition of curvilinear concrete ter-races in cool blues and whites, separated to accommodate sunbathers below and spectators of the arena-like space within or views of the town without. The regular rhythm of pillar and void in the four ranges of open changing cubicles on all sides of the pool echoes, perhaps unconsciously, ancient Egyptian temple terraces, and the double staircases into the sacred water pools.

RAILWAY STATION, Station Road. The most south-westerly station in Britain, 326 miles from Paddington by the original route through Bristol. 1879–80, of rock-faced granite, replacing the original timber station opened by the West Cornwall Railway in 1852, which had marked the completion of the standard gauge route from Truro. Two-storey range at the W end, single-storey range to the side facing the sea. The principal feature is the long, curved roof of the train shed covering the W end of the platforms, rebuilt several times but still impressive as the Cornish counterpart to the London terminus.

PENZANCE HARBOUR. One of the most interesting, complete and extensive of all Cornish harbours with an unusually complete range of structures. The SOUTH PIER had an excep-tionally complex evolution: eleven phases of post-medieval development have been identified, and its outer face is worth studying for evidence of its varied builds. A major reconstruc-tion in 1745–6 of the 'inner pier' (nearest Battery Rocks) prob-ably encased the medieval pier. It was extended first NNE between 1764 and 1812, and then ENE in 1853, and terminated by the sturdy LIGHTHOUSE. The long arm of the ALBERT PIER (1845–8) stretches S to enclose the large harbour, the construction of Wharf Road in 1866 bringing much improved access, and the opening of the ROSS SWING BRIDGE in 1881 gave good communication between the piers for the first time; the original scale of the harbour has been considerably reduced by infilling to construct the present car park. The FLOATING DOCK inside the SW part of the harbour is of 1882–4. W of Wharf Road are the C18 and C19 ABBEY QUAYS, SLIP and ABBEY WAREHOUSE, and the 1881 DRY DOCK, a rebuild of the first dry dock on the site of 1814.

PERAMBULATIONS

*1. The town centre**

The railway station (*see* Public Buildings) makes a good starting point. Noting the spread of the harbour to which this tour will return, go up STATION ROAD past solid-looking former warehouses into MARKET JEW STREET. Its gracious curving climb up towards the Market House makes for good townscape, with lanes and opes off both sides, those on the s with glimpses down towards the sea. When examined in detail, however, it is a street whose sides are of somewhat unequal architectural interest. The s side's devastation by redevelopment in the second half of the C20 is all too obvious with some of the most lamentable commercial buildings of that period in any major historic street in Cornwall. Thankfully the N side retains its coherence and dignity, the buildings rising above THE TERRACE, a wide raised walkway paved with patterned granite and bounded by good cast-iron railings.

The street begins near the station with modest two-storey mid- to late C19 buildings (the LONGBOAT INN started as the Railway Hotel) but soon ramps up to larger properties with good architectural detail. On the l. the relatively low-key entrance to the WHARFSIDE CENTRE, by *Lyons, Sleeman & Hoare*, a large 1990s retail development whose interior scale is handled competently enough but whose elevations to WHARF ROAD betray its massive bulk and painfully unresolved jumble of styles. Nos. 84–86 of 1902 by *N. C. Whear Jun.* are distinguished by the use of white, brown and green glazed bricks. On the r., one of the most attractive opes is the steep steps of THE ARCADE, 1880, leading to BREAD STREET and the grid of mid to late C19 terraces to the N. The buildings above The Terrace are tall, three-storey and mostly mid to late C19, with the interesting interjection of BARCLAYS BANK (1963), a competent period piece by *Cowell, Drewitt & Wheatly*. On the l. the POST OFFICE of 1883, classical with granite pilasters and pediments, skilful enough to be by *James Hicks*. In front of the Market House (*see* Public Buildings) a fine white marble STATUE on a monumental granite plinth of Humphry Davy, 1872 by *Wills* of London.[†] On the l. the STAR INN with a mid-C19 front, its centre broken forward with a segmental pediment on consoles above the parapet over the centre window, and an earlier wing to the rear. It is worth a short diversion l. down NEW STREET for a sense of the more intimate scale of the older streets leading down to the harbour area, mostly lost in the C20, and also to see an exemplary early C20 housing scheme, ST MICHAEL'S COTTAGES, 1932 by *Cowell, Drewitt & Wheatly*, a serenely composed group of semi-detached cottages.

---

*This is indebted to Peter Laws' excellent account of Penzance's architecture in P. A. S. Pool *History of the Borough of Penzance* (1974).
[†]Davy was born at No. 4 The Terrace in 1778.

Now back to the main streets as Market Jew Street gives way to MARKET STREET which extends around the W end of the Market House complex. A highlight is No. 3, 1888 by *James Hicks* as the Devon & Cornwall Bank, with a red Aberdeenshire granite column to the ground floor and a first-floor oriel above. Then Nos. 6, 7 and 8, of 1960 by *Alec French & Partners*, an unworthy blank façade for such a site. Closing the view coming up the street are Nos. 23–24, 1850 for Samuel York, a draper, with massive Corinthian half-columns, capitals, entablature, and balustrade. No. 27A is a fine late C19 corner building, nicely detailed, and, beyond, No. 27B, 1905 for the Public Benefit Boot Company (see monograms PBBC), an extravagantly ornate free Baroque front of red and white terracotta with masks and swags. The GREENMARKET, originally part of the vast historic market area of the town, has more good three-storey mid-to late C19 buildings.

On the N side of MARKET STREET the beginning of the pedestrianized CAUSEWAYHEAD, one of the most visually enjoyable streets in the town. It starts on the l. with HSBC (the former London, City & Midland Bank), of 1922 by their usual architect, *T. B. Whinney*, well-mannered classical in pink elvan and grey granite with excellent detailing. On the opposite corner another lacklustre commercial building of 1971. Just into Causewayhead, a short diversion r. into BREAD STREET for many good examples of careful conversion of the former warehouses, workshops and factories that lay just behind the principal streets of the town. Causewayhead has buildings in a plethora of architectural styles, including the Modernist façade of No. 73 with its curved windows and on the other side the modest grandeur of the SAVOY CINEMA, adapted in 1912 from the former Victoria Hall by *Cowell & Drewitt*, and the charming Art Deco shopfront of WAVES café (No. 29), built in 1926 as the Penzance & District Electricity Supply Company's showroom (actually a front to a former chapel). Black Vitrolite surround to a bronze frame and a geometric pattern of small leaded panes in textured glass forming a band over the windows and door.

Now S of Market Square towards Chapel Street, but first diverting l. into PRINCES STREET for the remarkably large scale of the MASONIC ROOMS, with giant stucco Ionic pilasters and huge sash windows above a granite ground floor. Opposite, the serpentine glazed front to THE EXCHANGE, the former Telephone Exchange, with art gallery, 2007 by *MUMA* (*McInnes Usher McKnight Architects*).

CHAPEL STREET (so named after St Mary's Chapel on the site of the present church) is architecturally the outstanding street in Penzance with some excellent later C18 buildings, a number of them in brick, unusual for Cornwall at that period.

96   The EGYPTIAN HOUSE makes an astonishing start. It was built in 1835–6 for John Lavin as a showroom for his mineral and fossil dealership and other products including artefacts by the Lizard serpentine Company. It is exceptional, a brightly

coloured façade modulated by torus mouldings and a bold cavetto cornice into the semblance of an Egyptian temple pylon. Setting aside the many Egyptian-inspired funerary monuments of the time, it is the outstanding early C19 survival of Egyptianizing commercial architecture in Britain: despite the eclectic mix of elements, motifs derived directly from Egyptian forms without the mediation of classical or Renaissance influences come through strongly. Though the work of an unknown hand, the design clearly takes inspiration from Robinson's Egyptian Hall in Piccadilly (1812, demolished 1905), and the somewhat plainer Civil and Military Library of 1823 in Devonport. The latter, designed by John Foulston, housed a large library and mineral collection donated by Sir John St Aubyn of St Michael's Mount, perhaps no coincidence. The design of these buildings, associated with learning and the display of natural and human-made wonders, seems to have been consciously chosen to reflect the conception of Egypt as a source of esoteric knowledge.* Three-bay, three-storey façade, the central door flanked by fat closed papyrus bud columns reminiscent of the inner courts of Egyptian temples and shrines. Stepped central window at first-floor level flanked by classically inspired female terms, and stepped showroom windows flanking the entrance. Torus mouldings, shaped *in situ* in a natural cement and decorated to represent bundles of reeds lashed together, imitating examples found widely in Egyptian tombs and temples. Blank cartouches decorating the upper cornice and small lower one above the central first-floor window appear to be derived from Denon's illustration of the temple of Hathor at Dendera. Other elements are non-Egyptian, e.g. the centrally placed royal arms and naturalistic eagle, while the stepped windows and fancy geometric glazing bars are a fantastical extrapolation hinting at pyramids, uraei and sun discs. The whole exuberant effect completed by a warm colour scheme with gilded highlights, reinstated in the late C20.

In complete contrast No. 9 in the neo-Greek manner, with four Doric half-columns. The stucco front of the UNION HOTEL is early C19 with fluted Ionic pilasters and volutes but behind is an older building (e.g. the C16 fireplace in the front bar), and behind that the fine assembly room ante-room dating from 1791 with high vaulted ceiling, balustraded gallery, Regency staircase, fireplaces with columns and large semicircular-headed windows. To the rear, the remarkable survival of the shell of a late C18 THEATRE (now converted to flats) of almost exactly the same dimensions as that at Richmond, Yorkshire. The OLD CUSTOM HOUSE is late C18

*All also appear to have drawn directly on motifs made available through the *Description de l'Egypte*, the huge and meticulous record created by Napoleon's scientific and scholarly expedition to Egypt first published between 1809 and 1818; the separate publications of Dominque Vivant Denon, also a member of the expedition; or possibly the works of C18 explorers such as Richard Pococke, Frederick Norden and Carsten Niebuhr.

stucco with Doric porch and good interior. Then a group of excellent late c18 brick houses, some painted: CROWNLEY (No. 15) with a pediment, TREVELYAN (No. 16), No. 18 with a five-window front, Ionic doorcase and again a pediment, Nos. 19 and 20, three-storey, with Doric doorcase, brick aprons below the windows and modillion eaves, and further down on the opposite side Nos. 45 and 45A, with the porch in a central projection. The sequence is interrupted by the granite ashlar of No. 47, two-storey over a basement with Doric porch to the l. and two-storey canted bays. Opposite, the grand Methodist church and school (*see* Churches) set back in a railed forecourt. Set back behind the houses, BELL COURT, dated 1834, the former National School, its central slim campanile very prominent from the Abbey Slip area below. THE VICARAGE (No. 24) is tall, three storeys and five windows, with a granite ashlar front, but the porch in a side projection on fluted Ionic columns. Good interior including staircase, panelling and ceilings. Opposite, No. 38 has a monumental granite classical front of *c.* 1840 with Doric half-columns to the porch. Nos. 33–37 have pleasant three-storey stuccoed fronts and Nos. 30–32 have two storeys over a basement in granite ashlar, the double doorways approached by a flight of steps. Opposite is St Mary's church (*see* Churches). The handsomely proportioned CHAPEL HOUSE makes a good end to the street, its five-bay front at right angles to the road with the central three bays advanced under a wide pediment.

Continue down QUAY STREET towards the HARBOUR, noting the tactful modern infill of CHAPEL MEWS, past BARBICAN LANE and the DOLPHIN TAVERN, the adjoining former warehouses giving some impression of the area before c20 clearances. The development of the harbour area is described above, and it is worth exploring, the character of the working harbour especially compelling with large ships cheek-by-jowl with THE QUAY. Along The Quay, TRINITY HOUSE with the CUSTOM HOUSE behind, the SHIP REPAIR YARD and DRY DOCK, and then ROSS BRIDGE. From the road a good view of ABBEY SLIP and ABBEY WAREHOUSE, worth a diversion up ABBEY STREET to the ABBEY HOTEL with its pretty 1825 Gothick front fronting a c17–c18 building with good staircase with square newel, and panelled room. Then the former LIFEBOAT STATION of 1885 with oriel window and bellcote. Further along the road some well-mannered later c20 and early c21 housing developments at HARBOUR COURT, OCEAN BLUE, and HANOVER COURT. Return along WHARF ROAD towards the railway station.

2. The resort town

The Jubilee Pool (*see* Public Buildings) makes a splendid start, strongly evoking the spirit of modernity of the 1930s resort. Just to the E at BATTERY POINT, the WAR MEMORIAL of 1922 by *Edward Warren*, on the octagonal base of the BATTERY of 1739–40.

Immediately inland from the pool behind Gardens, another touch of the *moderne* is the YACHT INN of 1936 by *Colin Drewitt* for the St Austell Brewery, with streamlined proportions in white stucco and curved corner windows. It contrasts strongly with the adjoining SAILORS' INSTITUTE of 1908 by *Oliver Caldwell* with its octagonal tower, but the 1930s reassert themselves again in the streamlined façade of the PZ GALLERY, built as car showrooms and garage.

On the seafront BATTERY ROAD gives way to THE PROMENADE as it proceeds w. The promenade was built in 1843 by the corporation, and extends for about ½ m. At the w end, at a lower level, a new walk of 1887, paved with Penlee granite. REGENT TERRACE is the start of Penzance's early to mid-C19 residential suburb which, in its extensive spread and the sustained quality of what are mostly relatively modest buildings, is one of the most charming and important survivals of seaside architecture of its type anywhere in England. The terrace is typical, two-storey stucco fronts with classical detailing. w of Regent Terrace is QUEEN STREET, and uphill are the NATIONAL SCHOOL of 1871 with its bellcote, and PENHALE HOUSE, neat early C19. Then e again to REGENT SQUARE. One of the most delightful ensembles of buildings and spaces anywhere in Cornwall, twenty-one early C19 stucco houses around a perfect small square with a serpentine road running through it and its luxuriantly planted gardens. The houses are simply but handsomely detailed, with open porches on slender columns incised pilasters and either recessed or relief window architraves, some semicircular to the ground floor. The first dozen near the sea are the earliest, of the Regency, those at the e end completed 1836–9.

Return to the w end of the Square and Queen Street. More but plainer mid-C19 terraces in COULSON'S PLACE, COULSON'S BUILDINGS and small terraced housing in DANIEL PLACE. Near the seafront end of Queen Street, JUBILEE HOUSE, 1935 by *Colin Drewitt* of *Cowell, Drewitt & Wheatly*, one of the best buildings of that decade in Cornwall. Built as a new frontage onto existing buildings, three-storey with large-radius curved corners onto Queen Street with a sun terrace and small sun room on a flat roof. Curved corner windows and original bronzed shopfront, front door and garage door on ground floor.

Then n again towards the exotic Morrab Gardens with the library (*see* Public Buildings), bounded to the e by ST MARY'S TERRACE, a pleasant mix of stucco houses with the grander AUBREY VILLAS of 1864 towards its upper end, paired under pedimental gable, and then a handsome granite ashlar pair with pilasters to the upper storeys.

Crossing the n end of the terrace is PARADE STREET, the principal early C19 route from Chapel Street (*see* Perambulation 1) to this area, with the Acorn Theatre (*see* Public Buildings) and

No. 8, a good late C18 brick house like those in Chapel Street. At this point the vast bulk of PENLOWARTH looms above these little streets, a 1967 government office block of brutal intensity in this intimate context. A pedestrian walk N off PARADE STREET leads to NORTH PARADE of 1815–26, similar in scale to Regent Square, the middle section demolished when MORRAB ROAD was constructed by the corporation in 1879. SOUTH PARADE is a handsome terrace of five three-storey granite ashlar houses of 1815 divided by wide plain pilasters, the windows with recessed architraves. It is worth exploring this area around Morrab Gardens at leisure to see similar terraces, mostly in stucco, like MORRAB TERRACE, MORRAB PLACE and VICTORIA PLACE.

Now N into ALVERTON STREET and the grandiose presence of the Public Buildings (St John's Hall) (*see* Public Buildings). Further E in Alverton Street ALVERE, an excellent C18 town house in granite ashlar, two-storey over basement and accessed by gracious steps. Then N up CLARENCE STREET. On the corner with Alverton Street, BRANWELL HOUSE of 1989 by *Poynton Bradbury Associates*, a well-composed building that handles its relatively large scale successfully. The E side of Clarence Street starts with the surprising but splendid Romanesque stucco front of the Baptist church (*see* Churches). Beyond, a long stucco terrace of 1829–40 ending with St Paul's church (*see* Churches). Opposite, CLARENCE HOUSE, a granite villa of *c.* 1830, CLARENCE TERRACE, fine stucco houses of *c.* 1830, and CLARENCE PLACE: six elegant stucco houses of 1829–30 and CLARENCE COTTAGE, a mid-C19 villa with wide eaves and trellis veranda.

Return down Clarence Street, across Alverton Street and S down MORRAB ROAD with late C19 and Edwardian terraces of hefty granite, following down from the the Penzance School of Art (*see* Public Buildings). Part-way down is the entrance to the PENLEE GALLERY, an 1860s stucco villa, outside which stands the early C11 MARKET CROSS, so called because it was first recorded standing in the Greenmarket. Of unusual interest for its decoration, with four triangular features carved into the head to create an equal-limbed cross, and decoration on the shaft which includes an (undecipherable) inscription.

3. Outside the town centre

W of the centre ALVERTON STREET becomes ALVERTON TERRACE, Nos. 7–10 three-storey late C18 ending in the bow-windowed front of STANLEY HOUSE. Then come larger villas in landscaped grounds along ALVERTON ROAD, e.g. ALVERNE HILL of *c.* 1820–30. ALEXANDRA ROAD to the S was built in 1865 for the corporation by *John Matthews* with typical late C19 and Edwardian granite terraces and the occasional villa, like the bulky half-timbered TREHURST of 1902 by *Oliver Caldwell* for a prosperous grocer. Caldwell also designed the PENZANCE CLUB of 1896 at the S end overlooking the seafront. ROSEVALE is early C19 with large two-storey centre bay. Off the N end of Alexandra Road, HAWKINS ROAD has four houses in two pairs of 1879–80, TRENANCE and FERNLEIGH by *J. W. Trounson* and LYNWOOD and SUNNYSIDE by *William Berryman*.

Circling the NW fringe of the town, most now separated by the by-pass, a ring of larger villas of the late C18 and early C19 in spacious settings. CASTLE HORNECK, Castle Horneck Road, was a Borlase house, now a youth hostel. Granite, five-bay front with pediment. Nearby, ROSEHILL, a pretty ashlar granite villa with bowed portico of 1814, the best house of that time in the town, built for Richard Oxnam, a Penzance banker. Very fine interior, the entrance hall with segmental domed ceiling, rear stair hall with geometric staircase with ornate iron balustrade and a lantern with colonettes, and Ionic screen to landing. The principal rooms have marble chimneypieces, plaster cornices and ceiling roses, and panelled doors. NAN-CEALVERNE, Heamoor, has a long six-bay front and central pilastered porch. ROSECADGEHILL, Rosecadghill Road, said to have been built 1699, is of five bays, again in ashlar granite, with pilastered and pedimented Doric porch. Good interior including panelled room with fluted Ionic pilasters.

Former COASTGUARD STATION, Coastguard Crescent, above Chy-andour Cliff. 1886, a most attractive if quirky composition of cottages flanking a three-storey central tower with ornate quasi-Venetian details.

At HEAMOOR, 2 m. NW. St Thomas, 1892, a simple but well-built mission church with steeply pitched roof and W bellcote, with hall etc. attached on N side.

PERRANARWORTHAL

To the casual visitor travelling the Truro–Falmouth road through the wooded Kennall valley there is little to show of the once busy port with quays, limekilns and mills that developed around Perran Foundry, of huge significance in the C18 to late C19 industrial history of Cornwall. PERRAN WHARF is the now silted-up port along the River Kennal, PERRANARWORTHAL the medieval settlement around the churchtown above, and PERRANWELL the nearby village that expanded in the industrial era, all now conjoined by C20 expansion.

ST PIRAN. C16 tower of granite ashlar, three stages without buttresses with its pinnacles on supporting angel corbels, and embattled parapet. The rest of the church is an indifferent rebuilding of 1882 by *J. P. St Aubyn* in his usual Perp style, with a six-bay five-aisle arcade and arch- and wind-braced roofs. Over the S door a resited Norman tympanum: lamb and cross with an outer leaf-scroll moulding. – FONT. Octagonal, granite, possibly late medieval but reworked in the later C19. – STAINED GLASS. – Chancel E by *Heaton, Butler & Bayne*, 1907. – s aisle by *Joseph Bell*, 1853. – Classical marble wall MONUMENT to Benjamin Sampson †1840, of Tullimar (*see* below).

PERRAN FOUNDRY. The second largest foundry in the county after Harveys of Hayle, established in 1791 by the Fox family of Falmouth, also owners of the larger foundry at Neath Abbey. Like Harveys, the foundry built large beam engines, and cast cylinders up to 100 in. (2.5 metres) in diameter. It closed in 1879 with the end of mining in Gwennap and lay derelict in the late C20 and early C21 until conversion and extension to residential use 2012–13. Substantial remains include the COUNT HOUSE on the road, and in the main foundry area a long building range, formerly OFFICES and HAMMER MILL, with two cast-iron lintels over the entrance lettered PERRAN 1791 FOUNDRY. Behind, the massive MOULDING SHOP.

Opposite the Foundry, Nos. 1–3 RIVERSIDE, late C18 industrial housing and offices, partly weatherboarded and, just E, the mostly C19 NORWAY INN, Norway being the source of timber landed here in the C18. In COVE HILL the pretty early C19 Gothic ROSE LODGE, and GOONVREA TERRACE and FIR COTTAGE, early C19 industrial housing. Of the larger houses of the industrial entrepreneurs, the best survival is TULLIMAR, ½ m. E, built *c.* 1828 for Benjamin Sampson, agent to Perran Foundry, who established the Kennal Vale gunpowder works. Neoclassical style, a four-square plain stucco building with chaste plaster ornament inside. Rev. Francis Kilvert stayed here in 1870 when he wrote his evocative description of the Cornish industrial landscape on his journey to Hayle (*see* p. 467), and in the C20 it became the home of William Golding.

7050

PERRANPORTH

Miles of fine sandy beaches backed by the towering dunes of Perran Sands make Perranporth a popular holiday resort. It grew after the arrival of a branch line of the G.W.R. in 1903–5 with terraces of Edwardian boarding houses with yellow brick dressings on the slopes above the valley that leads to the beach. Its later C20 expansion was considerable but undistinguished.

ST MICHAEL, Boscawen Road. 1872 as a chapel of ease to Perranzabuloe. Plain E.E. style with lancets.

CHRIST THE KING (R. C.), Wheal Leisure. Small timber-framed church clad in cedar shingles, with monopitched-roofed SE turret lit by *dalle-de-verre* glass by *Father Charles Norris* of Buckfast.

Former PASSMORE EDWARDS CONVALESCENT HOME, Granny's Lane. Late C19, a substantial presence on an elevated site looking towards the sea. Two-storey three-bay centre with pretty cast-iron balcony to the flat roof (for patients to take the sea air), flanked by three-storey wings with half-hipped gables.

PERRANUTHNOE

5020

St Piran. A small, low church, with the usual C15 W tower of regular granite blocks, three-staged and unbuttressed. The rest much restored and rebuilt by *J. P. St Aubyn* 1883. S doorway with three medieval heads in hoodmould. The S side has no aisle but a transept on plain three-eighths respond, C12 but rebuilt. The four-bay N arcade is of square piers with demi-shafts. – FONT. C13, granite, square, with trefoil-headed blank niches. – The best feature of the interior is the chancel, enriched 1925–30, especially the ALTAR, REREDOS and COMMUNION RAILS by the *Pinwills* with good figure carving, and CHANCEL SCREEN and CHOIR STALLS, good enough to be by the same firm. – STAINED GLASS. Chancel E and S transept S, 1883 by *Lavers, Barraud & Westlake*. – MONUMENT. H. Cole †1775, conventional design of its period by *C. Regnart* of London, 1800.

CHURCHTOWN HOUSE, N of the church. Former rectory. C17 origins with good early C18 features including open-well stair with unusually heavy column-turned balusters and moulded ramped handrail, and fine plaster barrel-vaulted ceiling with moulded cornice in chamber.

ACTON CASTLE, 2 m. SE. Now a hotel. Castellated mansion of 1775 for John Stackhouse, the eminent botanist. The similarities with the contemporary Tregenna Castle, St Ives, suggest *William Wood* of Truro as architect. The original house is three bays and three storeys over a basement, on a two-room plan with large central stair hall. Identical late C18 two-storey wings. All classical with medievalized detail: a quirky composition, e.g. the tripartite windows flanked by blind cruciform gun loops. C18 stair.

PERRANZABULOE

7050

St Piran. Built 1804, reusing the arcade, tower, tracery and much else from the earlier church of St Piran near his oratory (*see* p. 601). Made more Cornish medieval in a restoration of 1873 but conspicuously lacking mellowness. Two-stage W tower with set-back buttresses, embattled parapet with pinnacles over the corners. Substantial body – nave, chancel, N aisle, S transept and S porch. The five-bay arcade has standard Cornish piers and capitals. Arch- and mid-braced roofs of 1873, wagon roofs over the chancel. – FONT. C12 base and shafts, C15 octagonal bowl, a piece of *Volkskunst*, with little figures of the Virgin and three apostles in niches. – BENCH-ENDS made into a screen at the W end, early C16 with one motif for each end: three similar bench-ends incorporated into the pulpit. – STAINED GLASS. Chancel E, 1883 by *Ward & Hughes*. – S aisle E, 1909 by *Fouracre & Son*. – MONUMENTS. Several good slate plates, e.g. Perryn Hoskyn †1675, by the same hand as the Lawrence plate at Cubert (q.v.). – Nicely lettered inscription plate to the subscriptions for the building of the church, by *J. Isbell* of Truro.

PERRAN ROUND, 1½ m. NNE. An enigma. An almost perfect circle – 130 ft (40 metres) diameter – with an earth rampart 12 ft (3.7 metres) high surrounded by a 6-ft (1.8-metre) deep ditch. It may have a long history – an Iron Age fortification? – but there is no record of it until the mid C18. It was subsequently used for preaching, including by Wesley, and for Cornish wrestling, drama etc.

CHYVERTON, 1½ m. ESE in a generous landscape setting. A medieval property of the Arundells but the present house is of the mid C18, extended *c.* 1770. Approached across the SE end of a sinuous lake NE of the house by a single-span humped-back BRIDGE of *c.* 1780. The original brick house was of an almost square double-pile plan of basement and two storeys, five bays with pediment and small lunette window, flanked by two set-back pavilions, their fronts linked to the rear wall of the house by high screen walls. Both links were subsequently converted into wings, the W *c.* 1790, the E *c.* 1920. The interior was largely remodelled between 1832 and 1850 in classical style. Large stair hall with open-well stair with cast-iron balustrade and three-bay Doric colonnade between stair hall and axial passage. Attractive Neoclassical wall and ceiling plaster-work in the principal rooms. Good late C18 STABLE BLOCK of two-storey parallel ranges; later single-storey link with high flanking walls and a central gateway.

ST PIRAN'S ORATORY AND CHURCH. *See* p. 601.

PHILLACK

Though its history from the mid C18 is about the rise of Hayle (q.v.), Phillack retains its distinct identity, the churchtown pleasantly situated on the N side of the estuary above Copperhouse Pool against the extensive sand dunes of The Towans. Probably of Iron Age origin, it has a long continuity as a religious centre, with evidence of pre-Christian graves and an important group of early Christian memorial stones in the churchyard.

St Felicitas (St Felec). Three-stage w tower, with set-back buttresses to the lower stages, battlements, and a pyramidal slate roof. It is C15 but the rest of the church was rebuilt by *William White* in 1865–7, mostly in E.E. style: he incorporated older fragments including a C5 stone with XP (chi-ro) monogram into the porch gable, a C12 carved head in the N gable of the N vestry and some cusped tracery in its S wall, with other features inside. The interior is profoundly satisfying, White skilfully articulating the spaces of a relatively small building (e.g. how the low Dec piers are employed in wide bays in the nave and narrower bays in the chancel and the addition of a dramatic sanctuary arch) to create an atmosphere of quiet mystery. The original large chancel arch is enhanced by a later but delicate iron screen. – FONT. Medieval, but so thoroughly re-tooled that nothing worth having survives in what now looks like a late C19 reproduction. Square bowl with sloping sides and motifs of rosette, cross, etc., in medallions (cf. Gwithian). – PULPIT. Made up from panels of a rood screen with the same vertical foliage Serpentines as at Gwinear (q.v.). – C15 carved fragments in porch. – Norman ALTAR SLAB with incised consecration crosses, built into High Altar. – C12 or C13 TOMB-LID set into E wall of vestry, which also has two fragments of the undersides of CANOPIES, 'groined in the most delicate manner' (Sedding), probably originating as part of a shrine or tabernacle. – STAINED GLASS. A good mid-C19 to early C20 ensemble. Three by *William Wailes*, the earliest the E window of the N aisle, 1850 (perhaps this was the E window before the rebuild?), and the two easternmost windows of the S aisle. – Chancel E, 1911, and S aisle E, 1905, by *Curtis, Ward & Hughes*. – Chancel S by *Lavers, Barraud & Westlake*, 1858.

The CHURCHYARD is full of interest, bounded by a WALL of cast scoria blocks and copings with a C19 lychgate with buttressed front walls. To the E the OLD VESTRY, a striking example of a whole building in scoria, the vitreous black set off by white pointing. Against its W wall a somewhat mutilated WHEEL-HEAD CROSS and an INSCRIBED STONE. The inscription reads CLOTVALI MOBRATTI. The date (*see* the Hiberno-Saxon letters) may be anything between C7 and C10. – On the S side of the churchyard a WHEEL-HEAD CHURCHYARD CROSS, the principal face with an elongated figure with irregular three-cord plaitwork below and similar plaitwork on the reverse and sides. One of the Penwith series of pre-Conquest sculpture (cf. Paul, St Buryan and St Erth). – Between the lychgate and the tower a CROSS-HEAD with an equal-limbed cross in relief. – Some CAST-IRON MEMORIALS (cf. Helston and St Erth), probably from Harveys foundry. – COPED STONE. Outside the S wall of the church. Only half of it is preserved. One of four surviving examples (cf. Lanivet, St Buryan, St Tudy).

The Cornwall Copper Company's domain is represented by RIVIERE HOUSE, 1791, for John Edwards, the manager. A dignified three-storey three-bay house with tall sash windows

to the ground and first floors and wide bracketed eaves. COP-
PERHOUSE POOL is crossed by a CAUSEWAY and the BLACK
BRIDGE, of scoria blocks, built *c.* 1790 to give access to Riviere
House. A small BRIDGE of three equal spans over a narrow
stream on the footpath along the N side of Copperhouse Creek
dates from 1837 and marks the route of the Hayle Railway that
went over the swing bridge towards the original Foundry
Square terminus (cf. Hayle).

8030

PHILLEIGH

ST FILI. Sturdy C14 W tower of two and a half storeys with
buttresses only to the S and W on the lower stage and simple
battlemented parapet. Nave and chancel under one roof, N
transept, S aisle and S porch. Extensively restored in 1867 by
the *Rev. C. W. Carlyon* (cf. St Anthony-in-Roseland and St
Just-in-Roseland) with mostly C19 Perp windows; low C13
pointed-head door and late C15 to early C16 square-headed
windows with cinquefoil lights and hoodmoulds survive in the
W and E walls of transept. Aisle arcade of seven bays on circular
piers with four attached shafts, with four rather low capitals.
The entrance arches to tower and transept unmoulded. C19
arch-braced roofs with cavetto cornices enriched with ballflow-
ers and rosettes and Carlyon's favourite dog-tooth decoration
to the trusses. – FONT. Octagonal, C13, with two flat blank
niches with pointed heads in each side. – Arcaded brattished
SCREEN, C19, between nave and transept. – Other Carlyon
furnishings include pews with scroll shaped ends, tiled flooring
in the nave and glazed tiles in the chancel. – ROYAL ARMS, of
George II, 1735, painted, on tower screen. – REREDOS. 1915.
– STAINED GLASS. E window, 1867 by *J. Powell & Sons.*

GLEBE HOUSE, S of the church. Early to mid-C18 rectory,
extended in later C18 and C19. A fine example of a largish early
Georgian house, the slate-hung E front especially pleasingly
proportioned: of five bays symmetrically arranged around a
wide central door, the ground-floor windows with pointed-
arched lights; tall early C19 sashes above, and a hipped roof
with pedimented gabled dormers and tall end stacks. The
interior has much good C18 detail including an open-well stair,
fielded dado panelling to the vestibule, and panelling and
cornices.

ROUND COTTAGE, opposite the church. A delightful little *cottage
orné* of *c.* 1820. Two semicircular wings like corner turrets
linked by a central vestibule and stair, with pointed-headed
arched windows with Gothick tracery. Interior with arched
door to stairs, panelled doors, and other good details. The
strong similarities with the round-houses at nearby Veryan
(q.v.) suggest it may be associated with the same patron, the
Rev. Jeremiah Trist.

PILLATON

St Odulph. A splendidly strong w tower of very regular granite blocks, c15, of three stages on a high plinth with buttresses set back from the angles, embattled parapet and pinnacles. Porch and s transept also of granite blocks. The porch has a fine four-centred and wave-moulded arched doorway and c15–c16 wagon roof with moulded ribs, carved bosses, and wall-plate richly carved with pomegranates and flowers. The plan of the church – nave and chancel, s transept, and n aisle – suggests that the transept is left over in plan, if not elevation, from an earlier cruciform layout. It has a square-headed e window. n aisle of six bays with very slim piers, of the same profile as at Callington and its neighbourhood, that is square with four attached demi-shafts. The e end of the nave and n aisle have image-niches, partly projecting on corbels, partly carved into the wall. An exceptionally large squint, at the same time the entrance to the roof-loft staircase and connecting transept and chancel (cf. Quethiock). Late c15 wagon roofs in n aisle and s transept, the transept roof with the wall-plate set on a moulded granite cornice. A restoration of 1878 by *Henry Elliott* renewed the nave and chancel roofs. – royal arms, of 1663 and 1729. – stained glass. Chancel e, geometric patterns, aisle e, 1878, by *J. T. Fouracre*. – monuments. In the s transept three memorials to the Tillies of Pentillie Castle (q.v.), the finest to James Tillie †1772, classical, in the best London style of the moment; no figures. The others to Robert Tillie, 1742, and James Tillie, 1746.

Paynters Cross. *See* Pentillie Castle.

POLKERRIS

A small port for the Rashleighs of Menabilly; the arm of a crescent-shaped single pier reaches across the bay to protect a little beach between a natural amphitheatre of cliffs. The happy result of this estate history is a rare, nearly intact c18 and c19 village group, almost uncompromised by later development. There are small groups of modest cottages, a former Methodist church of 1850 of the simple plain sort and the c19 Rashleigh Arms. To the middle and e of the beach, the substantial remains of c18 fish cellars and net lofts, once some of the largest pilchard curing chambers in Cornwall, now roofless and reduced so that, especially from the sea, the former openings appear charmingly like the battlements of a folly. Also an c18 limekiln jauntily sports a Second World War pillbox on top.

Tregaminion, ¼ m. e. A chapel of ease to Tywardreath on the Rashleighs' estate. 1815. The carved stone bearing the

Rashleigh arms in the wall over the porch was found when the foundations were dug. Small, simple building, its chief feature a bellcote over the w end, square-headed windows to side elevations, Perp tracery to e and w ends. – STONE CROSSES. One immediately sw of the church, a tall wheel-head cross and shaft, Greek cross on each face with widely extended limbs. The other immediately nw of the church, a small wheel-head cross and shaft, Greek cross on one face framed by a sunken panel between the arms.

KILMARTH, ½ m. N. C18 rebuild by the Rashleighs of an earlier mansion of the Baker family, probably of medieval origin. Present house* two-storey five-window front, slate-hung, with two-storey wing l. and single-storey wing r. Two classical two-storey PAVILIONS, 2011 and 2013 by *Craig Hamilton Architects* in the early C21 garden.

GRIBBIN TOWER, Gribbin Head, 1½ m. sw. Day navigation beacon built 1832 by Trinity House. Very tall tower on square plan, slightly tapered, rising to a corbelled parapet. Dramatic painted red and white stripes.

MENABILLY. *See* p. 347.

See p. 347.

2050

POLPERRO

If Polperro is perhaps the most famous of all the small Cornish fishing ports, it is also the most enigmatic. Approached by road it is the epitome of what tourism has made of Cornwall, its extreme picturesqueness deservedly charming those seeking the place idealized in poster, postcard and painting. From the sea it is utterly different, a slash in the cliffs offering a narrow inlet through jagged rocks that curves round into a wooded gorge towards the small harbour, with the little settlement at its head. This dramatic setting defines Polperro, a network of narrow streets either side of a small but fast-flowing river, its modest buildings closely packed and rising in random tiers up the steep valley sides. Many of Polperro's buildings are of C17–C18 origins with later dressings especially of the later C19. There is plenty of whitewashed render, slate roofs and slate cladding, large end chimneystacks on buildings sometimes gable-end to the street, flights of steps, and external stairs, and the occasional example of folk-art shell decoration. Even the one large building, the church of ST JOHN, 1838, sited high on the s side above Lansallos Street, has to be sought out: its distinctive feature, good in silhouette, is its n transept, whose tall narrow lancets are flanked by octagonal corner turrets with crenellated parapets and crowned by an octagonal timber bell-

---

* Daphne du Maurier moved here from Menabilly and used it as the inspiration for *The House on the Strand* (1969).

cote. – STAINED GLASS. 1956 by *Margaret Aldridge Pope* in the Arts and Crafts tradition.

The working HARBOUR is the *raison d'être* of Polperro. The fishing port was recorded as early as 1303, a full century before neighbouring Mevagissey. The present harbour walls, quays and piers show sequential improvements from the late C17 to the late C19. Earliest are the walls of the inner basin, pierced by the river BRIDGE built after 1854. The basin's N side was built on from the late C18 for fish sheds and houses in The Warren. PRINCE ALBERT PIER, running SW–NE, was first built *c.* 1740 and successively rebuilt, repaired and extended during the C19: it now encloses the mouth of the outer harbour with a much shorter pier extending S from The Warren. Seaward from these, the DUKE OF CORNWALL'S PIER, added 1861 from the N side of the harbour. The significance of the pilchard industry is recorded by the former L'TEGLIOS FISH CELLARS (now Heritage Museum of Smuggling and Fishing) on The Warren, a simple single-storey late C19 building; the Teglio brothers settled here in the early C20 and exported pilchards to Italy. THE LOFT, a former net loft, now a store, sits alone high above the S side of the harbour. Other buildings began as fish cellars or net lofts, or had living accommodation above. Examples of the former are the late C18 house on QUAY ROAD overlooking the harbour and the early C19 CAPTAIN'S CABIN and THE PORCH in Lansallos Street; and of the latter, ISLAND HOUSE, The Warren, its impressive elevation to the harbour of four storeys and attic. For the rest, it is best to perambulate the little streets, most no more than lanes, and enjoy the myriad visual delights of a place that ultimately defies exact description.

HOLY WELL, Landaviddy Lane. Field spring issuing from rock, the well-house now gone. In the field above the well the chapel of St Peter Porthpyne was recorded in 1392.

POLRUAN

1050

ST SAVIOUR. 1890–1, by *W. Smith* of Truro, in rubble stone with brick dressings. The unprepossessing exterior disguises a spacious, dignified interior, wide and lofty, with S transept and S aisle of three arcades with square chamfered piers and capitals, and simple timber roof. But its chief interest is the STAINED GLASS. Four windows by *C. E. Kempe*, 1893–1905, and two circular windows of the S wall by *William Morris & Co.* They are all of 1892, brought here from St David's School Chapel, Wray Park, Reigate, in 1958–9 (Michael Swift).

The guidebooks recommend Polruan chiefly as a viewpoint for Fowey – and indeed the layout of the town and its medieval defences is wonderfully set out from across the estuary – but by approaching the town by ferry one can appreciate the dramatic cluster of small streets sprinkled with former chapels and old inns rising in steep tiers from the waterfront. At river level one can also forget the dreadful toll c20 housing took on its skyline. Polruan was probably the busiest harbour on the estuary in the early medieval period before being overtaken by Lostwithiel and Fowey (qq.v.). FORE STREET, climbing steeply uphill, and EAST and WEST STREETS running along the hillside, are full of visual interest. In East Street, Nos. 8 and 9, a smart mid-c19 front of Plymouth limestone with ribbed brick segmented arches to windows, panelled doorcase, and limestone curbs and walls with granite gateposts and ball finials. West Street has the READING ROOM AND LIBRARY of 1875 and the former WESLEYAN CHAPEL, 1880 by *Hicks* of Redruth, with pinnacled octagonal turrets. The street leads to THE BLOCKHOUSE (Polruan Castle), of a pair with the ruinous blockhouse on the Fowey side (q.v.), built after the French raid of 1437, but far more impressive in its massive scale and features. As well as a chain tower, it was a watch tower and had a first floor with c16 fireplaces, stairs and doorways, and mullioned windows of later adaptation. Up BATTERY LANE to the fragmentary but eloquent remains of the medieval ST SAVIOUR'S CHAPEL, on the hilltop. Return via the top of FORE STREET. The POLRUAN CROSS is a fragment of a granite Latin cross on a Pentewan stone shaft.

7010

POLTESCO

½ m. E of Ruan Minor

This beautiful place, hidden among bamboos and trees as the Poltesco valley and its little stream give into Caerleon Cove, was the early centre of the serpentine cutting and polishing industry, at one time employing nearly one hundred people. The remains of the factory buildings can still be traced over the extensive site in low walls, wheel pits, a partly collapsed chimney and one tall structure dated 1866. There is also a round WINCH HOUSE, evidence of the fishing cove before the industry arrived. The serpentine works closed in 1893, after which small serpentine workshops began to be established in Lizard Town and at Lizard Point, Landewednack (q.v.).

7030

PONSANOOTH

In the c18 and c19 this part of the Kennal valley was one of the busiest industrial areas in Cornwall (cf. Perranarworthal), with mining activity alongside a diverse range of mills – corn, grist, textile, paper and gunpowder among them.

ST MICHAEL AND ALL ANGELS, St Michael's Road. A mission church (to St Gluvius). 1880, plain Gothic with bellcote. – STAINED GLASS. E window by *G. Maile*, 1963.

PONSANOOTH METHODIST CHURCH, Chapel Hill. One of the best and most complete chapels in Cornwall. Datestone 1843. The granite and ashlar entrance front is approached by a semicircular forecourt bounded by ashlar granite walls, with a flight of steps between monolithic granite piers: it is the more imposing because of the steeply rising site with an extensive burial ground behind. Three-bay symmetrical design, the central bay broken forward, surmounted by a triangular pediment curiously truncated by a shaped apex. The first-floor windows have intersecting glazing bars. The interior has galleries on all four sides on columns, with panelled fronts cantilevered out on shaped brackets.

In ST MICHAEL'S ROAD, Nos. 31–41 are three pairs of council houses of 1922 by *P. Edwin Stephens*, in an Arts and Crafts-influenced style, pleasant, modest, and well detailed with swept hipped roofs, probably the last granite council houses built in Cornwall.

VIADUCT, ¼ m. E. Loftiest in this section of the GWR at 140 ft (42 metres) high and 650 ft (198 metres) long, a 1930 replacement of Brunel's original, the piers of which stand alongside.

LYNHER DAIRY, ½ m. NNW. 2003 by *Sutherland Hussey Architects* of Edinburgh. Simple, functional, with steep monopitch roof to the E range and timber cladding.

KENNAL VALE, 1 m. W. A magical setting for a major industrial site, the numerous water-powered 'incorporating' MILLS spaced out and almost hidden along the steep wooded valley of the Kennal. Set up by Benjamin Sampson (cf. Perranarworthal) in 1811 it soon became the largest gunpowder producer in the county, supplying mines and manufacturers of safety fuses. The square mill buildings were paired, with a waterwheel between, driving shafts below the main floor. The risk of explosion was minimized by well-spaced buildings, lightweight roofs and large windows. Systems of leats supplied water from the river to mills, the tail water sometimes then working the next mill down the valley.

POOL

6040

The sprawling C20 development that links Camborne with Redruth has long since engulfed Pool, a large and important industrial village in the later C18 and C19 including major mines, engineering works, iron foundries and the locomotive and carriage works of the Hayle Railway established here in 1837.

TREVENSON CHURCH (ST JOHN), Church Road. A small Gothick chapel of ease to Illogan built by the Bassets of Tehidy (q.v.) 1806–9: the thin castellated W tower is a later addition. The tall rectangular nave has two large and widely spaced two-centred arched windows to the N and S elevations and a stepped triple lancet E window: the dainty intersecting tracery, geometrical in intention, is in cast iron and incorporates trefoil and quatrefoil heads, diagonal glazing below, and narrow margin lights. Plain W gallery on two cast-iron columns. – GLASS. Quatrefoil in W tower of Italian enamelled glass.

POOL METHODIST CHURCH, Fore Street. Dated 1862. The symmetrical three-bay front has tall round-headed windows flanking a wide basket-arched central doorway with a round-headed window above. The interior has a horseshoe-shaped gallery on cast-iron Tuscan columns and good mid-C19 detail. Sunday school added 1881.

EAST POOL & AGAR MINE. The road towards Redruth runs between two old copper mines that rose to greater importance with tin in the C19 and were incorporated into South Crofty in the mid C20. S of the road, originally part of East Pool mine, a small WINDING ENGINE, and N, marked by its 110-ft (36-metre) stack, the larger pumping ENGINE HOUSE on Taylor's Shaft at Wheal Agar; the mines amalgamated in 1896, the lettering on the stack EPAL (East Pool & Agar Ltd. Mine). Both engines and houses were saved by the Cornish Engine Preservation Society and, now owned by the National Trust, are open to the public. The pumping engine, the largest preserved steam engine in Cornwall, was built by Harvey's of Hayle in 1892 for Carn Brea mines and moved here in 1924, where it worked until 1954. The WINDING ENGINE at Mitchell's Shaft on East Pool Mine is small by comparison.

CORNWALL COLLEGE, ¼ m. NW. The major development of this site, formerly the house and grounds of TREVENSON HOUSE, 1779 for the steward to Lord de Dunstanville, was of the 1960s by the *County Architect's Department*. The METHOD system gave some consistency to the campus, punctuated by the seven-storey tower of *c.* 1968 with much exposed concrete and Brutalist detailing, now hidden behind smart flush cladding of 2012. Further development to the N of the original site of the late C20 and early C21 by various architects.

HEARTLANDS (SOUTH CROFTY), ½ m. SW. At the centre of this major area of regeneration, ongoing in 2013, is the last Cornish BEAM ENGINE to operate a mine. Built at Copperhouse in 1854, it worked four mines before arriving at South Crofty in 1903 and working here until 1955. Some use made of retained buildings for museum and visitor centre among new industrial-style buildings, but it lacks the context of the surrounding buildings at Geevor (q.v.).

PORT ELIOT *see* ST GERMANS

PORT GAVERNE

Like neighbouring Port Isaac and nearby Port Quin, Port Gaverne developed as a fishing settlement at the head of a narrow inlet between the steep cliffs of the hostile N coast. In the C19 it also exported large quantities of slate from the Delabole quarry, and imported limestone and coal: the slate was brought down by the specially constructed Slate Road to the N and loaded into sea ketches which were too wide for Port Isaac but could rest on the beach here between tides. When in 1893 the North Cornwall Railway Company linked Delabole to Launceston and Plymouth, Port Gaverne lost the slate trade but, paradoxically, boosted its pilchard industry by virtue of the great improvement the new rail link made to the rapid export of fish products.

The little settlement is comprised of a few houses, a hotel and four large FISH CELLARS, an important group in a county that has lost so much evidence of this once vital industry. The early C19 RASHLEIGH and UNION cellars near the beach survive largely intact, both partly cob-walled. The former is especially instructive, retaining the characteristic rectangular pattern around an open court. A two-storey SE main range is flanked by a narrow two-storey wing on the SW side and a narrow single-storey wing on the NE, with a smoking house with louvred openings on the W front. Both front and side display brick niches that housed pressing poles. Just inland are the now converted VENUS and LIBERTY cellars. Fine C19 LIMEKILN between Rashleigh and Union.

PORT ISAAC

The most important of the trio of ports – cf. Port Gaverne and Port Quin – along this inhospitable stretch of coast. Like its neighbours, it is gathered around the head of a small inlet but here the surrounding cliffs are so high and sheer that the settlement seems to hang precipitously above the harbour in steep streets of small houses and cottages piled one above the other. It is irresistible, quintessential picturesque Cornwall, but it is also a place where one can still sense something of the authentic small Cornish fishing port with that industry still thriving here.

ST PETER, Church Hill. 1882–4. Possibly by *Hine & Odgers*, but, if so, disappointing compared to their better work. Plainest E.E. with lancets, the original granite, elvan and Bath stone exterior now rendered. Interior of austere simplicity. – STAINED

GLASS. Chancel E, 1921 by *Jones & Willis*, chancel N, 1901 by *Fouracre & Sons* in Kempe style.

Former METHODIST CHURCH AND CHURCH ROOMS, Roscarrock Hill. One of the most strikingly sited chapels in Cornwall, standing immediately behind the harbour and its fish cellars, and presenting an especially attractive front elevation seaward. The original chapel on the l. was erected in 1837 and converted to schoolrooms when the adjoining chapel was built in 1869. Both are two-storey with hipped slate roofs. The earlier smaller building had a two-window front with brick round-arched heads, a central oculus, and a bellcote, an unusual feature for a chapel. The later building has a five-window front, again with brick round-arched heads, and radiating glazing bars in cast iron. The interior has a gallery on three sides on cast-iron columns and retains many of its original fittings that suit its use as an art gallery.

Former SCHOOL, Fore Street. 1877 by *Silvanus Trevail*. Its strong vertical proportions and an emphatic Gothic style with asymmetrically placed gables admirably suit its position precipitously perched above the harbour, offering picturesque elevations all round. It originally comprised two large schoolrooms on a U-shaped plan, with a central entrance in a three-stage tower surmounted by a turret. The r. side was later extended as the schoolmaster's house. Contemporary railings and gatepier.

PERAMBULATION. The best place to start is the harbour, though the narrow streets leading down to it offer a succession of good vistas that should be savoured. From the harbour, the essence of Port Isaac can be appreciated in one sweep, r. to l., with the former COASTGUARD COTTAGES on the steep slope above; next the long convex curve of the slate-roofed FISH CELLARS immediately above the beach with the former Methodist church (*see* above) rising behind; then the concave curve of the PENTUS WALL AND STORES rising from the beach; slate-hung houses all around; and finally high on the cliff the Gothic pile of the former school (*see* above). The fish cellars, still in use, are of early C19 origin, on an irregular courtyard plan fronted by a two-storey range with a wide central opening. To the l. a range of former stables and salt pits, open-fronted to the yard with an arcade of timber and granite posts and with net lofts above. To the r., a later smoking house and more open-fronted sheds. The Pentus Wall leads to a row of five lean-to former fish cellars, now stores.

As in Polperro, the only way to appreciate the buildings of Port Isaac is to walk its closely packed streets, with the densest concentrations of older houses and cottages in FORE STREET, DOLPHIN STREET, MIDDLE STREET and CHURCH HILL. Most are C18 and C19 with much slate cladding and scantleslate roofs (Delabole slate was exported from here from the C16), sash windows, and nice C19 shopfronts; there are also many examples of former small fish cellars converted to stores and garages. One might note the slightly grander early C18

GOLDEN LION INN at the corner of The Platt and Fore Street;
the timber-framed front of No. 10 Fore Street jettied out over
the street like those in Fowey and Looe; and the quirkily
shaped slate-hung BIRDCAGE, No. 11 ROSE HILL. But no one
building is outstanding, all contributing harmoniously to a
truly delightful and visually enjoyable place.

PORT QUIN   *9080*

2¼ m. NW of St Endellion

One of the most delightful places in Cornwall. Sheltered at the
head of a small inlet between steep cliffs is a hamlet of former
fishermen, market gardeners and miners' cottages, the latter
employed in the Doyden antimony mine, important in the C19:
one of the gardens was known as the Hop Garden, probably
associated with the C19 brewing enterprise at Roscarrock
(q.v.). The outer wall of a former fish cellar of the late C18
survives, with a line of brick niches used for housing pressing
poles with associated slip to the beach. Romantically placed
above on Doyden Point is DOYDEN CASTLE (National Trust).
An especially picturesque folly, built 1839 by Samuel Symms
of Gonvena, Egloshayle (q.v.), for his recreation. Two-storey,
built into the cliff, above a basement wine cellar, ground floor
with two-light windows with square heads, first floor two-
light with two-centred arched headers rising to battlemented
parapet with crocketed pinnacles. The very exposed position
has weathered its stonework to interesting textures. From the
castle are extensive views W along the magnificent cliff scenery
towards the silhouette of Pentire Head and The Rumps promontory castle (*see* below). The National Trust's stewardship of
the area from Port Quin to Polzeath has sustained its sublime
character untarnished by C20 development of the kind that in
1936 saw the entire Pentire headland divided into building
plots and put up for sale.

THE RUMPS, 3½ m. W. Later Iron Age CLIFF CASTLE with three
ditched ramparts cutting off at its narrowest point a flaring
promontory with two rounded hills, The Rumps. Excavations
in the 1960s produced artefacts from the last centuries B.C.
and the first A.D.; some post-Roman amphorae sherds were
also found. Between middle and inner ramparts are traces of
round-houses.

PORTH NAVAS   *7020*

A good example of a small estuary port. A late C18 QUAY, enlarged
in the early to mid C19, of massive granite blocks from the

granite quarries of the parish of Constantine on the W side of Porth Navas Creek, some late C18 cottages, and a former READING ROOM and WASHHOUSE.

PORTHCURNO

The once quiet valley, where fishing took place from its idyllic beach, was transformed in 1870 when the first telegraphic cable from Gibraltar and Lisbon was landed, followed by cables linking places across the world: it became a centre of worldwide communications and a vital link in governing the British Empire, and played an important part of the defence of Britain during the Second World War. Competition from Marconi's wireless telegraph (cf. Mullion and Landewednack) resulted in the amalgamation of companies in 1928 to form what became Cable & Wireless Ltd. After the company's closure in 1993, many of the buildings were demolished but the most important survive and now form the MUSEUM OF SUBMARINE TECHNOLOGY. The most striking is the long, two-storey flat-roofed slab on the E side of the valley, built in phases from 1904 as the offices of the Eastern Telegraph Company. Dug into the hillside behind, and also part of the museum, are two interconnected parallel TUNNELS, rock-cut and concrete-block lined, constructed 1940–1. The CABLE HUT of 1929 stands on the edge of the beach. All contain much original equipment.

MINACK THEATRE, Minack Point. A magical site for an open-air theatre on the cliffs above the beach. *Rowena Cade* started its construction in 1931 and continued its evolution until her death in 1983. Working with her gardener *Billy Rawlings* and his mate *Charles Thomas Angrove*, the walls of the terraces that form an amphitheatre facing the sea were made from hand-cut granite from boulders, and the terraces infilled with earth; later she used cement decorated by her (using an old screwdriver) with lettering and intricate Celtic designs. Arches, balconies and flights of steps moulded almost seamlessly into the cliff face combine with the sublime seascape that forms the backdrop to the stage, perched right on the cliff edge, to create a unique setting for drama. A visitor centre of 2000 by *Hocking & Newton* was tactfully created above the theatre, the roofs of its three buildings of irregular shape looking like the clustered cottages of a fishing cove.

PORTHILLY

ST MICHAEL. Small, humble, and in a lovely setting overlooking the wide Camel estuary. A chapelry of St Minver from the C12. Of the cruciform Norman building, nave, chancel and S transept, the latter widened to the w in the c13 and a lancet placed in its e wall; the foundations of a corresponding n transept are known from excavation. In the c15 a narrow one-bay s chancel chapel was added with standard piers and a four-centred arch, and an arch inserted into the e wall of the transept to give on to the the newly built chapel. c15 wagon roofs, heavily restored. The church was rescued from ruin in 1865–7 by Rev. W. Hart Smith, who also restored St Enodoc (q.v.), under the generally sympathetic supervision of *J. P. St Aubyn*. He rebuilt the modest two-stage tower with its saddleback roof, unusually placed not at the w but over the s porch. – FONT. Simple Norman, with circular bowl and round shaft with cable mould-ing, similar to St Enodoc. – ROOD SCREEN. Only the lower framework survives, the moulded and chamfered stiles carved with rosettes and the bases stopped with ornate carvings of vases and floral trails. – PULPIT. Early c16, of high quality with moulded stem and hexagonal drum carved with linenfold pan-elling. – Two PISCINAS, one c13 in e wall of the s transept, another of the c14 in the chancel. – STAINED GLASS. e window 1867 by *Michael O'Connor*, pretty and richly coloured. – ETCHED GLASS. In s transept s window, beautifully lettered inscription by *David Peace*, 1976 (cf. St Merryn). – MONU-MENT. Fine slate ledger slab to William Rounsenall †1659, with border inscription, decorated verse and panel. – CROSS-HEAD. Near s side of s door. Massive four-holed cross pierced from both sides with central boss and decoration on all four sides of the shaft.

At the approach to the churchyard, LYCHGATE, probably by *St Aubyn*, like that at St Minver, and PORTHILLY FARM-HOUSE and PORTHILLY GREYS, late c16 or early c17 houses originally of three-room and cross-passage plan.

At ROCK, ¼ m. N, an c18 QUAY projecting into the Camel estuary with a c19 warehouse, converted to a sailing club house, at its s end. LIFEBOAT STATION. 1997 by the *Bazeley Partnership*. Nicely reticent, tucked in below the dunes, with a wave roof. Among the rapidly redeveloping sites, RADOON, 2004 by *ECD Architects*, a large holiday house designed with sustainable technology, with curved zinc roof overhanging the balcony to the first-floor living area.

JESUS WELL, ½ m. N. Well-house to a holy well. Medieval origins, possibly rebuilt late c19, restored in c20. Gable-end entrance with four-centred arch and a corbelled stone roof. Slate stone in threshold inscribed JESUS SAITH UNTO HER GIVE ME TO DRINK Timor Domini Fons Vitae M. L. ('The fear of the Lord is the fruition of life').

PORTHLEVEN 6020

Porthleven's strong character reflects its transformation in the c19 from a small fishing settlement into an industrial port town, especially after the harbour was acquired by Harvey's of Hayle in 1855 to service the copper, tin and china clay trade, powerfully expressed in its fortress-like sea defences and its range of public buildings.

St Bartholomew, Church Row. 1839–42 by *Sampson Kempthorne*. Restored 1891 by *G. H. Fellowes Prynne*, who added the baptistery. Lady Chapel, 1934, by *C. R. Corfield*. The plain but pleasingly proportioned Romanesque exterior is a prelude to a fine interior that owes much to its embellishment by Fellowes Prynne, including a splendid low chancel SCREEN with brasswork that curves towards the altar seraphim MURALS in the sanctuary, possibly by *E. A. Fellowes Prynne*, CHOIR STALLS by *Harry Hems* of Exeter, and an anchor-shaped ROOD. Specially delightful are the brass stencils of fish, starfish and anchors on the PULPIT. – STAINED GLASS. E window by *Powells*, 1863.

Methodist church, Fore Street. 1881–3 by *James Hicks*. An ambitious Wesleyan chapel in an exuberant Gothic style, its spiky profile visible all over the town. Its strong verticality is reinforced on the street elevation with buttresses flanking the large central traceried window that rise to open bellcotes with pinnacles, end buttresses to the flanking stair bays rising to pinnacles, and paired central entrance doors also buttressed and pinnacled. To the r. the contemporary CHAPEL-KEEPER'S HOUSE in complementary style with buttressed porch and corners and nice detailing like the pierced bargeboards and crested ridge tiles.

Methodist chapel, Peverell Road. 1863, a rebuilding of an earlier chapel, enlarged with W porches 1876. Two-storey with round-headed windows to the first floor. Interior with gallery on slender cast-iron columns.

Wesley chapel and schoolroom, Chapel Terrace. 1840 datestone, wings added 1867 and 1868. Thinly coursed ashlar granite front, two-storey, two-bay with round-headed windows with Y tracery.

Bickford Smith Institute, Institute Hill. Now the Town Council offices. 1882, by *James Hicks* for William Bickford Smith of Camborne (cf. Tuckingmill) as a scientific and literary institute and library, with its three-stage Italianate clock tower the most striking building in the town. Dramatically sited on the E headland at the start of the long arm of the harbour wall that stretches out into the sea, it has tall paired lancets to the middle stage and the upper clock-face stage corbelled out with a crenellated parapet surmounted by a copper-clad spire: it is a memorable image.

The Wharf, including the inner and outer harbours, E and W wharfs, inner jetties, and main pier. The scale of the construction is monumental, mostly of vast granite blocks and copings giving the harbour an embattled, almost military, character. It is of two major phases, the first 1811–25 with the building of the outer harbour (the Porthleven Harbour and

Dock Company was first incorporated in 1811), the second 1855–58 the large inner basin by Harveys of Hayle. Between the two are slots and a hoisting derrick to lower huge timber bulks to protect the basin. Several large granite bollards.

PERAMBULATION. Porthleven is well worth a gentle exploration, especially around the harbour. The older fishing village was on the E side of the harbour and the streets behind. In LOE BAR ROAD, a rare example of a simple FISHERMAN'S CABIN, single-storey over basement, one-room plan, looking out to sea. Off FORE STREET, mostly C19 terraced housing with a few C18 survivors: CHURCH ROW is a nice modest example. The most prominent is BAY VIEW TERRACE, a rather splendid Edwardian row of mostly semi-detached houses, 1902–5 by *Abraham Dellbridge* of Camborne, looking surprised to be here rather than a London suburb. Below on THE WHARF, the HARBOUR INN, early C19 with later C19 extension with round-arched doorways and two oriel windows, and the former CUSTOM HOUSE, datestone 1840, built as an account house, with an imposing ashlar granite front. Between them tightly planned HOUSING, 2004 by *Form Design Group*. At the corner of SALT CELLAR HILL a three-storey warehouse of 1816. On BREAGSIDE, the W side of the harbour, the best sense of Porthleven's C19 industrial character with a CHINA CLAY STORE, 1893, probably by Harvey's of Hayle, with three round-arched ground-floor openings; a three-storey WAREHOUSE, early C19, with a wide doorway in the centre of each floor; a C19 LIMEKILN; the C18 SHIP INN on the headland; a Second World War PILLBOX; and the former LIFEBOAT STATION, 1893, converted to an artist's studio 2010. Returning to Breagside, on the l. a small but stylish housing development by *Conran & Partners*, 2008, a two-storey white-rendered terrace terminating with a three-storey block of warehouse form.

METHLEIGH, Breage Road, ½ m. NNW. C17 house extended and refronted in the C19. Good example of a late C19 MODEL FARM on a courtyard plan with the principal BARN forming a corner and a three-storey farm MILL on higher ground behind. Range of PIGSTIES E of the mill. A special feature is the way water is channelled and used throughout the farmstead.

PORTHPEAN

ST LEVAN, Higher Porthpean. 1884–5 by *J. Reeves* for Lady Graves-Sawle of Penrice (*see* below). Small church in Pentewan ashlar, nicely composed on its steeply sloping site and in well detailed E.E. style. Pretty W front with a projecting pointed-arched loggia, lancet window and bellcote on corbels; the loggia has carved family shields and inscription 'Jesus Came to Them Walking on the Seas'. – REREDOS. 1895 by Reeves in Devon marble. – STAINED GLASS. A good and complete set by *Clayton & Bell*, 1904–36. In the churchyard a fine entrance with wrought-iron overthrow and lantern between gatepiers.

PENRICE, ½ m. N. Large mid-C18 country house, now a hospital. Pentewan ashlar with granite dressings. Courtyard plan with service ranges to rear. Entrance front two-storey with five-window centre range flanked by projecting wings; the central three bays broken forward under a triangular pediment with a pedimented porch on square columns. High quality mid-C18 interior, the stair hall with open-well cantilevered staircase, the inner hall with central oval and many moulded and carved cornices.

PORTHPEAN HOUSE, Lower Porthpean. A charming marine villa created by two phases of C19 extension of an C18 house, resulting in a grand stucco front facing the sea: two-storey between semicircular end bays except for a middle three-storey section which represents the older house, also seen as a rear wing on the entrance front where it is Pentewan ashlar.

On Black Head, 2 m. S, the MEMORIAL to A. L. Rowse. 1999, a massive granite monolith with exquisite incised lettering designed by *Gerry Breeze* and carved by *Anthony Fanshawe*.

PORTHTOWAN

6040

Former C19 ENGINE HOUSE, almost on the beach. For Wheal Lushington mine. Built for a small enclosed winding engine, with no projecting beam and so gables built to roof height. It was converted *c.* 1960, an early example of reuse as a house and sometime café.

Taking the road inland towards Redruth, the valley meanders through a bleak mining landscape, the ENGINE HOUSES of TYWARNHAYLE copper mine perched on the steep E side. Buildings adjoining the road date from the Royal School of Mines' use of Tywarnhayle (1911–2005) for training surveying students. Where the valley widens stands WHEAL ELLEN ENGINE HOUSE, a distinctive design with a projecting string course of grey brick dividing the modest red brick section of the stack, and an elaborate castellated top.

PORTLOE

9030

2 m. E of Veryan

Still one of the most intact of small Cornish fishing harbours, with limekilns mixed in with former fishermen's cottages.

CHURCH. *c.* 1890. W front with two pointed windows flanking a central pointed-arch doorway, their wooden tracery with trefoil heads surmounted by cusped tympanum arches with side-lights. Octagonal open bellcote with steep roof. Four-bay arcade of round piers on octagonal bases and four-centred arches. – FONT. Late C19, Norman style with two carved heads.

METHODIST CHURCH, E of the harbour. Plain mid-C19. Pointed-arch windows to the chapel over a basement schoolroom.

PORTREATH

A private bathing place for the Bassets of Tehidy (it was originally called Basset Cove, and six small rock-cut baths survive), before becoming a port, like Hayle, for their Camborne–Redruth mines. It was connected to the mining area by the Poldice Tramway from 1812 and from 1837–8 by a branch from the Hayle Railway, Cornwall's second standard-gauge railway and the future GWR mainline. By 1840 it was shipping 100,000 tons of copper ore per year and importing vast quantities of coal. There is still tangible evidence of this history in the modern holiday place.

METHODIST CHURCH, Penberthy Road. Dated 1858, a plain rectangle with tall round-headed windows.

The HARBOUR was begun in 1760 and improved in 1778–81 and 1824. It has curved sides formed by excavation of natural rock, with a short outer bullnose on the N side and a long curved pier on the S, both mostly of large granite blocks. A gated slipway at the SW corner represents the last phase of building in the 1860s. At the inner end a short passage leads to the 'new basin' begun in 1800. Another passage at its inner end opens into the 'inner basin' of 1846, with a slipway in the centre of its landward end.

SE of the basin, and rising impressively S, is the PORTREATH INCLINE of 1837, which formed the final descent of the Hayle Railway, operated by a steam winding engine. The raised lower section crosses Glenfeadon Terrace by a semicircular bridge with granite voussoirs, with another smaller bridge across a stream nearer the bottom.

W of the bridge in Glenfeadon Terrace is GLENFEADON HOUSE, built in the mid C19 for the Bassets. The striking façade is the result of the addition, by the Bain family, shipowners and merchants, of a swanky loggia in the later C19. It rises from a raised ground floor (which is supported on rusticated piers) as an arcade of seven round-headed arches on Tuscan columns mounted on a balustrade and balustraded parapet. The central entrance is approached by a flight of double-returned steps with cast-iron ornamental balusters. The GAZEBO on the corner of the road, once belonging to the house, is a Gothick semicircular turret with triangular-headed lancet windows and an embattled parapet.

PORTWRINKLE

WHITSAND BAY HOTEL. Originally built in 1871 by Lord Graves in Thanckes Field, Torpoint, where it replaced the Graves family mansion and took the name Thanckes House. It was demolished stone by stone in 1909 and re-erected here, opening as a hotel in 1910. Best seen when descending the road from Crafthole, when its four-storey embattled porch tower strikes a dramatic note: otherwise the exterior is rather dull Elizabethan with a symmetrical three-gabled façade to the sea. Remarkably complete ground-floor interior, the fine stained-glass window to the stair showing two galleons in full sail.

On the hotel's golf course near Crafthole a circular DOVE-COTE, C17 with a corbelled stone roof, a striking feature in the landscape.

POUGHILL

ST OLAF. A church of more than usual interest, especially for the evidence of its evolution from the C14 to the C16. C15 W tower of three stages with buttresses leaving the corners free, NE stair-turret and tall crocketed pinnacles: W face decorated with quatrefoils above plinth, E face with image niche at second stage with trefoil head (both a lesser version of Week St Mary). Unceiled wagon roof, richly carved, to S porch and trefoil-headed nodding ogee image niche above S doorway, the late C15 to early C16 plank door on square framing with wrought-iron strapwork. The church, probably originally cruciform, was extended in the C14 with a narrow N aisle on a low four-bay arcade of thick yellow limestone piers: they are of a section inserting a keeled projection l. and r. of each of the standard hollows (cf. St Veep) and with capitals of quatrefoils in roundels. The chancel bay has a slightly lower arch. The E bay of the S aisle is similar, though with trefoil-headed arches to the capitals, indicating perhaps that a matching S aisle was intended but not executed: it was finished in the late C15 or early C16 on taller granite piers of Cornish standard section, the adjustment of height made by an engaged demi-pier supported on the capital of the C14 pier. Curiously, the W respond is also of limestone but of the same Perp design. N chantry chapel widened and re-roofed with Tudor heads facing in different directions as late at 1530–40. Good wagon roofs with some traces of original colouring, the nave–chancel division noteworthy for its decorative carving. Restored 1873, 1882–91 and

1928–29. – FONT. Of table-top type, but with two tiers of blank arcades (cf. Poundstock, St Tudy). The heads of the arches are pointed. – C13 PISCINA. – ALTAR. Replaced with Lord's Table 1550, top renewed 1941. – BENCH-ENDS. A rich array (cf. Kilkhampton and Launcells nearby), some with original benches, of the early C16, and mid to late C16: the former deeply carved with Instruments of the Passion, the latter less numerous with armorial motifs or IHC initials. – Large plasterwork ROYAL ARMS of Charles I with some strapwork decoration (cf. Boconnoc, Kilkhampton, Launcells, Marhamchurch, Poundstock and Stratton). – WALL PAINTINGS. Two large St Christophers, entirely and stridently repainted by *Frank Salisbury*, 1894. – STAINED GLASS. Chancel E by *Clayton & Bell*. – S aisle E, 1860 by *John Hardman*. – Good N aisle window, 1914 by *Kempe & Co.* – N aisle E 1887, by *Frederick Drake*.

Across the road opposite the church, former CHURCH HOUSE, now residential and subdivided. Of early C16 origin but extensive C19 and C20 alterations. Interior retains heavily moulded beams and bressumer with foliage carving.

POUNDSTOCK

2090

The church and medieval guildhouse make a very pretty group, beautifully situated in a little hollow and surrounded by trees.

ST WINWALOE. Fine unbuttressed W tower of three stages, with trefoil-headed statue niche on W wall at second stage and large octagonal turrets with crocketed pinnacles, just as at Jacobstow (q.v.) and similarly late C15 to early C16. Nave, S transept, and N aisle, probably the ghost of a Norman cruciform plan, its N arm incorporated into the N aisle. The aisle is C15, of six bays built in two stages, the two E bays slightly later; the former are Cornish standard, the latter octagonal monoliths with rustic octagonal capitals. *Otho B. Peter* prepared plans for a restoration in 1884 but it was a long campaign of 1892–8 by *G. H. Fellowes Prynne* that gave the interior its attractive character, the church arch with pierced tracery and large angel corbels, with more angels on the chancel wall-plate, familiar from his other work (cf. St Austell and St Columb). – ROOD SCREEN, 1903, LADY CHAPEL SCREEN, 1917, the latter by *Violet Pinwill*. – FONT. Large, square, with two tiers of blank niches with pointed heads, probably C13 (cf. Poughill). – PULPIT. Octagonal, Jacobean. – BENCH-ENDS. A few in the chancel. – CHEST of *c.* 1530–50 in the N aisle, from Parnham House, Dorset, with panels of profile heads in medallions. – WALL PAINTINGS on the N wall. Very faded but iconographically interesting: the Tree of Deadly Sins, the Warning to Sabbath Breakers, and the Weighing of Souls. – PAINTED PANELS of saints, early C16, on board fixed to N wall of nave, formerly part of the medieval rood screen, restored 1985 by *Anna Hulbert*. – STAINED GLASS. Two good medieval fragments in N chancel chapel and S transept. – MONUMENTS. Wall monument, 1638, with moulded cornice and pediment flanked by obelisks and Penfound arms (*see* below). – Several fine slate memorials in N aisle, especially delightful that to William and John Trebarfoote †1628 and 1630 (*see* below) on W wall. – Also Elizabeth Peanet †1720, John Harvey †1669 and Charles Manaton †1732.

60 GUILDHOUSE (locally gildhouse). An exceptionally significant survival of a church house, a once common building type familiar from other SW counties, particularly Devon: this is both an unusually large and extraordinarily well-preserved example. Long two-storey range built into the SW slope of the churchyard so that the upper floor is accessed from ground-floor level. Highly picturesque buttressed elevations with timber four-light mullioned windows, ogee-headed on the ground floor, early C16-looking but mostly repaired 1919 in a meticulous restoration by *E. H. Sedding*. N end has a C16 timber door frame flanked by small two-light windows with ogee heads, the l. one original. Original plan of ten-bay open hall: most of the medieval roof trusses survive, of principals with short curved feet, three tiers of threaded purlins and diagonally set ridge, with traces of smoke blackening throughout. First floor and stack inserted mid C16 (the massive crossbeams dendrologically dated to 1543). It later became the parish poor house, was subdivided for eight families, and partly used as a schoolroom in the C19. In disrepair by the time of Sedding's restoration which gave it much of its present character. Carefully restored again 2005–9 by *Jonathan Rhind Architects*. The outstanding feature of the present interior is the spectacular ROYAL ARMS with strapwork decoration (cf. Kilkhampton, Launcells, Marhamchurch, etc.), originally of Charles I (date 1638 revealed during its restoration), later altered to George IV. It was removed from the church in the 1980s for conservation and restoration by *Hugh Harrison* because of fears of damage by vibration from the sonic boom from Concorde: fitted with a new surround, it was found to be too large to remove through the door to return it to the church.

PENFOUND MANOR, I m. E. One of the oldest inhabited secular buildings in Cornwall. A Domesday manor, held by the wife of Edward the Confessor before it passed to the Count of Mortain. William Penfound was MP for Bodmin in 1431–2, and in 1588 Carew records the family as 'among the chief gentry of the County'. The picturesque front elevation, approached by a courtyard, contains the medieval hall range, with stone of very small dimensions; an off-centre porch with four-centred doorway with inscription in spandrels IN THE YEAR 1642 and C17 sundial in the gable; and a l. projecting gabled wing with four-light ground-floor mullioned window and massive lateral stack. The still open hall has a roof of four C15 smoke-blackened trusses of a base-cruck derivative type, with a further truss at the E end of the 'little hall'. This suggests an original hall length of six or seven bays. Many C16 and C17 features. Also a BATHROOM entirely painted and signed by *David Gentleman*, 1950.

At PENFOUND FARM just to the N a good example of a Victorian planned FARMYARD, built for Edward Mucklow *c.* 1880. Imposing entrance to the yard, the buildings with canted corners, the gateposts with pyramidal caps, and contemporary iron gates. The buildings include the usual wide range of specialist structures.

TREBARFOOTE MANOR, 1 m. W. Former manor house. Early C17 remodelling of earlier building with the S front altered in the C19. Approached through C18 gatepiers and walls. Long seven-window S front incorporating an original three-room through-passage-plan house with rear wings. Roof trusses over lower end of the early C17 with cranked collars. Unusually complete C17 interior including plaster chimneypiece in hall with Trebarfoote quartering Burgoyne and canted ceiling of moulded plasterwork to chamber above. Datestone, not *in situ*, in porch carved WT MY 161 (last number missing), for William and Mary Trebarfoote.

VIADUCT, NE of Woolston Farm, 2 m. NE of church. 1898, carrying the Holsworthy–Bude railway. Rusticated concrete block in Flemish bond, an early use of this material in bridge construction.

PRIDEAUX PLACE *see* PADSTOW

PROBUS

8040

ST PROBUS AND ST GRACE. The glory is its tower, the tallest in Cornwall at over 125 ft (38 metres) high, of three stages, and lavishly decorated, though with more tact and taste than in the Trecarrel buildings in and around Launceston. The leading squire here was John Tregian of Golden (q.v.), and work was in progress in 1523. Its plinth has the not unfamiliar quatrefoil decoration, and another strip of ornament above. The hood-mould of the W door is the upper moulding of this second strip conducted round. On the N and S sides the ground floor has three statue niches. The first string course is again ornamented; so is the second; so are the buttresses, set back from the angles (with pinnacles in relief). The second stage has windows with narrowly decorated belfry windows. But on the third stage are two windows on each side, again with the same ornamentation as the belfry windows. Above are another eight little blind windows and then the decorated battlements and the pinnacles, each with four little sub-pinnacles, a most satisfying fullness of orchestration. The ensemble is not at all Cornish: it is entirely Somerset, especially similar to North Petherton. The body of the church is surprisingly generously spaced. It has two aisles of identical design, buttressed, with not specially interesting side windows, and more elaborate E windows. No transepts, but N and S porches. The arcades are tall, unifying the spatial effect of the church, which is in itself by no means tall. They are of seven bays and have the same Devonshire section of the piers as St Ives of the same date – instead of the usual hollow between the two attached shafts, a wavy curve – and an exceptionally complex moulding of the arches. Tower arch also very tall and has responds with large panelling. Strong late C19 character inside restored by *G. E. Street* 1849–51; chancel elaborately embellished by *J. P. St Aubyn* in 1886 and 1888; S aisle and porch re-roofed in 1893, and extended S as a chapel in 1904. – ALTAR SLAB with five consecration crosses. – PISCINA. Norman pillar piscina in sanctuary, with zigzag decoration. – REREDOS. By St Aubyn, the *opus sectile* work by *J. Powell & Sons*, 1886. – BENCH-ENDS. C16, worked into a rood screen by St Aubyn, 1897, and also incorporated in N parclose screen, choir stalls, and tower screen. – STAINED GLASS. In N chapel, an ambitious 1904 window by *Clayton & Bell*. – Two N aisle windows by *Wailes*, 1858 and 1861. – MONUMENTS. Brass to John Wulvedon †1514 and wife, two figures with inscription beneath, as usual. – Thomas Hawkins †1766, a very good epitaph with a seated mourning figure holding a medallion with Hawkins's portrait, a flying angel above, the whole against the usual pyramid. Attributed to *Nicholas Read* (GF).

In the churchyard, monument to the Hawkins family, 1914, with four kneeling pall-bearers at the corners, as in the Villiers monument in Westminster Abbey.

The large village centres on a steeply sloping triangle of pleasant C18 and C19 houses in front of the church. The schools by *Street* and the parsonage by *Wightwick* have been demolished.

TREHANE HOUSE, 2 m. W. Ruins of red brick country house, dated 1703, gutted by fire 1946 and retained as a garden feature.

TREWITHEN. *See* p. 656.

PRUSSIA COVE

7 m. E of Penzance

So named by John Carter, born 1738, the eldest son of a family of smugglers, because of his admiration for Frederick the Great; Carter became known as the King of Prussia because of his daring encounters with the revenue. Today it remains a miraculously unspoiled microcosm of the old Cornwall so well portrayed by Betjeman in his *Shell Guide*, thanks to the careful stewardship of the Behrens estate.

PORTH-EN-ALLS. The centrepiece of the estate, by *Philip Tilden*, 1910–14 for T. T. Behrens, on the site of the small thatched house of John Carter: this had been replaced 1903–5 by a new villa by *Oliver Caldwell* which Tilden considered wholly inadequate but which he had to build around. A remarkable design of great originality that takes full advantage of its spectacular cliff-edge site overlooking the sea. Approached down a lane along the side of Prussia Cove, the house is completely hidden until, at the last moment, the drive arrives into a low-key vernacular-feeling circular court with the concave-fronted CHAUFFEURS' LODGE on the inland side and the concave walls of the entrance terrace to seaward. But even this is just an announcement, because all that can still be seen of the house is the front door and part of the roof which is clad in Forest of Dean stone slates. The entrance hall too is modest, so that the surprise of the considerable scale of the house is only revealed in the principal rooms on the floor below, which are carried on a three-bay Romanesque-style arcade with three-light bay windows over. This, and the other seaward elevations of the Y-shaped plan, have irregularly disposed features in a kind of free Tudor style, creating a lively composition that sits perfectly on what is an almost sheer cliff face. The interior is of equally varied detail and sustained quality with C17-style joinery, C15 and classical-style features, and unpainted and unrendered walls. Brilliantly conceived and skilfully executed as the house is, with Tilden living on site and famously recalling in his autobiography that it was 'built on lobster and hock', it is only the 'essentials' part of his original grand design, which envisaged the 'wonders', including a great hall with an elaborate arched roof and minstrel's gallery, a grand staircase, a balcony jutting out over the sea, and a subterranean boathouse, never built because of the onset of the Great War: the toothing for the continuation of the house is visible in the ashlar walling at the E end.

The delight of Prussia Cove is, of course, primarily to be found in the natural world but it is subtly enhanced by the picturesque scatter of modest buildings including C18 and C19 houses and cottages like CLIFF COTTAGE, SEA VIEW and WILLIE'S COTTAGE, a terrace of C19 COASTGUARD COTTAGES, and FISHERMEN'S HUTS and FISH CELLARS, the latter partly thatched. At the top of the lane, TRENALLS HOUSE and OLD FARMHOUSE, a small C18 house grandiosely extended by *Oliver Caldwell* of Penzance including a three-storey tower.

QUETHIOCK

3060

ST HUGO. Of more than usual interest for both its pre-C15 features (cf. nearby St Ive and South Hill, and Sheviock) and its later C19 embellishment. A most remarkable and early-looking W end, with a thin W tower rising above the roof of a broader nave, and a staircase tower with a saddleback roof coming up on the r. to the height of the foot of the tower. It has battlements but no pinnacles. The w front is heavily buttressed at the corners. The date is probably C13. The church was appropriated to the Archpriest of Hacombe, Devon, in 1336, and rebuilt in 1344, and there is still a strong sense of the C14 cruciform church with much to be seen: the whole s transept with its angle buttresses, and with a good strong arch connecting it with the nave, and the N transept with the same buttresses, although only a little of it projects out beyond the later aisle. Inside the N transept is an early C14 funeral recess, an ogee arch with crocketed finials (cf. St Ive), finely moulded but badly preserved. The four-bay N aisle is standard Cornish C15. Low undecorated funeral recess in s wall of s transept. The old wagon roofs are specially well preserved. An exceptionally large squint connects s transept and chancel. One can walk into it, for at the same time it gives access to the rood-loft staircase just as at nearby Pillaton. The attractive character of the interior owes much to a sustained campaign of restoration between 1878 and 1888 by *Rev. William Willimott*, who came here from St Michael Caerhays where he had undertaken accomplished embellishment. He worked with *Henry Elliott* as architect. A great deal of the characteristically vigorously carved furnishings are by Willimott, including the ALTAR FRONT, CHANCEL SCREEN and CHAIRS. His also the ambitious and charming scheme of STAINED GLASS with interesting iconography including St Cadoc preaching by a Celtic cross – a few medieval fragments incorporated in the N aisle E window; the TILES and PAINTING of the E wall and REREDOS; and the richly painted CHANCEL CEILING. All of this is appealing, and skilfully fashioned, and, as a complete ensemble of its date, remarkable. – MONUMENTS. Large brass to Roger Kyngdom †1471, his wife and sixteen children. – Brass of 1631 to Richard Chiverton and family, not good. – Tomb-chest with slate top and backplates to Hugh Halkinow †1599.

The churchyard, probably a *lann*, has the tallest WHEEL-HEAD CROSS above ground level in Cornwall, found in the churchyard in pieces and re-erected by Willimott in 1881. Interlace and scrollwork on the shaft and trefoil openings in the head between the arms of the cross, which looks curiously Gothic. Hencken believes a C13 date and a kind of Celtic revival (cf. Padstow).

RAME

ST GERMANUS. Remote, in an exposed position on the peninsula. Bishop Bronescombe consecrated a rebuilt cruciform church in 1259, which was followed by a re-dedication in 1321. Of both periods there is still much to see. The slender w tower, unbuttressed, with no w door, long lancets on its w face, and the pointed arch towards the nave inside are likely to be C13, and the octagonal broached spire with its small lucarnes an addition of the early C14. It is all remarkably similar to Sheviock where, as here, the nave is wider than the tower. The chancel also has C13 work: cf. its two much repaired N lancets, and both this and the N transept may incorporate walling of this date. The N wall of the nave has a two-light Dec window. The rest of the church is mostly C15–C16, with the exception of a Norman tympanum decorated with three circles with four-spoked wheel and four-petalled flower resited on the W wall of the S aisle (cf. Launceston St Thomas). The S aisle of five bays has an exceptional pier profile, circular, with four demi-shafts and simple moulded capitals: the aisle windows are straight-headed. A squint high up connects N transept and chancel. The aisle has a good ceiled wagon roof, the porch roof also C15. The church was restored in 1845 and 1884–5. Wagon roofs to nave, chancel and N transept with moulded ribs and bosses, and ROOD SCREEN, by *Harry Hems* of Exeter. – BENCH-ENDS. The old ones mostly with tracery in the Devon way, not the usual Cornish motifs of shields with initials or Instruments of the Passion, again as at Sheviock. – MONUMENT to Roger Ashton, vicar of St Andrew, Plymouth, †1677, good robust workmanship of its date, with a large cherub's head at the foot.

CHAPEL OF ST MICHAEL, Rame Head. Dramatically sited on the tip of the promontory with commanding seaward views, and used therefore as a watch tower from the medieval period. Probably of Norman origin, perhaps on an earlier hermitage site. Simple, solid, of slatestone rising from a battered plinth, with a stone-vaulted roof. Single cell, possibly once with a W gallery. Large E and S windows, small W window. Within a later Iron Age CLIFF CASTLE marked by a single ditch with causewayed entrance and vestigial bank where the neck of the promontory is at its narrowest.

POLHAWN BATTERY, ¼ m. W. Perched halfway up the cliffs at Whitesand Bay's E end. Built 1861–3 to defend against landings to the rear of Tregantle and Scraesdon forts to which it was linked by the military road (the present coast road). Two-storey, with two wings, limestone and granite exterior, brick vaulting to the interior. The exterior is protected by rock-cut dry ditches. Released by the War Office in 1928, it was in private residential use and is now a hotel.

QUEEN ADELAIDE'S SEAT, Penlee Point, 1 m. ESE. A Gothick grotto at the furthest point of Mount Edgcumbe's landscape. Open pointed arches with rubble voussoirs. Richard Hewlings suggests it might be mid C18.

REDRUTH

7040

The sea of C20 development that swept Redruth up with Camborne and the settlements between into Cornwall's largest

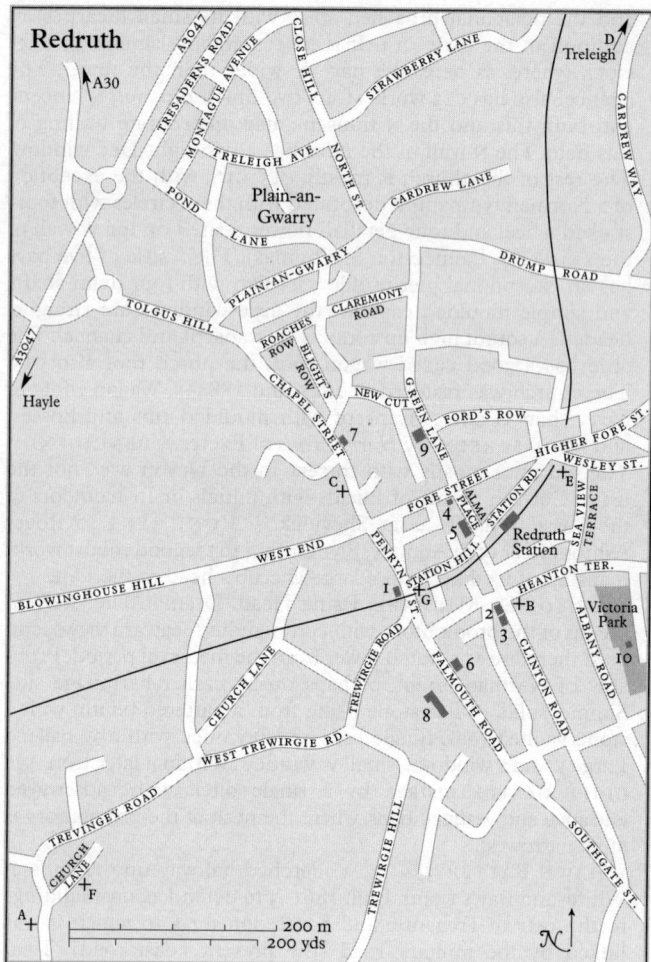

Redruth

A30

Treleigh

Plain-an-Gwarry

Hayle

Redruth Station

Victoria Park

200 m
200 yds

A   St Euny
B   St Andrew
C   St Mary (former)
D   St Stephen, Treleigh
E   Redruth Methodist Church
F   Quaker meeting house (former)
G   Baptist chapel

1   Town Hall (former)
2   Passmore Edwards Free Library
3   School of Science and Art
4   Clock tower
5   Town Market
6   Fire station (former)
7   Police station (former)
8   Trewirgie School
9   Masonic Hall
10   War memorial

conurbation, with a population of over 45,000, provides an unprepossessing setting for one of the county's most singular historic towns. Its plan shows its origins as a planted medieval settlement, and its role as the capital of the greatest of all the mining areas in the industry's C18 and C19 heyday is well represented, but what is most memorable is its distinctive architectural personality, which reflects an extraordinary renaissance in the later C19 after mining had collapsed and the pervasive influence of one architect, *James Hicks*.

Redruth lies below the granite heights of Carn Brea (q.v.) to the SW and Carn Marth to the SE on part of the mineralized shelf sloping N to the sea that is shared with the rest of the conurbation. The church, a mile SW of the town centre, may have been settled from the C6 on an early Christian *lann*. The C14 new town was located at an early river crossing in a deep N–S valley and the intersection of two major land routes: the E–W spinal road and the N–S Portreath to Falmouth road, the modern junction of Fore Street, West End, Chapel Street and Penryn Street. The town developed as one long street running E–W down a steep hill as Fore Street and up again as West End, with other early streets off the lower part of Fore Street.

Though Redruth's first market and fair charters are of 1533, it never attained borough status. Tin streaming was significant from the medieval period and Redruth became an important market town in the later C16 and C17, but the early C18 saw it develop as the administrative and financial hub of the burgeoning mining industry, as new technology allowed ever deeper mine working: Tonkin, writing in 1739, reported 'This town is of late years grown very considerable. It owes its rise to the great confluence of people drawn together by the mines of tine and copper with which it is surrounded . . . it is chiefly of one large street, nearly half a mile in length.'* A new settlement had also developed N of the town at Plain-an-Gwarry by that time. Ancillary metal industries expanded within the town, including iron and brass foundries, wire works, stamps, blowing houses and hammer mills. Its early C19 expansion was stimulated by improvements in transport brought about by the advent of the railways. An early initiative was the railway to the quays at Devoran (q.v.), horse-drawn from 1826 with steam locomotives from 1854, followed, more importantly, by the beginnings of what was to develop into the present mainline railway. This opened in 1837, mainly to carry copper ore from its terminus at the W end of the town to Hayle harbour, with branches serving mines and the quays at Portreath (qq.v.). Passengers were carried along its main route. Growth continued through the economic peak of mining in the 1850s when the area was producing two-thirds of the world's copper, assisted by a second phase of the development of the railway network, to Penzance and Truro in 1852 with a new station near the top of the town, and connection to the national system in 1859. It was on the railway from Perranarworthal to Hayle in 1870 that Francis Kilvert memorably wrote in his diary of 'the bowels of the earth ripped open, turned inside out in the search for metal ore, the land defiled and cumbered with heaps and wastes of slag

---

*Davies Gilbert, *The Parochial History of Cornwall, founded on the manuscripts of Mr William Hals and Mr Thomas Tonkin* (1788).

and rubbish, and the waters poisoned with tin and copper washings'.

From the 1870s, just when the economic downturn hit many other mining towns hard, Redruth began a remarkable transformation. The explanation for this 'apparent paradox of a growing town at the epicentre of the mining collapse' has been ably demonstrated by Ronald Perry and Sharron Schwartz.* The town's diverse industrial and commercial base meant it was not solely dependent on mining, allowing the development of other enterprises, including the processing of agricultural products and tourism, which had been impossible when mining dominated all: for example, the West of England Bacon Curing Factory, the largest in Cornwall, was located here in the early 1890s, and the Redruth Brewery was operating nearly two hundred public houses, inns and hotels all over Cornwall by 1895. The other explanation is the inflow of money from abroad. The spread of Cornish mining expertise and manpower overseas generated substantial mining investments by Cornishmen who either remained in Cornwall or retained strong links with their native county. Substantial funding was remitted to Redruth both from migrant workers and from investors in foreign mines.†

The result was a building boom. New banks, mining offices and a Mining Exchange, shopping emporia and a rebuilt market house were matched by churches and chapels, schools, a public library, the largest Masonic Hall in Cornwall, and other social and cultural buildings like the Temperance Coffee Tavern in Alma Place. Many were designed by *James Hicks* who, as chief agent for Lord Clinton, also laid out one of the most ambitious residential developments of that period in Cornwall on Clinton's land on the town's SE outskirts, around Clinton Road and Albany Road, for Redruth's significant managerial, professional and trading class: such was Hicks's dominance that this part of Redruth was dubbed 'Hicksville'. It is Hicks's rich, stylistically diverse and largely intact architectural achievement that recent regeneration has allowed to shine out once again after the town had suffered decades of decline in the C20.

CHURCHES

ST EUNY. Outside the town in its churchtown, set within a lovely embowered churchyard. The tall, elegant late C15–C16 W tower of granite ashlar has buttresses set back from the angles and angel corbels to the corners of the embattled parapet, from which crocketed pinnacles crown slender turrets. In surprising

---

*'James Hicks, Architect of Regeneration in Victorian Redruth', *Journal of the Royal Institution of Cornwall Journal* (2001).
†This is reflected in the names of many terraces and houses, e.g. Akankoo Place in Southgate Street, named after mines on the Gold Coast of Africa; Huasco House in Falmouth Road after a rich silver mining district in Chile; Kolar Villa at Pool, Balaghat House at Southgate, and Mysore Villa at Mount Ambrose, all connected to Indian mines; and Montana at Portreath New Road and Phoenix Villa in North County, which show United States connections.

contrast, the body of the church, of nave and N and S aisles, is a classical building of 1768, of a distinctly urban character eloquently expressive of the town's prestige at that time. It is externally of two storeys divided by a low first-floor band with small sashes below and tall round-headed windows above, mostly small-paned, surmounted by a dentilled cornice: the triple-gabled E end has matching fenestration to the aisles and a Venetian window in the wider centre. The interior is charming, simple Georgian, spacious and lofty, the aisles of five bays of Doric columns on tall stylobates with square entablatures supporting the heavily moulded longitudinal beams to a panelled flat ceiling. The double-chamfered two-centred tower arch has semi-octagonal responds. Restored by *James Hicks* in 1878 when the W gallery was removed. – FONT, granite, presented by Hicks. – C18 polychrome on slate DECALOGUE, LORD'S PRAYER and CREED. – MONUMENTS. Mostly of the 1820s and 1830s, including a good relief bust and tablet to William Davey †1827 by *Chantrey*: Davey did much to improve the working conditions of miners. – Other wall monuments by *Theakston* of Pimlico and *Pearce* of Truro. Against the N wall of the tower is a primitively carved demi-figure from a Norman corbel table, a reminder of the original Norman church, the plan of which (with an apse) has been excavated.

The CHURCHYARD is approached through a splendid C18 Gothic LYCHGATE, the wide semi-elliptical entrance archway surmounted by an embattled parapet with obelisk finials. The granite coffin rest is of such extraordinary length that it protrudes at the W end, presumably for multiple burials after mining accidents. The extensive churchyard contains the graves of many emigrant miners, and a modest gravestone to James Hicks †1896, with wide mossy paths leading out towards the slopes of Carn Brea.

ST ANDREW, Clinton Road. 1881–6 by *James Hicks* with *J. P. Seddon* of London and *Sydney Toy*, Seddon's Redruth-born assistant; completed 1937–8 to a design of 1927 by *R. F. Wheatly* of *Cowell, Drewitt & Wheatly* of Truro. Free E.E. style, completed in strict E.E. As Canon Alan Dunstan observed, compared with the sober and solid Nonconformist chapels and the simple classicism of St Euny, St Andrew 'represented in 1883 just what people thought a church should be, with worship developing along Tractarian lines'.* Plan of nave, N and S aisles, and N transept. Partly in pink Carn Marth elvan from Hicks's quarry, but mostly polychrome killas with granite dressings. Built into the steeply E–W sloping site, deployed to great effect in the gabled W end which is a splendid two-storeyed presence to Clinton Road. It rises between prominent angle buttresses flanking a shallow porch set against a slightly projecting screen with small coupled lancets and blank arcading. Above is a large five-light window with circular tracery, surmounted by a

* 'The Church among the People', *Journal of the Royal Institution of Cornwall Journal* (2000), pp. 125–41.

stepped triple lancet in the apex of the gable. The composition is supported by the w ends of the N and S aisles which have stepped parapets, slightly set back. The nave and aisles are of seven bays, the w four original, the E three added, the buttressed aisles with small windows with trefoil heads, the pilastered nave with stepped triple lancets, but simple lancets in the added bays. The N transept has set-back buttresses, a tall single lancet in the gable wall, and an octagonal turret at the junction with the nave. The added two-bay chancel, in similar style, has two lancets each side and an E window of three cusped lancets. The fine interior is richly articulated: the aisle arcades of two-centred arches are slightly recessed behind granite piers, quatrefoil to the springing, the inner shafts continuing as coupled engaged columns terminating in massive rough-hewn granite capitals below the level of the windows: the upper windows are set behind an arcade of two-centred arches between which the line of the piers is continued as slender coupled sunk shafts with a simplified version in the added bays. At the w end an elaborate FONT on a stepped platform in front of a three-bay arcade opening on to steps to the basement. The basement houses many facilities – crypt, vestries, Sunday School and meeting rooms – missing in earlier churches.

Former ST MARY, Chapel Street. 1827–8 by *Charles Hutchens*, as a chapel of ease to St Euny and the Anglican presence in the town centre. Plain Commissioners' Gothic, the street elevation modestly enlivened by a slightly projecting centre that rises above the gable to battlements, a four-centred window with cusped tracery and thin diagonal buttresses at the corners with set-offs and pinnacles. The windows introduced for conversion to residential use strike a discordant note.

ST STEPHEN, Treleigh. 1865–7 by *J. P. St Aubyn*. E.E. on a cruciform plan with shallow transepts and apsidal chancel. Lancet windows, gabled bellcote, and a low porch with diagonal buttresses and good details.

REDRUTH METHODIST CHURCH, Wesley Street. Dated 1826 in the gable. A proud, plain rectangle of six by eight round-headed windows, an enlarged edition of the typical Cornish Methodist chapel. The pedimented façade has a four-bay ground-floor arcade on slender Tuscan columns between projecting porches. The interior, which seated over 1,300, has a continuous gallery on fluted iron columns with foliated capitals, the gallery front with rounded open panels with cast bronze openwork. Ornate late C19 pulpit and organ case on a gallery above. Adjoining it, and more than holding its own, is the WESLEYAN CENTENARY MEMORIAL HALL, dated 1891, by *James Hicks*. A strong façade in free classical style, symmetrical with an open-pedimented centre reinforced by a rock-faced plinth, rusticated rock-faced quoins, and banded rock-faced pilasters to the centre. The wide and slightly projecting centre forms a porch with two Doric columns flanking steps to the large round-headed doorway. First-floor Venetian window.

Former QUAKER MEETING HOUSE, Church Lane. 1814. A plain, solid rectangle with sash windows, much like St Austell and Truro. A nice example of a modest Quaker chapel.

BAPTIST CHAPEL, Penryn Street. 1876 by *James Hicks*. Nicely proportioned plainish Gothic with a strong vertical emphasis that stands up well against the towering viaduct behind.

PUBLIC BUILDINGS

Former TOWN HALL, Penryn Street. 1850 by *Robert Blee*, a Redruth-born architect. An elegant classical front in granite ashlar with a wide recessed porch with Doric columns, and a frieze of triglyphs and wreaths.

PASSMORE EDWARDS FREE LIBRARY, Clinton Road. 1894 by *James Hicks*, perhaps his best civic building. Part of an imposing group with the adjacent buildings by the same architect (*see* below), and a worthy counterpoint to his St Andrew's church opposite. A splendid composition in a castellated baronial style, two-storey and four bays, the ground floor much buttressed. The two-bay centre is flanked l. by a projecting gable with a canted oriel window on a buttressed column and r. by a three-storey octagonal tower rising to an embattled parapet and surmounted by a pyramidal roof with elaborate weathervane. The tower houses the former main entrance, approached via wide sweeping walls and a flight of steps. The reading room was formerly the Thomas Collins School, 1891, where Collins, the ex-headmaster of Trewirgie School, taught children of emigrant Cornish parents alongside local children. Now linked to the l. by a poor 1970s entrance foyer to the former OFFICE built by *Hicks* for his own use, a fanciful confection of granite and pink terracotta in charmingly eclectic Renaissance style, the attic stage with a shaped gable, and a nice contrast with its more assertive neighbours.

Next to this is the former SCHOOL OF SCIENCE AND ART. 1882–3, also by *Hicks*, with extensive additions for its subsequent use as the School of Mines. A simplified and even more robust version of castellated baronial with buttressed ends to the front elevation. Strong central entrance between large granite columns carried up as corbels to support a tall canted bay with a round-headed tripartite central window under a large gable. Smaller gables to flanking windows. The r. wing (now a restaurant) was added in 1889 by the Miners Association of Devon and Cornwall as a MUSEUM in memory of Dr Robert Hunt, Keeper of the Mining Record Offices, London.

CLOCK TOWER, Fore Street. *See* Perambulation 1.

TOWN MARKET, Station Hill. Rebuilt 1877, possibly by *Hicks*. The plain exterior encloses a delightful rectangular market with open arcades on slender granite columns with workshops above, and a more substantial market house with a formerly open four-bay arcade on square granite piers. A further arcade leads through to Fore Street.

Former FIRE STATION, Falmouth Road. Built *c.* 1900. Tall single storey with two large wagon doorways and a small octagonal turret with pyramidal cap.

Former POLICE STATION, Chapel Street. 1908. An innovative complex built as a court room, two cells and houses for an inspector and six constables.

TREWIRGIE SCHOOL, Falmouth Road. 1886. An enlarged version of the usual plan but distinguished by an unusually picturesque bell-turret, rising through an octagonal middle stage to a delicate flèche over the open-arched bell housing.

MASONIC HALL, Green Lane. 1876 by *James Hicks*. Then the largest in Cornwall. Striking street elevation in an eclectic style containing classic pilasters with triglyphs and stiff-leaf capitals and Gothic pointed-head windows above, and incorporating finely sculptured panels depicting different trades, flanked by heraldic arms. The most richly decorated, and successful, component is the entrance to the r., a wild mix of architectural motifs around an ogee-arched doorway, flanked by pink inset columns, which breaks into a panelled first floor, the arch crowned by a figure sculpture.

RAILWAY STATION, Station Hill. Opened in 1852. One of the best-preserved stations in Cornwall, with surviving canopies both sides, the down-side waiting room restored, and linked by the latticed footbridge of 1888. w of the station is the VIADUCT, also 1888, by *P. J. Margary* for the GWR. The tall battered piers support eight segmental-headed arches in rock-faced granite blocks from Hick's Carn Marth quarry, carrying the railway line 80 ft (24 metres) above the Falmouth Road and Penryn Street. The piers of *Brunel*'s fan viaduct remain alongside.

WAR MEMORIAL, Victoria Park. Of *c.* 1920, octagonal obelisk on a tall square pedestal with a chamfered base and diagonal buttresses.

PERAMBULATIONS

1. Fore Street to West End and adjoining streets

For a prospect of the essential topography of the historic centre on its long spinal E–W route, start at the top of FORE STREET at its junction with Higher Fore Street, Station Road and Wesley Street, where the Methodist church and Wesley Centenary Memorial Hall are an emphatic presence (*see* Churches). Fore Street quickly begins its steep descent w with mostly mid- to late C19 shops and houses on both sides. On the r., tall granite GATEPIERS are all that survives of the late C19 United Methodist Free Church, one of the largest in Cornwall, demolished in 1973. Further down, evidence of the former hotels and coaching inns of the C18 town. First the RED LION HOTEL, probably late C18, remodelled in the C19. Six-bay stucco front with banded corner pilasters. Next the LONDON HOTEL, late C18, with a central carriage passage and a wide

Doric porch to the r. topped by decorative ironwork. On the corner of Fore Street and Alma Place (*see* Perambulation 2), Nos. 70 and 72, one of the finest buildings of late C19 Redruth's commercial zenith, built in 1870 by *James Hicks*, his first commission in the town, as a three-storey SHOP AND WAREHOUSE for Samuel Trounson. It was extended l. in 1890. Granite ashlar ground floor and red, buff and yellow brick above in a robust Venetian Gothic. Elaborately detailed, the extension with squat bulgy columns in pink granite, with bands of blind arcading between the floors, the upper floors having giant composite pilasters, the windows with set-in shafts, and crowned by a large modillioned cornice topped by white brick pedestals bearing carved stone finials. On the opposite corner with Alma Place, the CLOCK TOWER, the indisputable centrepiece of the town, visible at every turn and like a Cornish version of the Palazzo Vecchio tower. It is of 1828, but altered 1836 and rebuilt and raised 1900. Ashlar granite in four stages, the ground floor with diagonal buttresses and large, formerly open, two-centred arches, each succeeding stage slightly set back above a weathered band and surmounted by a slightly oversailing embattled parapet.

Running s, GREEN LANE has a few pleasant early to mid-C19 houses, the Masonic Hall (*see* Public Buildings) and the former RADICAL CLUB, 1886, with a two-storey, three-window front and vermiculated quoins. Off Green Lane too, a small diversion l. to SYMONDS TERRACE, with nice early to mid-C19 houses in two paired terraces.

Return to Fore Street. On the r. Nos. 23 and 24 are two *c.* 1700 houses, the first floors slate-hung, with long rear wings. The street widens slightly downhill as the ghost of the former market place around the former KINGS ARMS HOTEL. Mid to late C18 three-storey symmetrical five-bay front, the centre between narrow single-bay projecting wings, all sash windowed. The central entrance has a ground-floor arcade formed by a carriage entrance under a semi-elliptical arch flanked by square-headed doorways. Further down, the NATWEST BANK was built as the Devon & Cornwall Bank in 1888 by *James Hicks*. Tall three-storey Renaissance front, central first-floor oriel with a balustraded parapet and Ionic pilasters to the second floor enriched with palmettes. Next door Nos. 9 and 10, another splendid late C19 pair of shops in an eclectic style, the upper floors in red and yellow terracotta, with large semicircular-headed windows to the first floor, and a turret to the l. corner finished with an octagonal lantern with a copperclad cap and finial. To the n off CROSS STREET is MURDOCH'S HOUSE, the home of William Murdoch, inventor of gas lighting and builder of the first working model steam locomotive. A plainish two-storey house with an external stair to the first floor. In front is a medieval cross with stubby limbs, and behind are the ruins of DRUIDS HALL, the C19 town's principal library and assembly rooms, destroyed by fire in the early 1980s. Finally in Fore Street, the splendid REGAL

CINEMA of 1935 by *W. H. Watkins* of Bristol, with a striking Art Deco façade complete with tower and the cinema name set between horizontal streamlining. The circular foyer, with its original Art Deco floor, disguises the angled set-off of the auditoria behind. Just before this on the r., LEMIN's COURT, a rare survival of the formerly numerous crowded courts behind Fore Street.

The ascent of WEST END begins w of Chapel Street and Penryn Street. It developed strongly in the mid C19 around the terminus of the railway to Hayle (now the car park opposite the entrance to the Penventon Hotel) as the business and banking quarter of the town. On the l., No. 3 is an early pair of three-storey houses in plain classical style with a shared recessed porch. On the r. and l., the former REDRUTH DRAPERY STORES, 1886, rebuilt 1916, the grandest example of the emporia built at the peak of Redruth's late C19 flowering as a retail centre: the premises on the l. have full-height glazing to ground- and first-floor showrooms, those on the r. giant granite columns to the entrance. On the l., Nos. 9 and 10, a handsome very early C19 pair of former houses and offices; No. 11 was the studio of James Chenall, an early photographer, who lived here from 1875. Tall three-storey front of granite and Pentewan ashlar in classical style with giant pilasters to the upper floors rising to a panelled parapet interspersed with short balustrades. The entrance retains its original wrought-iron railings. Opposite, Nos. 55–57, and further up on the l. more Edwardian emporia. On the r. the OLD TRAM OFFICE, the terminus of the Camborne–Redruth Tramway, the only street tramway in Cornwall, which ran from 1902 to 1927.* Then the character of the street changes as the terraces give way to the former larger houses of the local magnates. TOLVEAN, 1870, remodelled by *James Hicks* for Alfred Lanyon, with Hicks's name on the front door, has an elaborately detailed front with slim colonettes with foliate capitals to its plethora of windows, including a two-storey central canted bay with six lights on each floor. Off West End to the r., in spacious grounds, the PENVENTON HOTEL, 1830–5 for John Penberthy Magor, proprietor of the Redruth Brewery, purchased by Arthur Carkeek in 1891. The original stucco classical building is almost subsumed in modern extensions. Nearby ST JOSEPH's CONVENT. Mid-C19, fine classical elevations, the s front with a wide pedimented centre broken forward with a prominent bay window below, the outer windows with pedimented architraves. Beyond, on the r. above the road, is the impressive pile of the former GRAMMAR SCHOOL, 1907. Opposite, behind Penventon Terrace, two buildings remain from the former Redruth Hospital: the MINER'S HOSPITAL, 1863, and the WOMEN'S HOSPITAL, 1890, with inscriptions over their entrance doors. They are now absorbed into an 'urban village', developed 2002–6,

---

*Uniquely in Britain, goods traffic was also carried, ore being taken for processing at Tolvaddon. This continued until 1934.

in the quaint style of Poundbury, Dorset, with the familiar faux motifs.

Back down West End with good views of the steep rise of Fore Street opposite, then l. at the crossroads into CHAPEL STREET with the former St Mary's church (*see* Churches) prominent on the l. Beyond a good trio of early C19 villas with neat classical fronts and hipped roofs with deep projecting eaves. Opposite, the ROSE COTTAGE TAVERN, probably mid-C18, extended and altered: long, low two storeys. Return to the crossroads into PENRYN STREET, created in its present form in 1763 as part of the turnpike to Falmouth. It begins well with the BRITISH LEGION CLUB, a former house of *c.* 1800, of plain classical design. The ruins of Druids Hall (*see* above) are opposite. The best building here is the former Town Hall (*see* Public Buildings). Off into STATION HILL l., Nos. 1–4 form a good group of early to mid-C19 houses in simple classicism. No. 1 is lower and slate-hung; No. 2, the former SAVINGS BANK, stucco with channelled corner pilasters and a wide ground-floor loggia with two pairs of Doric columns *in antis*, and swept and ramped wrought-iron railings between the columns. Nos. 3 and 4 in Pentewan ashlar on a slope so that the basement of No. 3 is exposed, with a shallow recessed porch with a semi-elliptical arched architrave containing coupled doorways and ground-floor windows in shallow recesses. Return downhill where, as the railway viaduct (*see* Public Buildings) soars above, FALMOUTH ROAD begins with Nos. 2 and 4, a pair of mid-C19 shops, No. 4 slate-hung with good C19 shopfronts, a feature of the town generally. Then the old fire station (*see* Public Buildings), and further down on the r. the flèche of Trewirgie School beckons, making a good end point (*see* Public Buildings).

2. The late nineteenth-century town and 'Hicksville': Alma Place, Station Road, Station Hill and Clinton Road

Begin at the N end of ALMA PLACE, created as a major concentration of late C19 civic buildings to shift the commercial focus of the town from West End to near the new railway station, opened in 1852. Like the warehouse and clock tower already described on Fore Street, at the entrance to Alma Place, most of the buildings are by *James Hicks*, beginning with the former COFFEE TAVERN on the W side, dated 1880, as part of the Temperance establishment. Lively medieval-style front, two-storey, with a tall gabled centre breaking slightly forward with a wide entrance and set-in colonettes; large two-centred arched window above and surmounted by an apex finial with flanking pinnacles. The ogee cresting over the entrance arch is flanked by large panels, the inscription with foliation interlacing raised lettering. The other first-floor windows have triple-arched lights with colonettes. The r. end is chamfered and has a highly decorative corbelled oriel rising to a conical roof. Next the

former POST OFFICE and BAIN & FIELD's BANK, also possibly by *Hicks*. Two-storey eight-bay stylish Renaissance front.
Alternate bays have round-headed doorways, the intermediate
bays large tripartite windows to the ground floor, and two
canted oriels above. Then the former MINING EXCHANGE of
1880, built as one with the adjoining OFFICES on the l. of the
Wheal Peevor mine. Single-storey symmetrical classical façade,
of charmingly small scale, the large round-headed central
doorway with set-in colonettes with carved foliated capitals
and foliated panels in the soffit. Above the dentilled cornice
and the entablature, the inscription is surmounted by a segmented pediment with the Cornish arms and rising to a ball
finial. The adjacent offices are similar but with a panelled
entablature with a central roundel and a triangular pediment
with an apex finial. At the S end of Alma Place, up STATION
ROAD to the station (*see* Public Buildings), and, opposite, a
pair of former OFFICES, single-storey, in a delightful eclectic
style. The l. office has large symmetrical-head sashes, the central
door with an elaborate architrave surmounted by a pediment
breaking the eaves with the date 1891. The r. office, of the Malayan
Tin Dredging Co., is similar but with coupled segmental-headed
windows and a central Jacobean-style gablet containing stepped
triple recesses and flanked by pedestals bearing small urns.

Now S of the railway bridge along BOND STREET towards
CLINTON ROAD. On the l., the two-bay corrugated-iron
former GWR BUS GARAGE, 1904, and then a nice run of
modest two-storey shops and houses makes a good approach
to Clinton Road, spacious and tree-lined. At the start, the view
up BASSET STREET, a good street of modest late C19 houses,
with the CHIMNEY of the Pednandrea Mine still forming an
eyecatcher on the hill behind, although much reduced from its
original 145 ft (44 metres). Clinton Road begins with the
definitive Hicks ensemble of St Andrew's church, the Passmore
Edwards Free Library and former School of Mines (*see*
Churches and Public Buildings). Then the VILLAS, of excellent
quality, much variety and nicely detailed with porches, bays
and gables in an enjoyable mix of Gothic and classical styles:
they were known as 'Clinton Castles' when first erected.
PENARTH, next to the church, in French Renaissance style,
was Hicks's own house. The villas were built by redundant
miners and funded by public subscription. It is well worth
exploring the grid of more modest streets built parallel to
Clinton Road along and across the contours for a sense of the
social gradations of the late C19 town.

PLAIN-AN-GWARRY. ½ m. N. Tonkin wrote in 1739: 'to the south
of Treleigh are a long row of houses belonging to the barton, on
a level piece of ground called Plain-an-Gwarry (a level for sports)
from a round in the middle for a public playing place'.*

* Davies Gilbert, *The Parochial History of Cornwall, founded on the manuscripts of Mr
William Hals and Mr Thomas Tonkin*, 4 vols., London, (1788).

The main street, of an almost rural character, is of modest two-storey houses set back behind long front gardens with the MINER'S ARMS on the N side and the looming bulk of the METHODIST CHAPEL at the E end. This is of 1883–4 by *James Hicks*. Large Italianate front with rusticated ground floor, tall first-floor windows, the eyecatchers the pyramidal finials to the central pediment and balustraded flanking bays. The hamlet continued to grow throughout the C18 and C19 with further rows of cottages along KING STREET, BLIGHT'S ROW and FOUNDRY ROW. To the W off CHAPEL STREET the extensive site of the former REDRUTH BREWERY, founded in 1742, which prospered from serving thirsty miners to become regionally important. It was closed in 2002, but the offices, c. 1860, originally built by the British & Foreign Safety Fuse Co. and set at right angles to TOLGUS HILL, remain. In the late C19, CLAREMONT ROAD was developed with semi-detached and terraced housing linking the settlement with Redruth.

TOWN MILL, Tolgus place. ¾ m N. A former corn mill converted for foundry use in 1860 by William Sara. It was worked by his family until the end of the C20. A complex of buildings and sheds, of simple rough stone and slate, corrugated iron and timber weatherboard construction, as was once typical of small industrial sites all over Cornwall. The foundry was water powered and became known for the manufacture of waterwheels. Tin stream works existed all the way down to Portreath. They survived at TOLGUS TIN, still water powered, until 1968. Much of the equipment is similar to that at King Edward Mine (*see* Camborne), but here it is housed in a series of corrugated-iron and timber-clad sheds. The impressive CORNISH STAMPS, probably the only surviving, show how tin ore after initial crushing was further reduced to the consistency of sand before being separated out by its physical property of being heavier. The drum is turned by a 14-ft (4.3-metre) overshot WATER-WHEEL, probably built by Sara's Tolgus foundry.

RESTORMEL CASTLE   *1060*

Standing high on the E slope of the Fowey valley, Restormel was   51
long considered by far the most perfect example of medieval military architecture in Cornwall. But more recent analysis of its fabric and landscape setting has suggested that by as early as the end of the C13 its function was less as a military stronghold and more as a magnificent fortified hunting lodge, which overlooked an extensive deer park that stretched down the valley to the new administrative centre of Cornwall at Lostwithiel (q.v.).* It had

*This account is indebted to *Restormel Castle, Cornwall: A Reappraisal*, by N. Thomas with E. Berry and O. Creighton (1993–4), a research report for English Heritage.

originated as a relatively small ringwork-and-bailey in the late
CII or early CI2 to guard a crossing of the Fowey. At this time it
belonged to the Cardinhams but, after briefly passing to Simon
de Montfort in 1265, it was granted to Richard, Earl of Cornwall,
the younger brother of Henry III, in 1268. Richard, who died in
1272, initiated the rebuilding of the keep in its present form, and
his son Edmund, who died in 1300, completed the project as a
symbol of the family's power and status in Cornwall.

Even in its ruined state, the castle still evokes its original dominance of the landscape, sitting on a natural spur of which the
SHELL-KEEP occupies the high point. From the W (bailey) side
the castle can be easily approached but on the other sides the
slopes are steep, especially E to the river. The spur has been
artificially scarped and a circular ditch or moat dug, about
60 ft (18.3 metres) wide and 30 ft (9.1 metres) deep, around
the keep. Nevertheless the defences at Restormel, and especially those of the bailey, are much less substantial than those
at Launceston, Trematon and Totnes. The circular keep is
110 ft (33.5 metres) in diameter within, the original height
27½ ft (8.4 metres). Outside there is a sheer wall all the way
round, except for the gate to the W, and the chapel tower nearly
opposite to the NE that projects a little into the moat. The
whole inner face of the keep was covered by a complete range
of domestic buildings typical of a major medieval house but
fitted into this circular space instead of on the usual rectangular plan, with partition walls radiating from the centre of the
ward. That these, and the projecting chapel, are not later additions to the outer wall as previously supposed but constructed
with it, is suggested by the bonding of the structures with the
wall and proved by the existence of large original window
openings in the outer walls of the hall, solar and chapel, the
latter's E window built not of stone but timber.
   Surviving traces of the earlier castle include the bailey
rampart, building platforms within the bailey, and the well and
three stone-built structures, possible bases for towers, within
the keep. The earliest standing fabric is the early CI3 GATE-
HOUSE, its fine inner arch of Pentewan stone clearly a later CI3
addition to the original build. From the gatehouse, the principal rooms, at first-floor level and mostly above cellars or small
rooms, follow each other round anticlockwise. The first room
was either the GUEST CHAMBER or GUARD HALL, only accessed
from the stair to the wall-walk, lit by two two-light windows
with seats overlooking the courtyard, but with no fireplace. The
next room, the most northerly, was the most private CHAMBER
in the castle, lit by two windows overlooking the courtyard and
a larger arched window in the outer wall. It was only accessible
from the adjoining ante-chapel and originally had an elaborate
fireplace in its W wall. The ANTE-CHAPEL was lit by a window
to the courtyard, and led to the CHAPEL with its large and
originally decorative three-light E window (subsequently
blocked during the Civil War), two blocked openings or niches

in the N and S walls, and a piscina. Next was the SOLAR or INNER HALL, lit by a large window with window seat in the external wall. It would have been heated by a fireplace in the lost radial wall and had stairs within the thickness of the keep wall which allowed access to the wall-walk, possibly for watching the chase. This room was connected by a doorway to the HALL, which had two large arched external windows and a fireplace in the inner face of the keep wall. The main access was from a wide first-floor doorway from the courtyard, leading into the SCREENS PASSAGE and adjoining a small SERVICE ROOM above the SERVERY and KITCHEN.

The way in which the shell-keep at Restormel was, at least in part, consciously reconstructed in its late C13 form as the centrepiece of a designed medieval landscape has regional parallels with Tintagel, where the dramatic coastal scenery was harnessed to the Arthurian legend in the C13 rebuild, also by Richard, and Launceston, with its C13 cylindrical *donjon* also commanding views over its deer park (qq.v.). And the rebuilding of Okehampton Castle, Devon, in the early C14 similarly created a stronghold on the principal approach road but a domestic face where it looked into the deer park. By the C16 the castle was in poor repair and, apart from a brief flurry of activity during the Civil War, the subsequent history was of neglect until in the late C18 it was incorporated as a picturesque ruin into the romantic landscaped garden of Restormel Manor (*see* below).

RESTORMEL FARMHOUSE. Immediately E and below the castle. The striking feature is the early to mid-C18 BARN, in brick and architecturally treated: U-plan with shallow wings to front l. and r. with hipped roofs over each, segmental-headed door and cart openings, blind windows for symmetry, modillion cornice and pigeon holes.

RESTORMEL MANOR. Further E and close to the river. Pretty early Gothic Revival (*c.* 1760s) refronting of the mid- to late C17 house, battlemented and with white Gothick sash windows (cf. Tregenna Castle, St Ives). Fine mid-C18 open-well stairs with contemporary decorative plaster ceiling over earlier plasterwork. The garden was created by William Masterman *c.* 1784.

RIALTON MANOR

1 m. SE of St Columb Minor

The remains of the once substantial house of Prior Vivian of Bodmin (q.v.), who liked to spend his time here, and of great charm inside and out. A manor of Bodmin Priory, it is of C15 origin extensively altered and enlarged by Vivian in the early C16 but later reduced to a farmhouse with C18–C20 alterations. The main feature of the exterior is the impressive porch,   55 two-storey, wide, and crenellated, added in front of the medieval hall range. It has a four-centred arched doorway on standard Cornish piers and inside a tunnel-vaulted roof of moulded ribs which, owing to the closeness of the transverse arches, looks like a wagon roof in stone. At first floor, three mullion-and-transom windows, all of three lights. Between the two l. windows is a wide mullion with two vertical panels with blind cusped arches, the mullion to the r. similar, with only one vertical panel. Lattice glazing with early C16 iron stanchions. Below the l. window a stone quatrefoil originally lighting the stair.

Inside, the former cross-passage and room to the r. are all now one. Three heavily roll-moulded beams. To the l., a room with three chamfered beams and basket-arch fireplace. Narrow doorway to former stair-tower with chamfered surround and four-centred arch. Four bays of the hall's wagon roof survive; carved ribs and wall-plate and carved bosses, with cross-braces between the ribs. The room over the porch has a stud partition with a four-centred arch to the former stair at the front. In the window, early C16 armorial stained glass.

The front of the house is enclosed by a courtyard of slate-stone walls with granite dressings, incorporating some medieval masonry, entered through a four-centred arched door with recessed spandrels and roll-moulding, probably resited. Two other four-centred arch doors.

The courtyard also contains a little free-standing HOLY WELL. C15 with corbelled stone-roofed well-house with gable-ends: the front gable has a four-centred arched opening with roll moulding and hollow chamfers, the roof with moulded granite coping. Inside, the whole floor is the well, with an image niche at the rear.

INSCRIBED STONE in the wall of a farm building: BONE MIMORI ILLI (FILI?) TRIBUNI, in Roman capitals, C5 or C6.

ROCHE

So called from the fantastic outcrop of jagged schorl to the SE of the village, a phenomenon as impressive now in an industrial landscape as it must have been in the solitude of the Middle Ages. The cliff rises almost vertically against the backdrop of the vast spoil heaps of the china clay workings as if it were some C19 Victorian play of fantasy in a public park.

Perched on top of the cliff is the roofless ST MICHAEL's CHAPEL, licensed in 1409, the fusion of building and rock so complete that it is initially difficult to see where the living rock ends and the walls begin. It consisted of a lower room with alcove and piscina and the chapel proper above. The whole looks very much like a three-stage Cornish tower with the usual string courses between. The carrying up of the blocks remains a feat to be wondered at. No ornamental detail of importance survives but the stark simplicity of the ensemble is unforgettable.

St Gomonda (St Gonand). There was a cruciform church here by the mid C13 but it was extensively altered to a rectangular plan in 1822 and then restored to its original form by *J. D. Sedding* in 1890. Tall w tower of three stages, C15, granite, with buttresses set back from the angles: of the same proportions as St Stephen's, Launceston. It rises to large angel corbels as at St Mabyn (q.v.) to support pinnacles, now lost. The body of the church is essentially medieval: the lower half of the N wall of nave and chancel may be C13, the N transept and its arch C14, the s wall of the s aisle Perp. Sedding's achievement is in the interior, plain and uncluttered, even austere, but in its honest simplicity striking and successful. The six-bay arcade, removed in 1822, was reconstructed by him in Polyphant stone, the wagon roofs reinstated and the fine large E window inserted, of six cusped lights and Y-tracery; similar but smaller window in the E end of the s aisle. Other windows of 1822, with intersecting tracery. – FONT. Norman, almost exactly like   23 Bodmin, circular bowl with angels' heads at the corners, and between them interlaced snakes (and on the w side a curious motif like an oblong envelope). Below them stylized lilies. Repaired by Sedding. – PULPIT. Large octagon in smooth Polyphant on a plinth with a flight of steps, open-sided with moulded piers and decorated panels. Probably by Sedding.

On the s side of the churchyard, a tall CROSS, wheel-head type but with an almost square head, very primitive decoration with four irregular circular depressions. Shaft decorated with groups of small holes of crude form with incised lines separating the groups. In field E of the churchyard, another wheel-head WAYSIDE CROSS, equal-centred cross, with plain shaft. In the garden of the former rectory, a short Latin WAYSIDE CROSS.

HOLY WELL, ½ m. NW of the railway station. Of medieval origin, built into the bank, simple Gothic-arched well-house.

CARBIS WHARF, 1 m. E of the village. Rare survival of three beehive KILNS of the late C19 Carbis brick and tile works. Only one retains its domed brick roof. Square chimney. Two other chimneys also survive.

ROSCARROCK

2 m. w of St Endellion

9070

A cluster of stone and slate farmstead buildings in a fold in the open landscape above Port Quin shelters one of Cornwall's most memorable houses. Roscarrock, the home of the eminent family of that name from the C11 until 1673 (cf. St Endellion), is a large late medieval gentry house on a courtyard plan with main ranges facing SE, SW and NE, and the NW side closed by an embattled curtain wall.[*] The play of patinas of its weathered building materials on its many-faceted elevations make it immediately loveable.

The SOUTH EAST RANGE, by which the house is approached, has a polite symmetrical front with decorative banding of alternate courses of granite ashlar and squared slatestone, a contrast with plain rubble walls to the E. This range contains the principal rooms that resulted from an extensive remodelling of the whole house in the 1840s, with decorative joinery and plasterwork of that period. The refitting, however, completely conceals one of the best early C16 roofs in Cornwall, originally over an open hall, the upper end to the W, the service end to the E with an unheated service room beyond. Of thirteen trusses, it is of cruck-like appearance but technically comprised of principals with short curved feet. The principals have cambered collars and are joined at the apex by unnotched mortice-and-tenon joints held by a single peg. Each truss has upper arch braces, with the lower sections of the arches fashioned from the curved feet of the principals. Each bay originally had three sets of curved wind-braces, the top tier to the ridge. This is comparable to the roofs of Cotehele and Trecarrel (qq.v.).

The NORTH EAST RANGE comprises an unusually large kitchen with a very high ceiling, lit by a long sash window, and with an impressive range of three fireplaces in an axial stack that backs onto a former brewhouse, both dating from the mid-C19 refurbishment.

The SOUTH WEST RANGE is of great interest with several features without close parallels in Cornwall. Built at the same time as the SE range, it was improved in the mid to late C16 to provide highly prestigious accommodation at first-floor level at its N end. In the 1840s almost the whole of this wing was converted into a malthouse, the existing floor and fittings stripped out and two floors inserted (using some decorative joinery from the SE range), with a kiln provided by re-fitting a pre-existing small block adjoining to the N.[†] It has recently been returned to domestic use in a thoughtful restoration by Robert and Kate Sloman that has retained evidence of the building history. The range has a central cross-passage with wide and high opposing doorways large enough to take a mounted rider. The door arches are not exactly Tudor, three-centred with spandrels carved with a distinctively angular three-leaf motif. The courtyard wall, like the inner face of the adjoining N curtain wall, was built to a high standard in contrasting colours of green and purple-grey volcanic and slatestone. The external wall is plainer,

---

[*] This account is much indebted to the report of 1997 by John Thorp of John Thorp's Keystone Consultants.

[†] The malthouse, kiln and brewhouse, combined with the cultivation of hops in the sheltered market gardens at Port Quin (q.v.), make the brewing operation at Roscarrock a highly unusual, large-scale enterprise.

apart from an exceptionally fine bay window which projects   69
from its N end and originally overlooked pleasure gardens to
the W with views out over Port Quin bay. This is part of the
mid- to late C16 re-fitting which also provided a fireplace in
the gable-end wall and other first-floor windows. The window,
of granite ashlar, has four main lights and single sidelights, with
hollow-chamfered mullions and round-headed lights with
sunken spandrels below a frieze of zigzag ornament. Above this
the frame has a moulded cornice. The zigzag frieze is repeated
around the granite ashlar chimneyshaft. Inside, the original
roof survives from end to end, of twelve bays and similar in
design and construction to the SE range, though smaller and
not as consistently decorated. It was unequally divided into a
seven-bay S section and a five-bay N section by a full-height
stone wall. The S section was the plainer, the N section richer
with cranked collars with a curving soffit which continues into
the principals to create a continuous arch and, originally, wind-
braces. Both sections were built two-storey, the ground floor
for stables and storage. The function of the upper rooms
remains uncertain but what is indisputable is the superior
quality of the smaller N room behind the bay window.

The original purpose of the small adjoining NORTH BLOCK is
also unclear. It adjoins the handsome NORTH WEST CURTAIN
WALL which has massive ashlar granite crenellations. Both
have small squint windows, strategically placed for defensive
purposes: although the defensive efficacy of this arrangement
was limited, it demonstrates a common design feature of
Cornish houses of this period.

Directly W of the SW wing is an impressive court of C19 PIGSTIES,
and beyond a WALLED GARDEN with high walls except on the
S side which is formed by a RAISED WALK, similar to those at
Godolphin (q.v.), part of the C16 pleasure grounds.

ROUGHTOR   *1080*

3 m. SE of Camelford

PREHISTORIC REMAINS. A remarkably well-preserved series on
the hill that was the focus of the positioning and design of
prehistoric monuments over much of east Cornwall.

The remains can be described in the form of a 4 m. perambulation beginning at the car park ¾ m. SE of Roughtor Farm.
From here the hill's three peaks run N to S: Showery Tor, Little   4
Roughtor and Roughtor. Note a broad stony bank on lower
slopes to l. and numerous round-houses and enclosures to r.:
the 419-yd (383-metre) long bank has three straight stretches,
the lowest-lying and longest aligned on Showery Tor's cheesewring (a natural stack of granite slabs). Prehistoric PASTURE
BOUNDARIES attached to it confirm an early date. Much wider
than a boundary (up to 14 ft (4.3 metres) between kerbs), this

later Neolithic BANK CAIRN was probably walked along. After 250 yds (230 metres) it narrows slightly (suggesting a second-ary phase) and changes course towards Little Roughtor, with its own cheesewring. The final 90 ft (27 metres) points, less certainly, to a third cheesewring between Little Roughtor and Roughtor. Walking uphill, ENE, l. of Showery Tor, past numer-ous oval and round Early Bronze Age CAIRNS, some superim-posed on early, possibly Neolithic, FIELDS. One can continue to a large solitary CAIRN on a rimmed platform on the ridge of the rounded Roughtor Downs. Extensive views include Bodmin Moor's most famous cheesewring, on distant Stowe's Hill. Head S towards Showery Tor's own cheesewring (soon obscured by intervening rocks) and enjoy its sudden reappear-ance when climbing to the top. A Bronze Age RING CAIRN respectfully encircles the remarkable stack, which may have been regarded as the work of giant ancestors. Cross to Little Roughtor's beautifully kerbed CAIRN (Bronze Age) apparently deliberately obscuring its cheesewring, a very different response to Showery Tor. Notice three sinuous stony banks skirting the top edge of natural clitter on the hill's NW side linking Little Roughtor to Roughtor. They, and others on the SE side, form a fine TOR ENCLOSURE, apparently not a defended space, but a special hilltop area, probably used for community gatherings. HOUSE PLATFORMS are visible towards the S end. Climb to more CAIRNS and broad-banked ENCLOSURES at Roughtor's summit. Here are footings of the late C14 CHAPEL (St Michael) erected by Sir Hugh Peverell, Lord of Hamatethy. Downhill from the tor enclosure to the SE side is a line of small Bronze Age CAIRNS running along the contour and then curving SW to a large Middle Bronze Age SETTLEMENT. Some ROUND-HOUSES are conjoined; others have smaller later prehistoric huts, probably used by seasonal herders, built inside. Several ovoid and curvilinear enclosures, those to the E overlain by later medieval strip fields containing narrow lazy beds (plant-ing ridges). On the return to the car park along the lower W slope are an early modern granite STONE WORKING (cider mill stones, troughs, millstones, gateposts, etc.) and small sub-rectangular early medieval TRANSHUMANCE HUTS. Pass two CAIRNS, to reach a straggling Bronze Age SETTLEMENT with over one hundred ROUND-HOUSES within or edging sub-circular enclosures. At each house the bank cairn is seen on the distant skyline. The MEMORIAL downstream from C19 Roughtor Ford granite bridge is to Charlotte Dymond, mur-dered here in 1844.

LOUDEN HILL LONG CAIRN, ¼ m. SW. Early Neolithic. Stony mound on hill's lower NE slopes, overtowered by Roughtor. Oriented N–S, 115 ft (35 metres) long with low kerb slabs and hints of internal structures or compartments, now resembling rooms. Downhill from ruined medieval farming settlement with two LONGHOUSES, outhouses and corn-drying barn, pos-sibly associated with Henry Cauvel, free tenant at 'Lauedon' in 1288.

FERNACRE STONE CIRCLE, ½ m. s. Early Bronze Age. Cornwall's largest stone circle, 153 ft (46.5 metres) diameter. Irregular, with stretches almost straight and the sixty-three surviving stones (thirty-eight still standing) varying considerably. Carefully placed on a broad plain so that the peaks of Roughtor, Brown Willy and Garrow are due N, E and S respectively. Low outlying standing stones to E and SE and low platform CAIRN to S.

GARROW TOR SETTLEMENTS, ½ m. s. Over 180 prehistoric ROUND-HOUSES in seven discrete groups, several demonstrably multi-period. This description runs roughly anticlockwise from S. A medieval field system covers most of the S and E slopes: low stony banks define irregular strips running downhill and containing spade-dug lazy beds and stone clearance heaps. Above the track at the S end a small group of Middle Bronze Age ROUND-HOUSES reused in the Iron Age, possibly by transhumants, who built the ENCLOSURE wall linking most houses. More ROUND-HOUSES and irregular fields on higher SE slopes.

Garrow farmstead, downhill from a ruined medieval hamlet, has a small C17 FARMHOUSE on the lower end of a medieval LONGHOUSE; collapsing early modern BEEHIVE HUT SW of farmhouse. The post-medieval enclosure above the farmhouse contains a remarkable sequence of dwellings whose dates extend occupation back more than 3,000 years. Five other ruined longhouses in the lower part include one excavated with hearthstone in the dwelling room, and mangers complete with hand-drilled tethering holes in the lower room, the cowhouse. Entry passage's opposed doors now partly blocked. Uphill is a medieval CORN-DRYING BARN and a probably early medieval sub-rectangular TRANSHUMANCE HUT. In the enclosure's upper half are several typical Middle Bronze Age ROUND-HOUSES and three Iron Age or Roman period houses of a form peculiar to Garrow, termed by their excavator CORRIDOR-HOUSES. Outer rings of upright slabs are concentric to what are probably inherited Bronze Age houses; the function of the narrow, tightly curving spaces remains unclear. Climb W to the summit ridge and another settlement, with ROUND-HOUSES and 'CORRIDOR-HOUSES' within very small banked enclosures, all overlain by modern drystone pasture and field boundaries. More prehistoric settlements on NE and W slopes. The beautiful summit tors may have been manipulated by prehistoric people.

RUAN LANIHORNE

ST RUMON. On a wooded promontory of the Fal near a small quay. Low single-stage W tower with buttresses only at the foot and meeting at the corners, with battlemented parapet and crocketed pinnacles: it is C13 with two tiers of single-light windows, the upper part rebuilt in 1675. Nave, chancel, N aisle, S transept with S porch added 1699. C13 two-light lancet to S wall of nave (probably re-set), four C15 Perp windows in N wall of nave and W window, E windows C19 Dec. The interior reflects extensive but thoughtful restoration of 1866 by *Edmund Sedding* that included rebuilding of the aisle arcade, re-roofing throughout, and rearrangement and re-flooring of the chancel. The two-centred tower arch is low and unmoulded. Aisle arcade of six bays with standard Cornish piers with four capitals and bands of decoration between capital and abacus, the detail different on each capital; the arches four-centred. The C19 arch-braced roofs incorporate carved bracing from the original wagon roof and carved wall-plates; the porch roof of reused common rafters. – FONT. Square, with quatrefoil and ogee arch decoration: C14. The cover is made up of wall-plates from the old roof. – PULPIT. Hexagonal, of bench-ends of *c.* 1530 with Renaissance shell motifs. – COMMANDMENT TABLES and CREED painted in a *Volkskunst* manner: probably early C19. – The ALTAR and LECTERN also incorporate C15 roof carpentry. – MONUMENT. Fine effigy of priest with hands in prayer under a trefoil arch, no doubt C13.

OLD PARSONAGE, NNE of the church. Former rectory, 1850, by *William White*. 'One might almost mistake the perspective we have seen of it for an old building; it is so irregular and picturesque. We have some fears that this might, in reality, appear exaggerated.' This was the comment of *The Ecclesiologist* in February 1850. The anxiety was unfounded. White's achievement is a building of well-proportioned ranges and romantic silhouette in his inventive Gothic that bears comparison with his intended bishop's palace at St Columb Major (*see* p. 523). It is on a lesser scale, and on an L-shaped rather than quadrangular plan, but there is the same variety of elevation and architectural detail to convey the purpose of different parts of the building as well as implying a complex historical evolution. Here the touches include cusped windows to the staircase and ventilators to the kitchen to indicate their varied function as Pugin had advocated. The stucco and timberwork on the garden front are unfortunate later additions but the interior retains excellent detail including a stair with a two-centred arch springing from two levels and a corbelled and arched fireplace to the W room.

METHODIST CHAPEL and MANSE, 1 m. SE. Dated 1869, the ensemble on a characteristic road-junction site. Gothic style, apsidal E end and ramp linking chapel to first-floor doorway of manse. The W front is especially appealing with its pointed-arch door, flanking single-light trefoil-headed lancets, diagonal corner buttresses and rose window, set behind granite-coped boundary walls and railings.

RUAN MAJOR

ST RUMON. In an unassuming way one of the most memorable
churches in Cornwall, not so much for its architecture as its
elegiac ambience. Deserted during the C20 (cf. Merther), its
tower and bare ruined walls lie embowered in fields and trees
among the luxuriant wild flowers of its churchyard, with only
farm buildings nearby.* There was a church here by 1208 but
its character was drastically altered in a radical reconstruction
of 1866–7 when the late C15 to early C16 S and N aisles were
removed, their blocked arcades now forming the external walls,
and the S porch moved. The arcades are standard Cornish but
the porch has panelled jambs just like Breage, Constantine,
Cury, Mullion, and the great hall at Godolphin. The low doorways interrupting the arcades gave access to the rood screen,
portions of which were still in place sixty years ago. W tower of
serpentine and granite blocks; plain and unbuttressed, like the
neighbouring towers on the Lizard. It may have a C14 lower
stage and a C15 upper part. The font is at Ruan Minor (q.v.).

RUAN MINOR

ST RUMON. A tiny church, first mentioned in 1277, in an exposed
position near the S tip of the Lizard. Solid little C15 tower of
only one stage built of great blocks of serpentine, and creeper-
clad (a welcome exception in Cornwall). It is very plain, unbuttressed and has no W door. Much of C14–C15 character remains
in the body of the church though there was a thorough restoration of 1853–4 with re-roofing, re-flooring and re-seating, and
in 1879 the chancel was extended and raised to a higher roof
level than the nave. The nave is very low, the N aisle of only
four small bays of standard Cornish design and the detailing
of minimum elaboration; the diminutive scale of the arcade
(the arches are no more than 10 ft (3 metres) high) is partly
the result of the pier bases being buried by the raised floor
level. Before the restoration the E bay of the arcade was narrower and lower, usually associated with a former rood loft.
The two-light Dec window at the W end of the aisle was originally the E window of the chancel and when it was rebuilt the
mullion was turned inside out. There is also a simpler and less
restored window of similar C14 date in the centre of the N wall,
presumably *ex situ* as the other detail of the aisle is C15,
including a blocked N doorway with a late C15 or early C16
head. – FONT. Norman, small, with a simple chevron motif,

---

*Pevsner in 1947 found it 'so little visited that at the time of writing a white owl
was nesting in the timbers of the S porch roof'.

much re-cut. – C13 PISCINA with chip-carved saltire crosses, set in a later chamfered arch, as if formerly a pillar-piscina, remodelled when the chancel was extended in the C14. – LECTERN. 1893, of polished red and green serpentine from the former serpentine manufactory at nearby Poltesco (q.v.). – In the tower COMMANDMENT BOARDS, dated and signed 'Oliver Hill 1677'. – STAINED GLASS. Chancel E, 1909 by *Kempe & Co.*, commemorating the death of a sixteen-year-old boy from a fall from the cliffs near Carleon Cove. – S nave 1926, by *E. M. Stevenson Rex & J. Vicat Cole*, a lovely composition with excellent figures and exquisite detail including local scenes as background. – S nave 1947, by *Wippell*, indifferent. – FONT. Outside the porch. C19 in C14 style, from Ruan Major (q.v.).

ST AGNES

The large parish was one of the great tin and copper mining districts with eight other settlements, like Mithian (q.v.), outside the main centre of St Agnes village, which is gathered around the churchtown. From the C17 it had its own harbour at Trevaunance Cove, which was repeatedly damaged by Atlantic storms and eventually washed away in the early C20. The population peaked at nearly 8,000 in 1841 but sunk to 2,500 by 1881, a collapse still strikingly evoked by the thick scatter of abandoned chimneys and engine houses in the almost treeless landscape, some in, or very near, the heart of the village, and visible at every turn.

CHURCHES AND PUBLIC BUILDINGS

St AGNES, Churchtown. A medieval chapelry to Perranzabuloe (q.v.). Excavations in 1931 revealed the foundations of a pre-C15 aisleless church but this was replaced by a second church in 1481. This was itself completely rebuilt in 1848 by *J. P. St Aubyn*, except for the tower and spire. W tower of two stages with diagonally set corner buttresses and embattled parapet from which rises a broach spire (rebuilt in 1905). St Aubyn's work is in the Cornish Perp tradition with traceried granite windows, four-centred arched doorways, and five- and six-bay arcades to N and S aisles. – FONT. C15, octagonal, of Catacleuse, with quatrefoil motifs. – LECTERN. 1906, a fine Art Nouveau angel. – POOR BOX held up by the figure of a hungry man, probably Elizabethan, with traces of paint. – STAINED GLASS. Good N aisle window of St Agnes, 1936 by *Theodora Salusbury*, in the Arts and Crafts style. – By the S porch, which is linked to the vestry by a timber slype, a pre-Conquest

WHEEL-HEAD CROSS with cross pattae, the top and r. side mutilated.

METHODIST CHURCH, British Road. 1860 datestone. A large chapel, two-storey with two tiers of round-headed windows and a handsomely proportioned front with a triangular pediment. The gallery was floored over in 1964 to create a still gracious first-floor worship area retaining the tiered seating, with parish rooms beneath. Adjacent is the village's extensive GARDEN OF REST and park.

CHURCH HALL, Vicarage Road. Late C19. An Arts and Crafts composition, the E end with three-light traceried window flanked by trefoil-headed single-light windows at lower level, a timber-framed S porch, stone lateral stack and bellcote near the centre of the roof.

MINERS AND MECHANICS INSTITUTE, Vicarage Road. Dated 1893, by *W. J. Wills* for J. Passmore Edwards as reading, billiard and committee rooms. Elaborate symmetrical front of three bays, the central door bay with pinnacles and shaped finial, the flanking window bays with stepped tripartite mullioned windows with round heads. The interior is planned around a central lightwell. The front is bounded by ornate cast-iron railings on rock-faced granite walls.

OLD SCHOOL, British Road. Built *c.* 1874, possibly by *J. D. Sedding*. An impressive design, satisfyingly composed with engaging Gothic detail. Steeply pitched roofs crowned by an octagonal bellcote with spirelet and a Dec traceried gable-end window, and prominent tapering lateral stacks in diagonally set brick. Fine cast-iron railings surmounting the granite coped walls to the road.

MUSEUM, Penwinnick Road. 1877 by *E. R. Jones* of Plymouth. Built as a pair of mortuary chapels. A small-scale pretty Gothic composition, with tall gables to each elevation embellished with cusped and pierced bargeboards. The front has single lancet windows and twin porches with scissor-braced gables and cross-braced and arch-braced sides.

PERAMBULATION

CHURCHTOWN has good groupings of late C18–C19 buildings around the W end of the church, with several good shopfronts. By the lychgate, BANK HOUSE, early C19, built as the Capital & Counties Bank (founded 1834), of two storeys over a basement, the central door approached by a flight of steps. Opposite, the three-storey sash-windowed ST AGNES HOTEL, probably C18, remodelled *c.* 1830. N of the church the former VICARAGE, late C19, of the plainest Gothic with a pointed-arched doorway. To the NE on Town Hill, STIPPY-STAPPY is a nice terrace of nine virtually identical early to mid-C19 two-bay cottages stepping steeply downhill. They were built by the harbour company of Trevaunance Cove. SE of the church behind the Old School in British Road (*see* above), a terrace

of Edwardian COASTGUARD COTTAGES and a smart COACH-
HOUSE with office above.

Of the former mining industry, WHEAL KITTY, ¼ m. E, is an
exemplary conversion of 2005 of a former mine, including an
ENGINE HOUSE into office and workshop accommodation
with shed-like WORKSHOPS added tactfully between the original buildings by *Lilly Lewarne* of Truro. Numerous scattered
engine houses and stacks can be seen from this high point. On
the opposite side of the deep and wooded Trevaunance valley,
WHEAL FRIENDLY, and rich tin mines, known as ROYAL
POLBERRO CONSOLS after Queen Victoria's visit in 1846. On
Turnavore shaft the house, still roofed, is built of the usual
rough killas with granite and brick dressings but has a red brick
pointed-arch window in the back wall. Further W, WEST
WHEAL KITTY, near the Methodist church, is now surrounded by bungalows, and looking inland, GOONINNIS, a
trial mine that produced nothing, but left a fine engine house
with distinctive castellated stack of 1899, set in fields (its 50-in.
(1.25-metre) cylinder engine was built in 1863 by Harvey's of
Hayle, and later worked at a china clay pit until 1955). A
further ¼ m. NE down steep hills leads to TREVELLAS
COOMBE, with tin stream-workings right down to the sea. The
engine house of BLUE HILLS MINE remains, and a short way
upstream the remains of one stream works has been developed
and opened to the public to illustrate the processing of tin with
water-powered stamps, through to smelting and casting small
items in Cornish tin.

WHEAL COATES, 1 m. W, below St Agnes Beacon. One of the
best places to appreciate the remnant coastal industrial landscape, with spectacular views and the shell of the TOWAN-
ROATH ENGINE HOUSE perched dramatically on the cliffs
below, now restored by the National Trust. Never prosperous – for
tin or copper – the mine finally closed in 1889, leaving remains
of the WINDING ENGINE and STEAM STAMPS above the cliffs.
The drainage adit can be seen from the beach at low tide.

ST ALLEN

ST ALLEN. In a lovely remote position. A tall W tower in three
stages with buttresses set back from the angles: an exceptionally tall crenellated NE stair-turret rises above the crenellated
parapet and terminates in a conical spirelet. The N side has a
remarkable blocked late C12 or early C13 doorway with remains
of colonettes of one order and round-arched head with chamfer
enriched with nailheads. The r. capital belongs to the lively
kind of stiff-leaf as it is familiar at Wells, Somerset. On the N
side of the chancel also is an E.E. lancet window: Sedding
regarded the W doorway of the tower as E.E. too. There is a
pretty early C16 porch. After such a fine exterior the interior

disappoints: it was the subject of a major restoration including new roofs, floors and furnishings in 1873–4 and more recent additions at the w end. s aisle running almost the full length of the church with a six-bay arcade of Cornish standard design with four-centred arches; it was added by 1508–11 and then used as the Bevill family chantry. – FONT. Octagonal, re-cut and remounted in the C19, with C17 ogee cover with ball finial and enclosed in an early C19 balustrade with narrow pointed arches. – READER'S DESK has front of c. 1570–1600 from a three-decker pulpit of 1638, panelled and carved with three flat consoles. – ROYAL ARMS of Charles II, dated 1660. – STAINED GLASS. Chancel window, 1862 by *Lavers & Barraud.* N window of nave, 1889 by *A. L. Moore & Co.* – MONUMENTS. John Martin †1626, a slate slab unusually cut to fit the sloping sill of the N middle window, with excellent foliage decoration and lengthy inscription. – COFFIN SLAB, C13, with elaborate cross. – In the churchyard, three early medieval CROSSES, the best s of the s aisle, a tapered monolith wheel-head with a cross pattae on each side and groove running down the shaft to form a margin. Two other wheel-head cross-heads, one exceptionally large s of the tower, the other near the e end. Sturdy LYCH-GATE of C15 origin.

ST ANTHONY-IN-MENEAGE

7020

ST ANTHONY. In a delightful waterside location among trees and a few cottages, best approached by the narrow lane alongside the little Gillan Creek. The w tower, of elegant proportions and rising serenely almost from the water's edge, is Perp, three stages of very fine-grained ashlar granite blocks, and boldly embattled with the pinnacles on angel corbels (cf. Mawgan-in-Meneage etc.). Of the cruciform C13 church, the chancel with an E.E. window and portions of the s wall of the nave and s transept survive. The C15 s porch is attached to the transept, also as at Mawgan. The buttressed N aisle has a five-bay arcade on plain octagonal piers with plain double-chamfered arches, probably late C14 or early C15, and an external door to the rood stair. Fine wagon roofs in nave, chancel and N aisle, richly carved. – FONT. C15, circular, with shield-holding angels, but not as severely hieratic as, for example, at St Ives. The inscription reads: 'Ecce Karissimi De Deo Vero Baptizabuntur Spiritu Sancto' (Behold the beloved of the true God shall be baptized with the Holy Spirit). Between the angels are the initials QP, BM, BV, PR. The base of a C12 font found in the churchyard is nearby. – REREDOS in N chancel chapel, a panel depicting the Last Supper, said to be from Newstead Abbey, C14 or C15. – In the E wall of the transept, relief CARVING of the Last Supper, C15, German. – C13 STOUP, resited in porch. – PULPIT. 1950 by *Violet Pinwill.* – GLASS. Chancel E, fragment of medieval glass but otherwise 1890 by *Heaton, Butler & Bayne*. – S aisle, 1994 by *David Peace*, etched, a charming composition of a set of bells in ringing position with ropes and sallies and inscription (cf. St Merryn and Porthilly). – By the SW corner of the tower the resited remains of a medieval cross-head with face carved on one side.

ROSKRUGE BARTON, 1 m. S. Late C17 gatepiers announce a late medieval house that evolved from the late C16 to early C18. Picturesque elevations with C17 chambered porch and mullioned windows: one small C16 window with ogee head. Irregular plan but with a recognizable through passage, hall, parlour and rear service wing with cellar. Late C17 open-well staircase, C17 barrel ceiling in one chamber, and C18 panelled doors with a mix of Mannerist and classical motifs.

ST ANTHONY-IN-ROSELAND

8030

ST ANTHONY. Set in a lovely location at the head of a small creek opposite St Mawes but, except for its spire, hidden from view by Place, the home of the Sprys (*see* below), which lies like a screen between it and the water. Much restored in 1850 for Sir Samuel Spry by his cousin, the amateur architect the *Rev. C. W. Carlyon*, in his engaging version of Gothic. It is still the best example in Cornwall of what a parish church might have looked like in the C12 and C13, unique in the county as the only medieval church to retain its original crossing tower on a cruciform plan, and the only one to be physically attached to a house.

This was originally the church of a small Augustinian priory, a dependent of Plympton Priory. It was re-dedicated by Bishop Bronescombe in 1259, the likely date of the crossing tower and N transept. The walls of the tower were slightly heightened in 1850 and carry a broach spire with four lucarnes. The outstanding feature of the exterior is the Norman S doorway, greatly restored and re-set but with those at Kilkhampton, St Germans and Morwenstow one of the finest in Cornwall: one scalloped colonette each side, an outer ring of zigzags (cf. St Cleer and St Martin-by-Looe), an outer and an inner order of crescents filled with stylized foliage, and an Agnus Dei in the centre. Other than blocked windows in the tower, all the windows are 1850 in the E.E. style. Inside, the E and W tower arches are genuine C13: inner chamfered orders carried on slender shafts with roll-moulded bases and beautifully carved stiff-leaf foliage capitals, both arches terminating in small heads. The N and S arches have chamfered orders carried on foliate corbels without shafts below. In each arm of the transept a trefoil-headed PISCINA, the S one re-set. In the S transept also the rear arches and jambs with nook-shafts of the E and W windows seem C13, re-set. Carlyon's roofs are arch-braced with exaggerated dog-tooth detail to the wall-plates, the tower roof a fine piece of mid-C19 carpentry, springing from carved corbels. The character of the interior owes much to the coloured glazing in rich reds and blues in interlaced and rounded designs, the complete scheme of floor tiling, and the furnishings of octagonal PULPIT, PEWS, COMMANDMENT TABLES and REREDOS, all designed by Carlyon. – Nice Art Nouveau ALTAR RAILS. – Ten Spry MONUMENTS in the N transept including: Mary Gayer †1656, black marble tablet. Arthur Spry, 1685, an elaborate marble composition. Sir Richard Spry by *Richard Westmacott*, 1755, with Britannia leaning on an urn with the Spry arms, and a low relief of one of his ships. Thomas Spry, Admiral of the Red, †1828 and wife, 1835. Impressively large, by *H. Hopper* of London, in white marble with figures of barefoot sailor and a girl supporting the memorial tablet, the Spry arms above surmounted by flags and naval trophies.

In the churchyard, E of the church, granite monolith COFFIN, round-headed and tapered. Medieval.

The priory buildings have gone except for some fabric in the adjoining wing of PLACE, to which the church is connected by the N transept and by a door at the E end of the nave, from where a short flight of steps leads to a room with massive cross-beams of the late C15 or early C16. Otherwise the complex structural history of the house is unclear. After the Reformation, Place was successively owned by the Godwin, Fortescue and Vyvyan families until becoming the home of the Sprys from 1649: Sir Samuel Spry, MP for Bodmin, thoroughly remodelled and extended the house *c.* 1840 and later,* giving it its copy-book but somewhat lifeless French Gothic façade. The eye-catching feature of the front, especially from across the estuary, is the central porte cochère rising three storeys to a square-plan spire designed no doubt to complement the church: it has pointed-arched openings and diagonal buttresses. Central doorway with Gothic fanlight and detail. All the windows have arched lights and moulded hoodmoulds, some incorporating the Spry family motto; the ground-floor windows have central mullions with carved capitals.

The lawn in front of the house was a mill pond for a tide mill. Its DAM of *c.* 1856 has in its N wall a stream exit arch with granite voussoir and flanking pilaster piers with granite quoins rising above wall level.

St ANTHONY's LIGHTHOUSE. 1834–5, by *James Walker*, engineer of Trinity House, the builder *Olver* of Falmouth. A pretty composition of octagonal tower on four floors surmounted by a twelve-light lantern with weathervane and paired chimneys to the landward side; there were living quarters for two keepers. Moulded spray-deflecting cornice with simple parapet balustrade. Above the lighthouse is St ANTHONY BATTERY, an artillery battery and magazine in use from the early C19 until

---

*Tenders were invited for alterations in the *Royal Cornish Gazette* of 15 October 1858; the architect was *W. G.* or *E. Habershon* of London.

the Second World War. Single-storey officers' quarters just beneath the summit, with panoramic views over the Fal estuary and Carrick Roads.

ST AUSTELL

Situated on the southern edge of the vast spoil heaps of the china clay country, St Austell is Cornwall's largest town and displays more vividly than any other the enduring relationship between mining and the county's urbanization. While other mining industries have gradually declined and vanished, the development and continued success of the china clay industry allowed the town to

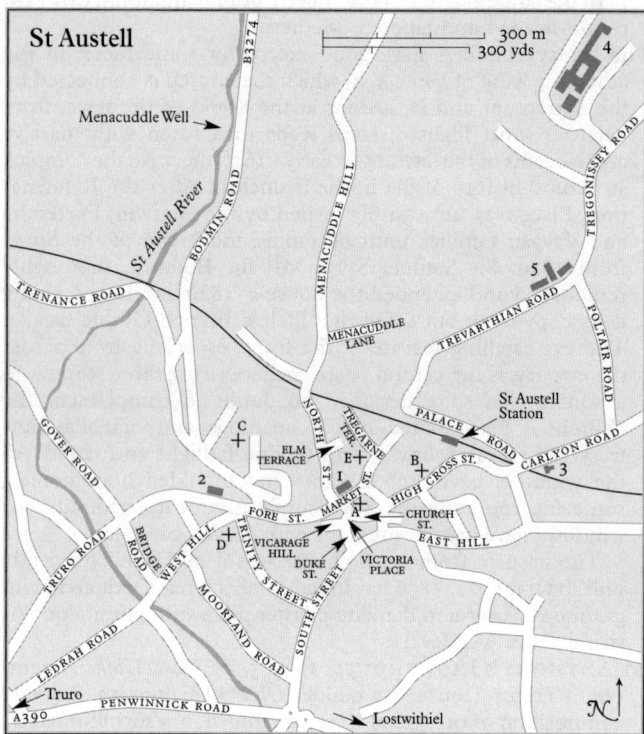

St Austell

A	Holy Trinity
B	Friends meeting house
C	St John's Methodist Church
D	Baptist church
E	Bible Christian chapel (former)
I	Town Hall and Market Hall
2	Public Assembly Rooms (former)
3	Public Library
4	Cornwall College
5	Poltair School

prosper through the second half of the C19 and well into the C20, and it remains important today. But there is more to St Austell than china clay: as A. L. Rowse wrote of his native parish,[*] 'There is a sense in which it is not invidious to say that the parish of St Austell is the heart of Cornwall. At least it is the most representative, for it has everything of Cornwall in it.'

Unlike most other pre-C19 Cornish towns that were deliberately promoted around a medieval market or planned as an industrial settlement, St Austell's growth seems to have been more organic. It started as a churchtown for an exceptionally large rural parish that embraced within its boundaries both its own quarries, such as Pentewan, and eventually even its own harbours at Charlestown, Par and Pentewan. At Domesday the area of modern St Austell was divided between three medieval manors, the principal one being gifted to Tywardreath Priory by the Cardinham family in the early C12. The oval raised churchyard of Holy Trinity echoes early Christian *lann* enclosures elsewhere in Cornwall and the early network of roads radiating from the church site and its enclosure is still the basic framework of the settlement's layout. At the meeting points of the three manors, the plan of the streets to the s of the church suggests the gradual and piecemeal infilling of a former open market area. During the C15 and C16 the town was an important centre for tin streaming and mining, and became a stannary court: the scale and quality of Tywardreath Priory's late C15 rebuilding of Holy Trinity suggest an attempt to create a prestigious urban centre at this period. The town petitioned for a market in 1638 and was granted a Friday market in 1661.

As the scale and industrialization of Cornish ore mining increased during the C18, St Austell continued to prosper as a commercial centre for the mining industry, 'the Peru of England' to Shaw, writing in 1788.[†] Its prestige had been enhanced by the building of the new turnpike road between Truro and Plymouth through the centre of the town via West Hill, Fore Street and East Hill in 1760 and Charles Rashleigh's development of Charlestown (q.v.) as its port in 1792. But it was the C19 that saw the town's meteoric rise, first through copper and then through the rapid expansion of the china clay industry. Its population doubled between 1811 and 1828, and china clay output increased from 13,000 tones in 1828 to 66,000 in 1850 and 550,000 in 1900. The arrival of the railway in 1859 with its impressive viaducts w of the town further boosted its commercial pre-eminence, while an earlier link of 1825 via a mineral tramway from the bottom of West Hill to Pentewan ensured that the mineral output of the area continued to be exported through the centre. And from 1869 it could boast Walter Hicks's renowned and pioneering steam brewery.

It is this period that is best represented in the buildings of St Austell today: not only the major buildings of the centre and

[*] A. L. Rowse, *St Austell Church: Town: Parish* (1960).
[†] Stebbing Shaw, *A Tour to the West of England in 1788* (1789).

the enrichment of the parish church, but the building of Truro Road as a new western entrance to the town and the development of several residential suburbs spanning the social scale. While there had been few earlier villas, now there grew an encircling ring of Late Victorian villas in extensive grounds on the higher slopes of the town, while in the industrial valley to the w there was purpose-built industrial housing. As with Henry Rice at Liskeard and James Hicks at Redruth, one architect was pre-eminent: here it was *Silvanus Trevail* who ranged from banks, public assembly rooms and the Liberal Club to villas and workers' housing. Add the plethora of chapels (Henderson counted nineteen in 1898), and the thick scatter of industrial settlements like Mount Charles and Holmbush outside the centre, and this was indeed 'clayopolis'.

c20 St Austell continued to develop, with the county's first pedestrian shopping precinct and first tower block of the 1960s and major residential expansion reflecting its continuing if relative economic buoyancy compared with much of industrial Cornwall. With the town's population approaching 30,000, the 1960s precinct was redeveloped in the early c21 to suit contemporary aspirations. This process of continuous development, reinforced by the modern road network and in recent decades given another boost by proximity to the Eden Project, gives an initial impression that historic St Austell has been swallowed up in its coalescence with neighbouring settlements and a sea of c20 building. Persistence is required to reach the heart of the place, but it is well rewarded.

CHURCHES

HOLY TRINITY. The late c15 w tower of richly decorated Pentewan stone at the centre of the old town's steeply sloping streets is one of Cornwall's architectural high points. The most noteworthy feature is its enrichment on all four sides by figure sculpture in niches, with iconography of unusual interest. On the N, E and S are four apostles each, on the w a striking pyramidal group: the Trinity at the top, Annunciation below with the lily as an isolated motif between the two kneeling figures, and the risen Christ between two saints at the foot. The style is that familiar from c15 alabaster work, rather hard and stocky but memorable. The richest decoration is reserved for the top (as at Probus, q.v., and in Somerset towers) where beneath the usual pinnacles there are four strips of ornament of the type found at Launceston and Fowey. This high-level distinction is further emphasized by the change to polygonal buttresses at belfry level and intricately patterned and pierced slate louvres of 1823 to the bell chamber. The tower can be dated by the coat of arms of Bishop Courtenay (i.e. before 1472): there are also fleurs-de-lys, a flowering branch and a plain shield possibly connected with an early c19 restoration. CLOCK FACE on w face of the tower with twenty-four bosses for the hours, probably c16. The exterior of the body of the church, particularly the s elevation, is highly attractive, with Pentewan stone supplemented by granite in battlemented aisles and a battlemented, buttressed two-storey s porch. The latter has a curious doorway with openwork tracery: an ogee arch inserted into a round one (cf. Mylor and St Just-in-Roseland), a motif originated at Gloucester and found, for example, in tomb canopies at Tewkesbury. There are also shield-holding angels and an elaborate scheme of c16 shield mounted iconography including Instruments of the Passion, Crucifixion, Ascension and Christ in Glory.

In contrast to the exterior, the interior is almost all granite. Nave of five bays, chancel of two bays, N and s aisles, s porch and N vestry. It is mainly c15–c16, the result of major rebuilding by Tywardreath Priory, but the e end is a more complex sequence of c13–c16 work under c19 re-roofing of the chancel. There is significant survival of pre-c15 work: the circular pier of the s chancel arcade, the two responses of the arches, and the double-chamfered arches themselves are early c13; the N chancel arcade is also E.E. but later, with a handsome octagonal pier with four slim attached shafts in the diagonals, a motif which comes from Dartmouth and its neighbourhood. The chancel e window and the N aisle e window have intersecting tracery and pointed quatrefoils: can they and the N chancel aisle be of *c.* 1290, the date recorded for the endowment of a chantry chapel of St Michael? Slender nave piers of standard Cornish section with moulded capitals and on the s side some decoration of the abaci. The aisles have wide Perp windows giving an even light. Except in the chancel, the wagon roofs are c16, the aisles in particular set out in unusually small panels: they rest almost immediately on the arcades.

Successive campaigns of c19 restoration and early c20 embellishment have contributed strongly to the character of the INTERIOR, a reflection of St Austell's prosperity at that period. The result is a significant ensemble of Late Victorian ecclesiological art. It began in earnest in 1870–2 under *J. P. St Aubyn* and included re-roofing the chancel, re-seating the church, and a new REREDOS by *Earp*. This was later enlarged and enriched by *Luscombe & Son* under *G. H. Fellowes Prynne* in 1890. The 1880s and 1890s saw the most sustained campaign including: PULPIT by *Harry Hems* of Exeter; colouring and regilding of bosses again by *St Aubyn*; oak CHOIR STALLS designed by *G. H. Fellowes Prynne*, executed by *J. Northcott* of Ashwater, Devon; and the 'illumination' of the e wall in 1891 to Prynne's design, with two panels painted by his brother, *E. A. Fellowes Prynne* (now partly overpainted). Oak CHANCEL ARCH and PARCLOSE SCREENS also by *Luscombe & Sons* to Prynne's design. Early c20 additions include the TOWER SCREEN, 1914 in memory of Walter Hicks, heavy oak arches with huge angel corbels in the N and s aisles, and the elaborate BAPTISTERY of 1923, of five different granites, alabaster and marble. – FONT. Norman, of Bodmin type, with faces at the corners of remarkable freshness, trees of life and dragons. –

PILLAR PISCINA. Norman, and of interesting design; another CI2 PISCINA in the S porch. – BENCH-ENDS re-erected as panelling inside the base of the tower. – MONUMENT to Joseph Sawle †1769 by *Isbell*. Free-standing, about 6 ft (1.8 metres) high, black urn on a square base. – STAINED GLASS. E window, middle window of St Michael's Chapel and window over tower doorway by *Mayer* of Munich. – Four S aisle windows by *Suffling*. – S window in St Michael's Chapel by *Clayton & Bell*. – Baptistery window by *Kempe & Co.*, 1908. – CHURCHYARD. Cast-iron railings with arrowhead shafts and shaped stanchions of 1886 by *J. P. St Aubyn*, partially replaced to NW. – CROSS. Found in 1879 at Treverbyn, re-erected in 1891 to E of chancel.

FRIENDS MEETING HOUSE, High Cross Street. Dated 1829. Dignified Quaker simplicity, 'an honest and solid shelter for quiet worship'. Long ashlar front with four sash windows. Inside two meeting rooms divided by a wide paved passage with screen walls of vertically sliding shutters. The Society of Friends had early and important connections with St Austell, probably arriving *c.* 1650 through the Laver family, related by marriage to its founder George Fox. The present building supersedes earlier houses of *c.* 1690 and 1788 on other sites.

ST JOHN'S METHODIST CHURCH, Bodmin Road. Built in 1828 to seat 1,000, designed by *George Michael*, and altered, mainly internally by *Silvanus Trevail*, in 1892. A large Wesleyan chapel approached by a sweeping drive, with five-bay front and prominent end bays. The open Ionic porch, surround to central upper window and small raised pediment to the centre bay appear to be Trevail additions.

BAPTIST CHURCH, West Hill. Dated 1899, by *F. C. Jury* of St Austell, standing large and proud, a good example of the late chapel style mixing classical and Gothic: exaggerated pediment to central double door and round-headed arched windows with plate tracery above. Uphill is its *c.* 1833 predecessor, a small stucco gabled building now in commercial use.

Former BIBLE CHRISTIAN CHAPEL, Tregarne Terrace. 1891, to design by *F. C. Jury*, opposite the older chapel begun 1828. St Austell was an important Bible Christian centre with conferences held here in 1836 and on five subsequent occasions in the C19.

MAJOR BUILDINGS

TOWN HALL AND MARKET HALL, Market Street. 1844, in an accomplished Italian Renaissance palazzo style by *F. C. Cope* and *Christopher Eales* (architect of the City Hall, Truro, q.v.), and at a cost of £7,000 very expensive. The interior is equally impressive but because of its contrasting austerity. Stone-vaulted bays from Market Street lead into a surprising two-level space dictated by the steeply sloping site to form a galleried first floor over the ground-floor arcade. Plain cast-iron columns give a character that seems more derived from industry than architecture. The Town Hall occupied a large plain public room over the entrance.

Former PUBLIC ASSEMBLY ROOMS, Truro Road. Now a shop. 1895 by *Silvanus Trevail*. Originally large hall, offices, smaller function rooms, and the fire station of the Urban District Council. Two-storey seven-bay front, the central five bays flanked by slightly projecting end bays. Round-headed arched windows with granite dressings. The larger scale and heavy detailing of the first floor have the effect of making the building ponderous rather than dignified.

PUBLIC LIBRARY, Carlyon Road. 1959–60 by *F. K. Hicklin*, County Architect, job architect *Michael Kirkbride*. Small but carefully planned and well detailed. T-plan with single-storey wing projecting from the rear of the two-storey main range. Steel frame construction with rock-faced granite walling and turquoise-tinted clerestory glazing. The full canted clerestory lighting of the main double-height lending area creates a spacious volume from a relatively confined ground floor but still manages to incorporate a mezzanine level.

CORNWALL COLLEGE, off Tregonissey Road. 1965 by *Bazeley & Barbary*. Formerly English China Clay's offices, now college, community centre etc. Vast sprawling mid-C20 building on a very prominent site. Well-detailed concrete frame construction expressed externally and accentuated by darker exposed aggregate panels below windows. The top floor originally provided executive dining rooms with spectacular views over St Austell Bay. Much of the structure, cladding and textured grey blockwork was manufactured using waste material from china clay production as aggregate.

SANDY HILL COMMUNITY PRIMARY SCHOOL, Sandy Hill. 1972 by *County Architect's Department*, project architect *Lionel Aggett*. One of the best primary schools of the period. Strong horizontal lines created by deeply projecting flat roof broken by bastion-like towers.

POLTAIR SCHOOL, Poltair Road/Trevarthian Road. A cluster of buildings, all substantial additions to the civic pride of the early C20 town. The former County Secondary School, (now West Block) is of 1906 by *B. C. Andrew* in a stripped-down Baroque style with central cupola, enlarged 1926. Assembly Hall, 1925. Girls' School in Neo-Georgian, 1933.

RAILWAY STATION. The railway arrived in 1859, but the earliest surviving station buildings are on the up platform and the footbridge is of 1882: the down platform is, in contrast, a pleasingly simple shelter structure of 2001 by *Lacie Hickie Caley*.

PERAMBULATIONS

There is much in St Austell's intriguing morphology as well as its buildings and architecture that displays the town's evolution, especially the zenith of its prosperity and civic pride in its public and private buildings of the second half of the C19.

1. Church Street, Victoria Place, High Cross Street and north-eastwards

A logical start is opposite the lavish DRINKING FOUNTAIN set against the S wall of the churchyard. 1890, marble with polished pink granite bowl and columns with pointed arch niche surmounted by an elaborate cast-iron lamp standard. Along CHURCH STREET, VICTORIA PLACE, VICARAGE HILL and EAST HILL are pleasant three-storey stucco buildings, mostly with C19 fronts. PROVINCIAL HOUSE, Church Street, dated 1865, is commercial showrooms with tall round-headed arched windows at second floor and pretty decoration. More typical are Nos. 6–12 VICTORIA PLACE with modified Corinthian pilasters, moulded architraves, sash windows in moulded cases and shopfronts with fluted Doric columns to their entrances. Behind and with a canted front to turn the corner and balustraded parapet are FRY DAYS and MOUNT EDGCUMBE HOSPICE SHOP, datestone 1893, also date of 1705 and motto 'one and all'. Built by *Silvanus Trevail* as the YMCA with reading room, gym etc. At the SE corner of the churchyard, the WHITE HART HOTEL. Originally built as the C18 town house of the Rashleighs, it was trading as an inn by 1735 and prospered especially after the new turnpike road passed its door from 1760. The main block has a clearly added storey of 1925, the adjoining extension is accomplished later C18, elegantly turning the corner to East Hill with a Venetian window at the rear. This part was purpose-built as a suite of function rooms; its original panoramic wallpaper of the Bay of Naples by *Dufour, c.* 1800, is now in the Victoria and Albert Museum. Later Italianate rear extension of the 1860s with round-headed arched windows. Opposite, at No. 1 Church Street, the startling former St Austell Bank (now NATWEST and partly converted to residential use) of 1898–1900: *Silvanus Trevail's* most confident assertion of his reputation in St Austell, and redolent of its boom-town character at the turn of the century. Known locally as the 'Red Bank', the colour of its brick and terracotta spectacular for a stone town. Trevail designed the building to take full advantage of its pivotal position at the intersection of four of the town's major streets and at the eastern end of the churchyard. Eclectic style, three-storeyed, central section carried up into elaborate attic gable between corbelled-out pilasters; flanking rounded corner sections with strongly corbelled and arched Venetian cornices surmounted by Oriental pepperpot roofs with finials; and then plainer end sections. Central and end sections have geometric patterned terracotta panels over first- and second-floor windows. Interior has elegant full-height staircase.

Opposite, at the entrance to HIGH CROSS STREET, the former Devon & Cornwall Bank (now NATIONWIDE) is also by Trevail but a complete contrast in Bath stone of *c.* 1900. Further up some early C19 houses including BIBS AND BOBS, a pair of houses dated WF 1804 built around a central entrance

with staircase. Then the remarkable POST OFFICE of 1920 by
A. R. Myers of *H. M. Office of Works* (cf. Bodmin and Falmouth), a confident solid Luxulyan granite building. A rigorous yet subtle street elevation with controlled use of materials:
the plinth and window surrounds are in lighter stone, the walls
of darker stained stone. Deeply set windows, the smaller
windows on the first floor grouped above uniformly spaced
long ground-floor windows, surmounted by a pared-down
modillion cornice. Further up again, the STATION HOTEL,
built 1908 as the offices of the West of England China Clay
Company from 1919 to 1965.

*2. Northwards via North Street, Market Street, Tregonissey Road
and Menacuddle Hill*

Starting from the w end of the churchyard, past the early C19
QUEEN'S HEAD HOTEL with elevations to Market Street and
North Street and the splendidly showy Market Hall of 1844
(*see* above). In NORTH STREET, the OLD MANOR HOUSE.
Late C17 and C18, mullioned-and-transomed leaded-light casement windows, first-floor modillioned cornice and contemporary staircase. In MARKET STREET, No. 5, of 1898, was designed
by *Silvanus Trevail* as a pioneering hairdressing salon with
separate floors for ladies and gentlemen, now woefully pebble-
dashed. Next door is TREGONISSEY HOUSE, one of St Austell's most distinctive and historically significant buildings. It
was here that Walter Hicks founded his famous, and enduring,
St Austell Brewery in 1869. Hicks took advantage of the innovations revolutionizing the brewing industry at that time to
build a steam brewery, that is to say a brewery which used
steam rather than direct heating by furnaces to heat up the
mash. Two separate blocks, the prestigious three-storey offices
to the street, the brewery with its massive chimney and roof
ventilators behind. The front block is smart brick with tall
paired windows subdivided by slender stone columns. The
brewery was so successful that Hicks was looking for another
site by 1893 (*see* below).
On up TREGONISSEY ROAD are the 1828 and 1891 Bible Christian chapels (*see* Churches) that stand either side of the
entrance to TREGARNE TERRACE, another achievement of
Silvanus Trevail, substantial terraced houses now mostly converted to offices, built in two phases during the 1890s, and
showing Trevail's typical subtle variation of scale and detail. At
the top TREGARNE LODGE, also by Trevail, for the developer
Sir F. L. Barratt's own use. Returning to Tregonissey Road, the
footbridge over the railway offers panoramic views over the
town centre, and an impression of the sylvan quality of the
Late Victorian suburbs. N is TREVARTHIAN ROAD which leads
to the ST AUSTELL BREWERY, where Walter Hicks moved in
1893 from the original brewery in the town centre. It is by
Davison, Inskipp & Mackenzie, who also designed Charrington's

Anchor Brewery and Taylor Walker's Barley Mow Brewery in east London. A large but effectively massed cluster of specialist buildings culminating in the tall brick tower added in the early C20, still the heart of the present brewery. Front three-storey central block with hipped roof flanked by two-storey wings with round-headed brick arches set within gables, the three-storey gabled main range set behind. Brick dressing to Pentewan stone. Much original brewing equipment, including coppers and tuns, still in use. Beyond, the County Schools of 1906 onwards (*see* Major Buildings). Returning down Trevarthian Road, it is possible, and rewarding, to negotiate a route across MENACUDDLE HILL via Menacuddle Lane. Just before the railway is TREMENA ROAD which offers a taste of St Austell villadom of the late C19 and glimpses of some of the larger pre-railway villas set in heavily wooded grounds, like NORTH HILL HOUSE with its prominent glazed look-out (the lodge is visible from the road) and TRESLEIGH. Back down Menacuddle Hill, with ELM TERRACE, quiet two-storey stucco of the 1890s, on the l. near the bottom, before reaching the town centre again.

3. West: Fore Street to West Hill, Truro Road and Bodmin Road

The pedestrianized FORE STREET, still the main shopping area of the town, has the huge advantage in a centre comprised of small, steeply sloping streets of being almost level throughout, and is further enhanced by taking the long gentle curve of the natural contour; at the E end too, its focal point is the tower of Holy Trinity. This was one of the most important commercial streets in St Austell, and its admixture of mostly plain C19 fronts with more showy later C19 and early C20 buildings in brick with stone dressings gives it a coherence that relies on the whole rather than its components. There are earlier buildings behind at least some of these late fronts: an obvious example is the town house of the Tremaynes that lurks behind the present shopfront of WARRENS THE BAKERS, the older roof-line clearly visible. The street is enlivened by several narrow passages or opes leading off uphill or downhill, rising or falling sharply as the steeply sloping terrain dictates. But the C20 was not kind to Fore Street, and it suffered particularly from the worthy intention of creating links to the former 1960s Aylmer Square SHOPPING CENTRE along its S side: alas it resulted in the irruption into this gentle street of crude concrete structures at key points. One building of interest near the W end is the THIN END RESTAURANT, another *Silvanus Trevail* special, built as the former Liberal Club 1889–90. Here he used a Free Renaissance style in banded Bath stone and brick above a ground floor of solid granite; central entrance lobby entrance for clubrooms with Ruabon tiles and Luxulyan granite steps. The W end of the street at the junction with WEST HILL, BODMIN ROAD and TRURO ROAD is one of the principal historic entrances to the town centre and is marked by the C18 ABEDA TOYS, formerly the General Wolfe public house, and the major public buildings – the Baptist church in West Hill, Public Assembly Rooms in Truro Road and St John's Methodist Church off Bodmin Road. In Truro Road, BLAYLOCK OPTICIANS, *c.* 1880 with unusual canted bay across ground floor and elaborate sculptured alcove rising between first- and second-floor windows.

It is worth venturing further along Bodmin Road, past a group of 1840–60 villas, to enjoy views of the TRENANCE VIADUCT and distant prospects of the china clay tips as well as the vast spread of C20 infill in the main valley below and opposite. Down LEDRAH ROAD, the OLD BRIDGE, C16 and C17, three spans with cutwaters and round-headed arches. Also good view of Cornwall's first tower block, PARK HOUSE on Bridge Road, of 1967 by *Wimpey.*

Back on West Hill, the land falls sharply to the valley bottom, the terminus of the mineral tramway to Pentewan marked by the survival of a small part of a CHINA CLAY CELLAR once over 200 ft (61 metres) long, and into MOORLANDS ROAD, a coherently planned development of industrial housing, again by *Silvanus Trevail.* Simple but dignified terraces in stone with red brick dressings, articulated by Trevail's occasional slightly projecting bays and other attention to detail especially on corners. The return to the town centre by SOUTH STREET is now dominated by WHITE RIVER PLACE, a redevelopment of the 1960s shopping precinct in 2007–9 by *Chetwoods Architects.* A missed opportunity, its larger scale militating against successful integration into the historic townscape, especially on the S approach where the TRINITY STREET elevation presents a fortress-like wall. It rises to eight storeys in a pseudo-tower flanked by an angular, awkward cinema squatting to the l. and an intimidating flight of steps to the r. The interior achieves a more comfortable scale. Beyond, the solid MASONIC HALL of 1900, DUKE STREET and EAST HILL mark a return to C19 St Austell.

URBAN VILLAGE. 2007 by *Alan Leather Associates.* Mixed-use development on a brownfield site, consciously drawing on historic elements of the area to create townscape of convincing urban character.

HOLY WELL, Menacuddle, about 1 m. N off the Bodmin Road. Almost hidden below the road, set against its retaining wall, is one of Cornwall's most endearing places. The chapel and well are specially romantically placed among rocks, overshadowing trees, and flowing water in the remains of gardens laid out by the Rashleighs of Menabilly after 1795. C15, entirely of granite with groined barrel-vaulted roof and two late C15 arched doorways to a small room with a sunken well trough.

WILLIAM COOKWORTHY BRIDGE, approximately 2 m. N over the Bodmin Road. 2002 by *David Sheppard,* architect, and *Simon Ballantine,* engineer. 82-ft (25-metre) long cycle and pedestrian bridge with distinctive long slim vertical fins giving it a graceful lightness of touch.

WHEAL MARTYN CHINA CLAY MUSEUM, 3 m. N, near Carthew. Based on a small late C19 clayworks where the visitor can trace the refining process and walk to the edge of the CLAY PIT being worked some 500 ft (152 metres) below. The main drying KILN or DRY is over 200 ft (61 metres) long. Entrance area built around the ruins of GOMM CLAY WORKS, the dry left roofless but with impressive rough granite pillars that once supported the roof. Some smaller structures, typical of the industry, are the WORKMEN'S SHELTER, CRIB HUT (canteen), and BLUEING HOUSE (where Reckitt's Blue was added to brighten the clay), all simple weatherboarded or corrugated-iron-clad huts. A 35-ft (11-metre) WATERWHEEL demonstrates the transmission of water power by reciprocating flat-rods or cables from valley streams to pump clay pits on higher ground.

At CARLUDDON, 3 m. NE, one of the archetypal pyramidal china clay tips, prominent in the landscape for miles around.

0060

ST BENET'S
½ m. s of Lanivet

Founded as a chapel in 1411, referred to in Bishop Vesey's register in 1535, and apparently dissolved in 1549. Early C16 gatehouse and domestic range with detached C16 tower from former chapel, the relationship not fully understood. It was purchased c. 1855 by the rector, Reverend W. Phillips Flamank, who spent lavishly on alterations and additions. The HOUSE is dominated by its unrefined Regency and Gothic makeover of the mid C19, but the least altered part on the l. of the main range is immediately recognizable as the gatehouse to the medieval establishment. It retains an octagonal corner stair-turret, a four-centred arched pedestrian doorway with deep mouldings, and, to its r., a broad carriage archway of similar character, now a window with mid-C19 timber Gothic tracery. Above the arch is a good carved oriel window with three ogee-arched heads flanked by two ogee niches. Similar carriage arch to the rear, now blocked, and a first-floor granite window with cusped lights. The ground floor of the main range has C15 window heads with cusped lights elongated almost to ground floor in the mid C19. The interior is of mostly of mid- to late C19 character but the gatehouse retains a basket-arched doorway and first-floor corridor with fragments of stained glass with figure work and panels of arms, removed from Lanivet church during the restoration of 1865.

The TOWER is offset at an angle to the rear of the house. Remains of two stages of the original three. The E side has the tower arch and line of the gable that lead into the nave, the piers standard Cornish, and a stair in the NW corner; the W side a four-centred arched door and remains of a Perp window.

Round-headed CROSS in front of the house. Small incised Latin cross enclosed in a bead on a tapered modern shaft.

ST BLAZEY

0050

ST BLAISE. Built *c.* 1440 but extensively restored, by *E. B. Moffatt* of *Scott & Moffatt* in 1839, and *E. H. Sedding* in 1897. The W tower, nave, chancel, S aisle and S porch are reworked Perp, all faced in regular granite blocks. Tower in three stages, without buttresses, embattled and with short stumpy pinnacles; on the second stage a little ogee-headed niche with finials l. and r. The interior is lofty and airy with tall standard Cornish piers to the S aisle decorated on plain capitals and abaci with a castellated or fleur-de-lys cresting. The N aisle was built in 1839 in imitation of the S aisle, and extended W in 1897. C19 wagon roofs with carved ribs. – STAINED GLASS. In the porch, St Blaise and the Good Shepherd, by *E. R. Suffling*, 1899. – MONUMENTS. Slate plate of 1701 with Father Time looking like a benevolent churchwarden. – Henry Scovell †1727 and his wife. Wall tablet with columns l. and r. and inscription framed by draperies. At the foot an oval relief of the Last Judgement, with the two dedicatees being carried up by angels. It is by *Weston* of Exeter.[*]

The main road village has streets of plain early C19 cottages with a few nice houses close to the church. In Fore Street, former MARKET HOUSE, on granite columns, early C19.

TREGREHAN. *See* p. 640.

EDEN PROJECT. *See* p. 179.

ST BREOCK

9070

A small churchtown of slatestone cottages and former rectory above the church, which is exquisitely set at the foot of a steep valley by a tiny stream under old trees.

ST BREOCK. Important to the medieval bishops of Exeter as part of the great episcopal manor of Pawton, now only marked by a farmhouse. Bishop Bronescombe dedicated the church in 1259 and Bishop Stapledon dedicated the high altar in 1318. Sturdy three-stage tower, the lower parts C14 without

[*]The triptych memorial by *H. Hopper* to Sir Thomas Carlyon †1831, described by Pevsner in 1951, is no longer *in situ.*

buttresses but with a NE square stair-turret and battlemented parapet: the third storey is Perp. Nave and chancel in one, S aisle, N and S porches and small N and S transept chapels. Of the C13 the rebuilt N transept arch and traces of an original cruciform plan. Of the early C14 still the two doorways (the S door re-set when the aisle was added) and the two Catacleuse nave windows next to the tower which are C13 lancets enlarged by the insertion of two lights. The aisle arcade is of six bays of standard Cornish granite piers with finely carved capitals and four-centred arches in Beer stone: it seems entirely C15 with Catacleuse windows. In a petition of 1662 the parishioners stated that 'the decay of the timber and leaning of the walls and pillars was in so much danger that we have been forced to take it down to the ground': the petition was granted in 1677. A restoration by *J. P. St Aubyn* in 1878 included complete re-roofing except for the aisle roof, removal of the galleries, re-seating and reglazing. The remaining plaster was stripped from the walls in the 1950s. – FONT. A lovely little C15 Catacleuse octagon, each side with well-executed panels of tracery and quatrefoils. – HIGH ALTAR by *E. H. Sedding* with transparent alabaster REREDOS carved by the *Pinwills*, 1908. – STAINED GLASS. S chancel chapel, *Heaton, Butler & Bayne*, feeding of 5,000, wedding at Cana etc., 1879. – S transept, *Lavers, Barraud & Westlake*, 1873. – S aisle, fragments of medieval saint and inscriptions. – MONUMENT of the C13 with foliated cross and inscription in French: 'Thomas P . . . gist ici' (Thomas P . . . e Vicar of Nansent lies here: God on his Soul have mercy). – BRASS to a member of the Tredeneck family, two wives (one lost) and several children; *c.* 1510. – Smaller brass, to Christopher Tredeneck, 1531. – Large slate slab to Charles Tredenick, 1578, with strapwork and two excellent Michelangelesque putti. – Large slate wall monument to a member of the Prideaux-Brune family, 1598, with kneeling figures and plenty of heraldry. – Another slab with coats of arms, Viell impaling Arundell, presumed to commemorate William Viell and Jane his wife, daughter of Sir John Arundell of Trerice.

The CHURCHYARD is exceptionally attractive and extensive, the land rising steeply to N, S and W, full of C18 and C19 slate headstones reflecting St Breock's role as the mother church of Wadebridge.

PILLAR STONE used as gatepost at Nanscowe Farm, about 1 m. SW of St Breock. Inscriptions in Roman capitals: ULLAGNI FILI and SEVERI. Date probably C5 or C6.

ST BREOCK LONGSTONE, at the summit of St Breock Downs. Early Bronze Age. 'Mene-gurta', the stone of waiting. Massive quartzy rock, its weight estimated at 17 tons; now 10 ft (3 metres) high, it was 13½ ft (4.1 metres) before it fell in 1945. Excavation preceding re-erection in 1956 revealed low cairn of quartz stones surrounding stone. Probably associated with several other quartz menhirs and dozens of large BARROWS, mainly simple round mounds, along the rolling ridge separating N and central Cornwall.

ST BREWARD

A large parish on the w slopes of Bodmin Moor, its landscape dominated by Brown Willy and Roughtor (qq.v.), Cornwall's highest peaks, rich in features from prehistory onwards and in more recent centuries the location of some of Cornwall's most famous granite quarries. The medieval churchtown lies at the N end of a long, straggling village that was considerably developed after the opening in 1834 of a branch of the Southern Railway for goods and minerals.

ST BREWARD. In spite of the remote moorland location there was a Norman church here of sizeable dimensions with narrow aisles, and transept(s) were added in the C13. The sturdy w tower may incorporate Norman work in its lower two stages which are unbuttressed: the third storey is later and recessed so that buttresses could be formed at the corners. The most striking feature is the distinctive banding of the lower stages where long flat slabs of granite alternate with courses of square slabs. Recessed w door with carved heads as label stops. There is C12 masonry in the walls of the narrow N aisle, the E and N sides of the chancel and at the w end of the nave on the s side, where a small Norman window remains. The s aisle has a good set of early C16 windows of four lights with late Perp tracery like Egloshayle, the E window is of five lights. s porch is C16 too with wagon roof. The N aisle retains five circular Norman piers (cf. Morwenstow and North Petherwin), notable for their capitals, scalloped, and one with odd stylized tree motifs, two to a side, like candelabra. The first three piers (in white elvan) are shorter than the fourth and fifth, and the N transept does not correspond exactly with them: there is some uncertainty about the extent of work to them in a drastic restoration of 1863–5 by *J. P. St Aubyn*.* The s aisle arcade is of standard Perp design, the capitals and abaci finely moulded, the arches almost segmental. Fine wagon roof to s aisle, the rest replaced by St Aubyn. – FONT. Made up of Norman fragments, the bowl possibly originally the base of a font, the present base the capital of a pier, reversed. – PARCLOSE SCREEN to the N chancel incorporating C15 pieces. – BENCH-ENDS. A few displayed on the front of the nave pews and the back of the choir stalls. – ALTAR. 1985 of granite carved by craftsmen from the local quarries. – ROYAL ARMS, painted wood, 1700 WR. – STAINED GLASS. Chancel E, 1883 by *Beer & Driffield*. – N chapel, 1933 by *Clayton & Bell*. – Other windows with patterned glass of 1867. – MONUMENTS. Good C17 slates in the s chancel chapel. – Christopher Rogers †1609 with two kneeling figures in relief, originally part of a tomb-chest of which other plates are displayed. – William Billing †1654 and

---

*He may have left the piers alone but rebuilt some of the arches, though Sedding considered three bays of the aisle to have been reconstructed in the C17.

Nicholas Borrough †1651. – On the N wall of the chancel slate to Lewis Adams †1607 with figures similar to the Rogers memorial.

In the churchyard to the S of the church a large medieval WHEEL-HEAD CROSS with pierced trefoils, on a C19 shaft, restored and resited here 1890.

HOLY WELL, Chapel Farm, ½ m. SW. Late medieval well-house with corbelled granite roof which stood close to the former chapel of St James, first mentioned in 1422.

LEAZE, 2 m. ENE. Rare example of a small late C17 upland farmhouse, originally simply a hall heated by a gable-end stack with a chamber above, with a lean-to porch on the l. side of the hall. The continuous outshut at the rear is a later addition.

HAMATETHY, 1 m. N. Large house, possibly on the site of a medieval manor, mostly of 1924 reusing many features from the demolished house at Trewinnow, Davidstow, including granite arched doorway dated 1678. Good farmyard buildings.

DE LANK QUARRY, ½ m. SSE. Entered from the W through a narrow defensive-feeling defile carved through the living rock, the quarry reveals a working industrial landscape where the silver-grey of extracted stone and active quarry faces contrasts with the overgrowth of quarries long disused, including that from which the blocks of the Eddystone Lighthouse were extracted. De Lank was one of the most prolific of Cornish quarries in the late C19 and early C20, its even-textured hard biotite granite proving popular for both appearance and durability in London projects including Tower Bridge, New Scotland Yard, Trafalgar Square and the Royal Opera House, and docks in Britain and Bombay. Blocks were moved out by tram to the mainline railway at Wenford Bridge, and thence to Wadebridge Quay for export.

CARWETHER, 1½ m. N. A deserted medieval hamlet of four LONGHOUSES, each with yards, gardens and outhouses, and detached CORN-DRYING BARNS at each end, as at Brown Willy. The largest longhouse was occupied at least as late as the mid C17. Low banks and ridge and furrow are visible around the hamlet in the slanting morning or evening sunlight.

STANNON STONE CIRCLE, 1 m. SE of Highertown. Early Bronze Age. Large stone circle similar to Fernacre (Roughtor). Ring not circular; four virtually straight sections, and diameter ranges from 128 ft to 141 ft (39 to 43 metres). Mix of large and small stones, some nearly touching; thirty-nine still upright, twenty-nine fallen. Arc of four stones to NW appear related, with the circle impressively skylined from it. Brown Willy's summit is due E.

KING ARTHUR'S HALL, ¾ m. E of Candra. Early medieval. Peculiar sub-rectangular earthwork aligned due N, 154 ft by 66 ft (47 by 20 metres) internally, too large to have been roofed. Later gaps in SW and NE corners. Asymmetrically profiled heavy bank faced internally with large vertically set granite slabs, many slumped inwards. A lack of close parallels has encouraged speculation: some see a unique prehistoric ritual or ceremonial monument; others an early medieval pound for trespassing livestock.

ALEX TOR CAIRN, 1½ m. NE. Early Bronze Age. Summit cairn incorporates a natural tor and continues its line with massive inward-leaning granite kerb slabs.

For the archaeology of ROUGHTOR, GARROW TOR and BROWN WILLY *see* pp. 483, 485 and 126.

ST BURYAN

4020

ST BURYAN. One of the proudest churches of west Cornwall, all Perp, all granite, in a fairly high position, its four-stage tower 92 ft (28 metres) high, a landmark from far away. It dominates its small village within which it sits raised on a walled *lann* that was circular until a thoughtless road-widening scheme of the 1980s straightened its s boundary. The reason for its surprisingly ambitious scale and lavishness of plan – nave and chancel with identical N and S aisles and chancel aisles of six wide bays – is that, like Crantock, this was a collegiate church, traditionally founded by King Athelstan, and re-founded by Bishop Brewer of Exeter in 1238; it had a dean and three prebendaries, and chapelries at St Levan and Sennen. The latter arrangement lasted until 1864 when the three parishes became independent.

Of the Norman church there are only limited, yet eloquent, remains: two blocked arches in the N wall of the chancel, visible internally and from outside. The arcade of two bays has a circular pier and semicircular responds with rough reeded capitals of early C12 character. It probably separated the quire of the canons from a chapel containing the shrine of St Beriana. The Norman church had at least a nave, chancel, and N chancel aisle or chapel, but only this evidence survived the almost complete rebuilding of the early C16 to its present plan and architectural form, a plan type (with wide aisles under parallel roofs) originating in Cornwall at St Petroc, Bodmin (q.v.). The stately W tower has a NE stair-turret rising above the pinnacles, and buttresses set back from the angles. There is a battlemented, buttressed and pinnacled S porch, a grander version of the one at St Just-in-Penwith (q.v.). The staircase to the rood loft projects from the S wall. Most of the windows are of three lights without cusping or tracery. The interior is impressively lofty, spacious, and light, with a high proportion of clear glazing. The four-bay nave arcades and two-bay chancel arcades are tall, slim, of standard section, with very finely moulded capitals. There were restorations in 1814, 1854 and 1874–81, the latter by *William Butterfield* who introduced the three higher floor levels of the chancel.

66   The glory of the church, however, is its early C16 ROOD SCREEN: it had been mostly dismounted in 1825 but was reassembled and restored in an exemplary manner by *E. H. Sedding* in 1910, the missing elements copied from surviving fragments or based on other close parallels. The quality of the original work invites comparison with some of the best Devon screens of this period rather than local examples. The screen runs right across nave and aisles. Each of the three sections has a central opening and two panels l. and two r. of it. Each panel, within richly carved uprights and top rail, has four narrow upright motifs, with foliage arranged in undulating, zigzag, or patera fashion; it is mostly complete, with much beautiful red, blue and green paint and gilding surviving. Only a short section of a fan-vaulted canopy is original, but the rood beam, with an upper trail of vine and a lower trail with birds, fish, beast, grotesque heads, etc., all hiding in and peeping out of foliage scrolls, is almost entirely late medieval, also with much lovely colouring: the lower trail incorporates a slightly abbreviated version of the Godolphin arms, and another a large hound with very long tongue.* – FONT. With shield-holding angels at three of the corners, rudely carved, on a pier-like shaft resembling the standard Cornish design: probably also early C16. – ALTAR and REREDOS, *c.* 1920, designed by *Sedding*, carved by *Violet Pinwill*, of good quality. – BENCH-ENDS made into a litany desk. Note the mermaid on one of them. – MISERICORDS in the choir. A rare survival of four medieval stalls of very simple design with plain shields; they have been moved from their original position as return stalls backed against the screen. – STAINED GLASS. Chancel E, 1875 by *Alexander Gibbs*. S chancel E, 1897 by *Ward & Hughes*. – MONUMENT to Clarice de Bolleit, with cross and inscription in Norman-French, coffin-shaped, C13.

    In the churchyard, set up on a base stone and four-stepped base on the S path to the church, a CHURCHYARD CROSS-HEAD, by far the most impressive of the Penwith group of pre-Conquest crosses. The principal face shows Christ with arms outstretched and feet turned outward, the figure with a tunic rather than a loin cloth. The expanded limbs of the cross-head are decorated with a double bead on the lower section and a single bead on the upper half, and are joined by a ring pierced with four holes. The reverse face displays five bosses representing the five Wounds of Christ, enclosed by a double bead. Wheel-headed WAYSIDE or MARKET CROSS to the S of the churchyard.

At CROWS-AN-WRA, 1½ m. NNW, a pretty C18 GUIDE POST, triangular with pyramidal cap and incised inscriptions with place names written as round-headed arches.

---

*I owe this discovery and attribution to John Schofield, who points out that the incorporation of the Godolphin arms means the screen must date from *c.* 1530 onwards.

ALSIA MILL, 1 m. WSW. C17 mill on earlier site, remodelled C18–C20, built into the bank. Surviving overshot waterwheel and complete C19 mill machinery. GOOSE HOUSES nearby.

TRESIDDER MILL AND MILLHOUSE, 1½ m. SW. C18, extended C19, integrated mill and miller's house. Overshot waterwheel. Original C19 machinery inside.

BOSKENNA, 1½ m. SE. Large irregular plan house, dated 1678, 1858 and 1888. The 1678 building survives as the NW wing of the present house. Much rebuilt in 1888, the exterior with many replications of C17 features alongside some originals, though some of these are not *in situ*. Interior retains C17 parlour with bolection-moulded panelling and fine ribbed plaster ceiling, and C17 open-well stair with heavy turned baluster and pendants.

TREWOOFE MANOR, 2 m. E. Farmhouse, mainly C17, but incorporating the doorway (*c.* 1490) of a larger medieval house with arms of Trewoofe and Levelis families within carved pilaster panels.

PENBERTH, 2 m. SSW. Mostly 1921–8 by *Cowell, Drewitt & Wheatly*, radically extending a modest late C19 villa into a spreading butterfly plan house with a bedroom range and outbuildings to the rear. The result is a pleasing composition in an Arts and Crafts style skilfully articulated on a sloping site with a two-storey W entrance range that gives into the single-storey central and E ranges: the latter, a library, has fittings brought from Sheffield including a timber chimneypiece inscribed 1655 WB. The two storey gatehouse, dramatically spanning a stream, is also by Drewitt.

The unspoiled PENBERTH COVE below the house with a PILCHARD HOUSE, FISH CELLARS and a restored CAPSTAN.

The parish is exceptionally rich in prehistoric and medieval evidence, including eighteen crosses. Of prehistoric remains:

MERRY MAIDENS STONE CIRCLE, 1½ m SE. A true circle, 79 ft (24 metres) in diameter, with nineteen equally spaced stones, most with flat tops, grading in height from SSW to NNE. The eastern gap is where a twentieth probably stood. Part of a complex of early prehistoric monuments (cairns, standing stones, entrance grave, cists, etc.) in a loose band running NE to SW in land that was unenclosed until a few hundred years ago.

THE PIPERS, 1½ m. SE, ¼ m from Merry Maidens. Later Neolithic or Early Bronze Age. Cornwall's tallest surviving STANDING STONES, at 5.05 and 4.2 m. The NW stone now leans towards the SW one and may have guided people towards the Merry Maidens stone circle, which are on line and probably contemporary, but not visible. Their name may also link them with the maidens petrified for Sabbath dancing. Also known as the Hurlers (being a goal in St Buryan's cross-country hurling matches).

TREGIFFIAN ENTRANCE GRAVE, 100 yds W of Merry Maidens. Late Neolithic entrance grave whose chamber broadens slightly at inner N end. Reused and adapted in the Bronze Age with a secondary orthostatic kerb that blocks the cham-

ber's s entrance. Excavated in 1868 and 1967–8. The eastern
entrance stone (now a replica) was covered with prehistoric
cupmarks – thirteen circles and twelve long ovals – and a
second CUP-MARKED STONE was found on the chamber's
floor.

5   BOSCAWEN-UN CARVED STANDING STONE and STONE
CIRCLE, 1½ m. N. A ring of nineteen stones, probably originally twenty (gap on W side), in an ellipse that nevertheless
appears circular on site. The stones are all granite except for
one quartz one to WSW, are unevenly spaced and vary in shape
and height. Excavated in the 1860s when a bisecting hedge was
removed; this confirmed that the stone just SW of the centre
was apparently deliberately angled. Tall and shaped like a Neolithic stone axe-head, it appears to be chopping the ground.
Carved in relief on its NE face are two stone axe-heads, again
of Neolithic form. The circle and a possible cist grave in NE
part of the ring appear later, probably Early Bronze Age. Views
dominated by Creeg Tol to N and Chapel Carn Brea to NW.
Encircling ha-ha built in 1860s.

TATER DU LIGHTHOUSE, 3 m. SE. 1965, Cornwall's newest
lighthouse. Built after the wreck of the *Juan Ferrer* in 1963
when eleven people died. Designed by Trinity House, built by
Messrs Humphreys Ltd of Knightsbridge, and fully automatic.

2060   ST CLEER

Few landscapes convey the richness of Cornwall's prehistoric,
medieval and industrial past so vividly as this large parish on the
s slopes of Bodmin Moor. It was transformed during the C19
boom in tin and copper mining and granite quarrying on Caradon
Hill and Minions Moor: its population rose fourfold to over
4,000 between 1801 and 1860, the medieval churchtown expanded
into a small market town, and several substantial settlements like
Minions and Pensilva developed.

ST CLAIR. An exceptionally fine C15 W tower of regular granite
blocks in three stages, with buttresses set back from the angles,
and decorated with pinnacles in relief. In addition the third
stage has another set of little relief pinnacles at the corners.
Above these rise the big main pinnacles of the tower. Of the
Norman church one doorway remains re-set in the N wall, with
one order of colonettes and a chevron outer voussoir, nothing
very spectacular since much detail was lost in its resiting. The
church has N and s aisles, both buttressed and both consisting
of four bays and a lower one for the chancel. The s aisle
windows have Perp tracery, the N windows are straight-headed,
that is later. The N arcade on the other hand is earlier, say
c. 1400, with octagonal piers and a fairly simple profile of the
arch. The richer s arcade of green Polyphant has an unusual
profile of the piers, with a fillet on each side of the standard

hollow (cf. Lewannick), and a very complex moulding. There is a squint between N aisle and chancel. Nave, aisles and S porch have C15–C16 wagon roofs with moulded ribs and bosses. Chancel has late C19 wooden chancel arch and wagon roof, both with angel corbels, part of an excellent ensemble from a restoration of 1904 by *G. H. Fellowes Prynne* which included the REREDOS, ALTAR FRONT, ROOD and PARCLOSE SCREENS, CHOIR STALLS, BENCH-ENDS and black and white marble FLOOR. – PULPIT. 1896 by *Harry Hems* of Exeter. – FONT. C13, Purbeck (?) table-top type, with five flat pointed blank niches on each side. – PAINTINGS. Verses from the Bible with crude C18 cartouche work, probably originally in the spandrels of the arcade. – ROYAL ARMS dated 1708. – STAINED GLASS. Chancel E, 1920 by *Clayton & Bell*. – S aisle windows, 1904 by *Fouracre & Watson*, panels of saints. N aisle W, Faith, Hope and Charity with interesting photographic faces. – MONUMENTS. Robert Langeford †1614, a chest tomb with fine carved slate top and thirteen kneeling figures. – Nicholas and Mary Connock †1804, by *R. Isbell* of Stonehouse.

A good group of buildings around the churchyard includes the C17–C19 VICARAGE, and the former POLICE STATION, and MARKET HOUSE, both of 1859. In the village street NE of the church a HOLY WELL, a pretty Breton-looking C15–C16 building, of more architectural finesse than most Cornish holy wells. Restored 1864 by *Henry Rice* of Liskeard. Square, of granite, with a steep-pitched roof and stumpy pinnacles like Dupath, on two-bay arcades to the front and sides, round-headed and on granite piers with slightly decorated capitals. Inside a pointed barrelvault and a solid back wall with openings and niches. Beside it a WAYSIDE CROSS, C15, probably in its original position, unusually with a Latin cross cut in relief on both faces.

HOCKING HOUSE CHAPEL and SUNDAY SCHOOL, ¼ m. W. A good group, the chapel of 1846 with an exceptionally complete interior with gallery and fine fittings including box pews and leaders' pews. The school is of 1870 at first-floor level, accessed by external steps above a coachhouse and stable.

KING DONIERT'S STONE, 1 m. NW. The decorated pedestal of a large memorial cross, with a mortice to receive a cross-shaft. Its principal face is inscribed in Anglo-Saxon miniscules 'Doniert rogavit pro anima' (Doniert has asked prayers for his soul). King Doniert is reputedly Dungarth, who drowned in A.D. 875. The reverse face has interlace panels of the same period, four knots, and on the sides four-cord plait interlace on one face, also of the same date.

LONG TOM or LONGSTONE CROSS, 2 m. NE. Prominently sited on the open moor, a tall monolith with an equal-limbed cross in relief, with small projections at the neck, and an incised rectangular panel below. It may have been carved from a pre-historic menhir.

TRETHEVY QUOIT, 1 m. NE. One of Britain's best-preserved Neolithic PORTAL DOLMENS. The long sides of the rectangular chamber project beyond the E end stone, where a small ante-chamber was created with two additional uprights; one now missing. The rear w support fell before 1850 leaving the capstone more steeply tilted than originally designed, and the ante-chamber higher. Door-like rectangular gap in e support, apparently natural, allowed crawling access to main chamber, presumably to perform rituals. Small circular hole in capstone's NE corner not yet adequately explained. Low stone mound surrounding quoit probably secondary, perhaps Bronze Age.

For MINIONS and THE HURLERS STONE CIRCLES *see* p. 356.

ST CLEMENT

ST CLEMENT. In its small churchtown far away from the village (which is now a suburb of Truro), in a lush landscape on the shore of the Tresillian River. Probably occupying an earlier *lann* site. Dedicated 1259. Tall w tower, three stages, with the buttresses towards N and s from the NW and SW corners. The buttresses reach up only to the second stage and end in prominent gargoyles of a man, sheep, ox and bird. Lesser gargoyles at the base of the crenellated parapet from which rise tall corner pinnacles with crocketed finials. The tower is unlikely to be as early as the doubtful 1326 F.K.I. inscription (probably C19) on a stone inside the ringing chamber, and the top stage is later. The body of the church was largely reconstructed in a severe restoration of 1865 by *H. Michell Whitley* during which frescoes including St Christopher found on the N and E window splays were destroyed. The C15–C16 s aisle of six bays has an arcade of standard piers with elaborately moulded capitals and nearly semicircular arches; it has a good set of Perp windows. The N transept has an arch of the same details towards the nave. The roofs are 1865 but with some applied details from the C15 originals of which there are more in the porch roof, in the tower screen, and in the partition in the N transept arch. – FONT. C14, octagonal, with tracery and interlace panels on a C19 pedestal. – PULPIT. serpentine, *c.* 1870. – GLASS. 1861–2. A rare and striking set of fourteen enamel-painted windows by *Rev. Clement Carlyon* in lively geometric patterns with heraldic motifs. – Pillar ALMS BOX in N transept, date 1728. – STOCKS, in porch. – MONUMENTS. Samuel Thomas †1796, signed by *Bacon*, 1799. Two standing allegorical figures against the usual obelisk, whose top, however, is going curiously Gothic; excellent workmanship, one of the finest marble sculptures in Cornwall. – Rear-Admiral Robert Carthew Reynolds †1811, signed *Micali direxit* (not fecit!) *Liburni* (i.e. at Leghorn), 1816. A young soldier and two women: he points to a monument with a naval battle; his portrait medallion higher up.

In the churchyard outside the s aisle an impressively tall CROSS. The sign of the cross in a circle; on the shaft the main inscription VITALI FILI TORRICI (Vitalus son of Torricus), above which in smaller characters the (probable) personal name IGNIOC. Date any time between the C5 and C7, the second inscription possibly later, the cross-head carved in the C12. – The church is approached by a charming group of thatched cottages and through a LYCHGATE, with slate-hung upper room and built on to a cottage; early C19 Gothick windows to the churchyard, no doubt a vestry room or school-room as at Kenwyn (q.v.). Exceptionally handsome lettering on C18 slates on the walls, complete with endearing mistakes in spelling and spacing.

The parish has a number of country houses, reflecting its proximity to Truro, mostly of relatively modest architectural interest.

LAMBESSOW BARTON, ½ m. NW. C17 and early C18 and earlier, with C20 wing. Two-storey SW front, 1:2:1 bays. Good C17 and C18 fittings including dog-leg stair with turned finials and pendants to newels, plaster cornices and mouldings, and late C18 chimneypiece with festoons in first-floor room in back wing. The house of John Foote, C17 mayor of Truro.

PENCALENICK HOUSE, 1 m. NE. 1881 (dated rainwater heads) by *J. P. St Aubyn* for Michael Williams, son of Michael Williams of Caerhays (q.v.). Paul Holden says it 'deserves the title of the last great Victorian house built in Cornwall: over two thirds of the house were given over to service functions and staff quar-ters'. Splendidly situated in an elevated position overlooking the Tresillian River and highly visible from the Tregothnan estate. Eclectic Palladian style on a rectangular plan around courtyard. The W entrance has a heavy Tuscan porte cochère, the S garden front three central bays broken forward with pedi-ment over between flanking canted bays. Chimneys with scrolled buttresses. The interior has a wide open-well stair and plasterwork including arabesque and geometric strapwork designs; other features draw on Adam style, Elizabeth and Jacobean precedents. The NORTH LODGE is a pretty early C19 *cottage orné* with the thatched roof carried over a veranda on rustic wooden posts with half-round arches.

BODREAN MANOR, 2 m. N. Early C19 with C18 sections to rear and late C19 service wing. Stucco with brick chimneys, sym-metrical two-storey S front of 3:3:3 bays and flanking canted bays. Gable pediment over W entrance front with granite doorcase.

For KILLAGORDEN, PENMOUNT CREMATORIUM and POL-WHELE *see* Truro, Other Buildings.

ST CLETHER

2080

ST CLETHER. The church lies W and away from the village. C15 W tower, unbuttressed and unpinnacled. The rest was rebuilt

1863–6 by *John Hayward* of Exeter in E.E. style, reusing the scalloped capitals of three thick circular Norman piers (cf. Morwenstow, North Petherwin and St Breward), and a few feet of impost moulding in the three w bays of the five-bay arcade between nave and s aisle: a square pier divides the two E bays. – FONT. The most elementary Norman with round bowl and round shaft with rope band. – STAINED GLASS. Chancel E and one aisle window.

HOLY WELL AND CHAPEL OF ST CLETHER, ¼ m. NW. Only accessible by a footpath across a ferny meadow above the little River Inny and below rock outcrops. In this remote setting, with no house visible anywhere, the chapel and well-house evoke perhaps more powerfully than anywhere in Cornwall a sense of the medieval religious landscape. The well chapel is the largest in the county, with the well-house set into the hillside on its N side. The tall, narrow well-house has a steeply gabled roof of large granite slabs and a rectangular basin. The chapel, of about 11 ft by 20 ft (3.4 by 6.1 meters), is of the simplest character within and without, with w and N doors, a rude altar table, and a plain late C19 roof. A spring feeds the well-house from which water runs underground into and across the E end of the chapel and flows out on the s side into a niche in the wall, expressed externally as another holy well. There is a small shelf to the rear of the niche with a door above: Sedding suggests the shelf was for thanksgiving donations from pilgrims, the door allowing the priest to collect donations from inside the chapel. Another niche to the rear of the altar, possibly for housing a relic of the saint. Both well-house and chapel are essentially C15–C16, thoughtfully restored 1897 (before which the chapel was roofless) by *Rev. Sabine Baring-Gould* et al., with 'every stone replaced where it had fallen': the result is authentic and enchanting.

THE OLD VICARAGE, opposite the church. Early C17, slate-hung front elevation with end-stacks, probably originally of two-room through-passage plan with C17–C19 rear extensions.

BASIL MANOR, ¼ m. S. A large courtyard-plan house with a gatehouse range and hall range parallel to it. Of early C16 origin, extended in the later C16 and C17, and extensively restored and partly rebuilt *c.* 1870s–80s by *J. P. St Aubyn*. Nearby a WHEEL-HEAD CROSS close to the River Inny, and two more on the road leading w. All are of similar design with projections at the neck.

ST COLUMB MAJOR

A small hilltop town dominated by the tall tower of its medieval church commanding the valley of the River Menalhyl and the Vale of Lanherne. The medieval town plan is still clearly readable, essentially one long main street running NE–SW along a ridge from the church to the southern end of Fair Street, with a northern extension downhill to the river at Bridge, an early crossing point of the Menalhyl. There are a few minor streets but no pre-C20 suburbs or major redevelopment to disrupt the intactness of the historic town centre.

St Columb, one of the largest parishes in Cornwall, owes its medieval growth to the patronage of the Arundells of Lanherne, one of the great Cornish families of the period, who promoted it as a separate manor from Lanherne by the early C15. In 1409 they established a manor mill at Bridge, near the medieval moated rectory, and were granted a charter for a market and fair in 1533. They were also instrumental in the development of the church, one of the finest in Cornwall. Sir John Arundell (†1435), five times Sheriff of Cornwall, founded a college of five priests for a chantry chapel in 1428, the largest ever founded in the county. The college survived the Dissolution and is still mentioned in early C19 records but all visible traces have gone: it probably stood immediately W of the church tower.

But St Columb never became a borough and in 1670 the Arundells leased the rights to the market and fair to a John Kinge of St Columb. The town became a staging point on the N–S route from Camelford and Wadebridge to Truro. John Ogilbys road atlas of 1675 records over 100 houses and notes that courts were regularly held there, while Joel Gascoyne's map of 1699 shows it as the largest place after Padstow in the hundred of Pydar. But thereafter its growth seems to have been modest and its population was in decline as late as between 1841 and 1851.

The town then suddenly burst into life again in a later C19 period of prosperity that lasted into the early C20. A new Market House had been erected in 1848 which also served as the magistrates' and county courts. Now the town built on its historic market and fair functions – and associated activities such as hurling, wrestling and Morris dancing – to become the administrative, financial and social hub of an extensive hinterland. Lake's parochial history of 1867 notes the construction of 'many good residences and places of business'. Among these were several by *William White*: his striking Venetian Gothic at Bank House and the sublime Victorian romanticism of his rebuilt rectory are two of the small-scale highlights of the Gothic Revival in Cornwall.

This was the town's high noon, its ambition perfectly symbolized by the then rector (and doomed London property speculator) Dr Samuel Walker's zealous but unsuccessful promotion of St Columb as the see of the proposed new diocese of Cornwall. The town changed only slowly during the C20. The market was moved to the southern end in 1906, well away from the cluster of genteel late C19 villas just N of the centre. The 1970s by-pass helped divert later C20 development away from the town centre to the surrounding lower land, though as a consequence a sea of modern houses now washes over the originally sylvan setting of White's rectory. But the strong identity of the town on the hill prevails.

St Columba. Impressively sited and visible for miles around as befits one of Cornwall's greater churches. The tall w tower of four, not the usual three, stages (the fourth possibly a c15 addition), the body of the church wide and spreading with nave and chancel both aisled N and S, large transepts, and two-storeyed porches N and S, the latter embattled. The tower is the more memorable for being open at ground level, allowing N–S passage as formerly at Lostwithiel and Tavistock, possibly here because the former college buildings (*see* above) hemmed it in so closely W as to prevent processions; its buttresses are set back from the angles, the first three stages rendered, the fourth with three-light Perp bell openings with slate louvres.

The interior is strikingly spacious, the nave arcades only three bays long but of wide span and imposing height, the two-centred arches rising from short square piers with four demi-shafts attached, the capitals of Caen stone. Nave and transepts are connected by arches of the same height but narrower. The S chancel arcade continues the style of the nave; the N has standard Cornish piers. The chancel aisles open back into the transepts by lower arches. The transepts are early to mid-c14 but it is most likely that the main structure represents a grand scheme of rebuilding, including the provision of chantry chapels, undertaken from *c.* 1433, the date of the will of Sir John Arundell, who requested burial 'in the middle of the new chapel annexed to the chancel', i.e. the S chancel aisle. There were two other chantries: the Jesus chantry founded in *c.* 1480 in the existing S transept and the chantry of the Holy Trinity in the N chancel aisle, founded as a guild chapel before 1484; the latter has tall niches with carvings of saints and prophets in Beer stone flanking the E window. The c14 S doorway with its ballflower ornament, rare in Cornwall, must have been re-set after the present wide aisles replaced earlier narrow aisles; the Arundell chantry is recorded as requiring the rebuilding and extension of the existing S chancel aisle. The embattled parapets of the S porch and the S aisle anticipate the Tudor style of the later c15 or early c16.

As to window tracery, the most reliable is the much restored S transept window of *c.* 1320 in Geometric Dec, a four-light lancet with three circles and fluted nook-shafts. Most of the other windows were replaced in a series of major c19 restorations, sometimes using sections of original tracery, that began under Rector Samuel Walker in 1845 in pursuit of his campaign for the church to become the cathedral of the proposed new diocese. He cleared out the pews, monuments and two W galleries. The next in the 1860s under *J. P. St Aubyn* included the rebuilding of the chancel and chancel aisles and new Dec windows in the three eastern gables and the S chancel aisle; he may also have been responsible for the curiously domestic arched-braced roof of the N chancel aisle. But it was the scheme under *G. H. Fellowes Prynne* of 1902–6 that has left the most tangible stamp on the church as seen today. It cost £10,000, a vast sum for the time, and was intended to ensure that 'some of the mischief done by previous "restorations" was put right'. It included more extensive re-windowing, this time in Perp, including the replacement of the E window of the chancel again, as well as the renewal of nave, aisle and transept roofs using old ribs and bosses 'as far as possible'. Much is therefore the result of skilful re-invention rather than original work, but good enough to convince.

The character of the interior also owes much to this period, including the REREDOS carved by *H. H. Martyn & Co.* of Cheltenham, richly carved chancel arch and ROOD SCREEN with figures, pulpit, wall-plate angels in the nave, panelling of the baptistery and Arundell chantry, and the flooring of the chancel and baptistery. A vestry was also added to the N transept. This echoes the similar late embellishment at St Austell and the same later C19 prosperity of the town sustained into the early C20. – FONT. Of *c.* 1300, octagonal bowl on a central stem with clustered outer shafts, large crude faces on five sides in quatrefoils (four *en face*, one in profile) and tracery motifs otherwise. – BENCH-ENDS. Thirty-eight of the usual early to mid-C16 type with two shields with initials, Instruments of the Passion etc. – PISCINAS in chancel and S chancel aisle, beautifully carved early C14. – BRASSES in the Arundell chantry N and S of the altar (and presently carpeted over), some of the best in Cornwall: Sir John Arundell †1545, two wives, children and armorial shields set in Purbeck slab; Sir John Arundell and John Arundell, wives, children and armorial shields including hirondelles, 1633 set in black marble (cf. the Arundell brasses at Mawgan-in-Pydar). On the parclose screen Dame Frances Gifford †1752, lozenge-shaped. – MONUMENT in N chancel aisle to Edward Heale †1796 by *Robert Isbell* of Stonehouse, slate tablet surrounded by shield of arms with putti on apron. – BRONZE PLAQUE. The New Birth on W wall of baptistery by *Rev. Allan Wyon.* (cf. Newlyn) – STAINED GLASS. Four windows by *Percy Bacon Bros*, the most impressive the chancel E, 1906. S transept, 1895 by *Clayton & Bell*.

The town's hilltop site is most apparent N of the church as the land falls steeply away towards the river, accentuated by the N LYCHGATE pointing downhill towards the former rectory: an elaborate cusped arch surmounted by gable with finial and supported by piers with pyramidal caps. – Near the E end of the church a large WHEEL-HEAD CROSS, the finest of its type in Cornwall and deserving a more dignified base; another RECTANGULAR CROSS-HEAD near the S porch, early but crude. – Attached to the W wall of the tower a tapered stone COFFIN SLAB, the remains of a carved STONE CROSS and another WHEEL-HEAD CROSS. – Good granite C18 and C19 CHEST TOMBS and slate HEADSTONES: e.g. of the former, William Tremain †1818, S of S aisle, and group of five late C18 and early C19 N of church; of the latter, John Williams †1740, S of S transept, fine primitive cherub's head with wings and good lettering.

MARKET HOUSE, Market Place. Dated 1848 in granite ashlar and the most notable example of classicism in the town. Two-storey symmetrical five-bay front to Market Place, rusticated ground floor, moulded cornice and parapet, round-headed windows with voussoirs and keystones. The E end with central bay broken forward rises to a square clock tower surmounted by an open cupola. Restored from near-dereliction in 1992 to provide a library on the ground floor but retaining a spacious staircase hall and the open granite stairs to the meeting rooms above.

ST COLUMB GALLERY AND MUSEUM, Bank Street. Dated 1874, formerly the St Columb Institute and opened in 1875 as the Mechanics Institute, Temperance Hall and New Vestry Room. Brick with granite dressings in Gothic style, but a pale shadow of Bank House, White's masterly essay opposite (*see* below). Planned around an entrance hall/central room with large rooms either side. Two-centred arched doors and windows, the tall central double doors with good ironwork.

ST COLUMB MAJOR SCHOOL AND SCHOOL HOUSE, Newquay Road. By *Silvanus Trevail*, 1876; a little-altered ensemble, good strong composition, the end bays advanced with three-light triple lancets and complete with arrowhead railings and pyramid gatepiers.

PERAMBULATION. From the churchyard the essential character of the town centre is clear, substantial mid- to late C19 institutional and commercial buildings soon giving way to modest houses with shops, much slate cladding, and hardly anything of the C20. The slate cladding is often applied to timber-framed walling, characteristic of south-west town building and also seen, for example, at Launceston and Padstow. Most is C18–C19 but an earlier example can be seen in GLEBE HOUSE, Market Place, with picturesque gabled and slate-hung elevations to the S side of the churchyard and to Market Place. The 1638 dated lead rainwater head may record a major reordering which adapted the stair hall and added a service wing at the rear of the two-storey range. Opposite, and in complete contrast, is the Market House (*see* above) and to its S, eleven cast-iron BOLLARDS with fluted shafts, emblems of hurling and shields of fifteen besants (the tinners' arms), and acorn finials.

E of the Market House, COLUMB HOUSE (Nos. 1–12 Market Place), an 1882 row of shops with integral warehouse to the rear. They speak of St Columb's later C19 commercial renaissance which finds its apogee in the building just across in NORTH STREET: *William White*'s St Columb Bank (now BANK HOUSE) of 1856–7. Founded by a group of local merchants, its presence is as eye-catching today in its use of Venetian Gothic at the heart of a modest slate-clad town as the architect and his clients must have originally intended, yet its presence is quietly impressive rather than dominant. The quality of White's design is sustained through meticulous detailing and execution on all the elevations of the L-shaped plan and carried through the interior. Main front to North Street two-storey, raised above cellars and surmounted by a steeply gabled attic: the cellars are protected by exquisite Ruskinian wrought-iron grilles, the rainwater pipes by granite bollards. Garden walls and gateways to both East Street and North Street carefully crafted into the overall design, the former skilfully resolving the swift change of scale from town centre to back lane. The polychromy of the exterior is all the more memorable for its subtlety, principally using a varied palette of Cornish building stones. The main wall surface Pentewan, also used for some dressings. More of the decoration is in St Stephen granite, e.g. the quoins and a double band at first-floor window-sill level, accentuated by contrast with thin bands of red brick at first-floor level and at the springing of the ground-floor window arches. Most of the window arches display combinations of all these materials and those of more than one light have colonnettes of grey Catacleuse, the three-light ground-floor windows' spandrels filled with polychromatic tiles.

The interior is a remarkably complete survival of a building type now almost vanished – the local private bank: banking hall, vault, offices and service accommodation are all still intact. Main entrance from North Street by a granite-vaulted vestibule with granite ribs and bosses with carved stone masks. To the r. is the banking hall with Gothic granite chimneypiece with polychromatic tiles, and windows with grey Catacleuse columns set behind the outer mullions and shutters rising from the floor. The bank vault is set behind the vestibule. A separate garden entrance from North Street gives into the spacious staircase hall with open-well stair and leads to the most impressive room in the building at the rear, presumably for the reception of major clients: its walls have blank arcades, the window has columns between the lights and at each side in different marbles, and the chimneypiece is a more elaborate version of that in the banking hall with side columns. There is a similar chimneypiece in the adjoining front room and lesser but still high-quality pieces on the first floor. As at the Old Rectory (see below), White's assured handling of Gothic is remarkable, using highly stylized detail in an almost Mannerist way with strong simple motifs executed in a variety of different stones and finishes.

s along North Street to the small C19 enclave of UNION SQUARE. The LIBERAL CLUB, dated 1812, was originally a house but much altered; symmetrical three-window front and central portico with square columns and diluted classical detail. Former BARLEY SHEAF INN, early to mid-C19, two-storey asymmetrical front angled along the line of the street, now residential. Turning the corner between Union Hill and Broad Street, the three-storey hipped-roofed mid-C19 ALLIANCE PHARMACY. A rare classical note is struck by the CONSERVATIVE CLUB, mid-C19, three-storey four-bay front, rusticated quoins and cornice. Off the square's E side, GLENCAIRN, one of the large mid- to late C19 villas built around the

NE slopes of the town. At the entrance to its drive, grandiose
GATEPIERS. Down UNION HILL, and presenting double
gables to the street, is TREVANTON, 1860, with alterations by
Silvanus Trevail in 1879 including a loggia and billiard room at
the rear, bay windows and service rooms. The staircase with
its barley-sugar newel posts with pyramid finials and the
Gothic arch on the landing must also be his.

Back up the hill, at BROAD STREET's junction with FORE
STREET is BARCLAYS BANK, established 1873 as the Miners'
Bank and later becoming the Consolidated Bank of Cornwall.
Splendidly showy in a Free Jacobethan style, red brick with
yellow diapers and granite dressings, shaped gables, strapwork
etc. culminating in a polygonal tower on the corner with spire
and finials. Opposite, the RED LION HOTEL, 1810, the grandest of the town's ten hostelries at the end of the C19. Granite
ashlar front, originally with double-depth plan and dining and
assembly rooms to rear. Much altered after a fire in 1953 and
subsequently partly rebuilt. A marble plaque commemorates
James Polkinghorne, champion wrestler in 1826, and the centenary of Cornish wrestling 1826–1926. Further down Fore
Street, LLOYDS BANK of 1891 is by *Silvanus Trevail*. In granite
ashlar and classical style, originally a pair of attached banking
halls with separate entrances at either end. Doric columns to
doors, central four bays with rock-faced rusticated pilasters
between windows. Nos. 24–26 are three late C19 shops with
granite pilasters at ground floor and elaborate capitals and
patterned yellow tilework above. Set back on E side behind
other houses a former CONGREGATIONAL CHAPEL, originally
built *c.* 1795 but subsequently enlarged and now mostly early
C19. Central entrance with three round-arched windows above.
Now a workshop. On the street frontage another former chapel,
now the YOUTH CLUB, brick with granite dressings and
pointed-head windows. Pointed-arch entrance with paired
lancets above, with tablet N of doorway dated 1812. On W side,
again set behind other buildings, BIBLE CHRISTIAN CHAPEL
dated 1842, also now in other use. Fore Street has some C18
houses remodelled in the C19.

Return to the centre by WEST STREET with its medley of
slate-hung cottages, workshops and stores, to the steeply
gabled former SUNDAY SCHOOL of 1866 with pointed windows
and intersecting timber tracery. Then N down BANK STREET.
After the Museum (*see* above), pretty C18–C19 terraced houses
of two and three storeys running down the hill, soon giving
way to C19 villas. ASHLEIGH is *Silvanus Trevail*'s 1896 refronting of an earlier house with heavy transomed-and-mullioned
windows and embattled parapet. Almost opposite, and gracefully accomplished on a steep site, is PENMELLYN, *c.* 1855 by
William White, announced by gatepiers with steep pyramidal
caps with finials. Another example of White's dexterity, this
time a blend of Victorian Gothic and Vernacular Revival.
Asymmetrical L-shaped plan, the porch set in the angle of the
two ranges, the door with pointed arch. High-quality detail

throughout, the varied features held effortlessly together in the overall design.

Further down at BRIDGE are the C19 TOLL HOUSE, the early C19 BRIDGE of one round arch with dressed voussoirs and parapet walls with granite copings and TOWN MILLS: the present buildings on this historic site of water-powered industry are C19, with gabled timber hoist housing and small ridge ventilator on the main range. Just up the hill on the other side of the River Menalhyl is ROSEMELLYN, dated 1871, two-storey symmetrical front with central three-storey porch tower rising to a pyramidal roof and obelisk finials, faintly reminiscent of nearby Trewan Hall (*see* below). First and second floors of both porch and tower have a string course of brick in a chevron pattern.

OLD RECTORY, Bridge. 1851 by *William White*, one of his earliest and most important buildings. Its original setting, sequestered, low-lying and moated in the Menalhyl valley below the church, may have been diminished by C20 housing, but White's achievement of what Mark Girouard has called 'a charming and sympathetic exercise in Victorian Romanticism' still shines out. Presented at the time as a 'restoration', he almost completely rebuilt the previous medieval hall house on the site using elements of the original plan, at an expensive £7,000, in pursuit of Rector Samuel Walker's ill-fated ambition that it should be the bishop's palace for the new Cornish see.

White's composition of the house is consummate, the original approach along the tree-lined valley crossing a bridge over the moat towards the many gabled, rambling elevations arranged around a courtyard plan: the intended effect of long, cumulative history lightly worn is achieved instantly. The style is C14 Gothic, carried out in a gentle structural polychromy using three different stones – dark blue Catacleuse, white St Stephen's granite and brown St Columb, the latter the main walling material. The asymmetrical E entrance front is especially loveable, the two-storeyed gabled porch flanked to the l. by a polygonal tower and a single bay, to the r. by three gabled bays. The l. hand bay has a four-light window to the ground floor, three-light above, both cusped. The r. has large cusped and traceried first-floor windows above smaller windows between buttresses on the ground floor, reflecting the distinctive planning of the house which places the principal rooms on the first floor; the larger end bay has a five-light window above two lancets, the window lighting the drawing room which runs along the r. side of the house. Other delightful touches are the corbelled oriel window supported by a (later) granite pillar on the s front, tall ashlar chimneystacks all of different designs, an octagonal bellcote with weathervane and beautifully crafted delicate iron brackets for the rainwater gutters.

The interior sustains the high promise of the exterior. The two-storeyed entrance hall with arch-braced roof leads directly across the tiled floor to a straight granite stair, rising dramatically between stone walls through the whole width of the hall and leading up to the main hall with two-bay arch-braced roof with collars and queen struts, a stone chimneypiece and a gallery. The drawing-room has a four-bay arch-braced roof on stone corbels. The room to the l. of the main hall is the former library with two-bay roof with cranked arch-braces, collars and queen struts. White's characteristically meticulous attention to detail is everywhere apparent with fine Gothic doors, wainscotting and dado rails, door and window fittings and stained glass in several windows.

The ground floor has some of the best and most original features of the house. Immediately l. of the entrance is the waiting room with one stone column with ring mouldings. The former dining room is to the r. of the entrance hall, now partitioned, with chamfered beams resting on stone corbels. Beyond are two small rooms, the wine cellar and the beer cellar, the latter with three-bay arcades of plain stone piers with two central arches and brick vaulted ceiling. To the rear of the dining room is the first service stair, a striking feature with chamfered piers forming the balustrade and chamfered stone arches. A second service stair backs on to the courtyard which has a timber gallery at first-floor level and a (formerly external) timber stair. One of White's major skills is his ability to reduce Gothic to its bare essentials to reveal its moving simplicity, and the detail throughout the house, but especially of the vaulted undercroft and the first service stair, is of an elegant austerity reminiscent of French Cistercian monasteries. It is an understated masterpiece.

THE RETREAT, off Union Hill. 1838 by *Scott & Moffatt* as the former workhouse, then hospital. Successfully converted to residential use in 1993 by *Hocking & Newton* though its setting is somewhat compromised by a clumsy new block in front of the main elevation. Strong classical design, the single-storeyed front range symmetrical around a tall entrance arch with pediment with large modillions; and a fine pair of cast-iron gates with knob finials. It leads through to the courtyard and the main central range with the central octagonal three-storey tower with canted bays, flanked by six bay wings of two storeys and a cross-wing at the end of each wing. The plan is standard for a C19 workhouse but this is an early and architecturally impressive example.

TREWAN HALL, ¾ m. N. A large gentry house, of C15 origin but substantially remodelled and enlarged in the early C17. Though partly rebuilt in the C18 and thoroughly restored *c.* 1870, possibly by *William White*, the overall character of the C17 house prevails. It is of U-shaped plan, the central double-depth hall range flanked by far-projecting symmetrical wings. The l. wing, which extends to the rear as a cross-wing, seems to have been rebuilt in the late C19. The r. wing was partly reconstructed in the C18 but terminates in an early C17 gatehouse. The result is a fine asymmetrical front elevation, the main range with an embattled parapet, the wings with shaped stepped gables, with many Gothic (Perp or Perp-style) windows with cusped lights and some tracery.

The outstanding feature of the house is the GATEHOUSE, in granite ashlar, probably of the same date as the hall fireplace of 1635 (*see* below). It shows clear parallels with the gatehouse at Lanhydrock (q.v.), with which it is a close contemporary, in a similar transitional style between Gothic and classical. It has a moulded plinth with a four-centred arch double doorway with roll mouldings and recessed spandrels with carved leaves. Ionic columns to l. and r. support a moulded string course with three diamond dies, a sill string at first floor, and four-light windows with hollow-chamfered mullions and three columns with convex caps. The frieze above has carved dies and cornice. As at Lanhydrock, the crowning glory is the richly embellished roof, a shaped gable with three columns of a primitive Ionic order with two blind round-headed lights, carved frieze and cornice, adorned with obelisk finials set on four balls, three over the centre of the gable of which two have carved strapwork.

The evidence for White's involvement is unproven, but the extensive C19 refurbishment has close parallels to his other work at St Columb Major around the same time. The entrance hall seems to have been reconstructed on the line of the medieval through passage, and to the rear of this is a stone vault very similar to the vestibule vault at Bank House (*see* above). Similarly the three-arched stone screen to the hall is reminiscent of some of his work at the Old Rectory (*see* above). The hall, open to the roof, is also C19, of four bays with arch braces. On the inner wall is the granite fireplace with a segmented arch, roll mouldings and a vestigial ogee dated 1635.

NANSWHYDEN, 2 m. w. The Palladian mansion, built in 1740 by *Thomas Edwards* (cf. Trewithen, Tehidy, etc.) of Greenwich for Robert Hoblyn, MP for Bristol, was destroyed by fire in

St Columb Major, Nanswhyden. Engraving after W. Borlase, 1758

1803. A diary account of 1757 records: 'at the entrance of the house are stone steps on each side after the manner of Lord Tilney's on Epping Forest and our Mansion House for the Lord Mayor of this City . . . the staircase [is] very magnificent'. A COACHHOUSE and GRANARY remain as part of Nanswhyden Farm. The coachhouse has three elliptically arched carriage entrances with dressed granite lunettes above; the granary is, unusually, of red brick, on brick piers.

CASTLE-AN-DINAS, 2 m. ESE. Large Iron Age HILLFORT overlooking Goss Moor and any spinal prehistoric routeway through Cornwall. Two Bronze Age ROUND BARROWS within enclosure surrounded by four concentric ramparts. Excavations and geophysical and phosphate analyses in the 1960s suggested limited settlement activity. The enclosure may instead have been used for important community gatherings. The ditch of the slightest and apparently earliest rampart (probably earlier Iron Age), second from ouside, had silted up before the later Iron Age ramparts were built.

NINE MAIDENS, 2¼ m. NNE, in a field. Until the late C19 this STONE ROW's large, slender quartz stones, up to 6 ft 10 in. (2.1 metres) high, marched through heathy grassland. The 350-ft (107-metre) long line has five unevenly spaced stones still erect, another leaning, one fallen (and split) and two stumps; a tenth stone (fallen) is recent. Probably once much longer.

ST COLUMB MINOR

The mother parish of Newquay and now absorbed into the town's C20 suburbs but at its heart still rural and villagey.

ST COLUMBA. A proud C15 W tower, of four stages rather than the usual three, its noble proportions enhanced by tall pinnacles corbelled out on carved figures at the level of the top string course above the usual buttresses set back from the angles. Three-light bell-openings with Perp tracery and slate louvres at the fourth stage. The surprise is the interior and the strong C14 character of the nave and chancel arcades; nave with four bays of piers consisting of four major and four minor shafts, the arcades two-centred and their detail similar to St Columb Major (q.v.); chancel with two bays with four central arches and similar piers – the aisles seem to have been extended early on to the full length of the chancel. A blocked window on the N side of the W end of the nave may pre-date the addition of the N aisle. Door to former rood screen in N aisle with stone newel stair and upper doorway. Restoration of 1785 and a major reconstruction in 1884 by *J. D. Sedding*. He altered the floor levels to suit a High Anglican arrangement, heightening the chancel and sanctuary, lowering the nave and aisle floors – hence the odd heights of the pier bases – renewed most of the roofs except for the C15 wagon roofs with carved ribs, wall-plates and bosses over the aisle chapels, and replaced most of the windows in Perp. Exceptions are the four-light window in the N aisle with two tall lights and flanking lower lights and one in the S aisle. – FONT. Norman, of Bodmin type, circular bowl with chevron carving, four outer shafts surmounted by faces, much worked over. – BENCH-ENDS. Several were found in 1896, some with the usual two shields to an end, some with the later composition of only one larger motif; they had an inscription stating they had been erected out of the poor's stock in 1525 but none are now visible. – ROYAL ARMS of Charles II in N aisle, painted plaster with ancient colour mounted on a panel with strapwork, cherub and pinnacles. – STAINED GLASS. N aisle E by *Gibbs & Howard*, 1885. – MONUMENTS. A good local ensemble in the N aisle; all of slate: monument with robust low relief carving of a woman with inscription around the border dated 1640; slate tablet to Richard Budd †1787; slate tablet with fine vigorous carving in relief of a male figure initialled RE, *c*. 1640. In S aisle, another slate monument, to Henry Minnow †1697, with central panel with verses and border with flower carving.

Over the C15 S porch fine slate SUNDIAL, with gnomon, dated 1826. – LYCHGATE. Late C19, possibly part of Sedding's campaign. Elegant tall pointed chamfered arch with coping and cross finial flanked by pinnacles with pyramidal tops and with contemporary iron gates. The CHURCHYARD has many excellent C18 and C19 memorials including headstones in granite and slate, chest tombs, and a slate ledger stone attached to the S wall, C17 with carved flowers and strapwork and vale-dictory verses.

CHURCH STREET has pleasant groups of C18 and C19 cottages, especially immediately SE of the church, which sustain the settlement's village character. Towards Newquay the street is more Victorian with the former METHODIST CHAPEL, late C19 Gothic, front gable with central single light and flanking lower lights, gabled porches and stone pinnacles at either end.

RIALTON HEIGHTS, on a wedge-shaped plot of land E of the church. 1974 by *Feilden & Mawson*, an exemplary housing scheme for the elderly, one of the few post-war local authority schemes of note in Cornwall. The ingenious layout exploits the difficulties of the site to great effect, arranging the development around a pedestrian street that points to the church tower in one direction and the open countryside in the other. The houses, of varied scale and clad in Forticrete (much now painted), are close on both sides of the street but relieved by openings off to small parking courts and a road behind; the latter area has a very open character with gardens and ample landscaping. Despite some attrition of the detailing, the clarity of the design has stood the test of time well.

TREVELGUE HEAD PROMONTORY FORT, 1 m. WNW. Seven ramparts, in three groups, with deep inland ditches, isolate and subdivide a long elegant headland broken in two in post-prehistoric times. Porth Island, now reached by footbridge, contained fragmentary fields and at least twelve round-houses. Excavations in 1939 produced remarkably rich finds indicating interrupted occupation and metalworking activity from the C3 B.C. to the C6 A.D. Two large Bronze Age BARROWS, one dramatically perched above sea-cut chasm on Porth Island, the other on N edge of inland part of promontory.

ST DAY

7040

In an unassuming way one of the most atmospheric places in Cornwall. It first grew as a pilgrimage centre on the great E–W land route to St Michael's Mount and by the C15 was the county's second greatest shrine. What the special miracle or relic was is unknown and the site of the shrine chapel of the Holy Trinity is uncertain, but the street pattern of the medieval settlement survives. It is, however, St Day's later C18 and C19 industrial history that is all-pervasive, from the time the town became the market and service centre for the 'copper kingdom' of the Gwennap area, then the most famous copper mining district in Cornwall. It is set on a low hilltop in a landscape shaped by the legacy of mining, the mines once infiltrating the town and with engine houses on the horizon. With its attractive mix of C18 and C19 buildings on its main streets, St Day has the faded dignity of a place that went quietly to sleep after its boom years, and has yet to fully awaken.

HOLY TRINITY, Church Street. 1826–8 by *Charles Hutchens* (cf. St Mary, Penzance, and St Mary, Redruth). There could be no more poignant symbol of St Day's decline from its C19 peak than the roofless church. Today, when approached through the long straight avenue sloping down from the churchyard gate to the w front and seen among trees against the wide landscape beyond, it appears as a loveable and fanciful Gothick folly. The style is entirely that of Commissioners' churches all over England. All the motifs are thin – even the granite appears like paper – yet highly successful, especially the show w front: two tiers of Perp windows to the aisles flank a lean w tower not projecting forward but given strong verticality by octagonal corner shafts finishing in tall pinnacles and surmounted by a low octagonal spire rising to a flèche. There are similar shafts and pinnacles to the corners. The E end windows contain the remains of stained glass. The church was abandoned in 1956 in favour of the former mission hall opposite the w entrance to the churchyard, converted to the present church by *Giles Blomfield*.

The CHURCHYARD, most of which lies E of the church with views out over the open landscape, has a number of specially impressive granite tomb-chests and headstones. On the w approach to the church is a small medieval WHEEL-HEAD CROSS.

The town is gathered around the CLOCK TOWER in Fore Street, *c.* 1830 in E.E. style. Of three stages successively set back with two-centred arched openings rising to an embattled parapet and surmounted by a tall octagonal wooden bellcote. On the s side a large porch, also embattled.

An exploration of the pretty town centre is as much about the intriguing morphology of the settlement as its mostly modest buildings. The basic plan is triangular, like Breage, and incorporates the ancient E–W pilgrim route along Telegraph Hill and Street, West End, and Vogue Hill, with streets like Mills Street representing later industrial growth. It has been suggested that the site of the medieval shrine chapel was adjacent to Trevean Cottage on the w side of the small square in front of Buckingham Terrace, possibly within an early Christian *lann*. There is a striking contrast between the densely built-up centre and the spacious and verdant outer streets with paths into the open countryside. Of the building stock, there are many attractive mid-C18 to mid-C19 houses, former shops and cottages, several larger houses in walled gardens, some good early to mid-C19 shopfronts, and outbuildings like the former CARPENTER'S SHOP in Telegraph Street, with a boarded upper storey, and WILTON'S WORKSHOP behind No. 6 Church Street, where the finest underground surveying instruments were made. Nos. 1–25 MILLS STREET are a specially well-preserved development of workers' housing, *c.* 1840, built as a speculative development for the mining industry. Among other features of interest are PEBBLES, Fore Street, a former count house; VOGUE SHUTE, Vogue, a C17–C19 water shute with its retaining wall built alongside the ramped access for carts; and excellent granite paving, kerbstones and cobbles.

The best view of the former industrial landscape is from the churchyard looking E, where much of the hillside is still devoid of vegetation nearly 150 years after mining ceased. This was the site of CONSOLIDATED MINES, with the world's richest copper lode working from 1819 to 1840 employing nearly two thousand workers. The ore was taken by railway to Devoran (q.v.) for shipping to Swansea for smelting. Little remains apart from a few engine houses or solitary stacks: the prominent very squat tapered chimney is actually a clock tower.

SCORRIER HOUSE, 1 m. NW. The larger C18 house of the Williams family was destroyed by fire except for part of the service wing in 1908 and rebuilt *c.* 1910 in classical style. Two-storey four-bay entrance front with large square single-storey porte cochère. The interior is planned around a sumptuous and extravagant entrance hall and staircase, the imperial stair rising between fluted columns on tall parallel pedestals.

At the s end of the garden, two medieval CROSSES. The taller example, formerly on the Helston–Penryn road and erected here *c.* 1849, has an equal-limbed cross within a double bead to both faces, with two crosses within circles on the principal face; and covering the rest of the shaft, some excellent zigzag decoration, also on the reverse and one side, with latticework on the remaining side. The other has a figure on the principal face and a Latin cross on the reverse enclosed in a broad bead.

ST DENNIS

St Denis. As a vantage point to view the crazy scenery of the china clay country, this church should be visited. It lies about 700 ft (200 metres) up inside an Iron Age hillfort and its dedication may have originated in the Cornish word for fort: *dinas*. The land around is bare with cyclopic granite walls separating road from field, bleak terraces of workers' houses and the cones and flat-topped hills of china clay workings all around. Late C15 tower, two-stage, of ashlar granite, without buttresses. NE stair-turret, embattled with circular panelled pinnacles and pyramidal lead roof. The rest of the church was substantially rebuilt in 1847 (not very correctly as the odd window shapes show), and the S aisle arcade removed (to Nanpean, q.v.), the nave and aisle roofed as one. The S porch with its pedimented panelled gable and obelisk finials records the rebuilding date. N aisle rebuilt after a fire in 1986, with octagonal piers. Arch-braced roofs of the same date.

In the churchyard. – FONT. W of S porch. Circular, C15 on modern base. – CROSS. S of S porch. Fine tall granite head and shaft with Latin crosses on both faces, a double bead surround running down the shaft with three incised symbols similar to those at Nine Maidens Down Cross, Crowan (q.v.), either depicting hourglasses or chalices.

Parkandillick Engine House, 1 m. N. Three-storey *c.* 1900 engine house with attached boiler house and detached chimney, complete with its 50-in. (1.27-metre) bore engine and machinery.

cottage at Enniscaven, 2 m. NE. Small cob and thatch cottage of single storey and attic and two unit plan. A rare survival of a once common building type.

ST DOMINIC

A delightful Tamar-side parish, of great scenic beauty.

St Dominica. A strange three-stage W tower with a corbelled-out top stage, somewhat domestic-looking. The top stage retreats again some distance below the parapet, and in the space so formed, on the E, S and W sides, are three sunk panels each containing a curious little figure, rudely carved but probably of the twelve apostles, like South Hill. The buttresses are diagonal, as usual in early Cornish towers, and a broad, flat stair-turret rises on the SE side, ending like a buttress. Embattled parapet and pinnacles. As to date, the lower two stages must be C14: Sedding suggested the tower had a parapet which was incorporated into the top stage added in the C15, hence the corbelling. C15 S porch with four-centred arched outer doorway with clustered piers with plain abaci, ceiled wagon roof with moulded ribs, carved bosses and wall-plate. Nave and N and S aisles of five bays presenting three equal gables to the E end. The S aisle is earliest, which comes out in the design of the piers: square with four attached demi-piers, whereas the N side has the later Cornish standard shape. Also the arches on the S side are simply double-chamfered, on the N side four hollows instead of the chamfers. Tall narrow four-centred tower arch. Late C15 wagon roofs to nave, chancel and aisles, ceiled, with finely carved moulded ribs, bosses and wall-plate with pomegranates, leaves and flowers: the aisle wall-plates are brattished. A restoration of 1873 by *Henry Elliott* included re-flooring, re-pewing, and stencilled decoration of the chancel roof. – STAINED GLASS. Chancel E, 1871. Tower W, 1903 by *Clayton & Bell*. N aisle E, 1894, and N aisle W, 1895, by *Fouracre & Watson*. N aisle N, 1963 by *Brian D. L. Thomas*, made by *Whitefriars Glass*, with local agricultural scenes including reaper and various farm produce. – MONUMENTS. The outstanding feature of the interior, though not immediately apparent because it is obscured by the organ, is the CHEST TOMB to Sir Antony Rous †1622 and his son †1620. The two men lie side by side, in armour facing their shields of arms. Only one of the twelve columns that once formed its rich canopy survives. – John Clarke, 1749, marble tablet on corbels with slate pilasters, cornice, and shield of arms, by *J. R. Veale*. – William Brendon, 1700, oval slate convex tablet with stone-carved wreath surround, putti and grotesque mask.

At the NW corner of the churchyard and built into its bank, a pretty little former SUNDAY SCHOOL, early to mid-C19 with pointed-arched lights with diamond glazing.

HALTON QUAY, 2 m. SSE. One of the ports of Callington. The wharf, a CHAPEL (built as an office for the quay) and a large LIMEKILN remain in poignant isolation on the banks of the wide reaches of the tidal Tamar.

ST ENDELLION 9070

ST ENDELIENT. The church stands sentinel over its coastal parish, low-roofed, secure against Atlantic gales, and imbued with a profound serenity. By 1291 it was staffed by four prebendaries: three of the clergy were suppressed in 1548 but reinstated from 1555 and the four were made into a collegiate body in 1928. The three-stage C16 W tower of large blocks of 'Lundy' granite is unbuttressed, with banded quatrefoil decoration to the plinth, and crowned by an embattled parapet: its distinctive octagonal pinnacles with ball finials appeared to Betjeman 'like hare's ears peeping over the hill'. The body of the church dates from the early C15 with nave, N and S aisles, and a chancel that spreads beyond the aisle arcades. The S doorway has fleurons in the jambs and voussoirs.

The interior is light and spacious, enhanced by its clear glazing. The nave is low and wide with five-bay arcades of Cornish standard design with four-centred arches, the capitals with varied motifs including the large horizontal leaves familiar from Devon; the aisle windows are of three lights, again standard Cornish Perp. The wide E end is pleasingly proportioned, the E window of five lights; the E windows of the aisles are of four. Fine C15 wagon roofs throughout, with carved bosses and carved angels against the wall-plates at the foot of the principals. The roofs were taken down and re-erected in 1937. Some of the bosses (e.g. in the S aisle) are original, as are five of the angels, the rest c. 1900–40. – FONT. Norman, very small and simple. – BENCH-ENDS. In the nave, of the standard Cornish Perp type, one of arms of Roscarrock impaling Granville of Stowe. – Good, solid 1930s pews in the nave and N and S aisles, locally carved by *Arthur Dustow*. – C17 CHAIRS in chancel and C17 BENCH in S aisle. – MONUMENTS. Tomb-chest in the S aisle, c. 1475–1500, of Catacleuse stone and of superb quality. It has three deep niches on each of the long sides, and more on each of the short ones. The niches have ogee arches on colonettes and inside beautifully designed and sculpted little vaults. The detail, such as the cusping, is as delicate as if it were of cast iron. There are close similarities with the other outstanding sculpture of this date in this area (cf. Padstow, St Issey and St Merryn). By the same hand is the STOUP inside the S door, also of Catacleuse, and also excellent, with carved arms of Roscarrock, Chenduit or Cheney and Pentire, and some acorn motifs. – C16 LEDGER STONE of John Roscarrock in N aisle with marginal inscription and cross in relief; other good C18 ledger stones in the floor of the S aisle. – CURIOSUM. C18 ringers' rhymes (the same as St Kew) with pictures of ringers in the belfry.

In the CHURCHYARD a remarkable ensemble of C18 and C19 headstones, almost an illustrated history of inscription-writing. Excavations in 1977 revealed graves on the S side of the road fronting the church, the remains of a large cemetery probably dating from the C8. Immediately N of the churchyard, the RECTORY, possibly originating from one of the four prebendal houses. Early C17, remodelled c. 1840 when the eaves were raised, c. 1860 when the cross-wing was added, and c. 1960.

TRESGUNGERS, 1 m. NE. A substantial late C16 gentry house, once in the possession of the Vyvyans of Trelowarren. The striking feature of its front elevation is the central three-storey entrance tower with an embattled parapet, added in 1660 for I. and M. Matthews (datestone). Many granite mullion windows with hoodmoulds, that to the hall of eight lights with alternating king mullions, and a similar arrangement in the six-light ground-floor window of the cross-wing to the l. and in the first-floor four-light windows. It originally comprised a central range with a through passage, the hall on the r. and a parlour on the l. with a service wing beyond; there seems to have once been a matching r. cross-wing. Some C17 fittings, the parlour remodelled in the early C18 with moulded plaster cornice. Late C16 roof to main range and cross-wing, the former of seven bays, the latter of seven bays with principals with slightly curved feet like those at nearby Roscarrock.

CROSS-SHAFT, 2 m. W on the road to Port Quin. Inscription: XP and BROCAGNI HIC IACIT NADOTTI FILIUS. Date probably C6 or C7; lettering transitional between Roman and Hiberno-Saxon.

ROSCARROCK. *See* p. 481.

ST ENODER

8050

ST ENODER. A large church, especially impressive its S elevation of W tower, S aisle and S porch all in large granite blocks and battlemented. The tower, entirely of the Cornish type with corner buttresses and pinnacles, was rebuilt in 1711 after a collapse of 1686, the date demonstrated only by the remarkable Baroque scrolls that replace the set-offs and by the odd tracery of the W window. The S aisle, which had been damaged by the fall of the tower, has quatrefoil panels, which include the date 1686 at battlement level, repeated in the plinth. The two-storey S porch is, however, C16: it has set-back buttresses and crocketed finials, quatrefoil panels like the S aisle, demi-figures of angels in the doorway and shield carrying angels on the buttresses. The S and N windows of four lights are of the same Perp design, some renewed in the C19. The N window of the N transept is puzzling: it is a rare C14 design of wavy lattice tracery; is it reused? Light and spacious interior, clear-glazed except for the E window of the chancel with one C15 head in the tracery of the SE window. The S arcade of four bays is C14 with octagonal piers and two-centred arches. The N arcade and N transept are C15 of standard design – see also the much lower three-bay arcades of the N and S chancel aisles. Both nave aisles and the N transept have wagon roofs, the chancel and E end of the S aisle C19 arch-braced roofs with wind-braces. – FONT. Norman, circular, with four crude corner faces and a crisscross pattern around the rim. – BENCH-ENDS. C16, partly with one, partly with two shields for an end, on C19 benches. Further C16 fragments in C19 pulpit and base of lectern. – ROOD SCREEN. A delightful C19 filigree of Gothic tracery on slender single and paired colonettes, the dado incorporating four C16 bench-ends. – MONUMENT. Very infantile slate plate to Dorothy Tanner †1634, with kneeling figures in low relief.

ST ENODOC

9070

'. . . And all things draw towards St Enodoc'* wrote the younger Betjeman of his spiritual home in Cornwall and final resting place. There is indeed something quietly compelling about this unassuming medieval chapelry to St Minver sheltered behind Daymer Bay below Brea Hill and once, like St Piran's Oratory and Church (q.v.), almost lost in the dunes. Even though it has a little C13 spire, rare in Cornwall, it must still be sought out in a dip among the golf links in its tamarisk-protected churchyard. It was dug out in 1863 by Rev. W. Hart Smith, the vicar of St Minver, and restored by *J. P. St Aubyn*, a partnership reprised at Porthilly (q.v.) two years later. The church is essentially Norman: N wall of nave, N transept, and ground storey of the N tower (with a N window and arch into the transept). The position of the tower is unusual (but *see* Blisland and Bodmin not too far away). The S door is C14 with two-centred arches and moulded jambs. There is no aisle to the nave but a C15 S chancel aisle of three bays, low, small, and of standard Cornish design which probably absorbed the S transept; a S porch was added at the same time. – FONT. Simple C12, with a round bowl, shaft with cable moulding and round base, very like Porthilly. – ROOD SCREEN. The base of the C15 screen survives, the uprights moulded and carved with a floral trail; restored panels with blind tracery. – Holy water STOUP re-set in S wall with C15 arch above. – STAINED GLASS. S aisle E window with grisaille glass with angel, 1851 by *Toms* of Wellington. – MONUMENTS. In S porch, incised slate slab of John Mably and daughter Alice, 1687, a very late example of incised effigies. – E. E. Betjeman, father of Sir John, of Undertown, Daymer (*see* below), †1934, on S wall. – Slate tablet, 1995, with fine relief by *Philip Chatfield*, a survivor of a brig wrecked nearby on The Rumps with the loss of three lives. – Also in S porch, CROSS of the wheel-head type with an equal-limbed cross in relief with slightly expanded ends enclosed in a narrow bead. Just inside the churchyard by the lychgate is the Delabole slate HEADSTONE to Sir John Betjeman †1984, by *Simon Verity*. Wonderfully spirited Gothick inscription surrounded by entwined flora and fauna, exquisitely executed, and lovely in all weathers.

On BREA HILL four Bronze Age round BARROWS on summit ridge. Early modern circular stone-walled look-out imposed on E cairn.

---

*From 'Sunday Afternoon Service in St Enodoc Church, Cornwall', in *New Bats in Old Belfries* (1945).

At nearby DAYMER and TREBETHERICK, several houses of the earlier C20 that demonstrate Arts and Crafts influence on the genteel immigrants to Cornwall at that period. For example UNDERTOWN, Daymer Lane, 1928 by *Robert Atkinson* for E. E. Betjeman. Large projecting stone stack with inglenook fireplace and steeply pitched slate roof sweeping down to first-floor level on the front elevation over a veranda, and large semicircular stair-tower at rear. Extended in the late C20. DAYMER HOUSE, 1910, by *A. Allen*, a striking design with seven-window fronted house, first-floor slate clad, with battered corner buttresses in stone rising to the eaves and tall stone stacks. On the cliffs overlooking Greenaway Beach, a group of HOUSES by *C. Cowles-Voysey*, son of C. F. A. Voysey, white-rendered with steep slate roofs, in a simple but dignified vernacular style. TREEN in Daymer Lane was John Betjeman's holiday home with an extension by *John Brandon Jones* of the 1960s.

ST ERME

ST HERMES. The church is set within an oval churchyard or *lann*. The imposing C15 W tower of broad proportions is of granite ashlar in three stages, with buttresses leaving the corners free, a stair in the NW angle, and tall crocketed pinnacles above the crenellated parapet. The rest was radically remodelled by *John Foulston* in 1819–20 using much C15 fabric, like the stumpy pinnacles that crown the buttresses along the body of the church and N and S transepts, and bestowing a pretty early C19 character to the interior. Foulston widened the nave and chancel giving into narrow N and S aisles only 7 ft (2.1 metres) wide, under a single-span roof. Most of the carved ribs, purlins and bosses from the C15–C16 roofs were retained and refixed in new segmental barrel-vaulted ceilings which have wider panels than the originals. Foulston also reused the six-bay S aisle arcade, of standard Cornish design with four plain capitals to each pier and heavy semicircular arches; the N arcade is a copy. Two very large mask corbels re-set above the original roof-line. S porch added 1867. A thoughtful restoration in 1908 by *E. H. Sedding* slightly re-arranged the panels of the roof, added new carved wall-plates, and inserted new window tracery; the church was also re-seated and re-furnished. – FONT. Norman, circular, of unusual ornamentation with a large foliage scroll along the top of the bowl and four motifs of lilies, conventionally treated, below; cf. the later and richer type of font decoration at Bodmin, St Austell, etc., of which Sedding considered this to be the prototype. – ROYAL ARMS of George IV dated 1827, painted on metal sheet. – STAINED GLASS. E window, 1911 by *Mary Lowndes*, Christ's call to the fishermen, in the Arts and Crafts tradition. – BRASS. Robert

Trencreeke †1594 and his wife and family in civil dress, not in its original form or setting.

TRUTHAN BARTON, 1 m. NW. Early C18 house incorporating parts of an earlier building. Main block with five-bay front and central heavy doorcase with slight pediment flanked by square late C19 bay windows with elongated sashes and crenellated parapets. GATEPIERS at SE corner of yard, late C17 or early C18, of megalithic character with ball finials.

TREGASSOW HOUSE. 1 m. SE. Late C17 house, five-window front with central six-panelled door and twelve-pane sashes with much crown glass. Good late C17 to early C18 stair.

ST ERNEY

ST ERNEY (St Terney). Recorded either as a chapelry to Landrake, first mentioned in 1269 (Henderson), or its mother church: the two have always been closely related. Its late C14 two-stage W tower, with massive buttresses to the top of the first stage, no W door and crowned by stumpy pinnacles, is as charmingly diminutive as Landrake's tower (q.v.) is strikingly elegant. Two late medieval carved heads above N door. The plain interior has an intimate character with a C15 N aisle of four bays with Cornish granite standard piers. A restoration of 1872 installed simple arch-braced roofs. – FONT. C13, though Sedding suggests c. 1680. Thick circular font and square bowl. The top half has a section with three plates and two hollows, the lower half the most elementary line decoration. – FURNISHINGS of 1928, good quality. – STAINED GLASS. Chancel E, 1882.

ST ERTH

ST ERTH. A small church among trees near the river at the foot of the village, of unusual interest for the quality of the late C19 to early C20 restorations. The early C15 W tower is of three stages, unbuttressed, and has grotesque heads below the battlements. The fine late C15 S porch, like that at Lelant, is buttressed, the jambs of its entrance with octagonal panels (cf. Breage) and heavily moulded bases and caps, and the upper stages of the buttresses with blind trefoil-headed panels. The body of the church was extensively rebuilt by *J. D. Sedding* in 1873–4 reusing much original material including Perp windows in the N aisle and the E window of the S aisle, and carved timbers and bosses for the wagon roofs of the aisles and the porch roof, with new work in Sedding's version of Cornish medieval. The restorations were continued into the early C20, until at least 1916, by *E. H. Sedding* and *Cowell, Drewitt &*

Wheatly and included the reconstruction of the Trewinnard chapel. Betjeman lauds the result as 'one of the first really sensitive restorations in Britain', a verdict endorsed by the passage of time. The s aisle has six bays of standard Cornish granite design, with plain capitals: its E end forms the Trewinnard chapel. The N arcade starts in the same way as the W, but is continued with taller piers with moulded capitals and leaf decoration around the abaci. In 1874 and 1911 dormer windows were put into the roofs to give more light, and they look very pretty now. The character of the interior is mysterious and serene, enhanced by Sedding's use of green Polyphant for the walls, open benches of pitch pine, BENCH-ENDS in C15 style, and a chancel with decorated roof, encaustic tiles, and a REREDOS of 1903. The embellishment reaches its peak in the Trewinnard chapel with its richly carved ROOD SCREEN in the C15 style, an exquisitely carved and coloured ALTAR and REREDOS, and TAPESTRIES, reproductions from Trewinnard Manor. Much of the work in the various phases of the church's restoration was carried out by *Harry Hems* and his workshop. – FONT. Norman, square, of unusual design, each side with two saltire crosses. – LECTERN. 1907 by *Herbert Read*. – ROYAL ARMS of George I. Painted. – Parts of a pre-Norman CHURCHYARD CROSS with plaitwork shaft, in the NW corner of the s aisle. – STAINED GLASS. Six windows by *Clayton & Bell* of the late C19 to early C20 including the s window of the Trewinnard chapel, 1912, showing Bishop Benson with a model of Truro Cathedral. – One in the N aisle, 1949 by *Wippell*.

In the embowered and luxuriant churchyard, entered by an elaborate Gothic LYCHGATE of 1925: three WHEEL-HEAD CROSSES; some C18 headstones with good lettering; some later examples signed by *John Trevaskis*, sculptor of St Erth; a WAR MEMORIAL, early C20 by *Sir Ninian Comper*, finely proportioned with a large square stepped base rising through an octagonal tapered shaft to a Crucifixion; and some cast-iron MEMORIALS, presumably from Harvey's foundry at Hayle.

METHODIST CHAPEL, Chapel Hill. 1827 with additions and alterations, the final major phase 1906 by *Oliver Caldwell* of Penzance who raised the roof and Gothicked the windows.

CHURCH HALL. 1921, probably by *F. G. Drewitt*. Now residential but retaining the barrel ceiling of the auditorium.

ST ERTH BRIDGE. Bridge and causeway. Early C19 rebuilding of C17 and medieval bridges, the datestone 1879 recording its later W extension. Three spans over the main channel with triangular refuges over the cutwaters. The W end has a wide single span with parapet walls that continue to flank the causeway.

In the village the pleasant FORE STREET has a number of modest late C18–C19 houses and cottages like Nos. 1, 2 and 3 ROCK CLOSE TERRACE, datestone 1791, CARPENTER'S SHOP, ANVIL HOUSE and BLACKSMITH'S SHOP. The VILLAGE HALL, The Green Lane, was built 1841 as the National School, with pretty latticed iron windows.

St Erth Station, ½ m. NW. A station, known as St Ives Road, was originally built here in 1852 for the West Cornwall Railway. The present buildings date from the opening of the branch line to St Ives in 1877, and constitute a rare survival of a complete station. The branch terminus is L-shaped containing offices, luggage and waiting rooms. On the s platform a small shelter and guard's hut. Footbridge, open-sided but roofed. Canopies to the platforms on a double colonnade of chamfered wooden posts surmounted by pierced iron brackets.

The prosperity of this area close to Hayle is reflected in a number of substantial manor houses and large farmhouses that were modernized during the C18 to mid C19 and survive intact, especially:

Trewinnard Manor, ½ m. s. Early C18, built away from the earlier medieval courtyard plan house, for the Hawkins family. Double-depth plan, contemporary sash windows, resited granite oriel window, and unaltered interior including panelling, open-well stair, chimneypieces and cornices. Fine entrance with granite gate-piers and garden walls: the low walls are surmounted by old wooden railings with turned finials. To the NW of the house, early to mid-C18 COACHHOUSE and STABLES with central pedimented gable over the two-bay coachhouse, flanked by identical servants' accommodation either side. Extensive former FARM BUILDINGS to the w.

Trelissick Manor, ½ m. N. Medieval on a pre-Conquest site, remodelled 1688 for James Paynter and in the C18, extended in the early C19. L-shaped plan, front range of five rooms, rear wing with stair hall, back parlour and large kitchen. The l. hand part of the front range (and wing) is taller and contains a principal parlour and principal chamber above with good late C17 features, and has granite and timber mullioned-and-transomed windows, rare for Cornwall. Paynter was the man who proclaimed James Francis Edward Stuart as king in 1715. In the C19 the house was rented by William Harvey (1805–93), son of John Harvey and nephew of Henry Harvey (cf. Hayle). To the w and NW an especially large range of C17–C19 farm buildings with several BARNS, a COVERED YARD, and a slate-hung GRANARY.

Tredrea Manor, ¼ m. SW. C17, but largely rebuilt c. 1856. Smart granite ashlar front of five bays with some C18 sashes and good interior with much original carpentry, joinery and plasterwork, including plaster ceiling in r. parlour divided by double bands into a central round panel with leaf centre rose and corner panels with arabesques in shallow relief. Behind the fashionable front, a very traditional service wing.

Gear Farmhouse, 1½ m. ESE. Early C18, double-depth plan with equal-sized parlours flanking a wide central entrance hall leading to a rear stair hall between kitchen and pantry. Symmetrical five-bay front with wide central doorway and eighteen-pane sashes with much crown glass. Good interior carpentry, joinery and plasterwork.

ST ERVAN

The church sits low in its remote churchtown with a large former rectory of 1853 in the Domestic Revival style, former school, and farm.

ST HERMES. The upper stage of the unbuttressed C15 W tower was rebuilt in reinforced concrete in 1955 and given a pyramidal roof, with the original W window re-set. The body of the church is of nave, N and S transepts and chancel, all probably C13 (cf. the N door), the nave and chancel conspicuously not aligned: the chancel was rebuilt 1665. It was re-windowed from the C15. Despite a sweeping restoration of 1887–9 that renewed all the roofs and rebuilt the tower, chancel and transeptal arches, its small scale, cruciform plan and unusually thick walls strongly suggest the character of a typical Cornish church before 1400. – FONT. Octagonal, plain, late C12 or early C13. – PULPIT. C18 of fielded panels with fluted pilasters at the corners. – CORBEL. Late C15, in E wall of N transept. The church is notable for its good C17 slate MONUMENTS that have never been banished to the outside walls. – In the chancel, Richard Harvey †1666 and Richard Russell †1654. – In the S transept William Pomeroye †1622 with figure in contemporary dress, and Humphrey Arthur †1696 with floral decoration around a central inscription panel, and another slate to his wife, Elizabeth. – In the N transept an unidentified slate with ten kneeling figures and date 1627 or 1629. – More early to mid-C17 slates in the nave.

At RUMFORD a simple former METHODIST CHAPEL of 1830 with slate-hung front with two narrow pointed-arch windows, and the later C19 METHODIST CHURCH with unusually chunky Gothic trefoil-headed lancets on the front.

At PENROSE, I m. W. METHODIST CHAPEL, dated 1861. The best surviving example in Cornwall of the simplest form of wayside chapel, tiny and humble, of rectangular plan with a slightly later lean-to trap house to the l. Virtually unaltered interior with panelled box pews ramped up towards the rear, a rare (if not unique) panelled musicians' or choir area with benches to the sides in front of the preaching rostrum, and a prominent row of hat pegs.

ST EVAL

ST UVELUS (St Eval). The church lies all on its own on a high plateau, with bleak former military housing and a transmitter station on the former Second World War airfield as its nearest neighbours; its churchtown was demolished in 1938 for the runway. Its tall unbuttressed three-stage tower is so prominent at a long distance that after it fell Bristol merchants helped pay for its rebuilding in 1727 (in the old style) as a seamark before the erection of Trevose Head Lighthouse. It is banded with Catacleuse blocks for this purpose and the decorative contrast of this stone is also used in the porch, windows, and some quoining. The interior is low and whitewashed, with a Norman N wall and a (rebuilt) N transept with a deeply splayed Norman window in the nave wall: *J. D. Sedding*, who restored the church in 1889, identified Norman masonry in the tower arch which reuses rude impost mouldings and jambs. C15–C16 with Perp windows: it is of six bays, of which the first four belong to the nave, then a curiously low four-centred arch, and then the sixth high again. The arcade is of standard Cornish design with stylized leaf decoration of the abaci; similar arches on the N side, and a triangular space for the staircase of the rood screen, E of the N transept. Nave, chancel and s aisle have C15–C16 wagon roofs with moulded ribs and wall-plates, and carved bosses. – FONT. The plainest Norman cup design. – PULPIT. Octagonal, dated 1688. – ROOD SCREEN. Only the base of the screen survives: this has traceried panels, those in the s aisle finely carved with Renaissance influence, the section across the nave with some remnant colour. – BENCH-ENDS. A good set of the C16, reused in Sedding's re-seating, of the usual motifs with initials, Instruments of the Passion, etc., two shields with symbols to each end. Some parts of bench-backs with arcading also remain. – Re-set engaged Catacleuse CAPITAL, C15, in s aisle with stylized floral decoration, finely carved. – STAINED GLASS. 1989 by *Crear McCartney* to commemorate the RAF station. Striking colours and strong composition incorporating RAF symbolism around a crown of thorns. – MONUMENTS. Three good rural slate monuments in the N transept, the best to Simon Leach †1672 carved in relief, the inscription in an oval flanked by pilasters with large acanthus leaves on the shafts and his arms above flanked by vases of flowers.

ST EWE

ALL SAINTS. A church of unusual interest, in its most striking parts – tower, spire and s aisle – of the C13 and C14, earlier than most. w tower and spire almost diminutive in comparison to the body of the church, accentuated by being built into the steeply sloping site. Two-stage tower an almost solid square of masonry with narrow C14 w window, restored in the C19, and diagonal buttresses, surmounted by an octagonal spire with small broaches, small windows at its foot, and a band of quatrefoil decoration halfway up (cf. Gerrans). The exterior shows how extensive later intervention has been. A major restoration by *J. P. St Aubyn* of 1881, 'severe' according to Cox in 1912, involved remodelling the chancel, extensive re-roofing and almost complete re-windowing; a painting in the church shows much larger s aisle windows with keystones which date from an earlier rebuilding of 1767. Also deliberate incorporation of antiquarian features e.g. into the N wall of the chancel, the datestone WP 1636 on the extension of the E window, and the fragment of castellated leadwork dated 1727 IS and CP on the s side of the church. Now to the interior. The arch to the N transept has chamfered imposts and is C13; the roof is a C19 reconstruction with bosses imported from St Keyne. The s aisle belongs to the end of the C14. The arcade of six bays has piers consisting of four major and four minor shafts, capitals decorated with stylized flowers, and castellated abaci, the arches four-centred. Here, as at Gorran, the arch opposite the N transept is significantly wider than the rest of the arcade, possible evidence of a former s transept and original cruciform plan. Wagon roof with exceptionally rich foliage decoration to ribs, and large bosses. – FONT. Norman, on five supports, with a plain bowl with four badly carved (or cut away) corner faces. – ROOD SCREEN. The most important object in the church. It goes across the nave only, with three sections on each side of the opening. Each section has two panels of blank tracery, then the real tracery of four lights, and above the coving an elaborate cornice with beasts, birds, a naked boy, etc. all scrambling through foliage (cf. St Buryan), a quirky but engaging composition. – PULPIT. C19 incorporating medieval bench-ends. – More MONUMENTS than usual, above all William Mohun †1737, excellent London work, attributed to *Sir Henry Cheere* (GF); with a life-size bust, above a broken pediment and below a broken pediment. The fruit and flower decoration is also first-rate. – William Williams †1785. Urn, etc. by *R. Isbell* of Stonehouse. – John Hope †1813 (of Amsterdam and Trevorrick), and his son (drowned while at Eton), inscription and classical frame only, by *Bedford* of 256 Oxford Street, 1821. – CURIOSUM. – The copy of a SEATING PLAN of 1676. A remarkable survival.

The compact church town of small cottages, with the CROWN INN, formerly an C18 house, endures at the heart of the modern village around a C15 CROSS on a curiously over-sized base.

ST GENNYS

1090

ST GENNYS. A remote, romantic setting not far back from high cliffs that give wide views across Bude Bay from the churchyard. Yet the church lies sheltered against a small hill in its little churchtown so that the w tower seems diminutive when first seen: it is in fact of three stages, the lower two Norman with small windows deeply splayed inside. The upper stage 1910 by *E. H. Sedding*, who also added the buttresses of the type that leave the angles free and have pinnacles applied in relief at the second stage. The N and S walls of the chancel are Norman too, as is the tower arch to the nave with its simple imposts. The nave is of four bays, low, with low arcades. The S arcade is on octagonal granite piers with double-chamfered four-centred arches. On the N aisle the W bay is the same but the other three are of Polyphant on Cornish standard piers with capitals and abaci with flat, stylized flower motifs and uncommonly manifold mouldings (for Cornwall) to the arches: the penultimate W arch sites incongruously on the one octagonal N pier. Extensively restored 1871 by *St Aubyn*, somewhat mitigated by Sedding's later work. – FONT. Square, C12 of the Purbeck table-top type, with six (in the W seven) blank niches with pointed heads. – BENCH-ENDS. A few fragments made into a litany desk. – STAINED GLASS. S aisle E, 1921 by *Heaton, Butler & Bayne*. In the churchyard, late C16 chest tomb to Benet Mill and Christopher Bligh, related to Bligh of the *Bounty*. Moulded granite pilasters with recessed panels; inscription in large rustic letters without serifs. – Delabole slate HEADSTONE to Percy Walter White †1938, finely proportioned and inscribed by *Eric Gill* 1931. – Other more recent slate memorials of unusually good and simple design and lettering.

NANCEMELLAN, Crackington Haven, ½ m. SW. 1905 in Arts and Crafts tradition with steep slate roof, massive lateral stack, porch and bay window under pent slate roof and segmentally arched window openings. Well-detailed interior.

ST GERMANS

The memorably picturesque ensemble of church, house and park is of the highest architectural and historic interest.

ST GERMANS. Other medieval Cornish churches are closely associated with great houses (cf. Boconnoc, Lanherne and Lanhydrock) but none can compare in importance with St Germans, a priory church surviving more fully than any other monastic foundation in the county. It was the cathedral of Anglo-Saxon Cornwall. Bishops are known between 931 and 1050, but no architectural fragments remain. In 1050 the bishopric, with that of Crediton, was merged in a new diocese with its see in Exeter. Between 1161 and 1184 Bishop Bartholomew reorganised St Germans as a priory of Augustinian canons. Of this building, finally consecrated in 1261 by Bishop Bronescombe, so much is still in existence that no other church in Cornwall can vie with it as an example of Norman planning and architecture.

The Norman building had two W towers, a nave of 102 ft (31 metres), two narrow aisles with lean-to roofs, and a monks'

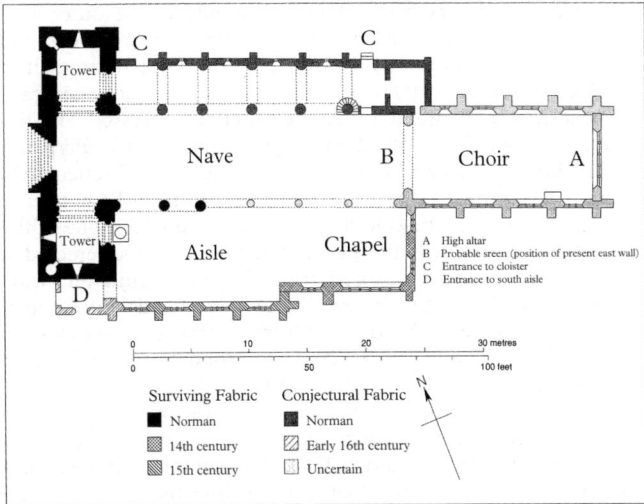

A	High altar
B	Probable screen (position of present east wall)
C	Entrance to cloister
D	Entrance to south aisle

St Germans, church, plan

choir at the E end,* but no transept and no crossing tower. Of the E part nothing is left after the church's length was reduced by 55 ft (16.8 metres) in the late C15 and a new E wall constructed. The WEST FRONT, however, stands complete up to roof height. The aisle width and height can be read from traces against the N tower outside and the E walls of the S tower inside. The W front, mostly built of the beautiful sage-green stone from Tarten Down near Landrake, is uncommonly plain and powerful for its date. With the wide flat buttresses of the two towers it is more reminiscent of Franco-Norman work of a hundred years earlier (say St Étienne at Caen) than the livelier Transitional which more central parts of England practised towards the end of the C12. The N tower is built on lower ground so that its bottom stage is lower than that of the S tower. Between the towers is a porch under a gable (with the rare feature of a cross), with two small round-headed windows slightly above, and on the upper floor three round-headed windows with the centre light higher than the others. These latter windows are provided with nook-shafts. The towers have other small Norman windows, and the S tower Perp work, higher up. The N tower turns into octagonal shape on the second storey (cf. Jumièges, Normandy) and ends in a C13 octagon. The W portal under the gable is unrivalled in Cornwall. It is of seven orders, with three of the orders and voussoirs having uncommonly vivid chevron; whether the innermost order possessed different ornaments cannot now be said, as the stone

19

*The choir was probably aisled on its N, but not its S, side. See L. Olson and A. Preston Jones, 'An Ancient Cathedral of Cornwall?', *Cornish Archaeology*, 37–8 (1998–9).

has weathered very badly. The hoodmould of the outer arch exhibits foliage decoration. Nice Art Nouveau ironwork and bronze door furniture by *Henry Wilson* on the w door itself.

After this, the SOUTH ELEVATION is a complete contrast. The aisle is battlemented (like the towers), buttressed, and has four large windows, all of four lights, three clearly Perp but with different tracery, the fourth (on the w) still reticulated, that is Dec. The aisle can be dated by the arms of Bishop Lacy (1420–55) among the shields on the hoodmoulds of one of the windows. To the E is the grand and lofty s chapel erected *c.* 1330, with one much restored original window and a very wide domestic-looking C16 window. To the w is a handsome s porch, of the same date as the aisle, with two entrance arches close to each other to w and s and a depressed tunnel-vault with a grid of thick granite ribs. An earlier head is built into its w face.*

The church is entered from the porch by a dramatically steep descent down a flight of steps. The ground floors of the towers were open to the nave and aisles by Transitional pointed arches of simplest design: two steps with an inserted roll moulding (cf. Morwenstow). On the first floor the towers were connected by a gallery, as indicated by the two remaining doors (currently hidden by late C20 fittings). The staircase of the s tower is the only Cornish staircase of Norman date. Nowhere else in Cornwall can one gain such a strong sense of the interior of a Norman church, especially striking when one stands under the s tower looking E past its majestic NE pier. At the SE corner of the N tower are a similar (formerly free-standing) pier and associated respond piers relating to the lost Norman N aisle, demolished in 1802. The pier capitals of the clustered shafts are of nine different types, mostly scalloped, but some also of a very primitive 'Ionic' kind. Of the Norman nave, the first two s bays survive. It had a clerestory with windows in line with the spandrels, not, as usual, with the apexes of the arches (cf. the upper N wall of the s aisle), a motif repeated at North Petherwin which such Gothic churches as Callington, Fowey and Lostwithiel took up; the windows have rich chevron ornament. The thick, short window piers have square, scalloped capitals and pointed arches of plain two-step moulding. The N wall was rebuilt after 1802 with the involvement of *Soane*, with a short N transept that contained the Eliot pew, the transept arch incorporating some Norman material.

With no more than these bays belonging to the original building of the C12 and C13 (and what has been reused of other Norman fragments in the other five bays after a partial collapse of the E end in 1592), the interior of St Germans is as much of interest for its domination by the work of the later Middle Ages and the C19. The proportions, with the aisle 6 ft (1.8 metres) wider than the nave, are unusual. The fine five-light chancel E window belongs to the 1592 rebuilding of the E end.

*The E and N walls are currently only viewable from the grounds of Port Eliot (*see* below) so are described as part of the interior.

St Germans, church, south aisle, east end. Lithograph, 1850

The s aisle is a mixture of four styles: the Norman of the first two bays, the interesting imitation-Norman of the rebuilding of 1592, the Dec of the E end, and the early C15 Perp of the rest. The E end is richly decorated and of high aesthetic quality, clearly derived in style from Exeter Cathedral. To get an impression of its pristine finesse of detail and unusual motifs St Ive near Liskeard, consecrated in 1338, may be compared. The E wall of the chapel has two three-light windows with a niche for an image between (cf. the niches of St Ive), and a higher three-light window, all incorporating roundels. The lower windows are original, the upper a restoration with C14 fragments salvaged from the grounds of Port Eliot. There is also a PISCINA. In the s wall are two C14 niches, the E one, a sedile, especially exquisite, the wider one with an ogee-headed canopy a funerary recess. Set further w in the s wall another fine C14 ogee-headed recess, and a niche with a traceried head. The C19 roofs are a disappointment, the result of restoration by *J. P. St Aubyn*, 1887–98.

FONT. Late Norman or early C13, re-assembled from fragments in 1840, badly damaged. – WOODWORK. Only minor medieval remains: one choir stall (misericord with a man called Dando, punished for hunting on Sunday), *c.* 1375–1400: fragment of the rood screen: a wooden figure of St Anthony (in the vestry), indifferent, *c.* 1500, brought over from Port Eliot. – The other generally good quality furnishings belong to the late C19 restoration: the excellent CHOIR STALLS and PARCLOSE SCREEN by *Harry Hems* of Exeter; the fine PULPIT, LECTERN, MOSAIC and black and white MARBLE FLOORS also of this date. – REREDOS, 1920. – STAINED GLASS. The largest single scheme of *Morris & Co.* glass in Cornwall (cf. Ladock, St Michael Penkevil and Polruan). – Chancel E window by *Edward Burne-Jones*, 1896. To see such exquisite work, after many less accomplished Victorian windows in Cornish churches, brings home most forcibly the value of William Morris's reform. Here are clear outlines, pleasing patterns, and simple colours in sufficiently large expanses to be taken in individually. No overcrowding, no competing with the art of painting, and yet a sentiment that is wholly of the C19. – Another fine set by the same in the S window of the S chapel, 1902, of six lights depicting Joy, Justice, Faith, Hope, Charity and Praise. – Chapel E, 1872–84. – Chapel S, 1886. – S aisle, 1877, probably by *Burlison & Grylls*, armorial with angels. – Nave W, 1889 by *Fouracre & Son*. – Chancel N, 1876 by *Clayton & Bell*, Transfiguration, and 1898 by *Fouracre & Son*, the latter clearly influenced by the Burne-Jones E window. – Coloured wooden STATUE of St Nicholas. – MONUMENTS. In the porch a C13 STONE COFFIN. – John Moyle †1661. Large TOMB-CHEST (in the vestry) with a heraldic device in bas relief on a

81 black marble slab. – Edward Eliot, 1722 by *Rysbrack*. A first-rate example of Rysbrack's art and the most ambitious C18 monument in Cornwall. Of white and black marble. Eliot is shown reclining on a sarcophagus in Roman costume with an allegorical figure on his l., mourning. Short pyramid in relief and putti in the background. – Many other C18 and C19 Eliot monuments including the 1st Earl of St Germans †1823 by *Sir R. Westmacott*, a sad maiden seated by a tall pillar with an urn.

91 PORT ELIOT. The priory was acquired after the Dissolution by the Eliots, later created Earls of St Germans. Their house occupies the N part of the priory site and sits serenely in parkland below the church, on a terrace in the slope down to what was once a tidal creek of the River Tiddy. Its long E–W axis represents the N range of the priory's conventual buildings that were one-room deep and two-storey: though not visible externally, what survives is the undercroft with three C13 lancet windows and the walls of the refectory above, now the saloon and drawing room of the present house. At its E end the range was attached to the prior's lodgings, demolished *c.* 1730–40 by Richard Eliot. There were other monastic buildings and a graveyard between the house and the church.

What the visitor sees on the main approach, however, is the W front of 1829 by *Henry Harrison* (cf. Heligan, Penrose, Trewarthenick, etc.). As an entrance front it is highly successful, indeed dramatic, boldly embattled, with a theatrically large-scaled central porte cochère, first-floor windows with Gothic glazing, and defined to the N side by a long, heavily buttressed

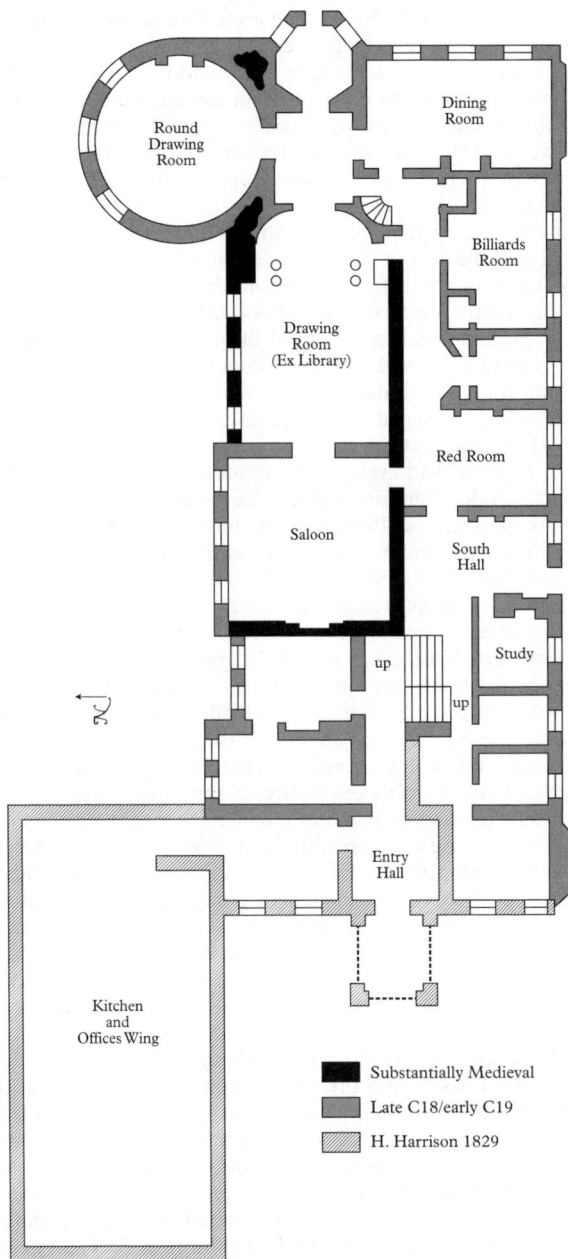

Round
Drawing
Room

Dining
Room

Billiards
Room

Drawing
Room
(Ex Library)

Red Room

Saloon

South
Hall

up

Study

up

Entry
Hall

Kitchen
and
Offices Wing

■ Substantially Medieval

█ Late C18/early C19

▨ H. Harrison 1829

St Germans, Port Eliot. Plan

and embattled service wing of two parallel blocks linked at the w end by a large Tudor-Gothic arch. The interior sustains the drama, the double-height entrance hall lit by clerestory windows leading to a dimly lit lobby and then, by a wide flight of stairs to the r., to the foot of an elegant staircase, the start of the Soanian interior. *Soane*'s remodelling of the house between 1804 and 1809 for the 2nd Lord Eliot was not as extensive as he had originally proposed. He had to confront several difficulties arising from his taking over an incomplete remodelling by *John Johnson*, the London architect, who had extended the s front and built the round room at the E end of the house in the late C18.* *Repton*, who had suggested Soane's employment, produced a Red Book for Edward, 1st Lord Eliot, in 1793, and was highly critical of Johnson who 'has done all the mischief he could by his Islington Gothic', proposed re-establishing the building link between house and church. Soane had envisaged instead removing the sprawling w wings of gallery and services that had been erected in a remodelling of *c.* 1730–40 and creating the main entrance by the w front, which would open into a magnificent *enfilade* down the entire length of the house. Both Repton's link and Soane's w entrance were rejected, and Soane's remodelling of the exterior seems to have been confined principally to the s and E elevations and the addition of battlements and Gothic windows. His influence on the interior, however, was transformational. He was able to realize part of his grand *enfilade* by repositioning the interconnecting doors of the rooms along the w–E axis to create a long view out into the parkland: his enfilade runs from the drawing room, where he created an apse at the E end, screened by two pairs of Ionic columns and an entablature similar to that at Aynho Park, Northamptonshire; continuing through a small vestibule divided by pilasters into symmetrical bays to accommodate existing door openings and given a bowed ceiling; and finally opening into a fully glazed conservatory of octagonal plan. To avoid this arrangement simply being a corridor he devised a circulation passage to the s to serve each of the rooms independently and contrived a new staircase rising from the basement that was constructed successively in granite from the basement, Portland stone for the first-floor landing, and timber for the upper floors.

By Soane also are the most striking interiors at Port Eliot, the Round Room and the dining room at the E end, not fully fitted out by Johnson. The elegant proportions of the ROUND ROOM, 40 ft (12 metres) in diameter, are skilfully enhanced by Soane's shallow dome, the shallowest of his career, radiating in crisply moulded ribs from a centre roundel with an incised Greek key pattern. Its walls are covered by a vast MURAL by *Robert Lenkiewicz*, commissioned by the 10th Earl and painted

---

*Johnson also created a new principal entrance at the E end, replacing the original in the basement of the N front. I am indebted to Ptolemy Dean's account of the development of the house in *Soane and the Country Estate* (1999).

between the late 1970s and the artist's death in 2002. Known as *The Riddle Mural* or *The Condition of Man*, one half shows death, destruction, unrequited love, the apocalypse, etc., the other half love, friendship and harmony. Though unfinished, it is a worthy enrichment of this splendid room, thrilling in its scale, ambition and the vivid depiction of its subject matter. In the DINING ROOM Soane introduced blind doors to create a symmetrical arrangement with timber entablatures above the doors and a chimneypiece with incised Greek key patterning. The reeded and fluted white marble shafts of the chimneypiece in the morning room are also his.

The charm of the relationship between church and house is immensely enhanced by their setting in the extensive PLEASURE GROUNDS that merge imperceptibly into the wider PARKLAND. From the house the STABLES and COACHHOUSE present a picturesque incident on the NW skyline. Built by Soane, 1802–6, they are arranged in paired ranges N and S of a central yard with gatepiers forming an entrance at the E end in which, as Christopher Hussey noted, 'Gothic, baronial, and Tuscan elements are fused in a characteristic unusual Soanian design'. Each range has a central two-storey block with a heavily corbelled embattled parapet flanked by single-storey asymmetrical wings. To the SE of the house the ORANGERY, a delightful and early type of conservatory of *c.* 1790 with Chinoiserie glazing, Greek pilasters and classical treatment of the back wall. To its S, a group of four Roman BUSTS on tapered piers and to the N an URN on a plinth. The orangery stands at the W end of a large WALLED KITCHEN GARDEN. Of the many commissions by the present earl in the late C20, wire SCULPTURES of the Minotaur and Elephant (the latter the Eliot symbol) by *Ryder* at the centre of a maze SE of the house, and a MONUMENT NE of the house above the quarry, a memorial to the 9th Earl (†1988) in the form of a PINNACLE re-erected from Westminster Abbey. Further into the park and forming a picturesque group on the N side of the lake, the buildings of the home farm including an early C19 ornamental DAIRY, CALF HOUSE, STABLE and PIGEON HOUSE, some of these possibly by Soane.

The extent of Repton's influence on the landscape was limited by Edward Eliot's own enhancements after his succession in 1748. These had included reclaiming the tidal creek for parkland and much planting in the pleasure grounds on the promontory NE of the house and on a ridge overlooking the river ½ m. N. It seems that Repton, impressed by his client's achievements (and strong views), felt it unnecessary, or unwise, to make radical proposals. In the event, though most of his Red Book recommendations were rejected, the planting of the wider landscape owes much to him.

Stretched out along the main road, St Germans has the indelible character of an estate village, with the TOWN LODGE and LYCHGATE announcing the presence of the great house and church. The former is of *c.* 1840 in showy Tudor-Gothic, a pair of two-storey square blocks linked by a carriage arch surmounted by the Eliot arms. The latter is a modest counterfoil in subdued Gothic. Both have walls of Tarten Down stone with granite dressings. The other lodges to the great estate – TIDEFORD, FURZE PARK and PENMADOWN – are of plainer mid- to late C19 Gothic. The most arresting buildings in the village are SIR WILLIAM MOYLES'S ALMSHOUSES, an unusually picturesque composition of 1583. Six houses with six gables and originally with miniature separate ground-floor and upper-floor flats. The gables project and are supported on plain stone piers. The space thus gained in front of the wall is used as a loggia on the ground floor and as a balcony on the upper floor. The balcony is reached by outer stairs. Restored and converted to four apartments in the late C20.

At the E end of the village down QUAY ROAD is ST GERMANS QUAY with a wharf and a row of cottages set below the thirteen high arches of the railway VIADUCT of 1908 which replaced the original 1855 structure.

ST HILARY

ST HILARY. A church of uncommon interest and arresting atmosphere, comfortably situated at the end of a tree-lined lane in its small churchtown. C13 tower of two stages with buttresses to the ground floor only, and a very noticeable batter, with very primitive carved faces along the top cornice. It is surmounted by a broached spire, one of the few in Cornwall, with statues in niches on all faces. The rest of the church was rebuilt 1853–5 by *William White* after a fire, and demonstrates his originality. The five-bay arcades to the nave arcades and three to the chancel are intersected by very shallow transepts, the intersection of the roofs creating a lantern over the crossing lit by eight tiny windows which shed a low and mysterious light at the centre of the church. The arcades have pointed arches on slender piers, the roofs are arch-braced. It was to provide the perfect setting for a rich array of art from the Newlyn School, created by *Father Bernard Walke*, vicar 1913–36. With his wife, *Anne Walke*, he developed close associations with the Newlyn artists and commissioned a programme of enrichment that became, and remains, the outstanding collection of early C20 religious art anywhere in Cornwall. Attacked by Protestant protesters against Walke's Anglo-Catholic ecclesiology in 1932, the ensemble was largely re-assembled and restored by the late C20. Walke's overall scheme was coordinated by *Ernest Procter* with an integrated design for the decoration of White's PULPIT SCREENS and STALLS. Procter himself contributed some of the major works including the striking large CRUCIFIXUS above the altar steps (with smaller versions for the PROCESSIONAL CROSS and ALTAR CROSS); an exquisitely tender painting of the Visitation in the REREDOS of the Lady Chapel; and the Deposition in All Souls' Chapel at the W end of the S aisle. He also painted the panels of the pulpit and clergy stalls with figures of the saints. – The painted panels of the CHOIR STALLS are worth studying in detail: they are by a number of other Newlyn artists including *Norman Garstin*, *Alethea Garstin*, *Gladys Hines*, *Harold Knight*, *Dod Procter* and *Anne Walke*. – Other PAINTINGS include a large St Francis by *Roger Fry* and St Joan of Arc and Virgin and child by Anne Walke. – Large CRUCIFIXUS on N wall by *Phyllis Yglesias*. – In St Joseph's Chapel, a REREDOS, an extraordinary granitic depiction of the City of God, with a Flemish painting of Christ blessing *c.* 1500; and on the S wall a STATUE of St Joseph, Spanish Baroque, C18. – STAINED GLASS. Mostly late C19 and early C20 including chancel E, 1902 by *Ward & Hughes* and others of 1902 by *Clayton & Bell*. – INSCRIBED STONES. One in the S aisle has an inscription which refers to Constantine the Great and, according to the titles used, 306–8: the stone was probably a milestone. The other (in the churchyard) reads NOTI. NOTI (the monument to Notus, son of Notus) and should from its lettering be C6–C7.

TREGEMBO, 2 m. ENE. Mid- to late C17. U-plan, with one shallow wing of one room carried on two-bay open colonnade of late C17 Doric columns, possibly reused from a former range closing the plan as at Godolphin (q.v.). Good C17 and C18 interior.

½ m. NW of Goldsithney on Tregurtha Downs mine a rare example of an architect-designed ENGINE HOUSE, reputedly by *J. P. St Aubyn*. A smaller version of that East Wheal Rose (cf. St Newlyn East), sensitively converted to residential use built for a second-hand copper house foundry 80-in. engine, later to become Robinson's engine at South Crofty, now preserved at Heartlands (cf. Pool).

ST ISSEY

ST ISSEY. Rebuilt in 1869–71 by *J. P. St Aubyn* after the collapse of the SE half of the C13 tower which also damaged the W bays of the nave. Large parts of the medieval fabric were incorporated but externally most of the detail is of the rebuild. The tower is of three stages, of severely plain design but incorporating the original Catacleuse W door with angels with shields as stops to the hoodmould. The handsome interior is of nave and two aisles. The N aisle of three bays has piers with four major and four minor demi-shafts (cf. St Columb Minor, St Wenn etc.), and two-centred arches: typical Cornish C14. The S aisle of three bays plus two lower bays for the chancel (cf. Bodmin) is Cornish standard, with horizontal leaves along the abacus of each shaft and four-centred arches. Late C19 arch- and wind-braced roof to the nave. The aisles have lean-to roofs. The chancel is elaborately and effectively decorated with stencilling: a green dado enriched with flowers and foliage patterns, and above this elaborate masonry patterning, the E wall with a diaper pattern into which are set roundels with sacred monograms. The decoration extends to the organ pipes, roof and the two easternmost piers of the nave. It is signed by *Whately*, Frome, Somerset, 1882 and *Fred James*, Frome, Somerset, 1882. – FONT. Plain, circular bowl on five supports with four motifs on flat decoration: cross, star, candelabra, etc. Sedding considered it a C17 copy of a C12 font. – The REREDOS and a PANEL on S aisle altar are the outstanding features of the church. The reredos is late C15, repaired at the lower l. end. Five panels of Catacleuse, richly carved with deep polygonal niches rising to ogee heads with miniature vaults inside: in the spandrels of the heads are little figures in low relief of ecclesiastics and laymen standing in pairs, twenty altogether. The panels are a more elaborate version of those of the simpler tomb at St Endellion (q.v.): no doubt they belonged to a similar tomb-chest. The PANEL is a small Pietà with two monks or priests in the spandrels. It may have formed part of the same monument but is by a conspicuously different hand: it is executed in a concise, stylized and very effective manner, the carving even more exquisite and in higher relief. These two pieces are without doubt the finest of the group of late C15 Catacleuse sculpture in north Cornwall. Henderson draws attention to an indulgence granted in 1399 to all those who would visit the tomb of Lady Matilde Chyverston in St Issey church. The date is not convincing. – STOUP. At the S door, also in Catacleuse, with a finely carved angel bearing a shield.

GATES to the N and SW entrances to the churchyard, 1870–1. In the churchyard, S of the church, tall granite MONUMENT crowned by a broken trefoil, one of a pair with a similar one to the N side with its original head.

ST IVE

ST IVO. One of the best Dec churches in Cornwall and so of unusual importance and interest. It can be compared with South Hill, a sister church in style though more elaborate in detail, and especially the S chapel at St Germans with its connections with the cathedral workshop at Exeter: Bartholomew de Castro, closely connected with Bishop Grandisson, was rector here *c.* 1330. The consecration of 1338 refers to most of what is to be seen now in nave, chancel and transept: the building was probably cruciform. Fine W tower with bold set-back buttresses: it may be C14 in its lower stages but its late C15 or early C16 top is richly embellished with twelve instead of the usual four pinnacles, two subsidiary pinnacles flanking the

St Ive, St Ivo, chancel. Lithograph, 1850

main pinnacle at each corner. The majority of the windows also of the Dec style, the tracery in Beer stone, simple, with pointed trefoils and quatrefoils in the tracery. The E window of five lights is especially beautiful, one of the very best of its date in Cornwall: if, as Street implied, it was restored by *Hayward*, it was most skilfully done. Inside it is flanked by graceful niches, richly crocketed, with nodding ogee arches placed diagonally. The tracery has pointed trefoils and pointed 'daggers' connected by straight bars so as to form star shapes (cf. St Germans). In the S wall a PISCINA and a triple SEDILIA, the latter with trefoils in the spandrels and bulbous foliage. The whole chancel is a very complete and satisfying example of early C14 style. The origin of all this is clearly Exeter Cathedral, contemporary with the motifs being employed there between 1320–40.* Pointed N transept arch has mouldings that die out to the jambs just as at South Hill, an ogee-headed funerary

---

*The E window has close similarities to the W window of the Cathedral and the interior decoration to work in the choir, e.g. the dragon heads at the base of the foliage decoration of the niches, just as on the bishop's throne. I am grateful to John Allan for this and other observations.

recess in the N wall with bulbous finial above as at Quethiock, and a piscina in its E wall, all early C14. The S aisle and S porch were added in the later C15 or early C16, the aisle with stepped buttresses between Perp windows that are reminiscent of Callington. The arcade has piers of standard Cornish pattern with carved capitals and four-centred arches. The wagon roofs of nave, aisle and porch are C15, the carved timber wall-plate of the nave set on a moulded stone plate. A sensitive restoration of 1883–4 by *R. M. Fulford* refurnished the church and laid new floors. – FONT. Octagonal, stem *c.* C14. – PULPIT. Dated 1700, yet entirely in the Tudor or Jacobean tradition, superbly carved, with *c.* 1700 octagonal tester. – ROYAL ARMS. 1660, painted plaster, yet still with strapwork ornament, of a design often to be found in north Cornwall (cf., for example, Launcells and Kilkhampton). – SCULPTURE. Fragment of a St Christopher, alabaster, of excellent quality and exquisite tenderness of expression, perhaps from one of the chancel niches. – STAINED GLASS. E window, 1897, by *Percy Bacon Bros.* – Chancel S, 1847. – Nave N, 1906, by *E. R. Suffling.* – MONUMENTS. J. Lyne †1791, large, by *Isbell.* – Slate ledger stones, Robert Soby, 1741, and others of the C17, in the chancel.

In the churchyard, two medieval CROSSES and, in the NE corner, a small building with a coursed granite front wall said to have been built as a C19 MORTUARY.

CHANTRY, S of the church across the road. The rectory of 1852–4 by *William White* for the Ven. Reginald Hobhouse. An interesting example of the evolution of White's design for parsonage houses in separating out the ecclesiastical and secular aspects. Boldly massed with striking verticality of outline with very steeply pitched roofs, and irregular elevations full of architectural incident, similar to Ruan Lanihorne rectory (q.v.). As there, the entrance front is to the N, with a pointed-head door and cusped window: the S front, in contrast, has eight-pane sashes with stone relieving arches in structured polychromy and first-floor windows of simple casements set close under the eaves, a White motif. The former kitchen window is a nice example of White's originality, with three ventilators placed above its four lancets. The service area was set in a cross-wing at the W end of the house with stables and coachhouse, all designed to be visible from the road.

ST IVES

Improbably blue sea, sands of white gold, and air of intense luminosity fuse with the backdrop of the ancient Penwith landscape to furnish St Ives with a setting of breathtaking natural beauty. The prospect of the slate-roofed old fishing town crowded into its narrow streets around the harbour and along its chapel-crowned promontory is unforgettable, the epitome of picturesque

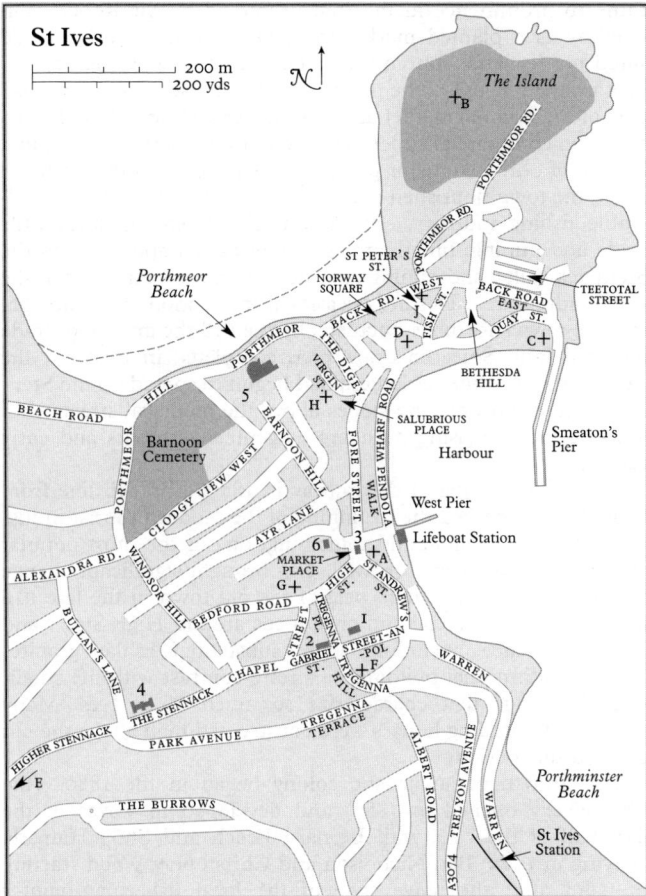

St Ives

200 m
200 yds

A	St Ia	I	Guildhall
B	Chapel of St Nicholas	2	Library
C	Chapel of St Leonard	3	Market House
D	Mariners' Church (former)	4	Stennack School (former)
E	St John-in-the-Fields	5	Tate St Ives
F	Church of the Sacred Heart & St Ia (R.C.)	6	Barbara Hepworth Museum and Sculpture Gallery
G	Bedford Road Methodist Church		
H	Zion Community Church		
J	Bible Christian Chapel		

Cornwall, and visually delightful throughout. It is also leavened with much of architectural and artistic interest, reflecting its long association with an artistic tradition of international importance that has made the town's name symbolic of Cornwall's contribution to modern English art.

Though probably a site of prehistoric human activity and the promontory, The Island, a pre-Roman cliff castle, St Ives first came to prominence in the C15, promoted by Sir Robert Willoughby as a planted market town after Lelant's harbour had silted up. Its large church was begun in 1410, with market and fairs granted in 1487. The present market house occupies a small part of the original market area W of the church with Fore Street, the main commercial street, backing onto the harbour and quay. As one of only two major ports (with Padstow) on the hostile N coast, the town flourished in subsequent centuries with a considerable fishing industry, especially pilchard seining, mercantile trade and mining: tin streaming was of early importance in the Stennack valley and mining later became more significant in the surrounding area. Despite occasional inundations by sand that saw the town's fortunes fluctuate, by the C18 the growth of trade required John Smeaton's new pier, completed in 1770. By the early to mid C19 the settlement had begun to spread up the Stennack valley and onto the slopes above the medieval streets with housing for increasing numbers of genteel residents and early visitors.

It was the coming of the railway in 1877, a branch line from St Erth, that marked the beginning of the modern tourist industry, St Ives becoming, and remaining, one of the most popular visitor destinations in Cornwall. This brought significant change to the character of a small part of the old town in the late C19 with a new commercial and civic focus around High Street and Tregenna Place, including some substantial ashlar granite-fronted institutional buildings, a strong contrast with the small-scale buildings that characterize so much of St Ives. Many terraces of boarding houses were constructed high above the old town in this period.

The growth of an artistic colony began in the 1880s (the first gallery opened in 1887) and developed in waves in the first half of the C20, with Bernard Leach and Shōji Hamada arriving in 1920; Ben Nicholson and Christopher Wood starting to paint after the naïve style of the local fisherman-painter Alfred Wallis from 1928; Nicholson, Barbara Hepworth and Naum Gabo coming in 1939 at the invitation of Adrian Stokes (cf. Little Parc Owles, Carbis Bay); and Wilhelmina Barns-Graham, John Wells, Sven Berlin, Peter Lanyon (the only native Cornishman), Bryan Wynter and Terry Frost gathering from 1945. By the time of the Festival of Britain in 1951, St Ives painters and sculptors, influentially linked to British architecture through Leslie Martin, dominated the English Modernist art scene. The international importance of their work is well represented in St Ives today, especially in Evans & Shalev's inspirational Tate St Ives but also evocatively in Hepworth's Trewyn Studio and Leach's Pottery. The inevitable danger of the town's undoubted success in widening its appeal as a cultural centre alongside the vibrant tourist trade is that the intimacy of the old town is eroded by over-large apartment developments. It was the small-scale and intimate in such a splendid setting so far west that first drew artists here and it is what St Ives should always be about.

CHURCHES

St Ia. The tall tower is glimpsed from all over the town but the   35
best view of the church is from the water, where its four gabled
ends spread out proudly. For the architectural historian one
important thing is that its dates are so safely established: a
Papal Bull of 8 September 1410 allowed the start of building,
the font was in place by 1428, and the church consecrated in
1434, so the features we see here are all certain to belong to
this period and the continuity of building is clearly visible. It
is remarkable to find a tall tower of four stages and a nave of
seven bays with identical N and S aisles as a mere chapel of
ease to Lelant (though the case is not unique; cf. for example
St Nicholas, King's Lynn, Norfolk). The tower is of rough
granite blocks with buttresses set back from the angles and the
unusual feature of pinnacles projected on corbels. The piers of
the arcades, of sandstone, are tallish, though the church is
rather low for its size, and not of Cornish but of Devon standard; they have four demi-shafts, connected with diagonals by
a concave–convex undulation. The arches are four-centred.
The capitals are more finely carved than usual, that of the E
respond of the S arcade a shield-bearing angel. S of the E parts
of the S aisle an outer S aisle of three bays, added by the Trenwith family c. 1500 with a rich decoration of vine leaves and   46
grapes on the capitals which also feature in the finely carved
wagon roof, enhanced by gilding and painting by *Herbert Read*,
1962. The other roofs, also of the wagon type, are handsomely
carved, the nave and chancel roof again with vine-pattern
decoration to the wall-plates and full-length angel figures,
strikingly streamlined, at the junction of the ribs and wall-
plates. The chancel roof has the pattern of ribs and purlins
intersected diagonally by a raised continuous moulding giving
a pretty net-like effect, with richly carved bosses at the intersections of the diagonals as well as of the purlins and ribs in the
sanctuary; both nave and chancel roofs tactfully gilded and
painted 1963 also by *Reed*. Restorations of 1853 by *William White*,
1866 by *F. C. Hingeston-Randolph* and 1897–1905 by *E. H.
Sedding* treated the church kindly. – FONT. Circular base with   48
attached corner bases of supports, decorated by lions *passant
gardant* (cf. Crowan). The circular bowl has severely stylized
angels at the corners, holding shields and joined by a band.
The material, granite, imposed so much restraint on detail that
the work looks modern, an especially appropriate resonance in
the town where Hepworth worked. It is set in the dignified
BAPTISTERY, 1956 by *Stephen Dykes Bower*, with excellent
woodwork by *John Williams* of St Austell and a chequered pavement of Delabole slates set on edge. – BENCH-ENDS. Mostly
of the standard design with two shields to an end, but in the
chancel two complete benches with large single motifs to each
panel and at the ends figures of saints with angelic shield-
bearers as 'poppyheads'. Renaissance ornament is hardly
apparent, except for certain profile portraits. – PULPIT. Each

side consists of a panel from a bench-end with one motif and a quatrefoil below. – ROOD SCREEN, 1933. – HIGH ALTAR AND REREDOS, 1897, with alabaster figures. – LADY CHAPEL SCREEN, 1932. – ORGAN CASE by *Violet Pinwill*, with nice wave and fish detail. – SCULPTURE. Madonna and Child of 1953 by *Barbara Hepworth* as a memorial to her son Paul. Exquisitely tender. – PAINTING. Three Angels, 1985 by *Bryan Pearce*. – Beautifully embroidered BANNER of St Ia, mid C20 by *Alice Moore*. – STAINED GLASS. Chancel E, 1906 by *C. E. Kempe*. – Lady Chapel s by *Heaton, Butler & Bayne* and *Fouracre & Sons*, both 1886. – Tower w, 1862 by *Powell & Sons*, designed by *E. J. Poynter*. – MONUMENTS. Fragments of a brass to Oto Trenwyth †1463, showing his wife kneeling with a smaller figure of St Michael on the l. – Slate slab to the Sise family, 1642. – Hitchens family monument, 1815 by *Garland & Fieldwick*.

In the churchyard near the s porch an exceptionally large granite LANTERN CROSS with a rectangular head on a tall octagonal tapered shaft. Principal face with the crucified Christ, the arms of the cross held by God; Madonna and Child on reverse. Narrow sides with images of bishop and possibly St Ia. Coeval with the building of the church. CHURCHYARD WALL PIERS AND ENTRANCE ARCH, NW of the church. 1910, strongly modelled and embattled.

CHAPEL OF ST NICHOLAS, The Island. Of immense importance to the St Ives townscape, on the summit of the promontory. Small, plain medieval chapel, demolished 1904 by the War Office but rebuilt in replica in 1911 for Sir Edward Hain. Interior restored 1971 by *J. F. Holman*.

CHAPEL OF ST LEONARD, Smeaton's Pier. Small simple building, much rebuilt. The fishermen's chapel, though it cannot be the medieval building and must post-date the pier.

Former MARINERS' CHURCH, Norway Square. 1903–5 by *E. H. Sedding*. Never completed, and since 1945 the gallery of the St Ives Society of Artists which gave many significant artists including Barbara Hepworth, Peter Lanyon and Bryan Wynter their first public exhibitions. Built into steeply sloping ground w–e, the single-storey w entrance end approached by a short flight of steps over a basement that is fully expressed at the E end, providing a large chapel above and reading and recreation rooms below. A strong Gothic composition, a striking presence among the small fishermen's terraces, especially the tall polygonal E end, its verticality accentuated by full-height buttresses and lancets at chancel level. A truncated bell-turret is set in the return between nave and chancel on the s side. The body of the church recedes behind, the s elevation plan with lancets and empty image niches, the w end more elaborately but still robustly detailed. Pleasingly simple, almost austere, interior that suits the reuse admirably.

ST JOHN-IN-THE-FIELDS, 1 m. w, off Higher Stennack. Now surrounded by modern housing but originally built to serve the mining communities at Halsetown and further s of the town. 1857–8 by *J. P. St Aubyn*. One of his best churches, 'impressively in the style of Butterfield' (Betjeman). An ambitious building of five-bay nave with buttressed N and S lean-to aisles. S porch and W tower with saddleback roof. E.E. style with steeply pitched roofs to nave and lower chancel. Lancets to the aisles and tower, small quatrefoils to the clerestory. Spacious interior with lofty nave, the roof springing impressively from corbels between the clerestory windows. – STAINED GLASS. Five windows of 1903–5 by *J. Jennings*.

SACRED HEART AND ST IA (R.C.), Tregenna Hill. 1908 by *Canon A. J. Scoles* with *B. G. Raymond*. Tightly fitted into the streetscape on a steeply sloping corner site, skilfully composed around an octagonal corner bell-turret at the SW corner of the church with the presbytery at right angles downhill. Typical Catholic interior of the period with tall fiddly tabernacles etc., competent but not moving. Memorial plaque on exterior commemorating the Western Rising of 1549, by *Fr. Charles Norris* of Buckfast, 1949.

BEDFORD ROAD METHODIST CHURCH, Bedford Road. 1898–9. An impressive presence in the street scene especially from High Street. Tall gable-end with Dec-style tracery window accentuated by corner tower rising in two linked stages, both with octagonal lanterns and surmounted by conical roofs.

ZION COMMUNITY CHURCH, Salubrious Place, off Fore Street. Former Countess of Huntingdon's Chapel of *c.* 1800, plain gabled front with two tall round-headed windows with marginal Gothic glazing.

BIBLE CHRISTIAN CHAPEL, St Peter's Street. Datestone 1858. Simple rectangular building with round-headed windows and central round-headed door.

St Ives was a strong centre of nonconformity (the first Methodist Society in Cornwall was formed here in 1743) and several other chapels and churches, some now in other uses, are noted in the perambulation.

PUBLIC BUILDINGS

GUILDHALL, Street-an-Pol. 1940 by *Geoffrey Drewitt*. Handsome five-bay classical front with single recessed bay to r. Tall sash windows to first floor with central balcony over lower, smaller-windowed, ground floor. Deep modillion eaves with hipped roof surmounted by slate cupola on a swept base. The forecourt is memorable for the striking large bronze SCULPTURE 'Dual Form', 1965 by *Barbara Hepworth*.

LIBRARY, Gabriel Street. 1896–7 by *John Symms & Son* of Blackwater as the Passmore Edwards Free Library. Completely remodelled inside 1968. Fine corner building, both elevations lively with buttressed bays rising to small turrets, transomed-and-mullioned windows, and a corner oriel turret rising to an elegant flèche from an embattled parapet.

MARKET HOUSE, Market Place. Datestone 1832. Round-ended rectangular building with hipped roof. Central cupola with ball finial.

THE HARBOUR. SMEATON'S PIER, designed by *John Smeaton*, was built 1767–70 to replace the smaller medieval pier. Contractor *Thomas Richardson*, the main contractor on the Eddystone Lighthouse. Its original extent is marked by the attractive LIGHTHOUSE, with a square granite plinth supporting a cantilevered octagonal gallery with an octagonal granite base to the circular lantern: it is often attributed to *James & Edward Harvey* and dated 1831 but is probably part of Smeaton's original design. Pier lengthened to its present extent in the 1890s with new lighthouse cast by *Stothert & Pitt* of Bath.

LIFEBOAT STATION, West Pier. 1994 by *Poynton Bradbury Wynter Cole*. A slightly heavy building, all in granite, with few windows. Central bay for the lifeboat with high, glazed roller door surmounted by a low pitch gable, with two smaller wings.

Former STENNACK SCHOOL, The Stennack. 1878–81 by *Silvanus Trevail* as the Board School. One of Trevail's best institutional buildings, a large, spreading composition of three gable-ended parallel ranges with linking ranges at the s front. Central range has wider gable and porch in the angle to the r. under a small bell-tower surmounted by a pyramidal spire. Good Gothic detailing throughout. Plans were exhibited in the 1878 Paris Exhibition and afterwards at the International Exhibition in Australia.

BARNOON CEMETERY, Porthmeor Hill. 1855 with two simple Gothic mortuary chapels, overlooking Porthmeor Beach. Includes grave of Alfred Wallis (†1942) with unusual tile design by *Bernard Leach* featuring a lighthouse.

124 TATE ST IVES, Porthmeor. 1989–93 by *Evans & Shalev*, their intention that 'the experience of visiting the gallery ought to be a natural extension of visiting St Ives and thus provide some insight into the artists' inspirations and aspirations'* realized in a reticent yet powerful building, the winning design of an architectural competition. White marble-dash clads a structure ingeniously contrived to rise in a series of broken planes around the vast cylinder of the entrance rotunda, an echo of the gasholder previously on the site. The concept is of an organic Modernism consciously drawing on the Modernist artistic tradition of St Ives and reprising some motifs from the architects' earlier Courts of Justice at Truro (q.v.).

The roof of the rotunda is carried seawards on two tall subtly canted columns, pierced by long rectilinear glazing, that form a huge window open to the Atlantic and the Penwith sky: at ground level the space within the rotunda takes the form of a small amphitheatre, with slender round columns above first-floor level. From here the spacious entrance hall is suffused with mauve light from a STAINED GLASS WINDOW by *Patrick Heron*, 1993, probably the largest such window in the world without leading: abstract coloured shapes with irregular

---

* *Tate Gallery St Ives: The Building* by David Shalev and Michael Tooby (1995).

boundaries enhanced by the natural irregularities of the German handmade glass. The disposition of spaces throughout the building is gracefully achieved. The four floors are accessed by a staircase with Mackintosh-like lattice detail and a wide handrail. The main gallery occupies the entire second floor, designed as a sequential series of rooms of different scales and proportions, sparse in detail and softly lit. A second gallery, semicircular and following the inner curve of the rotunda, was designed for sculpture and ceramics and is flooded with light. The placing of windows, rectangular and circular, gives unexpected glimpses of the sea and town culminating in panoramic views from the roof.

BARBARA HEPWORTH MUSEUM AND SCULPTURE GALLERY, Back Street. As Trewyn Studio the workplace of Barbara Hepworth from 1949 and her home from 1950; established as a museum of her work at her wish. Hepworth used the garden as a private viewing area, especially for her larger bronzes: she often kept an artist's cast of new sculpture for this purpose. The result is an astonishing assemblage of some of her best bronzes and other pieces that can be viewed in the environment in which they were created and often in the position the artist placed them. Hepworth's command of scale is especially well demonstrated, from the miniatures in the house to some of the largest of her *œuvre* in the garden. Among the bronzes familiar from elsewhere are smaller pieces like TORSO II (TORCELLO), CANTATE DOMINO, and GARDEN SCULPTURE (MODEL FOR MERIDIAN), all 1958, and RIVER FORM, 1965 (cast 1975); medium-scale forms such as FIGURE FOR LANDSCAPE, 1959–60; and the large FOUR SQUARE (WALK THROUGH), 1966, TWO FORMS (DIVIDED CIRCLE), 1969, and her last major work, CONVERSATION WITH MAGIC STONES, 1973, to accommodate which the garden was extended. Of stone, there is IMAGE, 1951–2, and STONE SCULPTURE (FUGUE II), 1956. Seen among her planting, and with glimpses of the sea and town beyond, the sculptures make Hepworth's artistic personality immediately tangible.

LEACH POTTERY, STUDIO AND MUSEUM, Higher Stennack. Established 1920 by Bernard Leach, with Shōji Hamada. The long low range fronting the road with a louvred ridge vent is the kiln shed, giving on to a throwing and glazing workshop in the centre and a cross-wing at the NE end, built 1921 as a workshop with Leach's studio above. In the kiln shed a THREE-CHAMBERED CLIMBING KILN, 1923, offering ascending firing temperatures, designed by the Japanese engineer, chemist and potter *Matsutayashi Tsurunoske*, the first in the western world. At the rear and parallel to the main range, studios, 2008, by *Gilmore Hankey Kirke* of Plymouth. A skilful complement to the original, taking its cue from the Eastern tradition that inspired Leach, raised on round concrete stilts like staddle stones with a covered walkway facing into a courtyard formed with the frontage buildings.

PERAMBULATION

It is worth taking advantage of the many views of St Ives from
above the town before starting an exploration because, once in
the maze of little streets, it is easy to lose one's orientation.
Apart from the streets mentioned below, the visitor should also
explore the numerous small lanes and opes, not least to enjoy
the textures of street paving and the wealth of slate cladding
of the buildings.

Within the town, the best place to start is The Island and St
Nicholas's Chapel (*see* Churches), from where the old town
centre stretches E around the harbour, while Porthmeor Beach
lies W on the other side of the isthmus of the promontory. Now
to Smeaton's Pier noting the diminutive St Leonard's Chapel
(*see* Churches), and The Harbour (*see* Public Buildings).
Behind The Quay is the network of densely packed streets and
small C18 and C19 houses that was the fishermen's quarter of
DOWN'LONG. This is the best place in Cornwall to get a sense
of what a typical fishing town looked like, with many good
survivals of former fish cellars and houses above identifiable
by their external stairs, e.g. in BACK ROAD, FISH STREET,
PORTHMEOR ROAD, THE DIGEY and VIRGIN STREET. Most
have been converted to other uses, few as imaginatively as the
OLD SAIL LOFTS, Bethesda Hill, to offices by *Poynton Bradbury Wynter Cole*, 1989. The remains of industrial fish cellars
have sometimes been incorporated or adapted into new structures, the best example BARNALOFT and PIAZZA, two residential blocks of 1963 by *Henry Gilbert* for Percy Williams based
on the granite walls of old pilchard cellars between BACK
ROAD WEST and PORTHMEOR BEACH: a good period piece,
an exemplary solution to building on restricted sites, with
balconies and large windows overlooking the beach. Adjacent
to this, PORTHMEOR STUDIOS, an early C19 pilchard cellar
extended when artists arrived in the 1880s to form studio space
above the net lofts, later occupied by Ben Nicholson, Francis
Bacon and Patrick Heron, among others. The cellars continue
in uses connected with the fishing industry, the floor above
supported on cast-iron pipes. Much of the upper structure is
timber-framed and clad with large north-light windows to the
beach. Meticulously restored 2010–12 by *Long & Kentish*. Of
other buildings, the most striking is the verticality of the former
Mariners' Church (*see* Churches) while the picturesque SLOOP
INN, C18- and C19-looking but incorporating earlier fabric, is
an interesting presence in the strongly teetotal fishing community (cf. TEETOTAL STREET and SALUBRIOUS PLACE):
the number of C19 chapels (e.g. the Bible Christian chapel, St
Peter's Street) also reflects this.

Now around the Harbour and along WHARF ROAD built 1922
as a relief road to FORE STREET behind: before its construction the only connection from Fore Street to the waterfront
was through narrow opes. The buildings overlooking the
harbour are generally unremarkable, though there are one or

two survivals of external stairs of former fish cellars and the early C19 former CUSTOM HOUSE retains some dignity among the many adaptations. At the s end WEST PIER, the Lifeboat station and St Ia's church with the Market House in MARKET PLACE to its w (*see* Churches and Public Buildings). The perambulation will return to Fore Street, but for now continue into HIGH STREET and adjacent streets, the C19–early C20 civic and commercial centre of the town with several sober Neoclassical banks in granite ashlar, the three-storey five-bay early C19 front of the QUEENS HOTEL, and the exuberant stucco front of BOOTS with its huge first-floor broken pediment, the former Scala Cinema, 1920. Uphill w the view is closed by the imposing front of the Bedford Road Methodist Church (*see* Churches), while the corner to TREGENNA PLACE is nicely returned by the former POST OFFICE of 1906 with pretty oriels. Turn l. into STREET-AN-POL for the Guildhall (*see* Public Buildings), and the heavily altered OLD VICARAGE. Back to Tregenna Place and the junction with GABRIEL STREET, with two fine corner buildings on opposite sides, the library (*see* Public Buildings) and the Neoclassical NATWEST BANK. Continue up TREGENNA HILL for the Church Of the Sacred Heart & St Ia and, beyond, the smart C18 front of No. 6 FERNLEA TERRACE. The summit of the road is marked by the MALAKOFF GARDEN with its panoramic views and SCULPTURE, Epidaurous, by *Hepworth*, 1961. A small-scale work but immensely powerful because of its spectacular positioning above the town overlooking St Ives Bay, strongly evocative of the influence of the Cornish seascape and landscape on the sculptor's work.

Return down Tregenna Hill and l. into GABRIEL STREET. At its upper end the handsome front of the WESTERN HOTEL, late C18 two-storey over basement, the centre bay advanced and pedimented, with rusticated quoins; the third storey and three-bay wing to the l. are mid-C19 additions. Adjacent, the tower and stepped front of the Art Deco ROYAL CINEMA of 1939 by *Cowell, Drewitt & Wheatly*. On the opposite side slightly further up CONNAUGHT VILLAS, a good early C19 three-storey-bay pair in granite ashlar with rusticated quoins, plain cornice and parapet, and large Doric porch serving both houses. Adjacent the former WESLEYAN SCHOOLS, dated 1845, very domestic-looking five-bay front in granite ashlar with a pediment, and then the former WESLEYAN CHAPEL, now the St Ives Theatre, its exceedingly plain elevations only relieved by small round-headed first-floor windows. To the r. of these in CHAPEL STREET a former early C19 CHAPEL, and then back along High Street past the Market, and into FORE STREET. The s end was substantially redeveloped in the C19 and is now characterized by taller three-storey buildings, while towards the N end, the former Countess of Huntingdon's Chapel (*see* Churches) and THE DIGEY return it to the smaller scale of the late C18 and early to mid C19. At this point it is possible either to continue to Porthmeor Beach along The Digey and adjacent streets, noting HARRY'S COURT at the w end of Back Road West where No. 3 was the home of Alfred Wallis, or to go back to the s end of Fore Street and r. up BACK STREET past the Barbara Hepworth Museum and Gallery (*see* Public Buildings), and climb BARNOON HILL to Porthmeor Beach. Whichever route is chosen, Tate St Ives (*see* Public Buildings) makes a fitting finale.

TREGENNA CASTLE HOTEL, Trelyon Avenue. Spectacularly sited overlooking the town and St Ives Bay. Built *c.* 1773 'by *Samuel Stephens* under the direction of Mr Wood, architect of Bath' (Kellys) but more likely to have been by *William Wood* of Truro, and enlarged by *George Wightwick* in 1845 and later. Swete, visiting in 1780, described it as a 'pleasant seat, decorated with battlements'. Though much altered and extended, the E entrance front is original, a two-storey five-bay square block with battlemented parapet and chimneys as corner turrets. It is flanked by single-storey wings, set back and similarly detailed. Two-storey four-window square block in the same style set back to the N: with later additions the N front has thirty-one windows. Very little of the original interior remains.

KNILL'S MONUMENT, Vorvas, 2 m. s. 1782 possibly by *William Word* for John Knill, former mayor of St Ives, and intended as his mausoleum. Tall granite pyramid on a square base, like a steeple in long views.

4050

ST JOHN

ST JOHN. One of the simplest and earliest-feeling churches in Cornwall, comparable in plan to Tremaine (q.v.). Norman W tower of two low stages, unbuttressed, the upper storey recessed. The N and s windows are clearly Norman: deep inner splay, slight outer chamfer. The tower has a pyramidal roof. The body of the church is nave, chancel and s porch only, with a low and narrow tower arch, a C12 s door, window of *c.* 1320 in the chancel s wall and C16 window on the N side of the nave. The other windows, roofs and furnishings are of a restoration by *William White* in 1867–8, as is most of the STAINED GLASS, a good and complete set, some (e.g. E window) possibly by *Hardman*. In the C16 window, gathered fragments of medieval glass including some C16 Flemish-looking pieces.

1090

ST JULIOT

ST JULITTA. In an isolated position, below the lane that passes it but high above the lovely Valency valley from which it should ideally be approached on foot from Boscastle. The character of the church can only be understood in the context of its restoration 1870–2 by *Thomas Hardy*, working as an architect before he devoted himself to literature. He inherited a commitment to the rebuilding of much of the old church which had become seriously dilapidated, and though he later regretted his part in such destruction supervised its radical remodelling. The strong C14-looking tower was reconstructed, the ambitious embattled s porch with its stone transverse vault and the s aisle retained, but the original nave, chancel and N transept were replaced by a new shorter N aisle, the s aisle becoming the new nave and chancel. The four-bay arcade and the Perp tracery of the aisle windows are Cornish standard: good early C16 wagon roof with decorated wall-plates and bosses. – FONT. C15 square, of granite. – STAINED GLASS. Chancel E, 1923–4 by *Powells of Whitefriars*. – ENGRAVED GLASS. Nave s, 2003 by *Simon Whistler*, an ethereal evocation of Hardy's literary imagination.

Three medieval CROSSES in the churchyard, that by the stile at the SW entrance especially well preserved and executed.

HENNET, just NE of the church. Rare example of a T-plan C16 house, possibly an open hall. Bedchamber in parlour wing with good plaster arms of Elizabeth I.

OLD RECTORY, ¼ m. NW. Mid-C19, entrance front asymmetrical with two gables and a central porch, all with ornate bargeboards. The house where Hardy met Emma, his first wife, sister of the rector's wife, while restoring the church.*

ST JUST-IN-PENWITH   3030

Perhaps more than any other part of Cornwall the St Just area makes the county's industrial history immediately tangible. The small town, the centre of the most productive of all the C17–C19 Penwith mining areas, is set on the narrow coastal plain seaward of the high moors. The landscape is thickly populated with ruined engine houses and small mining settlements, near some of the greatest mines like Botallack and Levant (qq.v.).

ST JUST. A large church, set back from the main square of the town centre, its tower and walls all of granite blocks. The tower is C15, of three stages, unbuttressed, embattled and pinnacled. The E windows of the N and s aisles have tracery of the flamboyant 'palm tree' pattern (cf. Padstow). Fine s porch with buttresses set back from the angles, also buttressed and pinnacled (cf. St Buryan), with pretty C18 sundial. The interior is unexpectedly low but spacious with identical six-bay aisle arcades of Beer stone, their Perp

---

*The church and rectory appear in his novel *A Pair of Blue Eyes* and the church as the background to many of his *Poems of 1912–13*, written after Emma's death.

windows also identical, with two alternating designs. The shafts are like those of St Ives, deviating from the Cornish standard, the capitals unusually richly sculpted including large horizontal leaves, fruit, flowers, shields, and shield-holding angels. The capital of the N arch of the chancel has three shields, the next W the shield of the angel has the letters J and M and bosses, a motif repeated on the label stops to the S aisle window E of the porch: the five bosses accompanying the J representing the five wounds of Christ, the seven bosses of the M the seven dolours of the Virgin. The craftsmanship is so similar to the Trenwith aisle at St Ives that the same masons must have been employed. A severe restoration of 1865–6 by *J. P. St Aubyn* installed his usual arch- and wind-braced roofs. – STONE with chi-rho (XP) monogram and inscription SELVS IC IACIT in the N aisle, found in the wall of the chancel when that was partly rebuilt in 1834: probably C5–C6. – CROSS-SHAFT with Hiberno-Saxon interlace built into the N wall of the N aisle, C8 or C9. – FONT. C19. The date C14 cannot be accepted. – Set of four CANDELABRA given in 1746 by John Edwards (inscription): Edwards was a wealthy mine owner. – WALL PAINTINGS. *St Aubyn* stripped the walls of their plaster with an effect even more destructive of the dignity of the interior than usual because of the strident black pointing.* In the process he discovered six paintings, of which two survive on the N wall of the N aisle, both very restored, a St George and a Warning to Sabbath Breakers (cf. Breage). – STAINED GLASS. S aisle E, 1886 by *Fouracre & Watson*, good. – Three windows in S aisle, 1927–8 by *Clayton & Bell*, indifferent.

Rudely carved WHEEL-HEAD CROSS lying outside the porch. – At the SW corner of the churchyard, WHEEL-HEAD CHURCHYARD CROSS with figure of Christ on an incised Latin cross.

METHODIST CHURCH, Chapel Road. 1833, enlarged and remodelled in 1860, partly re-fitted 1893. Highly prominent, because of its large scale, in the approach to the town from the coast road, and a dominant feature of the townscape as it closes the view from the centre down Chapel Street. One of the best and most important Methodist churches in Cornwall. Impressive three-bay classical front with large Tuscan porch, round-headed sash windows, the centre first-floor window tripartite, and moulded gable parapet. Side elevations with pretty inter-secting glazing. An especially good and complete interior, the oval gallery carried on slender Doric columns. Moulded and modillioned ceiling cornice with carved and painted ceiling rose. The square columns flanking the organ loft originally gave into the apsidal communion area, now partitioned off. Rare original bow-fronted PULPIT incorporated into ornate cast-iron rostrum, 1860s BOX PEWS in gallery, and many other features.

---

*If there is one church in Cornwall that should have its plaster restored it is St Just.

WESLEYAN REFORM UNION CHAPEL, Bosorne Terrace.
Opened 1860. A tall, plain, dignified rectangle with round-
headed sash windows. Central round-arched door with spoked
fanlight. Interior with gallery with original painted and panelled front and box pews.

LAFROWDA CLUB, Chapel Street. Built 1842 as the Literary
Institute. A surprise to find a Greek Revival front in this little
street of modest cottages. Tall two storeys, the wide central
bay advanced and pedimented and flanked by very narrow
bays, in turn flanked by pilasters. The central bay has fluted
Doric columns with triglyph entablature to ground floor, and
first floor with Ionic half-columns flanking a round-headed
window.

PLAIN-AN-GWARRY, Bank Square. A shallow-banked circular
enclosure about 150 ft (46 metres) in diameter surrounded by
stone and earth banks. Possibly a prehistoric round in origin
but later a place for the performance of medieval miracle plays
and other events (cf. Perran Round, Perranzabuloe).

PERAMBULATION. The small scale of the town, and its strongly
C19 industrial character, are quickly discernible. At its core is
the small medieval settlement of the original churchtown and
Plain-an-Gwarry with MARKET SQUARE between, subsumed
in the rapid expansion of the 1830s when mining was booming
and the built-up area more than tripled: St Just's population
peaked at over 9,000 in 1861 from under 3,000 in 1801. Some
sense of the scale of the pre-C19 settlement is offered by Nos.
2 and 3 CHURCH SQUARE, just W of the church, a C17 house
converted into two cottages in the C19 when the front wall was
mostly rebuilt but retaining its tall granite gable-end stacks,
gable coping, scrolled kneelers, and three blocked mullioned
windows in its E gable-end wall. The scrolled kneelers, a local
feature, can also be seen on No. 4 opposite, another C17 house.
More small houses in the area around the church.

The modest scale is maintained throughout the town, though
in MARKET SQUARE, the commercial heart of St Just, there
are several more substantial buildings, especially the dignified
ashlar granite front of the WELLINGTON HOTEL, c. 1840, with
its three wide elliptical arches to the ground floor, sash windows
with keystones over, and a modillion cornice under a hipped
roof. On the opposite side the COMMERCIAL HOTEL, early
C19 stucco enriched with a rusticated ground floor and scribed
end pilasters. The evidence of the westward expansion of the
town in the 1830s is clear N of Plain-an-Gwarry in BANK
SQUARE, and the buildings of CHAPEL STREET, CAPE CORN-
WALL STREET and MARKET STREET. A good route for a sense
of the later town is down Chapel Street to the Methodist
church, l. along CHAPEL ROAD, and r. into CAPE CORNWALL
STREET: between the latter and BOSONE ROAD are small cot-
tages laid out on a strict grid like VICTORIA ROW, QUEEN
STREET, PRINCES STREET, REGENT TERRACE and PLEAS-
ANT TERRACE. Return to the centre by CAPE CORNWALL
STREET past the BOARD SCHOOLS of 1877 and 1880, the

mid-C19 METHODIST SCHOOL AND MANSE, and the tall red
brick-dressed INSTITUTE of 1928.

Evidence of the parish's rich prehistory includes:

BARTINNEY CASTLE, 3 m. SE. Circular HILLTOP ENCLOS-
URE formed of a roughly kerbed low stony bank. No ditch and
the SW gap is not certainly an original entrance. It was probably a form of ritual or ceremonial gathering place and contains three close-spaced or touching ring cairns and several
other small cairns; probably Late Neolithic or Early Bronze
Age. The hill's convex profile provides few short views, but
dramatic long ones, to Land's End, the sea and the West
Penwith hills.

CHAPEL CARN BREA, 3 m. SSE. Cornwall's westernmost
hill, overlooking Land's End and with views to Scilly, has a
large kerbed summit CAIRN. 1879 excavations revealed at least
three concentric internal retaining walls and a central chamber,
probably an ENTRANCE GRAVE, with four capstones (no longer
visible). Higher in the mound, and visible on the SSE side, is
a secondary CIST with squarish capstone. By 1302 a CHAPEL
(now removed) to St Michael stood on top; its hermit maintained a light to guide shipping, but was murdered that year.
Smaller KERBED CAIRN to the S contains a large slab, possibly
the capstone of a cist, which yielded a large Middle Bronze
Age cremation urn when excavated in 1907. The summit tor
has an unusual Neolithic LONG CAIRN on its N side. This
mound of granite stones, kerbed in places, has a rounded
ridge-like back reaching and maintaining the height of the tor
and so incorporating it into its structure. Visible from SW and
SE of the hill, it resembles an axe-head when viewed from the
axe stone at Boscawen-Un stone circle (St Buryan).

TREGESEAL STONE CIRCLE, 1½ m. NE. The eastern of two
Early Bronze Age circles standing on moorland beyond Hail-
glower's fields, the working of which accounted for a third. Six
western stones were lost to Victorian shallow quarrying (possibly streamworking) but were replaced by 1932. Only one
stone of the W circle is now visible, embedded in a field boundary. Aerial photos suggest a possible third circle further W. The
skyline is dominated by Carn Kenidjack, 600 yards N across a
moorland that contains numerous other remains including an
ENTRANCE GRAVE, four HOLED STONES, and prehistoric
CAIRNS, ROUND-HOUSES and FIELDS. CARN VRES logan
stone is close by.

BALLOWBALL BARROW ENTRANCE GRAVE and CAIRN,
1 m. W. A complex cliff-top Neolithic and Bronze Age cairn
found beneath mining debris (now removed). Excavated and
partly reconstructed in 1878–9. The earliest element is part of
a paved Neolithic entrance grave oriented NNE that would have
been within a smaller cairn. It has two surviving capstones.
The SSW–NNE line was continued by five Bronze Age CISTS.
A domed cairn was built over the central three and a sixth cist
was inserted into the cairn's fabric. The entrance grave, still a

significant presence when the cists and central mound were built, seems to have always been kept open and accessible. It was later incorporated into a large encircling mound, forming a perimeter platform. A narrow corridor around the central mound was created by the excavator to display the two external cists.

CAPE CORNWALL. *See* p. 143.

BOTALLACK. *See* p. 121.

LEVANT MINE. *See* p. 303.

ST JUST-IN-ROSELAND

8030

ST JUST. An arm of Carrick Sound touches the churchyard on the w side of the St Mawes promontory, giving the church the most idyllic of settings, even for Cornwall. It is enhanced by lush tropic planting belonging to the garden of the Edwardian botanist John Treseder, which is now merged with the church-yard to form a curiously beautiful waterside park. On the landward approach the church lies at the very bottom of a richly wooded coombe so that even from the lychgate one is above the tower and looks down on the long parallels of nave and s aisle. The mother church of St Mawes, it was re-dedicated by Bishop Bronescombe in 1261 – the date of the chancel – having been in the ownership of Plympton Priory since 1140. The w tower of two stages has diagonal buttresses and a battlemented SE stair-turret rising above the battle-mented parapet: the top windows are two-light C15 with arched heads and cinquefoils. The N transept has walling that must belong to 1261. The s aisle is entirely Perp, as is the seven-bay aisle arcade resting on standard Cornish granite piers with plain capitals and nearly semicircular arches. The s porch has a carved wagon roof and a fine doorway like St Austell and Mylor (q.v.) but the openwork ogee tracery on top of the arch is broken off. The jambs still show their panelling. Energeti-cally restored in 1872 by the rector, the *Rev. C. W. Carlyon* (cf. St Anthony-in-Roseland and Philleigh): the arch-braced roofs, biblical texts, PEWS, PULPIT and CLERGY SEAT with coarse, vigorous carving are all by his hand. The roof BOSSES 1990 by *John Phillips*, carved by *Charles Moore*. – Double PISCINA in chancel, 1261. – FONT. C15, octagonal with uninteresting quatre-foil panels. – PAINTED PANEL of the Lord's Prayer, 1693, beside s door. – BRASS. E wall of aisle. A priest in choir cope, probably *c.* 1505, for rector William Perys. Excellent.

LYCHGATES at the s and E entrances to the churchyard, first built 1632, possibly rebuilt early C19, the s again in 2008. Low-pitched two-bay arch-braced roofs with cusped bargeboards and segmental-arched wooden lintels cover the walkways which have wooden-seated side ledges.

HOLY WELL OF ST JUST, E of the church. Medieval, rebuilt in
the C19. Built into the hillside with simple w-facing entrance
with slate slab cover.

Former RECTORY. Mid-C18, extended late C18 and early C19.
Originally a two-room central stair plan, now double-depth
with SW wing. Five-window front with twelve-pane sashes with
much crown glass. Interior has good C18 fittings including
open-well stair with heavy turned balusters and a completely
panelled room to the l.

ST KEVERNE

ST KEVERNE. The church lies by a square, which gives the place
something of the appearance of a small town rather than a
village, as befits the centre of the largest of the Lizard parishes.
There was a church here by the C10 and an early monastery,
acquired by Beaulieu Abbey in 1235. It has several unusual
features. First of all a spire, octagonal and ribbed; it was
renewed as late as 1770, probably because it was useful as a
landmark near the treacherous Manacles. It surmounts a two-
stage unbuttressed tower in the Lizard pattern with a fine W
door with a serpentine chequer surround and four shields (cf.
St Austell and St Enoder), a hoodmould with serpents' heads
as label stops and, within, a small barrel-vaulted vestibule with
stone benches. The second rare feature is the projection of the
two aisles forward to flank the tower and the tower opens into
them (cf. Lanteglos-by-Fowey). Finally there are three rood
stairs in the complex evolution of the N wall. The interior is
surprisingly spacious, though low: 110 ft (33.5 metres) long,
with N and S aisles of seven bays. The piers are of strikingly
banded green/grey/beige/pink stone, mostly elvan, with shields
in the corners of the capitals. The chronology of this is puzzling, the piers of the S aisle, of square section and attached
shafts, being earlier (late C14?) than the Cornish standard of
the N aisle (late C15 to early C16): perhaps the S aisle piers were
reused when the church was rebuilt by Beaulieu in the late C15,
because they do not comfortably fit their places. Their shape
is standard Cornish, but of larger, broader, heavier section than
later on: their date may be late C13 or early C14. The outer wall
of the N aisle is also buttressed, also a sign of early date, and
the first window from the W end, a lancet, and the N door
belong to the same period too. The rest, and especially the S
aisle windows, is clearly Perp, specially good on the E side. The
arches connecting chancel and aisles also have a decoration of
the abaci typical of a later date. The pretty S doorway has two
suspended shields carved at capital level. S and N chancel
chapels have wagon roofs; other roofs were replaced in a restoration of 1893 by E. H. Sedding when the E end of the chancel
was rebuilt above plinth level. – FONT. C15, with angels at the

corners holding shields with inscriptions between. – On the sill
of the N chapel window various fragments of medieval tracery
and two figures from a CRUCIFIXUS, probably from a reredos.
– PULPIT. Jacobean, with nice ornamental panels. – BENCH-
ENDS. Only a few of the standard Cornish type. – WALL
PAINTINGS. St Christopher, surrounded by scenes from the
life of the saint, very faint, on the N wall: *inter alia* a heron, fish
and mermaid are discernible. – STAINED GLASS. Chancel E
1898, commemorating the wreck of the SS *Mohegan* with the
loss of 106 lives. – In the NE corner of the churchyard are the
mass graves of wreck victims.

The Square and its immediate surrounds have a good array of
modest C17–C19 houses with much serpentine walling e.g. No.
8 LEMON STREET. ¼ m. N, a roadside SCULPTURE, 1996 by
Terence Coventry, a memorial to the Cornish uprising of 1497.
Two larger than life-size bronze figures, strongly modelled, of
Michael Joseph an Gof, the smith from St Keverne, and
Thomas Flamank, a lawyer from Bodmin.

THREE BROTHERS OF GRUGWITH, 2 m. WSW. Large Early
Bronze Age CIST whose large lumpy capstone is supported by
two parallel slabs, one leaning inwards, probably side stones.
End stones missing, no sign of covering mound.

COVERACK. *See* p. 165.

ST KEW

0070

ST JAMES (St Kewa). The archetypal late Perp Cornish church,
delightfully set in a sheltered valley among trees in its small
churchtown. Fine, tall C15 W tower of three stages whose buttresses leave the angles free, surmounted by an embattled
parapet with corner pinnacles and crocketed finials. Large rectangular SE stair-turret rising above the battlements. S doorway
of Polyphant stone, with C16 door triple-lapped and studded, its
inner face renewed. Lofty, light and spacious interior, the tall
nave and chancel matched by five-bay N and S aisles of equal
height; the arcades are of standard Cornish granite design with
four-centred arches. The capitals are of limestone and some
have a decoration of large horizontal leaves. Much Perp tracery,
some renewed: the E windows of the aisles have four and five
lights, the N and S windows three. Ceiled wagon roofs with
carved bosses, arcade and wall-plates with angels against the
wall-plate at the foot of the principals (cf. St Endellion). Wagon
roof in the C15 S porch too. – The most memorable feature of
the church is its STAINED GLASS which, although far less
extensive than the surviving scheme at St Neot (q.v.), is of
higher quality, equal to anything in SW England. The NE
window, dating from 1485–90, is preserved almost completely.
It tells in twelve episodes (three rows of four scenes) the story
of Christ's Passion from the Entry into Jerusalem to the

42, 43
44

Harrowing of Hell. Only two scenes in the lower panels are missing. At the bottom of the window is a strip of kneeling donor figures, and a tiny scene of the Nativity. In the tracery coats of arms: Pentire and Carminow, royal arms, Beare, and unknown, possibly Carminow, families. The SE window, which may be early C15, contains fragments of the Tree of Jesse: Jesse's hand gripping the vine, Solomon, David, and above, the Virgin and Child, with eight angels in the tracery; C15. Small fragments of medieval glass in the tracery of other windows. – FONT. Octagonal, late C14, Polyphant, with quatrefoil panels. – PULPIT. Uncommonly good, Elizabethan with ornamental panels. One panel with a man in a tree (a rebus?). – BENCH-ENDS. Four C16 examples survive. – ROYAL ARMS. 1661, plasterwork, with the usual strapwork decoration (cf. Kilkhampton). This is formed on an older oak panel and chamfered base, possibly a tympanum, mutilated when moved into its present position. – ALMS BOX. At the W end of the N aisle. – LANTERN CROSS. C15, of Catacleuse stone, carved on all four faces with the Crucifixion, the Virgin and Child and two single figures, either saints or bishops. It stands on a CROSS-SHAFT of a different stone, probably from a separate monument. – OGHAM STONE. An early Christian (C6 or C7) memorial stone with Latin inscription IUPTV, the name of Jesus, which is also rendered in Ogham, a script consisting entirely of straight lines. Ogham stones are common in SW Ireland but rare in Cornwall (cf. Lewannick, St Clement). – STOCKS in the porch. – MONUMENTS. At the E end of the nave are several C18 slate ledger stones of fine quality. – In the S aisle John Cavell, 1602, with arms of Cavell impaling Courtenay, Godolphin and Pomoroy. – In the N aisle, Honor Webber †1601, with lovely carved figures of mother and three children in high relief.

In the churchyard many C18 and C19 slate HEADSTONES with good lettering, and several fine ledger stones hung on the exterior walls of the church. – E of the S aisle, wheel-headed WAYSIDE CROSS, one side of the head cut off in its previous use as part of a footbridge over the Allen River. – On the N side of the church, another WAYSIDE CROSS, the wheel-head intact.

In the churchtown, the ST KEW INN. Probably of C16–C17 origin as a house, now of charming late C18 to early C19 vernacular appearance. Earlier central two-storey range with two-storey wings projecting forward l. and r. The large hall has an impressive C19 fireplace with expanding cast-iron grate in working order. Behind high walls TRESCOBEL, the early former C19 vicarage, with symmetrical two-storey front with sashes and Doric porch. Fine early C19 interior, the central entrance hall with plastered groin-vaulted ceiling of three bays.

The parish has a number of small hamlets. Among them, CHAPEL AMBLE, Methodist chapel, 1840, and Sunday School, c. 1820, the former church; TRELILL, 1812, former Methodist church of the simpler early type; and PENDOGETT, interesting conversion of Methodist chapel by *Robert Evans*, 1993.

The good-quality agricultural land of this large inland parish supported a number of C17–C19 farmhouses with an unusual occurrence of C19 slate-clad timber-framed granaries. There is also a handful of fine gentry houses including:

BOKELLY, 1 m. E. Pretty and complete former farmstead including C16 FARMHOUSE remodelled in the C18, rare C16 BARN with HORSE ENGINE HOUSE, C19 GRANARY and PIGSTIES, and early C20 SHELTER SHEDS. Home of William Carnsew in the late C16, who wrote about his visits to other important Cornish houses.

PENGENNA, 2 m. NE. Rare late C16 three-storey house, the former seat of the Mohun family. Early C17 front wing at higher end and two-storey cross-wing at lower end. Principal elevation with mullioned windows under hoodmoulds and four-centred arched doorway inscribed TM (Thomas Pocock). Plaster overmantel in parlour depicting Adam and Eve in the Garden of Eden.

ST KEYNE   2060

ST KEYNE. Prominently sited on the summit of a hill and within a pronounced raised oval churchyard or *lann*. C15 unbuttressed W tower of three stages with embattled parapet and crocketed pinnacles. The body of the church – nave, N aisle, S transept and S porch – was extensively rebuilt, especially on the S side, in restorations of 1868 and 1874–8 by *J. P. St Aubyn*. Scant evidence of an earlier, possible cruciform, church is offered by an ornamental hoodmould with three badly carved heads above the S door, and an early C14 cusped ogee-headed window high up in the N wall above a blocked N door, both re-set. Otherwise all the details are Perp, or renewed by St Aubyn. Three-bay arcade to N aisle with standard Cornish piers. C19 roof with scissor trusses and cambered collars with arch bracing. – FONT. C15, octagonal, plain. – STAINED GLASS. S aisle, St Peter and St Paul, 1906, and N aisle, Suffer the Little Children, 1913, by *Clayton & Bell*. – Two old armorials in N aisle tracery. – MONUMENTS. Well-engraved slate memorials on external N wall of N aisle, including John Edgcumbe †1770 and John Hicks †1800.

HOLY WELL OF ST KEYNE, ½ m. SSE. The well-house, made famous by Southey's poem which celebrated the tradition of bride and groom racing to the well after the wedding service, is delightfully set among trees below the lane. Of C16 origin, it was rebuilt in 1936 after the lane was widened. Simple building with granite ashlar walls and a gabled roof of large granite blocks.

ST LEVAN

ST LEVAN. Not far from Land's End, but, in contrast to Sennen, in a sheltered coombe set back from magnificent cliffs, resting against a hillside, with the E parts half buried in it. The W tower is of only two stages, unbuttressed. The N side of the church with the N transept (note its narrow C13 window) shows earlier masonry than the granite of tower, S aisle and S porch. The S aisle has six bays with octagonal piers and plain double-chamfered arches. At the time when the C15 S aisle was built, the N transept received two arches of the same design. C15 wagon roof to porch, restored wagon roof to S aisle with old black and yellow chevron decoration, and C19 wagon roof to nave and chancel. Restored 1872 by *J. D. Sedding** and 1891 by *J. P St Aubyn*. – FONT. An exceptional Norman type with a large circular bowl having a lower border of cable, an upper border of chip-carved saltire crosses, and four flat motifs of stars in circles on the sides; the bowl is similar to Phillack, the geometric decoration like Cury and Cubert. – ROOD SCREEN. The base survives, two panels l. and two r. of the central opening. Each panel has three narrow uprights carved with a shield sharing the same initials and symbols of the Passion as Cornish bench-ends, and a long, narrow ornamented motif above, mainly foliage, but also two dragons standing on their tails. – BENCH-ENDS. Some are old, and several of unusual, interesting designs, for example two profiles facing each other, two profiles turning away from each other, two fishes, two eagles, a St James *en face* with his pilgrim's hat, and two jesters. Only one of them has Renaissance candelabra in its frame. The date is probably *c.* 1535. – PULPIT. 1752, charming, solid oak panels with a little inlay work. – STAINED GLASS. Chancel E, 1880 by *Joseph Bell & Son*.

In the churchyard S of the S porch, a fine wheel-headed CHURCHYARD CROSS considered *in situ* (a great rarity), cruci-fied Christ on one face, an equal-limbed cross on the other, both enclosed in beading, and with zigzag and lattice decora-tion to the sides. Another WHEEL-HEAD CROSS and mutilated CROSS-SLAB at the NE entrance where there are also two sets of STEPS, STILE and COFFIN REST dated 1794.

HOLY WELL, BAPTISTERY, HERMITAGE and CHAPEL, ¼ m. S of the church overlooking Porth Chapel beach. The remains of the well-house and baptistery, a single-cell small square struc-ture, are immediately adjacent to the spring, from which a flight of steps leads to the ruins of the chapel and hermitage on the cliff edge below, two small roofless rectangular buildings

---

* Sedding found 'magic in the art of the place. In what does it consist? Clearly it is not size, not even proportion, nor any sense of scale and texture altogether, but because the structure is informed with a soul . . . the atmosphere of the place suggests it is not man, but other beings, that are its real owners and tenants-in-charge.'

set side by side, found in excavation and now obscured by vegetation and land slips. Probably C7 or C8.

DAYMARK, 1 m. SW. Dated 1821. A cone over a tapered shaft, black and white painted, looking like a squat rocket.

TRERYN DINAS, 1 m. E. Later Iron Age CLIFF CASTLE with three widely spaced separate lines of different forms and possibly different dates. The largest, simplest rampart with deep external ditch is at the promontory's neck. A central line on the headland's ridged back has two closely spaced ditched banks, the inner one stone-faced. The promontory tip is cut off by stone-faced bank with ditch that is in a poor position defensively, being overlooked by high ground. Encloses a dramatic granite rockscape including the large delicately poised LOGAN ROCK that could be set rocking by a finger until dislodged and inadequately repaired in 1824. Spaces enclosed by outer lines might have accommodated gatherings, but the inner line isolated a special place, perhaps with some symbolic meaning.

PORTHCURNO. *See* p. 452.

ST MABYN

0070

A hilltop settlement, with the churchtown clustered almost defensively around the parish church and its raised oval churchyard, which makes a good, coherent group with late C19 school, pub and surrounding small terraces and cottages.

ST MABYN. A large C15–C16 church of nave, N and S aisles, S porch and W tower. The strikingly tall tower, rising unbuttressed through three tiers, is a landmark for miles around and looks one build, after the S aisle and porch. W door arch of Catacleuse stone, like Egloshayle (q.v.), heraldic beasts on the corners of the first and second tier string courses, and the Evangelists below the parapet: the fourth figure displaced to the E face by the NE stair-turret. The extent of C19 structural work is uncertain, as the exterior of the E end demonstrates: the chancel projects forward with straight joints to both aisles and the E window looks C16, but is remarkably less weathered than the aisle windows – is it careful C19 reconstruction? Round granite rainwater heads. The interior offers a sense of the structure and spaciousness of the Perp church, albeit without its rood screen. Nave and aisles of seven bays with standard Cornish granite piers and two-centred arches, the capitals of lighter-coloured granite, their span less in the chancel than the nave (cf. Bodmin). Ceiled wagon roofs throughout, except for the chancel's slighter C19 replacement ribs above original wall-plates: in contrast the easternmost panels of the N and S aisle roofs are foliage-enriched. The late medieval atmosphere prevails over a series of C19 interventions, the latest of 1884–9 raising the chancel floor and re-seating and re-flooring throughout: the only really false note the dull parclose screens. – Norman FONT of Purbeck stone, combining a square bowl on a circular base. The bowl has eight flat blank niches with pointed heads in faint relief, the base in a star pattern – it never had shafts and the blank section suggests it might originally have stood against a column. – PISCINAS. One in chancel, re-cut, another in S aisle. – CREDENCE TABLE. One C16 panel possibly from an earlier pulpit. – STAINED GLASS. Fragments of medieval glass in top lights of aisle windows, including angel heads. – E window, 1880, excellent C16 style with expressive faces.

CHURCHYARD. Many good C18 and C19 slate headstones, including a notable group removed from the church in the early C19 and re-erected against the N wall of the tower and aisle. Much reduced pre-Conquest wheel-head MALTESE CROSS on C19 base.

COLQUITE, 1½ m. SSE. Below the present house, the fragmentary remains of a late C15 manor house, with two doorways and a window opening on the ground floor and five windows on the upper floor. It might have been a first-floor house.★

HELIGAN, 1½ m. ESE. Fragmentary remains of a house dated 1679.

TREGARDEN, ¾ m. W. The house successively of the Beres, Barnets, Godolphins and Mitchells. Large early C17 house, probably of earlier origin, of rare E-shaped plan, two-storey with central gabled porch and projecting wings l. and r. South front with four-light mullions with king mullions on ground floor and three-light mullions above. Roll-moulded four-centred arch to porch with carved spandrels, inner doorway also four-centred arch. Hall has large hollow-chamfered fireplace and fine, probably C17, plaster coat of arms on higher end wall. C18 stair to rear of hall with thick stick balusters, square newel, and deep moulded rail. A large four-centred arch with square hoodmould fronting the forecourt, probably the remains of a gatehouse.

ST MARTIN-BY-LOOE

1 m. NE of Looe

ST KEYNE AND ST MARTIN. The mother church of East Looe (*see* Looe), its earliest recorded dedication 1258 by Bishop Bronescombe. The two lower stages of the W tower are early C14 with diagonal buttresses and a rare C13 or C14 W door in Polyphant stone with nook-shafts, the rest of the tower Perp with pinnacled stair-turret in the SE corner rising above the battlement and pinnacled parapet. Nave of three bays with S

★A detailed study was made by F. Chesher in *Cornish Archaeology*, VI (1967).

aisle and chancel of two narrower bays, N and S transepts. Though the general impression of the exterior and interior is Perp, enough remains of the pre-Perp church to form some idea of its shape: fine Norman N door, one of the best in Cornwall (cf. Kilkhampton, Morwenstow, St Anthony-in-Roseland etc.), of four orders with rich deep moulding and zigzag and dog-tooth ornament, one narrow E.E. window towards the W end of the S wall, the walls of the transept chapels. Most of the piers are Cornish standard, but with fillets between the shafts and the hollows. Some of the piers have simple decorated abaci; some have not. The ceiled wagon roofs are C15: this is one of the few churches in Cornwall that has dendrochronological dating, suggesting the nave, chancel and S aisle roofs are of 1453–78, the N transept roof probably of the same date, and only the S transept roof slightly later, though the sequence is not fully understood. – FONT. Norman, with groups of four-petalled flowers, an unusual motif, and a tree of life on one side, considered by Henderson to be a C15 copy. It stands on a square Norman base with stoolings for corner shafts. – ALTAR RAILS. First half of the C17. – Aisle PARCLOSE SCREEN. 1612, and interesting in its continuation of a basically Perp composition, with three openings per section. – PULPIT. Late C18 or early C19 octagonal Regency Gothic with pointed-arched panels. – Remains of C14 PISCINA in E wall of chancel. – PEWS, 1923–48, and ROOD SCREEN, 1934, by *Violet Pinwill* and her school in their characteristic late medieval style. This is a specially good ensemble, the bench-ends with kneeling angel caps. – STAINED GLASS. Chancel E and S transept S by *Mayer*, 1909. – S aisle and chancel N by *Fouracre & Watson*, 1879–90. – N aisle by *William Morris & Co.* of Westminster, 1920. – MONUMENTS. Tomb-chest to Philip Mayow †1590, probably by *Peter Crocker* of Looe (cf. Lansallos, Pelynt and Talland), a flat slate figure in high relief in a handsome arched recess with intermittent ashlar rustication. Very traditional, medievalizing style. – Walter Langdon and wife †1667. By *Nicholas Abraham*, 1678. An ambitious but conservative work for its date. The painted figures face each other kneeling, with a prayer-desk between. Back wall with columns, broken pediment and swags. – Many minor early C19 monuments.

KEVERAL BARTON, 3 m. E. Front range is the remains of a C16 courtyard house. Large chimneystacks and wide four-centred arched doorway. Remodelled in the C17 with timber mullioned window in rear elevation and many interior features.

ST MARTIN-IN-MENEAGE

ST MARTIN. On its own a little S of the village. The church was rebuilt, except for the W tower, in 1830 after a fire. The C15 tower is of two stages with heads projecting from the top course. The body of the church is an aisleless rectangular auditorium with serpentine blocks prominent in the external walls. It was Gothicized in the later C19 with pointed-arch doors and windows with Y-tracery, the latter probably replacing earlier sashes. Most of the fittings are also of this date. – FONT. Norman, with corner shafts and rosettes in flat relief. – STAINED GLASS. Chancel E, 1918 by *Jones & Willis*.

MUDGEON FARMHOUSE, 1 m. N. An excellent example of the way the Cornish house evolved from the C16 to C18. Originally a three-room and through-passage hall house, the lower end lost, with a C17 parlour wing at the higher end and an early C18 service wing. Six-light parlour window retains much original glass. C18 staircase and bolection-moulded panelling to back parlour.

8030

ST MAWES

Guarded by its castle, the town enjoys a sublime setting on a sheltered S-facing bay at the mouth of the Percuil River looking towards St Anthony's Head. St Maw, a Breton saint, is said to have established himself here in the C6 and carved a chair of stone (cf. St Germoe): Leland, writing in 1542, describes 'a pretty village or fisher town with a pier called St Maws, and there is a chapel of him and his chair of stone a little without, and his well'. The chapel seems to have decayed by the C17 when the inhabitants unsuccessfully petitioned for its restoration (being forced to go to St Just-in-Roseland), the remains of the chapel being converted to a house. The town was made a parliamentary borough in 1562. It had had a quay since the early C15, one of the earliest in Cornwall, becoming a significant fishery, especially for supplying Falmouth's cured pilchard trade, and in 1854 an Act of Parliament was obtained to erect a new pier and deepen the harbour. The pier was destroyed by a storm in 1872 but rebuilt the following year with a sea wall under the supervision of the *Rev. C. W. Carlyon* (cf. St Just-in-Roseland). Its transformation from fishing port to genteel watering place began in the C19 but gathered pace from the 1930s, and the centre is now a mix of small houses, cottages and waterfront hotels now set against C20 development reaching to the skyline.

52   ST MAWES CASTLE. Aesthetically the trefoil leaves of the three lower bastions of Henry VIII's castle, stretching out on two levels to SW, SE and NW from the taller circular central tower, give an impression of all-round symmetry and harmony of composition strikingly un-medieval and convincingly of the Renaissance. If one compares St Mawes with Pendennis opposite across the Fal (q.v.), and with Deal, Walmer and Camber in Kent and Sussex, all ingenious variations on the theme of

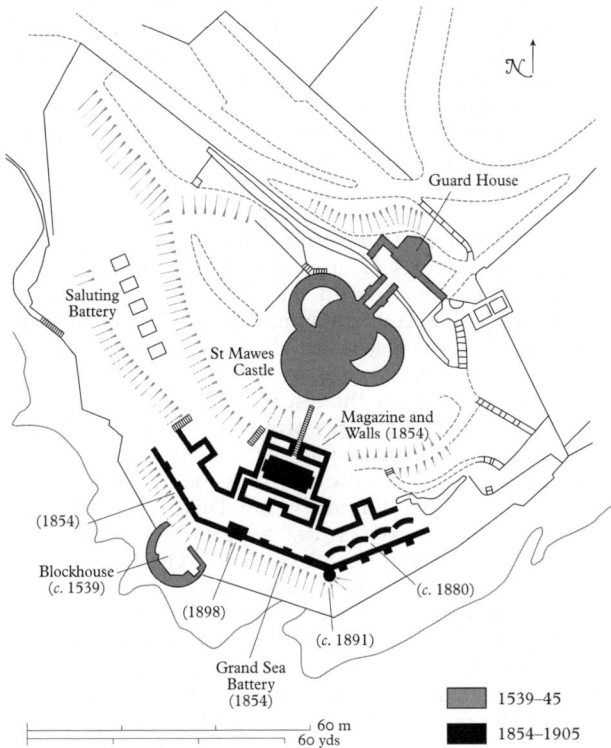

St Mawes Castle. Plan

the grouping of semicircular units, this impression is confirmed and enhanced. Yet these shapes were not devised for reasons of pleasure in geometrical play. They were considered by Henry VIII and his engineers (or devisors, as they were called) the most up-to-date fortifications. The art of defence had changed much since the Middle Ages owing to the introduction of cannon and gunpowder. Low bastions were now preferable to the high keeps and gatehouses of the past. In England few monuments of the C16 exist, because there was no warfare on land, and if Henry VIII had not, after a ten-year truce had been concluded in 1538 between the Emperor Charles V and the King of France, been rightly afraid of an attack by Francis I instigated by the pope, he would not have set up his chain of castles along the south coast. Their designers were probably foreigners (we know one of them, *Stefan von Haschenperg*, from Moravia, but he is not documentarily connected with the Cornish castles), and while their work must have appeared wonderfully new and ingenious to the English, it was in fact only moderately up to date. Round bastions, as recommended by Dürer in his book on fortifications in 1525 and much used in Italy about and after 1500, were just then being replaced in the most modern designs of Sammicheli by the angular bastion to which the future belonged.

To the visitor today the lobed shape of the terraces overlooking Falmouth Bay (the middle one larger and lower than the r. and l. ones) remains unforgettable, regardless of their functional qualities or shortcomings. St Mawes is also by far the most perfectly preserved and decorated of all the Henrician castles, with detail of a high standard of craftsmanship: gargoyles, carved coats of arms, and laudatory inscriptions of Henry and his son, Edward, later Edward VI. The latter were devised by John Leland, the antiquary and chaplain to the king, and carried out by masons familiar with the new Renaissance fashion. The panel above the entrance bearing the beautifully carved royal arms has the inscription over: SEMPER HONOS HENRICE TUUS LAUDESQUE MANEBUNT ('Henry, thy honour and praises will remain for ever'). Others read: GAUDEAT EDWARDO NUNC DUCE CORNUBIA FELIX ('Rejoice happy Cornwall now that Edward is her Duke') and EDWARDUS FAMA REFERAT FACTISQUE PARENTUM ('May Edward resemble his father in fame and deeds'). On the external wall of the main keep is a shield supported by a lion and dragon and surmounted by a crown. On either side are figures in full relief, perhaps tritons, holding scrolls with the inscription over: SEMPER VIVET ANIMA REGIS HENRICI OCTAUS QUI ANNO 34 RENGI HOC FECIT FIERI ('May the soul live for ever of Henry VIII who had this made in the 34th year of his reign'.)

St Mawes Castle was begun in 1540 and completed in 1545. It was approached by a drawbridge from the land side which led into the first floor of the KEEP. Close to the entrance a special staircase connected this floor with the octagonal upper room and, higher still, the roof (now a modern replacement) with a little (since rebuilt) watch tower. From the staircase and three further, shorter staircases the rampart walls of the bastions are reached, their courtyards accessed from the ground floor of the keep which was the mess room of the garrison (ceiling 1880). Below this in the basement was the kitchen. The granite piers of this room as well as some of the beams are original. The garrison, except at moments of danger, varied from sixteen to one hundred. Defence was by means of large cannon in the casements (with smoke-vents) and in the courtyards of the bastions, and light guns in socketed embrasures on the rampart walls of the bastions (the square recesses are for keeping ammunition). In the upper room of the keep are eight recesses for gunners, each with an ammunition cupboard and a smoke-vent. The drawbridge could be commanded by musketry fire from cross-slits in the NE wall of the keep.

Below SW on the shoreline are the remains of the lower fort which from the start augmented the castle, as Little Dennis did for Pendennis. It was originally roofed to provide a second, open gun deck, for a total of nineteen guns.

In 1646 the Royalists surrendered the castle to Parliament without a shot being fired. Its subsequent uneventful history has resulted in its remarkably unaltered form. Neglected for centuries, it saw minor changes during the Napoleonic wars, was given new gun emplacements and magazines in the late C19 and was reoccupied during the First and Second World Wars.

ST MAWES, Church Hill. First erected as a chapel of ease to St Just in the early C19, rebuilt 1881. A small but carefully detailed essay in the E.E. style. The slate roof is laid with alternate bands of plain and fish-scale decoration, surmounted by a two-stage slate-hung bellcote with pyramidal roof rising to a ball and cross finial. Three-light lancets between weathered buttresses to nave, two-light windows with quatrefoil tracery to chancel, the E window with three trefoils. The interior has a plain four-bay arch-braced roof springing from granite corbels with intermediate plain collared trusses. – STAINED GLASS. Geometric grisaille windows, chancel E window and W windows by *J. Powell & Sons*, 1884. – Three windows in S wall of nave by *F. W. Skeat*, 1960, depicting the story of St Maw. – FONT. Octagonal, in Perp style with quatrefoils.

The HARBOUR QUAY begins with an earlier part at right angles to the shoreline, the C19 extension at an angle to this. The SEA WALL is of 1859, supporting both Marine Parade and Lower Castle Road. On and behind the waterfront the SHIP AND CASTLE HOTEL, *c.* 1900 by *Silvanus Trevail*, and a good range of mostly small-scale houses of the C17 to early C19 with much stucco, some slate cladding and sash windows. LOWER CASTLE LANE has a number of houses of C17 origin with large stacks and some thatch. CHAPEL TERRACE has polite little houses of the early C18. In COMMERCIAL ROAD more C17 houses and ST MAWES HOLY WELL, medieval with restoration of 1939: pointed and chamfered doorway. The adjoining house, HOLY WELL COTTAGE, an early to mid-C19 remodelling of an earlier house, may incorporate some walling of the medieval chapel. Of the larger earlier villas, the best is BRAGANSA HOUSE of *c.* 1820, in a commanding position in its own grounds overlooking the harbour. Modest two-window W entrance front with simple Doric porch, the S front grander with full-height bay, ground-floor windows round-headed with hoodmoulds, the first floor with sixteen-pane sashes. Intact interior including geometric stair with wreathed handrail.

TREWITHIT, Polverth Point. 1967 by *John Crowther & Associates*. Among mid-C20 detached houses on rising ground is one of the best modern houses in Cornwall. A monopitch roof runs down as the site slopes up N, creating sun and views on two levels along the whole S elevation, the upper floor entirely glazed with an extensive balcony and projecting glazed sun-lounge.

ST MELLION

St Mellanus. Of the church dedicated by Bishop Bronescombe in 1259, perhaps traces incorporated into the cruciform building represented by the s wall of nave and chancel and s transept. What is visible on the s side, however, clearly belongs to the C14: see the (renewed) windows, Dec, just going Perp (the transept windows were sashes in 1849). Mid-C15 w tower of broad and short proportions of regular granite blocks in the usual three stages, with thin corner buttresses. The N aisle was added in the late C15, the s porch in the early C16. Five-bay N aisle arcade with piers of Cornish granite standard with a little stylized decoration of the abaci. C15 ceiled wagon roofs to nave and N aisle with moulded ribs and carved bosses and wall-plates. The church was restored in 1862 by *J. P. St Aubyn* including the s transept and chancel roofs. – Two *c.* 1330 PISCINAS with Dec ogee-cusped arches. – PULPIT. Jacobean. – STAINED GLASS. Chancel s, 1876, s transept, 1859. – MONUMENTS. The highlights of the church are the Coryton monuments (cf. Newton Ferrers and Pentillie), especially those to William Coryton †1651 and wife, and Sir William Coryton †1711 and wife: two large, grand, and utterly reactionary compositions. Their type, standing solidly on the ground, with figures, life-size and kneeling towards each other across a prayer-desk, with double columns flanking the figures, a coffer-vaulted arch above them, and small figures and a coat of arms on the entablatures and pediment, was in fashion about 1600. To find it used in Cornwall in the 1650s may not surprise, but to find it still in 1711 goes beyond belief. – BRASS. Peter Coryton †1551, with wife and twenty-four children, of a design that belongs to the *Fermer workshop.** – John Coryton †1803, with sarcophagus and urn, large and elegant. – William Coryton, 1836 by *Thomas & Edward Gaffin.* – John Tillie Coryton †1843, the same composition as John Coryton.

Former RECTORY. Good solid early C19 with two symmetrical curved bay windows.

PENTILLIE CASTLE. *See* p. 422.

ST MERRYN

St Merryn. The stocky w tower with stumpy pinnacles stands sentinel against Atlantic gales in the little churchtown away from the modern village. Its lower stage is Norman (with remains of a Norman arch into the nave) with buttresses set

---

*A group of over eighty mid-C16 English brasses named after two of this type to the Fermer family at Easton Neston, Northants; cf. also Crowan.

back from the corners: the upper storeys are C15. Relocated on top of the buttresses three probably C15 carved Catacleuse angel corbels holding shields which may, like the font, have come from the ruined church at Constantine (q.v.). Of the early medieval church the nave, N transept with its E.E. deeply splayed E window and E.E. arch into the nave, and chancel walling. C15 or C16 S aisle arcade of seven bays in lovely blue-grey Catacleuse, the most striking architectural use of this stone in any church in the county: it is of standard Cornish design with four-centred arches but the carving is notably sharper and fresher than granite allows. Unceiled wagon roofs with moulded ribs and carved wall-plates and bosses. – FONT. C15. Of the pillar type, almost a copy of that in Padstow, also in Catacleuse but reduced in size and execution of the figures of apostles and angels on the round bowl and the four octagonal shafts. Still sharply and finely carved. – BENCH-ENDS. Some C16 bench-ends here incorporated into re-seating of 1887. – ROYAL ARMS. Plaster, with strapwork decoration by *John Abbot*, 1662, for Thomas Peter of Harlyn House (q.v.); restored 1981. – ETCHED GLASS by *David Peace*, 1979 and 1987 in two windows in the S aisle. Lovely lettering running lightly across the glazing, like his work at St Michael, Porthilly (q.v.). – MONUMENTS. John Mitchell and family †1617, with seven kneeling figures: poor quality. – William Trevathvan of Porthcothen, 1695. – STOCKS, dated 1788, in porch. – CURIOSUM. Board with a poem of instructions for bellringers (cf. St Minver).

In the village, METHODIST CHAPEL, 1905, in Arts and Crafts style.

ST MEWAN

9050

St Mewan. The Perp W tower was intended to be tall and stately, but was not continued above the second stage. It is nevertheless finished off in style, its embattled parapet with masks on the merlons, pinnacles with cable moulding, and a C19 pyramidal roof: inside a tall four-centred tower arch reflects the original ambition. The rest of the originally C12 cruciform church was extensively rebuilt from the mid to late C15 and thoroughly restored c. 1851 by *G. E. Street*, with a further restoration in 1890–1. Of Norman date the lower part of the N nave wall and the chancel windows, the E window with nook-shafts with masks, probably re-set in the mid C19. To the mid-C15 S aisle of five bays (of the same design as St Stephen-in-Brannel, q.v.) corresponds a N chancel aisle of three bays. – FONT. Late C14 octagonal font, with tracery panels, standing on a Norman base with palmette-style carving. – Fragment of C12 font in nave. – PISCINA. C13, in chancel. – STAINED GLASS. Several *Heaton, Butler & Bayne* windows of the 1880s in s aisle. *O'Connor* window in tower of the 1860s *E. R. Suffling* in chancel N 1891.

GOVER VIADUCT, 1 m. N. Impressive in the landscape, one of the series of viaducts carrying the railway between St Austell and Truro. The stone piers of the 1859 original remain to the N of the 1898 viaduct, of eight round arches, corbelled and battered and with buttresses.

9040

ST MICHAEL CAERHAYS

ST MICHAEL. Overlooking the Luney valley above the castle and park within an oval churchyard or *lann*. C15 W tower of three stages, battlemented but unbuttressed and unpinnacled. Of the originally cruciform church some masonry on the N side, with the N transept, still exists. The N doorway has a Norman tympanum with a very worn *Agnus Dei* (cf. Egloskerry), very minor. The S aisle is of two bays only, of standard Cornish design with Devon horizontal leaf-frieze capitals: it was probably built as a chantry by the Trevanions in the early C16. Restored in 1864, and again in 1883 by *J. P. St Aubyn*. The earlier restoration, as recorded in the N window of the N transept, the work of *William Willimott*, rector 1852–78 before he moved on to Quethiock (q.v.). All but one of the STAINED-GLASS windows is by his hand, its rich colours and studied medievalism bestowing an authenticity to the whole interior, showing a remarkable growth in confidence and willingness to experiment with design and technique. The charming mosaic REREDOS is also his, as is the PARCLOSE SCREEN and probably the extremely pretty COMMANDMENT TABLETS. – FONT. Norman, circular, with large leaves in flat relief. – PISCINA. In the chancel, C14, with crocketed finials. – CORBEL. On the N side of the chancel, a C15 shield-holding angel. – MONUMENTS. William Trevanion, 1769, with three plain vases and drapery from above. – Charlotte Trevanion, 1810, aged twenty-seven: the most interesting object in the church, Gothic, with a correct crocketed gable *à la* Aymer de Valence in Westminster Abbey, but l. and r. of it two mourning putti of *Coade* stone, still entirely in the Baroque tradition. – STATUE, life-size, of Captain George Bettesworth †1808, in naval uniform, also by the *Coade* firm. He was the brother of J. Bettesworth-Trevanion of Caerhays Castle.

92 CAERHAYS CASTLE. A very picturesque mansion, in a superb position overlooking Porthluney Bay, so deeply hidden in its woods that the sudden revelation of the castle with its battlemented walls and square and round towers among ornamental trees and shrubs is breathtaking. Built in 1808 for J. Bettesworth-Trevanion by *John Nash*, his largest surviving essay in castellated Gothick. It replaced an earlier house and garden on the same site. Of the earlier house there is little

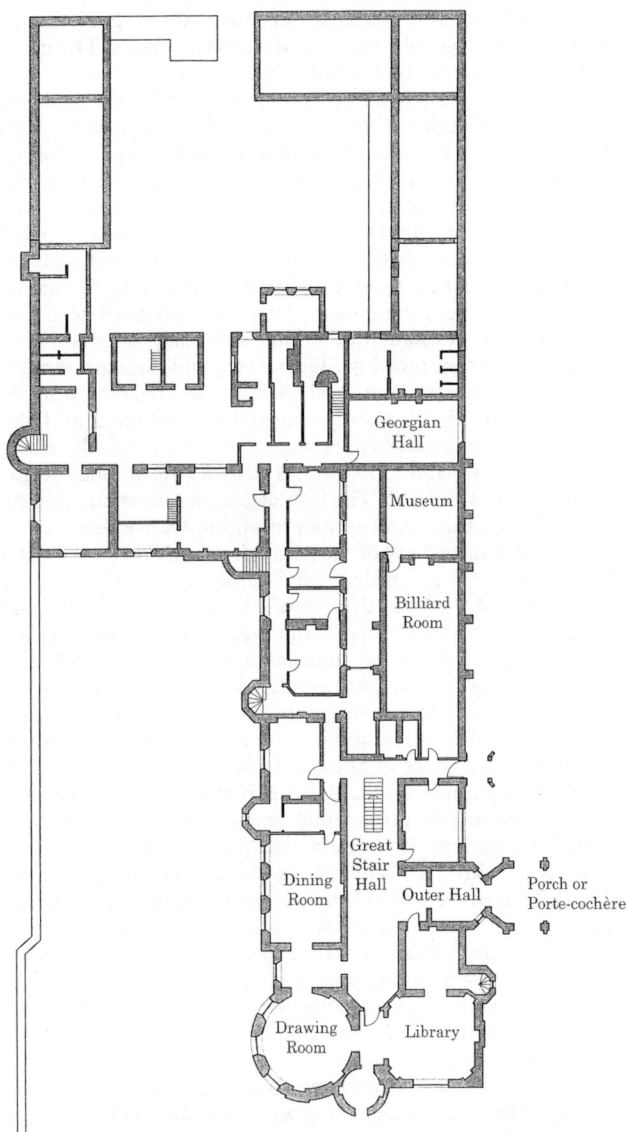

St Michael Caerhays, Caerhays Castle. Plan

visible (save one C16 door jamb reused as a lintel to the cellar), but the foundations of the present building may incorporate older fabric. Approximately L-plan, asymmetrically composed with the main range running SW–NE and culminating in a massive circular tower with an attached, higher, circular stair-tower. The other range extends SE from the SW end ending in a circular turret with the services and stables attached to the

w. The entrance front centres on a two-storey porte cochère
between a polygonal tower l. and a square tower r. The garden
front has two polygonal towers and a slender polygonal tower
with an ogee stone roof to complement the main NE corner
tower. The interior is planned around a long, wide gallery
through the main axis of the house, with a stair rising and
returning in two flights at the SW end; at the other a lobby
gives access to a circular closet with the library l. and a circular
drawing room r., the latter connecting with a suite of rooms
along the garden front. The gallery rises to the roof with long
skylights and an iron-railed balcony. Nash employs ornament
sparely but where the gallery joins the walls used his typical
arrangement of miniature groins springing originally from
round colonettes, now lost. The service buildings are arranged
around two courtyards with clock tower and bellcote: a smaller
inner court with offices, originally dairies, and servants' hall to
the N, the larger outer court with stables and coachhouses.

The GARDEN and PLEASURE GROUNDS are among the most
celebrated in Cornwall. The formal gardens are an integral part
of Nash's Gothick conception, in an impressive series of terraces to the SE and NW of the house; it is unclear to what extent
he incorporated the walls of the earlier garden shown on an
estate map of 1802 but they appear to survive best in the walls
of the terrace and towers to the rear of the house. The later
terraces are enclosed by crenellated walls, the SE wall facing
the sea battered and buttressed, breaking forward into two
small bastions, and climaxing in a tower rising in two gradu-
ated stages. The surrounding slopes around the house are
terraced into a series of grass and gravel walks with drives and
paths through the woodland, richly underplanted with important collections of ornamental trees and shrubs, especially
camellias, derived from early C20 plant-hunting expeditions
associated with J. C. Williams: his family bought Caerhays in
1852 and have continued to develop the garden's design and
planting from Nash's original layout. Another pleasure garden
walk descends s past an early C19 arch by Nash; SE towards
the sea is a serpentine lake formed by damming the River
Luney. Surrounding it all is the extensive PARK including a C19
deer park created by Michael Williams, replacing the Trevanions' earlier park of the C15.*

LOWER LODGE at Porthluney Cove. Another asymmetrical
arrangement around a gateway with a circular plan tower each
side and the screen wall running l. in a serpentine plan, and
to the r. in an arc with a square terminal tower. Above the park
to the W, HIGHER LODGE, again asymmetrically planned, of
a two-storey circular tower and a larger, octagonal two-storey
tower and circular stair linked by a Gothic carriage arch. Both
are Nash style but appear to be 1850s.

---

*I am indebted to Peter Herring, Stephen Tyrrell and Charles Williams for their
insights into the evolution of the house, gardens and landscape.

ST MICHAEL PENKEVIL   *8040*

The church and estate village of Tregothnan (q.v.).

ST MICHAEL. Of interest as much for *G. E. Street*'s rebuilding of 1863–5 as for the rich furnishing of the C13 and early C14 original. Strong s elevation overlooking the main entrance to the great house (q.v.), the w tower of two stages with massive corner buttresses with three offsets to above the first stage, and a high octagonal stair-turret, its verticality emphasized by Street's additions of a spirelet to the turret and a steep pyramidal roof to the tower. The vertical rhythm is taken up in the similarly buttressed porch and transept. Pointed w doorway, its stone and the porch inner doorway C13–C14. Also Dec windows; two and three lights, with intersecting tracery. Tower arch, N transept arch, and rear arch in s transept also *c.* 1300. As far as the details are concerned, not a square inch of surface is not tooled up. The furnishings are of outstanding quality. In the N and s transepts SEPULCHRAL NICHES with SEDILIA as one composition, the sedilia with cinquefoil heads and hood-moulds, on heads as label stops, all of noble, classical C13 proportions. In the s transept are two seats and a PISCINA, in the N transept three seats. The architectural detail tallies perfectly with the surviving consecration stone (chancel, N side) of 1261, and is in no way provincial. But Street dated the transepts to the early C14 and pointed out that their walls are not bonded with the nave walls and that the s transept arch contains a reused part of a C13 doorway. The enlargement and rich decoration are no doubt due to Sir John Trejague, who petitioned in 1319 for the repair of the church and the founding of an arch-presbytery or college for an arch-priest and four chaplains. Also two REREDOSES to the transept altars, on the s *c.* 1300, on the N C15, with flamboyant detail: behind them are tiny cells, possibly to house valuables. There is another ALTAR with a piscina on the upper floor of the tower, a very old tradition in churches dedicated to St Michael. – ALTAR SLAB on the N transept altar, originally on the floor of the s transept. – STAINED GLASS. Three-light E window by *Morris & Co.*, 1866. A lovely composition in jewel-like colours: with the E window at Ladock (q.v.) the best and earliest Morris glass in Cornwall. Centre light the Crucifixion, with angels holding the sun and moon above and two weeping angels below by *E. Burne-Jones*, St Michael by Morris in panel below; to l. three Marys and weeping angels by Burne-Jones, St Michael and the Devil by Morris below; to r. St John with Joseph and Nicodemus and praying angels by Burne-Jones, St Michael spearing the Dragon by Morris below. – Many of the other windows contain panels designed by *Lady Falmouth* in the 1860s. – MONUMENTS. Two coffin slabs with foliated crosses; C13. – Brass to John Trenowith †1497, biggish and good. – Brass to John Trembras, MA, parson, 1515, in academic robes. –

Unimportant brasses of 1619, 1622 and 1634. – Numerous monuments to the Boscawen family including Hugh Boscawen †1659, stiffly reclining on his elbow with a book in his hand against a background with triple Corinthian colonnade; Admiral Boscawen †1761, signed by *Rysbrack* 1763, designed by *Adam* – just a bust between trophies against the usual pyramid; Edward Hugh Boscawen †1774 by *Nollekens*, simple medallion; the Hon. Frances Boscawen, who died 'at the spa in Germany', also by *Nollekens*, just inscription and urn in relief; and the same composition exactly repeated for Elizabeth Ann, Viscountess Falmouth, †1783 (by *Nollekens*), George Evelyn Boscawen †1808 (by *J. Isbell* of Truro), Edward Boscawen, Earl of Falmouth, †1841 (by *Pearce* of Truro), and two others. The family has apparently not had great confidence in monumental memorials.

The attractive early to mid-C19 estate village has a range of mostly mid-C19 COTTAGES, some like Nos. 11, 12, 19 and 20 with latticed iron glazing. SCHOOL, ½ m. N, of *c.* 1888 in Tudor Gothic with transomed-and-mullioned windows and an octagonal bellcote, and SCHOOL HOUSE and COTTAGE in similar style.

5030

ST MICHAEL'S MOUNT

53   Every prospect of the Mount presents a memorable fusion of the spectacular and picturesque: a granite cone rising steeply from the sea, crowned by its medieval church and castle, and wrapped around on its SE flank by the dramatic architecture of the late C19 mansion of the St Aubyns. Its extraordinarily rich history endows it with a powerful and enduring mystique amply represented in its buildings, landscape, and seascape and long celebrated by artists, writers and travellers. Even for Cornwall, this is an enchanting place.

An island for most of the time but linked to the mainland by a causeway at low tide, the Mount has been a prestigious possession throughout history. A naturally defensible site, surrounded by water and with precipitous cliffs to the S and W and steep slopes to the N and E, it commands Mount's Bay and its tin-rich hinterland. Its good sheltered harbour, near an important navigable passage between Marazion and Hayle (until historically recent silting up), made it the Iron Age tin-trading port of Ictis and a centre of power from earlier prehistory.

Though there is little documentary evidence of a monastery on the site before the C12, future archaeological investigation may confirm an earlier religious foundation. The site was granted by Edward the Confessor to the abbey of Mont-Saint-Michel in Normandy before 1050, and it was Abbot Bernard who founded a priory between 1135 and 1144 intended for between six and twelve Benedictine monks. The later medieval priory church still

St Michael's Mount. Drawing by W. Borlase, 1762

dominates the summit, with the other main elements of the monastery (not on the standard plan because of the cramped summit site) absorbed into the later medieval and post-medieval castle and house. From the CII to the CI6 the Mount became the most popular place of pilgrimage in Cornwall, enhanced by the recording of three miracles in 1262 and after 1400 by the legend that St Michael had made one of his three earthly appearances here. There were also an unusually large number of holy relics. Pilgrims came from as far away as London and East Anglia, and some went on from here to Compostella.

That Bernard's priory was always defended (like other similar French monasteries) is confirmed by the surviving buildings of the castle. The main W range with its N and S towers guarding the W door (the only entry to the castle before the CI9 house was built) is substantially late CI2. Two other rectangular towers stood behind to the SE, with a curtain wall that incorporated natural outcrops and cliffs entirely encircling the summit. The castle protected both priory and harbour, the priory buildings tucked in behind the towers and themselves embattled. There are a large number of other military remains elsewhere on the Mount, from prehistoric earthworks to C20 pillboxes and gun emplacements. But its military importance declined from the later medieval period so that by the Civil War, when its defences had been reinforced, it capitulated without a struggle and was soon afterwards deserted as 'not worth the taking or keeping'.

The priory was suppressed as alien in 1425 and Henry VI gave the property to his favourite Brigittine nuns at Syon. After the Reformation it belonged to the Crown which appointed governors there. In the CI7 it changed hands three times, first to the Earls of Salisbury, then to Francis Basset of Tehidy, and finally in 1659 to the St Aubyns. The St Aubyns first made the buildings on the Mount into a summer residence and subsequently into a permanent residence. In the late 1740s the semi-detached Lady Chapel at the NE corner of the church became the Blue Drawing

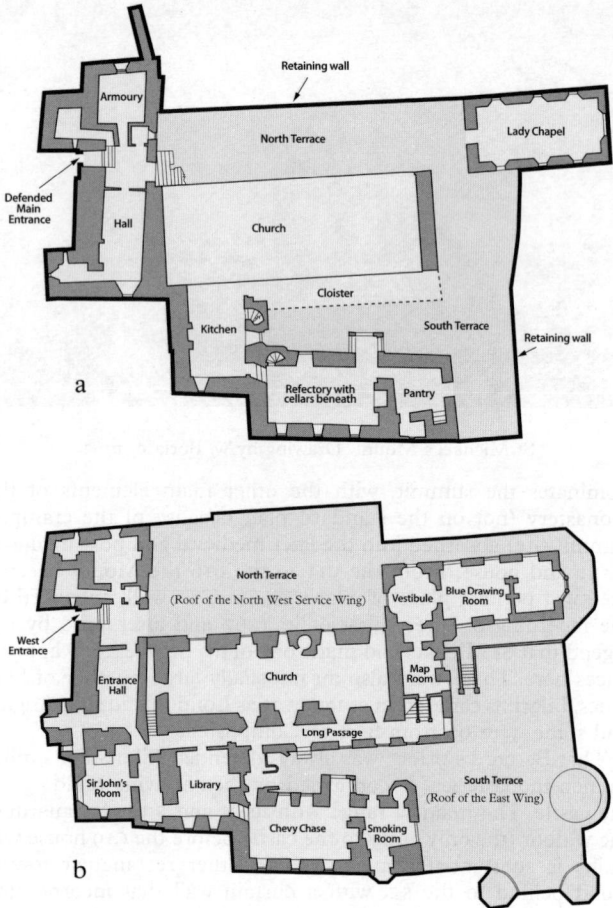

St Michael's Mount.
a) Monastery, probable plan in early C16 b) Late C19 plan

Rooms and the s tower Sir John's Room and the Library. Relatively minor changes were made in the early to mid C19 before *J. P. St Aubyn*, cousin of John St Aubyn who had been created a baron as 1st Lord St Levan in 1887, designed the spectacular E wing and a NW service wing to provide extensive modern accommodation for the family, with significant alterations to the existing buildings. Most of the Mount was given to the National Trust by the 3rd Lord St Levan in 1954.

The Mount is most satisfyingly approached on foot following in the steps of the medieval pilgrims across the CAUSEWAY from Marazion, passing CHAPEL ROCK near the mainland end, the site of a chapel of the Blessed Virgin Mary demolished by Royalists in 1645. About two-thirds along the causeway on the

l. is a CROSS BASE, its large rectangular socket evidence of a huge cross swept away in the C18. The HARBOUR probably dates from the early C14 and incorporates early C15 walling, though it was extensively repaired in 1726–7 and again in 1823. Immediately behind is the VILLAGE, largely a late C19 planned replacement of the streets, courtyards, cellars and lofts of the former fishing settlement, built to service the Mount's tourist industry. A few C18 buildings survive, notably the former ST AUBYN'S ARMS and the COTTAGE immediately W, and the former CHANGE HOUSE and FISH CELLAR to the E. Gothic style LYCHGATE to the cemetery, 1899. A Tudor-style LODGE and arched GATEWAY of 1877 guard the entrance to the Mount, with ELIZABETH TERRACE to the SW and further W the ENGINE HOUSE and TUNNEL ENTRANCE of the tramway to the castle.

Now begin the steep ascent up the footpath to the summit, announced by the pretty former DAIRY by St Aubyn, modelled on the kitchen at Glastonbury Abbey. Further up a WELL, the site of the legend of Cormoran the Giant. Then evidence of Civil War defences in the remains of a WATCH TOWER and GUARDROOM. Finally the path reaches the platform for the GUN BATTERIES, probably C18 in their present form.

The approach to the W front of the CASTLE is up a steep flight of wide granite steps. Despite the considerable interventions by St Aubyn (1878 datestone) which included adding the lower NW service wings and a mansard roof to the N tower, and enlarging or replacing many windows, the WEST RANGE still has the authentic air of the medieval stronghold. The low arched DOORWAY, a Tudor replacement of the C12 original, is set in a slight projection between the NORTH and SOUTH TOWERS and is defended by interior drawbar slots and a port-cullis. As shown in a Borlase drawing of 1762, the towers were once of a similar size but the N tower was expanded in the C18. The doorway opens into an entrance hall that originally gave access to the church through a now blocked W door: to its S a large rectangular room, almost certainly the original hall of the castle; to the N the N tower, which probably contained service rooms in the late medieval period. In other words, this is the typical medieval plan of cross-passage linking the domestic end of the castle to the S with the service end to the N.

The SOUTH RANGE, its S wall rising sheer from the steep slope below and the least altered elevation of the Mount's buildings, incorporates the principal domestic quarters of the priory. The refectory is represented by the CHEVY CHASE ROOM, mostly rebuilt in the early to mid C16, above the much thicker walls of the Garrison Room below, the original monastic cellars. The Chevy Chase Room is one of the most impressive in the castle with an arch-braced roof of the early to mid C16, a pretty plaster frieze of 1641 depicting the Chevy Chase (with bull-baiting, boar-hunting, hare and hounds, stag-hunting and ostrich hunting), some fine C18 Gothic-style plasterwork, and Gothick dado and doors. A collection of mostly Continental

STAINED GLASS in the bay recess. A three-storey section to the
E contained a garderobe, and a three-storey tower to the W, the
likely location of the kitchen and priest's lodging, is now
the LIBRARY and CHINTZ ROOM.

Now around the E end of the CHURCH OF ST MICHAEL to the
NORTH TERRACE to the N door of the church, the principal
entrance since this Tudor door was formed. Though standing
on the footprint of the C12 building, the present structure is
largely the result of late C14 to early C15 rebuilding, with a
major restoration by St Aubyn who gave it a new roof, rebuilt
at least the upper part of the E end, and removed some of the
window tracery. The tower rises like a crossing tower (though
there are no transepts) and is surmounted by a five-sided
lantern known as St Michael's Chair: two original bells were
made by *William Dawe*, a London founder, who worked
between 1358 and 1408, giving a final date for the tower's
construction. The character of the interior is still evocative of
a pilgrimage destination, plain, even sombre, with relatively
low light levels and much late C19 to early C20 STAINED
GLASS, much of it by *John J. Jennings*. – Behind the altar three
English ALABASTERS (Mass of St Gregory, Head of St John,
Pilate washing his hands). – Six Flemish alabasters on the S
wall. – ORGAN. 1786 by *John Avery* of Bristol, with Gothic
Revival screen below. – CHANDELIER. Brass, an C18 replica of
a Flemish design of the type which so often appears in early
Flemish paintings. – Two exceptionally fine pieces of late medi-
eval figure sculpture in Catacleuse on a LANTERN-HEAD
CROSS (pinnacles renewed 1827) and a large CORBEL. –
BRONZE of St Michael defeating Lucifer by *Lyn Constable
Maxwell*. – CRUCIFIXUS above the altar, 1987 by *John Miller*,
tenderly carved.

NE of the church, the former LADY CHAPEL, founded 1463,
completed before 1500 and ruinous by 1731. Rebuilt in the late
1740s as the suite of BLUE DRAWING ROOMS. Their detail is
of the most charming pre-Strawberry-Hill Rococo Gothic. The
entrance hall with vaulted plasterwork, the large drawing room
with a barrel-vaulted ceiling and a trefoiled arcade to the
cornice, and small drawing room with panelled plaster ceiling
and vaulted plasterwork to the bay window. Exceedingly pretty
fireplaces and other details. A quite remarkable ensemble, the
earliest and best example of its period in Cornwall, and especially surprising in such a remote place.

St Aubyn's E wing must be regarded as the best work of this
prolific but by no means always sympathetic architect. The
challenge, to design a vast new building on such a celebrated
but highly constrained site, was wholly successfully achieved.
Skilfully devised under an extended terrace in the SE corner
of the summit buildings, it does not interfere with the
silhouette of monastery and castle. Yet, seen from the E, it is
an entirely worthy addition to the Mount with its own strong
character, 'a sight', as Pevsner observed, 'from some positions
reminiscent of Mount Athos or Tibetan monasteries'. The

accommodation is on four floors, designed in a free Baronial style, its principal feature a semicircular stair projection rising to the parapet level of the terrace and an embattled walkway on pseudo machicolations, and then rising still further to an embattled turret with a large false gable, and finally surmounted by multi-flue stacks. Projecting on the SE corner is a two-storey octagonal oriel.

The magnificent natural setting of the Mount's buildings is further enhanced by extensive TERRACED GARDENS and PLEASURE GROUNDS developed in the mid C18 but much evolved in the C19 with exotic tropic planting. The formal terraced gardens lie on the SE slope, informal gardens to the S and SE, and pleasure grounds to the E, N and W. Among many other features of interest in the grounds are a number of MEDIEVAL CROSSES and an octagonal CROSS-SHAFT.

ST MINVER   9070

ST MENFRE. The church stands in its small churchtown on the highlands of its large parish. It has a spire, a rarity in Cornwall, octagonal, in granite ashlar with plain broaches at the corners and tall narrow gabled lucernes in the sides between, rising from a three-stage tower with stepped angle buttresses and NE stair projection. Both tower and spire were rebuilt in a restoration of 1870–5 by *J. P. St Aubyn*. Of the C12 church only possible fragments of masonry in the N walls of the N aisle and chancel. The four-bay N arcade is early C13; short, thick octagonal piers with the plainest of capitals and double-chamfered two-centred arches. The tower arch is similar. The N aisle itself is uncommonly narrow and has a (renewed) lean-to roof, a rare survival of the pre-C15 form. The C15 S aisle is of seven bays and standard Cornish, the five W with two-centred arches, the two E lower and four-centred. C15 wagon roof in porch, the rest replaced, arch-braced with two tiers of wind-braces to nave and S aisle. – FONT. Octagonal, C15, with traceried panels. – ROOD SCREEN. Removed in 1837 and part re-set into the tower arch. Each panel has two lights, two forming one arch; the tracery is Perp. – Many good BENCH-ENDS in the nave, probably of *c.* 1530–40, finely carved with secular subjects, with a strong Italian Renaissance flavour. – COMMUNION RAILS. C17, of plain balusters. – Against the W wall a Norman CAPITAL, found in 1927. It has three scallops, the crescents ornamented as, for example, at St David's and in Cornwall at St Germans and St Teath. – STAINED GLASS. Fine E window by *Michael O'Connor*, 1870: bright, lively and very rich in the German Renaissance way, plenty of deep blues, pinks and purples (cf. Porthilly). – N window of chancel by *Toms* of Wellington, Somerset, 1851. Good sharp colours. – MONUMENTS. S aisle. Brass to Roger

Opy †1517, a small figure with a long scroll upwards from his head. – Epitaph to John Roe †1657, still kneeling in profile, though with more realism and courtliness than fifty years before. – Classical monument to Thomas Darell †1697. – N aisle. Remains of slate altar tomb of Thomas Stone †1604, decorated with figures and arms in high relief.

In the churchyard s of the porch, small Latin CROSS and many C19 headstones by *Robert Olver*, born in this parish, worked in north Cornwall, †1872. LYCHGATE, probably by St Aubyn, with decorative slate hanging in the gable-ends of the steeply pitched roof, the slates shaped to form trefoil arches: similar to that at Porthilly.

The church is approached from the se by a path lined with small cottages. Nearby GATEPIERS to the former VICARAGE, C19 with reused C17 capitals with large ball finials; the house early C18, remodelled 1789 (datestone) and extended *c.* 1830s. Two-storey, almost symmetrical three-window w front, the 1830 wing to rear.

The parish has an unusually rich and varied range of buildings, including two medieval chapelries at St Enodoc and Porthilly (qq.v.). At Tredrizzick, ½ m. w, METHODIST CHURCH, 1872 datestone. Unusual, faintly Italianate design. Tapered and round-ended walled forecourt. The FRIENDS BURIAL GROUND, ½ m. NW, has high walls enclosing a small square cemetery dating from *c.* 1690, partly rebuilt in 1883 (datestone). There were sufficient Quakers in late C17 St Minver for a meeting house on this site, though the building had vanished by 1879.

That there were also a number of large houses in the late C16 and early C17 is demonstrated by a remarkable survival at TREVELVER, 1 m. s. The house itself is a fragment of a larger U-plan manor house, much remodelled, but the parlour is a complete late C17 room with bolection-moulded panelling, cornice and double doors with raised and field panelling, decorated with topographical sketches and painting of *c.* 1690. The cornice has fine depictions of buildings in the neighbourhood including parish churches, a windmill and Wadebridge bridge. Above the fireplace a cruder painting of Trevelver and the adjacent houses, now farms, Carlyon and Dinham. The round tower of CANT WINDMILL, prominently sited nearby, is probably that illustrated.

TREWORNAN, 1½ m. SE. First recorded in 1211, the present building incorporating the remains of a large early C17 manor house, partly demolished about the C18 and extensively remodelled in the C19. A late C17 painting shows a s front with central two-storey porch with flanking wings and an e wing beyond: the e end of this s range survives, with adapted wings. Fine early C17 dog-leg stair with moulded rail, turned balusters and newels. To the s GATEPIERS, probably C17, slender piers, surmounted by ball finials.

TREWORNAN BRIDGE, ¼ m. SW of the house, across the River Amble. 1791, built by Rev. William Sandys to a medieval design. Handsome four-span bridge with pointed arches and cutwaters to each side, the parapets carried out over the cutwaters as refuges.

ROSERROW, ¾ m. NW. A fragment of another former large manor house, belonging to the Penkevills in the early C16 and then the Carews, survives in a building that became a farmhouse (now in the centre of a holiday village). There are some C16 ceiling beams and a hall with an exceptionally large fireplace and a bay with lintel dated 1553.

THE RUMPS. *See* Port Quin.

ST NECTAN   *1060*

ST NECTAN. A chapel of ease to St Winnow since 1281 in a remote position W of Boconnoc. There was a chapel here from 1281. C15, but its unusual appearance expresses a chequered history: it was enlarged in the C19 but reduced to nave and chancel in 1962. Tower severely damaged in the Civil War, and cut down to the first stage and part of the second (see the pinnacle reused as a gatepost) surmounted by a pyramid slate roof with a slate-hung bellcote. Hints of its former stature are buttresses set back from the angles and the tower arch with shafts of the usual Cornish type and octagonal capitals. Four-centred doorway to the S porch, which has its original wagon roof. Plastered wagon roof to nave. – FONT. Bowl possibly C13, with later octagonal shaft. – WHEEL-HEAD CROSS at E entrance to the churchyard. Equal-limbed cross in relief, the arms expanded at their ends, the whole enclosed in a narrow head.

ST NEOT   *1060*

A large parish on the SE slopes of Bodmin Moor with a rich medieval tin-mining history. The churchtown is gathered comfortably around the parish church set in a bend in a wooded valley.

ST NEOT. There was a church here by *c.* 890, dedicated to the saint most of whose bones were removed to St Neots, Huntingdonshire, in the late C10, and still collegiate in the C11. The plan is C15 Cornish standard – W tower, nave, N and S aisles and S porch – and is consciously designed to show its most spectacular side to those arriving up the valley: unusual stress is placed on the splendid seven-bay S aisle and two-storey S porch, both built of large regular granite blocks and richly embellished with buttresses, clasping and crocketed pinnacles between each bay, and crenellations very similar to Liskeard and North Hill. The aisle has large four-light Perp s windows and a five-light E window. The interior of the porch has triple shafts forming two panels and a remarkable stone tunnel-vault with heavy ribs forming a purely geometrical repeating pattern; five bosses, the centre one decorated with four faces. The oldest part of the church is the three-stage tower with thick diagonal buttresses surmounted by crocketed pinnacles and an embattled parapet, and has Dec windows; the ground floor has a stone vault of pointed tunnel shape with transverse arches, unique in Cornwall. Spacious, lofty interior with tall piers of the standard pattern to N and S aisles, the capitals sketchily ornamented, the arches four-centred. Nave and aisles have wagon roofs, ceiled with moulded ribs and bosses. Squint from the E end of the N aisle into the chancel. – FONT. C15 bowl on C13 shaft, the E side in its design still derived from the Egloshayle type. – ROOD SCREEN, PARCLOSE SCREEN, CHOIR STALLS from a restoration of 1889–1900 by *G. H. Fellowes Prynne* that included the chancel arch, chancel flooring and the wagon roofs of nave and chancel, painted and decorated with angels on the wall-plates in the chancel, by *J. Northcott* of Ashwater, Devon. – MONUMENTS. William Bere and family, kneeling figures, 1610, slate, excellent quality in high relief, comparable to the monuments at St Tudy (q.v.). – Recess in N wall of chancel, partly restored, with no monument but traces of painting and lettering.

The glory of the church is its STAINED GLASS, a remarkable survival of a complete pre-Reformation glazing scheme, at its best comparable in quality to Fairford, Gloucestershire.* Though much renewed and restored in 1825–30 by *John Hedgeland* and later, here we can gain an all too rare impression of the original colour character of Perp churches. One must have been inside in St Neot in sunshine as well as dull weather to appreciate how the stone changes its hues as the colours of the windows are strongly or softly reflected on it.

Fourteen of the seventeen windows contain medieval glass, mostly dating from 1480 to 1530 but perhaps incorporating some components from a mid-C15 scheme (in the original E window) suspended when the church was enlarged in stages from 1480 onwards, beginning with the E end of the S aisle, its W end completed *c.* 1515, and followed by the N aisle *c.* 1520–30 with its square-headed cusped windows. There were various losses before Hedgeland's intervention but his work, assisted in London by *James Nixon*, glass painter, and *B. Baillie*, glazier, and paid for by a former vicar and patron, Rev. R. W. Grylls, is apparent everywhere except for the Creation window in the S chapel, which had survived almost intact; six windows were moved around in whole or in part. In 1918 two of Hedgeland's

*This account is greatly indebted to Michael Swift's comments and Joanna Mattingly's assessment, 'Stories in the Glass – reconstructing the St Neot pre-Reformation glazing scheme, *Journal of the Royal Institution of Cornwall* (2000), where the windows are described in detail and the dating sequence documented.

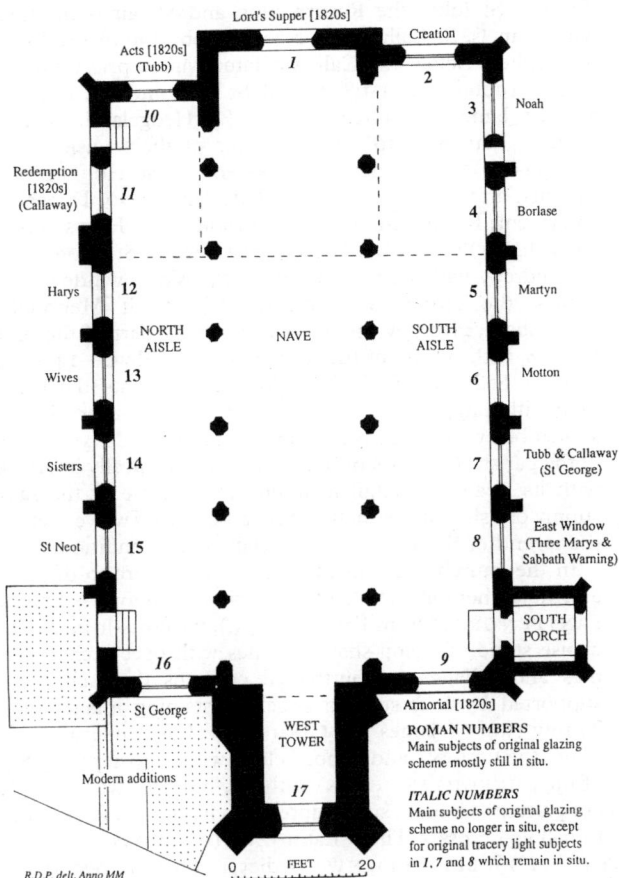

Plan labels:
- Lord's Supper [1820s]
- Creation
- Acts [1820s] (Tubb)
- Noah
- Redemption [1820s] (Callaway)
- Borlase
- Harys
- Martyn
- NORTH AISLE
- NAVE
- SOUTH AISLE
- Motton
- Wives
- Sisters
- Tubb & Callaway (St George)
- St Neot
- East Window (Three Marys & Sabbath Warning)
- SOUTH PORCH
- St George
- WEST TOWER
- Armorial [1820s]
- Modern additions

ROMAN NUMBERS
Main subjects of original glazing scheme mostly still in situ.

ITALIC NUMBERS
Main subjects of original glazing scheme no longer in situ, except for original tracery light subjects in *1*, *7* and *8* which remain in situ.

R.D.P. delt. Anno MM

0 FEET 20

St Neot, parish church. Plan of stained glass

windows were moved to the NE chapel, with a further restoration in 1937–8.

The sequence described, shown above, starts with the E window of the chancel – 1. Tracery, the Annunciation flanked by female saints. Main panels, the Last Supper by Hedgeland, 1830, after a German woodcut. – 2. Creation window. Tracery, the nine orders of Angels. Below, the Creation from the beginning to God commanding the making of the Ark. – 3. The story of Noah. From his cutting down trees for making the Ark to his drunkenness and death; eight of the twelve scenes original. – 4. Borlase window. Above, St Christopher, St Neot, St Leonard, St Katherine. Below, Nicholas Borlase and family. – 5. Martyn window. Above, Virgin and Child, Rood (head replaced), St John the Evangelist and St Stephen. Below, the Martyn family. – 6. Motton window. Four Evangelists; the inscription mentions John Motton as donor. – 7. Tubb window.

68

Tracery, St John, the Resurrection and St James the Great. Main panels, St Lalluwy, St Neot, St John the Evangelist and St Stephen. Below, the Callaway family and a priest, probably Robert Tubbe, vicar 1508–44. – 8. St Peter and St Paul, Christ and St James the Greater. – 9. By Hedgeland, armorial, 1830. – Returning to the E window of the N aisle, 10. By Hedgeland. Main panels, the Descent of the Holy Spirit, St Stephen and St Paul. – 11. By Hedgeland, 1830. Deposition, Interment, Resurrection and Ascension. – 12. Harys window. Main light, St John the Baptist, St Gregory, St Leonard and St Andrew, with donors below. – 13. Wives window. Main panels, the Virgin, St Mabenna, Christ, St Meubred of Cardinham, given by the wives from the W part of the parish in 1528, with twenty of the wives depicted below. – 14. Sisters window. St Petroc, St Clair, St Manac, All Saints, depicted as God with a napkin full of souls, given by the 'Sisters' in 1529, shown below. – 15. St Neot window, given by the young men of the parish. The story of St Neot, iconographically interesting with its wealth of detail including the miracle of the saint's supply of fish and the theft of his cattle. – 16. Twelve scenes of the legend of St George. In especially good condition.

In the churchyard, outside the S porch, a group of crosses assembled here in 1918–19 from various locations. – Late C15 LANTERN CROSS from Trewarne (q.v.), the cross-head in Catacleuse stone of trefoil-shaped niches with ogee-arched canopies and foliage and buttressed columns on each corner, supported by four stylized angels containing images of the Trinity (W), St James the Great dressed as a pilgrim (E), St James the Less (N), and a robed cleric with a crozier (S). – Shaft of the CHURCHYARD CROSS with fine interlace work in different patterned panels, surmounted by a fragment of a (separate) four-holed cross. – Three Latin WAYSIDE CROSSES.

ST NEOT'S WELL, ½ m. NW. Medieval holy well, restored and dated 1852, endearingly situated at the back of a meadow built into the bank of a wooded hillside. The four-centred arched door with hoodmould and Maltese cross above leads down two steps into the well, roofed with granite slabs.

The parish has a number of medieval bridges, the best PANTER'S BRIDGE over the River Bedalder 2 m. W and TREVERBYN OLD BRIDGE over the River Fowey 2¼ m. S, both with two wide four-centred arches with triangular cutwaters.

TREVERBYN VEAN, 2 m. S. Of c. 1858–62. The house was designed, or at least conceived, in part by *Col. Lygon Cocks*. However it was *George Gilbert Scott* and *Henry Rice* of Liskeard who oversaw the plans and building, the former probably using *Richard Coad* as his agent. Fine Tudor Gothic composition with irregular elevations all round, the SE/SW sides especially accomplished with two-storey canted bay, first-floor oriel, and a large external stack. The interior has a full-height hall with C15-style arch-braced collar-truss roof with wind-braces, a gallery with cusped braces and pierced panels, and spectacular French Gothic style fireplace with attached columns and a tall tapering hood. Elsewhere panelled ceilings with carved bosses and four-centred doorways with linenfold panelled doors and original door furniture. A magnificent plasterwork overmantel depicting the legend of St Neot was removed and destroyed in the C20.*

ST NEWLYN EAST

8050

In former mining country high above Newquay: it was to export minerals from its mines that J. A. Treffry constructed his tramway to Newquay (q.v.) in the 1840s. One end of the settlement is marked by two Methodist chapels, the other by the imposing parish church set in its raised churchyard or *lann*.

ST NEWLYN. C15 W tower of three stages with buttresses set back from the corners to the second stage, clasping buttresses to the third stage, and finishing in thin pinnacles with battlements and a square NE stair-turret. Perp S porch, battlemented, and, as the staircase shows, meant to have an upper chamber as at Bodmin. There is Norman masonry in the chancel and N transept with reused and widened Norman window, part of a probably cruciform building. The church was re-dedicated in 1259. N doorway C14. The S aisle is of six bays of Cornish standard design plus two lower, two-centred ones for the chancel, as at Bodmin, with wave-moulding instead of the usual hollow between the shafts throughout. The chancel aisle must be C14 according to this arcade, as is the piscina next to its altar. Also in the C15–C16 the N transept was separated from the nave by two standard arches, no doubt replacing earlier arches, the first instalment of a planned N aisle. The convincing medieval character of the interior owes much to a comprehensive but sensitive restoration by *J. D. Sedding* in 1883.[†] It included the introduction of much excellent carved woodwork and new roofs for the nave, chancel and S aisle reusing bosses; the chancel ceiling is richly panelled and painted. The N transept roof with foliate decoration survived. – FONT. Norman, of the rich Bodmin type, with angel faces at the corners, the lower shafts replaced in green serpentine in 1883. The bowl is decorated with intertwined floriated scrolls above stylized lilies interspersed with four feline figures, a lively and varied composition (cf. Callington and Luxulyan). – ROOD SCREEN. An impressive reinvention by Sedding with an elaborately carved rood loft: four columned traceried panels of the original have been reused in the parclose screen between chancel and

---

*LEWARNE, a rich Victorian seat of the Grylls family, built in 1869 in a Neo-Tudor style has been demolished.

[†]It has many resonances with E. H. Sedding's reinvention of Crantock a decade later (q.v.).

S aisle. – BENCH-ENDS. Many, of Cornish standard, eight capped by delightful crouching beasts. – ROYAL ARMS. Of Charles I. Plaster with strapwork decoration. – STAINED GLASS. The E window of the N nave by *Kempe*, 1904. – MONUMENT. Lady Arundell †1691: simple, but with her bust at the top in an open segmented pediment. Attributed to *William Stanton* (GF). Originally in the S chancel aisle, the chapel of the Arundells of Trerice (q.v.). – LANTERN-HEAD CROSS. Near the font. Much eroded Crucifixion on front, Virgin and Child on the reverse, single figures on the other faces, one probably St Newlina.

NEWLYN PREACHING PIT, Cargoll Road. The smallest and most intimate of the three surviving Wesleyan preaching pits in Cornwall (cf. Gwennap and Indian Queens). Built 1846, formed from a former stone quarry. Circular with seven tiers of seating and topped by a Cornish bank. On the E a semicircular preaching platform. It is said to have held two thousand people. Small storeroom with hearth inside the entrance. Late C19 iron gates with overthrow.

CARGOLL FARM BARN, 1 m. W. Late C14, all that remains of the medieval palace of the Bishops of Exeter, purchased by Bishop Bronescombe in 1269. Eight-bay barn, buttressed on the E side and S end. Raised cruck-trusses to each bay supporting square-set arcade plates, subdivided by intermediate trusses of raised base crucks and long carved wind-braces to each bay. A rare survival of a medieval roof in Cornwall, the intermediate trusses unique in the county except for the fragmentary remains of the roof at Maer, Bude (q.v.).

EAST WHEAL ROSE MINE, 1 m. SE. A dramatic grouping in the landscape of the exceptionally tall ENGINE HOUSE with its free-standing chimney, 100 ft (30.5 metres) tall: it was reputedly designed by *J. P. St Aubyn*, a larger version of that at Tregurtha Downs, St Hilary (q. v.). The engine was the famous Harvey's 100 inch, the largest ever made, for lead and silver mining to a maximum of 170 fathoms.

TREWERRY MILL, 1 m. E. 1690 for the Arundells, incorporating fabric and features from Trerice including inscription 1639 IA MA (John Arundell). Re-set overshot cast-iron waterwheel, 16 ft (4.9 metres) in diameter, inscribed 'Jabez Buckingham, North Hill'.

ST PINNOCK

ST PINNOC. On the E side of a small square in its remote-feeling churchtown. Though probably of Norman cruciform origin, the church is mostly C15. W tower of three stages with angle buttresses set back on the N and S faces and a three-eighths NE stair-turret, and embattled with pinnacles and crocketed finials. Nave and four-bay N aisle with standard Cornish granite piers with Pentewan stone capitals. C16 S porch. Extensively restored between 1876 and 1882, begun by *Hine* and completed with *Odgers*, including the rebuilding of the S transept and part of the E end. C19 Perp window tracery throughout. Wagon roof to nave, N aisle and porch with moulded ribs and moulded stone wall-plate, partly restored with new bosses carved by *Moutrie* of Tavistock. – FONT. Norman, of an uncommon type, with corner heads and arms supporting the heavy, wide, square top. – C15 PISCINA under a basket arch (N aisle). – Late C19 furnishings with SCREENS and PULPIT by *Hems* of Exeter. – FLOOR TILES by *Maw & Co.*, increasing in ornamentation E. – MONUMENTS. Slate to Ames Copplestone †1629, and Jane, daughter of Emmanuel Ganbe, †1629. – On exterior chancel wall, slate to Thomas Hockin †1767 with heraldic arms in roundels.

The parish has two of the series of VIADUCTS in quick succession in this stretch of the GWR. ST PINNOCK, 1½ m. NNW, 1854–5 by *I. K. Brunel*, heightened in 1882, is at 151 ft (46 metres) the highest of Brunel's timber fan viaducts in Cornwall and is 633 ft (193 metres) long. A dramatic structure, its nine piers of five battered stages with pointed openings piercing the upper four stages. The additional sixth stage is of a slightly cruder tapering design, with the original iron girders still carrying the mainline. WESTWOOD, just to the E, was the more usual masonry replacement built parallel to the original, 88 ft (27 metres) high and 372 ft (113 metres) long, in 1879.

ST PIRAN'S ORATORY AND CHURCH   7050
4½ m. N. of Perranzabuloe

Even for a county imbued with the legends of the Celtic saints, the remoteness and solitude of the little oratory and church lost in the Penhale Sands is evocative and compelling.

The ORATORY, probably C6 or C7, was of modest size – 29½ ft by 16½ ft by 19 ft (9 by 5 by 5.8 metres) – and had a pitched roof with E and W gables, only one small window (not splayed inside) on the S, a stone seat running all round, and an altar with canopy. It had been inundated by the sand by 960, by which time a new church had been built (*see* below). Excavated in 1835, sheltered in a concrete structure from 1910, it was reburied in 1980, at which time twelve cists were discovered in the area of its former churchyard. In 2014 being re-excavated and consolodated.

The CHURCH that succeeded the oratory was erected ¼ m. E inland. The whole site is enclosed by a large curvilinear earthwork and possibly represents an early monastic enclosure or *lann*. In turn it too was lost to the sand and c. 1805 much of it was dismantled and reused in the new church of St Piran at

Perranzabuloe (q.v.). The foundations were excavated in 1912, and re-cleared of sand as recently as 2005. Remains of nave, chancel and N transept, built *c.* 1150, and a S aisle, transept and porch added in 1462. One C15 capital remains, inverted, at the W end of the nave. The large scale reflects the importance of the cult of St Piran in the later medieval period when veneration of the saint spread from here to other churches in Cornwall (cf. Perranarworthal and Perranuthnoe) and beyond, and shows the plan of a typical medieval Cornish church.

11 Immediately S of the church is the CROSS, a massive granite monolith originally standing nearly 9 ft (2.7 metres) tall, its circular head of the four-holed type, the lower hole not pierced right through, with small projections at its neck. It is decorated with punch-dots in tight horizontal lines.

9050

ST STEPHEN-IN-BRANNEL

ST STEPHEN. Stately granite W tower, visible for miles against the china clay spoil heaps, of three stages with set-back buttresses, an embattled parapet and large crocketed pinnacles. That a Norman church preceded the present building is clear from the fine C12 S doorway of simple but striking design of two chamfered orders in banded dark and pale stone with small roundels carved on the chamfer of each arch. The spacious interior has a wide N aisle of eight bays with standard Cornish piers: early to mid C15. S chancel aisle of three bays with similar piers. The other roofs and most of the Perp style windows are the result of two C19 restorations, one begun in 1854, and another in 1893 by *G. H. Fellowes Prynne*. – STAINED GLASS. E window by *George Cooper-Abbs* for *Wippell* of Exeter, 1947. Expressive local scenes, including the china clay industry, pottery, farming and domestic life, with lively figures and good colours. – FONT. Late Norman, of the Bodmin type, on five supports with C13-looking bases, the bowl with demi-figures at the corners (two with arms, two bearded) and between them trees of life, two facing animals, etc. – PULPIT. C19, incorporating C17 carving. – CHOIR STALLS and PRAYER-DESKS. C19 Gothic with stencilled decoration, matching the SCREENS to N and S. – COMMUNION RAIL. Early C17.

CROSS. On S side of churchyard. Found at the end of the C19 in a field on nearby Tencague Farm, which had a licensed chapel in 1381. The cross-head, on a modern shaft, displays an equal-limbed cross on both faces.

The churchtown is all granite cottages; the QUEENS HEAD INN, smart early C19 granite ashlar, and an adjoining terrace form a modest but charming square in front of the church.

ST STEPHEN'S BEACON, 1¼ m. E. Unusual oval enclosure on steep-sided hill. Terrace with inner scarp follows contour 33 ft (10 metres) below summit. Low inner and outer banks, but no certain ditch. Probable entrance at NE. Two large secondary enclosures on NW and SE slopes, with heavy stone banks, again ditchless. Unlike any known Iron Age hillfort; possible Neolithic HILLTOP ENCLOSURE. Robbing of Bronze Age summit CAIRN for stone for nearby mine engine house in 1860s revealed long CIST (no longer visible) containing ashes. Cairn reused for fire beacon.

ST TEATH

ST TETHA. The large church stands in its round churchyard at the centre of a substantial churchtown. It was first recorded *c.* 1190 and by the 1260s was supporting two prebendaries and a vicar. Sturdy three-stage W tower with NE stair-turret of three-eighths plan, the lower stage probably Norman, with walls nearly 6 ft (1.8 metres) thick, the upper stages not as massively built and with Perp windows, the W doorway dated 1630. Wide nave and N and S aisles, both dendrochronologically dated to *c.* 1540. Both aisles are of six bays with piers of standard Cornish granite design, plain capitals and plain four-centred arches. There is some evidence of the Norman church at the W end in the traces of a respond built into the walling between the tower and the N aisle (visible from the aisle only), and parts of two Norman capitals reused as the base for an altar in the N aisle. Good early and late Perp tracery, mostly in Catacleuse stone, the aisle windows of three lights, the E window of the S aisle of five lights. In the two easternmost windows on the N side are image niches with ogee heads. Ceiled wagon roofs in N and S aisles with high-quality carving of the wall-plate in the N aisle. Porch roof probably made of timbers from former nave and chancel roofs with delicately carved wall-plates. – FONTS. C14, Dec, Catacleuse. – Near the N door an C11 font found in 1978. – The arch stones of a C13 STOUP survive in the porch, the bowl lost. – BENCH-ENDS. Good C16 examples with shields in N and S aisles, some of the rest moved to Tintagel in 1879 (q.v.). – C17 carved panels incorporated in CHOIR STALLS and PULPIT, with arms of Carminow family, dated 1630. – Painted Jacobean pedestal ALMS BOX. – STAINED GLASS. A few fragments of medieval glass including one of the Five Wounds incorporated in the chancel E window. – MONUMENT to a priest, C14, in window base in S aisle, badly preserved but of high quality, with angels l. and r. at the head and lions at the feet. – Slate ledger to Francis Bennet †1636 with finely cut figures in contemporary costume in low relief.

Within the churchyard NW of the church, the former CHURCH HOUSE. C16, two-storey, one of the best surviving Cornish examples despite alteration. The churchyard elevation has one two-light mullioned window and the remains of others.

The interior has finely moulded beams, evidence of former partitions and roof with raised cruck trusses, only the feet visible.

The centre of the village is marked by a CLOCK TOWER in THE SQUARE, built *c.* 1920 as a First World War memorial. Two stages under a pyramidal roof with clock face on all four elevations, rectangular lancets above and long rectangular windows with hexagonal glazing bars on the SW and NE sides. At the entrance to the modern cemetery a former CHURCHYARD CROSS (the third tallest in Cornwall after Mylor and Quethiock) with a four-holed head, re-assembled in 1883. Much pleasant building and some slate cladding (e.g. GREYSTONES, Fore Street, with unusual slate fillet slips over the slate joints). Of larger buildings the mid-to late C19 VICARAGE W of the church in treed grounds; METHODIST CHURCH, 1869, Trevilly Lane; and COUNTY PRIMARY SCHOOL, 1878 by *Silvanus Trevail*, almost exactly the same as Delabole (q.v.).

ST TUDY

ST TUDA. The churchtown is gathered around the large C15 church in its round churchyard. Tall unbuttressed three-stage W tower surmounted by embattled parapet with crocketed finials. Blind tracery to belfry windows. Proud E end where the large Perp windows of nave and N and S aisles with four and five lights appear. The S aisle accompanies nave and chancel the whole way, with six bays, the N aisle only for the three E bays. S porch with Perp doorway and roof, finely decorated. The arcades are identical, of Cornish granite standard, the mostly Catacleuse windows are of three lights, mainly with standard Cornish Perp tracery. The wagon roofs are original with moulded ribs, carved wall-plates, and bosses, with carved ribs in the N aisle. C19 chancel roof, part of a restoration of 1873–4 by *J. P. St Aubyn* when the C16 benches were moved to Michaelstow (q.v.); there were further restorations later that century and in 1932 when the chancel was reordered and re-furnished. – FONT. Norman, Polyphant stone. Square table-top type with the blank arcading on one side in two tiers (cf. Egloshayle, Poughill, St Cleer, St Mabyn etc.). – In the wall between nave and S aisle, a primitively carved figure, probably from a Norman CORBEL TABLE. – In the S aisle, a pre-Norman COPED STONE from the churchyard, hog-back shaped with elaborate decoration: blind arcading on the sides, interlaced cable, and foliage scrolls on the top (cf. Lanivet, St Buryan, Phillack). – ALTAR RAILS by *Violet Pinwill*. – PAINTING. Last Supper, late C16 Flemish. – STAINED GLASS. Tiny fragments of medieval glass in the tracery of the S aisle E window of chalice and rose. – S aisle window, 1894 by *Frederick Drake* of Exeter. – N aisle, 1864 by *Lavers & Barraud*. Chancel E, 1879 by *Ward & Hughes*. –

MONUMENTS. Many good Delabole slate plates, some with kneeling figures, especially well cut: Sacheverell Sitwell described them as 'something rare and peculiar to that far country outside and beyond England'. – Against S wall of S aisle, probably Alice Reskyner *c.* 1563–4, four figures in high relief with shields above. – Against W wall of S aisle, Humphrey Nicholls †1597, with effigies of parents and children in high relief, and another of Humphrey Nicholls and wife. – The motif of two kneeling figures facing each other with a prayer-desk between and small figures of kneeling children below is still preserved in the ambitious monument to Antony Nicholls †1659 below E window of S aisle: the main figures are almost life-size, limestone, the architecture of the monument grey marble.

THE CLINK. On the N edge of the churchyard. Former church house (cf. St Teath). Probably of C16 or C17 origin, refurbished C18 and later. Two-storey, plain, with external stair to first floor from road and churchyard.

OLD RECTORY, near the church, 1909–11 by *E. H. Sedding* in a restrained Arts and Crafts style.

The parish is rich in small former manor houses. Among them:

HENGAR, 2 m. NE. Now in a holiday park. A regular visiting place for Thomas Rowlandson when painting his Cornish landscapes and townscapes. Totally destroyed by fire 1904, rebuilt 1906 in a robust Elizabethan style with huge entrance hall and impressive imperial stair.

LAMELLEN, 2 m. NW. First built 1698, almost entirely but handsomely rebuilt 1849 in Picturesque Elizabethan style with irregular elevations, steeply pitched roofs and tall brick chimneys grouped in threes. Very complete mid-C19 interior with good details.

TINTEN, 1¼ m. S. The chapel of the old manor house, now an outbuilding of the farm, is still recognizable with its C15 E window of three lights with cusped heads. The interior retains evidence of a piscina in the S wall and aumbry in the N wall. The chapel was first licensed in 1330.

TREMEER, ¾ m. NW. C16 origins, rebuilt 1798 and partly 1899. Complex triple-pile plan. Remodelled in Arts and Crafts style.

WETHERHAM, 1¼ m. SW. The main elegant late C17 or early C18 elevations, remodelling an earlier building, have tall, narrow eighteen-pane sashes. Later C18 or early C19 wing and rambling service ranges to the rear that may incorporate earlier fabric.

ST VEEP

ST CIRICUS AND ST JULETTA. High above the Fowey within its oval churchyard or *lann*. Nothing remains of the originally cruciform church which belonged to Montacute Priory by 1269, and although a dedication of 1336 is recorded, it is difficult to attribute much of the present building to that date. Only the sturdy W tower is that early looking, of two stages with unusual thick clasping buttresses, no pinnacles, and a shallow rectangular NE stair-turret: its arch to the nave is steep, two-centred, and unmoulded. Otherwise the interior has a mid-C15 to mid-C16 character. The S aisle is separated from the nave by an arcade whose piers have four demi-shafts and four sharply keeled minor shafts between (cf. Poughill). The capitals are heavily moulded, the first four arches steeply pointed. It was extended E one bay in the early C16 for a S chancel chapel. The cusped windows may have been altered to their square-headed form in the mid C16. On the N side piers with four major and four minor shafts (cf. St Columb Major, St Issey) with the large horizontal leaf decoration of Devon. Squint from N chancel aisle to chancel. Wagon roofs with richly moulded wall-plates, also rich S porch roof. This is one of the few Cornish churches with dendrochronological dating, suggesting *c.* 1460 for the nave and chancel roofs, almost immediately followed by the S aisle roof, but as late as *c.* 1540 for the N aisle roof: the gap suggests the original intention for a N aisle could not be afforded until just before the Reformation. – FONT. C15 with geometric pattern decoration. – ALTAR STONE. Marble, with consecration crosses. – PULPIT. Simple C17, ornamented with elaborate classical foliage festoons, cartouches and crossed keys, of the second half of the C17; said to originate from Corpus Christi, Oxford. – BENCHES. Five C16, in S chancel chapel. – ROYAL ARMS. 1661 of Charles II, in chancel; *c.* 1780 of George III in S aisle. – MONUMENTS. Two slate plates to Nicholas Courtenay †1589 and his brother †1598.

To S of the churchyard, THE CLOSE, part of the former vicarage, *c.* 1820s with later alterations. Pretty symmetrical S front with two storey canted bays.

GIANT'S HEDGE. Probably post-Roman. Long linear earthwork winding for over five miles and through three parishes E from the River Lerryn's tidal limit to Muchlarnick, possibly to St Nonna's Camp, a probably Iron Age hillfort, just N of West Looe River's tidal limit. Has a ditch on the N side (usually downhill) of a broad bank 8½ ft (2.6-metres) high. Appears defensive, but more likely delineating territory and asserting status. Possibly continued another four miles SE from Muchlarnick to West Looe.

ST WENN

ST WENNA. In windswept country N of Castle-an-Dinas. The W tower, though reduced to two stages from three after partial collapse in 1825, still displays its C15 ambition in rising from a tall moulded plinth with quatrefoil and chevron decoration similar to Fowey and St Austell, and with buttresses set back from the angles with demi-shafts and crocketed finials above the first stage. Also fine W doorway and window, the former with moulded surround, recessed spandrels and square hood-mould, the latter of four narrow lights, C15. At the second stage an offset three-light bell-opening. Chancel rebuilt at the same time as the tower. Major restoration under *J. P. St Aubyn* 1886–9 but the church is charming in its intimate scale and interesting detail. Short N and S aisles of three bays, the piers in St Stephen's granite of four major and four minor shafts with Devon horizontal leaf-frieze capitals and four-centred arches, C15 or early C16. C19 roofs throughout, the nave and chancel arch- and mid-braced. – FONT. C12 style, Bodmin type, exactly as at Mawgan-in-Pydar and St Columb Major, probably a copy; there is a fragment of the original in the vestry. Good scheme of later C19 decoration at the E end of the chancel with REREDOS, The Last Supper, commandments etc., in tile and mosaic, and E window STAINED GLASS, painted grisaille with the Good Shepherd in the centre, both by *J. Powell & Sons*, 1873. – SUNDIAL. On S face of the tower, slate with punning inscription 'Ye know now when', 1860.

ST WINNOW

1050

ST WINNOW. In the loveliest of settings beside the tranquil Fowey with wide vistas of woods and fields along the estuary, and all alone except for the barton and former vicarage. The church is essentially Cornish Perp standard with nave and chancel, S aisle of six bays, S porch and W tower, though the N side contains Norman remains, suggesting the usual cruciform plan. Tower of three stages with buttresses to second stage only, set back from the corners though reaching very close to them, and embattled parapet. S aisle arcade piers are granite and have the usual Cornish profile and capitals with ornamental carving. Wagon roofs to nave, S aisle and porch with moulded ribs and carved bosses and elaborately carved wall-plate to E end of S aisle. The Norman transept arch was reconstructed in the C13: cf. the window W of it. Restoration by *E. H. Sedding*, begun 1874, completed 1907. – FONT. Granite with Perp carving of smiling angels holding hands and inscription 'Behold the beloved of the true God shall be baptized with the Holy Spirit' (cf. Treslothan, St Anthony-in-Meneage, with the same inscription). – BENCH-ENDS. Partly the usual Cornish Perp type, partly *c.* 1525–35, partly Elizabethan. Among the motifs a man drinking and a St Catherine's Wheel. – Jacobean ALTAR TABLE and later C17 PULPIT (on short C19 bulbous legs). – ROOD SCREEN. A rare and important survival for

14

Cornwall, sensitively restored under Sedding by *Violet Pinwill* (cf. Lanteglos-by-Fowey) in 1907. The nave part is essentially original, except for the coving and the cornice. The base has four tall narrow panels for each section, carved with individual stylized flowers or leaves above each other instead of the undulating scrolls of, for example, Morwenstow and St Buryan. – STAINED GLASS. An exceptionally significant late C15 ensemble in the E window of the S aisle. It was assembled from several windows in 1867 with the insertion of skilful and sympathetic work of that date. There are important parallels with the contemporary glass at St Kew and St Neot (qq.v.) and more locally with the figures at Lanteglos-by-Fowey (q.v.). More widely there are also similarities with the Exeter workshop and the Exeter Cathedral glass. The window is of four lights and tracery with eight full-length figures of saints, two rows of donor figures, and armorials in the tracery and at the bottom of the main lights; the S aisle was built as a chantry for the Kayles who developed nearby Ethy. – In the E window, Crucifixion figures re-set, also late C15. – MONUMENT. Slate to William Sawle †1651, of pretty curved shape.

QUAY, 100 yds W. Late C18 and earlier with dressed stone from St Winnow Barton. Leland described it *c.* 1538: 'By this church is a warfe to make shipes by.'

ST WINNOW BARTON. Of *c.* 1840, reusing stonework and walls from the earlier C15–C16 mansion: e.g. in the gable front projection a C16 moulded doorway with ferns carved in the spandrels.

Former VICARAGE. Above the church and barton. Of *c.* 1740 with extension and remodelling *c.* 1800 by *Robert Walker*. Almost asymmetrical seven-window front of three storeys, centre three bays projected forward with gabled roof, in the extension.

4050

SALTASH

A borough by 1201 with a rich history but so badly treated by the second half of the C20 as to be almost unrecognizable from the town Pevsner described thus in 1951: 'The thrill of Saltash is the excessive contrast between the small scale and the variety of the small shapes of the fishing town along the waterside and climbing up the steep hill, and the sheer height of the granite piers . . . of Brunel's Royal Albert Bridge.' Sadly no more. Gone are the buildings of fishing and commerce along the waterfront, gone too whole streets of little houses behind and climbing the hill, and though Brunel's bridge remains a monumental presence it no longer dominates the place in the way Pevsner found so memorable.

The extent of the erosion of the town's history, the worst of any in Cornwall's impressive array of intact historic towns, had several causes. Bomb damage in 1941 destroyed many buildings in the Fore Street area. The picturesque housing around the waterside was declared unfit for habitation and cleared between 1957 and 1966. The construction of the new Tamar Bridge taking the A38 into Cornwall in 1959–62 required a further loss of buildings, consolidated by the demolition of yet more buildings behind Fore Street when a tunnel was constructed in 1986 for the Saltash by-pass. And the post-war redevelopment of the upper parts of Fore Street and around the waterfront was of a depressingly lacklustre kind. The Tamar Bridge did, however, bring about the town's rapid expansion because of easy access to Plymouth and it now encompasses St Stephens-by-Saltash, the mother church. There remains much of interest including two medieval churches, a fine guildhall, some good groups of buildings in Fore Street, one of the best post-war buildings in the county, and, above all, views of the two bridges that mark out Saltash as the S gateway to Cornwall.

CHURCHES

St Nicholas and St Faith, Alexandra Square. Only a chapel of ease to St Stephen until 1881, yet the building belongs to the foundation of the borough, for the three-stage tower is Norman, unbuttressed and adjoining the N transept (like the Norman towers at Blisland and St Enodoc), the blocked S door with blind tympanum is Norman, and most of the masonry of the chancel with two windows, nave, S transept (including the transept arch), and W wall is Norman too. In the early C14 a N chancel chapel was added. Then, at the usual time, in the C15, came a N nave aisle. S porch with early C17-looking outer door frame with moulded label and carved spandrels but with a canopied niche over, which must be before 1558. Lofty interior, the arcade to the N chapel simply double-chamfered, the responds with moulded capitals, the aisle arcade of five bays with a Cornish standard arcade and wagon roof. The wagon roof of the nave is of the same date, and also the five-light E window of the chapel. A squint connects S transept and chapel. – Restored 1869, probably by *J. Ambrose* of Plymouth, and 1930 by *A. S. Parker*. – FONT. Probably Norman, of an unusual vague shape, with corner ribs and a centre rib on each side; possibly of domestic origin. – STAINED GLASS. Chancel E, 1880 by *A. Gibbs*. – Other late C19 and early to mid-C20 glass, some much restored after war damage, including S aisle windows of St Nicholas and St Germans, 1908 by *Fouracre & Watson*, and First World War soldier, 1920 by *William Morris & Co.* of Westminster. – N aisle, 1910 by *Fouracre & Watson* and 1958 by *Hugh Easton*. – N chapel E, 1905 with interesting facial painting. – MONUMENT. John and James Drew and J. W. Drew, two captains and one acting lieutenant, drowned in 1798 and 1799, with three portrait medallions against the usual pyramid and reliefs of shipwrecks. – William Bailey by *R. Isbell* of Stonehouse.

ST STEPHEN, St Stephen's Road. A large and ambitious church
with a stately tower standing in a most unusual position N of
the W end of the nave and facing the W end of an obviously
later N aisle. It is tall, three-staged, with buttresses set back
from the angles and a stair-turret on a three-eighths plan rising
to the height of the pinnacles: the latter may have been added
by *G. H. Fellowes Prynne* who restored the tower in 1895. The
church had been previously restored by *Ewan Christian* in
1872. The exterior of the body of the church is Perp except
that at the E end joints are visible showing that the nave was
there before both aisles. The aisles are not of the same date,
though both C15–C16, their windows large. S porch with elaborate joints and diagonal buttresses, quite a decorative piece. The
interior is lofty and exceptionally light. Four-bay arcades to
nave, one bay to chancel; the piers of standard section, but the
capitals and the mouldings of the arches differ characteristically. They show the N arcade to be older than the S arcade.
Ceiled wagon roofs, including to porch, some restoration. –
FONT. Norman, large, of the Bodmin type, on five supports
with busts at the corners and trees of life and animals on the
sides. – REREDOS, *c.* 1900 by *Harry Hems* of Exeter. Seven-bay,
Gothic style, very brightly painted. – STAINED GLASS.
Five windows in the N aisle, 1903–12 by *Fouracre & Son*. –
MONUMENTS. Very stiffly semi-reclining woman in a flat
niche, *c.* 1600–20. – W. Hitchens with wife and ten children,
tomb-chest with large elaborate slate top, and backplates; Elizabethan. Next to it G. Wadham †1606 and wife (Hitchens's
daughter). The corner position of the two monuments is due
to C19 restoration. – An *Isbell* monument of 1806 in the N tower
arch, to Sarah Traill. – In the large raised churchyard NE of the
church, family VAULT of Benjamin Tucker and family, early
C19, a rectangular single-storey mausoleum with blind Gothic
recesses. – Immediately SE of the church, CHURCHYARD
CROSS, of the lantern type, much eroded, the canopied faces
with the Crucifixion on its principal face and the Virgin and
Child on the reverse.

OUR LADY OF THE ANGELS (R.C.), New Road. 2007 by *Lacie
Hickie Caley*. A dramatic sculptural form complementing its
hillside setting on the Saltash skyline. The saddleback zinc roof
is echoed in the curved walls of the church with its central
cedar-shingle clad nave.

PUBLIC BUILDINGS

GUILDHALL, Fore Street. A handsome presence alongside the
parish church. Built *c.* 1780, extended and restored 1925. Ten-bay
ground-floor arcade on Doric columns, originally open, and five-
bay first floor with round-headed windows with projecting keystones, surmounted by a shallow-pitched roof with wide modillion
eaves. Two-bay W front with large round-headed porch on

columns. Carved tympanum and the Saltash arms in pedimented tablet breaking the eaves.

SALTASH LIBRARY, Callington Road. 1963 by the *County Architect's Department*, job architect *Royston Summers*. One of the most innovative of the County Architect's post-war *œuvre*, worth comparing with the different but equally striking library at St Austell (q.v.). A powerful presence among later mediocre public buildings, the roof sweeping steeply up to the entrance front to double height from the low rear, fully glazed entrance screen and hall, gallery to rear. The design is based on the proportions of the human figure of Le Corbusier's modular system. Extended at the rear but not in a way that spoils the impact of the original.

BISHOP CORNISH EDUCATION CENTRE, Lynher Drive. 2010 by *ARCO2 Architects Ltd* of Bodmin. An excellent example of a sustainable building using relatively new technology that is excitingly designed and attractively finished. Timber-framed with straw bales and lamb's wool insulation, green roof and solar heating and lighting. Its hillside site is skilfully deployed to lead from a relatively low-key entrance through the interior spaces to a gracefully curved veranda and terrace on stilts with views out over the town.

ST BARNABAS COMMUNITY HOSPITAL, Higher/Lower Port View. 1887 by *G. H. Fellowes Prynne*. Hospital in domestic style with the appearance of a country house. Red brick with stone facing, decorative tilework and timber verandas to the first and second floors of the main elevation. Small apsidal first-floor chapel, intimate and colourful, with external stairs.

RAILWAY STATION, Albert Road. The up platform retains its 1859 building, at present sadly neglected. Single-storey, stuccoed symmetrical five-bay front with bracketed cast-iron brackets to porch over central entrance, flanked by small recessed bays. Later twelve-bay single-storey down side building with lower E bay.

ROYAL ALBERT BRIDGE. 1847–59 by *Isambard Kingdom Brunel*. The bridge was an engineering feat for its date, a combined suspension and arched bridge. The technical reason for the two by no means elegant sausage-shaped tubular arches is that their outward thrust on to the abutments counteracts the inward drag of the chains. The oval section of the arches increases their stiffness and gives enough width for the single line of the railway between the vertical chains hanging from the arches: not a handsome, but a safe and sound solution. The high granite shafts on the other hand are still spectacular from the waterside. The inscription 'I K Brunel Engineer' was placed after Brunel's death.

TAMAR BRIDGE. 1959–61 by *Mott, Hay & Anderson*. When opened the largest suspension bridge in the United Kingdom, with a central span of 1,100 ft (335 metres) and side spans of 374 ft (114 metres). The reinforced concrete towers have legs at 50-ft (15.2-metres) centres. In 2001 it became the first bridge in the world to undergo strengthening and widening from three to five lanes using cantilevers while remaining open to traffic.

PERAMBULATION

It is worth going down to the waterside to see the scale of Brunel's achievement and the faintest hint of what Pevsner saw in the siting of the BOATMAN INN at the foot of the bridge's piers. The missed opportunity of the redevelopment is clear in the surreal decision to incorporate a doorway dated 1584 into the standard 1960s council house (No. 10 TAMAR STREET) next door. Nothing alas now needs to be said about the rest of this area that climbs up to FORE STREET. In CULVER STREET, MARY NEWMAN'S COTTAGE, C17 and later, and the station in Albert Road (see Public Buildings). Fortunately some nice C18 and C19 buildings, some incorporating C17 and earlier fabric, survive around the Guildhall (see Public Buildings), including No. 30A with a re-set C16 doorway. In CALLINGTON ROAD Nos. 2 and 4, early C19 three-storey slate-hung houses.

At ANTONY PASSAGE, 1 m. SSW, a former TIDAL MILL, C17 with C19 alterations, with a small quay, sluices and mill pond, and MILL HOUSE. Also FERRY HOUSE, early to mid-C19 former inn, where the ferry from Antony landed, all below the RAILWAY VIADUCT of c. 1880.

SANCREED

ST SANCREED. The church sits secluded in its remote church-town. Given to Tewkesbury c. 1125, transferred to the Dean and Chapter of Exeter 1242. All granite with unbuttressed W tower of a single stage with a rectangular NE stair-turret, C14. Blocked Norman N door with plain tympanum. N transept with narrow lancets. C15 S porch with restored wagon roof and trefoil-headed niche above S door. The S aisle is C15, of five bays of variant Cornish design. Good five-light E window of the chancel of the same date. The N transept is screened off from the nave by two arches. The interior bears the imprint of an extensive but thoughtful restoration of 1881–91 by *J. D. Sedding* that included new wagon roofs and furnishings: of special note the highly decorative chancel roof in geometric patterns. – FONT. Of the St Ives type, with four angels holding shields, C15. – ROOD SCREEN. The base of the C16 screen survives with traces of original colouring. The carving of the panels is especially entertaining: a jester blows a trumpet, with a snake winding up it, a goat among thistles, an owl, the *signum triciput*, etc. – Pillar POOR BOX dated 1739. – STAINED GLASS. Chancel E, 1940 by *Townsend & Howson*, strong design, good colours, scenes of local life. – REREDOS, now on N wall of chancel, by *Sedding*, a Nativity panel, carved by *S. Trevenan*: it is the same design as St Clement, Bournemouth. – MONUMENT. To William Alexander Stanhope Forbes †1916, within a classical frame, a very fine bronze half-portrait in relief by his father, *Stanhope Forbes*, exquisitely executed.

In the churchyard two of the best and most important wheel-headed CHURCHYARD CROSSES. One, to the S of the porch, has a figure of a haloed Christ, and a shaft decorated with two panels, the lower panel with interlace work; below this in the small panel the name 'Runho' is inscribed. More interlace work to the reverse face of the shaft and the sides. The other, by the S path to the church, is considered *in situ*, and has a Christ figure with arms outstretched on the head and a decorated shaft with two panels: the upper panel has an arrow-like symbol with a long vertical bar terminating in a vase. The sides of the shaft have zigzag and triangular key pattern decoration. Other CROSSES throughout the parish.

HOLY WELL and BAPTISTERY, ¼ m. E. Steep flight of steps leading to spring-fed well, roofed with granite lintels. Probably medieval. The ruins of the baptistery are immediately N, of rectangular plan, partly built into the bank at the rear.

TREGANNICK, I m. N. 1935 by *Geoffrey Bazeley*. A rare Modernist house in this part of Cornwall, its flat roof and white rendered walls very visible from the road, though it is only of modest size. On the garden elevation the l. bay projects to act as a stop for the balcony, with the main block recessed at the corner but the roof continued over. Interior unaltered at time of writing.

CARN EUNY, I m. W. Long-lived farming settlement excavated and consolidated 1964–72. Iron Age timber round-houses were replaced by at least five Roman-period COURTYARD HOUSES and several free-standing oval or circular stone-walled houses, now a dense complex of overlapping and interlocking structures. Beneath is a remarkable FOGOU complex. A passage to a C5 B.C. subterranean circular chamber, corbelled and paved, was truncated the following century by the slightly serpentine main fogou running NE–SW, whose original entrance was a steeply sloping side creep passage.

CAER BRAN, ¾ m. WSW. Circular Iron Age HILLFORT with single rampart and ditch, strong and continuous to N and E where bank is partly stone revetted, but discontinuous and lower on S and W sides; possibly unfinished. Its builders left unharmed a smaller concentric inner HILLTOP ENCLOSURE with ditchless bank, possibly Late Neolithic or Early Bronze Age, which contains three circular features, probably RING CAIRNS.

BOSWENS MENHIR, 3 m. NNW. Prominent Early Bronze Age STANDING STONE, an 8-ft (2.4-metre) high skylined finger, strangely scooped on its NW and SE faces, standing on a low platform CAIRN. The sea, Chun Quoit, Carn Galva and Carn Kenidjack are dramatically visible from it.

SCRAESDON FORT *see* ANTONY

SENNEN

3020

ST SENNEN. The westernmost church of England, in an exposed position on the hill, not down in the cove, with its w tower facing the New World. The tower is unbuttressed, of three stages. The small, low church consists of nave, N transept (with a narrow lancet), chancel and an added s aisle of five bays. This has square piers with four attached demi-shafts and four-centred arches. A re-dedication of 1441 may refer to this addition. Restored 1867 by *J. P. St Aubyn* with new arch- and wind-braced roofs and much replaced tracery. – FONT. With inscription of 1442 on the pedestal. – PULPIT. 1929 by *Pinwill & Co.*, the carving including crabs, fish and lobsters. The same firm refurbished the chancel in 1939 with fine CHOIR STALLS with crowning angels and provided the ALTAR, REREDOS and PANELLING in 1953: the latter incorporate charming scenes of local life and work, flanking angels above the altar. Altogether a fine ensemble of their work. – SCULPTURE. A figure of the Virgin and Child, of good quality and late C13 date; the head is modern. – STAINED GLASS. Chancel E, s aisle E and two windows in s aisle s, 1878–9 by *Clayton & Bell*. – In the church-yard NW of the church a WHEEL-HEAD WAYSIDE CROSS with Latin crosses on both faces, and another CROSS-HEAD near the s gate with the cross formed by the carving out of four triangular grooves.

In the little churchtown the FIRST AND LAST INN with a low C17 range nearest the church and large C18 and C19 extensions, and CHURCHTOWN HOUSE, early C19 with a smart ashlar granite front of three bays with central round-headed doorway that has rusticated long and short voussoirs over impost cornices.

At SENNEN COVE a picturesque group above the 1908 BREAK-WATER that shelters the slipway, beach and lifeboat station. Several C18 cottages near the ROUND HOUSE, the most complete capstan house relating to the fishing industry to survive in Cornwall. The capstan room, which retains its original eight-barred capstan, is on the rubble-walled ground floor, with the former net loft clad in vertical tarred boards and with a conical slate roof above. Within the loft the original C18 kingpost roof structure, the weight of the roof carried on angled struts that bear on the basement walls. Further up behind a row of early C19 COASTGUARD COTTAGES, three pairs of double-depth plan, each pair originally sharing a front door.

PENROSE FARMHOUSE, 1 m. E. The Penroses are first recorded at Penrose in 1302. The farmhouse is a good example of C18 refronting to a C16 and C17 house. Within a cross-wing to the r. is a C16 roof structure, and in the room below a carved plaster panel in low relief thought to represent the C16 burial site of the young son of Squire Penrose who died at sea while attempting to rescue members of his crew. Within the FARM BUILDINGS are the remains of a C17 former terrace of six one-room plan cottages, probably the oldest example of purpose-built workers' housing in Cornwall.

MAEN CASTLE, I m W. Early Iron Age CLIFF CASTLE with unusual stone-built rampart. Orthostats and laid slabs form inner and outer faces and subdivide its length into rubble-filled compartments. Entrance passage marked by tall granite jambs and guarded by low external wing walls. A kink at the rampart's N end is created by reusing an earlier field boundary. Steep-sided, flat-bottomed ditch with counterscarp bank echoes rampart line. Rampart and ditch run deep to N but peter out on southern slopes, as if for display rather than defence; excavations in 1939 and 1948–9 failed to find convincing evidence of settlement.

LONGSHIPS LIGHTHOUSE, 1¼ m. W of Land's End. Established on a group of rocks called Carn Bras in 1795. Present lighthouse 1872–5 built by *James Douglass*. Circular grey granite tower 45 ft (13.7 metres) above high water, 86 ft (26.2 metres) high to the gallery with a lantern 18 ft (5.5 metres) high.

WOLF ROCK LIGHTHOUSE, 9 m. SW of Land's End. 1869–76, designed by *James Walker*, built by *James Douglass*. 135-ft (41-metre) granite tower, the blocks dovetailed, bolted and cement-grouted; there are seven floors beneath the lantern. The substantial landing stage was necessary for its construction. The first lighthouse in the world to have a helicopter landing platform fitted above the lantern, in 1972.

FLAG CABLE TERMINAL, 1¼ m. SSE. Almost hidden from view by trees, and set down behind a bund on three sides, stands one of the most sophisticated large sheds in the county, by *Poynton Bradbury Wynter Cole*, 2002. The British terminal of an international fibre-optic communications network, a massive shallow arched roof gives a clear open space, supported on cellular beams supported by mass concrete bases built into the inner side of the surrounding bund. The roof sails over the set-back walls of silver flush insulated panels, there being no requirement for windows.

SHEVIOCK 3050

THE BLESSED VIRGIN MARY. Unlike the usual Cornish village church that is predominantly of the C15, Sheviock is memorable for substantial fabric and features of the C13 and early C14, probably the work of the Dawnay family, tenants of Tavistock Abbey. The two-stage unbuttressed W tower is evidently C13–C14, slender (in fact narrower than the nave whose roof appears to the l. and r.), with long narrow lancet windows (an upper one cusped), no W door, and slim octagonal broached spire with small lucarnes, all very like nearby Rame (q.v.)

whose spire was dedicated in 1321. Carved medieval mask high up on the W face of the tower. The S side in its exterior and interior is all early C14. The S buttressed transept, the windows of three and four lights, the S and E windows of the equally heavily buttressed chancel (the latter of five lights), and the W window of the N aisle, no doubt reused when in the C15 the N transept was broken up and replaced by the usual N aisle, are all of this date and of Beer stone. The windows all have cusped lights, pointed and cusped little quatrefoils, and, except for the chancel E window, as their main motif a five-pointed star in a large circle. In the interior also the C14 dominates over the C15: *see* the S transept arch, the inner arches to all the S windows, the fine slender shafts supporting the inner arch in the case of the chancel E window, the diagonally placed ogee-headed niche on the l. of this window, and especially the twin funeral recesses at the S end of the transept. That these are also all executed in Beer stone and are of unusually high quality reinforces the C14 links with St Germans, St Ive, South Hill and the Exeter Cathedral workshop.

In the FUNERAL RECESSES on plain tomb-chests with quatrefoil decoration lie a knight and lady of *c.* 1375: some colour survives. Above the figures is a ribbed coving, and then a strip of blank cusped arches. They are Sir Edward Courtney †1370 and his wife, Emmeline, heiress of the Dawnays, †1371. The N aisle has Perp windows and an arcade of six bays with Cornish standard piers and some decoration of the abaci. On the N wall, opposite the S transept, on an identical TOMB-CHEST is another knight of about the same date, probably a brother of Emmeline Dawnay, and no doubt transferred from the N transept. If one tries to forget about the N aisle and replaces it in one's mind with a N transept, one will have a good picture of a C14 church in Cornwall. – Three plain SEDILIA, a corbel used as a CREDENCE, and PISCINA in the chancel; another PISCINA in the S transept. Wagon roof to N aisle with moulded ribs and wall-plate and carved bosses. The other roofs, more steeply pitched and of honest, simple design and construction, belong to an excellent restoration of 1850 by *G. E Street*, which was judged 'one of the most satisfying of modern times' by *The Ecclesiologist*, and also included the refurnishing of the chancel with its *Minton* tiled floor. Street also relocated the slate TABLETS of the Lord's Prayer and the Creed from the chancel to the N aisle. – FONT. Plain, circular, C13. – BENCH-ENDS. A few with tracery decoration (not the shields or Instruments of the Passion as usual in Cornwall; cf. Rame again) and some in the first and last pews of each section with Renaissance motifs. – STAINED GLASS. A fine E window by *William Wailes* to designs by Street with rich colouring and good figures under C14-style canopies. The S windows of the chancel also belong to this partnership, one incorporating the Courtney arms in the tracery. – Tower W, 1961 of John Wesley, an unusual and delightful Anglican depiction with a globe and inscription over

'The world is my parish'. – MONUMENT. Brass cross on black marble plate to Alphonse Charles de Morel †1849.

TREHILL, ½ m. SE. 1836–40 by *George Wightwick* for Rev. S. M. Roberts. Fine Italianate villa in a lovely elevated but sheltered position not far from the sea. Two-storey, graciously proportioned, the S garden front with tripartite sashes to the ground floor, tripartite round-headed windows to the first floor, and deep eaves under a slightly pitched hipped roof. The interior is similarly accomplished, the rooms arranged on a double-depth plan around a central entrance and staircase hall, all sparingly but finely detailed. Nearby the STABLES and COACH-HOUSE, also by Wightwick.

TREWIN, 1 m. WNW. A small square brick house of *c.* 1750, doubled by a similar square range in the C19. The Georgian front is two-storey and five-bay with plain end pilasters and a central doorcase with Doric pilasters and entablature. Central passage and stair hall, one room with fielded panelling and a chimneypiece with egg-and-dart ornament flanked by arched niches. The C19 extension is plain and stuccoed.

SHILLINGHAM

4050

The MANOR HOUSE, of medieval origin and *c.* 1700 remodelling, has been so altered as to make its history almost unintelligible. Its CHAPEL stands on its own a little further E, in ruins. It was first recorded in 1318. The W wall with a door just like Henry Trecarrel's chapel at Trecarrel is now missing but the other three walls still stand, with the N window retaining tracery of *c.* 1300 and image brackets on each side of the E window. It is possible that the window in the E wall of the house with a pair of foil-headed lancets originated in the W wall of the chapel. Walled GARDEN with a fine four-centred granite gateway within a moulded rectangular arch with carved spandrels and a label with large square carved stops and a heraldic shield.

SITHNEY

6020

ST SITHNEY. C15 W tower of regular granite blocks, unbuttressed, embattled parapet with slender corner pinnacles set on sculptured figures, possibly the Evangelists. The plan of the church with N and S aisles and N and S transepts is similar to neighbouring Breage, though not as ambitious or finely executed. Good C15 Perp window tracery with bulbous cusps (cf. Cury, Gunwalloe, Mullion etc.). S porch with panelled jambs (cf. Breage, Godolphin and other Lizard churches), Norman fragments with chevron decoration, built into the SE corner, and wagon roof. Inside, nave and aisles of six bays, both with standard Cornish granite piers, those on the S with undecorated capitals, those on the N with the familiar decoration of large horizontal leaves. The two arches between chancel and aisle on the N side are lower than the others. There are differences in the mouldings of the arches too. The arch to the N transept belongs to the type of the N arcade, that to the S transept of the C16. The outstanding feature of the church is the inner face of the W window of the N aisle, C14, with the inner arch panelled and decorated with quatrefoils and Tudor roses, uncommonly good. Restoration 1878 by *J. D. Sedding*. – FONT. Norman, circular, small and indifferently decorated. – STAINED GLASS. Medallions of C15 and C16 glass in baptistery. – MONUMENTS. Coffin-shaped slab with cross, *c.* 1240. – In the NE part of the churchyard a pillar on a pedestal to John Oliver, erected by his son, Dr Oliver of Bath, in 1741. The inscription is probably by Pope. It reads: 'William Oliver, from a filial sense that the blessings he now enjoys were, under the conduct of Providence, owing to the piety and tenderness of his mother and to the goodness and generosity of his father, erected this monument to their memorys'. – To the S, a wheel-headed WAYSIDE CROSS with an equal-limbed cross in relief, the reverse face hollowed out for a feeding bowl for cattle.

TREVARNO, 1 m. NE. 1834 by *George Wightwick*, conceived, along with Pencarrow, as his most ambitious classical work in Cornwall. Enlarged by *William Bickford Smith* after 1874, but reduced in the late C20. Plain elevations, the garden front five-bay and two-storey, the centre bay advanced and gabled. Extensive gardens, parkland, lake and BOATHOUSE, *c.* 1870 with ornate bargeboards and bellcote with spire.

TRUTHALL. *See* p. 685.

3070

SOUTH HILL

ST SAMSON. The mother church of Callington (q.v.). Lonely but serene, within a large churchyard, itself surrounded by a larger sub-rectangular enclosure, probably a *lann*, that witnesses the early Christian origins of the site – it may also have been an early medieval religious settlement. Moreover, the church is earlier than most Cornish churches, the re-dedication of 1333 by Bishop Bronescombe referring to the greater part of the present building – the two lower stages of the tower, nave, chancel and N transept, all of which are strongly buttressed with a continuous plinth and have interesting Dec features. At that date the church was cruciform, that is in the Norman and E.E. tradition of Cornwall (cf. nearby St Ive, Quethiock and Sheviock): the foundations of the former s transept, removed for the C15 s aisle, were identified in excavations of 2005.* The tower, whose upper stage was added in the C15 in large granite blocks, has a w door with triple cavetto moulding with fillets between, carved heads below the hoodmould of the w window, and, as at St Dominic (q.v.), its parapet supported by a frieze with the twelve apostles, three on each face, carved in relief, and shield-holding angels at the corners; there are corresponding smaller angels at the top of the second stage. C15 porch with ceiled wagon roof with carved bosses and brattished.

The interior is lofty and spacious, with a very tall, narrow four-centred tower arch. Fine pointed arch to the N transept with multiple mouldings dying out to the jambs as at St Ive. The chancel E window is especially fine late Dec, of graceful and elegant proportions with finely executed geometrical tracery with 'daggers' and pointed trefoils and quatrefoils in Beer stone; the internal window arch is richly and boldly moulded, springing from plain capitals supported by octagonal shafts attached to the jambs. It bears comparison with the E window at St Ive and several of the windows at Sheviock. By its side an ogee-arched PISCINA, cinquefoiled, originally with crockets. On the S wall of the chancel the Dec window overlaps an earlier SEDILIA, E.E. looking. The N windows of the chancel are late C19 replacements, tall and pointed; the wall below has two ogee-arched tomb-recesses with cusping and bulbous finials, the E one heavily restored, and a squint from the transept (the Manaton chapel) cutting into the w recess. The fourbay aisle arcade has tall standard Cornish piers and moulded capitals. C15 ceiled wagon roofs to chancel and S aisle. A thoughtful restoration of 1871–2 by *J. D. Sedding* renewed the nave and transept roofs on simple kingpost trusses with arch braces and respected the substantially Dec character of the church. – Another PISCINA with cusped head, much eroded, in the E wall of the Manaton chapel. – FONT. Norman, a fine example of the St Austell type, with corner faces, trees of life, and long animals in profile. – STAINED GLASS. N transept, 1912 by *Fouracre & Son*, St Sampson with archbishops Temple and Benson. – Elsewhere much pretty ornamental diapering. – MONUMENT. In the Manaton chapel, the incised slab of 1507 to John Manaton and wife is no longer present, but fine monument on E wall to Michael Hill and wife, 1663, with figure in relief, half kneeling at a library table, his head resting on his hand, his elbow on a skull, with remains of ancient colour and verse inscription below.

Near the entrance to the churchyard, an INSCRIBED STONE, CVMREGNI/FILI MAVCI, '[the stone] of Cumregnus, son of Maucus', with traditional lettering with Roman and early Saxon features, the inscription topped by two curved lines,

*The excavations also revealed seven cist graves, radiocarbon-dated to between 1010 and 1280, thus substantially pre-dating the re-dedication.

above which is a stone carved with XP motif. Four feet (1.2 metres) of the stone are below ground.

SOUTH PETHERWIN

St Paternus. The large church stands at the centre of the village within a probable *lann*, its W tower of 1456 prominent in the local landscape. The tower is of three stages, not tall but finely proportioned with buttresses set back from the angles, large octagonal corner turrets with crocketed finials, and deeply recessed and moulded W door and window: all very similar to other local towers (cf. Lezant, North Hill, Stoke Climsland, etc.). There must have been a very large aisled Norman church here (it was appropriated to St Germans before 1269), for the scalloped Norman capital displayed outside the N porch is nearly 3 ft (0.9 metres) across: it belonged originally to a circular pier (cf. North Petherwin, St Breward and St Teath). The N door is also Norman, though modest in dimensions and design (one order of colonettes and a crenellated motif on the voussoirs), and mutilated by the insertion of a C16 arch. The STOUP by its side is Norman too, the only one in Cornwall. Finally, in 1889 the original Norman W respond of the N arcade was discovered, good granite blocks, vertically tooled, and a plain capital. The interior is rather low but spacious with N arcade of the earlier type, the piers square with demi-shafts and moulded capitals, some of Polyphant, still with fairly simple heavy detail, and simple double-chamfered arches (cf. St Stephen-by-Launceston). The N chancel aisle of two more bays was added later, to the same design as that of the S aisle: standard Cornish piers with a little decoration on the abaci. The three E windows have the typical four-light design of this district (cf. Launceston). The N aisle windows are not very large and were renewed as part of an extensive restoration of 1888–9 by *G. H. Fellowes Prynne* when the N aisle was rebuilt and the roofs renewed (some C15 fragments in S aisle). – FONT. Late C12, circular, unusually on octagonal shafts, with flat pointed arches all round (a development of the square type at Egloshayle and Madron). – Some remains of the ROOD SCREEN, including parts of a vine cornice, incorporated in the tower screen of 1902. – PULPIT. 1631, octagonal, with linenfold panels, standing on one not very thick shaft branching out into eight scrolls with caryatids. – READING DESK. Made up of pieces of Jacobean pews. – Some old BENCH-ENDS on the front of the 1903 choir stalls. – ROYAL ARMS of James I, painted on board. – STAINED GLASS. Chancel E, 1895. Two medieval armorials, one of Tremayne, in the tracery of the S aisle window. Another S aisle window of 1912, possibly by *Drake*. – MONUMENTS. Two early C13 sepulchral slabs in tower. – Ambrose Manaton of Trecarrell †1651, aedicule with Ionic columns and scrolled pediment with arms. – Chevity (Probat?) †1676, finely carved slate.

METHODIST CHAPEL ¼ m. W of St Paternus. 1872. Unusually architecturally ambitious Gothic. Apsidal E and W ends and short transepts, tall lancets, and steeply pitched patterned-slate roof. To N, attached former SUNDAY SCHOOL. Also former STABLES and GIGHOUSE.

TREGUDDICK, 2 m. WNW. Inscription above porch door 'Anno Domini 1576 N.T.', i.e. Nicholas Treguddick. Though remodelled and extended in 1878 after a fire, much of the C16 house survives. The five-window front, all mullioned, steps up from the lower end to the two-storeyed porch and higher upper end. Large royal arms of Elizabeth I dated 1593 at high end of hall.

HOLYWAY CROSS, 2½ m. WNW. Fine wheel-head cross standing beside the eastbound carriageway of the A30. Equal-limbed cross with widely expanded ends, the lower limb extending down beyond a band towards the base of the shaft.

STITHIANS

7030

ST STITHIAN. An all-granite church with a fine C15 W tower of three stages with buttresses set back from the angles, embattled, and with panelled and crocketed pinnacles rising from shield-carrying angel corbels. A drastic restoration of 1873, following an earlier campaign in 1862, replaced all the windows (except the W tower window) and roofs, and added a N porch; there is no S porch. Inside, the N aisle has a C14 arcade of six bays with piers of non-standard Cornish design but heavy proportions. The S aisle has thin square piers with four attached shafts and less pointed arches than the N aisle. The tower arch has shafts attached to the responds as at Mawgan-in-Meneage and Constantine. – FONT. Plain, octagonal. – PULPIT. Nice plain Georgian. – PISCINA. On a Norman corbel with two animals facing each other, part of a Norman Bodmin-type font. – STAINED GLASS. Chancel E, 1899 by *Clayton & Bell*.

In the churchyard at the E end of the church, a tall wheel-headed WAYSIDE CROSS with a figure of Christ on the principal face, and a broad-limbed Latin cross on the reverse.

TRETHEAGUE, ¼ m. SW. Small country house, early C18, with lovely rusticated granite ashlar front of five bays and two storeys above basement; incongruous C20 battlements distracting from the classical perfection. The central doorway is approached by a flight of granite steps with original wrought-iron railings. Virtually unaltered interior on double-depth plan with finely detailed entrance hall and stair hall. Good Rococo plasterwork. To the rear a contemporary WALLED GARDEN and ICE HOUSE.

TREVALES, ½ m. SE. Small country house, mid-C18, but over-powered by late C19 extension and remodelling.

STOKE CLIMSLAND

Much of the parish has long been in the ownership of the Duchy of Cornwall, reflected in its good C20 estate-village housing planned around the large green.

ALL SAINTS. A large church sitting well in the landscape above the upper reaches of the Tamar valley, its fine W tower visible for miles. The tower is C15, of regular granite blocks in three stages with the buttresses set back from the angles and large octagonal corner turrets with crocketed pinnacles, all very like Lezant, North Hill, South Petherwin, etc. Of the church dedicated in 1321 nothing is visible except the E responds of the arcades with typically complex profiles. The rest is C15–C16 with buttressed N and S aisles and Perp windows (some replaced in the C19 in Dec), and an especially large and handsome E window in the N chancel chapel. S porch with fine panelled and studded door. The interior is graciously proportioned, light and spacious, with six-bay N and S arcades. The nave piers are square with four attached demi-shafts as at Callington (in the S aisle Polyphant, in the N aisle granite with Polyphant capitals), and simple double-chamfered arches: they are older than the lower chancel arcades with piers of Cornish standard profile. Ceiled wagon roofs with bosses at intersections. Rather thoroughly restored 1856–8 by *J. H. Hakewill* of London. – STAINED GLASS. Chancel E, 1851 and chancel N, 1837 by *William Wailes*. – MONUMENTS. Three fine early C17 slates, unfortunately relegated to the vestry at the rear of the N aisle. – John Bagwell †1623, rector and chaplain to James I. He is kneeling with hands clasped on a prayer-desk with the figure of Death behind about to shoot a dart into him. – Clara and Maria Harrington †1603, two kneeling figures within the two arches of a round-headed pilastered arcade. – Another without inscription showing husband and wife and kneeling children.

VILLAGE HALL, 80 yds NW. By *Richardson & Gill, c.* 1919. Modestly scaled. Neoclassical front with cupola over.

WHITEFORD TEMPLE, ½ m. SSW. A folly in the form of a small classical temple, the most substantial evidence of the former mansion and estate of Sir John Call of 1779, built on his return from India; the house was demolished in 1913. Granite ashlar front with triple round-headed arcade and pediment flanked by two lower lean-to wings: both lean-tos have recessed *Coade* stone plaques of a reclining female figure, the r. with a sheaf of corn, the l. a stack of bales with sailing ship background. Some GARDEN WALLS and a much altered SERVICE RANGE survive just to the S.

DUCHY COLLEGE, ½ m. w. Part of the Whiteford estate which became the home farm of the Duchy of Cornwall from 1913 when the substantial farmhouse, lodges, cotttages, and a handsome range of farm buildings on a courtyard plan were built by *Richardson & Gill*: the house incorporates some of the fabric and fittings from Whiteford. From 1984 it was the county agricultural college, it is now the independent Duchy College as part of Cornwall College, with a campus evolved around the original home farm buildings. The CAMPUS CENTRE is the courtyard range of former farm buildings, the main front with a two-bay two-storey gabled centre dated 1913 with the Duchy insignia, surmounted by a slender cupola, and flanked by five-bay wings, the l. originally an open arcade. The more recent buildings, some by the *Trewin Design Partnerhsip* (e.g the PENDRAY BUILDING of 1998) are clustered around in a manner reminiscent of a prosperous farmstead, well judged in scale and reticence of design, and mostly timber-clad.

HORSE BRIDGE, 2½ m. E. 1457, remarkably similar to Greystone Bridge, Lezant. Bridge over the Tamar and the border with Devon. Five segmental arches, recessed in the simple chamfering and double ring of voussoirs, between cutwaters that rise to refuges at the parapet.

KIT HILL. *See* p. 262.

STRATTON

2000

A medieval settlement that became a substantial market town and administrative centre, flourishing until the end of the C19 when the arrival of the railway in 1898 fuelled the rapid rise of Bude as a seaside resort. Its gentle decline in the C20 has ensured the survival of its charming, coherent character, its narrow little streets climbing up the hill to the church.

ST ANDREW. A fine church, the mother church of Bude. Tall stately w tower of three stages with unusual polygonal set-back buttresses, embattled parapet, and crocketed pinnacles on grotesques in Ham Hill stone. Good w doorway, window and statue niche in Ham Hill stone, like the pinnacles a late C19 replacement of the C14 Polyphant original; it is very similar in design to the arrangement at Lewannick. The decoration is unusually elaborate for Cornwall with small pilasters to the doorway rising to frame the window, and culminating in tall gabled and crocketed pinnacles and an ogee hoodmould rising to a crocketed finial. The statue niche appears medieval. Most of the window tracery in the body of the church renewed in the late C19. N aisle C14, financed 1348 by Sir Ralph de Blanchminster, who expressed a wish in his will to be buried in this aisle. Square Polyphant piers with four attached demi-shafts, and double-chamfered pointed arches: only the three w bays are original, the eastern bays rebuilt late C19. s arcade granite, Cornish standard. Good wagon roofs throughout. The character of the interior is much influenced by the church's enrichment in a series of late C19 and early C20 restorations: the most striking is the ROOD SCREEN, 1901–13 by *E. H. Sedding*, erected in stages but eventually running right across the church. – FONT. Plain, Norman, circular. – PULPIT. Plain Jacobean with panels of round-headed blind arches. – BENCH-ENDS, mostly in the N aisle, not as interesting as many others of more diverse patterns in the neighbourhood. – Exceptionally large plaster ROYAL ARMS, Charles I, with strapwork decoration, like those at Boconnoc, Kilkhampton, Launcells, Marhamchurch, Poundstock and Poughill. – Large chamfered arched recess in N wall of chancel, unlikely to be an EASTER SEPULCHRE as often reported as it is too small and plain. – STAINED GLASS. A splendid array of late C19 and early C20 glass with several of the leading firms represented. Of special note: chancel E by *Morris & Co.* with figures by *Burne-Jones*, and w windows of tower and N aisle, 1906 and 1904 by *Kempe & Co.* – s aisle windows, 1888 by *Ward & Hughes*. – N aisle E and easternmost window of N aisle, 1896 by *Clayton & Bell*. – MONUMENTS. – EFFIGY of a cross-legged knight, preserved on the sill of a N window, probably Sir Ralph de Blanchminster. – BRASS. Sir John Arundell of Trerice †1561 and two wives: three brass figures, inscription and armorial bearings set in stone matrix, formerly the top of an altar tomb. – In the churchyard NE of the church TOMB of Anca Winand van Wulfften †1922 by *Tom Rosandic*, a large bronze of a harping youth; and N of the lychgate early C17 CHEST TOMB of Nicholas Westlake †1620.

It is well worth exploring the main streets – Church Street, Fore Street and Market Street – and the smaller lanes and drangways leading off them, to gain a sense of the old town, with specially good survivals of C19 shopfronts. Nos. 1 and 2 CHURCH SQUARE may have originated as a guildhouse, late C15 to early C16 with five-bay arch-braced roof. On the s side of the square the POST OFFICE, DWELLING HOUSE and THE DRANGWAY, originally a three-room and cross-passage C16 house, the passage surviving as the rear of the drangway between the square and Gibraltar Square behind, marked by two granite arched doorways. Many good C16 and C17 interior features including rich C17 plasterwork and C16 linenfold panelling. GIBRALTAR HOUSE, Church Square, late C18, has large sixteen-pane sashes and two plaques, RS GIBR 1785 and 12th REGT FOOT. In Fore Street a nice group on the w side including THE TREE INN, C16 in origin, the house adjoining downhill, and KERSONE COTTAGES, late C18 brick in Flemish bond.

MEMORIAL, ½ m. N, to the Civil War battle of Stamford Hill. Erected 1713 by Lord Lansdown using a late C15 church pinnacle.

TALLAND

St Tallanus. Set high on the cliffs above Talland beach, the mother church of West Looe (*see* Looe) and the E half of Polperro (q.v.). It was in the possession of Launceston Priory *c.* 1200 and apparently C13 fabric survives at the W end of the nave, with three lancet windows with cusped heads, and three buttresses. Of the same date the E wall of the church and perhaps the lower storey of the tower. This is of three storeys, built into the hillside, with set-back buttresses on the S face, and battlements. What is remarkable is its very unusual position, detached from the church to the S but connected with it by a wagon-roofed late C15 or early C16 porch: is it in this position better to act as a daymark? The main body of the church is probably also late C15 to early C16: nave of six bays, spacious six-bay S aisle and N transept chapel. The piers are of granite and standard Cornish section on tall moulded bases, with horizontal leaf decoration to the capitals, the arches four-centred. Most of the other windows are Perp too, except the chancel with its C13 three-light lancet with cusped heads, partly restored. Fine carved wagon roofs to S aisle, restored 1907. Nave roof largely replaced in clumsy restoration of 1848–50 by *Charles Walcott*, using some medieval material. The church is very completely pewed. – FONT. C15, ornamented with quatrefoils in panels and nice lead lining of 1672. – BENCH-ENDS. A fine collection, partly *c.* 1525, partly *c.* 1600 (cf. Lansallos), including intertwined foliage, carved figureheads and Renaissance detailing. The bench-ends at the corners of each block have angels with scroll, chalice, etc., as crowning features. The bench-ends in the N transept are Jacobean with names of Sir Bernard and Lady Elizabeth Grenville. – CHOIR STALLS made up of fragments from Bernard Grenville's pew, with remains of the early C17 rood screen taken down in the mid-C19 restoration. – PULPIT and READING DESK, Jacobean with carved panels. – MONUMENTS. Two of the most outstanding slate monuments in Cornwall. – Tomb-chest and inscription panel of John Beville †1578, signed by *Peter Crocker* of Looe (cf. Pelynt and St Martin-by-Looe). Remarkably fine figure in high relief on the top and bull on the W end of the chest, inscriptions and arms all incised in slate with rich iconography, including herms and columns in the early Egyptianizing style. – Slate slab to Joanne Mellow †1625 and her baby, who both died in childbirth: the touching carving in shallow relief represents mother and baby sitting in a four-poster bed and is executed in unusually sharp perspective for its date.

TEHIDY

The former seat of the Bassets, one of the great Cornish mining dynasties, who acquired the manor *c.* 1150 through marriage

Tehidy. Engraving after W. Borlase, 1758

to a Dunstanville heiress. Though of great historic interest as
the hub of mining entrepreneurship (cf. Camborne, Redruth
and adjoining parishes), what survives after the sad depletions
of the C20 is hardly enough to evoke a real sense of the wealth
and prestige of the family in its prime. That is perhaps best
conveyed by the proud Dunstanville monument on the summit
of Carn Brea (q.v.), to which the estate looked s.

Nothing is known of the houses on this site before 1736 when a
new house for John Pendarves Basset was begun. It was
designed by *Thomas Edwards* of Greenwich, his first Cornish
project from which he went on to build or remodel a string of
other Cornish houses (cf. Carclew; the Mansion House and
Princes House, Truro; Nanswhyden, near St Columb; Trelowarren; and Trewithen). He also rebuilt Helston church.
Tehidy was an imposing Palladian mansion with a main pedimented block set at the centre of four detached quadrant
pavilions. The main block was destroyed by fire in 1916 but
three of the pavilions survived (the NE pavilion had been lost
in a remodelling and extension of the 1860s by *William Burn*),
and were incorporated into a rebuilding as a hospital in 1922.
The site was redeveloped between 1997 and 2000 with an
estate of new houses built so close to the main approach as to
rob the old house of much of its remaining dignity.

The main elevation is now a curious composition with the 1922
rebuild in classical style making an awkward link between the
SE and NE pavilions, its proportions not helped by an exag-
geratedly tall central clock tower. The pavilions are of scored
stucco, rectangular, with twelve-pane sashes at the ground
floor and four-pane sashes above, all with raised surrounds and
keystones. They rise rather impressively by hipped rectangular
roofs to four tall chimneys gathered around central lanterns
with a large keyed oculus in each face. The SE pavilion has a
large round-arched recess containing a statue of Flora in *Coade*
stone. The NW pavilion is similar.

A section of the former parkland is now a country park. The KEEPER'S COTTAGE, Cot Road, single-storey with a steeply pitched pyramidal thatched roof and apex chimney, and the EAST and SOUTH LODGES with similar thatched roofs, are nice examples of the Picturesque style of the late C18. The lodges have very prominent one-and-a-half-storey gabled porches in granite ashlar rising to wider gables carried on moulded corbels, and lozenge-and-diamond leaded glazing.

TEMPLE

1070

ST CATHERINE. The Knights Templar acquired a large block of land on Bodmin Moor *c.* 1150 and the place was named after the order. The church, of diminutive scale but strangely impressive in its remote moorland location, was reconstructed from ruins in 1882–3 by *Silvanus Trevail*. At least some of the foundations of the earlier building were reused, with the w tower rebuilt above the C12 and C13 lower stage. The tower is a remarkable example of how thick the language of the Middle Ages becomes in the hands of one of the more original later Victorians: of special note is Trevail's unusual, and highly successful, use of proportions in which the second stage is recessed and the top corbelled out as a heavy battlemented parapet. One- and two-light lancet windows to nave, chancel and N transept with reused cusped head and spandrels on N side of nave. The interior is of striking simplicity with whitewashed walls under a plain arch-braced roof. – FONT. Plain, circular Norman bowl on restored stem and square base. – STAINED GLASS with subjects largely relating to Knights Templar and Hospitaller (the latter held Temple by 1332). – Chancel E, 1883 by *Lavers, Barraud & Westlake.* – Tower N, 1883, includes a Templar on horseback.

To the s of the church, a late C19 STORE, probably contemporary with the rebuilding and by *Trevail*, since it incorporates fragments of the earlier church and several crosses including the emblems of the Knights Hospitaller on the N wall, a granite wheel-head cross as a finial on the W gable-end and Latin cross on the E gable-end.

BROCKBARROW COMMON, 1 m. NE. Around sixty ruined houses and huts among small enclosures on the open moor. Larger buildings up to 42½ ft (13 metres) in diameter are perfect ROUND-HOUSES, probably Middle Bronze Age; large upright granite slabs define inner and outer faces. Smaller less circular huts, some just 13 ft (4 metres) across, formed of stony banks, may be summer homes of early medieval transhumants. Location and lack of extensive fields suggest the prehistoric settlement was pastoral.

STRIPPLE STONES, 1¼ m. N, on natural shelf s of Hawk's Tor Important later Neolithic regional meeting place, the south-west's only CIRCLE HENGE. Large stone circle, 151 ft (46 metres) in diameter, with around twenty-eight stones originally (thirteen survive, of which four are still upright), and a taller central stone, around 10 ft (3 metres) high when standing. Encircled by a ditch with bank beyond.

TRIPPET STONES, 1¼ m. NW. Impressive Early Bronze Age STONE CIRCLE, 108 ft (33 metres) diameter, with originally around twenty-seven evenly spaced stones, of which twelve remain. Victorian bound stone near centre. Carefully selected stones, most with fairly flat tops. Placed precisely on line with the entrance to Stripple Stones henge, whose circle is visible on E skyline.

3050

TIDEFORD

The parish was created from St Germans in 1852.

ST LUKE. 1845 by *George Wightwick*, a very competent Gothic essay with good Perp style window tracery. The slate-hung bellcote now stands somewhat curiously, though still housing the bell, by the S porch. Nave with four-bay hammerbeam roof rising from stone corbels, with a stepped four-centred arch to the lower roofed chancel. – FONT. Norman, with long well-carved faces at the four corners and large rosettes in circles. It comes from the chapel of St Luke near Bolventor on Bodmin Moor, established by the priories of Montacute and Launceston before 1340. It is indeed of the same Altarnun type as that of St Thomas, Launceston, which may come from the priory.

HESKYN MILL, ¼ m. N. Formerly part of the Port Eliot estate (*see* St Germans). On an early mill site. A rare example, powered by two wheels, one either side of the mill building, and a later C19 engine house for a steam engine with a free-standing chimney. Remarkably complete set of machinery, retained after conversion to a restaurant. Nearby is TIDEFORD BRIDGE, widened in the C18 but incorporating the moulded ribs of the medieval bridge, perhaps of the C14.

0080

TINTAGEL

The experience of Tintagel is unforgettable – 'Black cliffs and caves and storm and wind' Tennyson noted in his diary. Here is scenery of supreme majesty richly infused with history and legend since 1136 when Geoffrey of Monmouth made this windswept headland the birthplace of Arthur in his colourful *History of the Kings of Britain*.

Tintagel possibly started as a small settlement in the Roman period and was a major Dark Age stronghold of a Cornish king or prince long before Richard Earl of Cornwall built his castle here in the C13, no doubt exploiting the Arthurian legend to strengthen his claim to the loyalties of the Cornish. The castle was soon abandoned, but even in ruins it attracted early travellers like Leland 1533–42 and Norden in the early C17. Publication of the first large-scale map of Cornwall in 1699 identifying the headland as 'King Arthur's Castle' stimulated a flow of visitors throughout the C18, but it was only the later C19 that saw Tintagel's rise as a significant part of the rapidly developing Cornish tourist industry, enhanced by the popularity of the Arthurian legend which had been brought to a wider audience through the publication of Tennyson's epic poem *The Idylls of the King* between 1859 and 1869. By the end of the century it could boast one of Cornwall's largest and most luxurious new hotels, and the little village of Trevena, realizing where its future lay, had changed its name to Tintagel. The Arthurian story continued into the C20 with the building of the extraordinary King Arthur's Halls of Chivalry in the centre of the village in the 1920s. Tintagel remains, deservedly, one of the most visited places in Cornwall.

St Materiana (St Metherian). All on its own on a bleak treeless headland, a setting that only enhances the best small Norman church in Cornwall. Excavations in the NW of the churchyard have revealed C6 burials linking it with the early medieval settlement on the island of Tintagel Castle (*see* below) and evidence of one or possibly two much smaller and earlier chapels on this site. The present building is predominantly Norman, Early Norman too with certain features reminiscent of the Anglo-Saxon. Cruciform plan with chapel to N of chancel and sturdy three-stage C15 W tower. The low, narrow, sparsely windowed nave and chancel, their massively thick walls, and the dark interior impart an authentic Norman character throughout. The earliest part is the N wall of the nave with a very Saxon-looking doorway and two tiny windows l. and r. in Catacleuse. The S door is Norman, of modest size, with one order of columns with scalloped capitals. W of it another early window. The N chancel chapel is a slightly later Norman addition of great interest as a chapel of such early date in a relatively small church. All the windows have deep inner splays and a slight chamfering on the outside. More Norman details in the chevron moulding of the chancel arch and the arch connecting the S transept and the nave, the latter with its imposts at a curiously low level. The N transept and the longer S transept seem to have been first planned in the C12 but not built until the C13. E.E. lancet three-light window in the E wall of the N transept, late C13 E windows to the S transept, plain C14 N porch and C14 canopied sepulchral niche in the S arch of the chancel. There was extensive restoration in 1868–70 by *J. P. St Aubyn* which replaced the medieval roofs with arch- and wind-braced roofs throughout, rebuilt the W walls of the S and N transepts and the S porch, installed a three-light window to replace the previous Norman E window of the chancel, and removed the medieval bench-ends. FITTINGS. – FONT. Norman, mid-C12. Square and plain except for faces at the corners, on five feet, the four in the corners octagonal. Also possible Norman font bowl at the W end of the nave brought from the chapel on the island. – ROOD SCREEN. *c.* 1500 with Perp. tracery. – REREDOS. Made of the C16 bench-ends, with some from St Teath. Usual symbols of the Passion and heraldic devices. More pieces in the READING DESK. – STONE BENCH. C15, runs continuously around the W and S walls of the S transept. – ALTAR. Pre-Reformation stone altar in N chancel chapel. – STAINED GLASS. E window, 1991, by *Alfred Fisher*. A medley of Eucharistic themes, wild flowers and children. – MONUMENTS. Fine C13 slab with head *en face* above a foliated cross. – BRASS. Joanna Kelly, *c.* 1430, set in W wall of S transept. – DOOR HINGES. Re-set in the N door. Original C12 ironwork, among the earliest in Cornwall. – INSCRIBED STONE. Round stone at W end of S transept inscribed IMP C G VAL LIC LICIN. The inscription refers to the Emperor Licinius, A.D. 308–24.

10　TINTAGEL CASTLE. The prospect of the ruinous castle improbably set half on a sheer cliff, half on an island, joined only by a narrow neck of land between, is dramatic and memorable. These are the remains of the castle built by Earl Richard from 1233, overlaying the C5 and C6 stronghold. The site is best viewed from either the church or Camelot Castle Hotel (*see* below) before approaching the castle itself by a narrow path below high walls on a high crag to the l. and the Great Ditch to the r. The Ditch, following the line of a natural fault visible on the hill opposite, was first dug as part of the Dark Age defences, and it was the narrowness of this approach that gave the site its name *Dim Tagell*, the Fortress of the Narrow Entrance.

The entrance is through the remains of the gate-tower into the lower part of the outer courtyard, originally larger before about a quarter of it collapsed into the sea. The upper courtyard, reached by stairs in the cliff face, has similarly been reduced, by probably a half. In the curtain wall the remains of two latrines, and on the floor of the courtyard a group of stone-floored rooms of late medieval date with the lower grass-topped walls of earlier buildings, possibly of the early medieval period. Steep steps lead down to the modern bridge over the isthmus, with views of the Haven where ships were beached and unloaded.

At the top of the steps to the island, the inner castle court is entered through a battlemented wall, built in 1852 by Richard Kinsman, vicar of Tintagel, after the castle had become a tourist attraction. This area was the heart of the C13 castle with the remains of Earl Richard's Great Hall and service rooms built on a heavily buttressed platform clinging limpet-like to the side of the cliff; even so, one end has been lost to the sea. Opposite, a two-roomed building with steps to the former upper floor, probably a private chamber. As early as 1272 the buildings were reported as being in disrepair and in the early C14 the roof of the Great Hall was removed and a new two-storey house built within its walls.

Through the archway in the battlemented wall at the N end of the courtyard is a path to the Iron Gate, a defended rock-wharf. The main path leads to the top of the Island and its spectacular sea and cliff views, and the best place to see the sheer daring of the siting of the outer court. In this area is much visible evidence of both Dark Age and later medieval settlement. Along the more sheltered eastern slopes are four small groups of ruined buildings, C5 and C6, with another group at the N end, from which more Mediterranean ware has been found than from all other early medieval sites in Britain put together. Remains, now grassed over, have also been revealed of over 150 other buildings of the same period. Of the later medieval period there is a small walled enclosure for a garden, a well, a rock-hewn tunnel (probably a medieval larder) and the remains of the late C16 St Juliot's Chapel.

PERAMBULATION. The village has an enjoyable variety of build-ings, reflecting the honourable place that tourism, ancient and modern, has in Cornwall's history. In FORE STREET, there are good examples of small C18 cottages with rag slate roofs and gabled dormers hidden among the larger C19 buildings. Of particular significance is the OLD POST OFFICE, apparently the 59 archetypal and picturesque Cornish cottage – low, dark, with rag slate roofs like a cluster of hills and of a slatey hue like elephant hide – but originally a substantial town house of medieval origin with mid-C16–C17 improvements.* It was acquired by the National Trust in 1900 with funds raised by local artists and extensively repaired in 1896 by *Detmar Blow*, and again in the late C20. The medieval house may have origi-nated as a three-room plan: a hall and inner hall divided by a through passage from a lower-end room, all originally open to the roof. In about the mid C16 the eaves were heightened and the building was re-roofed. Floors were inserted to the rooms at either end during the C17 and a winder stair-turret was added to link the hall with the chamber above the inner room. The three-bay hall remained open to the roof until floored in the C19: it was later removed. The upper floor at the lower end is now accessed by a late C19 staircase. What is remarkable is the survival of the open hall's display of C16 roof carpentry: raised cruck-trusses with curved feet and cranked collars, the princi-pals only joined at the apexes by being stepped and abutted, with a threaded diagonal ridge and threaded purlins. The large lateral stack was first added to the front in the C16 but rebuilt in its present stepped form in the late C19. The gabled two-storey former porch at the higher end was added post-1862 (based on evidence in an engraving from a sketch by Maclean) but

*This account draws on research by Eric Berry, Joanna Mattingly and Nigel Thomas.

incorporates a mullioned window of reused C17 fragments. The porch fronting the passage is also post-1862 but incorporates a doorway made up from C16 doorway fragments. Several reused small single-light windows of C15 round-headed form are of solid pieces of local greenstone. The ancient appearance of this building is therefore partly an illusion, but the late C19 'earlying-up' work adds to the extraordinary vernacular character.

Further along Fore Street, in front of Kays Mews, a STONE CROSS, removed here from Trevillet in 1875. Round head, much eroded, of a very unusual form. Long inscriptions on both sides: Matthew – Markus – Lucas – John on the one, 'Aelnat ficit hanc crucem pro anima sua' on the other, a remarkable instance of the dedication of a cross. Aelnat is a Saxon, not a Celtic name: the miniscules are Hiberno-Saxon. Next door, TREVENA HOUSE, three-window front with canted bays, built 1860 for J. D. Cook, founder-editor of the *Saturday Review*, but from 1928 remodelled by *Frederick Glassock* as the headquarters of his Fellowship of the Knights of the Round Table of King Arthur,* opened in 1933. Two halls at the rear: an inner hall with large paintings of the Arthurian legend by *William Hatherell*, and beyond the spectacular HALL OF CHIV-ALRY. This dramatic space, tall and wide with aisle-like cor-ridors, culminates at its E end in a round table and vast canopied and columned throne approached by a flight of steps, all in different Cornish granites. A rich variety of Cornish building stones elsewhere – walls of Polyphant and Tintagel stone, floor of Polyphant inset with patterns of the round table in red porphyry and the cross of the knights in white elvan, shields of different colours around the walls. The hall's char-acter is, however, defined by a major ensemble of STAINED GLASS by *Veronica Whall*. Seventy-three windows in the Arts and Crafts tradition, a complete scheme at different scales and with varied motifs. Three large round-headed windows at the E and W ends with scenes from the life of King Arthur; nine clerestory windows on both N and S sides of the knightly virtues; and forty-one smaller windows in the aisles of the devices of the knights. The strong figurative work, colours, textures and glazing techniques are exquisitely executed.

CAMELOT CASTLE HOTEL, Atlantic Road. Formerly King Arthur's Castle Hotel. 1896 by *Silvanus Trevail*, the epitome of his ambition and vision as the driving force behind the devel-opment of Cornish tourism in the later C19, here harnessing the Arthurian legend to his cause and linking his hotel as closely as possible to the county's most renowned historic site. From its western terrace, there is no better place to appreciate the castle, especially against the setting sun. The hotel is con-ceived as the keep of a medieval castle, tall and square on the

116

*The fellowship was modelled on Freemasonry and had a worldwide membership of over 17,000 by the early 1930s: it was wound up in 1937 after Glassock's death. He was the founding partner of Monk and Glass Custard of Clerkenwell, London.

headland above the C13 castle ruins and visible for miles along the north Cornish coast. The entrance front is pure showmanship, using all the devices of the archetypal castle to create the desired dramatic effect: battered walls, a central entrance tower rising to five storeys with octagonal turrets, and projecting four-storey corner towers above the main three-storey build, all crenellated with machicolations and arrowslits. To this medieval artifice Trevail adds a medieval porte cochère, a practical necessity on such a windswept site. The other elevations are more domestic with round and square bays and balconies and more obviously hotel-like. The interior, almost unaltered, offers an unparalleled opportunity to experience the heady mix of Arthurian drama and late C19 luxury that Trevail intended for the visitor. A relatively modest entrance lobby with mosaic tiled floor and panelled walls opens up first into the staircase hall from which the imperial staircase rises majestically through three full storeys, and then into the vast GREAT HALL. This is designed around Trevail's replica of the C14 Round Table at Winchester, set between five-bay round-arched Romanesque arcades with Italian marble piers with cushion capitals supported by short corbelled colonettes. The DINING ROOM is of similarly impressive scale, planned to enjoy unsurpassed views of the castle, cliffs and sea. All the ground-floor rooms display rich decoration, the outstanding features the elaborate Gothic chimneypieces (the largest at either end of the Great Hall), in limestone with darker sandstone bands, marble colonettes and decorative tiles – Arthurian knights in the Great Hall, the seasons in the dining room, floral elsewhere. Melodramatic it may be, but as a stage set for Trevail's tourist theatre it is a triumph.

TINTAGEL VICARAGE, Vicarage Hill. Pretty C19 fenestration to older house. In the garden a DOVECOTE, medieval, round with conical roof, built into the bank. Low domed vaulted roof, and 250 rectangular stone nesting boxes arranged in three tiers. The potence has been removed.

At BOSSINEY, ½ m. E, METHODIST CHAPEL. 1860, with pretty Gothick windows.

PRINCE OF WALES QUARRY, 2 m. SE. ENGINE HOUSE, completed 1872, restored 1976. Dramatically sited above the former quarry. Unusual plan with the chimney attached at the SW corner, and used for both pumping out the quarry and winding, in this case hauling trucks from the Borthwick quarry across the valley.

TONACOMBE MANOR

½ m. SSE of Morwenstow

In Sedding's estimation 'the most delightful medieval home left in the county'. A romantic survival of a largely C16 house in remote country that has retained its genteel charm. Like nearby Marsland, it was of double courtyard plan in the C16 and even today its surrounding walls and s gatehouse range give it a fortified appearance. Entered through an arched granite doorway, the chamber of the gatehouse is accessed by stone steps in a lean-to projection within a narrow courtyard with the main range opposite. It consists of three rooms and through passage with open hall and parlour at the higher end heated by rear lateral stacks, and a second smaller parlour with solar above to the rear of the large parlour. A rear range, demolished in the C19, may have been the C16 service range. There was extensive late C16 refurbishment and the addition of two parlours to the rear of the main range in the early C18. Picturesque elevations with many mullioned windows. The interior retains its open hall and gallery with a five-bay roof of moulded arch-braced trusses with slightly cranked collars and two tiers of threaded purlins. The E end of the hall has 1578 wainscot panelling with frieze and fluted pilasters, and there is extensive similar panelling in other rooms. The immediate environment of the house is equally charming, the surrounding walls creating a pleasance to the E. A lower courtyard and carriageway to the W are probably C17 in origin, the latter with gatepiers at either end, surmounted by the Waddon falcon. At least some of the materials at Tonacombe may have come from the demolished house at Stowe (*see* Kilkhampton).

TORPOINT

The town was created in the late C18 to house workers from the Plymouth Dock (now Devonport Dockyard). Its design, on a strong grid-iron pattern, was commissioned by Reginald Pole-Carew of Antony in 1774 and its building supervised by *Samuel Harvey*: in 1787 there were only forty-four houses but by 1821 there were over 240. The establishment of the Royal Navy's major training facility at nearby HMS *Raleigh* boosted its population during the C20. Despite substantial later C20 depredations enough survives of the town plan in Fore Street and adjacent streets and around the waterside to convey something of the character of the historic settlement.

St James the Great, Salamanca Street. Built 1816–17 as a chapel of ease to Antony to serve the rapidly expanding town. A plain rectangle with small bellcote and clock at E end, altered and extended with a Gothic E end in 1884–6 by *William White*, who had worked at Antony earlier (q.v.). The original windows were Gothick, of which one survives, now internal, of three lights with cusped tracery in cast iron, and the church was galleried on the N, W and S sides. White installed E.E.

lancets, removed the N and S sections of the gallery, and built a new chancel with gabled N chancel aisle, cross-gabled choir vestry, and lean-to clergy vestry. From the outside White's additions look rather awkward against the bulky box of the nave, but the interior effect is surprisingly pleasing and effective. The W gallery, nicely curved back in the centre, stands on iron columns. The chancel arch is four-centred with a narrower arch to the N chapel: a second arch within the chancel and single arches to the N and S sides create the effect of a crossing tower. Four-bay arch-braced chancel roof on corbels.

TORPOINT METHODIST CHURCH. Prominently sited at the junction of Fore Street and Quarry Street. Dated 1795 on the Quarry Street entrance front; extended along Fore Street in 1908. Entrance front with rusticated pilasters, pediment, central pair of recessed doors and two-light round-headed windows with roundels. Round-headed windows to Fore Street. The gallery over the vestibule is of 1795, on cast-iron fluted piers. At the opposite end the rostrum has cast-iron panels in fish-scale pattern, and some pews with cast-iron panels.

TOR HOUSE, Salamanca Street, facing the W front of the church. Dated 1792, built for Joshua Rowe, proprietor of the Crinnis mines near St Austell. It stands on a terrace and is approached by a central flight of fourteen granite steps. Block-shaped, three-storey and three-bay elevations with central Doric porch on the entrance front. French windows to l. and r. with Gothick margin glazing and overlights, sash windows above, a fenestration pattern repeated on the return elevation. The interior, on a double-depth plan, is uncommonly richly detailed. The entrance hall has a double vault with decorative plasterwork and a vaulted open-well staircase, the stair with Doric newel and cast-iron balusters with a lyre pattern baluster to alternative steps. The rest of the house has much fine detail including plasterwork decoration that unusually extends to the attic storey.

THANCKES PARK, to the N of the town. The former grounds of Thanckes House, the late C19 house of Lord Graves that was moved to Portwrinkle (q.v.) in 1909–10.

TORPOINT CHAIN FERRY, across the Tamar to Devonport. In 1831 the sailing-boat service, in regular use since 1791, was replaced by a 'floating bridge' designed by *James Meadows Rendel*, engineer, who had pioneered the bridge for Dartmouth. It was later used at Saltash. Engines drive teethed wheels engaging with permanent fixed chains, shore to shore, that run on board the ferry but otherwise hang down in the river allowing other shipping to pass. Behind the ferry the early C20 FERRY OFFICES in an austere Georgian by *Thomas Percy Endean*.

CAREW WHARF, just S of the ferry. Late C18 and early C19 former WAREHOUSES, converted to housing c. 2000. The two-storey twelve-bay warehouse with heavy raking buttresses that juts out into the river was the Western Counties & General Manure Co.

stores supplying fertilizer and guano to the market gardens of the Tamar valley.

Further s on Marine Drive the Torpoint Yacht Harbour incorporating the BALLAST POND, 1783, built by the Admiralty with French prisoners of war for barges to load or unload ballast for the navy.

4030

TOWEDNACK

St WINWALOE. Loveable and diminutive, in fields below the Penwith moorland. A chapelry of Lelant until 1902, but the Norman ALTAR SLAB with consecration crosses (recovered in 1934), and a large stone with incised cross used as a BENCH in the s porch, show evidence of an early church in this place. Low, two-stage w tower without buttresses or pinnacles, possibly C14: the NE stair-turret is accessed up steps from the w end of the nave. C13 nave and chancel (cf. the N wall, especially thick in the chancel). The most remarkable feature is the double-chamfered chancel arch of *c.* 1300, unique so far west in Cornwall. A s aisle was added in the C15, the four-bay arcade with octagonal piers and four-centred arches. The intersecting tracery of the E window and its cusping point to the end of the C13 (cf. Zennor). All the other windows renewed, most of the originals having gone before *J. D. Sedding*'s restoration of 1869–70, which also replaced all the roofs in a plain, dignified form that suits the simplicity of the interior. – FONT. Granite, octagonal, with faces at the corners, dated 1720. Its base is the inverted bowl of a Norman font. – BENCH-ENDS. On N wall. With the profiles of James Trevella and Matthew Trenwith and dated 1633, remarkably late. In the churchyard, a wheel-headed WAYSIDE CROSS and a small GABLE CROSS.

Former SCHOOLROOM, ¼ m. E. Plain, sash-windowed, early C19, remodelled mid C19.

3070

TRECARREL
1½ m. WSW of Lezant

What survives is eloquent testimony to the ambition of the great house of Henry Trecarrel, Mayor of Launceston in 1536 and 1543, who rebuilt St Mary Magdalene at Launceston and died 1544. Probably originally on a courtyard plan but either reduced or never completed. Its s elevation of granite ashlar has a large window with ogee tracery to light the high end of the Great Hall, two high-set ogee-headed lights (cf. Cotehele), and a four-centred arched doorway to the screens passage with Trecarrel's arms impaling those of Kelway, his wife's family, over. The splendid roof has been restored as an open hall of ten arch-braced trusses with one bay of re-set wind-braces: it bears comparison with the roofs of similar date at Cotehele and Roscarrock (qq.v.). Rear lateral fireplace with cusped lintel. Off the lower end a wing with early C16 arch-braced roof, extended E: its E front incorporates reused C17 windows and doorway.

The early C16 CHAPEL, also in granite ashlar, stands SE of the house, of small scale but high quality, with angle buttresses, traceried E window, and a four-centred arched W doorway. The interior, with a wagon roof, has evidence for a W gallery incorporating a priest's lodging chamber accessed by a former stone stair with its own fireplace and garderobe. C16–C19 FARM BUILDINGS of strong vernacular character.

TREGAMINION see POLKERRIS

TREGANTLE FORT see ANTONY

TREGONY   *9040*

An early medieval port until the river silted up and a borough before 1086 – it sent two members to Parliament before 1832. Of the castle, church of St James and chapel of St Anne noted by Leland, nothing remains. In 1934 it was merged with St Cuby parish. Now a little town of pleasant early to mid-C19, mostly terraced, houses and cottages. From the causeway and bridge over the diminutive Fal the settlement winds up Tregony Hill to Fore Street as one long street, curving gently and widening out at its centre around the eyecatcher of a clock tower, much like Grampound (q.v.).

ST CUBY. Low W tower in two stages with diagonal buttresses and a two-centred arch to the W door, early C15. The N wall of the nave and the N transept show medieval masonry but large sections of the upper walls were rebuilt during major C19 restorations, starting in 1828 and finished by J. P. St Aubyn in 1899; the tracery is typical of the pre-antiquarian early C19. The outstanding feature is the C15 S porch added on to the S aisle: it has a pointed tunnel-vault with transverse arches, closely comparable to Creed and Luxulyan (qq.v.), with two heads of kings as a boss in the apex of the middle arch. Its S wall is a charming antiquarian confection using Norman capitals, a round-headed arch and more kings' heads as label stops. Strong C19 character inside with arch-braced roofs of that date and rebuilt six-bay S arcade with octagonal piers and four-centred arches, reusing two C15 pier shafts at the E end. – FONT. Late Norman, Bodmin type, with the same heads at the corners, and motifs of animals, knots, and trees of life between. – PULPIT. Hexagonal, incorporating C16 bench-ends. – ROYAL ARMS. Of James II, painted, one of only four in Cornwall, and another, of 1831. – MONUMENT. Hugh Pomeroy †1644, broad crucifix with bead-and-reel enriched oval border surrounding shield and inscription. – INSCRIBED STONE. On the exterior of the SW corner of the S aisle: NONNITA ERCILINI RIGATI . . . TRIS FILI ERCILINI; C6 or C7.

CONGREGATIONAL CHURCH, Fore Street. Set back, small and elegant inside and out. Pretty early C19 front with pointed-arched windows with interlaced glazing: interior with three-sided gallery on wooden columns. Its Gothic panelled front carried out on shaped brackets.

METHODIST CHURCH, Fore Street. 1824. Plain, rectangular with round-headed windows with marginal glazing.

CLOCK TOWER, Fore Street. Five stages rising to a timber cupola with ogee lead roof and ball and spirelet finial with weathervane. Dated 1833 at second stage, 1864 at the fourth.

SCHOOL and SCHOOL HOUSE, Fore Street. 1878 by *James Hicks*, extended *c.* 1918. Central range with school house as l. wing, classroom to r., in Gothic and Tudor styles.

ALMSHOUSES, Tregony Hill. Erected 1696 by Hugh Boscawen, extensively rebuilt 1895 by *Silvanus Trevail*. The street front has a wooden-fronted gallery on six short plain granite columns forming a passage to the ground-floor rooms; their windows have lost their mullions. The rear elevation is very different, with two massive lateral stacks, granite mullioned windows to ground and first floor, and the end stacks combining to offer a fine essay in late C17 Cornish vernacular.

8040

TREGOTHNAN

The spectacular mansion of the Falmouths, i.e. the Boscawen family, is immeasurably enhanced by the splendour and scale of its romantic setting. Miles of private drives, most notably from the Tresillian entrance to the N, offer frequent glimpses of sheets of water between hills and wooded valleys before arrival at the formal entrance from the neat estate village of St Michael Penkevil (q.v.). Here the great house sits at the heart of its estate on the crest of a secluded peninsula between the Fal and Truro rivers, looking down S through a Reptonian landscape towards the estuary and Carrick Roads.

Tregothnan was acquired by John Boscawen in 1334. The medieval house, of which a sketch is preserved in a deed of 1611, was of courtyard plan with a prominent gate-tower. Hugh Boscawen (†1701) built a new house adjoining to the NE *c.* 1650, preserving the earlier house as the kitchen court. In turn Hugh Boscawen's house was largely rebuilt by *William Wilkins* in

1816–18 for the 4th Viscount Falmouth, encasing some of the mid-C17 building, of which two complete rooms survive. This was followed by a major enlargement by *Lewis Vulliamy* for the 2nd Earl in 1845–8. Before Wilkins came on the scene there were a number of other more or less castellated designs proposed for Tregothnan including one possibly by *Wyattville* and one by *Humphry Repton*, who produced a Red Book for the estate in 1809.

The combined achievement of Wilkins and Vulliamy is a house of extreme picturesqueness in an elaborate East Anglian Tudor Gothic: the style was, of course, that of Norfolk, Wilkins's native county, but it may also have been influenced by the decision to retain the medieval house as the kitchen court. Vulliamy's extensions, which dramatically elongated the N and S elevations (and in the process finally removed the medieval building), are in the same style and greatly increase the picturesque effect. The plan became a long rectangular range running E–W with a central spine corridor. The irregular elevations, with large mullioned-and-transomed windows, towers, polygonal angle turrets rising to chimneys, battlements and a profusion of tall Tudor terracotta and stone stacks of different designs, are magnificent. As Christopher Hussey remarked, 'the entire conception exemplifies romantic Regency taste keyed up to the same pitch as were George IV's coronation ceremonies and the exotic imperialism of the Royal Pavilion – where Nash's dome and minarets are the contemporaries of Tregothnan's towers'.

The long and astonishing N entrance front, approached from a spacious forecourt enclosed by mid-C19 wrought-iron railings, completely disguises the existence of the mid-C17 house. The three central bays are by Wilkins, the middle one projecting as a two-storey pointed-arched porch behind which rises his four-storey stair-tower. They are flanked to the E by Wilkins's library, extended by one bay by Vulliamy; and to the W by a three-storey tower added by Vulliamy, then two Wilkins bays, a two-storey projecting porch by Vulliamy, and finally a kitchen range connecting through to the office court. The E front is mostly Wilkins though the NE corner is masked by Vulliamy's library extension. The S front is supremely picturesque: it starts at the W end with a projecting gabled bay by Vulliamy, next the five bays with much plainer windows that front the remains of the 1650 house, then an irregular eight bays by Wilkins culminating in a slightly projecting eight-light bay window.

From the two-storeyed gatehouse porch the main entrance leads to Wilkins's impressively tall STAIR HALL in a form of Gothic that appears to have been influenced by Wyatt's at Ashridge, Herts. The staircase is of cantilevered imperial design with a cast-iron balustrade incorporating trefoils and quatrefoils, lit by a clerestory with three three-light windows on both sides of the tower and separated from the upper corridors by Gothic screens. The compartmented ceiling has elaborate heraldic decoration. Wilkins's other interior work is mainly classical, in the Greek style, of fairly restrained design but good quality craftsmanship of which the decoration of the BALLROOM and DRAWING ROOM are notable examples. The two rooms of the 1650 house are the COMMON PARLOUR with a broad-banded geometric and foliated plaster ceiling and a wooden chimneypiece with caryatids, and the room above it, with a plaster ceiling looking somewhat earlier and a chimneypiece looking somewhat later, i.e. typical 1650–60. Compact fruit bundles, thick volutes, very pronounced lugs. The chimneypiece is especially fine with a painted panel, drapery festoons and bolection mouldings. The extent of the survival of other fabric of the mid-C17 house is unclear.

There are extensive service ranges NW of the house in the double courtyard plan of the STABLE YARD and OFFICE YARD, and the CLOCK TOWER. The smaller office yard is by *Wilkins*, the larger stable yard by *Vulliamy*, a lesser version in yellow brick of his additions to the entrance front. The main entrance to the house from the village is announced by C17 GATEPIERS surmounted by ball finials just S of the church. To the l. of the entrance within the estate two early C19 Gothic LODGES. The most distant herald of what is to come is the entrance adjoining the church at Tresillian (q.v.). A pair of gabled LODGES linked by a massive Tudor Gothic ARCH with Tudor roses in the spandrels is surmounted by a huge shaped pediment enclosing the Falmouth arms within a pointed-arch tympanum. The arch contains traceried timber doors. The lodges are flanked by quadrant walls with carved lions, the drive lined with granite bollards linked by chains. Probably 1835 by Vulliamy.

The estate embraces extensive gardens and pleasure grounds giving into parkland, ornamental woodland and carriage drives: the formal gardens lie to the S and SE of the house, the pleasure gardens to the SE and SW. Most of the disposition of woodland, parkland and drives is derived from *Repton*'s proposals of 1809. The arrangements for the drive entrance near the house were altered by *W. A. Nesfield* in the mid C19. He also altered the formal gardens below the S front, subsequently redesigned in the late C20 by *Robert Myers* as a highly successful parterre with reflecting pools. Built into the kitchen garden wall a reused ARCHWAY of *c.* 1675–80 with similarities to the entrance arches at Godolphin and Collacombe, Devon.

0050

TREGREHAN

1 m. SW of St Blazey

The house of the Carlyon family since 1676; the core is of *c.* 1680, built for Thomas Carlyon I. Unusually for the date it was a double-pile house, nearly symmetrical, and planned so that the best rooms faced the sea. Its present appearance is the result of successive remodellings, principally in the late C18 by *William Wood* of Truro and a classical transformation in 1848–9 by *George Wightwick*. The principal elevation is the s front, transformed by Wightwick by the addition of a two-storey range in front of the original. It is of Pentewan ashlar, symmetrical of 1:5:1 bays, the ends broken forward. The mid-C19 Ionic colonnade along the front was removed in 1969 and two of the columns reused for the central doorcase. Set back to l. and r. of this front are pavilion wings added by Wood; of the same period the canted bays. Wightwick moved the entrance to the w front where he created a splendid entrance hall, expanding an existing lobby E by replacing the original wall with a colonnade, doing the same to the N to incorporate a magnificent staircase, and throwing a coved ceiling with intersecting plaster ribs above a reeded band up into the room above. The hall has a fine chimneypiece of red and white marble with detached Ionic columns, and a Vitruvian scroll frieze; a similar chimneypiece in the sw room. In the E range two fine early C18 plaster ceilings in the ground-floor rooms, both with intersecting geometrical figures, probably representing a second campaign by Thomas Carlyon I; the passage to the rear of these rooms has a late C18 moulded ceiling cornice. Above in the attic a granite bressumer in the fireplace inscribed T.C. 1680.

In the 1840s, Edward Carlyon employed *W. E. Nesfield* to design major improvements to the gardens and park. The sweeping approach drive from the w and the forecourt to the entrance front are Nesfield's, as is the Italian parterre to the s with its terrace, walls, a central fountain, urns and statues of the Four Seasons: the spire of St Mary the Virgin, Par (q.v.), is an eye-catcher from the terrace, the land for Street's new church being given by the Carlyons.

To the NE, the service court. On the w, the detached STABLE. Two-storey pedimented block with two-bay wings, the centre with granite pilasters supporting an open pediment with datestone WC 1836. The KITCHEN GARDEN was probably also part of Nesfield's scheme. Datestone 1844 in walls of English bond red brick with granite copings and two mid-C19 GREENHOUSES with S-curve half-hipped end gables to the central block and ribbon pattern cast-iron braces. In the centre, a fountain basin with four entwined dolphins set on a rocky base supporting a shell basin and putto on their raised tails, attributed to Nesfield.

SOUTH LODGE. Pretty Tudor Gothic with lozenge pattern glazing. 1853 by *Thomas J. Colling*.

TRELAWNE

1 m. SE of Pelynt

The former Trelawny mansion, seat of the Royalist Bishop Jonathan Trelawny (1650–1721) buried at Pelynt (q.v.). Now the centre of a holiday park. A Domesday manor, it passed through the Cardinhams, Champernownes and Bevilles before being purchased by the Trelawnys from the crown in 1600. The house's complex history is reflected in its rambling ranges evolved from a standard medieval courtyard plan overlain by the predominantly mid-C19 character imposed by *J. P. St Aubyn*'s thorough rebuilding and remodelling of 1860–2 (there was a previous substantial restoration in 1780 after a major fire). Imposing N entrance range, an irregular composition around the large three-storey entrance tower of the mid C15 with NE stair-turret with quatrefoil lights and a wide two-centred C19 arch. To the l., the chapel raised over a vaulted basement: it was dedicated in 1701 having been rebuilt by Bishop Trelawny on the site of an earlier chapel, and rebuilt again in 1860. To the r., the front of the former hall, rebuilt with C19 windows. A cross-wing at the higher end of the hall incorporates medieval fabric, extended and remodelled *c.* 1700 with C20 extensions masking the W elevation; a stair projection with a *c.* 1700 stair in the angle between hall and wing serves both ranges. Three-storey E elevation with C19 double-gable wing to the l. and single-gable wing to the r. projecting from the earlier range, itself remodelled in the C19. The interior retains *c.* 1700 fittings in the former hall including bolection-moulded panelling and fireplace, the latter incorporating a painted shield with heraldic quartering of the Trelawny marriages, and decorative plasterwork. In the W wing more late C17 or earlier C18 panelling and plasterwork. The chapel has a C19 hammerbeam roof with timber- and stone-carved angels on corbels, some possibly from the medieval chapel.

TRELISSICK

8030

In a sublime position on an elevated site falling away s towards the Fal estuary and commanding fine vistas over Carrick Roads. Soon after 1750 John Lawrence built a new house within a small park, designed by *Edmund Davey*. This was radically remodelled and extended for Thomas Daniell (whose mother was the niece and heiress of Ralph Allen of Prior Park, Bath) by *P. F. Robinson* *c.* 1825 onwards: Robinson's design was published as an example of a 'Residence in the Grecian Style' in his *Designs for Ornamental Villas* of 1827. Further additions were made by *J. P. St Aubyn* in the later C19.

93   The mansion contains the core of the mid-C18 house which comprised a central block of double-depth plan with a ground-floor classical loggia on the s front, flanked E and W by single storey wings for dining and drawing rooms, illustrated on an estate plan of *c.* 1821. Robinson transformed this into the severest neo-Grecian mansion in Cornwall by adding a giant six column Ionic portico after that of the Erechtheion at Athens

to the centre of the s front which screens the recessed five-window front of the original: the result would have appeared especially temple-like when viewed from the river because the flanking wings remained single storey. Robinson also added a single-storey Doric portico on the w entrance front and inserted a top-lit staircase hall behind the entrance hall. The building assumed its present form after St Aubyn added a games room above the portico, lit by dormers, and first floors to the e and w wings. To the e of the house is a solarium with a central Ionic doorway added in 1933 by *M. Joubert* to replace an earlier conservatory.

The house has a very complete C18 and C19 interior. The W ENTRANCE HALL has panelled walls and plaster ceiling divided into six panels with two shell roses and a doorway flanked by two Doric columns that leads to the STAIR HALL. This has a fine open-well open-string stair with iron balusters, some with trailing vine and rose decoration. The ground-floor rooms show some early C19 remodelling of the C18 rooms. The LIBRARY, formerly the dining room, has a chimneypiece and doorcase with enriched pulvinated friezes, cornices with dentils, and other mid-C18-style detail. The DRAWING ROOM is similarly richly decorated with a deeply coved cornice and band, mahogany doors with fluted friezes over, and a fine chimneypiece with caryatids.

In the KITCHEN GARDEN N of the house and enclosed by brick walls is a striking three-storey Flemish Gothic-style former WATER TOWER with a conical slate roof. Also a GAME LARDER, late C19, of octagonal plan with slate roof rising to a ventilator. The mid-C19 former STABLES and CARRIAGE HOUSE and two mid-C19 BARNS have been tactfully converted to visitor facilities: the former is arranged around a courtyard with a central three-storey coachhouse surmounted by a clock with pyramidal roof, enclosed by a wall, all in brick. NE of the house are NEW LODGE, mid-C19 and two-storey Gothic, and NW OLD LODGE, a single-storey stucco building with a classical w pediment supported by Doric columns, *c.* 1825 by Robinson: they represent successive rearrangements of the entrance drives further N and W of the house.

The celebrated GARDENS, PLEASURE GROUNDS and PARK that surround the mansion and offer it the most generous of settings have been developed almost continuously by successive owners since Ralph Allen Daniell ('Guinea-a-Minute Daniel'), father of Thomas, expanded and developed the C18 park creating a network of walks, rides and carriage drives. The C20 reworking of the gardens by *Ida and Ronald Copeland* was definitive for the planting, and the National Trust, the owner of the gardens since 1955, has continued this fine tradition. The exceptionally beautiful wooded grounds have walks overlooking the Fal estuary and offer glimpses of the sumptuous Tregothnan (q.v.) across the water. At one viewpoint on a rocky outcrop to the SE of the house is a charming timber and thatch hexagonal SUMMERHOUSE, 1996 by *Paul Edwards*.

7020

TRELOWARREN

TRELOWARREN

86   Sequestered deep in richly wooded parkland, announced by
      Gothic lodges, and approached by long drives, the long, low-
      lying spread of the great house is historically much more
      complex than it first appears. Mentioned in Domesday, it has
      been the home of the Vyvyans since 1427 and a heavily dis-
      guised medieval and Tudor range lies at the centre of its
      U-shaped plan. The wings projecting w were first built in
      the C17 but the house owes its present appearance principally
      to two later phases of remodelling, one of the mid C18, the
      second of the early C19. Both were remarkable exercises in
      architectural antiquarianism: indeed 'the key to architectural
      appreciation of Trelowarren is provided by the romantic
      backward-looking tradition of the family. The Vyvyans were
      Royalists in the C17, Jacobite in the C18, and ultra-Tory in the
      C19: this consistency is demonstrated in the conscious archa-
      ism of the house.'*

      Norden's map of Cornwall of 1584 shows the C16 house set in
      its deer park: John Vyvyan had married into the Courtenays,
      Earls of Devon, in 1561, whose wealth funded a major recasting
      of the house and chapel. It was the first baronet, Sir Richard
      Vyvyan (1611–65), a loyal Royalist, who extended the house
      with the wings which flank the w entrance court. The s wing
      was a new chapel for which a licence was granted in 1636, and
      of which the four E bays survive: they have windows with
      cinquefoil-headed lights and quatrefoil tracery, four to the N,
      three to the s, and there is a four-centred granite doorway with
      decorated spandrels and a bracket-shaped hoodmould up to
      the string course. The w ends of both wings were returned N
      and s so that their fronts were symmetrical, with steep gables
      and scrolled kneelers. Sir Richard celebrated the Restoration
      with a splendid pair of Jacobean gatepiers dated 1661 that first
      stood at the w end of the entrance court and by adding polyg-
      onal granite bay windows dated 1662 to the s and w sides of
      the main range.

      But it was to a later Sir Richard (1732–81) that Trelowarren
      owes the introduction of *Thomas Edwards* of Greenwich and
      the house's predominant motifs of Georgian antiquarianism.
      Edwards had developed a substantial Cornish practice,
      almost certainly through the influence of Rev. William Borlase
      (cf. Tehidy, Trewithen etc.): several drawings of Trelowarren
      before and after Edwards's interventions were published in
      Borlase's *Natural History of Cornwall* in 1758 that show multi-
      gabled and irregularly windowed E and w elevations. Between
      1756 and 1760 Edwards transformed the house without and
      within. He regularized the elevations by reproducing the extant

*John Martin Robinson, 'Trelowarren' in *Country Life* (22 July 1999). His account,
and this, is greatly indebted to Sir Ferrers Vyvyan who has generously made his
extensive research available.

Trelowarren, west front. Engraving by R. Polwhele, 1816

Tudor mullioned windows, square-headed on the ground floor, round-headed on the first; introducing a shallower hipped roof with a continuous crenellated parapet; and rendering and colour-washing the rubble walls. The chapel was extended W, its exterior clad in Bath stone (also used by Edwards, through the connection with Ralph Allen, at Mansion House, Truro). In the main range the hall was subdivided and a new entrance hall, accessed from the E, was provided with an elegant cantilevered stone stair and ogee-headed plaster panelled walls derived from Batty Langley; the parlour was decorated with similar trefoil-headed panelling.

The second great transformation was undertaken by Sir Richard Rawlinson Vyvyan (1800–79) in the 1830s. His impact was especially radical on the W front and its approach. The SW return wing was demolished and the chapel extended W to occupy the extra bays with a new Gothic W gable with an ogee-headed and traceried blank window. Its interior was decorated with elaborate Gothic plasterwork with richly crocketed canopies, exactly matched at Prideaux Place, Padstow (q.v.), and a Gothic plaster vault with bosses and a panelled dado. At its E end double doors opened into the library with a fine Neoclassical marble chimneypiece. The N range was remodelled to provide family accommodation with a large new kitchen to the rear with Tudor gables to the W elevation. The old W entrance porch beneath the 1662 bay window was blocked and adapted into a bay window. This was part of a wholesale reorganization of the approach to the house from the W through the resited 1662 gatepiers, the drive then leading along a castellated wall past the S end of the stables and the arcaded wall of the Lady Garden that Sir Richard had brought in 1832 from Nanswhyden, another Edwards house. It continued past the S side of the house to end up at the E front. All this necessitated excavation of the ground near the house, burying the parterres on the E side and creating a long, wide terrace above the S elevation that Sir Ferrers Vyvyan is now recovering as part of wider landscape renovation.

To the W of the house the former STABLES, dated 1698 but rebuilt in 1882 (datestone) on a larger scale, and looming rather uncomfortably over the lower-set house. Alongside NW more former STABLES and CARRIAGE HOUSES and an extensive set of brick WALLED GARDENS, all early to mid-C18. New building to provide RECEPTION and RECREATION FACILITIES has been sensitively inserted by *Gale & Snowden* of Barnstaple, who have also designed eco-housing of exemplary simplicity using local materials in the adjacent wooded landscape.

The DEER PARK (or Great Park), on rising ground to the E of the house, is enclosed N, E and S by park pales. The mid-C19 landscaping of GARDENS, PLEASURE GROUNDS and PARKLAND was undertaken to the designs of *Dionysus Williams* who introduced the drive from the W and built the DOUBLE LODGES to the S. In the 1830s Sir Richard Rawlinson Vyvyan more than doubled the size of the estate and gave Trelowarren its connections to the wider landscape, introducing the long Reptonian approach drives similar to those at Tregothnan, and using far-off landmarks like Constantine church as points-in-view. The approach from Gweek is now a public road, though its start is marked by the COTTAGE ORNÉ, the former lodge, on the S side of the village. The present main entrance from the W is by the mid-C19 Tudor CARAVONE LODGE, the part Gothic POND LODGE and ORNAMENTAL POND.

Further E towards the house the complex Iron Age HALLIGYE FOGOU, one of the best examples of a fogou in Cornwall. The fogou was originally entered from the ditch of an ENCLOSED SETTLEMENT. A curving NE–SW passage narrows at the NE end on meeting a shorter straighter NNW–SSE passage. The longer passage is only entered from the shorter one, itself only entered in the earliest phase (C5 or C4 B.C.) by a low narrow 'creep' passage at the N end, which was entered from the ditch. Major C1 B.C. changes saw the creep entry lengthened and a second narrow creep added, providing access from within the enclosure.

TREMAINE

2080

ST WINWALOE. In remote country alone on a hilltop among beech trees and with views for miles around. The church sits within an oval earthwork or *lann* and is a rare survival in Cornwall of a simple two-cell church: nave and chancel together are only 45 ft (14 metres) long. Low W tower of two stages with buttresses only to the first stage and the N and S sides, battlemented parapets and crocketed pinnacles. Norman N wall with a little blocked doorway and a damaged tympanum. Partly rebuilt in the C13–C14; windows replaced in the C15–C16: of the latter date the square-headed s windows. Interior of charming simplicity with C15 ceiled and plastered wagon roof with moulded ribs, carved bosses and carved wall-plate, and plain plastered walls. A curious feature is the narrow flight of steps visible in the N wall – are they to a former rood loft? – FONT. Norman, circular with cable mouldings, like nearby Egloskerry.

TREMATON

4050

TREMATON HALL. The house presents a fine Palladian s front, stuccoed, two-storey and five bays, the central three bays surmounted by a wide pediment. This is by *George Wightwick* who remodelled the late C18 house *c.* 1830; the earlier house incorporated a C17 building. Elegant late C18 open-well staircase to the rear of the entrance hall. Across the rear courtyard a late C18 two-storey BARN.

TREMATON CASTLE, 1½ m. SE. One of the most extensive castles in Cornwall, more impressive than Launceston, if not as perfect as Restormel. The position is superb with wide views towards the Hamoaze and the Sound. The castle is mentioned in Domesday and has been owned by the Duchy of Cornwall since 1337. The original motte-and-bailey was reconstructed with a stone keep and curtain wall in the mid C12 and a gatehouse added in the C13.

The GATEHOUSE, 'one of the most beautiful and untouched examples of its period' (S. Toy), was defended by two portcullises and a gate on the ground floor. Above, reached by a stone newel stair at the NW corner, are two guard chambers above each other with two loopholes defending the approach, each room with a fireplace flanked by C13 columns with excellent stiff-leaf capitals. The windows have been enlarged. The CURTAIN WALL survives intact on the w with smaller sections on the s and NE. It is 7 ft (2.1 metres) wide and 15 ft (4.6 metres) high to the parapet walk with battlements in places almost complete: there is a sally-port through the wall to the N. The SHELL-KEEP on the mount, of the same type at Launceston, Restormel and Totnes, is vaguely oval, 57 ft by 71½ ft (17.4 by 21.8 metres) high to the rampart, the walls 15 ft (4.6 metres) wide at the base and steeply battered. The parapet is complete with the merlons solid, except for one. Traces of former buildings are visible on the inner face with roof corbels above the gateway.

The hall was somewhere in the inner bailey. It was built *de plaustro* by Edward Duke of Cornwall in the C14 and has entirely disappeared, as have traces of the chapel and other buildings. Instead there is now a pretty castellated HOUSE with regularly disposed Georgian windows in the six-bay w front, the first-floor windows taller, the centre four bays broken forward from the flanking single bays. The interior is graciously proportioned and detailed with almost Soanian purity, the plan arranged with strict symmetry around the central top-lit and galleried entrance hall. The hall is marked off from the porch by a flat Soanian arch, the staircase accessed by a smaller but similar arch in the E wall with niches in its curved wall and stairs of elegant simplicity. The mouldings are everywhere of the most restrained form, finely executed. It is likely that this accomplished design can be attributed to *Benjamin Tucker*, Surveyor General to the Duchy, who built the house for himself in 1807–8; it was he who, understandably, pulled down the W part of the curtain wall to obtain the sublime sea views.

TRENEGLOS

2080

ST GREGORY. With its chapelry at Warbstow, the church belonged to Tywardreath Priory in the C12. A drastic restoration of 1858 rebuilt the body of the church and probably the tower. The chief feature of interest is the Norman tympanum, in unusually high relief, above the S door: it has two beasts facing each other with a tree standing between them, the composition not especially Cornish. The workshop may have been the same which made the tympanum for nearby Egloskerry. The porch has a C15 wagon roof. Late C15 or early C16 tracery re-set in N aisle. – FONT. Norman. Small circular bowl on one shaft, with faces unusually at the corners of the base.

26

TREREIFE

4020

87 The home of the Nicholls and Le Grice families from at least the Elizabethan period. The Nicholls were yeomen farmers and minor gentry but John Nicholls (1663–1714) became a successful Middle Temple barrister and substantially remodelled Trereife by 1711. Later C18 to early C20 alterations and extensions have built on the early C18 work to result in one of the most charming houses in Cornwall. The earlier building seems to have been of a main range with two wings, the latter still showing C17 mullioned windows and a large fireplace. Nicholls added a well-proportioned seven-bay front, of two storey and attics in a hipped roof: an impressive staircase hall running up to the attics at the rear of the entrance hall probably belongs to this phase although its design is very conservative. Central doorway with simple door with pediment on carved brackets. The interior is full of good detail of engagingly disparate periods in panelling, plasterwork, chimneypieces and various

patterns of Gothic glazing. To the far r. of the main front the former STABLES, good Early Georgian, with a hipped-roofed infill block of mid-Georgian style that shows its original face to the stable courtyard with Gothic glazing to the front. Projecting forward from the stable block on the front elevation a fine C18 brick-walled KITCHEN GARDEN.

TRERICE

8050

3 m. SE of Newquay

The excellent Elizabethan house of the Arundells, cousins of the   70
Arundells of Lanherne (q.v.), lies in a quiet tributary valley of the Gannel.

In the early 1570s John Arundell V rebuilt the core of a substantial mid-C15 to early C16 courtyard-plan house, adding a delightful show front to the SE in a warm local ashlar elvan. This is the prettiest in Cornwall, almost symmetrical with a three-storey porch between slightly projecting end wings, set off by highly decorative scrolly gables with carved mask corbels at their bases, and with large trefoil gables between. To the l. of the porch, the vast Great Hall window going through two floors, a lattice of twenty-four sections subdivided by a central king mullion, six other mullions, two tiers of transoms, and 576 panes, many of them original glass.

The history of the house is more complex than this front suggests.* It is hinted at in what is now the plain SE gable-end of the SW range. This end of the house is shown in a painting of 1811 with string courses, windows and an apparently scrolly gable to match the rest of the front, but seems to have been rebuilt by 1818 (*see* the blocked openings). The string courses, evidence for originally similar mullioned windows later replaced by sashes, and ashlar elvan facing are continued in the SW elevation, indicating that it too is part of the 1570s rebuild. It also has a large bay built as a staircase tower in the 1570s but slightly later converted to a magnificent window at first-floor level to light the great chamber: its window mouldings are later than those of the SE front. Further evidence of the house's evolution is visible in the rear wall of the front range where the l. jamb to the screens passage is straight in contrast to the moulded late C16 jamb to the r: this and the walling immediately above is the only remnant of the pre-1570s house, the rest of the range to the l. having been rebuilt in the early 1950s, replacing an early C20 rebuild, long after the collapse of the roof at the NE end of the house in 1860; the original NE range of the courtyard has vanished without trace. The rear

*This account owes much to Eric Berry, Jo Sturgiss and Nigel Thomas's research of 2008.

wall also has four surviving windows, originally open, to the
ground-floor corridor behind the Great Hall, and an early C17
staircase-turret built to replace that on the SW elevation after
its conversion to a bay window.

Inside is some of the most important early plasterwork in the
county. The GREAT HALL is flooded with light from the great
E window and rises to a fine plasterwork ceiling in a large open
strapwork pattern of thin ribs ornamented with oak leaves and
scroll designs, supported on corbels decorated with medallions, and with spherical pendants: curiously it does not exactly
fit the space, especially over the window. Between the pendants, the initials J.A., K.A. and M.A., probably of John Arundell
V, his first wife, Katherine, and his sister Margaret. The fireplace with its scrolled plaster overmantel, supported by finely
modelled terms, is dated 1572: the crispness of the plasterwork
in the hall reflects its restoration c. 1840 after the Aclands of
Killerton, Devon, acquired the house. Over the N end of the
hall, a gallery lit by small recessed arches set high in the
cornice. The present STAIR is a C20 invention, occupying one
of the projecting wings of the 1570s façade, the imported staircase incorporating both C17 and C18 elements, and late C16-
style replica plasterwork in simple strapwork. On the first floor
in the GREAT CHAMBER one of the richest displays of late
C16 plasterwork anywhere in Cornwall, lit by the bay window:
the room would originally have been lit by a window in the SE
wall. Elaborate barrel ceiling in fine interconnecting strapwork
with Tudor rose motifs and scroll designs, large pendants, and
a deep frieze. On the W wall the coat of arms of Henry
FitzAlan, 12th Earl of Arundel. Massive fireplace overmantel
incorporating the Arundell arms supported by telamones, the
arms in the central cartouche probably of John Arundell V's
father, flanked by those of his wives' families, and the date 1573
in a mixture of Roman and Arabic numerals. The LONG
GALLERY along the N side of the house, not much more than
a narrow corridor, has simpler early C19 strapwork. The excellence of the Trerice plasterwork bears close comparison with
parallels in Devon, including Collacombe, and probably
reflects Arundell's connection with Edmund Tremayne of Collacombe, Clerk to the Privy Council.

S of the house and stepping up the hillside to its main elevations,
a suite of three Elizabethan GARDEN TERRACES in the Orchard,
Front Court and Bowling Green Terrace: an important survival
of late C16 garden history. The Front Court contains two
crouching Arundell lions brought from Kenegie Manor,
Gulval, in the early C19, and the granite caps and balls from
the gatepiers from Tresmarrow, near Launceston, in the 1970s.
At the rear a good range of FARM BUILDINGS on a U-shaped
plan centring on the tall great barn, of bank barn type built
into the slope with cattle shelter below the barn floor. These
ranges are some of the earliest structures on the site: there are
slit windows in the NE wall and the barn entrances show clearly
the addition of the porches in the early C17 to the original

openings to the threshing floor, with the pintels of the earlier
door hanging still extant.

TRESILLIAN   8040

HOLY TRINITY. The eye-catching bellcote, especially striking
approached over the bridge from Truro, heralds the principal
entrance to the Tregothnan estate (q.v.). It is by *W. D. Caröe*,
1904, in picturesque Arts and Crafts Gothic, with the rubble
buttresses soaring to the apex of the nave and then tiered in
ashlar to enclose three bells within cusped arches. Caröe incorporated an existing mission church of 1878 as the nave of his
new building after Tresillian replaced Merther (q.v.) as the
parish church. The bellcote is part of an asymmetrical composition with a two-light cusped window and quatrefoil to the w
end of the nave, flanked to the r. by the gable-end of the s aisle
with a cusped lancet. The roofs are steeply pitched, the gables
coped. The interior is simple but powerful with an arcade of
pointed arches corbelled out and supported on octagonal piers,
with a larger version for the chancel arch, a scissor-braced roof
to the nave, and arched-braced roof to the aisle. The notable
fittings are from Merther. – FONT, probably C12 with octagonal
shaft. – PULPIT. C17, Jacobean, polygonal with carved panels.
– FIGURE. C15, of St Anthony, in Catacleuse. The r. hand BELL
is from the detached bell-tower at Lamorran (q.v.), the others
from Merther.
CROSS. Outside w front of the church. Wheel-head only, probably
pre-Norman, with Latin crosses to both sides.
RECTORY, above the church. 1904, also by *Caröe*. Accomplished
Arts and Crafts-influenced house with irregular elevations and
nice details including round chimneystacks.
BRIDGE. At the head of the creek, carrying the Truro–St Austell
road. Widened in 1903. In 1646 a treaty was made here between
Fairfax and Lord Hopton by which Cornwall was surrendered
to the Parliamentarians.
WHEEL INN. Long, low, thatched, C17 and earlier.

TRESLOTHAN   6030

A charming model hamlet is all that remains of the great estate
of the Pendarves family (cf. the monuments in Camborne
church) whose Georgian mansion was demolished in 1955. All
the buildings were designed and built as a piece 1840–5 by *George
Wightwick*.

ST JOHN. 1840–2. Built as the chapel to Pendarves House.
Restored 1880, and altered in 1899. E.E. style, well executed.

The six-bay nave has clasping granite pilasters to the corners, lesenes, tall side lancets, a stepped triple-lancet w window, and a gabled w bellcote. The small one-bay chancel also has a stepped triple lancet. The interior has a wagon roof with large queenpost trusses on corbelled wall-plates with arch bracing. – ALTAR STONE. In s chapel, *c.* 1000–50, with inscription 'Aegured' and a rectilinear pattern enclosed by a T-fret border. – FONT. C15, from Camborne church, granite, with four angels holding shields and an ornamental band connecting them, with inscription 'Behold the beloved of the true God shall be baptized with the Holy Spirit', cf. St Anthony-in-Meneage, St Winnow. So summary and bold is the treatment of the granite that it looks decidedly modern (cf. St Ives). – SCULPTURE. In the vestry a late C14 or early C15 alabaster panel. – STAINED GLASS. *Clayton & Bell* windows from Troon mission church.

In the churchyard, outside the E end of the chancel, a WHEEL-HEADED CROSS with a figure with arms outstretched and feet apart enclosed by a bead (cf. the similar cross outside The Institute, Camborne). – s of the church, the PENDARVES MAUSOLEUM. Late C19, of granite ashlar with a roof of granite slabs. E.E. style with diagonal buttresses to the corners and matching side-wall buttresses. The gabled E front is almost filled by a large two-centred arch with cusped arches on slender shafts and a cusped light above. – Near the mausoleum, TOMB of John Harris, the Cornish poet, †1884.

The rest of the buildings show Wightwick's skill in varying scale and style. A pretty little WELL on the corner of BACK LANE is in the form of a Gothic gabled porch above a water trough. TRESLOTHAN HOUSE, built 1843 as the vicarage, is, like the other houses, in Tudor style, on an irregular rectangular plan with mullioned-and-transomed windows and prominent, tall stacks.

TRESLOTHAN LODGE, 1842, the former schoolmaster's house, is on a T-plan with the porch in the angle. The first-floor windows are in gableted half-dormers treated as oriels. TRESLOTHAN CHURCH COTTAGES, dated 1845, were built as a pair on an H-plan formed by a short central range with cross-wings. The side walls each have a gabled porch with a Tudor-arched outer doorway.

CARWYNNEN QUOIT, ¼ m. s. Early Neolithic CHAMBERED TOMB; large capstone supported by three uprights. Collapsed in 1842 and re-erected 'in much the same position' as a romantic antique focus of the Pendarves designed landscape between 1853 and 1872. It fell again in 1967.

TRESMEER

ST NICHOLAS. Low two-stage unbuttressed C15 w tower. The rest rebuilt 1878–81 reusing some early fabric, especially the late C13 three-light lancet windows of the chancel and s wall of nave. Top of a wheel-head cross re-set in e wall of porch. – FONT. Norman, circular with one cable moulding close to the top.

TRETHEVY

0080

St Piran. Probably of medieval origin – one trefoil-headed window survives in the N wall. Long used as a farm building until restored as a chapel of ease to Tintagel in 1942, it retains a simple barn-like character. Restored HOLY WELL opposite in the lane.

TREVALGA

0080

St Petroc. Not far from the cliffs, the unbuttressed, unpinnacled w tower faces the ocean. It may be C13 in origin but has a Perp three-light window above the w door. The plain interior has the atmosphere of an early outpost chapel, low, unaisled, and unwindowed on the N side except for a small lancet in the N transept; the lower masonry of nave, chancel and transept may be Norman. N transept with C13 arch, two-light e window transept and squint with Norman piscina and niche. Five late C19 single lancets light the s side with a triple-lancet e window. Medieval roofs survive over chancel and transept but the nave roof was renewed in a restoration of 1875 by *J. P. St Aubyn.* – REREDOS. A composite. Altarpiece a carved triptych, C16, Flemish, of the Annunciation, Visitation and Crucifixion, flanked by C17 panelling and with medieval bench-ends below. – STAINED GLASS. Two windows by *Clayton & Bell,* 1893. – MONUMENT. Samuel Roscarrock †1640, small but exquisite. – WHEEL-HEAD CROSS near s door. CHEST TOMB. Elizabeth Richard †1740, unusually good lettering.

Thanks to a far-sighted former owner and a local trust, the VILLAGE is a miraculous pre-C21 survival – a cluster of small manor house, farmstead and cottages, all yellow lichen-covered slate roofs, slatestone walls and huge slate fences – leading one inexorably down towards the cliffs and the sea.

REDEVALLAN, 1½ m. SE. A more elaborate version of the typical Cornish vernacular house. On an E-plan with symmetrical front, the central range with two-storey porch and two bays projecting forward. Date 1642 in the plaster frieze above the bay window in the parlour.

TREVERBYN

St Peter. Like Charlestown and Par (qq.v.), the church of a
newly created ecclesiastical parish of 1847 to serve the rapidly
expanding population of the china clay country. 1848–50 by
G. E. Street, the second church designed in his own name,
immediately following Par. The Builder called it 'plain but
good'. It is indeed good early Street, smaller in scale and
simpler in concept than Par but with the same accents: skilled
use of local materials, strong design and simplification of
detail. The modest exterior has steep-pitched slate roofs over
the nave and slightly lower chancel, with Dec tracery to small
two-light windows in the N and S walls and larger four-light
windows to the E and W ends. Bellcote over the W end. The
bold internal space of the interior therefore comes as a surprise: it is lofty and dignified, especially memorable the great
barn-like arched and wind-braced roof of the nave with its
soaring pointed chancel arch. The chancel roof is similar, the
sanctuary roof boarded and painted. The effect is enhanced by
Street's subtle use of levels and lighting to give prominence to
the altar. The vocabulary is simple early Dec employed not to
be decorative but purely architectural. – STAINED GLASS. Two
windows in the S wall of the nave, 1898 and 1902, and one in
the N wall, 1897, by E. R. Suffling.
Good contemporary wrought-iron GATES to the churchyard. The
church was the centrepiece of a group of buildings by Street
including the former VICARAGE, 1858, solid and workmanlike,
and enlivened by a circular stair-turret; and SCHOOLROOM
and SCHOOL HOUSE, plain but strong compositions.

TREVONE

St Saviour. 1959 by Peter Falconer. Charming and unusually
late mission church built to serve Trevone's development as a
holiday resort, simply designed yet finely detailed, e.g. the
excellent carving to the bowl of the font.
Atlantic Terrace, a classic row of former small hotels
and boarding houses, shows that development started in the
late C19.

TREVOSE HEAD
2¼ m. NW of St Merryn

LIGHTHOUSE. 1847. Built by *Jacob & Thomas Olver & Sons* of
Falmouth. Circular white tower 87 ft (26.5 metres) high with

lantern surmounted by a weathervane, flanked by two low single-storey blocks.

POLVENTON, Mother Ivey's Bay. 1936. By *Crowe & Careless* for R. H. Stein, close to the cliff edge for extensive sea views. Very streamlined Modernist house, one, two, and three storeys, with first-floor windows arranged on the corners, and curved windows to the single-storey range that wraps around the three seaward-facing sides. Skilfully refurbished and extended 1980–2000 by *Amanda Le Page* of *Gilmore Hankey Kirke Architects* with glazed semicircular three-storey stair-tower and NW wing.

LIFEBOAT STATION, on the N side of Mother Ivey's Bay. 1996 by *Poynton Bradbury Wynter Cole* of St Ives, project architects, with *Haskoning UK Ltd*, consulting engineers. Dramatically sited on tall tubular pilotis, its wave-like profile making the building seem as if it is surging against the sheer cliffs behind.

TREWARNE

2 m. NE of St Kew

0070

One of the most interesting smaller C17 gentry houses in Cornwall whose evolution is yet to be fully elucidated. L-shaped plan with main S and E ranges and a rear stair-tower in the angle between; a N service wing has been demolished. The S and E fronts are of a quality rare in the county, the result of the mid-C17 rebuilding of an earlier house by the Nicholls family who had acquired the estate in the early C16. Symmetrical S front, the central entrance with a four-centred arch flanked by pairs of unusually tall four-light windows with king mullions and transoms, and with five smaller three-light windows above; the E elevation has two similarly tall ground-floor windows, the r. window even grander with six lights. What is odd for such an imposing arrangement is that the first-floor windows on the S front are uncomfortably tightly positioned under the eaves. That this was originally a three-storey house is strongly suggested by the E elevation, where the walling continues above the first-floor string course, and the evidence of the stair-tower: it is of very substantial dimensions and, even though it has been truncated, still rises above the main ranges with the stair continuing to climb to the lost floor. The hipped roof also looks slight for such a house, the original form probably gabled (as is the N end of the E wing), indicated by the survival of scrolled kneeler stones and apexes in the garden that are similar to those on the gables at Trerice and the nearby Mansion House at Blisland (qq.v.). An early C19 description describes the rooms as 'spacious and lofty with rich ceilings and cornices beautifully wrought and walls highly ornamented with emblems of sacred and profane history in figures two to

five feet high in Plaster of Paris'.* The gracious proportions
of the principal rooms and the surviving fine-quality plasterwork in high relief still reflect such a sumptuous interior. Two
armorial pieces, one in the E ground-floor room with the arms
of Nicholls impaling Mohuns (removed from the chamber
above the parlour), another in a chamber with a pretty cornice,
and a lively scene of Abraham about to sacrifice Isaac in the
principal chamber.

The house sits on a steep s-facing slope and is entered through
a delightful walled raised garden with four-centred headed
doorways. At the centre of the s garden wall is a TOWER of two
storeys from the ground level below with a doorway curiously
positioned above at the higher (garden) level and thus in the
air (the present external steps are an addition). Its function is
unknown. In the gardens to the E of the house CUSPED
TRACERY likely to be fragments of a former chapel (the
lantern cross now at St Neot (q.v.) came from here), and a
HOLY WELL.

2080

TREWEN

ST MICHAEL. Small chapel with no W tower, only a gabled
bellcote. C15 and early C16, thoroughly restored by *J. P.
St Aubyn* 1863–4. Nave and N aisle only with blocked door
and straight-headed windows in the N wall, the E window of
three lights with standard Cornish tracery. s porch with two
re-set C15 multiple-moulded jambs and a C15–C16 wagon roof
with carved bosses. The simple interior has great charm, the
aisle arcade on four low piers of Cornish standard, the plain
Norman FONT square with chamfered corners, and the homely
C19 furnishings.

9040

TREWITHEN

The plain and stately house of the Hawkins family sits on a gentle
slope in pleasure grounds giving onto generous parkland. Its
origins are in a house of at least C16 date which was acquired
in 1728 by Philip Hawkins, son of Philip Hawkins of Pennans
(Creed). A design for replacing it with a fashionable Palladian
mansion with pavilion wings is in the County Record Office
and is attributed to *James Gibbs*. A second scheme again
possibly by Gibbs for reusing the existing buildings to achieve
the same ends was adopted, however, and Trewithen's graceful
symmetry is, as a result, more reminiscent of the comfortable

*F. Hitchens and S. Drew, *History of Cornwall* (1817).

scale and proportions of the Cornish gentry house rather than a purer Palladian form.

The precise dates of the phases of Trewithen's development remain uncertain, along with the nature of the relationship between the several architects who worked on the house.* By 1730 it seems that work was underway, either on an addition to the existing house or implementation of the Gibbsian scheme, and this was continued by *Thomas Edwards* of Greenwich from *c.* 1738. When Philip Hawkins died in the same year the work was carried on by his executors until at least 1743. It resumed after 1756 for the newly-married Thomas Hawkins, nephew of Philip. Edwards departed in 1761, but a reference in a letter of 1764 shows that by that time Thomas had engaged *Sir Robert Taylor,* who may have been working on the interior from the late 1750s. Surprisingly Hawkins seems at the same time to have commissioned new plans for remodelling his house from either *Matthew Brettingham the Elder* (1699–1769) or his son *Matthew Brettingham the Younger* (1725–1803). But what, if anything, had been done by the time of Hawkins's death in 1766 from a smallpox vaccination?

The N entrance front is a quietly assured composition, nine bays wide with a recessed five-bay centre and an arched doorway. It seems to have been executed as part of the works completed by 1742. Set at right angles, flanking the forecourt, are detached brick pavilions, the W of 1738 and the E of 1758. They housed dairy/brewhouse-washhouse and stables/coach-house respectively and have matching five-bay fronts and octagonal cupolas. The house was also originally brick on this side but in 1948 was rendered to match the Pentewan stone of the additions made by Edwards. It is believed that he began by infilling the courtyard of the house with the S range of five bays.† This most closely follows Palladian rules, being the dominant component of the composition with the lower, two bay, ends of the E and W ranges set back to l. and r.: it has windows twice as high as wide, a classical cornice, and architrave surrounds to windows and doors. After Philip Hawkins's death, this range seems to have remained in carcase for twenty years. The E range was rebuilt in 1758. It is of seven bays, the central three a canted bay with central door. The W service range was much altered and extended during the C19.

The completion of the interior is due to Taylor. He created the splendid dining room with its arcaded screens to the E and W ends of three slightly depressed semicircular arches springing

*I am most grateful to Paul Holden for his help with my understanding of Trewithen's development: his Trewithen and the Brettingham Plans, *Georgian Group Journal* XXI 2013 is essential reading. Richard Garnier has been generous with his research on the question of Sir Robert Taylor's contribution. Pamela Dodd's important work on Thomas Edwards is represented in The Hawkins of Trewithen and Thomas Edwards of Greenwich *JRIC* 1998.
†Richard Garnier has however suggested to me that this infilling might date from the first phase of work *c.* 1728–30.

from capitals with Ionic entablatures in the Roman manner and plaster groin-vaulted ceilings behind. Its stucco decoration includes Rococo arabesques on the fireplace wall and one of his typical Rococo chimneypieces. He also redesigned the main staircase with an oval skylight over a cantilevered staircase in a semicircular open well with a wreathed hand rail: this is evidently incomplete in comparison with a surviving drawing which confirms that the adjacent secondary stair with a geometric Chinese Chippendale balustrade by Edwards was to have been replaced with a corkscrew stair. Among the many other fine rooms, the pine-panelled central E canted-bay room may owe its Ionic doorcase to Taylor while the SE oak-panelled room with good Ionic detail may survive from the Gibbsian design: likewise the decoration of some bedrooms. Taylor also intended a double-height Palladian entrance hall which was not executed, perhaps due to Thomas Hawkins's early death.

In the W courtyard STABLES AND COACHOUSE to a design found (by Paul Holden) in pencil on the back of the Brettingham plan, based loosely on Palladio's Villa Maser and part of the scheme to re-develop the W side of the house. Long fifteen-bay range (reduced from the seventeen shown on the plan), all blocked, with double-height pavilions and pediment gable, all in brick in Flemish bond.

The informal woodland GARDENS AND PLEASURE GROUNDS are situated principally to the S and W, with lawns on the E-facing slope of the house and an C18 walled garden to the W: the GARDEN HOUSE in the style of a Chinese pavilion, echoes what Taylor was doing inside. In 1824 Henry St Aubyn was commissioned to plan the extension of the park to the N, E and W of the house, including a picturesque circuit ride that provides its present setting.

Near the Home Farmhouse, an C18 BARN with two ENGINE HOUSES. The horse engine house is of 1800. The steam engine house was added in 1811 for an engine designed by Richard Trevithick and built at the Hayle Foundry (q.v.). It was the first steam engine made for threshing and the earliest surviving agricultural steam engine in the world, now in store at the Science Museum, London.

TRURO

The prospect of Pearson's cathedral with its towers and spires soaring above the roofs of the small city is both memorable and emblematic of Truro's pre-eminence. The choice of the town as the seat of the new Cornish diocese in 1876, the granting of city status the following year (making it the only city in Cornwall) and the consecration of the unfinished cathedral in 1887 set the seal on an urban history that began in the C12, flourished in the

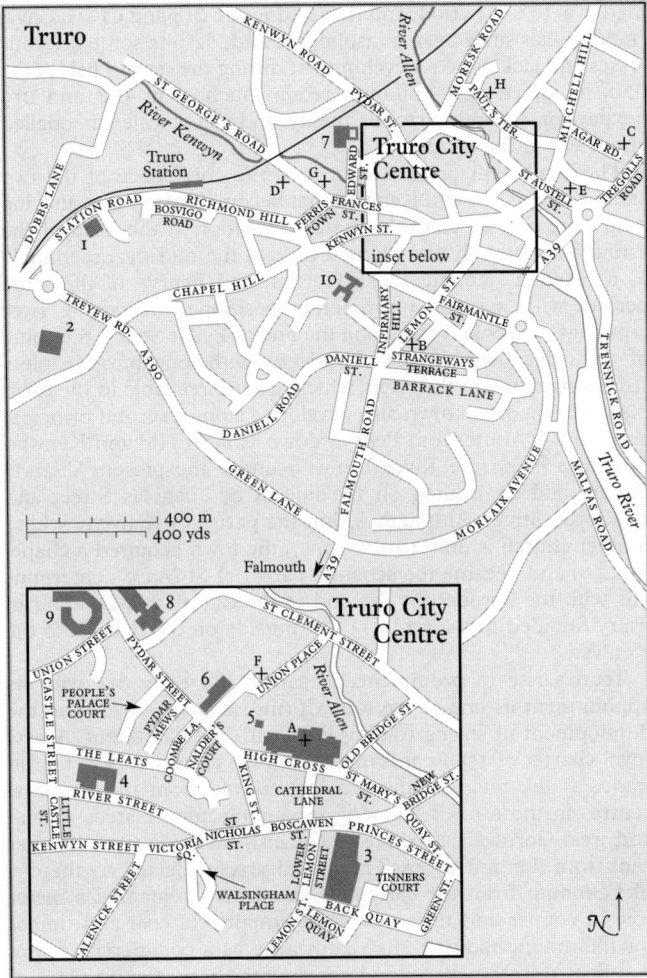

Truro

A	Cathedral
B	St John
C	St Paul
D	St George
E	Our Lady of the Portal and St Piran (R.C.)
F	Truro Methodist Church (St Mary Clement)
G	St George's Methodist Church
H	Friends meeting house

1	Old County Hall
2	New County Hall
3	City Hall (Hall for Cornwall)
4	County Museum and Art Gallery
5	Assembly Rooms (former)
6	Public Library
7	Courts of Justice
8	Council offices
9	Government offices
10	Infirmary (former)

medieval to C17 period, and flowered in the C18 and C19. Its civic standing has since been consolidated and, despite some grievous losses and lacklustre redevelopment during the second half of the C20, its streets and buildings retain much of its C18 and C19 heyday, of an architectural quality and on a scale unequalled elsewhere in the county.

The settlement originated around the confluence of the two small Rivers Allen and Kenwyn that become Truro River, flowing s into the Fal, an enviable strategic position at the head of the estuary. A borough was planted here in the mid C12, seemingly as a planned settlement like Helston and Penryn of the same period, with a castle prominently positioned above the river crossings. It was laid out along the line of Pydar Street, the spine of the ridge between the two rivers, with long burgage plots stretching down to the rivers which are still readable in the town plan. The medieval town also developed along a second principal axis, an E–W route from Penryn down Chapel Hill and Kenwyn Street, crossing the River Kenwyn under the present Victoria Square and continuing on the line of St Nicholas Street and Boscawen Street. Although within the parish of Kenwyn, whose mother church is only 1 m. N (q.v.), the town acquired a chapel by 1259 and became the separate parish of St Mary's coterminous with the borough by the end of the C13, with a Dominican friary founded in the mid C13 just outside on the w bank of the Kenwyn.

Truro's rise to prominence began in the early C14 with its appointment as one of the four Cornish coinage towns and the development of strong trading links with the Continent. A new royal charter of 1589 confirmed Truro's leading status in the tin trade, as the focus of the industry moved from the medieval centres in the E to the rapidly developing mining areas of mid and west Cornwall: its share of Cornish tin coinage was 60 per cent from the mid 1660s. Though adversely affected by the rise of Falmouth from the early C18, the town maintained a major role in copper and tin exports and imports of coal and timber for the mining industry. Its significance as a commercial centre is reflected in the cluster of large country houses and estates of leading Cornish families – above all the Earls of Falmouth at Tregothnan – in its immediate hinterland, as well as the wealth of urban building that transformed it into an elegant Late Georgian town.

The C18 architectural achievement is remarkable for Cornwall. The surviving mid-C18 town mansions, Princes House and Mansion House, are of metropolitan quality, as is the façade of the Assembly Rooms of c. 1780. A dignified central space was created in the 1790s by the demolition of the row of buildings in the middle of Boscawen Street. In 1794 Lemon Street, the most gracious street in Cornwall, was started, rising serenely from the water's edge to the Falmouth Road. Writing in 1795, W. G. Maton found Truro 'unquestionably the handsomest town in Cornwall, the streets regular and commodious and the houses of a very neat appearance',* while in 1806 another observer concluded 'this elegant little town holds out a temptation little inferior to Bath or Bond Street'.

Almost until the close of the C18 Truro had not spread significantly beyond the medieval street pattern but the next fifty years saw rapid expansion. New bridges constructed S E of the medieval crossings opened up the development of the river frontages, like Lemon Quay on the S bank on the Kenwyn, while a new line of the turnpike was constructed E in 1828–30 along the line of Tregolls Road. The grandest expression of the town's mid-C19 prestige is the classical City Hall, 1847, providing a splendid centrepiece to Boscawen Street and a handsome façade to Back Quay. The population rose from around 5,000 in 1801 to near 11,000 in 1851, with new houses, mostly in stucco, built right across the social range. The most ambitious is Strangeways Terrace off the top of Lemon Street but much of the most enjoyable building of this period is more modest, like the pretty crescent of Walsingham Place and the humbler terraces of the suburbs around and above the centre, like Ferris Town, Frances Street, River Street and Richmond Hill to the w and Fairmantle Street, Carclew Street and Daniel Street to the s.

The second half of the C19 saw Truro consolidate its role as the cultural and civic heart of Cornwall. The opening of the mainline railway first to Penzance in 1852 and then to London via Plymouth and the GWR network in 1859 was another boost to the town's economy, its import expressed in the twenty-eight arches of the magnificent viaducts of 1904 over the Allen and Kenwyn valleys (replacing Brunel's originals) that form the northern backdrop to the city. Cathedral city status not only brought the first new cathedral for a new Anglican diocese since the Reformation but a plethora of large new religious, public and commercial buildings, many by good local architects like James Hicks and Silvanus Trevail, following mid-century work by Philip Sambell, which added powerful new architectural character to the town. There was major suburban expansion, especially to the w around the station, to the s w in Falmouth Road and to the N E in terraces and villas overlooking the city and its cathedral. And splendid new public spaces, Waterfall Gardens and Victoria Park, were laid out alongside and above the Kenwyn in the 1890s.

Despite the decline of its industrial base in the C20, Truro's function as a regional, civic, commercial and administrative centre continued to develop strongly, with two major civic buildings on prominent sites, the New County Hall, 1966, on the S W edge of the city, and the Courts of Justice on the castle site in 1988. Major road construction for a by-pass and inner relief road of the 1960s and 1970s retained the integrity of the historic centre's street pattern at the high cost of severing the city from its river. A comprehensive development scheme for the city centre in the late 1960s prepared by *MWT Architects* was implemented

*W. G. Maton, *Observations on the Western Counties of England* (1795).

only in a piecemeal fashion, mostly around Pydar Street, and resulted in buildings of at best only mediocre quality; the re-development of other prominent sites in the post-war period was generally architecturally undistinguished. Lessons are being learned and a conservation plan prepared by *Robert Thorne* of *Baxter Associates* in 2008 is currently evolving into a masterplan intended, *inter alia*, to improve the standard of new development and safeguard the setting of the historic centre from further extensive suburban growth. The city that offers the most reward-ing of urban architectural explorations in Cornwall deserves no less.

CATHEDRAL

From his appointment as first bishop to the new see of Truro in 1877 Edward White Benson, later Archbishop of Canter-bury, was determined on a new cathedral. It was to symbolize the resurgence of the Anglican Church in Cornwall, provide an appropriate setting for the revived ritual of the Oxford Movement which he wished to promote, and dominate its city in the manner of the great medieval cathedrals. The commis-sioning of *John Loughborough Pearson* after a limited competi-tion in 1878 that included Bodley, Burges, R. P. Pullan, St Aubyn, John Oldrid Scott and Street was to prove inspired: Pearson did not enter the competition but had worked with Benson at Lincoln, where Benson had been chancellor before his preferment and where Pearson had been cathedral architect since 1870.[*] The E parts were built before Pearson's death in 1897, the nave and central tower between 1898 and 1903, and the W towers between 1903 and 1910, all by *F. L. Pearson* to his father's design.

Truro is J. L. Pearson's masterpiece. Here he created not a copy but the ideal of the C13 cathedral. The sources are both French and English: there were protests about the un-Cornishness of the design, exacerbated by the architect's desire to build the exterior entirely in limestone. As a compromise, Pearson built in a combination of Carnsew granite for the exterior ashlar and Bath stone (Box) or Doulting for the carved work and the spires, while the interior was St Stephen's granite with Bath stone dressings, a mix that slightly militates against the purity of Pearson's design.

The EXTERIOR especially resonates with influences from Nor-mandy, the cathedral rising sheer from its surrounding streets of modest buildings, achieving through its verticality the domi-nance that Benson sought and overcoming the problem of its highly constricted site at the lowest part of the town: its con-struction necessitated the demolition of a number of buildings on the N side of the site as well as most of the parish church

[*]Benson's vision of what a cathedral should be, based mostly on evidence from Lincoln's history, is set out in his book *The Cathedral: Its Necessary Place in the Life and Work of the Church* (1878).

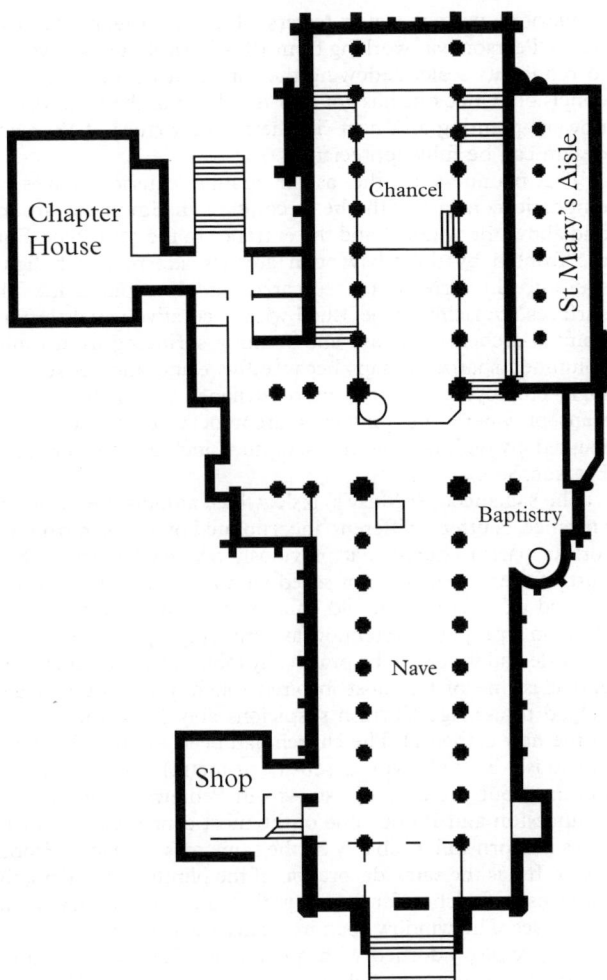

Truro, Cathedal. Plan

of St Mary. It is, however, a picturesque dominance, the towers and spires pure Normandy Gothic (cf. Coutances and St Étienne Abbey, Caen), especially on the W front where their ascendancy is accentuated by spirelets and gabled lucarnes clustered around their bases, and square turrets with pyramidal roofs in Norman French style that flank the rose window of the nave; a similar and larger turret with a pyramidal copper roof rises from the SE corner of the S transept. Yet the most pervasive influences are English, especially Lincoln: the cathedral is similarly cruciform with double transepts, twin W towers, a larger central tower over the main crossing, and a square E end. The gable on the W front is also an obvious relation to Lincoln while the towers and spires show some similarities with the stair-towers of Peterborough's W front where Pearson was working from 1883. Everything is reworked to reduce its scale, endowing the cathedral with an attractive concision. Once one has got over the shock of the compressed, upward-pointing and neat silhouette, the virtues of Pearson's design can be fully appreciated.

The plainness of the ashlar granite exterior makes an emphatic contrast with the decoration in limestone around and above the W doors and the entrance to the S transept. Both are fronted by three-bay open arcades adorned with figure sculpture in turreted niches carried up into pinnacles. The surfaces are richly embellished with decorative panels around pointed-arched doorways and vaulting springing from multi-columned shafts. Perhaps because this elaboration is so sparingly employed, it is the more striking, especially to the S transept where the pinnacles are crocketed, the doorways flanked by sedilia, and the sculpture includes the figure of Pearson Sen.

The S chancel (St Mary's) aisle, which adjoins the S transept entrance, is utterly different, incorporated by Pearson from the former parish church that previously occupied most of the E part of the site. It was not saved without a fight: Benson had wanted all traces of the old church swept away and regarded Pearson's proposed retention as 'tinkering up rotten stones'; the aisle had indeed to be practically rebuilt. Pearson prevailed, and it is one of his most inspired touches: no doubt it also helped to assuage Cornish suspicions about the 'foreignness' of the new cathedral. The church had been extensively rebuilt previously in 1768, with a 128-ft (39-metre) spire by *Thomas Edwards*, but the aisle of 1504–18 in Pentewan stone is with Launceston and Probus one of the most ornate Gothic structures in Cornwall, probably by the same masons as the Probus tower. It has the same decoration of the plinth in two tiers, the same use of niches for statuary, the same decorating of the buttresses. The window spandrels have tracery, and the battlements are also adorned with quatrefoils. The S wall windows are large, seven of two lights, one of five, and the E window is of five.

105 The cathedral INTERIOR, of soaring height and ever-changing vistas, is in many ways a *beau ideal* of the E.E. style, perfected as against the proportions of, say, Salisbury and purged of the loveable irregularities of other E.E. cathedrals. Truro is vaulted throughout. Pearson knew better than any other architect of his generation how necessary stone vaults are to Gothic perfection and here he offers a masterclass in their design and variety. While most are quadripartite rib-vaults, he chose sexpartite vaults for the nave, a French (from Caen) rather than an English tradition, an eight-part vault for the baptistery and a twelve-part vault over the central crossing. The crypt is, in contrast, of massive late C12-style vaulting. Other English characteristics are evident everywhere: the gallery (which France in the C13 had given up), the straight E end with its lancets

(like Whitby), the moulded capitals. The E parts have more decoration, the nave is almost bare: throughout, the various elements of the design are differentiated by simple mouldings and shafts that demonstrate the structural logic of Gothic rather than being only adornment.

The quality of the architectural motifs is consistently impressive. Specially successful are the tall W tower halls opened towards the nave, the niches in which the aisle windows are placed, and the circular BAPTISTERY, E.E. at its richest and most compact. This is one of the most accomplished and satisfying parts of the interior especially in its relationship to the aisles, from which it is experienced as a logical extension. It has eight slender piers and is vaulted with eight decorated principal ribs and intermediate and ridge ribs, with carved bosses at each intersection: the pattern of the vault is similar to the apse vault at Pershore, Worcs. In sharp contrast to the disciplined purity of the nave the wall arcading is enriched with shafts of green and red Lizard serpentine★ as a setting for the FONT, the bowl and plinth in rich red marble rising from a richly patterned floor and surmounted by a font cover suspended from the central boss.

The interior of the SOUTH CHANCEL AISLE (St Mary's Aisle) has an arcade with piers of standard Cornish design with plain capitals and nearly semicircular arches. The resolution of the relationship between the aisle and the new cathedral shows Pearson's genius. It is accomplished by aligning the choir with the aisles, which requires it to be at a slight angle from the nave, and by varying the handling of the vaulting to the S side of the choir: the thrust from the choir vault is carried by massive transverse arches over an outer aisle in front of the chancel aisle by arcade piers separating it from neighbouring aisles. The result is a thrilling vista of shafts and vaults looking E from the baptistery and S transept, given further emphasis by an acutely pointed outer arch. The lower level of the aisle floor, well below the nave floor and therefore dramatically lower than the floor of the choir, adds to the effect. The bosses are late C20, designed by *John Phillips* and carved by *J. W. Harvey*.

The FURNISHINGS of the cathedral generally meet the exacting expectations created by their architectural setting and demonstrate Benson's determination that every component should enrich the liturgical experience. – The font, described above, is dramatic in its colours and suitably sumptuous for its rich baptistery context. – The REREDOS fulfils Pearson's intention that it should be the culmination of the design of the cathedral interior, the carving by *Nathaniel Hitch* of Kensington highly competent if not truly inspired. When first seen from the W entrance it is strangely moving, the more so perhaps because it is clearly unfinished. The central panels of the

---

★Many imported varieties of building stones were used in the interior of the cathedral, but it is still one of the best places to see the range of Cornish materials (*see* Introduction, p. 3).

Crucifixion and Christ in Glory are flanked by eight pairs of angels in tiered niches, in turn flanked by panels of Old Testament scenes and lesser tiered niches of saints, martyrs, apostles and Evangelists. – Either side of the reredos, SEDILIA with nodding ogee arches. – CHOIR STALLS and BISHOP'S THRONE, designed by Pearson, their spiked Dec canopies finely conceived and enriched with figures of the Cornish saints by *Violet Pinwill*. – Iron SCREENS around the sanctuary and choir, copying C13 work. – INLAID PAVEMENT of the sanctuary, of Italian marble of the highest quality. As with the exterior and the baptistery, so here the concentration of embellishment in a small area makes the contrast with most of the interior the more striking. – PULPIT, in St Mary's aisle, of a comfortably bulgy shape and with inlay of good local workmanship. – Hopton Wood stone pulpit in the Choir. – Hanging PYX in the S aisle by *Ninian Comper*, made for Caldey Abbey, Pembrokeshire, and donated by Athelstan Riley (cf. Little Petherick). – REREDOS in the NW tower Jesus Chapel by *Anne Walke*, 1923, showing Cornish miners and market gardeners. – The STAINED GLASS for the new cathedral designed by Pearson represents the largest single scheme of Late Victorian glass in England, and is one of the finest. It is all by *Clayton & Bell*. The series consists of three rose windows, the window of the SE transept, the baptistery (a sub-set of its own) and the thirty-eight lights around the nave, choir and transepts, climaxing in the great E window. The colours are rich, the iconography dense, the whole effect authentically medievalizing. Among the most striking depictions are the execution of Charles I in the S aisle, and Newlyn fishermen and Dolcoath miners in the W tower windows. The unusual design of the tracery of the N transept rose window reflects its adaptation by Pearson to accommodate Benson's desire to show the complete biblical genealogy of Christ.* – In the S chancel aisle is an E window with centre panels of 1911 by *Kempe & Co.* and six good windows by *William Warrington* dating from 1847–50. – PIETÀ. The best and earliest sculpture in the cathedral. In the S aisle, C14 from Brittany, powerful in its directness and simplicity. – C14 sculpture of St Nicholas, also from Brittany. – MONUMENTS. In the N transept, Richard Roberts †1614 ('of his age seventy or thereabouts') and wife below, a large affair with the two effigies reclining stiffly and uncomfortably, double columns l. and r., and on their entablatures two small figures of Father Time and Death. The carving of the larger figures is by no means good. – Some late C18 and early C19 monuments to Vyvyans, too high up to be seen. – At the W end on the S side WAR MEMORIAL, to the South African War, an unusually large essay in carved Polyphant by *F. L. Pearson*.

On the small area of land to the N Pearson had proposed a cloister like Salisbury with an octagonal chapter house. A single bay

---

*I am grateful to Michael Swift for this and other information about Benson's influence.

of the cloister was built in the 1930s and the responds for its N end were provided in the late Gothic former CATHEDRAL SCHOOL opposite, by *Frank Pearson*, 1908, with a four-storey embattled tower and multi-windowed main elevation. Between them a CHAPTER HOUSE was added in 1967 by *John Taylor* of *MWT Architects*. The hall itself is cruciform. The building is of concrete with surfaces of grit-blasted granite aggregate. The heaviness of the horizontal concrete members is in total contrast to the verticalism of the cathedral, and the tiny round arches of the vertical slit windows cut into the top slab – a fashionable motif initially derived from Le Corbusier's Maisons Jaoul – have no more convincing relation to the pointed arches of Pearson's building. Such extreme nonconformity initially strikes one as overstated (not that imitation of Pearson's C13 style would have been preferable, but it would have been equally valid to employ modern forms more consistent in vertical emphasis), yet somehow it works as a low, solid base from which the majesty of the cathedral rises dramatically above. A neat gabled SHOP, in granite, was tucked in discreetly on the N side near the W end by *W. P. Rookley* in 1987.

CHURCHES

ST JOHN, Lemon Street. 1828 by *Philip Sambell* in the Greek style. A plain rectangle with apsidal chancel. The W front is a striking presence in the upper part of Lemon Street, its three bays with corner pilasters and parapet with a central projecting bay surmounted by a cupola on six slender columns, and with a bowed porch with blind arcade of round arches and moulded parapet. Central rose window over. Interior has a gallery on columns painted *à la grecque* to resemble Doric columns. Otherwise much altered in 1893–1900. – STAINED GLASS. Ten windows by *Heaton Butler & Bayne*, 1886–7, excellent colours.

ST PAUL, Tregolls Road. 1868 by *J. D. Sedding*. Chancel, N aisle and tower base begun 1882–4, tower finished 1909–10 to design by *E. H. Sedding*. The exterior is highly accomplished, richly ornamented with the elder Sedding's original variations on Perp tracery themes, the gabled centre with battlemented turrets l. and r. and straight parapets to the aisles. The three-stage tower is dramatically placed close to the SE corner above the road and is especially effective, broad, strong, with angle buttresses and corner statues for pinnacles. The interior does not quite live up to expectations. Tall, six-bay aisles with standard Cornish piers, four-centred arches to N side, round arches to S; two-bay arcades with engaged shafts and four-centred arches between choir and chancel transepts and tower; round choir and chancel arches. – STAINED GLASS. E window and three vestry windows 1884 by *Lavers Barraud & Westlake*. N aisle window by *A. Gibbs*, 1890.

ST PAUL'S CHURCH HALL, Agar Road, possibly by *E. H. Sedding*. Simple Perp style with four-light E window, and three-light traceried windows to the N and S elevations between buttresses. Later giant concrete flying buttresses to the SE corner and N side.

ST GEORGE, St George's Road. The parish was taken out of Kenwyn (q.v.) in 1846 and a new church consecrated in 1854. It is by the *Rev. William Haslam*, with assistance from *Joseph Clarke* of London. Cruciform plan with apsidal-ended chancel, N porch and square W tower. E.E. style with many lancets. The interior is of excellent quality, lofty and well lit with fine scissor- and wind-braced roof, the principal trusses springing from posts on stone corbels and a high moulded chancel arch springing from shafted abutments with carved imposts. It is richly coloured and decorated with much polychromy. The oak and vine capitals of the chancel arch by *Clemens* of Truro are painted and gilded. Windows surrounded by painted trails and angels with musical instruments in the spandrels. *Minton* tiles to Haslam's design. – STAINED GLASS. Mostly by *Horwood Bros* of Frome.

TRURO METHODIST CHURCH (ST MARY CLEMENT), Union Place. The centre of Cornish Methodism. 1829–30 by *Philip Sambell* to replace an earlier preaching house in Kenwyn Street, enlarged 1868 and 1884, interior reordered 2000. Handsome classical front, with faintly Egyptianizing motifs in granite ashlar in three bays, has giant double pilasters to the central bay and pediment with ornamental circular ventilating panel. Central doorway flanked by fluted Doric columns, side entrances with eared architraves. Upper windows to front and side walls are round-arched with rectangular windows in the side walls. The impressive interior, formerly seating over 1,500, has a continuous round-ended gallery with late C19 panelled front, supported on cast-iron columns, and a good ensemble of coloured glass in geometric patterns. At the rear former SCHOOLROOM, dated 1866, in similar classical style with giant pilasters rising to a broken pediment through which rises a large moulded round-headed window. Also former WESLEYAN SCHOOL, datestone 1887, in same style but plainer, with 1:3:1 bay front and triangular pediment with oculus over three stepped lights of central bay.

Former ST GEORGE'S METHODIST CHURCH, St George's Road. 1881. Gothic Revival with Free Style influences. Tall W gable with central four-light window with geometrical tracery flanked by single lancets and buttresses carried up as flat-capped turrets above modelled gablets. To each side a set-back portico. Good cast-iron gates and railings in square panels embellished with quatrefoils.

FRIENDS MEETING HOUSE, Paul's Terrace. The Friends acquired a building for a meeting house in 1704 but this was built in 1825, a plain, dignified rectangle (cf. St Austell and Redruth) with a hipped slate roof and tall windows with flat-arched heads. In plan it is typical of its period with a large meeting room and a smaller women's meeting room at opposite ends of the building, separated by a through passage flanked by wooden shutters which permit the whole of the interior to be made into one room. Nearby is the BURIAL GROUND, 1825, with freestone ashlar gatepiers.

OUR LADY OF THE PORTAL AND ST PIRAN (R.C.), St Austell Street. 1973 by *MWT*. The exterior is fortress-like, the almost unpierced high white-rendered walls enclosing a courtyard of church, hall and presbytery accessed by steep steps. Impressively spacious church interior, monopitch roof sloping dramatically down towards the altar, which is lit only by sidelights with *dalle-de-verre* glass by *Father Charles Norris* of Buckfast Abbey.

PUBLIC BUILDINGS

OLD COUNTY HALL, Station Road. 1911, by *T. B. Silcock*, in a rather heavy Edwardian Baroque, to signify the arrival of the then relatively new County Council. Enlarged 1925. Large plan enclosing two small courtyards with the council chamber placed centrally. N entrance front of symmetrical 1:4:1:4:1 bays, two storeys, with end and central bays broken forward with pediments, and a central cupola. Central entrance fronted by a bowed porch carried on Doric columns with balustrade to parapet. Interior has open-well stair and vaulted ceilings to corridors. Permission has been granted in 2013 for conversion as a hotel by *Poynton Bradbury Wynter Cole*.

NEW COUNTY HALL, Treyew Road. 1963–6 by *F. K. Hicklin*,   122
succeeded by *A. J. Groves*, County Architects: Hicklin's design team was *K. M. G. Kirkbride* (chiefly responsible with Hicklin), *A. H. M. Linscott* and *J. R. Coward*. Lavish in scale, austere in design, and excellent in finishes, it ranks among the very best of mid-C20 county halls and is the most ambitious and successful of the council's considerable Modernist *œuvre* in the post-war period, often described in terms of its resemblance to Le Corbusier's monastery of La Tourette, 1953–60. *Sir Geoffrey Jellicoe* was highly influential in the evolution of the project, choosing the site and advising on the design, layout and landscaping.* The building is dramatically set on a steep s-facing slope in informal parkland on the SW edge of the city. Unfortunately the present approach to the NE front of offices is a far less effective introduction than the original entrance further E which allowed the first prospect to be of the SE elevation, where the principal architectural feature, the COUNCIL CHAMBER, boldly cantilevered forward from the strict discipline of the main building line in a pitched lozenge shape, could be seen against the landscape beyond. The plan is a large rectangle enclosing a spacious open courtyard that steps down as the site falls to the s, the s range on tall slender pilotis and the w range on pilotis of diminishing size, allowing the building to float over the slope and maintain views s, and the landscape

---

*This account is much indebted to Jeremy and Caroline Gould's history of the project in their *New County Hall: Management Guidelines* (2008).

to flow into the courtyard. The skyline, in spite of the fall, could thus be kept even. The frontages are even too, except for a slight variation where the staircases are and the conspicuous change in the SE range for the council chamber. The rigorous and consistent design employs a reinforced concrete frame construction clad with pre-cast concrete members, making a grid of relatively tall and narrow openings. The finishes are of strongly textured board-marked and exposed aggregate concrete, except for the council chamber which is clad in Derbydene limestone and has a copper roof.

The quality of the interior spaces is highy impressive, reflecting the influence of a study tour of Scandinavian post-war civic buildings undertaken by Hicklin and his associates in 1960 in preparation for the design. The principal formal entrance is beneath the council chamber into a spacious light-filled entrance hall, from which the staircase rises to a long gallery running the length of the range and from which the council chamber is accessed. The chamber is the high point of the building on which the most design effort, most exacting detailing, and most resources were lavished. Though square on plan, the seating and desks are arranged in symmetrical circles on five descending levels. The only natural light comes from a chequerboard pattern of square windows on the N and S walls set deep within angle reveals. It is especially Scandinavian in its cool, collected character, conducive to serious debate. But everywhere the finishes, furnishings and fittings are of consistently considered standard and materials.

The COURTYARD is imaginatively designed and planted to allow the flow of the landscape in and around the building. It steps down from the second- and first-floor levels on the N, where its arrangement is formal, to the S where it blends into the grassland of the park. The formal part originally included a reflecting pool and a water garden with similarities to Jellicoe's design for Plymouth Civic Centre. On a terrace sits the elegiac tall pierced SCULPTURE, Rock Form, Porthcurno, by *Barbara Hepworth*, 1965.

CITY HALL, Boscawen Street. 1846–7 by *Christopher Eales*. The suite of buildings designed to house civic, judicial and market functions originally comprised the N range fronting Boscawen Street, another range behind separated by a court, a large market, and a S range to Back Quay. The Boscawen Street elevation is very up to date, that is in the Italian Renaissance style, a grander version of Eales's palazzo market hall at St Austell, the two-storey front with an originally completely open arcade on tall vermiculated columns on the frontage giving into an interior of Piranesian proportions. First-floor sash windows with consoles to sills and alternate triangular and round pediments. Thick modillion cornice and tall pedimented clock tower. The Back Quay elevation is quieter but still dignified, of seven bays of sash windows with round arches, the central bays breaking forward. The market halls were

demolished in 1994 to make way for the HALL FOR
CORNWALL, its large bulk and fly tower quite tactfully inserted
by *Hocking & Newton* and linked to the Back Quay range. Fine
interiors to the N ranges include moulded and plastered ceilings, chimneypieces, doorcases and cast ironwork; especially
notable the first-floor council chamber, mayor's parlour and
former courtrooms in the front ranges. There is a re-set inscription of 1615 on the ground floor.

COUNTY MUSEUM AND ART GALLERY (ROYAL INSTITUTION
OF CORNWALL), River Street. 1845, by *Philip Sambell*, as
the Truro Savings Bank, adapted to current use 1912–14 by
Sampson Hill of Redruth. W wing and central hall built 1914–
17, opened 1919. Imposing classical front in granite ashlar, the
symmetrical five-window front articulated by giant Ionic pilasters with the three central bays broken forward and surmounted
by a triangular pediment. Doric porch with entablature. The
interior is remarkably intact. The plan is rectangular, the
central entrance hall leading to a spacious stair hall with an
imperial stair to a balcony on pairs of Ionic columns. The side
galleries have panelled ceilings with moulded ribs. To the r.,
now integrated with the museum by a slightly recessed and
thoughtfully understated linking façade of 1997–8 by *Poynton
Bradbury Wynter Cole*, the former BAPTIST CHAPEL, 1849–50,
also by *Sambell*. The street elevation in granite ashlar also has
giant pilasters dividing its three bays, with round-arched openings recessed to the first floor, the tall central window rising
into an open pediment. The altered interior retains round
ceiling rose with carved acanthus and reused cast-iron balustrades to the balcony.

Former ASSEMBLY ROOMS, No. 13 High Cross. of *c.* 1780 by
Christopher Ebdon, a pupil of James Paine. Little more than the
façade remains after radical reconstruction for offices in the
1970s, but what survives demonstrates that when first built it
must have been the best secular building in the town, of
remarkably high quality and not at all provincial. The façade
in fine Pentewan ashlar is a compact design of two tall storeys
and only three bays wide with a pediment over the whole, as
Paine would have done it. Ground floor of two round-headed
doorways with delicate Adamesque fanlights in the arches
which have moulded surrounds and keystones and above them
entablatures and paterae in the spandrels. They flank a central
Venetian window within a relieving arch, its sill dropped to
ground level during the 1950s. The first floor has three tall
windows with well-executed circular medallions of Garrick and
Shakespeare l. and r. and a rectangular panel bearing a sphinx-
and-urn design at the centre. There is another circular medallion, of Minerva, in the pediment. The paterae and medallions
are in unglazed ceramic.

PUBLIC LIBRARY, Pydar Street. 1896, as the Free Library, and
extended as the Central Technical Schools for Cornwall in
1897–9, by *Silvanus Trevail* on both occasions. The most

prestigious Cornish benefaction of Passmore Edwards working with his favourite architect, and showing Trevail at his inventive best, here skilfully deploying a mixture of Renaissance Classical and Domestic Gothic. The LIBRARY, striking in its use of a vibrant pink-veined stone as the main walling material with Bath stone dressings, is two-storey with central doors to both elevations of its corner site, large mullioned-and-transomed windows to the ground floor and round-headed to the first floor, and a projecting two-storey bay to Pydar Street. The former TECHNICAL SCHOOL, now integrated with the library, is more elaborate with richer detail. Its central round-arched doorway with spoked fanlight is set between pairs of pilasters in the manner of a Gibbs surround. The upper stages are more complex with projecting central and outer bays surmounted by pedimented gables: the recessed bays between have two-light gabled windows flanked by three-light blind partitions with traceried heads. Fine frieze of Cornish trades and craftsmen over the first-floor windows of the central bay. The interior layout of both buildings is relatively unaltered, the library with an entrance hall leading to a stair hall with an open-well stair, the technical school also with an open-well stair.

123 COURTS OF JUSTICE, Edward Street. 1986–8 by *Evans & Shalev*, marking the architects' shift from their New Brutalist style towards Postmodernism. Of the highest calibre in concept, architectural composition, and immaculately controlled detail. A large complex on a prominent site (the medieval castle) yet so skilfully modulated that it never intimidates whether from a distance, on approach, or inside: its relationship to the city, as well as its immediate neighbourhood of modest mostly stucco houses, seems one of natural integration, helped by its sparkling white render and the absence of a dominant external feature. The scale is diffused in a low-rise structure spread around two conically capped rotundas, which rise up from the flat roof-line to mark the two major assembly areas inside the court house: these almost disappear on the approach, the entrance marked by a large portico with a triangular pediment that signifies the dignity of the court without being overbearing. The fine interior, which accommodates three courtrooms and follows conventional courtroom design with separate circulation patterns for judiciary, jury, defendants and public, is the high point. It is brilliantly lit by natural light through sandblasted glass blocks in the curved clerestory windows of the rotundas, supported by slender columns, and echoed in screen walls of glass blocks at lower levels: these motifs were successfully reprised and developed in the architects' Tate St Ives (q.v.). Other detail reinforces the cool and lofty character of the assembly spaces: white-glazed tiles with intersecting black inserts cover the full floor area to the stair flights, constructed in contrasting blue-black Staffordshire bricks. The formal garden, overlooking the city, is given definition by a semicircular enclosing wall at its E end framed by giant paired columns with heavy horizontal lintels.

COUNCIL OFFICES, Pydar Street. 1979, by *MWT Architects*, in a style used in several other buildings in the area. The redeeming feature is that the mass of the large complex is subdivided into separate blocks with monopitch roofs sloping up from the street with neat grouping of openings. The set-back from the street line helps to integrate the offices into the street scene, important as they frame the approach to the cathedral.

GOVERNMENT OFFICES (PYDAR HOUSE), Pydar Street. 1986, by *MWT Architects*. A poor composition of seven blocks weakly linked by glazing to form an incomplete octagon, on a steeply sloping site near the top of the street.

Former INFIRMARY, Infirmary Hill. Now part of a large residential development. 1799, by *William Wood*. Remarkably stately, though plain. Three-storey symmetrical 3:3:3 bay N front, the central bays broken forward and rising to four storeys into the open pediment; similar pediment to projecting cross-wing to r. Central doorway with 1799 date in frieze; above is a sash with round-arched recess over an apron with Cornish arms flanked by swags.

Former ST CLEMENT'S HOSPITAL, Tregolls Road. Now converted to residential use and surrounded by housing in Penair Crescent. Built 1851 as the Truro Union Workhouse, by *William Harris*. A good example of its type and date, on a large plan arranged around three courtyards with a central four-storey octagonal tower. The handsome entrance front is two-storey with a single-storey entrance porch and two projecting wings all under the same eaves board, with windows in tall round arches with voussoirs and key blocks.

TRURO STATION, Station Road. 1897. Single-storey, with two taller roofed bays broken forward of central booking hall with decorative ironwork to their flat roofs, a standard GWR design.

VIADUCTS, E of the station. The first is Carvedras, of eighteen spans and 1,329 ft (405 metres), the longest in Cornwall, over the Kenwyn valley; the second Truro, of eleven spans over the Allen. Both were rebuilt in 1904. Beside them are the redundant piers of Brunel's 1858 viaducts, 60 ft (18 metres) apart and originally spanned by fan-shaped timber constructions.

PERAMBULATIONS

1. West and north-west of the cathedral: High Cross and Pydar Street

The best starting point for an exploration of Truro is HIGH CROSS at the W front of the cathedral. The CROSS-HEAD, found in St Nicholas Street in 1958, and now on a shaft of 1988, is a typical wayside cross, not the elaborate version that might once have stood in such an important position. The sophisticated façade of the former Assembly Rooms (*see* Public Buildings) is a reminder that this was the heart of the late C18 town and an area of good town houses. No. 18A, mid to late C18 with a possibly C17 range to its rear. The frontages along

PYDAR STREET, SW, notably No. 24 and No. 25 KING STREET, late C19 purpose-built commercial premises, by *Silvanus Travail* and his assistant *Alfred Cornelius*, illustrate the area's later commercial prestige. No. 25 is three storeys, with a splendid front in an early Northern Renaissance style with Ionic pilasters to the shopfront, tall wide windows to the first and second floors, and a balustraded parapet on carved consoles with a panel inscribed 'Burton' in relief, surmounted by a triangular pediment. No. 24 is brick and terracotta, three storeys, the central bay broken forward from the second floor and rising to a triangular pedimented gable with panel inscribed 'Harvey' in relief below. The W side of High Cross is unfortunately now framed by a large and ungainly retail development of 1980 by *Norman Jones, Sons & Rigby* of Southport, its front faceted to the corner of High Cross and Pydar Street, the first floor jettied out, the bland reconstituted Bath stone façade articulated by recessed brick panels echoed in the roof recesses.

Of the medieval borough, of which Pydar Street was the main axis, the original burgage plots survive in the property boundaries and narrow passages like COOMBE LANE and PEOPLE'S PALACE COURT opening off the SW side. They are fronted by late C18 and early C19 town houses, subsequently converted to commercial use, mostly in stucco with slate-hanging at No. 8 and the occasional ashlar, like No. 7 in Pentewan and No. 17 in granite, three-storey diminishing to two as the street rises NW. Good architectural detail, including giant fluted pilasters to No. 19 and a variety of cornices and eaves treatment. NALDER'S COURT, 1989 by *Bruges Tozer*, is a minor retail essay in Postmodernism neatly inserted behind the late C18 façade of No. 6: the roofs are supported by fans of slender posts springing from first-floor bays and pilotis.

The NE side starts with Trevail's library (*see* Public Buildings) which forms a splendid corner building to UNION PLACE, which has the stately front of Truro Methodist Church (*see* Churches) as its focal point. But much of the rest is of the second half of the C20, part of the development planned by *MWT Architects*. Some façades were retained to alleviate the impact of the large retail development of the 1970s (job architect *Roger Hocking*), which spreads around into St Clement Street. Its scale is mitigated to the street frontages by MWT's trademark motif, reprised in later developments further up the street, of segmenting the building façade into separate blocks with monopitch roofs.

The upper part of Pydar Street is dominated by a cluster of civic and government buildings of the later C20, first on the r. the council offices, then on the l. government offices, also by *MWT Architects*, in variations on the segmented theme. The view NW is framed by the railway viaducts, and the fitting climax is *Evans & Shalev*'s splendid Courts of Justice, off Castle Rise. All are described under Public Buildings above.

2. South and south-west of the cathedral: King Street, Boscawen Street, St Nicholas Street and River Street

Begin in High Cross, where KING STREET continues the line of Pydar Street SE, with more good former C18 town houses, e.g. No. 18, with a five-window front in brick with tall sashes spanned by double-ogee heads. The building height ramps up through No. 16, probably originally two early C19 town houses of three storeys with a regular six-window front and good stucco detail, to BARCLAYS BANK, on the corner of St Nicholas Street and Boscawen Street. This is of 1888 by *James Hicks*, as the West Cornwall Bank, one of his most accomplished designs in a roguish Baroque, perfectly symbolizing the commercial self-confidence of late C19 Truro. A robust entablature breaks forward over the ground floor where fat pilasters divide the bays, from which paired Composite columns rise to divide pairs of round-headed windows, to an even heavier parapet entablature surmounted by obelisks with ball finials. Hicks is still not finished, for above again are dormer windows with elaborately shaped gables surmounted by open round pediments.

The wide, spacious BOSCAWEN STREET is cobbled and flanked by granite-lined water channels that are a feature throughout the town centre. The street has been important throughout Truro's history. In the C17 it contained the great town houses of the Robartes and Foote families on the N side (both gone), with properties on the S side originally having direct access to the River Kenwyn. There were more serious losses in the later C20, especially the demolition of the C16–C17 Red Lion Hotel* on the N side, replaced by the triple-gabled façade of the CO-OP, 1969 by *Inskip & Wilczynski*: like other rebuilds of this period in the street, the intentionally stark contrast has not worn well. The grand centrepiece is the City Hall (*see* Public Buildings) but drawing the eye to the E end is COINAGE HALL, a building of *c.* 1850 on the site of the former coinage hall demolished in 1840. In Tudor style with tall gabled elevations, transomed-and-mullioned windows, and a two-storey porch bay facing down the street. In front the WAR MEMORIAL, *c.* 1920 by *Joseph Whitehead* of London. A tall tapered chest rising from a stepped moulded base, mostly in rock-faced granite, with stepped capstones as a base for a fine bronze statue of a foot soldier in battledress raising his helmet in the air. Large former town houses of the late C18 and early C19 include Nos. 9, 11 and 12 on the S side and Nos. 27 (four-storey), 28 and 29 on the N side, all with excellent classical detail in stucco. No. 31 has a smart late C18 Pentewan ashlar front. On the corner with CATHEDRAL LANE is an exuberant

---

*The hotel, which had been converted from the Foote house in 1769, was demolished in 1967. Sidney Schofield rescued the 1671 staircase and stored it at Godolphin.

essay in eclectic Elizabethan vernacular of 1905 by *Alfred Cornelius*, the second floor jettied out with elaborate timber framing above the first floor of glazed white bricks. On the corner with Lower Lemon Street is LLOYDS BANK, built 1890 by *Silvanus Trevail*, his first Devon & Cornwall Bank commission, and linked to the smaller and plainer pre-existing bank of the 1840s next door by *Henry Rice* of Liskeard. An accomplished classical building making excellent use of its site, the corner accentuated by its use as the entrance flanked by columns in pink granite, carried up into bowed sash windows and surmounted by a domed cupola. The upper floors are articulated by giant Ionic pilasters. Two later C20 buildings in LOWER LEMON STREET stand out: No. 6, 1963 for W. H. Smith by *John Crowther*, with its white mosaic-tiled and windowless three-storey façade floating above the continuous receding glazed ground floor; and No. 4, 1958 by *Taylor & Crowther*, more restrained, with carefully detailed slate panels and stone cladding.

ST NICHOLAS STREET, the continuation of Boscawen Street w, suffered some C20 disruption, but No. 1 is a good early C19 stucco town house and No. 15 another example of purpose-built commercial premises of the late C19, this by *James Hicks*: Italianate, four-storey and three bays, the most striking feature the full-height central arch flanked by narrow arches carried on giant fluted pilasters with stiff-leaf foliate capitals through the first and second floors. It was built for Messrs Cridle & Smith, art furnishers. VICTORIA SQUARE follows, an engaging mix of building styles including one tall Art Deco front (Malletts). Off the s side of the square is WALSINGHAM PLACE, one of the most delightful examples of the modest graciousness that must have characterized late C18 Truro, a terrace of stucco houses on a gentle curve with simple pilasters and lion-head corbels to the door hoods, the w side sadly stripped of its stucco.

Continuing w, KENWYN STREET has more stucco building of the late C18 and C19. On the N side the former PRIMITIVE METHODIST CHAPEL of 1878, its tall front in Gothic style, buttresses surmounted by tall pinnacles, a rose window over the porch, and three stepped lights in the central gable. No. 107 on the corner with Little Castle Street is a curiosity, a large late C19 off-licence and depot, now shops, by *Leonard Winn*, single-storey with original shopfront rounding the corner with slender mullions and small-paned overlights under a moulded entablature with incised nameplate 'The Redruth Brewery Company Limited'.

Now N along LITTLE CASTLE STREET across River Street up into CASTLE STREET. Above, THE LEATS, a good group of villas and a terrace of the early C19, probably all by *Philip Sambell*, with nice stucco decoration including panelled corner pilasters and round-headed niches. Pleasant extensions of this perambulation could include continuing w along The Leats and the WATERFALL GARDENS into VICTORIA GARDENS

with its pretty bandstand of 1898, and then returning via St
George's Road or into Frances Street, the w extension
of River Street, and thence into the early and mid-C19 suburb
of Ferris Town and Richmond Hill leading up towards
the later C19 development around the station (*see* Public
Buildings). Return to the centre via River Street, developed
in the 1840s, mostly lined with three-storey mid-C19 town
houses and shops: No. 3 and Nos. 4–8 have anthemion and
shell decoration to their first-floor window heads. On the N
side is the red brick façade of *Silvanus Trevail*'s premises for
Nankivell & Co, wine merchants, of 1891. The County Museum
and Art Gallery Royal Institution of Cornwall (*see* Public
Buildings) make a fitting centrepiece.

*3. East of the cathedral: Old and New Bridge Streets, Quay Street
and Princes Street*

The topography of the area E of the cathedral towards Truro
River is intriguing. It reflects the successive bridgings eastward
of the Allen and Kenwyn tributaries and the accompanying
shift of the working waterfronts, the culverting of the Kenwyn,
the infilling of the historic quays, and the construction of the
inner relief road, Morlaix Avenue, which breaks the connection
with the modern waterfront. Fortunately some sense of the
historic waterways can still be found in the crossings of the
Allen in Old Bridge Street, dating from the C13, and New
Bridge Street, from the later C18, an area of intimate scale
especially striking so close to the cathedral, with an enjoyable
variety of small later C18 and C19 houses and shops: No. 1 Old
Bridge Street is a rare example for Truro of late C18 red brick
in Flemish bond.

In contrast Princes Street, and to a lesser extent Quay Street
into which it runs, demonstrate wealth and prestige from the
early C18 right through to the close of the C19: it is not a long
street and is best described in the historical sequence of buildings to explain their exceptional interest. Of the early C18 are
Nos. 5–7 Princes Street which originated as three town houses
of double-depth plan, with deep eaves over a modillion and
moulded cornice. The Old Mansion House, Quay Street,
of 1709, is brick (now painted) and also of double-depth plan
with a smart symmetrical seven-window front, with a slightly
projecting centre bay over which the deep cornice with heavy
modillions is broken forward and surmounted by a triangular
pediment. Towards the E end of Princes Street Penhaligon
House is contemporary but much larger, of three storeys with
a wide five-window front, much restored but with fine mid-C18
plasterwork ceilings.

Good as they are, these houses are outshone by Princes House
and Mansion House, the finest town houses in Cornwall,
of a quality that, as an C18 gazetteer recorded, 'within as well
as without would not ill become the best square in London or

Westminster'. Princes House is of 1739 for William Lemon (1696–1760), who rose from humble origins to make a fortune from tin and copper mining; Mansion House is of 1755–62 for Thomas Daniell, who started as clerk to William Lemon and later took over his business to become a leading figure in the Cornish mining industry in his own right. Both houses originally had private quays on the Kenwyn, which lies to their rear. They are both by *Thomas Edwards* of Greenwich (cf. Trewithen), and of complementary yet distinctive design, the former Gibbsian outside and Baroque inside, the latter Palladian outside, Rococo within.

The front of Princes House is a neat, simple design, five bays and two-and-a-half storeys, built most unusually for Cornwall of yellowish brick (now painted over) with stone dressings, over a granite semi-basement. The central door is approached up a broad flight of steps. Ground-floor windows have Gibbs surrounds, those above moulded architraves. There are plain string courses at first-floor level and under the first-floor eaves, and the front is surmounted by a modillion cornice and flanked by rusticated quoins. Heavy Italianate C19 porch; the original door is round-headed and flanked by Corinthian half-columns. It is, however, the opulence of the interior that is exceptional, with a splendid combined entrance and staircase hall separated by a screen of Ionic columns, the staircase an extremely heavy mahogany piece with turned balusters. Walls and ceiling are decorated with fine plasterwork in Italian Baroque style with ornate swags, garlands and flowers, the ceiling of almost overpowering boldness and vigour and of unusual design consisting of a central ellipse and four half-ellipses. On the first floor at the rear a good room with rich Baroque ceiling, fireplace, overmantel and enriched doors, doorcases and shutters. Another room on this floor has an Ionic columnar screen. All the main rooms have original fittings with varying degrees of enrichment.

Mansion House is every bit as good, perhaps even better in that the equally rich interior decoration is more refined and delicate. Daniell had married a niece of Ralph Allen of Bath and above a granite basement the building is of Bath stone, a wedding present from Allen's Combe Down quarries. Its plain symmetrical front, of five bays and two and a half storeys, has a broad flight of steps to a central entrance retaining original cast-iron railings and lamp-standards. Doorcase of Doric half-columns supporting a pediment, the cornice of which is broken to admit a Rococo fanlight. The internal planning is an advance on Princes House. Square entrance hall to the r. from which a round-headed archway in its rear wall leads to a small circular domed vestibule with similar openings l., r., and straight on to the main staircase, lit by a Venetian window above. The staircase is the most notable feature of the rich interior, similar to the former staircase at Carclew (q.v.) also by Edwards. The wooden steps are cantilevered, the tread-ends enriched with scrolls and Greek key ornament and coved beneath, and the balustrade is of wrought-iron scrolls. The Venetian window is fully orchestrated with Ionic piers, entablatures and balusters below, the walls with enriched plaster frames. Three ceilings of fine late Baroque plasterwork, that in the entrance hall coved. A wealth of enriched detail throughout, one fireplace especially fine with Aesop's fable plaque. Even the back staircase is noteworthy with a balustrade of a simple Chippendale-Chinese fretwork design.

The two houses are separated by No. 10, WEAR HOUSE, 1888 by *Silvanus Trevail*, built as Polkinhorne's warehouse and assertively placed right on the street line and in Jacobean style. Other buildings show the continued importance of the street in the mid to late C19. At the W end No. 2, *c.* 1850 in Tudor-Gothic style, has a tall front with pointed-arched doorway and four-light transomed windows with trefoil heads. No. 7 Quay Street, late C19 by *Alfred Cornelius*, is a large corner shop with offices above, exuberant in polychrome brick and terracotta in a mixture of high Victorian and Baroque with enormous lunette windows lighting the first floors. The high point of the E end of the street is the former BISHOP PHILPOTTS LIBRARY AND PUBLIC ROOMS of 1867–9, in Tudor Gothic with tall and dignified elevations to both Princes Street and Back Quay. The library is at the W end, the S elevation with an elaborate stone oriel above the door with traceried windows and a bracket below lettered HEN. PHILPOTTS EP EXON DD 1869. The N elevation is multi-bayed and richer in detail. The interior has good Gothic and High Victorian detail, the library with massively over-engineered bookcases.

4. Lemon Street, Strangeways Terrace and Falmouth Road

The sequence of building from the junction of Lemon Street with Boscawen Street to the top of Falmouth Road shows more clearly than anywhere else in Truro the city's development from the closing years of the C18 to the beginning of the C20. LEMON STREET developed outside the framework of the medieval street pattern on land owned by the Lemon family and is named after its founding father, William Lemon (*see* Princes House, above). It provided an easier route up the valley side for the road to Penryn and Falmouth and opened up development of the S bank of the Kenwyn, with a new bridge across the river in 1798 and a new street, Lower Lemon Street, taken through to the S side of Boscawen Street. Though constructed piecemeal between *c.* 1790 and *c.* 1810, the basic design and construction elements were specified in the building plot leases, with many of the builders and their clients known and much of the work overseen by *William Wood.*★

★I am grateful to the Truro Buildings Research Group, founded by Veronica Chesher, and their excellent publications on the city for this and much other valuable information.

Begin in LOWER LEMON STREET at Trevail's bank on the corner
with Boscawen Street and the three-storey former town houses
on the E side. On the W side the ROYAL HOTEL by *Wood*. Three
storeys, eight-window range; the original symmetrical building
has 1:3:1 fenestration with the central bays broken forward and
a large royal coat of arms above the central doorway. It later
incorporated two other houses to the r., slightly set back. The
street proper begins after the junction with Back Quay and
Lemon Quay (*see* p. 681). Of generous width and gentle ascent
towards the eyecatcher of the Lander Monument (*see* below)
on the skyline, its graciousness is reminiscent of Bath and
Bristol, though not as grand. The terraces of two- and three-
storey houses are of a restrained and dignified Late Georgian
design largely in ashlar Pentewan (with some granite and
repairs in Ham Hill stone) that bestows a lovely mellow character to the whole street composition. The W side starts with
three-storey houses, the S with two-storey houses over basements in granite ashlar, with stepped bridges to the central
entrances often enclosed by original latticed wrought-iron railings. The subtle variations in detail, especially in porches, doorcases and doors, are delightful, reflecting the street's
development by individual owners, and add to the enjoyment
of the most architecturally coherent street in Cornwall: its
strength is such that it readily absorbs a few later rebuilds and
even the large *moderne* façade of the PLAZA CINEMA of
1935–6. Between Nos. 72 and 73 a former carriage entrance to
the LEMON STREET MARKET, 2006 by *CAD Architects,* a successful insertion of a simple market hall, galleried internally,
connecting through to Lemon Mews Road and Walsingham
Place (*see* p. 676).

As the street rises, the houses diminish to more modest terraces
of two storeys: off to the l., CARCLEW STREET is a good
example of smaller terraced housing of the early C19 with
paired round-headed doorways. Towards the top the character
of Lemon Street changes. On the r. are detached villas, first
LEMON LODGE, 1818, by *John Chappell*, builder, in stucco
with full-height canted bays flanking a central porch, and then
LEMON HOUSE, 1815, with a two-storey symmetrical three-
bay front range in stone with Tuscan porch. On the l. ST JOHN'S
CHURCH (*see* Churches) and LEMON VILLAS, before 1840,
opposite the beginning of STRANGEWAYS TERRACE of
1837. Five pairs of town houses of three storeys over basements, linked by ground-floor porches with paired doorways,
almost severe in plain stucco unadorned except for rusticated
ground floors. Beyond are STRANGEWAYS VILLAS, two
c. 1840 two-storey pairs over basements with canted oriel
windows and good ironwork. They are similar to UPPER
LEMON VILLAS of the same date which turn the corner from
Strangeways Terrace into Falmouth Road, these with deep
moulded eaves on central and end consoles and more original
ironwork to the street boundary. In front rises the splendid

LANDER MONUMENT, 1835 by *Philip Sambell*. A tall fluted Doric column in granite rising from a square plinth, surmounted by a figure of Richard Lander (the explorer who with his brother John discovered the source of the Niger in 1827) by *Neville Northey Burnard* of Altarnun. Erected by *Bowden* of Helston.

At the start of FALMOUTH ROAD to the r. is DANIELL STREET, one of the best and most complete streets of early C19 planned terraces, the houses like those in Carclew Street with round-headed arched paired doorways. Then in Falmouth Road a short terrace of mid-C19 houses opposite Nos. 1–21, a long terrace of similar date, mostly in stucco with quoins and a mid-floor decorative band. On the r., in dramatic contrast, rises a terrace of five former houses of 1856, now FARLEY HOUSE, CLIFDEN GATE and GLENBANK. Tall, in ornate Elizabethan style with four shaped gables breaking forward flanked by the stepped gables of two projecting wings with finials. Later C19 houses follow, including No. 32, *c.* 1880, a former vicarage, its plainness a contrast to the exuberant French Renaissance/ Baronial style of Nos. 40–46 COLCHESTER VILLAS, 1883 by *James Hicks*. Terrace of four houses, the end houses L-shaped with three-storey towers over porches in the angles, the smaller middle houses with five-bay loggia surmounted by a decorative balustrade. Even more Baronial is the main building of TRURO HIGH SCHOOL beyond. 1896 by *E. R. Robson*, of two storeys with a splendidly quirky three-storey tower which has an embattled parapet on a cornice with brackets like machicolations, a bowed oriel, and a projecting three-storey bay. The return down to the centre offers good views of the city and cathedral.

5. *Back Quay, Lemon Quay, Malpas Road and the riverside*

Lemon Quay and Back Quay come as an anti-climax after the graciousness of Lemon Street. Where one expects to find the city's historic waterfront is a large and usually desolate open space, created from the infilled quay, and all that is visible of the river is a small section of the Kenwyn under the shadow of the bridge carrying Morlaix Avenue across its SE end. The quays were infilled in the 1930s, and the rest of the C20 was a story of missed opportunities as the redevelopment of the quaysides proceeded.

The N side of this public piazza is formed by the buildings of BACK QUAY which starts strongly from its junction with Lemon Street, its high point the restrained classicism of the HALL FOR CORNWALL (*see* City Hall above). It is flanked to the l. by the jolly polychrome front of the MARKET INN, *c.* 1900, in terracotta and glazed tiles, its name panel surmounted by a triangular pediment with scrolled abutments and ball finials. To the r. POUNDLAND, built *c.* 1935 as Wool-worths, has a nice *moderne* brick façade. The rest of the street represents the rebuilding of the former private quays to the grand Princes Street houses at this period, all faintly stream-lined: behind Nos. 21–27, TINNERS COURT, a discreet late C20 retail development, offers a good view of the rear elevation of Mansion House. The long, low corner building to GREEN STREET was built in the mid 1930s as a state-of-the-art service station and showrooms. The bus station occupies the site of The Green, a former public open space in front of the Bishop Philpotts Library (*see* p. 679).

The buildings along the S side of the piazza, opposite, were LEMON QUAY, almost completely redeveloped between *c.* 1970 and the early C21, and this is the greatest disappoint-ment. It begins at the Lemon Street end with LEMON QUAY HOUSE, 1973 by the *Douglas Feast Partnership* of London, its large scale at least mitigated by strong vertical articulation. Next WETHERSPOON'S, built as the West Briton newspaper offices, has a decent 1950s brick façade with a clock flèche. The rest of the street is a large single development of 2001 stretching back to FAIRMANTLE STREET and culminating in the MARKS & SPENCER store on the corner with Morlaix Avenue. It is by *Lyons, Sleeman & Hoare*, revised by *Kensington Taylor Architects*. The faux industrial style is hopelessly uncon-vincing, the façades dressed up with flimsy warehouse motifs like the shallow triple gables of the lower section and the steel-framed bays of the corner building, the latter each incongru-ously sporting a small first-floor bay supported on a spindly colonette. Such a prime site so prominent in views across the city towards the cathedral from Morlaix Avenue deserved far better than this clumsy monolith.

For a sense of Truro's waterfront it is necessary to venture under Morlaix Avenue via the subway, past the bleak spread of the blocky TESCO, 1979 by *MWT Architects* (project architect *Roger Hocking*), to view TOWN QUAY at the confluence of the Allen and Kenwyn and the start of Truro River. It is the most visible of the former quays. Early C18 and later, the oldest part vertically set killas, otherwise roughly carved killas with granite copings. Its S end is rounded with battered walls. From here too are good views across to the E bank where a series of early C21 developments displays consistently thoughtful and contex-tual design. Something of the character of the historic water-front has been retained in the mix of converted buildings and new structures echoing warehouse forms with much timber cladding along MALPAS ROAD, their best elevations to the waterside. Several good examples are by the *Lilly Lewarne Practice*; the 1978 conversion of the HTP Mill of 1911 by *Alfred Cornelius*; the VICTORIA WAREHOUSE, converted to offices, 2001; WEST BRITON OFFICES, 2002; and OSPREY HOUSE, 2003. Above Malpas Road is THE PARADE, a delightful terrace of eighteen modest early to mid-C19 houses, an appropriate finale.

OTHER BUILDINGS

ALVERTON MANOR HOTEL, Tregolls Road. Formerly the Convent of the Epiphany. In a secluded setting above the modern dual carriageway. It began as a large mid-C19 house, was converted *c.* 1880 to a convent, and became a hotel in 1984. A complex but attractive ensemble in a medley of different styles. The original house forms the N–S range, its hall to the W. For the convent, the hall was converted to a chapel, the first-floor rooms subdivided for cells, and a clock tower and main entrance added by *Ninian Comper* in 1897–1900 to the original entrance. *E. H. Sedding* added a N wing in free Gothic in 1903–4 and a new chapel in E.E. style in 1908–10: the W wing in a free Tudor style is probably also by him. The HALL has a five-bay canted roof with much moulded and carved timber and a bay window with richly moulded columns and mullions, filled with STAINED GLASS by the *Hardman Co.*, memorial date 1889. In the N–S range much Gothick detail including staircase with Gothic pierced balusters and fleur-de-lys stencilling. The former CHAPEL is a striking presence, with a five-bay nave, five-sided buttressed apsidal E end with undercroft, N projecting bay and polygonal stair, and slype. Fine interior with vaulted stone roof with quadripartite bays and moulded ribs carried on columns with three shafts and moulded bases. Three N windows and apse windows by *Kempe & Co.*, N bay by *Clayton & Bell*, slype windows by *Hardman*. Some of the fittings from the chapel are now at Epiphany House, Kenwyn (q.v.).

BOSVIGO HOUSE, Bosvigo Lane. Small country house, early to mid-C18, extended *c.* 1780 and remodelled early C19. Seven-window front, three centre bays of the earlier building with central door with open porch. The l.-hand wing has late C18 sashes with thick glazing bars and tall mid-C19 sashes above, the r. wing late C18 to early C19 sashes. Good C18 chimneypieces and other fittings including Gothic-style fittings to front l. room.

TRURO SCHOOL, Trennick Road. Set high above the Truro River and prominent in many views out of the city. Founded 1880, on this site since 1882 of which the main building is by *Elliot Ettwell* of West Bromwich with tall straight main façade looking higher than its two storeys with dormers. To the r. a square tower, four-storey with steep slate roof suggesting French Gothic Revival influence. To the r. of the tower an elevated classroom like a Gothic chapel. The school chapel follows, 1928 by *George Withers* in a simple modern Gothic style, forming a prominent end to the range: it has some attractive Art Deco windows of 1927 and good *dalle-de-verre* glass of 1980. Major additions behind, including the *Burrell Theatre*, 2002 by the *Lilly Lewarne Practice*.

KILLAGORDEN, 1 m. N. Central two-room C18 plan with long service wing to rear and early C19 wings. Symmetrical two-storey SE front of 3:3:3 bays, central doorway with porch with granite columns and frieze. Good interior, including open-well stairs of late C18 with wreathed mahogany handrail over newel and contemporary plaster cornices. Early C19 ENTRANCE LODGE, ½ m. E, single-storey, Gothic details.

PENMOUNT CREMATORIUM, 1 m. N. An C18 and C19 house, adapted in 1956. Stucco S entrance front of 2:1:2 bays with central bay broken forward and porch, now enclosed and partly hidden by C20 porte cochère. C18 and C19 details in several rooms including entrance hall which has pedimented doorcases, Vitruvian scroll frieze and gallery to one side. Back stair early C18, main early C19 stair now at Polwhele (*see* below). Once the home of Charles Henderson, the Cornish historian. CHAPELS of 1956 and 1978.

POLWHELE SCHOOL, 1 m. NE. The home of Richard Polwhele (1760–1838), the Cornish historian. C16 core but mostly early C19 and 1870 when it was remodelled and extended either by *George Gilbert Scott* or his assistant *Richard Coad*. Dull Tudor Gothic around three sides of a courtyard; medieval fabric survives in the gable and inner side wall of the W wing and front wall and central axial wall of the main range. The E wing and the whole of the E front are of 1870. Interior has open-well stair with stone treads said to be from Penmount (*see* above), with painted canopied ceilings over with crests of Polwhele marriages.

ROYAL CORNWALL HOSPITAL, 2 m. W. Planned as a partial replacement for the Royal Cornwall Infirmary of 1799; now a critically overcrowded site, hemmed in by other developments all round. The initial major building, a five-storey concrete slab block, by *Adams, Holden & Pearson*, now surrounded by developments spread over fifty years in varying unrelated architectural styles. The three-storey KNOWLEDGE SPA is by *Nightingale Associates*, 2004, on a narrow wedge of land facing the roundabout off which the hospital is entered. Sweeping curved end, the two bands of white brise-soleil set against dark tinted glazing, following the curve with a screen of conifers behind. However, most of the remainder is a disappointment, the major and dominant central Trelawny wing, 1998, a bulky and uninspired complex in fair-faced concrete block. Many of the later developments are individual buildings by different architects using different materials, plainly unrelated to each other, sitting on their own cramped sites.

TRELISKE SCHOOL, 1 m. W. Built *c.* 1880 as a small country house. Classical style with Mannerist detail. Two-storey with flanking single-storey wings. Symmetrical entrance front of 2:1:2 bays, the central bay broken forward and surmounted by a steep triangular pediment with oculus. Elaborate porch with blind arcaded frieze on large moulded brackets above. The interior has very high-quality fittings, virtually complete as built.

TRURO COLLEGE, 3 m. W. First phase 1993 by the *Stanley Partnership*, a modest and refined two-storey building with overhanging eaves and brise-soleil. Now almost lost in later, much larger and bulkier buildings of three and four storeys where most have a single curving roof. Adapted to various plan forms – triangular, square, or parallelogram – with one corner sailing over, another almost dropping to the ground. Large walls of glass alternate with circular windows and buildings end in sharp corners. Perhaps too many exciting shapes for one site.

Massive residential expansion, particuarly since 2000, N and W of the city has been universally mediocre–poor. Few examples merit attention though the Arts and Crafts influences on both local authority housing and detached bungalows from the 1930s are worth spotting: examples of the work of *P. Edwin Stephens* and *Alfred Cornelius*, spreading from Truro to Falmouth, are characterized by sweeping roofs, overhanging eaves, roughcast render, and even occasionally a raking buttress or chimney.

The best large estate was REDANNICK, off Chapel Hill, on a steeply sloping site looking NE to the cathedral. 1950s by *John Taylor*, one- and two-storey houses along winding roads using simple geometric shapes and Scandinavian influence, with painted rendered walls and some monopitch roofs. Off Mitchell Hill NE of the city, ALVERTON COURT, 1963 also by *Taylor*, took the same concept to a more refined level. Well-planned traffic-pedestrian segregation accesses well-landscaped grounds in which are set two terraces of three two-storey houses and five varied single-storey houses, which, carefully articulated, complete the corners.

TRUTHALL

6030

1½ m. NE of Sithney

Mentioned in Domesday, acquired by the Arundells of Lanherne and Trerice (qq.v.) in 1557. Announced from the road by fine C17 gatepiers fronting a courtyard. To the r. a rare survival of a late medieval hall, extended at its lower end in the late C16. In the centre a virtually unaltered wing of 1642, and to the l. another wing rebuilt in the late C19 but incorporating earlier fabric. The principal elevation faces away from the courtyard and retains two Beer stone two-light transomed-and-mullioned windows with cinquefoil heads. The mid-C17 range has a symmetrical frontage with mullioned windows and a plaque above the door inscribed 1642 and IA and MA. The hall retains its smoke-blackened base-cruck derivative roof, exceptionally rare in Cornwall. The room over the entry is slightly jettied over the hall and a first-floor chamber has a plaster barrel ceiling.

TUCKINGMILL

The parish is contiguous with the E side of Camborne (q.v.).* It lies in the valley of the Red River which in the C18 and C19 was a network of mills, foundries, tin-stream works, tail-works, arsenic works, manufactures and some of the most important Cornish mines.

ALL SAINTS, Pendarves Street. 1843–6, by *John Hayward* of Exeter, an early church in his career. Funded by the Bassets of Tehidy to serve the mining district. A most attractive composition in the Norman style, built of a lovely warm pink killas with granite dressings, the W end especially finely grouped and detailed. The four-stage W tower, with half-height angle buttresses to the NW corner and a cylindrical stair-turret to the SW, is surmounted by a pyramidal lead roof above a corbel table. The tower is attached to the S aisle instead of the nave, allowing the W end of the tall nave to show impressively set back alongside: it has two single light windows and in the gable above a triple-light window which has shafts with cushion capitals. Five-bay nave with granite lesenes and a Lombard frieze to each bay, and single-light windows like the W end. A gabled N porch has a Norman-style doorway including set-in shafts and a carved extrados. The five-bay S aisle matches the N. The interior is of striking simplicity with white-painted unplastered walls and splayed window embrasures, the aisle arcade of cylindrical columns with scalloped caps and chamfered semicircular arches, the chancel arch semicircular with slender set-in shafts and dog-tooth ornament. Arch-braced collar-truss roof supported on slender wall-posts on large scalloped corbels. – FONT. Fine Norman bowl of *c.* 1100 with interlaced inverted semicircles below two ropework bands and incised chevron around the rim. From the former chapel of St Derwa at Menadarva (cf. Penponds; Professor Charles Thomas). – STAINED GLASS. Chancel E, 1847 by *Joseph Bell*. Exceptionally bright and dazzling. – The rest of the 1890s by *Fouracre & Watson* or *Fouracre & Son*, Plymouth.

Former WESLEYAN METHODIST CHAPEL, Chapel Road. Dated 1843 in pediment, and altered by conversion. The symmetrical four-bay pedimented front has raised quoins and round-headed windows with rusticated surrounds.

Former BICKFORD SMITH'S FUSEWORKS, Pendarves Street. The invention of the safety fuse by William Bickford in the early C19 was of great significance for the mining industry. Manufacture commenced at Tuckingmill in 1831; a hundred years later one thousand miles of fuse were produced every week. Production ceased in 1961. The buildings are partly mid-C19 but mostly rebuilt and refronted in 1910 as the site

---

*See also Redruth, Carn Brea, Pool and Portreath for the wider picture of the Camborne–Redruth conurbation.

expanded to over six acres, taking in adjoining buildings including the former Tuckingmill Foundry Co. At the corner with Chapel Road, a two-storey three-bay office range to the factory and, after a wide entrance, the impressive eight-bay north-light spinning shed, almost unique in Cornwall, with two round-headed cast-iron windows in each bay, set in rusticated stonework. The factory has a rusticated façade with a tall central gabled entrance with a keyed semicircular arch, and rusticated outer arches surmounted by elaborate occuli. The offices have full-height canted bays flanking the slightly projecting entrance with rusticated pilasters surmounted by a Dutch gable.

TUCKINGMILL HOTEL, No. 109, Pendarves Street. Mid- to late C19. Plain, symmetrical, like other similar villas along the road from here through Roskear to Camborne.

CHAPEL ROAD continues S up the Red River valley, once lined with streamworks extracting the last grains of tin running out of South Crofty, l., and the Dolcoath mines, r. The road up the side of the valley towards Carn Brea (q.v.) offers fine views of the remains of the huge mining endeavour of this area.

TYWARDREATH   *0050*

Nothing survives of the Benedictine priory founded between about 1088 and 1150 by Richard Fitz Turold. The family later became Lords of Cardinham at Restormel and immensely powerful in the C13–C15. With Glasney College (Penryn) and the two priories of Bodmin and Launceston, the priory at Tywardreath was one of the most important monastic foundations in Cornwall. Its buildings were pulled down at the Dissolution but their site was just below the S side of the present churchyard. Some fragments are scattered in later buildings, notably a carving of the Virgin and Child above the door of No. 13 Church Street, and there is a monument to the last prior in the church.

ST ANDREW. A large imposing church, the C14–C15 W tower of four stages rather than the usual three with SE stair-turret and no pinnacles. The rest was rebuilt in 1880–7 to the C15 plan and using original features and materials. The architect was *Richard Coad* at a cost of £4,000, expensive for the time. Nave and chancel under one roof, S aisle, N transept, N and S porches and late C19 vestry added E of the transept with tall stone stack. Traceried windows throughout except a square-headed cusped window between transept and porch. The interior is lofty and spacious. Seven-bay S arcade on standard Cornish piers with moulded capitals and steep four-centred arches. Rood stair with basket-arched lower doorway and four-centred arch to former screen. Unpainted oak wagon roofs with carved bosses and boarded panels, the E end with extra panels. – FONT. Octagonal, C15, with shields in quatrefoils in circles. – PULPIT. Made up of C16 bench-ends and fragments of the former rood screen, a large figure of the resurrection of Christ, and smaller figures of St Andrew and St Lawrence. – BENCH-ENDS. Incorporated into the pew-ends of the N transept, mostly symbols of the Passion; they come from the same workshop as the series at Golant. Others by *Harry Hems* of Exeter, late C19, attached to the screen on the E side of the Lady Chapel. ALTAR STONE. The High Altar, of Caen stone with C14 consecration crosses. – MONUMENTS. In the N transept, Thomas Colyns †1534, the last prior. Slate plate with foliated cross. – Jane (otherwise indecipherable) †1636. Slate plate with good inscriptions and ornament. – Jane Pole †1795, graceful relief of woman by an urn, by *C. Regnart* of Cleveland Street, Fitzroy Square. – Caroline Rashleigh †1842, interred at Kensal Green, Gothic with name etc. in Gothic capital letters by *Pierce* of Truro.

The large village centre is pleasant and almost unspoiled, its character predominantly honest early to mid-C19: it more than tripled its population between 1811 and 1831, peaking at over 3,000 in 1851. The streets are lined with plain Late Georgian and Early Victorian houses and cottages, mostly terraced, and a good range of modest public buildings. Of note is the handsome former BUTTER MARKET, datestone 1860, E of the church in Church Street, with three first-floor sash windows over six smaller windows in round-headed openings to the originally open ground floor. Also the NEW INN in Fore Street with sash windows and open Doric porch with slender fluted columns. Adjoining it and parallel to the street a building with round-headed windows dated 1862 and shown as the TOWN HALL on contemporary maps: it has the look of a plain Nonconformist chapel.

Former VICARAGE, Vicarage Road. Quirky early to mid-C19. W elevation has a projecting pedimented bay with tall two-light mullion-and-transom window and wide Tudor arch doorway, S elevation two-light mullion windows and a central ground-floor niche with the coat of arms of the former priory.

NANSAVELLEN, Mount Bennett Road. 1988 by *Architecton* (project architects *Colin Harvey* and *Robert Organ*). Small single-storey house, imaginatively designed to take full advantage of its old quarry site and to give easy level access. The approach is deliberately low key through a gravelled courtyard defined by a house elevation with few windows. This accentuates the surprise of the main elevation, planned around the garden with much boldly articulated glazing including a small conservatory seamlessly integrated with the house.

TREVERRAN, 1 m. N. Small but exceptionally interesting house of *c.* 1720. The outstanding feature is the four granite Ionic columns with dosserets rising the full height of the façade and through the continuous moulded granite eaves cornice: there are two at the angles, two enclosing the door and windows over it. On the dosserets are plinths, suggesting the giant order once carried a balustrade. Central doorway with segmented broken pediment. The fine interior has contemporary fielded panelling with moulded cornices, fireplace with large fluted Ionic pilasters, and an C18 staircase.

TRENYTHON, 1 m. E. Small country house, now an hotel. 1860. Large rectangular plan plus service wing set back. Two storeys, 1:3:1-bay garden front with canted side bays. The rear entrance front has central tetrastyle Doric porte cochère. Fine interior with moulded and richly carved plaster ceiling cornice, moulded architraves and panelled doors. Large stair hall with imperial staircase and parallel balcony to each side carried on large brackets. Carved screens either side of the staircase. Central front room has rich reused C17 panelling.

VERYAN

ST SYMPHORIAN. A most unusual plan. Nave, N aisle, S transept, tower to the S of the transept (cf. Mawgan-in-Pydar, Duloe), and W porch. Three-stage tower with angle buttresses, early Dec windows to top stage, and battlements with crocketed pinnacles; carved heads and symbols in cove under parapet. The body of the church was extensively restored 1847–50, including rebuilding of the W front and S transept. The doorway to the W porch has the oddest of capitals, scalloped, with six heads in a row above the tops of the scallops. Remains of heads of a Norman corbel table, two in the porch, one above the apex of the porch entrance (wrongly restored). A *c.* 1300 window in the W wall of the S transept and many re-set C15 windows. The aisle arcade is eight bays long (an unusual length), white granite, of standard Cornish profile, with limestone capitals and large horizontal leaves, etc., to decorate the abaci. Arch-braced roofs, the nave incorporating braces, bosses and purlins of wagon roofs. – FONT. Bodmin type with carved faces over the four shafts and odd ornament between (the local reactionary continuation of Norman conventions, or a self-conscious late medieval copy?). – ROOD SCREEN. Two sections of the base, each with two panels; undistinguished carving. – MONUMENTS. John Trevanian †1712, Baroque with cherubs and coats of arms. – Jeremiah Trist, vicar for fifty-three years, †1829.

In the churchyard, Trist family TOMB-VAULT, dating from 1802 but the solemn façade is much later C19. Very shallow Doric portico with pediment and sans-serif curving legend RESURGEMUS forming enriched architrave to vault.

ST SYMPHORIAN'S WELL. In the village centre. Medieval core with mid-C19 decoration, restored 1913. Doorway set low with impost blocks of C12 or C13 and another made up of C15 cusped fragments under a C13-style hoodmould. The well-head has rocky abutments and a tapered octagonal granite shaft capped by a reused trefoil roll gable finial. Interior with half-dome corbelled roof.

The churchtown sheltered among trees and richly planted gardens is the perfect setting for its distinguishing feature, five Gothick ROUND-HOUSES (cf. the similar Round Cottage at Philleigh). They were built before 1820 by *Rev. Jeremiah Trist*, squarson and agricultural improver, based on an idea of Charles Penrose with whom Trist had collaborated on the Board of Agriculture's survey of Cornwall. Penrose had built a round cottage on his estate at Ethy Barton and had published the ground plan as suitable for a workman's cottage. Trist's were designed as single-storey buildings with two bedrooms facing E and the kitchen W (to allow sun as long as possible), their loftiness considered wholesome and their round plan easier to keep clean. Four are thatched with wooden cross finials. BEEHIVE COTTAGE has reused medieval tracery and a conical slate roof with octagonal central chimney. The OLD SCHOOL HOUSE was built with an enlarged ground-floor plan, its roof overhanging a veranda supported on two Doric granite columns where pupils could sit in the open air. Converted to a schoolmaster's house in 1872. PARC BEHAN, NW of the village, was built as a private dwelling 1802–10. Two-storey villa, double-depth central stair plan, pretty centre bay of 2:1:2. S front broken forward with rusticated quoins and bullseye window, r. hand bay added *c.* 1930.

HOMEYARD HOMES, Sentry Lane. Almshouses of 1956 by *Dawber, Fox & Robinson* for Cornish Seamen's Widows, endowed by Maria Laetitia Kempe Homeyard †1944. The round-house form is employed as the distinguishing feature of a delightful Arts and Crafts composition. Two 'houses' act as towers flanking a central veranda, skilfully linked to single-storey splayed wings which have steep hipped slate roofs with dormers.

CRUGSILLICK, 1 m. W. C17 house, remodelled and extended *c.* 1710. U-shaped plan of central hall with projecting wings. Interior has good early C18 detail with many plaster cornices, the parlour with a double heart and fleur-de-lys design, panelling and doorways.

WADEBRIDGE

A town defined by its magnificent medieval bridge across the Camel, built at the then highest navigable point of the river and the lowest point at which it could be forded. It was part of the important episcopal manor of Pawton which embraced St Breock 1 m. inland: the town had no medieval churches, those being at St Breock and the bridgetown of Egloshayle across the estuary (qq.v.). A market and two fairs were granted in 1312 but little is known of the town's C14–C17 development. By the C18 it was one of the principal corn-exporting ports of the county but its most significant growth, strongly reflected in the town's present character, came during the second half of the C19. This was stimulated by the opening of the railway between Wadebridge and Wenford in 1834, one of the earliest in England, which laid the basis for the town's development as a commercial centre for a large area of north Cornwall after the railway was successively linked to Bodmin, Launceston and Padstow by the end of the century. The remnant warehouses, quays and commercial buildings of its late C19 and early C20 heyday are still just discernible in the rapidly changing C21 town.

TOWN HALL, The Platt. 1888, from designs by *C. E. Collins*. The eye-catching clock tower promises much from the other side of the estuary but a clumsy remodelling of 1962 sadly depleted what was originally an expression of municipal self-confidence in a robust Renaissance style. The two-storeyed main range with the Molesworth arms and a balcony above the central entrance has lost its tall gabled roof and large stained-glass window to utilitarian flat-roofed offices. Quirky three-storey block to the l. with a pyramid roof from which the lead-clad clock tower rises awkwardly to a flèche of faint oriental inspiration.

WADEBRIDGE BRIDGE. Built *c.* 1468 at the expense of John Lovebond, vicar of Egloshayle (q.v.), and mentioned by William of Worcester in 1478 and Leland in 1542. Although widened downstream in 1853 and upstream in 1962–3, it remains one of the best medieval bridges in England. At 320 ft (97.5 metres) long it is the longest in Cornwall with thirteen of the original seventeen arches still visible: the rest have been built around at either end. The original pointed arches, recognizable from river level between the C19 and C20 extensions, are 18½ ft (5.6 metres) wide between piers of 12 ft (3.7-metre) width. The 1853 alterations under the direction of *William Pease*, surveyor of bridges for east Cornwall, inserted granite segmental arches across the original deep cutwaters to widen the carriageway by 3 ft (0.9 metres) either side. The 1962–3 work, to the designs of *Posford, Pavoy & Partners* for the Ministry of Transport, almost doubled the original width to 36 ft (11 metres): it employed pre-cast concrete ribs between new piers and 'masonry faced to Ancient Monuments standards'.

Former RAILWAY STATION, ¼ m. SE of the bridge in Southern Way. Now the Betjeman Centre. A fragmentary evocation of the once extensive railway network of north Cornwall. Booking hall, waiting room and canopy for platform 1, built *c.* 1895 when the London & South Western Railway link from Launceston was finally opened. Single-storey, the ends set slightly forward, the canopy of cast-iron columns with wrought-iron spandrels.

PERAMBULATION. It is worth walking the length of the bridge to appreciate the medieval achievement. Its NE end offers the best views from river level via steps down to the fragmentary

walls of the C18 BRADFORD QUAY. At the S end is the beginning of MOLESWORTH STREET, the principal street in the
town, which continues in a gentle curve uphill through the
centre right up to the Late Victorian and early C20 villas at
the town's NW edge. It is pleasant, modestly gracious townscape, the buildings almost all stucco and sash windows of the
later C18 and C19 with good later C19 and early C20 shopfronts.
Of the more notable buildings the former chapel-like LITER-
ARY INSTITUTE and LIBRARY, 1839, on the corner with
HARBOUR ROAD. There are several buildings (e.g. Nos. 27–29,
29–33 and 39) that look late C18, remodelled in the mid C19
with late C19 shopfronts, their parapets with moulded cornices
and blind rectangular panels. No. 36 has large twelve-paned
sashes with heavy moulded architraves above a late C19 shopfront and moulded cornice with parapet above. At mid-point
in the street the wide central porch with Doric columns and
moulded cornice of the MOLESWORTH ARMS, a former
coaching inn of C17 origin with C18 and especially C19 major
alterations. No. 41 has incised corner pilasters above a late C19
shopfront, No. 54 early C19 sashes and entrance hall which has
a C19 plaster cornice with egg-and-dart moulding. A dramatic
stop to the quiet stucco streetscape is provided by the sturdy
Edwardian POLICE STATION at the junction with Whiterock
Road, its main range behind a two-storey projecting wing: its
curved window sills impart a suitably defensive character.
Opposite, the former CONGREGATIONAL CHAPEL, 1874,
large, tall and plain with lancets. Then one of the prettiest-
looking buildings in the town, THE ELMS and PRIDHAM
HOUSE, mid- to late C17 with slate-hung front and two-storey
porch with Doric columns. Opposite a fine row of late C19
villas and further up the former WADEBRIDGE BOARD
SCHOOL, 1878 by *Silvanus Trevail*.

Back down to Whiterock Road and about ¼ m. up on the
r. a good group of early C19 houses on the road to St Breock
in Nos. 1–4 WHITEROCK TERRACE, 1830–40, with open
porches, canted and square bays, and sash windows. On the
road itself, GLANILDOR and GREYSTONES, slate-hung with
hipped roofs and sash windows. Returning down Whiterock
Road into PARK ROAD and then into FOUNDRY TERRACE, a
good row of plain stone cottages with round-headed doorways
behind the former foundry buildings, now FOUNDRY SQUARE:
small foundries were an important component of later C19 and
early C20 Wadebridge's commercial life. This area still gives an
impression of the pre-C21 town.

WARBSTOW

ST WERBURGH. In its small churchtown, within a likely *lann*.
A chapelry to Treneglos in the C12, both belonging to

Tywardreath Priory. A plain, humble, unbuttressed W tower of two stages, but a surprisingly ambitious C15 N porch in ashlar granite blocks, the gabled roof with C17 scrolled kneelers, and an inner door of Polyphant with fleurons and a cinquefoil-headed niche over. Nave and C15 N aisle only, the S transept was removed at a restoration of 1861. Good three-light Perp tracery especially the E chancel window: chancel has a trefoil-headed lancet in S wall that may be the earliest part of the church. The aisle arcade is low with Cornish standard piers and four-centred arches. – FONT. A fine example of the Altar-nun type with faces at the four corners (here unbearded) and stylized six-petal flowers in niches on the four sides. – STAINED GLASS. S wall of nave, 1998 by *Arthur Bradley (Minster Glass)*. In the S gable wall of a farm building just NE and below the church a small two-light late medieval WINDOW.

WARBSTOW BURY, ½ m. NW. HILLFORT, one of the largest and best preserved in Cornwall, its summit affording spectacular views. Three bank and ditch ramparts, the more substantial inner and outer ones probably later Iron Age, with entrances to SW and SE. Slighter central rampart may be earlier, possibly Late Bronze Age or Early Iron Age. Giant's Grave, a low rect-angular mound with shallow side ditches at the hillfort's centre, appears later than slight cultivation ridges: more likely a medi-eval pillow mound for rabbits than a Neolithic long barrow.

WARLEGGAN   *1060*

ST BARTHOLOMEW. A small, low church on the lonely SW fringe of Bodmin Moor, approached through an avenue of old beech trees. The sturdy C15 W tower, of two unbuttressed stages with N stair-tower and surmounted by embattled parapet and pin-nacles, originally had a spire which fell on the body of the church in 1818. The nave and chancel are essentially C13 with one single-cusped lancet in the N wall of the nave; the chancel E window is of three cusped lights. Wide C15 S aisle of five bays on standard Cornish granite piers, the abaci carved with geo-metric and natural designs, one with the carving of a man with a spear, one of a bear, and another with a hare and her young. – FONT. C14. Octagonal stone bowl on octagonal shaft with ring marking. – C18 baluster ALMS BOX. – Fine plasterwork ROYAL ARMS of 1664 (but still with Jacobean strapwork). – STAINED GLASS. Chancel E by *Fouracre & Watson*, 1882. – MONUMENTS. Slate ledger stone to Richard Bere, 1618, with shield of arms and inscription with strapwork.

Outside the SW corner of the church, a WHEEL-HEAD CROSS, brought here in the C19 from the moor.

VILLAGE PUMP. C19, within a small walled enclosure. Wooden housing to the pump, spout and handle, and granite trough.

Near Pantersbridge, 1 m. s, BARLEY SPLATT, 1970 by *Graham Ovenden*. A rare Cornish example of domestic Postmodernism, the architectural motifs especially varied, the detail well executed, the overall effect, including its colours, striking.

0060

WASHAWAY

ST CONAN. 1883, as a chapel of ease to Egloshayle, by *W. J. Jenkins* of Bodmin. Charming, small and simple Gothic with cusp-headed lancets and a central gabled bellcote supported by a sturdy buttress. Nave, chancel and N transept. – FONT. Of outstanding importance, one of the oldest in Cornwall, rescued from the rectory garden at Lanteglos-by-Camelford in the late C19. Of the same size and indistinct vaguely circular shape as Morwenstow, but with plenty of decoration of a Celtic character, not easily distinguishable now; interlacings and probably intertwined animals too, *c.* 1100 or earlier. – Fine C16 PULPIT carved with New Testament scenes, brought from Germany by Sir William Molesworth in the early C19 and presented to the church in 1928. – STAINED GLASS. Three windows by *Heaton, Butler & Bayne*, 1920 and 1930.

WASHAWAY CROSS. ¼ m. SE of the church. Cross-head with fleurs-de-lys on both faces; re-erected on a tall new shaft in 1935.

2090

WEEK ST MARY

The origins of the village as a small medieval borough are evident in the plan, with the centre of the settlement the former market place, traces of burgage plots and the faint but readable earthworks of a former castle immediately to the w of the medieval church.

ST MARY THE VIRGIN. Large and dignified, standing comfortably in a spacious churchyard N of the village square. The best feature is the fine C15 w tower of granite ashlar, unbuttressed but with an unusual degree of decoration. There are carved figures on the plinth and above and below each of the three string courses: the motifs are squares with trefoil, quatrefoil, star, etc., set in (cf. North Tamerton, Jacobstow). There is decoration also to the jambs of the canopied niche at the second stage on the s face, with simpler niches on the other faces, and below the sill of the w window. Nave and aisles, s aisle late C14, N aisle C15 of standard Cornish type, the s arcade with shorter, thicker piers of Polyphant, the N arcade slim and of granite as usual; the E bays on the s also belong to this later phase (cf. North Tamerton). The aisle wagon roofs remain, though much restored 1877–81 by *J. P. St Aubyn*: he left his mark on the character of the interior which, as Henderson remarked, 'presents a cold appearance'. – FONT. Octagonal, late Gothic, with coarse carving. – STAINED GLASS. N aisle, 1887 by *Kempe*, of St Catherine, St Cecilia and St Agnes, and centre light of another 2003 by *Minster Glass (Arthur Bradley)*.

CASTLE. The field was named Castle Hill, apparently from the earthworks of a low motte, C11, or ringwork, in its NW corner, probably built by Richard Fitz Turold, Robert of Mortain's steward and forebear of the powerful Cardinham family. The low circular mound's encircling ditch was crossed by an entrance causeway in the NE. Earthworks to the S may include a bailey, as well as the mounds of building platforms and enclosures left on a shrinkage of the small town.

THE COLLEGE. Enough survives of the foundation of 1508 by Dame Thomasina Bonaventure, a local girl who became the wealthy widow of a former Lord Mayor of London, to illustrate both the status of the settlement at that period and the sizeable scale of her enterprise. It is announced by a battlemented wall to the village street which incorporates the gable-end of a house, the principal surviving building of a much larger complex. Four-centre door in the N wall with shield in tympanum and floral motifs in the spandrels, and a lot of detail in the S wall including lateral chimney, stair-turret and three-light mullioned windows. The house continued E in what became a shippon when the building became a farmhouse after the foundation was appropriated to Launceston. The adjoining NEW COLLEGE to the N incorporates a further two tympana in the gable-end wall facing The College, and HAYESCROFT to the S has cusped masonry in its gable wall also; both were originally part of the foundation. A WELL-HOUSE in the courtyard, of tall polygonal plan, has a moulded cornice likely to be the base of a more elaborate roof.

PENHALLAM MANOR (or Bury Court), 1 m. W. A rare Cornish medieval moated manor house site, home of the Cardinham and then Champernowne families. Squarish courtyard building complex on a platform within a roughly circular moat with four substantial ranges entered via a drawbridge and gatehouse on the S side. Apparently developed in three main phases, late C12 to mid C14, the eastern domestic range first. Northern hall and southern chapel ranges of the early C13 were followed in the early C14 by the western kitchen and service range. Abandoned in the later C14. Located in landscape redolent of medieval and earlier power, at the N end of a deer park in a valley below the Iron Age hillfort of Ashbury.

MARHAYES MANOR, 1¾ m. N. A Domesday manor, rebuilt in the late C17 incorporating fragments of the earlier building, and of exceptional interest for its late C17 plasterwork: the rebuilding may be connected with John Rolle of Marhays, born 1626, who was made a Knight of the Bath for assisting with the Restoration. Outwardly rather plain in late C17 Flemish bond brickwork, square on double-depth plan, the main rooms at first-floor level with long windows over low ground-floor service rooms. Accessed from the N by a flight of steps, from the E by a ground-floor door. The plasterwork is in two of the first-floor rooms: the smaller in the SE corner has a ceiling with a quatrefoil layout and undercut naturalistic sprays of foliage and fruit. The NE room's plasterwork is a sumptuous composition of branches, leaves, fruit, flowers and birds, all deeply undercut and supremely skilfully executed, comparable to the best work in Devon of the period. The house may have been intended to be larger, or was truncated subsequently.

WENDRON

6030

There were once four churches or chapelries in this large mining parish, at Churchtown where the surviving church stands, Porkellis, Carmenelis and Franchise Farm. The landscape is still redolent of its mining past with deserted engine houses and a scatter of former Methodist chapels.

ST WENDRON. The church is approached through the low wide arch of its unusual two-storey C18 LYCHGATE with parish room over. Granite ashlar W tower, C15, of three stages, the middle stage curiously compressed, with diagonal buttresses and embattled parapet with pinnacles. Fine embattled S porch with pinnacled buttresses set back from the corners and four-centred doorway with moulded joints with bases and imposts. It and the early C15 S aisle are also granite ashlar. Most of the windows are C15, save for the N window of the chancel which is C13, and the E window of the chancel, C14, both remodelled in the C19: the chancel is certainly the oldest part of the church. The attractive interior has a five-bay nave S arcade between plus two lower bays at the E end, separated by one yet lower, narrow arch, where the rood screen went across. Two bays of late C14 pointed arches between the nave and N transept. The piers are all Cornish standard, the S aisle with plain capitals except for the responds which have shield-bearing angels as does the N transept arcade. Medieval wagon roofs over S aisle and N transept. The church was restored 1867–9 by *Edmund & J. D. Sedding*: theirs are the nave and chancel roofs, the rebuild of the nave arcades and the raising of the E window. – FONT. C14? With quatrefoils and very crude corner shafts. – TOMB-RECESS. In N wall of chancel, C13 or C14 with wide arch. Below is a CROSS-SLAB with incised cross, the head encircled. Langdon regarded this as the earliest of all Cornish crosses. – PILLAR POOR BOX, dated 1702. – MONUMENTS. Brasses in chancel. – To Warin Penhalluryk, vicar, 1535; headless. – To an unknown Elizabethan family, *c.* 1580, with seven sons and eight daughters. – Handsomely lettered stone wall tablet to Canon Doble †1945, the great expert on Cornish hagiology.

On opposite sides of the path between lychgate and church, an unusual SUNDIAL, dated 1770 in the form of a round column, and a four-holed CHURCHYARD CROSS, badly mutilated, but unusual with five bosses on each face, the only one in Cornwall. Also a WHEEL-HEAD CROSS by the tower. There are eight other crosses in the parish.

HOLY WELL OF ST WENDRON, 2 m. s, near Trelill Farm. Probably C15, with pointed-arch doorway to the interior, which has a corbelled granite roof; stone seats at the sides, and a shallow pointed-arched well niche in the w wall. One of the best-preserved medieval holy wells in Cornwall.

Former WESLEYAN CHAPEL, Porkellis. Date plaque 1866. Symmetrical three-window entrance front with triangular stucco pediment and round-headed openings to tall windows. Complete and unaltered interior with cantilevered panelled gallery on paired brackets over Doric columns and rostrum with canted front. Adjacent is the CHAPEL of 1814 (now in use again) with pretty traceried fanlight above its door.

TRENETHICK BARTON. 1½ m. SSW, now on the outskirts of Helston but still in a secluded embowered setting. The former house of the Hill family whose coat of arms is above the main door. An exceedingly attractive ensemble of medieval house, gatehouse and courtyard walls, one of the best in Cornwall. The house shows complex C16–C19 evolution, and may incorporate earlier fabric, but the unforgettable image is the approach through its delightful two-storey GATEHOUSE with Tudor arch and heavy hoodmould and three-light mullioned window above. The gatehouse opens on to the garden court, enclosed by high walls, and faces the HOUSE which is gabled with a projecting two-storey porch and many fine mullioned windows; the other elevations are also full of incident and interest with more mullioned windows. Large hall on the l. of the cross-passage, C17 inner parlour or buttery within a small axial wing on the far l., and a large service room to the r. of the passage. Above the service room is a large chamber with two closets at the front with a window bay between. The rear wings are C16 and C17 service ranges, subsequently adapted, probably on the sites of earlier wings. The interior, largely unaltered since the C18, retains good C16–C18 features including a coffered ceiling in the hall covered with fine C18 plasterwork, C16 moulded beams, a late C17 stair with heavy turned balusters, and C16–C17 fireplaces. To the l. of the house, late C17 former STABLES. To the rear, tall KITCHEN GARDEN WALLS.

NINE MAIDENS, 3 m. N. Two small Bronze Age STONE CIRCLES. Best-preserved is the SW circle with five flat-topped stones. NE circle now has just two stones, embedded in field hedge.

POLDARK MINE, ½ m. NE. The site, with evidence of medieval mining, is now a mining-based centre with visitor access to underground workings. Among the collection, the last BEAM

ENGINE to work in Cornwall: the little *c.* 1830 30-inch cylinder engine from Greensplat China Clay Works continued in use near Wheal Martyn (*see* St Austell) until 1958.

WERRINGTON

WERRINGTON PARK. A residence of the abbots of Tavistock, given by Henry VIII, like other Tavistock property, to John Lord Russell, but acquired and rebuilt by the Drakes. In 1651 it came into the hands of Sir William Morice, later Charles II's Secretary of State. His family added the C18 front range. The rooms here are listed in an inventory of 1763, but the excellent interior decoration may only have been completed after 1775, when the estate was bought by the Duke of Northumberland.

The house is admirably sited on an eminence overlooking a landscaped valley. The C18 part is most interesting, a crisp white stucco front of seven bays with a canted centre. Ornament is confined to a little restrained stonework: pediment over the central garden door, two side windows with flat architraves and false balconies. Such features betray an awareness of mid-C18 Palladian practice, but in Palladian terms the balance is odd, chiefly because there is no basement. The main rooms are at ground-floor level; the first-floor bedroom windows are low, of attic proportions. It is almost as if the top half only of an architect's elevation was used – service rooms at ground-floor level being superfluous because the older house behind served for the purpose (cf. Sharpham). The large hipped roof above a dentilled cornice also appears incongruous. Entrance at the side, through a later porch.

The plan of the C18 range is eminently simple: three front rooms, a wide corridor or gallery behind, ending in a Venetian window, with the stair hall at the end near the entrance. The corridor has a shallow barrel vault. It was intended as a sculpture gallery, as the 1763 inventory makes clear. At either end screens of green marbled wooden Ionic columns; above them medallions of the Duke and Duchess of Northumberland, which must have been added after 1775. The staircase is arranged around a rectangular well. It has a wrought-iron balustrade with lyre pattern, and plasterwork panels in the style of the mid C18 with a lively variety of devices: musical instruments, brushes and palettes, and hawking trophies, and below these winged and bearded heads with garlands of flowers. The three reception rooms have exquisite plaster ceilings in a more delicate Rococo style, in which the French rocaille motif appears, together with musical instruments (central room) or cornucopias with flowers in high relief (corner rooms). Excellent fireplaces in the Kent style, especially the one in the central room, with voluted jambs, frieze of red marble, and richly ornamented overmantel with painting of the Judgement of Paris. Enriched doorcases and shutters. In the SW room a showy Italian fireplace, a late C19 import. First-floor passage with attractive overdoors with pulvinated friezes; at the ends, overdoors with open pediments.

Behind this C18 range, three wings around a small courtyard. The W one has the oldest visible fabric, with a wall not at right angles to the rest; it incorporates a massive stone stack adjacent to the present kitchen, and several late medieval granite doorways. The back wing was the 'old house' of the C18 inventories, i.e. Late Tudor to early C17. Now very plain, gutted by fire in 1974, and with few features of interest left. Three-storey porch with the date 1641; projecting crude early C19 Gothic corridor on either side. Behind this, three storeys to the l. with large kitchen at the end; two-storeyed part to the r., with ground-floor old hall, which remained the main dining room until it became the servants' hall in the later C19. Remains of early C18 panelling, an C18 staircase, and a room with fielded panelling E of the hall. The low E range was remodelled after 1882 for the Williams family to provide for typical Late Victorian needs. It houses a library with mullioned windows (original fittings, including an C18 fireplace brought from Italy), a small smoking room, and a billiard room beyond, also very complete.

Landscaped GROUNDS with a lake, four LODGES, and the C18 WHITE BRIDGE over the River Attery, carrying one of the drives. On a hill an eyecatcher, a FOLLY with a seat in a deep round-arched recess and with three Indian sugarloaf excrescences on top. The former may well be derived from the Daniells' Indian drawings and aquatints, which would date this addition to the alterations of Werrington Park c. 1800 or shortly after.

ST MARTIN. Built on a new site in 1742, as part of the replanning of the house and park. The old tower was reused (diagonal buttresses and pinnacles) but the façade was considerably widened by a screen wall with angle turrets, all castellated and provided with the typical blank quatrefoils of C18 Gothicism. In niches in the façade and on the other sides of the church contemporary statues of the crudest style, yet at the same time quite impressive in their wild attitudes. The interior completely altered in a radical restoration of 1891 by *J. P. St Aubyn* that bestowed a sombre dignity to its well-proportioned spaces. – FONT. Norman, undecorated, but on a base with heads at the corners. – Another FONT with a small bowl on a baluster shaft is contemporary with the building of the church, as is the PULPIT. – STAINED GLASS. Chancel E, 1891, and chancel N and S by *James Powell & Sons*. – Nave S, 1872, very Pre-Raphaelite. – Nave N, 1949 by *Rosemary Smith-Marriott* in the Arts and Crafts tradition. – Nave NE, 1896 by *Fouracre*. – MONUMENT to members of the Drake family: kneeling figures in relief in a strapwork frame, early C17, on the outside of the E wall of the chancel. – On the N exterior wall of the chancel, headstone to Philip Scipio †1734, a black servant, touchingly worded.

CULLACOTT, 2 m. w. A rare survival of a complete medieval open-hall house, originally a longhouse, with C16 parlour wing and other C16 extensions, recorded in an inscribed lintel over the parlour window ANNO DOM 1579 BY WATER BLYGHTE. At that time the house was turned back to front, the original hall window blocked and a new mullioned window fitted to the new front. Long lower end, through passage fronted by a single-storey porch, a long chambered porch at the rear and a room over the entry jettied over the open hall as well as the wings. Late medieval roof with trenched purlins dovetailed-jointed over the trusses at the lower end of the hall. Three C16 latrines, including one with a fireplace. Rare scheme of C16 wall painting of two phases that includes a coat of arms and a faux tapestry at the high end of the hall. Remnants survive on other walls and there is another wall painting at the lower end of the room over the entry of St George and the dragon. It is likely the house continued to function as a longhouse long after the higher end had been extended and improved *c.* 1579.

YEOLMBRIDGE, 1 m. w. 'The oldest and most perfectly finished bridge in Cornwall' (Henderson). Probably mid-C14, widened late C19. Two four-centred arches with unusual early ribbed vaulting, three to each arch. Flood arches on the s side rebuilt late C19 and C20.

WHITSTONE

ST ANNE. In a delightful situation outside the village against the hillside. It is approached from the higher ground to the NE through the handsome LYCHGATE and past the HOLY WELL OF ST ANNE built into the lower SE corner of the churchyard. Unbuttressed three-stage W tower, the NE stair-turret rising above the battlements with a higher pinnacle; the tracery of the W window is of one piece of granite. C19 S door, possibly incorporating part of a re-cut C12 doorway. Interior of five bays with N and S aisles, the piers of standard Cornish type with plain capitals and four-centred arches. Extensively restored 1881–2 by *Samuel Hooper* of Hatherleigh: he replaced the windows in Bath stone and renewed the roofs to nave and chancel, reusing C15 ribs, bosses and wall-plates in the N and S aisle. The character of the interior belongs strongly to the restoration, which was good of its kind with simple well-designed pine pews, encaustic floor tiles and richly furnished chancel with cinquefoil headed sedilia, piscina and aumbry. – Early C16 BENCH-ENDS incorporated into chair. – FONT. Norman, circular, with a simple undulating leaf frieze along the top of the bowl. – STAINED GLASS. S aisle E, 1895 and S aisle S, 1886 by *Lavers, Barraud & Westlake*. – MONUMENTS. Slates to John Cornish †1610 with rustic letter-ing. – George Hele †1652, large slate used as N chapel altar front with three arches of blind arcading in relief. – Outside against S wall pretty slate with scrolly decoration to Thomas Edgcumbe †1712.

The LYCHGATE of 1882 is also by *Hooper*, with steep gabled roof carried on boldly moulded wooden brackets supported on slightly battered walls of polychromatic stonework. Hooper probably also reconstructed the HOLY WELL using C15 masonry for the fleuron-decorated coping and the base of the cross at the apex.

FROXTON, 1¼ m. NW. Former manor house with C15 core and C16 and C17 alterations. A Domesday manor, it was illustrated in the Spoure Book of 1698 where the extant buildings are clearly shown as part of a courtyard plan, of which two ranges have gone. The surviving main range shows evidence of original open-hall plan with rebuilding to l. of through passage and roof with four smoke-blackened arch-braced trusses, trenched purlins, and yoke ridge, perhaps C14.

WITHIEL

9060

ST CLEMENT. A large church at the W end of a wide street of granite cottages. Stately three-stage tower of the late C15 or early C16 with buttresses set back from the angles and a NE stair-turret surmounted by battlemented parapet and tall octagonal pinnacles with crocketed finials. Nave and chancel in one, probably of the C14, N chancel aisle probably begun as a chantry for the Bevills of Brynn, S aisle added by 1533 since it incorporates the arms of Prior Vivian (the church was part of Bodmin Priory's extensive estate). The tall narrow N door is C13. The E end of the chancel was remodelled, probably as part of a thoughtful restoration of *c.* 1820: it has pilasters surmounted by tall panelled piers with crocketed pinnacles. The S porch has an outer door with tall four-centred arch, hollow-chamfered with nook-shafts, carved wagon roof and large stoup with carved shield. Unusual S door with tall three-centred arch, roll-moulded with reused spandrels, tympanum with carved shield and leaves and wave-moulded surround; there are parallels with Cotehele, Pengersick and Trecarrel – it may be an early C16 prototype. S aisle arcade of six bays with standard Cornish piers and four-centred arches and a carved wagon roof; a similar but lower three-bay N arcade with a C19 screen. The early C19 restoration imparted a distinct and charming Gothick character to the interior with clear glass, plain wagon roofs to nave and chancel (cf. the similar workmanship at Cardinham), wooden benches in nave and wooden pulpit. – FONT. Octagonal bowl with carved panels on carved stem with panels, cable moulding and coarsely chip-carved ornamental motifs. The date is probably 1476 as the decoration includes St Clement's anchor and Clement was not named as

patron until this date: it is set against painted Gothick panelling with the commandments and biblical texts. – STAINED
GLASS. C16 fragment in E window of the S aisle with the arms
of Prior Vivian. – MONUMENT. Henry Vyvyan †1811. Slate
headstone with carved figures in Gothic style. Nice C19 cast-
iron GATES to churchyard, that on the S side with PRIVY with
pointed-arched door.

OLD RECTORY, S of the church. Said to have been built by
Prior Vivian but in its present form early C19 with a pretty
Gothick front: it is asymmetrical with pointed-arched lights
and Y-tracery and square hoodmoulds, embattled parapet, and
two-storey porch with pointed-arched doorway. The interior
has good Gothick detail; the E entrance has nice Gothick cast-
and wrought-iron gate.

SWINDON VILLA, 1 m. SSE. A curiosity. A late C19 GWR railway
carriage brought from the Swindon works c. 1935, now with
corrugated-iron roof over the original but with the interior
partitions and fittings preserved.

RUTHERNBRIDGE, 1 m. NE. On the old road from Bodmin to
Padstow, fine mid-C15 bridge, two-span with four-centred
arches and cutwaters continued upwards as refuges. Beside the
bridge, METHODIST CHAPEL, a good example of the later
but still plain wayside chapel, dated 1879, with single lancet
windows with cast-iron glazing bars; and small SUNDAY
SCHOOL dated 1899.

4030

ZENNOR

An especially lovely and unspoiled churchtown, its modest buildings gathered unassumingly around the church and churchyard
and giving immediately into the fields of the rich prehistoric and
medieval Penwith landscape.

ST SENAR. Given in 1150 to Tywardreath Priory but appropriated to Glasney College by Bishop Bronescombe in 1270. Late
C15 W tower of three stages, unbuttressed. Most windows C19
in Perp style but some straight-headed windows and the S
window of the S transept with intersecting and cusped tracery,
possibly a copy of the c. 1300 original. The S side of the nave
at least is partly Norman, with a narrow window of deep inner
splay. The transept and chancel are later, but still earlier (C14?)
than the late C15 to early C16 N aisle of six bays. The arcade of
the N aisle has octagonal piers and plain double-chamfered
arches: curiously, the two-bay arcade of the transept is similar,
perhaps demonstrating a start on a S aisle never completed.
There is a squint from the transept into the chancel. Restored
1890 by F. C. Hingeston-Randolph with wagon roofs. – FONT.
In Beer stone, possibly a gift from Glasney where much of the
stone was also used. Octagonal on five supports, the four outer

supports corbelling out like stove pipes to make corner shafts. Difficult to date: probably late C13 rather than C14. – BENCH-ENDS. Only two, made into a seat, but one of them the pretty mermaid of Zennor (*en face*). – STAINED GLASS. Six windows of 1890, possibly by *Ward & Hughes*. – SUNDIAL, dated 1737, with very nice slate cutting. In the churchyard three wheel-headed WAYSIDE CROSSES. – In the NE of the churchyard FIRST WORLD WAR MEMORIAL by *Ursula Edgcumbe*, an unusual design of a square pier surmounted by four carved figures looking out to seaward and landscape. – Set in the SW wall of the churchyard, another WAR MEMORIAL, 1922 by *G. L. Kennedy*, mason *James Thomas* of Nancledra, a Celtic-style cross with relief on head and shaft.

To the NE of the churchyard the former mid to late C19 VILLAGE SCHOOL, now the village hall, a simple rectangle with hipped roof and sash windows. Across the lane the former VICARAGE, late C18 or early C19 with C19 extensions including stable and trap house to the r. of the front and C19 wrought-iron gates with hooped bracing. Adjacent to the W the former FARM-HOUSE and COTTAGE, and nearby a delightfully miniature cottage, VICARAGE MEADOW, originally the vicarage coach-house with groom's accommodation. Beyond, GERARD'S COTTAGES, a row of four C18 and early C19 houses. SW of the church, The TINNERS ARMS, C18 with C19 and C20 extensions, a picturesque rambling composition. Further S the MILL with original machinery and the ZENNOR WAYSIDE MUSEUM, the former miller's house, late C17 or early C18.

At TREMEDDA, ½ m. NE, a C17 farmhouse around which are grouped planned FARM BUILDINGS, highly unusual for Cornwall, of *c.* 1910 by *George Kennedy*. The most impressive is a long symmetrical 2:3:2 fronted range of a T-plan, the centre broken forward with three-bay ground-floor arcade for wagons on square piers with massive lintels, and an oculus at first-floor level over each bay. The l. hand bays form a round-headed arcade as a link to the farmhouse with an open loggia above, with front and rear dairy behind; both loggia and front dairy have plaster vaulted ceilings. The complex included a granary and stabling.

At PORTHMEOR, 2 m. WSW, a multi-farmstead hamlet dramatically straddling a hairpin bend in the coast road, with houses of the C17–C19 and extensive farm buildings of the C19. Of special interest adjoining the road a pigsty range with swill kitchen.

ZENNOR QUOIT, 1½ m. SE. A large, complex Early Neolithic CHAMBERED TOMB, comprising two chambers defined by massive upright granite slabs. The larger W trapezoidal one widens W to E. Smaller E antechamber entered by a narrow gap between two broad, roughly symmetrical façade stones, the northern one partly split by the C19 builder of the adjacent field barn. An C18 drawing shows its capstone, the largest in Cornwall, fairly horizontal. By the mid C19 the rear W upright had fallen and the capstone had slipped to rest partly on the ground. C19 and C20 diggings produced Neolithic and Bronze Age potsherds, the latter perhaps associated with a low cairn surrounding the quoit, now largely removed. Diggings also produced human bone, radiocarbon-dated to the later fourth millennium B.C., a few centuries later than the more modest SPERRIS QUOIT, ¼ m. NE.

CLIFF CASTLE, Gurnard's Head, 2 m. W. Iron Age. Three ditched ramparts grip the narrowest part of the neck of a slender promontory of metamorphic rock projecting from higher granite cliffs. Vulnerable to attack from higher ground immediately inland; may not have been defensive, but instead cut off a symbolically important headland. Neolithic entrance graves at Treen, Pennance and Trewey were all sited precisely where a promontory's furthest, tallest rockpile appears, rounded and cairn-like, above the coastal plateau's rim. Simple sub-circular scoops on the promontory's sloping E side are small round-houses; a few are ringed with low stone walls, some partly lost to cliff erosion. Excavations of houses and ramparts produced mainly later Iron Age artefacts, some Romano-British and a few, intriguingly, Neolithic.

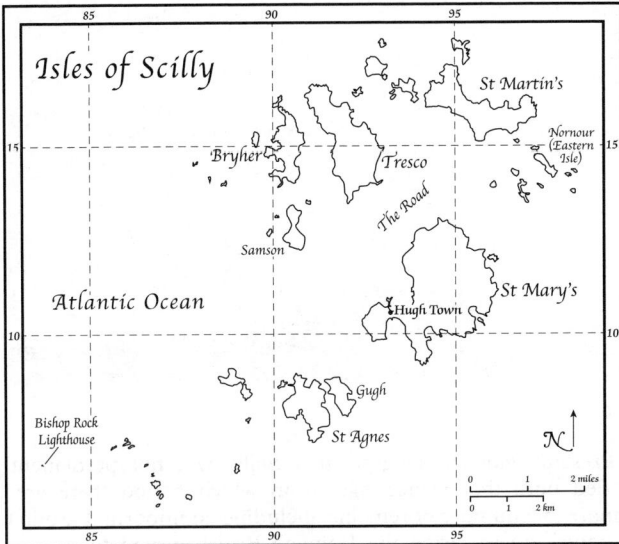

Map of the Isles of Scilly

ISLES OF SCILLY

Such are the enchantments of the natural world on Scilly – sub-tropical gardens that flourish in its virtually frost-free climate, abundant flora and fauna, and beaches of white sand washed by a turquoise sea – that the wealth of evidence of its human occupation stretching back over four thousand years is sometimes overlooked. Yet this archipelago of two hundred rocks and islands 28 m. w of Land's End has over a thousand archaeological sites with rich concentrations of prehistoric and medieval remains, as well as extensive fortifications reflecting the islands' role in the defence of Britain from the mid C16 until the mid C20. It also offers a surprisingly varied range of architecture and buildings for a place with such a relatively small population and only one urban settlement, Hugh Town on St Mary's.

Part of the fascination of Scilly is its history as a relatively recent 'drowned landscape'. At the end of the last ice age the archipelago may have been a single land mass but, as the ice melted, rising sea levels submerged low-lying areas which by 3000 B.C. formed separate islands, the main one comprising the modern islands of St Mary's, Bryher, Tresco and St Martin's, with St Agnes, Annet and the Western Rocks three smaller and separate tracts of land. It was probably not until the end of the Roman period that the present islands began to appear, and even as late as the C11 most of them were joined at low water, leaving prehistoric and medieval sites lying between high and low water still visible, as for example on Samson Flats.

The EAST Prospect

Present evidence suggests that Scilly was not permanently settled until the Bronze Age, from which period there are a remarkable number of remains, including an important group of entrance graves. From the Romano-British period there is the courtyard house at Halangy Down, St Mary's, comparable to the courtyard houses at Chysauster and Carn Euny in West Penwith (qq.v.), and the Roman altar in Tresco Abbey gardens, as well as a wealth of artefacts from a shrine on Nornour. But there is scant evidence of early medieval building apart from the ruins of three chapels on Tean, St Martin's and St Helen's (the only one with internal features). Shortly after the Conquest the islands became Crown property, from 1141 part of the earldom, and after 1337 the Duchy of Cornwall, where they have remained.

From the C12 most of Scilly was administered by Tavistock Abbey from St Nicholas' Priory on Tresco where remains of the priory church survive in the abbey gardens. In the medieval period the secular centre was at Old Town, then known as Ennor, on St Mary's, where a small settlement grew around the sheltered natural harbour of Old Town Bay: the remains of the stone quay survive. But it was the realization of the strategic position of the Scillies in the Western Approaches that, from the mid C16 onwards, led to the islands becoming a major fortification, with the Godolphins (*see* Godolphin) becoming lessees from 1570. Between 1548 and 1554 the defences constructed included King Charles's Castle and blockhouse on Tresco, and Harry's Walls, begun 1551 but never completed, on St Mary's. The threat of a second Spanish invasion after the Armada led Francis Godolphin to build Scilly's most extraordinary building, Star Castle, St Mary's, in 1593, accompanied by a curtain wall across the neck of the headland of The Hugh. The defences were strengthened during the Civil War when the islands were a Royalist stronghold. In the early C17 the War of the Spanish Succession prompted a thirty-year programme of re-fortification with the rebuilding and extension of the curtain wall around Star Castle and its extension around

Scilly Isles, St Mary's, drawing by Col. C. Lilly, 1715

most of the headland as what became known as The Garrison. Many of the older buildings of The Garrison and Hugh Town date from this period when the quay at Hugh Town was also rebuilt. During the Napoleonic Wars two circular gun towers were constructed on St Mary's on The Garrison and Telegraph Hill, and Scilly's defences were again augmented during the two C20 world wars.

Despite all this military activity, the islands were historically always impoverished and it was not until Augustus Smith took over the lease of Scilly in 1834 that the economy began to improve. His energetic, if sometimes autocratic, programme of reform saw many new buildings, often designed by him, including his own house on Tresco, and a new quay and church at Hugh Town. His successor, Thomas Algernon Dorrien-Smith, continued to promote new ventures, including the flower industry, as well as designing buildings that range from the dignified Gothic of St Nicholas, Tresco, to the quirky Post Office in Hugh Town with its chunky granite front. The C20 saw significant new building on Scilly, especially in Hugh Town where the duchy rebuilt much of Hugh Street in the 1920s. Local authority housing of good quality post-war build and other nice period pieces have added to the gentle architectural charms of the islands' main settlement.★

BISHOP ROCK LIGHTHOUSE
8000
4 m. w of St Agnes

The first lighthouse was swept away in 1850. *James Walker*, engineer in chief to Trinity House, started reconstruction 1852. Circular tower of Carnsew granite blocks, 35 ft (10.7 metres) at base, 70 ft (21.3 metres) high, completed 1857–8. *James*

★This account is indebted to Peter Laws's excellent *The Buildings of Scilly* (1980).

Douglass, Walker's successor, modified the tower in 1881, encasing it in a granite sleeve extended upward to raise the lantern 144 ft (44 metres) above mean high water. The granite blocks were dovetailed horizontally and vertically, the lower courses secured by Muntz bolts to the block in the course below; the work was completed in 1887. Steel helicopter deck added 1977.

8010

BRYHER

ALL SAINTS. Rebuilt 1821–2 by *Christopher Strick*, enlarged 1882 and 1887. Rectangular single-cell plan with narrow sanctuary end and SW tower with pyramidal roof. Good C19 fittings and furnishings. – STAINED GLASS. Four windows 2007 by *Oriel Hicks*, strikingly simple design incorporating flora and fauna of Scilly with excellent lettering.

SHIPMAN HEAD. A complex of prehistoric monuments at Europe's wild western extremity. Unusual CLIFF CASTLE, probably Iron Age, on a long low rocky promontory. It has a simple roughly kerbed stony outer rampart incorporating natural boulders when twisting down from the prominent cliff-top outcrop to the lower W cliff edge. Within is bare and lumpy Badplace Hill (with two Bronze Age kerbed CAIRNS) and beyond that, separated by a sheer-sided chasm, is the rocky island of Shipman Head itself. Second stony rampart on The Gulf's far edge, probably built before the rise in sea level separated Shipman Head from Bryher's mainland. The cliff castle appears designed to celebrate rock, weather and sea. Views W over Hell Bay take in the Norrard Rocks, resembling great cairns set on the sea, and to the S is Shipman Head Down, covered with around 150 small platform CAIRNS, most kerbed with upright slabs, and some absorbing large natural boulders. More than mere stone clearance heaps, a few contain remains of burial cists or chambers. Low stony banks linking many cairns contain numerous upright slabs, some possible robbed from cairn kerbs.

SAMSON HILL. Large ENTRANCE GRAVE on natural bench below granite outcrop of Works Carn with S views towards Samson. Kerbed oval mound incorporates natural boulders and contains chamber entered from NNE; two capstones in place and three more collapsed into chamber.

9000

GUGH

OLD MAN OF GUGH, on the island's E side. In an area rich in Bronze Age CAIRNS and ENTRANCE GRAVES is this 8½-ft

(2.6-metre) long STANDING STONE on Kittern Hill's lower SE slopes. Despite packing stones at its base, the stone leans eastward towards St Mary's Sound, as if wind-blown.

NORNOUR

One of the uninhabited eastern isles with a multi-phase PREHISTORIC SETTLEMENT by the S beach. Excavated and consolidated in the 1960s and 1970s. Eleven closely spaced and overlapping rounded stone structures of Middle Bronze Age origin; the surviving structures are mostly later Bronze Age and Iron Age. Occupation was possibly continuous for 1,500 years, with earlier buildings reused, adapted or overlain, usually only one or two occupied at any time, and separated by pathway into W and E homesteads. The ruins of the last, westernmost house were the focus of activity in the Roman period. Masses of apparently votive offerings – brooches, Roman coins, glass beads, small goddess figurines and trinkets – suggest that this remote ruin at the very edge of Rome's empire, but on western sea routes, was used as a SHRINE for perhaps over two hundred years. The island's distinctive rocky crest drew sailors to it.

ST AGNES

St Agnes. Early C19, a simple unpretentious single-cell building with two-stage W tower which has round belfry windows and oversailing pyramidal roof. Charmingly plain interior with woodwork in white, fawn and black. – STAINED GLASS. Chancel E, 1967, designed by *Marigold Hicks* and made by *Moira Forsyth* as an RNLI memorial, an excellent example of mid-C20 glass.

The most memorable monument on the island is the well-proportioned gleaming white former LIGHTHOUSE. 1680 for Trinity House, one of the earliest, lantern rebuilt by *Samuel Wyatt* in 1805–6. Three-storey to lantern, with projecting eaves with cast-iron stanchions tied to the glazing with square panes under a curved conical roof.

ST MARTIN'S

One of the best places to see the little fields protected by hedges or walls for the protection of early crops that are characteristic of Scilly.

St Martin. 1866 for Augustus Smith, on the site of an earlier church. Rectangular single-cell plan with W bellcote and W

porch flanked by mid-C20 extensions. – STAINED GLASS. S
aisle E, 1869 by *Clayton & Bell*.

METHODIST CHAPEL. Built *c.* 1845, with gallery and white, fawn
and black woodwork, as in the church on St Agnes.

Terrace of three COTTAGES near the shop/Post Office, 1964 by
Geoffrey Drewitt, decent and well judged.

The outstanding monument is the DAYMARK, a conical tower,
banded red and white, of 1687, erected by Thomas Elkins, first
steward of the Godolphins to live on the islands.

9010

ST MARY'S

OLD CHURCH OF ST MARY, Old Town. A restored fragment of
the original C12 foundation. Rebuilt in 1666 (datestone in N
wall) and 1743 but ruinous in the 1820s, and though restored
by *Augustus Smith* in the 1830s, its present appearance is principally the product of yet another major campaign of 1890. W
gable with bellcote. Possible C12 N door with roll-moulded
joints and scalloped capitals to round arch with solid stone
tympanum. – STAINED GLASS. Chancel E, 1891.

NEW CHURCH OF ST MARY, Church Street, Hugh Town.
1836–8 by and for *Augustus Smith*. Competent Gothic Revival
style. Three-stage N tower with buttresses framing recessed
bays. Wide nave and chancel in one rectangle, also buttressed. Lancets throughout. Simple interior with collegiate-
style seating, three ranks of stalls either side of the central aisle,
returned against the W gallery. – Coloured and gilded wooden
LION from the flagship of Sir Cloudesley Shovell, wrecked
1707. – STAINED GLASS. Chancel E 1887 by *C. E. Kempe*. – W
window, 1937 by *A. C. Ward*. – Two N windows, 1967 by *Alfred
Wilkinson* commemorating the lighthouse and lifeboat. –
Against the S wall of the chancel two fine LEAD CISTERNS
dated 1727 with maker's mark of *Hezekial Walker*, Master
Plumber of the City of London, the fronts with a strapwork
pattern of ribs decorated with winged cherubs' heads, the
cipher of George I, and the crest of the Board of Ordnance.
They originated at Star Castle.

ST MARY'S METHODIST CHURCH, Church Street. 1899–1900
by *A. J. Trenear*. A plain rectangle with lancets. Gallery on cast-
iron columns. Some fittings from the former chapel in Garrison Lane (*see* below).

Former WESLEYAN METHODIST CHAPEL, Garrison Lane.
1828. Handsome granite ashlar front with round-headed sash
windows.

TOWN HALL, The Parade. 1889 by *G. Goodfellow*, 'honorary
architect'. A plain, chapel-like building that dominates
The Parade. Classical style, two-storey three-bay front with
pediment.

HARBOUR QUAYS, Hugh Town. The OLD QUAY, protecting the N side of the inner harbour, was begun by Francis Godolphin soon after 1601, and rebuilt 1740 and 1748. The NEW QUAY extending N to Rat Island was built 1835–8 for Augustus Smith, and lengthened 1889 for the flower trade and in the 1990s to accommodate larger vessels. Partly vertically coursed granite to the early arm, shaped granite blockwork to the later arms, and large concrete panels to the late C20 section.

THE GARRISON and STAR CASTLE,* Hugh Town. The GARRISON GATEWAY forms an impressive outer entrance to the castle. The walls and bastion across the neck of The Hugh were begun by *Francis Godolphin* soon after 1601 but were substantially reinforced and extended around the headland 1716–46 by *Abraham Tovey*, Master Gunner, after a report by Colonel Christian Lilly in 1715 drawing attention to the inadequacy of the defences. The large moulded arched doorway is set in a wall of fine granite blocks, above which is a plaque inscribed AT; above that is another plaque dated 1742 with the GR monogram, and finally a bellcote. Just outside are an early C17 powder MAGAZINE and BLAST WALLS, just inside to the r. the GUARD HOUSE and to the l. GATEHOUSE COTTAGE, both shown on Lilly's plan of 1715. To the N NEWMAN HOUSE, the former Garrison stores, *c.* 1716–18 with porch and internal alterations of 1927 by *Richardson & Gill*.

From here, a steep ascent to STAR CASTLE, a hotel since 1933. 1593–1600 by *Francis Godolphin* with *Robert Adams*, one of the leading military architects of the late C16. A stone BRIDGE across the ditch gives access to the castle's GATEWAY, slightly broken forward from the outer face of the rampart, with a granite ashlar square-headed doorway dated 1593 on the lintel with the initials of Robert Adams (l.) and Francis Godolphin (r.) at the base of each jamb and a large plaque above inscribed ER. The massive RAMPART rises to first-floor level beyond a narrow lower walkway around the castle house, its outer wall taking the form of an eight-pointed star which gives the castle its name. On each of the cardinal points on the rampart is a small single-storey BARRACK ROOM; on the SE point a SENTRY BOX; on the SW the ruins of a small building (the LATRINE); on the NE a BELLCOTE; on the NW a LOOK-OUT PLATFORM AND FLAGPOLE. The rampart is encircled by a dry moat, much shallower than its original depth. A tunnel of dog-leg plan leads through the rampart to the lower walkway with housing for a PORTCULLIS at the back of the tunnel and a GUARDHOUSE built into the rampart. Off the centre of the N side of the walkway is a SALLY-PORT, one of three, the others blocked.

The CASTLE HOUSE is more a defensible dwelling than anything like the keep of a medieval castle: square on plan,

54, p. 712

---

*This account is much indebted to *Star Castle* by Jo Cox and John Thorpe of Keystone Consultants (1993).

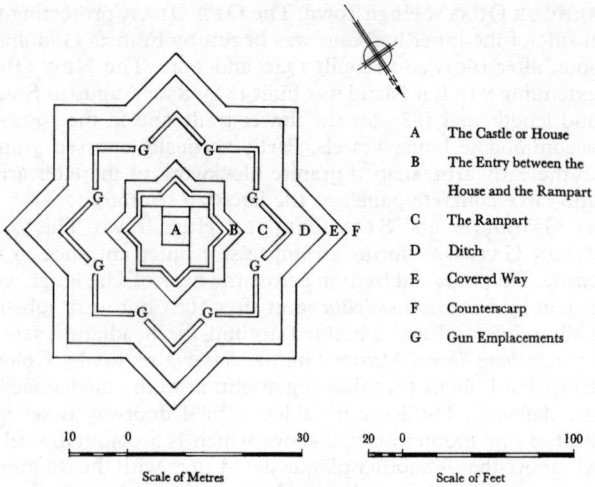

A	The Castle or House
B	The Entry between the House and the Rampart
C	The Rampart
D	Ditch
E	Covered Way
F	Counterscarp
G	Gun Emplacements

Scilly Isles, St Mary's, Star Castle. Plan as surveyed in 1600

two-storey with cellars and attic, with small canted full-height projections in the middle of each side. The three CELLARS are cut into the bedrock, two now used as the hotel bar, one a store. The ground floor is the least altered part of the building after a major internal reconstruction of 1700, the two original doorways set opposite each other in the E and W walls. The front doorway has a richly moulded surround with semi-urn stops and hoodmould. The internal carpentry is anchored to a massive square central masonry core which incorporates two vast chimneystacks, serving the former GREAT HALL to the E (now the main part of the hotel dining room) and the KITCHEN to the W: it seems as if only the masonry shell was retained in the early C18 rebuild. The staircase is of that date, the most impressive internal feature, of dog-leg form, running from the ground floor to attics with closed-string, square-section newel posts and moulded flat handrail. Most of the first floor and attics are of later date, with a few earlier features reused. The main roof is of 1700.

The highly unusual design of Star Castle does not fit neatly into any fort typology: as David Evans has observed, 'It can perhaps most usefully be considered as old-fashioned: a belated successor to the quirky Henrician coastal defence fortresses, for its defensive arrangements function (to use Cornish examples) more in the way of St Mawes than Paul Ives' bastioned trace at Pendennis, where Adams had been working immediately prior to his posting to Scilly.'* Godolphin was well aware of the weakness of his design, for example the lack of a drawbridge, the thinness of the parapet walls, and the fact that

_____

*'Some Observations on the Design of Star Castle', in Cox and Thorpe (1993).

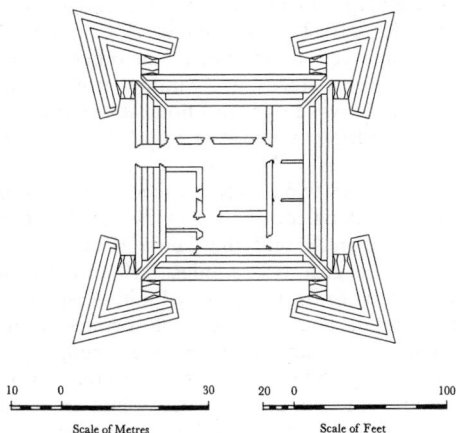

Scilly Isles, St Mary's, Harry's Walls.
Plan as projected in 1551

several parts of the ditch were not flanked. He therefore proposed as 'most needful' extensive outworks that were never constructed. The odd design and incomplete defences explain its dismissal by Charles I's surveyors in 1637 as 'so ill contrived that the least assault of the enemy could easily carry it'. It nevertheless remains Scilly's most memorable building.

The extensive defences of THE GARRISON are spread all around the promontory, with major earthworks of the BREASTWORKS and BATTERIES. The latter are mostly angular in plan and located in BASTIONS with some finely constructed granite walls: major examples at Morning Point, Steward Point and Woolpack Point. There is also much evidence of the reinforcement of the defences in the C20, readily visible at Woolpack. The SIGNAL GUN TOWER, a three-storey circular building, was a C16 windmill converted to a gun tower in 1803, later used as a signal station: it was at this tower that Marconi heard wireless signals from Porthcurno about 1898.

HARRY'S WALLS, on the summit of Mount Flagon. Only one side and two corners of the projected square artillery fort were built, but even this is impressive enough to demonstrate that it was in the vanguard of military design of the 1550s and would have been a formidable fortification if completed. The massive stone curtain wall terminated in a pointed bastion at each end facing S and W. The NW side is defined by an unfinished rock-cut ditch. Its abandonment was caused by the passing of the threat of French invasion.

BUZZA TOWER, Buzza Hill. The last windmill to be built on St Mary's, begun 1820, restored late C20.

PERAMBULATION. An exploration of HUGH TOWN should start from The Garrison and Star Castle, with good views of the intimate scale of the little town built over the isthmus between

The Hugh and the main part of the island with beaches on both sides. HUGH HOUSE (Duchy of Cornwall offices), in Garrison Walk, was built in 1792 as the officers' mess. Austere but dignified three-storey five-window front, granite ashlar above the rubble-walled ground floor. A few hundred yards s, Nos. 1 and 2 TRINITY COTTAGES, 1858, two pairs of light-house keepers' houses. Along the N side of Parson's Field, a range of one- and two-storey local authority houses, nicely articulated and detailed, of 1951 by *Bazeley & Barbary*. Now down to The Parade and the Town Hall (*see* above). The Parade has good groups of modest C18 and C19 houses that are typical of the town. Excellently built, of island granite, left plain or plastered. Their low elevation is suited to the exposure of the island. Often admirable in severe simplicity of design and in detail (bay and bow windows, iron railings, trellis work, porches, door panelling), they are miniatures with a local accent of the Cornish town architecture of their time. Along CHURCH STREET, with more early to mid-C19 terraces that step up to a group of three-storey stucco houses in the middle. Past the MUSEUM, Modernist of 1967 by *Geoffrey Drewitt*, and the Methodist church to the parish church of St Mary (*see* above) that forms the focal point of the street. Just to the SE of the church THE CHAPLAINCY, the 1830s rectory, stucco with simple pilasters. Return E along The Strand overlooking Town Beach with some very small early C19 cottages in Nos. 1–10 EAST STRAND. At the junction with Silver Street, the BISHOP AND WOLF pub, built *c.* 1700 for Thomas Elkins, first land steward of the Godolphin estate, resident on the islands from 1683. Two-storey five-window front, the full-length ground-floor bay of 1952 by *Geoffrey Drewitt*. Into Hugh Street, where Nos. 1–8 were rebuilt *c.* 1926 by *Richardson & Gill* for the Duchy of Cornwall, a striking contrast with the traditional character of the town but wholly successful. Two storeys of coursed and dressed granite with flat roofs behind parapet, the corner shop (MUMFORD'S) with half-columns an especially delightful accent. Beyond, the gabled front of the POST OFFICE with its granite monoliths and blocky walling of 1897 and initials AS (Augustus Smith). On the N side, a plain late C18 terrace of four houses, much remodelled in the early C20 by the duchy, probably by *Richardson & Gill*. BARCLAYS BANK of 1935 by *Frederick Drewitt* is a thoughtfully designed period piece of good proportions and well detailed. The ATLANTIC HOTEL is late C18 and early C19 but remodelled in 1927 by *Richardson & Gill*. The Harbour (*see* above) makes a fitting finale.

At Old Town, LAUNCESTON CLOSE is a well-mannered housing scheme for the Duchy of Cornwall by *Louis de Soissons*, 1966. Also MIDDLE CARN, 1935 by *Thomas Hughes*.

AIRPORT TERMINAL. 1975 by *R. E. Nugent* of British European Airways, extended 1988–9.

GIANT'S CASTLE, 1¾ m. E. Iron Age CLIFF CASTLE on a small rocky promontory. Four concentric earth and stone ramparts, incorporating natural boulders and with shallow external ditches, take up the whole of the N slope, but leave a tor prominently displayed above. Very small enclosed area; just 82 ft (25 metres) across. Iron Age pottery was recovered when a Second World War firing target was cut into the W end of the outer rampart.

BANT'S CARN and HALANGY DOWN, 2 m. NNE. Bant's Carn is an atypical ENTRANCE GRAVE, excavated in 1900 and 1970. The oval central cairn (probably Neolithic) is encircled by a lower Early Bronze Age platform. The stone-lined passage across that led to the main chamber is unusually high at 5 ft (1.5 metres) though its entrance is constricted by jamb stones and a lower capstone, forcing a crouched entry: it expands within. The Halangy Down SETTLEMENT comprises interconnected ruined houses, huts and smaller structures, all set among prehistoric brick-shaped fields defined by stony lynchets. Excavations (1930s, 1950s, 1960s) suggest the site developed from another first used in the Early Bronze Age: Halangy Porth, closer to the present cliff. Halangy Down itself flourished from the Iron Age to the early medieval period; most surviving structures, including a COURTYARD HOUSE, date from C2 to C4 A.D.

PORTH HELLICK DOWN, 2 m. ESE. Large Bronze Age ENTRANCE GRAVE on the NW crest of Porth Hellick Down. Northernmost of a group of seven. Kerbed earth and rubble mound in the centre of a much lower platform. E of the mound's centre is a chamber covered by four large capstones reached by an entrance passage (now roofless) from the cairn's NW side. Transverse slabs constrict entrances to both passage and chamber. Restored in the C20.

INNISIDGEN, 2½ m. NNE. Two ENTRANCE GRAVES on a ridge below Innisidgen Carn. The highest is an ovoid kerbed mound with a central chamber entered from the E and closed at the WNW end by a single upright slab. Incorporated into an early field system (banks and lynchets), as is the lower entrance grave on the hill's N slope, a circular kerbed mound whose central chamber is entered from the S.

SAMSON

8010

Long among the most impoverished of the islands, Samson was depopulated in 1855 when Augustus Smith evicted the last families. The poignant remains of their humble COTTAGES are still visible on South Hill.

TRESCO

9010

ST NICHOLAS. 1877–9 by *Thomas Algernon Dorrien-Smith* as a memorial for his uncle, Augustus Smith. Built by *Richard & Thomas Chudleigh*, masons, and *William Nicholls*, carpenter. Based on the cruciform plan of the medieval priory church (*see* below) with SE tower with pyramidal roof behind parapet.

Three-bay nave with W rose window, otherwise lancets. Arch-braced roof springing from stone corbels. – Fine oak PANEL by *Claud Phillimore* commemorating five Dorrien-Smith sons who died in the Second World War. – STAINED GLASS. Excellent set by *C. E. Kempe*, 1879–1905. – N transept by *Kempe & Co.*, 1919.

TRESCO PRIORY, ABBEY AND GARDENS. In the magnificent sub-tropical gardens of C19 Tresco Abbey, the significant remains of the Benedictine PRIORY CHURCH of St Nicholas. The priory was extant by 1066, granted to Tavistock Abbey in 1114, and dissolved 1538. What survives are parts of the nave and chancel, visible as a roofless rectangular building with walls of varying heights pierced by large opposed openings in the N and S walls marking the crossings to the former N and S transepts. The S crossing has a broad pointed arch, probably C13, with stepped and chamfered moulding, and a smaller doorway to the W that linked the nave to the cloisters. Blocked openings are evident in other parts of the walls. In the S doorway an early Christian MEMORIAL STONE used as a sill slab, with an inscription '. . .(?T)HI FILI' on the upper line and '. . . COLINI' or 'COGI' or 'COCI': it probably originated in an early Christian cemetery in the vicinity of the later priory. Built into another garden wall the fragment of a FONT, Norman, with blank arcading. On the Long Walk, simple squared ROMAN ALTAR, less than 3 ft 3 in. (1 metre) high, with relief carvings of sacrificial axe and cleaver on sides, but front and rear blank – no inscription, but it was possibly originally painted. Brought from near The Garrison on St Mary's to Tresco in 1870 by Augustus Smith, presumably from a shrine, perhaps on a small hill called Mount Hollis.

On the edge of the gardens the VALHALLA of 1871 by *Augustus Smith*, to serve as an entrance for visitors who had first come in appreciable numbers *c.* 1860. Extended 1960 by *T. M. Dorrien-Smith*. An L-shaped structure with a two-storey gabled cottage to the W and a single-storey range to the E. The garden façades have loggias supported by rustic stone piers, the walls decorated with sea shells. The loggias house an extravaganza of figureheads and other ornamented fragments of wreckage, an astonishing sight.

Breaking with tradition, *Augustus Smith* built his residence here rather than on St Mary's. He began TRESCO ABBEY in 1836 with a modest two-storey granite house which over the next sixty years was gradually enlarged, in 1843, 1861, and with a massive four-storey tower in 1891, by which time the work had been taken over by *Thomas Algernon Dorrien-Smith*. The scale is large, the complex plan reflecting the evolution of the house, with irregular elevations that appear picturesque enough from a distance because of the articulation of the building into many different components around a square main block. The varied fenestration – mullioned windows, central bays and oriel – and a second, slender three-storey tower with pyramidal roof create a somewhat restless composition. Interior with many original features including Chinese wallpapers brought to England by Smith's grandfather, Samuel, a merchant with connections in the Orient. At the SE end of Abbey Road the charming GATEHOUSE with pyramid-roofed tower of 1843.

CROMWELL'S CASTLE, 1 m. N of the abbey. 1651–2, superseding King Charles's Castle (*see* below) in the defence of New Grimsby Harbour. The 60-ft (18-metre) circular tower, finely placed near the water's edge to command the channel between Bryher and Tresco, is one of the most memorable sights on Scilly. Entrance high up, to be reached by ladders. Below it the principal living room with a rib-vault. Open platform on top: six gunports in the wall. *Abraham Tovey* added a six-gun battery on the seaward side *c.* 1740.

KING CHARLES'S CASTLE, just E inland of Cromwell's Castle. The not very eloquent remains of a fortification of 1550–4. Cruciform in plan with domestic quarters to rear of semi-hexagonal battery, originally of two storeys with gun-ports to the centre of each of the sides. Four-centred doorway at E end.

THE BLOCKHOUSE, ¾ m. NNE above Old Grimsby. Constructed 1554. A small fort, rectangular in plan, high on a natural carn reached by stone steps.

SMITH MONUMENT, Abbey Hill. 1872. Rough granite rubble obelisk 15 ft (4.5 metres) high with plaques to Augustus Smith and Thomas Algernon Dorrien-Smith.

GLOSSARY

Numbers and letters refer to the illustrations (by John Sambrook)
on pp. 728–735.

ABACUS: flat slab forming the top of
a capital (3a).

ACANTHUS: classical formalized leaf
ornament (4b).

ACCUMULATOR TOWER: see Hydraulic power.

ACHIEVEMENT: a complete display
of armorial bearings.

ACROTERION: plinth for a statue or
ornament on the apex or ends of a
pediment; more usually, both the
plinth and what stands on it (4a).

AEDICULE (*lit.* little building):
architectural surround, consisting
usually of two columns or pilasters
supporting a pediment.

AGGREGATE: *see* Concrete.

AISLE: subsidiary space alongside
the body of a building, separated
from it by columns, piers, or posts.

ALMONRY: a building from which
alms are dispensed to the poor.

AMBULATORY (*lit.* walkway): aisle
around the sanctuary (q.v.).

ANGLE ROLL: roll moulding in the
angle between two planes (1a).

ANSE DE PANIER: *see* Arch.

ANTAE: simplified pilasters (4a),
usually applied to the ends of the
enclosing walls of a portico *in antis*
(q.v.).

ANTEFIXAE: ornaments projecting
at regular intervals above a Greek
cornice, originally to conceal the
ends of roof tiles (4a).

ANTHEMION: classical ornament
like a honeysuckle flower (4b).

APRON: raised panel below a window or wall monument or tablet.

APSE: semicircular or polygonal end
of an apartment, especially of a
chancel or chapel. In classical architecture sometimes called an *exedra*.

ARABESQUE: non-figurative surface

decoration consisting of flowing
lines, foliage scrolls etc., based on
geometrical patterns. Cf. Grotesque.

ARCADE: series of arches supported by piers or columns. *Blind
arcade* or *arcading*: the same
applied to the wall surface. *Wall
arcade*: in medieval churches, a
blind arcade forming a dado
below windows. Also a covered
shopping street.

ARCH: Shapes *see* 5c. *Basket arch* or
anse de panier (basket han-
dle): three-centred and depressed,
or with a flat centre. *Nodding*:
ogee arch curving forward from
the wall face. *Parabolic*: shaped
like a chain suspended from
two level points, but inverted.
Special purposes. *Chancel*: dividing chancel from nave or crossing.
Crossing: spanning piers at a crossing (q.v.). *Relieving or discharging*:
incorporated in a wall to relieve
superimposed weight (5c). *Skew*:
spanning responds not dia-
metrically opposed. *Strainer*:
inserted in an opening to resist
inward pressure. *Transverse*: spanning a main axis (e.g. of a vaulted
space). *See also* Jack arch, Triumphal arch.

ARCHITRAVE: formalized lintel, the
lowest member of the classical entablature (3a). Also the moulded
frame of a door or window (often
borrowing the profile of a classical architrave). For *lugged* and
shouldered architraves *see* 4b.

ARCUATED: dependent structurally
on the arch principle. Cf. Trabeated.

ARK: chest or cupboard housing the

tables of Jewish law in a synagogue.

ARRIS: sharp edge where two
surfaces meet at an angle (3a).

ASHLAR: masonry of large blocks
wrought to even faces and square
edges (6d).

ASTRAGAL: classical moulding of
semicircular section (3f).

ASTYLAR: with no columns or
similar vertical features.

ATLANTES: *see* Caryatids.

ATRIUM (plural: atria): inner court
of a Roman or C20 house; in a
multi-storey building, a toplit
covered court rising through all
storeys. Also an open court in
front of a church.

ATTACHED COLUMN: *see* Engaged
column.

ATTIC: small top storey within
a roof. Also the storey above the
main entablature of a classical
façade.

AUMBRY: recess or cupboard to
hold sacred vessels for the Mass.

BAILEY: *see* Motte-and-bailey.

BALANCE BEAM: *see* Canals.

BALDACCHINO: free-standing canopy, originally fabric, over an
altar. Cf. Ciborium.

BALLFLOWER: globular flower of
three petals enclosing a ball (1a).
Typical of the Decorated style.

BALUSTER: pillar or pedestal of
bellied form. *Balusters*: vertical
supports of this or any other form,
for a handrail or coping, the whole
being called a *balustrade* (6c).
Blind balustrade: the same applied
to the wall surface.

BARBICAN: outwork defending the
entrance to a castle.

BARGEBOARDS (corruption of
'vergeboards'): boards, often
carved or fretted, fixed beneath
the eaves of a gable to cover and
protect the rafters.

BAROQUE: style originating in Rome
*c.*1600 and current in England
*c.*1680–1720, characterized by
dramatic massing and silhouette
and the use of the giant order.

BARROW: burial mound.

BARTIZAN: corbelled turret, square
or round, frequently at an angle.

BASCULE: hinged part of a lifting (or
bascule) bridge.

BASE: moulded foot of a column or
pilaster. For *Attic* base *see* 3b.

BASEMENT: lowest, subordinate
storey; hence the lowest part of a
classical elevation, below the *piano
nobile* (q.v.).

BASILICA: a Roman public hall;
hence an aisled building with a
clerestory.

BASTION: one of a series of defensive semicircular or polygonal projections from the main wall of a
fortress or city.

BATTER: intentional inward inclina-
tion of a wall face.

BATTLEMENT: defensive parapet,
composed of *merlons* (solid) and
crenels (embrasures) through
which archers could shoot; sometimes called *crenellation*. Also used
decoratively.

BAY: division of an elevation or
interior space as defined by regular
vertical features such as arches,
columns, windows etc.

BAY LEAF: classical ornament of
overlapping bay leaves (3f).

BAY WINDOW: window of one or
more storeys projecting from the
face of a building. *Canted*: with
a straight front and angled sides.
Bow window: curved. *Oriel*: rests
on corbels or brackets and starts
above ground level; also the bay
window at the dais end of a medieval great hall.

BEAD-AND-REEL: *see* Enrichments.

BEAKHEAD: Norman ornament
with a row of beaked bird or beast
heads usually biting into a roll
moulding (1a).

BELFRY: chamber or stage in a
tower where bells are hung.

BELL CAPITAL: *see* 1b.

BELLCOTE: small gabled or roofed
housing for the bell(s).

BERM: level area separating a ditch
from a bank on a hill-fort or
barrow.

BILLET: Norman ornament of small
half-cylindrical or rectangular
blocks (1a).

BLIND: *see* Arcade, Baluster, Portico.

BLOCK CAPITAL: *see* 1a.

BLOCKED: columns, etc. interrupted by regular projecting

blocks (*blocking*), as on a Gibbs surround (4b).

BLOCKING COURSE: course of stones, or equivalent, on top of a cornice and crowning the wall.

BOLECTION MOULDING: covering the joint between two different planes (6b).

BOND: the pattern of long sides (*stretchers*) and short ends (*headers*) produced on the face of a wall by laying bricks in a particular way (6e).

BOSS: knob or projection, e.g. at the intersection of ribs in a vault (2c).

BOWTELL: a term in use by the C15 for a form of roll moulding, usually three-quarters of a circle in section (also called *edge roll*).

BOW WINDOW: *see* Bay window.

BOX FRAME: timber-framed construction in which vertical and horizontal wall members support the roof (7). Also concrete construction where the loads are taken on cross walls; also called *cross-wall construction*.

BRACE: subsidiary member of a structural frame, curved or straight. *Bracing* is often arranged decoratively e.g. quatrefoil, herringbone (7). *See also* Roofs.

BRATTISHING: ornamental crest, usually formed of leaves, Tudor flowers or miniature battlements.

BRESSUMER (*lit.* breast-beam): big horizontal beam supporting the wall above, especially in a jettied building (7).

BRICK: *see* Bond, Cogging, Engineering, Gauged, Tumbling.

BRIDGE: *Bowstring*: with arches rising above the roadway which is suspended from them. *Clapper*: one long stone forms the roadway. *Roving*: *see* Canal. *Suspension*: roadway suspended from cables or chains slung between towers or pylons. *Stay-suspension* or *stay-cantilever*: supported by diagonal stays from towers or pylons. *See also* Bascule.

BRISES-SOLEIL: projecting fins or canopies which deflect direct sunlight from windows.

BROACH: *see* Spire and 1c.

BUCRANIUM: ox skull used decoratively in classical friezes.

BULL-NOSED SILL: sill displaying a pronounced convex upper moulding.

BULLSEYE WINDOW: small oval window, set horizontally (cf. Oculus). Also called *œil de bœuf*.

BUTTRESS: vertical member projecting from a wall to stabilize it or to resist the lateral thrust of an arch, roof, or vault (1c, 2c). A *flying buttress* transmits the thrust to a heavy abutment by means of an arch or half-arch (1c).

CABLE OR ROPE MOULDING: originally Norman, like twisted strands of a rope.

CAMES: *see* Quarries.

CAMPANILE: free-standing bell-tower.

CANALS: *Flash lock*: removable weir or similar device through which boats pass on a flush of water. Predecessor of the *pound lock*: chamber with gates at each end allowing boats to float from one level to another. *Tidal gates*: single pair of lock gates allowing vessels to pass when the tide makes a level. *Balance beam*: beam projecting horizontally for opening and closing lock gates. *Roving bridge*: carrying a towing path from one bank to the other.

CANTILEVER: horizontal projection (e.g. step, canopy) supported by a downward force behind the fulcrum.

CAPITAL: head or crowning feature of a column or pilaster; for classical types *see* 3; for medieval types *see* 1b.

CARREL: compartment designed for individual work or study.

CARTOUCHE: classical tablet with ornate frame.

CARYATIDS: female figures supporting an entablature; their male counterparts are *Atlantes* (*lit.* Atlas figures).

CASEMATE: vaulted chamber, with embrasures for defence, within a castle wall or projecting from it.

CASEMENT: side-hinged window.

CASTELLATED: with battlements (q.v.).

CAST IRON: hard and brittle, cast in a mould to the required shape.

Wrought iron is ductile, strong in tension, forged into decorative patterns or forged and rolled into e.g. bars, joists, boiler plates; *mild steel* is its modern equivalent, similar but stronger.

CATSLIDE: *See* 8a.

CAVETTO: concave classical moulding of quarter-round section (3f).

CELURE OR CEILURE: enriched area of roof above rood or altar.

CEMENT: *see* Concrete.

CENOTAPH (*lit.* empty tomb): funerary monument which is not a burying place.

CENTRING: wooden support for the building of an arch or vault, removed after completion.

CHAMFER (*lit.* corner-break): surface formed by cutting off a square edge or corner. For types of chamfers and *chamfer stops see* 6a. *See also* Double chamfer.

CHANCEL: part of the E end of a church set apart for the use of the officiating clergy.

CHANTRY CHAPEL: often attached to or within a church, endowed for the celebration of Masses principally for the soul of the founder.

CHEVET (*lit.* head): French term for chancel with ambulatory and radiating chapels.

CHEVRON: V-shape used in series or double series (later) on a Norman moulding (1a). Also (especially when on a single plane) called *zigzag*.

CHOIR: the part of a cathedral, monastic or collegiate church where services are sung.

CIBORIUM: a fixed canopy over an altar, usually vaulted and supported on four columns; cf. Baldacchino. Also a canopied shrine for the reserved sacrament.

CINQUEFOIL: *see* Foil.

CIST: stone-lined or slab-built grave.

CLADDING: external covering or skin applied to a structure, especially a framed one.

CLERESTORY: uppermost storey of the nave of a church, pierced by windows. Also high-level windows in secular buildings.

CLOSER: a brick cut to complete a bond (6e).

CLUSTER BLOCK: *see* Multi-storey.

COADE STONE: ceramic artificial stone made in Lambeth 1769–*c.*1840 by Eleanor Coade (†1821) and her associates.

COB: walling material of clay mixed with straw. Also called *pisé*.

COFFERING: arrangement of sunken panels (coffers), square or polygonal, decorating a ceiling, vault, or arch.

COGGING: a decorative course of bricks laid diagonally (6e). Cf. Dentilation.

COLLAR: *see* Roofs and 7.

COLLEGIATE CHURCH: endowed for the support of a college of priests.

COLONNADE: range of columns supporting an entablature. Cf. Arcade.

COLONNETTE: small medieval column or shaft.

COLOSSAL ORDER: *see* Giant order.

COLUMBARIUM: shelved, niched structure to house multiple burials.

COLUMN: a classical, upright structural member of round section with a shaft, a capital, and usually a base (3a, 4a).

COLUMN FIGURE: carved figure attached to a medieval column or shaft, usually flanking a doorway.

COMMUNION TABLE: unconsecrated table used in Protestant churches for the celebration of Holy Communion.

COMPOSITE: *see* Orders.

COMPOUND PIER: grouped shafts (q.v.), or a solid core surrounded by shafts.

CONCRETE: composition of *cement* (calcined lime and clay), *aggregate* (small stones or rock chippings), sand and water. It can be poured into *formwork* or *shuttering* (temporary frame of timber or metal) on site (*in-situ* concrete), or *pre-cast* as components before construction. *Reinforced*: incorporating steel rods to take the tensile force. *Pre-stressed*: with tensioned steel rods. Finishes include the impression of boards left by formwork (*board-marked* or *shuttered*), and texturing with steel brushes (*brushed*) or hammers (*hammer-dressed*). *See also* Shell.

CONSOLE: bracket of curved outline (4b).

COPING: protective course of masonry or brickwork capping a wall (6d).

CORBEL: projecting block supporting something above. *Corbel course*: continuous course of projecting stones or bricks fulfilling the same function. *Corbel table*: series of corbels to carry a parapet or a wall-plate or wall-post (7). *Corbelling*: brick or masonry courses built out beyond one another to support a chimney-stack, window, etc.

CORINTHIAN: *see* Orders and 3d.

CORNICE: flat-topped ledge with moulded underside, projecting along the top of a building or feature, especially as the highest member of the classical entablature (3a). Also the decorative moulding in the angle between wall and ceiling.

CORPS-DE-LOGIS: the main building(s) as distinct from the wings or pavilions.

COTTAGE ORNÉ: an artfully rustic small house associated with the Picturesque movement.

COUNTERCHANGING: of joists on a ceiling divided by beams into compartments, when placed in opposite directions in alternate squares.

COUR D'HONNEUR: formal entrance court before a house in the French manner, usually with flanking wings and a screen wall or gates.

COURSE: continuous layer of stones, etc. in a wall (6e).

COVE: a broad concave moulding, e.g. to mask the eaves of a roof. *Coved ceiling*: with a pronounced cove joining the walls to a flat central panel smaller than the whole area of the ceiling.

CRADLE ROOF: *see* Wagon roof.

CREDENCE: a shelf within or beside a piscina (q.v.), or a table for the sacramental elements and vessels.

CRENELLATION: parapet with crenels (*see* Battlement).

CRINKLE-CRANKLE WALL: garden wall undulating in a series of serpentine curves.

CROCKETS: leafy hooks. *Crocketing* decorates the edges of Gothic features, such as pinnacles, canopies, etc. *Crocket capital*: *see* 1b.

CROSSING: central space at the junction of the nave, chancel, and transepts. *Crossing tower*: above a crossing.

CROSS-WINDOW: with one mullion and one transom (qq.v.).

CROWN-POST: *see* Roofs and 7.

CROWSTEPS: squared stones set like steps, e.g. on a gable (8a).

CRUCKS (*lit.* crooked): pairs of inclined timbers (*blades*), usually curved, set at bay-lengths; they support the roof timbers and, in timber buildings, also support the walls (8b). *Base*: blades rise from ground level to a tie- or collar-beam which supports the roof timbers. *Full*: blades rise from ground level to the apex of the roof, serving as the main members of a roof truss. *Jointed*: blades formed from more than one timber; the lower member may act as a wall-post; it is usually elbowed at wall-plate level and jointed just above. *Middle*: blades rise from half-way up the walls to a tie- or collar-beam. *Raised*: blades rise from half-way up the walls to the apex. *Upper*: blades supported on a tie-beam and rising to the apex.

CRYPT: underground or half-underground area, usually below the E end of a church. *Ring crypt*: corridor crypt surrounding the apse of an early medieval church, often associated with chambers for relics. Cf. Undercroft.

CUPOLA (*lit.* dome): especially a small dome on a circular or polygonal base crowning a larger dome, roof, or turret.

CURSUS: a long avenue defined by two parallel earthen banks with ditches outside.

CURTAIN WALL: a connecting wall between the towers of a castle. Also a non-load-bearing external wall applied to a C20 framed structure.

CUSP: *see* Tracery and 2b.

CYCLOPEAN MASONRY: large irregular polygonal stones, smooth and finely jointed.

CYMA RECTA and CYMA REVERSA: classical mouldings with double curves (3f). Cf. Ogee.

DADO: the finishing (often with panelling) of the lower part of a wall in a classical interior; in origin a formalized continuous pedestal. *Dado rail*: the moulding along the top of the dado.

DAGGER: *see* Tracery and 2b.

DALLE-DE-VERRE (*lit.* glass-slab): a late C20 stained-glass technique, setting large, thick pieces of cast glass into a frame of reinforced concrete or epoxy resin.

DEC (DECORATED): English Gothic architecture *c.* 1290 to *c.* 1350. The name is derived from the type of window tracery (q.v.) used during the period.

DEMI- or HALF-COLUMNS: engaged columns (q.v.) half of whose circumference projects from the wall.

DENTIL: small square block used in series in classical cornices (3c). *Dentilation* is produced by the projection of alternating headers along cornices or stringcourses.

DIAPER: repetitive surface decoration of lozenges or squares flat or in relief. Achieved in brickwork with bricks of two colours.

DIOCLETIAN OR THERMAL WINDOW: semicircular with two mullions, as used in the Baths of Diocletian, Rome (4b).

DISTYLE: having two columns (4a).

DOGTOOTH: E.E. ornament, consisting of a series of small pyramids formed by four stylized canine teeth meeting at a point (1a).

DORIC: *see* Orders and 3a, 3b.

DORMER: window projecting from the slope of a roof (8a).

DOUBLE CHAMFER: a chamfer applied to each of two recessed arches (1a).

DOUBLE PILE: *see* Pile.

DRAGON BEAM: *see* Jetty.

DRESSINGS: the stone or brickwork worked to a finished face about an angle, opening, or other feature.

DRIPSTONE: moulded stone projecting from a wall to protect the lower parts from water. Cf. Hoodmould, Weathering.

DRUM: circular or polygonal stage supporting a dome or cupola. Also one of the stones forming the shaft of a column (3a).

DUTCH or FLEMISH GABLE: *see* 8a.

EASTER SEPULCHRE: tomb-chest used for Easter ceremonial, within or against the N wall of a chancel.

EAVES: overhanging edge of a roof; hence *eaves cornice* in this position.

ECHINUS: ovolo moulding (q.v.) below the abacus of a Greek Doric capital (3a).

EDGE RAIL: *see* Railways.

E.E. (EARLY ENGLISH): English Gothic architecture *c.* 1190–1250.

EGG-AND-DART: *see* Enrichments and 3f.

ELEVATION: any face of a building or side of a room. In a drawing, the same or any part of it, represented in two dimensions.

EMBATTLED: with battlements.

EMBRASURE: small splayed opening in a wall or battlement (q.v.).

ENCAUSTIC TILES: earthenware tiles fired with a pattern and glaze.

EN DELIT: stone cut against the bed.

ENFILADE: reception rooms in a formal series, usually with all doorways on axis.

ENGAGED or ATTACHED COLUMN: one that partly merges into a wall or pier.

ENGINEERING BRICKS: dense bricks, originally used mostly for railway viaducts etc.

ENRICHMENTS: the carved decoration of certain classical mouldings, e.g. the ovolo (qq.v.) with *egg-and-dart*, the cyma reversa with *waterleaf*, the astragal with *bead-and-reel* (3f).

ENTABLATURE: in classical architecture, collective name for the three horizontal members (architrave, frieze, and cornice) carried by a wall or a column (3a).

ENTASIS: very slight convex deviation from a straight line, used to prevent an optical illusion of concavity.

EPITAPH: inscription on a tomb.

EXEDRA: *see* Apse.

EXTRADOS: outer curved face of an arch or vault.

EYECATCHER: decorative building terminating a vista.

FASCIA: plain horizontal band, e.g. in an architrave (3c, 3d) or on a shopfront.

FENESTRATION: the arrangement of windows in a façade.

FERETORY: site of the chief shrine of a church, behind the high altar.

FESTOON: ornamental garland, suspended from both ends. Cf. Swag.

FIBREGLASS, or glass-reinforced polyester (GRP): synthetic resin reinforced with glass fibre. GRC: glass-reinforced concrete.

FIELD: see Panelling and 6b.

FILLET: a narrow flat band running down a medieval shaft or along a roll moulding (1a). It separates larger curved mouldings in classical cornices, fluting or bases (3c).

FLAMBOYANT: the latest phase of French Gothic architecture, with flowing tracery.

FLASH LOCK: see Canals.

FLÈCHE or SPIRELET (lit. arrow): slender spire on the centre of a roof.

FLEURON: medieval carved flower or leaf, often rectilinear (1a).

FLUSHWORK: knapped flint used with dressed stone to form patterns.

FLUTING: series of concave grooves (flutes), their common edges sharp (arris) or blunt (fillet) (3).

FOIL (lit. leaf): lobe formed by the cusping of a circular or other shape in tracery (2b). Trefoil (three), quatrefoil (four), cinquefoil (five), and multifoil express the number of lobes in a shape.

FOLIATE: decorated with leaves.

FORMWORK: see Concrete.

FRAMED BUILDING: where the structure is carried by a framework – e.g. of steel, reinforced concrete, timber – instead of by load-bearing walls.

FREESTONE: stone that is cut, or can be cut, in all directions.

FRESCO: al fresco: painting on wet plaster. Fresco secco: painting on dry plaster.

FRIEZE: the middle member of the classical entablature, sometimes ornamented (3a). Pulvinated frieze (lit. cushioned): of bold convex profile (3c). Also a horizontal band of ornament.

FRONTISPIECE: in C16 and C17 buildings the central feature of doorway and windows above linked in one composition.

GABLE: For types see 8a. Gablet: small gable. Pedimental gable: treated like a pediment.

GADROONING: classical ribbed ornament like inverted fluting that flows into a lobed edge.

GALILEE: chapel or vestibule usually at the W end of a church enclosing the main portal(s).

GALLERY: a long room or passage; an upper storey above the aisle of a church, looking through arches to the nave; a balcony or mezzanine overlooking the main interior space of a building; or an external walkway.

GALLETING: small stones set in a mortar course.

GAMBREL ROOF: see 8a.

GARDEROBE: medieval privy.

GARGOYLE: projecting water spout often carved into human or animal shape.

GAUGED or RUBBED BRICKWORK: soft brick sawn roughly, then rubbed to a precise (gauged) surface. Mostly used for door or window openings (5c).

GAZEBO (jocular Latin, 'I shall gaze'): ornamental lookout tower or raised summer house.

GEOMETRIC: English Gothic architecture c. 1250–1310. See also Tracery. For another meaning, see Stairs.

GIANT or COLOSSAL ORDER: classical order (q.v.) whose height is that of two or more storeys of the building to which it is applied.

GIBBS SURROUND: C18 treatment of an opening (4b), seen particularly in the work of James Gibbs (1682–1754).

GIRDER: a large beam. Box: of hollow-box section. Bowed: with its top rising in a curve. Plate: of I-section, made from iron or steel plates. *Lattice*: with braced framework.

GLAZING BARS: wooden or sometimes metal bars separating and supporting window panes.

GRAFFITI: *see* Sgraffito.

GRANGE: farm owned and run by a religious order.

GRC: *see* Fibreglass.

GRISAILLE: monochrome painting on walls or glass.

GROIN: sharp edge at the meeting of two cells of a cross-vault; *see* Vault and 2c.

GROTESQUE (*lit.* grotto-esque): wall decoration adopted from Roman examples in the Renaissance. Its foliage scrolls incorporate figurative elements. Cf. Arabesque.

GROTTO: artificial cavern.

GRP: *see* Fibreglass.

GUILLOCHE: classical ornament of interlaced bands (4b).

GUNLOOP: opening for a firearm.

GUTTAE: stylized drops (3b).

HALF-TIMBERING: archaic term for timber-framing (q.v.). Sometimes used for non-structural decorative timberwork.

HALL CHURCH: medieval church with nave and aisles of approximately equal height.

HAMMERBEAM: *see* Roofs and 7.

HAMPER: in C20 architecture, a visually distinct topmost storey or storeys.

HEADER: *see* Bond and 6e.

HEADSTOP: stop (q.v.) carved with a head (5b).

HELM ROOF: *see* 1c.

HENGE: ritual earthwork.

HERM (*lit.* the god Hermes): male head or bust on a pedestal.

HERRINGBONE WORK: *see* 7ii. Cf. Pitched masonry.

HEXASTYLE: *see* Portico.

HILL-FORT: Iron Age earthwork enclosed by a ditch and bank system.

HIPPED ROOF: *see* 8a.

HOODMOULD: projecting moulding above an arch or lintel to throw off water (2b, 5b). When horizontal often called a *label*. For label stop *see* Stop.

HUSK GARLAND: festoon of stylized nutshells (4b).

HYDRAULIC POWER: use of water under high pressure to work machinery. *Accumulator tower*: houses a hydraulic accumulator which accommodates fluctuations in the flow through hydraulic mains.

HYPOCAUST (*lit.* underburning): Roman underfloor heating system.

IMPOST: horizontal moulding at the springing of an arch (5c).

IMPOST BLOCK: block between abacus and capital (1b).

IN ANTIS: *see* Antae, Portico and 4a.

INDENT: shape chiselled out of a stone to receive a brass.

INDUSTRIALIZED or SYSTEM BUILDING: system of manufactured units assembled on site.

INGLENOOK (*lit.* fire-corner): recess for a hearth with provision for seating.

INTERCOLUMNATION: interval between columns.

INTERLACE: decoration in relief simulating woven or entwined stems or bands.

INTRADOS: *see* Soffit.

IONIC: *see* Orders and 3c.

JACK ARCH: shallow segmental vault springing from beams, used for fireproof floors, bridge decks, etc.

JAMB (*lit.* leg): one of the vertical sides of an opening.

JETTY: in a timber-framed building, the projection of an upper storey beyond the storey below, made by the beams and joists of the lower storey oversailing the wall; on their outer ends is placed the sill of the walling for the storey above (7). Buildings can be jettied on several sides, in which case a *dragon beam* is set diagonally at the corner to carry the joists to either side.

JOGGLE: the joining of two stones to prevent them slipping by a notch in one and a projection in the other.

KEEL MOULDING: moulding used from the late C12, in section like the keel of a ship (1a).

KEEP: principal tower of a castle.

KENTISH CUSP: *see* Tracery and 2b.

KEY PATTERN: *see* 4b.

KEYSTONE: central stone in an arch or vault (4b, 5c).

KINGPOST: *see* Roofs and 7.

KNEELER: horizontal projecting stone at the base of each side of a gable to support the inclined coping stones (8a).

LABEL: *see* Hoodmould and 5b.

LABEL STOP: *see* Stop and 5b.

LACED BRICKWORK: vertical strips of brickwork, often in a contrasting colour, linking openings on different floors.

LACING COURSE: horizontal reinforcement in timber or brick to walls of flint, cobble, etc.

LADY CHAPEL: dedicated to the Virgin Mary (Our Lady).

LANCET: slender single-light, pointed-arched window (2a).

LANTERN: circular or polygonal windowed turret crowning a roof or a dome. Also the windowed stage of a crossing tower lighting the church interior.

LANTERN CROSS: churchyard cross with lantern-shaped top.

LAVATORIUM: in a religious house, a washing place adjacent to the refectory.

LEAN-TO: *see* Roofs.

LESENE (*lit.* a mean thing): pilaster without base or capital. Also called *pilaster strip*.

LIERNE: *see* Vault and 2c.

LIGHT: compartment of a window defined by the mullions.

LINENFOLD: Tudor panelling carved with simulations of folded linen. *See also* Parchemin.

LINTEL: horizontal beam or stone bridging an opening.

LOGGIA: gallery, usually arcaded or colonnaded; sometimes freestanding.

LONG-AND-SHORT WORK: quoins consisting of stones placed with the long side alternately upright and horizontal, especially in Saxon building.

LONGHOUSE: house and byre in the same range with internal access between them.

LOUVRE: roof opening, often protected by a raised timber structure, to allow the smoke from a central hearth to escape.

LOWSIDE WINDOW: set lower than the others in a chancel side wall, usually towards its w end.

LUCAM: projecting housing for hoist pulley on upper storey of warehouses, mills, etc., for raising goods to loading doors.

LUCARNE (*lit.* dormer): small gabled opening in a roof or spire.

LUGGED ARCHITRAVE: *see* 4b.

LUNETTE: semicircular window or blind panel.

LYCHGATE (*lit.* corpse-gate): roofed gateway entrance to a churchyard for the reception of a coffin.

LYNCHET: long terraced strip of soil on the downward side of prehistoric and medieval fields, accumulated because of continual ploughing along the contours.

MACHICOLATIONS (*lit.* mashing devices): series of openings between the corbels that support a projecting parapet through which missiles can be dropped. Used decoratively in post-medieval buildings.

MANOMETER or STANDPIPE TOWER: containing a column of water to regulate pressure in water mains.

MANSARD: *see* 8a.

MATHEMATICAL TILES: facing tiles with the appearance of brick, most often applied to timber-framed walls.

MAUSOLEUM: monumental building or chamber usually intended for the burial of members of one family.

MEGALITHIC TOMB: massive stone-built Neolithic burial chamber covered by an earth or stone mound.

MERLON: *see* Battlement.

METOPES: spaces between the triglyphs in a Doric frieze (3b).

MEZZANINE: low storey between two higher ones.

MILD STEEL: *see* Cast iron.

MISERICORD (*lit.* mercy): shelf on a carved bracket placed on the underside of a hinged choir stall seat to support an occupant when standing.

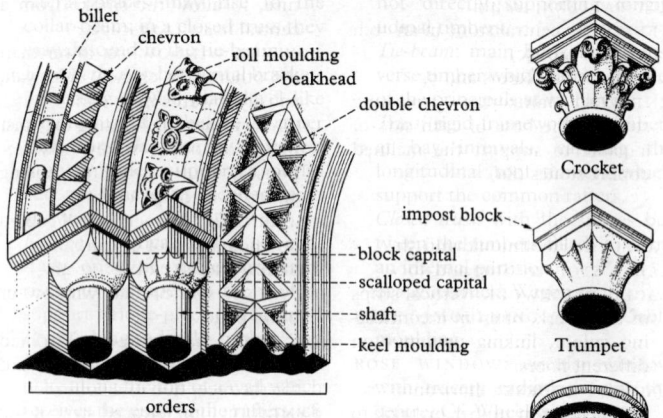

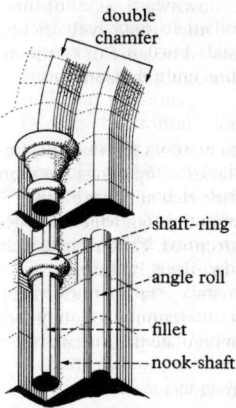

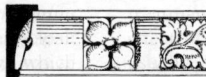

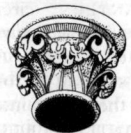

a) MOULDINGS AND ORNAMENT

b) CAPITALS

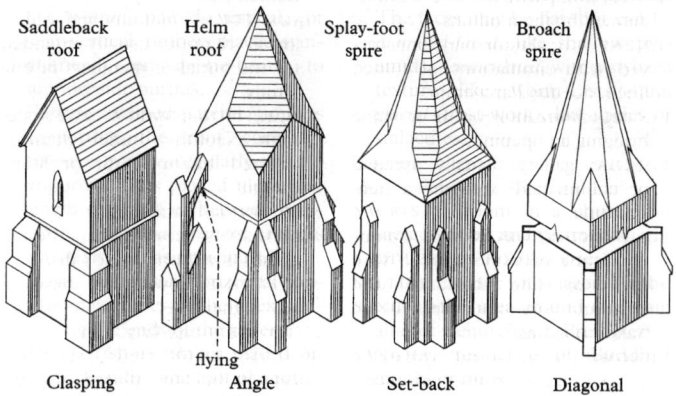

c) BUTTRESSES, ROOFS AND SPIRES

FIGURE I: MEDIEVAL

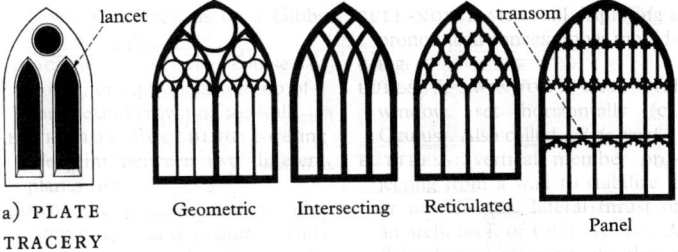

lancet

transom

a) PLATE TRACERY

Geometric   Intersecting   Reticulated   Panel

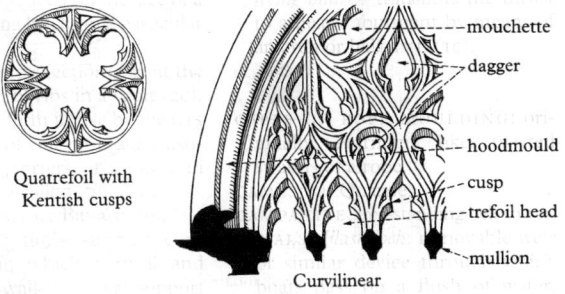

Quatrefoil with Kentish cusps

mouchette
dagger
hoodmould
cusp
trefoil head
mullion

Curvilinear

b) BAR TRACERY

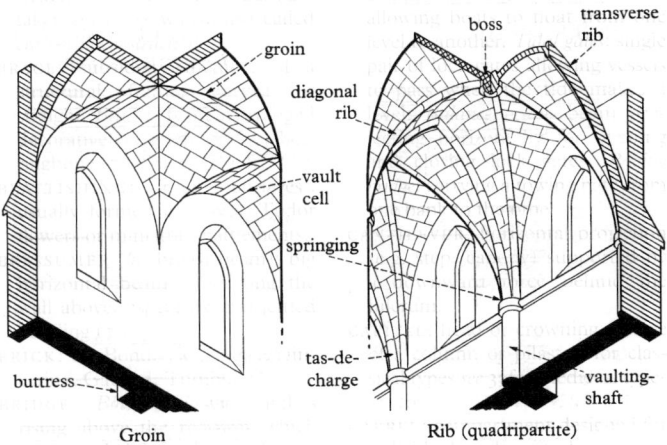

groin
diagonal rib
vault cell
springing
buttress
tas-de-charge

boss
transverse rib
vaulting-shaft

Groin   Rib (quadripartite)

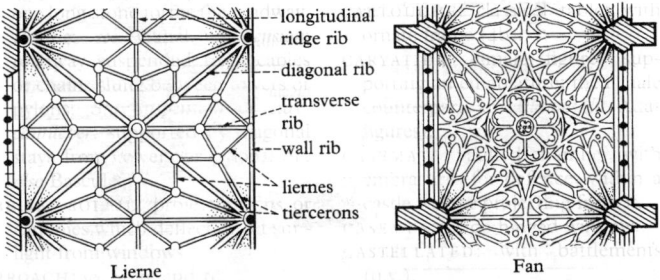

longitudinal ridge rib
diagonal rib
transverse rib
wall rib
liernes
tiercerons

Lierne   Fan

c) VAULTS

FIGURE 2: MEDIEVAL

ORDERS

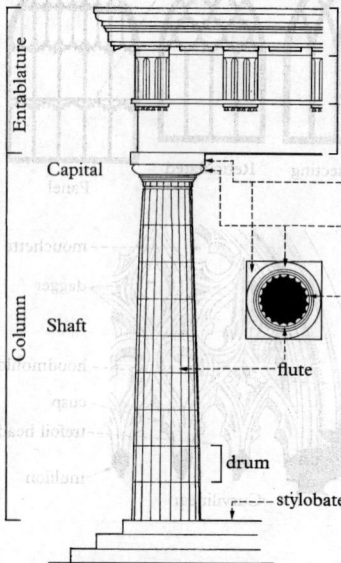

a) GREEK DORIC

	cornice
Entablature	frieze
	architrave
Capital	abacus
	echinus
	arris
Shaft (Column)	flute
	drum
	stylobate

Cyma recta

Cyma reversa with
waterleaf-and-dart

Ovolo: Egg-and-dart
Astragal: Bead-and-reel

Cavetto   Scotia

Torus: bay leaf

f) MOULDINGS AND
ENRICHMENTS

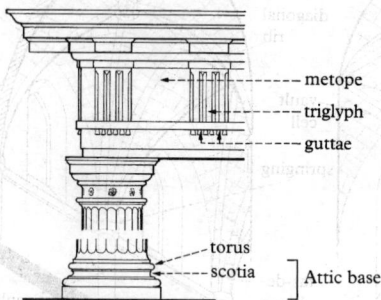

b) ROMAN DORIC

- metope
- triglyph
- guttae
- torus
- scotia } Attic base

e) TUSCAN

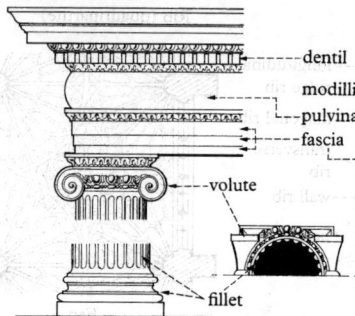

c) IONIC

- dentil
- modillion
- pulvinated frieze
- fascia
- volute
- fillet

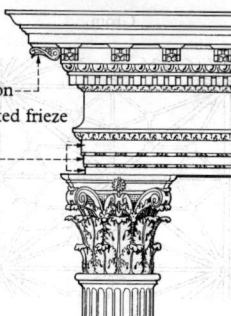

d) CORINTHIAN

FIGURE 3: CLASSICAL

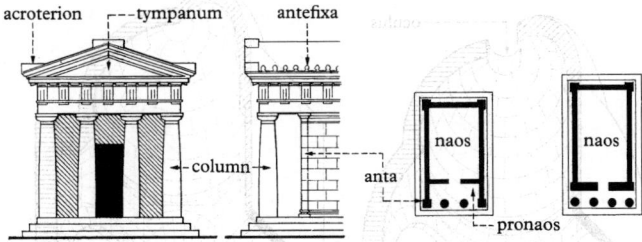

a) PORTICO

Distyle in antis   Prostyle

Anthemion & Palmette

Guilloche

Key pattern

Rinceau

Husk garland

Vitruvian scroll

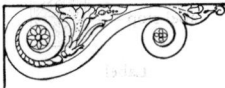

Console

Diocletian window

Acanthus

Broken pediment

Segmental pediment

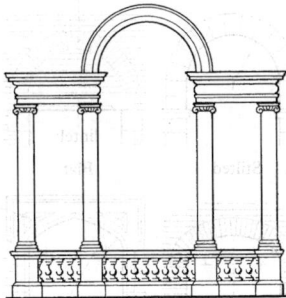

Venetian window

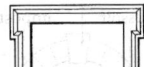

Lugged architrave

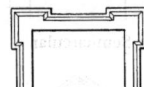

Shouldered architrave

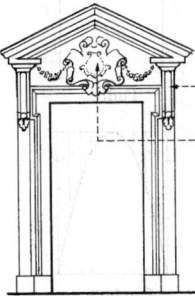

Open pediment

Swan-neck pediment

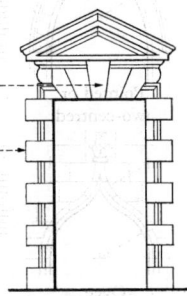

Gibbs surround

b) ORNAMENTS AND FEATURES

FIGURE 4: CLASSICAL

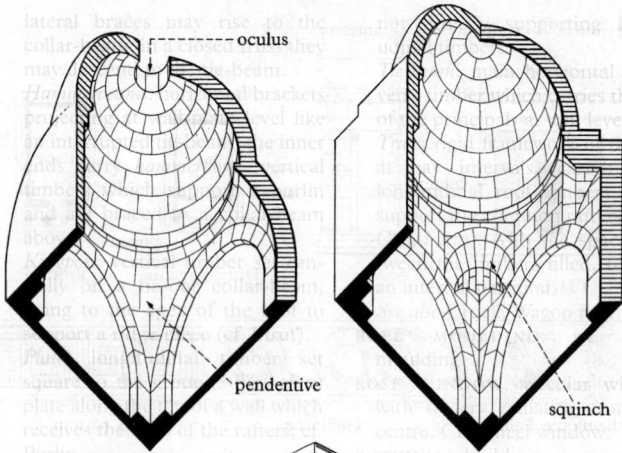

a) DOMES

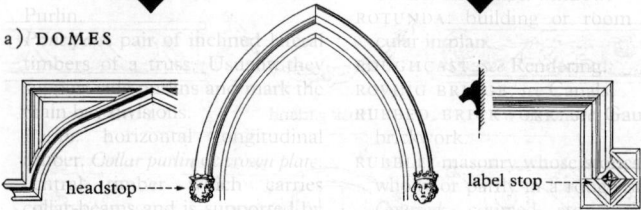

b) HOODMOULDS

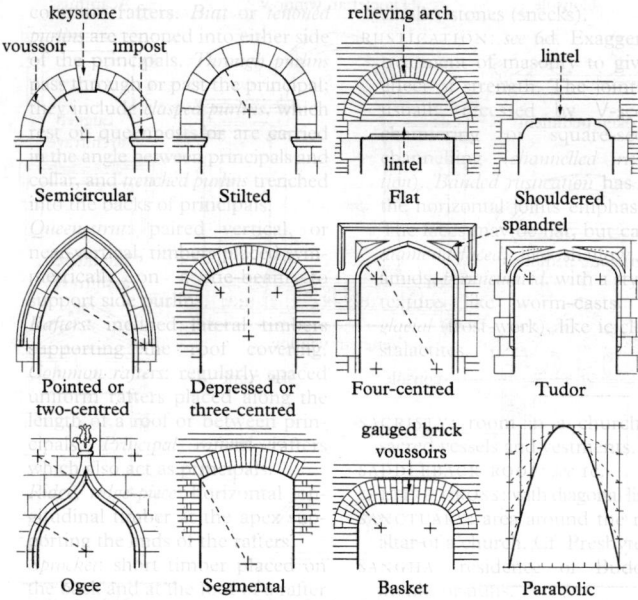

c) ARCHES

FIGURE 5: CONSTRUCTION

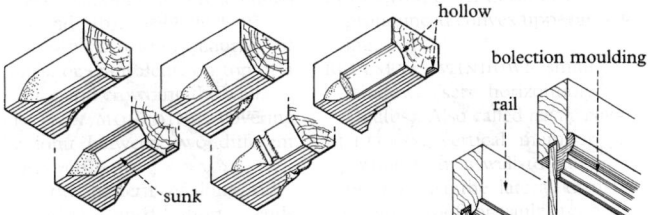

a) CHAMFERS AND CHAMFERSTOPS

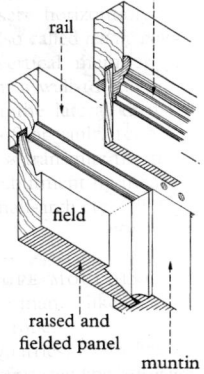

b) PANELLING

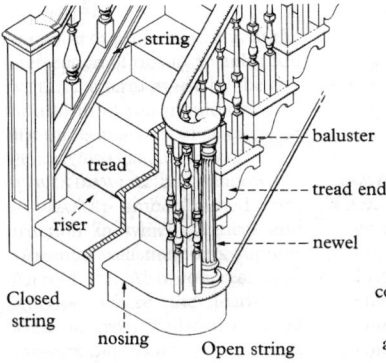

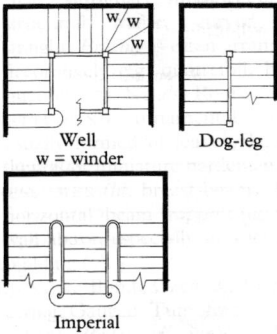

c) STAIRS

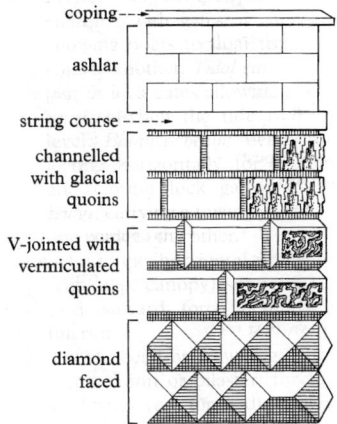

d) RUSTICATION

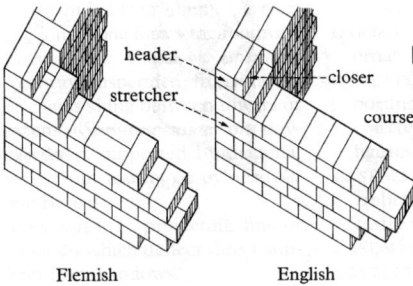

e) BRICK BONDS

FIGURE 6: CONSTRUCTION

common rafter
principal rafter
purlin
collar
tie-beam
queen-strut

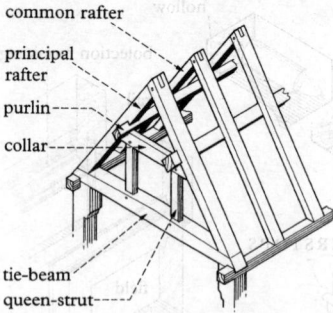

Queen-strut roof with clasped purlins

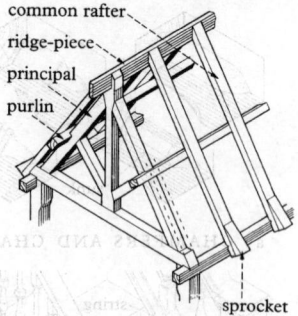

common rafter
ridge-piece
principal
purlin
sprocket

Kingpost roof with trenched purlins

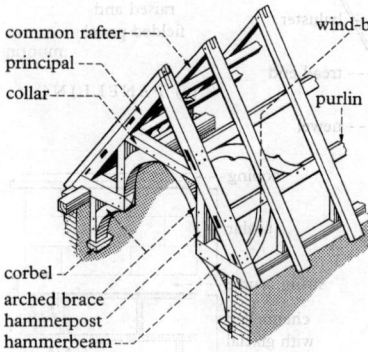

common rafter
principal
collar
wind-braces
purlin
corbel
arched brace
hammerpost
hammerbeam

Hammerbeam roof with butt purlins

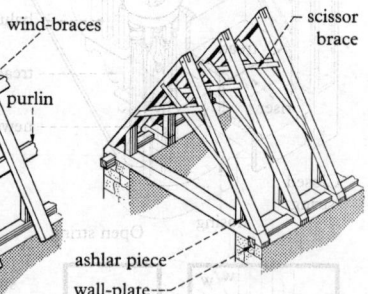

scissor brace
ashlar piece
wall-plate

Scissor truss roof

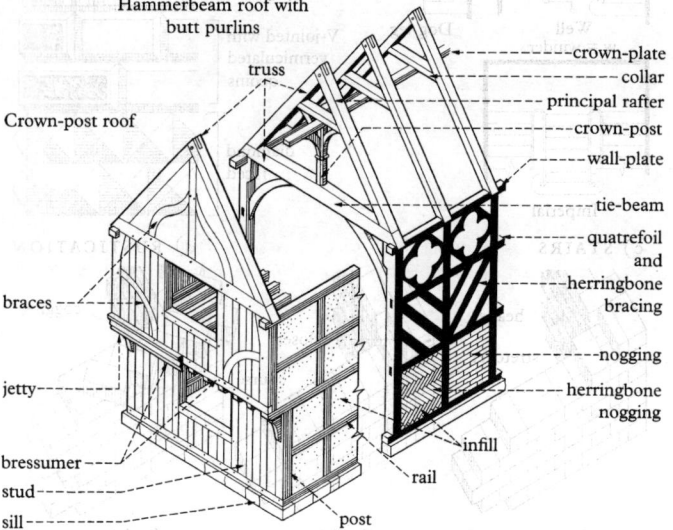

Crown-post roof

truss
crown-plate
collar
principal rafter
crown-post
wall-plate
tie-beam
quatrefoil and herringbone bracing
nogging
herringbone nogging
infill
rail

braces
jetty
bressumer
stud
sill
post

Box frame: i) Close studding   ii) Square panel

FIGURE 7: ROOFS AND TIMBER-FRAMING

Hipped with dormer

Half-hipped with catslide

Mansard

Double-pitched

Gambrel on a Wealden house

Kneelered

Flemish or Dutch

Tumbled

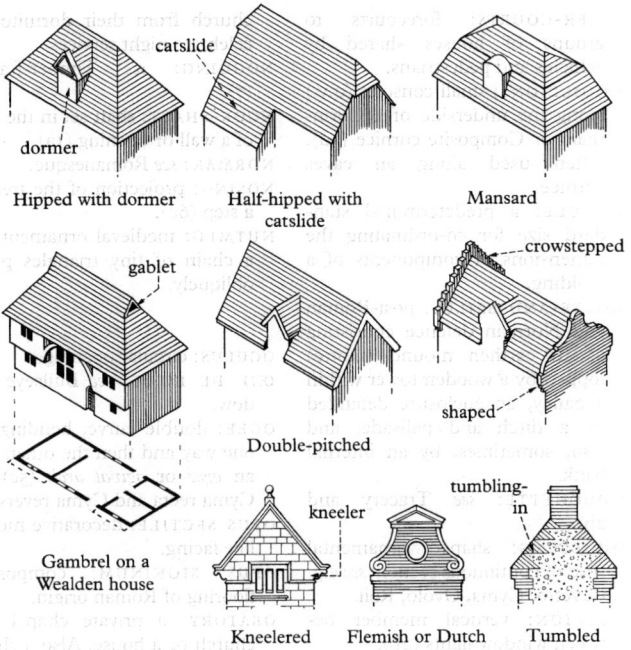

a) ROOF FORMS AND GABLES

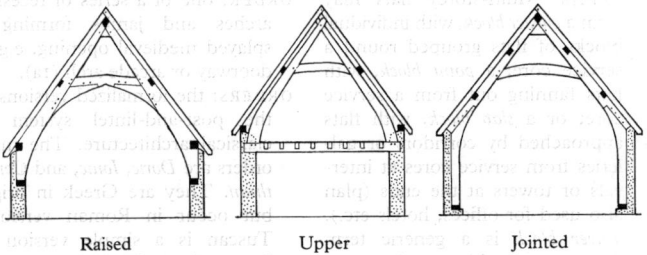

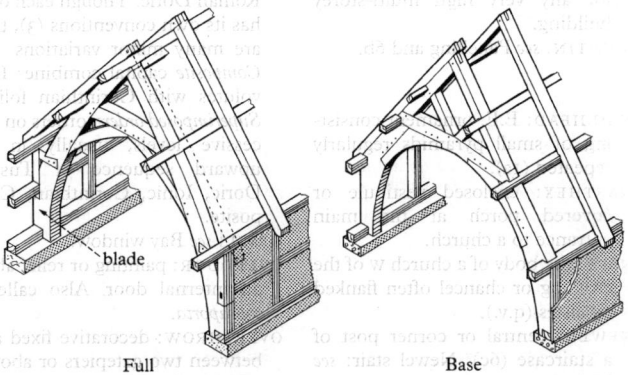

Raised

Upper

Jointed

Full

Base

b) CRUCK FRAMES

FIGURE 8: ROOFS AND TIMBER-FRAMING

MIXER-COURTS: forecourts to groups of houses shared by vehicles and pedestrians.

MODILLIONS: small consoles (q.v.) along the underside of a Corinthian or Composite cornice (3d). Often used along an eaves cornice.

MODULE: a predetermined standard size for co-ordinating the dimensions of components of a building.

MOTTE-AND-BAILEY: post-Roman and Norman defence consisting of an earthen mound (motte) topped by a wooden tower within a bailey, an enclosure defended by a ditch and palisade, and also, sometimes, by an internal bank.

MOUCHETTE: see Tracery and 2b.

MOULDING: shaped ornamental strip of continuous section; see e.g. Cavetto, Cyma, Ovolo, Roll.

MULLION: vertical member between window lights (2b).

MULTI-STOREY: five or more storeys. Multi-storey flats may form a *cluster block*, with individual blocks of flats grouped round a service core; a *point block*, with flats fanning out from a service core; or a *slab block*, with flats approached by corridors or galleries from service cores at intervals or towers at the ends (plan also used for offices, hotels etc.). *Tower block* is a generic term for any very high multi-storey building.

MUNTIN: see Panelling and 6b.

NAILHEAD: E.E. ornament consisting of small pyramids regularly repeated (1a).

NARTHEX: enclosed vestibule or covered porch at the main entrance to a church.

NAVE: the body of a church W of the crossing or chancel often flanked by aisles (q.v.).

NEWEL: central or corner post of a staircase (6c). Newel stair: see Stairs.

NIGHT STAIR: stair by which religious entered the transept of their church from their dormitory to celebrate night services.

NOGGING: see Timber-framing (7).

NOOK-SHAFT: shaft set in the angle of a wall or opening (1a).

NORMAN: see Romanesque.

NOSING: projection of the tread of a step (6c).

NUTMEG: medieval ornament with a chain of tiny triangles placed obliquely.

OCULUS: circular opening.

ŒIL DE BŒUF: see Bullseye window.

OGEE: double curve, bending first one way and then the other, as in an *ogee* or *ogival arch* (5c). Cf. Cyma recta and Cyma reversa.

OPUS SECTILE: decorative mosaic-like facing.

OPUS SIGNINUM: composition flooring of Roman origin.

ORATORY: a private chapel in a church or a house. Also a church of the Oratorian Order.

ORDER: one of a series of recessed arches and jambs forming a splayed medieval opening, e.g. a doorway or arcade arch (1a).

ORDERS: the formalized versions of the post-and-lintel system in classical architecture. The main orders are *Doric*, *Ionic*, and *Corinthian*. They are Greek in origin but occur in Roman versions. Tuscan is a simple version of Roman Doric. Though each order has its own conventions (3), there are many minor variations. The *Composite* capital combines Ionic volutes with Corinthian foliage. *Superimposed orders*: orders on successive levels, usually in the upward sequence of Tuscan, Doric, Ionic, Corinthian, Composite.

ORIEL: see Bay window.

OVERDOOR: painting or relief above an internal door. Also called a *sopraporta*.

OVERTHROW: decorative fixed arch between two gatepiers or above a wrought-iron gate.

OVOLO: wide convex moulding (3f).

PALIMPSEST: of a brass: where a metal plate has been reused by turning over the engraving on the back; of a wall painting: where one overlaps and partly obscures an earlier one.

PALLADIAN: following the examples and principles of Andrea Palladio (1508–80).

PALMETTE: classical ornament like a palm shoot (4b).

PANELLING: wooden lining to interior walls, made up of vertical members (*muntins*) and horizontals (*rails*) framing panels: also called *wainscot*. *Raised and fielded*: with the central area of the panel (*field*) raised up (6b).

PANTILE: roof tile of S section.

PARAPET: wall for protection at any sudden drop, e.g. at the wall-head of a castle where it protects the *parapet walk* or wall-walk. Also used to conceal a roof.

PARCLOSE: see Screen.

PARGETTING (*lit.* plastering): exterior plaster decoration, either in relief or incised.

PARLOUR: in a religious house, a room where the religious could talk to visitors; in a medieval house, the semi-private living room below the solar (q.v.).

PARTERRE: level space in a garden laid out with low, formal beds.

PATERA (*lit.* plate): round or oval ornament in shallow relief.

PAVILION: ornamental building for occasional use; or projecting subdivision of a larger building, often at an angle or terminating a wing.

PEBBLEDASHING: see Rendering.

PEDESTAL: a tall block carrying a classical order, statue, vase, etc.

PEDIMENT: a formalized gable derived from that of a classical temple; also used over doors, windows, etc. For variations see 4b.

PENDENTIVE: spandrel between adjacent arches, supporting a drum, dome or vault and consequently formed as part of a hemisphere (5a).

PENTHOUSE: subsidiary structure with a lean-to roof. Also a

separately roofed structure on top of a C20 multi-storey block.

PERIPTERAL: see Peristyle.

PERISTYLE: a colonnade all round the exterior of a classical building, as in a temple which is then said to be *peripteral*.

PERP (PERPENDICULAR): English Gothic architecture *c.* 1335–50 to *c.* 1530. The name is derived from the upright tracery panels then used (see Tracery and 2a).

PERRON: external stair to a doorway, usually of double-curved plan.

PEW: loosely, seating for the laity outside the chancel; strictly, an enclosed seat. *Box pew*: with equal high sides and a door.

PIANO NOBILE: principal floor of a classical building above a ground floor or basement and with a lesser storey overhead.

PIAZZA: formal urban open space surrounded by buildings.

PIER: large masonry or brick support, often for an arch. See also Compound pier.

PILASTER: flat representation of a classical column in shallow relief. *Pilaster strip*: see Lesene.

PILE: row of rooms. *Double pile*: two rows thick.

PILLAR: free-standing upright member of any section, not conforming to one of the orders (q.v.).

PILLAR PISCINA: see Piscina.

PILOTIS: C20 French term for pillars or stilts that support a building above an open ground floor.

PISCINA: basin for washing Mass vessels, provided with a drain; set in or against the wall to the S of an altar or free-standing (*pillar piscina*).

PISÉ: see Cob.

PITCHED MASONRY: laid on the diagonal, often alternately with opposing courses (*pitched and counterpitched* or *herringbone*).

PLATBAND: flat horizontal moulding between storeys. Cf. stringcourse.

PLATE RAIL: see Railways.

PLATEWAY: see Railways.

PLINTH: projecting courses at the

foot of a wall or column, generally chamfered or moulded at the top.

PODIUM: a continuous raised platform supporting a building; or a large block of two or three storeys beneath a multi-storey block of smaller area.

POINT BLOCK: *see* Multi-storey.

POINTING: exposed mortar jointing of masonry or brickwork. Types include *flush*, *recessed* and *tuck* (with a narrow channel filled with finer, whiter mortar).

POPPYHEAD: carved ornament of leaves and flowers as a finial for a bench end or stall.

PORTAL FRAME: C20 frame comprising two uprights rigidly connected to a beam or pair of rafters.

PORTCULLIS: gate constructed to rise and fall in vertical grooves at the entry to a castle.

PORTICO: a porch with the roof and frequently a pediment supported by a row of columns (4a). A portico *in antis* has columns on the same plane as the front of the building. A *prostyle* porch has columns standing free. Porticoes are described by the number of front columns, e.g. tetrastyle (four), hexastyle (six). The space within the temple is the *naos*, that within the portico the *pronaos*. *Blind portico*: the front features of a portico applied to a wall.

PORTICUS (plural: porticūs): subsidiary cell opening from the main body of a pre-Conquest church.

POST: upright support in a structure (7).

POSTERN: small gateway at the back of a building or to the side of a larger entrance door or gate.

POUND LOCK: *see* Canals.

PRESBYTERY: the part of a church lying E of the choir where the main altar is placed; or a priest's residence.

PRINCIPAL: *see* Roofs and 7.

PRONAOS: *see* Portico and 4a.

PROSTYLE: *see* Portico and 4a.

PULPIT: raised and enclosed platform for the preaching of sermons. *Three-decker*: with reading desk below and clerk's desk below that. *Two-decker*: as above, minus the clerk's desk.

PULPITUM: stone screen in a major church dividing choir from nave.

PULVINATED: *see* Frieze and 3c.

PURLIN: *see* Roofs and 7.

PUTHOLES or PUTLOG HOLES: in the wall to receive putlogs, the horizontal timbers which support scaffolding boards; sometimes not filled after construction is complete.

PUTTO (plural: putti): small naked boy.

QUARRIES: square (or diamond) panes of glass supported by lead strips (*cames*); square floor slabs or tiles.

QUATREFOIL: *see* Foil and 2b.

QUEEN-STRUT: *see* Roofs and 7.

QUIRK: sharp groove to one side of a convex medieval moulding.

QUOINS: dressed stones at the angles of a building (6d).

RADBURN SYSTEM: vehicle and pedestrian segregation in residential developments, based on that used at Radburn, New Jersey, USA, by Wright and Stein, 1928–30.

RADIATING CHAPELS: projecting radially from an ambulatory or an apse (*see* Chevet).

RAFTER: *see* Roofs and 7.

RAGGLE: groove cut in masonry, especially to receive the edge of a roof-covering.

RAGULY: ragged (in heraldry). Also applied to funerary sculpture, e.g. *cross raguly*: with a notched outline.

RAIL: *see* Panelling and 6b; also 7.

RAILWAYS: *Edge rail*: on which flanged wheels can run. *Plate rail*: L-section rail for plain unflanged wheels. *Plateway*: early railway using plate rails.

RAISED AND FIELDED: *see* Panelling and 6b.

RAKE: slope or pitch.

RAMPART: defensive outer wall of stone or earth. *Rampart walk*: path along the inner face.

REBATE: rectangular section cut out of a masonry edge to receive a shutter, door, window, etc.

REBUS: a heraldic pun, e.g. a fiery cock for Cockburn.

REEDING: series of convex mouldings, the reverse of fluting (q.v.). Cf. Gadrooning.

RENDERING: the covering of outside walls with a uniform surface or skin for protection from the weather. *Limewashing*: thin layer of lime plaster. *Pebbledashing*: where aggregate is thrown at the wet plastered wall for a textured effect. *Roughcast*: plaster mixed with a coarse aggregate such as gravel. *Stucco*: fine lime plaster worked to a smooth surface. *Cement rendering*: a cheaper substitute for stucco, usually with a grainy texture.

REPOUSSÉ: relief designs in metalwork, formed by beating it from the back.

REREDORTER (*lit.* behind the dormitory): latrines in a medieval religious house.

REREDOS: painted and/or sculptured screen behind and above an altar. Cf. Retable.

RESPOND: half-pier or half-column bonded into a wall and carrying one end of an arch. It usually terminates an arcade.

RETABLE: painted or carved panel standing on or at the back of an altar, usually attached to it.

RETROCHOIR: in a major church, the area between the high altar and E chapel.

REVEAL: the plane of a jamb, between the wall and the frame of a door or window.

RIB-VAULT: *see* Vault and 2c.

RINCEAU: classical ornament of leafy scrolls (4b).

RISER: vertical face of a step (6c).

ROACH: a rough-textured form of Portland stone, with small cavities and fossil shells.

ROCK-FACED: masonry cleft to produce a rugged appearance.

ROCOCO: style current *c.* 1720 and *c.* 1760, characterized by a serpentine line and playful, scrolled decoration.

ROLL MOULDING: medieval moulding of part-circular section (1a).

ROMANESQUE: style current in the C11 and C12. In England often called Norman. *See also* Saxo-Norman.

ROOD: crucifix flanked by the Virgin and St John, usually over the entry into the chancel, on a beam (*rood beam*) or painted on the wall. The *rood screen* below often had a walkway (*rood loft*) along the top, reached by a *rood stair* in the side wall.

ROOFS: Shape. For the main external shapes (hipped, mansard, etc.) *see* 8a. *Helm* and *Saddleback*: *see* 1c. *Lean-to*: single sloping roof built against a vertical wall; lean-to is also applied to the part of the building beneath. Construction. *See* 7. *Single-framed* roof: with no main trusses. The rafters may be fixed to the wall-plate or ridge, or longitudinal timber may be absent altogether. *Double-framed* roof: with longitudinal members, such as purlins, and usually divided into bays by principals and principal rafters. Other types are named after their main structural components, e.g. *hammerbeam, crown-post* (*see* Elements below and 7). Elements. *See* 7. *Ashlar piece*: a short vertical timber connecting inner wall-plate or timber pad to a rafter. *Braces*: subsidiary timbers set diagonally to strengthen the frame. *Arched braces*: curved pair forming an arch, connecting wall or post below with tie- or collar-beam above. *Passing braces*: long straight braces passing across other members of the truss. *Scissor braces*: pair crossing diagonally between pairs of rafters or principals. *Wind-braces*: short, usually curved braces connecting side purlins with principals; sometimes decorated with cusping. *Collar* or *collar-beam*: horizontal transverse timber connecting a pair of rafter or cruck blades (q.v.), set between apex and the wall-plate. *Crown-post*: a vertical timber set centrally on a tie-beam and supporting a collar purlin braced to it longitudinally. In an open truss lateral braces may rise to the collar-beam; in a closed truss they may descend to the tie-beam.

Hammerbeams: horizontal brackets projecting at wall-plate level like an interrupted tie-beam; the inner ends carry *hammerposts*, vertical timbers which support a purlin and are braced to a collar-beam above.

Kingpost: vertical timber set centrally on a tie- or collar-beam, rising to the apex of the roof to support a ridge-piece (cf. Strut).

Plate: longitudinal timber set square to the ground. *Wall-plate*: plate along the top of a wall which receives the ends of the rafters; cf. Purlin.

Principals: pair of inclined lateral timbers of a truss. Usually they support side purlins and mark the main bay divisions.

Purlin: horizontal longitudinal timber. *Collar purlin* or *crown plate*: central timber which carries collar-beams and is supported by crown-posts. *Side purlins*: pairs of timbers placed some way up the slope of the roof, which carry common rafters. *Butt* or *tenoned purlins* are tenoned into either side of the principals. *Through purlins* pass through or past the principal; they include *clasped purlins*, which rest on queenposts or are carried in the angle between principals and collar, and *trenched purlins* trenched into the backs of principals.

Queen-strut: paired vertical, or near-vertical, timbers placed symmetrically on a tie-beam to support side purlins.

Rafters: inclined lateral timbers supporting the roof covering. *Common rafters*: regularly spaced uniform rafters placed along the length of a roof or between principals. *Principal rafters*: rafters which also act as principals.

Ridge, ridge-piece: horizontal longitudinal timber at the apex supporting the ends of the rafters.

Sprocket: short timber placed on the back and at the foot of a rafter to form projecting eaves.

Strut: vertical or oblique timber between two members of a truss,

not directly supporting longitudinal timbers.

Tie-beam: main horizontal transverse timber which carries the feet of the principals at wall level.

Truss: rigid framework of timbers at bay intervals, carrying the longitudinal roof timbers which support the common rafters.

Closed truss: with the spaces between the timbers filled, to form an internal partition.

See also Cruck, Wagon roof.

ROPE MOULDING: *see* Cable moulding.

ROSE WINDOW: circular window with tracery radiating from the centre. Cf. Wheel window.

ROTUNDA: building or room circular in plan.

ROUGHCAST: *see* Rendering.

ROVING BRIDGE: *see* Canals.

RUBBED BRICKWORK: *see* Gauged brickwork.

RUBBLE: masonry whose stones are wholly or partly in a rough state. *Coursed*: coursed stones with rough faces. *Random*: uncoursed stones in a random pattern. *Snecked*: with courses broken by smaller stones (snecks).

RUSTICATION: *see* 6d. Exaggerated treatment of masonry to give an effect of strength. The joints are usually recessed by V-section chamfering or square-section channelling (*channelled rustication*). *Banded rustication* has only the horizontal joints emphasized. The faces may be flat, but can be *diamond-faced*, like shallow pyramids, *vermiculated*, with a stylized texture like worm-casts, and *glacial* (frost-work), like icicles or stalactites.

SACRISTY: room in a church for sacred vessels and vestments.

SADDLEBACK ROOF: *see* 1C.

SALTIRE CROSS: with diagonal limbs.

SANCTUARY: area around the main altar of a church. Cf. Presbytery.

SANGHA: residence of Buddhist monks or nuns.

SARCOPHAGUS: coffin of stone or other durable material.

SAXO-NORMAN: transitional Romanesque style combining Anglo-Saxon and Norman features, current *c.* 1060–1100.

SCAGLIOLA: composition imitating marble.

SCALLOPED CAPITAL: *see* 1a.

SCOTIA: a hollow classical moulding, especially between tori (q.v.) on a column base (3b, 3f).

SCREEN: in a medieval church, usually at the entry to the chancel; *see* Rood (screen) and Pulpitum. A *parclose screen* separates a chapel from the rest of the church.

SCREENS or SCREENS PASSAGE: screened-off entrance passage between great hall and service rooms.

SECTION: two-dimensional representation of a building, moulding, etc., revealed by cutting across it.

SEDILIA (singular: sedile): seats for the priests (usually three) on the S side of the chancel.

SET-OFF: *see* Weathering.

SETTS: squared stones, usually of granite, used for paving or flooring.

SGRAFFITO: decoration scratched, often in plaster, to reveal a pattern in another colour beneath. *Graffiti*: scratched drawing or writing.

SHAFT: vertical member of round or polygonal section (1a, 3a). *Shaft-ring*: at the junction of shafts set *en delit* (q.v.) or attached to a pier or wall (1a).

SHEILA-NA-GIG: female fertility figure, usually with legs apart.

SHELL: thin, self-supporting roofing membrane of timber or concrete.

SHOULDERED ARCHITRAVE: *see* 4b.

SHUTTERING: *see* Concrete.

SILL: horizontal member at the bottom of a window or door frame; or at the base of a timber-framed wall into which posts and studs are tenoned (7).

SLAB BLOCK: *see* Multi-storey.

SLATE-HANGING: covering of overlapping slates on a wall. *Tile-hanging* is similar.

SLYPE: covered way or passage leading E from the cloisters between transept and chapter house.

SNECKED: *see* Rubble.

SOFFIT (*lit.* ceiling): underside of an arch (also called *intrados*), lintel, etc. *Soffit roll*: medieval roll moulding on a soffit.

SOLAR: private upper chamber in a medieval house, accessible from the high end of the great hall.

SOPRAPORTA: *see* Overdoor.

SOUNDING-BOARD: *see* Tester.

SPANDRELS: roughly triangular spaces between an arch and its containing rectangle, or between adjacent arches (5c). Also non-structural panels under the windows in a curtain-walled building.

SPERE: a fixed structure screening the lower end of the great hall from the screens passage. *Spere-truss*: roof truss incorporated in the spere.

SPIRE: tall pyramidal or conical feature crowning a tower or turret. *Broach*: starting from a square base, then carried into an octagonal section by means of triangular faces; and *splayed-foot*: variation of the broach form, found principally in the southeast, in which the four cardinal faces are splayed out near their base, to cover the corners, while oblique (or intermediate) faces taper away to a point (1c). *Needle spire*: thin spire rising from the centre of a tower roof, well inside the parapet: when of timber and lead often called a *spike*.

SPIRELET: *see* Flèche.

SPLAY: of an opening when it is wider on one face of a wall than the other.

SPRING or SPRINGING: level at which an arch or vault rises from its supports. *Springers*: the first stones of an arch or vaulting rib above the spring (2c).

SQUINCH: arch or series of arches thrown across an interior angle of a square or rectangular structure to support a circular or polygonal superstructure, especially a dome or spire (5a).

SQUINT: an aperture in a wall or through a pier usually to allow a view of an altar.

STAIRS: *see* 6c. *Dog-leg stair*: parallel flights rising alternately in opposite directions, without an open well. *Flying stair*: cantilevered from the walls of a stairwell, without newels; sometimes called a *Geometric* stair when the inner edge describes a curve. *Newel stair*: ascending round a central supporting newel (q.v.); called a *spiral stair* or *vice* when in a circular shaft, a *winder* when in a rectangular compartment. (Winder also applies to the steps on the turn.) *Well stair*: with flights round a square open well framed by newel posts. *See also* Perron.

STALL: fixed seat in the choir or chancel for the clergy or choir (cf. Pew). Usually with arm rests, and often framed together.

STANCHION: upright structural member, of iron, steel or reinforced concrete.

STANDPIPE TOWER: *see* Manometer.

STEAM ENGINES: *Atmospheric*: worked by the vacuum created when low-pressure steam is condensed in the cylinder, as developed by Thomas Newcomen. *Beam engine*: with a large pivoted beam moved in an oscillating fashion by the piston. It may drive a flywheel or be *non-rotative*. *Watt* and *Cornish*: single-cylinder; *compound*: two cylinders; *triple expansion*: three cylinders.

STEEPLE: tower together with a spire, lantern, or belfry.

STIFF-LEAF: type of E.E. foliage decoration. *Stiff-leaf capital see* 1b.

STOP: plain or decorated terminal to mouldings or chamfers, or at the end of hoodmoulds and labels (*label stop*), or stringcourses (5b, 6a); *see also* Headstop.

STOUP: vessel for holy water, usually near a door.

STRAINER: *see* Arch.

STRAPWORK: late C16 and C17 decoration, like interlaced leather straps.

STRETCHER: *see* Bond and 6e.

STRING: *see* 6c. Sloping member holding the ends of the treads and risers of a staircase. *Closed string*: a broad string covering the ends of the treads and risers. *Open string*: cut into the shape of the treads and risers.

STRINGCOURSE: horizontal course or moulding projecting from the surface of a wall (6d).

STUCCO: *see* Rendering.

STUDS: subsidiary vertical timbers of a timber-framed wall or partition (7).

STUPA: Buddhist shrine, circular in plan.

STYLOBATE: top of the solid platform on which a colonnade stands (3a).

SUSPENSION BRIDGE: *see* Bridge.

SWAG: like a festoon (q.v.), but representing cloth.

SYSTEM BUILDING: *see* Industrialized building.

TABERNACLE: canopied structure to contain the reserved sacrament or a relic; or architectural frame for an image or statue.

TABLE TOMB: memorial slab raised on free-standing legs.

TAS-DE-CHARGE: the lower courses of a vault or arch which are laid horizontally (2c).

TERM: pedestal or pilaster tapering downward, usually with the upper part of a human figure growing out of it.

TERRACOTTA: moulded and fired clay ornament or cladding.

TESSELLATED PAVEMENT: mosaic flooring, particularly Roman, made of *tesserae*, i.e. cubes of glass, stone, or brick.

TESTER: flat canopy over a tomb or pulpit, where it is also called a *sounding-board*.

TESTER TOMB: tomb-chest with effigies beneath a tester, either free-standing (tester with four or more columns), or attached to a wall (*half-tester*) with columns on one side only.

TETRASTYLE: *see* Portico.

THERMAL WINDOW: *see* Diocletian window.

THREE-DECKER PULPIT: *see* Pulpit.

TIDAL GATES: *see* Canals.

TIE-BEAM: *see* Roofs and 7.

TIERCERON: *see* Vault and 2c.

TILE-HANGING: *see* Slate-hanging.

TIMBER-FRAMING: *see* 7. Method of construction where the structural frame is built of interlocking timbers. The spaces are filled with non-structural material, e.g. *infill* of wattle and daub, lath and plaster, brickwork (known as *nogging*), etc. and may be covered by plaster, weatherboarding (q.v.), or tiles.

TOMB-CHEST: chest-shaped tomb, usually of stone. Cf. Table tomb, Tester tomb.

TORUS (plural: tori): large convex moulding usually used on a column base (3b, 3f).

TOUCH: soft black marble quarried near Tournai.

TOURELLE: turret corbelled out from the wall.

TOWER BLOCK: *see* Multi-storey.

TRABEATED: depends structurally on the use of the post and lintel. Cf. Arcuated.

TRACERY: openwork pattern of masonry or timber in the upper part of an opening. *Blind tracery* is tracery applied to a solid wall.
Plate tracery, introduced *c.* 1200, is the earliest form, in which shapes are cut through solid masonry (2a).
Bar tracery was introduced into England *c.* 1250. The pattern is formed by intersecting moulded ribwork continued from the mullions. It was especially elaborate during the Decorated period (q.v.). Tracery shapes can include circles, *daggers* (elongated ogee-ended lozenges), *mouchettes* (like daggers but with curved sides) and upright rectangular *panels*. They often have *cusps*, projecting points defining lobes or *foils* (q.v.) within the main shape: *Kentish* or *split-cusps* are forked (2b).
Types of bar tracery (*see* 2b) include *geometric(al)*: *c.* 1250–1310, chiefly circles, often foiled; *Y-tracery*: *c.* 1300, with mullions branching into a Y-shape; *intersecting*: *c.* 1300, formed by interlocking mullions; *reticulated*: early c14, net-like pattern of ogee-ended lozenges; *curvilinear*: c14, with uninterrupted flowing curves; *panel*: Perp, with straight-sided panels, often cusped at the top and bottom.

TRANSEPT: transverse portion of a church.

TRANSITIONAL: generally used for the phase between Romanesque and Early English (*c.* 1175–*c.* 1200).

TRANSOM: horizontal member separating window lights (2b).

TREAD: horizontal part of a step. The *tread end* may be carved on a staircase (6c).

TREFOIL: *see* Foil.

TRIFORIUM: middle storey of a church treated as an arcaded wall passage or blind arcade, its height corresponding to that of the aisle roof.

TRIGLYPHS (*lit.* three-grooved tablets): stylized beam-ends in the Doric frieze, with metopes between (3b).

TRIUMPHAL ARCH: influential type of Imperial Roman monument.

TROPHY: sculptured or painted group of arms or armour.

TRUMEAU: central stone mullion supporting the tympanum of a wide doorway. *Trumeau figure*: carved figure attached to it (cf. Column figure).

TRUMPET CAPITAL: *see* 1b.

TRUSS: braced framework, spanning between supports. *See also* Roofs and 7.

TUMBLING or TUMBLING-IN: courses of brickwork laid at right-angles to a slope, e.g. of a gable, forming triangles by tapering into horizontal courses (8a).

TUSCAN: *see* Orders and 3e.

TWO-DECKER PULPIT: *see* Pulpit.

TYMPANUM: the surface between a lintel and the arch above it or within a pediment (4a).

UNDERCROFT: usually describes the vaulted room(s), beneath the main room(s) of a medieval house. Cf. Crypt.

VAULT: arched stone roof (sometimes imitated in timber or plaster). For types see 2c.
Tunnel or *barrel vault*: continuous semicircular or pointed arch, often of rubble masonry.

Groin-vault: tunnel vaults intersecting at right angles. *Groins* are the curved lines of the intersections.

Rib-vault: masonry framework of intersecting arches (ribs) supporting *vault cells*, used in Gothic architecture. *Wall rib* or *wall arch*: between wall and vault cell. *Transverse rib*: spans between two walls to divide a vault into bays. *Quadripartite* rib-vault: each bay has two pairs of diagonal ribs dividing the vault into four triangular cells. *Sexpartite* rib-vault: most often used over paired bays, has an extra pair of ribs springing from between the bays. More elaborate vaults may include *ridge ribs* along the crown of a vault or bisecting the bays; *tiercerons*: extra decorative ribs springing from the corners of a bay; and *liernes*: short decorative ribs in the crown of a vault, not linked to any springing point. A *stellar* or *star* vault has liernes in star formation.

Fan-vault: form of barrel vault used in the Perp period, made up of halved concave masonry cones decorated with blind tracery.

VAULTING SHAFT: shaft leading up to the spring or springing (q.v.) of a vault (2c).

VENETIAN or SERLIAN WINDOW: derived from Serlio (4b). The motif is used for other openings.

VERMICULATION: *see* Rustication and 6d.

VESICA: oval with pointed ends.

VICE: *see* Stair.

VILLA: originally a Roman country house or farm. The term was revived in England in the C18 under the influence of Palladio and used especially for smaller, compact country houses. In the later C19 it was debased to describe any suburban house.

VITRIFIED: bricks or tiles fired to a darkened glassy surface.

VITRUVIAN SCROLL: classical running ornament of curly waves (4b).

VOLUTES: spiral scrolls. They occur on Ionic capitals (3c). *Angle volute*: pair of volutes, turned outwards to meet at the corner of a capital.

VOUSSOIRS: wedge-shaped stones forming an arch (5c).

WAGON ROOF: with the appearance of the inside of a wagon tilt; often ceiled. Also called *cradle roof*.

WAINSCOT: *see* Panelling.

WALL MONUMENT: attached to the wall and often standing on the floor. *Wall tablets* are smaller with the inscription as the major element.

WALL-PLATE: *see* Roofs and 7.

WALL-WALK: *see* Parapet.

WARMING ROOM: room in a religious house where a fire burned for comfort.

WATERHOLDING BASE: early Gothic base with upper and lower mouldings separated by a deep hollow.

WATERLEAF: *see* Enrichments and 3f.

WATERLEAF CAPITAL: Late Romanesque and Transitional type of capital (1b).

WATER WHEELS: described by the way water is fed on to the wheel. *Breastshot*: mid-height, falling and passing beneath. *Overshot*: over the top. *Pitchback*: on the top but falling backwards. *Undershot*: turned by the momentum of the water passing beneath. In a *water turbine*, water is fed under pressure through a vaned wheel within a casing.

WEALDEN HOUSE: type of medieval timber-framed house with a central open hall flanked by bays of two storeys, roofed in line; the end bays are jettied to the front, but the eaves are continuous (8a).

WEATHERBOARDING: wall cladding of overlapping horizontal boards.

WEATHERING or SET-OFF: inclined, projecting surface to keep water away from the wall below.

WEEPERS: figures in niches along the sides of some medieval tombs. Also called mourners.

WHEEL WINDOW: circular, with radiating shafts like spokes. Cf. Rose window.

WROUGHT IRON: *see* Cast iron.

INDEX OF ARCHITECTS, ARTISTS, PATRONS AND RESIDENTS

Names of architects and artists working in the area covered by this volume are given in *italic*. Entries for partnerships and group practices are listed after entries for a single name.

Also indexed here are names/titles of families and individuals (not of bodies or commercial firms) recorded in this volume as having commissioned architectural work or owned, lived in, or visited properties in the area. The index includes monuments to members of such families and other individuals where they are of particular interest.

INDEX OF PLACES

Principal references are in **bold** type; demolished buildings are shown in *italic*.
IS = Isles of Scilly